DISCOVERING COMPUTERS
A Link to the Future
World Wide Web Enhanced

Gary B. Shelly
Thomas J. Cashman
Gloria A. Waggoner
William C. Waggoner

Contributing Authors

Misty E. Vermaat
Tim J. Walker
Tom L. Hall
John F. Repede

SHELLY CASHMAN SERIES®

COURSE TECHNOLOGY
ONE MAIN STREET
CAMBRIDGE MA 02142

an International Thomson Publishing company   ITP®

CAMBRIDGE · ALBANY · BONN · CINCINNATI · LONDON · MADRID · MELBOURNE
MEXICO CITY · NEW YORK · PARIS · SAN FRANCISCO · TOKYO · TORONTO · WASHINGTON

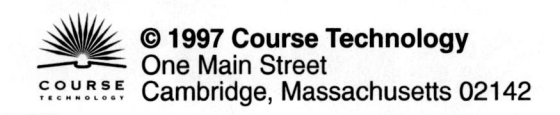

© 1997 Course Technology
One Main Street
Cambridge, Massachusetts 02142

I(T)P® International Thomson Publishing
The ITP logo is a registered trademark
of International Thomson Publishing.

Printed in the United States of America

For more information, contact Course Technology:

Course Technology
One Main Street
Cambridge, Massachusetts 02142, USA

International Thomson Publishing Europe
Berkshire House
168-173 High Holborn
London, WC1V 7AA, United Kingdom

Thomas Nelson Australia
102 Dodds Street
South Melbourne
Victoria 3205 Australia

Nelson Canada
1120 Birchmont Road
Scarborough, Ontario
Canada M1K 5G4

International Thomson Editores
Campos Eliseos 385, Piso 7
Colonia Polanco
11560 Mexico D.F. Mexico

International Thomson Publishing GmbH
Konigswinterer Strasse 418
53227 Bonn, Germany

International Thomson Publishing Asia
Block 211, Henderson Road #08-03
Henderson Industrial Park
Singapore 0315

International Thomson Publishing Japan
Hirakawa-cho Kyowa Building, 3F
2-2-1 Hirakawa-cho, Chiyoda-ku
Tokyo 102, Japan

All rights reserved. No part of this work may be reproduced or used in any form or by any means—
graphic, electronic, or mechanical, including photocopying, recording, taping, or information and retrieval systems—
without prior written permission from the publisher.

ISBN 0-7895-1297-1 (Perfect bound)
ISBN 0-7895-2848-7 (Case bound)

SHELLY CASHMAN SERIES® and **Custom Edition**® are trademarks of International Thomson Publishing, Inc. Names of all other products mentioned herein are used for identification purposes only and may be trademarks and/or registered trademarks of their respective owners. International Thomson Publishing, Inc. and Course Technology disclaim any affiliation, association, or connection with, or sponsorship or endorsement by, such owners.

Library of Congress Catalog Card Number: 97-65049

1 2 3 4 5 6 7 8 9 10 BC 10 9 8 7

Contents

DISCOVERING COMPUTERS
A Link to the Future, World Wide Web Enhanced

Preface	x

CHAPTER 1
An Overview of Using Computers

Objectives	1.1
Computer and Information Literacy	1.2
What Is a Computer?	1.4
What Are the Components of a Computer?	1.4
Input Devices	1.4
System Unit	1.6
Output Devices	1.6
Storage Devices	1.7
Communications Devices	1.7
Peripheral Devices	1.7
What Does a Computer Do?	1.7
Why is a Computer so Powerful?	1.8
Speed	1.8
Reliability	1.8
Accuracy	1.8
Storage	1.8
Communications	1.8
Connectivity	1.9
Categories of Computers	1.10
Personal Computers	1.10
Servers	1.13
Minicomputers	1.14
Mainframe Computers	1.14
Supercomputers	1.15
Computer Software	1.16
System Software	1.17
User Interface	1.17
Application Software	1.18
What Are the Elements of an Information System?	1.19
An Example of How One Company Uses Computers	1.20
Reception	1.20
Sales	1.21
Marketing	1.21
Shipping and Receiving	1.22
Manufacturing	1.22
Product Design	1.23
Accounting	1.23
Human Resources	1.24
Information Systems	1.24
Executive	1.25
Summary of How One Company Uses Computers	1.25
Summary of an Overview of Using Computers	1.25
Computers at Work: Shopping for an Auto Online	1.26
In the Future: From the Global Village to the Local Village	1.27
review	1.28
terms	1.30
yourTurn	1.31
hotTopics	1.32
outThere	1.33
winLabs	1.34
webWalk	1.35

SPECIAL FEATURE
TIMELINE
Milestones in Computer History   1.36

CHAPTER 2
Software Applications: User Tools

Objectives	2.1
The Operating System and User Interface	2.2
Software Applications	2.4
Word Processing Software	2.4
Desktop Publishing Software	2.12
Spreadsheet Software	2.14
Database Software	2.21
Presentation Graphics Software	2.24
Communications Software and Web Browsers	2.26
Electronic Mail Software	2.27
Personal Information Management Software	2.28
Personal Finance Software	2.29
Project Management Software	2.29
Accounting Software	2.30
Groupware	2.30
Computer-Aided Design (CAD) Software	2.31
Multimedia Authoring Software	2.32
Integrated Software and Software Suites	2.32
Object Linking and Embedding (OLE)	2.34
Learning Aids and Support Tools for Application Users	2.36
Summary of Software Applications	2.37
Computers at Work: Shortcuts to Creating Documents	2.38
In the Future: Software by Subscription	2.39
review	2.40
terms	2.42
yourTurn	2.43
hotTopics	2.44
outThere	2.45
winLabs	2.46
webWalk	2.47

iv CONTENTS

CHAPTER 3
The System Unit

Objectives	3.1
What Is the System Unit?	3.2
How Data Is Represented in a Computer	3.3
ASCII and EBCDIC	3.4
Unicode	3.4
Parity	3.5
The Components of the System Unit	3.6
Motherboard	3.7
Microprocessor and the CPU	3.7
The Control Unit	3.8
The Arithmetic/Logic Unit	3.8
Registers	3.8
The System Clock	3.8
Word Size	3.9
Microprocessor Comparison	3.10
Upgrade Sockets	3.10
Memory	3.11
RAM	3.11
ROM	3.13
CMOS	3.13
Memory Speed	3.13
Coprocessors	3.14
Buses	3.14
Expansion Slots	3.15
Ports and Connectors	3.16
Parallel Ports	3.16
Serial Ports	3.18
Bays	3.18
Power Supply	3.18
Sound Components	3.18
Summary of the Components of the System Unit	3.19
Machine Language Instructions	3.19
Types of Processing	3.21
Pipelining	3.21
Parallel Processing	3.21
Neural Network Computers	3.22
Number Systems	3.22
The Decimal Number System	3.22
The Binary Number System	3.23
The Hexadecimal Number System	3.24
Summary of Number Systems	3.24
How Computer Chips Are Made	3.25
Summary of the System Unit	3.27
Computers at Work: How Many Computers Do You See Each Day?	3.28
In the Future: 2,000 MIPS by the Year 2000	3.29
review	3.30
terms	3.32
yourTurn	3.33
hotTopics	3.34
outThere	3.35
winLabs	3.36
webWalk	3.37

CHAPTER 4
Input and Output

Objectives	4.1
What Is Input?	4.2
The Keyboard	4.2
Pointing Devices	4.5
Mouse	4.5
Trackball	4.6
Touchpad	4.6
Pointing Stick	4.7
Joystick	4.7
Pen Input	4.8
Touch Screen	4.9
Light Pen	4.10
Digitizer	4.10
Graphics Tablet	4.11
Source Data Automation	4.12
Image Scanner	4.13
Optical Recognition	4.14
Magnetic Ink Character Recognition (MICR)	4.17
Data Collection Devices	4.17
Terminals	4.18
Other Input Devices	4.19
Sound Input	4.19
Voice Input	4.19
Biological Feedback Input	4.21
Digital Camera	4.21
Video Input	4.22
Electronic Whiteboards	4.22
What Is Output?	4.23
Types of Output	4.23
Reports	4.23
Graphics	4.25
Audio Output	4.25
Video Output	4.26
Display Devices	4.27
Monitors	4.27
Flat Panel Displays	4.29
Resolution	4.30
How Images Are Displayed on a Monitor	4.31
Printers	4.32
Impact Printers	4.32
Nonimpact Printers	4.34
Plotters	4.38
Special-Purpose Printers	4.39
Other Output Devices	4.40
Data Projectors	4.40
Computer Output Microfilm	4.41
Facsimile (Fax)	4.42
Multifunction Devices	4.42
Summary of Input and Output	4.43
Computers at Work: Helping People with Special Needs	4.44
In the Future: The Widespread Use of Voice Input	4.45

review	4.46
terms	4.49
yourTurn	4.50
hotTopics	4.51
outThere	4.52
winLabs	4.53
webWalk	4.54

CHAPTER 5

Data Storage

Objectives	**5.1**
What Is Storage?	**5.2**
Magnetic Disk Storage	**5.3**
Floppy Disks	5.3
Hard Disks	5.8
Disk Cartridges	5.11
Maintaining Data Stored on a Disk	5.12
CD-ROM and Optical Disks	**5.14**
Magnetic Tape	**5.16**
Cartridge Tape Devices	5.16
Reel-to-Reel Tape Devices	5.17
Storing Data on Magnetic Tape	5.18
Other Types of Storage Devices	**5.19**
PC Cards	5.19
RAID Storage Systems	5.19
Mass Storage Systems	5.21
Special-Purpose Storage Devices	5.21
Summary of Storage	**5.23**
Computers at Work: HSM: Hierarchical Storage Management	**5.24**
In the Future: Holographic Storage	**5.25**
review	5.26
terms	5.28
yourTurn	5.29
hotTopics	5.30
outThere	5.31
winLabs	5.32
webWalk	5.33

CHAPTER 6

Communications and Networks

Objectives	**6.1**
What Is Communications?	**6.2**
Examples of How Communications Is Used	**6.2**
Electronic Mail (E-mail)	6.2
Voice Mail	6.2
Facsimile	6.2
Telecommuting	6.2
Videoconferencing	6.3
Groupware	6.4
Electronic Data Interchange	6.4
Global Positioning Systems (GPSs)	6.5
Bulletin Board Systems (BBSs)	6.5
Online Services	6.6
The Internet	6.7
A Communications System Model	**6.8**
Transmission Media	**6.9**
Twisted-Pair Cable	6.9
Coaxial Cable	6.9
Fiber-Optic Cable	6.10
Microwave Transmission	6.11
Wireless Transmission: Radio and Light Waves	6.12
An Example of a Communications Channel	6.14
Line Configurations	**6.14**
Point-to-Point Lines	6.14
Multidrop Lines	6.15
Characteristics of Communications Channels	**6.16**
Types of Signals: Digital and Analog	6.16
Transmission Modes: Asynchronous and Synchronous	6.17
Direction of Transmission: Simplex, Half-Duplex, and Full-Duplex	6.18
Transmission Rate	6.18
Communications Software	**6.19**
Communications Equipment	**6.19**
Modems	6.19
Multiplexers	6.20
Front-End Processors	6.21
Network Interface Cards	6.21
Wiring Hubs	6.22
Gateways	6.22
Bridges	6.22
Routers	6.22
Communications Networks	**6.23**
Local Area Networks (LANs)	6.23
Wide Area Networks (WANs)	6.26
Network Configurations	**6.27**
Star Network	6.27
Bus Network	6.28
Ring Network	6.29
Communications Protocols	**6.29**
Ethernet	6.30
Token Ring	6.31
An Example of a Communications Network	**6.32**
Summary of Communications and Networks	**6.33**
Computers at Work: GPS: Tool of the Modern Traveler	**6.34**
In the Future: Anywhere, Anytime Voice and Data Communications	**6.35**
review	6.36
terms	6.39
yourTurn	6.40
hotTopics	6.41
outThere	6.42
winLabs	6.43
webWalk	6.44

CONTENTS

CHAPTER 7

The Internet and the World Wide Web

Objectives	**7.1**
What Is the Internet?	**7.2**
History of the Internet	**7.3**
How the Internet Works	**7.4**
Internet Addresses	**7.6**
The World Wide Web (WWW)	**7.7**
How a Web Page Works	7.7
Web Browser Software	7.9
Multimedia on the Web	7.11
Searching for Information on the Web	7.16
Intranets and Firewalls	**7.17**
Other Internet Services	**7.19**
E-mail	7.19
FTP	7.20
Gopher	7.21
Telnet	7.22
Usenet	7.23
Internet Relay Chat (IRC)	7.24
Network Computers	**7.25**
Network Computers for Business	7.25
Network Computers for the Home	7.26
Summary of Network Computers	7.27
How to Connect to the Internet and the World Wide Web	**7.28**
Computers at Work: Doing Business on the World Wide Web	**7.30**
In the Future: The Future of the Internet and the World Wide Web	**7.31**
review	7.32
terms	7.35
yourTurn	7.36
hotTopics	7.37
outThere	7.38
winLabs	7.39
webWalk	7.40

SPECIAL FEATURE

Guide to World Wide Web Sites   7.41

CHAPTER 8

Operating Systems and System Software

Objectives	**8.1**
What Is System Software?	**8.2**
What Is an Operating System?	**8.2**
Functions of an Operating System	**8.4**
Process Management	8.4
Memory Management	8.7
Input and Output Management	8.8
System Administration	8.10
Loading an Operating System	**8.12**
Popular Operating Systems	**8.14**
DOS	8.14
Windows 3.x	8.15
Windows 95 and Beyond	8.16
Windows CE	8.16
Windows NT	8.17
Macintosh	8.17
OS/2	8.18
UNIX	8.18
NetWare	8.19
Utilities	**8.19**
Language Translators	**8.23**
Summary of Operating Systems and System Software	**8.23**
Computers at Work: The Social Interface	**8.24**
In the Future: The Next User Interface	**8.25**
review	8.26
terms	8.28
yourTurn	8.29
hotTopics	8.30
outThere	8.31
winLabs	8.32
webWalk	8.33

SPECIAL FEATURE

How to Purchase, Install, and Maintain a Personal Computer   8.34

CHAPTER 9

Data Management and Databases

Objectives	**9.1**
Data Management	**9.2**
Data Accuracy	9.3
Data Security	9.3
Data Maintenance	9.3
The Hierarchy of Data	**9.4**
Types of File Organization	**9.5**
Sequential File Organization	9.5
Indexed File Organization	9.6
Direct File Organization	9.7
Summary of File Organization Concepts	9.8
How Is Data in Files Maintained?	**9.9**
Adding Records	9.9
Changing Records	9.10
Deleting Records	9.11
Summary of How Data Is Maintained	9.12
Databases: A Better Way to Manage and Organize Data	**9.12**
What Is a Database?	**9.12**
Why Use a Database?	**9.13**
Types of Database Organization	**9.15**
Hierarchical Database	9.15
Network Database	9.16
Relational Database	9.17
Object-Oriented Database	9.18
Database Management Systems	**9.18**
Query Languages: Access to the Database	**9.20**
Querying a Relational Database	9.21
Structured Query Language	9.22
Database Administration	**9.22**
The Role of the Database Administrator	9.23
The Role of the User in a Database System	9.24
Guidelines for Designing Database Files	9.25
Summary of Data Management and Databases	**9.25**
Computers at Work: Data Warehouses and Data Mining	**9.26**
In the Future: Storing All Types of Data	**9.27**
review	9.28
terms	9.31
yourTurn	9.32
hotTopics	9.33
outThere	9.34
winLabs	9.35
webWalk	9.36

CHAPTER 10

Information Systems

Objectives	**10.1**
Why Is Information Important to an Organization?	**10.2**
How Do Managers Use Information?	**10.4**
Management Levels in an Organization	**10.5**
Senior Management – Strategic Decisions	10.6
Middle Management – Tactical Decisions	10.7
Operational Management – Operational Decisions	10.7
Nonmanagement Employees – On-the-Job Decisions	10.7
Functional Areas in an Organization	**10.8**
Other Approaches to Management Organization	10.10
Qualities of Valuable Information	**10.11**
Types of Information Systems	**10.13**
Office Systems	10.13
Transaction Processing Systems	10.13
Management Information Systems	10.14
Decision Support Systems	10.16
Expert Systems	10.17
Integrated Information Systems	**10.18**
The Role of Personal Computers in Information Systems	**10.19**
Summary of Information Systems	**10.19**
Computers at Work: Executive Information Systems	**10.20**
In the Future: The Cyber Corporation	**10.21**
review	10.22
terms	10.25
yourTurn	10.26
hotTopics	10.27
outThere	10.28
winLabs	10.29
webWalk	10.30

CHAPTER 11

Information Systems Development

Objectives	**11.1**
What Is the System Development Life Cycle?	**11.2**
Phases in the System Development Life Cycle	11.2
Guidelines for System Development	11.3
Who Participates in the System Development Life Cycle?	11.3
Project Management	11.4
Feasibility Assessment	11.5
Documentation	11.6
Data and Information Gathering Techniques	11.7

What Initiates the System Development Life Cycle?	**11.7**
North Harbor State Bank – A Case Study	11.9
Planning Phase	**11.9**
Planning at North Harbor State Bank	11.10
Analysis Phase	**11.11**
The Feasibility Study	11.11
Feasibility Study at North Harbor State Bank	11.12
Detailed Analysis	11.12
Structured Analysis and Design Tools	11.13
The Build-or-Buy Decision	11.19
What Is Commercial Application Software?	11.19
What Is Custom Software?	11.20
Detailed Analysis at North Harbor State Bank	11.20
Design Phase	**11.21**
Acquiring Essential Hardware and Software	11.21
Identifying Technical Specifications	11.21
Soliciting Vendor Proposals	11.22
Testing and Evaluating Vendor Proposals	11.23
Making a Decision	11.24
Software Acquisition at North Harbor State Bank	11.24
Detailed Design	11.25
Prototyping	11.27
CASE Tools	11.28
Quality Review Techniques	11.29
Detailed Design at North Harbor State Bank	11.29
Implementation Phase	**11.30**
Develop Programs	11.30
Install and Test the New System	11.30
Train and Educate Users	11.30
Convert to the New System	11.31
Implementation at North Harbor State Bank	11.32
Support Phase	**11.33**
Support at North Harbor State Bank	11.33
Summary of the System Development Life Cycle	**11.33**
Computers at Work: System Development Methodologies – What Are the Differences?	**11.34**
In the Future: The Virtual Classroom	**11.35**
review	11.36
terms	11.39
yourTurn	11.40
hotTopics	11.41
outThere	11.42
winLabs	11.43
webWalk	11.44

CHAPTER 12

Program Development and Programming Languages

Objectives	**12.1**
What Is a Computer Program?	**12.2**
The Program Development Life Cycle	**12.2**
What Initiates the Program Development Life Cycle?	12.3
Step 1 – Analyze Problem	**12.4**
Step 2 – Design Program	**12.4**
Top-Down Design	12.5
Structured Design	12.6
Proper Program Design	12.8
Design Tools	12.9
Quality Review Techniques	12.12
Step 3 – Code Program	**12.13**
Step 4 – Test Program	**12.13**
Step 5 – Formalize Solution	**12.15**
Step 6 – Maintain Program	**12.15**
Summary of the Program Development Life Cycle	**12.16**
What Is a Programming Language?	**12.16**
Categories of Programming Languages	**12.16**
Machine Language	12.17
Assembly Language	12.18
Third-Generation Languages	12.19
Fourth-Generation Languages	12.20
Natural Languages	12.21
Object-Oriented Program Development	**12.21**
Object-Oriented Programming	12.23
Popular Programming Languages	**12.23**
BASIC	12.23
Visual Basic	12.24
COBOL	12.25
C	12.26
C++	12.26
FORTRAN	12.27
Pascal	12.27
Ada	12.28
RPG	12.28
Other Programming Languages	12.29
How to Select a Programming Language	**12.29**
Program Development Tools	**12.30**
Application Generators	12.30
Macros	12.31
RAD Tools: Visual Basic, Delphi, and PowerBuilder	12.32
HTML	**12.34**
Script and Scripting Languages: Java and PERL	12.36
Summary of Program Development and Programming Languages	**12.37**
Computers at Work: COBOL: Conversion of the Century	**12.38**
In the Future: Verbal Program Development	**12.39**
review	12.40
terms	12.42
yourTurn	12.43
hotTopics	12.44
outThere	12.45
winLabs	12.46

SPECIAL FEATURE

Careers in the Information Age   12.48

CHAPTER 13
Security, Privacy, and Ethics

Objectives	**13.1**
Computer Security: Risks and Safeguards	**13.2**
Computer Viruses	13.2
Virus Detection and Removal	13.4
Unauthorized Access and Use	13.5
Hardware Theft	13.9
Software Theft	13.10
Information Theft	13.11
System Failure	13.13
Backup Procedures	13.15
Disaster Recovery Plan	13.17
Developing a Computer Security Plan	13.19
Information Privacy	**13.20**
Unauthorized Collection and Use of Information	13.20
Employee Monitoring	13.22
Ethics and the Information Age	**13.23**
Information Accuracy	13.23
Codes of Conduct	13.24
Internet Security, Privacy, and Ethics Issues	**13.25**
Internet Security and Privacy	13.25
Objectionable Materials on the Internet	13.27
Summary of Security, Privacy, and Ethics	**13.28**
Computers at Work: Active Badges	**13.30**
In the Future: Taking People at Face Value	**13.31**
review	13.32
terms	13.35
yourTurn	13.36
hotTopics	13.37
outThere	13.38
winLabs	13.39
webWalk	13.40

CHAPTER 14
Multimedia

Objectives	**14.1**
What Is Multimedia?	**14.2**
Text	14.2
Interactive Links	14.3
Still Graphic Images	14.4
Animation	14.5
Audio	14.5
Video	14.6
Multimedia Applications	**14.7**
Computer-Based Training	14.7
Special Education	14.8
Electronic Books and References	14.9
How-To Guides	14.10
Magazines	14.11
Entertainment	14.12
Virtual Reality	14.12
Information Kiosks	14.14
Electronic Marketing and Sales	14.15
The Internet and the World Wide Web Applications	14.15
Multimedia Equipment	**14.16**
Multimedia Personal Computer	14.16
Overhead Projection Systems	14.19
Video Capture Card	14.20
Scanners, Digital Cameras, and Photo CDs	14.20
Laser Disks	14.22
Video Overlay Cards	14.22
Developing Multimedia Applications	**14.23**
Analysis	14.23
Design	14.24
Production	14.25
Multimedia Authoring Software	14.25
Summary of Multimedia	**14.31**
Computers at Work: Multimedia Marketing Hits the Slopes	**14.32**
In the Future: Hybrid CD-ROMs Will Never Be the Same	**14.33**
review	14.34
terms	14.37
yourTurn	14.38
hotTopics	14.39
outThere	14.40
winLabs	14.41
webWalk	14.42

SPECIAL FEATURE

Virtual Reality   14.43

Index   I.1
Photo Credits

PREFACE

Discovering Computers: A Link to the Future, World Wide Web Enhanced is intended for use in a one-quarter or one-semester introductory computer course. No experience with computers is assumed. The material presented provides the most in-depth treatment of introductory computer subjects ever found in a textbook. Students will finish the course with a complete understanding of computers, how to use computers, and how to access information on the World Wide Web. The objectives of this book are as follows:

- Present the fundamentals of computers and computer nomenclature, particularly with respect to personal computer hardware and software and the World Wide Web
- Make use of the World Wide Web as a repository of the latest information in an ever-changing discipline
- Present the material in a visually appealing and exciting, easy-to-understand manner with a format that invites students to learn
- Give students an in-depth understanding of why computers are essential components in the business world and society in general
- Use a fully integrated, hands-on approach to foster an appreciation of the World Wide Web
- Focus on the computer as a valuable productivity tool
- Recognize the personal computer's position as the backbone of the computer industry and emphasize its use as a stand-alone and networked device
- Provide exercises and lab assignments that allow students to interact with a computer and actually learn by using the computer and the World Wide Web
- Present strategies for purchasing, installing, and maintaining a personal computer system

Distinguishing Features

The distinguishing features of this textbook include the following:

The Proven Shelly and Cashman Pedagogy

More than two million students have learned about computers using Shelly and Cashman computer fundamentals textbooks. This new and exciting book is our best work ever. With World Wide Web integration, extraordinary visuality, currency, and the Shelly and Cashman touch, students and teachers alike will find this to be the finest textbook they have ever used.

World Wide Web Enhanced

Each of the Shelly and Cashman computer fundamentals books has included significant educational innovations that have set them apart from all other textbooks in the field. *Discovering Computers* continues this tradition of innovation with its integration of the World Wide Web. The purpose of integrating the World Wide Web into the book is to: (1) offer students additional information on a topic of importance; (2) provide currency; and (3) underscore the relevance of the World Wide Web as a basic information tool that can be used in all facets of society. The World Wide Web is integrated into the book in two central ways:

- Throughout the text, marginal annotations titled *inCyber* provide suggestions on how to obtain additional information via the World Wide Web on an important topic covered on the page.
- Every end-of-chapter page in the book has been stored as a Web page on the World Wide Web. While working on an end-of-chapter page, students can display the corresponding Web page to obtain additional information on a term or exercise and to study for exams. See page xv for more information.

This textbook, however, does not depend on Web access in order to be used successfully. The Web access adds to the already complete treatment of topics within the book.

Visually Appealing

Using the latest technology, the pictures, drawings, and text have been artfully combined to produce a visually appealing and easy-to-understand book. Pictures and drawings reflect the latest trends in computer technology. The pictures, which were chosen for their pedagogical value, allow students to see the actual hardware, software, and other subjects being described in the book. The state-of-the-art drawings are geared toward simplifying the more complex computer concepts. Finally, the text on each page was set to make the book easy to read. This combination of pictures, drawings, and text sets a new standard for computer textbook design.

Latest Computer Trends

The terms and technologies your students see in this book are those they will encounter when they start using computers. Only the latest application software packages are shown throughout the book. New topics and terms include MMX™ technology, network computers, intranets, firewalls, HTML, Java, VBA, Windows CE, T1 lines, ISPs, TCP/IP, MAEs, IP address, MPEG compression, "cookies," and much more.

Chapters on The Internet and the World Wide Web, and on Multimedia

Chapter 7 covers the Internet and World Wide Web, which is the fastest growing area of computer technology. Topics include how the Internet works; browsers; URLs; search tools; firewalls; intranets; and Internet services. Chapter 14 introduces students to the latest in multimedia technology. Topics include multimedia applications and the types of media used in the applications; multimedia hardware and software; and a discussion of leading multimedia software packages.

Computers at Work and In the Future

Each chapter ends with two full pages devoted to features titled *Computers at Work* and *In the Future*. *Computers at Work* presents an example of how the concepts in the chapter are being used today. *In the Future* describes an application that will be available in the future using concepts presented in the chapter.

Shelly Cashman Series Interactive Labs

Eighteen unique, hands-on exercises, developed specifically for this book and free to adopters, allow students to use the computer to learn about computers. Each Lab exercise takes students about 15 minutes to step through. Assessment is available. The exercises are described in detail on page xvi. These same exercises are available with audio for purchase under the title, *Exploring Computers: A Record of Discovery 2nd Edition* (ISBN 0-7895-2839-8).

End-of-Chapter Exercises

Unlike other books on the subject of computer fundamentals, a major effort was undertaken in *Discovering Computers* to offer exciting, rich, and thorough end-of-chapter material to reinforce the chapter objectives and assist you in making your course the finest ever offered. As indicated earlier, each and every one of the end-of-chapter pages is stored as a Web page on the World Wide Web to provide your students in-depth information and alternative methods of preparing for examinations. Each chapter ends with the following:

- **review** This section summarizes the chapter material for the purpose of reviewing and preparing for examinations. Links on the Web page provide additional current information.
- **terms** This listing of the key terms found in the chapter together with the page on which the terms are defined will aid students in mastering the chapter material. A complete summary of all key terms in the book, together with their definitions, appears in the Index at the end of the book. On the Web page, students can click terms to view a definition of the term and a picture of the term.

- **yourTurn** Fill-in and short-answer questions, together with a figure from the chapter that must be labeled, reinforce the material presented within the chapter. Students accessing the Web page can click a question to see a suggested answer.
- **hotTopics** The computer industry is not without its controversial issues. At the end of each chapter, several scenarios are presented that challenge students to critically examine their perspective of technology in society. The Web pages provide links to further challenge students.
- **outThere** Computers are found everywhere. This section provides many out-of-the-classroom projects that send students to the World Wide Web or out of the academic area where interesting discoveries about computers will take place.
- **winLabs** To complete their introduction to computers, students must interact with and use a computer. A series of Windows 95 Lab exercises are presented for student use. Many of these exercises also can be completed in a Windows 3.1 environment. Beginning with the simplest exercises within Windows, students are led through a series of activities that, by the end of the book, will enable them to be proficient in using Windows. Also included in this section are exercises that have students complete the Shelly Cashman Series Interactive Labs.
- **webWalk** In this section, students gain an appreciation for the World Wide Web by visiting interesting and exciting Web pages and completing suggested tasks. The last exercise sends students into a Chat room where they can discuss topics presented in the book with other students throughout the world.

Timeline: Milestones in Computer History

A colorful, highly informative eight-page timeline following Chapter 1 steps students through the major computer technology developments over the past 50 years, including the most recent advances and a glimpse of the future.

Guide to World Wide Web Sites

More than 100 popular Web sites are listed and described in a new guide to Web sites that follows Chapter 7.

Student Guide: How to Purchase, Install, and Maintain a Personal Computer

A nine-page student guide following Chapter 8 introduces students to purchasing, installing, and maintaining a desktop or laptop personal computer.

Special Feature: Careers in the Information Age

This special feature following Chapter 12 provides students with practical information on careers in the computer field, covering planning and prerequisites to maximize their potential opportunities.

Special Feature: Virtual Reality

Following Chapter 14, an eight-page special feature introduces students to the amazing world of virtual reality and how computers are used to create artificial environments they can experience.

Instructor's Support Material

A comprehensive instructor's support package accompanies this textbook in the form of two CD-ROM packages. The two packages, which are titled Instructor's Resource Kit (IRK) and Course Presenter, respectively, are described in the following sections. Both packages are available free to adopters. Two additional products also are available for purchase — a *Study Guide* and *Exploring Computers: A Record of Discovery 2nd Edition*. These products are described on the following pages.

PREFACE xiii

Instructor's Resource Kit (IRK)

The Instructor's Resource Kit (IRK) includes teaching and testing aids. The CD-ROM (ISBN 0-7895-1299-8) is available through your Course Technology representative or by calling 1-800-648-7450. The contents of the IRK are listed below.

- **ElecMan (Electronic Instructor's Manual)** ElecMan is made up of Microsoft Word files. The ElecMan files include the following for each chapter: chapter objectives; chapter overview; detailed lesson plans with page number references; teacher notes and activities; answers to the *winLabs* exercises; test bank (100 true/false, 50 multiple-choice, and 70 fill-in-the-blank questions per chapter); and transparency references. The transparencies are available in Figures on CD-ROM. The test bank questions are numbered the same as in Course Test Manager. You can print a copy of the chapter test bank and use the printout to select your questions in Course Test Manager. You also can use your word processor to generate quizzes and exams from the test bank.
- **Figures on CD-ROM** Illustrations for every picture, table, and screen in the textbook are available in electronic form. Use this ancillary to present a slide show in lecture or to print transparencies for use in lecture with an overhead projector. If you have a personal computer and LCD device, this ancillary can be a powerful tool for presenting your lectures.
- **Course Test Manager** This comprehensive LAN-based testing and assessment system helps instructors design and administer pretests, practice tests, and actual tests. This Windows-based program permits students to take tests online, where test results are available immediately after completion of the exam. Online test scheduling, automatic statistics collection and analysis, and printed tests are only a few of the features.
- **Offline Web Companion** The Offline Web Companion includes a fully functional copy of the Microsoft Internet Explorer 3 Web browser and all the *inCyber* Web pages referenced in the margins of the book. This system allows your students to access the *inCyber* Web pages without being connected to the Internet.
- **Interactive Labs** Eighteen hands-on Interactive Labs exercises that take students about fifteen minutes each to step through help solidify and reinforce computer concepts. Student assessment requires students to answer questions about the contents of the Interactive Labs.
- **winLabs Solutions** These files contain the solutions to the *winLabs* exercises including answers to the assessment questions for the Shelly Cashman Series Interactive Labs.

Course Presenter

Course Presenter (ISBN 0-7895-4262-5) is a multimedia lecture presentation system for *Discovering Computers* that provides PowerPoint slides for every subject in each chapter. Use this presentation system to present well-organized lectures that are both interesting and knowledge-based. Fourteen presentation files are provided for the book, one for each chapter. Each file contains PowerPoint slides for every subject in each chapter together with *optional choices* to show any figure in the chapter as you step though the material in class. More than 40, current, two- to three-minute video clips that reinforce chapter material also are available for *optional presentation*. Course Presenter provides consistent coverage for multiple lecturers.

Study Guide for Discovering Computers: A Link to the Future, World Wide Web Enhanced

This highly popular supplement includes a variety of activities that help students recall, review, and master introductory computer concepts. The *Study Guide* compliments the end-of-chapter material with short answer, fill-in, and matching questions and other challenging exercises (ISBN 0-7895-2849-5).

Exploring Computers: A Record of Discovery 2nd Edition

Exploring Computers: A Record of Discovery 2nd Edition is a supplement to *Discovering Computers*. It may be used in combination with the textbook to augment your students' learning process. With this journal and CD-ROM, students chronicle, analyze, and extend their experiences with an audio version of the Interactive Labs (ISBN 0-7895-2839-8).

Shelly Cashman Online

Shelly Cashman Online is a World Wide Web service available to instructors and students of computer education. Visit Shelly Cashman Online at http://www.scseries.com. Shelly Cashman Online is divided into four areas:

- **Series Information**   Information on the Shelly Cashman Series products.
- **The Community**   Opportunities to discuss your course and your ideas with instructors in your field and with the Shelly Cashman Series team.
- **Teaching Resources**   This area includes password-protected data, course outlines, teaching tips, and ancillaries such as ElecMan.
- **Student Center**   Dedicated to students learning about computers with Shelly Cashman Series textbooks and software. This area includes cool links and much more.

Acknowledgments

The Shelly Cashman Series would not be the most successful computer textbook series ever published without the contributions of outstanding publishing professionals. First, and foremost, among them is Becky Herrington, director of production and designer. She is the heart and soul of the Shelly Cashman Series, and it is only through her leadership, dedication, and untiring efforts that superior products are produced.

Under Becky's direction, the following individuals made significant contributions to this book: Ginny Harvey, series administrator and manuscript editor; Peter Schiller, production manager; Ken Russo, Mike Bodnar, and Greg Herrington, graphic artists; Stephanie Nance, graphic artist and cover designer; Patti Koosed, editorial assistant; Nancy Lamm, proofreader; Sarah Evertson of Image Quest, photo researcher; and Cristina Haley, indexer.

Special thanks go to Jim Quasney, our dedicated series editor; Lisa Strite, senior product manager; Lora Wade, associate product manager; Scott MacDonald, editorial assistant; and Sarah McLean, marketing director.

Our sincere thanks go to Dennis Tani, who together with Becky Herrington, designed this book. In addition, Dennis performed all the layout and typography, executed the magnificent drawings contained in this book, and survived an impossible schedule with goodwill and amazing patience. We are in awe of Dennis's incredible work.

Thanks go to Barbara Ellestad, Michael McQuead, Harry Rosenblatt, and Tim Sylvester, for reviewing the manuscript and to Mike Waggoner for his assistance with Chapter 7.

The efforts of our three contributing authors, John Repede, Misty Vermaat, and Tim Walker, on the chapter-ending material helped make this book extraordinary. Also, thanks to Misty Vermaat for Chapters 11 and 12 and Tom Hall for Chapter 14.

We hope you find using this book an exciting and rewarding experience.

Gary B. Shelly
Thomas J. Cashman
Gloria A. Waggoner
William C. Waggoner

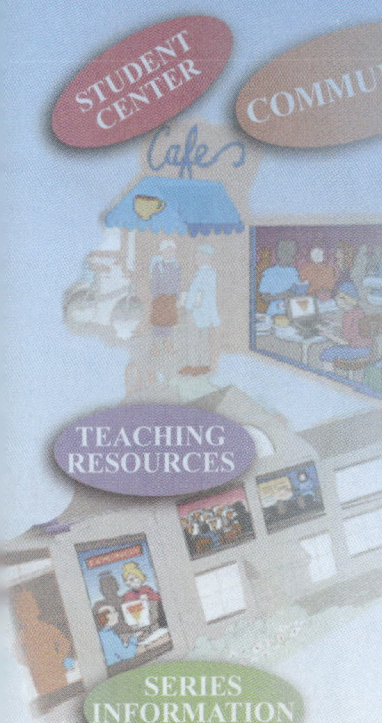

Notes to the Student

If you have access to the World Wide Web, you can obtain current and additional information on topics covered in this book in two ways:

1. Throughout the book, marginal annotations called *inCyber* specify subjects about which you can obtain additional current information. Enter the designated URL and then click the appropriate term on the Web page.

2. Each chapter ends with seven sections titled *review*, *terms* (Figure 1), *yourTurn*, *hotTopics*, *outThere*, *winLabs*, and *webWalk*. The pages in your book are stored as Web pages on the Web. You can visit them by starting your browser and entering the URL in the Shelly Cashman address box at the top of the page. When the Web page displays, you can click any of the links on the page to broaden your understanding of the topics discussed and to obtain the most current information about the topic.

You also can use the sections titled *terms* and *yourTurn* to prepare for examinations. In the *terms* section, display the Web page in your browser and then scroll through the terms. If you do not know the definition of a term, click the term on the Web page for its definition and a picture relating to it. If you click the rocket ship, a Web page will display additional current information about the term. In the *yourTurn* section, determine your answer to a question and then click the blank line to see the suggested answer.

Each time you reference a Web page from *Discovering Computers*, a navigation bar displays (Figure 1). To display a section within a chapter, click the chapter number and then click the section name. For instance, in Figure 1, to display the *outThere* page for Chapter 5, click chapter number 5 and then click outThere. If the chapter number you want already displays in the navigation bar (example: chapter number 1 in Figure 1), then simply click the section you want.

The exercises link displays a page containing links to all exercises in all chapters of the book. The news link displays pages that contain daily news about topics in each chapter of the book. The home link displays the home page for the *Discovering Computers* book. On the home page, if you click any of the section names, a page displays that contains links to the section for all chapters in the book. The index link contains an index/glossary for the entire book, together with definitions and appropriate pictures.

inCyber annotations provide additional current information on a topic

inCyber

For information on aspects of the Internet, including search tools, chat rooms, and home page creation, visit the Discovering Computers Chapter 1 inCyber page (http://www.scsite.com/dc/ch1/incyber.htm) and click Internet.

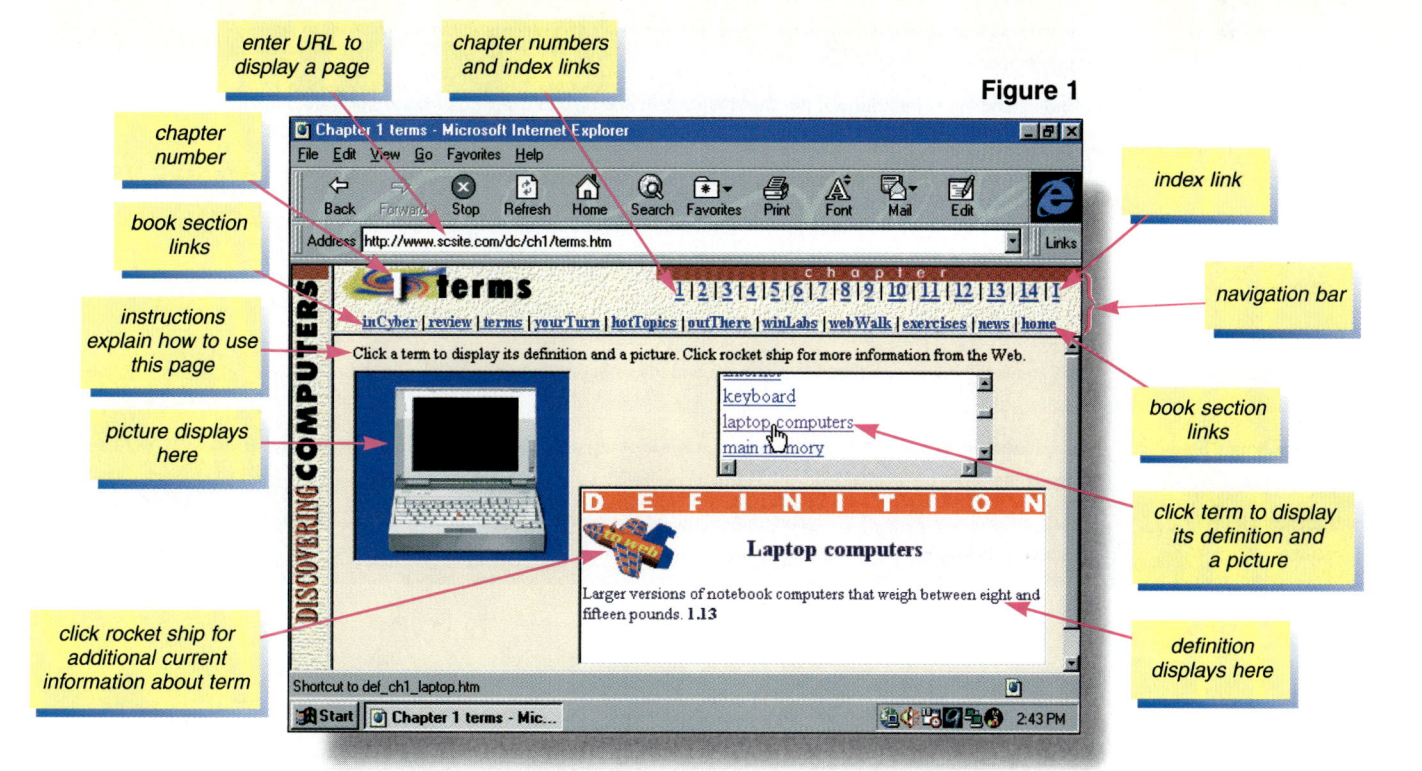

Figure 1

Shelly Cashman Series Interactive Labs

Each of the fourteen chapters in this book includes the *winLabs* hands-on exercises. The 18 Shelly Cashman Series Interactive Labs described below are included in the *winLabs* section. These Interactive Labs, which each take the students approximately 15 minutes to complete using a personal computer, help them gain a better understanding of a specific subject covered in the chapter.

Shelly Cashman Series Interactive Labs

Lab	Function	Page
Using the Mouse	Master how to use a mouse. The Lab includes exercises on pointing, clicking, double-clicking, and dragging.	1.34
Using the Keyboard	Learn how to use the keyboard. The Lab discusses different categories of keys, including the edit keys, function keys, ESC, CTRL, and ALT keys and how to press keys simultaneously.	1.34
Word Processing	Gain a basic understanding of word processing concepts, from creating a document to printing and saving the final result.	2.46
Working with Spreadsheets	Learn how to create and utilize spreadsheets.	2.46
Understanding the Motherboard	Step through the components of a motherboard and build one by adding components. The Lab shows how different motherboard configurations affect the overall speed of a computer.	3.36
Scanning Documents	Understand how document scanners work.	4.53
Setting Up to Print	See how information flows from the system unit to the printer and how drivers, fonts, and physical connections play a role in generating a printout.	4.53
Configuring Your Display	Recognize the different monitor configurations available, including screen size, display cards, and number of colors.	4.53
Maintaining Your Hard Drive	Understand how files are stored on disk, what causes fragmentation, and how to maintain an efficient hard drive.	5.32
Exploring the Computers of the Future	Learn about computers of the future and how they will work.	6.43
Connecting to the Internet	Learn how a computer is connected to the Internet. The Lab presents using the Internet to access information.	7.39
The World Wide Web	Understand the significance of the World Wide Web and how to use Web browser software and search tools.	7.39
Evaluating Operating Systems	Evaluate the advantages and disadvantages of different categories of operating systems.	8.32
Working at Your Computer	Learn the basic ergonomic principles that prevent back and neck pain, eye strain, and other computer-related physical ailments.	8.32
Designing a Database	Create a database structure and optimize a database to support searching.	9.35
Choosing a Programming Language	Differentiate between traditional languages and the newer object-oriented languages.	12.46
Keeping Your Computer Virus Free	Learn what a virus is and about the different kinds of viruses. The Lab discusses how to prevent your computer from being infected with a virus.	13.39
Understanding Multimedia	Gain an understanding of the types of media used in multimedia applications, the components of a multimedia PC, and the newest applications of multimedia.	14.41

An Overview of Using Computers

OBJECTIVES

After completing this chapter, you will be able to:

- Explain the difference between computer literacy and information literacy
- Define the term computer
- Identify the major components of a computer
- Explain the four operations of the information processing cycle: input, process, output, and storage
- Explain how speed, reliability, accuracy, storage, and communications make computers powerful tools
- Identify the categories of computers
- Explain the difference between system software and application software
- Describe how the six elements of an information system work together

CHAPTER 1

Computers play a key role in how individuals work and how they live. Even the smallest organizations have computers to help them operate more efficiently, and many individuals use computers at home for educational, entertainment, and business purposes. Computers also affect people's lives in many unseen ways. Buying groceries at the supermarket, using an automatic teller machine, or making a long-distance phone call all require using computers. The ability to use computers to communicate with other computers also is changing the way people work and live. Today, most computers have communications capabilities that enable them to access information and services around the world 24 hours a day, seven days a week.

As they have for a number of years, personal computers continue to make an increasing impact on our lives. At home, at work, and in the field, these small systems help us do our work faster, more accurately, and in some cases, in ways that previously would not have been possible.

Computer and Information Literacy

Today, most people believe that knowing how to use a computer, especially a personal computer, is a basic skill necessary to succeed in business or to function effectively in society. Given the increasing use and availability of computer systems, such knowledge will continue to be an essential skill. But is just knowing how to use a computer, sometimes called **computer literacy**, enough? Many people now believe that a person should be *information literate* as well as *computer literate*. **Information literacy** is defined as knowing how to find, analyze, and use information. It is the ability to gather information from multiple sources, select the relevant material, and organize it into a form that will allow you to make a decision or take a specific action.

For example, in shopping for a new car, you simply could visit several car dealers and talk to the salespersons about features of the model car in which you are interested. Even if you ask thorough questions and take written notes, your information will be limited to what you are told. As an information literate person, however, you will recognize the need to obtain relevant information about specific vehicles from a variety of sources before making any purchase decision. Such information might include vehicle list price, dealer cost, available options, repair history, and whether or not any recalls have been issued. This type of information is available in several consumer-oriented publications and automobile magazines. With these facts, you will be able to make a more *informed* decision on what car to buy (or not buy). So how do computers relate to information literacy? They relate because, increasingly, information on cars and other products, as well as information on finances, upcoming events, travel, and weather, is available from information sources that can be accessed using computers.

Figure 1-1
Today, most occupations require the use of computers. New applications are being developed every day. Computers help people find, analyze, and use information.

With communications equipment, computers can connect with online information service providers and the **Internet**, which is a global network of computers that houses information on thousands of subjects. Using a computer allows you to obtain up-to-the-minute information in a fast, efficient, and cost-effective manner. Computers have become the tools people use to access and manage information.

The purpose of this book is to give you the knowledge you need to understand how computers work and how computers and resources such as the Internet are used by people and organizations to gather, analyze and use information to make better decisions.

Chapter one will give you an overview of computer concepts. You will begin to learn what a computer is, how it processes data into information, and what elements are necessary for a successful information system. You also will begin to develop a basic vocabulary of computer terminology. While you are reading, remember that this chapter is an overview, and many of the terms and concepts that are introduced will be discussed in more detail in later chapters. Figure 1-1 shows a variety of computers, including personal computers, and their applications. As the photographs illustrate, many occupations now require the use of computers.

Computers affect your life every day and will continue to do so in the future. New uses for computers and improvements to existing technology are being developed continually. Learning about computers and their applications will help you to function effectively in society.

What Is a Computer?

The first question related to understanding computers and their impact on our lives is, "What is a computer?" A **computer** is an electronic device, operating under the control of instructions stored in its own memory unit, that can accept data (input), process data arithmetically and logically, produce results (output) from the processing, and store the results for future use. Most computers also include the capability to communicate by sending and receiving data to other computers and to connect to the Internet. While different definitions of a computer exist, this definition includes a wide range of devices with various capabilities. Often the term computer or **computer system** is used to describe a collection of devices that function together to process data. An example of a computer system is shown in Figure 1-2.

What Are the Components of a Computer?

Data is input, processed, output and stored by specific equipment called computer **hardware**. This equipment consists of input devices, a system unit, output devices, storage devices, and communications devices.

Input Devices

Input devices are used to enter data into a computer. Two common input devices are the keyboard and the mouse. As the data is entered using the **keyboard**, it is temporarily stored in the computer's memory and displayed on the screen of the monitor. A **mouse** is a type of pointing device used to select processing options or information displayed on the screen. The mouse is used to move a small symbol that appears on the screen. This symbol, called a **mouse pointer** or **pointer**, can be many shapes but is usually in the shape of an arrow.

---

inCyber

For details on new opportunities in the information age, visit the Discovering Computers Chapter 1 inCyber page (http://www.scsite.com/dc/ch1/incyber.htm) and click Opportunities.

Figure 1-2
A typical personal computer system.

Monitor
Temporary visual display of information. Most work similarly to televisions by using electrical signals to illuminate dots on the screen that combine to form text and images. (output)

Speaker
Used to amplify audio output such as music. (output)

System Unit
Horizontal or vertical case that contains most of the computer system electronics including the main circuit board (motherboard), central processing unit (CPU), and memory.

Floppy Disk Drive
Used for removable storage media called floppy disks or diskettes. The most common floppy disk size is 3 1/2 inches, which can store up to 1.44 million characters. (storage)

CD-ROM Drive
Most CD-ROM drives use low-powered laser light to read information that has previously been stored on a high-capacity CD-ROM. Some CD-ROM units also can write information on a disk. CD-ROMs can store up to 680 million characters. (storage)

Modem
A communications device that converts signals to and from the computer so that they can travel over telephone lines to other computers. (communications)

Hard Disk Drive
A hard disk drive stores data on spinning non-removable platters. Hard disks come in different sizes that allow them to store more than a billion characters. A panel light indicates when the hard disk is storing or retrieving data. (storage)

Keyboard
The primary input device of most users. The keyboard consists of letter, number, function, and control keys. (input)

Mouse
A type of pointing device that controls the movement of a symbol on the screen called the mouse pointer. Moving the mouse pointer on the screen and pressing buttons on the mouse causes processing actions to take place. (input)

Printer
Produces a permanent copy of computer-generated text and images on paper or other materials. (output)

System Unit

The **system unit** is a box-like case that contains the electronic circuits that cause the processing of data to occur. The electronic circuits usually are part of or are connected to a main circuit board called the **motherboard** or **system board**. The system board includes the central processing unit, memory, and other electronic components. The **central processing unit (CPU)** contains a **control unit** that executes the instructions that guide the computer through a task and an **arithmetic/logic unit** (ALU) that performs math and logic operations. The CPU is sometimes referred to as the **processor**. Figure 1-3 shows an example of a CPU of a personal computer.

Memory, also called **RAM (Random Access Memory)** and **main memory**, temporarily stores data and program instructions when they are being processed.

Other electronics in the system unit include components that work with the input, output, and storage devices. Storage devices and communications devices often are mounted inside the system unit case.

inCyber

For an overview of PC hardware, including discussions of the CPU and memory, visit the Discovering Computers Chapter 1 inCyber page (http://www.scsite.com/dc/ch1/incyber.htm) and click Hardware.

Figure 1-3
This Intel Pentium Pro is used as the CPU for many personal computers. Its microscopic electronic circuits contain 5.5 million transistors that can process instructions in billionths of a second.

Output Devices

Output consists of the results of processing. **Output devices** convert the results into a form that can be understood by the user. Three commonly used **output devices** are a **printer**, a **monitor**, and **speakers**. The printer produces a permanent hard copy while a monitor produces a temporary onscreen display. Speakers are used for audio output.

Storage Devices

Storage devices, sometimes called **secondary storage** or **auxiliary storage devices**, store instructions and data when they are not being used by the system unit. Storage devices often function as an input source when previously stored data is read into memory. A common storage device on personal computers is a **floppy disk drive**, which stores data as magnetic areas on a small removable plastic disk called a **floppy disk**. Another secondary storage device is called a hard disk drive. A **hard disk drive** contains a high-capacity disk or disks that provide greater storage capacities than floppy disks. A **CD-ROM drive** uses a low-powered laser light to read data from removable CD-ROMs.

Communications Devices

Communications devices enable a computer to connect to other computers. A **modem** is a communications device used to connect computers over telephone lines. A **network interface card** is used with communications cable to connect computers that are relatively close together, such as those in the same building. A group of computers connected together is called a **network**.

Peripheral Devices

The devices just discussed are only some of the many types of input, output, storage, and communications devices that can be part of a computer system. Different types of devices will be discussed in more detail in later chapters. A general term for any device connected to the system unit is **peripheral device**.

What Does a Computer Do?

Whether small or large, computers can perform four general operations. These four operations are **input**, **process**, **output**, and **storage**. Together, they comprise the **information processing cycle**. Each of these four operations can be assisted by a computer's ability to communicate with other computers. Collectively, these operations describe the procedures that a computer performs to process data into information and store it for future use.

All computer processing requires data. **Data** refers to the raw facts, including numbers, words, images, and sounds, given to a computer during the input operation. In the processing phase, the computer manipulates and organizes the data to create information. **Information** refers to data that has been processed into a form that has meaning and is useful. The production of information by processing data on a computer is called **information processing**. During the output operation, the information that has been created is put into some form, such as a printed report, that people can use. The information also can be stored electronically for future use.

The people who either use the computer directly or use the information it provides are called **computer users**, **end users**, or simply **users**.

---

inCyber

For details on hard disk drives, visit the Discovering Computers Chapter 1 inCyber page (http://www.scsite.com/dc/ch1/incyber.htm) and click Hard Disk.

Why Is a Computer so Powerful?

The input, process, output, and storage operations that a computer performs may seem very basic and simple. The computer's power, however, is derived from its capability of performing these operations with speed, reliability, and accuracy, and to store large amounts of data and information. A computer's capacity to communicate with other computers increases its input, processing, output, and storage capabilities.

Speed

In a computer, operations occur through the use of electronic circuits contained on small chips. When data flows along these circuits, it travels at close to the speed of light. This allows processing to be accomplished in billionths of a second.

Reliability

The electronic components in modern computers are very reliable due to a low failure rate. The high reliability of the components enables the computer to produce accurate results on a consistent basis.

Accuracy

Computers can process even complex data precisely and accurately, and output error-free information. In fact, most instances of computer error usually can be traced back to other causes, often human mistakes.

Storage

Computers can store enormous amounts of data and keep that data readily available for processing. Using modern storage methods, the data can be quickly retrieved and processed and then re-stored for future use.

Communications

A computer that can communicate with other computers has many more options than a stand-alone computer. If a computer is able to communicate with a remote computer, it can share any of the four information processing cycle operations, input, process, output, and storage, with that remote computer. Communications capability is sometimes referred to as connectivity.

> **inCyber**
> For more information on time and frequency issues, visit the Discovering Computers Chapter 1 inCyber page (http://www.scsite.com/dc/ch1/incyber.htm) and click Speed.

Figure 1-4
*Use of the Internet has been made easier with browser programs such as Microsoft Internet Explorer. Browsers allow you to access World Wide Web sites that have text, graphics, video, and sound and have hypertext links to other information and Web sites. This screen shows how Microsoft Internet Explorer displays the first page of information (called a **welcome page**) located at the Web site of Microsoft Corporation, the developer of Microsoft Internet Explorer.*

CONNECTIVITY 1.9

Connectivity

Connectivity refers to the ability to connect a computer to other computers. The connection may be temporary, such as when a computer is connected to an online information service provider such as America Online, or permanent, such as when a computer is connected to a network of other computers. Connectivity has had a significant impact on the way people use computers. For many years, computers were used as stand-alone devices, limited to the hardware and software resources contained in that computer. Stand-alone computers, however, are becoming the exception.

Most business computers are connected to other computers as part of a network. Even home computers are increasingly used to access other computers to transfer data and to obtain information on practically any subject.

Today, millions of people use a global network of computers, called the **Internet**, to gather information, send messages, and obtain products and services (Figure 1-4). The **World Wide Web (WWW)** portion of the Internet consists of **Web sites**, which are computer sites that can be accessed electronically for information on thousands of topics. Web sites usually present their information in a **multimedia format** that combines text and graphics and can include video and sound. Internet **Web browser programs** enable users to display information and quickly connect to other Internet sites.

---

inCyber

For more information on how various companies are benefiting from connectivity, visit the Discovering Computers Chapter 1 inCyber page (http://www.scsite.com/dc/ch1/incyber.htm) and click Connectivity.

inCyber

For information on aspects of the Internet, including search tools, chat rooms, and home page creation, visit the Discovering Computers Chapter 1 inCyber page (http://www.scsite.com/dc/ch1/incyber.htm) and click Internet.

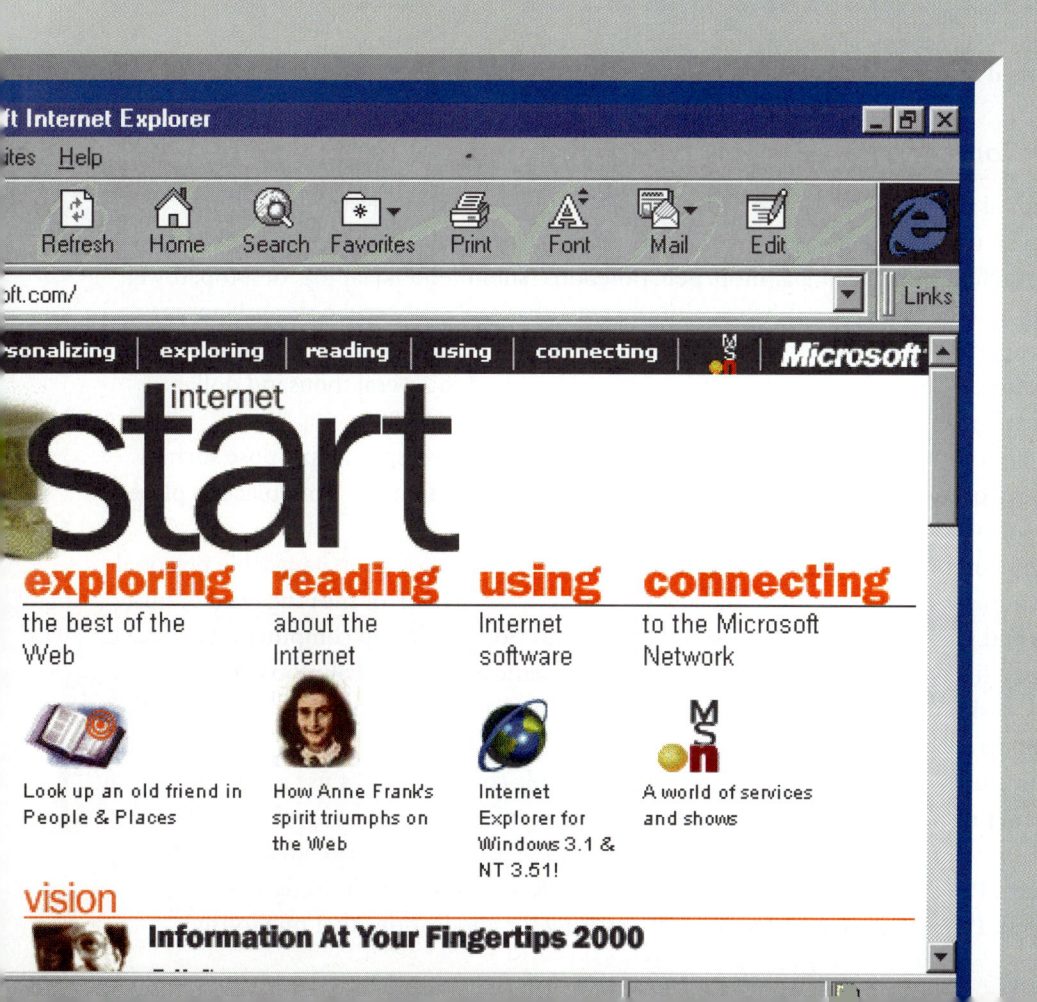

Categories of Computers

The five major categories of computers, which are personal computers, servers, minicomputers, mainframe computers, and supercomputers, are summarized in Figure 1-5.

Computers generally are classified according to their size, speed, processing capabilities, and price. Rapid changes in technology, however, make firm definitions of these categories difficult. This year's speed, performance, and price classification of one catagory may fit next year's classification of another category. Even though they are not firmly defined, the categories are frequently used and should be generally understood.

Category	Physical Size	Speed*	Number of Online Users	General Price Range
Personal Computer	hand-held to desktop or tower	1 to 200 MIPS	usually single user	hundreds to several thousand $
Server	tower or small cabinet	100 to 300 MIPS	2 to 1,000 users	$5,000 to $150,000
Minicomputer	small cabinet to several large cabinets	hundreds of MIPS	2 to 4,000 users	$15,000 to several hundred thousand $
Mainframe	partial to a full room of equipment	hundreds of MIPS	hundreds to thousands of users	$300,000 to several million $
Supercomputer	full room of equipment	thousands of MIPS	hundreds of users	several million $ and up

*speed rated in MIPS; each MIP equals one million instructions per second

Figure 1-5
This table summarizes some of the differences among the categories of computers. Because of rapid changes in technology, these should be considered general guidelines only.

Personal Computers

A **personal computer** (PC), also called **microcomputer** or **micro**, is a small system designed to be used by one person at a time. Classifications within this category, shown in Figure 1-6, include hand-held, palmtop, pen, notebook, subnotebook, laptop, desktop, tower, workstation, and network. Hand-held, palmtop, pen, notebook, subnotebook, and laptop computers are considered portable computers. Depending on their size and features, personal computer prices usually range from several hundred to several thousand dollars. The most expensive personal computers generally are less than $10,000.

Hand-held computers (Figure 1-6a) usually are designed for a specific purpose such as meter reading or inventory counting and are used by workers who move from place to place instead of sitting at a desk.

Palmtop computers (Figure 1-6b) often have several built-in or interchangeable personal information management functions such as a calendar to keep track of meetings and events, an address and phone file, and a task list of things to do. Some palmtop computers also have limited capabilities for typing notes and performing financial analysis. Palmtop computers do not have disk storage devices and usually have a non-standard keyboard, meaning that the keys are not arranged like a typewriter.

Pen computers (Figure 1-6c) are specialized portable computers that use a pen-like device to enter data. Sometimes the pen is used to write information on a special input screen and sometimes it is used as a pointing device to select a processing choice presented on the screen. Pen systems have special software that allows the system to recognize hand-written input. Pen systems have been used successfully for applications that previously

---

inCyber

For information on hand-held computers, visit the Discovering Computers Chapter 1 inCyber page (http://www.scsite.com/dc/ch1/incyber.htm) and click Hand-held.

CATEGORIES OF COMPUTERS **1.11**

required the user to fill out a paper form or checklist. One type of small pen input system is called a **personal digital assistant (PDA)** or **personal communicator** (Figure 1-6d). These hand-held devices are designed for workers on the go and often have built-in communications capabilities that allow the PDA to use voice, fax, or data communications.

Notebook computers (Figure 1-6e) are small enough to be carried in a briefcase but often are transported in their own carrying case. Notebooks are considered general-purpose computers because they can run most application software packages. They have standard keyboards and usually have at least one disk drive for storage. Notebooks usually weigh between four and eight pounds.

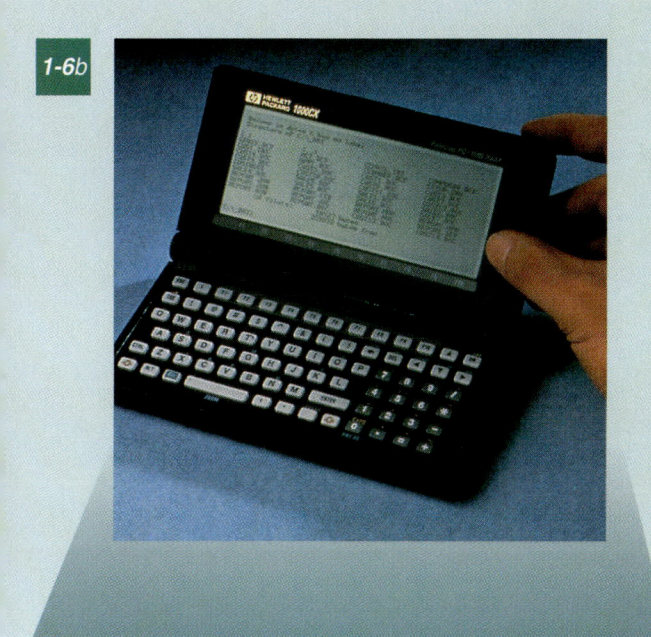

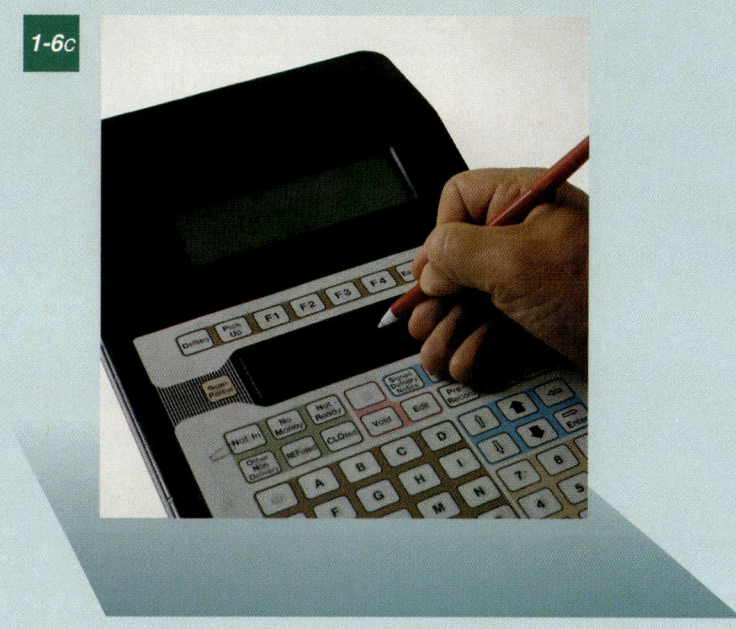

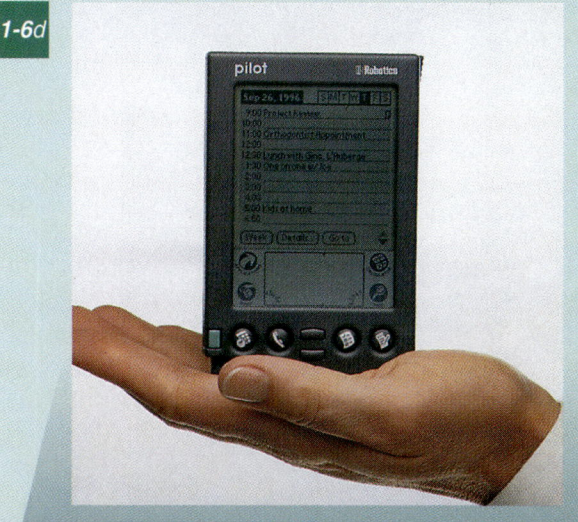

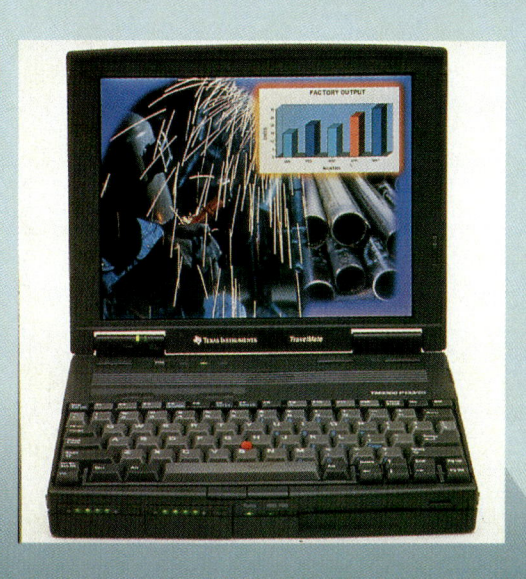

1-6a

1-6b

1-6c

1-6d

1-6e

Figure 1-6
These photographs show the many different types and sizes of personal computers. Shown are (a) hand-held, (b) palmtop, (c) pen, (d) personal digital assistant (PDA), (e) notebook,

(continued on next page)

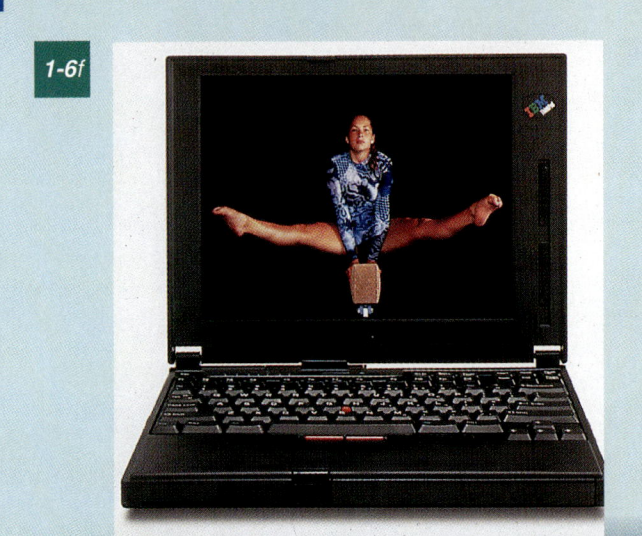

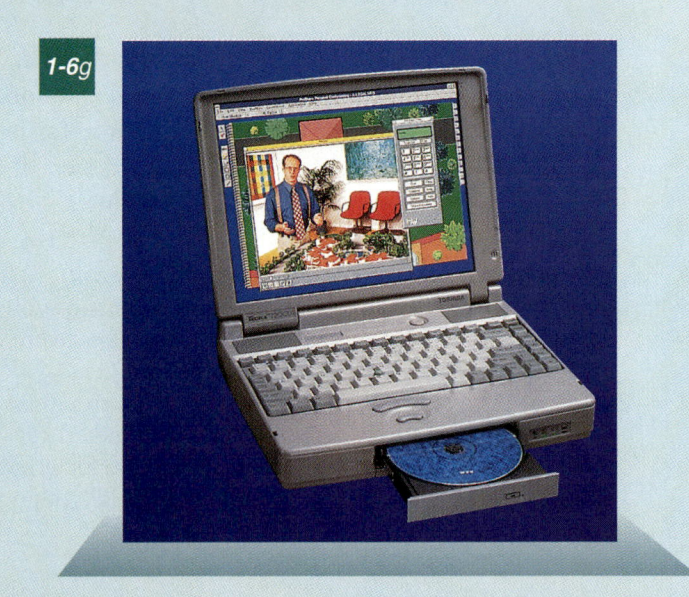

Figure 1-6 *(continued)*
(f) subnotebook (g) laptop, (h) desktop, (i) tower, (j) workstation, (k) network.

Subnotebook computers (Figure 1-6f) are smaller versions of notebook computers and generally weigh less than four pounds. To save weight and space, some subnotebooks do not have disk drives and use special-purpose memory cards for storage.

Laptop computers (Figure 1-6g) are larger versions of notebook computers that weigh between eight and fifteen pounds. The extra weight comes primarily from hard disk storage devices and larger display screens.

Desktop computers (Figure 1-6h) are the most common type of personal computer and are designed to fit conveniently on the surface of a desk or workspace. Desktop computers have separate keyboards and display screens.

Tower computers (Figure 1-6i) are personal computers in an upright case. A full-sized tower case provides more room for expanding the system and adding optional equipment. The more powerful personal computers sometimes are only available in tower cases. A mini-tower case, approximately half the height of a full-sized tower case, usually has less expansion room than a desktop computer but takes up less room on the desk.

Workstations (Figure 6-j) are expensive, high-end personal computers that have powerful calculating and graphics capabilities. Workstations are frequently used by engineers to aid in product design and testing. The term **workstation** also is sometimes used to refer to a personal computer or terminal connected to a network.

Network computers (NC) (Figure 1-6k) are low-cost computers designed to work while connected to a network but not as stand-alone computers. Network computers have limited processing capability and little, if any, storage because these tasks are performed on the network server to which it is attached. Some network computers are designed to use a television monitor as their display device.

inCyber

For more information on servers and network computers, visit the Discovering Computers Chapter 1 inCyber page (http://www.scsite.com/dc/ch1/incyber.htm) and click Server.

Servers

Server computers, shown in Figure 1-7, are designed to support a computer network that allows you to share files, application software, hardware, such as printers, and other network resources. The term **server** really describes how a computer is used. Technically, the term could be applied to any of the other categories of computers if they were used to support a network of other computers. In recent years, however, manufacturers have built computers specifically designed for network use and the term server is becoming widely used to describe this type of computer. Server computers usually have the following characteristics:

- designed to be connected to one or more networks
- the most powerful CPUs available
- multiple CPUs to share the processing tasks (one manufacturer's server can use up to 32 CPUs)
- large memory capacity
- large disk storage capacity
- high-speed internal and external communications capabilities

Small servers look like high-end personal computers and are priced in the $5,000 to $20,000 range. The more powerful servers look and function much like minicomputers and are priced as high as $150,000.

Figure 1-7
Server computers are designed to support a network of other computers. Servers allow the other computers to share data, application software, hardware resources such as printers, and other network resources. Small servers are powerful personal computers dedicated to a server function. The more powerful servers, however, are similar to minicomputers and are specifically designed for use on networks. The more powerful servers contain multiple CPUs, numerous hard disk drives, and large amounts of memory.

Minicomputers

Minicomputers, such as the one shown in Figure 1-8, are more powerful than personal computers and can support a number of users performing different tasks. Originally developed to perform specific tasks such as engineering calculations, their use grew rapidly as their performance and capabilities increased. Today, many businesses and other organizations use minicomputers to support their information processing requirements. These systems can cost from approximately $15,000 up to several hundred thousand dollars. The most powerful minicomputers are called superminicomputers.

Mainframe Computers

Mainframe computers, shown in Figure 1-9, are large systems that can handle hundreds of users connected at the same time, process transactions at a very high rate and, store large amounts of data. Mainframes usually require a specialized environment including separate air conditioning, cooling, and electrical power. Raised flooring is often built to accommodate the many cables connecting the system components underneath. The price range for mainframes is from several hundred thousand dollars to several million dollars.

Figure 1-8
Minicomputers are widely used in businesses to support multiple users.

Figure 1-9
Mainframe computers are large, powerful machines that can handle thousands of users concurrently and process immense volumes of data.

CATEGORIES OF COMPUTERS **1.15**

Supercomputers

Supercomputers, shown in Figure 1-10, are the most powerful category of computers and, accordingly, the most expensive. The capability of these systems to process hundreds of millions of instructions per second is used for such applications as weather forecasting, engineering design and testing, space exploration, and other jobs requiring long, complex calculations (Figure 1-11). These machines cost several million dollars.

inCyber

For general information on supercomputer vendors, visit the Discovering Computers Chapter 1 inCyber page (http://www.scsite.com/dc/ch1/incyber.htm) and click Supercomputer.

Figure 1-10
Supercomputers are the most powerful and expensive computers. They often are used for applications that require complex calculations.

Figure 1-11
This simulated weather pattern was calculated on a supercomputer.

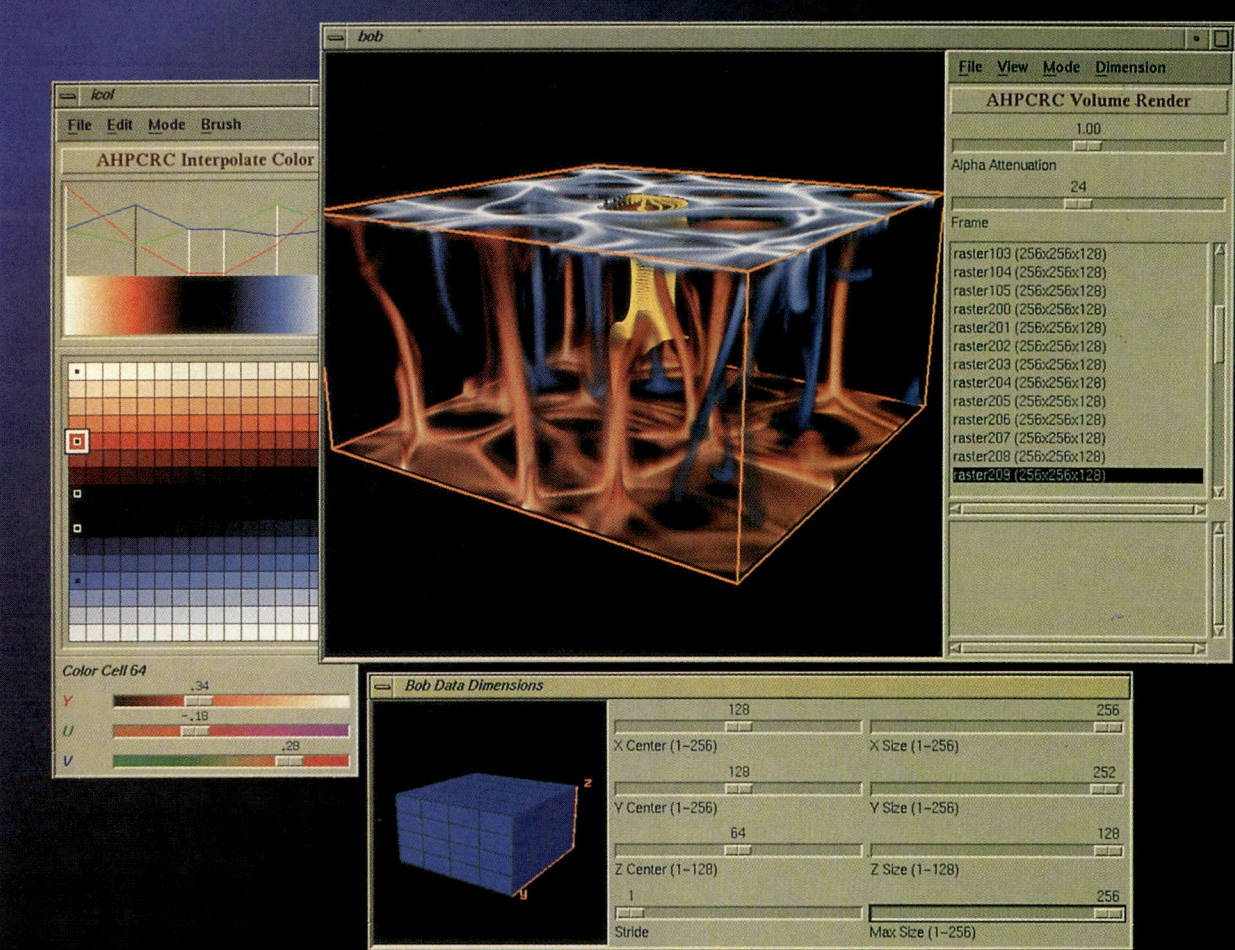

Computer Software

A computer is directed by a series of instructions called a **computer program** (lower screen in Figure 1-12b) that tells the computer what to do. Computer programs are commonly referred to as **software**. Before they can be performed, the program instructions must be loaded from disk into the memory of the computer. Many instructions are used to direct a computer to perform a specific task. For example, some instructions allow data to be entered from a keyboard and stored in memory; some instructions allow data in memory to be used in calculations such as adding a series of numbers to obtain a total; some instructions compare two values stored in memory and direct the computer to perform alternative operations based on the results of the comparison; and some instructions direct the computer to print a report, display information on the screen, draw a color graph on a screen, or store data on a disk.

Most computer programs are written by people with specialized training. These people, called **computer programmers**, write the instructions necessary to direct the computer to process data into information. The instructions must be placed in the correct sequence so the desired results will occur. Complex programs may require thousands of program instructions. Programmers often follow a plan developed by a **systems analyst** who works with both the user and the programmer to determine and design the desired output of the program.

Computer software is the key to productive use of computers. With the correct software, a computer can become a valuable tool. Software can be categorized into two types – system software and application software.

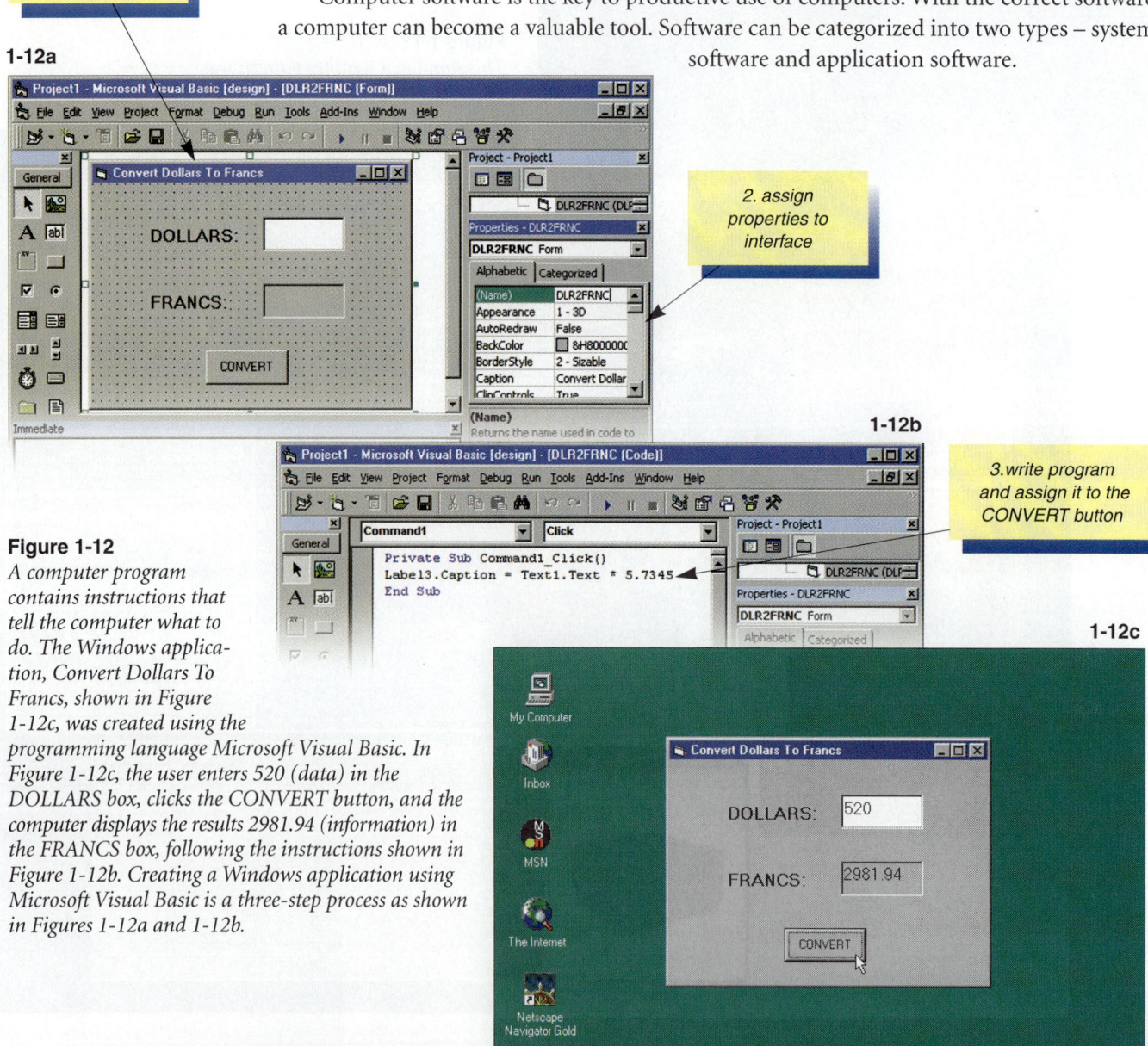

Figure 1-12
A computer program contains instructions that tell the computer what to do. The Windows application, Convert Dollars To Francs, shown in Figure 1-12c, was created using the programming language Microsoft Visual Basic. In Figure 1-12c, the user enters 520 (data) in the DOLLARS box, clicks the CONVERT button, and the computer displays the results 2981.94 (information) in the FRANCS box, following the instructions shown in Figure 1-12b. Creating a Windows application using Microsoft Visual Basic is a three-step process as shown in Figures 1-12a and 1-12b.

System Software

System software consists of programs that are related to controlling the actual operations of the computer equipment. An important part of the system software is a set of programs called the operating system. The instructions in the **operating system** tell the computer how to perform functions such as load, store, and execute a program and transfer data among the system devices and memory. For a computer to operate, an operating system must be stored in memory. Each time a computer is turned on, or restarted, the operating system is loaded from the hard disk and stored in memory. Many different operating systems are available for computers. An important part of the system software is the user interface.

User Interface

The **user interface** determines how you will interact with the computer. The user interface controls how information is presented on the screen and how you enter data and commands. Today, most computers use a graphical user interface. A **graphical user interface (GUI)** provides visual clues like small pictures, or icons, to help you. Each **icon** represents an application software program such as a word processor or a file or document where data is stored. Microsoft Windows 95 (Figure 1-13) is the latest version of Microsoft Windows, the most widely used graphical user interface for personal computers. Apple Macintosh computers also have a graphical user interface that is built into the Macintosh operating system.

inCyber
For more information on the Windows 95 graphical user interface, visit the Discovering Computers Chapter 1 inCyber page (http://www.scsite.com/dc/ch1/incyber.htm) and click GUI.

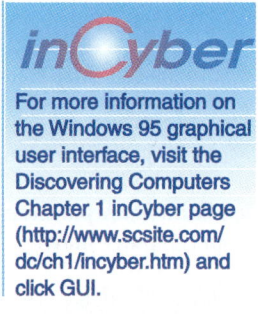

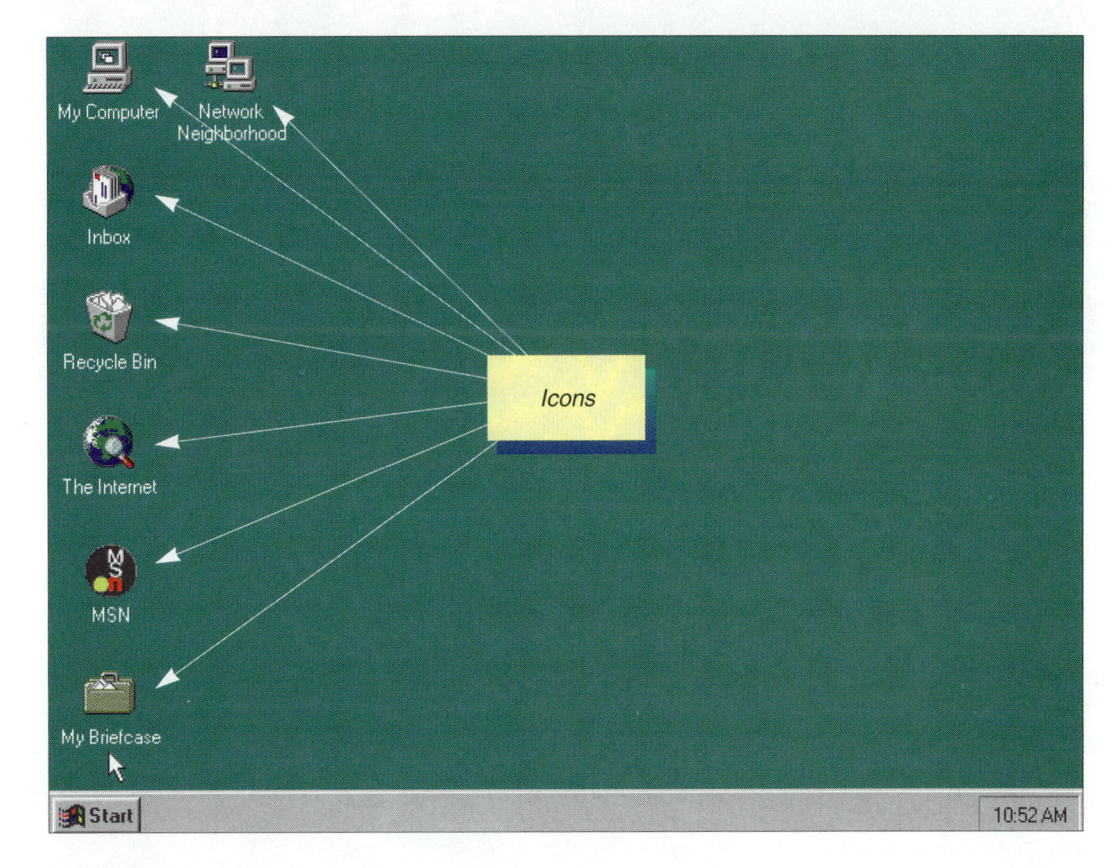

Figure 1-13
A graphical user interface, such as Microsoft Windows 95, makes the computer easier to use. The small pictures, or symbols, on the screen are called icons. The icons represent different processing options that you can choose. The icons (and the processing options) are selected by using a mouse or other pointing device.

1.18 CHAPTER 1 – AN OVERVIEW OF USING COMPUTERS

Application Software

Application software consists of programs that tell a computer how to produce information. Application software resides permanently in storage, such as disk. You load a program into memory when you need to use it. When you think of the different ways that people use computers in their careers or in their personal lives, you are thinking of examples of application software. Business, scientific, and educational computer programs are all examples of application software.

Most computer users do not write their own programs. In some corporations, the information systems department develops custom software programs for unique company applications. Programs required for common business and personal applications can be purchased from software vendors or stores that sell computer products (Figure 1-14). Purchased programs often are referred to as **application software packages**, or simply **software packages**. Some of the more widely used personal computer software packages are word processing, desktop publishing, electronic spreadsheet, presentation graphics, database, communications, and electronic mail (e-mail) software.

> **inCyber**
> For more information on application software packages, visit the Discovering Computers Chapter 1 inCyber page (http://www.scsite.com/dc/ch1/incyber.htm) and click Microsoft.

Figure 1-14
Many programs used for personal and business applications are purchased from computer stores.

1. Software

2. Hardware

3. Data

4. Users

5. Procedures

6. Information Systems Personnel

What Are the Elements of an Information System?

Obtaining useful and timely information from computer processing requires more than just the equipment and software described so far. Other elements required for successful information processing include accurate data, trained information systems personnel, knowledgeable users, and documented procedures. Together, these six elements – software, hardware, data, users, procedures, and information systems personnel – are referred to as an **information system** (Figure 1-15).

For an information system to provide accurate, timely, and useful information, each element in the system must be present and all of the elements must work together. The equipment must be reliable and capable of handling the expected workload. The software must have been carefully developed and tested, and the data entered for processing must be accurate. If the data is incorrect, the information produced from it will be incorrect.

Properly trained information systems personnel are required to run most medium and large computer systems. Even small networks of personal computers usually have a system administrator to manage the system. Users are taking increasing responsibility for the successful operation of information systems. This includes responsibility for the accuracy of both the input and output. In addition, users are taking a more active role in the development of computer applications. They work closely with information systems personnel in the development of computer applications that relate to their areas of work. Finally, all information processing applications should have documented procedures covering not only the computer operations but any other related procedures as well.

Figure 1-15
Six elements combine to make an information system: (1) software, (2) hardware, (3) data to be processed, (4) users who input the data and receive the output, (5) procedures to ensure data is processed accurately and consistently, and (6) information systems personnel to manage the computers.

An Example of How One Company Uses Computers

To show you how a typical mid-sized company might use computers, this section will take you on a visual and narrative tour of Dalton Corporation, a bicycle parts manufacturer. All of the computers at Dalton are joined together in a network that allows the computer users to communicate with one another and share information. In addition, Dalton operates an Internet Web site that provides product and selected company information (Figure 1-16). Customers, vendors, and other interested parties can access this information directly without having to speak to a Dalton employee.

Figure 1-16
Dalton's Internet Web site allows direct access to company and product information.

Reception

Before the installation of a computerized telephone system, a full-time operator was required to answer the telephone and direct the calls. Now, the computerized telephone system routes the calls to the appropriate person or department. If a caller does not want to leave a voice message or requests to talk to an operator, the call is routed to the receptionist (Figure 1-17). The receptionist can use the computer to determine the location of an employee. When employees leave their work areas for a meeting, lunch, or to travel away from the office, they record their destinations or reasons for being away using their computers. The employees can also record any special instructions to the receptionist, such as when they will return or to please hold their calls. If a caller wishes to leave a voice message, the computerized telephone system can play it back for the employee when he or she returns or calls in for messages.

Figure 1-17
The receptionist uses the computer system to locate employees away from their desks, to record messages, and to help with general administrative tasks.

Sales

The Dalton sales department consists of two groups: in-house sales representatives, who handle phone-in and mail-in sales orders and the field sales force, who make sales calls at customer locations. The in-house sales staff use headset telephones (Figure 1-18) so their hands are free to use their computer keyboards. Using the computer while they are on the telephone with a customer allows them to check product availability and the customer's credit status. A computer program also recommends products that complement the products ordered by the customer and displays information on special product promotions.

Outside sales representatives use notebook computers and special communications equipment and software to communicate with the Dalton main office. As with the in-house sales staff, they also can check product availability and customer credit status. If they receive a customer order, they can enter it into the Dalton computer system while they are still at the customer site. In addition, the field sales representatives can use the e-mail capability to check for or send messages.

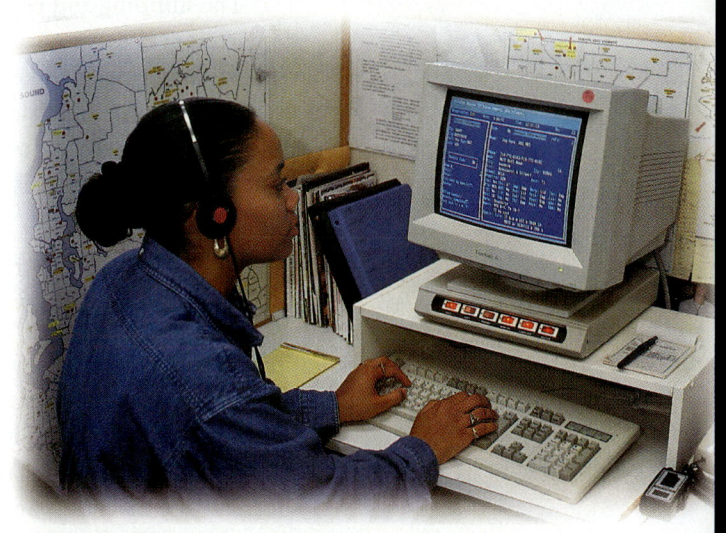

Figure 1-18
Order entry personnel use the computer to check product availability for customers. The system automatically displays additional products the customer may need and information on special product promotions.

Marketing

The marketing department uses the computer system for a number of purposes. Desktop publishing, drawing, and graphics software are used to develop all marketing literature (Figure 1-19). Product brochures on bicycle parts, advertising materials, and product packaging are all produced in-house, saving considerable time and money. The customer service representatives all have computers that allow them to record a variety of customer inquiries. Recording the nature of each customer service inquiry provides for better follow-up (less chance of forgetting an unresolved inquiry) and enables the company to summarize and review why customers are calling. This helps the company identify and resolve potential problems at an early stage. The marketing department also uses a calendar program to schedule product promotions and attendance at trade shows (Figure 1-20).

Figure 1-19
The marketing departments of many companies use desktop publishing and drawing software to create product literature and advertising materials.

Figure 1-20
Calendar programs help users plan their schedules.

Shipping and Receiving

The shipping and receiving department uses the computer system to enter transactions that keep Dalton's inventory records accurate (Figure 1-21). Inventory receipts are first checked against computer records to make sure that Dalton receives only what was ordered. If the received goods match what was ordered, only a single entry has to be made to update the on-hand inventory and purchasing records.

Shipping transactions are also efficient. If all requested items are in stock, only a single entry is required to decrease the inventory and create the information that will be used to prepare the billing invoice. Shipping information, such as the method and time of shipment, can be added to the transaction record so the computer system can be used to provide an up-to-the-minute status of the customer's order.

Figure 1-21
Computers help companies maintain accurate inventory records.

Manufacturing

The manufacturing department uses the computer to schedule production and to record the costs of the items produced. Special manufacturing software matches the availability of production resources such as people, machines, and material against the desired product output. This information allows Dalton to schedule production efficiently and tells them when and how much to buy of the raw materials they need to produce their products. Actual labor, material, and machine usage is recorded on the manufacturing floor using special workstations designed to be used in industrial environments (Figure 1-22). This information is entered into the computer system automatically to update inventory, production, payroll, and cost accounting records.

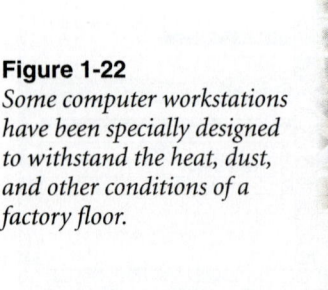

Figure 1-22
Some computer workstations have been specially designed to withstand the heat, dust, and other conditions of a factory floor.

Product Design

The product design department uses computer-aided design (CAD) software to design new products (Figure 1-23). CAD software allows the designers to create and review three-dimensional models of new products on the computer before expensive molds are required. If a design is approved, the CAD software can automatically produce a list of the required parts.

Figure 1-23
Computer-aided design (CAD) software is used to design new products. As with word processing software, CAD programs make the design process easier by allowing you to make changes until you are satisfied.

Accounting

The accounting department is one of the largest computer system users. Many of the accounting records are the result of transactions entered in the user departments, such as shipping and receiving and manufacturing. These records are used to pay vendor invoices, bill customers for product sales, and process the Dalton employee payroll (Figure 1-24). The accounting transactions are summarized automatically to produce Dalton's financial statements, which are used internally to monitor financial performance and given to outside organizations such as banks.

Figure 1-24
Accounting departments were one of the first users of computer systems and still rely heavily on computers to summarize financial transactions.

Human Resources

The human resources department uses the computer system to keep track of information on existing, past, and potential employees (Figure 1-25). Besides the standard information required for payroll and employee benefits, the system keeps track of employees job skills and training. This information enables the human resources department to review the records of existing employees first when a new job becomes available.

Figure 1-25
Human resources departments use computers to keep track of past, present, and potential employees.

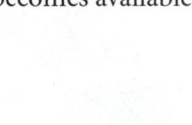

Figure 1-26
Information systems personnel help maintain the computer system by using performance measurement software to monitor system use.

Information Systems

A primary responsibility of the information systems department is to keep the existing system running and determine when and if new equipment or software is required. To help answer these questions, the information systems personnel use diagnostic and performance measurement software that tells them how much the system is being used and if system problems are being encountered (Figure 1-26). A systems analyst works with users to design custom software for user applications for which application software packages do not exist. A computer programmer then uses this design to write the program instructions necessary to produce the desired processing results and output.

Executive

The senior management staff of Dalton Corporation (the president and three vice presidents) use the computer as an executive information system (EIS). The EIS summarizes information such as actual sales, order backlog, number of employees, cash on hand, and other performance measures into both a numeric and graphic display (Figure 1-27). The EIS is designed specifically for executives who may not work regularly with computers and want only to see summarized information.

Figure 1-27
Executive information system (EIS) software usually presents summarized data and often uses charts and graphs to convey information.

Summary of How One Company Uses Computers

The computer applications just discussed are only some of the many potential uses of the computers within Dalton Corporation. In addition, employees in each of the departments can use the computer for preparing correspondence, project and task management, budgeting, and sending messages via electronic mail. As shown in the Dalton Corporation example, computers are used throughout an organization. Employees use computers to perform a variety of tasks related to their job areas. Because of the widespread use of computers, most organizations prefer to hire employees with computer experience and knowledge.

Summary of an Overview of Using Computers

This chapter presented a broad introduction to concepts and terminology that are related to computers. You now have a basic understanding of what a computer is, how it processes data into information, and what elements are necessary for a successful information system. You also have seen some examples of different types of computers and how they are used. Reading and understanding the overview of using computers this chapter should help you to understand these topics as they are presented in more detail in following chapters.

COMPUTERS AT WORK

Shopping for an Auto Online

Figure 1-28a

Shopping for a car or truck used to be a time-consuming process. Time was spent traveling to and from car dealers or locating the hard-to-find owner selling a used vehicle. Now, with a computer and a communications link, much of the work can be done online.

All of the major online services provide many resources for obtaining information on new and used vehicles. One of the best-looking references is CarPoint available on The Microsoft Network (MSN). CarPoint contains information and color photographs of more than 250 models from nearly 50 manufacturers. With CarPoint, you can browse through the models randomly or use built-in search capabilities to create a list that meets your specific desires. Once you have narrowed your choice to a specific model, you can request a report that gives detailed information on prices and other features. While the basic CarPoint information is free to MSN subscribers, the detailed reports cost $4.95 to download onto your computer.

Figure 1-28b

Not ready for a new car? Don't worry, even more information is available on used cars on various Internet Web sites. A good way to start gathering information is to do a keyword search on "cars" or "automotive." One Web site that may be familiar to vehicle shoppers is operated by the company that publishes the *Auto Trader* magazines (http://www.traderonline.com). Auto Trader® Online lets you search for a vehicle based on specific model and price range information. With Auto Trader® Online, you also can specify a beginning and ending year range. To localize the search, you can request to see only vehicles in a particular telephone area code, state, or region. The Auto Trader search returns a list of vehicles with two to four lines of description. Not shown are the seller's phone numbers. For $1.00, you can purchase the list with the phone numbers included. Auto Trader® Online also has information on new cars and has links to the Web sites of all the major car manufacturers. To verify that a used car price is reasonable, or to help

Figure 1-28c

determine the value of your car or truck, you can review the values published by *Edmund's Automobile Buyer's Guide* at its Internet site (http://www.edmunds.com/). Edmund's provides pricing and other information on the last ten years of most models.

If you are ready to buy or lease a new vehicle, Auto-By-Tel operates an Internet buying and leasing service (http://www.autobytel.com). Enter the features and options of the vehicle you want, and Auto-By-Tel will find a local dealer willing to sell or lease it to you at a wholesale price.

You may not get as much exercise, but the ability to research, compare, locate, and finance a vehicle from the comfort of your computer chair does offer some advantages. About the only thing you cannot do online is kick the tires!

IN THE FUTURE

From the Global Village to the Local Village

Much of the information written about the Internet focuses on specific Web sites that provide specialized information or services. These Web sites are literally spread around the world and have contributed to the concept of an "electronic global village" where Internet citizens, sometimes called *netizens,* can access worldwide information resources. Another, however, more local trend is developing, that may offer more value to the average person.

Numerous cities are now establishing community networks whose primary goal is to provide information to local citizens. One of the leaders of this movement is Blacksburg, in southwestern Virginia. The Blacksburg Electronic Village (BEV) (http://www.bev.net) was started in 1994. The goal of the BEV is to link its citizens to each other and to local business, civic, and government organizations.

One of the widely used services is e-mail, which allows BEV users to keep in touch with each other and register their opinions on local issues with city and county representatives. The BEV Village Mall has almost 200 businesses, each with its own custom-designed presentation of products or services. Some businesses advertise and others allow users to place orders online. The Community Events and News section lists information about upcoming arts and entertainment. Other sections of the BEV offer information on health services, area museums, and local schools. To encourage people to use the network and to help struggling users, BEV offers an online Help Desk to anyone experiencing problems.

Although Blacksburg is recognized worldwide as the leading electronic community, others are not far behind. Other leading electronic communities include Palo Alto, California (http://www.city.paloalto.ca.us), Taos, New Mexico (http://laplaza.taos.nm.us), and Boulder, Colorado (http://bcn.boulder.co.us). The list of communities that offer at least some online information is growing rapidly. An Internet Web site exists that keeps track of community pages by state and provides information on how to create a community Web site.

What are the social implications of the electronic communities? Some people are concerned that the substitution of electronic meetings for face-to-face gatherings is not healthy. Others say that networks such as BEV make communicating with new people easier and often lead to face-to-face meetings. These same issues were raised in the past with other technological changes such as the telephone and television. You still may not be able to fight city hall, but at least in the future you can bombard them with e-mail.

Figure 1-29a

Figure 1-29b

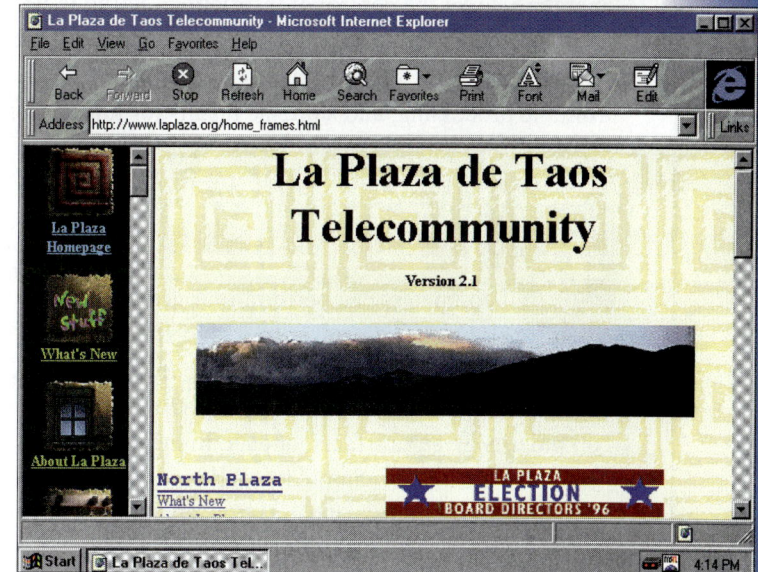

Figure 1-29c

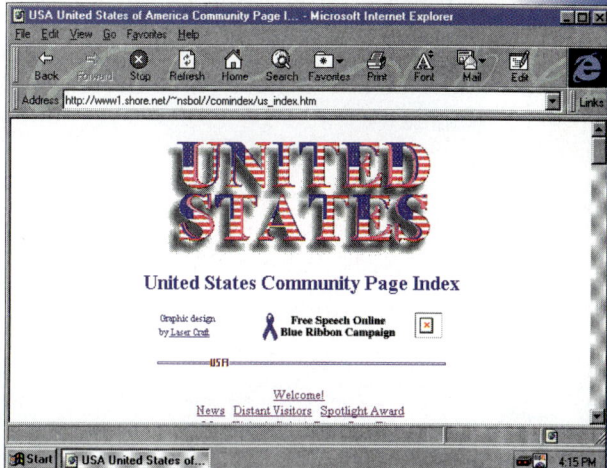

review

inCyber | review | terms | yourTurn | hotTopics | outThere | winLabs | webWalk | exercises | news | home

INSTRUCTIONS: *To display this page from the Web, launch your browser and enter the URL, http://www.scsite.com/dc/ch1/review.htm. Click the links for current and additional information.*

1. Computer Literacy vs. Information Literacy

Most people believe knowing how to use a computer, sometimes called **computer literacy**, is a basic skill necessary to succeed in business or to function in society. Many people feel, however, that a person should be *information literate* as well as *computer literate*. **Information literacy** is defined as knowing how to find, analyze, and use information.

2. Computers

Increasingly, the information people need is available from sources that can be accessed using computers. A **computer** is an electronic device, operating under the control of instructions stored in its memory unit, that can accept data (input), process data arithmetically and logically, produce results (output) from the processing, and store the results for future use.

3. Computer Systems

The term **computer system** frequently is used to describe the collection of devices that functions together to process data. This equipment, often called computer **hardware**, consists of input devices, a system unit, output devices, storage devices, and communications devices. **Input devices** are used to enter data. The **system unit** contains the electrical circuits that cause the processing of data to occur. **Output devices** convert the results of processing into a form that can be experienced by the user. **Storage devices** store instructions and data when they are not being used. **Communications devices** enable a computer to connect to other computers.

4. Information Processing

All computers can perform four general operations: **input**, **process**, **output**, and **storage**. Together, these operations comprise the **information processing cycle**. During the input operation, a computer is given raw facts, or data. In the processing phase, the computer manipulates and organizes the data to create information — data in a form that is useful and has meaning. The production of information by processing data on a computer is called **information processing**. During the output operation, the information created is put into a form that people can use. Informa-tion also can be stored electronically for future use.

5. Computer Power

A computer's power is derived from its capability of performing the operations of the information processing cycle with speed, reliability, and accuracy, and its capacity for storing large amounts of data and information. Data travels at close to the speed of light and processing is accomplished in billionths of a second.

6 Connectivity

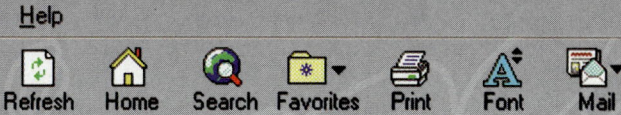

A computer's ability to communicate with other computers increases its input, processing, output, and storage capabilities. **Connectivity** refers to the ability to connect a computer to other computers, either temporarily or permanently. Today, millions of people use the **Internet**, a global network of computers, to gain information, send messages, and obtain products or services. The **World Wide Web (WWW)** portion of the Internet consists of computer sites, called **Web sites**, that can be accessed electronically for information on thousands of topics.

7 Personal Computers

Computers generally are classified according to their size, speed, processing capabilities, and price. Although rapid changes in technology make firm definitions difficult, computers can be grouped into five major categories: personal computers, server computers, minicomputers, mainframe computers, and supercomputers. **Personal computers** are small systems intended to be used by one person at a time. Classifications within this category include **hand-held, palmtop, pen, notebook, subnotebook, laptop, desktop, tower, workstation,** and **network**.

8 Other Computer Categories

Server computers are a category of computers designed to be part of a computer network. **Minicomputers** are more powerful than personal computers and can support a number of users performing different tasks. **Mainframe** computers can handle thousands of users at the same time, store large amounts of data, and process transactions at a very high rate. **Supercomputers**, the most powerful and expensive category of computers, are capable of processing hundreds of millions of instructions per second.

9 Computer Programs

A computer is directed by a series of instructions called a **computer program**, or **software**. Software can be categorized into two types: system software and application software. **System software** consists of programs related to controlling the actual operations of computer equipment. Important parts of system software are the **operating system**, which tells the computer how to perform basic functions, and the **user interface**, which determines how the user interacts with the computer. **Application software** consists of programs that tell a computer how to produce information. Purchased programs are called **application software packages**, or simply **software packages**.

10 Information Systems

Obtaining useful and timely information from computer processing requires equipment, software, accurate data, trained information systems personnel, knowledgeable users, and documented procedures. Together, these six elements are referred to as an **information system**. All of the elements must work together. Equipment has to be reliable and capable of handling the workload. Software must be carefully developed and tested. Data needs to be entered correctly. Trained information systems personnel are necessary to manage the system. Users are responsible for the accuracy of both input and output and are taking an active role in the development of computer applications. Finally, all information processing applications should have documented procedures covering computer and related operations.

1.30 terms

Shelly Cashman: http://www.scsite.com/dc/ch1/terms.htm

chapter 1 terms

1 | 2 | 3 | 4 | 5 | 6 | 7 | 8 | 9 | 10 | 11 | 12 | 13 | 14 | 1

inCyber | review | terms | yourTurn | hotTopics | outThere | winLabs | webWalk | exercises | news | home

INSTRUCTIONS: To display this page from the Web, launch your browser and enter the URL, http://www.scsite.com/dc/ch1/terms.htm. Scroll through the list of terms. Click a term for its definition and a picture. Click the rocket ship for current and additional information about the term.

laptop computers

DEFINITION

laptop computers
Larger versions of notebook computers that weigh between eight and fifteen pounds. **(1.13)**

application software (1.18)
application software packages (1.18)
arithmetic/logic unit (ALU) (1.6)
auxiliary storage devices (1.7)

CD-ROM drive (1.7)
central processing unit (CPU) (1.6)
communications devices (1.7)
computer (1.4)
computer literacy (1.2)
computer program (1.16)
computer programmers (1.16)
computer system (1.4)
computer users (1.7)
connectivity (1.9)
control unit (1.6)

data (1.7)
desktop computers (1.13)

end users (1.7)

floppy disk (1.7)
floppy disk drive (1.7)

graphical user interface (GUI) (1.17)

hand-held computers (1.10)
hard disk drive (1.7)
hardware (1.4)
home page (1.8)

icon (1.17)
information (1.7)
information literacy (1.2)

information processing (1.7)
information processing cycle (1.7)
information system (1.19)
input (1.7)
input devices (1.4)
Internet (1.3, 1.9)

keyboard (1.4)

laptop computers (1.13)

main memory (1.6)
mainframe computers (1.14)
memory (1.6)
micro (1.10)
microcomputer (1.10)
minicomputers (1.14)
modem (1.7)
monitor (1.6)
motherboard (1.6)
mouse (1.4)
mouse pointer (1.4)
multimedia format (1.9)

network (1.7)
network computers (NC) (1.13)
network interface card (1.7)
notebook computers (1.11)

operating system (1.17)
output (1.6, 1.7)
output devices (1.6)

palmtop computers (1.10)
pen computers (1.10)

peripheral device (1.7)
personal communicator (1.11)
personal computer (PC) (1.10)
personal digital assistant (PDA) (1.11)
pointer (1.4)
printer (1.6)
process (1.7)
processor (1.6)

RAM (Random Access Memory) (1.6)

secondary storage (1.7)
server (1.13)
server computers (1.13)
software (1.16)
software packages (1.18)
speakers (1.6)
storage (1.7)
storage devices (1.7)
subnotebook computers (1.13)
supercomputers (1.15)
system board (1.6)
system software (1.17)
system unit (1.6)
systems analyst (1.16)

tower computers (1.13)

user interface (1.17)
users (1.7)

Web browser programs (1.9)
Web sites (1.9)
workstations (1.13)
World Wide Web (WWW) (1.9)

Start | terms | 1:02 AM

yourTurn

chapter 1 | 2 | 3 | 4 | 5 | 6 | 7 | 8 | 9 | 10 | 11 | 12 | 13 | 14 | I

inCyber | review | terms | yourTurn | hotTopics | outThere | winLabs | webWalk | exercises | news | home

INSTRUCTIONS: *To display this page from the Web, launch your browser and enter the URL, http://www.scsite.com/dc/ch1/turn.htm. Click a blank line for the answer. Click the links for current and additional information.*

Label the Figure

1. _____
2. _____
3. _____
4. _____
5. _____
6. _____

Instructions: Identify each element of an information system

Fill in the Blanks

Instructions: Complete each sentence with the correct term or terms.

1. A(n) _____ is an electronic device, operating under the control of instructions stored in its memory unit, that can accept input, process the input arithmetically and logically, produce output from processing, and store the results for future use.
2. The information processing cycle is comprised of four operations: _____, _____, _____, and _____.
3. During information processing, a computer manipulates and organizes _____ to create _____.
4. The _____ portion of the Internet consists of computer sites that can be accessed electronically for information on thousands of topics.
5. _____ write the instructions necessary to direct a computer to process data into information, often following a plan developed by a(n) _____.

Short Answer

Instructions: Write a brief answer to each of the following questions.

1. What is the difference between computer literacy and information literacy? _____
2. What are the components of a computer system? How does each component contribute to information processing? _____
3. What capabilities make a computer a powerful tool? Describe each. How does a computer's ability to communicate enhance a computer's power? _____
4. According to what characteristics are computers generally classified? Describe each category of computers. _____
5. What is computer software? How is system software different from application software? _____

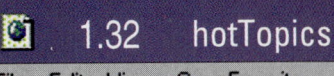

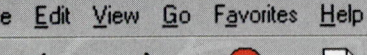

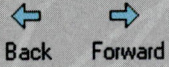

hotTopics

chapter 1 | 2 | 3 | 4 | 5 | 6 | 7 | 8 | 9 | 10 | 11 | 12 | 13 | 14 | I

inCyber | review | terms | yourTurn | hotTopics | outThere | winLabs | webWalk | exercises | news | home

INSTRUCTIONS: *To display this page from the Web, launch your browser and enter the URL, http://www.scsite.com/dc/ch1/hot.htm Click the links for current and additional information to help you respond to the hotTopics questions.*

1 *Most people feel that knowing how to use a computer is an essential skill.* Nevertheless, when one thousand Americans were asked in a recent MIT poll which of eight inventions they could not live without, the personal computer tied for last, along with the blow-dryer. The automobile, lightbulb, telephone, television, aspirin, and microwave oven were all perceived as more indispensable than the personal computer. Is the belief in the importance of computer literacy inconsistent with the results of this poll? Why or why not? How might the characteristics of the people questioned have affected the results? How would you rank the importance of computers compared to the other inventions in the list? Why?

2 *Many technological innovations have been "double-edged swords," with both positive and negative* effects on society at large. The automobile, for example, has allowed people to travel freely and extended the availability of goods and services; at the same time, however, it has increased air pollution and contributed to thousands of serious accidents. Together with a classmate, present a debate on the effect computers have had on society. One of you should argue that their impact primarily has been positive, while the other should contend that their impact primarily has been negative. When the debate is over, see if you, together with all of your classmates, can reach a consensus regarding the overall impact of computers on society.

3 *Not only has computer literacy become an integral part of school curriculums, the* use of computers also has affected other areas of study. For example, an increasing number of elementary schools has abandoned the teaching of cursive writing, instead promoting keyboarding skills. Many students are learning how to type in first grade, even as they discover how to print. A noted educator points out that if something has to be eliminated — printing, cursive, or keyboard — then cursive is the logical choice. Many systems have rejected the traditional loops and flourishes of cursive in favor of a simpler style that can keep pace with computer keyboards. In what other ways might the use of computers change what schools teach? How will computers make your son's or daughter's elementary school education different from yours? In general, are these changes positive or negative? Why?

4 *In 1995, a problem-plagued computer system in Albany, New York, finally "crashed," losing* almost 26,000 photo driver's licenses. Affected motorists were given extensions and temporary licenses and asked to have their pictures retaken, at no additional cost and without having to wait in line again. Although the company leasing the system corrected the problem at no cost to the state, both motorists and state workers were inconvenienced by the system's failure. Despite the reliability of computers, everyone has heard of similar computer errors. Describe a situation with which you are familiar where a similar computer error occurred. Who, or what, was responsible for the error? What steps could be taken to ensure that the error does not happen again?

5 *Your school has been given a grant to purchase a supercomputer, a mainframe computer,* several minicomputers, and a number of personal computers. How do you think each category of computer would be best used in your school? Who should have access to each computer? If the money for personal computers had to be spent on three different types of personal computers, what kind do you think should be purchased and how should they be used?

DISCOVERING COMPUTERS

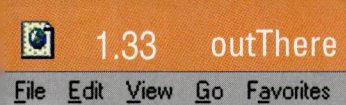

outThere

chapter
1 | 2 | 3 | 4 | 5 | 6 | 7 | 8 | 9 | 10 | 11 | 12 | 13 | 14 | I

inCyber | review | terms | yourTurn | hotTopics | outThere | winLabs | webWalk | exercises | news | home

DISCOVERING COMPUTERS

INSTRUCTIONS: To display this page from the Web, launch your browser and enter the URL, http://www.scsite.com/dc/ch1/out.htm. Click the links for current and additional information.

1 *For a few people, using a computer is still a novel experience. Increasingly,* however, computer use is becoming a fact of life. Does familiarity really breed contempt (as the old saying maintains)? Perhaps instead it engenders affection or only fosters indifference. Interview a person who uses a computer every day at work, and prepare a brief report on that person's feelings about computers. How does the person use the computer? Did he or she experience any initial anxiety when first confronting the computer? If so, did he or she overcome it? What type of training did the individual receive? With hindsight, what type of training would be recommended? How does a computer make the job easier or more difficult? Overall, how does the individual feel about computers?

2 *Computers have changed the way people access information. For example,* once avid newspaper readers now can turn instead to sites on the World Wide Web offered by their favorite tabloids. Some of the more recognizable names include *The New York Times,* the *Boston Globe, The Wall Street Journal,* the *San Francisco Chronicle,* and *USA TODAY.* How is the online rendering of a periodical different from the printed version? Purchase a newspaper that is represented on the World Wide Web and compare the printed paper to its Web site. How are they similar? How are they different? What are the advantages and disadvantages of each? In general, which do you prefer? Why?

3 *Are computers purchased by individuals from a broad spectrum, or does a certain type represent* most computer buyers? Visit a computer vendor and interview the manager or a salesperson about computer purchasers. Based on the interview, prepare a report on the demographics of computer buyers at that store. What gender are most buyers? In what age range do they fall? What is the average age group? What seems to be the typical educational level? What is the approximate average income of a typical buyer? Do buyers share any other characteristics? Why do most purchasers buy a computer?

4 *As the automobile led to the end of the horse and buggy, does* the growth of the Internet herald the demise of printed media? Probably not; in fact, many booksellers are turning to the Internet to promote their wares. Three of the largest bookstores online are Amazon, Chapter One, and Book Stacks Unlimited. Visit a bookstore Web site and compare searching for a book online to seeking a book in a traditional bookstore. Try looking for a particular title, a book by a certain author, and books on a specific subject. What are the advantages and disadvantages of shopping for a book online? How likely would you be to buy a book through a bookstore Web site? Why?

5 *Computers have had an important part in some major movies. How does Hollywood view* computers? Rent a videotape in which a computer plays a significant role — some examples are *2001: A Space Odyssey, War Games, Short Circuit, Virtuosity, Hackers,* and *The Net.* Watch the videotape, and then prepare a report on how the movie maker seems to view computers. What part do computers play in the movie? In general, are computers heroes, villains, or simply tools (for good or evil) of human characters? Why? What was the theme of the movie? What role, if any, did computers have in promoting the movie's theme?

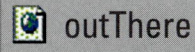

winLabs

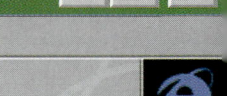

chapter 1 | 2 | 3 | 4 | 5 | 6 | 7 | 8 | 9 | 10 | 11 | 12 | 13 | 14 | I

inCyber | review | terms | yourTurn | hotTopics | outThere | winLabs | webWalk | exercises | news | home

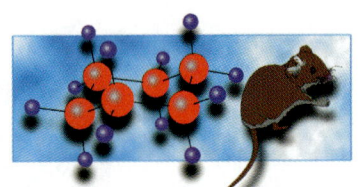

INSTRUCTIONS: *To display this page from the Web, launch your browser and enter the URL, http://www.scsite.com/dc/ch1/labs.htm. Click the links for current and additional information.*

1. Shelly Cashman Series Mouse Lab

Click the Start button on the taskbar; point to Programs on the Start menu; point to Shelly Cashman Series Labs on the Programs submenu; and then click Interactive Labs on the Shelly Cashman Series Labs submenu. When the Shelly Cashman Series Labs screen displays (Figure 1-30), if Using the Mouse is not selected, press the UP ARROW or DOWN ARROW key to select it. Press ENTER. Carefully read the objectives. With your printer on, press the P key on the keyboard to print the questions. Fill out the top of the Questions sheet and then answer the questions.

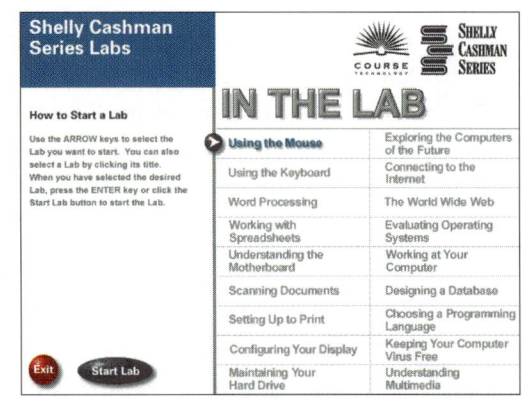

Figure 1-30

2. Shelly Cashman Series Keyboard Lab

Follow the instructions in winLab 1 above to display the Shelly Cashman Series Labs screen. Click Using the Keyboard. Click the Start Lab button. When the initial screen displays, carefully read the objectives. With your printer on, click the Print Questions button. Fill out the top of the Questions sheet and then answer the questions.

3. Learning What's New in Microsoft Windows 95

Click the Start button on the taskbar, and then click Help on the Start menu. Click the Contents tab in the Help Topics: Windows Help dialog box. Double-click the Introducing Windows book; double-click the Welcome book; double-click the A List of What's New book (Figure 1-31); and then double-click the A new look and feel topic. Click each topic in the Windows Help window and then read the information. Answer the following questions as you step through the topics: (1) What are two uses of the Start button? (2) Where is the My Computer icon located? (3) How do you start Windows Explorer? (4) Are spaces legal characters in a file name? (5) How do you display a shortcut menu for an item? Click the Close button.

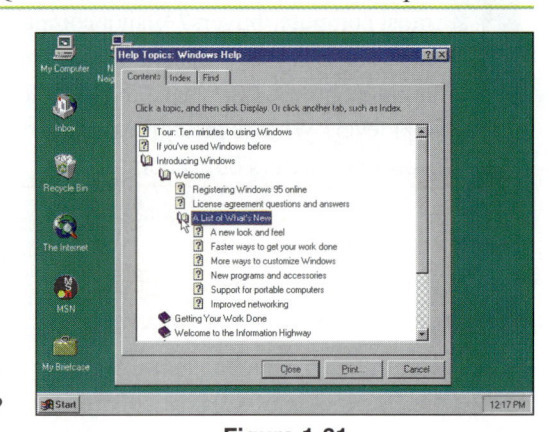

Figure 1-31

4. Improving Mouse Skills

Click the Start button on the taskbar; point to Programs; point to Accessories on the Programs submenu; point to Games on the Accessories submenu; and then click Solitaire on the Games submenu. When the Solitaire window displays, click its Maximize button. Click Help on Solitaire's menu bar, and then click Help Topics. Click the Contents tab, and then double-click the How to play Solitaire topic. Read and print the topic by clicking the Solitaire Help window's Options button, clicking Print Topic, and then clicking the OK button. Close the Solitaire Help window by clicking its Close button. Play the game of Solitaire. Quit Solitaire by clicking its Close button.

webWalk

chapter 1 | 2 | 3 | 4 | 5 | 6 | 7 | 8 | 9 | 10 | 11 | 12 | 13 | 14 | I

inCyber | review | terms | yourTurn | hotTopics | outThere | winLabs | webWalk | exercises | news | home

INSTRUCTIONS: *To display this page from the Web, launch your browser and enter the URL, http://www.scsite.com/dc/ch1/walk.htm. Click the exercise link to display the exercise.*

1. Information Literacy
Today, most people believe that knowing how to use a computer is a basic skill necessary to function successfully in society. Information literacy is knowing how to find, analyze and use information. You can increase your information literacy by completing this exercise.

2. PDA Enhancements
One type of small pen input computer system is called a personal digital assistant (PDA). These hand-held devices often have built-in communications capabilities that allow the PDA to use voice, fax, or data communication. To learn about products designed to enhance PDAs, complete this exercise.

3. Supercomputers
Supercomputers are the most powerful and expensive category of computers. These systems are capable of processing hundreds of millions of instructions per second. To view pictures of supercomputers (Figure 1-32) and learn more about them, complete this exercise.

Figure 1-32

4. Computer Glossary
RAM, ROM, MIPS, FLOPS. If you are perplexed by all the computer buzzwords, you can complete this exercise to help you sort it all out (Figure 1-33).

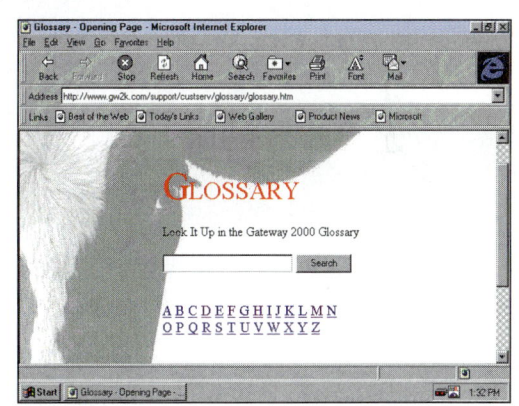

Figure 1-33

5. Information Mining
Complete this exercise to improve your Web research skills by using a Web search engine to find information related to this chapter.

6. Communications
A computer's ability to communicate with other computers increases its information retrieval capabilities. Complete this exercise to search a large database for information.

7. Web Commerce
Today, millions of people use the Internet to gain information, send messages, and purchase products and services. Complete this exercise to learn more about commerce on the Web.

8. Connectivity
Connectivity has had a significant impact on the way people use computers. To see some future possiblities of coupling connectivity with the latest software technology, complete this exercise.

9. Web Chat
Complete this exercise to enter a Web Chat discussion related to the issues presented in the hotTopics exercise.

TIMELINE

Milestones in Computer History

1937

Dr. John V. Atanasoff and his assistant Clifford Berry designed and began to build the first electronic digital computer during the winter of 1937-38. Their machine, the Atanasoff-Berry-Computer, or ABC, provided the foundation for the next advances in electronic digital computers.

1943

During the years 1943 to 1946, Dr. John W. Mauchly and J. Presper Eckert, Jr. completed the ENIAC (Electronic Numerical Integrator and Computer), the first large-scale electronic digital computer. The ENIAC weighed thirty tons, contained 18,000 vacuum tubes, and occupied a thirty-by-fifty-foot space.

1945

Dr. John von Neumann is credited with writing a brilliant report in 1945 describing several new hardware concepts and the use of stored programs. His breakthrough laid the foundation for the digital computers that since have been built.

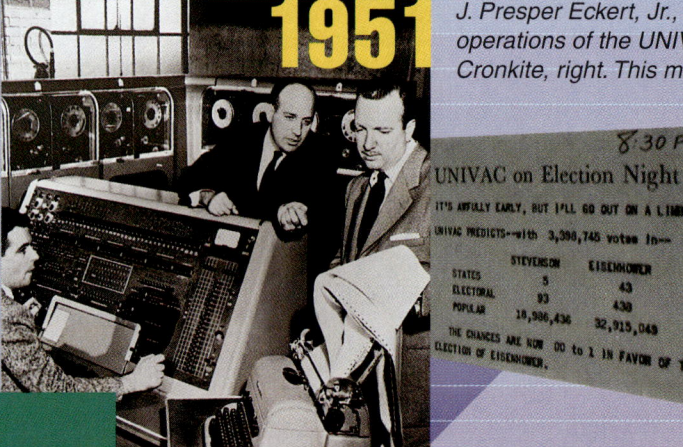

1951

J. Presper Eckert, Jr., standing left, explains the operations of the UNIVAC I to newsman Walter Cronkite, right. This machine was the first commercially available electronic digital computer.

Public awareness of computers increased when, in 1951, the UNIVAC I, after analyzing only 5% of the tallied vote, correctly predicted that Dwight D. Eisenhower would win the presidential election.

IN 1951-52

after much discussion, IBM decided to add computers to its line of business equipment products. This led IBM to become a dominant force in the computer industry.

MILESTONES IN COMPUTER HISTORY 1.37

In 1952, Dr. Grace Hopper, a mathematician and commodore in the U.S. Navy, wrote a paper describing how to program a computer with symbolic notation instead of the detailed machine language that had been used.

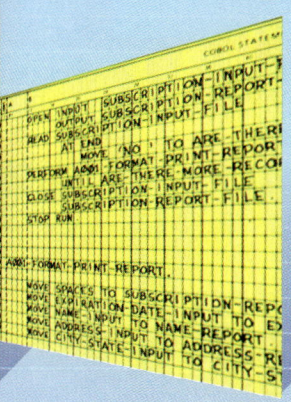

Dr. Hopper was instrumental in developing high-level languages such as COBOL, a business application language introduced in 1960. COBOL uses English-like phrases and runs on most computers, making it one of the more widely used languages in the world.

1952

The IBM model 650 was one of the first widely used computer systems. Originally, IBM planned to produce only 50 machines, but the system was so successful that eventually it manufactured more than 1,000.

1953

Core memory, developed in the early 1950s, provided much larger storage capacities and greater reliability than vacuum tube memory.

1957

FORTRAN (FORmula TRANslator) was introduced in 1957, proving that efficient, easy-to-use programming languages could be developed. FORTRAN is still in use.

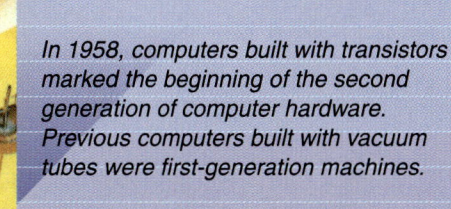

In 1958, computers built with transistors marked the beginning of the second generation of computer hardware. Previous computers built with vacuum tubes were first-generation machines.

1958

BY 1959 more than 200 programming languages had been created.

MILESTONES IN COMPUTER HISTORY

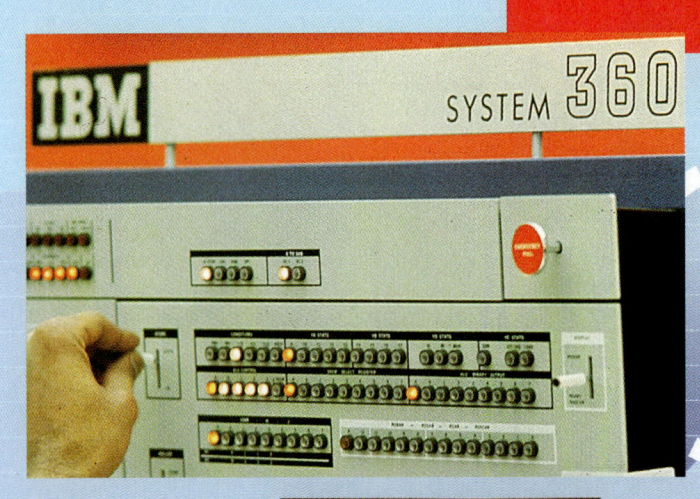

1960 From 1958 to 1964, the number of computers in the U.S. grew from 2,500 to 18,000.

1964 Third-generation computers, with their controlling circuitry stored on chips, were introduced in 1964. The IBM System/360 computers were the first third-generation machines.

In 1965, Dr. John Kemeny of Dartmouth led the development of the BASIC programming language. BASIC still is used widely on personal computers.

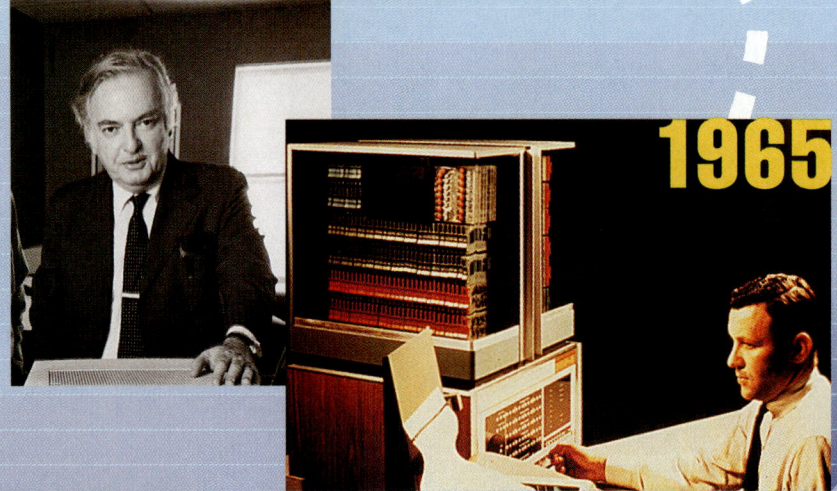

1965 Digital Equipment Corporation (DEC) introduced the first minicomputer in 1965.

1967 Pascal, a structured programming language, was developed by Swiss computer scientist Niklaus Wirth between 1967 and 1971.

1968 The software industry emerged in the 1960s. In 1968, Computer Science Corporation became the first software company to be listed on the New York Stock Exchange.

1969 ARPANET network established. Predecessor of the Internet.

MILESTONES IN COMPUTER HISTORY   1.39

1969 In 1969, under pressure from the industry, IBM announced that some of its software would be priced separately from the computer hardware. This "unbundling" allowed software firms to emerge in the industry.

1970 The fourth-generation computers built with chips that used LSI (large-scale integration) arrived in 1970. The chips used in 1965 contained as many as 1,000 circuits. By 1970, the LSI chip contained as many as 15,000.

In 1971, Dr. Ted Hoff of Intel Corporation developed a microprocessor, or microprogrammmable computer chip, the Intel 4004.

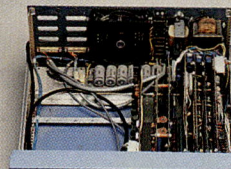

1971

1975 The MITS, Inc. Altair computer, sold in kits for less than $400, was the first commercially successful microcomputer.

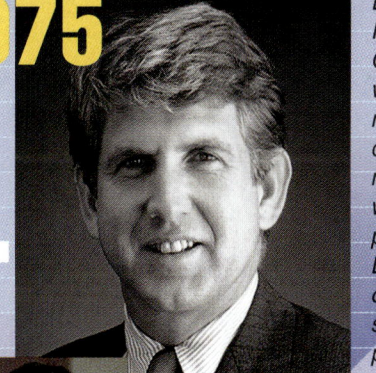

Ethernet, developed at Xerox PARC (Palo Alto Research Center) by Robert Metcalfe, was the first local area network (LAN). Originally designed to link minicomputers, Ethernet was later extended to personal computers. The LAN allows computers to communicate and share software, data, and peripherals such as printers.

1975

In 1976, Steve Wozniak and Steve Jobs built the first Apple computer.

1976

1.40 MILESTONES IN COMPUTER HISTORY

1979 The first public online information services, CompuServe and the Source, were founded.

The VisiCalc spreadsheet program written by Bob Frankston and Dan Bricklin was introduced in 1979. This product originally was written to run on Apple II computers. Together, VisiCalc and Apple II computers rapidly became successful. Most people consider VisiCalc to be the singlemost important reason why personal computers gained acceptance in the business world.

1980 In 1980, IBM offered Microsoft Corporation's founder, Bill Gates, the opportunity to develop the operating system for the soon-to-be announced IBM personal computer. With the development of MS-DOS, Microsoft achieved tremendous growth and success.

1981 The IBM PC was introduced in 1981, signaling IBM's entrance into the personal computer marketplace. The IBM PC quickly garnered the largest share of the personal computer market and became the personal computer of choice in business.

1982 More than 300,000 personal computers were sold in 1981. In 1982, the number jumped to 3,275,000.

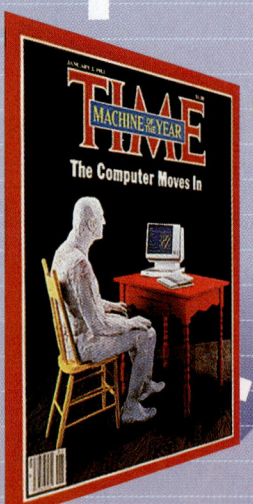

1983 Instead of choosing a person for its annual award, TIME magazine named the computer "Machine of the Year" for 1982. This event acknowledged the impact of the computer on society.

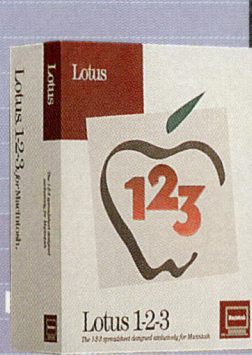

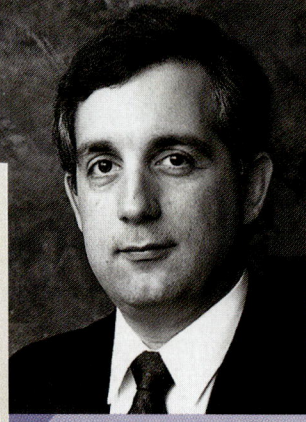

The Lotus 1-2-3 integrated software package, developed by Mitch Kapor, was introduced in 1983. It combined spreadsheet, graphics, and database programs in one package.

MILESTONES IN COMPUTER HISTORY   1.41

1984

IBM introduced a personal computer, called the PC AT, that used the Intel 80286 microprocessor.

Apple introduced the Macintosh computer, which incorporated a unique graphical interface, making it easy to learn.

1987

Several personal computers utilizing the powerful Intel 80386 microprocessor were introduced in 1987. These machines handled processing that previously only large systems could handle.

1989

The Intel 486 became the world's first 1,000,000 transistor microprocessor. It crammed 1.2 million transistors on a sliver of silicon that measured .4" x .6" and executed instructions at 15 MIPS (million instructions per second) – four times as fast as its predecessor, the 80386 chip. The 80 designation used with previous Intel chips, such as the 80386 and 80286, was dropped with the 486.

1990

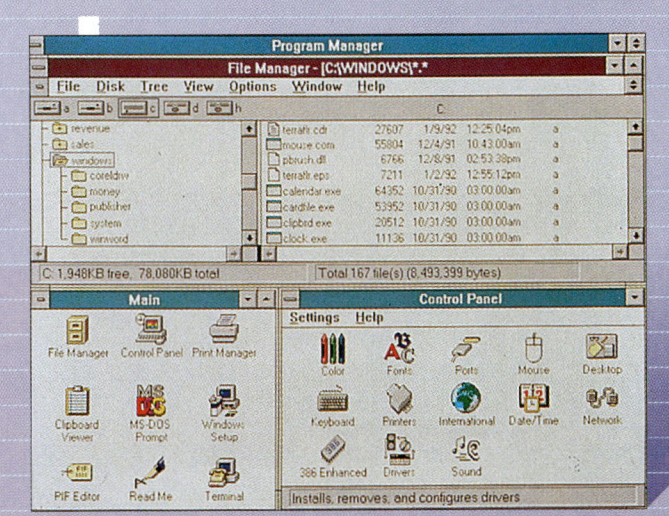

Microsoft released Windows 3.0, a substantially enhanced version of its Windows graphical user interface first introduced in 1985. The software allowed users to run multiple applications on a personal computer and more easily move data from one application to another. The package became an instant success, selling hundreds of thousands of copies.

1.42 MILESTONES IN COMPUTER HISTORY

BY 1990
more than 54 million computers were in use in the United States.

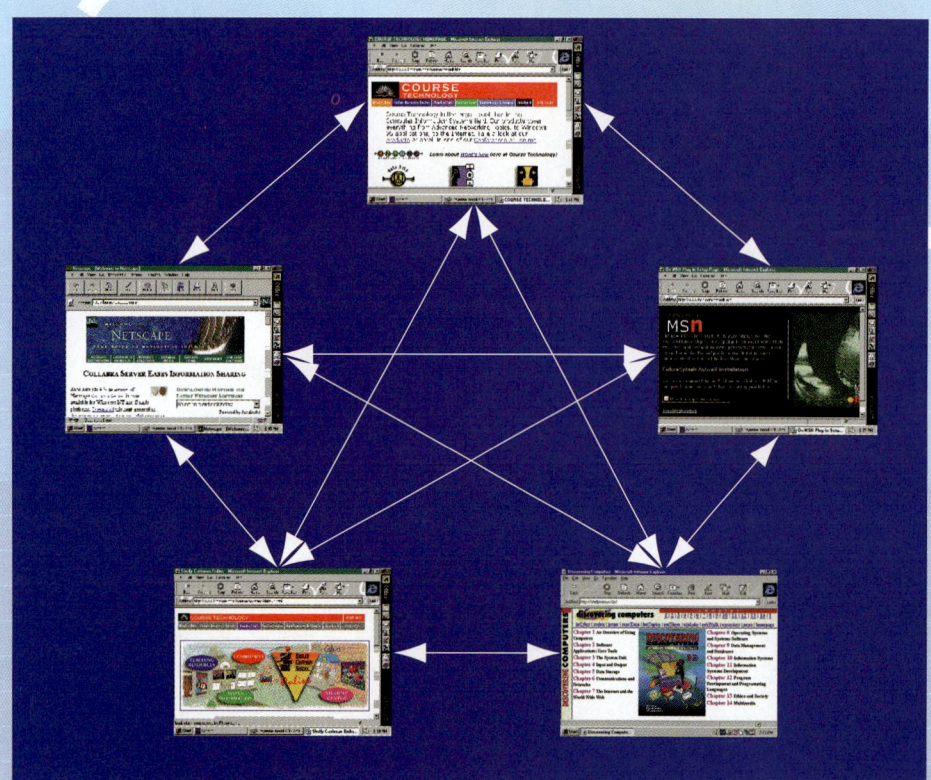

1991
World Wide Web standards released describing the framework for linking documents on different computers.

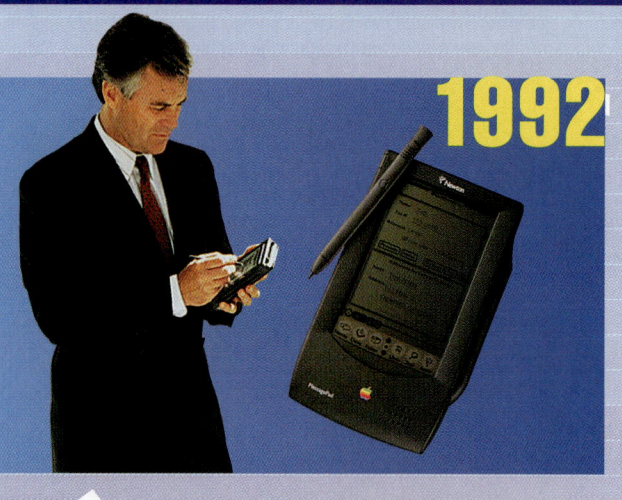

1992
Apple introduced a personal digital assistant (PDA) called the Newton MessagePad. This 7 1/4-by-4 1/2-inch personal computer incorporates a pen interface and wireless communications.

1993
Several companies introduced computer systems using the Pentium microprocessor from Intel. The Pentium chip is the successor to the Intel 486 microprocessor. It contains 3.1 million transistors and is capable of performing 112 million instructions per second (MIPS).

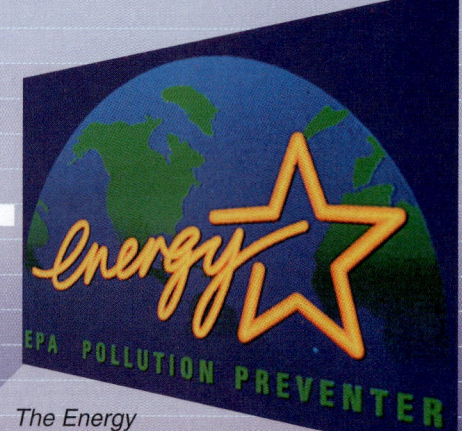

The Energy Star program, endorsed by the Environmental Protection Agency (EPA), encouraged manufacturers to build computer equipment that meets strict power consumption guidelines. Manufacturers meeting the guidelines then can display the Energy Star logo on their products.

MILESTONES IN COMPUTER HISTORY 1.43

1993 — Mosaic graphical Web browser was created by Marc Andreesen. This success ultimately led to the organization of Netscape Communications Corporation.

1995 — Intel begins shipment of the Pentium Pro microprocessor, the successor to its widely used Pentium chip. The Pentium Pro microprocessor contains 5.5 million transistors and is capable of performing 250 million instructions per second (MIPS).

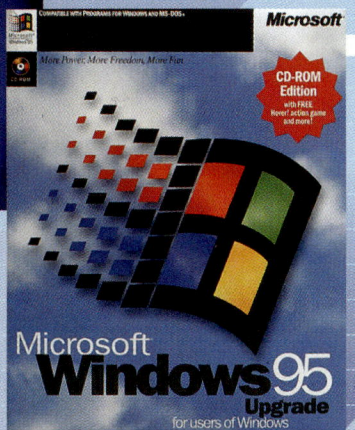

Microsoft releases Windows 95, a major upgrade to its Windows operating system, the leading graphical user interface for PCs. Windows 95 consists of more than 10 million lines of computer instruction developed by 300 person-years of effort. More than 50,000 individuals and companies tested the software before it was released.

IN 1996 — 2 out of 3 employees in the United States have access to a PC. 1 out of every 3 homes has a PC.

MORE THAN 50 million PCs were sold worldwide. More than 250 million are in use.

1997 — 50 million Internet and World Wide Web users; 15 million Internet host computers; Microsoft releases Office 97 with major Web enhancements integrated into Word, Excel, PowerPoint and Access.

"BY THE YEAR 2011, the microprocessor could have one billion transistors and might be capable of performing 100 billion instructions per second."

Dr. Andrew Grove, Chairman and CEO
Intel Corporation
"A Revolution in Progress"
COMDEX/Fall '96 Keynote Address

Software Applications: User Tools

OBJECTIVES

After completing this chapter, you will be able to:

- Define and describe a user interface and a graphical user interface
- Explain the key features of widely used software applications
- Explain the advantages of integrated software and software suites
- Explain object linking and embedding
- List and describe learning aids and support tools that help you to use personal computer software applications

CHAPTER 2

Today, understanding the applications commonly used on personal computers is considered a part of being computer literate. In fact, a working knowledge of at least some of these applications is now considered by many employers to be a required skill. Because of this, personal computer software applications are discussed early in this book. Learning about widely used applications will help you understand how people use personal computers in the modern world. Before discussing the applications, the operating system and the user interface are explained. The user interface controls how you work with the software and applies to all the applications. After learning about individual applications, you will learn about integrated software and software suites that combine several applications. The section on object linking and embedding will explain how data can be shared between applications. Finally, some of the aids and tools that are available to help you learn and use software applications are discussed.

The Operating System and User Interface

Before any application software is run, the operating system must be loaded from the hard disk into the memory of the computer and started. The **operating system** tells the computer how to perform functions such as processing program instructions and transferring data between input and output devices and memory. The operating system usually is loaded automatically from the hard disk when a computer is turned on and is always running until the computer is turned off. Once the operating system is loaded, application programs such as productivity software can be run.

All software, including the operating system, is designed to communicate with you in a certain way. The way the software communicates with you is called the user interface. A **user interface** is the way you tell the software what to do and the way the computer displays information and processing options to you. One of the more common user interfaces is the graphical user interface (GUI). The **graphical user interface**, or **GUI** (pronounced gooey), combines text and graphics to make the software easier to use. Graphical user interfaces include several common features such as icons, windows, menus, and buttons.

Icons are small pictures that are used to represent processing options, such as an application or a program, or documents, such as a letter (Figure 2-1).

A **window** is a rectangular area of the screen that is used to present information (Figure 2-1). Many people consider windows to be like multiple sheets of paper on top of a desk. In the same way that each piece of paper on the desk contains different information, each window on the screen contains different information. Just as papers can be moved from the bottom of a pile to the top of the desk when they are needed, windows can be displayed on a screen and moved around to show information when it is needed. The term Windows, with a capital W, refers to **Microsoft Windows**, the most popular graphical user interface for personal computers.

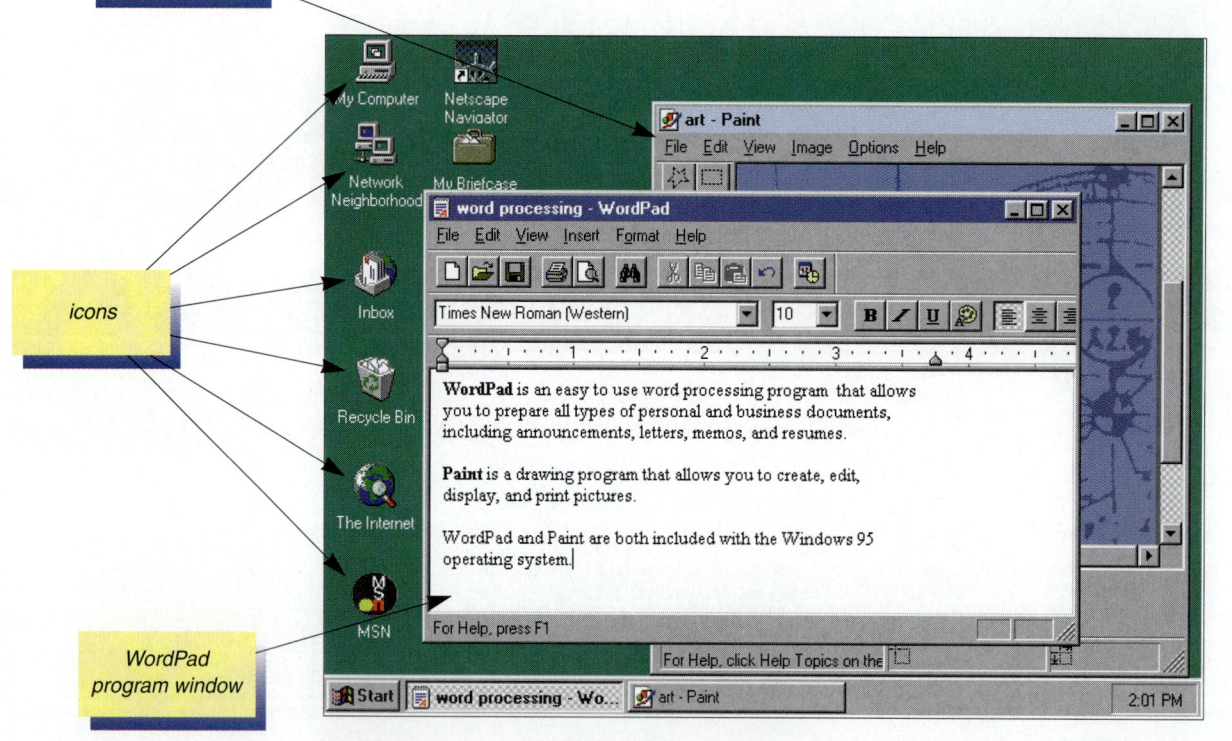

inCyber

For information on Windows 95, visit the Discovering Computers Chapter 2 inCyber page (http://www.scsite.com/dc/ch2/incyber.htm) and click Windows 95.

Figure 2-1
Two key features of a graphical user interface (GUI) are windows and icons. Windows are rectangular areas that present information. Icons are symbols that represent processing options or documents. In this screen, two windows are open: the WordPad program window in the foreground and the Paint program window in the background. Several windows can be open at the same time and moved from back to front so that all information on a window can be seen. The icons along the left side of the screen represent other applications that can be started.

A **menu** is a list of options from which you can choose. In a graphical user interface, menus often contain a list of related commands. **Commands** are instructions that cause the computer software to perform a specific action. For example, the menu shown in Figure 2-2 displays commands associated with the Windows 95 Start menu.

A **button** is an icon (usually a rectangular or circular shape) that when clicked, causes a specific action to take place. Buttons usually are clicked using a pointing device such as a mouse but some buttons such as OK and Cancel also can be activated by using the keyboard. Figure 2-3 shows several different types of buttons.

The features of a user interface make it easier for the user to communicate with the computer. You will see examples of these features and how they are used as you learn about the various personal computer applications.

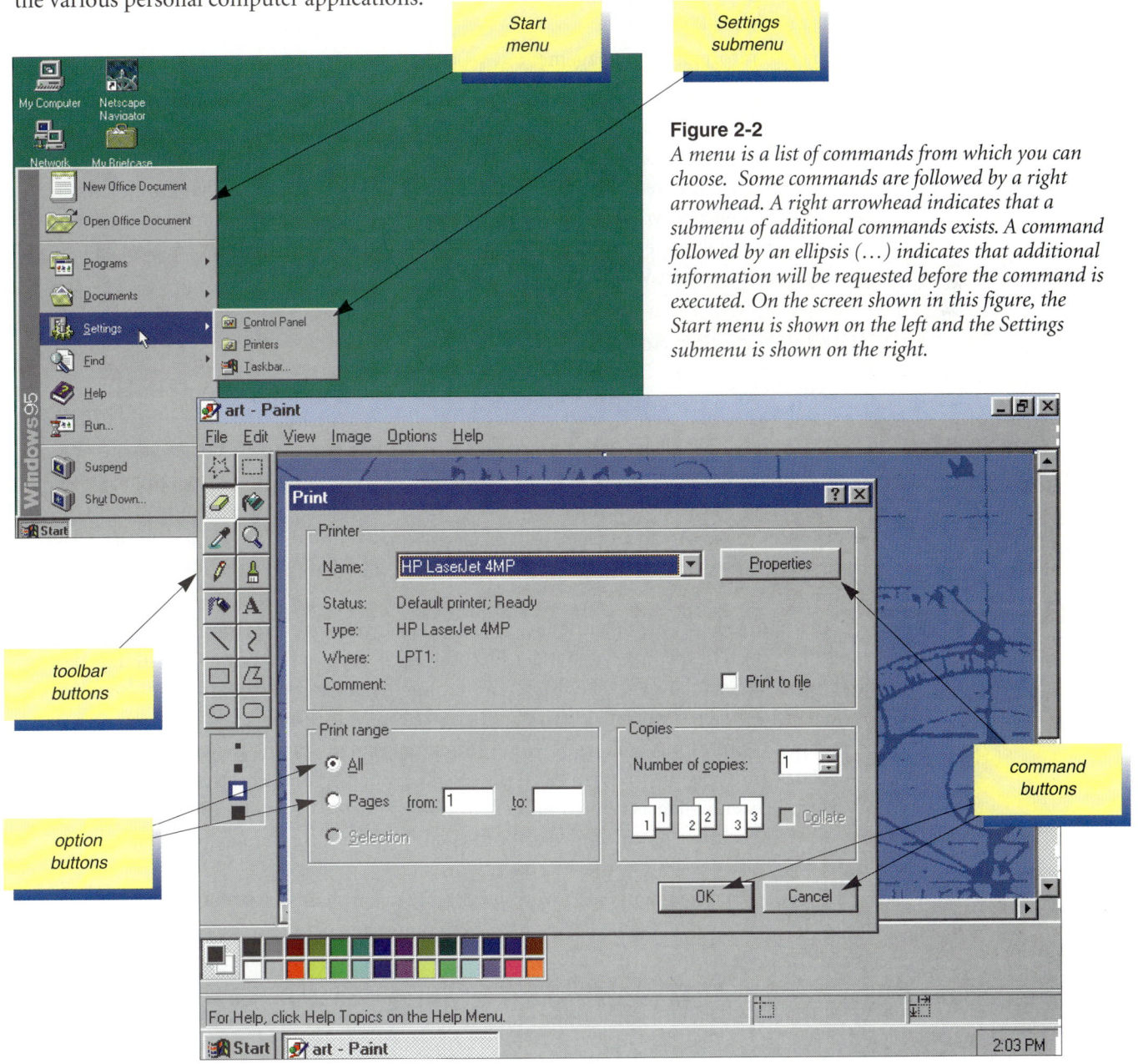

Figure 2-2
A menu is a list of commands from which you can choose. Some commands are followed by a right arrowhead. A right arrowhead indicates that a submenu of additional commands exists. A command followed by an ellipsis (...) indicates that additional information will be requested before the command is executed. On the screen shown in this figure, the Start menu is shown on the left and the Settings submenu is shown on the right.

Figure 2-3
A button is an icon that causes a specific action to take place. This screen shows several types of buttons. Many applications contain a row of buttons with icons called a toolbar. The icon indicates what happens when the button is clicked. For example, the selected button on the toolbar shown in this screen allows you to erase objects from a picture. The last two buttons allow you to add ellipses and rounded rectangles, respectively. Option buttons modify the action that will take place, such as printing all or a range of pages. Stand-alone buttons can contain text or icons and are referred to as command buttons.

Software Applications

The following sections of this chapter will introduce you to fifteen widely used personal computer software applications:

- Word processing
- Desktop publishing
- Spreadsheet
- Database
- Presentation graphics
- Web communications and browsers
- Electronic mail (e-mail)
- Personal information management
- Personal finance
- Project management
- Accounting
- Groupware
- Computer-aided design (CAD)
- Multimedia authoring
- Integrated software and software suites

With the exception of personal finance, which is primarily used by individuals, some organizations use all of the listed applications. Even though you personally may not use all of these applications, you should be at least familiar with their capabilities. These applications are discussed as they are used on personal computers, but most are available on computers of all sizes. The concepts you will learn about each application package on personal computers will also apply if you are working on a larger system. A software product within a category, for example, Microsoft Word, is called a *software package*.

Word Processing Software

The most widely used computer application is word processing. **Word processing** involves the use of a computer to produce or modify documents that consist primarily of text. Millions of people use word processing software every day to create letters, memos, reports, and other documents. A major advantage of using word processing to produce a document is the ability to easily change what has been done. Because the document is stored electronically, you can add, delete, or rearrange words, sentences, or entire sections. Newer word processors even have *intelligent* features that make changes to the document automatically.

Once completed, the document can be printed as many times as you like with each copy looking as good as the first. With older methods such as using a typewriter, making changes and reprinting a document takes much more time. Using word processing software also is a more efficient way of storing documents, because many documents can be stored on a disk. If computers are connected in a network, stored documents can be shared among users.

Today, most people perform word processing using personal computers or larger computer systems such as minicomputers or mainframes. These computers also can be used for other applications. **Dedicated word processing systems**, that can be used only for word processing, also exist, but are less frequently used.

Producing a document using word processing usually consists of four steps: creating, editing, formatting, and printing. A fifth step, saving the document, should be performed frequently throughout the process so that work will not be lost. In fact, most word processor programs have an optional **AutoSave** feature that automatically saves open documents at specified intervals. In the process of producing a document, the user may switch back and forth between these five steps.

Creating a Word Processing Document Creating a word processing document involves entering text, usually by using the keyboard. To aid in the process of creating a document, most word processing programs allow you to display the document on the screen exactly as it will look when it is printed. This capability is called WYSIWIG (pronounced whiz-e-wig). **WYSIWIG** is an acronym for What You See Is What You Get. Other common word processing features used during the creating step include word wrap, scrolling, and moving the insertion point.

- Word Wrap. **Word wrap** provides an automatic line return when the text reaches a certain position on a line in the document, such as the right-hand margin. Unlike a typewriter, you can continue typing and do not have to press a return or line feed key; the entered text automatically flows to the next line. Word wrap also operates when text is added to or deleted from lines.

document in memory

word wrap provides automatic return so text continues on next line

window allows you to view any part of a document

Figure 2-4
Modern word processors allow you to create professional looking documents that are easy to read and understand. The limited size of the screen only allows you to see a portion of the document at one time. The document can be moved (scrolled) up or down and right to left so any portion of the document that will fit on one screen can be seen.

- Scrolling. **Scrolling** is the process of moving the document so you can view any portion. Think of multipage documents as having been created on a continuous roll of paper. The screen can be thought of as a window that only allows a portion of the document to be seen. The document can be moved (scrolled) up or down behind the screen window. For wide documents, the screen can be scrolled left and right, as well. **Scroll tips**, small page labels beside the scroll box, show the current page as you scroll through a document, so you know how far you have scrolled through the document (Figure 2-4).

- Moving the insertion point. The **insertion point**, sometimes referred to as the **cursor**, is a symbol, such as a flashing vertical bar, that indicates where on the screen the next character will appear. The insertion point is moved by using a pointing device, such as a mouse, or the keyboard. The arrow keys on the keyboard move the insertion point one character or one line at a time. If you hold down an arrow key, the movement is repeated until you release the key. More efficient ways to move the insertion point farther and faster include using the PAGE UP and PAGE DOWN keys to move a page (or screen) at a time and the HOME and END keys to move to the beginning or end of a line. You can use other key combinations to move to the beginning of words or paragraphs, or to the start or end of the document.

Editing a Word Processing Document   **Editing** is the process of making changes in the content of a document. Word processing editing features include inserting and deleting; cutting, copying, and pasting; and searching and replacing. Additional editing features include spell checking; using a thesaurus; grammar checking; and adding revision marks, annotations, and highlighting.

- Insert and Delete. When you **insert**, you add text to a document. When you **delete**, you remove text. Most word processors normally are in the *insert mode*, meaning that as you type, any existing text is pushed down the page to make room for the new text. Word processors can be placed in a *typeover mode* (also called *overtype mode*), however, where new text replaces any existing text.

- Cut, Copy, and Paste. To **cut** involves removing a portion of the document and electronically storing it in a temporary storage location called the **Clipboard**. Whatever is on the Clipboard can be placed somewhere else in the document by using the **Paste** command. The end result of cut and paste is to move a portion of a document somewhere else. When you **copy**, a portion of the document is duplicated and stored on the Clipboard.

- Search and Replace. The **search** feature lets you find all occurrences of a particular character, word, or combination of words. Search can be used in combination with **replace** to substitute new letters or words for the old. Some word processing programs have advanced search and replace features that understand the meaning of words and their different forms. For example, if a user replaces the word *make* with the word *create* throughout a document, search and replace also changes *making* to *creating* and *made* to *created*. Replacement can be automatic or require user confirmation. This is just one of the many intelligent features of newer word processors, some of which are shown in Figure 2-4.

- Spelling Checker. A **spelling checker** allows you to review individual words, sections of a document, or the entire document for correct spelling. Words are compared to an electronic dictionary that is part of the word processing software. Some spelling checkers contain more than 120,000 words. If a match is not found, a list of similar words that may be the correct spelling is displayed. You can then select one of the suggested words; ignore the suggestions and leave the word unchanged; or add the unrecognized but properly spelled word to the dictionary so it will not be considered misspelled in the future. Many users customize their spelling dictionaries by adding company, street, city, and personal names so the software can check the correct spelling of those words.

inCyber

For details on spelling bees, visit the Discovering Computers Chapter 2 inCyber page (http://www.scsite.com/dc/ch2/incyber.htm) and click Spell.

While most spelling checkers operate as a separate process that can be started by the user, many word processors continually check the spelling of words as they are entered. Possible errors are shown on screen with red wavy underlines. To correct the misspelled words, you right-click the word (Figure 2-5). You can select a correct spelling from the shortcut menu that contains suggestions from the spelling checker dictionary.

- AutoCorrect. The **AutoCorrect** feature corrects common spelling errors automatically in words as they are entered. For example, if you enter the word, *teh*, the word processor automatically changes it to, *the*. AutoCorrect also corrects errors in capitalization. It will add capital letters to the names of days, remove capitals from words mistakenly capitalized in the middle of a sentence, and change two initial capital letters to just one. AutoCorrect is *smart* enough, however, not to change abbreviations such as CDs, PCs, and MHz. While spelling checkers and AutoCorrect can catch some misspelled words and repeated words such as *the the*, they cannot identify words that are used incorrectly. A thesaurus and grammar checker will help you to choose proper words and use them correctly.

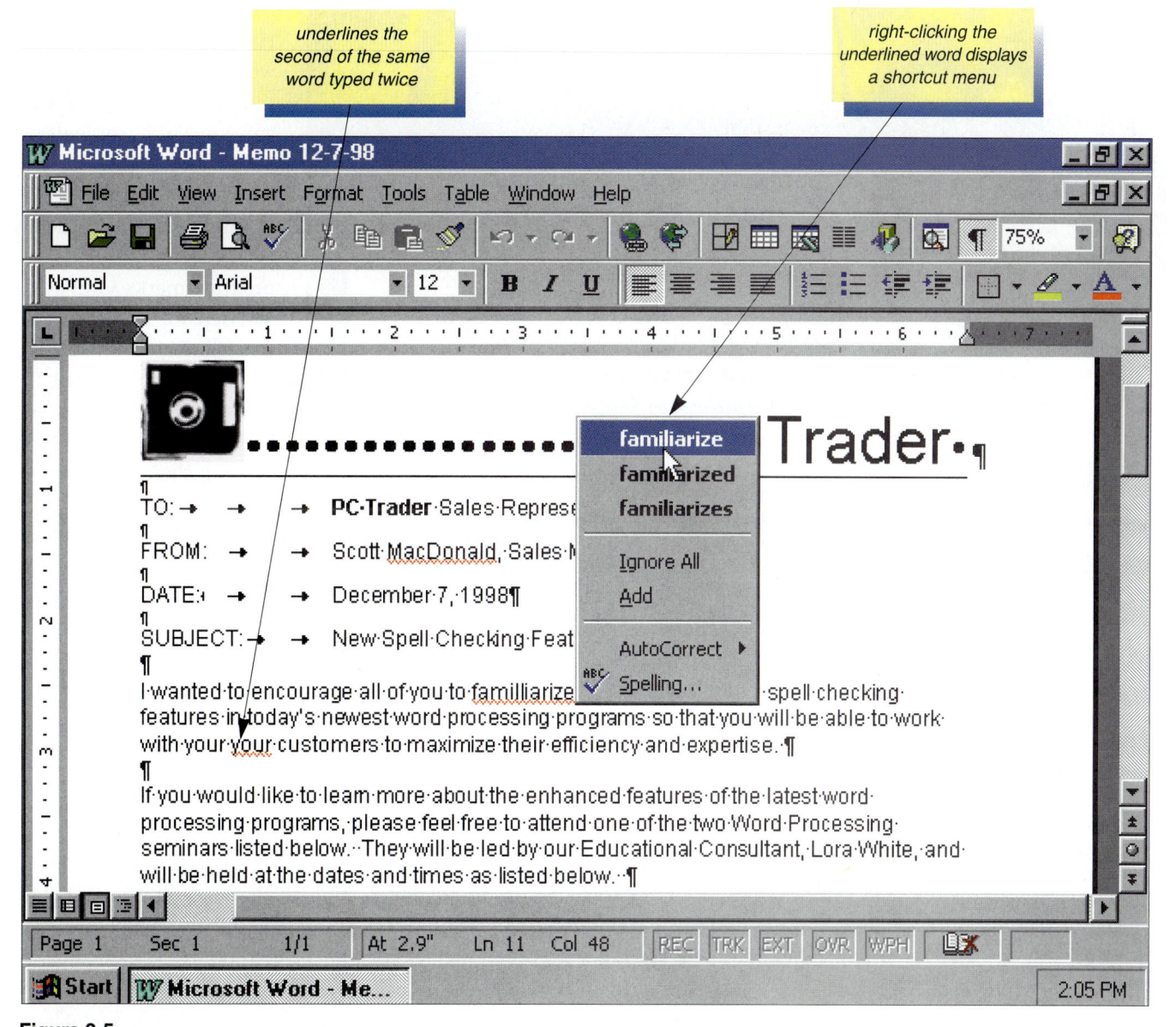

Figure 2-5
Some word processors check the spelling as you type. If you type a word that is not in the word processor's dictionary or you type the same word consecutively, the word processor marks the possible error with a red wavy underline or by some other means. If you right-click a marked word, the word processor displays a shortcut menu with a list of replacement words from which to select. The shortcut menu also includes a list of commands to help you correct the misspelled word in case the replacement words are not what you want.

To use writing tools, visit the Discovering Computers Chapter 2 inCyber page (http://www.scsite.com/dc/ch2/incyber.htm) and click Thesaurus.

- Thesaurus. A **thesaurus** allows you to look up synonyms (words with the same meaning) for words in a document while you are using your word processor. Using a thesaurus is similar to using a spelling checker. When you want to look up a synonym for a word, you click the word you want to check and then activate the thesaurus by using a keyboard command or a pointing device. The thesaurus software displays a list of possible synonyms. If you find a word you would rather use, you select the desired word from the list and the software automatically incorporates it in the document by replacing the previous word.

- Grammar Checker. A **grammar checker** is used to check for grammar, writing style, and sentence structure errors. This software can check documents for excessive use of a word or phrase, identify sentences that are too long, and find words that are used out of context such as *four* example.

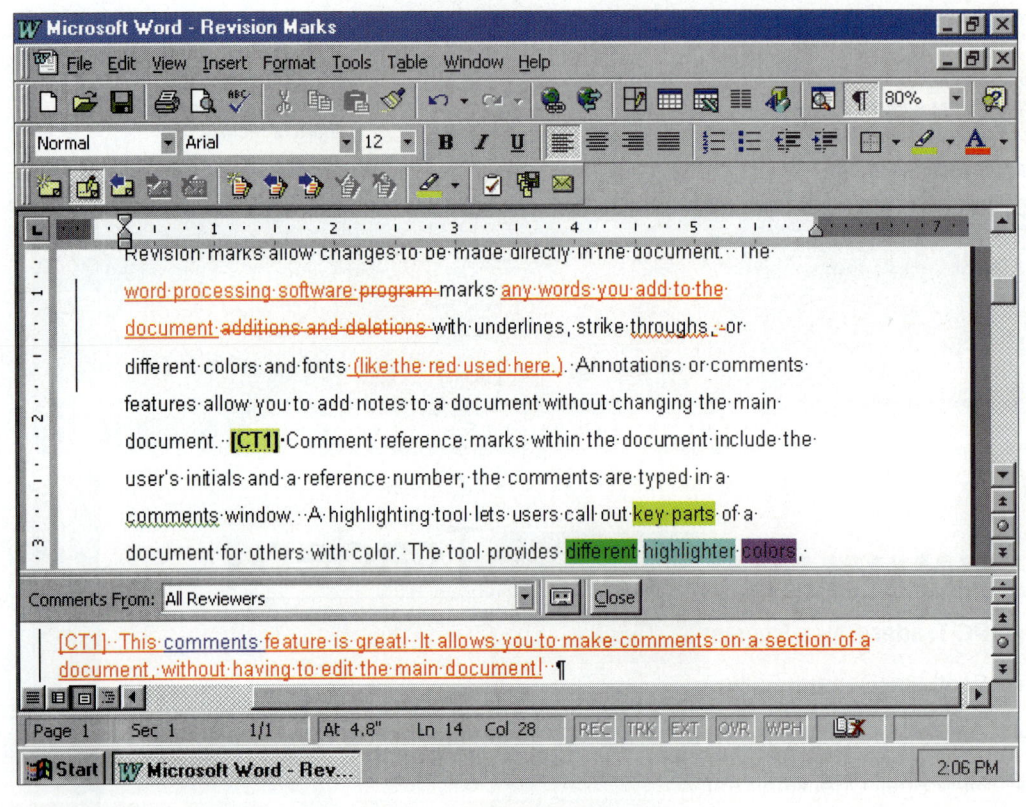

- Revision Marks, Annotations, and Highlighting Tools. Most word processors provide several revision features so you can edit documents online (Figure 2-6). **Revision marks** allow changes to be made directly in the document. The program marks additions and deletions with underlines, strikethroughs, or different colors and fonts. **Annotations** can be used to make comments without changing the document. Annotation marks include your initials and a reference number within the document; the annotations are typed in an annotation pane. A **highlighting tool** lets you use color to call out key parts of a document for others. The tool provides different highlighter colors, so that several users can highlight different sections of a document. When the document is routed, others can easily scan for revision and annotation marks or highlighted text.

Figure 2-6
Most word processors provide revision features that allow you to mark additions and deletions with underlines, strikethroughs, or different colors and fonts. Annotations can be used to make comments without changing the document. Highlighting tools allow you to call out key parts of the document.

Formatting a Word Processing Document To **format** means to change the appearance of a document. Formatting is important because the overall look of a document can significantly affect its ability to communicate. For documents that are going to be sent to clients, it is not unusual to spend more time formatting the document than was spent entering the text. The following word processing features can be used to format a document (Figure 2-7).

- Typeface, Font, and Style. A **typeface** is a specific set of characters that are designed the same. Helvetica and Times New Roman are examples of typefaces. The size of a typeface is measured vertically in points. Each **point** is approximately 1/72 of an inch high. The text you are reading in this book is ten point type. A specific combination of typeface and

SOFTWARE APPLICATIONS 2.9

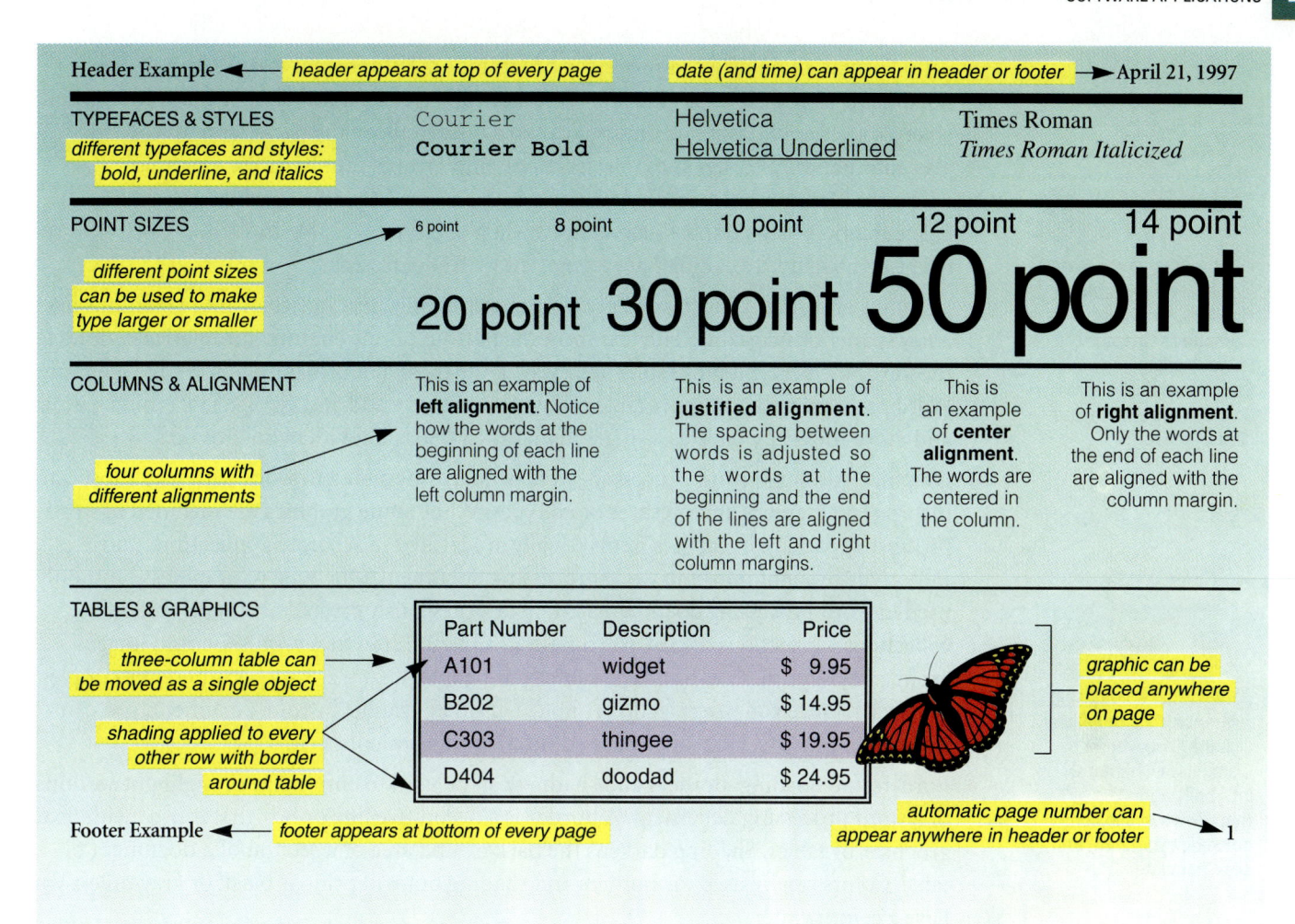

Header Example ◄— header appears at top of every page		date (and time) can appear in header or footer —► April 21, 1997		
TYPEFACES & STYLES *different typefaces and styles: bold, underline, and italics*	Courier **Courier Bold**	Helvetica <u>Helvetica Underlined</u>		Times Roman *Times Roman Italicized*
POINT SIZES *different point sizes can be used to make type larger or smaller*	6 point 8 point 10 point 12 point 14 point 20 point 30 point 50 point			
COLUMNS & ALIGNMENT *four columns with different alignments*	This is an example of **left alignment**. Notice how the words at the beginning of each line are aligned with the left column margin.	This is an example of **justified alignment**. The spacing between words is adjusted so the words at the beginning and the end of the lines are aligned with the left and right column margins.	This is an example of **center alignment**. The words are centered in the column.	This is an example of **right alignment**. Only the words at the end of each line are aligned with the column margin.
TABLES & GRAPHICS *three-column table can be moved as a single object* *shading applied to every other row with border around table*	Part Number Description Price A101 widget $ 9.95 B202 gizmo $ 14.95 C303 thingee $ 19.95 D404 doodad $ 24.95			*graphic can be placed anywhere on page*
Footer Example ◄— footer appears at bottom of every page			automatic page number can appear anywhere in header or footer —► 1	

Figure 2-7
Examples of word processing formatting features.

---

point size is called a **font**, though it is common to hear and read of typefaces being called fonts. A particular **style**, such as **bold**, *italics*, or <u>underlining</u>, can be applied to a font to make it stand out.

- Margins and Alignment. **Margins** specify the space in the border of a page and include the left, right, bottom, and top margin. **Alignment**, also called **justification**, deals with how text is positioned in relation to a fixed reference point, usually a right or left margin. **Justified alignment** aligns text with both the left and right margins. **Left alignment** and **right alignment** align text with the left and right margins only. **Centered alignment** divides the text equally on either side of a reference point, usually the center of the page.

- Spacing. **Spacing** deals with how far apart individual letters (horizontal spacing) and lines of text (vertical spacing) are placed. With **monospacing**, each character takes up the same amount of horizontal space. With **proportional spacing**, wide characters, such as W or M, are given more horizontal space than narrow characters, such as I. When a document uses monospace letters, two spaces should be inserted after a period at the end of a sentence. By contrast, when a document has proportional spacing, only one space is placed after *all* punctuation. **Line spacing** specifies the vertical distance from the bottom of one line to the next line. Single and double line spacing are the most common, but in some word processing software, exact distances also can be specified.

---

inCyber

For a look at original fonts, visit the Discovering Computers Chapter 2 inCyber page (http://www.scsite.com/dc/ch2/incyber.htm) and click Font.

- Auto Format. In many word processor programs an **AutoFormat** feature formats documents as you type. AutoFormat automatically creates numbered or bulleted lists and changes a series of dashes or underscores to a border above the paragraph. AutoFormat also automatically creates symbols, fractions, and ordinal numbers. For example,
  - The em dash symbol is created when you type, --, and the smiley when you type :).
  - The fractions $\frac{1}{2}$, $\frac{1}{4}$, and $\frac{3}{4}$ are created when you type 1/2, 1/4, and 3/4.
  - The ordinals 1st, 2nd, and 3rd are formatted with superscript.
- Columns and Tables. Most word processors can arrange text in two or more columns like a newspaper or magazine. The text from the bottom of one column automatically flows to the top of the next column. **Tables** are a way of organizing information in rows and columns. Word processors that support tables allow you to easily add and change table information and move the entire table as a single item, instead of as individual lines of text.
- Graphics. Although word processors were primarily designed to work with text, most can incorporate graphics and pictures of all types. While some **graphics** are included in word processing packages, graphics items usually are created in separate applications and imported (brought into) the word processing document. One type of graphics commonly used in word processing documents is **clip art**, previously created art that is sold in collections. Collections of clip art contain several hundred to several thousand images grouped by type, such as holidays, vehicle, or people. Figure 2-8 shows different examples of clip art. Once you insert a clip art image or other graphic in your document, you can move, resize, rotate, crop, and make some color adjustments to it.
- Borders and Shading. Borders and shading can be used to emphasize or highlight sections of a word processing document. A **border** is a decorative line or box that is used with text, graphics, or tables. **Shading** darkens the background area of a section of a document or table. Colors can by used for borders and shading but will print as black or gray unless you have a color printer.
- Page Numbers, Headers, and Footers. Most word processors can automatically apply page numbers to any location on the page. Page numbers can be started at a particular number and can appear in a font different than the main body of text. **Headers** and **footers** allow you to place the same information at the top or bottom of each page. A company name, report title, date, or page number, are examples of items that might appear in a header or footer.
- Built-in Styles. A **built-in style**, also called a **style sheet**, lets you save font and format information so it can be applied to new documents. Built-in styles usually are applied to a portion of a document, such as a heading, paragraph, or footnote. A **template** uses a

inCyber
For samples of clip art available on the Internet, visit the Discovering Computers Chapter 2 inCyber page (http://www.scsite.com/dc/ch2/incyber.htm) and click Clip Art.

inCyber
For information on using reference style templates, visit the Discovering Computers Chapter 2 inCyber page (http://www.scsite.com/dc/ch2/incyber.htm) and click Template.

Figure 2-8
Clip art consists of previously created illustrations that can be added to documents. Clip art usually comes in collections of graphic images that are grouped by type. These clip art examples are from an animals and nature collection.

Lion 1 · Iris · Puppy · Puffin · Conch 1 · Trout · Mammoth

SOFTWARE APPLICATIONS 2.11

Figure 2-9
Most correspondence is printed in portrait orientation; which is printing across the narrower portion of a sheet of paper. In landscape orientation, the printing goes across the wider portion of the paper.

Portrait Orientation

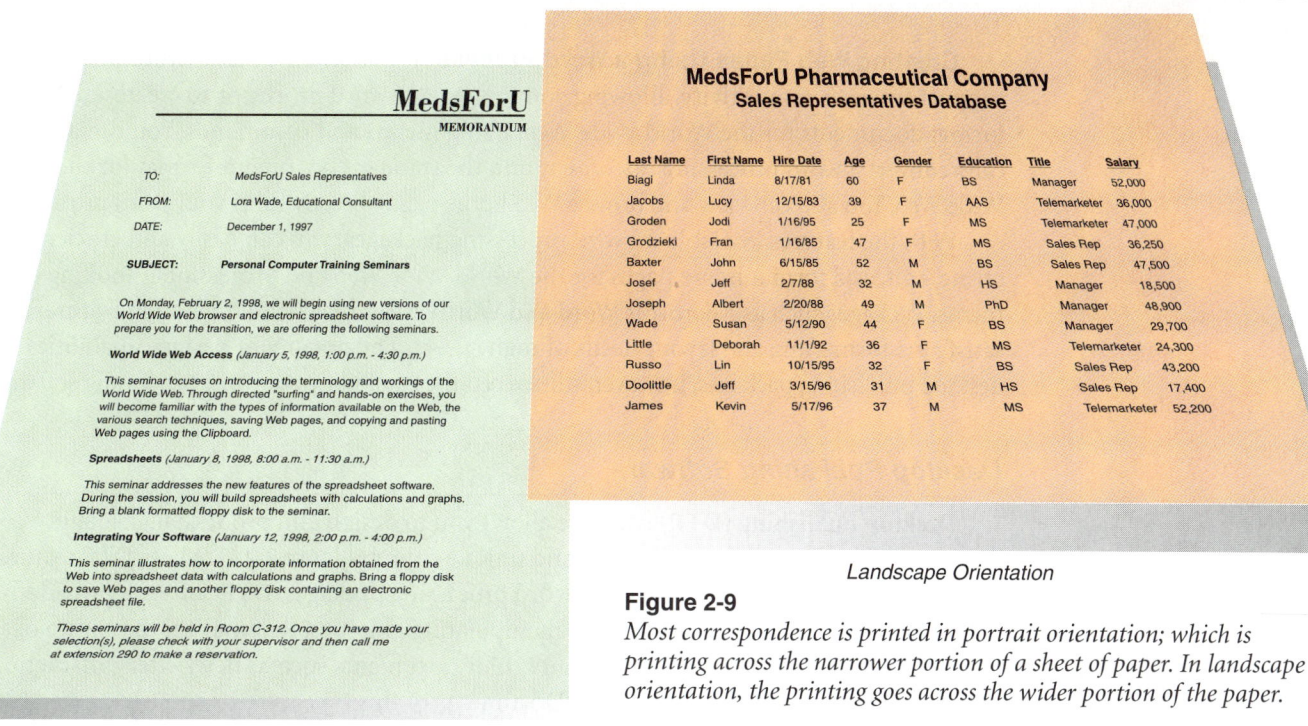

Landscape Orientation

predefined style sheet, which contains font, style, spacing, and formatting information and usually includes text that is always used, such as title and headings. A memo, a fax cover sheet, and a newsletter are examples of documents that often originate using a template.

Printing a Word Processing Document Most word processors give you many options other than printing a single copy of the entire document.

- Number of Copies and Pages. The ability to print individual pages and a range of pages (for example, pages 2 through 7) usually are available. In addition, you can specify how many copies are to be printed.

- Portrait and Landscape. **Portrait** printing means that the paper is taller than it is wide. Most letters are printed in portrait orientation. **Landscape** printing means that the paper is wider than it is tall. Tables with a large number of columns often are printed in landscape orientation. See Figure 2-9 for examples.

- Print Preview. **Print preview** (Figure 2-10) allows you to see on the screen how the document will look when it is printed. In print preview, you can see one or more entire pages. Even though the text may be too small to read, you can review the overall appearance and decide if the page needs additional formatting.

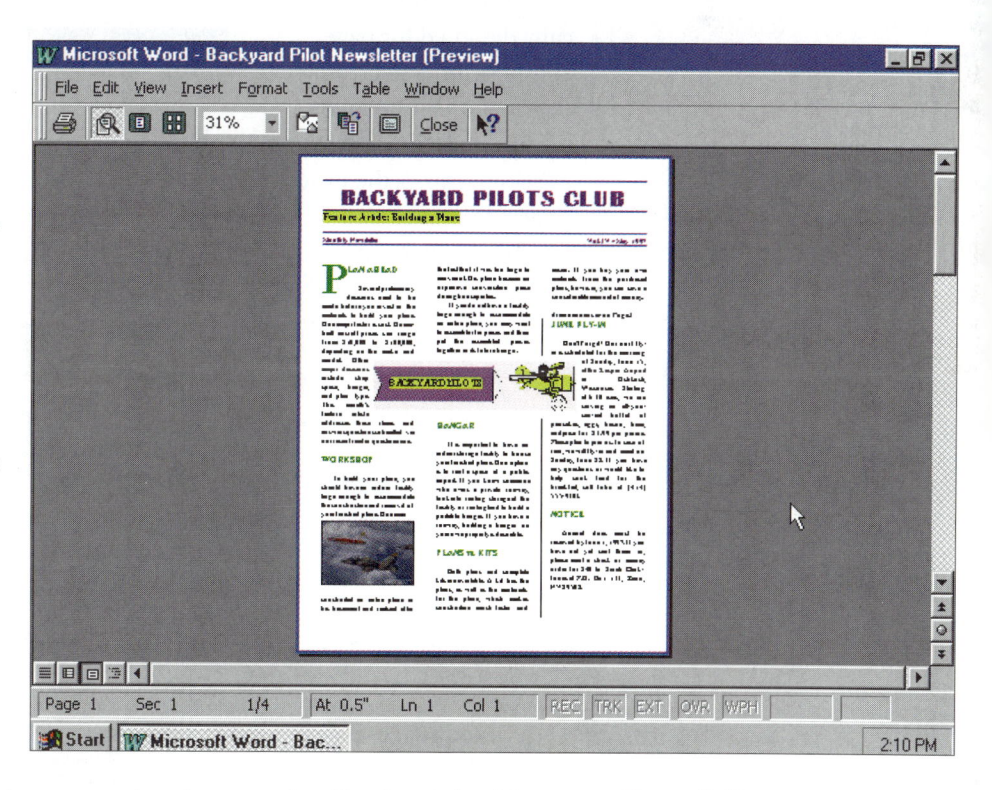

Figure 2-10
Print preview allows you to see on the screen how the document will look when it is printed. This feature helps you decide if the overall appearance of the document is acceptable or if the document needs additional formatting.

Creating Web Pages Using a Word Processor Today, the major word processors support Internet connectivity, allowing you to use your word processor to create, edit, and format documents for the World Wide Web. Using menus and commands, you can automatically convert a word processing document into the standard document format for the World Wide Web. You also can view and browse Web home pages directly from your word processor.

With the features available in word processing packages, you can easily and efficiently create, edit, and format home pages for the World Wide Web and professional-looking documents. Packages such as Microsoft Word and WordPerfect may contain enough features to satisfy the formatting and layout needs of many users. The document design capabilities of desktop publishing packages, however, still exceed the capabilities of word processing software.

Desktop Publishing Software

Desktop publishing (DTP) software allows you to design and produce high-quality documents that contain text, graphics, and unique colors (Figure 2-11). Many DTP features have been incorporated into the better word processing packages. DTP software provides additional tools, however, especially for manipulating graphics, that make it the choice of people who regularly produce high-quality color documents such as newsletters, marketing literature, catalogs, and annual reports. Documents of this type were previously created by slower, more expensive traditional publishing methods such as typesetting.

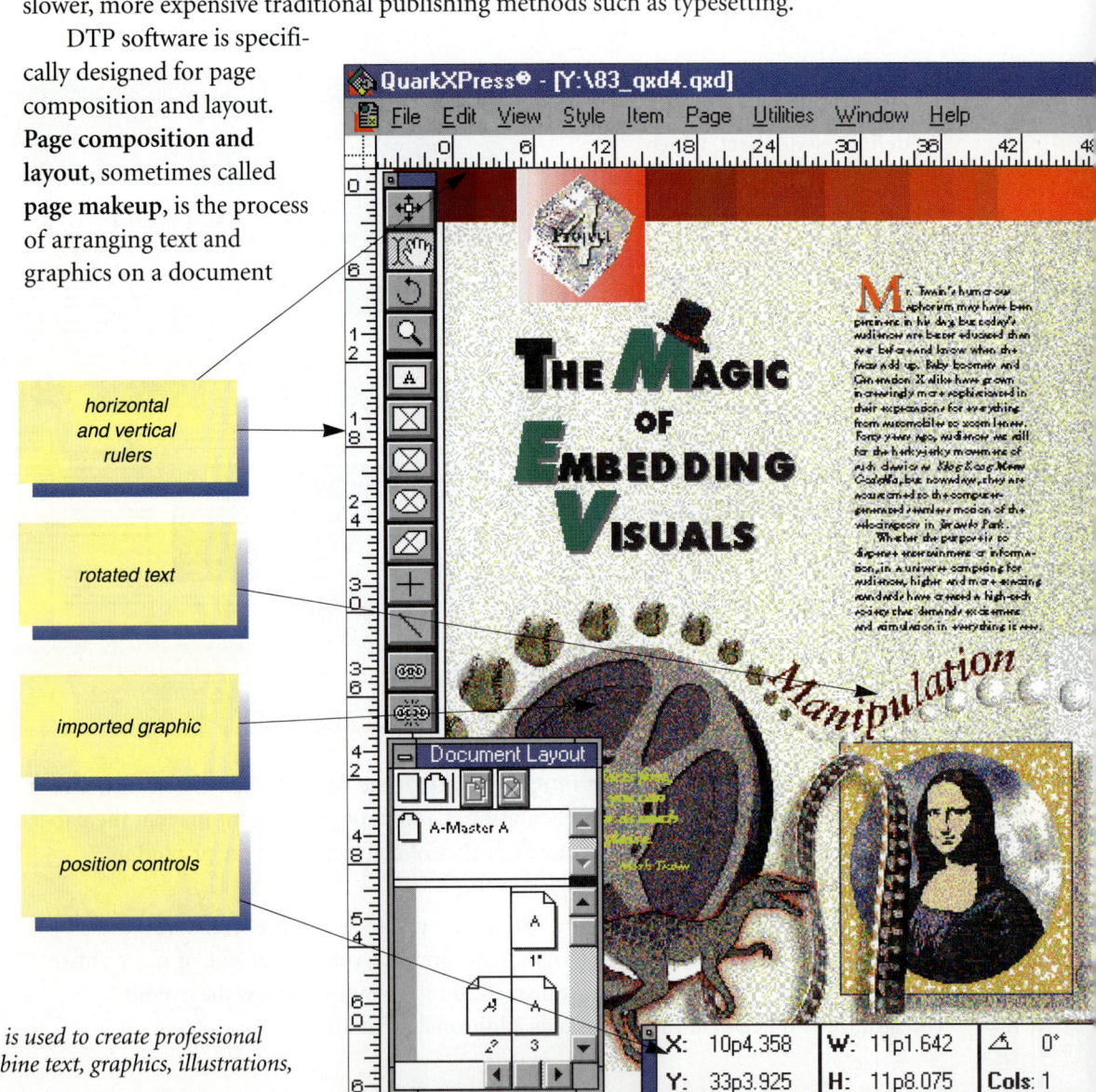

DTP software is specifically designed for page composition and layout. **Page composition and layout**, sometimes called **page makeup**, is the process of arranging text and graphics on a document

Figure 2-11
Desktop publishing software is used to create professional looking documents that combine text, graphics, illustrations, and photographs.

page. The text and graphics used by a DTP program are frequently imported from other software packages. For example, text is usually created with a word processor and then transferred into the desktop publishing package. Graphics objects, such as illustrations and photographs, also are imported from other software packages. **Illustration software** that is designed for use by artists, such as CorelDRAW! and Aldus Freehand, often is used to create graphics for DTP documents (Figure 2-12). Input devices, called scanners, can be used to convert photographs and art to import into DTP documents. Once a graphic is inserted in a document, a DTP program can crop, sharpen, and change the colors in the image.

DTP programs typically include **color libraries**, which are standard sets of colors used by designers and printers to ensure that colors will print exactly as specified. From these libraries, you can choose standard colors or specialty colors such as metallic or florescent colors. Tints or percentages of colors also can be added to any object or graphic.

Some of the other page composition and layout features that distinguish DTP software include the following (some of these features are illustrated in Figure 2-11):

- Ability to create master pages, which are non-printing pages that serve as templates
- Larger page sizes (up to 18" by 24")
- Page grids for aligning text and graphics
- Ability to stack and overlap multiple objects on a page
- Ability to *trap* objects to eliminate white space in a printed document

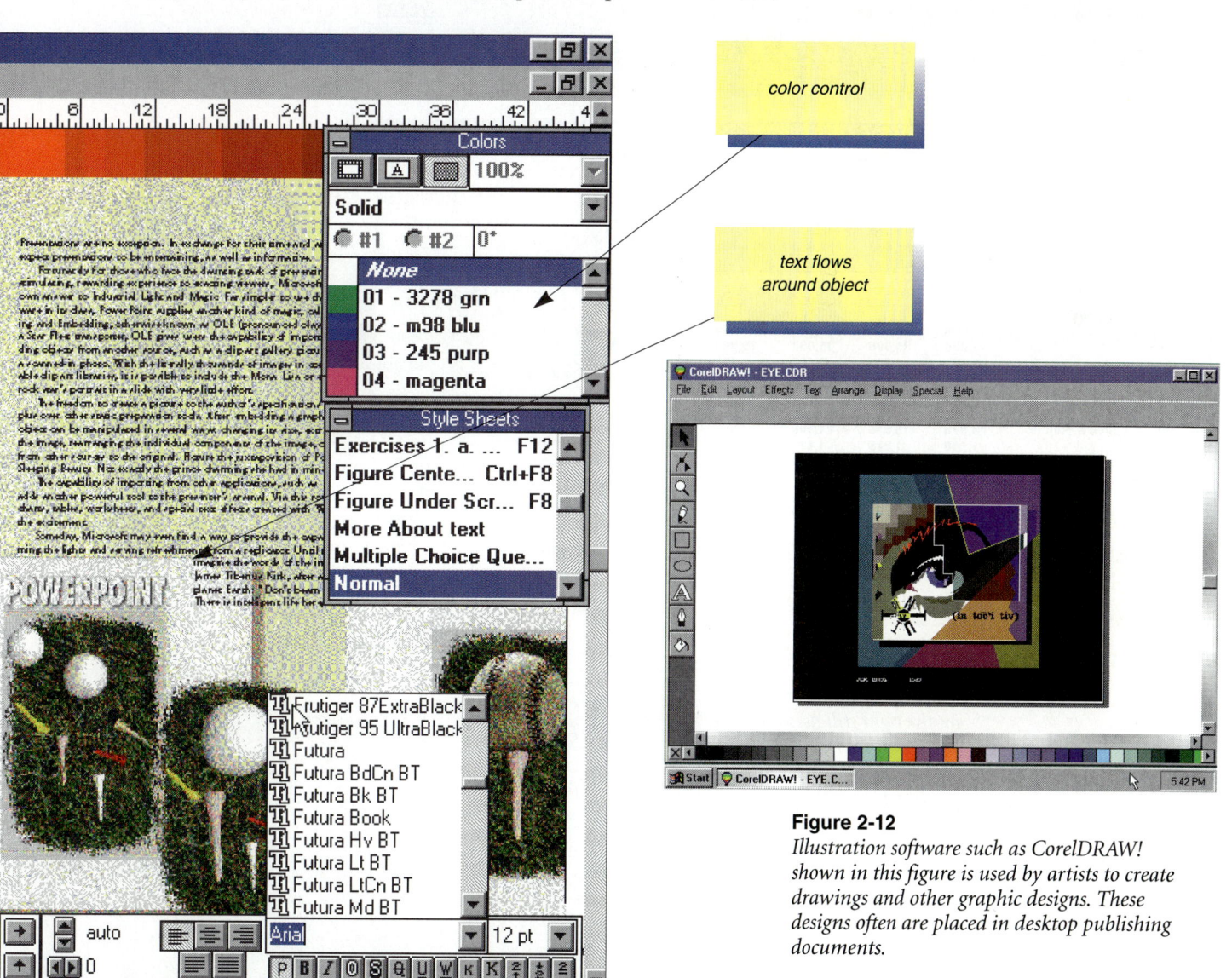

Figure 2-12
Illustration software such as CorelDRAW! shown in this figure is used by artists to create drawings and other graphic designs. These designs often are placed in desktop publishing documents.

The ability to print DTP documents relies on a page definition language. A **page definition language**, such as **PostScript**, describes the document to be printed in language the printer can understand. The printer, which includes a page definition language translator, interprets the instructions and prints the document. Using a page definition language enables a DTP document created on one computer system to be printed on another computer system with a different printer, so long as the second printer has a compatible page definition language.

With desktop publishing, you can create professional looking documents on your own computer and produce work that previously could be done only by graphic artists. By using desktop publishing, both the cost and time of producing quality documents are significantly decreased. Popular desktop publishing packages include PageMaker and QuarkXPress.

Spreadsheet Software

Spreadsheet software allows you to organize numeric data in a worksheet or in a tabular format called a **spreadsheet** or **worksheet**. Manual methods, those done by hand, have long been used to organize numeric data in this manner. You will see that the data in an electronic spreadsheet is organized in the same manner as it is in a manual spreadsheet (Figure 2-13).

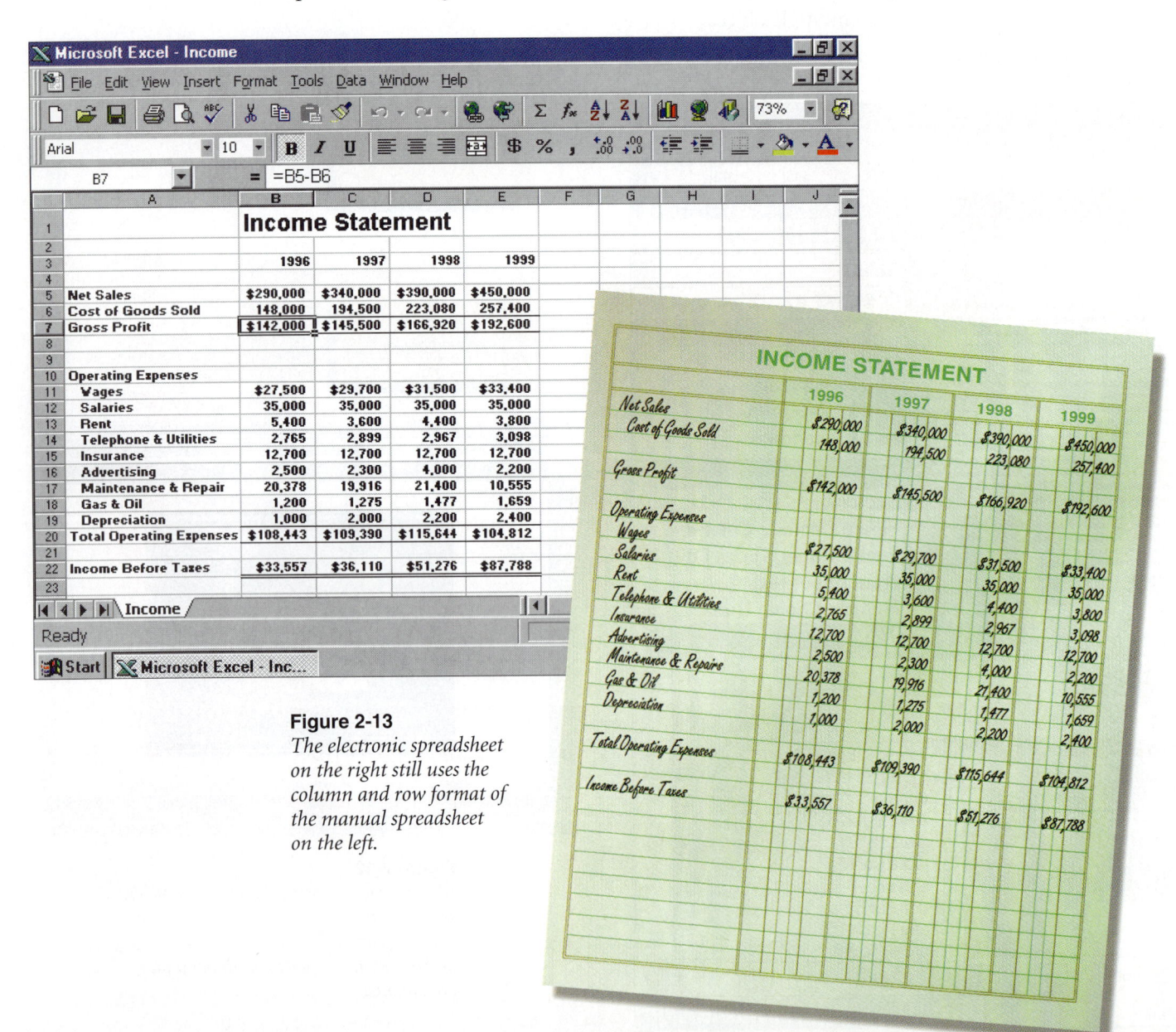

Figure 2-13
The electronic spreadsheet on the right still uses the column and row format of the manual spreadsheet on the left.

A spreadsheet file is like a notebook with up to 255 sheets (Figure 2-14). You access the different spreadsheets in a spreadsheet file by clicking the corresponding sheet tab. On each spreadsheet, data is organized vertically in **columns** and horizontally in **rows**. Columns are identified by a letter and rows by a number. Each spreadsheet has 256 columns and 16,384 rows. The column headings begin with A and end with IV. The row headings begin with 1 and end with 16,384. Only a small fraction of the active spreadsheet displays on the screen at one time. You can use the scroll bars, scroll arrows, and scroll boxes below and to the right of the window to view different parts of the active spreadsheet.

The intersection where a column and row meet is called a **cell** (Figure 2-14). Each of the spreadsheets in a spreadsheet file has more than 16,000,000 cells in which you can enter data. Cells are named by their location on the spreadsheet. As shown in Figure 2-14, the intersection of column E and row 7 is referred to as cell E7.

Cells may contain three types of data: labels (text), values (numbers), and formulas. The text, or **labels**, as they are called, identify the data and help organize the worksheet. Good spreadsheets contain descriptive titles. The rest of the cells in a spreadsheet may appear to contain numbers, or **values**. Some of the cells actually contain formulas, however. The **formulas** perform calculations on the data in the spreadsheet and display the resulting value

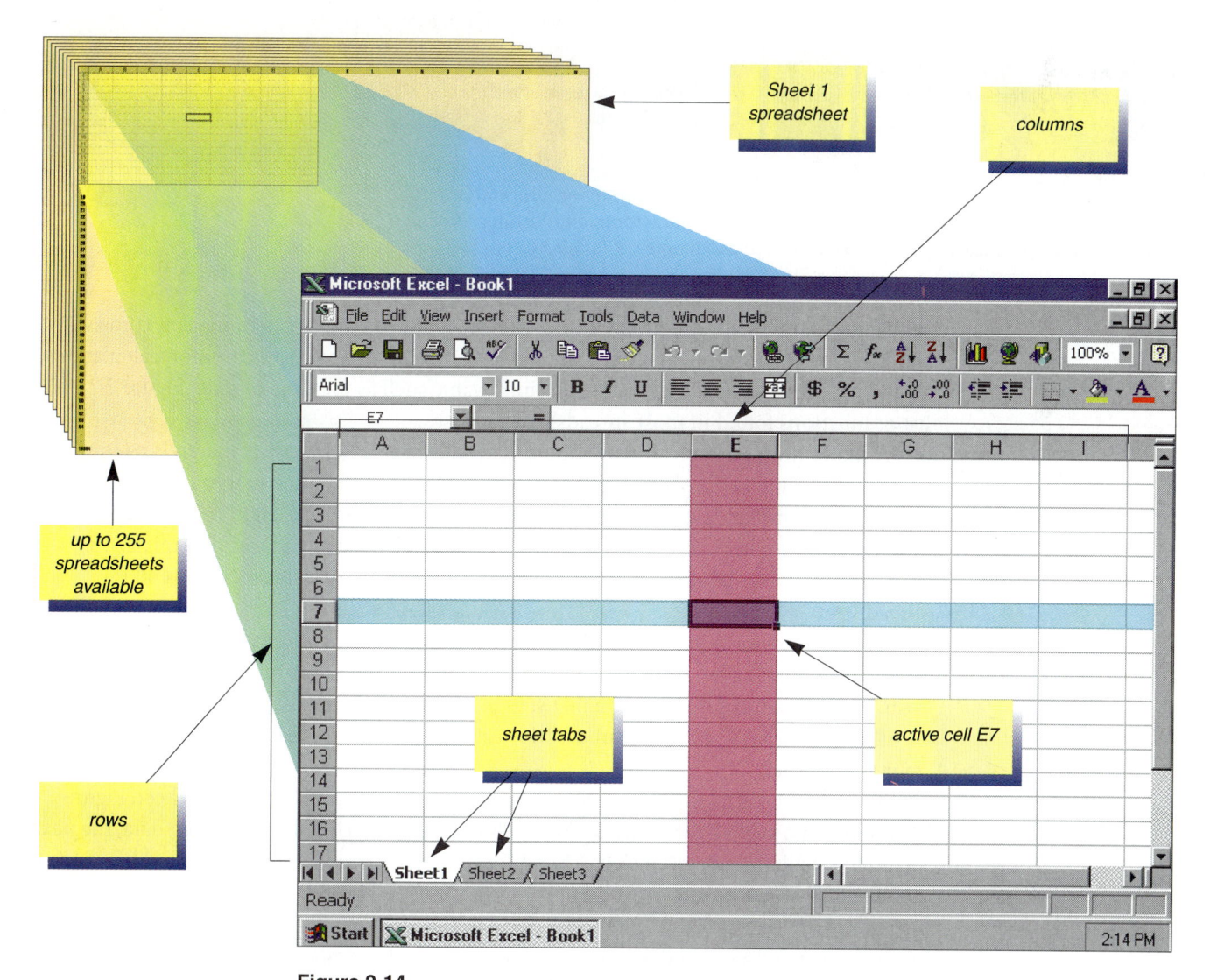

Figure 2-14
A spreadsheet file is like a notebook with up to 255 sheets. You view only a portion of a spreadsheet through a window which you can move to see other parts. On a spreadsheet, columns refer to the vertical lines of data and rows refer to the horizontal lines of data. Columns are identified by letters and rows are identified by numbers. The intersection of a column and row is called a cell.

SPREADSHEET FUNCTIONS

FINANCIAL
FV (rate, number of periods, payment)	Calculates the future value of an investment.
NPV (rate, range)	Calculates the net present value of an investment.
PMT (rate, number of periods, present value)	Calculates the periodic payment for an annuity.
PV (rate, number of periods, payment)	Calculates the present value of an investment.
RATE (number of periods, payment, present value)	Calculates the periodic interest rate of an annuity.

DAY & TIME
DATE	Returns the current date.
NOW	Returns the current date and time.
TIME	Returns the current time.

MATHEMATICAL
ABS (number)	Returns the absolute value of a number.
INT (number)	Rounds a number down to the nearest integer.
LN (number)	Calculates the natural logarithm of a number.
LOG (number, base)	Calculates the logarithm of a number to a specified base.
ROUND (number, number of digits)	Rounds a number to a specified number of digits.
SQRT (number)	Calculates the square root of a number.
SUM (range)	Calculates the total of a range of numbers.

STATISTICAL
AVERAGE (range)	Calculates the average value of a range of numbers.
COUNT (range)	Counts how many cells in the range have entries.
MAX (range)	Returns the maximum value in a range.
MIN (range)	Returns the minimum value in a range.
STDEV (range)	Calculates the standard deviation of a range of numbers.

LOGICAL
IF (logical test, value if true, value if false)	Performs a test and returns one value if the test is true and another value if the test is false.

Figure 2-15
Spreadsheet functions are predefined formulas that perform calculations or return information based on given data. This is just a partial list of some of the more common functions. Probably the most often used function is SUM, which is used to add a range of numbers.

in the cell containing the formula. You can create formulas or use functions that come with the spreadsheet software. **Functions** are stored formulas that perform common calculations, such as adding a range of cells or generating a value such as the time or date. Figure 2-15 is a list of functions found in most spreadsheet packages.

Another time-saving feature available in spreadsheets is a macro. A **macro** is a sequence of commands and keystrokes that are recorded and saved. When the macro is run, the sequence of commands and keystrokes is performed. Macros are used to reduce the number of keystrokes required for frequently performed tasks. Examples of tasks that might use macros are moving data from one spreadsheet to another or printing a portion of a spreadsheet.

This section illustrates how a spreadsheet works with steps to develop a simple spreadsheet to calculate the profit and profit percentage from four quarters of revenues and costs. As shown in Figure 2-16, the first step in creating the spreadsheet is to enter the labels, or titles. These should be short but descriptive, to help you organize the layout of the data in your spreadsheet.

The next step is to enter the values or numbers in the body of the spreadsheet. Figure 2-17 shows the value 125000 entered into cell B3. After entering the remaining data, the next step is to calculate the totals in cells F3 and F4. For some spreadsheets, formulas or functions are entered before the data.

In a manual spreadsheet, you would have to calculate each of the totals for the sales and cost in rows 3 and 4 by hand or with your calculator. To determine the sales totals in an electronic spreadsheet, you select the cells that you want to contain the totals (cells F3 and F4) and click the **AutoSum button** on the toolbar (Figure 2-18). The spreadsheet package is capable of determining that you want to sum by rows. The totals are calculated and displayed automatically (Figure 2-18).

SOFTWARE APPLICATIONS **2.17**

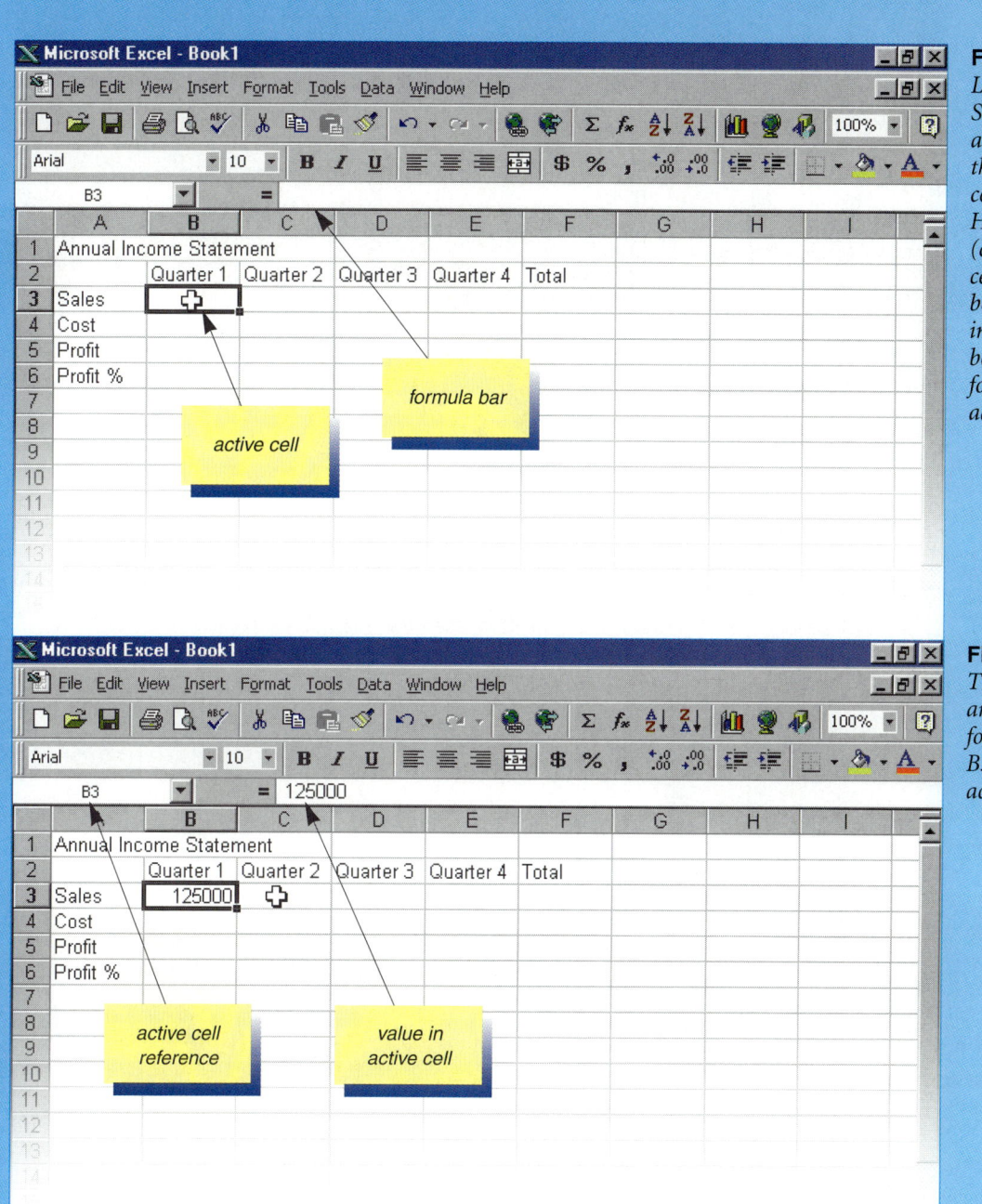

Figure 2-16
Labels such as Annual Income Statement, Quarter 1, Sales, and Cost are entered to identify the spreadsheet and the columns and rows of data. Here, the active cell is B3 (column B, row 3). The active cell is surrounded by a heavy border and its address displays in the formula bar. Nothing has been entered for this cell, so the formula bar shows only the cell address.

Figure 2-17
The value 125000 is entered and stored in cell B3. The formula bar shows the address, B3, and content, 125000, of the active cell.

Figure 2-18
The remaining values are entered in cells C3, D3, E3, B4, C4, D4, and E4. Cells F3 and F4 are selected. Clicking the AutoSum button on the toolbar assigns the formula =SUM(B3:E3) to cell F3 and =SUM(B4:E4) to cell F4. Cell F3 displays 615000, the sum of the values in the cells B3, C3, D3, and E3. Cell F4 displays 490000, the sum of the values in the cells B4, C4, D4, and E4. The SUM function assigned to cell F3 displays in the formula bar.

CHAPTER 2 – SOFTWARE APPLICATIONS: USER TOOLS

Figure 2-19
The formula to determine the Quarter 1 Profit in cell B5 is Quarter 1 Sales minus Quarter 1 Cost, or =B3 - B4. Thus, the formula =B3 - B4 is entered into cell B5 and the result 27000 displays. The formula to determine the Quarter 1 Profit % is Quarter 1 Profit divided by Quarter 1 Sales, or =B5 / B3 (the slash indicates division). Thus, the formula =B5 / B3 is entered into cell B6 and the result 21.60% displays. With cell B6 active, the formula =B5 / B3 displays in the formula bar.

Figure 2-20
This screen shows the completed spreadsheet. Once the formulas are assigned to cells B5 and B6, they are copied across rows 5 and 6 through column F. When you copy a formula, the spreadsheet program adjusts the cell addresses automatically. Hence, the formula in cell C5 is the same as the formula in cell B5, except that the cell addresses have been adjusted so the profit calculation in cell C5 pertains to the numbers immediately above cell C5.

Figure 2-21
The capability of a spreadsheet to recalculate totals automatically when data is changed is shown in this screen. This capability allows you to see quickly the total impact of changing one or more numbers in a spreadsheet. Using the spreadsheet shown in Figure 2-20, the value 150000 in cell C3 was changed to 110000. This one change results in five new values in cells containing formulas that use cell C3 directly or indirectly (cells C5, C6, F3, F5, and F6).

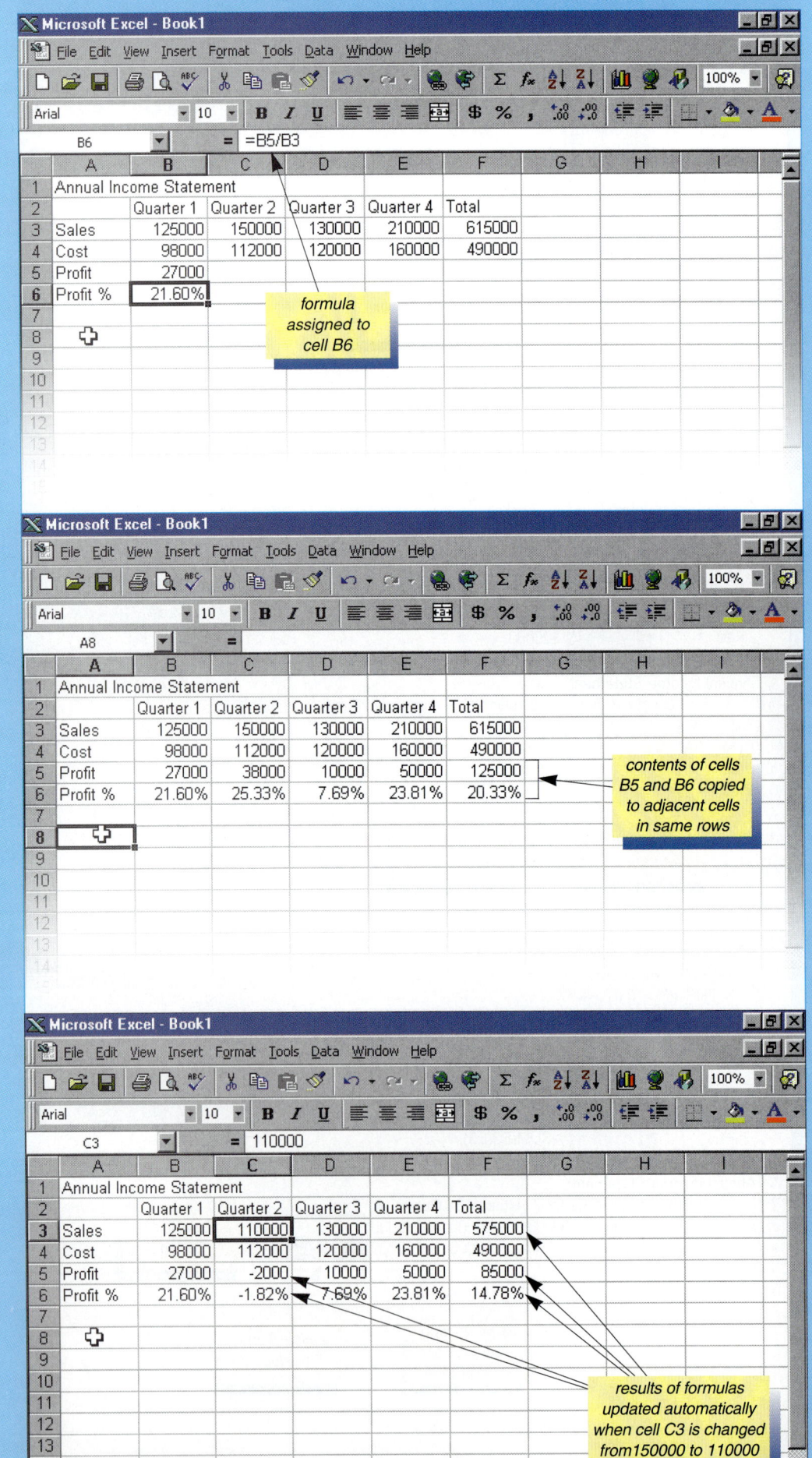

The next step is to determine the quarterly profits and total profits in row 5. The quarterly profit in cell B5 is equal to the first quarter sales in cell B3 minus the first quarter cost in cell B4. You can instruct the spreadsheet program to compute the first quarter profit by entering the formula =B3 - B4 in cell B5. The profit percent in cell B6 is equal to the first quarter profit in cell B5 divided by the first quarter sales or =B5 / B3. Figure 2-19 shows the results of entering these two formulas. With cell B6 selected, the formula =B5 / B3 displays in the formula bar.

Once a formula is entered into a cell, it can be copied to any other cell that requires a similar formula. Usually, when a formula is copied, the cell references are updated automatically to reflect the new location. For example, in Figure 2-20, when the formula in cell B5 is copied to cell C5, the formula changes from B3 - B4 to C3 - C4. This automatic updating of the formula is called **relative referencing**. If you are going to copy a formula but always want the formula to refer to the same cell location, you would use **absolute referencing**. For example, if you had a single tax rate that was going to be used to calculate taxes on the amounts in more than one cell, you would make an absolute reference to the cell containing the tax rate. To make a cell an absolute reference, you place a dollar sign in front of the column and row. In a formula, E5 would be an absolute reference to cell E5. As the formula is copied, the formula calculations are performed automatically. After copying the formula in cell B5 to C5, D5, E5, and F5 and copying the formula in cell B6 to C6, D6, E6, and F6, the spreadsheet is complete (Figure 2-20).

One of the more powerful features of spreadsheet software occurs when the data in a spreadsheet changes. To appreciate the capabilities of spreadsheet software, consider how a change is handled in a manual system. When a value in a manual spreadsheet changes, you must erase it and write a new value into the cell. You must also erase all cells that contain calculations referring to the value that changed and then you must recalculate these cells and enter the new result. For example, the row totals and column totals would be updated to reflect changes to any values within their areas. In a large manual spreadsheet, accurately posting changes and updating the values affected would be time consuming and new errors could be introduced. But posting changes on an electronic spreadsheet is easy. You change data in a cell simply by typing in the new value. All other values that are affected are updated automatically. Figure 2-21 shows that if you change the value in cell C3 from 150000 to 110000, five other cell values will change automatically. All other values and totals in the spreadsheet remain unchanged. On a computer, the updating happens almost instantly.

A spreadsheet's capability to recalculate when data is changed makes it a valuable tool for decision making. This capability is sometimes called **what-if analysis** because the results of different assumptions (*what-if we changed this ...*) can quickly be seen.

A standard feature of spreadsheet software is the ability to turn numeric data into a **chart** that graphically shows the relationship of numerical data. Visual representation of data in charts often makes it easier to analyze and interpret information. The types of charts provided by spreadsheet software are sometimes called **analytical graphics** or **business graphics** because they are used primarily for the analysis of numerical data by businesses. Figure 2-22 shows the chart types offered in one spreadsheet package. Most of these charts are variations on three basic chart types, line charts, bar charts, and pie charts.

Line charts are effective for showing a trend over a period of time, as indicated by a rising or falling line. If the area below or above a line is filled in with a color or pattern, it is called an area chart. **Bar charts** display bars of various lengths to show the relationship of data (Figure 2-23). The bars can be horizontal, vertical (sometimes called columns), or stacked on top of one another. **Pie charts**, so called because they look like pies cut into pieces, are effective for showing the relationship of parts to a whole. Pie charts often are used for budget presentations to show how much each part of the budget is a percentage of the total. To improve their appearance, most charts can be displayed or printed in a three-dimensional format.

Besides the ability to manipulate numbers, spreadsheet packages have many formatting features that can improve the overall appearance of the data. These features include the ability to change typefaces, sizes, and styles, add borders and lines, and use shading and colors to highlight data. Figure 2-24 shows the spreadsheet and chart with some of these features added.

Spreadsheets are one of the more popular software applications and have been adapted to a wide range of business and nonbusiness applications. Some of the popular packages used today are Microsoft Excel, Lotus 1-2-3, and Corel Quattro Pro.

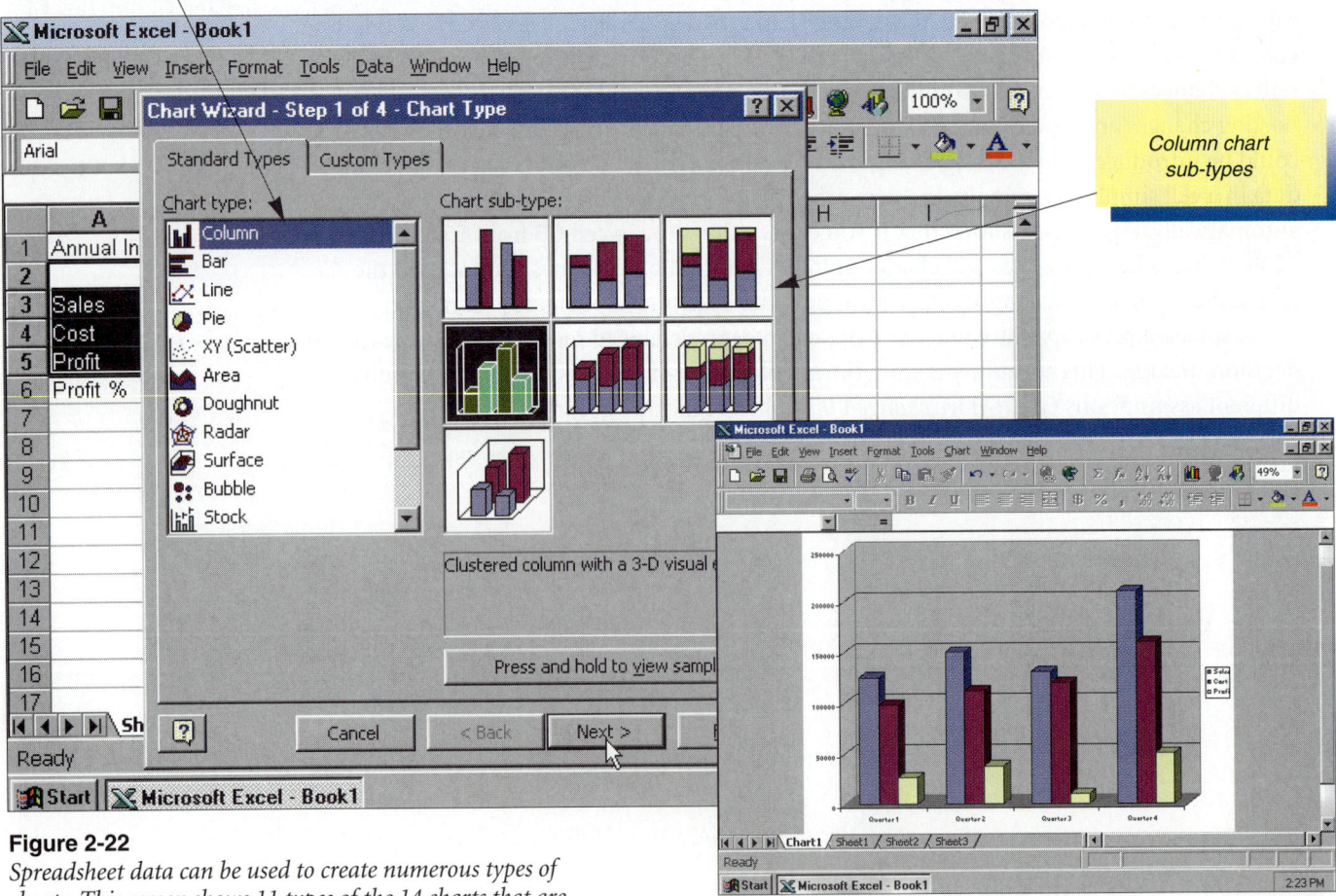

Figure 2-22
Spreadsheet data can be used to create numerous types of charts. This screen shows 11 types of the 14 charts that are available with the Microsoft Excel spreadsheet package.

Figure 2-23
A 3-D column chart can be created from spreadsheet data as shown on this Excel sheet.

SOFTWARE APPLICATIONS **2.21**

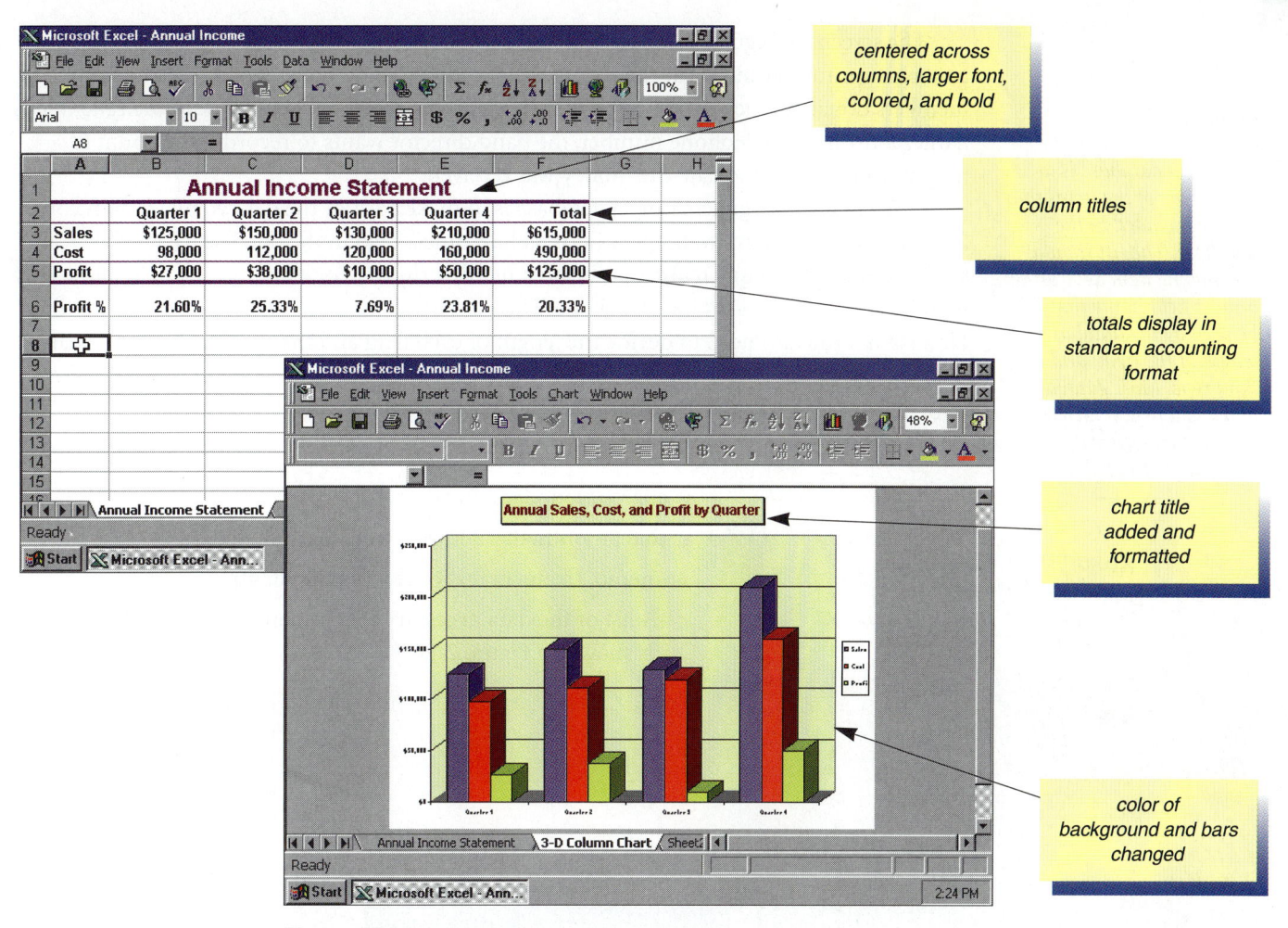

centered across columns, larger font, colored, and bold

column titles

totals display in standard accounting format

chart title added and formatted

color of background and bars changed

Figure 2-24
This spreadsheet and chart sheet show how the formatting features can improve the appearance of a spreadsheet and chart.

Database Software

A **database** refers to a collection of data that is stored in files. Although spreadsheet software can manage a small single-file database, most database applications require the use of database software. **Database software** allows you to create a database and to retrieve, manipulate, and update the data that you store in it. In a manual system (Figure 2-25), data might be recorded on paper and stored in a filing cabinet. In a database on the computer, the data will be stored in an electronic format on a storage device such as a disk.

When you use a database, you need to be familiar with the terms file, record, and field. Just as in a manual system, the word **file** is a collection of related data that is organized in records. Each **record** contains a collection of related facts called **fields**. For example, an address file might consist of records containing name and address information. All the data that relates to one name would be considered a record. Each fact, such as the street address or telephone number, is called a field.

Figure 2-25
A database is similar to a manual system, where related data items are stored in files.

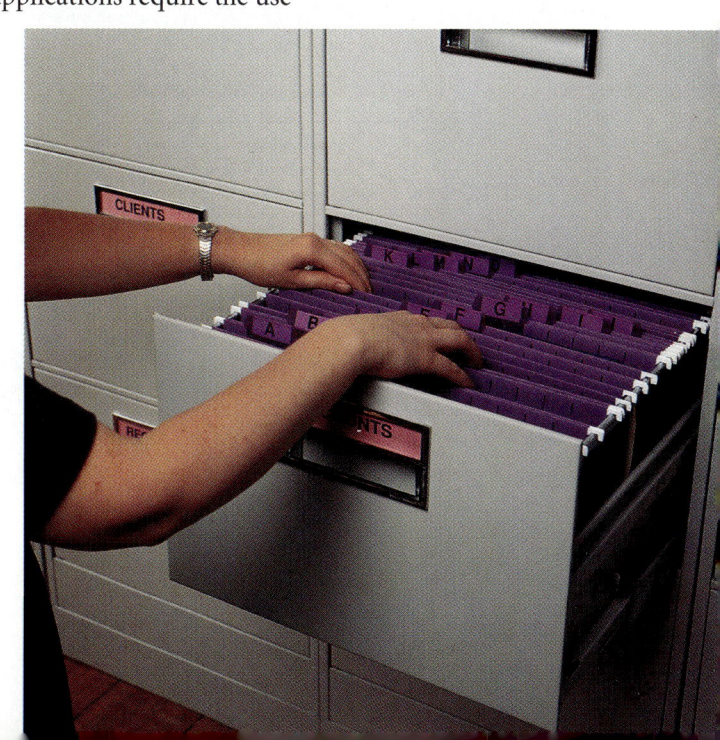

Figure 2-26
One of the first steps in creating a database is to make a list of the items that will be included in the database. The list should include the item description, a short field name that will be used by the database; the length of the item; and the data type. Most databases allow you to add, delete, or change fields after the database is created.

The screens in Figures 2-26 through 2-29 present the development of a database containing information about the members of a college band booster club. The booster club members donate money to help fund band activities. Besides keeping track of each member's name, address, and telephone number, the band director wants to record the amount of money donated and the date the money was received.

A good way to begin creating a database is to make a list of the data you want to record. Each item that you want to keep track of will become a field in the database. Each field should be given a unique name that is short but descriptive. For example, the field name for a member's last name could be Last Name. The field name for a member's first name could be First Name. You also need to decide the length of each field and the type of data that each field will contain. The type of data could be any of the following:

- **alphanumeric**, letters, numbers, or special characters
- **numeric**, numbers only
- **currency**, dollar and cents amounts
- **date**, month, day and year information
- **memo**, freeform text of any type or length

A list of the data necessary for the band booster club is shown in Figure 2-26.

Kokomo College Band Booster Club

ITEM	LENGTH	TYPE
Last Name	15	Text
First Name	15	"
Street	20	"
City	15	"
State	2	"
Zip	10	"
Phone	8	"
Amount	10	Currency
Paydate	8	Date/Time
Comments	50	Text

Figure 2-27
This screen shows how fields in a table are defined using the Microsoft Access database package.

Figure 2-28
Once the database fields are defined, data can be entered. Most database programs can create a data entry form automatically, based on information that was entered for the fields. This Microsoft Access data entry form lists each of the database fields in the order they were entered when the table was created, but they could have been arranged in any order.

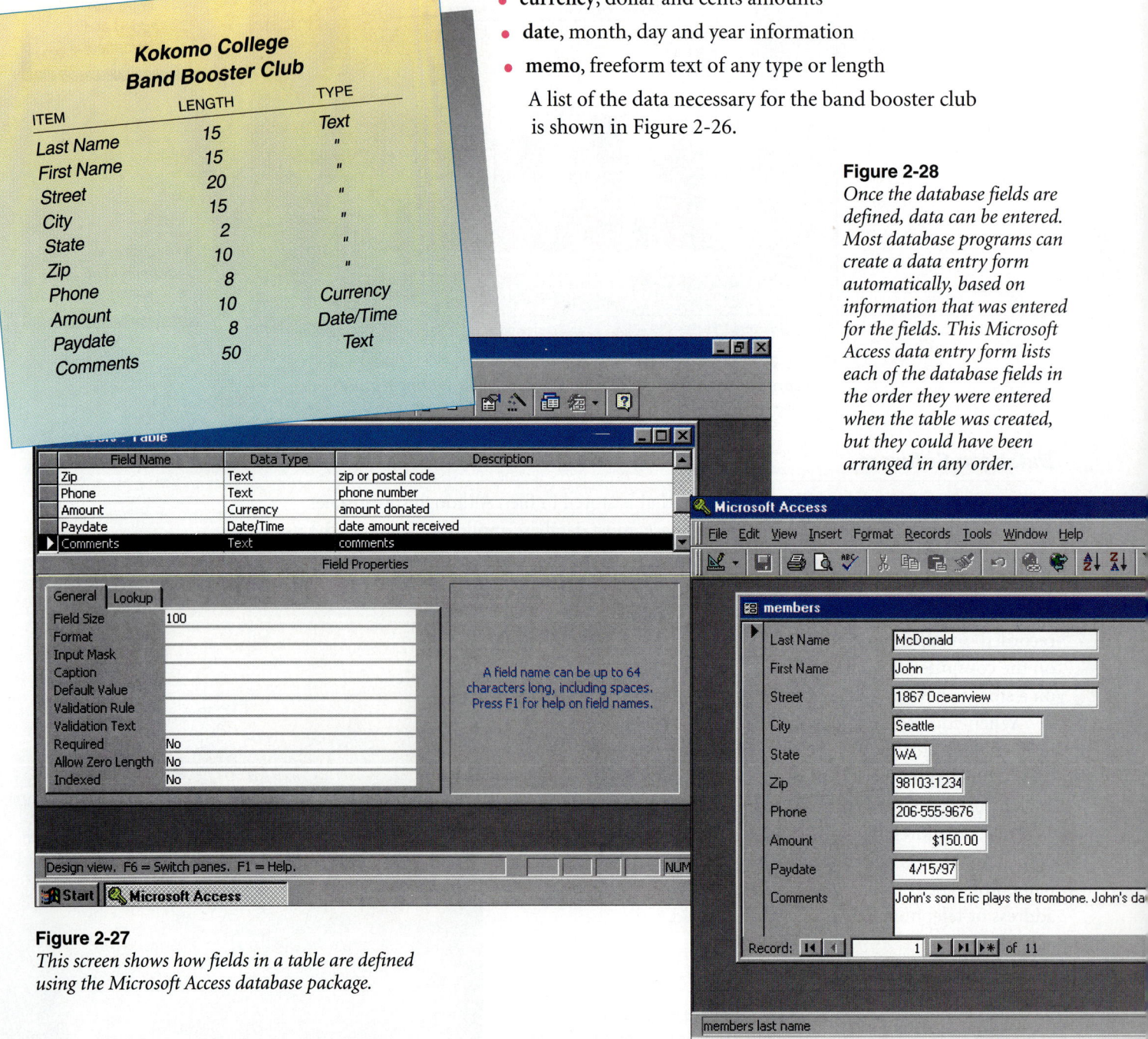

Each database program differs slightly in how it requires the user to enter, or define, fields. A field entry screen from Microsoft Access is shown in Figure 2-27.

After the database structure is created by defining the fields, individual database records can be entered. Usually, they are entered one at a time by using the keyboard. Most database programs, however, also have the ability to import data from other files. The field definitions specified for each field help you in entering the data. For example, designating the Paydate field as a date field prevents a user from entering anything other than a valid date. Comparing data entered against a predefined format or value is called **validation** and is an important feature of database programs. Figure 2-28 shows the entry screen for the band booster club data.

After the records are entered, the database can be used to produce information. All or some of the records can be selected and arranged in the order specified by the user. This is one of the more powerful features of a database; the ability to retrieve database information based on criteria specified by the user. For example, suppose the band director personally wanted to call and thank all the booster club members who donated more than $100. A report, called a **query** could be produced that listed the members names, phone numbers, and the amounts and dates donated. The report could be arranged so the largest donations were listed first. An example of such a report is shown in Figure 2-29.

As shown in the band booster club example, database software assists users in creating files and storing, manipulating, and retrieving data. Popular software packages that perform these functions include Microsoft Access, dBASE, FoxPro, and Paradox.

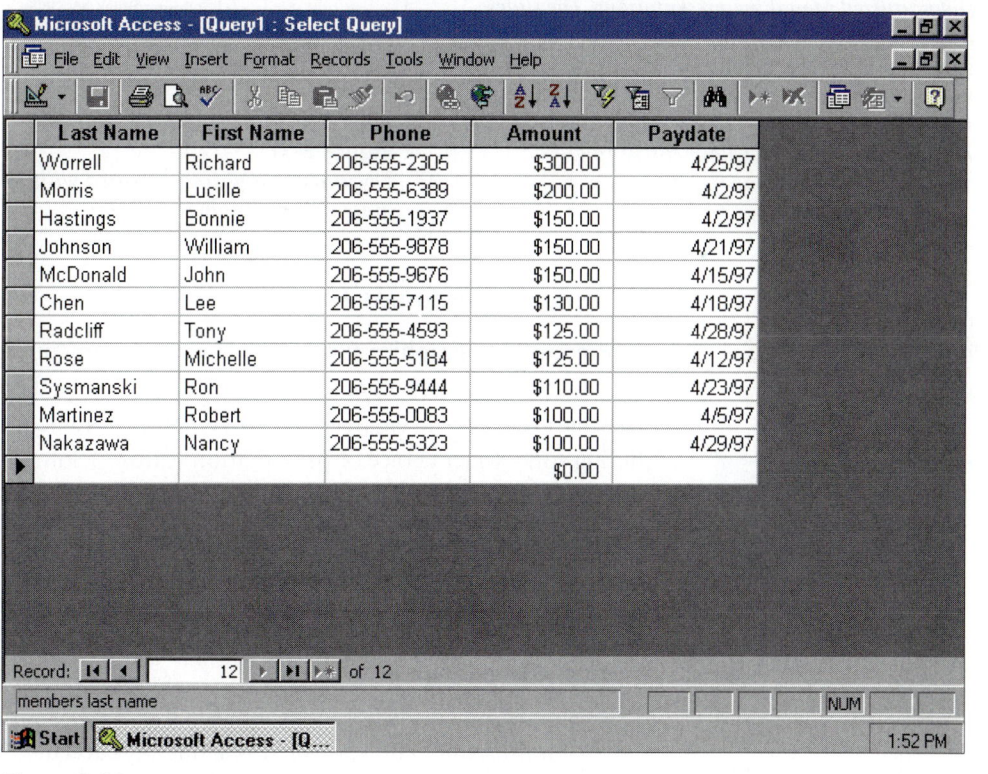

> **inCyber**
>
> For an example of how athletes use databases for training purposes, visit the Discovering Computers Chapter 2 inCyber page (http://www.scsite.com/dc/ch2/incyber.htm) and click Athlete.

Last Name	First Name	Phone	Amount	Paydate
Worrell	Richard	206-555-2305	$300.00	4/25/97
Morris	Lucille	206-555-6389	$200.00	4/2/97
Hastings	Bonnie	206-555-1937	$150.00	4/2/97
Johnson	William	206-555-9878	$150.00	4/21/97
McDonald	John	206-555-9676	$150.00	4/15/97
Chen	Lee	206-555-7115	$130.00	4/18/97
Radcliff	Tony	206-555-4593	$125.00	4/28/97
Rose	Michelle	206-555-5184	$125.00	4/12/97
Sysmanski	Ron	206-555-9444	$110.00	4/23/97
Martinez	Robert	206-555-0083	$100.00	4/5/97
Nakazawa	Nancy	206-555-5323	$100.00	4/29/97
			$0.00	

Figure 2-29
Database software can produce reports based on criteria specified by the user. For example, this screen shows the result of a request, called a query, that specified the name and phone number of each booster club member that contributed $100 or more. The records were sorted so the highest contributors are listed first. The results of the query can be displayed on the screen or printed.

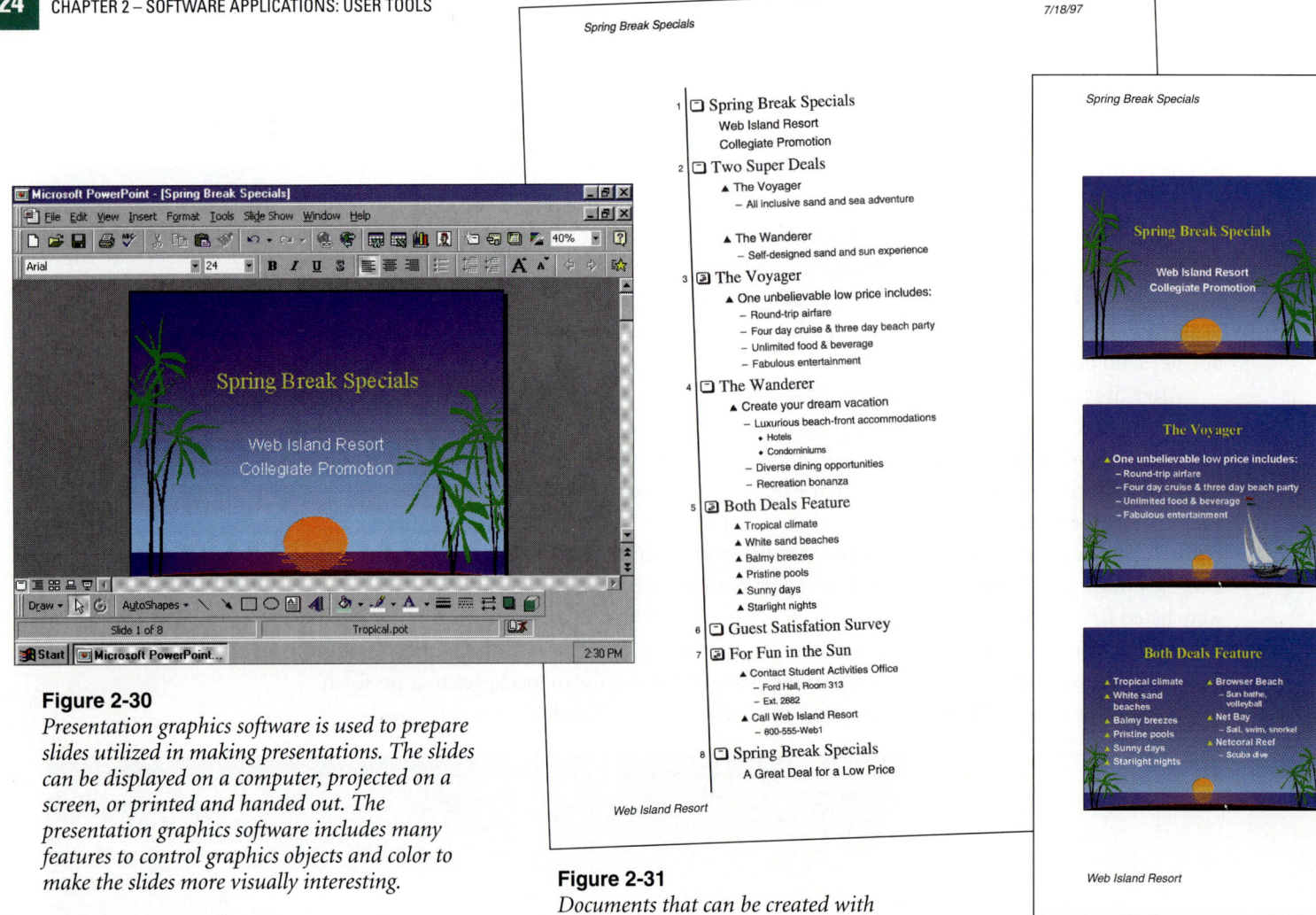

Figure 2-30
Presentation graphics software is used to prepare slides utilized in making presentations. The slides can be displayed on a computer, projected on a screen, or printed and handed out. The presentation graphics software includes many features to control graphics objects and color to make the slides more visually interesting.

Figure 2-31
Documents that can be created with presentation graphics software.

inCyber

For tips on using graphics effectively in a presentation, visit the Discovering Computers Chapter 2 inCyber page (http://www.scsite.com/dc/ch2/incyber.htm) and click Presentation.

Presentation Graphics Software

Presentation graphics allow you to create documents called **slides** that are used in making presentations before a group. The slides can be displayed on a large monitor or projected on a screen (Figure 2-30). Presentation graphics go beyond analytical graphics by offering you a wider choice of presentation features. Some of the features included with presentation graphics packages are:

- Numerous chart types
- Three-dimensional effects for charts, text, and graphics
- Special effects such as shading, shadows, and textures
- Sound and animation
- Color control that includes preestablished groups of complementary colors for backgrounds, lines and text, shadows, fills, and accents
- Image libraries that include clip art graphics that can be incorporated into the slides. Usually the image libraries are business-oriented and include illustrations of factories, people, money, and other business-related art.

Besides the slides, presentation graphics packages create several other documents that can be used in a presentation (Figure 2-31). Outlines include just the text from each slide, usually the slide title and the key points. A notes page is used by the speaker making the presentation and includes a picture of the slide and any notes the speaker wants to see when he or she is discussing the slide. Audience handouts include images of two or more slides on a page that can be given to people who attended the presentation.

SOFTWARE APPLICATIONS 2.25

notes page

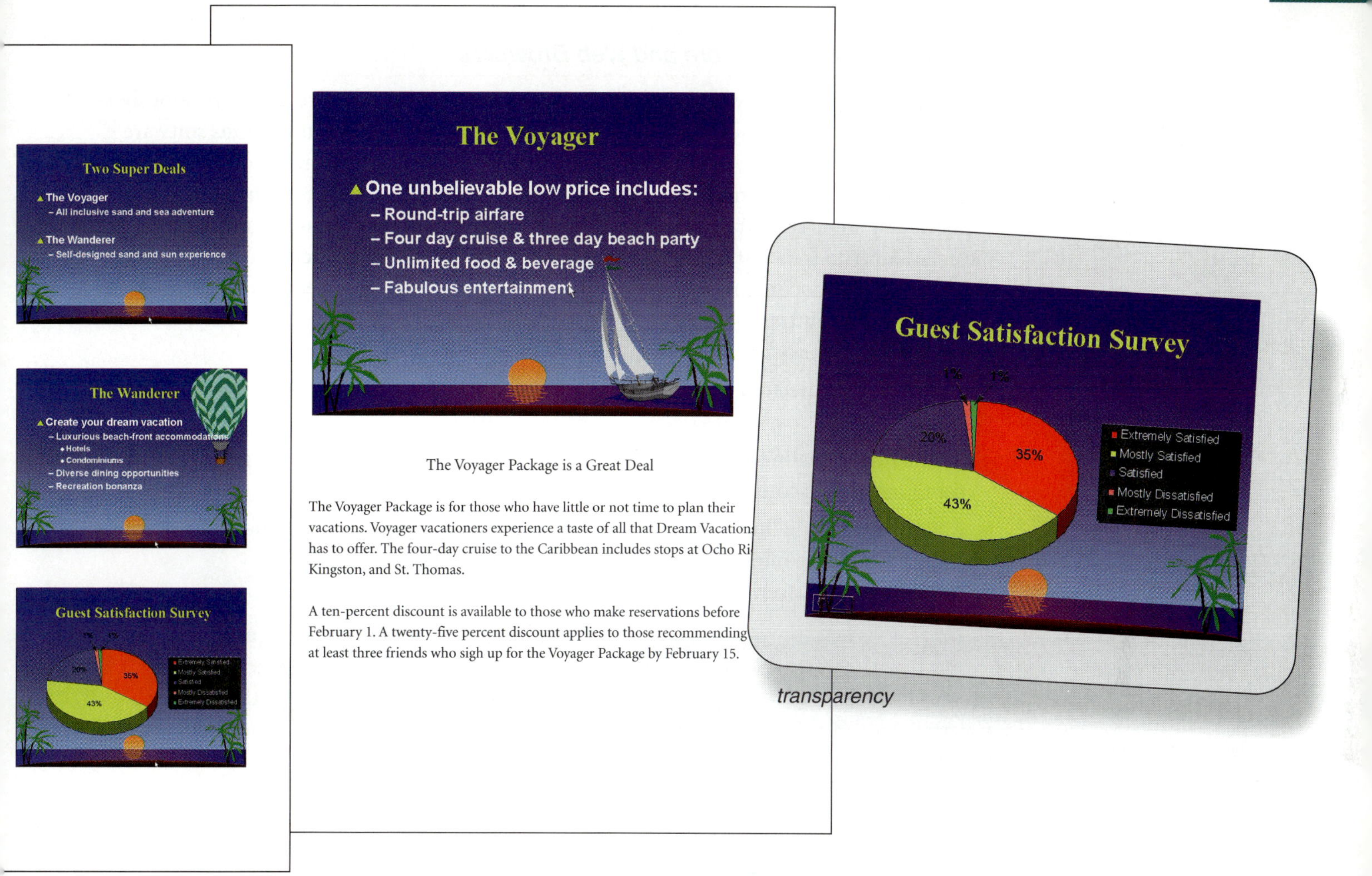

transparency

To help organize and present the slides, presentation graphics packages include slide sorters. A slide sorter presents a screen view similar to how 35mm slides would look on a photographer's light table (Figure 2-32). By using a mouse or other pointing device, you can arrange the slides in any order. When the slides are arranged in the proper order, they can be displayed one at a time by clicking the mouse or using the keyboard. The presenter also can set up the slides to be displayed automatically with a predetermined delay between each slide. Special effects also can be applied to the transition between each slide. For example, one slide might slowly dissolve as the other slide comes into view.

Using presentation graphics software allows you to efficiently create professional quality presentations that help communicate information more effectively. Studies have shown that people are more likely to remember information they have seen as well as heard and that they recall more information when it is presented in color. Popular presentation graphics packages include Microsoft PowerPoint, Aldus Persuasion, Lotus Freelance Graphics, and Compel.

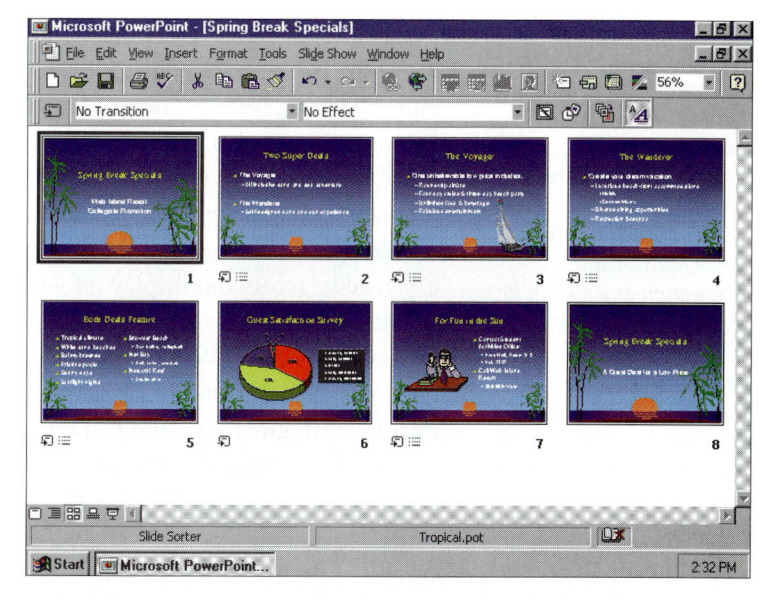

Figure 2-32
This slide sorter screen shows a miniature version of each slide. Using a pointing device or the keyboard, the slides can be rearranged to change their order of presentation.

Communications Software and Web Browsers

Perhaps more than any other application, communications software has tremendously changed the way people use computers in the last several years. **Communications software** is used to transmit data from one computer to another. For two computers to communicate, each must have data communications software, data communications equipment, and be connected by some type of link, such as a telephone line. Most communications packages have the ability to transmit and receive many different types of data, including text and graphics files, fax documents, and information obtained from online services or the Internet.

Besides transmitting and receiving the data, the communications software helps manage communications tasks by:

- Maintaining a directory of telephone numbers and settings for remote computers (Figure 2-33).
- Automatically dialing the number of the remote computer and establishing the communications connection.
- Automatically redialing if the line is busy. A time delay between communications attempts and a limit on the number of redial attempts also can be set.
- Automatically answering if another user calls your computer.

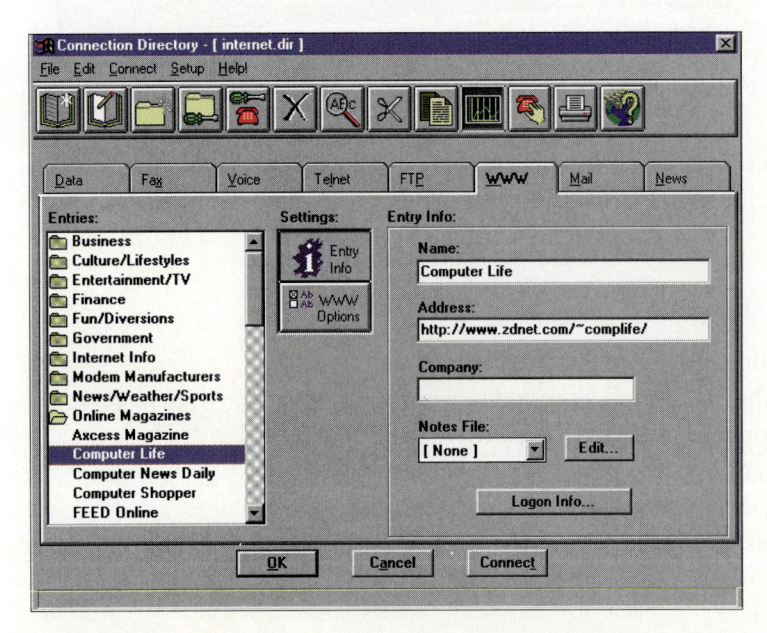

Communications software is frequently used by employees that are away from the office. Using communications software (and sometimes other packages such as electronic mail), remote employees can check their messages, send messages to other employees, check the quantity of inventory on hand, and enter orders that they have just received from customers.

Online Services Communications software also is used to access online services for news, weather, financial, and travel information. Online service companies such as The Microsoft Network and America Online provide a wide range of information and services for a small monthly fee. Other service companies provide detailed information in subject areas such as medicine, finance, or specific industries. Shopping is also available from several services. Online shoppers can read a description and, in many cases, see a picture of a product on their screen. Using a credit card, the product can be ordered. Most banks are now offering online banking. You can review recent financial transactions, transfer money from one account to another, and pay bills using your computer. All of these activities are made possible through the use of data communications software. Popular communications software packages are Procomm Plus and Crosstalk.

Figure 2-33
Communications software programs include directories that make it easier to connect with other computers. This screen shows the Procomm Plus communications software from Datastorm. Connection entries can be organized by type (e.g., data, fax, voice) and by category (e.g., business, finance, government). Clicking the Connect button at the bottom of the screen automatically makes the connection.

Web Browsers A **Web browser** is a special type of communications software that is designed to access and display information at Internet Web sites (Figure 2-34). Information at Internet Web sites is organized into what are called **Web pages**. The first page of information at each Web site is called the **home page**. The Web browser software interprets the Web page information and displays it on your computer screen in a format that usually includes text, graphics, sound, and video. Web browser software keeps track of Internet sites visited and can record the location of sites that you may want to revisit in the future. Netscape Navigator and Microsoft Internet Explorer are the most widely used browsers today.

SOFTWARE APPLICATIONS 2.27

Figure 2-34
Web browser software is used to access and display information at Internet Web sites. The site shown on this screen is used to search the Internet for information on a subject chosen by the user.

Electronic Mail Software

Electronic mail software, also called **e-mail**, allows you to send messages to and receive messages from other computer users (Figure 2-35). The other users may be on the same computer network or on a separate computer system reached through the use of communications equipment and software. Each e-mail user has an electronic mail box with an address to which the mail can be sent. To make the sending of messages more efficient, e-mail software allows you to send a single message to a distribution list consisting of two or more individuals. The e-mail software takes care of copying the message and routing it to each person on the distribution list. For example, a message sent to the Department Supervisors distribution list would be routed to each of the department supervisors. Most e-mail systems have a mail-waiting alert that notifies you by a message or sound that a message is waiting to be read even if you are working in another application.

Although e-mail was once used primarily within private organizations, today several communications

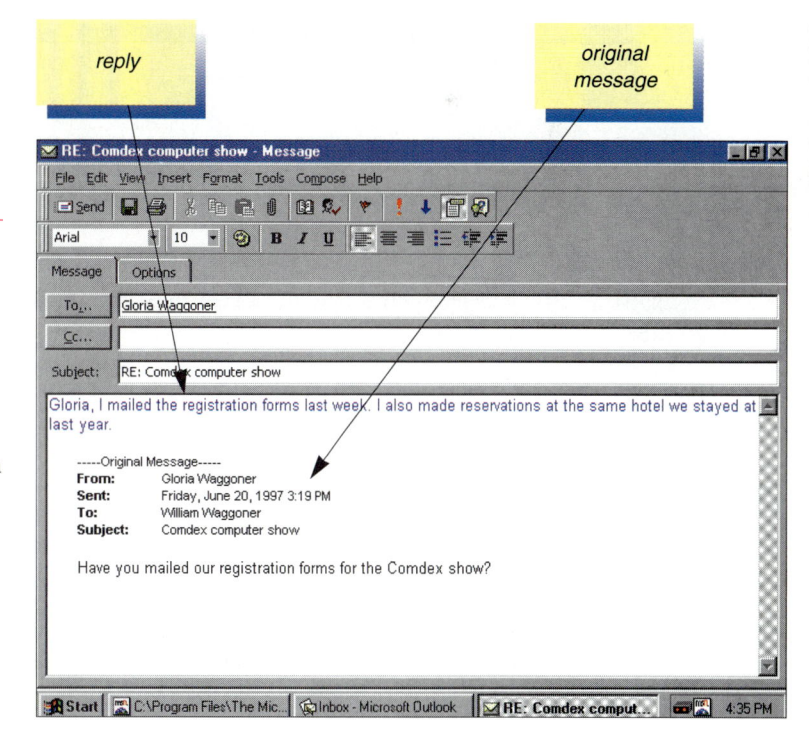

Figure 2-35
Electronic mail (e-mail) allows you to send and receive messages with other computer users. Each user has an electronic mail box to which messages are sent. This screen shows how a user can add a reply to a received message and then send the reply and a copy of the original message back to the person who sent the original message.

companies (such as MCI) and online services providers (such as America Online and CompuServe) provide public e-mail services for individuals. For a small monthly fee, you can receive mail from and send mail to others who have e-mail. Internet service providers such as the OnRamp Group and EarthNet offer e-mail as part of their standard service. Most Web browser software also includes e-mail capabilities. E-mail can be especially useful to people whose job keeps them away from the office. Remote workers can dial into their e-mail and send and receive messages at any time of the day. Because of its widespread use, informal rules, called e-mail etiquette, have been developed. These mostly common sense rules include:

- Keep messages short and to the point.
- Avoid using e-mail for trivia, gossip, or other non-essential communications.
- Keep the distribution list to a minimum.
- Avoid using all capitals letters – it is considered the same as yelling.
- It's okay (OK) for you (u) to (2) abbreviate as long as the abbreviation can be easily understood.
- Emoticons and acronyms also are used to show emotion (Table 2-1).
- Make the subject as meaningful as possible. Many e-mail systems list a summary of the mail and show only the subject, date, and sender.
- Read your mail regularly and clear messages that are no longer needed.

Popular e-mail packages are Microsoft Mail, Lotus cc:Mail, and Eudora.

EMOTICONS AND ACRONYMS	
:)	Happy
:(	Sad
;)	Wink/Sarcasm
:0	Shouting/Shocked
:I	Indifferent
:P	Sticking out tongue
:D	Laughing
<g>	Grin
BTW	By the way
IMO	In my opinion
LOL	Laughing out loud

Table 2-1

Personal Information Management Software

Personal information management (PIM) software can help you keep track of the miscellaneous bits of personal information that each of us deals with every day. This information can take many forms: appointments, lists of things to do, telephone messages, notes about a current or future project, and so on. Individual programs that keep track of this type of information, such as electronic calendars, have been in use for some time. In recent years, however, such programs have been combined so that one package can keep track of all of a user's personal information.

Because of the many types of information that these programs can manage, it is difficult to precisely define personal information software. The category can be applied to programs that offer any of the following capabilities and features, however: appointment calendars, outliners, electronic notepads, data managers, and text retrieval. Some personal information software packages also include communications software capabilities such as phone dialers and e-mail. Appointment calendars allow you to schedule activities for a particular day and time (Figure 2-36). Most of them will warn you if two activities are scheduled for the same time. Outliners allow you to *rough out* an idea by constructing and reorganizing an outline of important points and subpoints. Electronic notepads allow you to record comments and assign them to one or more categories that can be used to retrieve the comments. Data managers are simple file management systems that allow the input, update, and retrieval of related records such as name and address lists or telephone numbers. Text retrieval provides the capability of searching files for specific words or phrases such as *Sales Meeting*. Three popular personal information management packages are Microsoft Schedule+, Ecco Pro, and Lotus Organizer.

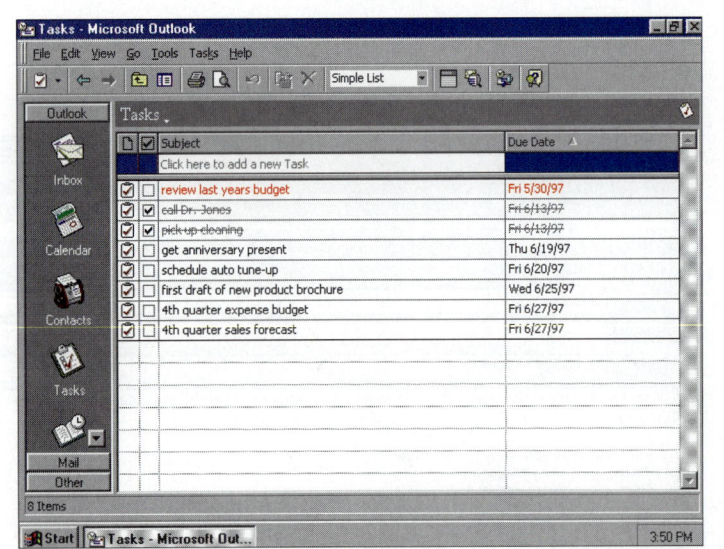

Figure 2-36
Personal information management (PIM) software helps organize and keep track of the many different types of information that people encounter each day. Microsoft Outlook, shown on this screen, allows you to keep track of appointments, events, task lists, and contacts.

Personal Finance Software

Personal finance software helps you track your income and expenses, pay bills, complete online transactions, and evaluate financial plans (Figure 2-37). Recording your financial transactions, especially expenses, helps you determine where, and for what purpose, your money is being spent. Reports can summarize transactions by category, by payee (such as the telephone company), or by time period (such as the last three months). Bill-paying features include the ability to print checks on your computer or have checks printed by an outside service. Several personal finance packages have agreements with credit card companies and banks that enable you to enter credit card transactions and bank account information automatically. You either receive a monthly transaction disk or download the data directly into your computer to obtain current credit card statements and account balances. Financial planning features include home and personal loan analysis, estimated income taxes, and how much money you should be saving for retirement. Other features included in many personal finance packages include home inventory, budgeting, tax related transactions, and investment tracking. Popular personal finance applications include Quicken and Microsoft Money.

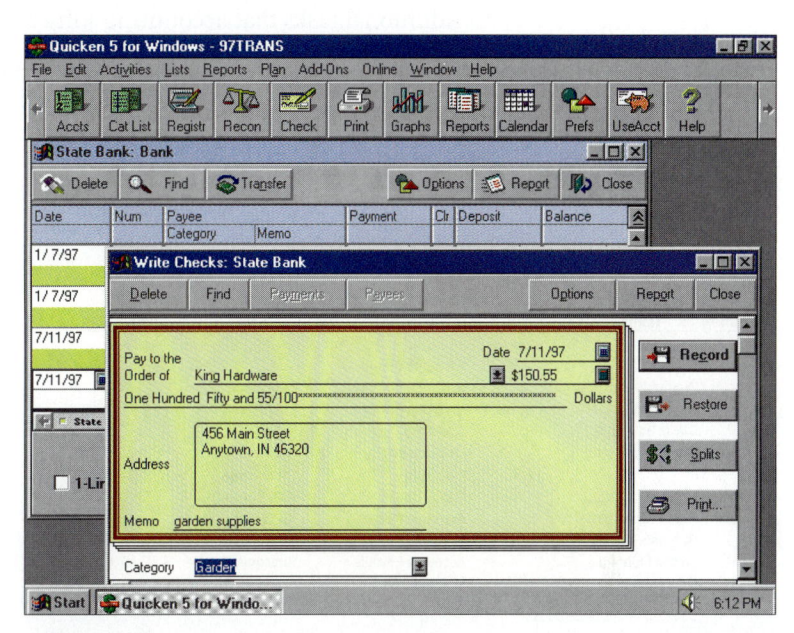

Figure 2-37
Personal finance software such as Quicken helps you track your income and expenses. This screen shows how checks are prepared.

Project Management Software

Project management software allows you to plan, schedule, track, and analyze the events, resources, and costs of a project (Figure 2-38). For example, a construction company might use this type of software to manage the building of an apartment complex or a campaign manager might use it to coordinate the many activities of a politician running for office. The value of project management software is that it provides a method for managers to control and manage the variables of a project to help ensure that the project will be completed on time and within budget. Popular project management packages include Timeline and Microsoft Project.

Figure 2-38
Project management software helps you plan and keep track of the tasks and resources necessary to complete a project. This screen shows part of a project plan for publishing a magazine. The more important tasks are listed in red. The bars in the upper right corner, called a Gantt chart, graphically indicate the duration of each task. The bottom portion of the screen identifies the resources required for the highlighted task; in this case, the hours needed from specific individuals.

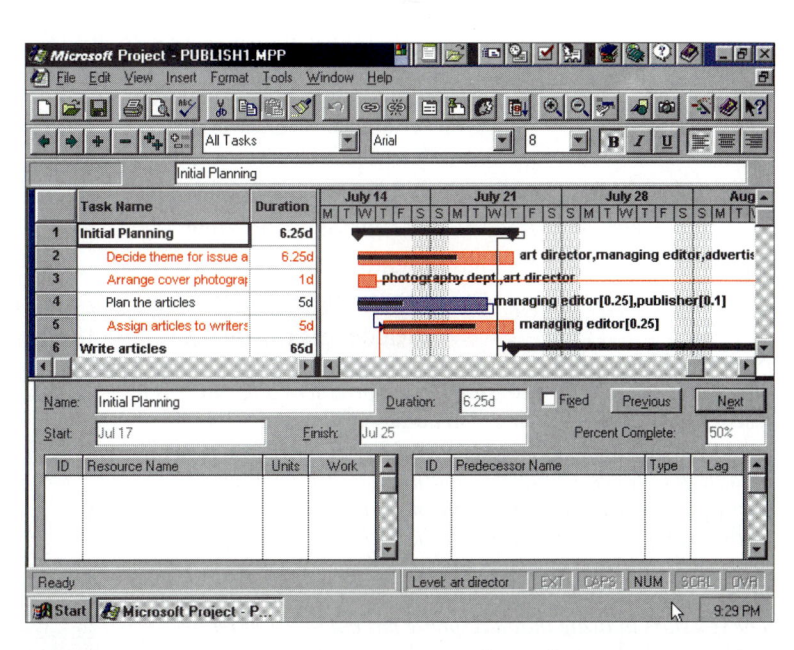

Accounting Software

Accounting software helps companies record and report their financial transactions (Figure 2-39). Some accounting tasks are similar to those handled by personal finance software: tracking income and expenses, writing checks, and recording transactions. Additional tasks that accounting software handles include the following:

- Invoicing; preparing bills for products or services sold
- Accounts receivable; amounts owed by customers
- Accounts payable; amounts owed to suppliers
- Purchase orders; purchase commitments
- Payroll; amounts owed to employees
- Job costing; costs associated with a specific task, contract, or project
- Inventory; keeping track of unsold products
- General ledger; financial transaction summary

The listed features are provided by most accounting software packages. Some packages offer more sophisticated features such as multiple company reporting, foreign currency reporting, tracking the value of company assets, and forecasting the amount of raw materials needed for products. Accounting packages for small businesses range from less than one hundred to several thousand dollars. Accounting packages for large businesses can cost several hundred thousand dollars. Popular small business accounting packages include Intuit QuickBooks and Peachtree Accounting.

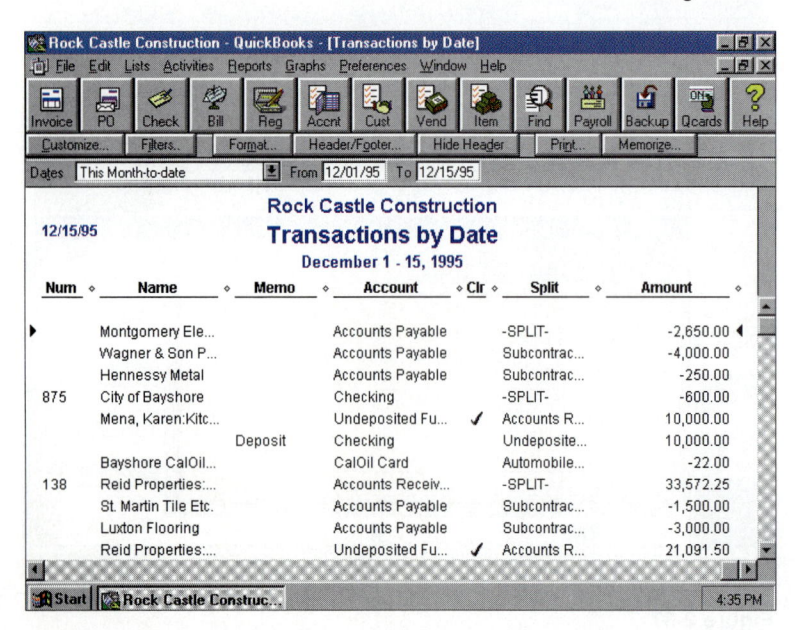

Figure 2-39
Accounting software helps businesses record and report financial transactions.

Groupware

Groupware is a loosely defined term applied to software that helps groups of people collaborate on projects and share information. Groupware is part of a broad concept called **workgroup technology** that includes equipment and software that help group members communicate, manage their activities, and make group decisions.

Some software applications discussed separately in this section, including e-mail and personal information management (PIM) software, also can be considered groupware. Other features and capabilities of groupware applications include:

- Group Editing; the ability for multiple users to revise a document with each set of revisions separately identified. Many word processing packages now include this capability.

Figure 2-40
One of the capabilities of the groupware product Lotus Notes is a discussion database. A discussion database allows multiple persons to add their comments to a subject in the database in an organized manner, similar to conducting a meeting that participants need not attend at the same time or the same place. In the example shown on this screen, the original message has 5/12/97 in the date column and is left-aligned. Responses are shown indented and one line below the item to which they refer. The red stars indicate that a response has not yet been read.

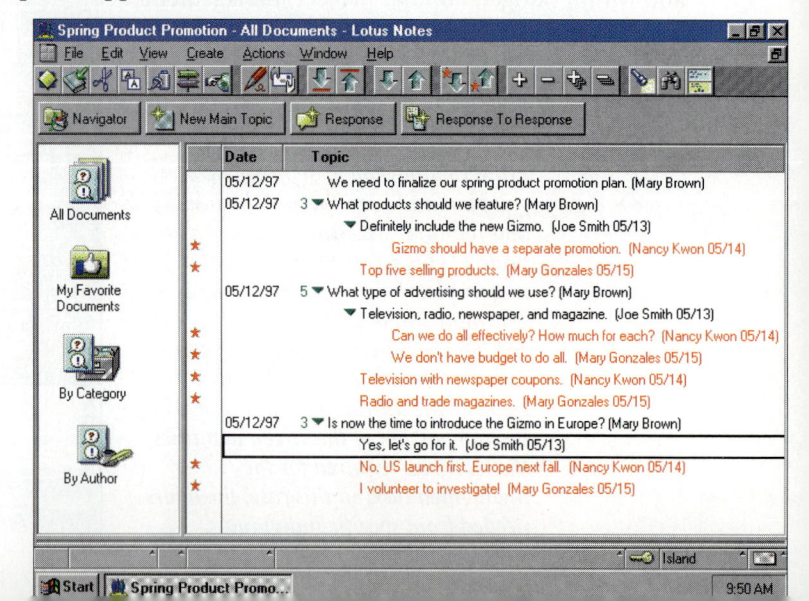

- Group Scheduling; a group calendar that tracks the time commitments of multiple users and helps schedule meetings when necessary.
- Workflow Support; software that automates repetitive processes such as processing an insurance claim, in which multiple persons must review and approve a document.
- Discussion Database; an organized way to keep track of responses to a particular topic or subject.

One of the more widely used groupware packages is Lotus Notes (Figure 2-40). Notes uses a shared database approach to groupware. In addition, Notes includes e-mail and a programming language that can be used to develop customized groupware applications.

Computer-Aided Design (CAD) Software

Computer-aided design (CAD) software assists a user in creating a design for a product, such as a bicycle, or a structure, such as a building (Figure 2-41). CAD software eliminates the laborious drafting that used to be required. Changes to some or all of the design can be made and the results viewed instantly. Three-dimensional CAD programs can rotate the item being designed so you can view it from any angle. Variations of CAD programs have been developed for applications such as electronic circuit design, home remodeling, landscape design, and office furniture layout. AutoCAD and Parametric are two widely used CAD packages.

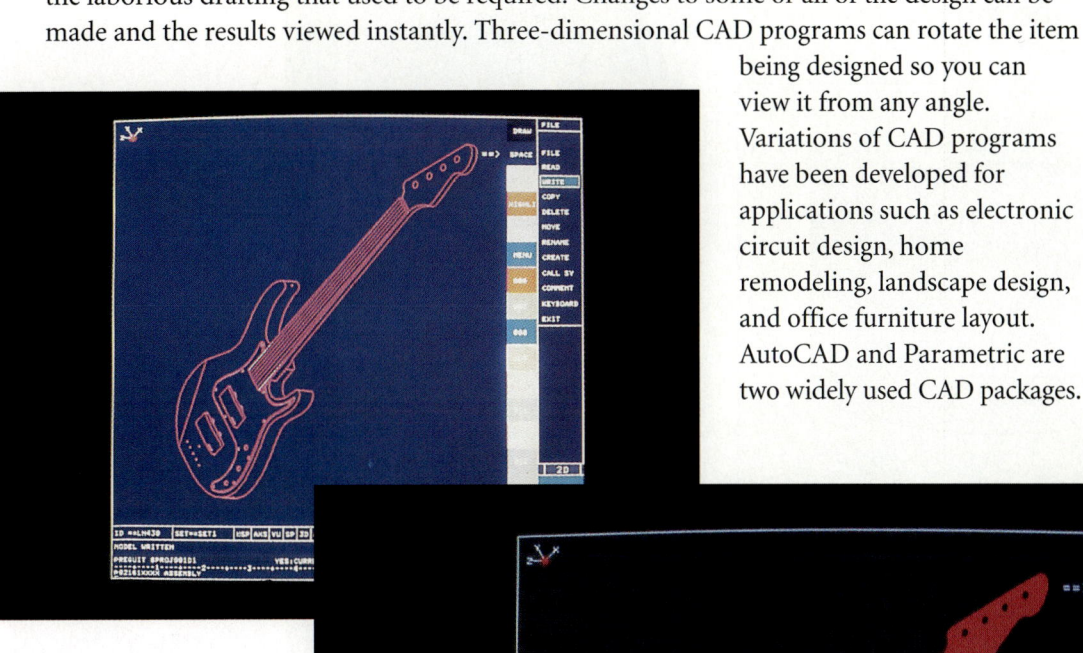

Figure 2-41
Computer-aided design (CAD) software helps users design products and structures.

Multimedia Authoring Software

Multimedia authoring software allows you to create a presentation that can include text, graphics, video, sound, and animation. A multimedia presentation is more than just a combination of these elements, however. A **multimedia presentation** is an interactive computer presentation in which you can choose what amount of material to cover and in what sequence it will be reviewed. For example, you may choose to click a video button to play a video or to skip the video and move to the next screen. Multimedia authoring software helps you create the presentation by controlling the placement of text and graphics and the duration of sounds, video, and animation. Multimedia ToolBook by Asymetrix Corporation is a widely-used multimedia authoring package (Figure 2-42).

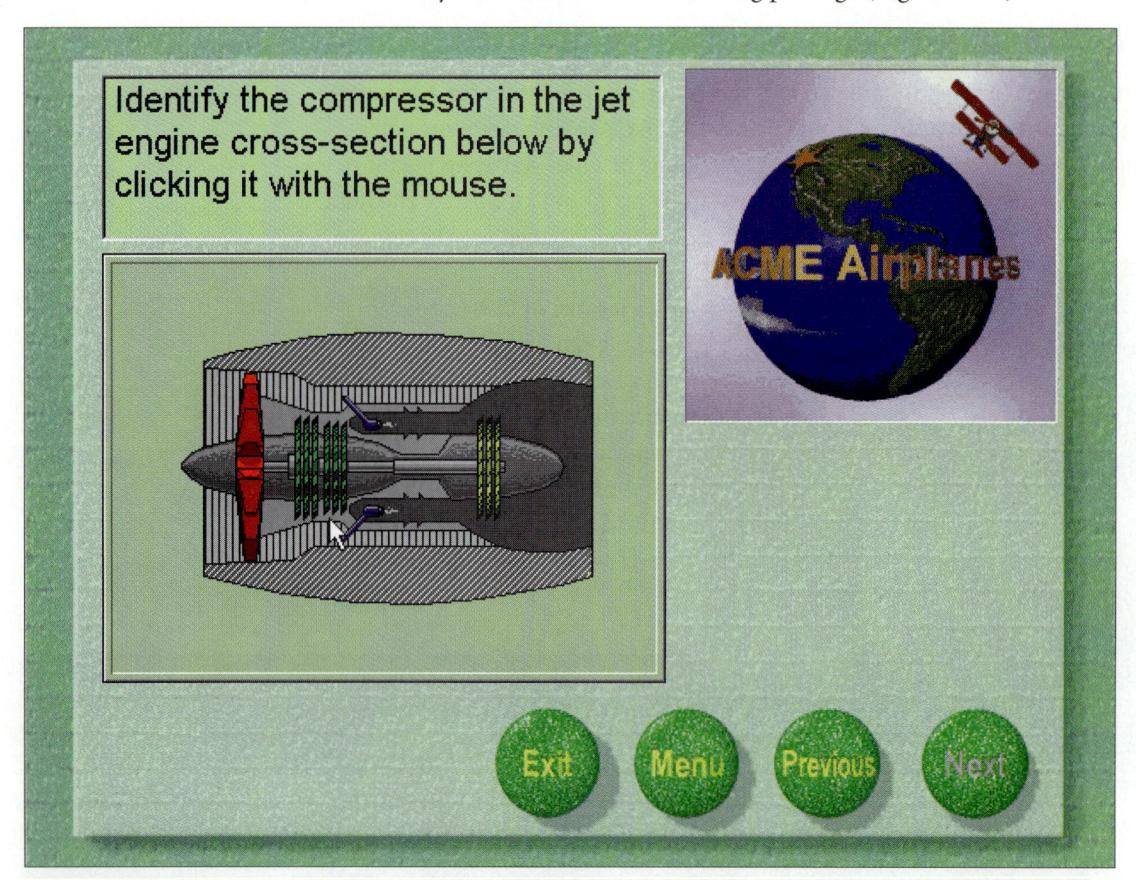

Figure 2-42
Multimedia authoring software enables a user to create a presentation using text, graphics, video, sound, and animation.

Integrated Software and Software Suites

Software packages such as databases and electronic spreadsheets are generally used independently of each other. But what if you wanted to place information from a database into a spreadsheet? You could reenter the database data in the spreadsheet. This would be time consuming, however, and errors could be introduced as you reentered the data. Integrated software and software suites are two approaches towards sharing information among applications.

Integrated software refers to software that combines applications such as word processing, spreadsheet, and database into a single, easy-to-use package. Many integrated packages also include communications capabilities. The applications that are included in integrated packages are designed to have a consistent command and menu structure. For example, the command to print a document looks and works the same in each of the integrated applications. Besides a consistent look and feel, a key feature of integrated packages is their capability of passing quickly and easily from one application to another. For example, revenue and cost information in a database on daily sales could be quickly loaded into a spreadsheet. The spreadsheet could be used to calculate gross profits.

Once the calculations are completed, all or a portion of the spreadsheet data can be passed to the word processing application to create a narrative report.

In their early days, integrated packages were criticized as being a collection of good but not great applications. To some extent this is still true. If you need the most powerful word processor or spreadsheet, you probably will not be satisfied with the capabilities of an integrated application. But for many users, the capabilities of today's integrated applications more than meet their needs. Besides the advantages of working well together, integrated applications are less expensive than buying comparable applications separately. Two popular integrated software packages are Microsoft Works (Figure 2-43) and ClarisWorks.

Similar to integrated software is a **software suite**, individual applications packaged in the same box and sold for a price that is significantly less than buying the applications individually. Although the use of suites was originally just a pricing strategy, suites are becoming more and more like integrated software. First the individual packages were just bundled together for a good price; now they are being modified to work better together and offer the same command and menu structures. For the developer, the advantages of products that look and work the same include shorter development and training time, and easier customer support. Another advantage is that customers who have learned one application package are more likely to buy a second package if they know it works in a similar manner. Popular software suites include Microsoft Office and Lotus SmartSuite.

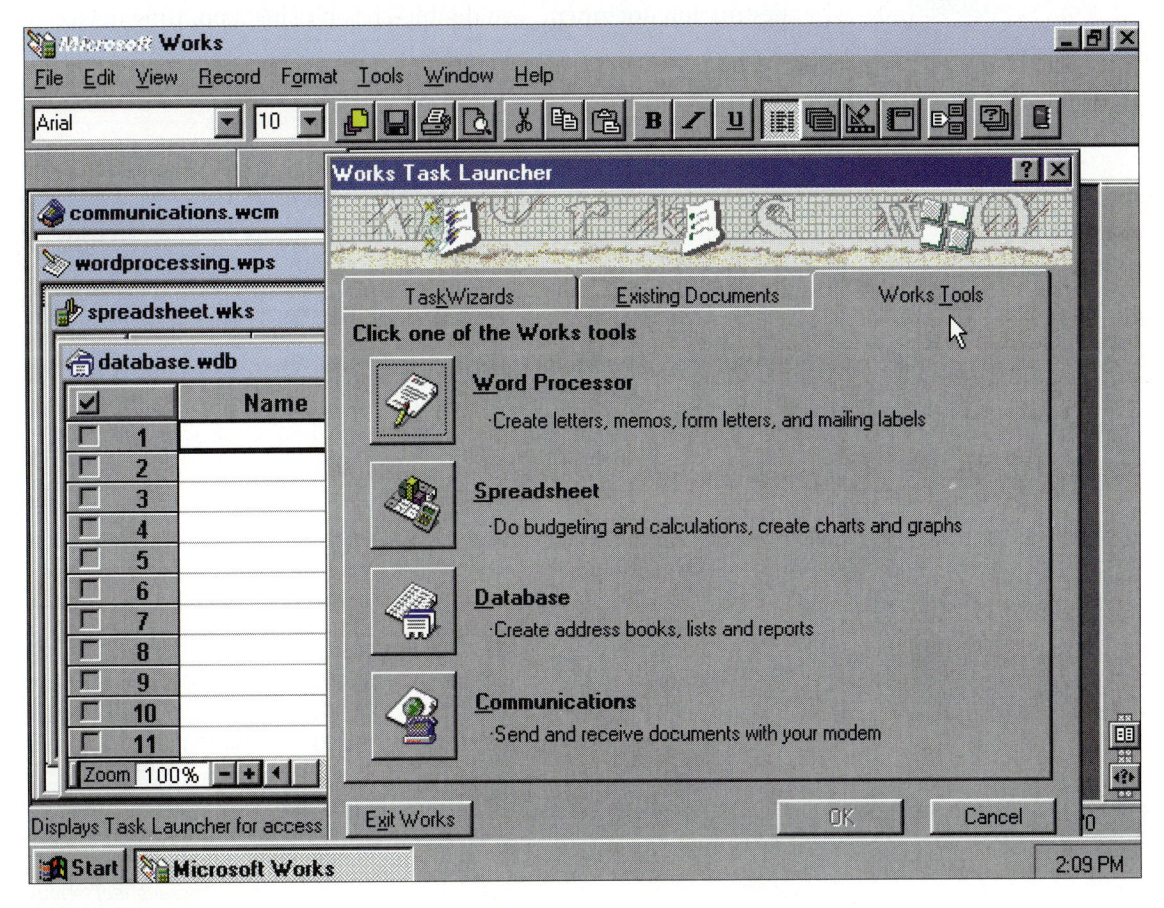

Figure 2-43
Microsoft Works provides word processing, spreadsheet, database, and communications capabilities in a single integrated software package.

Object Linking and Embedding (OLE)

Object linking and embedding, often referred to by the acronym **OLE** (pronounced oh-lay), are two ways to transfer and share information among software applications. To understand OLE, you first must understand something about objects. With regards to OLE, an **object** is any piece of information created with a Windows program. An object can be all or a portion of a document, a graphic, a sound file, or a video clip. Objects from one application, such as a spreadsheet document, can be placed in another application, such as a word processing document. When working with documents, the **source document** is the document from which the object originates, and the **destination document** is the document into which the object is placed. A document that contains objects from more than one application is called a **compound document**. The following numbers refer to Figure 2-44, which uses a spreadsheet and a word processing document to explain the difference between object embedding and object linking.

Figure 2-44
OLE (object linking and embedding).

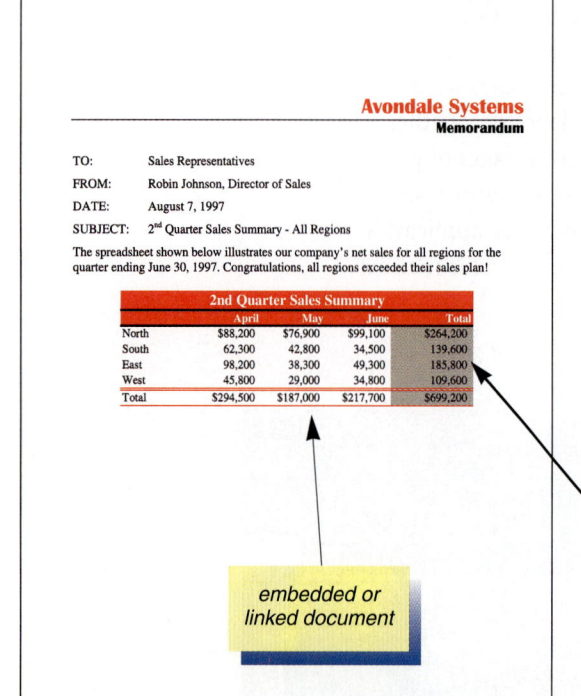

1. Both object linking and object embedding allow you to place all or a portion of a document into another document. This is similar to cut and paste using the Clipboard. With OLE, however, you have the added ability to make changes to the object while you are still working in the destination document. To select the object in the destination document, you double-click it using a pointing device.

embedded or linked document

2nd Quarter Sales Summary

	April	May	June	Total
North	$88,200	$76,900	$99,100	$264,200
South	62,300	42,800	34,500	139,600
East	98,200	38,300	49,300	185,800
West	45,800	29,000	34,800	109,600
Total	$294,500	$187,000	$217,700	$699,200

2. With an **embedded object**, you can make changes to the object in the destination document using tools from the application that originally created the object. Only the destination document is changed. The source document is not affected.

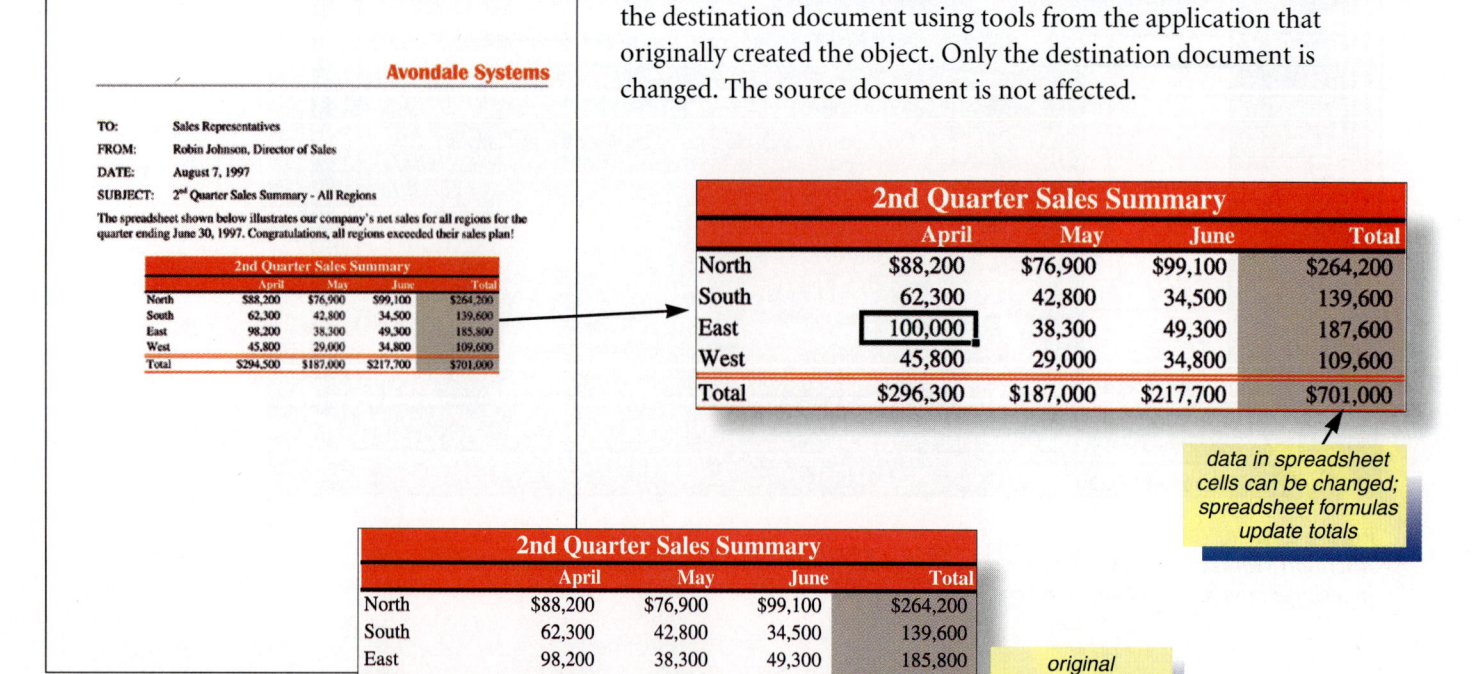

2nd Quarter Sales Summary

	April	May	June	Total
North	$88,200	$76,900	$99,100	$264,200
South	62,300	42,800	34,500	139,600
East	100,000	38,300	49,300	187,600
West	45,800	29,000	34,800	109,600
Total	$296,300	$187,000	$217,700	$701,000

data in spreadsheet cells can be changed; spreadsheet formulas update totals

2nd Quarter Sales Summary

	April	May	June	Total
North	$88,200	$76,900	$99,100	$264,200
South	62,300	42,800	34,500	139,600
East	98,200	38,300	49,300	185,800
West	45,800	29,000	34,800	109,600
Total	$294,500	$187,000	$217,700	$699,200

original spreadsheet is not changed

OBJECT LINKING AND EMBEDDING (OLE) **2.35**

3. With a **linked object**, you make changes to the source document using the original software application. When the object is selected, the original software application is opened. After you make changes and save the source document, changes are reflected in both the source document and the linked destination document.

spreadsheet application used to create spreadsheet opened

original spreadsheet is changed

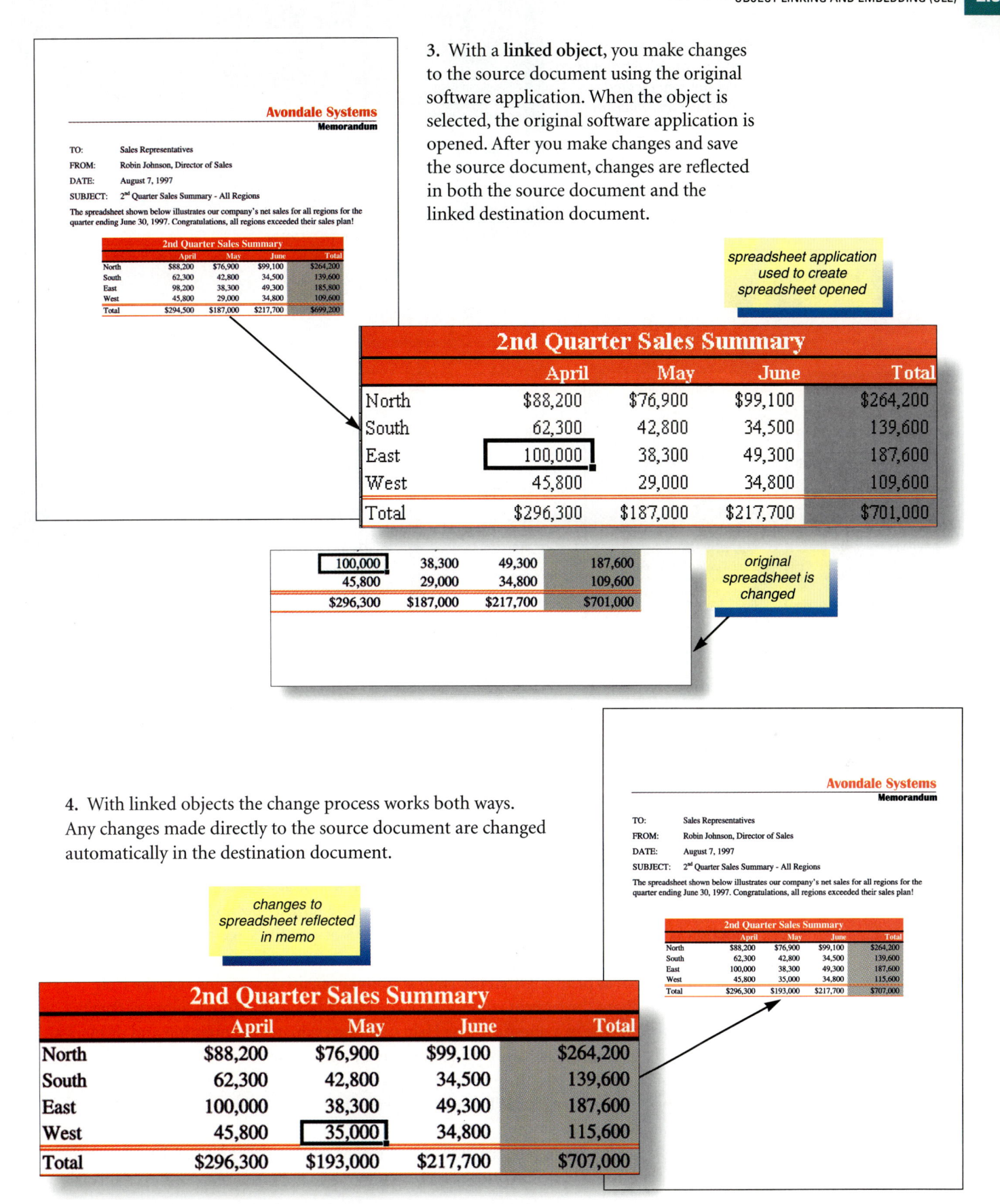

4. With linked objects the change process works both ways. Any changes made directly to the source document are changed automatically in the destination document.

changes to spreadsheet reflected in memo

OLE is particularly useful in situations where the overall form of a document stays the same, such as the memo in Figure 2-44, but the content of the document, such as the quarterly sales results, changes.

Figure 2-46
Software tutorials provide a step-by-step method of learning an application. This screen shows how the Quicken financial management tutorial explains how to set up a budget.

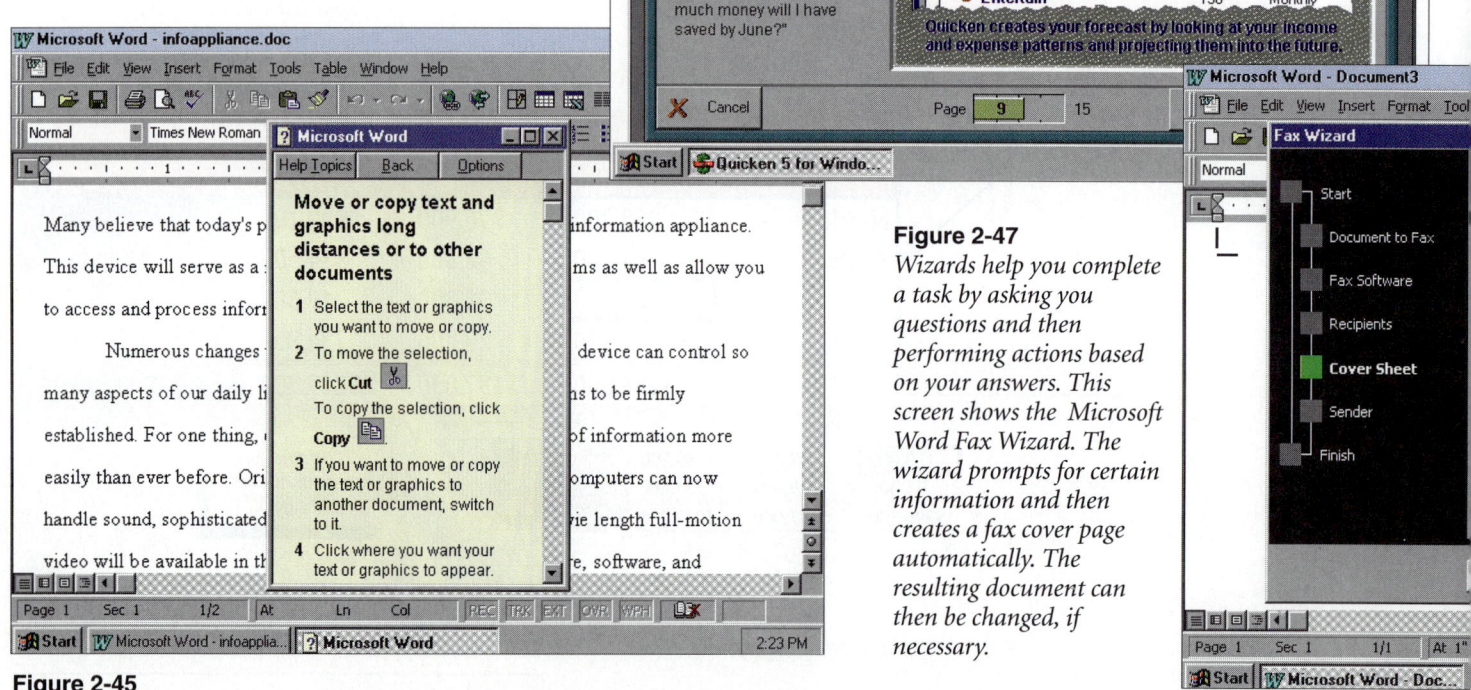

Figure 2-47
Wizards help you complete a task by asking you questions and then performing actions based on your answers. This screen shows the Microsoft Word Fax Wizard. The wizard prompts for certain information and then creates a fax cover page automatically. The resulting document can then be changed, if necessary.

Figure 2-45
Online Help provides assistance without having you leave your application.

Learning Aids and Support Tools for Application Users

Learning to use an application software package involves time and practice. In addition to taking a class to learn how to use a software application, several learning aids and support tools are available to help you, including online Help, tutorials, wizards, and trade books.

Online Help (Figure 2-45) refers to explanatory information that is available while you are using an application. In most packages, a function key or an on-screen button activates the Help feature. When you are using an application and have a question, using the help function key or button temporarily will overlay your work on the screen with information on how to use the package. Help topics can be accessed by topic, such as printing a document, or by keywords, such as printer. Often the Help is **context-sensitive**, meaning that the Help information is about the current command or operation being attempted. Some packages even allow you to type in a question. The Help software evaluates the question and displays a list of related topics. Many software developers believe that their online Help is so comprehensive that they have stopped shipping user's manuals along with the software. Many companies also have FAQs (Frequently Asked Questions) Web pages on the Internet to help you find answers to common questions.

Tutorials are step-by-step instructions using real examples that show you how to use an application (Figure 2-46). Some tutorials are written manuals, but more and more, tutorials are software-based, allowing you to use your computer to learn about a package.

A **wizard** is an automated assistant that helps you complete a task by asking you questions and then automatically performing actions based on your answers (Figure 2-47). Many software applications include wizards: word processing programs have wizards to help you create memorandums, meeting agendas, and letters; spreadsheet programs have chart and function wizards; and database programs have form and report wizards. These are just a few of the wizards available to help you learn and use these software programs effectively.

If printed documentation is included with a software package, often it is organized as reference material. This makes it helpful once you know how to use a package, but difficult to use when you are first learning it. For this reason, many **trade books** (Figure 2-48) are available to help you learn to use the features of personal computer application packages. These books can be found where software is sold and are usually carried in regular bookstores.

Summary of Software Applications

By reading this chapter, you have learned about user interfaces and several of the most widely used software applications. You have also read about some of the learning aids and support tools that are available for application software. Knowledge about these topics increases your computer literacy and helps you to understand how personal computers can help you in your career, school, and at home.

Figure 2-48
Trade books are available for all popular software applications.

COMPUTERS AT WORK

Shortcuts to Creating Documents

Before you invest the time to create a new document, you first should check to see if something similar already exists. Thousands of templates already have been created and are available from a variety of sources. Many of these templates are designed for general requirements common to many businesses, such as a fax cover sheet or a product invoice. Others templates are specific to particular professions such as legal or medical practices. The first place to look is in the template file included with your software application. Word processors usually have the most document templates, but spreadsheet, database, desktop publishing, and presentation graphics applications also include template files. If the standard templates do not represent your needs, ask your software supplier if add-on template packages are available. For example, Microsoft markets a Small Business Pack that consists of more than 40 easy-to-use templates, forms, and reports that assist businesses in everything from day-to-day operations to long range planning. Functional areas include financial, management, marketing, operations, planning, and sales.

Some documents, such as a contract or a lease agreement, need only a small amount of data changed each time they are prepared. Creation of these types of documents is made easier with document assembly programs that prompt you for the necessary data and insert it automatically in the document. Document assembly programs not only make preparation of routine documents faster, but they also reduce the possibility of leaving out key data.

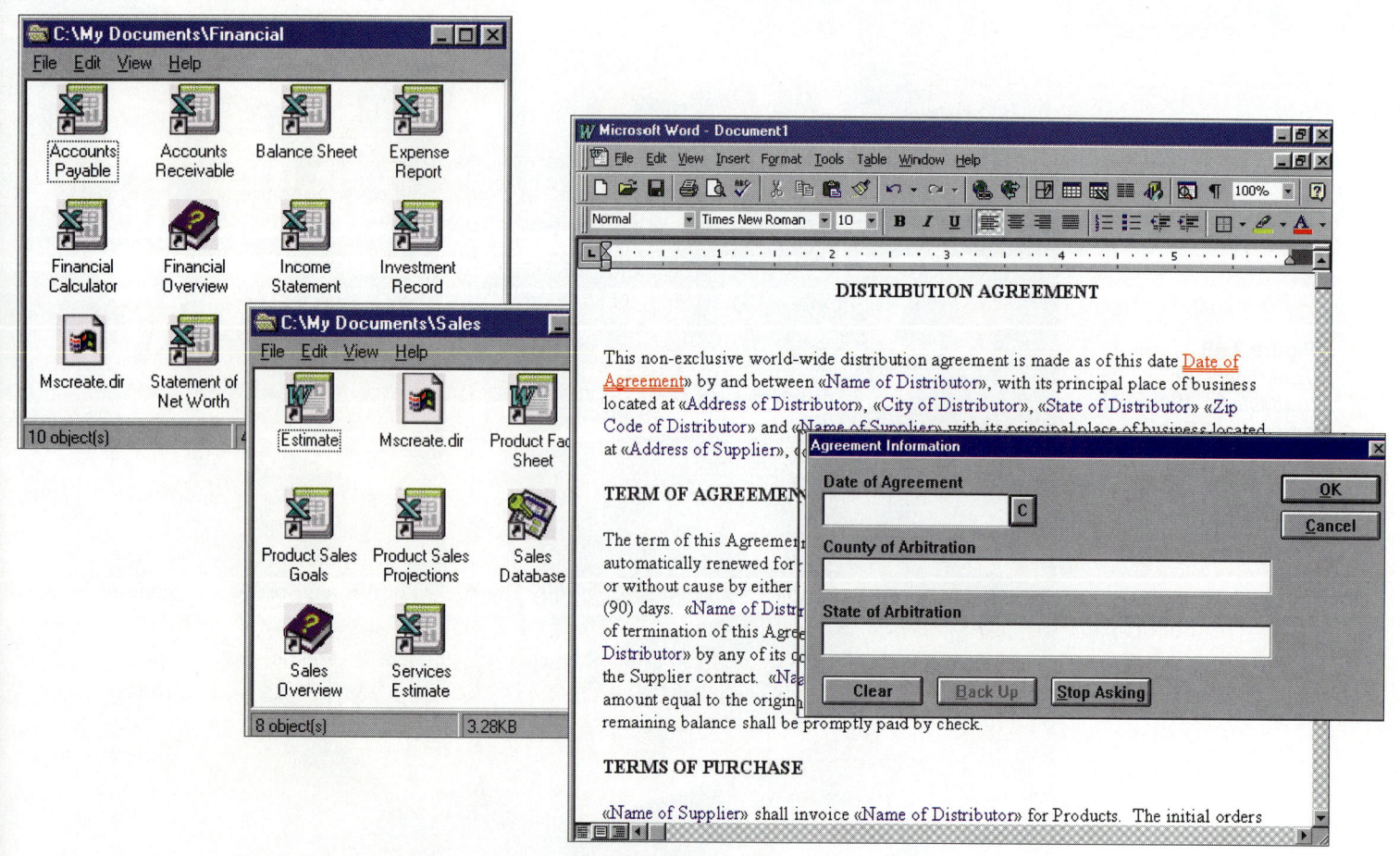

Figure 2-49

IN THE FUTURE

Subscription Software

In the future, will you pay an annual fee for application software packages, just as you pay for a magazine subscription? Some foresee this as the trend. Rather than paying a large one-time license fee for software, the vendor and the user may be better served by the user paying smaller amounts annually as long as he or she continues to use the software.

Software applications used to cost hundreds of dollars each. Some top-selling productivity applications had a list price of $500 or more. Intense competition lowered the prices of individual applications (and drove some developers out of business) and software suites have continued the downward per-package price trend. But today, software is even more expensive to produce and software developers have had to come up with other ways to generate revenue and lower support costs. One way to generate revenue is to charge maintenance or support fees. While some developers still provide toll-free support telephone numbers, most have gone to toll numbers. Even the toll-free numbers can be misleading. Often they connect to a person who will ask for a credit card number before you can talk to a technical support representative. Sometimes you are given the option of paying a flat fee; $25 is common, or paying $2 or $3 a minute for answers to your questions. You have to decide if it is a simple problem that is likely to be solved in a minute or two or if you would be better off with the flat fee. Some vendors use 900 area code numbers to charge your telephone number for pay-by-the-minute support. To lower costs, most vendors offer some type of online support. Some vendors offer online support from all of the following methods: dial-up bulletin boards, online service providers such as America Online, fax databases, and Internet Web sites. Many vendors now use these online methods to distribute software, especially corrections to known software problems.

Software Support Options

On the Internet • http://www.scseries.com
Answers to frequently asked questions (FAQs), technical bulletins, and other product support information are available 24 hours a day, 7 days a week at our Web site.

Fax Back • **(208) 555-9876**
Answers to many common installation and product questions are available 24 hours a day, 7 days a week from our fax-by-demand system.

Standard Support • **(208) 555-1234**
No charge support is available via a toll call Monday through Friday between 6:00 a.m. and 6:00 p.m. mountain time.

Priority Support
Priority support from support specialists is available 24 hours a day, 7 days a week. Two billing options are available:

(900) 555-4567 $2 per minute, $25 maximum. Charges appear on your telephone bill.

(800) 555-4321 $25 per incident. This service is billed to your credit card.

Figure 2-50

Upgrade fees are another way software companies generate revenues that help pay for ongoing development. Not too long ago, software upgrades came out every 18 to 36 months. Nowadays, some companies update their products several times a year. Many companies try for at least an annual upgrade. The upgrade fees usually are much less than the cost of buying the package new, but can still be substantial; sometimes more than $100. For a user with a lot of software, annual upgrade fees can be a significant ongoing expense. Some users are reluctant to upgrade each time the developer introduces a new version. Unless the new version has some feature the user needs, no practical incentive exists to upgrade. Most developers, however, stop supporting older versions of their product at some point in time. Usually, the last version is supported but versions two or more releases back often have limited or no support.

Overall, the tendency seems to be towards smaller but more frequent charges for software. Some developers have taken this approach to the point where they give away their software in hopes that you will install the product, become a dedicated user, and want to pay the subsequent upgrade and/or support charges. It's like the razor blade companies that give away their razors and make their profits selling replacement blades. To make it easier for the developer to receive the annual fees, some companies ask that you authorize the company to automatically charge a credit card. The annual fee has advantages to the user as well as the developer. If the developer has factored receiving annual fees into the software pricing, then you will obtain the product for a lower initial cost. Once the annual fee is paid, you do not have to worry about another $25 charge or speaking quickly to minimize a per-minute charge. All you have to worry about is whether the software vendor will answer the telephone!

2 review

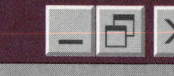

chapter
1 | 2 | 3 | 4 | 5 | 6 | 7 | 8 | 9 | 10 | 11 | 12 | 13 | 14 | I

inCyber | review | terms | yourTurn | hotTopics | outThere | winLabs | webWalk | exercises | news | home

INSTRUCTIONS: *To display this page from the Web, launch your browser and enter the URL, http://www.scsite.com/dc/ch2/review.htm. Click the links for current and additional information.*

1 User Interface

An operating system tells the computer how to perform functions such as processing program instructions and transferring data. Once the operating system is loaded into the memory of a computer, application programs can be run. The **user interface** is the way all software, including the operating system, communicates with the user. A **graphical user interface (GUI)**, one of the more common user interfaces, combines text and graphics.

2 Software Applications

Application software consists of programs that tell a computer how to produce information. Individual software products are called **software packages**. Understanding software applications commonly used on personal computers is part of being computer literate.

4 Desktop Publishing Software

Desktop publishing (DTP) software is used to design and produce high-quality documents that contain text, graphics, and unique colors. DTP software is designed specifically for **page composition and layout** (sometimes called **page makeup**), or the process of arranging text and graphics on the document page. A **page definition language** describes the document to be printed in language the printer can understand.

6 Database Software

A **database** is a collection of data stored in files. **Database software** is used to create a database and to retrieve, manipulate, and update the data kept in it. A **file** is a collection of related data stored in records. Each **record** contains a set of related facts called **fields**. The capability of retrieving information in a report, called a **query**, based on criteria specified by the user is one of the more powerful features of a database.

3 Word Processing Software

Word processing requires the use of a computer to produce or modify documents that primarily consist of text. Producing a document using word processing generally consists of four steps: creating, editing, formatting, and printing. Creating involves entering text. **Editing** is the process of making changes in the content of a document. **Formatting** means changing the appearance of a document. Printing can be done utilizing many different options. Diverse features are used during each step to create professional-looking documents or home pages on the World Wide Web.

5 Spreadsheet Software

Spreadsheet software organizes numeric data in a table format called a **spreadsheet** or **worksheet**. Data is arranged vertically in **columns** and horizontally in **rows**. A **cell** is the intersection where a column and row meet. Cells may contain **labels** (text), **values** (numbers), and **formulas** that perform calculations. A spreadsheet's capabilities of recalculating when data is changed, called **what-if analysis**, and creating a **chart** that graphically shows the relationship of numerical data make it a valuable tool for decision making.

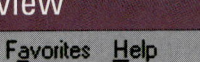

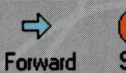

review

chapter 1 | 2 | 3 | 4 | 5 | 6 | 7 | 8 | 9 | 10 | 11 | 12 | 13 | 14 | I

inCyber | review | terms | yourTurn | hotTopics | outThere | winLabs | webWalk | exercises | news | home

7 Presentation Graphics Software

Presentation graphics allows the user to create documents called **slides** that are utilized in making presentations before a group. Presentation graphics packages offer numerous chart types, three-dimensional effects, special effects, sound and animation, color control, and image libraries. A slide sorter helps to organize and present the slides. Presentation graphics packages also can be used to create outlines, notes pages, and audience handouts.

8 Communications Software, Web Browser, and Electronic Mail Software

Communications software is used to transmit data from one computer to another. Most communications packages transmit and receive different types of data, maintain a directory, automatically dial, automatically redial, and automatically answer. A **Web browser** is a type of communications software designed to access and display information that is organized into **Web pages** at Internet Web sites. **Electronic mail software**, also called **e-mail**, allows users to send messages to and receive messages from other computer users.

9 Personal Information Management and Personal Finance Software

Personal information management (PIM) software helps individuals keep track of miscellaneous bits of personal information. These packages may offer appointment calendars, outliners, electronic notepads, data managers, and text retrieval. **Personal finance software** helps you track your income and expenses, pay bills, and evaluate financial plans.

10 Project Management Software, Accounting Software, and Groupware

Project management software allows users to plan, schedule, track, and analyze the events, resources and costs of a project. **Accounting software** helps companies record and report their financial transactions. **Groupware** is a term applied to software that helps multiple users work together by sharing information.

11 Computer-Aided Design (CAD) and Multimedia Authoring Software

Computer-aided design (CAD) software assists a user in creating a design for a product or structure. Changes can be made to all or part of the design and the results viewed instantly. **Multimedia authoring software** allows you to create a presentation that can include text, graphics, video, sound, and animation.

12 Integrated Software and Software Suites

Integrated software refers to software that combines applications into a single, easy-to-use package. The applications are designed to have a consistent command and menu structure, and data can be passed quickly from one application to another. In a **software suite**, individual applications are packaged in the same box and sold for a price that is significantly less than buying the applications individually. The packages are modified to work better together and offer the same command and menu structures.

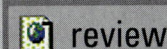

chapter 2 terms

1 | 2 | 3 | 4 | 5 | 6 | 7 | 8 | 9 | 10 | 11 | 12 | 13 | 14 | 1

inCyber | review | terms | yourTurn | hotTopics | outThere | winLabs | webWalk | exercises | news | home

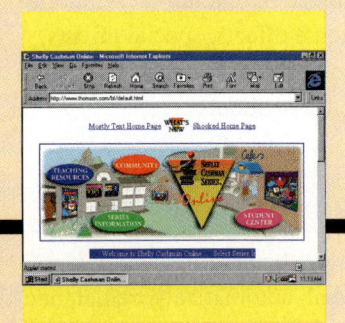

INSTRUCTIONS: To display this page from the Web, launch your browser and enter the URL, http://www.scsite.com/dc/ch2/terms.htm. Scroll through the list of terms. Click a term for its definition and a picture. Click the rocket ship for current and additional information about the term.

Web browser

DEFINITION

Web browser
Programs running on Internet-connected computers that enable users to access World Wide Web sites that have text, graphics, video, and sound and have hypertext links to other information and Web sites. (**2.26**)

absolute referencing (2.19)
accounting software (2.30)
alignment (2.9)
alphanumeric (2.22)
analytical graphics (2.20)
annotations (2.8)
AutoCorrect (2.7)
AutoFormat (2.10)
AutoSave (2.4)
AutoSum button (2.16)

bar charts (2.20)
border (2.10)
built-in style (2.10)
business graphics (2.20)
button (2.3)

cell (2.15)
centered alignment (2.9)
chart (2.20)
clip art (2.10)
Clipboard (2.6)
color libraries (2.13)
columns (2.13, 2.15)
commands (2.3)
communications software (2.26)
compound document (2.34)
computer-aided design (CAD) (2.31)
context-sensitive (2.36)
copy (2.6)
currency (2.22)
cursor (2.6)
cut (2.6)

database (2.21)
database software (2.21)
date (2.22)
dedicated word processing systems (2.4)
delete (2.6)
desktop publishing (DTP) (2.12)

destination document (2.34)

editing (2.6)
electronic mail software (2.27)
e-mail (2.27)
embedded object (2.34)

fields (2.21)
file (2.21)
font (2.9)
footers (2.10)
format (2.8)
formulas (2.15)
functions (2.16)

grammar checker (2.8)
graphical user interface (GUI) (2.2)
graphics (2.10)
groupware (2.30)

headers (2.10)
highlighting tool (2.8)
home page (2.26)

icons (2.2)
illustration software (2.13)
insert (2.6)
insertion point (2.6)
integrated software (2.32)

justification (2.9)
justified alignment (2.9)

labels (2.15)
landscape (2.11)
left alignment (2.9)
line charts (2.20)
line spacing (2.9)
linked object (2.35)

macro (2.16)
margins (2.9)
memo (2.22)
menu (2.3)
Microsoft Windows (2.2)
monospacing (2.9)
multimedia authoring software (2.32)
multimedia presentation (2.32)

numeric (2.22)

object (2.34)
object linking and embedding (2.34)
OLE (2.34)
online Help (2.36)
operating system (2.2)

page composition and layout (2.12)
page definition language (2.14)
page makeup (2.12)
paste (2.6)
personal finance software (2.29)
personal information management (PIM) software (2.28)
pie charts (2.20)
point (2.8)
portrait (2.11)
PostScript (2.14)
presentation graphics (2.24)
print preview (2.11)
project management software (2.29)
proportional spacing (2.9)

query (2.23)

record (2.21)
relative referencing (2.19)
replace (2.6)

revision marks (2.8)
right alignment (2.9)
rows (2.15)

scroll tips (2.6)
scrolling (2.6)
search (2.6)
shading (2.10)
slides (2.24)
software packages (2.4)
software suite (2.33)
source document (2.34)
spacing (2.9)
spelling checker (2.6)
spreadsheet (2.14)
style (2.9)
style sheet (2.10)

tables (2.10)
template (2.10)
thesaurus (2.8)
trade books (2.37)
tutorials (2.36)
typeface (2.8)

user interface (2.2)

validation (2.23)
values (2.15)

Web browser (2.26)
Web pages (2.26)
what-if analysis (2.19)
window (2.2)
wizard (2.36)
word processing (2.4)
word wrap (2.5)
workgroup technology (2.30)
worksheet (2.14)
WYSIWIG (2.5)

yourTurn

chapter 1 | 2 | 3 | 4 | 5 | 6 | 7 | 8 | 9 | 10 | 11 | 12 | 13 | 14 | I

inCyber | review | terms | yourTurn | hotTopics | outThere | winLabs | webWalk | exercises | news | home

INSTRUCTIONS: *To display this page from the Web, launch your browser and enter the URL, http://www.scsite.com/dc/ch2/turn.htm. Click a blank line for the answer. Click the links for current and additional information.*

Label the Figure

1. _____
2. _____
3. _____
4. _____
5. _____
6. _____
7. _____

Instructions: Identify each component of a graphical user interface.

Fill in the Blanks

Instructions: Complete each sentence with the correct term or terms.

1. A(n) _____ is the way the user tells the software what to do and the way the computer displays information and processing options to the user.
2. A(n) _____, which uses a predefined style sheet and usually includes standard text, can be used to produce certain types of word processing documents.
3. Spreadsheet cells may contain three types of data: _____ (text), _____ (numbers), and _____ that perform calculations and display the results.
4. With regard to OLE, a(n) _____ can be all or any portion of a document, a graphic, a sound file, or a video clip created with a Windows program.
5. Learning aids and support tools include _____, explanatory information available while using an application, _____, step-by-step instructions using real examples, _____, automated assistants that help complete a task, and _____, publications that help users learn features of personal computer application packages.

Short Answer

Instructions: Write a brief answer to each of the following questions.

1. What is a graphical user interface? Describe some common features of a graphical user interface. _____
2. How is desktop publishing software different from word processing software? _____
3. What spreadsheet capabilities make spreadsheet software a valuable tool for decision making? Why? _____
4. What are the advantages of integrated software and software suites? _____
5. What is object linking and embedding? How are linked objects different from embedded objects? _____

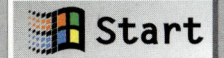

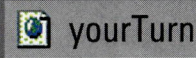

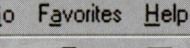

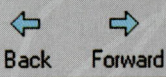

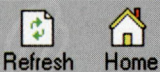

hotTopics

chapter
1 | 2 | 3 | 4 | 5 | 6 | 7 | 8 | 9 | 10 | 11 | 12 | 13 | 14 | I

inCyber | review | terms | yourTurn | hotTopics | outThere | winLabs | webWalk | exercises | news | home

INSTRUCTIONS: *To display this page from the Web, launch your browser and enter the URL, http://www.scsite.com/dc/ch2/hot.htm. Click the links for current and additional information to help you respond to the hotTopics questions.*

1 ***Increasingly sophisticated software applications not only have impacted*** business, but recreation as well. For ten years, chess grand masters have used databases to analyze and replay past games. As the databases expand and database tools become more powerful, some chess aficionados fear that tournament games eventually will be reduced to replays of extensive computer analysis. How might another game, sport, or pastime be affected by a software application described in this chapter? What attributes may be lost through computer use? What could you do to maintain the diversion's positive qualities despite the use of computers?

2 ***Many people believe that word processing software improves the quality*** of written work by making it easier to create and edit documents. Some people argue, however, that word processing software has become a crutch, eliminating the need to learn the rudiments and nuances of language. These people insist that much of the work produced with word processors is indeed *processed*, lacking the beauty, artistry, and individuality of great literature. How do you think word processing software has influenced written communication? Does it result in better work or simply more correct, mediocre work? What word processing features most enhance the quality of written material?

3 ***About 35 million people use e-mail while at work. Many of these people believe their*** communications are private, but employees have been fired for using e-mail to gripe about their bosses. Although this may seem an invasion of privacy, courts have ruled that companies have a right to all the data in their computer networks. On the other hand, corporations have been sued for harassment because of the disparaging remarks executives have made over e-mail. Who should have access to electronic mail messages and records? Why? If, on an e-mail system, you *overheard* an employee's insulting assertions about the boss or an executive's distasteful comments about an employee, would you tell anyone? What if you heard someone planning to steal a product or reveal company secrets? Where do you draw the line?

4 ***Over the past two decades, billions of dollars have been spent to computerize the classroom.*** Despite this, many students still are computer illiterate when they graduate from high school. Various reasons are given for this failure — inadequately trained teachers, classrooms unable to handle new equipment, machines made obsolete by rapidly changing technology, and so on. Perhaps the most telling problem is that educators are not sure of the best use for computers. Drill and practice? Problem solving? Games? A growing number of instructors feel that students should be taught the software applications they will have to know to succeed in the workplace. From the applications presented in this chapter, make a list of five applications you think every student should learn, from most important to least important. Explain your ranking. At what level should each application be taught? Why?

5 ***One of the catch phrases in education today is "learning styles," which is the belief that people*** learn things best in different ways. How do you learn things most effectively? If you had to learn one of the software applications described in this chapter, which of the learning aids and support tools (online Help, tutorials, wizards, or trade books) would fit your learning style best? Why? Would the type of software application you were learning affect your choice of learning aid? Why or why not?

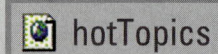

chapter 2 outThere

1 | 2 | 3 | 4 | 5 | 6 | 7 | 8 | 9 | 10 | 11 | 12 | 13 | 14 | I

inCyber | review | terms | yourTurn | hotTopics | outThere | winLabs | webWalk | exercises | news | home

INSTRUCTIONS: *To display this page from the Web, launch your browser and enter the URL, http://www.scsite.com/dc/ch2/out.htm. Click the links for current and additional information.*

1 ***Each software application is characterized by certain key features, but every software package*** in an application is not exactly the same. Different spreadsheet packages, for example, may use different methods to enter formulas, offer different functions, and have different ways to draw charts. People who use a software package at work often have strong feelings about the package's strengths and weaknesses. Interview someone who works with one of the software applications described in this chapter. Which software package does he or she use? Why was that package chosen? How did the person being interviewed learn to use the package? What does he or she like, or dislike, about the software? For what purpose does the individual use the package? If a friend of this person was choosing software to perform a similar task, would he or she recommend this software package? Why or why not?

2 ***The most popular Web browser is Netscape Navigator, which is used by almost eighty percent of*** people who surf the Web. Next in line is Microsoft's Internet Explorer, a distant second with a constituency of about ten percent. Internet Explorer is narrowing the gap, yet Netscape Navigator maintains that it is still a better browser. Information about both browsers can be found on the World Wide Web. Compare these two browsers, or another two browsers, and form your own opinion. What features are offered by both? What capabilities does one have that the other does not? What is the cost of each? Based on your evaluation, which Web browser do you think is better? Why?

3 ***The relative merit of integrated software versus individual software packages sometimes is*** perceived as quantity versus quality — integrated software provides more "bang for the buck" by combining several applications, but the capabilities of each component are eclipsed by individual software packages. Many feel, however, that integrated software is the best buy for average computer users. Visit a local computer software vendor and compare an integrated software package (such as Microsoft Works or ClarisWorks) to some individual software application packages. How much does the integrated software cost? How much would it cost to buy comparable application software packages individually? What are the differences, if any, between the capabilities of applications in the integrated software and those of individual software packages?

4 ***Users of desktop publishing software frequently enhance their work with*** scanned photographs or graphics. Now, the Internet is providing a new resource for desktop publishers. Companies such as Corbis, Picture Network International, Muse, and Liaison International offer archives of artwork and photographs. Information about all four companies can be found on the World Wide Web. What kind of illustrations are available? How are pictures on a specific subject located? How are the illustrations provided? What fees are involved? Would the cost be different for a high school student creating one paper than for a company? Which products do you prefer? Why?

5 ***Although most software packages can be learned with online Help or tutorials, many people*** prefer using trade books. Select a software application such as word processing, and visit a bookstore or software vendor to survey the trade books on that application. For what particular package (e.g., Word, WordStar, DisplayWrite, or WordPerfect) are the most titles available? How difficult would it be to learn each software package using the trade books at hand? Which trade book do you think is the best? Why? If you were going to purchase a software package solely on the basis of the related trade books, which package would you buy? Why?

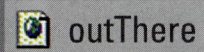

winLabs

chapter 1 | 2 | 3 | 4 | 5 | 6 | 7 | 8 | 9 | 10 | 11 | 12 | 13 | 14 | I

inCyber | review | terms | yourTurn | hotTopics | outThere | winLabs | webWalk | exercises | news | home

INSTRUCTIONS: *To display this page from the Web, launch your browser and enter the URL, http://www.scsite.com/dc/ch2/labs.htm. Click the links for current and additional information.*

1 Shelly Cashman Series Word Processing Lab

Follow the instructions in winLab 1 on page 1.34 to display the Shelly Cashman Series Labs screen. Click Word Processing. Click the Start Lab button. When the initial screen displays, carefully read the objectives. With your printer on, click the Print Questions button. Fill out the top of the Questions sheet and answer the questions.

2 Shelly Cashman Series Spreadsheet Lab

Follow the instructions in winLab 1 on page 1.34 to display the Shelly Cashman Series Labs screen. Click Working with Spreadsheets. Click the Start Lab button. When the screen displays, read the objectives. With your printer on, click the Print Questions button. Fill out the top of the Questions sheet and answer the questions.

3 Creating a Word Processing Document

Click the Start button on the taskbar; point to Programs on the Start menu; point to Accessories on the Programs submenu; and then click WordPad on the Accessories submenu. When the WordPad window displays, click its Maximize button. Type the first 2 paragraphs on page 2.4 under the heading Word Processing Software (see Figure 2-51). Press the TAB key to indent the first line of each paragraph. Press ENTER to begin a new paragraph. Do not bold or italicize any words. At the end of the second paragraph, press ENTER twice and then type your name.

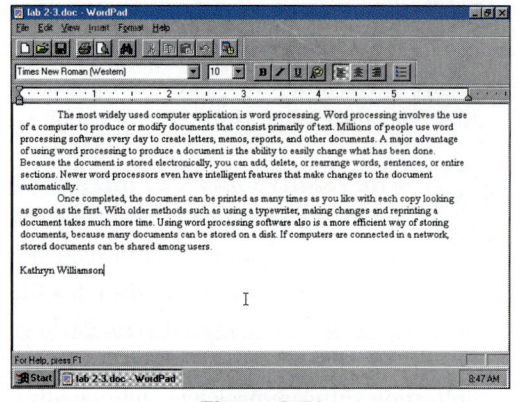

Figure 2-51

To correct errors in your document, move the I-beam mouse pointer to the location of the error and then click. Press the BACKSPACE key to erase to the left of the insertion point; press the DELETE key to erase to the right of the insertion point. To insert a character(s), click to the left of the point of insertion and then begin typing. If your screen does not display a toolbar, click View on the menu bar and then click Toolbar. When your document is correct, save it by inserting your student floppy disk into drive A and then clicking the Save button on the toolbar. In the Save As dialog box, type a:lab2-3 in the File name text box and then click the Save button. With your printer on, click the Print button on the toolbar to print the document. Close WordPad by clicking its Close button.

4 Using WordPad's Help

Open WordPad as described in winLab 3 above. Click Help on WordPad's menu bar and then click Help Topics. When the Help Topics: WordPad Help window displays, click the Contents tab, and then double-click the Working with Documents book. Click the Saving changes to a document topic; click the Print button; and then click the OK button. Click the WordPad Help window's Help Topics button to return to the Contents sheet. Click the Opening a document topic; click the Print button; and then click the OK button. Close any open Help windows and WordPad.

2 webWalk

chapter 1 | 2 | 3 | 4 | 5 | 6 | 7 | 8 | 9 | 10 | 11 | 12 | 13 | 14 | I

inCyber | review | terms | yourTurn | hotTopics | outThere | winLabs | webWalk | exercises | news | home

DISCOVERING COMPUTERS

INSTRUCTIONS: *To display this page from the Web, launch your browser and enter the URL, http://www.scsite.com/dc/ch2/walk.htm. Click the exercise link to display the exercise.*

1 Desktop Publishing
Desktop publishing software is designed specifically for page composition and layout. To increase your knowledge of desktop publishing software, complete this exercise.

2 Clip Art
Clip art consists of previously created illustrations that can be added to documents. A number of sources of clip art are available on the World Wide Web. To visit one of these sites, complete this exercise.

3 Online Help
Online Help refers to additional instructions that are available within application software. To learn more about your Web browser's online Help (Figure 2-52), complete this exercise.

4 Personal Information Management (PIM) Software
Personal information management (PIM) software helps you keep track of the miscellaneous bits of personal information that each of us deals with every day. You can learn about an innovative add-in to PIM software (Figure 2-53) by completing this exercise.

Figure 2-52

5 Information Mining
Complete this exercise to improve your Web research skills by using a Web search engine to find information related to this chapter.

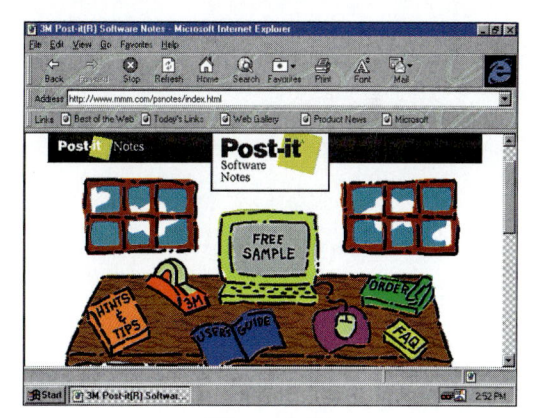

Figure 2-53

6 Interactive Assistance Services
Interactive assistance can help you perform tasks online. Complete this exercise to experience the way the World Wide Web can provide assistance to you.

7 Financial Information Online
Online services for up-to-the-minute financial news is widely available on the Web. Complete this exercise to see one example of a financial information service.

8 Weather Forecast
Online weather information is available for travelers, pilots, picnickers, and anyone else whose plans are dependent on weather. To see one example of unique weather forecasts, complete this exercise.

9 Web Chat
Complete this exercise to enter a Web Chat discussion related to issues presented in the hotTopics exercises.

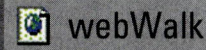

The System Unit

OBJECTIVES

After completing this chapter, you will be able to:

- Define a bit and describe how a series of bits in a byte is used to represent data

- Discuss how bit pattern codes are used to represent characters

- Identify the components of the system unit and describe their use

- Describe how the CPU uses the four steps of the machine cycle to process data

- Describe the primary use and characteristics of RAM and ROM memory

- Explain the difference between parallel and serial ports

- Describe a machine language instruction and the instruction set of a computer

- Describe various types of processing including pipelining, parallel processing, and neural networks

- Explain how computers use the binary number system

- Explain how a computer chip is made

CHAPTER 3

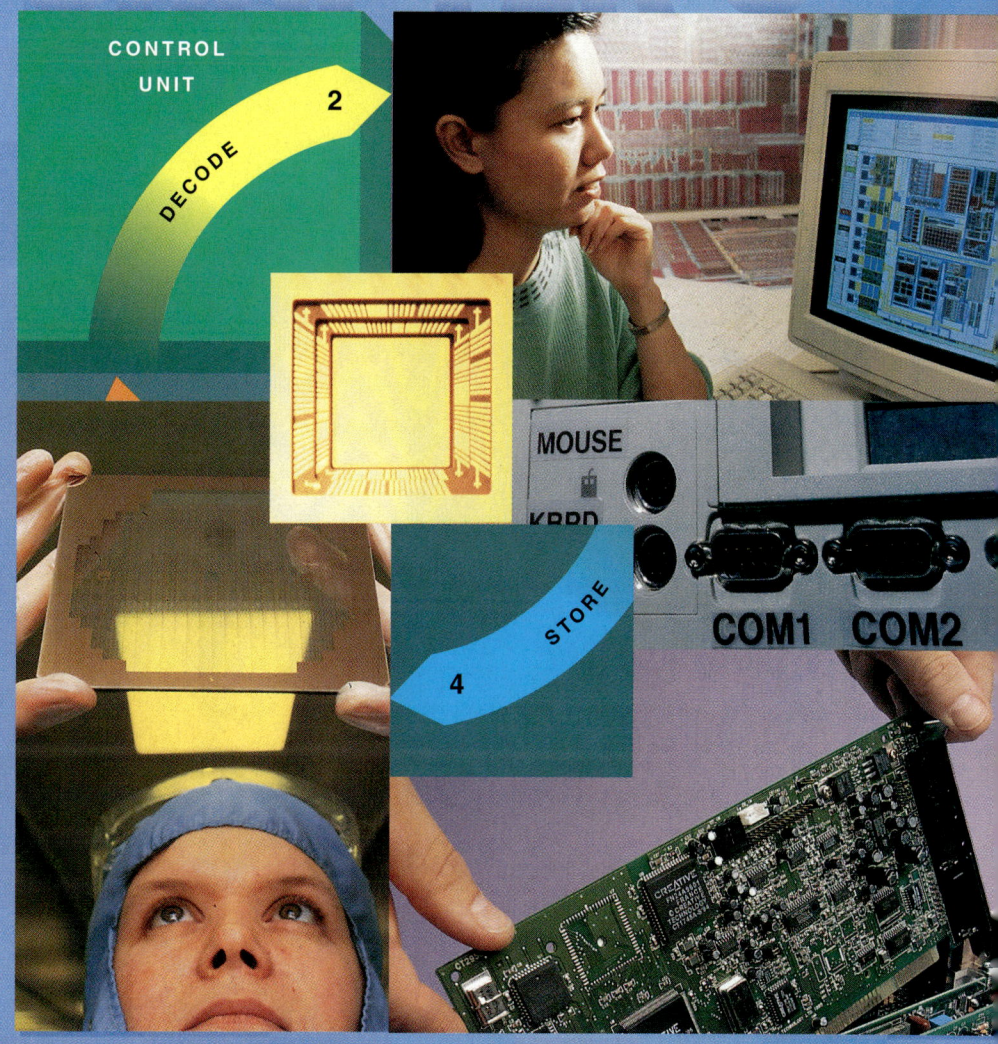

The information processing cycle consists of input, processing, output, and storage operations. When an input operation is completed and both a program and data are stored in memory, processing operations can begin. During these operations, the system unit executes, or performs, the program instructions and processes the data into information.

Chapter 3 examines the components of the system unit, describes how memory stores programs and data, and discusses the sequence of operations that occurs when instructions are executed on a computer. These topics are followed by a discussion of types of processing and number systems. How a computer chip is made is discussed at the end of the chapter.

What Is the System Unit?

The term computer usually means a combination of hardware and software that can process data and manage information. This term also is used more specifically to describe the system unit, because this is where the *computing* actually happens. It is in the **system unit** that the computer program instructions are executed and the data is manipulated. The system unit contains the central processing unit, or CPU, memory (also called random access memory, or RAM), and other electronics (Figure 3-1). To better understand how the system unit processes data, an explanation follows of how data is represented in a computer.

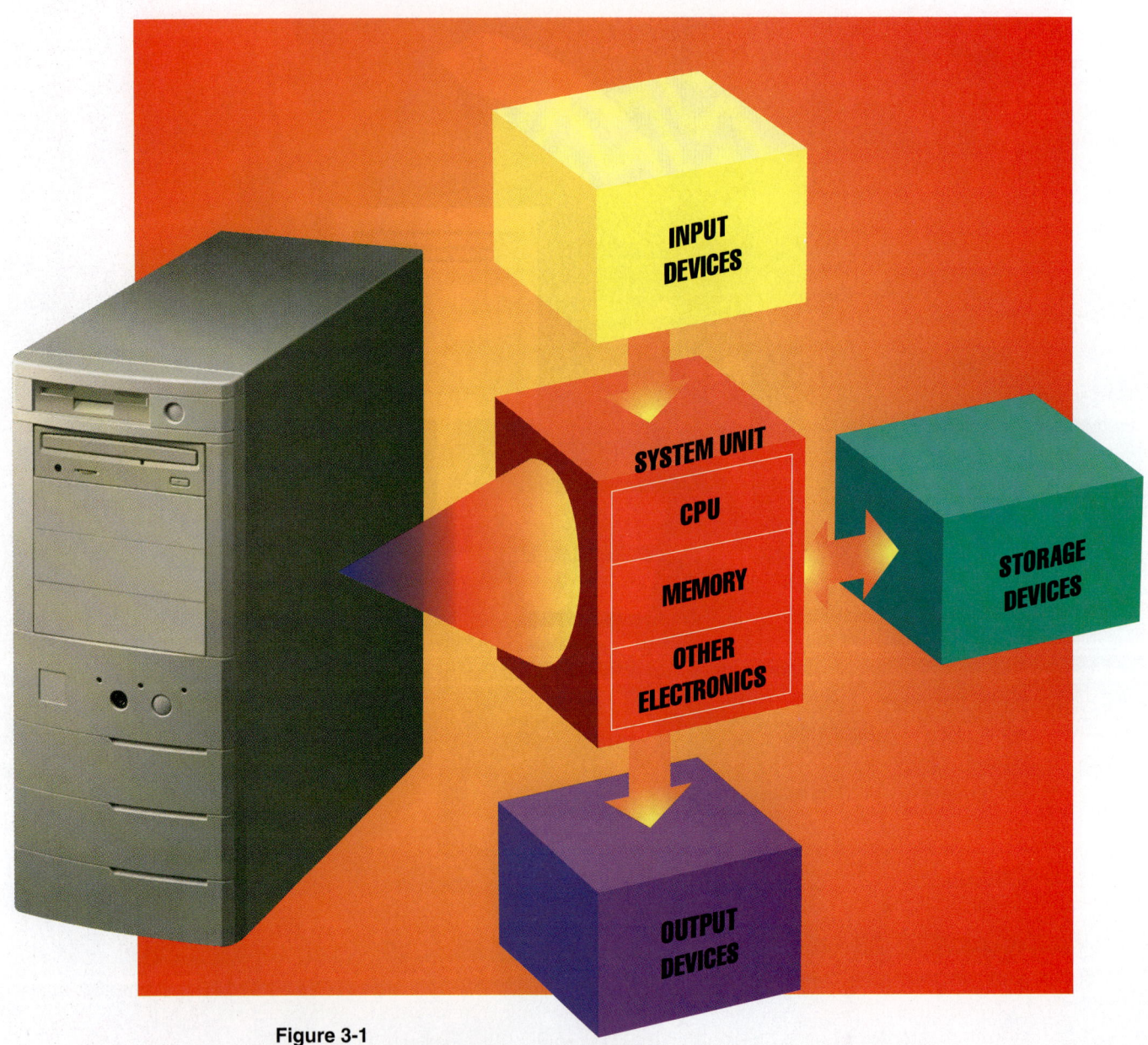

Figure 3-1
The system unit is the metal or plastic case that contains the central processing unit (CPU), memory, and other electronics. The system unit is connected to input devices such as a keyboard or mouse and output devices such as a monitor or printer. Storage devices such as a disk drive can be located either inside or outside the system unit case.

How Data Is Represented in a Computer

Most computers are **digital computers,** meaning that the data they process, whether it be text, sound, graphics, or video, is first converted into a digital (numeric) value. Converting data into a digital form is called **digitizing.** Other types of computers, called **analog computers,** are designed to process continuously variable data, such as electrical voltage.

You may be thinking that the digital values used by a computer are the digits 0 through 9. But in fact, only the digits 0 and 1 are used. Only two digits are used because they can be easily represented electronically by circuits in the computer being either off or on. A 0 is used to represent the electronic state of *off* and a 1 is used to represent the electronic state of *on*. Each off or on digital value is called a **bit**, the smallest unit of data handled by a computer. Bit is short for *bi*nary digi*t* (Figure 3-2). By itself, a bit cannot represent much data. But in a group of eight bits, called a **byte**, 256 different possibilities can be represented by using all the combinations of 0s and 1s (Figure 3-3). This provides enough combinations so a unique code can be assigned to each of the characters that are commonly used such as, the digits 0 through 9, the uppercase and lowercase alphabet, foreign characters that require accent marks such as umlauts (¨) and tildes (~), and special characters such as punctuation marks. Several different coding schemes are used on computers.

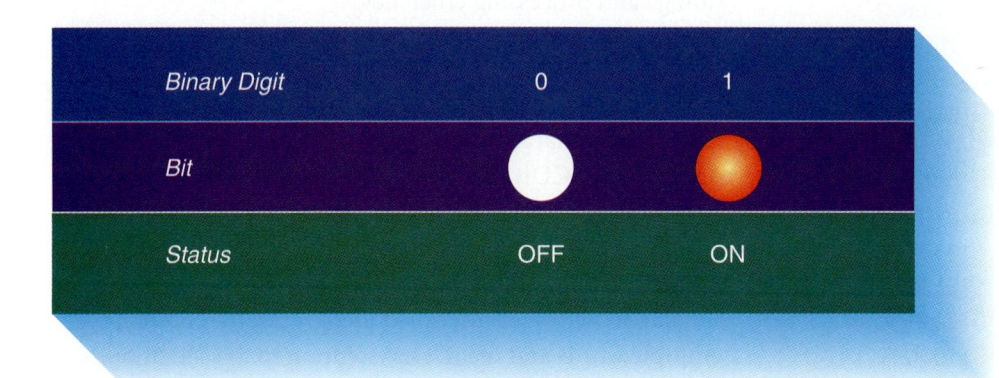

Binary Digit	0	1
Bit	○	●
Status	OFF	ON

inCyber
For details on digital computers, visit the Discovering Computers Chapter 3 inCyber page (http://www.scsite.com/dc/ch3/incyber.htm) and click Digital Computers.

Figure 3-2
A bit, the smallest unit of data handled by a computer, can represent either a 0 or 1 in the binary number system. A computer circuit represents the 0 or 1 electronically by being either off (representing the 0) or on (representing the 1).

Figure 3-3
A graphic representation of an eight-bit byte with four bits on and four bits off. The off bits (open circles) are represented by the binary digit 0 and the on bits (solid circles) are represented by the binary digit 1. This combination of bits represents the uppercase letter G.

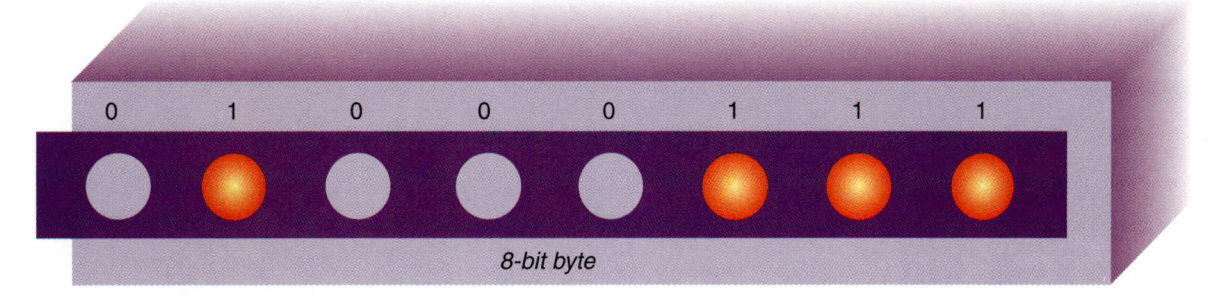

0 1 0 0 0 1 1 1

8-bit byte

ASCII and EBCDIC

Two widely used codes that represent characters in a computer are the ASCII and EBCDIC codes. The **American Standard Code for Information Interchange**, called **ASCII** (pronounced ask-ee), is the most widely used coding system to represent data. ASCII is used on many personal computers and minicomputers. The **Extended Binary Coded Decimal Interchange Code**, or **EBCDIC** (pronounced eb-see-dick) is used primarily on mainframe computers. Figure 3-4 summarizes these codes. Notice how the combination of bits (0s and 1s) is unique for each character.

When the ASCII or EBCDIC code is used, each character that is represented is stored in one byte of memory. Other binary formats exist, however, that the computer sometimes uses to represent numeric data. For example, a computer may store, or *pack,* two numeric characters in one byte of memory. These binary formats are used by the computer to increase storage and processing efficiency.

Unicode

The 256 characters and symbols that are represented by ASCII and EBCDIC codes are sufficient for English and western European languages but are not large enough for Asian and other languages that use different alphabets. Further compounding the problem is that many of these languages used symbols, called **ideograms**, to represent multiple words and ideas. One solution to this situation is Unicode. **Unicode** is a 16-bit code that has the capacity to represent more than 65,000 characters and symbols. Unicode represents all the world's current languages using more than 34,000 characters and symbols (Figure 3-5). In Unicode,

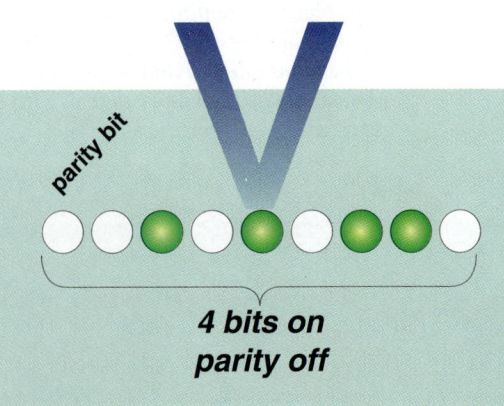

SYMBOL	ASCII	EBCDIC
0	01100000	11110000
1	01100001	11110001
2	01100010	11110010
3	01100011	11110011
4	01100100	11110100
5	01100101	11110101
6	01100110	11110110
7	01100111	11110111
8	01101000	11111000
9	01101001	11111001
A	01000001	11000001
B	01000010	11000010
C	01000011	11000011
D	01000100	11000100
E	01000101	11000101
F	01000110	11000110
G	01000111	11000111
H	01001000	11001000
I	01001001	11001001
J	01001010	11010001
K	01001011	11010010
L	01001100	11010011
M	01001101	11010100
N	01001110	11010101
O	01001111	11010110
P	01010000	11010111
Q	01010001	11011000
R	01010010	11011001
S	01010011	11100010
T	01010100	11100011
U	01010101	11100100
V	01010110	11100101
W	01010111	11100110
X	01011000	11100111
Y	01011001	11101000
Z	01011010	11101001
!	00100001	01011010
"	00100010	01111111
#	00100011	01111011
$	00100100	01011011
%	00100101	01101100
&	00100110	01010000
(	00101000	01001101
)	00101001	01011101
*	00101010	01011100
+	00101011	01001110

Figure 3-4
This chart shows numeric, uppercase alphabetic, and several special characters as they are represented in ASCII and EBCDIC. Each character is represented in binary using a unique ordering of zeros and ones.

4 bits on parity off

parity bit

30,000 codes are reserved for future use, such as ancient languages, and 6,000 codes are reserved for private use. Existing ASCII coded data is fully compatible with Unicode because the first 256 codes are the same. Unicode is currently implemented in several operating systems, including Windows NT and OS/2 and all major system developers have announced plans eventually to implement Unicode.

Parity

Regardless of whether ASCII, EBCDIC, or other binary methods are used to represent characters in memory, it is important that the characters be stored accurately. For each byte of memory, most computers have at least one extra bit, called a **parity bit**, that is used by the computer for error checking. A parity bit can detect if one of the bits in a byte has been inadvertently changed. While such errors are extremely rare (most computers never have a parity error during their lifetime), they can occur because of voltage fluctuations, static electricity, or a memory failure.

Computers are either odd- or even-parity machines. In computers with **odd parity**, the total number of *on* bits in the byte (including the parity bit) must be an odd number (Figure 3-6). In computers with **even parity**, the total number of on bits must be an even number. Parity is checked by the computer each time a memory location is used. When data is moved from one location to another in memory, the parity bits of both the sending and receiving locations are compared to see if they are the same. If the system detects a difference or if the wrong number of bits is on (e.g., an odd number in a system with even parity), an error message displays. Many computers use multiple parity bits that enable them to detect and correct a single-bit error and detect multiple-bit errors.

Figure 3-5
Unicode is a 16-bit character code developed to represent all the world's languages. This Cyrillic character set is part of the more than 34,000 characters that are currently represented in Unicode. The Unicode assigned code is along the top and left side of the chart.

inCyber
For an explanation of EBCDIC, visit the Discovering Computers Chapter 3 inCyber page (http://www.scsite.com/dc/ch3/incyber.htm) and click EBCDIC.

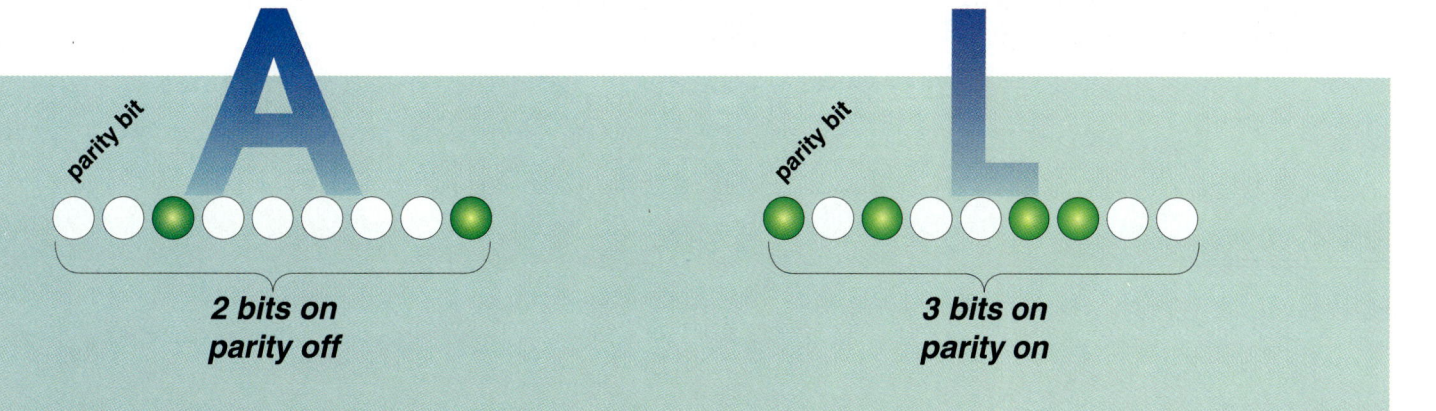

A — parity bit — 2 bits on parity off

L — parity bit — 3 bits on parity on

Figure 3-6
In a computer with even parity, the parity bit is turned on or off in order to make the total number of on bits (including the parity bit) an even number. Here, the letters V and A have an even number of bits so the parity bit is left off. The number of bits for the letter L is odd, so to achieve even parity, the parity bit is turned on.

3.6

The Components of the System Unit

The components of the system unit usually are contained in a metal or plastic case. For personal computers, all system unit components usually are in a single box. For larger and more powerful computers, the components may be housed in several cabinets. The components considered part of the system unit and discussed in the following sections include the motherboard, the microprocessor and CPU, upgrade sockets, memory, coprocessors, buses, expansion slots, ports and connectors, bays, the power supply, and sound components (Figure 3-7).

Figure 3-7
The components of the system unit are usually inside a plastic or metal case. This illustration shows how some of the components might be arranged in a typical PC.

MICROPROCESSOR AND THE CPU 3.7

Motherboard

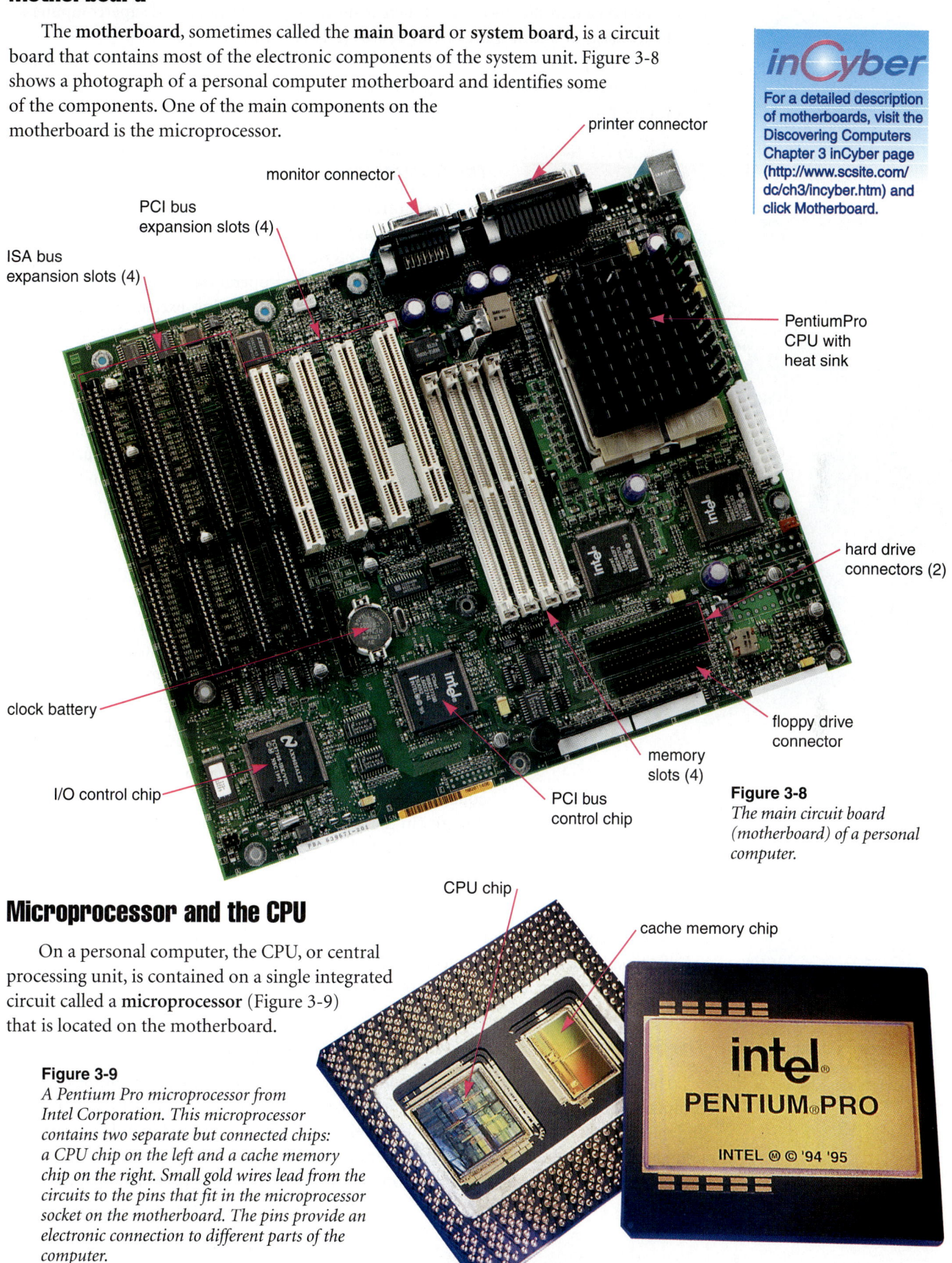

The **motherboard**, sometimes called the **main board** or **system board**, is a circuit board that contains most of the electronic components of the system unit. Figure 3-8 shows a photograph of a personal computer motherboard and identifies some of the components. One of the main components on the motherboard is the microprocessor.

inCyber

For a detailed description of motherboards, visit the Discovering Computers Chapter 3 inCyber page (http://www.scsite.com/dc/ch3/incyber.htm) and click Motherboard.

Labels on Figure 3-8:
- printer connector
- monitor connector
- PCI bus expansion slots (4)
- ISA bus expansion slots (4)
- PentiumPro CPU with heat sink
- hard drive connectors (2)
- floppy drive connector
- memory slots (4)
- PCI bus control chip
- I/O control chip
- clock battery

Figure 3-8
The main circuit board (motherboard) of a personal computer.

Microprocessor and the CPU

On a personal computer, the CPU, or central processing unit, is contained on a single integrated circuit called a **microprocessor** (Figure 3-9) that is located on the motherboard.

Figure 3-9
A Pentium Pro microprocessor from Intel Corporation. This microprocessor contains two separate but connected chips: a CPU chip on the left and a cache memory chip on the right. Small gold wires lead from the circuits to the pins that fit in the microprocessor socket on the motherboard. The pins provide an electronic connection to different parts of the computer.

Labels on Figure 3-9:
- CPU chip
- cache memory chip

intel PENTIUM®PRO
INTEL ® © '94 '95

An **integrated circuit**, also called a **chip** or an **IC**, is a complete electronic circuit that has been etched on a thin slice of material such as silicon. For mainframe and supercomputers, the CPU consists of one or more circuit boards (Figure 3-10).

The **central processing unit (CPU)** contains the control unit and the arithmetic/logic unit. These two components work together using the program and data stored in memory to perform the processing operations.

The Control Unit

The control unit can be thought of as the *brain* of the computer. Just as the human brain controls the body, the control unit *controls* the computer. The **control unit** operates by repeating the following four operations, called the **machine cycle** (Figure 3-11): fetching, decoding, executing, and storing. **Fetching** means obtaining the next program instruction from memory. **Decoding** is translating the program instruction into the commands that the computer can process. **Executing** refers to the actual processing of the computer commands, and **storing** takes place when the result of the instruction is written to memory. Fetching and decoding are called the **instruction cycle**. Executing and storing are called the **execution cycle**.

The Arithmetic/Logic Unit

The second part of the CPU is the **arithmetic/logic unit (ALU)**. This unit contains the electronic circuitry necessary to perform arithmetic and logical operations on data. **Arithmetic operations** include addition, subtraction, multiplication, and division. **Logical operations** consist of comparing one data item to another to determine if the first data item is *greater than*, *equal to*, or *less than* the other. Based on the result of the comparison, different processing may occur. For example, two part numbers in different records can be compared. If they are equal, the part quantity in one record can be added to the quantity in the other record. If they are not equal, the quantities would not be added.

Figure 3-10
With PCs, the CPU is contained in a single microprocessor chip. With larger computers, the CPU operations are split among several chips and sometimes more than one circuit board.

Registers

Both the control unit and the ALU contain **registers**, temporary storage locations for specific types of data. Separate registers exist for the current program instruction, the address of the next instruction, and the values of data being processed.

inCyber

For a discussion of the central processing unit components, visit the Discovering Computers Chapter 3 inCyber page (http://www.scsite.com/dc/ch3/incyber.htm) and click CPU.

The System Clock

The control unit utilizes the **system clock** to synchronize, or control the timing of, all computer operations. The system clock is not a conventional clock that tells time in hours and minutes, but rather a chip that generates electronic pulses at a fixed rate. The control unit and ALU are designed to complete their operations one step at a time with both starting each step at the same time. The pulses from the system clock set the pace. Think of the

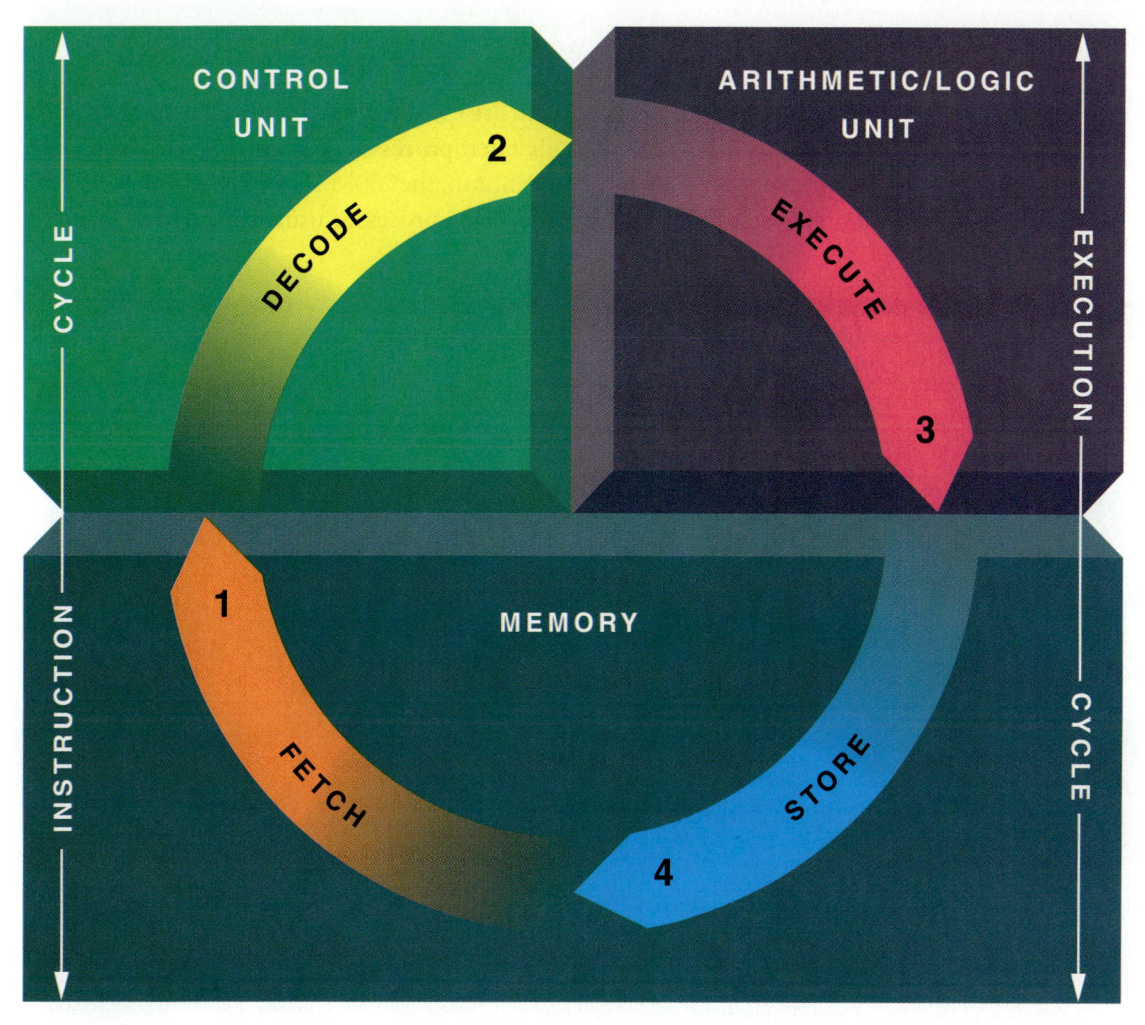

Figure 3-11
The machine cycle consists of four steps; fetching the next instruction, decoding the instruction, executing the instruction, and storing the result. Fetching and decoding are called the instruction cycle. Executing and storing are called the execution cycle.

control unit and ALU as members of a marching band that all take their steps to the beat of the system clock drummer. The pulse rate of the clock is measured in **megahertz** (abbreviated **MHz**). One megahertz equals one million pulses per second. The speed of the system clock varies among computers. Many personal computers can operate at speeds in excess of 100 megahertz.

Word Size

One aspect of the CPU that affects the speed of a computer is the word size. The **word size** is the number of bits that the CPU can process at one time. The word size of a machine is measured in bits. CPUs can have 8-bit, 16-bit, 32-bit, or 64-bit word sizes. A CPU with a 16-bit word size can manipulate 16 bits at a time. Sometimes, the word size of a computer is given in bytes instead of bits. For example, a word size of 16 bits may be expressed as a word size of two bytes because there are eight bits in a byte. Computers with a larger word size can process more data in the same amount of time than computers with a smaller word size.

Microprocessor Comparison

Personal computer microprocessors most often are identified by their model number or model name. Figure 3-12 summarizes some of the microprocessors currently in use. When discussing the three Intel processors prior to the Pentium, the "80" in the name/model number usually is not referred to. For example, the 80486 processor usually is referred to as a 486 processor.

Name	Date	Manufacturer	Word Size	Bus Width	Clock Speed (MHz)	MIPS*
Pentium Pro	1995	Intel	64	64	150-200	300
Pentium	1993	Intel	64	64	75-166	150
80486DX	1989	Intel	32	32	25-100	20-75
80386DX	1985	Intel	32	32	16-33	6-12
80286	1982	Intel	16	16	6-12	1-2
PowerPC	1994	Motorola	64	64	50-225	300
68040	1989	Motorola	32	32	25-40	15-35
68030	1987	Motorola	32	32	16-50	12
68020	1984	Motorola	32	32	16-33	5.5
Alpha	1993	Digital	64	64	150-333	275-1332

*MIPS: millions of instructions per second

Figure 3-12
A comparison of some of the more widely used microprocessors.

Upgrade Sockets

Some motherboards contain a type of receptacle for microprocessors, called an **upgrade socket** (Figure 3-13), that can be used to install a more powerful CPU.

The CPU upgrade sockets enable a user to install a more powerful microprocessor and obtain increased performance without having to buy an entirely new system. With a CPU upgrade socket, the old microprocessor does not have to be removed. When the new microprocessor is installed, the old microprocessor is automatically disabled. Many, but not all, systems can install a more powerful microprocessor even if they do not have a separate CPU upgrade socket. For these systems, the old microprocessor is removed and replaced with the new microprocessor.

Figure 3-13
This motherboard includes an upgrade socket that can accept a more powerful Intel microprocessor. This particular type of socket is called a zero insertion force (ZIF) socket. The ZIF socket uses a lever to clamp down on the microprocessor pins and makes the installation of the chip easier. Other types of upgrade sockets require the microprocessor pins to be forced into the socket.

ZIF socket

Memory

Memory refers to integrated circuits that temporarily store program instructions and data that can be retrieved. Memory chips are installed on the motherboard and also on similar circuit boards that control computer devices such as printers. Some memory is also designed directly into the CPU chip. Memory stores three items: the operating system and other system software that direct and coordinate the computer equipment; the application program instructions that direct the work to be done; and the data currently being processed by the application programs. Data and programs are transferred into and out of memory and data stored in memory is manipulated by computer program instructions.

The basic unit of memory is a byte, which, recall, consists of eight bits. Each byte in the memory of a computer has an address that indicates its location in memory (Figure 3-14). The number that indicates the location of a byte in memory is called a **memory address**. Whenever the computer references a byte, it does so by using the memory address, or location, of that byte.

The size of memory is measured in either kilobytes, megabytes, or gigabytes. A **kilobyte** (abbreviated as **K** or **KB**) is equal to 1,024 bytes, but for discussion purposes, is usually rounded to 1,000 bytes. A **megabyte** (abbreviated as **MB**) is approximately one million bytes or 1,000 kilobytes. A **gigabyte** (abbreviated as **GB**) is approximately one billion bytes or one million kilobytes. These terms are used when discussing the storage capacity of other devices such as disk drives, as well as discussing memory size. Three common types of memory chips are RAM, ROM, and CMOS.

> **inCyber**
> For an explanation of various memory chips, visit the Discovering Computers Chapter 3 inCyber page (http://www.scsite.com/dc/ch3/incyber.htm) and click Memory.

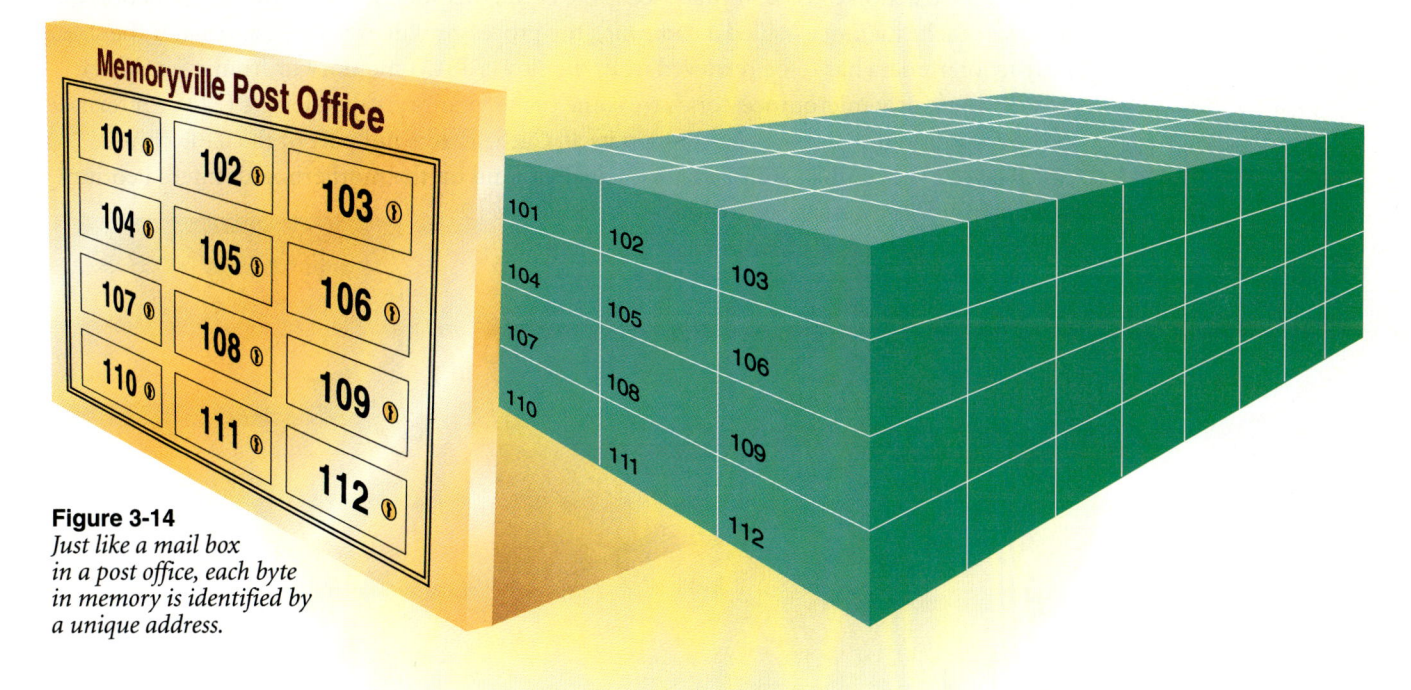

Figure 3-14
Just like a mail box in a post office, each byte in memory is identified by a unique address.

RAM

RAM (random access memory) is the name given to the integrated circuits, or chips, that can be read and written by the microprocessor or other computer devices. RAM memory is said to be **volatile** because the programs and data stored in RAM are erased when the power to the computer is turned off. As long as the power remains on, the programs and data stored in RAM will remain intact until they are replaced by other programs and data. Programs and data that are needed for future use must be transferred from RAM to secondary storage before the power is turned off. A relatively new type of memory called **flash RAM** or **flash memory** can retain data even when the power is turned off. Flash memory is sometimes used instead of a disk drive in small portable computers.

CHAPTER 3 – THE SYSTEM UNIT

Today, most RAM memory is installed by using a **SIMM** (**single in-line memory module**) or a **DIMM** (**dual in-line memory module**). A SIMM is a small circuit board that has multiple RAM chips on one side. Common SIMM sizes are 1, 2, 4, 8, and 16 megabytes of memory. A SIMM is installed directly on the motherboard. A DIMM is similar to a SIMM but has memory chips on both sides (Figure 3-15).

Many computers improve their processing efficiency by using high-speed RAM **cache** (pronounced cash) memory between the CPU and the main RAM memory to store the most frequently used instructions and data (Figure 3-16). When the processor needs the next program instruction or data, it first checks the cache memory. If the required instruction or data is in cache memory (called a *cache hit*), the processor will execute faster than if the instruction or data has to be retrieved from the slower RAM memory or from even slower storage. Most new microprocessors have some cache memory, called **level 1 (L1)** or **internal cache**, built into the microprocessor chip itself. Cache that is not part of the CPU chip is called **level 2 (L2) cache**. Level 2 cache is usually found on the motherboard. Intel's Pentium Pro microprocessor, however, includes a separate level 2 cache chip as part of its microprocessor package.

inCyber

For information on cache memory, visit the Discovering Computers Chapter 3 inCyber page (http://www.scsite.com/dc/ch3/incyber.htm) and click Cache.

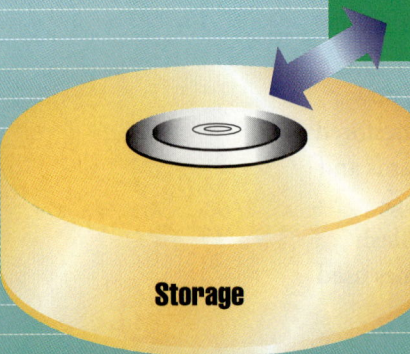

Figure 3-15
This photo shows a DIMM (dual in-line memory module). DIMMs contain memory chips mounted on a small circuit board. Each chip represents one of the bit positions in a byte. Common DIMM sizes are 1, 2, 4, 8, and 16 megabytes.

Figure 3-16
Many computers use high-speed cache memory to store frequently used instructions or data. If the required data or instructions are in cache, the processing will execute faster than if the instruction or data has to be retrieved from slower memory or from even slower storage. Cache memory can be included in the actual CPU chip (called level 1 cache) or can consist of a separate chip (called level 2 cache).

ROM

ROM (**read only memory**) is the name given to chips that store information or instructions that do not change. For example, ROM is used to store the startup instructions and data used when a computer is first turned on.

With ROM, instructions and data are recorded permanently in the memory when it is manufactured. ROM memory is described as **nonvolatile** because it retains its contents even when the power is turned off. The data or programs that are stored in ROM can be read and used, but cannot be altered, hence the name *read only*. Many of the special-purpose computers used in automobiles, appliances, and so on use small amounts of ROM to store instructions that will be executed repeatedly. Instructions that are stored in ROM memory are called **firmware** or **microcode**.

CMOS

CMOS (**complementary metal-oxide semiconductor**) memory (pronounced SEE-moss), is used to store information about the computer system, such as the amount of memory, the type of keyboard and monitor, and the type and capacity of disk drives. CMOS also operates the real-time clock on your computer that keeps track of the date and time. The system information in the CMOS memory is needed each time the computer is started. CMOS memory has very low electrical requirements and can be powered by a battery. Battery power enables CMOS memory to retain the stored information even when power to the computer is turned off (which is why your computer clock runs even when the computer is off). Unlike ROM memory, data in CMOS memory can be changed, such as when a new device is added to the computer system.

Memory Speed

Access speed is defined as the time it takes to find data and retrieve it. Because of different manufacturing techniques and materials, some types of memory are faster than others. The speed of memory is measured in **nanoseconds**, which is one billionth of a second (Figure 3-17). Most memory is comprised of **dynamic RAM (DRAM)** chips that have access speeds of 50 to 100 nanoseconds. RAM cache memory is faster and is comprised of **static RAM (SRAM)** chips with access times of 10 to 50 nanoseconds. Static RAM chips are not used for memory

Figure 3-17
Examples of a nanosecond (one billionth of a second).

How to Measure a Nanosecond
nanosecond = 1 billionth of a second

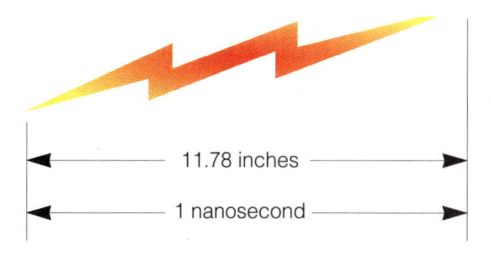

◄—— 11.78 inches ——►
◄—— 1 nanosecond ——►

Because electricity travels at close to 186,000 miles per second, it can travel 11.78 inches in one nanosecond.

It takes about $1/10$ of a second to blink your eye, the equivalent of 100 million nanoseconds. A computer can perform some operations in as little as 10 nanoseconds. Thus, in the time it takes to blink your eye, a computer can perform some operations 10 million times.

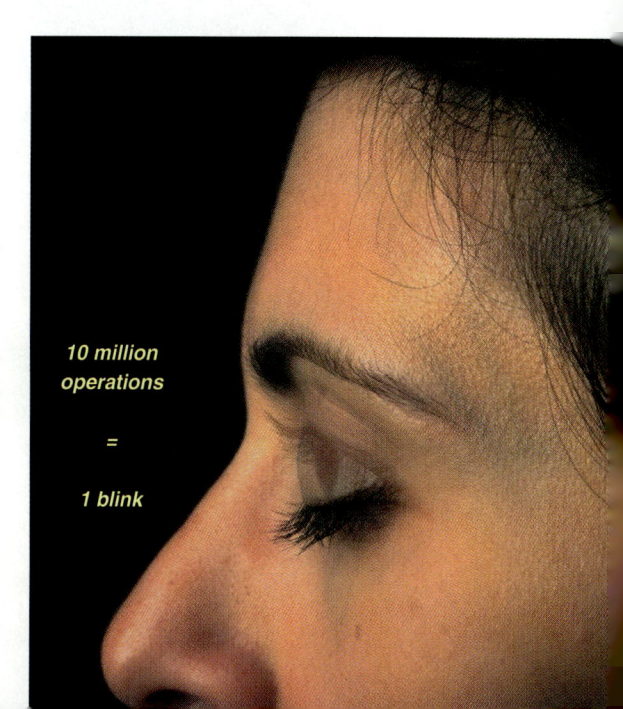

10 million operations
=
1 blink

because they are larger than dynamic RAM chips and because they cost significantly more to manufacture. ROM memory has access times between 50 and 250 nanoseconds. Registers and level 1 cache designed into the CPU chip are the fastest type of memory with access times of 1 to 10 nanoseconds. For comparison purposes, accessing data on a fast hard disk takes between 10 and 20 milliseconds. One **millisecond** is a thousandth of a second. Thus, accessing information in memory with a 70 nanosecond access time is 2,500 times faster than accessing data on a hard disk with a 15 millisecond access time.

Coprocessors

One way computers can increase their efficiency is through the use of a **coprocessor**, which is a special microprocessor chip or circuit board designed to perform a specific task. For example, math coprocessors can be added to computers to greatly speed up the processing of numeric calculations. Other types of coprocessors are used to speed up the display of graphics and for communications. Some computers have coprocessors designed into the CPU.

Buses

As previously explained, computers store and process data as a series of electronic bits. These bits are transferred internally within the circuitry of the computer along paths capable of transmitting electrical impulses. Sometimes these paths are actual wires and sometimes they are etched lines on the circuit board or within the CPU chip itself. Any path along which bits are transmitted is called a **bus**. Buses are used to transfer bits from input devices to memory, from memory to the CPU, from the CPU to memory, and from memory to output or storage devices. Separate buses are used for memory addresses, control signals, and data. One type of bus is called an expansion bus.

An **expansion bus** carries the data to and from the expansion slots where new system devices are added (Figure 3-18). Most expansion buses connect directly to memory. To obtain faster performance, some expansion buses bypass RAM and connect directly to the CPU. An expansion bus that connects directly to the CPU is called a **local bus**. Personal computers can have different types of expansion buses. Some computers have more than one type present. Figure 3-19 lists the more common expansion bus types on personal computers. It is important to know the type of expansion buses on your computer because some devices are designed to work with only one bus type.

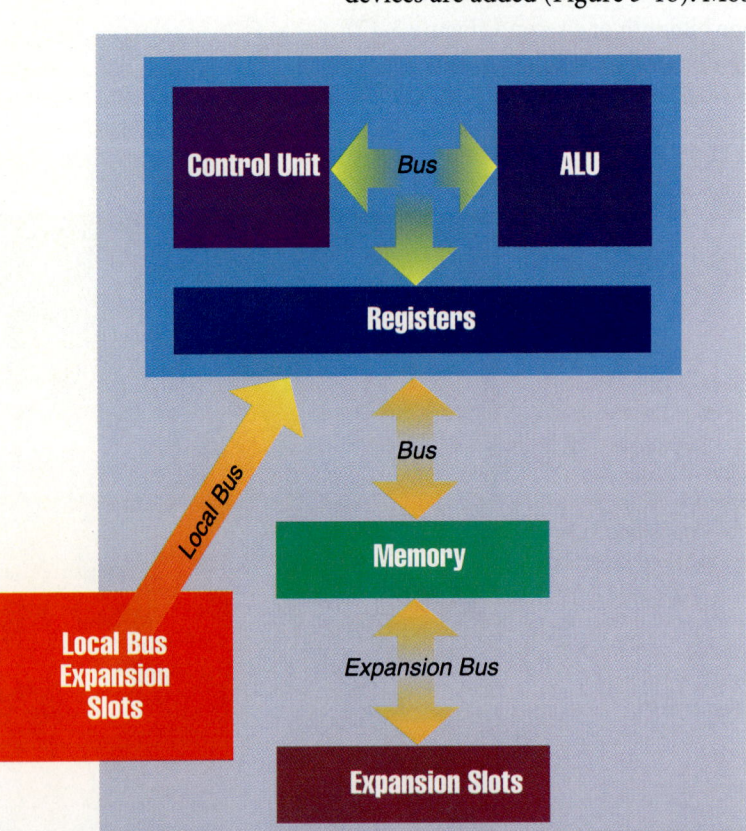

inCyber

For a description of coprocessors, visit the Discovering Computers Chapter 3 inCyber page (http://www.scsite.com/dc/ch3/incyber.htm) and click Coprocessor.

Figure 3-18
Buses are electrical pathways that carry bits from one part of the computer to another. Different buses exist for data, addresses, and control signals. The expansion bus carries data to and from the expansion boards that control peripheral devices and other components used by the computer. Many computers have a special type of expansion bus called a local bus. The local bus communicates directly with the CPU at a much faster rate than the standard expansion bus. The local bus is used for devices that require large amounts of data quickly such as monitors and disk drives.

Bus Name	Type	Bits	Description
PCI	local	32 or 64	Peripheral Component Interconnect local bus standard developed by Intel; also used on newer Macintosh computers
VESA or VL	local	32	local bus standard developed by Video Electronics Standards Association
EISA	standard	32	Extended Industry Standard Architecture developed by IBM clone manufacturers; backward compatible with ISA bus (ISA cards can run in EISA bus)
MCA	standard	16 or 32	Micro Channel Architecture developed by IBM for high-end PS/2 systems
ISA	standard	16	Industry Standard Architecture, sometimes called AT bus
XT	standard	8	developed for original IBM PC
NuBus	standard	32	high-performance expansion bus used in older Apple Macintosh computers

Figure 3-19
Types of expansion buses found on personal computers.

Buses can transfer multiples of eight bits at a time. A 16-bit bus has 16 lines and can transmit 16 bits at a time. On a 32-bit bus, bits can be moved from place to place 32 bits at a time, and on a 64-bit bus, bits are moved 64 bits at a time. The larger the number of bits that are handled by a bus, the faster the computer can transfer data. Think of a bus as a highway in which one 8-bit byte occupies one lane, and suppose a number in memory occupies four 8-bit bytes (32 bits). A 16-bit bus is like a two-lane highway; it can transfer data from memory to the CPU in two steps, transferring 16 bits at one time, 8 bits per lane. A 32-bit bus is like a four-lane highway; it can transfer the data from memory to the CPU in one step, transferring all 32 bits at one time, 8 bits in each of the four lanes. The fewer the number of transfer steps required, the faster the transfer of data occurs.

Expansion Slots

An **expansion slot** is a socket designed to hold the circuit board for a device such as a sound card that adds capability to the computer system. The circuit board for the add-on device is called an **expansion card** or **expansion board**. Expansion cards also are sometimes called **controller cards, adapter cards,** or **interface cards**. The expansion card usually is connected to the device it controls by a cable. The socket that holds the card is connected to the expansion bus that transmits data to memory or the CPU. Figure 3-20 shows an expansion card being placed in an expansion slot on a personal computer motherboard.

Figure 3-20
An expansion card being inserted into an expansion slot on the motherboard of a personal computer.

A special type of expansion slot is the PC Card slot. A **PC Card** is a thin credit card-sized device that can be inserted into a personal computer (Figure 3-21). PC Cards come in different thicknesses and often are used on portable computers for additional memory, storage, and communications capabilities. PC Cards conform to a specification developed by the Personal Computer Memory Card International Association, most often referred to by its initials, **PCMCIA**.

Ports and Connectors

A **port** is a socket used to connect the system unit to a peripheral device such as a printer or a modem. Most of the time, ports are on the back of the system unit (Figure 3-22), but they also can be on the front. Ports have different types of **connectors** that are used to attach cables to the peripheral devices. A matching connector is on the end of the cable that attaches to the port. Most connectors are available in two types, referred to as being male or female. Male connectors have one or more exposed pins, like the end of an electrical cord you plug into the wall. Female connectors have matching receptacles to accept the pins, like an electrical wall outlet. Figure 3-23 shows the different type of connectors you may find on a system unit. Ports can either be parallel or serial.

Parallel Ports

Parallel ports most often are used to connect devices that send or receive large amounts of data such as printers or disk and tape drives. **Parallel ports** transfer 8 bits (one byte) at a time using a cable that has eight data lines (Figure 3-24). The electrical signals in a parallel cable tend to interfere with one another over a long distance and therefore, parallel cables usually are limited to 50 feet. Personal computer parallel cables usually are 6- to 10-feet long. A special type of parallel port is the SCSI (pronounced scuzzy) port. **SCSI** stands for small computer system interface. A SCSI port can be used to attach seven to fifteen different devices to a single port. The devices are connected to the SCSI port and each other by a cable to form a continuous single line known as a *daisy chain*.

Figure 3-21
PC Cards are not much bigger than a credit card and fit in a small slot, usually on the side of a computer. PC Cards are used for additional memory, storage, and communications. Because of their small size, PC Cards often are used on portable computers. The card shown in this photo is a fax/data modem that can be connected to a telephone line.

inCyber
For an explanation of various PC Cards, visit the Discovering Computers Chapter 3 inCyber page (http://www.scsite.com/dc/ch3/incyber.htm) and click PC Card.

Figure 3-22
Ports are sockets used for cables that connect the system unit with devices such as a the mouse, the keyboard, and a printer. Usually, ports are on the back of the system unit and often are labeled.

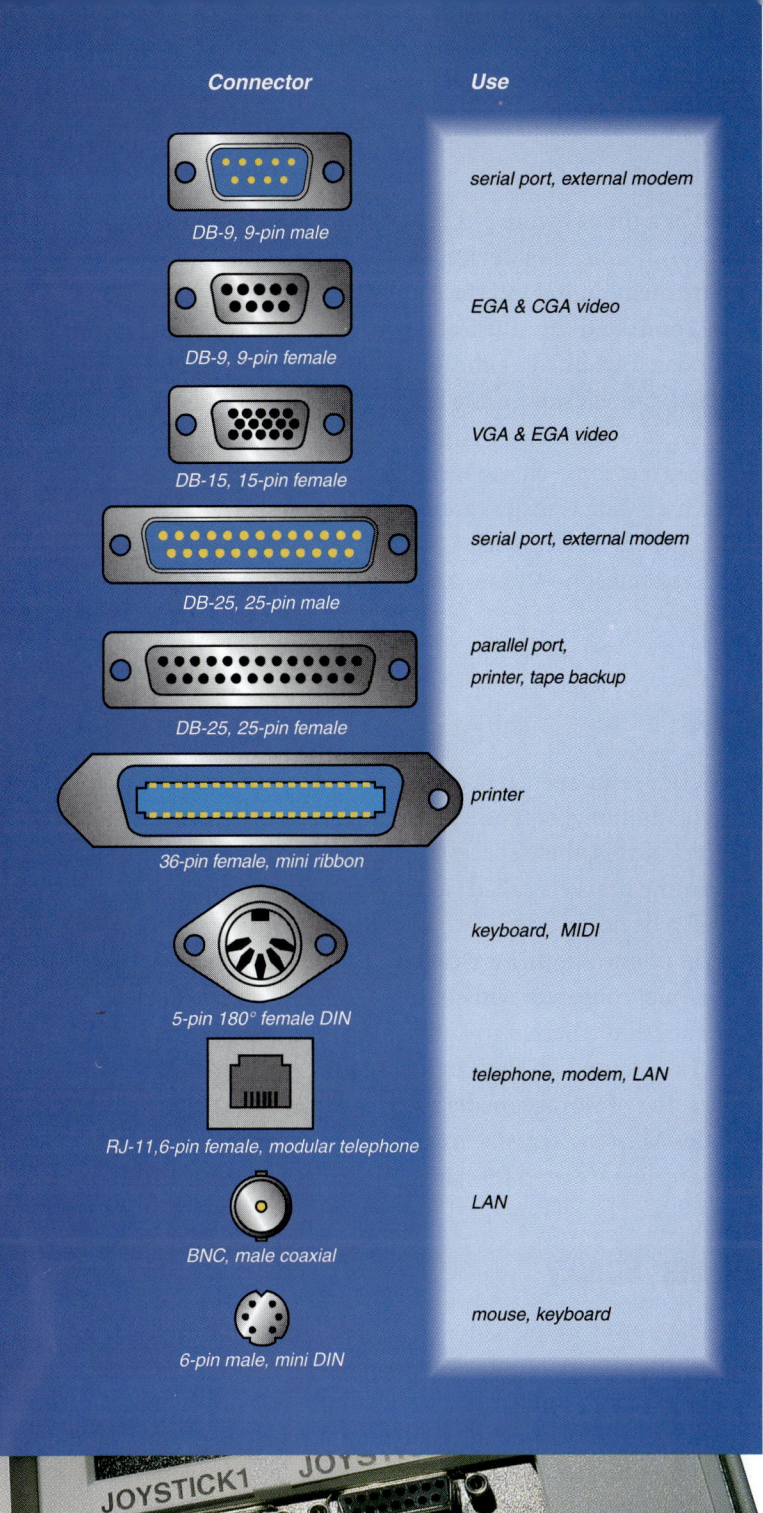

PORTS AND CONNECTORS **3.17**

Connector	Use
DB-9, 9-pin male	serial port, external modem
DB-9, 9-pin female	EGA & CGA video
DB-15, 15-pin female	VGA & EGA video
DB-25, 25-pin male	serial port, external modem
DB-25, 25-pin female	parallel port, printer, tape backup
36-pin female, mini ribbon	printer
5-pin 180° female DIN	keyboard, MIDI
RJ-11, 6-pin female, modular telephone	telephone, modem, LAN
BNC, male coaxial	LAN
6-pin male, mini DIN	mouse, keyboard

Figure 3-23
Examples of different types of connectors that are used to connect devices to the system unit. Adapters are available to join one type of connector with another.

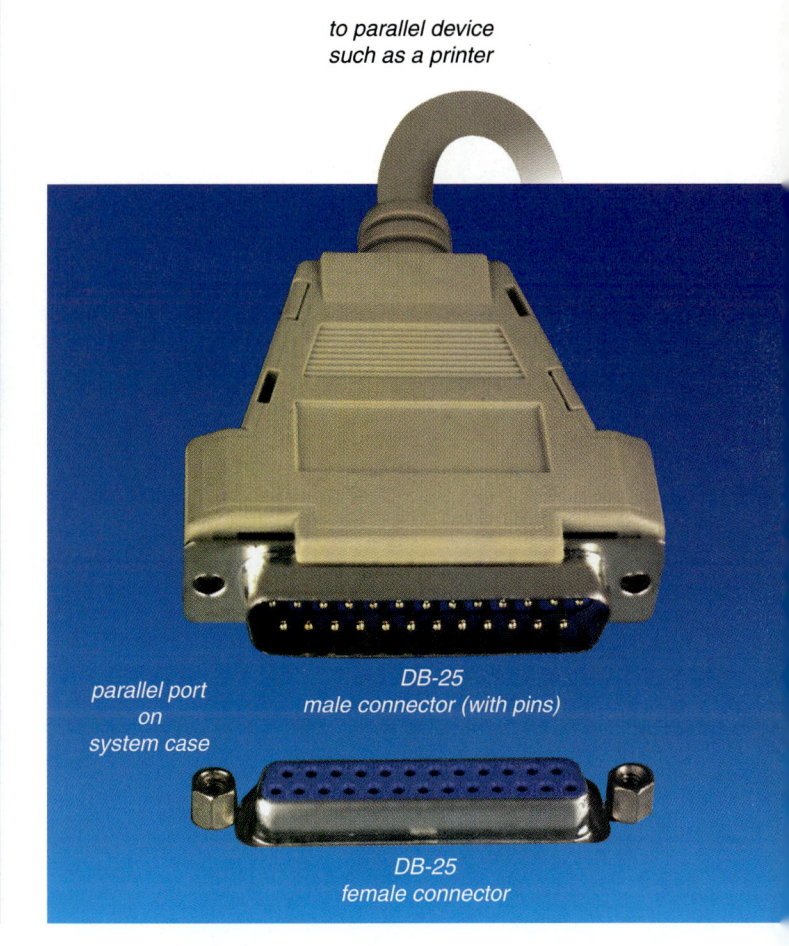

to parallel device such as a printer

parallel port on system case

DB-25 male connector (with pins)

DB-25 female connector

Figure 3-24
Parallel ports transfer eight bits at a time using a cable that has eight data lines.

Serial Ports

A **serial port** transmits data one bit at a time (Figure 3-25). Serial ports are used to connect the mouse, the keyboard, and communication devices such as a modem. A special type of serial port called a **musical instrument digital interface,** or **MIDI** (pronounced *midd-dee*) port is a serial port designed to be connected to a musical device such as an electronic music keyboard. Because they transmit data one bit at a time, older serial ports, sometimes called RS-232 serial ports, transfer data at a much slower rate than parallel ports. One advantage of these serial ports, however, is that because of reduced electrical interference, their connecting cables can be up to 1,000 feet long. Newer technology, such as the **Universal Serial Bus (USB)**, has significantly increased data transfer rates and allows up to 128 devices to be connected to a serial port. With USB, one device, such as a keyboard or monitor, plugs directly into the serial port. Other devices then connect into additional expansion sockets built into the keyboard or monitor.

Bays

A **bay** is an open area inside the system unit used to install additional equipment. Because they often are used for disk drives, these spaces also are called **drive bays**. Mounting brackets called **rails** are sometimes required to install a device in a bay. Two or more bays side by side or on top of one another are called a **cage**. Figure 3-26 shows a personal computer with a three-bay cage. *External bays* have one end adjacent to an opening in the case. External bays can be used for devices that require loading and unloading of storage media such as floppy disks, tapes, and CD-ROMs. *Internal bays* are not accessible from outside the case and are used for hard disk drives.

Power Supply

The **power supply** converts the wall outlet electricity (115-120 volts AC) to the lower voltages (5 to 12 volts DC) used by the computer. The power supply also has a fan that provides airflow inside the system unit to help cool the components. The humming noise you hear when you turn on a computer usually is the power supply fan. Personal computer power supplies are rated by wattage and range from 100 to 250 watts. Higher wattage power supplies can support more electronic equipment.

Sound Components

Most personal computers have the capability of generating sounds through a small speaker housed within the system unit. Software allows you to generate a variety of sounds including music and voice. Some computers also have built-in microphones that allow you to record voice messages and other sounds. As you will see in the chapter on output devices, many users enhance the sound-generating capabilities of their systems by installing expansion boards, called **sound boards**, and by attaching higher quality speakers to their systems.

---

inCyber

For samples of MIDI files, visit the Discovering Computers Chapter 3 inCyber page (http://www.scsite.com/dc/ch3/incyber.htm) and click MIDI.

to serial device such as a modem

DB-9 male connector (with pins)

DB-9 female connector

serial port on system case

Figure 3-25
Serial ports transfer only one bit at a time and generally are slower than parallel ports. Separate data lines are used to transmit and receive data. Pin 2 is used to receive data and pin 3 is used to send data.

Summary of the Components of the System Unit

The previous sections have presented information about the various components of the system unit. You should now be able to identify these components and have a more complete understanding about how they operate. The next section will explain how the system unit processes data by executing machine language instructions.

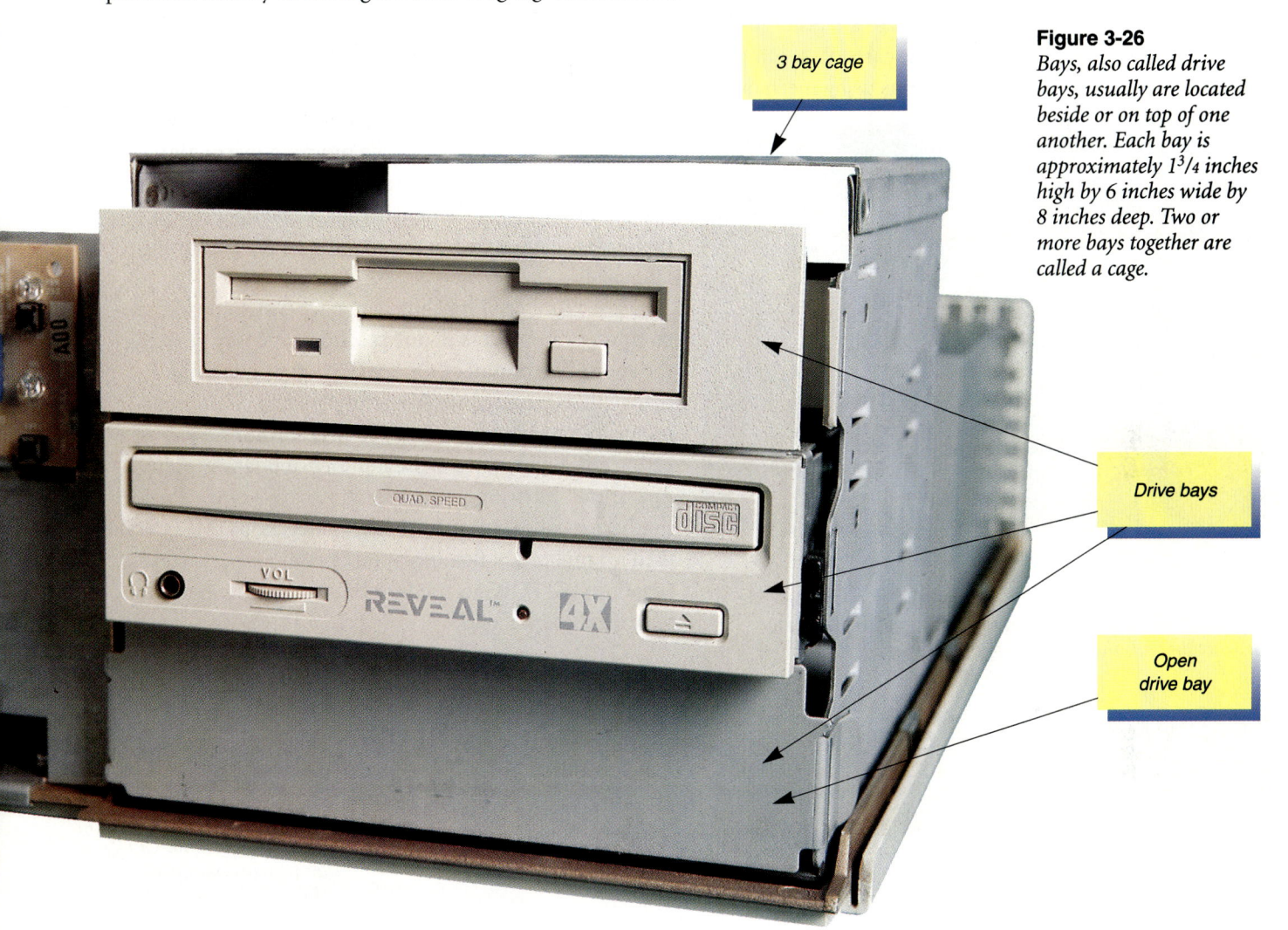

Figure 3-26
Bays, also called drive bays, usually are located beside or on top of one another. Each bay is approximately 1³/₄ inches high by 6 inches wide by 8 inches deep. Two or more bays together are called a cage.

Machine Language Instructions

The system unit gets its directions from programs permanently stored in ROM or temporarily stored in RAM. To be executed, program instructions must be in a form that the CPU can understand, called a machine language instruction. A **machine language instruction** is binary data that the electronic circuits in the CPU can interpret and convert into one or more of the commands in the computer's instruction set. The **instruction set** contains commands, such as ADD or MOVE, that the computer's circuits can directly perform. Most computers have hundreds of commands in their instruction sets and are referred to as **CISC** computers for complex instruction set computing (or computers). Studies have shown, however, that as much as 80% of the processing is performed by a small number of frequently used instructions. Based on these findings, some manufacturers have designed CPUs based on RISC technology. **RISC**, which stands for reduced instruction set computing (or computers), involves reducing the instructions to only those that are most frequently used. Because a RISC computer is designed to execute the frequently used instructions more quickly, overall processing capability, or throughput, is increased.

A machine language instruction is composed of two parts. The first part is called an operation code or opcode for short. An **operation code** tells the computer what to do and matches one of the commands in the instruction set. The second part of the machine language instruction is an operand. An **operand** specifies the data or the location of the data that will be used by the instruction. A machine language instruction may have zero to three operands. Figure 3-27 shows an example of a machine language instruction that adds the number 20 to a register in the CPU.

In the early days, computers actually had to be programmed in machine language instructions using mechanical switches to represent each binary bit. Today, program instructions are written in a readable form using a variety of programming languages. The program instructions then are converted by the computer into machine language instructions. Programming languages and conversion methods are discussed in the chapter on programming languages.

The number of machine language instructions that a computer can process in one second is one way of rating the speed of computers. One **MIPS** equals one million instructions per second. Powerful personal computers today are rated at more than 100 MIPS. Another way of rating computer speed is the number of floating-point operations. Floating-point operations are a type of mathematical calculation. The term **megaflops** (MFLOPS) is used for millions of floating-point operations per second. **Gigaflops** (GFLOPS) is used for billions of floating-point operations per second.

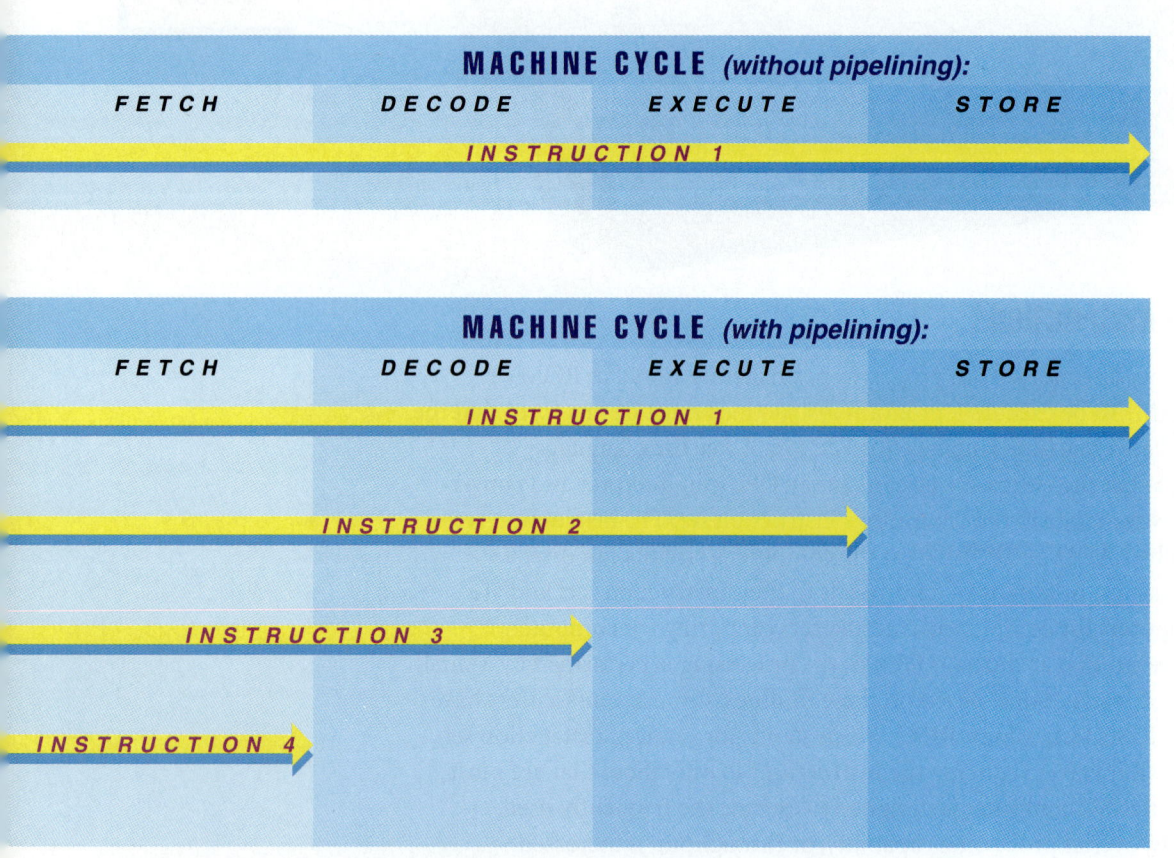

Figure 3-27
A machine language instruction consists of an operation code (opcode) and up to three operands. This machine language instruction adds the value 32 to a register.

MACHINE LANGUAGE INSTRUCTION

opcode	operand 1	operand 2
00000101	00100000	00000000
addition command	the value 32	data register in CPU

MACHINE CYCLE (without pipelining):
FETCH — DECODE — EXECUTE — STORE
INSTRUCTION 1

MACHINE CYCLE (with pipelining):
FETCH — DECODE — EXECUTE — STORE
INSTRUCTION 1
INSTRUCTION 2
INSTRUCTION 3
INSTRUCTION 4

Figure 3-28
With conventional CPUs, an instruction moves through the complete machine cycle before the next instruction is started. With pipelining, the CPU starts working on another instruction each time the preceding instruction moves to the next stage of the machine cycle. In this pipelining example, three other instructions are partially completed by the time instruction 1 is finished. Some CPUs have more than one pipeline.

Types of Processing

In the discussion thus far, the emphasis has focused on computers with single CPUs processing one instruction at a time. The following section presents variations from this approach.

Pipelining

The central processing unit (CPU) in most computers processes only a single instruction at a time. The CPU waits until an instruction completes all four stages of the machine cycle (fetch, decode, execute, and store) before beginning work on the next instruction. With **pipelining**, a new instruction is fetched as soon as the preceding instruction moves on to the next stage. The result is faster throughput because by the time the first instruction is in the fourth and final stage of the machine cycle, three other instructions have been fetched and are at various stages of the machine cycle (Figure 3-28). Some CPUs, called **superscalar CPUs**, have two or more pipelines that can process instructions simultaneously.

inCyber
For an explanation of pipelining, visit the Discovering Computers Chapter 3 inCyber page (http://www.scsite.com/dc/ch3/incyber.htm) and click Pipelining.

Parallel Processing

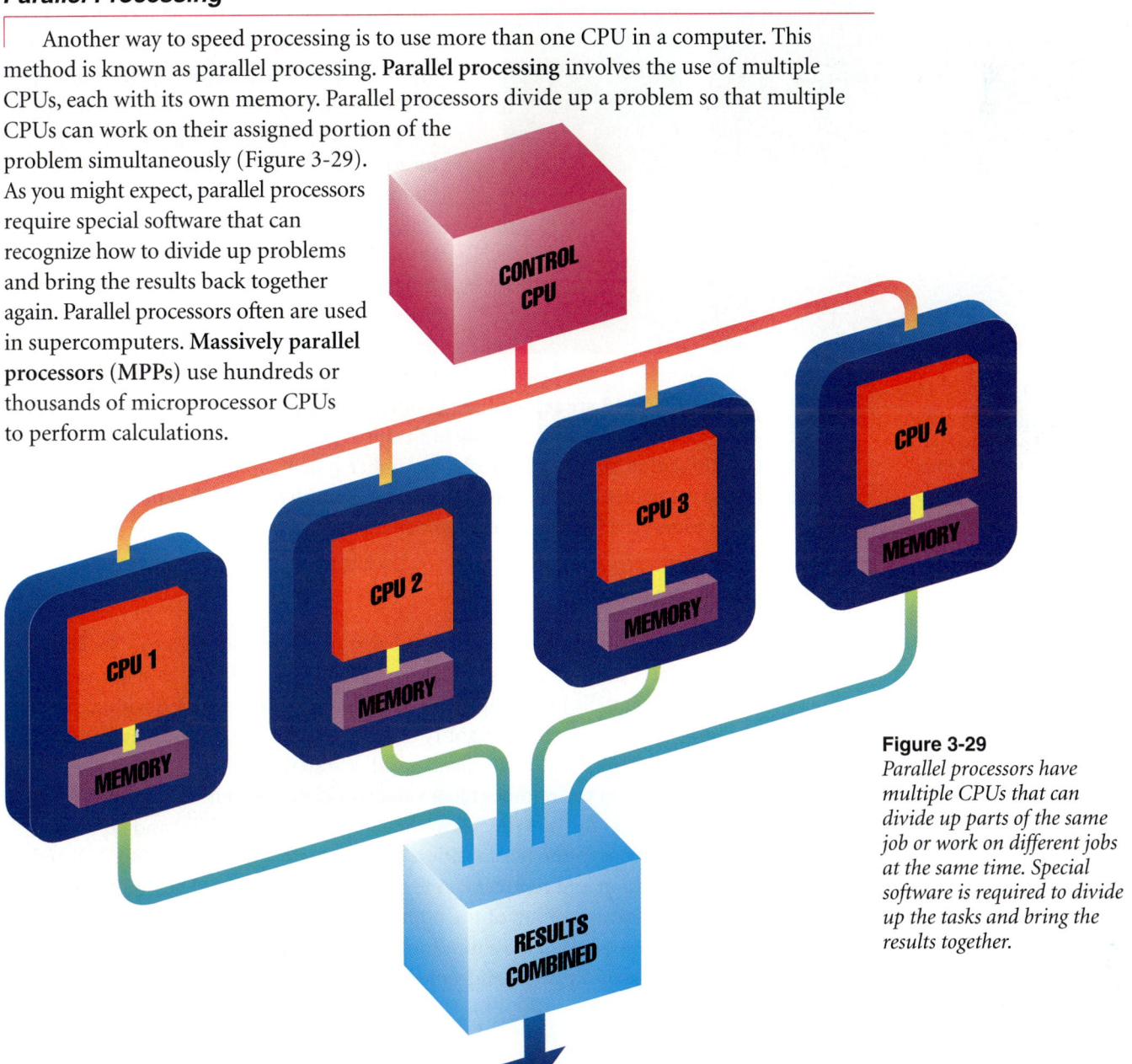

Another way to speed processing is to use more than one CPU in a computer. This method is known as parallel processing. **Parallel processing** involves the use of multiple CPUs, each with its own memory. Parallel processors divide up a problem so that multiple CPUs can work on their assigned portion of the problem simultaneously (Figure 3-29). As you might expect, parallel processors require special software that can recognize how to divide up problems and bring the results back together again. Parallel processors often are used in supercomputers. **Massively parallel processors** (MPPs) use hundreds or thousands of microprocessor CPUs to perform calculations.

Figure 3-29
Parallel processors have multiple CPUs that can divide up parts of the same job or work on different jobs at the same time. Special software is required to divide up the tasks and bring the results together.

Neural Network Computers

Neural network computers use specially designed circuits to simulate the way the human brain processes information, learns, and remembers. Neural network chips form an interconnected system of processors that learn to associate the relative strength or weakness of inputs with specific results (output). Neural network computers are used in applications such as pattern recognition to correctly guess the identity of an object when only hazy or partial information is available. Other applications that use neural network computers are speech recognition and speech synthesis.

Number Systems

This section describes the number systems that are used with computers. Whereas thorough knowledge of this subject is required for technical computer personnel, a general understanding of number systems and how they relate to computers is all most users need. As you have seen, the binary (base 2) number system is used to represent the electronic status of the bits in memory. It is also used for other purposes such as addressing the memory locations. Another number system that is commonly used with computers is **hexadecimal** (base 16). The hexadecimal system is used by the computer to communicate with a programmer when a problem with a program exists, because it would be difficult for the programmer to understand the 0s and 1s of binary code. Figure 3-30 shows how the decimal values 0 through 15 are represented in binary and hexadecimal.

DECIMAL	BINARY	HEXADECIMAL
0	0000	0
1	0001	1
2	0010	2
3	0011	3
4	0100	4
5	0101	5
6	0110	6
7	0111	7
8	1000	8
9	1001	9
10	1010	A
11	1011	B
12	1100	C
13	1101	D
14	1110	E
15	1111	F

Figure 3-30
The chart shows the binary and hexadecimal representation of decimal numbers 0 through 15. In hexadecimal, notice how letters A through F represent the numbers 10 through 15.

The mathematical principles that apply to the binary and hexadecimal number systems are the same as those that apply to the decimal number system. To help you better understand these principles, this section starts with the familiar decimal system, then progresses to the binary and hexadecimal number systems.

The Decimal Number System

The decimal number system is a base 10 number system (*deci* means ten). The *base* of a number system indicates how many symbols are used in it. Decimal uses 10 symbols, 0 through 9. Each of the symbols in the number system has a value associated with it. For example, you know that 3 represents a quantity of three and 5 represents a quantity of five. The decimal number system also is a *positional* number system. This means that in a number such as 143, each position in the number has a value associated with it. When you look at the decimal number 143, you know that the 3 is in the ones, or units, position and represents three ones or (3 x 1); the 4 is in the tens position and represents four tens or (4 x 10); and the 1 is in the hundreds position and represents one hundred or (1 x 100). The number 143 is the sum of the values in each position of the number (100 + 40 + 3 = 143). The chart in Figure 3-31 shows how the positional values (hundreds, tens, and units) for a number system can be calculated. Starting on the right and working to the left, the base of the number system,

power of 10	10^2	10^1	10^0	1		4		3	=	
				(1×10^2)	+	(4×10^1)	+	(3×10^0)	=	
positional value	100	10	1							
				(1×100)	+	(4×10)	+	$(3 \times 1\ )$	=	
number	1	4	3	100	+	40	+	3	=	143

Figure 3-31
The positional values in the decimal number 143 are shown in this chart.

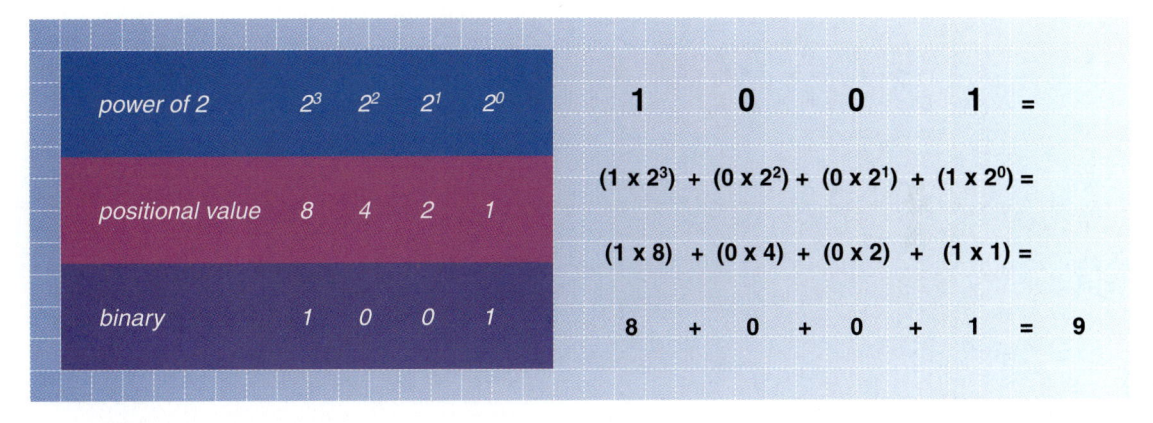

power of 2	2^3	2^2	2^1	2^0	1		0		0		1	=	
					(1×2^3)	+	(0×2^2)	+	(0×2^1)	+	(1×2^0)	=	
positional value	8	4	2	1									
					(1×8)	+	(0×4)	+	(0×2)	+	(1×1)	=	
binary	1	0	0	1	8	+	0	+	0	+	1	=	9

Figure 3-32
Each positional value in a binary number represents a consecutive power of two. Using the positional values, the binary number 1001 can be converted to the decimal number 9.

in this case 10, is raised to consecutive powers (10^2, 10^1, 10^0). These calculations are a mathematical way of determining the place values in a number system.

When you use number systems other than decimal, the same principles apply. The base of the number system indicates the number of symbols that are used, and each position in a number system has a value associated with it. The positional value can be calculated by raising the base of the number system to consecutive powers beginning with zero.

The Binary Number System

As previously discussed, binary is a base 2 number system (*bi* means two), and the symbols that are used are 0 and 1. Just as each position in a decimal number has a place value associated with it, so does each position in a binary number. In binary, the place values are successive powers of two (2^3, 2^2, 2^1, 2^0) or (8, 4, 2, 1). To construct a binary number, you place ones in the positions where the corresponding values add up to the quantity you want to represent; you place zeros in the other positions. For example, the binary place values are 8, 4, 2, and 1, and the binary number 1001 has ones in the positions for the values 8 and 1 and zeros in the positions for 4 and 2. Therefore, the quantity represented by binary 1001 is 9 (8 + 0 + 0 + 1) (Figure 3-32).

power of 16	16^1	16^0	A	5	=
positional value	16	1	(10×16^1) + (5×16^0)		=
			(10×16) + (5×1)		=
hexadecimal	A	5	160 + 5		= 165

Figure 3-33
Conversion of the hexadecimal number A5 to the decimal number 165. Notice that the value 10 is substituted for the A during calculations.

positional value	8421	8421
binary	0100	1101
decimal	4	13
hexadecimal	4	D

Figure 3-34
Conversion of the ASCII code 01001101 for the letter M to the hexadecimal value 4D. Each group of four binary digits is converted to a hexadecimal symbol.

The Hexadecimal Number System

The hexadecimal number system uses 16 symbols to represent values (*hex* means six, *deci* means ten). These include the symbols 0 through 9 and A through F (Figure 3-30). The mathematical principles previously discussed also apply to hexadecimal (Figure 3-33).

The primary reason why the hexadecimal number system is used with computers is because it can represent binary values in a more compact and readable form and because the conversion between the binary and the hexadecimal number systems is very efficient. An eight-digit binary number (a byte) can be represented by a two-digit hexadecimal number. For example, in the ASCII code, the character M is represented as 01001101. This value can be represented in hexadecimal as 4D. One way to convert this binary number to a hexadecimal number is to divide the binary number (from right to left) into groups of four digits; calculate the value of each group; and then change any two-digit values (10 through 15) into the symbols A through F that are used in hexadecimal (Figure 3-34).

Summary of Number Systems

As mentioned at the beginning of the section on number systems, binary and hexadecimal are used primarily by technical computer personnel. A general user does not need a complete understanding of numbering systems. The concepts that you should remember about number systems are that binary is used to represent the electronic status of the bits in memory and storage. Hexadecimal is used to represent binary in a more compact form.

---

inCyber

For an explanation of the hexadecimal number system, visit the Discovering Computers Chapter 3 inCyber page (http://www.scsite.com/dc/ch3/incyber.htm) and click Hexadecimal Number.

How Computer Chips Are Made

A computer chip is made by building layers of electronic pathways and connections by using conducting and nonconducting materials on a surface of silicon. The combination of these materials into specific patterns forms microscopic electronic components such as transistors, diodes, resistors, and capacitors; the basic building blocks of electronic circuits. Connected together on a chip, these components are referred to as an **integrated circuit**. The application of the conducting and nonconducting materials to the silicon base is done through a series of technically sophisticated chemical and photographic processes. Some of the manufacturing steps are shown in the following photographs.

A computer chip begins with a design developed by engineers using a computer-aided circuit design program (Figure 3-35). To better review the design, greatly enlarged printouts are prepared. Some chips take only a month or two to design while others may require a year or more. A separate design is needed for each layer of the chip. Most chips have at least four to six layers, but some have up to fifteen.

Although other materials can be used, the most common raw material used to make chips is silicon crystals (Figure 3-36) that have been refined from quartz rocks. The silicon crystals are melted and formed into a cylinder five to ten inches in diameter and several feet long (Figure 3-37). After being smoothed, the silicon ingot is sliced into **wafers** four to eight inches in diameter and 4/1000 of an inch thick.

Much of the chip manufacturing process is performed in special laboratories called **clean rooms**. Because even the smallest particle of dust can ruin a chip, the clean rooms are kept 1,000 times cleaner than a hospital operating

inCyber

For details on the Pentium chip, visit the Discovering Computers Chapter 3 inCyber page (http://www.scsite.com/dc/ch3/incyber.htm) and click Integrated Circuit.

Figure 3-35
Computer-aided design programs are used to create the chip design. Notice the enlarged design printouts in the background.

Figure 3-36
Silicon crystals are the most common raw material used to make the wafers that eventually will become computer chips.

Figure 3-37
Silicon crystals are melted and formed into a cylinder five to ten inches in diameter and several feet long. The ingot is sliced into wafers four to eight inches in diameter and 4/1000 of an inch thick.

Figure 3-38
To avoid contamination of the chip surface, manufacturing is performed in clean rooms 1,000 times cleaner than hospital operating rooms. Workers wear protective clothing called bunny suits.

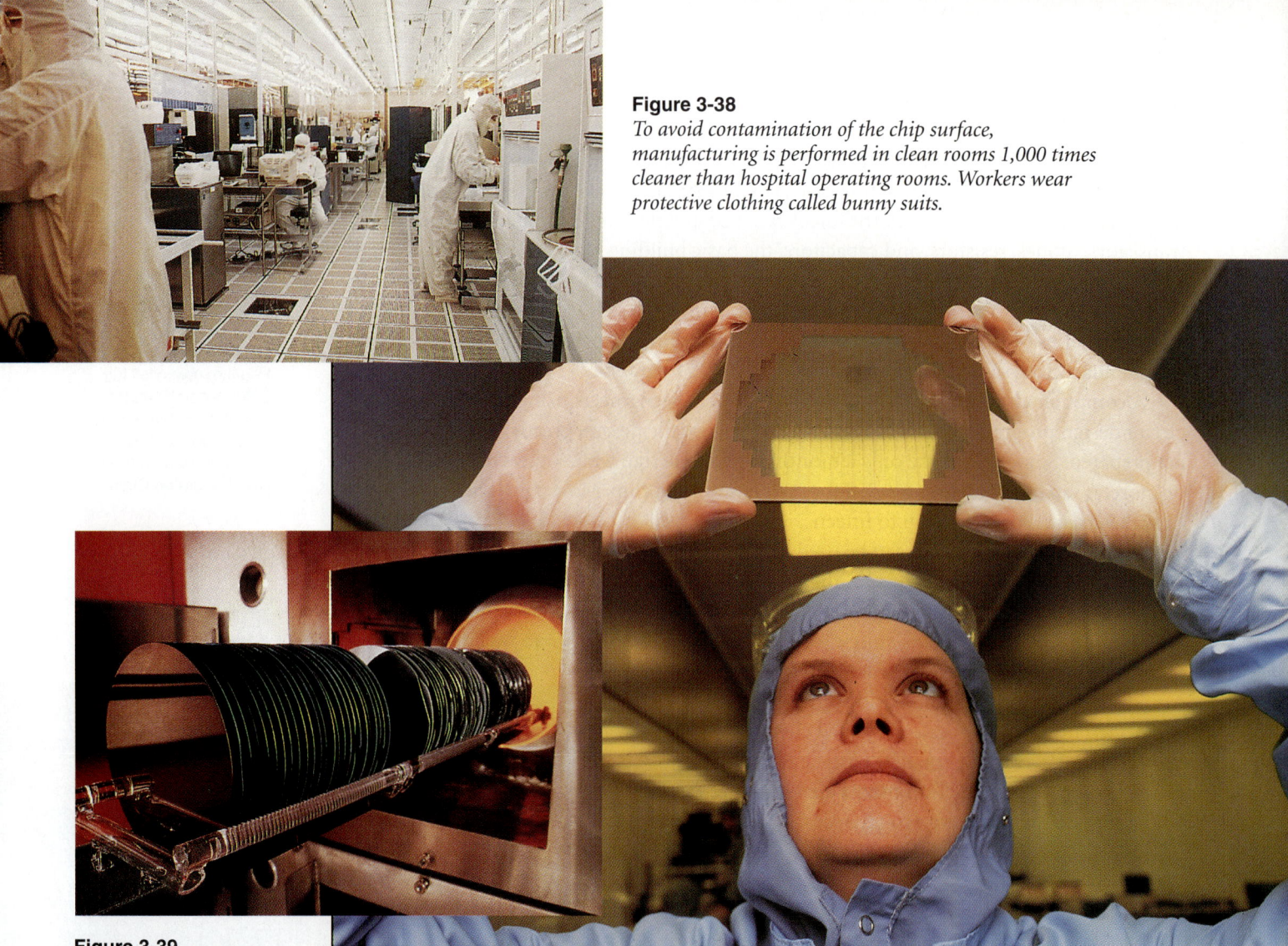

Figure 3-39
A high-temperature diffusion oven bakes chemicals into the wafer.

Figure 3-40
In the photolithography process, a mask with a layer of chip design is used as a negative. A different mask is used for each layer of the chip. The mask protects specific areas of the wafer from exposure to ultraviolet light. The areas not exposed to ultraviolet light will be removed in the next manufacturing step. The mask may contain up to 100 images of the individual chip.

room. People who work in these facilities must wear special protective clothing called **bunny suits** (Figure 3-38).

After the wafer has been polished and sterilized, it is cleaned in a chemical bath. After cleaning, the wafers are placed in a **diffusion oven** where the first layer of material is added to the wafer surface (Figure 3-39). Other materials, called dopants, are added to the surface of the wafer in a process called **ion implantation**. The **dopants** create areas that will conduct electricity. Channels in these layers of materials are removed in a process called **etching**. Before etching, a soft gelatin-like emulsion called **photoresist** is added to the wafer.

During **photolithography**, an image of the chip design, called a mask, is used as a negative (Figure 3-40). The photoresist is exposed to the mask using ultraviolet light. Ultraviolet light is used because its short wavelength can reproduce very small details on the wafer. Up to 100 images of the chip design are exposed on a single wafer. The photoresist exposed to the ultraviolet light becomes hard and the photoresist covered by the chip design on the mask remains soft. The soft photoresist and some of the surface materials are etched away with hot gases leaving what will become the circuit pathways (Figure 3-41). The process of adding material and photoresist to the wafer, exposing it to ultraviolet light, and etching away the unexposed surface, is repeated using a different mask for each layer of the circuit.

Figure 3-41
This microscopic view shows the electrical pathways that are created during the chip manufacturing process.

Figure 3-42
After the wafer manufacturing process is completed, the wafer is sliced into individual chips called die.

After all circuit layers have been added, individual chips on the wafer are tested by a machine that uses probes to apply electrical current to the chip circuits. In a process called **dicing**, the wafers are cut into individual chips called **die** (Figure 3-42). Die that have passed all tests are placed in a ceramic or plastic case called a **package** (Figure 3-43). Circuits on the chip are connected to pins on the package using gold wires (Figure 3-44). Gold is used because it conducts electricity well and does not corrode. The pins connect the chip to a socket on a circuit board.

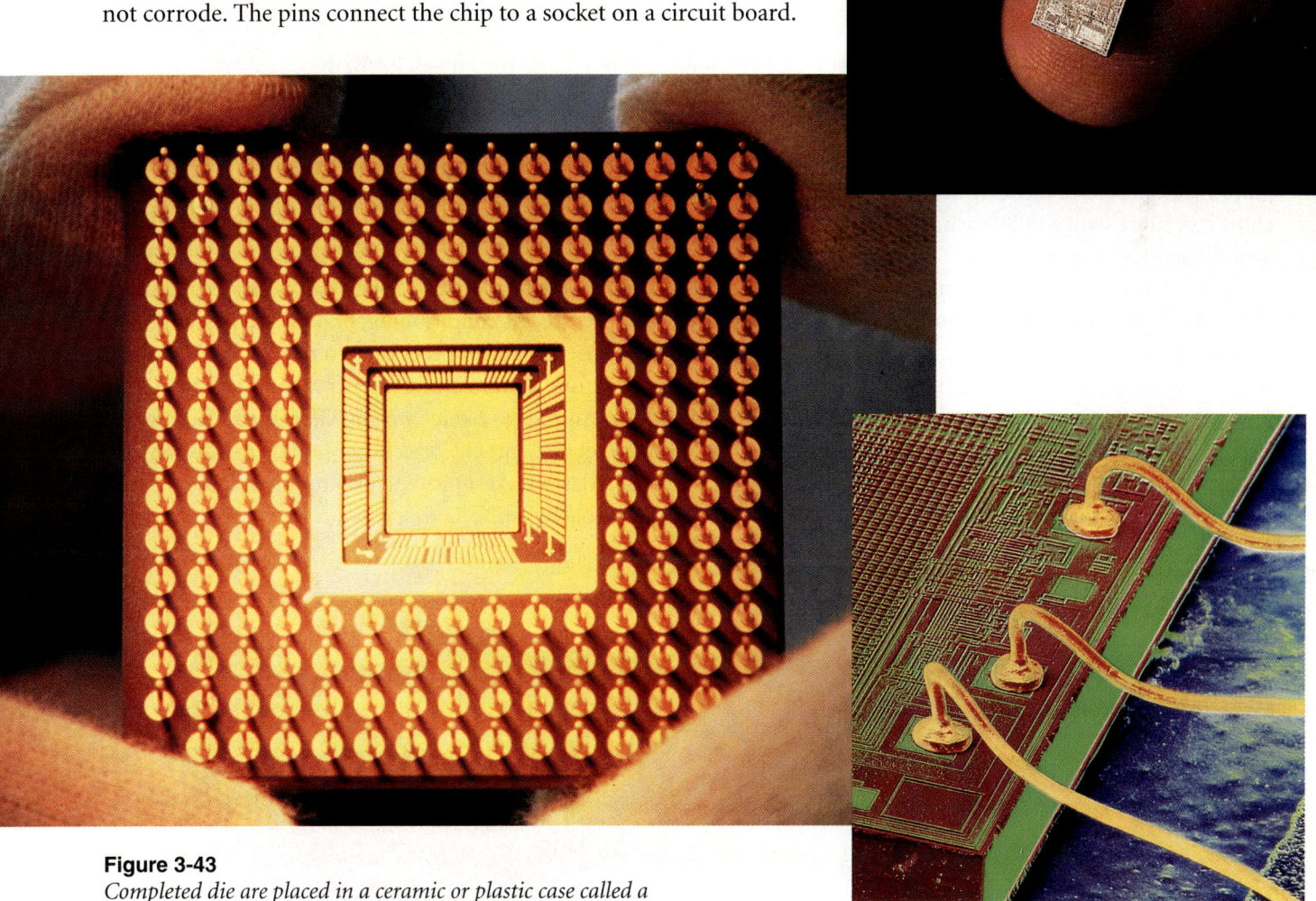

Figure 3-43
Completed die are placed in a ceramic or plastic case called a package. The gold-plated pins shown on the bottom of this package will connect to a socket on the computer motherboard.

Figure 3-44
Circuits on the chip are connected to the pins on the chip package with fine gold wires shown here in this microscopic photo.

Summary of the System Unit

This chapter examined various aspects of the system unit including its components, how programs and data are stored, and how the processor executes program instructions to process data into information. You also have studied various methods of processing, learned about the various number systems that are used with computers, and seen how computer chips are made. Knowing this material will increase your overall understanding of how processing occurs on a computer.

COMPUTERS AT WORK

How Many Computers Do You See Each Day?

If you ask someone how many computers he or she uses each day, the answer usually is one or two; a computer at work or school and possibly another computer at home. In reality, most people use dozens of computers each day. These other computers, called **embedded processors**, are built into equipment such as radios, cellular telephones, microwave ovens, copiers, automatic teller machines, and automobiles. We do not think of these processors as computers because we cannot see them and because they play a supporting role in the overall function of the device of which they are a part. In terms of volume, 90% of the processor chips produced are used for embedded applications; only 10% are used for personal and other general-purpose computers.

The capabilities and prices of embedded processors vary greatly. Kitchen appliances, such as a coffee maker, use simple 4- or 8-bit processors that cost less than a dollar. A programmable industrial robot may require a 16-bit processor that costs $20. More sophisticated devices such as communications switching equipment may use the same 32-bit processor as those installed in the more powerful personal computers and servers. These processor chips cost more than $1,000 each. Custom designed processor chips such as those used for aircraft flight control systems can cost even more.

Automobile manufacturers currently are the largest users of embedded processors. A new car has an average of six embedded processors to monitor and control ignition, fuel mixture, air conditioning, brakes, and passenger restraint systems such as air bags. Some luxury cars have more than 40 embedded processors to control lights, suspension, traction, and navigation systems automatically. In the future, auto manufacturers probably will use fewer but more powerful processors that will be connected with fiber optics to reduce weight. Consumer electronic devices also are heavy users. Think about how many appliances and entertainment devices contain digital displays and the capability of programming them to meet your desired use. Alarm wake-up times, programmed radio stations, and yes, the blinking 12:00 on your VCR, all are made possible by embedded processors.

Figure 3-45

IN THE FUTURE

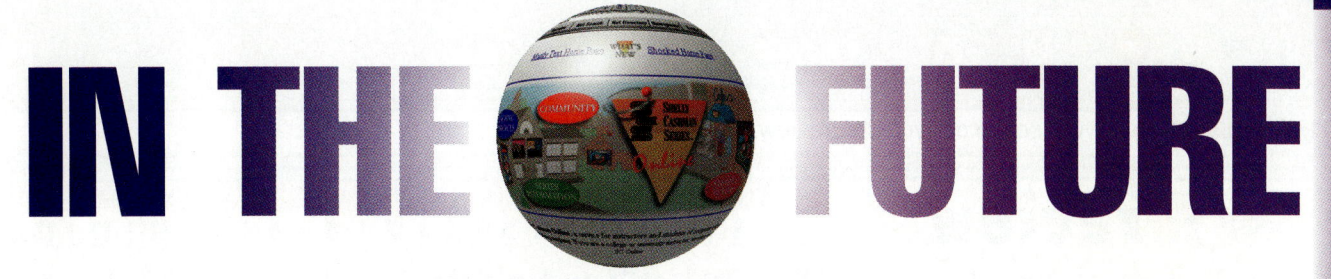

2,000 MIPS by the Year 2000

By the year 2000, Intel, the world's largest manufacturer of microprocessors, predicts it will have a CPU chip that can perform 2,000 MIPS; which is 2 billion instructions per second. This is almost seven times faster than most microprocessor CPUs currently available. To reach this performance level, Intel will have to continue to pack more transistors onto the slice of silicon that becomes the heart of the microprocessor. Intel's Pentium Pro processor has 5.5 million transistors. Its next generation processor, dubbed the P7, is estimated to have between 10 and 15 million transistors. The 2,000 MIPS processor will have between 50 and 100 million transistors spread among four or more integrated CPUs. To reach this level of transistor density, the size of the transistors will have to shrink below one-tenth of a micron. A micron is one-millionth of a meter. Current microprocessors have transistor sizes approximately .35 to .60 microns. For comparison purposes, an average human hair is 75 microns or approximately 150 times the size of current microprocessor transistors. The clock speed of the microprocessor also will have to improve, probably to more than 300 megahertz (each megahertz is one million cycles per second). Current microprocessors run at about 100 to 200 megahertz.

To reach these levels of transistor density and clock speed, microprocessor chip advances will have to continue to meet the prediction of Intel founder Gordon Moore. In 1965, Moore predicted that transistor density, and thus relative computing power, would double every 18 to 24 months. Called Moore's Law, this prediction has so far been amazingly accurate (Figure 3-46). To reach Intel's goal of the 2,000 MIPS chip by the year 2000, the law will have to hold true for a few more years.

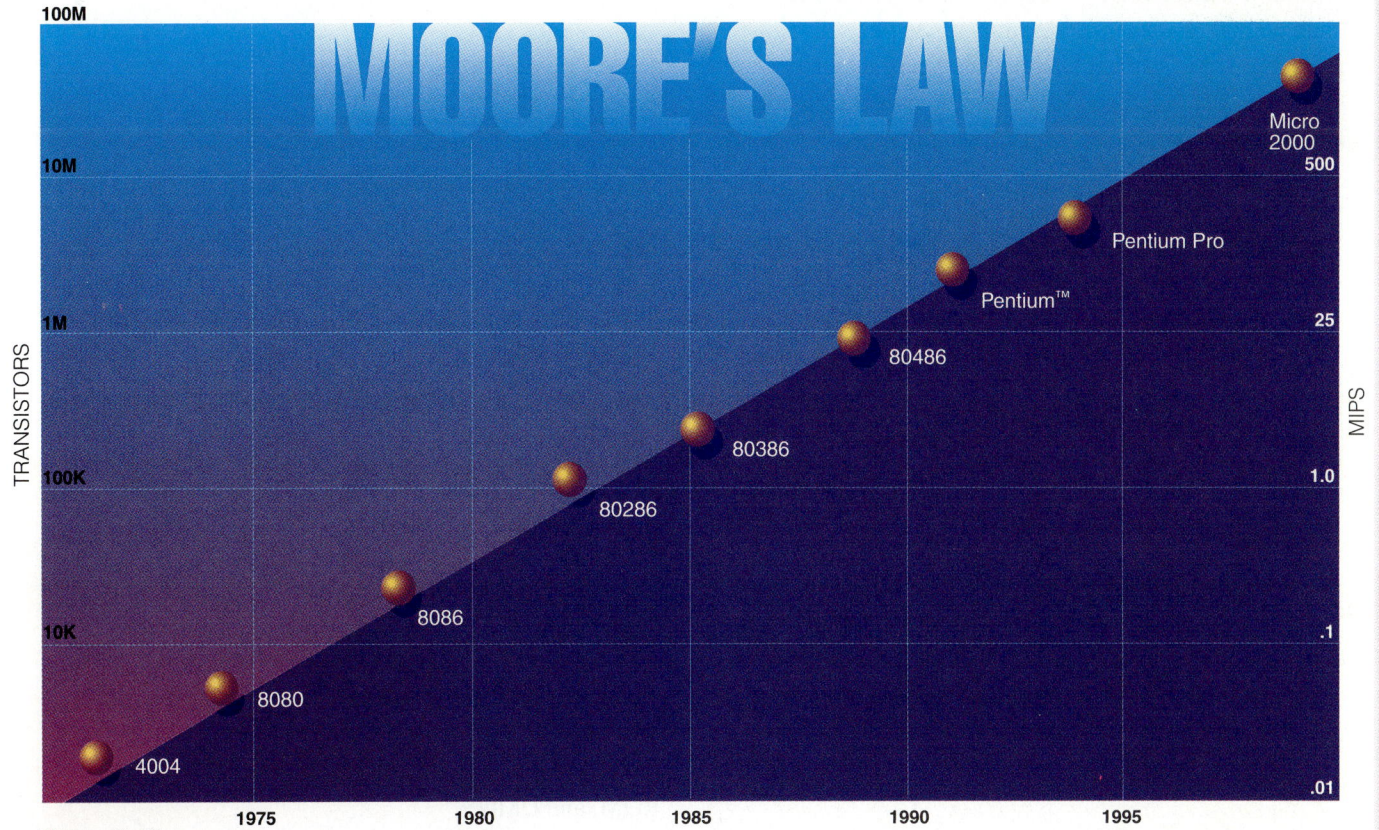

Figure 3-46

chapter 3 review

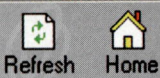

inCyber | review | terms | yourTurn | hotTopics | outThere | winLabs | webWalk | exercises | news | home

INSTRUCTIONS: *To display this page from the Web, launch your browser and enter the URL, http://www.scsite.com/dc/ch3/review.htm. Click the links for current and additional information.*

1 Bits and Bytes

Most computers are **digital computers**, meaning all the data they process is converted first into a digital (numeric) value. Only two digits are used because they can be represented by circuits being either off (0) or on (1). Each off or on digital value is called a bit, which is short for *bi*nary dig*it*. Using combinations of 0s and 1s in a group of eight bits, called a byte, a unique code can be assigned to 256 different data possibilities.

2 Bit Pattern Codes

Several different coding schemes are used on computers. The **American Standard Code for Information Interchange (ASCII)** is used on many personal computers and minicomputers. The **Extended Binary Coded Decimal Interchange Code (EBCDIC)** is used primarily on mainframe computers. With these codes, each character is stored in one byte (eight bits) of memory. **Unicode**, a 16-bit code that can represent more than 65,000 characters and symbols, can be used with all of the world's current languages. Every major system developer has announced plans to implement Unicode eventually.

3 Components of the System Unit

In the **system unit**, the computer program instructions are executed and the coded data is manipulated. Components considered part of the system unit include the motherboard, the microprocessor and CPU, upgrade sockets, memory, coprocessors, buses, expansion slots, ports and connectors, bays, the power supply, and sound components.

4 The Motherboard, Microprocessor, and CPU

The **motherboard** is a circuit board that contains most of the electronic components of the system unit. On a personal computer's motherboard is a single integrated circuit (chip), called a **microprocessor**, that holds the central processing unit. The **central processing unit (CPU)** contains the control unit and the arithmetic/logic unit, which work together to perform processing.

5 The Control Unit and the Arithmetic/Logic Unit

The **control unit** *controls* the computer by repeating four operations, called the **machine cycle**. The four operations are **fetching** program instructions from memory, **decoding** the instructions into commands the computer can process, **executing** the commands, and storing the results in memory. The **arithmetic/logic unit (ALU)** contains the electronic circuits to perform **arithmetic operations** (computations) and **logical operations** (comparisons) on data. Some motherboards contain a type of receptacle, called an **upgrade socket**, that can be used to install a more powerful CPU.

6 Memory

Memory refers to integrated circuits that temporarily store program instructions and data used by the CPU. Memory stores three items: the systems software, the application program instructions, and the data being processed. Memory size is measured in **kilobytes (K** or **KB)**, **megabytes (MB)**, or **gigabytes (GB)**. Three common types of memory chips are RAM, ROM, and CMOS.

3 review

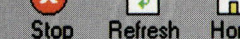

chapter 1 | 2 | 3 | 4 | 5 | 6 | 7 | 8 | 9 | 10 | 11 | 12 | 13 | 14 | I

inCyber | review | terms | yourTurn | hotTopics | outThere | winLabs | webWalk | exercises | news | home

7 RAM vs. ROM

RAM (random access memory) is the name given to the integrated circuits containing data that can be read and written by the microprocessor or other computer devices. RAM is volatile because the programs and data stored in RAM are erased when the power is turned off. **ROM (read only memory)** is the name given to chips that store information or instructions that can be read and used, but cannot be changed. ROM is **nonvolatile** because it retains its contents even when the power is turned off. **CMOS (complementary metal-oxide semiconductor)** memory is used to store information about the computer system that is needed each time the computer is started.

8 Coprocessors, Buses, and Explansion Slots

Computers can increase their efficiency with a **coprocessor**, which is a special microprocessor chip or circuit board designed to perform a specific task. Within the circuitry of a computer, any path along which bits are transmitted is called a **bus**. An **expansion bus** carries data to and from **expansion slots**, which are sockets designed to hold the circuit board for a device that adds capability to the computer system.

9 Parallel Ports and Serial Ports

A **port** is a socket used to connect the system unit to a peripheral device. **Parallel ports**, which transfer eight bits (one byte) at a time, are used most often to connect devices that send or receive large amounts of data, such as printers or disk and tape drives. **Serial ports**, which transmit data one bit at a time, are used to connect the mouse, the keyboard, and communication devices.

10 Bays, the Power Supply, and Sound Components

A **bay** is an open area inside the system unit used to install additional equipment. The **power supply** converts the wall outlet electricity (115 to 120 volts AC) to the lower voltages (5 to 12 volts DC) used by the computer. Most personal computers have the capability of generating sounds through a small speaker, and some have a microphone to record messages.

11 Machine Language Instructions

Program instructions must be in **machine language**, which is binary data that the electronic circuits in the CPU can interpret and convert into one or more of the commands in the computer's instruction set. The **instruction set** contains commands that the computer's circuits can perform directly. The first part of a machine language instruction, called the **operation code**, tells the computer what to do and matches a command in the instruction set. The second part of the instruction, called an **operand**, specifies the data or the location of the data that will be used by the instruction.

12 Types of Processing

The CPU in most computers processes a single instruction at a time. The CPU waits until the instruction completes all four stages of the machine cycle before beginning to work on the next instruction. **Pipelining** speeds throughput by fetching a new instruction as soon as the preceding instruction moves on to the next stage. **Parallel processing** uses multiple CPUs, which each work simultaneously on a portion of the problem. **Neural network computers** apply specially designed circuits to simulate the way the human brain processes information, learns, and remembers.

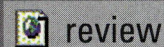

chapter 3 terms

1 | 2 | 3 | 4 | 5 | 6 | 7 | 8 | 9 | 10 | 11 | 12 | 13 | 14 | I

inCyber | review | terms | yourTurn | hotTopics | outThere | winLabs | webWalk | exercises | news | home

INSTRUCTIONS: *To display this page from the Web, launch your browser and enter the URL, http://www.scsite.com/dc/ch3/terms.htm. Scroll through the list of terms. Click a term for its definition and a picture. Click the rocket ship for current and additional information about the term.*

integrated circuit (IC)

DEFINITION

integrated circuit (IC)

Also called a chip, or IC, is a complete electronic circuit that has been etched on a thin slice of material such as silicon. For mainframe and supercomputers, the CPU consists of one or more circuit boards. **(3.8, 3.25)**

---

access speed (3.13)
adapter cards (3.15)
American Standard Code for Information Interchange (ASCII) (3.4)
analog computers (3.3)
arithmetic operations (3.8)
arithmetic/logic unit (ALU) (3.8)

bay (3.18)
bit (3.3)
bunny suits (3.25)
bus (3.14)
byte (3.3)

cache (3.12)
cage (3.18)
central processing unit (CPU) (3.8)
chip (3.8)
CISC (3.19)
clean rooms (3.25)
CMOS (complementary metal-oxide semiconductor) (3.13)
connectors (3.16)
control unit (3.8)
controller cards (3.15)
coprocessor (3.14)

decoding (3.8)
dicing (3.27)
die (3.27)
diffusion oven (3.26)
digital computers (3.3)
digitizing (3.3)
DIMM (dual in-line memory module) (3.12)

dopants (3.26)
drive bay (3.18)
dynamic RAM (DRAM) (3.13)

etching (3.26)
even parity (3.5)
executing (3.8)
execution cycle (3.8)
expansion board (3.15)
expansion bus (3.14)
expansion card (3.15)
expansion slot (3.15)
Extended Binary Coded Decimal Interchange Code (EBCDIC) (3.4)

fetching (3.8)
firmware (3.13)
flash memory (3.11)
flash RAM (3.11)

gigabyte (GB) (3.11)
gigaflops (GFLOPS) (3.20)

hexadecimal (3.22)

ideograms (3.4)
instruction cycle (3.8)
instruction set (3.19)
integrated circuit (IC) (3.8, 3.25)
interface cards (3.15)
internal cache (3.12)
ion implantation (3.26)

kilobyte (K or KB) (3.11)

level 1 (L1) cache (3.12)
level 2 (L2) cache (3.12)
local bus (3.14)
logical operations (3.8)

machine cycle (3.8)
machine language instruction (3.19)
main board (3.7)
massively parallel processor (MPP) (3.21)
megabyte (MB) (3.11)
megaflops (MFLOPS) (3.20)
megahertz (MHz) (3.9)
memory (3.11)
memory address (3.11)
microcode (3.13)
microprocessor (3.7)
millisecond (3.14)
MIPS (3.20)
motherboard (3.7)
musical instrument digital interface (MIDI) (3.18)

nanoseconds (3.13)
neural network computers (3.22)
nonvolatile (3.13)

odd parity (3.5)
operand (3.20)
operation code (3.20)

package (3.27)
parallel ports (3.16)
parallel processing (3.21)
parity bit (3.5)
PC Card (3.16)

PCMCIA (3.16)
photolithography (3.26)
photoresist (3.26)
pipelining (3.21)
port (3.16)
power supply (3.18)

rails (3.18)
RAM (random access memory) (3.11)
registers (3.8)
RISC (3.19)
ROM (read only memory) (3.13)

SCSI (3.16)
serial port (3.18)
SIMM (single in-line memory module) (3.12)
sound board (3.16)
static RAM (SRAM) (3.13)
storing (3.8)
superscalar CPUs (3.21)
system board (3.7)
system clock (3.8)
system unit (3.2)

Unicode (3.4)
Universal Serial Bus (USB) (3.18)
upgrade socket (3.10)

volatile (3.11)

wafers (3.25)
word size (3.9)

3 yourTurn

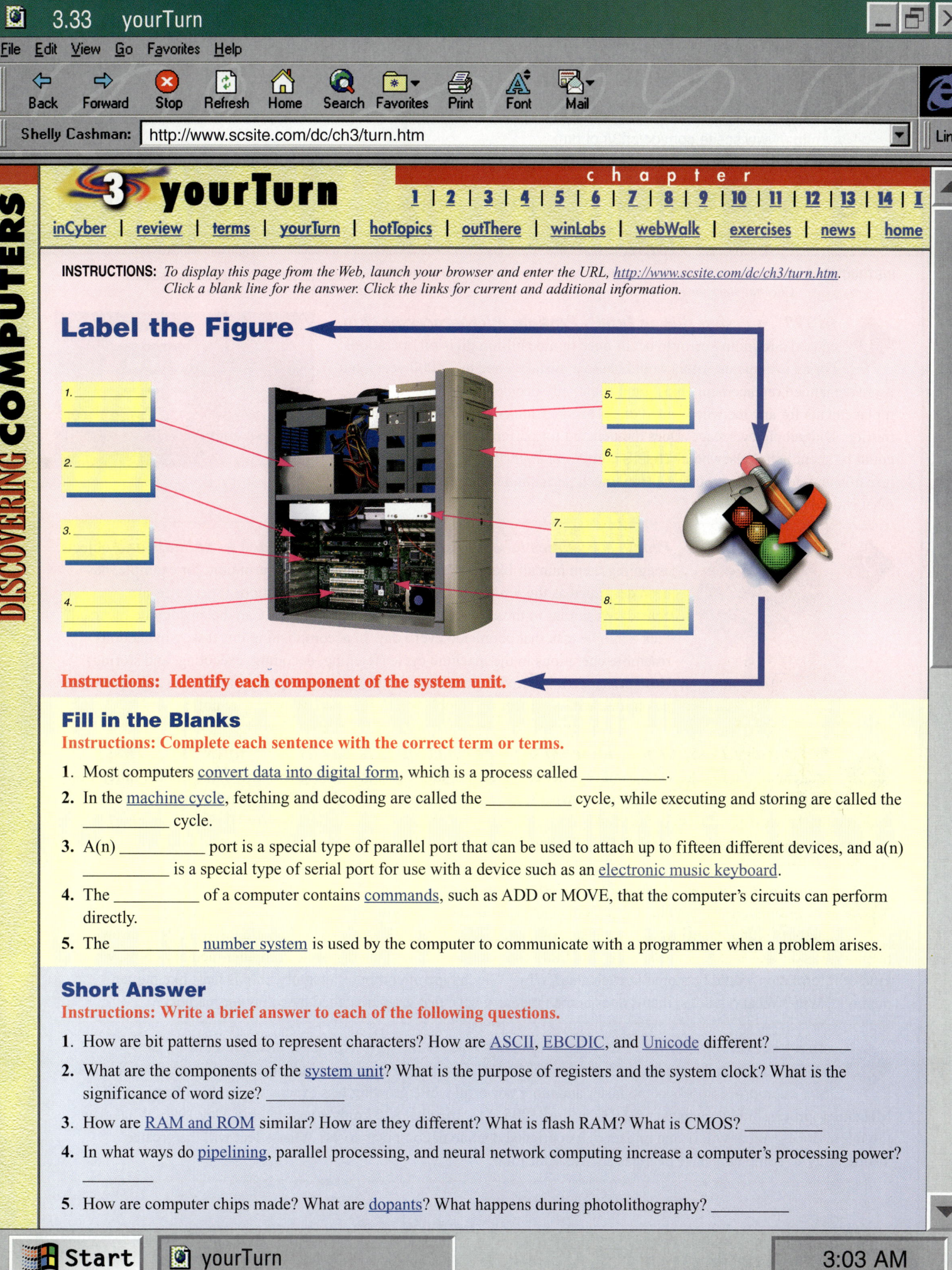

chapter 1 | 2 | 3 | 4 | 5 | 6 | 7 | 8 | 9 | 10 | 11 | 12 | 13 | 14 | I

inCyber | review | terms | yourTurn | hotTopics | outThere | winLabs | webWalk | exercises | news | home

INSTRUCTIONS: *To display this page from the Web, launch your browser and enter the URL, http://www.scsite.com/dc/ch3/turn.htm. Click a blank line for the answer. Click the links for current and additional information.*

Label the Figure

1. _____
2. _____
3. _____
4. _____
5. _____
6. _____
7. _____
8. _____

Instructions: Identify each component of the system unit.

Fill in the Blanks

Instructions: Complete each sentence with the correct term or terms.

1. Most computers convert data into digital form, which is a process called _____.
2. In the machine cycle, fetching and decoding are called the _____ cycle, while executing and storing are called the _____ cycle.
3. A(n) _____ port is a special type of parallel port that can be used to attach up to fifteen different devices, and a(n) _____ is a special type of serial port for use with a device such as an electronic music keyboard.
4. The _____ of a computer contains commands, such as ADD or MOVE, that the computer's circuits can perform directly.
5. The _____ number system is used by the computer to communicate with a programmer when a problem arises.

Short Answer

Instructions: Write a brief answer to each of the following questions.

1. How are bit patterns used to represent characters? How are ASCII, EBCDIC, and Unicode different? _____
2. What are the components of the system unit? What is the purpose of registers and the system clock? What is the significance of word size? _____
3. How are RAM and ROM similar? How are they different? What is flash RAM? What is CMOS? _____
4. In what ways do pipelining, parallel processing, and neural network computing increase a computer's processing power? _____
5. How are computer chips made? What are dopants? What happens during photolithography? _____

hotTopics

chapter 1 | 2 | 3 | 4 | 5 | 6 | 7 | 8 | 9 | 10 | 11 | 12 | 13 | 14 | I

inCyber | review | terms | yourTurn | hotTopics | outThere | winLabs | webWalk | exercises | news | home

INSTRUCTIONS: *To display this page from the Web, launch your browser and enter the URL, http://www.scsite.com/dc/ch3/hot.htm. Click the links for current and additional information to help you respond to the hotTopics questions.*

1. *In 1994, a design flaw in Intel's Pentium microprocessor chip* caused a rounding error to occur once in nine billion division operations. For an average user, this would cause a mistake once in 27,000 years, but users demanded replacement chips. Intel eventually decided to supply replacements for anyone who wanted one. This decision cost Intel almost $500 million. Did people overreact? Does the demand for perfection divert funds that could be spent better elsewhere? (Intel's costs were equivalent to half a year's research and development budget.) How much perfection should be expected, and what should be its price?

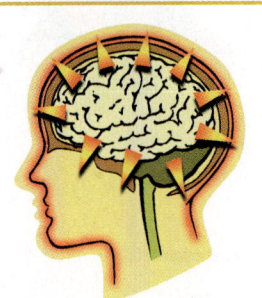

2. *People sometimes take an anthropomorphic approach to animals and* objects, assigning them human-like qualities and attributes. The control unit, for example, has been described as the *brain* of a computer because the functions it performs are considered similar to those discharged by the human brain. Can the analogy be reversed? Pick a simple task that people do every day. In accomplishing this task, what actions resemble operations in the machine cycle (fetching, decoding, executing, and storing)? How? What actions are different from any machine cycle operations? Can any operations be omitted without affecting completion of the task? Why or why not?

3. *In February 1996, the forerunner of the modern computers had its 50th anniversary. That* progenitor, the ENIAC (Electronic Numerical Integrator and Computer), weighed thirty tons, filled a thirty-by-fifty-foot room, and contained more than 18,000 vacuum tubes. Although the ENIAC performed several important tasks, its capabilities are dwarfed by today's notebooks. What will computers be like 50 years from now? Which components are most likely to change? How? Which components are least likely to change? Why?

4. *Computers have several different types of memory chips, each of which stores different kinds* of information. Do people also have distinct types of memory, with characteristics similar to computer memory chips? Consider, for instance, how RAM, ROM, cache RAM, and CMOS are different. If your own memory was divided into four areas, each with traits comparable to one of the disparate computer memory chips, what kind of information would be stored in each area? Why? Which type of computer memory chip is least like human memory? Why? What qualities, if any, does human memory have that are unmatched by computer memory?

5. *As a general marketing rule, higher quality results in higher prices, and the cost of new* products rises as the product becomes more popular. Computers appear to challenge these dictums, however, as new microprocessors become faster and more powerful while growing less expensive. An Intel Pentium 133 MHz microprocessor chip, which cost $935 in June 1995, was priced at $257 only a year later in May 1996. What drives the fall in prices? What will be the impact of a continued decline in computer costs? What effect will the greater affordability of computers have on areas such as education?

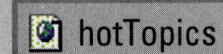

outThere

chapter 3

1 | 2 | 3 | 4 | 5 | 6 | 7 | 8 | 9 | 10 | 11 | 12 | 13 | 14 | I

inCyber | review | terms | yourTurn | hotTopics | outThere | winLabs | webWalk | exercises | news | home

INSTRUCTIONS: *To display this page from the Web, launch your browser and enter the URL, http://www.scsite.com/dc/ch3/out.htm. Click the links for current and additional information.*

1 *Many system unit manufacturers provide a toll-free telephone number* that customers can call with technical problems or questions. If the service technician determines a difficulty is a hardware problem that the customer can fix, the technician might ask the customer to open the system unit and make some adjustments. For this reason, every computer user can benefit by being familiar with the inside of the system unit. If you own a personal computer or have access to a personal computer, unplug the power supply and take the cover off the system unit. Make a sketch of the system unit and try to identify each part. Compare your sketch and list with a classmate who has done this exercise with a different computer. How are the computers similar? How are they different?

2 *In 1951, Remington Rand introduced the UNIVAC (UNIVersal Automatic Computer)* for commercial use by a few businesses and scientists. The invention of the microchip, by Jack Kilby and Robert Noyce (founder of Intel) in 1959 led to computers becoming an indispensable part of offices and laboratories. The World Wide Web offers several accounts of the story of microprocessors. Prepare a brief report on the history of microprocessors. What developments have been most significant? Why? What microprocessor chips are on the cutting edge of today's technology? Considering the microprocessor's past, what developments do you anticipate in the future?

3 *Perhaps the fastest growing portion of the personal computer market are* notebook computers. About 8% of personal computer sales in 1984, notebook computers are expected to make up more than 35% of sales in the year 2000. How do notebook computers compare with desktop models? Use a computer catalog, call a mail-order computer vendor, or visit a computer retailer and find a notebook computer and a desktop computer with comparable system units. What is the price of each computer? Describe the system units. How are they similar? How are they different? Which computer is the better buy? Why?

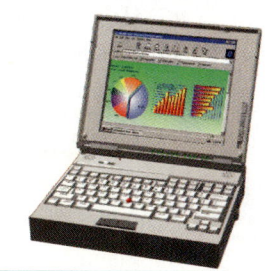

4 *Most authorities agree that* RISC *(reduced instruction set computing) processors are more* efficient than the traditional CISC (complex instruction set computing) processors. Perhaps because of the large number of CISC computers, however, debate continues on the World Wide Web over the merits of RISC. A few wonder if RISC has gone too far, but others argue that RISC has not gone far enough. CISC computers typically have more than one hundred instructions in their instruction sets, while RISC computers have about fifty. Compare CISC and RISC. What are the advantages of each? What are the disadvantages? Which type of computer eventually will prevail?

5 *Some people say that* Software drives hardware. *When purchasing a computer, this usually means* your system unit and peripheral devices (hardware) must be capable of running your application programs (software). Visit a store that sells computer software and make a list of application programs you would like now and those you may want in the future. Examine the software packages and note the capabilities required of the system unit (type of microprocessor, amount of memory, and so on). What are the minimum system requirements you would demand in a personal computer? What system requirements would be sufficient to provide a *cushion* so you could be sure the system also could run other, or new, application packages?

3 winLabs

chapter
1 | 2 | 3 | 4 | 5 | 6 | 7 | 8 | 9 | 10 | 11 | 12 | 13 | 14 | I

inCyber | review | terms | yourTurn | hotTopics | outThere | winLabs | webWalk | exercises | news | home

INSTRUCTIONS: *To display this page from the Web, launch your browser and enter the URL, http://www.scsite.com/dc/ch3/labs.htm. Click the links for current and additional information.*

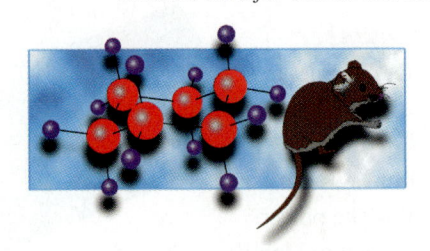

Shelly Cashman Series Motherboard Lab

Follow the instructions in winLab 1 on page 1.34 to display the Shelly Cashman Series Labs screen. Click Understanding the Motherboard. Click the Start Lab button. When the initial screen displays, carefully read the objectives. With your printer on, click the Print Questions button. Fill out the top of the Questions sheet and answer the questions. Close the Shelly Cashman Series Labs.

Setting the System Clock

Double-click the time on the taskbar. In the Date/Time Properties dialog box (Figure 3-47), click the question mark button on its title bar and then click the picture of the calendar. Read the information in the pop-up window and then click the pop-up window to close it. Repeat this process for the other areas of the dialog box and then answer the following questions: (1) What is the purpose of the calendar? (2) How do you change the time zone? (3) What is the difference between the OK and the Apply buttons? Close the Date/Time Properties dialog box.

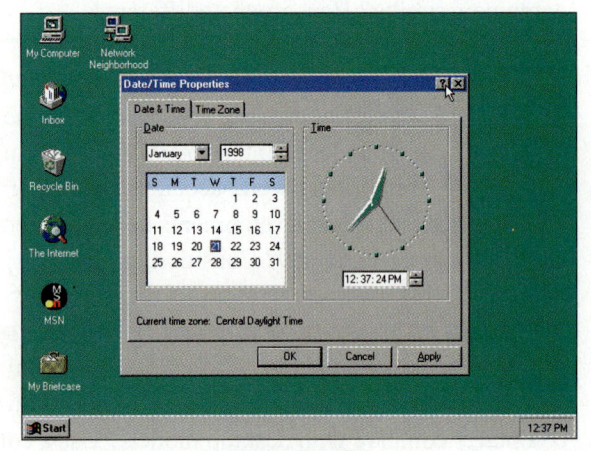

Figure 3-47

Using Calculator to Perform Number System Conversion

Click the Start button on the taskbar; point to Programs on the Start menu; point to Accessories on the Programs submenu; and then click Calculator on the Accessories submenu. Click View on the menu bar and then click Scientific to display the scientific calculator. Perform the following tasks: (1) Click Dec to select base 10. Enter **27843** by clicking the numeric buttons or using the numeric keypad. Click Hex. Write down the number that displays. Click Bin. Write down the result. Click C (the Clear button). (2) Convert the following decimal (base 10) numbers to hexadecimal (Hex) and binary (Bin) and write down each result: 5, 16, 33, 64, 2048, and 4000. (3) Convert the following hexadecimal (base 16) numbers to decimal (Dec) and binary (Bin) and write down each result: 42, 5AC, DDD, 97AE2, and 1D9A48. Close Calculator.

Using Help in a Dialog Box

Click the Start button on the taskbar; point to Settings on the Start menu; and then click Taskbar on the Settings submenu. In the Taskbar Properties dialog box, click the Taskbar Options tab; click the question mark icon on the title bar; and then click Show Clock. Right-click the pop-up window; click Print Topic on the shortcut menu; and then click the OK button to print the pop-up window contents. Click the pop-up window to close it and then close the Taskbar Properties dialog box. Answer the following questions: (1) How do you display and/or remove the clock from the taskbar? (2) When the clock displays on your taskbar, exactly what displays when you point to it?

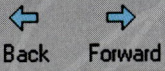

webWalk

chapter 3 | 1 | 2 | 3 | 4 | 5 | 6 | 7 | 8 | 9 | 10 | 11 | 12 | 13 | 14 | I

inCyber | review | terms | yourTurn | hotTopics | outThere | winLabs | webWalk | exercises | news | home

INSTRUCTIONS: *To display this page from the Web, launch your browser and enter the URL, http://www.scsite.com/dc/ch3/walk.htm Click the exercise link to display the exercise.*

1 Parallel Processing
In massively parallel processing (MPP), large numbers of processors divide the components of a problem into tiny fragments, with each processor working on a different fragment at the same time. Learn about applications of this technology by completing this exercise.

3 Memory Upgrades
Today's 32-bit operating systems, such as Windows 95 and Windows NT 4, require 16 MB of RAM just to run properly. Graphics and multimedia software can take as much as 32 MB or more to operate. Complete this exercise to learn about upgrading the memory of your PC.

4 PC Cards
The first credit-card sized PC cards were memory cards, but now, many PC cards are available, ranging from hard drives to network adapters. To learn about some of these cards, complete this exercise.

5 Information Mining
Complete this exercise to improve your Web research skills by using a Web search engine to find information related to this chapter.

7 RISC
As much as 80 percent of a PC's processing involves a small number of frequently used machine language instructions. Some manufacturers have taken advantage of this statistic by designing CPUs based on Reduced Instruction Set Computing (RISC). To learn more about RISC, complete this exercise.

9 Web Chat
Complete this exercise to enter a Web Chat discussion related to the issues presented in the hotTopics exercise.

2 Neural Networks
Artificial neural networks have become an accepted information analysis technology in a variety of disciplines. This has resulted in an assortment of commercial applications (Figure 3-48). To learn more about neural network applications, complete this exercise.

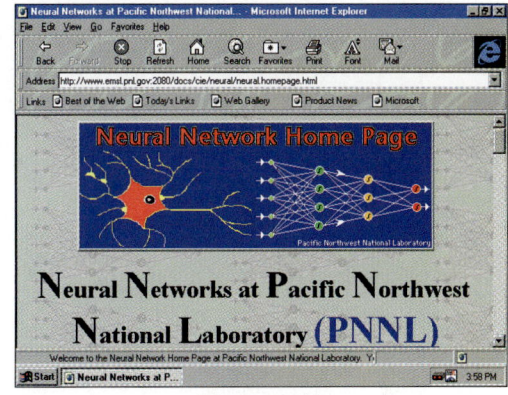

Figure 3-48

6 Microprocessors
Personal computer microprocessors most often are identified by their model number or model name. Complete this exercise to learn more about some of the widely used microprocessors.

8 Computer Chips
A computer chip is made by building layers of electronic pathways and connections using conducting and nonconducting materials on a surface of silicon. To learn how computer chips are made, complete this exercise.

Input and Output

CHAPTER 4

OBJECTIVES

After completing this chapter, you will be able to:

- Define the four types of input and how the computer uses each type

- Describe the standard features of keyboards and explain how to use the arrow and function keys

- Explain how a mouse and other pointing devices work and how they are used

- Describe several different methods of source data automation

- Define the term output

- Describe different types of printed output

- Identify different types of display devices

- Explain the difference between impact and nonimpact printers

- Explain how images are displayed on a screen

- List and describe other types of output devices used with computers

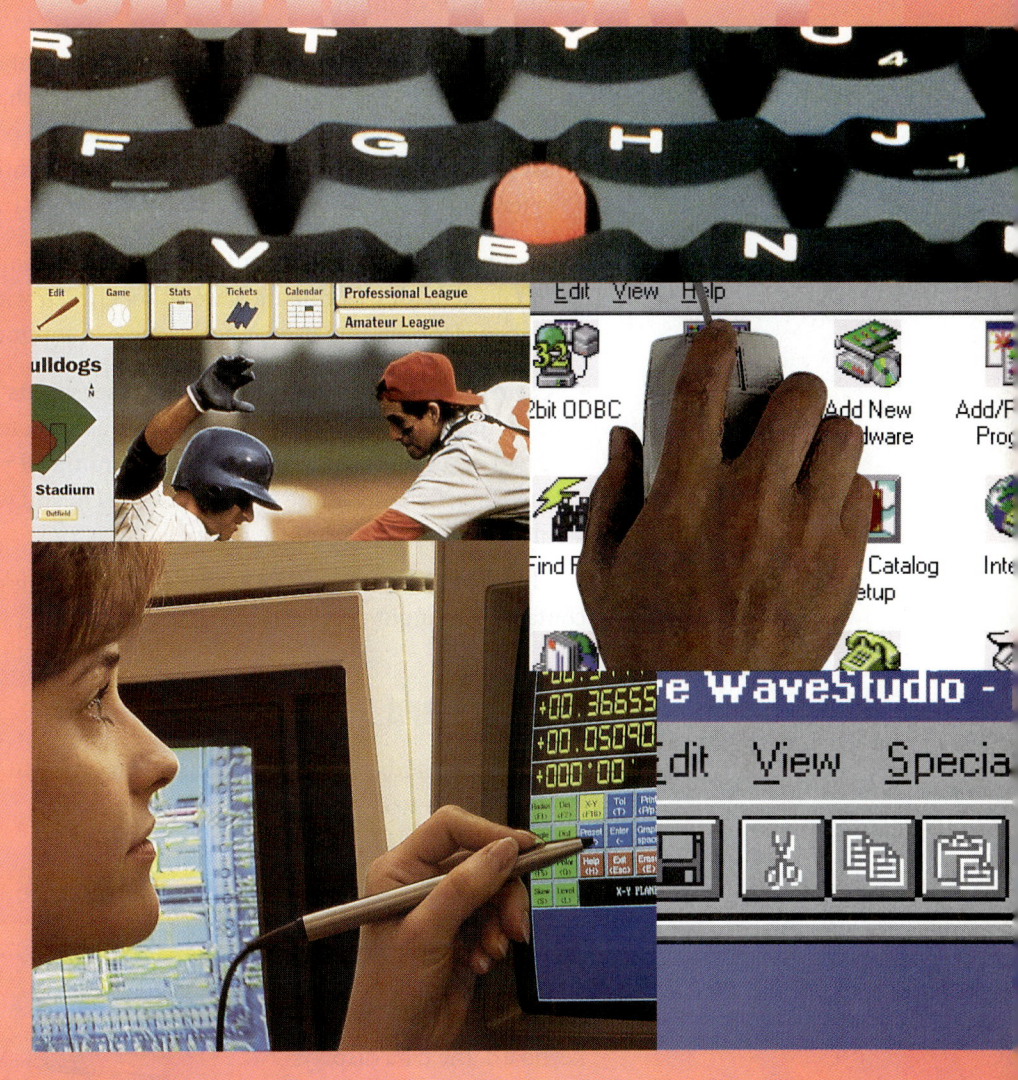

Input and output devices are essential to most computer tasks. Input devices convert data into a form that the computer can understand and process. Output devices take processed or stored data and convert it into a form that you can understand. This chapter describes many of the more commonly used input and output devices. Devices that can be used for both input and storage, such as disk and tape drives, will be covered in the storage chapter.

What Is Input?

Input refers to the process of entering data, programs, commands, and user responses into memory. These four types of input are used by a computer in the following ways:

- **Data** refers to the raw facts, including numbers, letters, words, images, and sounds, that a computer receives during the input operation and processes to produce information. Although technically speaking, a single item of data should be called a *datum*, it is common and accepted usage to use the word data to represent both singular and plural. Data must be entered and stored in memory for processing to occur. Data is the most common type of input.

- **Programs** are instructions that direct the computer to perform the operations necessary to process data into information. The program that is loaded from storage into memory determines the processing that the computer will perform. When a program is first created, usually it is input by using a keyboard and a pointing device. Once the program has been entered and stored on a storage device, it can be transferred to memory by a command.

- **Commands** are keywords and phrases that you input to direct the computer to perform certain activities. Commands are either chosen with a pointing device, entered from the keyboard, or selected using another type of input device.

- **User responses** refer to the data that a user inputs to respond to a question or message from the software. Programs sometimes ask you to answer "Yes" or "No" to a question. Based on the answer, the computer program will perform specific actions. For example, choosing Yes in response to the message, Do you want to save this file?, will result in the file being saved to a storage device.

Input also can refer to the media (e.g. floppy disks, tape cartridges, documents) that contain these input types.

The Keyboard

The **keyboard** is the most commonly used input device. You input data to a computer by pressing the keys on the keyboard. Keyboards are connected to other devices that have screens, such as a personal computer or a terminal. As you enter data through the keyboard, the data displays on the screen.

Most keyboards are similar to the one shown in Figure 4-1. The alphabetic keys are arranged like those on a typewriter. A **numeric keypad** is located on the right-hand side of most keyboards. The numeric keys are arranged in an adding machine or calculator format to allow you to enter numeric data rapidly.

Keyboards also contain keys that can be used to position the insertion point, or cursor, on the screen. An **insertion point**, or **cursor**, is a symbol, such as an underline character, rectangle, or vertical bar, that indicates where on the screen the next character entered will appear. The keys that move the insertion point are called **arrow keys** or **arrow control keys**. The arrow keys are the UP ARROW (↑), DOWN ARROW (↓), LEFT ARROW (←), and RIGHT ARROW (→). When you press any of these keys, the insertion point moves one space in the same direction as the arrow. In addition, many keyboards contain other control keys such as the HOME key, which you can press to move the insertion point to a beginning position such as the upper left position of the screen or document. The numeric keypad also can be used to move the insertion point. With most keys, if you hold them down, they will start to repeat automatically.

Most computer keyboards also contain keys that can alter or edit the text displayed on the screen. For example, the INSERT, DELETE, and BACKSPACE keys allow characters to be inserted into or deleted from data that displays on the screen. Pressing the CAPS LOCK key capitalizes all the letters you type.

The CAPS LOCK key is an example of a **toggle key**, which switches, or *toggles*, the keyboard between two different modes. The NUM LOCK key also is a toggle key. Pressing the NUM LOCK key turns the numeric keypad on or off. When the numeric keypad is on, you can use the keys to type numbers. When it is off, the same keys work like arrow keys and move the insertion point.

inCyber

For details on keyboards, visit the Discovering Computers Chapter 4 inCyber page (http://www.scsite.com/dc/ch4/incyber.htm) and click Keyboard.

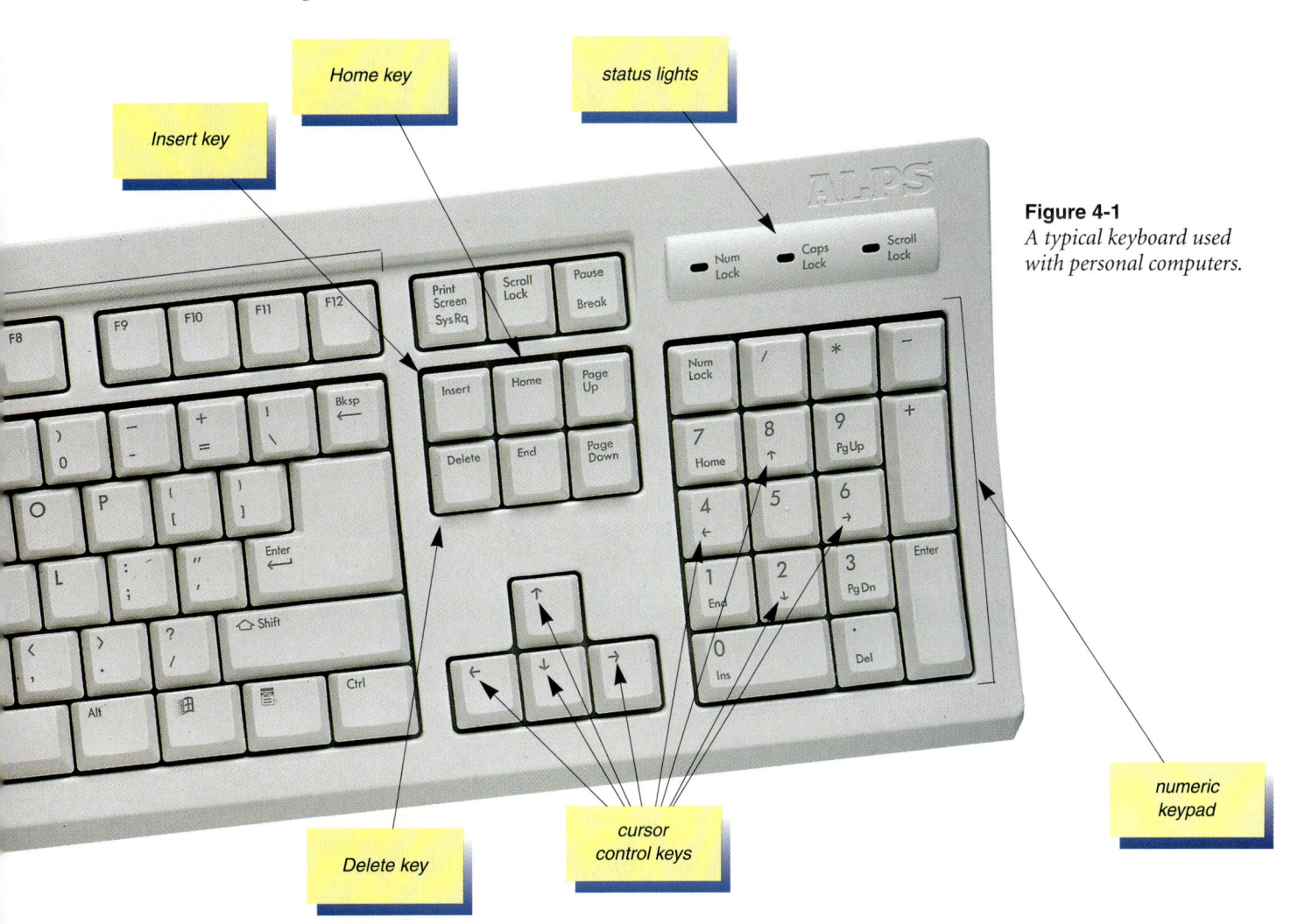

Figure 4-1
A typical keyboard used with personal computers.

Function keys are the keys located at the top of the keyboard that are programmed to initiate commands and accomplish certain tasks. Function keys are labeled with the letter F followed by a digit (Figure 4-1 on pages 4.2 and 4.3). When you are instructed to press F1, you should press function key F1, not the letter F followed by the number 1. For example, when you press the function key F1—which often is programmed as a Help key in word processor programs—the online Help window opens to provide assistance. Function keys also can save you time. For example, if you are typing on the keyboard, it may be faster to press the function key F7 than to move the mouse to click a button or menu command. Most application software packages are written so you can use a shortcut menu, a button, a menu, or a function key and obtain the same result.

Status lights in the upper right corner of the keyboard indicate if the numeric keypad, capital letters, and scroll lock are turned on.

The ESCAPE (ESC) key often is used by computer software to cancel an instruction or exit from a situation. The functions performed by the ESC key varies between software packages.

The disadvantage of using a keyboard as an input device is that training is required to use it efficiently. If you lack typing ability, you are likely to be at a disadvantage because of the time required to look for the appropriate keys. While other input devices are appropriate in some situations, you are encouraged to develop your keyboarding skills.

Figure 4-2
How a mouse works.

1. When you move the mouse, the ball rubs against rollers inside the mouse. One roller measures side-to-side motion and the other measures up-and-down motion.

2. The rollers are attached to encoder wheels that have metal contact points. Each time the encoder wheel contact points pass by the contact bar they send an electrical signal to the mouse software in the computer. The signals are translated into the direction and speed of the mouse and are used to move the on-screen mouse pointer.

3. Switches under each mouse button send a signal when a button is pressed. The mouse button signals are interpreted by the application software to select processing options or move on-screen objects.

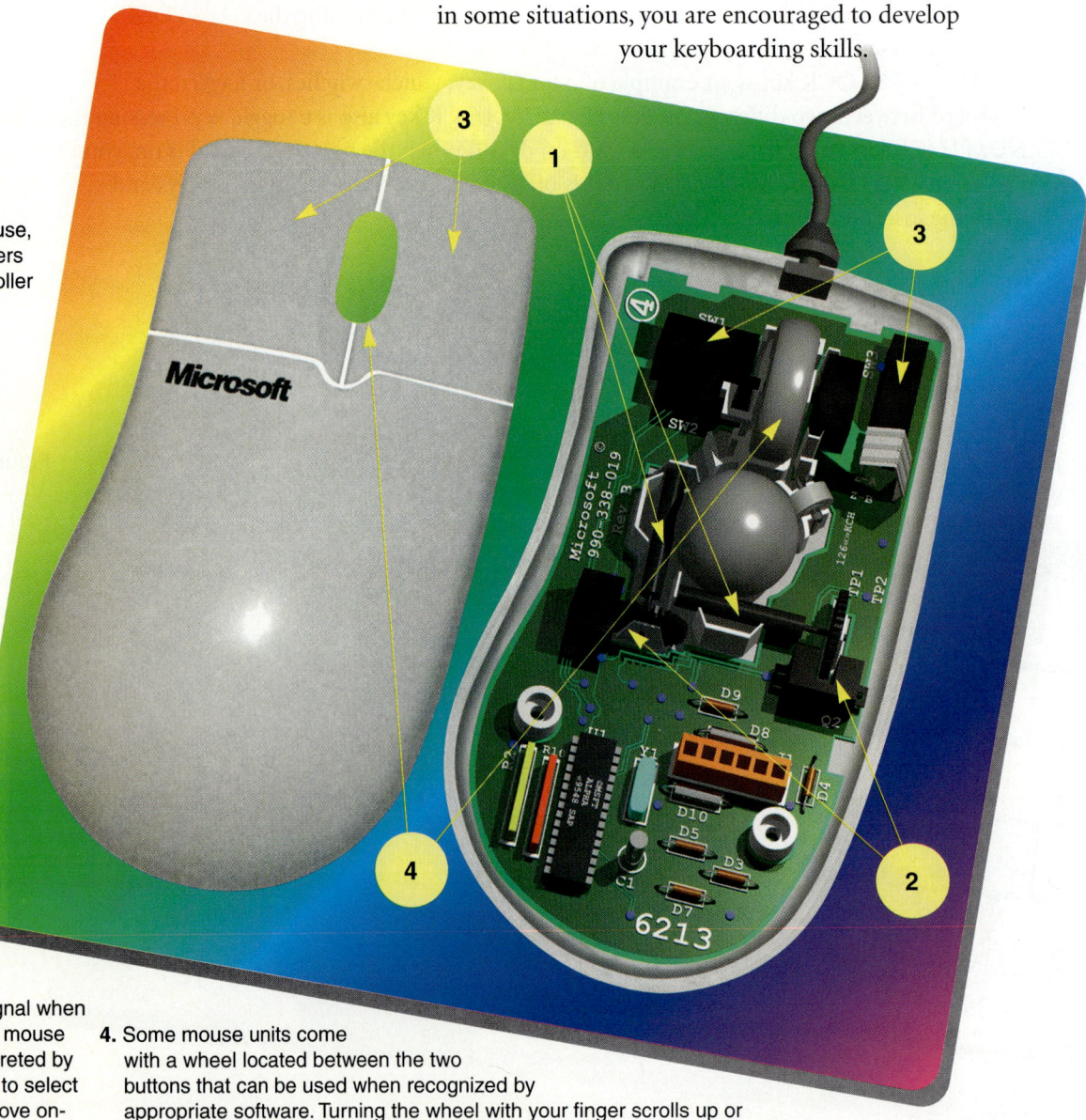

4. Some mouse units come with a wheel located between the two buttons that can be used when recognized by appropriate software. Turning the wheel with your finger scrolls up or down through a document. Pressing a key and turning the wheel, scrolls left or right. The wheel also can be pressed down, thus serving as a third mouse button.

POINTING DEVICES **4.5**

Pointing Devices

Pointing devices allow you to control an on-screen symbol, called the **mouse pointer** or **pointer**, that usually is represented by an arrowhead shaped marker (↖). You use the pointing device to move the insertion point to a particular location on the screen or to select available software options.

Mouse

A **mouse** is a small, palm-sized input device that you move across a flat surface, such as a desktop, to control the movement of the pointer on a screen. The mouse often rests on a **mouse pad**, which is a rectangular piece of cushioned material that provides better traction for the mouse than a desktop. On the bottom of the mouse is a mechanism, usually a small ball, that senses the movement of the mouse (Figure 4-2).

Electronic circuits in the mouse translate the movement of the mouse into signals that are sent to the computer. The computer uses the mouse signals to move the pointer on the screen in the same direction as the mouse (Figure 4-3). When you move the mouse left on the surface of the desktop or mouse pad, the pointer moves left on the screen. When you move the mouse right, the pointer moves right, and so on. The mouse usually is attached to the computer by a cable, but wireless mouse units also exist.

The top of the mouse contains one or more buttons. By using the mouse to move the pointer on the screen and then pressing, or **clicking**, the buttons on the mouse, you can perform actions such as pressing buttons, making menu selections, editing a document, and moving, or **dragging**, data from one location in a document to another. To press and release a mouse button twice without moving the mouse is called **double-clicking**. Double-clicking can be used to perform actions such as starting a program or opening a document. The function of the buttons can be changed to accommodate right- and left-handed people.

The primary advantage of a mouse is that it is easy to use. With a little practice, you can use a mouse to point to locations on the screen just as easily as using a finger.

Three disadvantages of the mouse exist. The first is that it requires empty desk space where it can be moved about. The second disadvantage is that you must remove a hand from the keyboard and place it on the mouse whenever the pointer is to be moved or a command is to be given. A third disadvantage is that mouse units must be cleaned to remove dust and dirt from the ball mechanism.

inCyber

For details of the mouse pointing device, visit the Discovering Computers Chapter 4 inCyber page (http://www.scsite.com/dc/ch4/incyber.htm) and click Mouse.

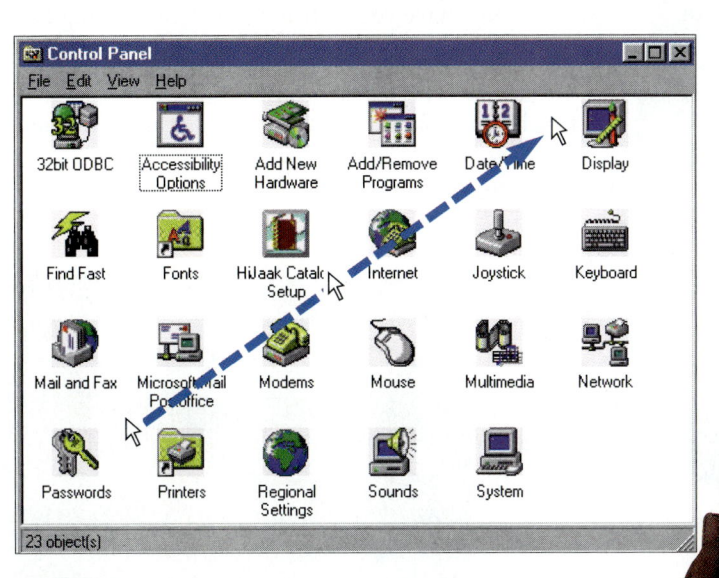

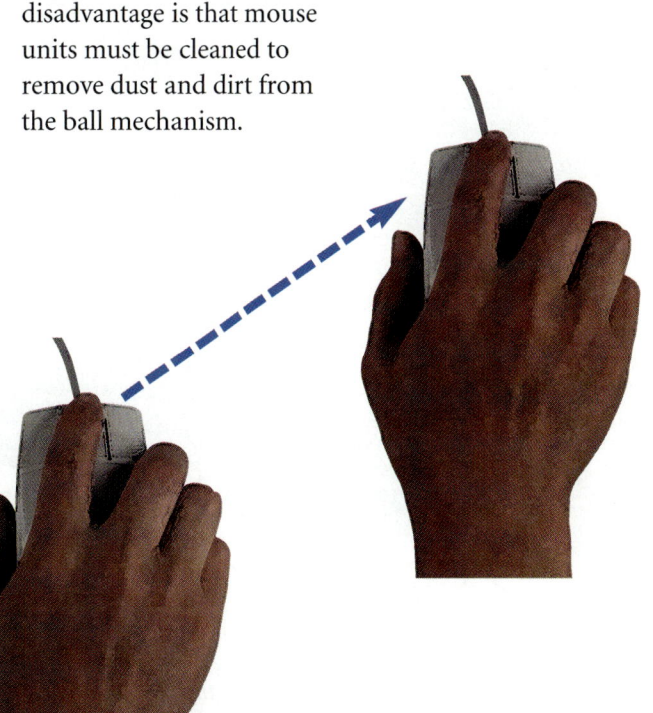

Figure 4-3
As the mouse is moved diagonally across a flat surface, the mouse pointer on the screen moves in a similar direction.

4.6   CHAPTER 4 – INPUT AND OUTPUT

Trackball

A **trackball** is a pointing device like a mouse only with the ball on the top of the device instead of the bottom (Figure 4-4). To move the pointer with a trackball, you rotate the ball in the desired direction. With a mouse, you have to move the entire device. To accommodate movement with both the fingers and palms of a hand, the ball on top of a trackball usually is larger than the ball on the bottom of a mouse. As with the mouse, the trackball occasionally needs to be cleaned. The main advantage of a trackball over a mouse is that it does not require clear desk space. Smaller trackball units have been designed for use on portable computers (Figure 4-5).

inCyber
For a detailed description of trackballs, visit the Discovering Computers Chapter 4 inCyber page (http://www.scsite.com/dc/ch4/incyber.htm) and click Trackball.

Figure 4-4
The trackball is like a mouse turned upside down. You rotate the ball to move the insertion point and then press one of the buttons on the side of the device.

Figure 4-5
Smaller trackball units often are used on portable computers.

Touchpad

A **touchpad**, sometimes called a **trackpad**, is a flat rectangular surface that senses the movement of a finger on its surface to control the movement of the insertion point (Figure 4-6). Most touchpads use an electronic grid underneath the surface of the pad to sense the location and movement of the finger. Some touchpads have buttons you can click like a mouse, while others have you indicate a click by tapping the finger on the touchpad surface. Touchpads often are built into portable computers, but stand-alone touch-pads that attach to any PC also are available.

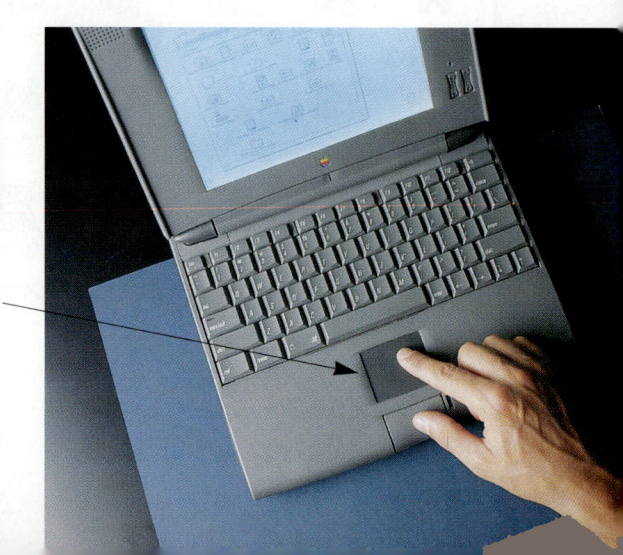

trackball

touchpad

Figure 4-6
Portable computers often use touch-pads to control the movement of the pointer. Electronics underneath the surface of the pad sense the movement of a finger and move the pointer in a corresponding direction.

POINTING DEVICES **4.7**

Pointing Stick

A **pointing stick**, sometimes called a **trackpoint** or **an isometric pointing device**, is a small device shaped like a pencil eraser that moves the insertion point as pressure is applied to the device (Figure 4-7). Pointing stick devices are used on portable computers because they require little space. Another advantage is they require no cleaning as mouse units and trackballs do.

Figure 4-7
Pointing stick devices move the on-screen pointer by sensing the direction and amount of pressure applied to a small eraser-shaped device located within the keyboard.

pointing stick

Joystick

A **joystick** uses the movement of a vertical stem to direct the pointer. Joysticks often are used with computer games and have buttons you can press to activate certain events, depending on the software (Figure 4-8).

Figure 4-8
Joysticks often are used with computer games to control the actions of a vehicle or player.

Pen Input

Pen input devices have become increasingly popular in recent years and eventually may be part of most if not all computers. Almost all of the personal digital assistant (PDA) class of personal computers use a pen. One advantage is that people who have never used a computer adapt naturally to using a pen as an input device (Figure 4-9).

Pen input devices can be used in three ways: to input data using hand-written characters and shapes that the computer can recognize, as a pointing device like a mouse to select items on the screen, and to gesture, which is a way of issuing commands.

Pen computers use special hardware and software to interpret the movement of the pen. When the pen touches the screen, it causes two layers of electrically conductive material to make contact. The computer determines the coordinates for the contact point and darkens that location on the screen. The darkened area on the screen is referred to as **ink**. Hand-written characters are converted into computer text by software that matches the shape of the hand-written character to a database of known characters or shapes. If the software is unable to recognize a particular character, it asks you to identify it. Most **handwriting recognition software** can be taught to recognize an individual's unique style of writing. In addition to working with character input, graphic recognition software used on pen input devices can improve drawings by cleaning up uneven lines. Wavy lines can be straightened and circles can be made perfectly round. Perhaps the most natural use of the pen is as a pointing device. When used this way, the pen functions like a mouse. Pressing the pen against the screen once or twice is the same as clicking the buttons on a mouse.

Gestures are special symbols made with the pen that issue a command, such as delete text. As shown in Figure 4-10, many gestures are identical to those used for manual text editing. Gestures can be more efficient than using a mouse or keyboard because they not only identify where you want to make a change but also the type of change to be made.

Pen input devices already have been adapted to many applications that were previously not computerized. Any application where a form has to be filled out is a candidate for a pen input device. One of the larger markets for pen input devices is mobile workers, who spend most of their time away from their desks or offices.

inCyber
For a discussion of pen input devices, visit the Discovering Computers Chapter 4 inCyber page (http://www.scsite.com/dc/ch4/incyber.htm) and click Pen Input.

Figure 4-9
Pen input systems allow you to use a pen to enter data or select processing options without using a keyboard. This method is easy to learn by individuals who have worked with a pencil and paper.

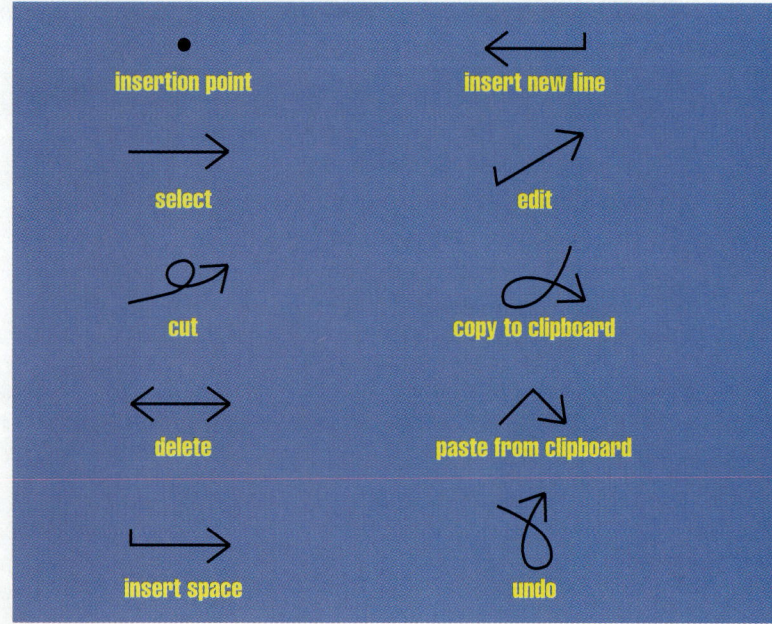

Figure 4-10
Gestures are a way of issuing commands with a pen. Gestures not only tell what you want done but also where you want to make a change. The arrows indicate the direction of the pen movement.

Touch Screen

A **touch screen** allows you to touch areas of the screen to enter data. They let you interact with a computer by the touch of a finger rather than typing on a keyboard or moving a mouse. You enter data by touching words or numbers or locations identified on the screen.

Several electronic techniques change a touch on the screen into electronic impulses that can be interpreted by the computer software. One technique uses beams of infrared light that are projected across the surface of the screen. A finger or other object touching the screen interrupts the beams, generating an electronic signal. This signal identifies the location on the screen where the touch occurred. The software interprets the signal and performs the required function.

Touch screens are not used to enter large amounts of data. They are used, however, for applications where you must issue a command to the software to perform a particular task or must choose from a list of options. Touch screens have been installed successfully in kiosks used to provide information in hotels, airports, and other public locations (Figure 4-11).

Figure 4-11
Touch screens frequently are used for information kiosks. Users touch the screen and receive information about the chosen topic.

inCyber

For an explanation of touch screens, visit the Discovering Computers Chapter 4 inCyber page (http://www.scsite.com/dc/ch4/incyber.htm) and click Touch Screen.

Light Pen

A **light pen** is used by touching it on the display screen to create or modify graphics (Figure 4-12). A light cell in the tip of the pen senses light from the screen to determine the pen's location. You can use the light pen to select processing options or draw on the screen.

Figure 4-12
The light pen can be used to make selections or to draw directly on the screen. A light cell in the tip of the pen can detect where on the screen the pen is touching. Light pens often are used in engineering applications.

Figure 4-13
Digitizers are used to create original drawings or to trace and reproduce existing drawings. When buttons on the hand-held device are pushed, the location on the drawing is input to the computer. Special software links the points together to create a drawing that can be modified.

Digitizer

A **digitizer** converts points, lines, and curves from a sketch, drawing, or photograph to digital impulses and transmits them to a computer (Figure 4-13). You indicate the data to be input by using a pen-like stylus or pressing one or more buttons on the hand-held digitizer device. Mapmakers and architects use digitizers for their precision tracing capabilities.

POINTING DEVICES **4.11**

inCyber

For information on graphic tablets, visit the Discovering Computers Chapter 4 inCyber page (http://www.scsite.com/dc/ch4/incyber.htm) and click Graphics Tablet.

Figure 4-14
The color template on the graphics tablet allows you to select processing options by placing a hand-held device over the appropriate location on the tablet and pressing a button.

Graphics Tablet

A **graphics tablet** works in a manner similar to a digitizer, but it also contains unique characters and commands that can be generated automatically by the person using the tablet (Figure 4-14).

The graphics tablet and the digitizer both use absolute referencing. That is, each location on the tablet and digitizer corresponds to a specific location on the screen. The previously discussed touchpad, which looks like a small graphics tablet, uses relative referencing. On the touchpad, it does not matter where you first place your finger; the touchpad measures only the direction of the finger movement. Graphics tablets commonly are used in computer-aided design applications by architects and designers.

Source Data Automation

Source data automation, or **source data collection**, refers to procedures and equipment designed to make the input process more efficient by eliminating the manual entry of data. Instead of a person entering data using a keyboard, source data automation equipment captures data directly from its original form, such as an invoice or an inventory tag. The original form is called a **source document**. In addition to making the input process more efficient,

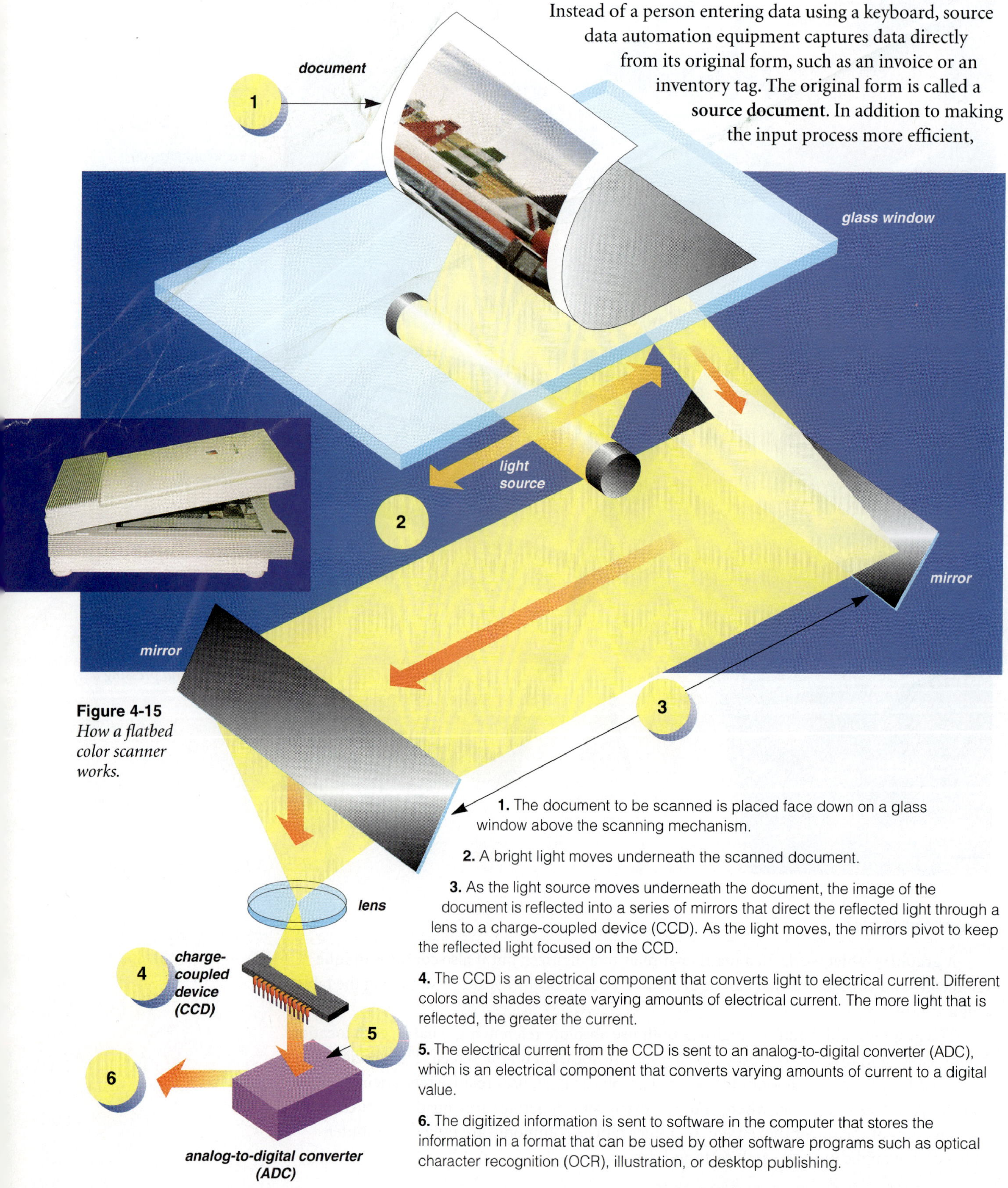

Figure 4-15
How a flatbed color scanner works.

1. The document to be scanned is placed face down on a glass window above the scanning mechanism.

2. A bright light moves underneath the scanned document.

3. As the light source moves underneath the document, the image of the document is reflected into a series of mirrors that direct the reflected light through a lens to a charge-coupled device (CCD). As the light moves, the mirrors pivot to keep the reflected light focused on the CCD.

4. The CCD is an electrical component that converts light to electrical current. Different colors and shades create varying amounts of electrical current. The more light that is reflected, the greater the current.

5. The electrical current from the CCD is sent to an analog-to-digital converter (ADC), which is an electrical component that converts varying amounts of current to a digital value.

6. The digitized information is sent to software in the computer that stores the information in a format that can be used by other software programs such as optical character recognition (OCR), illustration, or desktop publishing.

SOURCE DATA AUTOMATION 4.13

source data automation usually results in a higher input accuracy rate. The following section describes some of the equipment used for source data automation.

Image Scanner

An **image scanner**, sometimes called a **page scanner**, is an input device that can electronically capture an entire page of text or images such as photographs or art work (Figure 4-15).

Both monochrome and color units are available. The scanner converts the text or image on the original document into digital data that can be stored on a disk and processed by the computer. The digitized data can be printed, displayed separately, or merged into another document for editing. Hand-held devices that can scan a portion of a page also are available (Figure 4-16). **Image processing systems** use scanners to capture and electronically file documents such as legal documents or documents with signatures or drawings. These systems are like electronic filing cabinets that allow you to rapidly access and review exact reproductions of the original documents (Figure 4-17). Besides the actual image, these systems record information about the document such as the type of document, the date it was processed, and who submitted the document. This information can be used to retrieve the document image.

Figure 4-16
A hand-held scanner enters text or graphics less than a page wide. Software allows you to join separately scanned items to make up a complete page.

inCyber
For a description of image scanners, visit the Discovering Computers Chapter 4 inCyber page (http://www.scsite.com/dc/ch4/incyber.htm) and click Image Scanner.

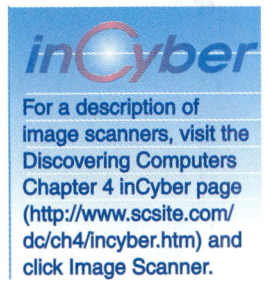

Figure 4-17
Image processing systems record and store an exact copy of a document. These systems often are used by insurance companies that may need to refer to any of hundreds of thousands of documents.

Optical Recognition

Optical recognition devices use a light source to read codes, marks, and characters and convert them into digital data that can be processed by a computer.

Optical Codes Optical codes use a pattern or symbols to represent data. The most common optical code is the bar code. A **bar code** consists of a set of vertical lines and spaces of different widths. The bar code usually is either printed on the product package or attached to the product with a label or tag. The bar code reader uses the light pattern from the bar code lines to identify the item. Several different types of bar codes exist, but the most familiar is the **universal product code** (**UPC**). The UPC bar code, used for grocery and retail items, can be translated into a ten-digit number that identifies the product manufacturer and product number (Figure 4-18).

Figure 4-18
Bar codes are a type of optical code found on most grocery and retail items. The universal product code (UPC) bar code is the most common. The numbers printed at the bottom identify the manufacturer and the product and can be used to input the item if the bar code reader fails.

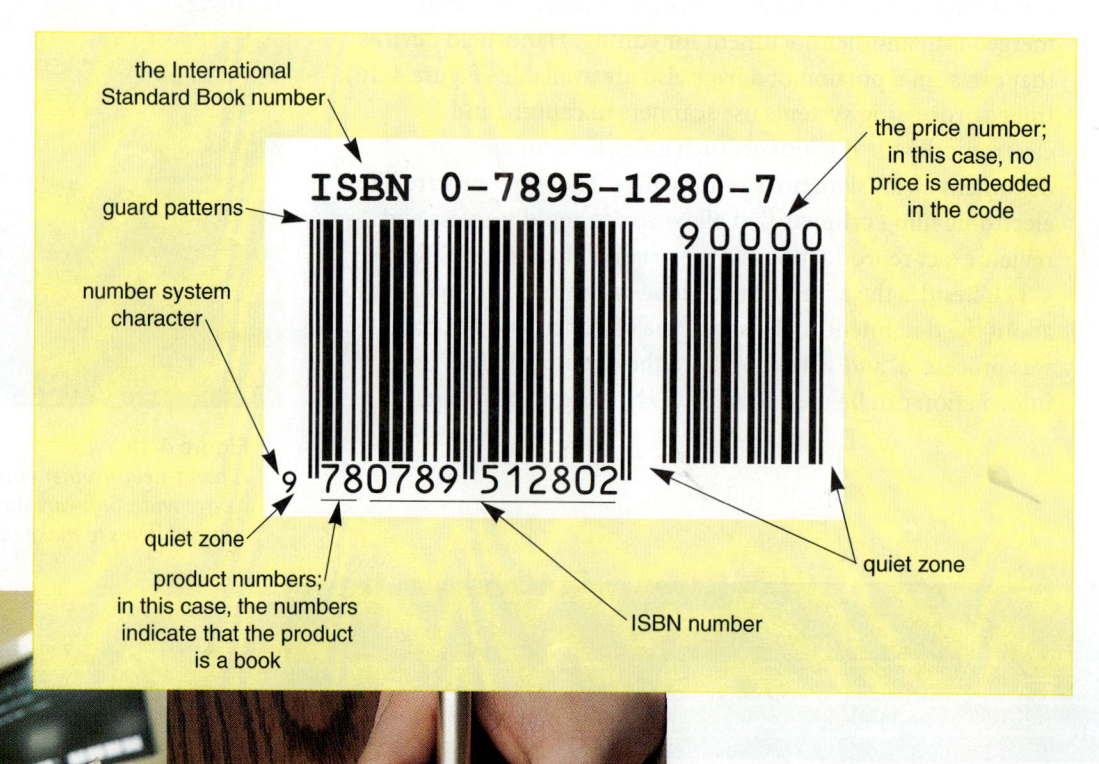

Figure 4-19
Three different types of bar code readers are shown here: a hand-held gun, a hand-held wand, and a stationary reader set in the counter of a grocery store.

Optical code scanning equipment includes light guns that can be aimed at the code and wands that are passed over the code. Grocery stores often use stationary units set in a counter. Figure 4-19 shows several different types of bar code readers.

Optical Mark Recognition (OMR)   Optical mark recognition (OMR) devices often are used to process questionnaires or test answer sheets (Figure 4-20). Carefully placed marks on the form indicate responses to questions and can be read and interpreted by a computer program and matched against a previously entered answer key sheet.

Optical Character Recognition (OCR)   Optical character recognition (OCR) devices are scanners that read typewritten, computer-printed, and in some cases hand-printed characters from ordinary documents. OCR devices range from large machines that can automatically read thousands of documents per minute to hand-held wands.

An OCR device scans the shape of a character, compares it with a predefined shape stored in memory, and converts the character into the corresponding computer code. The standard OCR typeface, called OCR-A, is illustrated in Figure 4-21. The characters can be read easily by both people and machines. OCR-B is a set of standard characters widely used in Europe and Japan.

inCyber

For an explanation of optical character recognition devices, visit the Discovering Computers Chapter 4 inCyber page (http://www.scsite.com/dc/ch4/incyber.htm) and click OCR.

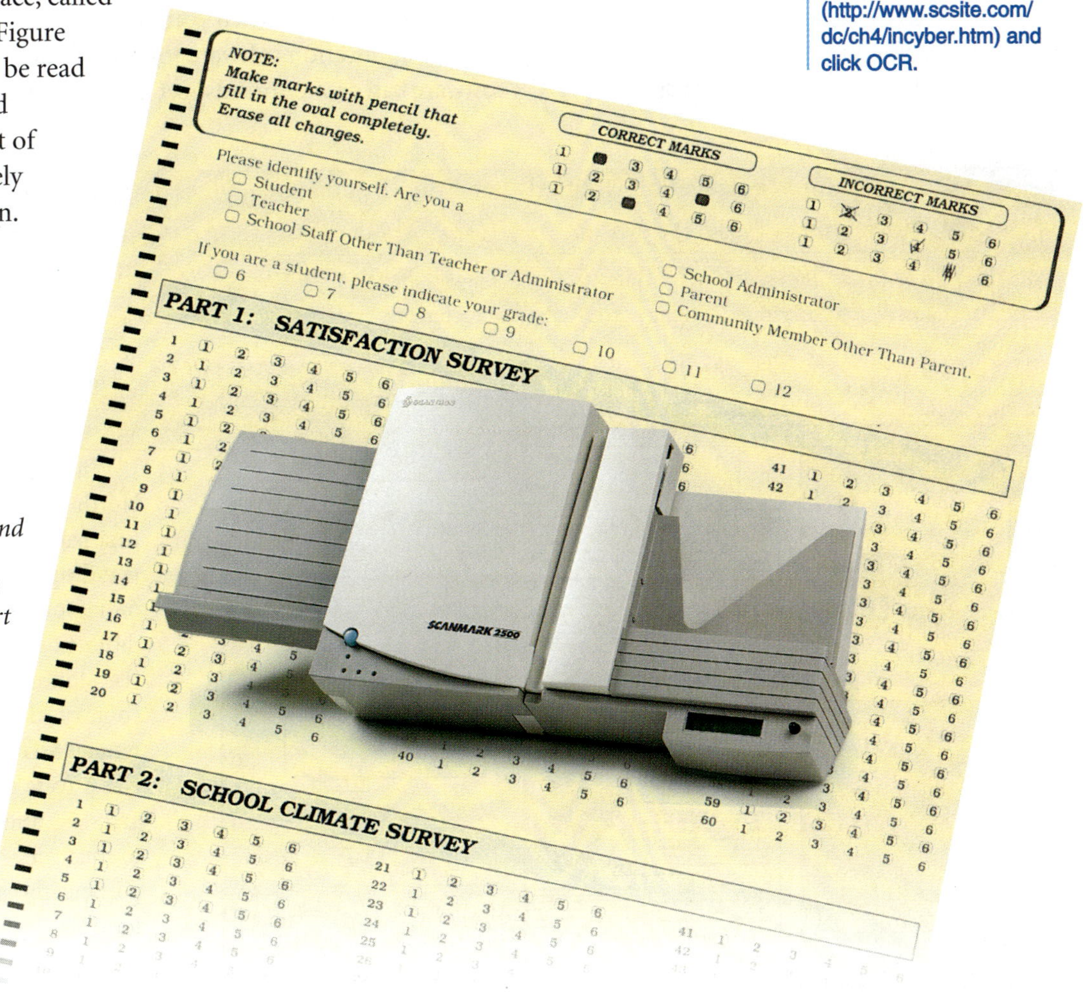

Figure 4-20
Optical mark recognition devices often are used for processing questionnaires and test answer sheets. For test scores, the reader can mark the incorrect answers, report the number of correct answers, and report the average score of all tests.

ABCDEFGHIJKLMNOPQRSTUVWXYZ
1234567890-=▮;',./

Figure 4-21
A portion of the OCR-A character set. Notice how the characters B and 8, S and 5, and the number 0 and the letter O, are designed differently so the reading device easily can distinguish between them.

OCR is frequently used for **turn-around documents**, which are documents designed to be returned (*turned around*) to the organization that created them. Examples of such documents are billing statements from credit card companies and department stores. The portion of the statement that you send back with your payment has your account number, total balance, and payment information printed in optical characters.

OCR Software OCR software is used with image scanners to convert text images into data that can be processed by word processing software. OCR software works as follows: First, the entire page of text is scanned. At this point, the page is considered a single graphic image, just like a picture, and individual words are not identified. Next, the software tries to identify individual letters and words. The methods used for word recognition are quite sophisticated and can include determining the most likely word based on previously identified words. Figure 4-22 shows how one OCR software package displays the status during the identification process. Modern OCR software has a very high success rate and usually can identify more than 99% of the scanned material. Finally, the OCR software displays the text that it could not identify. When you make the final corrections, the document can be saved in the application software format of your choice. Besides word processing files, OCR software can create spreadsheet and database files, as well.

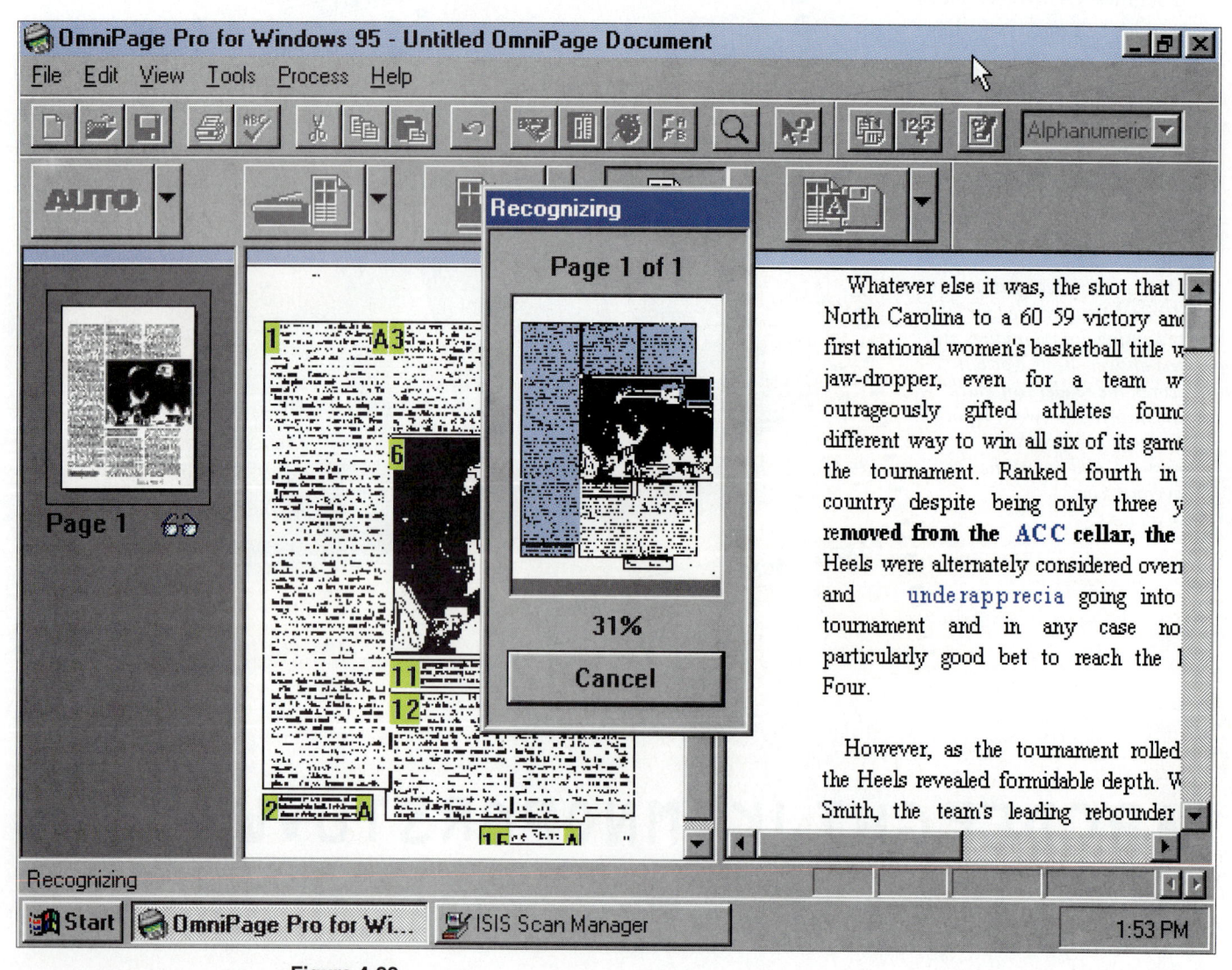

Figure 4-22
This screen shows OCR software in the process of converting a page of scanned text into data that can be input to word processing software. The entire page of text, including a photograph, was converted in less than ten seconds; much faster than the text could be entered using the keyboard.

SOURCE DATA AUTOMATION 4.17

Magnetic Ink Character Recognition (MICR)

Magnetic ink character recognition (MICR) characters use a special ink that can be magnetized during processing. MICR is used almost exclusively by the banking industry for processing checks. Blank (unused) checks already have the bank code, account number, and check number printed in MICR characters across the bottom. When the check is processed by the bank, the amount of the check is also printed in the lower right corner (Figure 4-23). Together, this information is read by MICR reader/sorter machines as part of the check-clearing process.

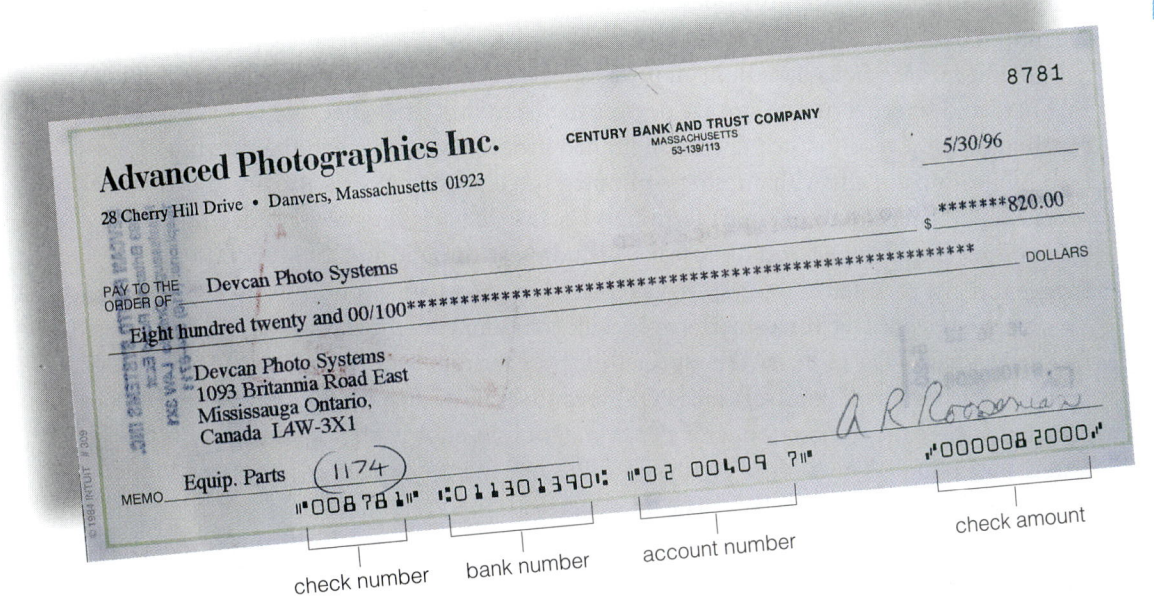

> **inCyber**
>
> For details on magnetic ink character recognition, visit the Discovering Computers Chapter 4 inCyber page (http://www.scsite.com/dc/ch4/incyber.htm) and click MICR.

Figure 4-23
The MICR characters printed along the bottom edge indicate the bank, account number, and amount of the check. The amount in the lower right corner is added after the check is cashed. The other MICR numbers are pre-printed on the check.

Data Collection Devices

Data collection devices are designed and used for obtaining data at the site where the transaction or event being reported takes place. Often, data collection equipment is used in factories, warehouses, or other locations where heat, humidity, and cleanliness is difficult to control (Figure 4-24). Data collection equipment must be rugged and easy to use because often it is operated by persons whose primary task is not entering data.

Figure 4-24
Data collection devices often are used in factories and warehouses where heat, humidity, and cleanliness is difficult to control.

Terminals

Terminals, sometimes called **display terminals** or **video display terminals (VDTs)**, consist of a keyboard and a screen. They fall into three basic categories: dumb terminals, intelligent terminals, and special-purpose terminals. The following sections explain each type.

A **dumb terminal** consists of a keyboard and a display screen you can use to enter and transmit data to or receive and display data from a computer to which it is connected. A dumb terminal has no independent processing capability or secondary storage and cannot function as an independent device (Figure 4-25). Dumb terminals often are connected to minicomputers, mainframe, or supercomputers that perform the processing and then send the output back to the dumb terminal.

Intelligent terminals have built-in processing capabilities and often contain not only the keyboard and screen, but also storage devices such as a disk drive. Because of their built-in capabilities, these terminals can perform limited processing tasks when they are not communicating directly with another computer. Intelligent terminals also are known as **programmable terminals** or **smart terminals** because they can be programmed by the software developer to perform basic tasks, including arithmetic and logic operations. In recent years, personal computers have replaced many intelligent terminals.

Special-purpose terminals perform specific jobs and contain features uniquely designed for use in a particular industry. The special-purpose terminal shown in Figure 4-26 is called a point-of-sale terminal. **Point-of-sale (POS) terminals** allow data to be entered at the time and place where the transaction with a customer occurs, such as in fast-food restaurants or hotels, for example. Point-of-sale terminals and serve as input to either computers located at the place of business or elsewhere. The data entered is used to maintain sales records, update inventory, make automatic calculations such as sales tax, verify credit, and perform other activities associated with the sales transactions and critical to running the business. Automatic teller machines (ATMs) are another kind of special-purpose terminal that allow you to complete financial transactions and other banking-related activities. You input data into the ATM using a bank card with a magnetic strip and a specialized keyboard. Both point-of-sale terminals and ATMs are designed to be easy to operate, requiring little technical knowledge.

Figure 4-25
A dumb terminal has no independent processing capability and cannot function as a stand-alone device. Dumb terminals usually are connected to larger computer systems.

Figure 4-26
Point-of-sale terminals usually are designed for a specific type of business, such as a restaurant, hotel, or retail store. Keys are labeled to assist the user in recording transactions.

Other Input Devices

Although characters (text and numbers) are still the primary form of input data, the use of sound and image data is increasing. To capture sound and image data, special input devices are required to convert the input into a digital form that can be processed by the computer. For personal computers, these input devices consist primarily of electronics contained on a separate card, such as a **sound card** or **video card**, that is installed in the computer. These cards convert the sound or video input into digital data that can be stored and processed by the computer.

Sound Input

Sounds usually are recorded with a microphone connected to the sound card or by directly connecting a sound device, such as an electronic music keyboard, to the sound card. Sound editing software (Figure 4-27) allows you to change the sound after it is recorded.

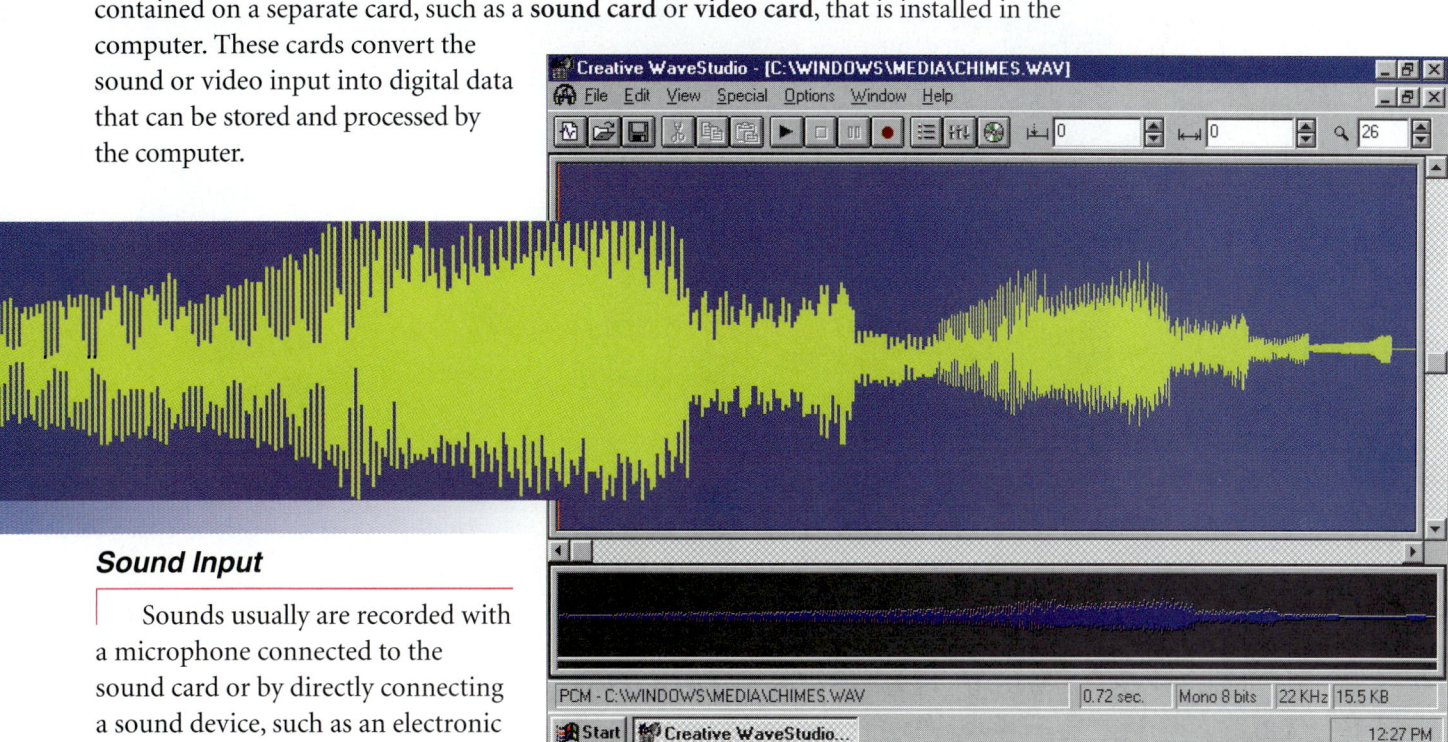

Figure 4-27
Sound editing software allows you to change sounds that have been digitally recorded. Sounds can be copied, speeded up, slowed down, or have special effects added, such as echo or fade. This screen represents the sound of chimes reversed with echo added.

Voice Input

Voice input, sometimes referred to as speech or voice recognition, allows you to enter data and issue commands to the computer with spoken words (Figure 4-28). Some experts think that eventually voice input may be the most common way to operate a computer. Their belief is based on the fact that people can speak much faster than they can type (approximately 200 words per minute speaking and only 40 words per minute for the average typist). In addition, speaking is a more natural means of communicating than using a keyboard, which takes some time to learn. Many telephone directory assistance services now use voice input. You are asked to give the city and name of the person or business you are calling, and your voice command starts a database search to locate the appropriate telephone number.

Figure 4-28
Many health professionals now use voice input to enter into the computer the numerous records that must be maintained on patients.

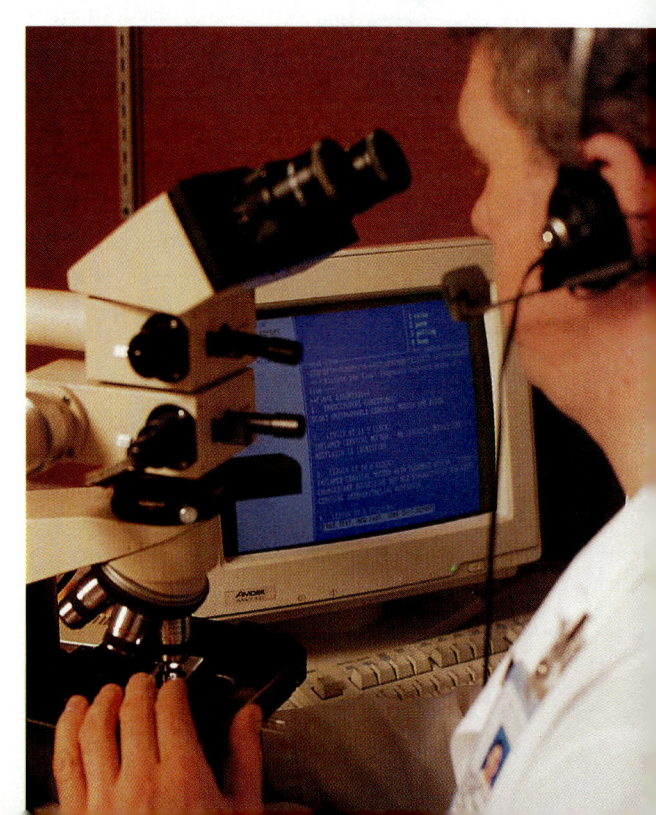

4.20 CHAPTER 4 – INPUT AND OUTPUT

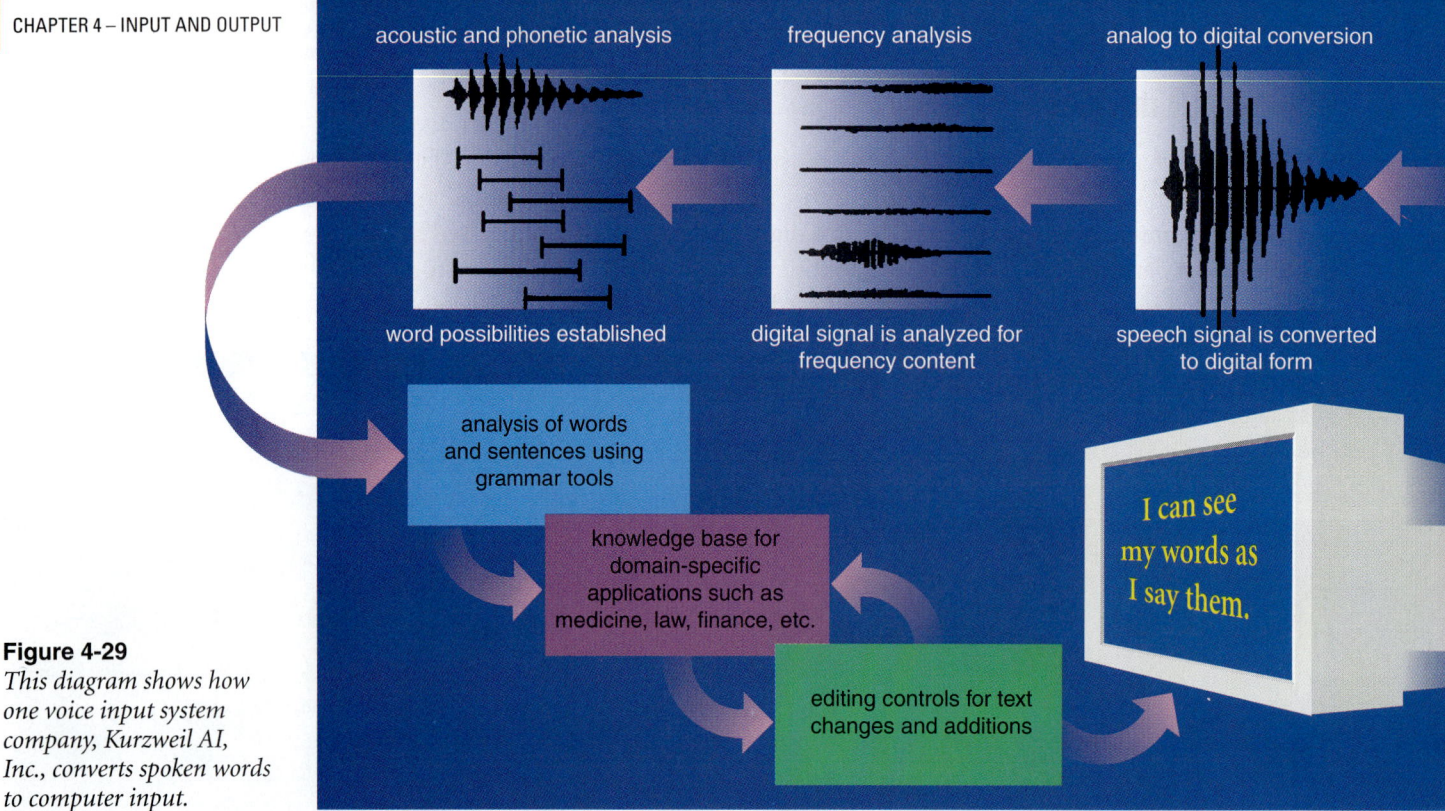

acoustic and phonetic analysis — word possibilities established

frequency analysis — digital signal is analyzed for frequency content

analog to digital conversion — speech signal is converted to digital form

analysis of words and sentences using grammar tools

knowledge base for domain-specific applications such as medicine, law, finance, etc.

editing controls for text changes and additions

I can see my words as I say them.

Figure 4-29
This diagram shows how one voice input system company, Kurzweil AI, Inc., converts spoken words to computer input.

inCyber
For an explanation of voice input systems, visit the Discovering Computers Chapter 4 inCyber page (http://www.scsite.com/dc/ch4/incyber.htm) and click Voice Input.

Most voice input systems use a combination of hardware and software to convert spoken words into data that the computer can process. The conversion process used by one voice input system developer, shown in Figure 4-29, is as follows:

1. Your voice, consisting of sound waves, is converted into digital form by **digital signal processing (DSP)** circuits that are usually on a separate board that has been added to the computer.

2. The digitized voice input is compared against patterns stored in the voice systems database.

3. Grammar rules are used to resolve possible word conflicts. Based on how a word was used, the computer usually can identify the correct word in cases of words that sound alike such as *to*, *too*, and *two*.

4. Unrecognized words are presented to you to identify.

With many voice input systems, especially the lower cost systems with limited vocabularies, you have to train the system to recognize your voice. For each of the words in the vocabulary, you speak the word. After each word has been spoken several times, the system develops a digital pattern for the word that can be stored on a storage device. When you later speak a word to the system to request a particular action, the system compares the word to the words that were previously entered. When it finds a match, the software performs the activity associated with the word. Such systems are referred to as **speaker dependent** because each person who wants to use the system has to train it to his or her voice. Larger vocabulary systems can contain up to 50,000 words and training on individual words is not practical. Instead, developers include multiple patterns, called **voice templates**, for each word. These templates include male and female voices as well as regional accents. These systems are called **speaker independent** because most users will not have to train the system to their speech patterns.

Most speech-to-text systems in use today use **discrete-speech recognition** that requires you to pause slightly between each word. **Continuous-speech recognition** systems that allow you to speak in a flowing conversational tone are not yet widely used because they require more complex software and hardware to separate and make sense of the words. Low-cost

Figure 4-30
This digital camera is used to record digital photographs of documents, products, or people. The camera is connected to a video board installed in the computer.

continuous-speech recognition systems are expected to be available for personal computers by the year 2000.

Beyond continuous-voice recognition is what is called natural language voice interface. A **natural language voice interface** allows you to ask a question and have the computer not only convert the question to understandable words but to interpret the question and give an appropriate response. For example, think how powerful and easy it would be to use a system if you simply could ask, How soon can we ship 200 red aluminum frame mountain bikes to Boston? Think about how many different pieces of data the computer might have to pull together to generate a correct response. Such natural language voice recognition systems are not commercially available now but are being developed using powerful computers and sophisticated software.

Biological Feedback Input

Biological feedback input devices work in combination with special software to translate movements, temperature, or even skin-based electrical signals into input. Devices such as gloves, body suits, and eyeglasses are used for biological feedback input. Still another device uses a sensor placed around a user's finger. As the user changes his or her thoughts, the electrical signals coming from the user's skin change and are deciphered into movements on the computer screen. Biological feedback input devices allow for even more natural input than voice recognition systems.

Digital Camera

Digital cameras record photographs in the form of digital data that can be stored on a computer. No chemical-based film is used. Some digital cameras, called field cameras, are portable and look similar to traditional film cameras. Other digital cameras, called studio cameras, are stationary and are connected directly to a computer (Figure 4-30). Many companies use digital cameras to record images of their products for online catalogs on the World Wide Web or to record photos of their employees for personnel records.

Video Input

Video material is input to the computer using a video camera or a video recorder using previously recorded material. Video data requires tremendous amounts of storage space, which is why video segments, or *clips*, in personal computer applications often are limited to only a few seconds. Improvements in video electronics and software, and larger capacity storage devices will enable movie length video data to eventually become available. Video applications currently under development include video repair manuals. Rather than just looking at a photo or diagram, you can view narrated video clips on how to disassemble and repair a piece of equipment.

Electronic Whiteboards

An **electronic whiteboard** is a modified conference room whiteboard that uses built-in scanners to record text and drawings in a file on an attached computer (Figure 4-31). The drawing is recorded and displayed as it is created and can be printed or stored for future use. Unique reflective collars near the tips of the dry-erase marking pens allow the sensors to identify and record different colors. The eraser also has an identifying collar that enables the computer to delete previously entered data in areas that the eraser covers. Communications software enables the drawing to be transmitted to a remote location.

The input devices discussed in this chapter are summarized in Figure 4-32.

Figure 4-31
An electronic whiteboard captures whatever is written on the whiteboard surface and saves it as a file on an attached computer. The file can be printed, modified, incorporated into other documents, or transmitted to other locations.

INPUT DEVICE	DESCRIPTION
Keyboard	Most commonly used input device; special keys may include numeric keypad, arrow keys, and function keys
Mouse, Trackball, Touchpad, Pointing Stick	Used to move pointer and select options
Joystick	Stem device often used as input device for games
Pen Input	Uses pen to input and edit data and select processing options
Touch Screen	User interacts with computer by touching screen with finger
Light Pen	Can be used to select options or draw on screen
Digitizer	Used to enter or edit drawings
Graphics Tablet	Digitizer with special processing options built into tablet
Image Scanner	Converts text, graphics, or photos into digital input
Optical Recognition	Uses light source to read codes, marks, and characters
MICR	Used in banking to read magnetic ink characters on checks
Data Collection	Used in factories and warehouses to input data at source
Sound Input	Converts sound into digital data
Voice Input	Converts speech into digital data
Digital Camera	Captures digital image of subject or object
Video Input	Converts video into digital data
Electronic Whiteboard	Captures anything drawn on special whiteboard

Figure 4-32
This table summarizes some of the more common input devices.

What Is Output?

Output is data that has been processed into a useful form called information that can be used by a person or a machine.

Types of Output

The type of output generated from the computer depends on the needs of the user and the hardware and software that are used. Two common types of output are reports and graphics. These types of output can be printed on a printer or displayed on a screen. Printed output is called **hard copy** and output that is displayed on a screen is called **soft copy**. Other types of output include audio (sound) and video (visual images). Each of these types of output are discussed in the following sections.

Reports

A **report** is information presented in an organized form. Most people think of reports as items printed on paper or displayed on a screen. For example, word processing documents can be considered reports. Information printed on forms such as invoices or payroll checks also can be considered types of reports. One way to classify reports is by who uses them. An **internal report** is used by individuals in the performance of their jobs. For example, a daily sales report that is distributed to sales personnel is an internal report because it is used only by personnel within the organization. An **external report** is used outside the organization. Sales invoices that are printed and mailed to customers are external reports.

Reports also can be classified by the way they present information. The four types of common reports are: narrative reports, detail reports, summary reports, and exception reports.

Narrative reports may contain some graphic or numeric information, but are primarily text-based reports. These reports, usually prepared with word processing software, include the various types of correspondence commonly used in business such as memos, letters, and sales proposals. Detail, summary, and exception reports are used primarily to organize and present numeric-based information.

In a **detail report**, each line on the report usually corresponds to one record that has been processed. For example, companies that sell products keep a sales log that shows specific information about each sale. Detail reports contain a great deal of information and can be quite lengthy. They are usually required by individuals who need access to the day-to-day information that reflects the operating status of the organization. For example, people in the warehouse of a distributor should have access to the location and number of units on hand for

DETAIL INVENTORY REPORT
by Part Number

Part#	Description	Location	Quantity On Hand
87143	ink-jet printer	Portland	1,400
87143	ink-jet printer	San Francisco	80
87143	ink-jet printer	Seattle	550
89620	laser printer	Portland	750
89620	laser printer	Seattle	250
93042	17-inch monitor	Portland	635
93042	17-inch monitor	San Francisco	240
93042	17-inch monitor	Seattle	50

one line printed for each part at each location

Figure 4-33
This detail report shows quantities for each part number and each location.

each product. The Detail Inventory Report in Figure 4-33 on the previous page contains a line for each warehouse location for each part number. Separate inventory records exist for each line on the report. Many software programs generate audit trails when they output detail reports. Audit trails provide a way to track changes made to data so you can backtrack to find the origin of specific information that appears on a report. For example, an audit trail could show that David Williams changed the inventory record for laser printers in the Seattle warehouse at 1:14 p.m. on November 27.

As the name implies, a **summary report** summarizes data. It contains totals for certain values found in the input records. The report shown in Figure 4-34 contains a summary of the total quantity on hand for each part. The information on the summary report consists of totals for each part from the information contained in the detail report in Figure 4-33. Detail reports frequently contain more information than most managers have time to review. With a summary report, however, a manager can review information quickly in summarized form.

An **exception report** contains information that is outside of *normal* user-specified values or conditions, called the *exception criteria*. Records meeting this criteria are an *exception* to the majority of the data. For example, if an organization wants to know when to reorder inventory items to avoid running out of stock, it would design an exception report. The report would tell which inventory items fell below the reorder points and therefore need to be ordered. An example of such a report is shown in Figure 4-35.

Exception reports help you focus on situations that may require immediate decisions or specific actions. The advantage of exception reports is that they save time and money. In a large department store, for example, more than 100,000 inventory items may exist. A detail report containing all inventory items could be longer than 2,000 pages. To search through the report to determine the items whose on-hand quantity was less than the reorder point would be a difficult and time-consuming task. The exception report, however, could select these items, which might number 100 to 200, and place them on a two- to four-page report that could be reviewed in just a few minutes.

Reports are also sometimes classified by how often they are produced. **Periodic reports**, also called **scheduled reports**, are produced on a regular basis such as daily, weekly, monthly, or yearly. **Ad hoc** or **on-demand reports** are created whenever they are needed for information that is not required on a scheduled basis.

Figure 4-34
The summary report contains the total on-hand quantity for each part. The report can be prepared using the same records that were used to prepare the report in Figure 4-33.

SUMMARY INVENTORY REPORT
by Part Number

Part#	Description	Location	Quantity On Hand
87143	ink-jet printer	***All***	2,030
89620	laser printer	***All***	1,000
93042	17-inch monitor	***All***	925

one summary line for each part

INVENTORY EXCEPTION REPORT

Part#	Description	Reorder Point	Quantity On Hand
89620	laser printer	1,200	1,000
93042	17-inch monitor	1,000	925

quantity on hand less than reorder point

Figure 4-35
The exception report lists inventory items with an on-hand quantity below their reorder points. These parts could have been selected from thousands of inventory items. Only these parts met the exception criteria.

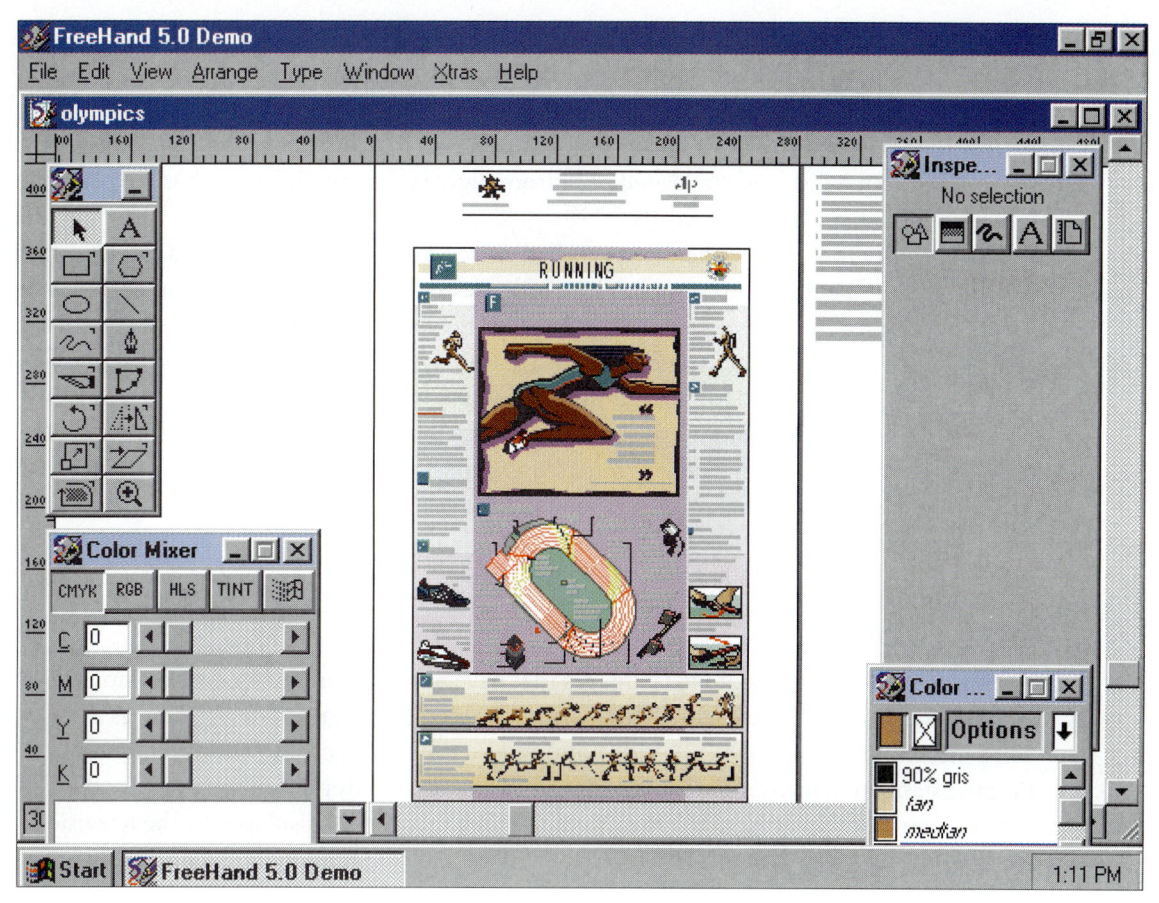

Figure 4-36
Computer drawing and paint programs often are used by professional artists to create advertising and marketing materials.

Graphics

Computer graphics are any non-text pictorial information. One of the early uses of computer graphics was for charts to help present and analyze numeric information. In recent years, computer graphics have gone far beyond charting capabilities. **Computer drawing programs** and **computer paint programs** allow an artistic user to create stunning works of art. These programs are frequently used for developing advertising and other marketing materials (Figure 4-36). Clip art and photographs also are considered types of computer graphics.

Audio Output

Audio output, consists of sounds, including words and music, produced by the computer. An audio output device on a computer is a speaker. Most personal computers come with a small (approximately two inch) speaker that usually is located behind an opening on the front or side of the system unit case. Increasingly, personal computer users are adding higher quality stereo speakers to their systems. The stereo speakers connect to a port on a sound card that works with sound, voice, and music software. Some PCs come with speakers built into the sides of the display unit.

Voice output is a type of audio output that consists of spoken words that are conveyed to you from the computer. Thus, instead of reading words on a printed report or monitor, you hear the words over earphones, the telephone, or other devices from which sound can be generated.

The data that produces voice output usually is created in one of two ways. First, a person can talk into a device that will encode the words in a digital pattern. For example, the words, *The number is*, are spoken into a microphone, and the computer software assigns a digital pattern to the words. The digital data is then stored on a disk. At a later time, the data can be retrieved from the disk and translated back from digital data into voice, so that the person listening will actually hear the words.

A second type of voice generation is called voice synthesis. **Voice synthesis** can transform words stored in memory into speech. The words are analyzed by a program that examines the letters stored in memory and generates sounds for the letter combinations. The software can apply rules of intonation and stress to make it sound as though a person were speaking. The speech is then played through speakers attached to the computer.

You may have heard voice output used by the telephone company directory assistance. Automobile and vending machine manufacturers are also incorporating voice output into their products. The potential for this type of output is great and it undoubtedly will be used in many products and services in the future.

Video Output

Video output consists of visual images that have been captured with a video input device, such as a VCR or camera, digitized, and directed to an output device such as a computer monitor (Figure 4-37). Video output also can be directed to a television monitor. Because standard televisions are not designed to handle a computer's digital signals, the video output has to be converted to an analog signal that can be displayed by the television. **High-definition television (HDTV)** sets are designed for digital signals and eventually may replace computer monitors.

Figure 4-37
This use of video output is like a video telephone system; it allows company employees to see the co-workers with whom they are talking.

Display Devices

A **display device** is the visual output device of a computer. The two most common types of display devices are monitors and flat panel displays.

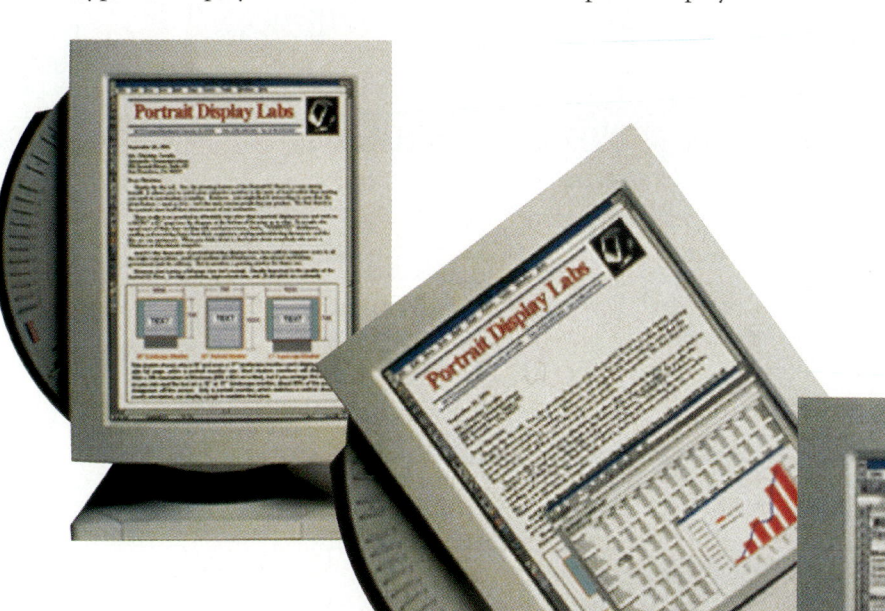

> **inCyber**
> For information on monitors, visit the Discovering Computers Chapter 4 inCyber page (http://www.scsite.com/dc/ch4/incyber.htm) and click Monitor.

Monitors

A **monitor** looks like a television and consists of a display surface, called a screen, and a plastic or metal case to house the electrical components. A monitor differs from a terminal, discussed earlier in the section on input devices, in that a terminal also has a keyboard. A monitor often has a swivel base that allows the angle of the screen surface to be adjusted. The term **screen** is used to refer to both the surface of any display device and to any type of display device. An older term sometimes used to refer to a monitor or terminal is CRT. A **CRT**, which stands for **cathode ray tube**, is actually the large tube inside a monitor or terminal. The front part of the tube is the display surface or screen.

The more widely used monitors are equivalent in size to a 14- to 17-inch television screen. Monitors designed for use with desktop publishing, graphics, or engineering applications come in even larger sizes that can display full-sized images of one or sometimes two $8^1/_2$-by-11-inch pages of data. One company even makes a monitor that can be tilted 90 degrees to display either long or wide pages or two pages side by side (Figure 4-38).

Figure 4-38
Portrait Display Labs manufactures a monitor that can be tilted 90 degrees to display long or wide pages or two pages side by side.

Figure 4-39
Color monitors are widely used because most of today's software is written to display information in color.

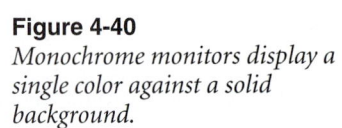

Figure 4-40
Monochrome monitors display a single color against a solid background.

A **color monitor** can display text or graphics in color (Figure 4-39). Color monitors are widely used with all types of computers because most of today's software is written to display information in color. The amount of colors a monitor can display at one time depends on the amount of memory installed on the video adapter board. The maximum number of colors that can be displayed is more than 16 million.

Monochrome monitors display a single color such as white, green, or amber characters on a black background (Figure 4-40) or black characters on a white background. Monochrome monitors are still used by business for order entry and other applications where color is not required and cost is a concern. Smaller, pen computers such as PDAs also often have monochrome monitors. Using a technique known as gray scaling, some monochrome monitors can display good quality graphic images. **Gray scaling** involves converting an image into different shades of gray like a black and white photograph.

Flat Panel Displays

A **flat panel display** is a thin display screen that does not use cathode ray tube (CRT) technology. Flat panel displays are most often used in portable computers, but larger units that can mount on a wall or other structure are also available. Two common types of technology used for flat panel displays are liquid crystal display (LCD) and gas plasma.

In a **liquid crystal display (LCD)**, a liquid crystal is deposited between two sheets of polarizing material. When an electrical current passes between crossing wires, the liquid crystals are aligned so light cannot shine through, producing an image on the screen. LCD technology also commonly is used in digital watches, clocks, and calculators. **Active matrix** LCD screens use individual transistors to control each crystal cell. **Passive matrix** LCD screens use fewer transistors; one for each row and column. **Dual scan** is a type of passive matrix LCD screen frequently used on lower cost portable computers. Active matrix displays cost more but display a sharper, brighter picture (Figure 4-41).

Gas plasma screens substitute a neon gas for the liquid crystal material. Any locations on a grid of horizontal and vertical electrodes can be turned on to cause the neon gas to glow and produce the pixels that form an image. Gas plasma screens offer better display quality than LCD screens but are more expensive.

Figure 4-41
Active matrix LCD screens produce the best color display by using individual transistors to control each crystal cell.

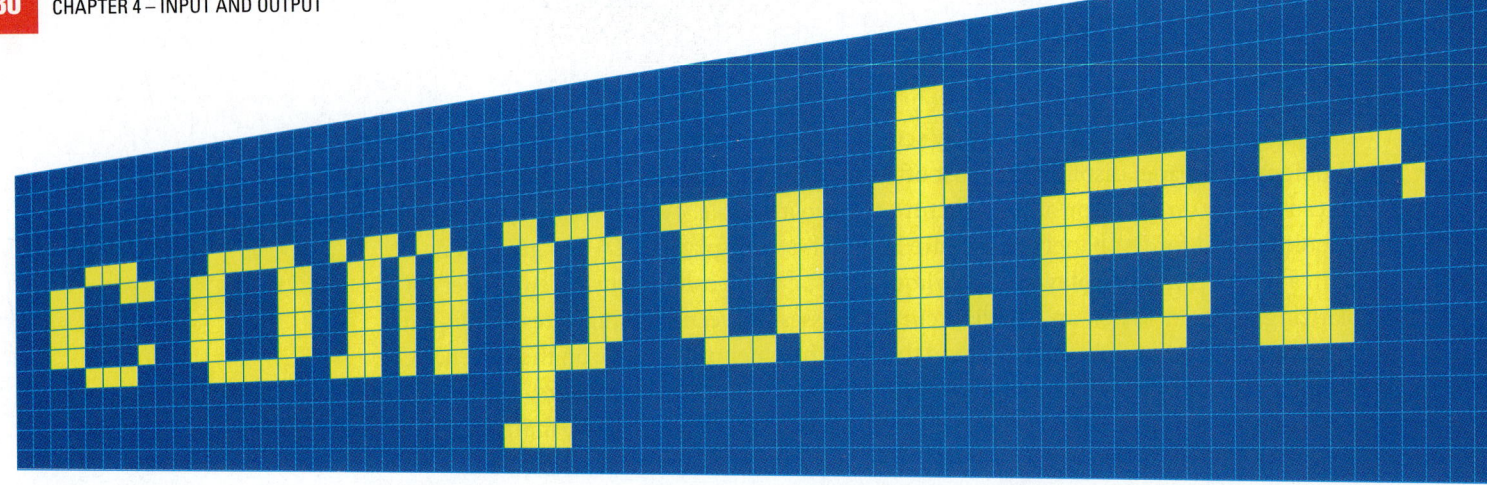

Figure 4-42
The word, computer, shown here is made up of individual picture elements (pixels). Each pixel can be turned on or off to form an image on the screen.

Resolution

Images are displayed on a monitor using patterns of lighted dots. Each dot that can be lighted is called a **picture element,** or **pixel** (Figure 4-42). The **resolution**, or clarity, of the image on a monitor is directly related to the number of pixels the monitor can display and the distance between each pixel. The distance between each pixel is called the **dot pitch.** In general, the greater the number of pixels and the smaller the dot pitch, the better the monitor resolution, because it means more pixels can be displayed. Pixels are the standard unit of measure for screen resolution. The number of pixels the monitor can display is expressed as the number of pixels horizontally and lines vertically on the screen, such as 640 (horizontal pixels) x 480 (vertical lines). The number of pixels actually displayed is determined by three things: the software program, the capability of the video adapter card, and the monitor itself.

Monitors and video adapter cards often are identified by the highest graphics display standard they support. Today, most monitors and video adapter cards support VGA and SVGA standards. **VGA (video graphics array)** devices can display a resolution of 640 x 480 pixels. **SVGA (super video graphics array)** devices can display resolutions even higher than 640 x 480 pixels. Common Super VGA resolutions are 800 x 600 and 1,024 x 768. Having a high-resolution monitor is important, especially when the monitor will be used to display graphics or other non-text information. High-resolution display can produce an image that is almost equivalent to the quality of a photograph (Figure 4-43).

Each of the video graphics standards have a specific frequency or rate at which the video signals are sent to the monitor. Some monitors are designed to only work with at a particular frequency and video standard. Other monitors, called **multiscanning** or **multisync monitors**, are designed to work within a range of frequencies and thus can work with different standards and video adapters.

Figure 4-43
High-resolution display devices can produce images that are equivalent to a photograph. These devices often are used in graphic arts, engineering, and scientific applications.

How Images Are Displayed on a Monitor

Most monitors used with personal computers and terminals use cathode ray tube (CRT) technology. To show color on a monitor, each pixel must have three colored phosphor dots. These dots are the additive primary colors red, green, and blue. A separate electron gun is used for each color. By varying the intensity of the electron beam striking the phosphors, and making some colored dots glow more than others, many colors can be generated. When a color monitor produces an image, the following steps occur (Figure 4-44):

1. The image to be displayed on the monitor is sent electronically from the CPU to the video circuits (located on a video graphics card) to the cathode ray tube.

2. Electron guns at the rear of the tube generate electron beams towards the screen. The beams pass through holes in a metal screen called the *shadow mask*. The shadow mask helps align the beams so they hit the correct dots on the screen. The screen is coated with colored phosphor dots. Phosphor is a substance that glows when it is struck by the electron beam.

3. The yoke, which generates an electromagnetic field, moves the electron beams across and down the screen. Older **interlaced monitors** illuminate every other line (e.g., lines 1, 3, 5, and so on) and then return to the top to illuminate the lines they skipped (e.g., lines 2, 4, 6, and so on). It is an inexpensive way to illuminate the entire screen, but causes flicker. In newer **noninterlaced monitors**, each line is illuminated sequentially (e.g., lines 1, 2, 3, 4, and so on) so the entire screen is lighted more quickly and in a single pass. The speed at which the entire screen is redrawn is called the **refresh rate**.

4. The illuminated phosphor dots create an image on the screen.

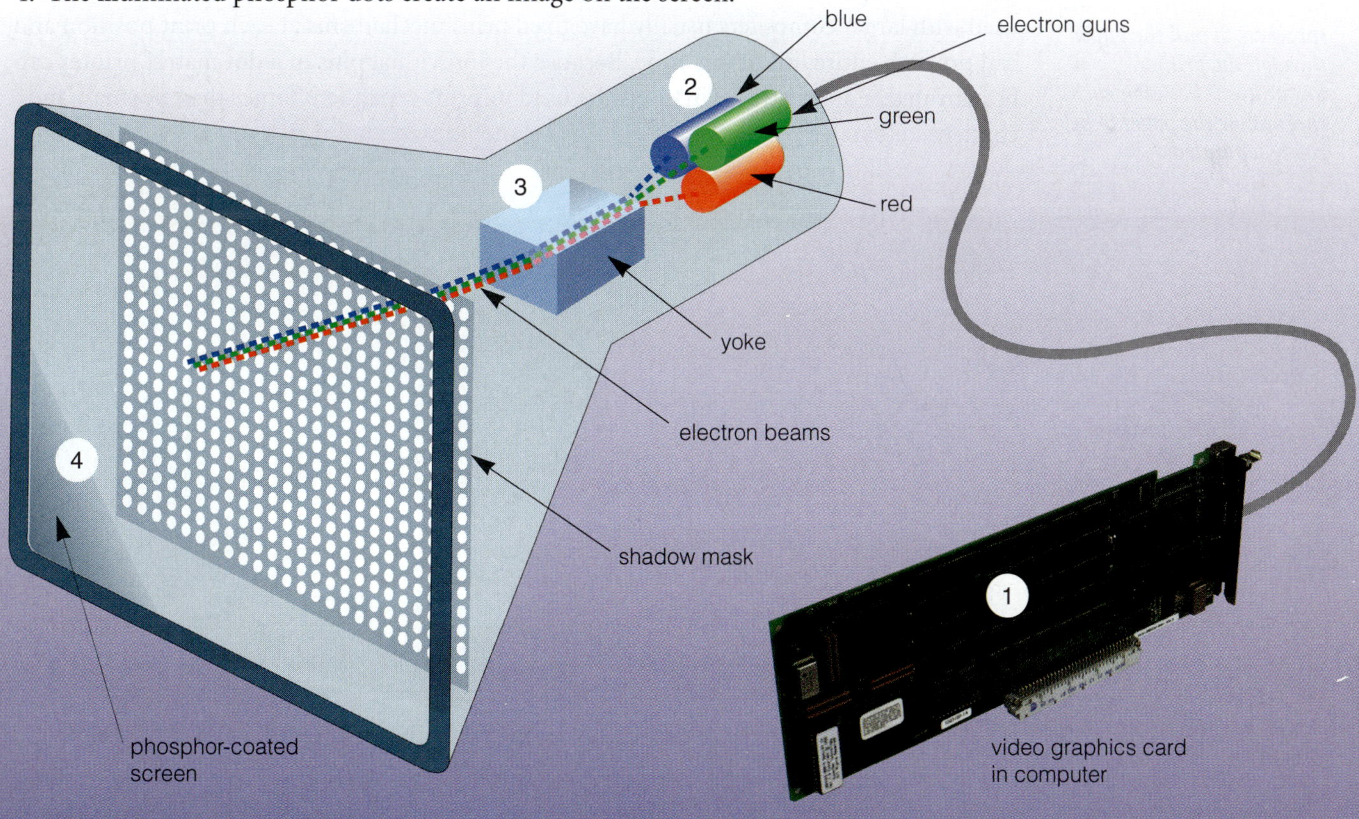

Figure 4-44
How an image is displayed. Each pixel on a color monitor screen is made up of three colored (red, green, and blue), phosphor dots. These dots can be turned on individually or in combinations to display a wide range of colors.

Printers

Printing requirements vary greatly among computer users. For example, home computer users might print only a hundred pages or fewer a week. Small business computer users might print several hundred pages a day. Users of mainframe computers, such as large utility companies that send printed bills to hundreds of thousands of customers each month, need printers that are capable of printing thousands of pages per hour. These different needs have resulted in the development of printers with varying speeds, capabilities, and printing methods. Generally, printers can be classified into two groups, impact or nonimpact, based on how they transfer characters to the paper.

Impact Printers

Impact printers transfer the image onto paper by some type of printing mechanism striking the paper, ribbon, and character together. Most impact printers use continuous-form paper. The pages of **continuous-form paper** are connected together for a continuous flow through the printer (Figure 4-45). The advantage of continuous-form paper is that it does not need to be changed frequently; thousands of pages come connected together. Some impact printers also use single-sheet paper. The advantage of using single-sheet paper is that different types of paper, such as letterhead, can be changed quickly.

Dot Matrix Printers A **dot matrix printer** produces printed images by striking wire pins against an inked ribbon. Its print head consists of a series of small tubes containing wire pins that, when pressed against a ribbon and paper, print small dots. The combination of small dots printed closely together forms the character. Most dot matrix printers used with personal computers have a single print head that moves across the page. Dot matrix printers used with larger computers usually have fixed print mechanisms at each print position and can print an entire line at one time. Because the individual pins of a dot matrix printer can be activated, a dot matrix printer can be used to print expanded (larger than normal) and condensed (smaller than normal) characters and limited graphics.

Figure 4-45
Sheets of continuous-form paper are connected together. Small holes on the sides of the paper allow sprockets to pull the paper through the printer. Perforations between each sheet allow the pages to be easily separated.

Dot matrix printers can contain a varying number of pins, depending on the manufacturer and the printer model. Print heads consisting of 9 and 24 pins (two vertical rows of 12) are most common. Figure 4-46 illustrates the formation of the letter G using a nine-pin dot matrix printer. The two rows of pins on a 24-pin print head are slightly offset (Figure 4-47) and can print overlapping dots that produce better quality output than a 9-pin printer.

The speed of impact printers with movable print heads is rated in **characters per second (cps)**. Depending on the printer model, this speed varies between 50 and 700 cps. The speed of impact printers that print one line at a time is rated in **lines per minute (lpm)**. High-speed dot matrix printers can print up to 1,400 lpm.

Dot matrix are the least expensive printers but are less frequently used because they do not offer a high-quality output. Dot matrix printers often are used when multiple copies of a document, such as an invoice or an airline ticket, must be printed. Dot matrix printers range in cost from under $200 for small desktop units to more than $10,000 for heavy-use business models.

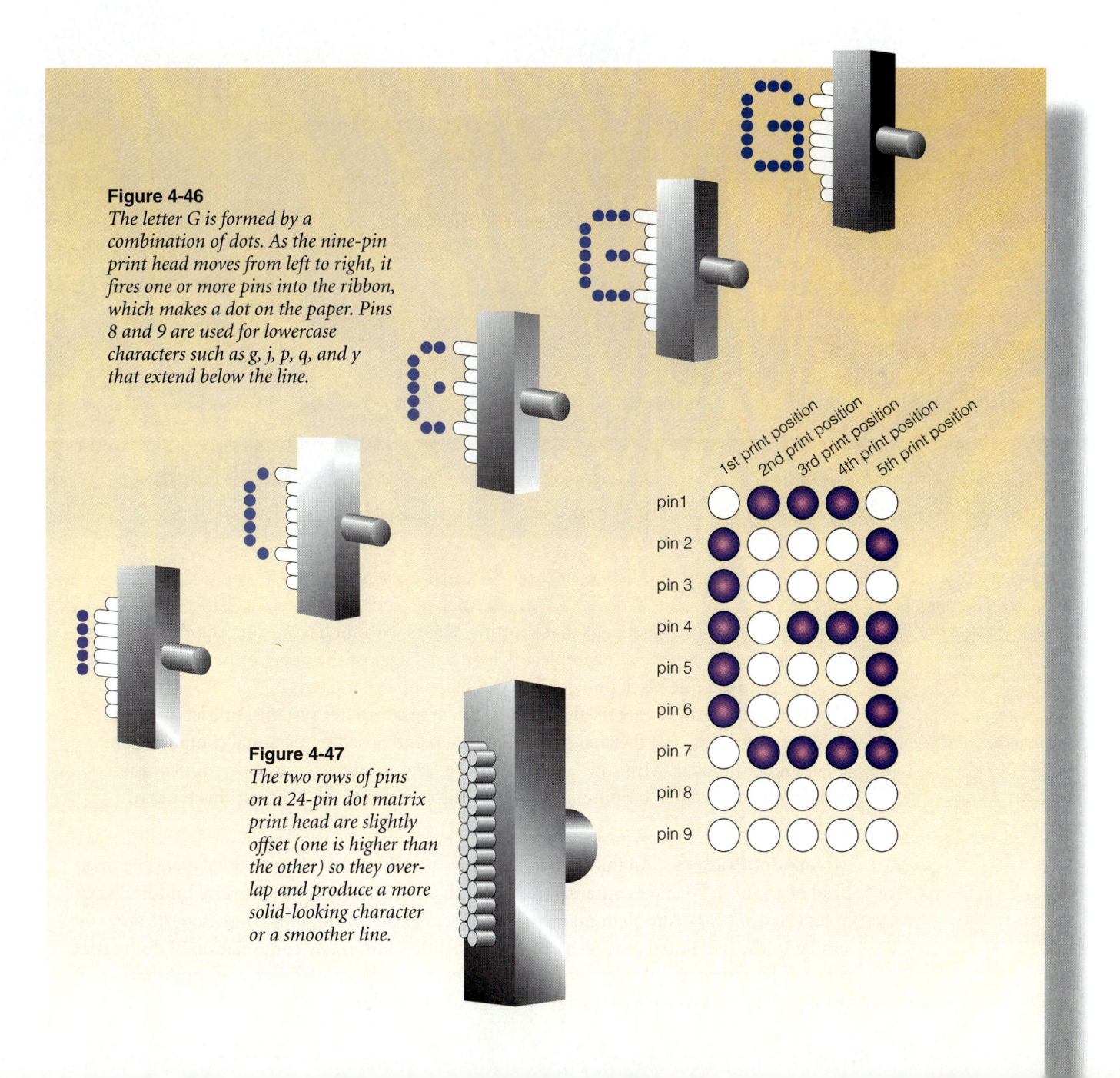

Figure 4-46
The letter G is formed by a combination of dots. As the nine-pin print head moves from left to right, it fires one or more pins into the ribbon, which makes a dot on the paper. Pins 8 and 9 are used for lowercase characters such as g, j, p, q, and y that extend below the line.

Figure 4-47
The two rows of pins on a 24-pin dot matrix print head are slightly offset (one is higher than the other) so they overlap and produce a more solid-looking character or a smoother line.

Band Printers Band printers are used for high-volume output on large computers systems. **Band printers** use a horizontal, rotating band containing numbers, letters of the alphabet, and selected special characters. The characters are struck by hammers located at each print position behind the paper and ribbon to create a line of print on the paper (Figure 4-48).

Interchangeable type bands with different fonts can be used on band printers. A band printer can produce up to six carbon copies, has good print quality, high reliability, and depending on the manufacturer and model of the printer, can print in the range of 600 to 2,000 lines per minute.

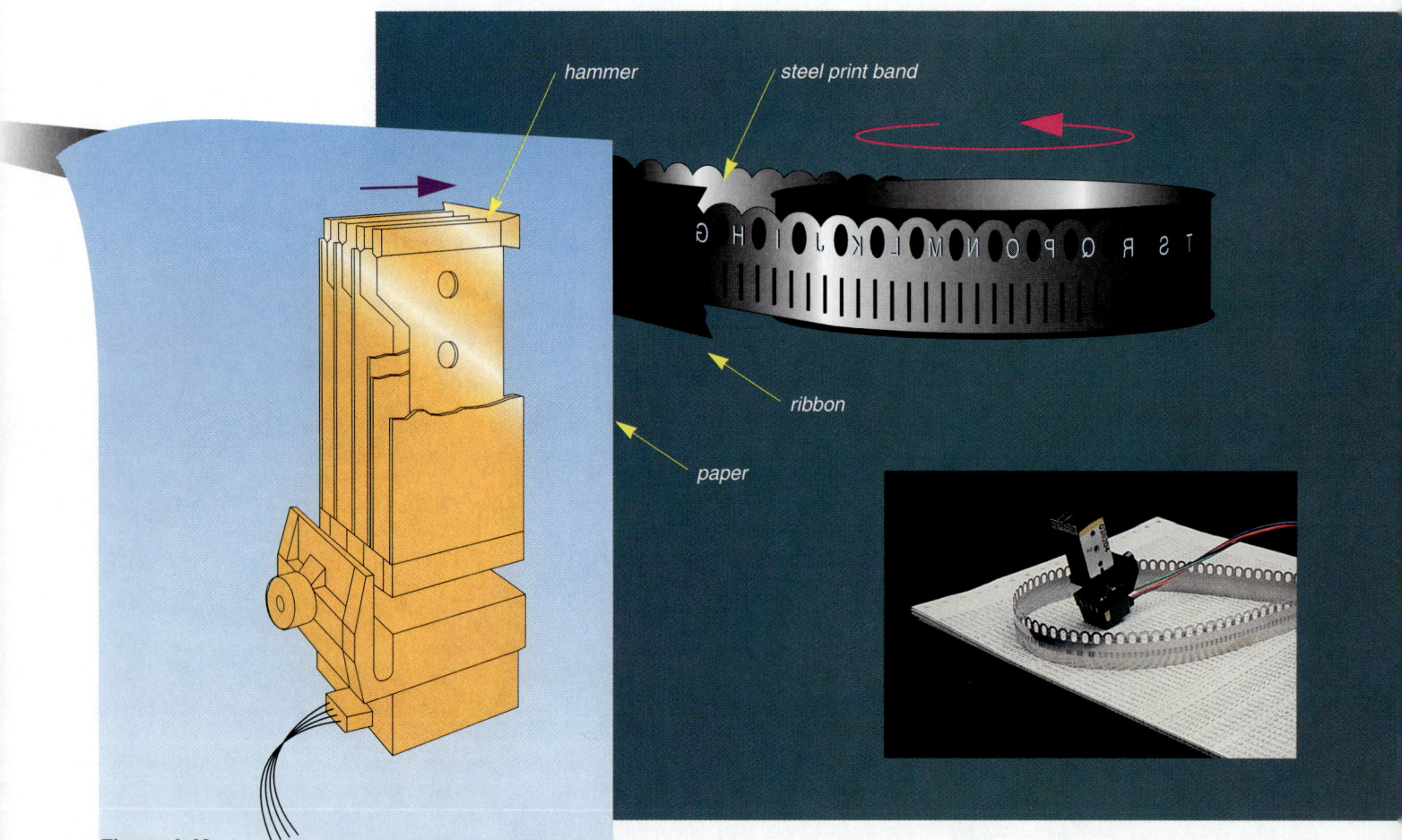

Figure 4-48
A band printer uses a metal band that contains solid characters. When the character to be printed on the band comes by, print hammers strike the paper and the ribbon, forcing them into the band to print the character.

Nonimpact Printers

Nonimpact printing means that printing occurs without having a mechanism striking against a sheet of paper. For example, ink is sprayed against the paper or heat and pressure are used to fuse a fine black powder into the shape of a character.

Nonimpact printers are used on small and large computer systems. Ink-jet printers, small laser printers, and thermal printers are frequently used on personal computers and small minicomputers. Medium- and high-speed laser printers are used on minicomputers, mainframes, and supercomputers. The following sections discuss the various types of nonimpact printers.

Ink-Jet Printers An ink-jet printer sprays tiny drops of ink onto the paper. The print head of an ink-jet printer contains a nozzle with anywhere from 50 to several hundred small holes (Figure 4-49). Although many more of them exist, the ink holes in the nozzle are similar to the individual pins on a dot matrix printer. Just as any combination of dot matrix pins can be activated, ink can be propelled by heat or pressure through any combination of the nozzle holes to form a character or image on the paper.

Ink-jet printers produce high-quality print and graphics and are quiet because the paper is not struck as it is by dot matrix printers. Standard weight copying machine paper is used for most ink-jet documents but heavier weight premium paper is recommended for better looking color documents. Lower quality paper can be too soft and cause the ink to bleed.

Figure 4-49
How a color ink-jet printer works.

1. The print head contains one black and at least one color ink cartridge. Some printers contain three separate color cartridges for the cyan (blue), yellow, and magenta (red) colors used for color printing.

2. An ink cartridge has anywhere from 50 to several hundred small ink nozzles, each less than half the width of a human hair. Each nozzle sprays only one color. Electrical contacts on the cartridge connect to the electronic circuits of the printer.

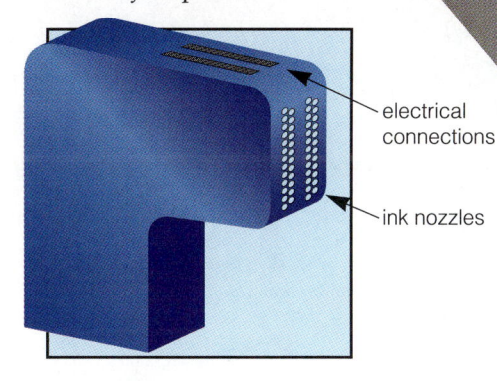

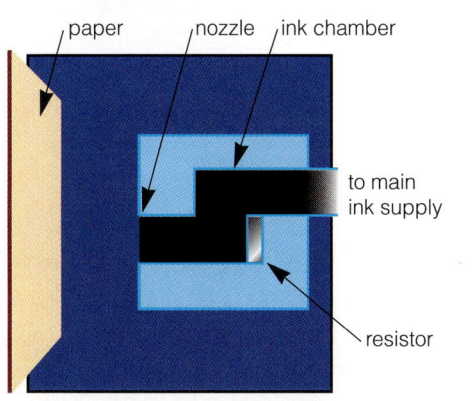

3. Each nozzle is connected to an ink chamber. The ink chambers are connected to the ink supply for each color.

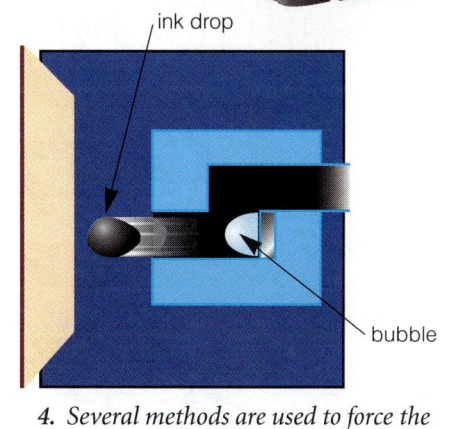

4. Several methods are used to force the ink through the nozzle and onto the paper. Using the thermal method illustrated here, a small resistor in the ink chamber is heated for several millionths of a second. The heat causes a bubble of ink to form and forces a drop out of the nozzle and onto the paper. Instead of the thermal method, some ink-jet printers use a vibrating crystal that forces the ink out the nozzle.

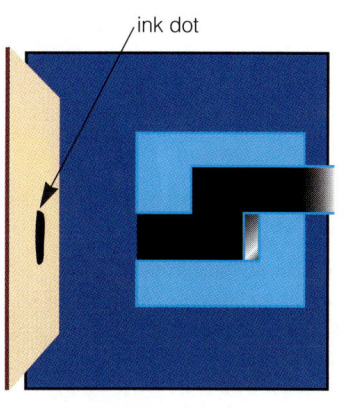

5. As the bubble collapses, fresh ink is drawn into the chamber from the main ink supply in the cartridge. Surface tension keeps the ink from dripping out of the nozzle.

Overhead projector transparency sheets also can be printed. Ink-jet printers print text at rates from two to eight pages per minute. Graphics and color print at a slower rate. In recent years, color ink-jet printers have become the most popular type of color printer (Figure 4-50). Good-quality color ink-jet printers are available for less than $500.

Laser Printers The **laser printer** is a nonimpact printer that operates similarly to a copying machine. A laser printer converts data from the computer into a laser beam that is directed to a positively charged revolving drum by a spinning mirror (Figure 4-51). Each position on the drum touched by the beam becomes negatively charged and attracts the toner (powdered ink). The toner is transferred onto the paper and then fused to the paper by heat and pressure to create the text or image.

Some laser-type printers use light emitting diode (LED) arrays or liquid crystal shutters (LCS). With these methods, the light can expose thousands of individual points on the drum. Although the light exposure methods of LED and LCS printers are different from laser printers, they often are referred to as and classified with laser printers. All laser printers produce high-quality text and graphics suitable for business correspondence (Figure 4-52). Color laser printers are available but are expensive and not yet widely used.

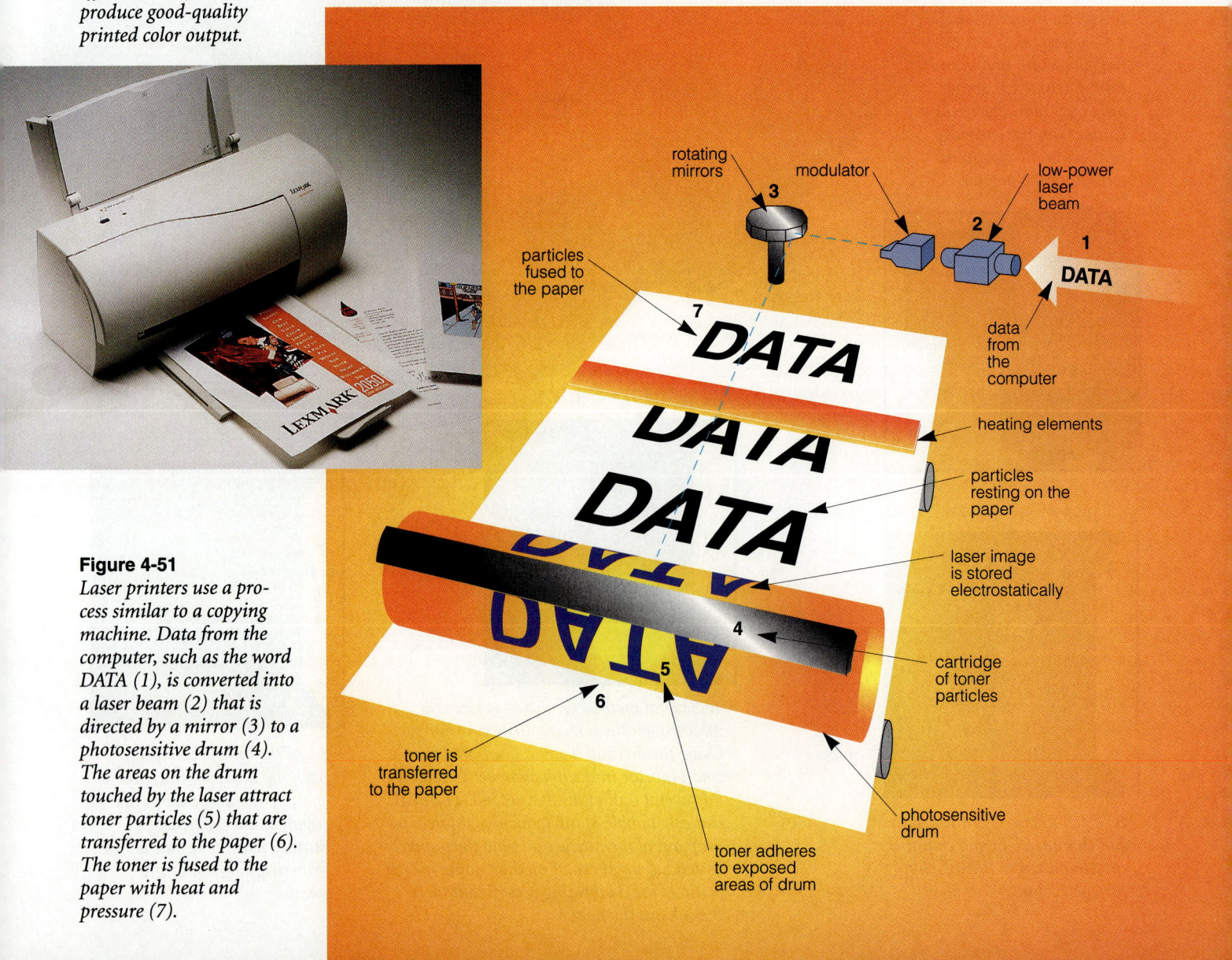

inCyber

For details on laser printers, visit the Discovering Computers Chapter 4 inCyber page (http://www.scsite.com/dc/ch4/incyber.htm) and click Laser Printer.

Figure 4-50
Color ink-jet printers have become an affordable way to produce good-quality printed color output.

Figure 4-51
Laser printers use a process similar to a copying machine. Data from the computer, such as the word DATA (1), is converted into a laser beam (2) that is directed by a mirror (3) to a photosensitive drum (4). The areas on the drum touched by the laser attract toner particles (5) that are transferred to the paper (6). The toner is fused to the paper with heat and pressure (7).

Laser printers are rated by their speed and resolution. Speed is measured in **pages per minute (ppm)**. Laser printers used with individual personal computers range from four to twelve pages per minute and start at less than $500. Laser printers supporting multiple users on a network or larger computer range from 16 to 50 pages per minute and cost from $10,000 to $100,000. High-speed laser printers costing as much as several hundred thousand dollars can produce output at the rate of several hundred pages per minute (Figure 4-53). Laser printer resolution is measured by the number of **dots per inch (dpi)** that can be printed. The more dots, the sharper the image. The resolution of laser printers ranges from 240 to 1,200 dpi with most printers currently offering 300 to 600 dpi. Laser printers usually use individual sheets of paper stored in a removable tray that slides into the printer case. Some laser printers have trays that can accommodate different sizes of paper while others require separate trays for letter and legal paper. Most laser printers have a manual feed slot where individual sheets and envelopes can be inserted. Transparencies also can be printed on laser printers.

Figure 4-52
Laser printers can produce high-quality text or graphics output.

Figure 4-53
High-speed laser printers can operate at speeds higher than 200 pages per minute. These printing systems can cost more than $200,000.

Thermal Printers Thermal printers, sometimes called **thermal transfer printers**, use heat to transfer colored inks from ink sheets onto the printing surface (Figure 4-54). Thermal printers can work with plain paper but produce the best results when higher quality smooth paper or plastic transparencies are used. A special type of thermal printer, using a method called **dye diffusion**, uses chemically treated paper to obtain color print quality equal to glossy magazine pages. Dye diffusion actually varies the color intensity of each dot placed on the page. Most color printers merely alter the pattern of cyan (blue/green), magenta (red/purple), yellow, and black dots to create the illusion of different colors. Thermal printers produce output at the rate of one to two pages per minute.

Figure 4-54
Thermal transfer printers are used to produce high-quality color output.

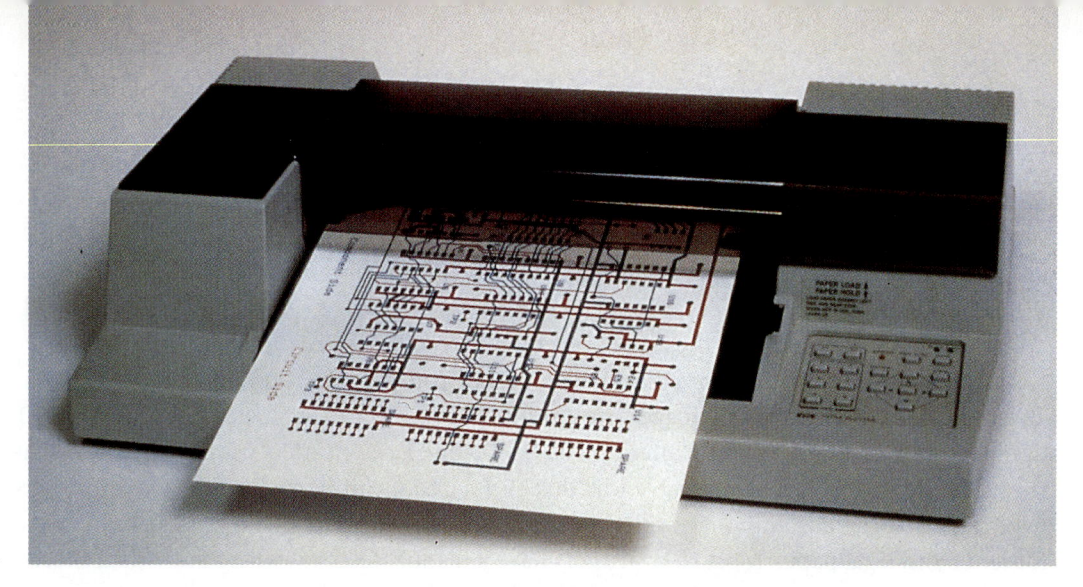

Figure 4-55
Color flatbed plotter.

Plotters

A **plotter** is an output device used to produce high-quality line drawings such as building plans, charts, or circuit diagrams. These drawings can be quite large; some plotters are designed to handle paper up to 40 inches by 48 inches, much larger than would fit in a standard printer. Plotters can be classified by the way they create the drawing. The two types are pen plotters and electrostatic plotters.

As the name implies, **pen plotters** create images on a sheet of paper by moving one or more pens over the surface of the paper or by moving the paper under the tip of the pens.

Two different kinds of pen plotters are flatbed plotters and drum plotters. When a **flatbed plotter** is used to plot, or draw, the pen or pens are instructed by the software to move to the down position so the pen contacts the flat surface of the paper. Further instructions then direct the movement of the pens to create the image. Most flatbed plotters have one or more pens of varying colors or widths. The plotter shown in Figure 4-55 is a flatbed plotter that can create color drawings.

A **drum plotter** uses a rotating drum, or cylinder, over which drawing pens are mounted. The pens can move to the left and right as the drum rotates, creating an image (Figure 4-56). An advantage of the drum plotter is that the length of the plot is virtually unlimited, because roll paper can be used. The width of the plot is limited by the width of the drum.

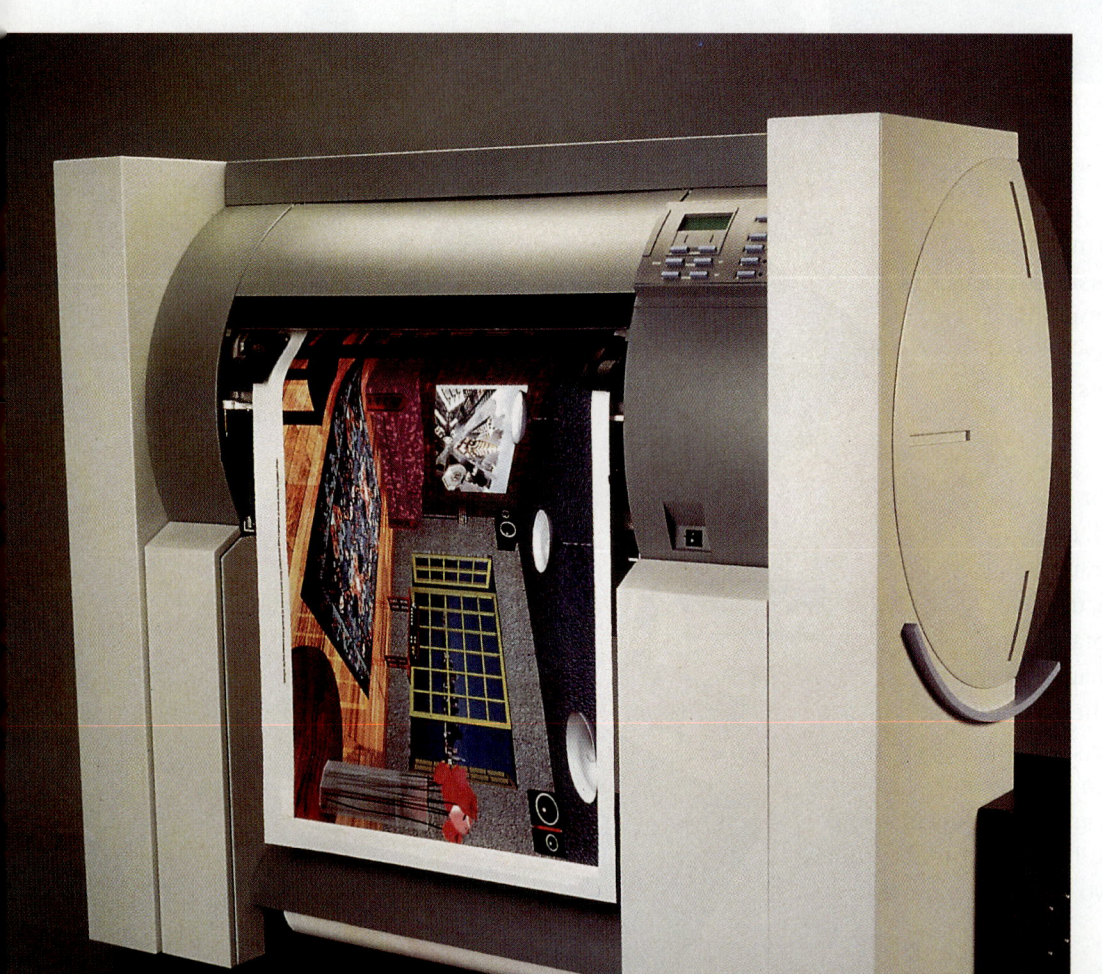

Figure 4-56
A drum plotter can handle larger paper sizes than a flatbed plotter.

With an **electrostatic plotter**, the paper moves under a row of wires (called styli) that can be turned on to create an electrostatic charge on the paper. The paper then passes through a developer and the drawing emerges where the charged wires touched the paper. The electrostatic printer image is composed of a series of very small dots, resulting in relatively high-quality output. In addition, the speed of electrostatic plotting is faster than with pen plotters.

Special-Purpose Printers

In addition to the printers just discussed, a number of other printers have been developed for special purposes. These include single label printers, bar code label printers, and portable printers. Figure 4-57 shows examples of these printers.

Figure 4-57
Other types of printers, from left to right, include a bar code label printer, a single label printer, and a printer designed for use with portable computers.

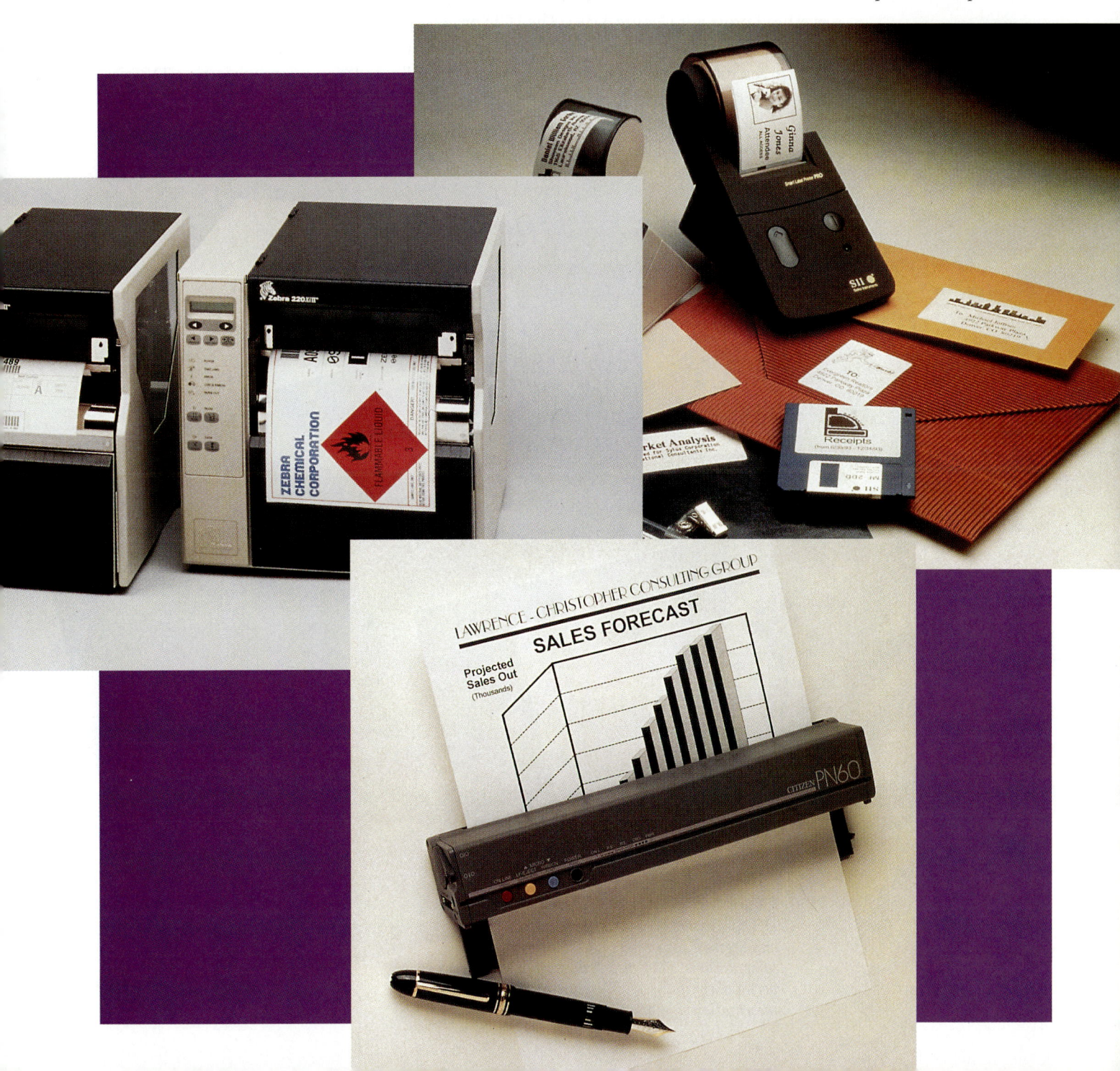

Other Output Devices

Although display devices and printers provide the majority of computer output, other devices are available for particular uses and applications. These include data projectors and computer output microfilm devices.

Data Projectors

A variety of devices are available to take the image that displays on a computer screen and project it so it can be clearly seen by a room full of people. Smaller, lower cost units, called **LCD projection panels**, use liquid crystal display (LCD) technology and are designed to be placed on top of an overhead projector (Figure 4-58).

Self-contained **LCD projectors** have their own light source and do not require a separate overhead projector (Figure 4-59). The LCD projection panels and projectors are easily portable and can be located at different distances from the projection screen.

Larger, more expensive units use technology similar to large-screen projection TV sets; separate red, green, and blue beams of light are focused onto the screen. These units are designed for larger areas such as meeting rooms or auditoriums. The three-beam projectors must be focused and aligned for a specific distance and thus once installed, usually are not moved.

Figure 4-58
Projection panels are used together with overhead projectors to display computer screen images to a group of people.

Figure 4-59
LCD projectors are portable and are well suited for small room presentations. They attach directly to a personal computer and display the same information shown on the computer screen.

Figure 4-60
Microfiche often is used for reports that must be kept on file but do not have to be referred to frequently.

Computer Output Microfilm

Computer output microfilm (COM) is an output technique that records output from a computer as microscopic images on roll or sheet film. The images stored on COM are the same as the images that would be printed on paper. The COM recording process reduces characters 24, 42, or 48 times smaller than would be produced on a printer. The information then is recorded on **microfiche** sheet film or on 16mm, 35mm, or 105mm roll film (Figure 4-60).

Microfilm has several advantages over printed reports or other storage media for certain applications. Some of these advantages are:

1. Data can be recorded on the film faster than printers; up to 30,000 lines per minute.

2. Costs for recording the data are lower. Studies have shown that microfilm can be as little as one-tenth the cost of printing a report.

3. Less space is required to store microfilm than printed materials. Microfilm that weighs one ounce can store the equivalent of ten pounds of paper.

4. The cost to store a megabyte of information is less on microfilm than it is on disk.

To access data stored on microfilm, a variety of readers are available. They utilize indexing techniques to provide a quick reference to the data. Some microfilm readers can perform automatic data lookup, called **computer-assisted retrieval (CAR)**, under the control of an attached computer. With the indexing software and hardware available for microfilm, you usually can locate any piece of data in a database in less than ten seconds, at a far lower cost per inquiry than using an online inquiry system consisting of a computer system that stores the data on a hard disk.

Facsimile (Fax)

Facsimile, or **fax**, equipment is used to transmit and receive an image of a document over telephone lines. The document can contain text and graphics, can be hand-written, or be a photograph. Fax equipment is available as an external stand-alone machine (Figure 4-61) or as part of an internal data communications package, such as a modem and fax software, that can send and receive data and fax transmissions. Stand-alone fax machines optically scan a document and convert the image into digitized data that is transmitted. A fax machine at the receiving end converts the digitized data and prints a copy of the original image. Internal fax equipment can transmit computer prepared documents, such as a word processing letter, or documents that have been digitized with a scanner. Documents received by internal fax equipment can be displayed on a monitor or sent to the printer.

Multifunction Devices

A **multifunction device** (**MFD**) is a single piece of equipment that can print, scan, copy, and fax (Figure 4-62). The MFD offers two primary advantages: it requires less space and costs less money than separate units. In fact, the cost of an MFD often is less than the total of any two devices it is designed to replace. Personal units are available for around $1,000. Higher volume business models are available for between $2,000 and $3,000.

Figure 4-61
A facsimile (fax) machine can send and receive copies of documents to and from any location with phone service and another fax machine. Fax capabilities often are built into personal computer communications equipment.

Figure 4-62
A multifunction device is a single machine that has the capabilities of a printer, scanner, copier, and fax machine.

Many MFDs are based on a printer because it is the device that is used the most. Both laser and ink-jet technology are available. Print speeds are comparable to stand-alone printers. Perhaps the second most important feature is the copier capability. Older units sometimes offered what was described as *convenience copying*; 200 dot per inch (dpi) resolution that was barely adequate for text and inadequate for most graphics. Newer models offer 300 to 600 dpi resolution, comparable to good-quality, stand-alone copiers.

Scanner capability usually will mirror the capabilities of the copier. Both features use the same components to capture the document image. Scanner use has significantly increased in recent years because of desktop publishing applications and the improvement of OCR software for automatically entering scanned text. Some scanner manufacturers offer limited MFD capability by providing software that turns a scanner into a copier. A separate printer must be available to output the copied document. Fax features usually include the capability of faxing to or from a PC or directly to another fax machine. Speed dialing and the capability of sending a fax to a distribution list also are common features.

The one obvious risk of an MFD is that if the machine breaks down you lose all four functions. But given the space and cost advantages of MFDs, more and more users are willing to take the risk.

The output devices discussed in this chapter are summarized in Figure 4-63.

Summary of Input and Output

The input and output steps of the information processing cycle use a variety of devices to allow you to enter data and provide you with information. After reading this chapter, you should have a better overall understanding of computer input and output.

OUTPUT DEVICE	DESCRIPTION
Display Devices	
Monitor	Visual display like TV set
Flat panel display	Flat visual display used with portable computers
Printers - Impact	
Dot matrix	Prints text and graphics using small dots
Band	High-speed rotating band text-only printer
Printers - Nonimpact	
Ink jet	Sprays tiny drops of ink onto page to form text and graphics; prints quietly; inexpensive color printer
Laser	Works like a copying machine; produces very high quality text and graphics
Thermal	Uses heat to produce high-quality color output
Plotter	Designed for line drawing; often used for computer-aided design; some units can handle large paper sizes.
Data Projectors	Projects display screen image to a group
COM	Stores reduced-size image on sheet or roll film
Facsimile (fax)	Transmits and receives text and image documents over telephone lines
Multifunction Devices	Combines printer, fax, scanner, and copier

Figure 4-63
Summary of the more common output devices.

COMPUTERS AT WORK

Helping People with Special Needs

For physically challenged and disabled individuals, working with standard computers either may be difficult or impossible. Fortunately, special software and hardware, called adaptive or assistive technology, enables many of these individuals to use computers productively and independently.

Adaptive technology covers a wide range of hardware and software products that help the user make the computer meet their special needs. For people with motor disabilities who cannot use a standard keyboard, a number of alternative input devices are available. Most of these devices involve the use of a switch that is controlled by any reliable muscle. One type of switch even can be activated by breathing into a tube. The switches are used with special software to select commands or input characters. For those who are unable to use their muscles to activate switches, a system exists that is controlled by eye movement. Called Eyegaze, the system uses a camera mounted on the computer and directed at one of the user's eyes. Using the movement of the user's eye, software determines where on the screen the user is looking to within 1/4-inch accuracy. To activate a choice on the screen, the user has to stare at it for approximately 1/4 of a second.

For blind individuals, voice recognition programs allow for verbal input. Software also is available that can convert text to Braille and send it to Braille printers. Both blind and non-verbal individuals use speech synthesis equipment to convert text documents into spoken words. For people with limited vision, several programs are available that magnify information on the screen.

The use of adaptive technology received further encouragement when the Americans with Disabilities Act (ADA) was enacted. Since 1994, the ADA requires that all companies with 15 or more employees make reasonable attempts to accommodate the needs of workers with physical challenges. Many employers are complying with the legislation by incorporating the use of personal computers and adaptive technology software and equipment.

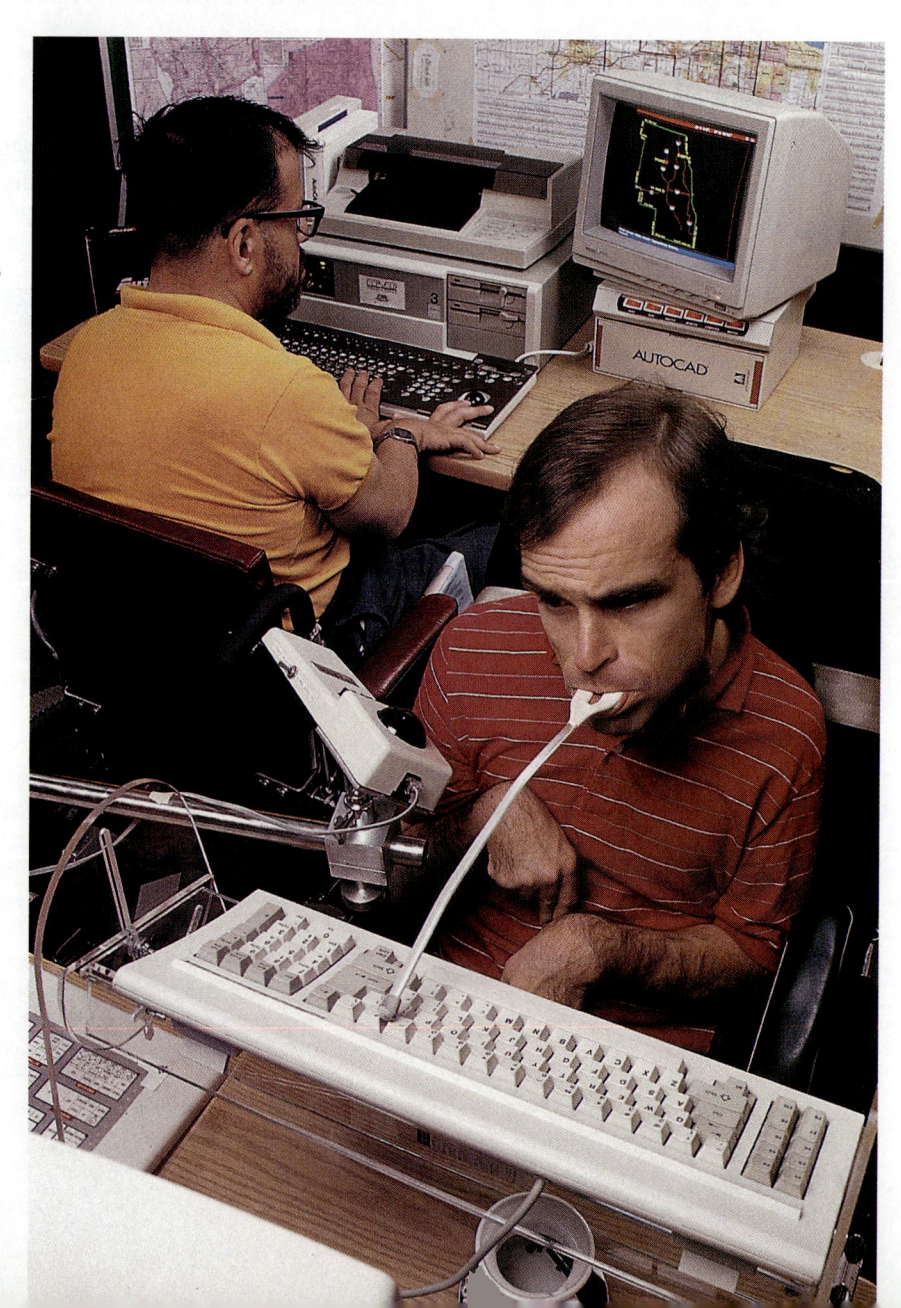

Figure 4-64

IN THE FUTURE

The Widespread Use of Voice Input

Although speech recognition programs have improved significantly in recent years, voice input still is used in only a limited number of applications, such as helping people with disabilities. These existing systems use discrete word recognition that requires the user to pause between each word. Discrete speech works well for commands that use one or two words, such as *print or shut down*, but it is unnatural and tiring to use for dictation. Most experts agree that for voice input to be used widely, continuous speech recognition systems that accept natural (conversational) speech will have to be developed. To provide continuous speech recognition, however, computers with more power are required. In addition, voice recognition software will have to be significantly improved.

To understand human speech, a computer has to go through four steps; sound analysis, word recognition, sentence or thought construction, and statement context. Sound analysis is the easiest part. Sound waves are converted into the smallest units of speech called phonemes. During word recognition, the phonemes are joined together to form words. This can be a difficult task because conversational speech often runs one word into another. The problem becomes more difficult during sentence and thought construction. During this process, the identified words are joined together to make a logical statement. As your high school English teacher may have told you, people do not always speak or write in a logical manner using correct grammar. Statement context involves using past statements to provide information about a current statement. For example, say the computer reservation agent just had told you that no flights were available on the day you wanted to leave, June 20. If you said, How about the next day?, the computer should know that you now want to check the flights on June 21.

Some experts think that significant breakthroughs in natural speech recognition are just a few years away and that affordable systems will be available by the year 2000. The optimists, however, already are talking about the next human interface challenge: how to read lips!

Figure 4-65

4 review

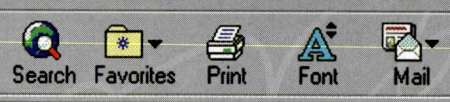

chapter 1 | 2 | 3 | 4 | 5 | 6 | 7 | 8 | 9 | 10 | 11 | 12 | 13 | 14 | I

inCyber | review | terms | yourTurn | hotTopics | outThere | winLabs | webWalk | exercises | news | home

INSTRUCTIONS: *To display this page from the Web, launch your browser and enter the URL, http://www.scsite.com/dc/ch4/review.htm. Click the links for current and additional information.*

1 Types of Input

Input refers to the process of entering data, programs, commands, and user responses into memory. **Data** refers to the raw facts that a computer receives and processes to produce information. **Programs** are instructions that direct the computer to perform the necessary operations to process the data. **Commands** are key words and phrases that direct the computer to perform certain activities. **User response** refers to the data a user enters to respond to a question or message.

2 Keyboards

The **keyboard** is the most commonly used input device. Users enter data by pressing keys. Alphabetic keys are arranged like those on a typewriter. Most keyboards also have a **numeric keypad**. Other keys include **arrow keys** or **cursor control keys**, which are used to move the cursor, and **function keys**, which can be programmed to accomplish certain tasks.

3 The Mouse

Pointing devices control the movement of an on-screen symbol called the **mouse pointer**, or **pointer**. A **mouse** is a palm-sized pointing device. A mechanism, usually a ball, on the bottom of the mouse senses its movement. Electronic circuits translate the mouse's movement into signals that are sent to the computer and used to direct the pointer. Various actions can be performed by moving the pointer and then pressing one of the buttons on top of the mouse.

4 Trackballs, Touchpads, Pointing Sticks, and Joysticks

A **trackball** is a pointing device like a mouse only with the ball on top. A **touchpad** is a flat surface that controls the movement of the pointer by sensing the motion of a finger on its exterior. A **pointing stick** is a device shaped like a pencil eraser that moves the pointer as pressure is applied. A **joystick** uses the movement of a vertical stem to direct the pointer.

5 Other Pointing Devices

Pen input devices can input data with hand written characters, select items by pressing the pen against the screen, and use gestures, which are special symbols, to issue commands. A **touch screen** allows users to touch areas of the screen to enter data. A **light pen** can be used to select processing options or to draw on the screen. A **digitizer** converts shapes from a drawing or photograph to digital impulses and transmits them to a computer. A **graphics tablet** is similar to a digitizer, but it also contains unique characters and commands.

6 Source Data Automation

Source data automation refers to procedures and equipment designed to make the input process more efficient by eliminating the manual entry of data, instead taking data directly from its original form. An **image scanner** electronically captures an entire page and converts the document into digital data that can be processed by a computer. **Optical recognition** devices use a light source to read optical codes, marks on forms, and characters from ordinary documents and convert them into digital data. **Magnetic ink character recognition (MICR)** uses a special ink that can be magnetized during processing. **Data collection devices** are designed and used for obtaining data at the site where the transaction or event being reported takes place.

7 Terminals

Terminals consist of a keyboard and a screen. **Dumb terminals** can be used to transmit data to or receive data from a connected computer, but have no independent processing capability. **Intelligent terminals** have built-in processing capabilities. **Special-purpose terminals** perform specific jobs and contain features uniquely designed for use in a particular industry.

8 Other Input Devices

Special input devices are required to convert sound and image data into digital form. For personal computers, these devices consist primarily of electronics contained on a **sound card** or a **video card**. Sounds usually are recorded with a microphone or by directly connecting a sound device. **Voice input** allows data and commands to be entered with spoken words. Digital cameras record photographs in the form of digital data. Video material is input using a video camera or a video recorder. An **electronic whiteboard** is a modified whiteboard that captures text and drawings in a file on an attached computer.

9 Types of Output

Output is data that has been processed into a useful form called information. A **report** presents information in an organized form. Reports can be classified by who uses them (**internal reports** or **external reports**), by the way they present information (**narrative reports, detail reports, summary reports,** or **exception reports**), or by how often they are produced (**periodic reports** or **ad hoc reports**). **Computer graphics** are any non-text pictorial information. **Audio output** consists of sounds, including words and music, produced by the computer. **Video output** consists of visual images that have been captured with an input device, digitized, and directed to an output device.

10 Display Devices

A **display device** is the visual output device of a computer. A **monitor** is a display device that looks like a television and consists of a display surface, called a **screen**, a plastic or metal case to house a **cathode ray tube (CRT)**, and the electrical components. A **flat panel display** is a thin display screen, most often used in portable computers, that does not employ CRT technology.

11 How Images are Displayed

When a color monitor produces an image, the image is sent electronically from the CPU to the video circuits and then to the cathode ray tube. Electron guns generate electron beams towards the colored phosphor dots that coat the screen. The beams pass through a shadow mask that helps align them so they hit the right dot. When struck by the electron beam, the phosphor dots glow. The yoke, an electromagnetic field, moves the beams across and down the screen, and the illuminated phosphors create the image.

12 Printers

Generally, printers can be classified in two groups. **Impact printers** transfer an image by some type of printing mechanism striking the paper, ribbon, and character together. Dot matrix printers and band printers are two types of impact printers. Nonimpact printers print without having a mechanism striking against a sheet of paper. Ink jet printers, page printers, and thermal printers are types of nonimpact printers.

13 Other Types of Output Devices

Plotters are used to produce high-quality line drawings. **LCD projection panels** and **LCD projectors** take the image that appears on a computer screen and project it. **Computer output microfilm (COM)** records output as microscopic images on roll or sheet film. **Facsimile (FAX)** equipment transmits and receives an image of a document over telephone lines. A **multifunctional device (MFD)** is a single piece of equipment that can print, scan, copy, and fax.

chapter 4 terms

1 | 2 | 3 | 4 | 5 | 6 | 7 | 8 | 9 | 10 | 11 | 12 | 13 | 14 | I

inCyber | review | terms | yourTurn | hotTopics | outThere | winLabs | webWalk | exercises | news | home

INSTRUCTIONS: *To display this page from the Web, launch your browser and enter the URL, http://www.scsite.com/dc/ch4/terms.htm. Scroll through the list of terms. Click a term for its definition and a picture. Click the rocket ship for current and additional information about the term.*

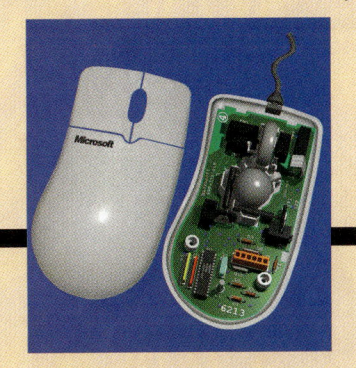

mouse

DEFINITION

mouse
A small, palm-sized input device that you move across a flat surface, such as a desktop, to control the movement of the pointer on the screen **(4.5)**

---

active matrix (4.29)
arrow control keys (4.3)
arrow keys (4.3)
audio output (4.25)

band printer (4.34)
bar code (4.14)
biological feedback input (4.21)

cathode ray tube (CRT) (4.27)
characters per second (cps) (4.33)
clicking (4.5)
color monitor (4.28)
commands (4.2)
computer-assisted retrieval (CAR) (4.41)
computer drawing programs (4.25)
computer graphics (4.25)
computer output microfilm (COM) (4.41)
computer paint programs (4.25)
continuous-speech recognition (4.20)
continuous-form paper (4.32)
CRT (cathode ray tube) (4.27)
cursor (4.3)

data (4.2)
data collection devices (4.17)
detail report (4.23)
digital cameras (4.21)
digitizer (4.10)
discrete-speech recognition (4.20)
display terminals (4.18)
dot matrix printer (4.32)
dots per inch (dpi) (4.37)
double-clicking (4.5)
dragging (4.5)
drum plotter (4.38)
dual scan (4.29)
dumb terminal (4.18)
dye diffusion (4.37)

electronic whiteboard (4.22)
electrostatic plotter (4.39)
exception report (4.24)
external report (4.23)

facsimile (4.42)
fax (4.42)
flat panel display (4.29)
flatbed plotter (4.38)
function keys (4.4)

gas plasma (4.29)
gestures (4.8)
graphics tablet (4.11)

hard copy (4.23)
high-definition television (HDTV) (4.26)

image processing systems (4.13)
image scanner (4.13)
impact printers (4.32)
ink (4.8)
ink-jet printer (4.34)
input (4.2)
insertion point (4.3)
intelligent terminal (4.18)
interlaced monitors (4.31)
internal report (4.23)

joystick (4.7)

keyboard (4.2)

laser printer (4.36)
LCD projection panels (4.40)
LCD projectors (4.40)
light pen (4.10)
lines per minute (lpm) (4.33)
liquid crystal display (LCD) (4.29)

magnetic ink character recognition (MICR) (4.17)
microfiche (4.41)
monitor (4.27)
monochrome monitor (4.28)
mouse (4.5)
mouse pad (4.5)
mouse pointer (4.5)
multifunction device (MFD) (4.42)
multiscanning monitors (4.30)
multisync monitors (4.30)

narrative report (4.23)
nonimpact printing (4.34)
noninterlaced monitors (4.31)
numeric keypad (4.3)

OCR software (4.16)
on-demand report (4.24)
optical character recognition (OCR) (4.15)
optical codes (4.14)
optical mark recognition (OMR) (4.15)
optical recognition (4.14)
output (4.23)

page scanner (4.13)
pages per minute (ppm) (4.37)
passive matrix (4.29)
pen input (4.8)
pen plotter (4.38)
periodic report (4.24)
picture element (4.30)
pixel (4.30)
plotter (4.38)
pointer (4.5)
pointing stick (4.7)
point-of-sale (POS) terminal (4.18)
programmable terminal (4.18)
programs (4.2)

refresh rate (4.31)
report (4.23)
resolution (4.30)

scheduled report (4.24)
screen (4.27)
smart terminal (4.18)
soft copy (4.23)
sound card (4.19)
source data automation (4.12)
source data collection (4.12)
source document (4.12)
special-purpose terminal (4.18)
summary report (4.24)
SVGA (4.30)

terminals (4.18)
thermal printer (4.37)
thermal transfer printer (4.37)
toggle key (4.3)
touch screen (4.9)
touchpad (4.6)
trackball (4.6)
trackpad (4.6)
trackpoint (4.7)
turn-around documents (4.16)

universal product code (UPC) (4.14)
user responses (4.2)

VGA (video graphics array) (4.30)
video card (4.19)
video display terminals (VDTs) (4.18)
video input (4.22)
video output (4.26)
voice input (4.19)
voice output (4.26)
voice synthesis (4.26)
voice templates (4.20)

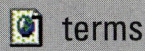

4 yourTurn

chapter 1 | 2 | 3 | 4 | 5 | 6 | 7 | 8 | 9 | 10 | 11 | 12 | 13 | 14 | I

inCyber | review | terms | yourTurn | hotTopics | outThere | winLabs | webWalk | exercises | news | home

INSTRUCTIONS: To display this page from the Web, launch your browser and enter the URL, http://www.scsite.com/dc/ch4/turn.htm. Click a blank line for the answer. Click the links for current and additional information.

Label the Figure

1. _____
2. _____
3. _____
4. _____
5. _____
6. _____
7. _____
8. _____

Instructions: Identify the components that produce an image.

Fill in the Blanks

Instructions: Complete each sentence with the correct term or terms.

1. Input refers to the process of entering _____, _____, _____, and _____ into memory.
2. The mouse, trackball, and touchpad are used to control an on-screen symbol called the _____ that usually is represented by a block arrow marker.
3. _____ is data that has been processed into useful information that can be used by a person or a machine.
4. _____ LCD screens, which use individual transistors to control each crystal cell, display sharper pictures than _____ LCD screens, which use one transistor for each row and column.
5. A(n) _____ is an output device that produces high-quality drawings such as maps, charts, or circuit diagrams.

Short Answer

Instructions: Write a brief answer to each of the following questions.

1. How is a computer keyboard like a typewriter? What keys can be found on most keyboards but not on traditional typewriters? What is the purpose of these keys? _____
2. What is source data automation? What is some of the equipment used for source data automation? For what purpose are optical codes, OMR devices, OCR devices, and OCR software used? _____
3. What is a report? What are three ways that reports can be classified? How are the types of reports within each classification different? _____
4. How are impact printers different from nonimpact printers? What are examples of each type of printer? How is the speed of each type of printer rated? _____
5. What are pixels? When purchasing a monitor, why are the number of pixels and the dot pitch important? _____

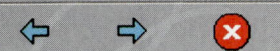

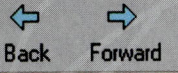

hotTopics chapter 4

1 | 2 | 3 | 4 | 5 | 6 | 7 | 8 | 9 | 10 | 11 | 12 | 13 | 14 | I

inCyber | review | terms | yourTurn | hotTopics | outThere | winLabs | webWalk | exercises | news | home

INSTRUCTIONS: *To display this page from the Web, launch your browser and enter the URL, http://www.scsite.com/dc/ch4/hot.htm. Click the links for current and additional information to help you respond to the hotTopics questions.*

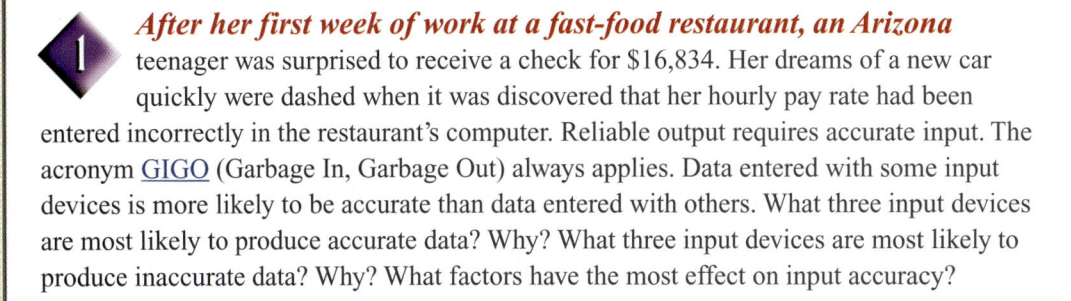

1. *After her first week of work at a fast-food restaurant, an Arizona* teenager was surprised to receive a check for $16,834. Her dreams of a new car quickly were dashed when it was discovered that her hourly pay rate had been entered incorrectly in the restaurant's computer. Reliable output requires accurate input. The acronym GIGO (Garbage In, Garbage Out) always applies. Data entered with some input devices is more likely to be accurate than data entered with others. What three input devices are most likely to produce accurate data? Why? What three input devices are most likely to produce inaccurate data? Why? What factors have the most effect on input accuracy?

2. *When Christopher Sholes invented the first practical commercial* typewriter in 1867, he purposely designed the keyboard to slow typists down and thus prevent keys from jamming. Having keys jam is no longer a problem, but more than a hundred years later, Sholes's sequence of letters, often called the QWERTY layout, continues to be used on most keyboards. Other arrangements have proved to be more effective. Trained typists using the Dvorak layout, which places the more used letters in the home row, can type up to three hundred percent faster than those using the QWERTY sequence. Why have these keyboards been slow to catch on? Will an arrangement other than the QWERTY layout ever become popular? Why?

3. *Almost everyone knows people who feel intimidated when forced to enter data into a computer.* Some input devices make it easy for even a novice to enter data, while others require instruction to be used efficiently. Which input device would be the easiest to use for someone who is uncomfortable with computers? Why? Which device requires the most training? Which input device would be the most important to learn how to use? Why? Which input device will be most commonplace fifty years from now? Will any device become an historical oddity, seen only in museums? Why?

4. *About 80 percent of today's movies are edited with a computer. Using video input devices,* directors can store more than a hundred miles of film on a hard drive. The click of a mouse then can access any scene, compare multiple versions, and seamlessly join the best shots. When the output is released, a scene might have a different background, or a group of a hundred may have been expanded into a crowd of thousands. Some directors, however, insist that the ease with which episodes can be cut and spliced has resulted in frenzied films that race too quickly from scene to scene. Perhaps worse, film editing, once a collaborative process, is now more of an individual effort. In general, do you think computers will have a positive or negative effect on movie making? Why? How else might the use of computers impact film making? What can be done to address the concerns of directors?

5. *When computers first were used in business, people predicted the "paperless office," where* nearly all documents would exist only electronically. Yet, much to the dismay of environmentalists, studies show that many of today's offices use more paper than in the past. Why, when it comes to paper, do you think computerized offices are often guilty of over-consumption? What impact might the World Wide Web have on paper use? What can be done to decrease the amount of paper used?

… 4.52 outThere

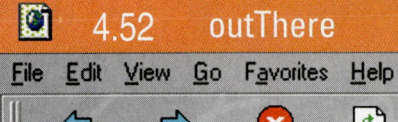

4 outThere

chapter 1 | 2 | 3 | 4 | 5 | 6 | 7 | 8 | 9 | 10 | 11 | 12 | 13 | 14 | I

inCyber | review | terms | yourTurn | hotTopics | outThere | winLabs | webWalk | exercises | news | home

DISCOVERING COMPUTERS

INSTRUCTIONS: *To display this page from the Web, launch your browser and enter the URL,* http://www.scsite.com/dc/ch4/out.htm. *Click the links for current and additional information.*

1 *Manufacturers of notebook computers work hard to reduce the size of their* machines. One problem they face is that, because of the size of the human hand, keyboard keys cannot be made much smaller or placed much closer together and still be practical. Therefore, many manufacturers reduce the number of keys. Most desktop computer keyboards have 101 or more keys, but notebook computers often use fewer keys by making some perform multiple functions. Visit a computer vendor and compare the keyboards of desktop computers to the keyboards of notebook computers. How many keys are on each keyboard? What keys are on the desktop computer keyboard that are not on the other keyboards? How do the notebook computer keyboards handle the functions of these keys? Try each keyboard. Is one keyboard easier to use, or more comfortable, than the other? Why?

2 *The computer mouse comes in a wide range of shapes with a variety of capabilities.* Among the types of mouse units are the cordless mouse, ergonomic mouse, whimsically designed mouse, ring mouse (worn on the finger like a ring), and even a tough mouse that can be dropped from a five-story building, plunged under water, or run over by a truck without damage. Visit several Web sites to find out more about the different types of mouse units. Which mouse do you think is the most unusual? Why? Which mouse has the most capabilities? Which mouse is least expensive? Which is most expensive? How is the difference in price justified? Which mouse would you like most to own? Why?

3 *Optical codes are used by retail stores, supermarkets, and libraries. Some people* mistakenly believe that the optical code contains the name of a product or its price, but optical codes are only a link to a database in which this information is stored. Visit an organization that utilizes optical codes to find out how the codes are used. How are the codes read? How can the optical code data be input if the reader fails? What information is obtained when the optical code is scanned? How is the information used? In what way does the information benefit the organization or its clientele? What are the advantages of using optical codes? The disadvantages?

4 *Recently, a monitor was developed with an extremely dense display screen—seven million pixels.* Of course, this achievement is important only if you understand pixels and how their density is related to picture quality. To purchase the best monitor for your needs, it is important to be familiar with a number of terms and to recognize the significance of each. Visit several Web sites to learn more about things to consider when buying a monitor. What is the best screen size? How are screen size and resolution related? What are focus and convergence? What issues are involved in monitor safety? When you have finished reviewing monitor characteristics, make a list of the five most important factors when purchasing a monitor.

5 *While printers produce an image on a page from top to bottom, plotters can draw on any part of* a page at random, and then move to any other part. This capability makes plotters particularly valuable to people who produce maps or blueprints. Arrange to interview someone in an organization that uses plotters. What kind of plotter does the organization use? Why? For what purpose is the plotter used? What is the advantage (or disadvantage) of using a plotter compared to creating a drawing by hand? If possible, ask to see a demonstration of the plotter or an example of its work. What size paper is used? How long does it take to produce an image? How clear is the final drawing?

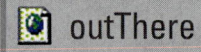

Start | outThere | 4:06 AM

winLabs

INSTRUCTIONS: *To display this page from the Web, launch your browser and enter the URL, http://www.scsite.com/dc/ch4/labs.htm. Click the links for current and additional information.*

1 Shelly Cashman Series Input Lab

Follow the instructions in winLabs 1 on page 1.34 to display the Shelly Cashman Series Labs screen. Click Scanning Documents. Click the Start Lab button. When the screen displays, read the objectives. With your printer turned on, click the Print Questions button. Fill out the top of the Questions sheet and then answer the questions.

2 Shelly Cashman Series Printer Lab

Follow the instructions in winLabs 1 on page 1.34 to display the Shelly Cashman Series Labs screen. Click Setting Up to Print. Click the Start Lab button. When the screen displays, read the objectives. With your printer turned on, click the Print Questions button. Fill out the top of the Questions sheet and then answer the questions.

3 Shelly Cashman Series Monitor Lab

Follow the instructions in winLabs 1 on page 1.34 to display the Shelly Cashman Series Labs screen. Click Configuring Your Display. Click the Start Lab button. When the screen displays, read the objectives. With your printer turned on, click the Print Questions button. Fill out the top of the Questions sheet and answer the questions.

4 Using the Mouse and Keyboard to Interact with an Online Program

Insert your Student Floppy Disk or see your instructor for the location of the Loan Payment Calculator program. Click the Start button on the taskbar, and then click Run on the Start menu to display the Run dialog box. In the Open text box, type the path and filename of the program. For example, type a:loancalc.exe and then press the ENTER key to display the Loan Payment Calculator window. Type 12500 in the LOAN AMOUNT text box. Click the YEARS right scroll arrow or drag the scroll box until YEARS equals 15. Click the APR right scroll arrow or drag the scroll box until APR equals 8.5. Click the Calculate button. Write down the monthly payment and sum of payments (Figure 4-66). Click the Clear button. What are the monthly payment and sum of payments for each of these loan amounts, years, and APRs? (1) 28000, 5, 7.25; (2) 98750, 30, 9; (3) 6000, 3, 8.75; and (4) 62500, 15, 9.25. Close Loan Payment Calculator.

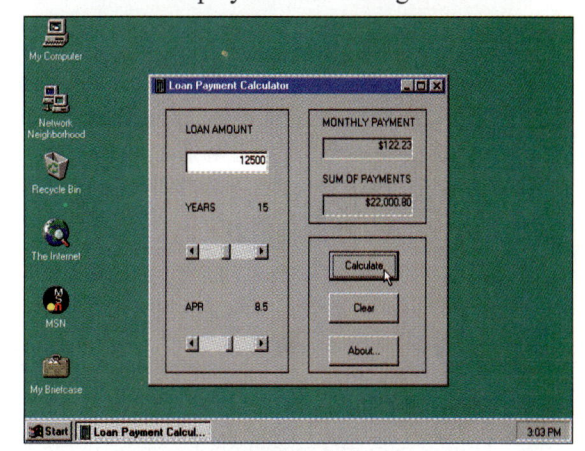

Figure 4-66

5 About Your Computer

Right-click the My Computer icon on the desktop. Click Properties on the shortcut menu. When the System Properties dialog box displays, click the Device Manager tab. Click View devices by type. Click the Print button. Click System summary in the Print dialog box and then click the OK button. Click the Cancel button in the System Properties dialog box.

4 webWalk

chapter 1 | 2 | 3 | 4 | 5 | 6 | 7 | 8 | 9 | 10 | 11 | 12 | 13 | 14 | I

inCyber | review | terms | yourTurn | hotTopics | outThere | winLabs | webWalk | exercises | news | home

INSTRUCTIONS: *To display this page from the Web, launch your browser and enter the URL, http://www.scsite.com/dc/ch4/walk.htm. Click the exercise link to display the exercise.*

1 User Responses
User responses refer to the data that a user enters to respond to a question or message from software. Learn about user responses to an automobile purchasing service (Figure 4-67) by completing this exercise.

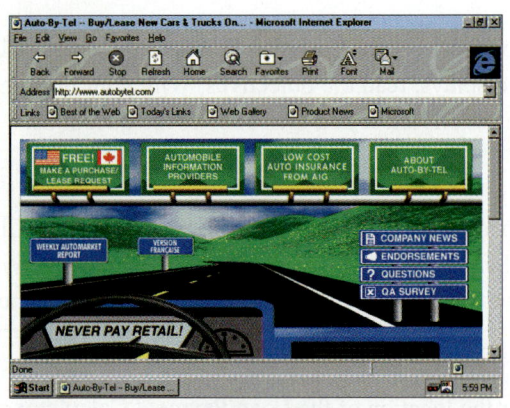

Figure 4-67

4 Output Devices
Output devices consist of hardware through which information can be communicated from the computer to the user. Complete this exercise to learn more about output devices.

5 Information Mining
Complete this exercise to improve your Web research skills by using a Web search engine to find information related to this chapter.

7 Digital Cameras
Digital cameras record photographs in the form of digital data. Complete this exercise to learn more about digital cameras and to see a "live" digital camera in action.

9 Web Chat
Complete this exercise to enter a Web Chat discussion related to the issues presented in the hotTopics exercise.

2 Input Devices
Input devices consist of hardware used to enter data, programs, commands, and user responses into computer memory. To learn about some unique input devices, complete this exercise.

3 Types of Output
The type of output generated from the computer depends on the needs of the user and the hardware and software that are used. To learn about the output of an interactive mapping service (Figure 4-68), complete this exercise.

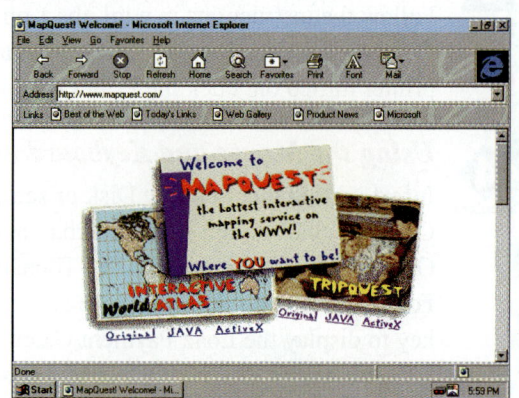

Figure 4-68

6 Displaying an Image
Each pixel on a color monitor screen is made up of three colored (red, green, blue) phosphor dots. These dots can be turned on in combinations to display a wide range of colors. Complete this exercise to learn more about RGB color values.

8 Computer Related Injuries
Keyboards are responsible for the vast majority of computer related injuries. Learn more about Carpal Tunnel Syndrome and other computer related injuries by completing this exercise.

Data Storage

OBJECTIVES

After completing this chapter, you will be able to:

- Define storage
- Identify the major storage devices
- Explain how data is stored on floppy disks and hard disks
- Explain how data compression works
- Explain how data is stored on optical disks such as CD-ROMs
- Explain how magnetic tape storage is used with computers
- Describe other forms of storage: PC Cards, RAID, and mass storage devices
- Describe how special-purpose storage devices such as smart cards are used

CHAPTER 5

Storage is the fourth and final operation in the information processing cycle. This chapter explains storage operations and the various types of storage devices that are used with computers. Combining what you learn about storage with your knowledge of input, processing, and output will allow you to complete your understanding of the information processing cycle.

What Is Storage?

It is important to understand the difference between how a computer uses memory and how it uses storage. As you have seen, memory, sometimes called RAM, temporarily stores data and programs that are being processed. **Storage**, also called **secondary storage** or **auxiliary storage**, stores data and programs when they are *not* being processed. Think of storage as a filing cabinet used to store files, and memory as your desk surface. When you need to work on a file, you take the file out of the filing cabinet (storage) and move it to your desk (memory). Although the term storage sometimes is used to refer to the temporary storage of data in memory, it commonly is used to refer to more permanent storage devices such as disk drives. Storage devices provide a more permanent form of storage than memory because they are **nonvolatile**, that is, data and programs held in storage are retained even when power is turned off. Most memory is **volatile**, which means that, when power is turned off, the data and programs stored in memory are erased.

The process of storing data is called **writing** or **recording data**, because the storage device records the data on the storage medium to save it for later use. The process of retrieving data is called **reading data**, because the storage device reads the data and transfers it to memory for processing.

Storage devices also can be used as both input and output devices. When a storage device transfers some of its stored data to the computer for processing, it is functioning as an input device. When a storage device receives information that has been processed by the computer, it is functioning as an output device.

Storage needs can vary greatly. Personal computer users might have a relatively small amount of data to be stored. For example, a database of names, addresses, and telephone numbers of two hundred customers of a small business might require only 100,000 bytes of storage (200 records x 500 characters per record). Users of large computers, such as banks or insurance companies, however, might need storage devices that can store trillions of bytes. In addition to data, software programs must be stored. Programs sometimes require tens to hundreds of megabytes of storage space. To meet the different needs of users, a variety of storage devices are available. Figure 5-1 shows how different types of storage devices and memory compare in terms of relative cost and speed. The storage devices named in the pyramid will be discussed in this chapter.

Figure 5-1
The pyramid chart compares the different types of computer storage and memory. Memory is faster than storage but is expensive and not practical to use for all storage requirements. Storage is less expensive per megabyte stored but is slower than memory. Many computer systems have two or more types of storage devices.

Pyramid levels (top to bottom):
- MEMORY (RAM)
- SOLID STATE
- HARD DISK
- OPTICAL DISK
- FLOPPY DISK
- TAPE
- MASS STORAGE

cost per megabyte: most expensive → least expensive
access speed: fastest → slowest

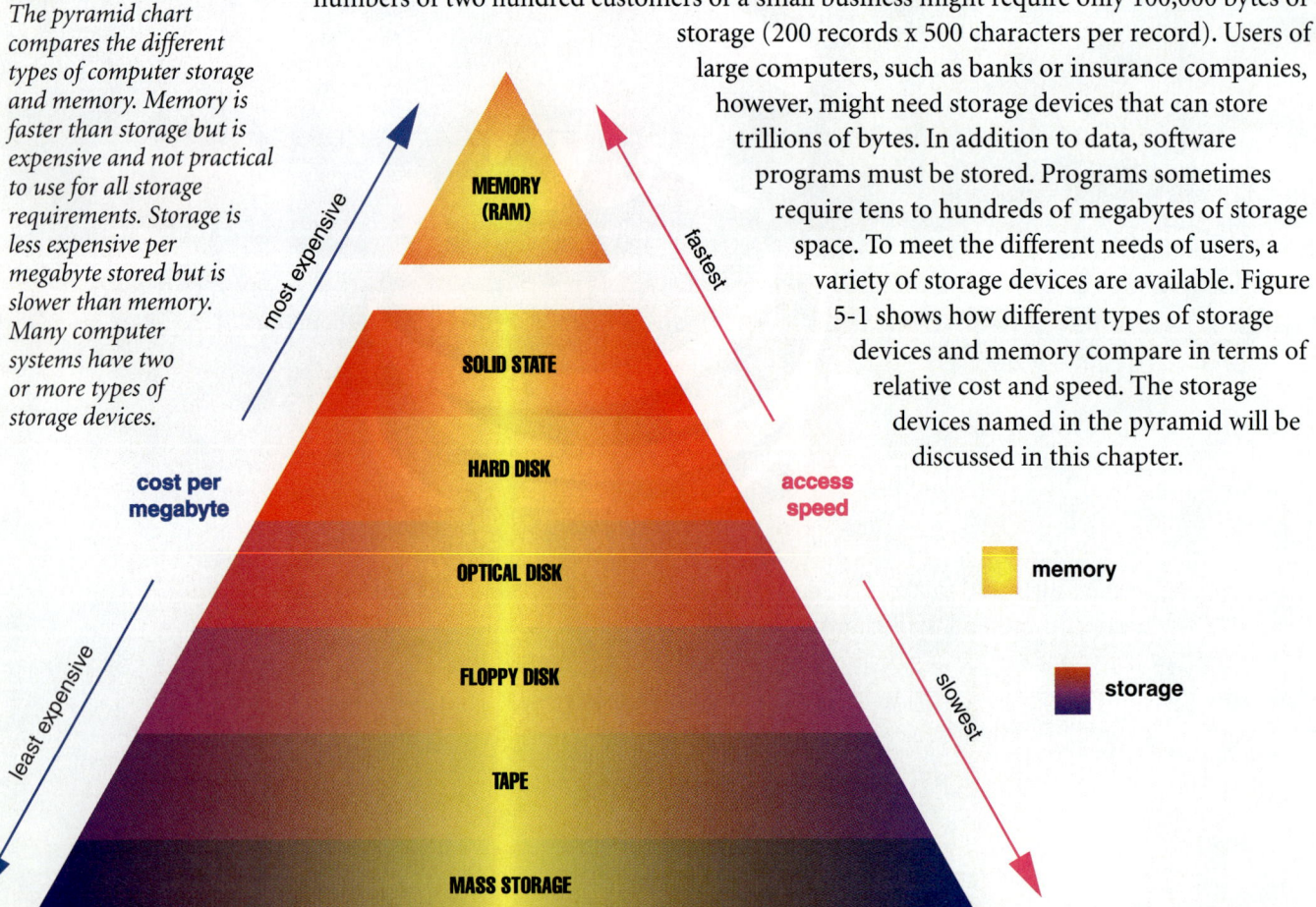

Legend: memory, storage

Magnetic Disk Storage

Magnetic disk is the most widely used storage medium for all types of computers. A **magnetic disk** consists of a round piece of plastic or metal, the surface of which is covered with a magnetic material. Data can be written to (recorded on) or read from the magnetic surface. Magnetic disk offers high storage capacity, reliability, and fast access to stored data. Types of magnetic disks include floppy disks, hard disks, and removable disk cartridges.

Floppy Disks

A **floppy disk**, also called a **diskette**, consists of a circular piece of thin mylar plastic (the actual disk), which is coated with an oxide material such as that used on audio and video recording tape. In the early 1970s, IBM introduced the floppy disk as a new type of storage. These early, eight-inch wide disks were called *floppies* because they were thin and flexible. The next generation of floppies looked much the same, but were only 5^1/$_4$ inches wide. Today, the most widely used floppy disk is 3^1/$_2$ inches wide (Figure 5-2). The flexible cover of the earlier disks has been replaced with a hard plastic outer covering. Although the 3^1/$_2$-inch disk is not very flexible, the term floppy disk still is used.

In a 3^1/$_2$-inch floppy disk, the circular piece of plastic used for recording is enclosed in a rigid plastic shell. Paper liners help keep the recording surfaces clean (Figure 5-3).

Figure 5-2
The 3^1/$_2$-inch floppy disk is the most widely used portable storage medium. A single floppy disk typically stores 1.44 MB of data.

Figure 5-3
In a 3^1/$_2$-inch floppy disk, the flexible plastic disk is enclosed between two liners that clean any microscopic debris from the disk surface and help to disperse static electricity. The outside cover is made of a rigid plastic material, and the recording window is covered by a metal shutter that slides to the side when the disk is inserted into the floppy disk drive.

inCyber

For details on floppy disks, visit the Discovering Computers Chapter 5 inCyber page (http://www.scsite.com/dc/ch5/incyber.htm) and click Floppy Disk.

A piece of metal called the shutter covers an opening in the rigid plastic shell. When the 3½-inch floppy disk is inserted into a floppy disk drive (Figure 5-4), the drive slides the shutter to the side to expose a portion of both sides of the recording surface.

Floppy disks are widely used with personal computers because they are convenient, portable, and inexpensive. Desktop PCs usually have permanently installed floppy disk drives. Portable computers often have removable floppy disk drives that can be replaced with other devices.

Figure 5-4
A user inserts a floppy disk into the floppy disk drive of a personal computer.

Formatting: Preparing a Floppy Disk for Use Before a floppy disk can be used for storage, it must be formatted. **Formatting** prepares the floppy disk for storage by defining the tracks, cylinders, and sectors on the recording surfaces of a floppy disk (Figure 5-5).

A **track** is a narrow recording band forming a full circle around the floppy disk. A **cylinder** is the set of tracks that occupy the same position on the top and the bottom of the disk and have the same number. Cylinder 3, for example, contains track 3 on side 1 of the floppy disk and track 3 on side 2 of the floppy disk. A **sector** is a pie-shaped section of the floppy disk. A **track sector** is a section of track within a sector. Each track sector holds 512 bytes. For reading and writing purposes, track sectors are grouped into clusters. A **cluster** consists of two to eight track sectors (the number varies depending on the operating system).

Figure 5-5
Each track on a floppy disk is a narrow, circular band separated from other tracks by a small gap. Floppy disks typically have eighty tracks with the track closest to the outside edge numbered 0. The tracks are divided into 18 sectors. Each sector of track holds 512 bytes of data. Two or more sectors form a cluster, the smallest amount of space used to record data.

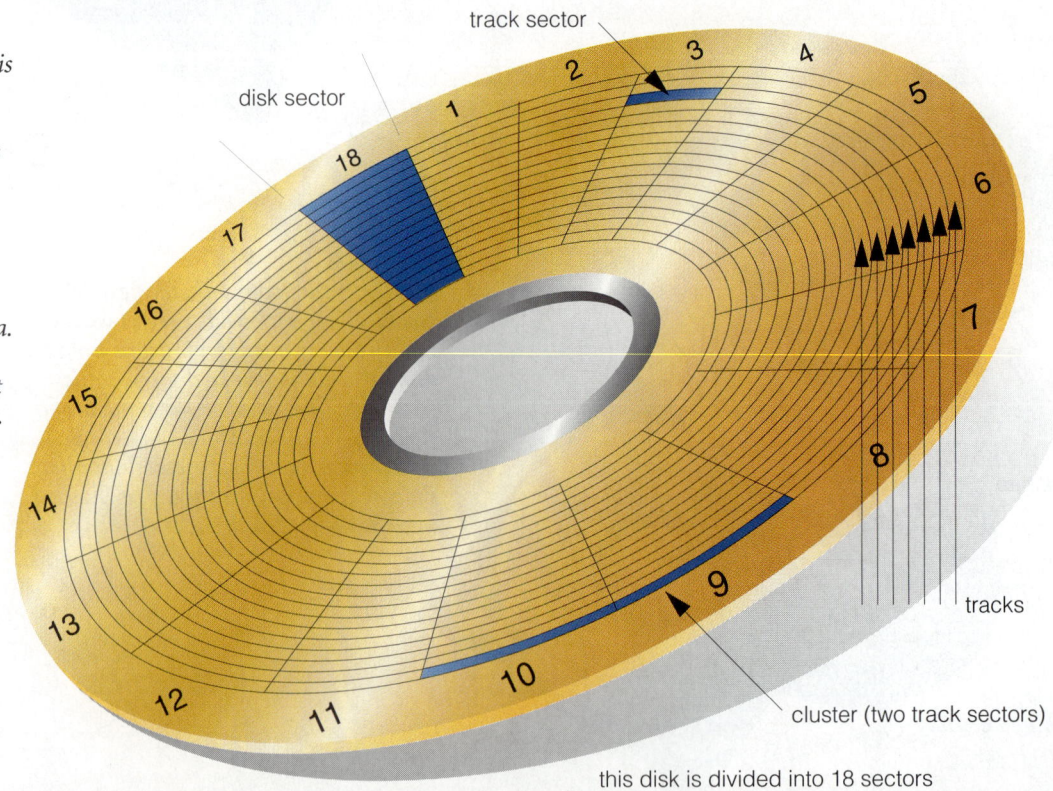

A cluster is the smallest unit of floppy disk space used to store data. Even if a file consisted of only a few bytes, one cluster would be used for storage. Although each cluster holds data from only one file, one file can be stored in many clusters.

The number of tracks and sectors created when a floppy disk is formatted varies according to the storage capacity of the floppy disk, the capabilities of the floppy disk drive used for formatting, and the specifications in the operating system software that does the formatting. An IBM-compatible system—one that is based on the design of the original IBM PC—usually formats 80 tracks and 18 sectors on each side of a 3^1/$_2$-inch floppy disk. Other computer systems, such as the Apple Macintosh, format disks differently than IBM-compatible systems.

The formatting process not only defines tracks on the recording surface, but also erases any data that is on the floppy disk, analyzes the recording surface for any defective spots, and establishes a directory that will be used to record information about files stored on the floppy disk. On most personal computers, this directory is called the file allocation table (FAT). For each file, the **file allocation table (FAT)** stores the file name, the file size, the time and date the file was last changed, and the cluster number where the file begins. On Windows 95 systems, the file allocation table is called the **virtual file allocation table (VFAT)**. When you ask a computer to list the files on a floppy disk, the information comes from the FAT file. FAT also keeps track of unused clusters and defective areas, if any, and is used when the computer writes new files to the floppy disk.

Figure 5-6
Data cannot be written on the 3^1/$_2$-inch floppy disk on the left, because the write-protect window in the corner of the floppy disk is open. A small piece of plastic covers the write-protect window of the 3^1/$_2$-inch floppy disk on the right, so data can be written on this floppy disk. The open hole at the opposite corner identifies this as a high-density disk.

open   closed

To protect data from being erased accidentally during formatting or other writing operations, floppy disks have a write-protect window. A **write-protect window** is a small hole in the corner of the floppy disk (Figure 5-6). A piece of plastic in the window can be moved to open or close the window. If the write-protect window is closed, the drive can write on the floppy disk. If the window is open, the drive cannot write on the floppy disk. The write-protect window works much like the recording tab on a video tape: if the recording tab is removed, a video cassette recorder (VCR) cannot record on the video tape. Another hole on the opposite side of the disk does not have the sliding plastic piece. This open hole identifies the disk as a high-density floppy disk.

Floppy Disk Storage Capacity The amount of data you can store on a floppy disk depends on two factors: (1) the recording density and (2) the number of tracks on the floppy disk.

The **recording density** is the number of bits that can be recorded on one inch of track on the floppy disk. This measurement is referred to as **bits per inch** (**bpi**). The higher the recording density, the higher the storage capacity of the floppy disk. Most floppy disk drives store the same amount of data in the longer outside tracks and the shorter inside tracks, despite the difference in size. Recording density, or bpi, is thus highest in the innermost track, and bpi is measured there. Some newer drives use a different recording method called multiple zone recording. **Multiple zone recording** (**MZR**) records data at the same density on all tracks. Because longer outside tracks must hold more data to achieve the same density as shorter inside tracks, the outside tracks sometimes contain extra sectors.

The second factor that influences the amount of data a floppy disk can store is the number of tracks on the recording surface. This measurement is referred to as **tracks per inch** (**tpi**). As previously explained, the number of tracks on the disk depends on the size of the floppy disk, the drive used for formatting, and how the floppy disk was formatted.

The capacity of floppy disks varies and increases every two or three years as manufacturers develop new ways of recording data more densely. A **high-density** (**HD**) **floppy disk**, the most widely used 3$\frac{1}{2}$-inch floppy disk, can store 1.44 MB of data—the equivalent of approximately 700 pages of 2,000 characters each. Higher and lower capacity 3$\frac{1}{2}$-inch floppy disks also exist but are not as widely used.

Storing Data on a Floppy Disk Regardless of the type of floppy disk or the way it is formatted, the process of storing data on a floppy disk is essentially the same. When you insert a floppy disk into a floppy disk drive, a shaft connected to the drive motor engages the notches in the metal hub (Figure 5-7). As the drive writes to or reads from the floppy disk, the drive motor spins the circular plastic recording surface at approximately 300 revolutions

Figure 5-7
When you insert a floppy disk into a floppy disk drive, the notches in the metal hub are engaged by a drive motor shaft. A lever moves the shutter to one side so a portion of the floppy disk surface is exposed. As the computer reads from or writes to a floppy disk, the drive motor shaft spins the floppy disk at approximately 300 rpm. Read/write heads above and below the recording surface move in and out to read or write data.

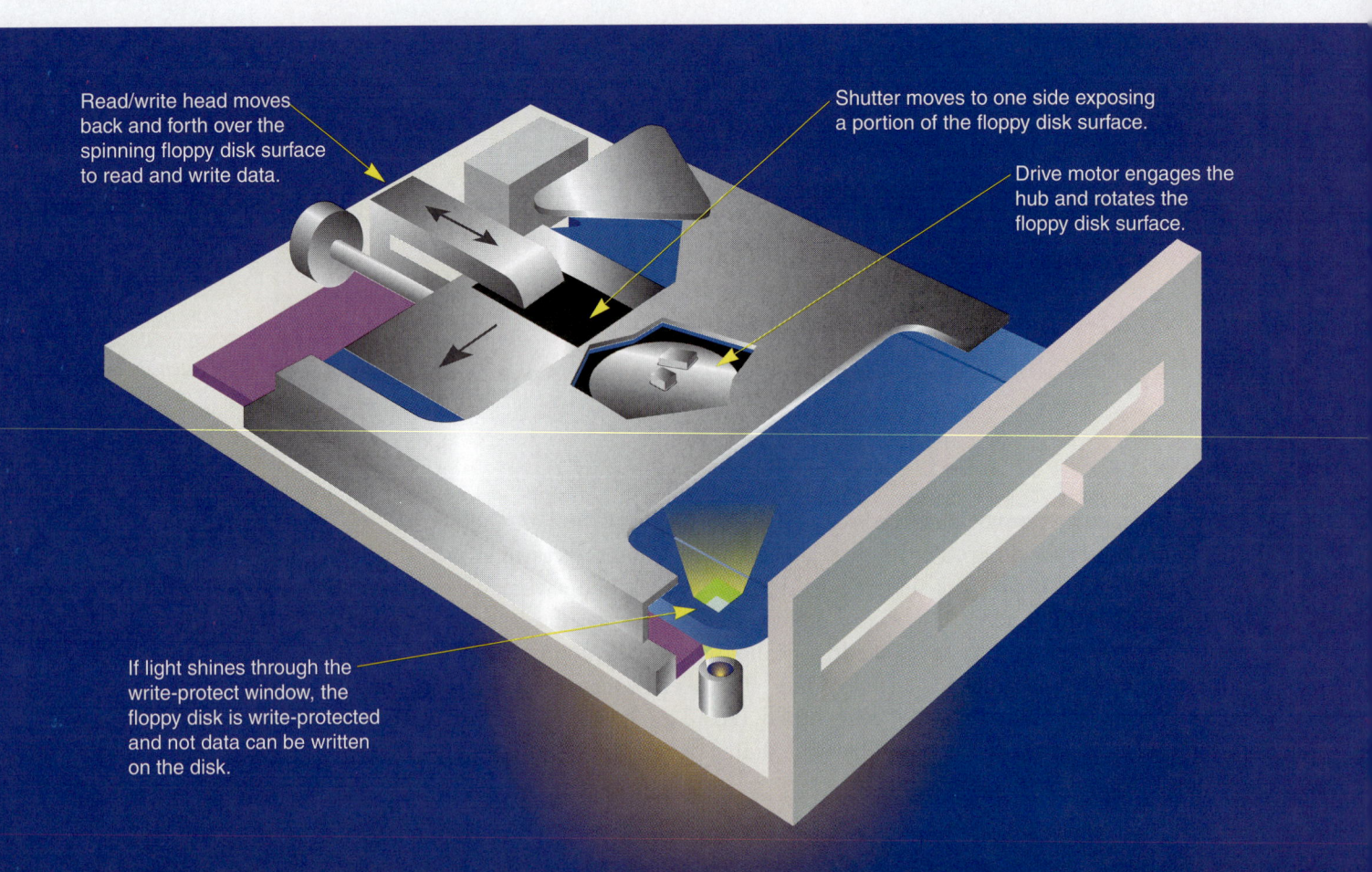

Read/write head moves back and forth over the spinning floppy disk surface to read and write data.

Shutter moves to one side exposing a portion of the floppy disk surface.

Drive motor engages the hub and rotates the floppy disk surface.

If light shines through the write-protect window, the floppy disk is write-protected and not data can be written on the disk.

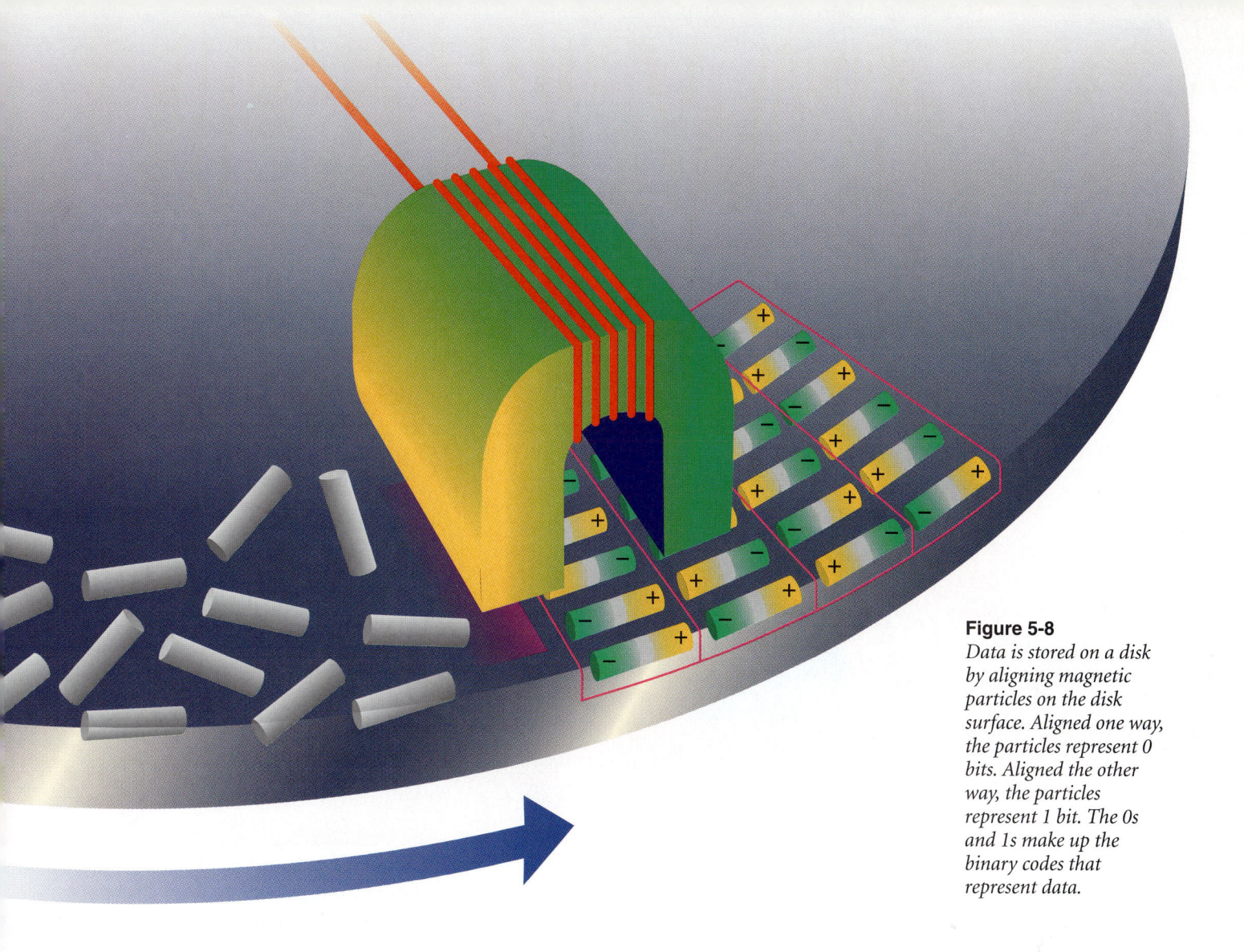

Figure 5-8
Data is stored on a disk by aligning magnetic particles on the disk surface. Aligned one way, the particles represent 0 bits. Aligned the other way, the particles represent 1 bit. The 0s and 1s make up the binary codes that represent data.

per minute (rpm). (If data is not being written or read, the disk does not spin.) A lever opens the shutter to expose a portion of the plastic recording surface.

Data is stored on tracks of the disk using the same binary code that is used to store data in memory, such as ASCII. To do this, a recording mechanism in the drive called the **read/write head** rests on the top and bottom surface of the rotating floppy disk, generating electronic impulses. These electronic impulses change the magnetic polarity, or alignment, of magnetic areas along a track on the disk (Figure 5-8). The plus or minus polarity represents the 1 or 0 bits being recorded. When reading data from the floppy disk, the read/write head senses the magnetic areas that have been recorded along the various tracks and transfers the data to memory. To access different tracks on the floppy disk, the drive moves the read/write head from track to track.

Data stored on a floppy disk must be retrieved and placed in memory to be processed. The time required to locate the data and transfer it to memory is called **access time**. Three factors determine the access time for a floppy disk drive.

1. **Seek time**, the time it takes to position the read/write head over the proper track.
2. **Rotational delay** (also called **latency**), the time it takes for the sector containing the data to rotate under the read/write head.
3. **Data transfer rate**, the time required to transfer the data from the disk to memory.

The access time for floppy disks is approximately 150 milliseconds—that is, data stored in a single sector on a floppy disk can be retrieved in about 1/6 of one second.

[Illustrations showing floppy disk care guidelines:]

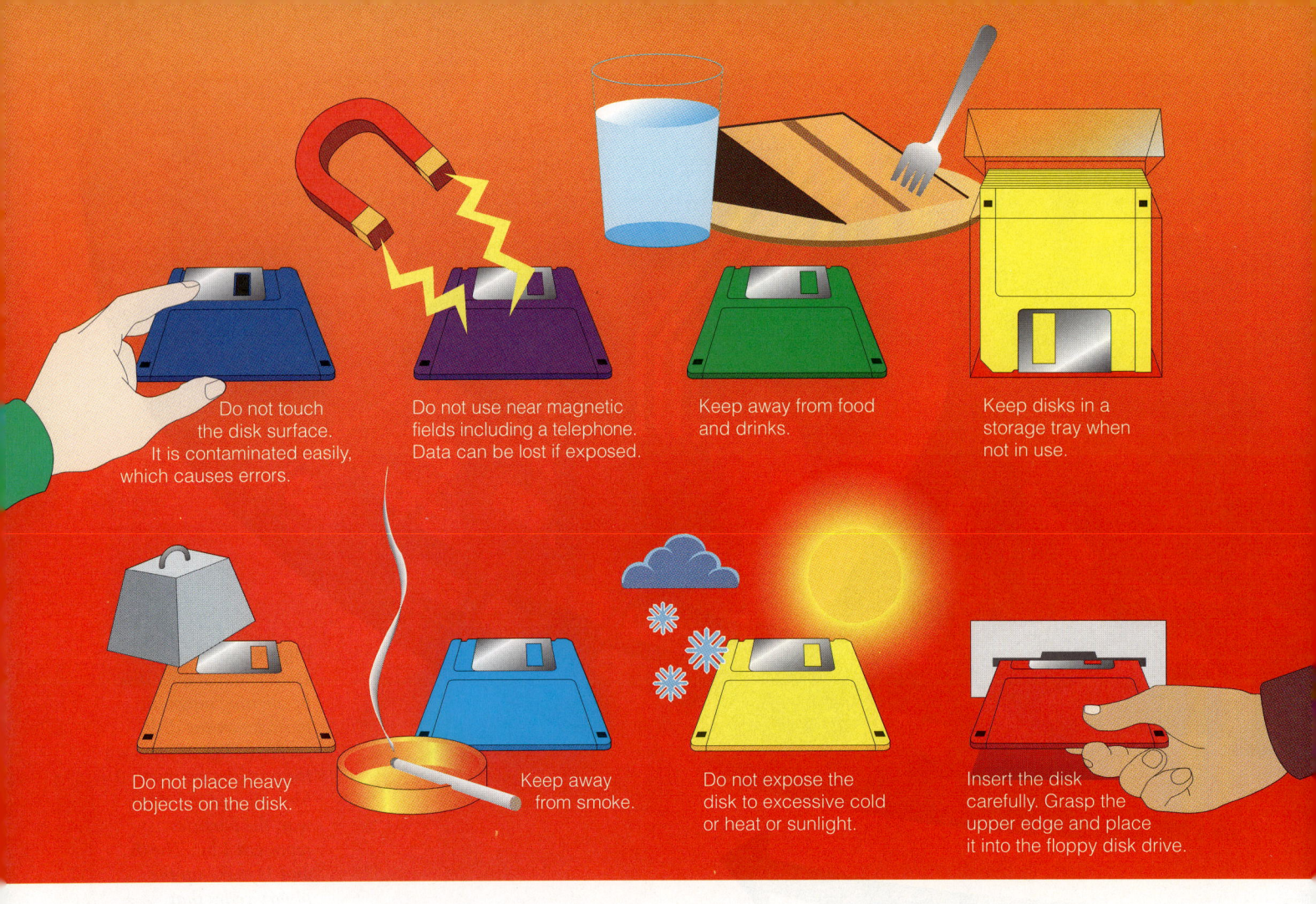

- Do not touch the disk surface. It is contaminated easily, which causes errors.
- Do not use near magnetic fields including a telephone. Data can be lost if exposed.
- Keep away from food and drinks.
- Keep disks in a storage tray when not in use.
- Do not place heavy objects on the disk.
- Keep away from smoke.
- Do not expose the disk to excessive cold or heat or sunlight.
- Insert the disk carefully. Grasp the upper edge and place it into the floppy disk drive.

Figure 5-9
Guidelines for the proper care of floppy disks.

The Care of Floppy Disks With reasonable care, floppy disks provide an inexpensive and reliable form of storage. When handling floppy disks, you should avoid exposing them to heat, cold, magnetic fields, and contaminants such as dust, smoke, or salt air. One advantage of the 3 1/2-inch floppy disk is that its rigid plastic cover provides protection for the data stored on the plastic disk inside. Figure 5-9 illustrates the guidelines for the proper care of floppy disks.

Hard Disks

Hard disks provide faster access times and larger storage capacities than floppy disks. **Hard disks** consist of one or more rigid **platters** coated with a material that allows data to be recorded magnetically on the surface of the platters (Figure 5-10). The platters most often are made of aluminum, but some newer hard disks use glass or ceramic materials. The platters, the read/write heads, and the mechanism for moving the heads across the surface of the disk are enclosed in an airtight, sealed case. This helps to ensure a clean environment for the disk. Unlike floppy disks, most hard disks are permanently mounted inside the computer and are not removable.

Figure 5-10
This high-capacity disk drive from Western Digital can store 4.3 GB of data. The data is stored on both sides of four platters. The top and bottom of each platter surface is read from or written to by a read/write head at the end of an access arm (such as the one shown over the top platter).

Minicomputers and mainframes use hard disks called **fixed disks** or **direct-access storage devices (DASD)**. These hard disks are often larger versions of the hard disks used with personal computers and can be mounted in the same cabinet as the computer or enclosed in their own stand-alone cabinet (Figure 5-11).

While most personal computers are limited to two to four disk drives, minicomputers can support eight to sixteen disk drives, and mainframe computers can support more than one hundred high-speed disk drives.

Hard Disk Storage Capacity Data is stored on both sides of a hard disk platter. If a drive has one platter, two surfaces are available for data storage; if a drive has two platters, four surfaces are available for data storage; and so on. Naturally, the more platters a drive has, the more data it can store. Just as with a floppy disk, a hard disk must be formatted before it can store data. Before a hard disk is formatted, it can be divided into separate areas called **partitions**. Each partition can function as if it were a separate disk. Separate partitions sometimes are used to store data belonging to different branches of a large company or even to separate the programs and data of a single user. Separate partitions also sometimes are used for different operating systems. On personal computers, hard disk partitions usually are identified by different letters, starting with the letter C. The letters A and B are reserved for floppy disk drives.

The storage capacity of hard drives is measured in megabytes, gigabytes, or terabytes. Figure 5-12 summarizes these terms and their abbreviations. Common storage capacities for personal computer hard disk drives range from 500 MB to several gigabytes. Five hundred megabytes of storage is the equivalent of 250,000 printed pages with about 2,000 characters per page—a stack of paper almost 85 feet high.

Figure 5-11
A high-speed, high-capacity fixed disk drive in a stand-alone cabinet.

inCyber
For information about hard disks, visit the Discovering Computers Chapter 5 inCyber page (http://www.scsite.com/dc/ch5/incyber.htm) and click Hard Disk.

Storage Terminology

term	abbreviation	number	number of bytes
kilobyte	KB	1,000	thousand
megabyte	MB	1,000,000	million
gigabyte	GB	1,000,000,000	billion
terabyte	TB	1,000,000,000,000	trillion

Figure 5-12
Common storage terms. Some larger storage devices can store terabytes of data.

Storing Data on a Hard Disk Storing data on hard disks is much like storing data on floppy disks, except that hard disks usually have multiple platters. Hard disks rotate at a high rate of speed, usually 3,600 to 7,200 revolutions per minute. Hard disk read/write heads are attached to **access arms** that swing out over the correct track on the disk surface. The read/write heads float on a cushion of air and do not actually touch the surface of the disk. The distance between the head and the surface is approximately ten millionths of an inch. As shown in Figure 5-13, this close clearance leaves no room for any type of contamination. If some form of contamination is introduced, or if the alignment of the read/write heads is altered by something jarring the computer, a head crash can occur. A **head crash** is when a read/write head collides with the disk surface. A head crash usually results in a loss of data.

Figure 5-13
The clearance between a disk read/write head and the disk surface is about 10 millionths of an inch. Because of this small difference, contaminants, such as a smoke particle, a fingerprint, a dust particle, or a human hair, could render the drive unusable. Hard disk drives are sealed to prevent contamination.

Access time for a hard disk is between ten and twenty milliseconds. This is significantly faster than a floppy disk for two reasons. First, a hard disk spins ten to twenty times faster than a floppy disk drive. Second, a hard disk spins constantly, while a floppy disk starts spinning only when it receives a read or write command.

Some computers improve the apparent speed at which data is written to and read from a disk by using disk cache. Similar in concept to RAM cache, **disk cache** is an area of memory set aside for data most often read from the disk. Every time the CPU requests data from the disk, disk cache software looks for the data in the disk cache memory area first. If the requested data is in disk cache, it is transferred immediately to the CPU, and the slower disk read operation is avoided. In addition to tracking the data requested from the disk, disk cache software also reads adjacent clusters on the assumption that they might be needed next. Disk cache memory is updated every time a disk read takes place. Disk cache software also makes disk write operations more efficient by temporarily holding data to be written until the CPU is not busy.

The flow of data to and from the hard disk is managed by a collection of electronic circuits called the **hard disk controller**. The controller can be built into the disk drive or it can be a separate board in an expansion slot. For personal computers, two types of controllers are common, IDE and SCSI. **Integrated drive electronics (IDE)** controllers can operate one or two hard disk drives. Most motherboards have built-in IDE connectors that use a cable to attach directly to the disk drive. IDE controllers can transfer data to the disk at a rate of up to 10 MB per second. **Small computer system interface**, or **SCSI** (pronounced *scuzzy*), controllers can support multiple disk drives or a mix of other SCSI-compatible devices. SCSI devices connect to each other in a chain, with a cable between each device. SCSI controllers usually consist of a circuit board mounted in an expansion slot. They are faster than IDE controllers and can provide up to 100 MB per second transfer rates.

Disk Cartridges

Some hard disk drives, called disk cartridges, are removable. **Disk cartridges** (Figure 5-14) provide both the storage capacity and fast access times of hard disks and the portability of floppy disks. High-capacity disk cartridges can store more than one gigabyte of data and can be used to transport large files or to make copies of important files. Disk cartridges also can be used when data security is an issue. At the end of a work session, you can remove the disk cartridge and lock it up, leaving no data on the computer.

One unique type of disk cartridge is called a Bernoulli disk. The **Bernoulli disk cartridge** works with a special drive unit that uses a cushion of air to keep the flexible disk surface from touching the read/write head. The flexible disk surface reduces the chance of a head crash but causes the cartridges to eventually wear out.

> **inCyber**
> For an explanation of disk cartridges, visit the Discovering Computers Chapter 5 inCyber page (http://www.scsite.com/dc/ch5/incyber.htm) and click Disk Cartridge.

Figure 5-14
This removable disk cartridge can hold more than 1 GB of data. It can be used to back up a hard disk or transport large files.

Figure 5-15
A fragmented disk has many files stored in non-contiguous clusters. This condition slows the retrieval of data from the disk. Defragmenting the disk reorganizes the files so they are located in contiguous clusters and speeds access time.

fragmented disk

disk after defragmenting

inCyber

For a discussion of backup procedures, visit the Discovering Computers Chapter 5 inCyber page (http://www.scsite.com/dc/ch5/incyber.htm) and click Backup.

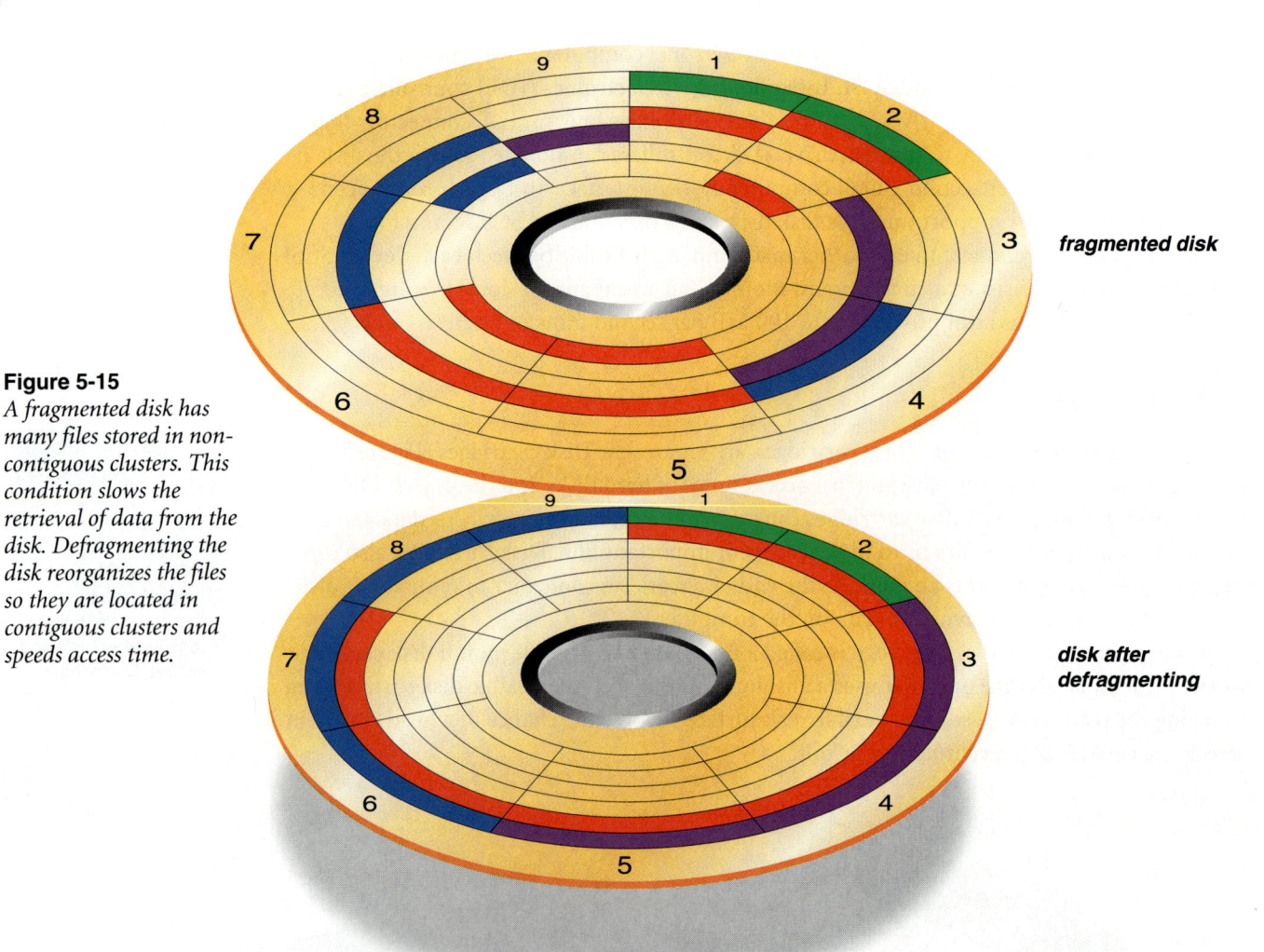

Maintaining Data Stored on a Disk

To prevent the loss of data stored on a disk, the two procedures that should be performed regularly are backup and defragmentation.

Backup **Backup** is the process of creating a copy of important programs and data. Backup should be performed regularly for all data and as needed for important files. To back up a floppy disk, simply copy the data on one floppy disk to another floppy disk. To back up a large number of files or an entire hard disk, tape cartridges or disk cartridges commonly are used.

Defragmentation When a computer stores data on a disk, it places the data in the first available cluster. While the computer tries to place data in clusters that are *contiguous* (all in a row), contiguous clusters are not always available. When a file is stored in clusters that are not next to each other, the file is said to be **fragmented**. The term fragmented also is used to describe the condition of a disk drive that has many files stored in noncontiguous clusters (Figure 5-15). Fragmentation causes the computer to run slowly, because reading data from several locations on the disk takes longer than if the data were all in one location. Defragmenting the disk solves this problem. **Defragmentation** reorganizes the data stored on the disk so that files are located in contiguous clusters. Defragmentation programs are available as part of system utility packages or as separate programs. Some operating systems also contain defragmentation programs.

MAGNETIC DISK STORAGE **5.13**

Data Compression   One way to store more data on a disk is to use data compression. **Data compression** reduces data storage requirements by substituting codes for repeating patterns of data. For example, consider the familiar Ben Franklin saying, "Early to bed, early to rise, makes a man healthy, wealthy, and wise." Including punctuation, this phrase includes 56 characters. As shown in Figure 5-16, by substituting special characters for repeating patterns, the original phrase can be compressed to only 30 characters, which is a reduction of 46%. Compression generally is stated as a ratio of the size of the original decompressed data divided by the size of the compressed data. The example shown, for instance, has a compression ratio of 1.9 to 1 (56 divided by 30). The codes substituted for the repeating patterns are filed in a table when the data is compressed. This substitution table is used to restore the compressed data to its original form, when necessary.

The type of compression described above is called *lossless compression* because no data is lost in the process. Lossless compression works best for text and numeric data that cannot lose data without losing some meaning. Compression ratios for lossless compression average 2 to 1 (the size of the data is reduced 50%). Other compression methods, called *lossy compression*, have higher compression ratios (up to 200 to 1), but do result in some data loss. Lossy compression methods typically are used to compress video images and sound. Video and sound both can lose data without a noticeable reduction in the overall quality of the output.

Lossy compression usually is performed with special hardware such as a video or sound expansion board. Disk compression programs such as Stacker can be installed to keep all files on a hard disk compressed automatically until they are needed for processing. Some file compression programs such as PKZIP compress and decompress data as directed by the user.

Compressed files often are used when files must be transferred over a communications line, such as a file that is downloaded from the Internet. Because it is smaller, a compressed file takes less time to transfer than a decompressed file.

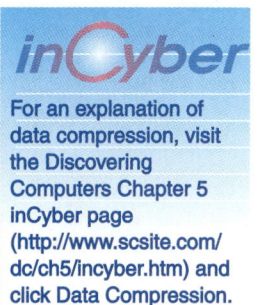

inCyber

For an explanation of data compression, visit the Discovering Computers Chapter 5 inCyber page (http://www.scsite.com/dc/ch5/incyber.htm) and click Data Compression.

DATA COMPRESSION

original uncompressed data
56 characters

*Early to bed,
early to rise,
makes a man healthy,
wealthy, and wise.*
Ben Franklin

pattern substitution

@   *early*
#   *to*
$ *ise*
%   *ma*
&   *ealthy*

compressed data
30 characters

*@ # bed,
@ # r$,
%kes a %n h&,
w&, and w$.*

compression results

characters reduced from 56 to 30;

46% reduction

compression ratio; 1.9 to 1

(56 divided by 30)

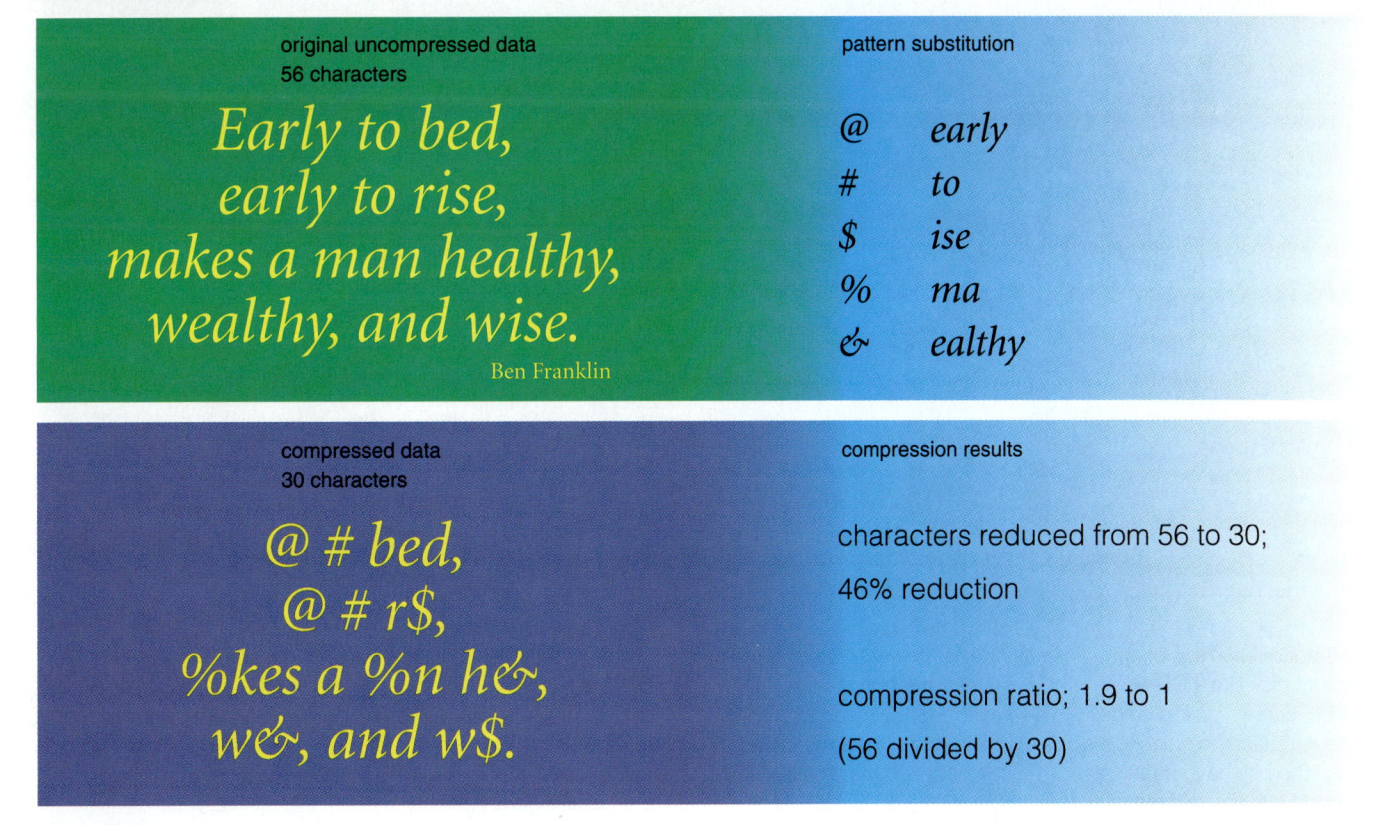

Figure 5-16
An example of data compression.

CHAPTER 5 – DATA STORAGE

CD-ROM and Optical Disks

Large quantities of data can be stored on **optical disks,** which use laser technology to read from and write data to a plastic disk or platter. Data is written on an optical disk by a high-powered laser that burns microscopic holes on the surface of the disk. A lower powered laser reads the data from the disk by reflecting light off the disk surface. The reflected light is converted into a series of bits that the computer can process (Figure 5-17).

A full-size, 14-inch optical disk can store 6.8 billion bytes of information. Up to 150 of these disks can be installed in automated disk library systems called jukeboxes that provide more than one trillion bytes of storage. A smaller optical disk, just under five inches in diameter, is called a **CD-ROM,** an acronym for **compact disk read-only memory** (Figure 5-18). CD-ROMs use the same laser technology as the audio compact disks that are used for recorded music. In fact, if a computer is equipped with a CD-ROM drive, a sound card, and speakers, audio compact disks can be played in the CD-ROM drive.

A CD-ROM can store almost 650 MB of information, or about 450 times the data that can be stored on a high-density $3^1/_2$-inch floppy disk. This is enough space to store approximately 325,000 pages of typed data. A revised format for CD-ROM disks, called **DVD** (**digital video disk**), eventually will increase the capacity of CD-ROM size disks to 4.7 gigabytes.

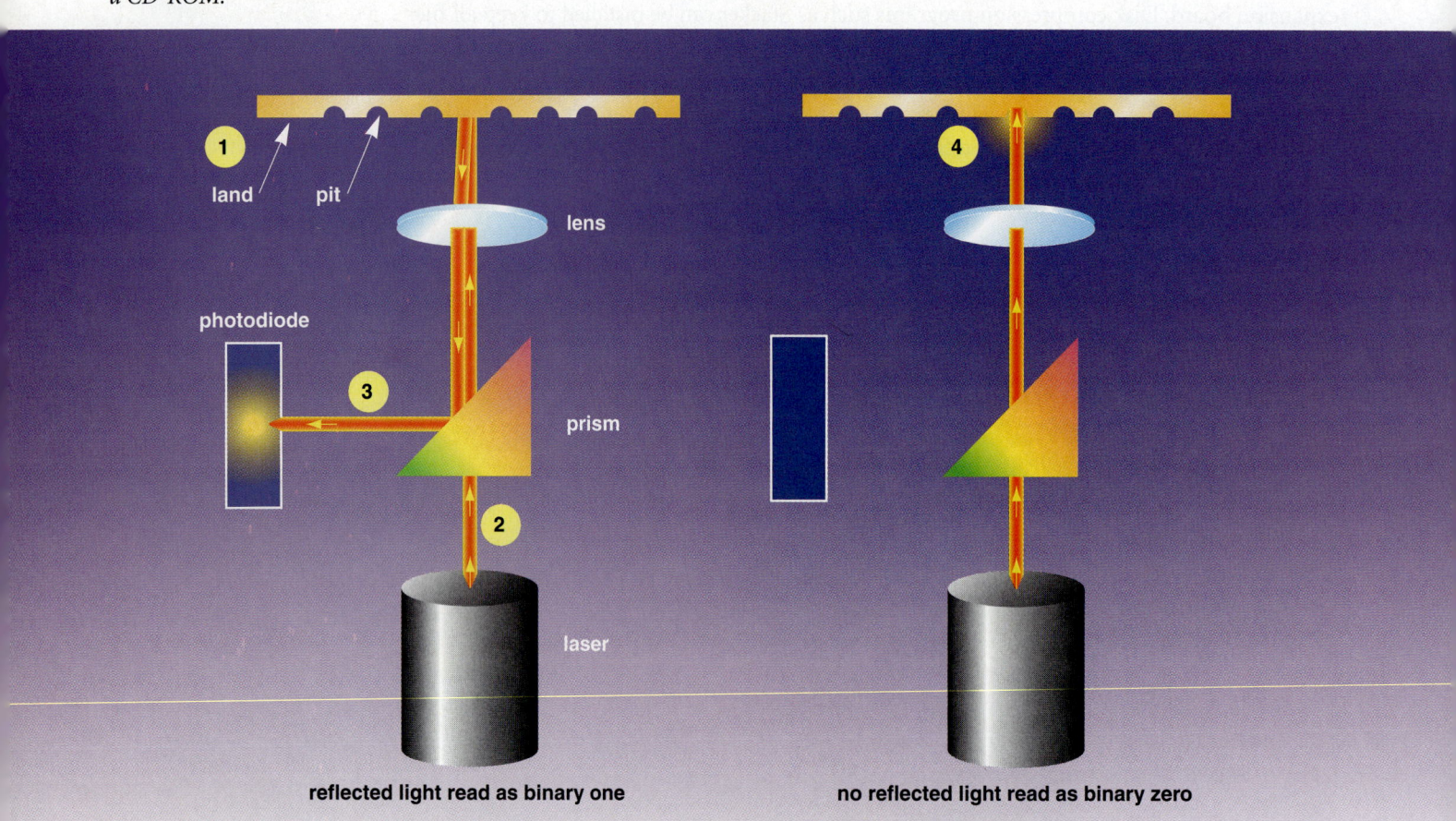

inCyber

For information about CD-ROMs, visit the Discovering Computers Chapter 5 inCyber page (http://www.scsite.com/dc/ch5/incyber.htm) and click CD-ROM.

Figure 5-17
How data is read from a CD-ROM.

reflected light read as binary one

no reflected light read as binary zero

1. The bottom surface of an optical disk like a CD-ROM has flat areas, called lands, and microscopic holes, called pits. The pits have been burned into the surface with a high-powered laser.

2. A lower powered laser is used to read the optical disk. The laser beam passes through a prism and a lens that focuses the beam on the disk surface.

3. Lands reflect the laser beam back to the prism, which then directs the light to a photo-diode, which is a component that converts light to an electrical signal. Reflected light is read as the binary bit 1.

4. Pits scatter the laser beam and no light is reflected to the photodiode. No reflected light is read as the binary bit 0.

The original CD-ROM drives were single-speed drives, but today, ten-speed, twelve-speed and sixteen-speed (abbreviated 10X, 12X, and 16X) are common. A CD-ROM drive's speed rating refers to how fast the drive can transfer data in relation to a standard established for CD-ROM drives used for multimedia applications. The original standard established a minimum transfer rate of 150 kilobytes per second (kbps). A 10X drive can transfer data at 1,500 kbps. A 12X drive can transfer data at 1,800 kbps and an 16X drive transfers data at 2,400 kbps, or 2.4 megabytes per second (mbps). The faster CD-ROM drives are especially useful for playing audio and video files.

Recordable CD-ROM drives, called **CD-R (compact disk-recordable)** drives, are growing in use. Multimedia developers who need the large storage capacities of CD-ROM and organizations that must store large volumes of data, for example, often use CD-R drives. A new type of erasable CD-ROM drive, called a **CD-E (compact disk-erasable)** drive, is not yet widely used because the technology is still relatively new.

Another type of erasable optical disk uses magnetic and optical technology to write and read data. **Magneto-optical (MO)** drives record data by using a magnetic field to change the polarity of a spot on a disk that has been heated by a laser. Another type of storage that combines optical and magnetic technologies is a special type of floppy disk, called a **floptical** disk. Flopticals use optical and magnetic technology to achieve higher storage rates (currently up to 120 MB) on a disk very similar to a standard $3^{1}/_{2}$-inch magnetic floppy disk. A floptical disk drive uses a low-powered laser to read the data that is stored in closely spaced tracks. The closely spaced tracks allow for higher bpi and tpi densities. Another advantage of a floptical drive is its capability of reading standard $3^{1}/_{2}$-inch floppy disks.

Figure 5-18
A CD-ROM can store hundreds of times as much information as a floppy disk of similar size. Many reference materials such as encyclopedias, catalogs, and telephone books now are published on CD-ROM instead of on paper.

inCyber

For an examination of recordable CD-ROM drives, visit the Discovering Computers Chapter 5 inCyber page (http://www.scsite.com/dc/ch5/incyber.htm) and click CD-ROM Drive.

Magnetic Tape

During the 1950s and early 1960s, magnetic tape was the primary method of storing large amounts of data. Today, even though tape is no longer used as a primary method of storage, it is still a cost-effective way to store data that does not have to be accessed immediately. In addition, tape storage serves as the primary means of backup for most systems and often is used to transfer data from one system to another.

Magnetic tape consists of a thin ribbon of plastic. One side of the tape is coated with a material that can be magnetized to record the bit patterns that represent data. Tape is considered a **sequential storage** media because the computer must write and read tape records one after another (sequentially). For example, to read the 1,000th record on a tape, the tape drive must first pass over the previous 999 records. The more common types of magnetic tape devices use cartridges that contain one-quarter- to one-half-inch wide tape (Figure 5-19). Some older computer systems use reel-to-reel tape devices.

inCyber
For a description of magnetic tape, visit the Discovering Computers Chapter 5 inCyber page (http://www.scsite.com/dc/ch5/incyber.htm) and click Magnetic Tape.

Figure 5-19
Magnetic tape cartridges contain tape one-quarter- to one-half-inch wide.

Cartridge Tape Devices

A **cartridge tape** contains magnetic recording tape in a small, rectangular plastic housing. Tape cartridges containing one-quarter-inch wide tape are only slightly larger than audio cassette tapes and frequently are used for personal computer backup. Faster, higher-capacity, one-half-inch cartridge tapes are used for larger system backup. For personal computers, cartridge tape units are designed to be mounted internally in a bay or externally in a separate cabinet (Figure 5-20).

Figure 5-20
One-quarter-inch cartridge tapes often are used to backup the hard disks of personal computers. Tape drives can be internal units mounted in a drive bay or external units.

MAGNETIC TAPE **5.17**

For larger systems, cartridge tapes usually are mounted in their own cabinet. Cartridge tapes for larger systems are designed so multiple tapes can be loaded and unloaded automatically so that tape storage operations can take place unattended (Figure 5-21).

Figure 5-21
Cartridge tape units used for larger systems have automatic loaders that allow multiple tapes to be loaded and recorded without the need of an operator.

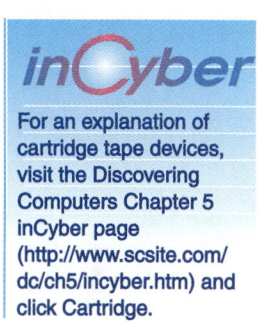

inCyber

For an explanation of cartridge tape devices, visit the Discovering Computers Chapter 5 inCyber page (http://www.scsite.com/dc/ch5/incyber.htm) and click Cartridge.

Reel-to-Reel Tape Devices

Reel-to-reel tape devices have been replaced almost completely by cartridge tape devices but still may be found on large computer systems. **Reel-to-reel tape** devices use two reels, a supply reel to hold the tape that will be read from or written to (Figure 5-22), and a take-up reel to temporarily hold portions of the supply reel tape as it is being processed. As the tape moves from one reel to another, it passes over a read/write head, which is the electromagnetic device that reads and writes data on the tape. When processing is complete, tape on the take-up reel is wound back onto the supply reel.

Figure 5-22
Older style tape units use reels of tape. A full-sized reel is 10 1/2 inches wide and contains more than 2,000 feet of one-half-inch tape. A reel this size can hold about 200 MB of data.

Storing Data on Magnetic Tape

Binary codes such as ASCII and EBCDIC are used to represent data stored on magnetic tape. As with disk drives, tape drives have an electromagnetic read/write head that can read or write magnetic patterns on the tape representing bits. Several different methods are used to record bits on the tape (Figure 5-23).

Quarter-inch-cartridge (QIC) tape devices, often used with PCs, record data in narrow tracks along the length of the tape. When the end is reached, the tape reverses direction, and data is recorded in another track in the opposite direction. This method of recording up and down the length of the tape is called **longitudinal**, or **serpentine**, **recording**. QIC cartridges have between nine and 144 tracks and can store from several hundred megabytes to more than 10 GB of data on a single tape. **Digital audio tape (DAT)** drives use **helical scan technology** to record data across the width of the tape at a six-degree angle. Instead of using a stationary read/write head, DAT tape drives use a rotating head similar to a video cassette recorder. Older one-half-inch reel-to-reel tape drives record data across the width of the tape in nine channels; eight channels for eight data bits (one byte) and one parity bit.

Tape density is the number of bits that can be stored on one inch of tape. As with disk drives, tape density is expressed in bits per inch, or bpi. Cartridge tape densities range from 6,000 bpi to more than 60,000 bpi. The higher the density, the more data that can be stored on a tape. Some cartridges used on large systems can hold in excess of 40 GB of decompressed data.

> **inCyber**
> For details on quarter-inch-cartridge (QIC) tape devices, visit the Discovering Computers Chapter 5 inCyber page (http://www.scsite.com/dc/ch5/incyber.htm) and click QIC.

Figure 5-23
Different methods of recording data on magnetic tape.

On most quarter-inch-cartridge (QIC) tapes, data is recorded in a single track along the length of the tape. When the end is reached, the tape reverses direction and data is recorded in another track in the opposite direction.

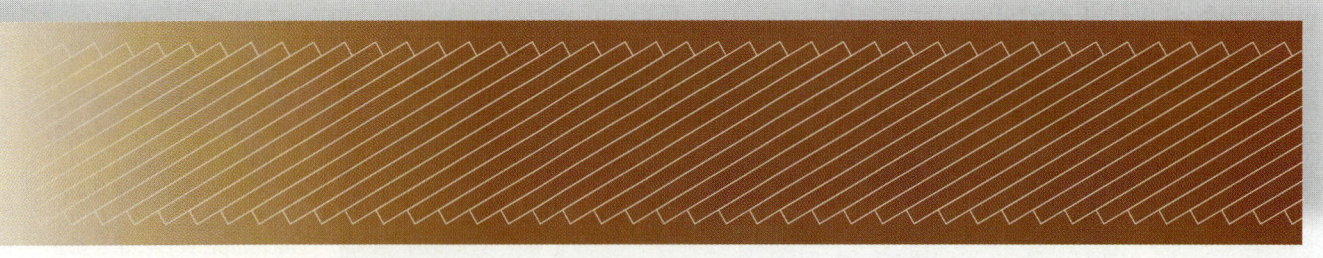

Digital audio tape (DAT) uses helical scan technology to record data in tracks at a six-degree angle to the tape.

Older, one-half-inch reel-to-reel tape drives record data in nine channels: eight channels for data bits and one channel for a parity bit.

Other Types of Storage Devices

The conventional disk and tape devices just described comprise the majority of storage devices and media, but other means for storing data sometimes are used. These include PC Cards, RAID storage systems, and mass storage devices.

PC Cards

PC Cards are small, credit card-sized cards that fit into PC Card expansion slots. Different types and sizes of the cards are used for storage, communications, and additional memory. Most often, PC Cards are used with portable computers, but they also can be used with desktop systems. PC Cards used for storage are only 10.5mm (about .4 inches) thick, but they contain small rotating disk drives, each 1.3 inches in diameter, that can store more than 300 MB of data (Figure 5-24).

PC Cards are useful for storage if you work with more than one computer or share a computer with others. Your data can be stored on a PC Card and moved quickly to a different computer.

RAID Storage Systems

As computers became faster, writing data to and reading data from increasingly larger disks became a hindrance. Computers spent a large percentage of time waiting for data to go to or from the disk drive. Rather than trying to build even larger and faster disk drives, some disk manufacturers began to connect several smaller disks into an integrated unit that acted like a single large disk drive. A group of integrated small disks is called a **RAID** storage system, which stands for **redundant array of inexpensive disks**. RAID technology can be implemented in several ways, called RAID levels.

Figure 5-24
Type III PC Cards are used as small removable disk drives that can hold more than 300 MB of data.

inCyber

For information about various PC Cards, visit the Discovering Computers Chapter 5 inCyber page (http://www.scsite.com/dc/ch5/incyber.htm) and click PC Card.

The simplest RAID method, called RAID level 1, uses one backup disk for each data disk (Figure 5-25). Each backup disk contains the same information as its corresponding data disk. If the data disk fails, the backup disk can be used as the data disk.

Because the disks contain duplicate information, RAID level 1 is sometimes called **disk mirroring**. RAID levels beyond level 1 divide data across more than one drive. Dividing a logical piece of data such as a record or word into smaller parts and writing those parts on multiple drives is called **striping** (Figure 5-26).

Parity information is an important part of RAID technology. It allows the system to rebuild, sometimes automatically, any information that is damaged on one of the data disks. Some RAID levels require a separate disk, called a parity or check disk, to track parity information. Other RAID levels store parity information directly on the data disk.

RAID storage systems offer a number of advantages over single large disk systems, called **SLEDs**, which stands for **single large expensive disks**. For one, data can be read from or written to RAID disks faster, because multiple read or write operations can take place at the same time. The biggest advantage, however, is the reduced risk of data loss. The ability to recreate damaged data is important to organizations that cannot afford to lose valuable stored information.

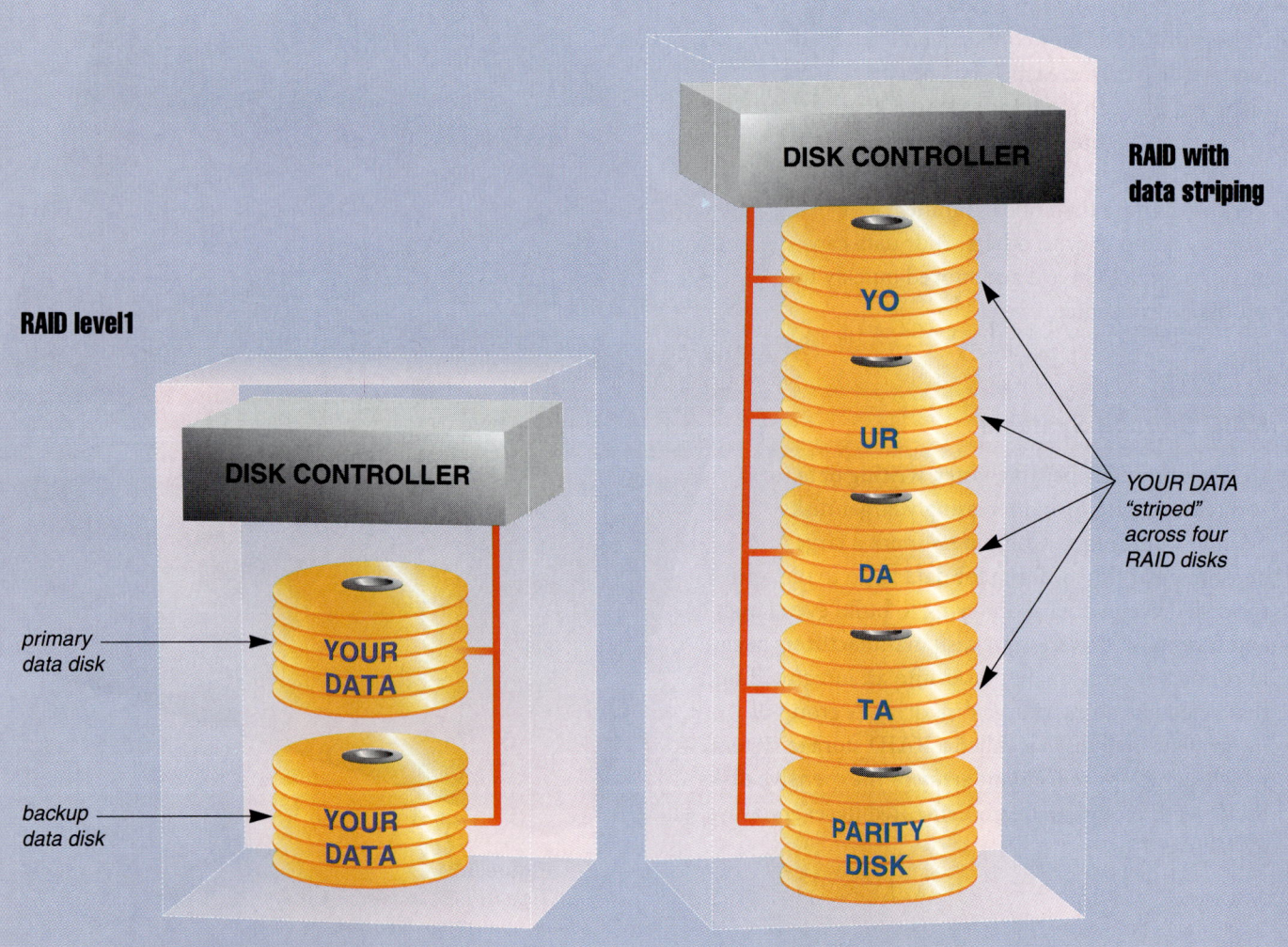

Figure 5-25
In RAID level 1, called disk mirroring, a backup disk exists for each data disk.

Figure 5-26
In RAID levels beyond level 1, data to be stored is divided into parts and written across several disks. This process is called striping. Some RAID levels call for additional parity disks that track information needed to recreate data if one of the data disks malfunctions.

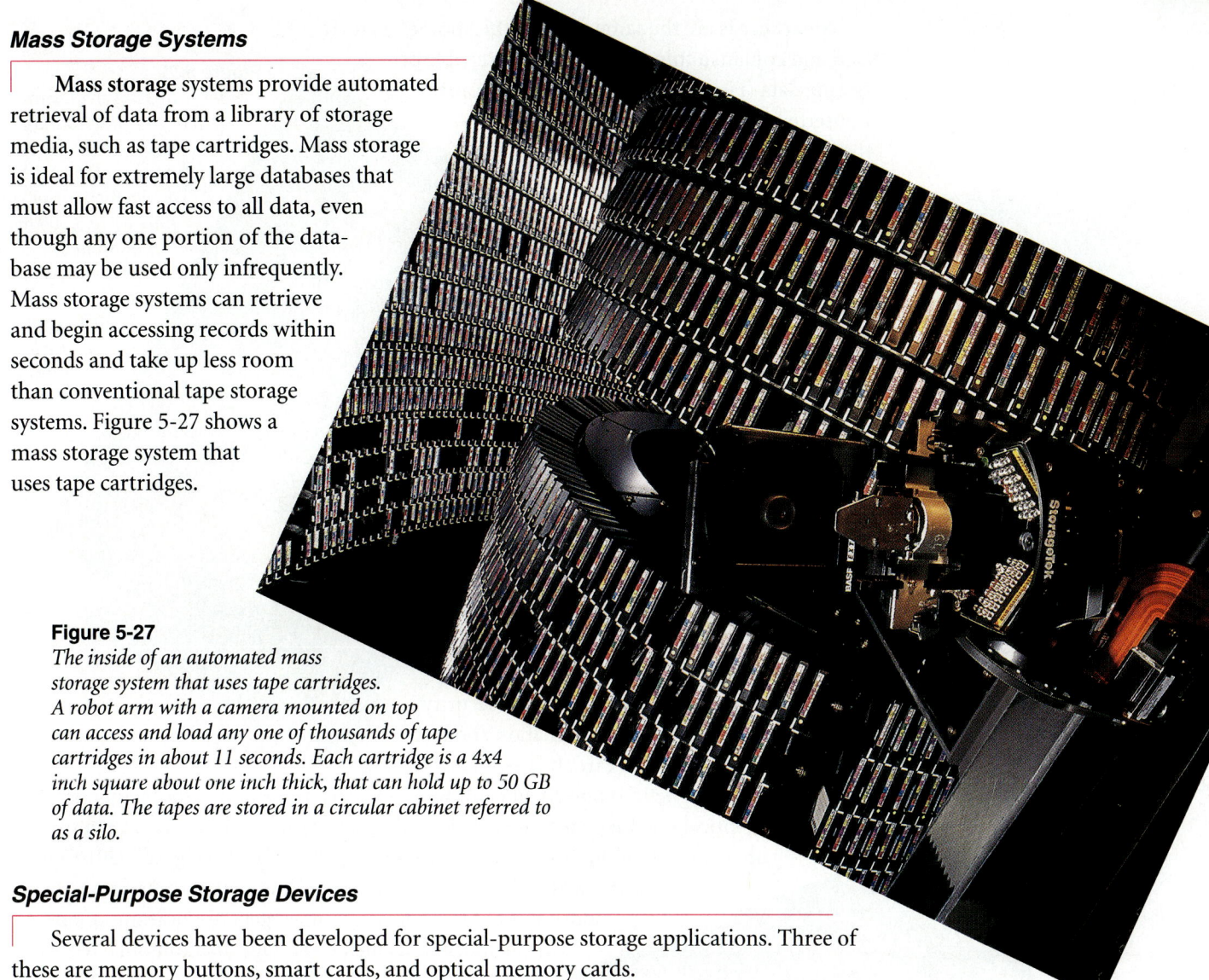

Mass Storage Systems

Mass storage systems provide automated retrieval of data from a library of storage media, such as tape cartridges. Mass storage is ideal for extremely large databases that must allow fast access to all data, even though any one portion of the database may be used only infrequently. Mass storage systems can retrieve and begin accessing records within seconds and take up less room than conventional tape storage systems. Figure 5-27 shows a mass storage system that uses tape cartridges.

Figure 5-27
The inside of an automated mass storage system that uses tape cartridges. A robot arm with a camera mounted on top can access and load any one of thousands of tape cartridges in about 11 seconds. Each cartridge is a 4x4 inch square about one inch thick, that can hold up to 50 GB of data. The tapes are stored in a circular cabinet referred to as a silo.

Special-Purpose Storage Devices

Several devices have been developed for special-purpose storage applications. Three of these are memory buttons, smart cards, and optical memory cards.

Memory buttons are small storage devices about the size of a dime that look like watch batteries (Figure 5-28). Memory buttons currently can hold up to 8,000 characters of data, but storage capacities are increasing rapidly. To read or update data in the button, you touch the button with a small pen-like probe, which is attached to a hand-held terminal. A sound is generated to indicate that the read or write operation is complete. Memory buttons are used in applications where information about an item must travel with it. Examples are laboratory samples, shipping containers, and rental equipment.

Figure 5-28
Memory buttons can hold up to 8,000 bytes of information. The buttons are ideal in situations where it would be difficult to have related information travel with an item in paper form. The buttons can be read or updated using a pen-like probe attached to a hand-held terminal.

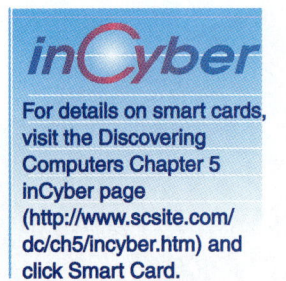

Smart cards are the same size and thickness of a credit card and contain a thin microprocessor capable of storing data (Figure 5-29). When a smart card is inserted into a specialized card reader, the information on the smart card can be read and, if necessary, updated. Smart cards often are used as prepaid telephone calling cards. Individuals buy smart cards with a specific amount of money stored in the card's microprocessor. Each time the card is used at a special pay telephone, the amount is reduced. An LCD display built into the phone indicates how much money remains in the card. Using smart cards provides convenience to the caller and eliminates the telephone company's need to collect coins regularly from the telephones. Smart cards also are used for employee time and attendance tracking (instead of time cards) and for security applications where detailed information about the card holder is stored in the card. It is estimated that 80% of conventional magnetic-stripe credit cards will be replaced by smart cards by the year 2001.

Optical memory cards are plastic cards the size of a credit card that can store up to 4.1 MB of digitized text or images using a laser beam (Figure 5-30). Optical memory cards are useful as a storage medium that permits data to be added but not to be erased or rewritten. Applications of optical memory cards include storage of automobile records, security identification data, and personal medical information for diagnostic use.

inCyber
For details on smart cards, visit the Discovering Computers Chapter 5 inCyber page (http://www.scsite.com/dc/ch5/incyber.htm) and click Smart Card.

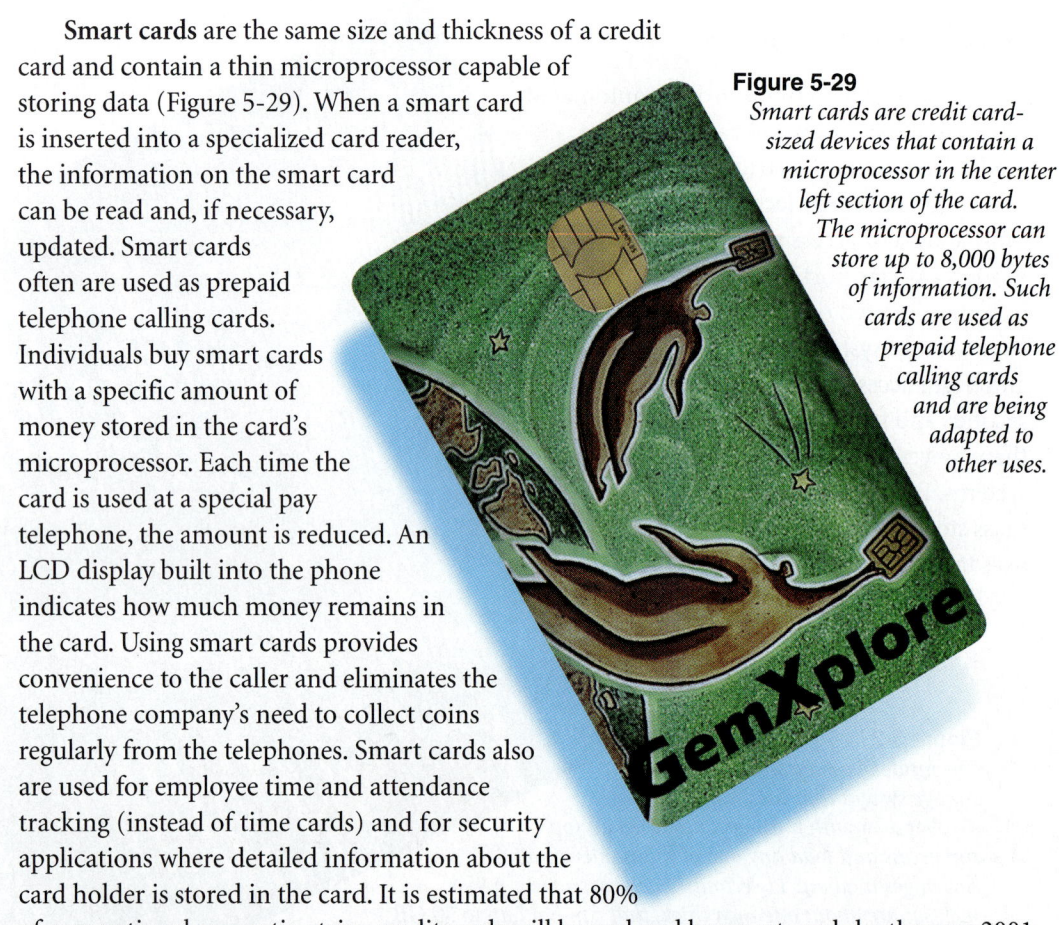

Figure 5-29
Smart cards are credit card-sized devices that contain a microprocessor in the center left section of the card. The microprocessor can store up to 8,000 bytes of information. Such cards are used as prepaid telephone calling cards and are being adapted to other uses.

Figure 5-30
This optical memory card can store up to 4.1 MB of data and images. It is the size and thickness of a credit card.

Summary of Storage

Storage is used to store data and programs that currently are not being processed by the computer. This chapter discussed the various types of storage used with computers. The chart in Figure 5-31 provides a summary of the storage devices covered. Adding what you have learned about these storage devices and storage operations in general to what you learned about the input, processing, and output operations will complete your understanding of the information processing cycle.

TYPE	SPACE WITH CAPACITY	DESCRIPTION
Magnetic Disk		
Floppy disk	1.44 MB	Thin, portable plastic storage media that is reliable and low cost.
Hard disk	500 MB to 5 GB	Fixed-platter storage media that provides large storage capacity and fast access.
Disk cartridge	100 MB to 1 GB	Removable hard disk unit that provides large storage capacity and is portable.
CD-ROM and Optical Disk	650 MB to 7 GB	High-capacity disks use lasers to read and record data.
Magnetic Tape		
Cartridge tape	120 MB to 4 GB	Tape enclosed in rectangular plastic housing.
Reel tape	200 MB	1/2-inch tape on 300- to 3,600-foot reel.
Other Storage Devices		
PC Card	40 MB to 300 MB	Credit card-sized disk used on portable computers.
RAID	5 GB to 40 GB	Multiple hard disks integrated into a single unit.
Mass storage	10 TB to 100 TB	Automated retrieval of storage media such as tape cartridges.
Special-Purpose Devices		
Memory button	8 KB	Stores data on chip in small metal canister.
Smart card	1 KB to 8 KB	Thin microprocessor embedded in plastic card.
Optical memory card	4 GB	Text and images stored in credit card-sized holder.

Figure 5-31
Summary of storage devices.

COMPUTERS AT WORK

HSM: Hierarchical Storage Management

Even though per-megabyte storage costs continue to decrease, the amount of data companies need to store is increasing more quickly than ever. While companies want and need to keep such vast amounts of data readily accessible, the costs of keeping all of this data stored on a hard disk are high.

This problem continues to occur, despite the fact that hard disk storage costs have dropped significantly over the past few years. In 1990, hard disk storage cost $2 per megabyte; by 1996, the cost was down to $ .20 per megabyte. Experts estimate that the cost will be $ .02 per megabyte by the year 2000. The main reason for the lower cost is the capacity increase of hard disks. In 1997, the average PC hard disk stored 1.2 GB. By the year 2000, 5 GB to 10 GB disk drives will be standard.

Lower per-megabyte costs and higher capacities have encouraged users to store more data. In addition, users are storing more complex data that requires more storage space, such as images, compound documents with embedded graphics, and sound and video files. The bottom line is that, even with dramatically lower storage costs, more data than ever exists to store, and companies cannot afford to store all this data on hard disks.

To help with this problem, many companies are turning to **hierarchical storage management** (HSM), which is a way of automating the transfer of data to lower cost, but slower, forms of storage. HSM addresses the storage issue by automating the transfer of data to different categories and speeds of storage devices. The top category is online storage. **Online storage** means the computer has fast, direct access to the data. Online storage mainly consists of hard disks, but some companies use RAM disks for even faster access. Accessing data stored on online devices is almost instantaneous. The next category is called near-line storage. **Near-line storage** usually consists of high-capacity optical disks. Accessing near-line storage may take 10 to 20 seconds while the system finds the appropriate optical disk and loads the requested data. The third category is off-line storage. **Off-line storage** usually consists of automated tape libraries. Tape libraries used for HSM may take up to several minutes to access requested data. The lowest category is shelf storage. **Shelf storage** means that the data has been stored on a tape or other removable media and stored in a cabinet or rack. Accessing this data requires the tape (or other media) to be retrieved manually and loaded on a storage device.

With HSM, files moved from online devices still have a reference, called a *placeholder*, stored online. The placeholder tells the system where to find the data, be it online or on the shelf. The user determines the criteria for transferring data from online storage and can change them at any time. A specific criterion, for example, might be to move any file not requested for ninety days to off-line storage.

Fine-tuning the criteria for moving data from one category to another takes time and experience. Users get very frustrated if data they need is not available because it has been moved to shelf storage too quickly. The goal of HSM is to store data on the lowest cost device but still provide an appropriate level of data availability.

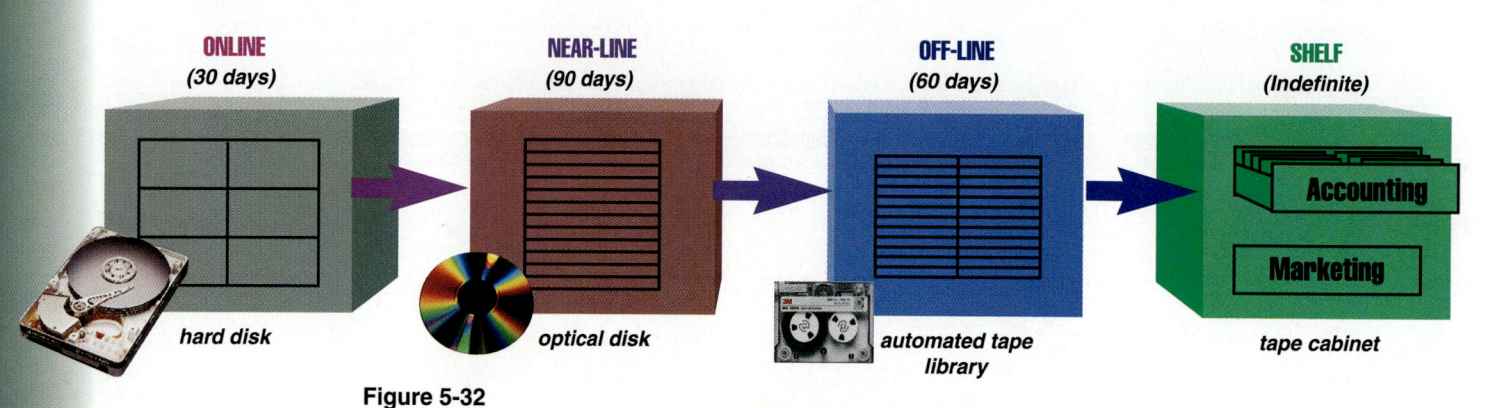

Figure 5-32
Hierarchical storage management (HSM) transfers data to different types and speeds of storage such as online, near-line, off-line, and shelf.

IN THE FUTURE

Holographic Storage

Early in the twenty-first century, around the year 2005, many experts believe that holographic storage devices will hold terabytes of data; the equivalent of a small library. These devices will store data as a hologram, which is a three-dimensional image in photosensitive material.

To record data, a single laser beam is split in two and directed toward the photosensitive material at right angles. Where the laser beams meet, the molecules are altered and the color changes from clear to blue. Blue molecules are considered 1 bits and the clear, unaltered molecules are considered 0 bits. To read information, a different colored laser beam is used. The reading laser beam interacts only with the blue molecules, making them briefly emit a red light. Sensors read the red light and transmit a 1 bit to the computer.

Several obstacles need to be overcome before holographic storage becomes commercially feasible. The first challenge is the size of the equipment required to record and read the material. The smallest size so far is approximately one-foot square. This may not seem that big but still it is much too large for personal computers. The second challenge is to find a suitable recording media. Early studies used chemically treated plastic cubes. The cubes have high storage capacities, more than six terabytes in the space of a sugar cube, but they require very low temperatures to retain their stored information. If the material is left at room temperature, it loses its information in a few hours. Even when it is cooled with liquid nitrogen, it retains its data only for a few months. Other materials lose data—it actually fades—when additional data is recorded. Recent research has focused on plastic discs similar to compact discs. These challenges are worth pursuing, however, because of the tremendous potential. In addition to storing large amounts of data in a small space, the estimated data transfer rates are more than 1,000 times faster than current magnetic disk drives.

Figure 5-33

review

chapter 1 | 2 | 3 | 4 | 5 | 6 | 7 | 8 | 9 | 10 | 11 | 12 | 13 | 14 | I

inCyber | review | terms | yourTurn | hotTopics | outThere | winLabs | webWalk | exercises | news | home

INSTRUCTIONS: *To display this page from the Web, launch your browser and enter the URL, http://www.scsite.com/dc/ch5/review.htm Click the links for current and additional information.*

1 Storage

Storage, also called **secondary storage** or **auxiliary storage**, stores data and programs when they are not being processed. The process of storing data is called **writing** or **recording data**, and the process of retrieving data is called **reading data**. Storage devices also can be used as both input and output devices. Because storage needs vary, a variety of storage devices is available.

2 Magnetic Disk Storage

Magnetic disks, the most widely used storage medium, consist of a round piece of plastic or metal, the surface of which is covered with a magnetic material. Types of magnetic disks include floppy disks, hard disks, and removable disk cartridges.

3 Floppy Disks

A **floppy disk** is a circular piece of thin mylar plastic that is coated with an oxide material. In a 3½-inch floppy disk, the circular piece of plastic is enclosed in a rigid plastic shell. **Formatting** prepares a floppy disk for storage by defining the **tracks**, **cylinders**, and **sectors** on the disk surface. When storing data, a **read/write head** resting on the surface of the rotating floppy disk generates electronic impulses. These impulses change the alignment of magnetic areas along a track to represent the binary code used to store data in memory. To read data, the read/write head senses the magnetic areas that have been recorded and transfers the data to memory. The time required to locate data and transfer it to memory is called **access time**.

4 Hard Disks

Hard disks consist of one or more rigid platters coated with a material that allows data to be recorded magnetically on the surface of the platters. The platters, read/write heads, and **access arms** that move the heads across the disk surface are all enclosed in an airtight, sealed case. Storing data on hard disks is much like storing data on floppy disks except that hard disks usually have multiple platters; and the read/write heads float on a cushion of air and do not touch the disk surface. Access time for a hard disk is significantly less than access time for a floppy disk because a hard disk spins faster and, unlike a floppy disk, a hard disk is spinning constantly.

5 Removable Disks

Disk cartridges are removable hard disk drives that provide both the storage capacity and fast access times of hard disks and the portability of floppy disks. The **Bernoulli disk cartridge** works with a special drive unit that uses a cushion of air to keep the flexible disk surface from touching the read/write head.

6 Maintaining Data Stored on a Disk

To prevent the loss of data stored on a disk, two procedures should be performed regularly: backup and defragmentation. **Backup** is the process of creating a copy of important programs and data. **Defragmentation** reorganizes the data stored on a disk so that files are located in contiguous (adjacent) clusters.

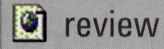

7 Data Compression

Data compression reduces data storage space requirements by substituting codes for repeating patterns of data. Compression most often is stated as a ratio of the size of the original data divided by the size of the compressed data. In *lossless compression*, which is used for text and numeric data, no data is lost in the compression process. In *lossy compression*, which is used for video images and sound, compression ratios are higher, but some data is lost.

8 CD-ROM and Optical Disks

Optical disks, which use laser technology, can store large quantities of data. A high-powered laser writes data on an optical disk by burning microscopic holes on the disk surface. A lower powered laser reads the data by reflecting light off the disk surface. The reflected light is converted into a series of bits. A **CD-ROM** (an acronym for compact disk read-only memory) is a smaller optical disk that can store about 450 times the data that can be stored on a 3fi-inch floppy disk.

9 Magnetic Tape

Magnetic tape consists of a thin ribbon of plastic, one side of which is coated with a material that can be magnetized to record the binary codes that represent data. Tape is a **sequential storage** media because the computer must write and read records one after another. The most common types of magnetic tape devices use **cartridge tape**, but some older systems use **reel-to-reel tape**. **Quarter-Inch-Cartridge (QIC)** tape devices, often used on PCs, record data in narrow tracks along the length of the tape. Tape storage serves as a primary means of backup, a method of transferring data between systems, and a cost-effective way to store data that does not have to be accessed immediately.

10 Other Types of Storage

PC Cards are small, credit card-sized cards that fit into PC Card expansion slots. Most often, PC Cards are used with portable computers, but they also can be used with desktop systems. A **RAID** storage system uses a group of integrated small disks that act like a single large disk drive. RAID storage systems read and write data faster than single large disk systems and reduce the risk of data loss. **Mass storage** systems provide automated retrieval of data from a library of storage media. Mass storage is ideal for large databases that must allow fast access to all data.

11 Special-Purpose Storage Devices

Memory buttons are small storage devices about the size of a dime that look like watch batteries. Memory buttons are used in applications where information about an item must travel with it. **Smart cards** are the same size and thickness of a credit card and contain a thin microprocessor capable of storing data. Smart cards often are used as prepaid telephone calling cards, as employee time and attendance tracking cards, and as identification cards for security applications. **Optical memory cards** are plastic cards the size of a credit card that can store up to 4.1 MB of digitized text or images using a laser beam. Optical memory cards are useful as a storage medium that permits data to be added but not to be erased or rewritten.

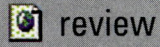

5 terms

chapter
1 | 2 | 3 | 4 | 5 | 6 | 7 | 8 | 9 | 10 | 11 | 12 | 13 | 14 | I

inCyber | review | terms | yourTurn | hotTopics | outThere | winLabs | webWalk | exercises | news | home

INSTRUCTIONS: *To display this page from the Web, launch your browser and enter the URL, http://www.scsite.com/dc/ch5/terms.htm. Scroll through the list of terms. Click a term for its definition and a picture. Click the rocket ship for current and additional information about the term.*

hard disks

DEFINITION

hard disks
Consist of one or more rigid platters coated with a material that allows data to be recorded magnetically on the surface of the platters. (5.8)

access arms (5.10)
access time (5.7)
auxiliary storage (5.2)

backup (5.12)
Bernoulli disk cartridge (5.11)
bits per inch (bpi) (5.6)

cartridge tape (5.16)
CD-E (compact disk-erasable) (5.15)
CD-R (compact disk-recordable) (5.15)
CD-ROM (5.14)
cluster (5.4)
compact disk read-only memory (5.14)
cylinder (5.4)

data compression (5.13)
data transfer rate (5.7)
defragmentation (5.12)
digital audio tape (DAT) (5.18)
direct-access storage devices (DASD) (5.9)
disk cache (5.10)
disk cartridges (5.11)
disk mirroring (5.20)
diskette (5.3)
DVD (digital video disk) (5.14)

file allocation table (FAT) (5.5)
fixed disks (5.9)
floppy disk (5.3)
floptical (5.15)
formatting (5.4)
fragmented (5.12)

hard disks (5.8)
hard disk controller (5.10)
head crash (5.10)
helical scan technology (5.18)
hierarchical storage management (HSM) (5.24)
high-density (HD) floppy disk (5.6)

integrated drive electronics (IDE) (5.11)

latency (5.7)
longitudinal recording (5.18)
magnetic disk (5.3)
magnetic tape (5.16)
magneto-optical (MO) (5.15)
mass storage (5.21)
memory buttons (5.21)
multiple zone recording (MZR) (5.6)

near-line storage (5.24)
nonvolatile (5.2)

offline storage (5.24)
online storage (5.24)
optical disks (5.14)
optical memory cards (5.22)

partitions (5.9)
PC Cards (5.19)
platters (5.8)

Quarter-Inch-Cartridge (QIC) (5.18)

RAID (5.19)
read/write head (5.7)
reading data (5.2)
recording data (5.2)
recording density (5.6)
redundant array of inexpensive disks (5.19)
reel-to-reel tape (5.17)
rotational delay (5.7)

secondary storage (5.2)
sector (5.4)
seek time (5.7)
sequential storage (5.16)
serpentine recording (5.18)
SLEDs (5.20)
small computer system interface (SCSI) (5.11)
smart cards (5.22)
storage (5.2)
striping (5.20)

tape density (5.18)
track (5.4)
track sector (5.4)
tracks per inch (tpi) (5.6)

virtual file allocation table (VFAT) (5.5)
volatile (5.2)

write-protect window (5.5)
writing data (5.2)

yourTurn

chapter 1 | 2 | 3 | 4 | 5 | 6 | 7 | 8 | 9 | 10 | 11 | 12 | 13 | 14 | I

inCyber | review | terms | yourTurn | hotTopics | outThere | winLabs | webWalk | exercises | news | home

INSTRUCTIONS: *To display this page from the Web, launch your browser and enter the URL, http://www.scsite.com/dc/ch5/turn.htm. Click a blank line for the answer. Click the links for current and additional information.*

Label the Figure

Instructions: Identify the types of computer storage and memory.

Fill in the Blanks

Instructions: Complete each sentence with the correct term or terms.

1. _____, also called _____ or _____, holds data and programs when they are not being processed.
2. Three factors determine access time for a floppy disk drive: _____, _____, and _____.
3. Before a hard disk is formatted, it can be divided into separate areas called _____, each of which can function as if it were a separate disk.
4. A group of integrated small disks that act as a single large disk drive is called a(n) _____ storage system.
5. _____, which are the same size and thickness as a credit card, contain a thin microprocessor capable of storing data.

Short Answer

Instructions: Write a brief answer to each of the following questions.

1. How does formatting prepare a floppy disk for storage? What is the file allocation table (FAT)? The amount of data that can be stored on a floppy disk depends on what two factors? _____
2. How is storing data on a hard disk different from storing data on a floppy disk? Why is access time faster for a hard disk than for a floppy disk? What is a disk cache? _____
3. What is data compression? How is lossless compression different from lossy compression? Why are compressed files often used when files are transferred over communication lines? _____
4. How is data recorded on and read from CD-ROMs? How are the speeds for CD-ROM drives rated? _____
5. For what purposes is magnetic tape used as a storage medium? Why is tape considered a sequential storage media? _____

hotTopics

chapter 5

1 | 2 | 3 | 4 | 5 | 6 | 7 | 8 | 9 | 10 | 11 | 12 | 13 | 14 | I

inCyber | review | terms | yourTurn | hotTopics | outThere | winLabs | webWalk | exercises | news | home

INSTRUCTIONS: *To display this page from the Web, launch your browser and enter the URL, http://www.scsite.com/dc/ch5/hot.htm. Click the links for current and additional information to help you respond to the hotTopics questions.*

1. *Some residents of Swindon, England, have replaced their cash with smart cards.* Special machines are used to transfer funds to the smart card's microprocessor, and purchases are made simply by running the card through a store's reader. Money can be moved from one card to another, and a small balance reader displays the amount remaining. Advocates claim that smart cards are less expensive than using cash, checks, or credit cards; provide greater security; offer increased control (parents can restrict the types of purchases that can be made on a dependent's card); and serve as a safe form of payment for purchases on the Internet. Opponents fear fraud by savvy counterfeiters, lack of anonymity in transactions, and possible invasion of privacy. What are the greatest advantages of using smart cards? What are the disadvantages? Do you think smart cards ever will replace money? Why or why not?

2. *The history of personal computer storage is a tale of increasing speed, capacity, and durability.* Until IBM invented the floppy disk in 1970, magnetic tape cartridges were the primary means of storage. Tape soon was replaced by the 5¼-inch floppy disk, a magnetic disk sheathed in a flexible cloth-like cover, that stored more data and allowed it to be accessed more quickly. Gradually, the 5¼-inch floppy disk has been supplanted by the sturdier, more capacious 3½-inch floppy disk. What does the future hold? Ten years from now, will the 3½-inch floppy disk, or a version it, still be an important storage medium? Why or why not? What storage medium, if any, might be used instead? Why?

3. *The National Gallery in Washington, D.C., is a remarkable collection that contains works by* Italian, French, and American masters. The Gallery has recorded its entire collection on an optical disk. The disk images offer startling clarity — even brush strokes are visible. Users can display any work in the collection almost instantaneously, locate works based on a range of criteria, and magnify portions of a work on the screen. Is this the beginning of a trend? Will all galleries, archives, and museums eventually take advantage of optical disk technology to catalog their holdings? Why or why not? Who is most likely to use the optical disks? Despite their advantages, how might optical disks pale when compared with a visit to the institution itself?

4. *A recent study has shown that data loss costs American businesses approximately $4 billion* every year. Despite this, another study discovered that less than 33% of all companies regularly backup their files. Many businesses that have backup policies learned from their mistakes; of the companies that backup their data, almost 30% confess to losing data in the past because of a computer crash. Why do so many businesses fail to backup their data? If you were a CEO of a company, what backup policy would you establish? How would you ensure that the policy was carried out?

5. *Recently, a cookbook was released on CD-ROM. Not only does this* cookbook offer a thousand recipes, but its search capabilities allow users to find dishes that meet specified criteria — ingredients, nutritional levels, cooking methods, ethnic origins, and so on — in seconds. The CD-ROM also includes video demonstrations of culinary procedures, such as trussing a turkey, along with a meal planner and glossary. What might be some disadvantages of the CD-ROM cookbook when compared with its traditional counterpart? Imagine another task that could be simplified using one of the storage media described in this chapter. What medium would you use? Why? How would the task be made easier? What might be some disadvantages of performing the task using a computer?

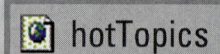

chapter 5 outThere

1 | 2 | 3 | 4 | 5 | 6 | 7 | 8 | 9 | 10 | 11 | 12 | 13 | 14 | I

inCyber | review | terms | yourTurn | hotTopics | outThere | winLabs | webWalk | exercises | news | home

INSTRUCTIONS: *To display this page from the Web, launch your browser and enter the URL, http://www.scsite.com/dc/ch5/out.htm Click the links for current and additional information.*

1 *The cost of floppy disks varies depending on such factors as recording* density, manufacturer, and whether or not the disk already is formatted for an Apple or IBM-compatible personal computer. What type of floppy disk is the best buy? Visit a computer vendor and compare three floppy disks: the least expensive, the most expensive, and one priced in the middle of the range. Who manufactures each disk? How are the floppy disks similar? How are they different? Which disk is recommended by the store's salesperson? Why? If you were purchasing a floppy disk for your own use, would you buy one of these floppy disks or a different one? Why?

2 *Digital video disks (DVDs) can store seven times as much information as* CD-ROMs — more than two million pages of text, seven hours of music, or multiple complete versions of a popular movie. The disks can be copied a thousand times, and each duplicate is as clear as the original. DVD technology has existed for awhile, but various commercial considerations delayed its introduction. Manufacturers had to agree on a unified format to avoid a conflict like that between VHS and Beta that once afflicted the videocassette industry. An understanding between movie makers, who feared counterfeiting if the disks could be copied, and software writers, who opposed restrictions on copying, had to be reached. Visit sites on the World Wide Web to find out about DVD. Who is most likely to purchase DVD technology? Why? What features of DVD are most important? How will DVD be used? What is a DVD-RAM drive? When will software be published on DVD-ROM disks?

3 *Some organizations, such as insurance companies, banks, libraries, and college registrars, are* information intensive, meaning they must keep track of and manipulate large amounts of data. For these institutions, choosing a suitable storage medium is a crucial decision. Care must be taken so the medium selected is adequate, reliable, cost-effective, and appropriate. Visit an information-intensive organization and interview someone responsible for maintaining the organization's data. What are the organization's storage requirements? What type of storage medium is used? In what way does that medium meet the organization's needs? Have any problems with storage ever existed? If so, how where the problems remedied? What kinds of backup procedures are employed?

4 *Many computer users support the saying "You never can have too much storage." Although* some turn to hardware solutions to address the problem of adequate storage, other users look to software answers, such as hard disk partitions or data compression. Information about both partition software and data compression software is available on the World Wide Web. Visit some Web sites to find out more about hard disk partitions and data compression. How do partitions increase the capacity of hard disks? What kind of data compression (lossy or lossless) is most suitable for communications devices? What are the most well known data compression algorithms? How can compression ratios of different algorithms be compared?

5 *As a result of expanding storage requirements for software and graphic files, new technologies* are being developed that offer even greater storage capacity. These technologies include DVD, flash memory cards, glass disks, glass-ceramic disks, and wet hard drives. Using current computer magazines and sites on the Web, prepare a brief report on one or more of these new technologies. What does the technology entail? What benefits does it offer? Why? When is the technology likely to be available for general use?

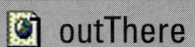

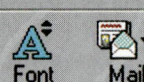

winLabs

INSTRUCTIONS: *To display this page from the Web, launch your browser and enter the URL, http://www.scsite.com/dc/ch5/labs.htm. Click the links for current and additional information.*

1 Shelly Cashman Series Secondary Storage Lab

Follow the instructions in winLabs 1 on page 1.34 to display the Shelly Cashman Series Labs screen. Click Maintaining Your Hard Drive. Click the Start Lab button. When the initial screen displays, read the objectives. With your printer turned on, click the Print Questions button. Fill out the top of the Questions sheet and then answer the questions.

2 Examining My Computer

Right-click the My Computer icon in the upper-left corner on the desktop. Click Open on the shortcut menu. What is the drive letter for the floppy disk on your computer? What letter(s) are used for the hard drives on your computer? If you have a CD-ROM drive, what letter is used for it? Double-click the drive C icon in the My Computer window. What are the names of the folders (yellow folder icons) on your drive C? Close all open windows.

3 Working with Files

Insert your student floppy disk into drive A. Double-click the My Computer icon on the desktop. When the My Computer window displays, right-click the 3½ Floppy [A:] icon. Click Open on the shortcut menu. Click View on the menu bar and then click Large Icons. Right-click the lab2-3 icon. If lab2-3 is not on your floppy disk, ask your instructor for a copy. Click Copy on the shortcut menu. Click Edit on the menu bar and then click Paste. A new icon titled Copy of lab2-3 displays in the 3½ Floppy [A:] window (Figure 5-34). Right-click the Copy of lab2-3 icon and then click Rename on the shortcut menu. Type lab5-3 and then press ENTER. Right-click the lab5-3 icon and then click Print on the shortcut menu. Close the 3½ Floppy [A:] window.

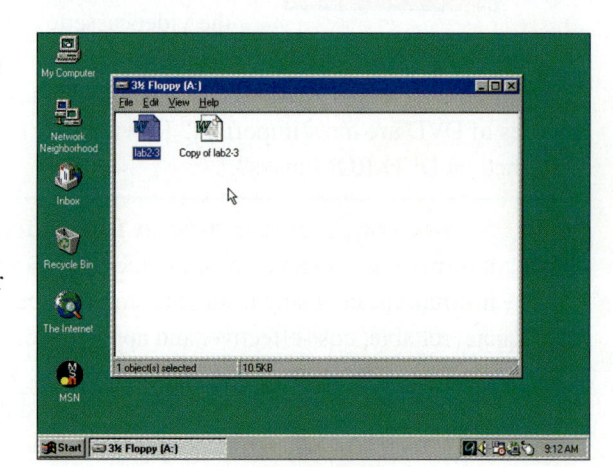

Figure 5-34

4 Using Help

Click the Start button on the taskbar, and then click Help on the Start menu to display the Help Topics: Windows Help dialog box. Click the Contents tab, double-click How To..., and then double-click Work with Files and Folders. Click Finding a file or folder. Click the Options button and then click Print Topic. Click the OK button. Click the Help Topics button. One at a time, print each of the remaining Work with Files and Folders topics. Close any open Help window(s). Read the printouts.

webWalk

INSTRUCTIONS: *To display this page from the Web, launch your browser and enter the URL, http://www.scsite.com/dc/ch5/walk.htm. Click the exercise link to display the exercise.*

1. Data Compression
One way to store more data on a disk is to use data compression. You can learn more about data compression by completing this exercise.

2. Audio File Storage
One common audio file format on the Web is the WAV format. Complete this exercise to learn about storage requirements for .wav sound files (Figure 5-35).

3. Video File Storage
One common video file format on the Web is the AVI format. To view some movie clips and learn about the storage requirements for .avi video files, complete this exercise.

4. Graphics File Storage
While GIF is still the dominant graphics format on the Web, JPEG is gaining ground fast. To view some dramatic pictures in .jpg format (Figure 5-36) and learn more about storage requirements for .jpg graphic files, complete this exercise.

Figure 5-35

Figure 5-36

5. Information Mining
Complete this exercise to improve your Web research skills by using a Web search engine to find information related to this chapter.

6. Web file formats
Multimedia files on the Internet come in many different formats. Some Web browsers need "helper" applications, also called "viewers," to be able to display certain file formats. Complete this exercise to learn more about different file formats and viewers for Web browsers.

7. Flash Memory
Digital cameras, PDAs, handheld PCs, navigation systems, digital voice recorders and even cell phones are targets for new storage technologies. Flash memory is electronically erasable, programmable, read-only memory, so it is non-volatile. Complete this exercise to learn more about Flash memory.

8. Digital Video Disk (DVD)
Twenty times more data can fit on a DVD than a CD. This translates into richer sound and images than ever heard or seen before. By some estimates, DVD optical drives will be a $4 billion market by the year 2000. Complete this exercise to learn more about DVDs.

9. Web Chat
Complete this exercise to enter a Web Chat discussion related to the issues presented in the hotTopics exercise.

Communications and Networks

OBJECTIVES

After completing this chapter, you will be able to:

- Define the term communications

- Describe several uses of communications technology

- Describe the basic components of a communications system

- Describe the various transmission media used for communications channels

- Describe the different types of line configurations

- Describe how data is transmitted

- Describe the functions performed by communications software

- Describe commonly used communications equipment

- Explain the difference between local and wide area networks

- Explain the use of communications protocols

When computers were first developed, they were designed as stand-alone systems. As computers became more widely used, equipment and software were designed to transfer data from one computer to another. Initially, this capability was available only on large systems. Today, even the smallest hand-held computers can communicate with other computers. This change has taken place because of several reasons. For one, communications equipment and software, once expensive options, now are standard components in most computer systems. In addition, opportunities to use communications to access information increase almost daily. Online services and the Internet, for example, allow you to send messages to friends, read magazines on the World Wide Web, and obtain research data, news, and product information, twenty-four hours a day.

This chapter provides an overview of communications with an emphasis on the communication of data and information. The chapter explains some of the terminology, equipment, procedures, and applications that relate to computers and their use as communications devices. It also discusses how computers can be joined together into a network, which is a group of connected computers that multiplies the power of individual computers by allowing them to communicate and share hardware, software, data, and information.

What Is Communications?

Communications, sometimes called **data communications** or **telecommunications**, refers to the transmission of data and information between two or more computers, using a communications channel such as a standard telephone line.

Examples of How Communications Is Used

The ability to instantly and accurately communicate information is changing the way people do business and interact with each other. The following applications rely on communications technology:

- Electronic mail (e-mail)
- Voice mail
- Facsimile (fax)
- Telecommuting
- Videoconferencing
- Groupware
- Electronic data interchange (EDI)
- Global positioning systems (GPSs)
- Bulletin board systems (BBSs)
- Online services
- The Internet

Electronic Mail (E-mail)

Electronic mail (e-mail), described in Chapter 2, allows you to use a computer to transmit messages to and receive messages from other computer users. The other users may be connected to the same computer network or to a separate network reached through the use of communications equipment.

Voice Mail

Voice mail allows callers to leave a voice message in a voice mailbox, much like leaving a message on an answering machine. The difference between voice mail and an answering machine is that a voice mail system digitizes the caller's message so it can be stored on a disk like other computer data. The party who was called then can listen to the stored message (by converting it from digital to audio form), reply to the message, or add comments and forward the message to another mailbox on the system.

Facsimile (Fax)

Facsimile, or **fax**, equipment, described in Chapter 4, is used to transmit a digitized image of a document over telephone lines. The document can contain hand-written or typed text, graphics, or even photographs. A fax machine scans the document and converts the image into digitized data, which is transmitted over a telephone line. The fax machine at the receiving end converts the digitized data back into its original image. Many PCs use fax equipment and a modem to send documents directly to a fax machine or to another PC. A person who receives the fax on his or her PC can print the document to create a hard copy.

Telecommuting

Telecommuting involves working at home and communicating with an office by using a personal computer and communications equipment and software (Figure 6-1). Using this equipment and software, a telecommuter can connect to the office's main computer or network to read and answer electronic mail, access databases, and transmit completed

---

inCyber

For a glossary of communications terms, visit the Discovering Computers Chapter 6 inCyber page (http://www.scsite.com/dc/ch6/incyber.htm) and click Communications.

Figure 6-1
Telecommuting allows you to work from your home or some other location away from the office.

inCyber
For details on telecommuting, visit the Discovering Computers Chapter 6 inCyber page (http://www.scsite.com/dc/ch6/incyber.htm) and click Telecommuting.

projects. Telecommuting provides flexibility, allowing companies to increase employee productivity and, at the same time, meet the needs of individual employees. Telecommuting can reduce the time used to commute to the office each week; eliminate the need to travel during poor weather conditions; provide a convenient and comfortable work environment for disabled employees or workers recovering from injuries or illnesses; and allow employees to combine work with personal responsibilities such as child-care. Some predict that by the year 2000, ten percent of the work force will be telecommuters.

Videoconferencing

Videoconferencing is the use of computers, television cameras, and communications software and equipment to conduct *electronic meetings* with participants at different locations (Figure 6-2). Special software and equipment are used to digitize and compress

Figure 6-2
Videoconferencing is used to transmit and receive video and audio signals over standard communications channels. This meeting is being transmitted to a video conference center at another location. The people at the other location also are being recorded and transmitted and can be seen on the TV monitor.

the video image so it can be transmitted along with the audio over standard communications channels. The video images of moving objects do not transmit as clearly as they do over television channels, but they are clear enough to contribute to the discussion. Images of nonmoving objects such as charts and graphs transmit more clearly.

Videoconferencing originally was developed for large groups holding meetings in a room specially outfitted with videoconferencing equipment. More recently, desktop videoconferencing equipment has been developed to allow individual users to conduct videoconferences using a personal computer (Figure 6-3).

Groupware

Groupware, described in Chapter 2, is software that helps multiple users to collaborate on projects and share information. Groupware is part of a broad concept called **workgroup technology**, which includes equipment and software used by group members to communicate, manage their activities, and make group decisions. Other features and capabilities of groupware include group editing, group scheduling, group decision support, workflow software, and discussion databases. Some software applications discussed separately in this section, including e-mail and videoconferencing, also can be considered groupware.

Electronic Data Interchange (EDI)

Electronic data interchange (EDI) is the direct electronic exchange of documents from one business's computer system to another. EDI frequently is used by large companies to transmit routine business documents such as purchase orders and invoices. In some industries, such as the automotive industry, EDI is the standard way of doing repeat business with suppliers. EDI offers a number of advantages over paper documents, including the following:

- Reduced paper flow
- Lower transaction costs
- Faster transmission of documents
- Reduced data entry errors, because data does not need to be reentered at the receiving end

Some companies have developed sophisticated EDI applications in which orders are created automatically based on sales or inventory levels, transmitted electronically to a vendor, and shipped to the customer. The entire process requires almost no human intervention.

---

inCyber

For information about videoconferencing, visit the Discovering Computers Chapter 6 inCyber page (http://www.scsite.com/dc/ch6/incyber.htm) and click Videoconferencing.

inCyber

For information about electronic data interchange (EDI), visit the Discovering Computers Chapter 6 inCyber page (http://www.scsite.com/dc/ch6/incyber.htm) and click EDI.

Figure 6-3
Desktop videoconferencing equipment allows individual users to communicate with other employees on their computer network. Some systems also can connect to remote locations.

Global Positioning Systems (GPSs)

A **global positioning system (GPS)** uses receivers that pick up and analyze transmissions from several satellites to determine the geographic location of the earth-based GPS receiver. Depending on the equipment used, a GPS system can be accurate to within 50 feet. GPS systems often are used for tracking and navigation by all types of vehicles, such as cars, trucks, boats, and planes. Small GPS systems even have been designed for use with portable personal computers. Some GPS systems work with map software, which can measure the distance between two points and display the user's exact location and direction of travel on a map (Figure 6-4).

Figure 6-4
Global positioning system (GPS) equipment communicates with satellites to provide an exact fix on the user's location.

Bulletin Board Systems (BBSs)

An electronic **bulletin board system (BBS)** is a computer system that maintains a centralized collection of information in the form of electronic messages. Once you access a bulletin board system using a personal computer and communications equipment, you can add or delete messages, read existing messages, or upload and download software. BBSs are run by a person called the **system operator**, or **sys op**, who maintains and updates the bulletin board.

More than 60,000 BBSs exist in the United States. Some of these bulletin boards provide specific services; for example, many hardware and software vendors have set up BBSs to provide online support for their products. Other bulletin boards function as electronic meeting rooms for special-interest groups that use the BBS to share information about hobbies such as stamp collecting, games, music, genealogy, and astronomy. Still other BBSs are strictly social; for example, users meet new friends and conduct conversations by posting messages on the bulletin board. While most BBSs are local and serve a relatively small number of users, some regional and national BBSs attract a larger user base.

inCyber

For an explanation of global positioning systems (GPSs), visit the Discovering Computers Chapter 6 inCyber page (http://www.scsite.com/dc/ch6/incyber.htm) and click GPS.

Online Services

Online services, sometimes called **information services**, make information and services available to paying subscribers. Once you subscribe to an online service, you can access it by using communications equipment and software to connect to the service provider's computer system. Services that are available include electronic banking, shopping, news, weather, hotel and airline reservations, and investment information. Some specialized online services provide very specific information, such as legal reports. Other online services (Figure 6-5) provide a wide variety of information. Figure 6-6 is a list of the major online service providers.

Figure 6-5
The leading online service providers. Each offers the latest news, weather, sports, and financial information along with shopping, entertainment, and electronic mail. They all offer Internet access.

America Online

NAME	DESCRIPTION	TELEPHONE NUMBER
America Online	Largest service provider. News, weather, shopping, finance, travel, and more.	800-827-6364
Prodigy	News, weather, shopping, finance, travel, and more.	800-776-3449
CompuServe	Most comprehensive of all services. Business oriented.	800-848-8199
The Microsoft Network	Newest service. News, weather, shopping, finance, travel, and more.	800-386-5550

Figure 6-6
The names and information telephone numbers of the major online information service providers.

The Internet

One of the more exciting uses of communications today is the Internet. The **Internet** is a global network of computer networks used daily by individuals and businesses to obtain information, send messages, order products and services, and more. Much like the telephone, the Internet is changing the way people communicate and share information. The history and uses of this growing communications application will be covered in more detail in Chapter 7.

A Communications System Model

Figure 6-7 shows the basic model for a communications system. This model consists of the following equipment:

- A computer or a terminal
- Communications equipment that sends (and usually can receive) data
- The communications channel over which data is sent
- Communications equipment that receives (and usually can send) data
- Another computer

The basic model also includes **communications software**, consisting of programs that manage the transmission of data between computers. For two computers to communicate with each other, each system must have compatible communications software. A **communications channel**, also called a **communications line**, **communications link**, or **data link**, is the path that the data follows as it is transmitted from the sending equipment to the receiving equipment in a communications system. Communications channels are made up of one or more transmission media.

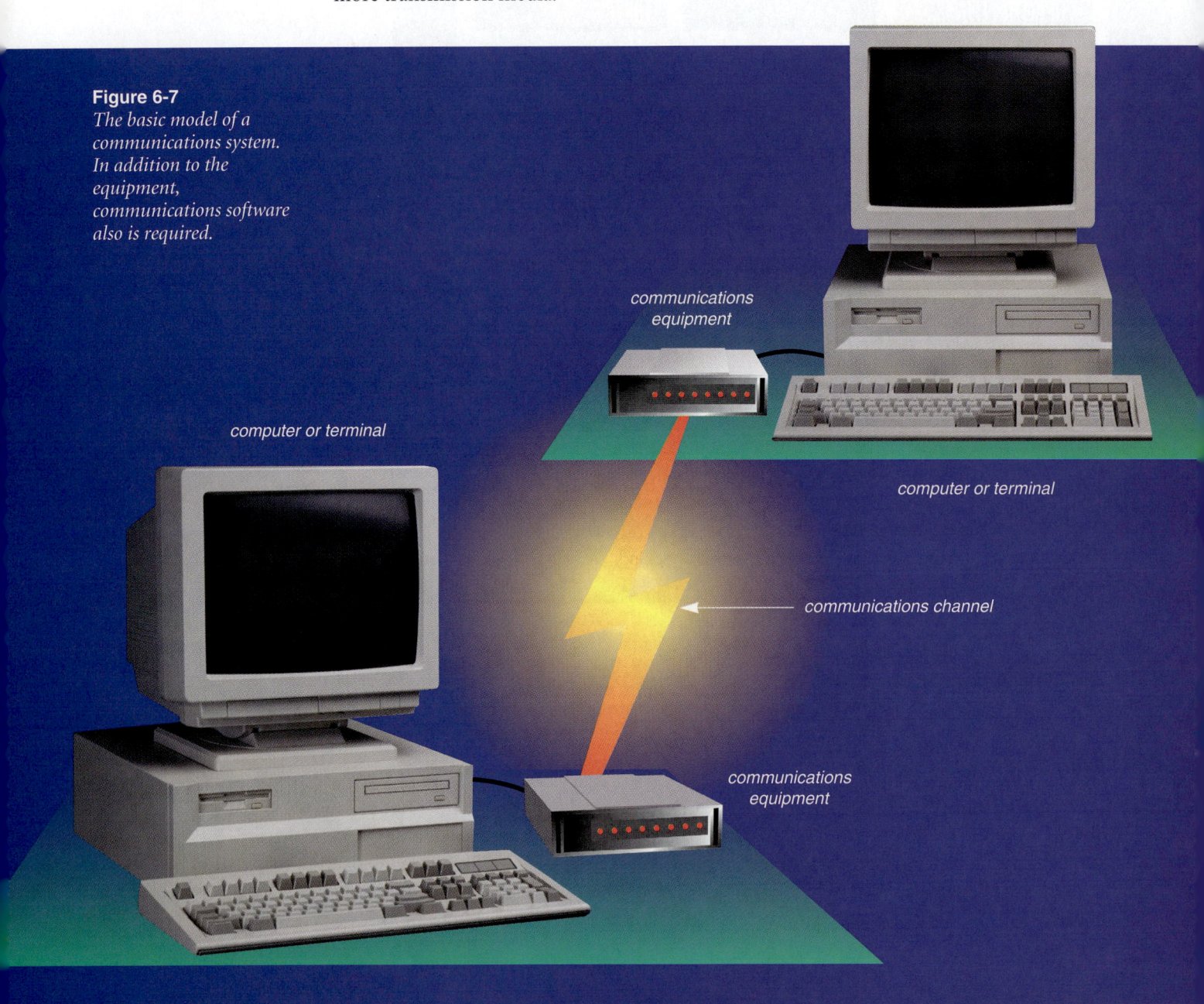

inCyber

For an example of how companies use communications systems, visit the Discovering Computers Chapter 6 inCyber page (http://www.scsite.com/dc/ch6/incyber.htm) and click Communications System.

Figure 6-7
The basic model of a communications system. In addition to the equipment, communications software also is required.

Transmission Media

Transmission media are the physical materials or other means used to establish a communications channel. The two types of transmission media are physical cabling media, such as twisted-pair cable, coaxial cable, and fiber-optic cable and wireless media, such as microwaves and other radio waves and infrared light.

Twisted-Pair Cable

Twisted-pair cable (Figure 6-8) consists of pairs of plastic-coated copper wires that are twisted together. A thin layer of colored plastic insulates and identifies each wire; the wires then are twisted to reduce electrical interference. **Shielded twisted-pair (STP) cable** has a foil wrapper around each wire that further reduces electrical interference. **Unshielded twisted-pair (UTP) cable**, also called **10baseT cable**, does not have the foil wrapper. Because twisted-pair cable is an inexpensive transmission medium that can be installed easily, it commonly is used for telephone lines and data communications between computers.

1. wires are twisted to reduce electrical interference
2. color coding identifies individual and pairs of wires
3. plastic sheath protects wires
4. modular connector; RJ11 (4-wire) connector used for voice and low-speed (up to 1 Mbps) data transmission; RJ45 connector (8-wire) used for high-speed (10 to 100 Mbps) data transmission

Figure 6-8
Twisted-pair cable often is used to connect personal computers with one another. It is inexpensive and can be installed easily.

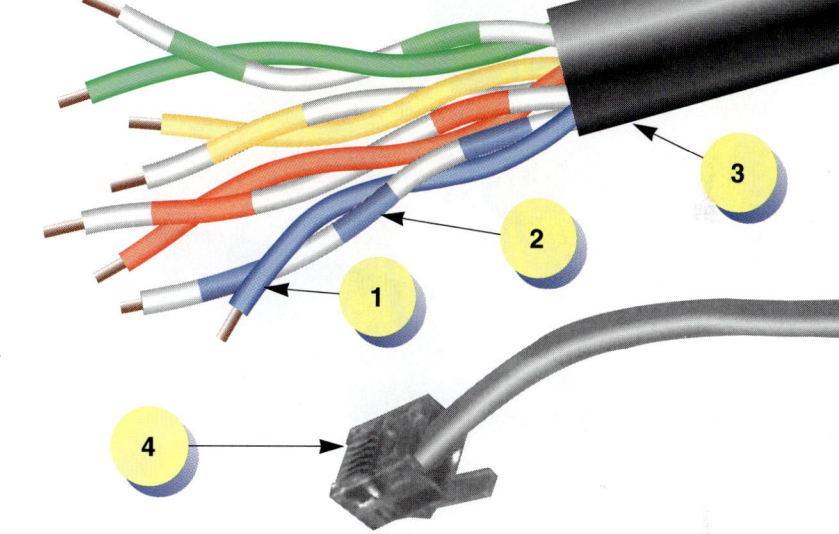

Coaxial Cable

A **coaxial cable**, often referred to as **coax** (pronounced *co-axe*), is a high-quality communications line that consists of a copper wire conductor surrounded by three layers: a nonconducting insulator surrounded by a woven metal outer conductor and a plastic outer coating (Figure 6-9). Because coaxial cable is more heavily insulated than twisted-pair, it is not susceptible to electrical interference and transmits data faster over longer distances.

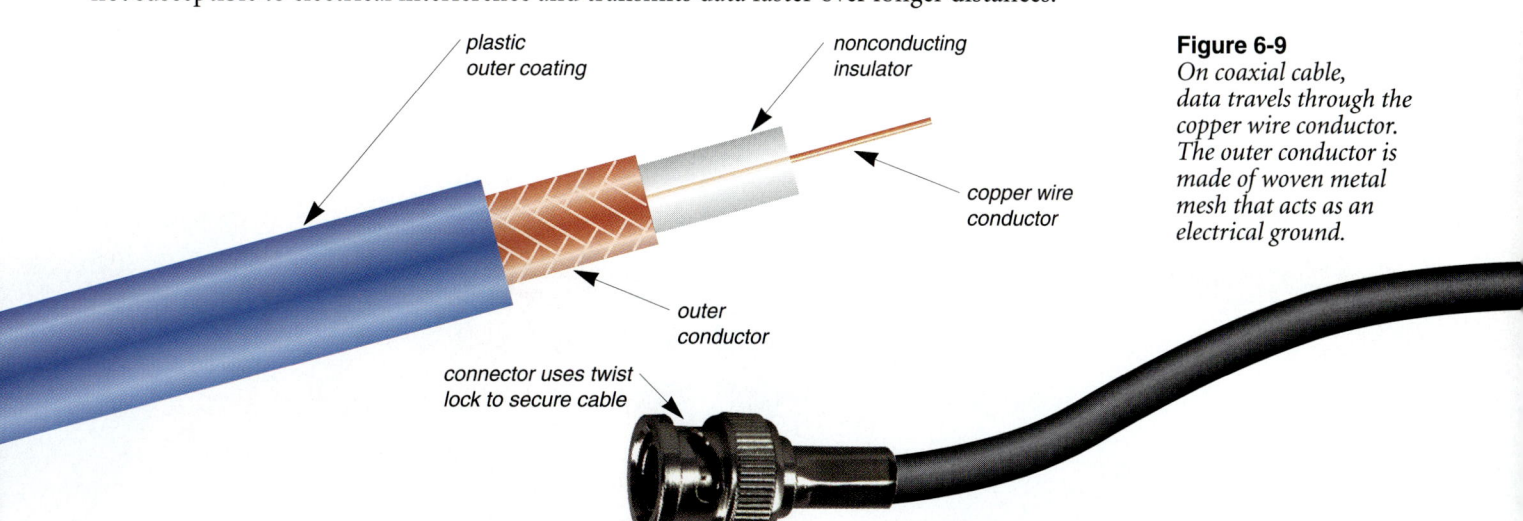

plastic outer coating
nonconducting insulator
copper wire conductor
outer conductor
connector uses twist lock to secure cable

Figure 6-9
On coaxial cable, data travels through the copper wire conductor. The outer conductor is made of woven metal mesh that acts as an electrical ground.

Different grades and sizes of coaxial cable exist. One type of coaxial cable, for example, is used for cable television. Another type called **thinnet**, or **10base2 cable**, is a small diameter coaxial cable that often is used with computer networks.

Fiber-Optic Cable

Fiber-optic cable uses smooth, hair-thin strands of glass or plastic to transmit data as pulses of light (Figure 6-10). The major advantages of fiber-optic cables over wire cables include substantial weight and size savings and reduced electrical and magnetic interference. Another advantage is increased speed of transmission. A single fiber-optic cable can carry several hundred thousand voice communications simultaneously. Fiber-optic cable does, however, cost more than twisted-pair or coaxial cable and can be difficult to install and modify. Despite these limitations, many telephone companies use fiber-optic cable for new telephone lines because of its high-carrying capacity.

Figure 6-10
Fiber-optic cable is made up of hair-thin strands of glass or plastic that carry data as pulses of light instead of electricity.

1. optical fiber is made up of an inner and outer core of glass or plastic; the inner core is 100 to 200 millionths of an inch in diameter
2. inner core layer carries light signals; the surrounding outer layer of glass acts as a boundary and keeps the light signal within the inner core
3. plastic buffer layer protects optical fiber against ultraviolet light and gives cable rigidity
4. several layers of high-strength fabric provide reinforcement and protection against cuts
5. plastic jacket surrounds inner materials and provides outer protection
6. fiber-optic connector has latching mechanism to prevent disconnection

inCyber
For information about fiber-optic cable, visit the Discovering Computers Chapter 6 inCyber page (http://www.scsite.com/dc/ch6/incyber.htm) and click Fiber-Optic.

Microwave Transmission

Microwaves are radio waves that can be used to provide high-speed transmission of both voice communications and digital signals. Earth-based microwave transmission, called **terrestrial microwave**, involves sending data from one microwave station to another, similarly to the way broadcast radio signals are transmitted (Figure 6-11). Microwaves are limited to line-of-sight transmission. This means that microwaves must be transmitted in a straight line and that no obstructions can exist, such as buildings or mountains, between microwave stations. To avoid possible obstructions, microwave antennas often are positioned on the tops of buildings, towers, or mountains.

Figure 6-11
The round antennas on the tower are used for microwave transmission. Microwave transmission is limited to line-of-sight. Antennas usually are placed 25 to 75 miles apart.

Communications satellites receive microwave signals from earth-based communications facilities, amplify the signals, and retransmit the signals back to the communications facilities. These communications facilities, called **earth stations**, use large, dish-shaped antennas to transmit and receive data from satellites (Figure 6-12). The transmission *to* the satellite is called an **uplink** and the transmission *from* the satellite to a receiving earth station is called a **downlink**.

Figure 6-12
Earth stations use large dish antennas to communicate with satellites.

6.12 CHAPTER 6 – COMMUNICATIONS AND NETWORKS

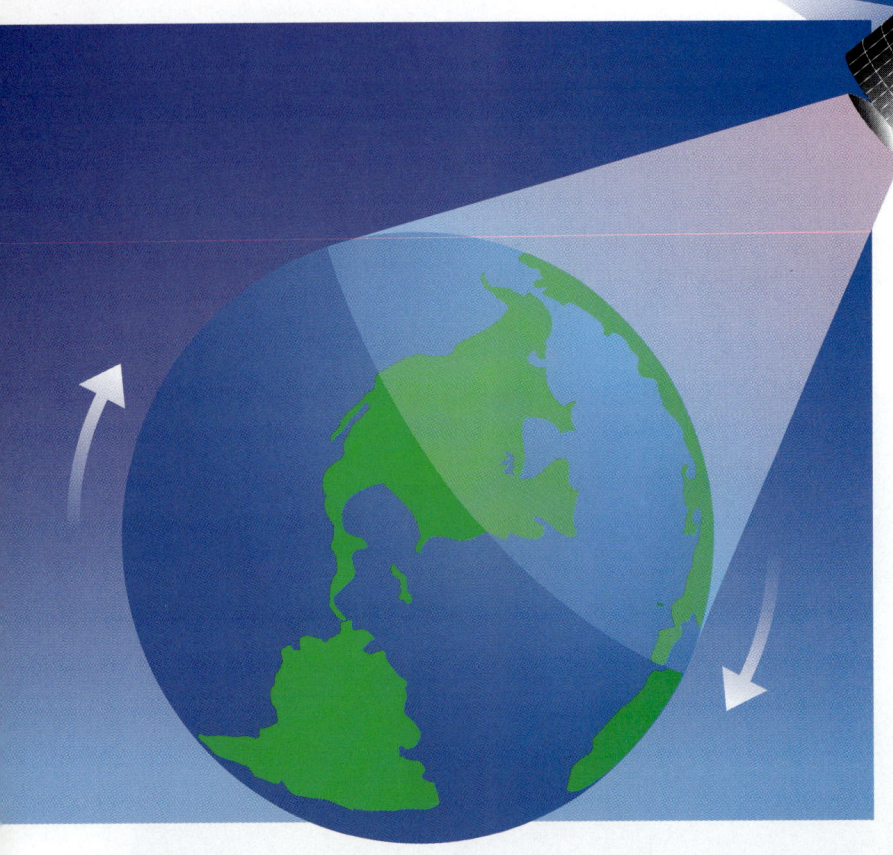

Communications satellites usually are placed about 22,300 miles above the earth in a **geosynchronous orbit** (Figure 6-13). This means that the satellite orbits at the same speed as the earth, so the dish antennas used to send and receive microwave signals remain fixed on the appropriate satellite at all times.

Businesses with operations in multiple locations often use private satellite systems to communicate information. If a business transmits only a small amount of information each day–say, daily sales results from a retail store–a small satellite dish antenna can be used. One such antenna, called a **very small aperture terminal** (VSAT) dish antenna, is only one to three meters in size, but transmits up to 19,200 bits per second. The cost of using a private satellite system with a VSAT antenna can be as low as $200 per month.

Figure 6-13
Communications satellites are placed in geosynchronous orbits approximately 22,300 miles above the earth. Geosynchronous means that the orbit of the satellite matches the rotation of the earth so the satellite is always above the same spot on the earth.

Wireless Transmission: Radio and Light Waves

Wireless transmission uses one of three techniques to transmit data: carrier-connect radio, infrared light beams, or radio waves. Carrier-connect radio and infrared light are used by companies to transmit data between devices that are in the same general area. Carrier-connect radio, for example, uses the existing electrical wiring of a building to act as an antenna, to transmit data within a building. Infrared light beams are used to transmit data between personal computer devices without connecting them with a cable (Figure 6-14). While such local wireless systems provide flexibility and portability, they are slower and more susceptible to interference than wired connections.

Figure 6-14
Many portable personal computers and printers come with infrared communications capabilities. This allows you to print a document without attaching the computer to the printer with a cable. The range is approximately ten feet.

infrared sensor

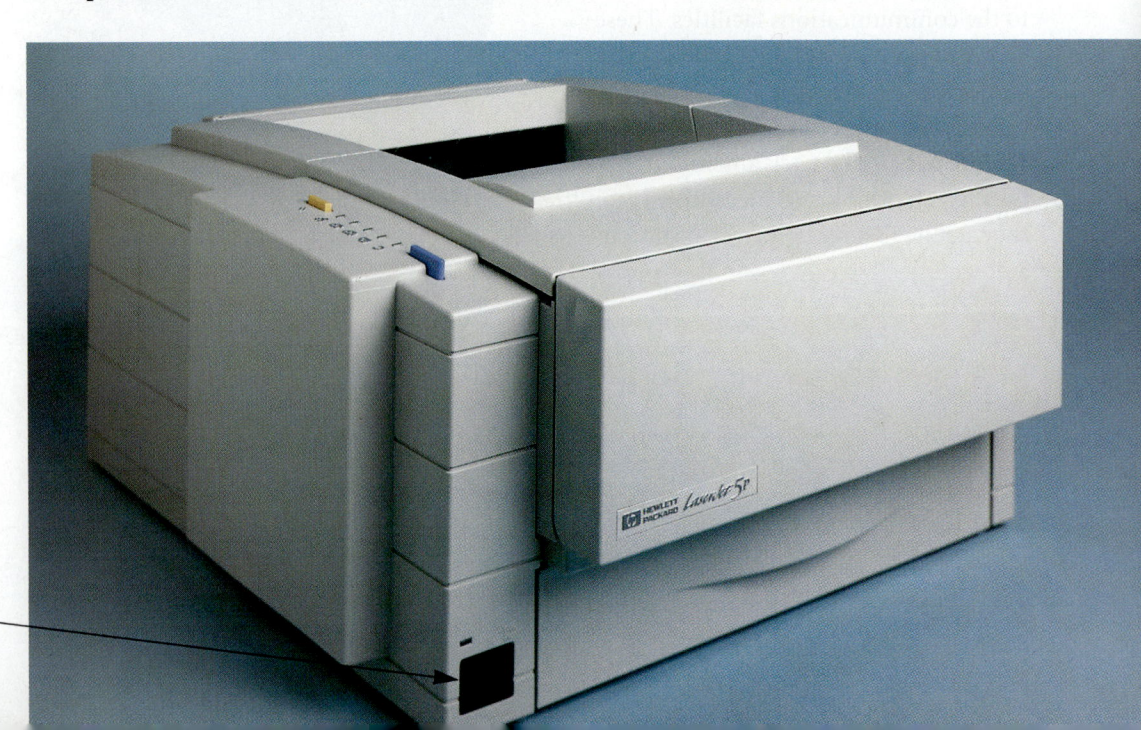

Radio-wave wireless systems are used to transmit data over longer distances such as cities, regions, and countries. Several companies run nationwide radio-wave networks to support mobile communications. Users include companies with large numbers of service personnel who need to access the company's databases while they are at a customer site. A repair technician, for example, might need to know the availability of a particular part. Using a portable radio data terminal (Figure 6-15), the technician can access the company's inventory database to determine the availability of the required part.

The cellular telephone system is another radio-wave wireless system widely used for mobile communications. A **cellular telephone** uses radio waves to communicate with a local antenna assigned to a specific geographic area called a cell (Figure 6-16). Individual cells range from one to ten miles in width and use between 50 and 75 radio channels. Suppose you make a call from a cellular telephone in your car. As you travel from one cell to another, a computer monitors the activity in each cell and switches the conversation from the current radio channel to an open radio channel in an adjacent cell. Cellular telephone channels can be used for both voice and digital data transmission.

Figure 6-15
This portable terminal uses radio waves to communicate with a base radio station that is connected to a host computer. Using such a terminal, service technicians can inquire instantly as to the availability of repair parts.

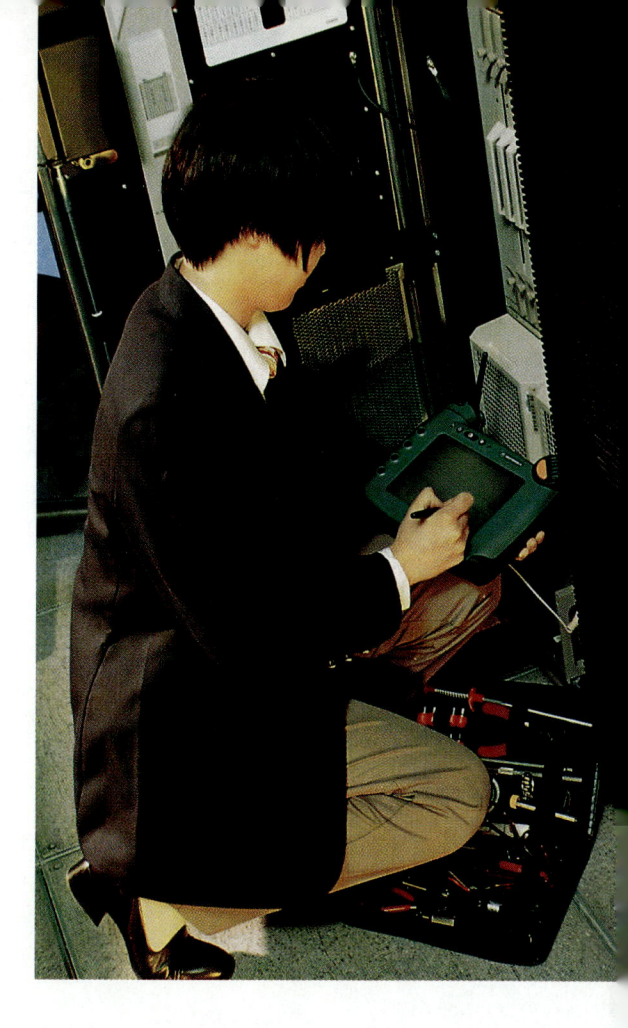

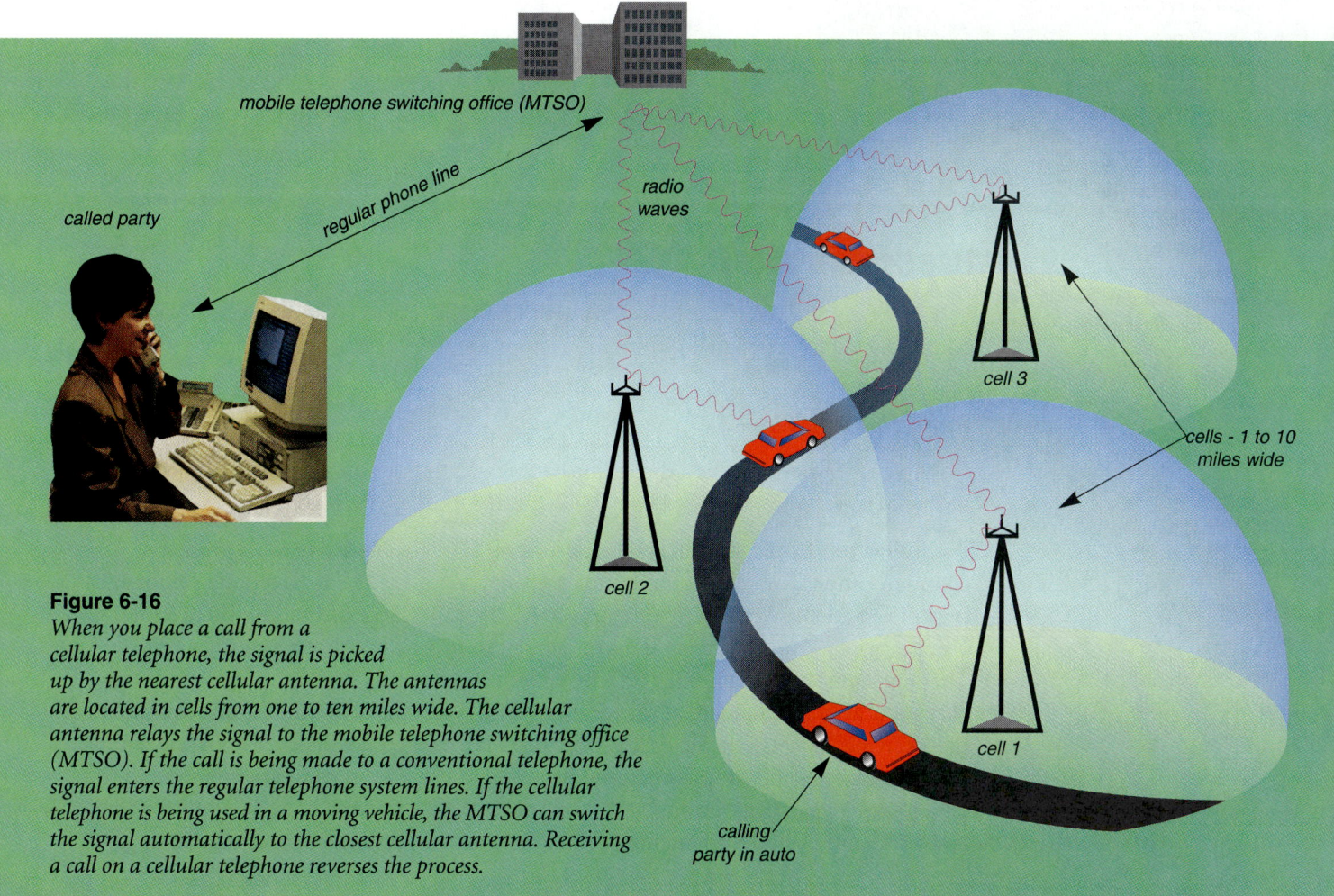

Figure 6-16
When you place a call from a cellular telephone, the signal is picked up by the nearest cellular antenna. The antennas are located in cells from one to ten miles wide. The cellular antenna relays the signal to the mobile telephone switching office (MTSO). If the call is being made to a conventional telephone, the signal enters the regular telephone system lines. If the cellular telephone is being used in a moving vehicle, the MTSO can switch the signal automatically to the closest cellular antenna. Receiving a call on a cellular telephone reverses the process.

An Example of a Communications Channel

Making a communications channel generally requires several different transmission media, especially when data is transmitted over long distances. Figure 6-17 illustrates a communications channel that uses several types of transmission media to transmit data from a personal computer to a large computer located across the country. The steps that would occur are as follows:

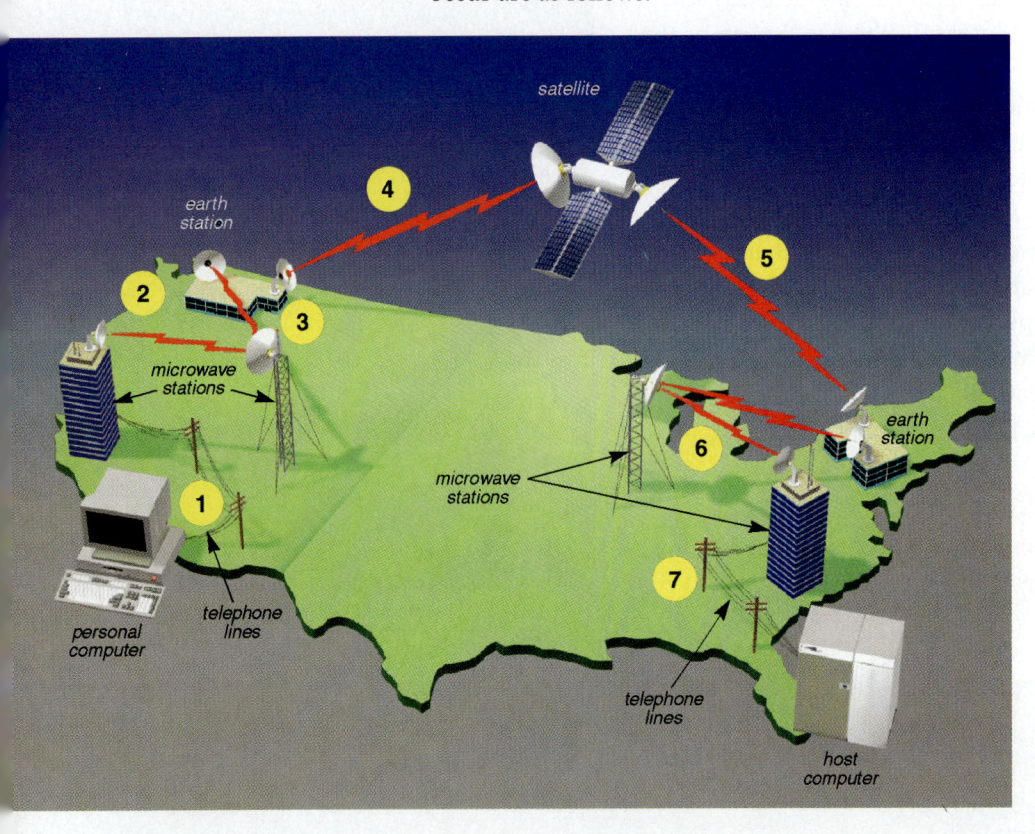

1. Data is input into the personal computer. The computer sends the data over telephone lines to a microwave station.
2. The microwave station transmits the data to another microwave station.
3. The last microwave station transmits the data to an earth station.
4. The earth station transmits the data to the communications satellite.
5. The satellite relays the data to another earth station on the other side of the country.
6. The earth station transmits the data to microwave stations.
7. The last microwave station sends the data over telephone lines to the large computer.

This entire transmission process would take less than one second.

Figure 6-17
Telephone lines, microwave transmission, and a communications satellite allow a personal computer to communicate with a large host computer.

Line Configurations

Two major **line configurations** (types of line connections) commonly used in communications are point-to-point lines and multidrop, or multipoint, lines.

Point-to-Point Lines

A **point-to-point line** is a direct line between a sending and a receiving device. It may be one of two types: a switched line or a dedicated line (Figure 6-18).

Switched Line A **switched line** uses a regular telephone line to establish a communications connection. Each time a connection is made, the telephone company switching stations select the line to be used for the call (hence the name switched line). Using a switched line to transmit data is similar to using a telephone to make a call. The communications equipment at the sending end dials the telephone number of the communications equipment at the receiving end. When the communications equipment at the receiving end answers the call, a connection is established and data can be transmitted. The process of establishing the communications connection is sometimes referred to as a **handshake**. When data transmission is complete, the communications equipment at either end terminates the call by hanging up, and the communications connection is ended.

Switched lines are relatively inexpensive. Using a switched line for data communications costs no more than making a regular telephone call. Another advantage of switched lines is that a connection can be made between any two locations with telephone service and communications equipment. For example, you could dial another computer to connect to the Internet and browse an online catalog. When you are done, you can hang up and place a second call to a different computer to check the balance in your checking account. One disadvantage of using switched lines is that line quality cannot be controlled because the line is chosen randomly by the telephone company switching equipment.

Dedicated Line A **dedicated line** is a line connection that always is established, unlike a switched line where the line connection is reestablished each time it is used. The communications device at one end always is connected to the device at the other end. Because dedicated lines maintain a constant connection, the quality and consistency of the connection is better than a switched line. You can create a dedicated line connection by running a cable between two points such as two offices or buildings; or you can lease a dedicated line from an outside organization such as a telephone company or some other communications service company. If the dedicated line is leased from an outside organization, it sometimes is called a **leased line** or a **private line**. The cost of dedicated lines varies based on the distance between the two connected points and the speed at which data will be transmitted. The charges for leased lines, however, usually are flat fees, meaning you pay a fixed monthly amount, regardless of how long you actually use the line.

Figure 6-18
A point-to-point line configuration using both switched telephone (dial up) lines (----) and dedicated lines ([solid line]) are connected to a computer in Denver. The dedicated lines are always connected, whereas the switched lines have to be connected each time they are used.

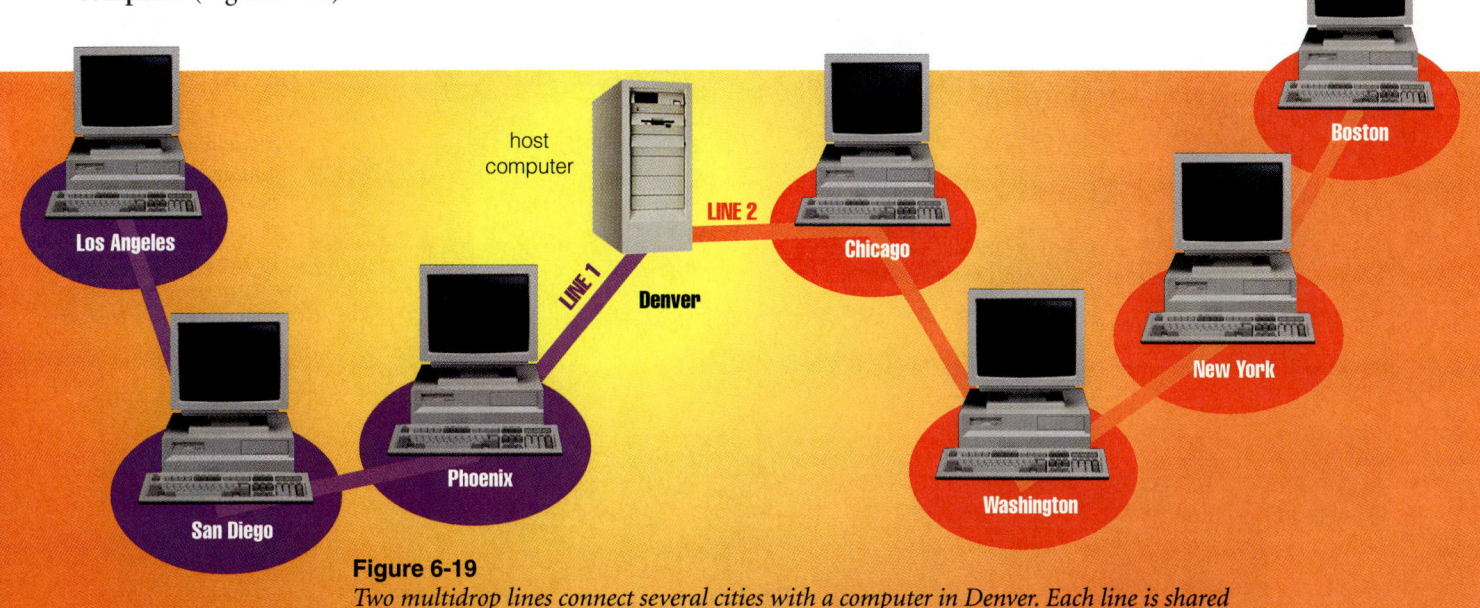

Multidrop Lines

The second major line configuration is called a **multidrop line** or **multipoint line**. Multidrop lines commonly are used to connect multiple devices such as terminals or personal computers along a single line to a main computer, sometimes called a **host computer** (Figure 6-19).

Figure 6-19
Two multidrop lines connect several cities with a computer in Denver. Each line is shared by computers at several locations. Multidrop line configurations are less expensive than individual lines to each remote location.

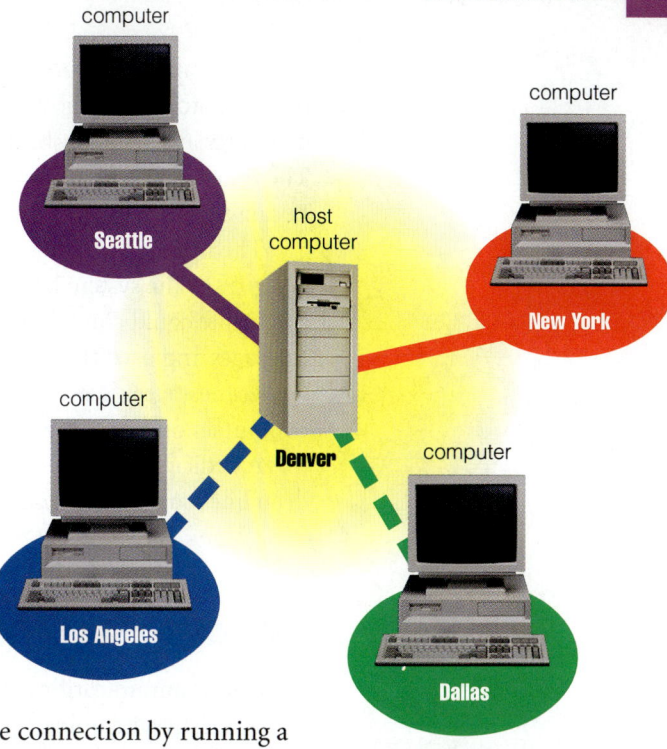

For example, suppose a ticket agent uses a terminal to request flight information from a database stored on a host computer. While the request is being transmitted to the main computer and the reply back to the terminal, other terminals on the line cannot transmit data. The time required to transmit the data, however, is short—most likely less than one second. Because the delays are so short, users cannot tell that other terminals are using the line.

The number of computers or terminals placed on one multidrop line is decided by the designer of the system based on the anticipated amount of traffic on the line. For example, a single line could connect 100 or more computers, provided each computer sent only short messages and used the communications line only a few hours per day. If the computers sent longer messages such as reports and used the line almost continuously, the number of computers on one line would have to be fewer.

A dedicated leased line almost always is used for multidrop line configurations. Using multidrop lines can decrease line costs considerably because many computers can share one line.

Characteristics of Communications Channels

The communications channels just described can be categorized by a number of characteristics including the type of signal, transmission mode, transmission direction, and transmission rate.

Types of Signals: Digital and Analog

Computer equipment is designed to process data as **digital signals**, which are individual electrical pulses that represent the bits that are grouped together in bytes. Telephone equipment originally was designed to carry only voice transmission, which is comprised of a continuous electrical wave called an **analog signal** (Figure 6-20). For telephone lines to carry digital signals, a special piece of equipment called a *modem* is used to convert between digital signals (0s and 1s) and analog signals. Modems are discussed in more detail later in this chapter.

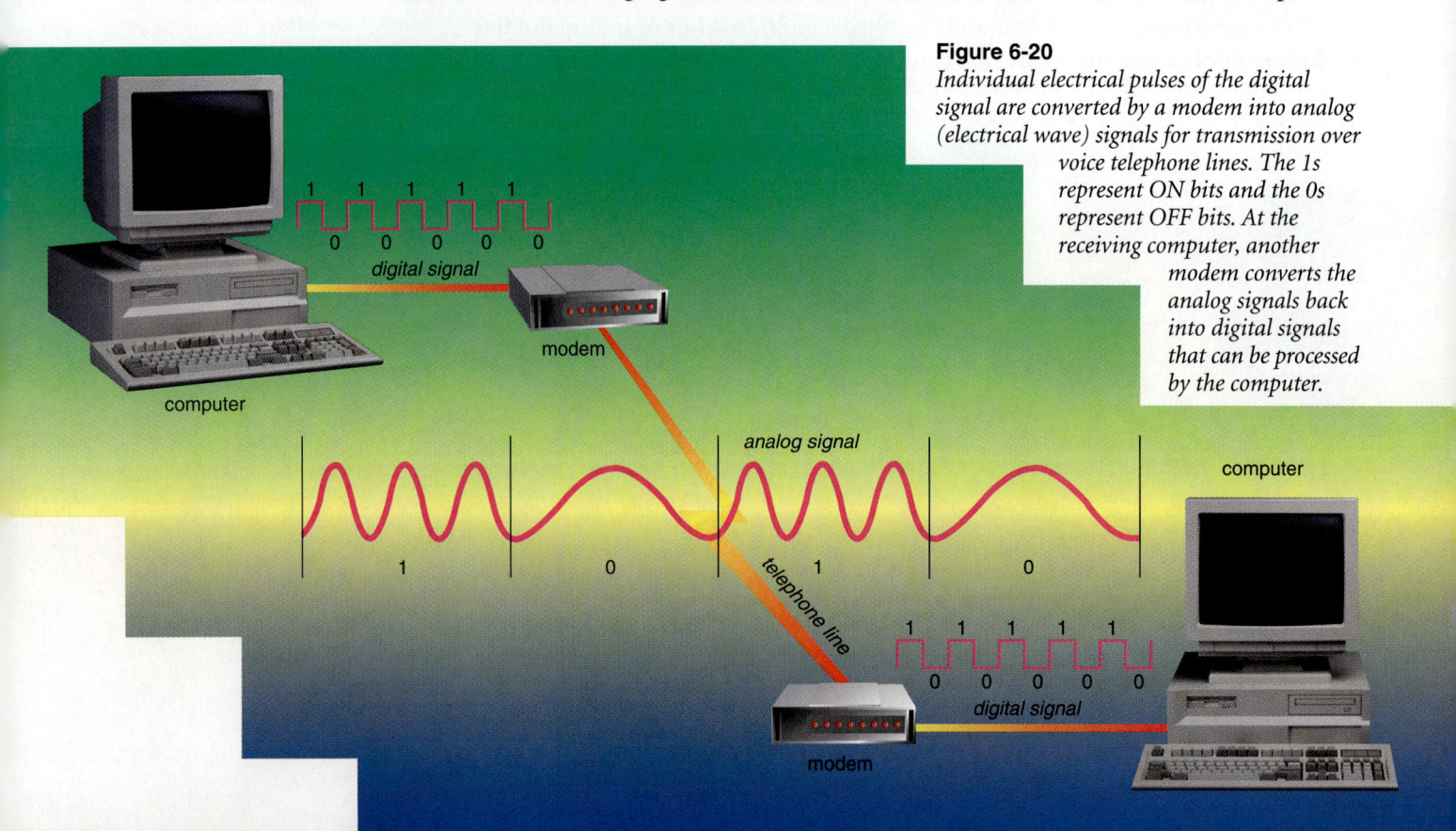

Figure 6-20
Individual electrical pulses of the digital signal are converted by a modem into analog (electrical wave) signals for transmission over voice telephone lines. The 1s represent ON bits and the 0s represent OFF bits. At the receiving computer, another modem converts the analog signals back into digital signals that can be processed by the computer.

To provide faster and clearer transmission of digital signals, many telephone companies now offer digital data service. **Digital data service** uses communications channels specifically designed to carry digital signals to provide higher speed and lower error rates than analog voice lines. Using the high-speed lines provided by digital data services is more expensive, however, than using a standard telephone line. A **T1** digital line, which transmits 1.5 megabits per second, costs several thousand dollars per month. A **T3** digital line, which transmits 45 megabits per second, costs more than $40,000 per month and requires a large investment in expensive equipment.

Digital data service, which now is available to customers in major metropolitan areas, typically is used by organizations with a consistent high-volume of communications traffic. Individuals who need fast digital data transmission can obtain an ISDN line. **ISDN (integrated services digital network)** is an international standard for the transmission of both analog voice and digital data using different communications channels and companies. Using ISDN lines, data can be transmitted over one or more separate channels at 128,000 bits per second, about four times as fast as an analog voice line. Future plans for ISDN include the use of fiber-optic cable that will provide transmission rates up to 2.2 billion bits per second—speeds high enough to allow the transmission of full-motion video images.

> **inCyber**
> For a review of ISDN lines, visit the Discovering Computers Chapter 6 inCyber page (http://www.scsite.com/dc/ch6/incyber.htm) and click ISDN.

Transmission Modes: Asynchronous and Synchronous

In **asynchronous transmission mode** (Figure 6-21) data is transmitted in individual bytes (made up of bits) at irregular intervals, such as when you enter data. Start and stop bits are used to distinguish where one byte stops and another byte starts. An additional bit called a *parity bit* sometimes is included at the end of each byte to check for errors and to detect if one of the bits was changed during transmission. Because only one byte is transmitted at a time, the asynchronous transmission mode is relatively slow and is best used to send only small amounts of data. This mode is efficient enough, however, for use with most personal computer communications equipment.

In the **synchronous transmission mode** (Figure 6-21), large blocks of data are transmitted at regular intervals. Timing signals synchronize the communications equipment at the sending and receiving ends, thus eliminating the need for start and stop bits for each byte. Error-checking bits and start and end indicators called *sync bytes* also are transmitted. While synchronous transmission requires more sophisticated and expensive equipment, it provides much higher speeds and accuracy than asynchronous transmission.

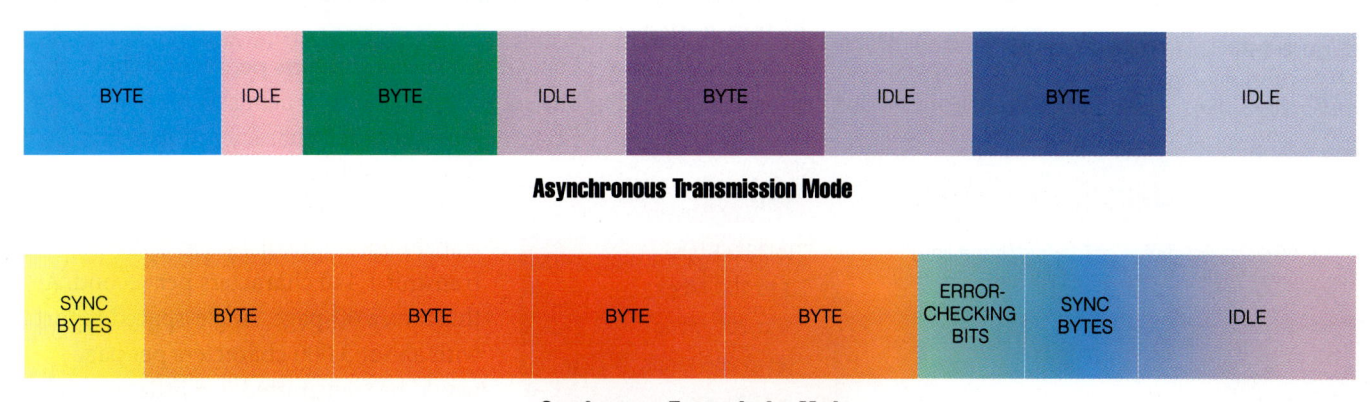

| BYTE | IDLE | BYTE | IDLE | BYTE | IDLE | BYTE | IDLE |

Asynchronous Transmission Mode

| SYNC BYTES | BYTE | BYTE | BYTE | BYTE | ERROR-CHECKING BITS | SYNC BYTES | IDLE |

Synchronous Transmission Mode

Figure 6-21
In asynchronous transmission mode, individual bytes are transmitted. Each byte has start, stop, and error-checking bits. In synchronous transmission mode, multiple bytes are sent in a block with sync bytes at the beginning of the block and error-checking bits and sync bytes at the end of the block. Synchronous transmission is faster and more accurate.

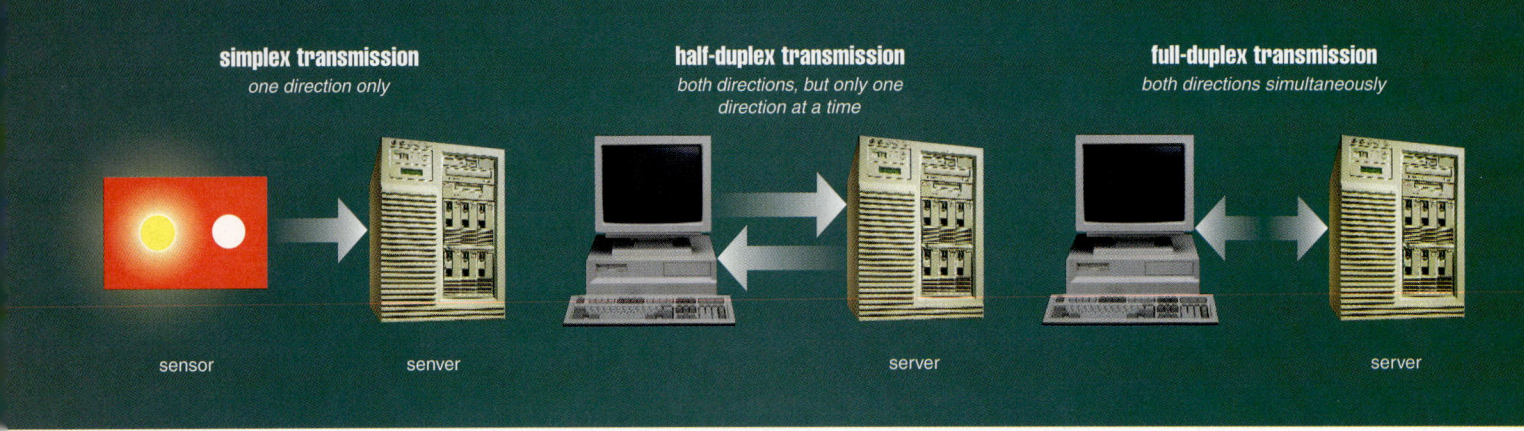

simplex transmission
one direction only

half-duplex transmission
both directions, but only one direction at a time

full-duplex transmission
both directions simultaneously

sensor — server — server — server

Figure 6-22
Simplex transmission allows data to flow in one direction only. Half-duplex transmission allows data to flow in both directions but not at the same time. Full-duplex transmission allows data to flow in both directions simultaneously.

Direction of Transmission: Simplex, Half-Duplex, and Full-Duplex

The direction of data transmission is classified in one of three ways: simplex, half-duplex, or full-duplex (Figure 6-22). In **simplex transmission**, data flows in one direction only. Simplex is used only when the sending device, such as a temperature sensor, never requires a response from the computer. For example, if a computer is used to control the temperature of a building, numerous sensors are placed throughout the building. Simplex transmission lines can be used to connect each sensor back to the computer because the computer needs only to receive data from the temperature sensors and does not need to send data back to the sensors.

In **half-duplex transmission**, data can flow in either direction, but can flow only in one direction at a time. Citizens band (CB) radio is an example of half-duplex transmission; you can talk or listen, but you cannot do both at the same time.

In **full-duplex transmission**, data can be sent in both directions at the same time. A normal telephone line is an example of full-duplex transmission; both parties can talk at the same time. Full-duplex transmission is used for most interactive computer applications and for computer-to-computer data transmission.

Tranmission Rate

The transmission rate of a communications channel is determined by its bandwidth and its speed. **Bandwidth** is the range of frequencies that a communications channel can carry. The larger the bandwidth of a channel, the more frequencies that channel can transmit. Because data can be assigned to different frequencies for transmission, a larger bandwidth means more data can be transmitted at one time.

The speed at which data is transmitted usually is expressed as **bits per second (bps)**, the number of bits that can be transmitted in one second. For example, using 10-bit bytes to represent each character (8 data bits, 1 start bit, and 1 stop bit), a communications channel with a transmission rate of 14,400 bps will transmit 1,440 characters per second. At this rate, a 60-page, single-spaced report with about 3,000 characters per page would be transmitted in a little more than two minutes. Figure 6-23 shows the range of transmission rates for different media. Each year, communications companies develop new methods and technologies to increase these rates.

Figure 6-23
Transmission rates of different media.

Media	Rate*
Twisted-pair wire (voice grade telephone line)	to 33.6 Kbps
Twisted-pair wire (direct connection)	1 to 100 Mbps
Coaxial cable	1 to 200 Mbps
Fiber-optic cable	up to 266 Mbps
Terrestrial microwave	5.7 Mbps
Satellite microwave	64 to 512 Kbps
Radio wave	4.8 to 19.2 Kbps
Infrared	1 to 4 Mbps

*****Rate:** bps — bits per second
Kbps — kilo (thousand) bits per second
Mbps — mega (million) bits per second

Communications Software

Some communications equipment is preprogrammed to accomplish its intended communications tasks. Other communications equipment must be used with a separate program to ensure proper transmission of data. These programs, referred to as **communications software**, manage the transmission of data between computers and have a number of features including dialing (if a switched telephone line is used), file transfer, terminal emulation, and Internet access.

The **dialing** feature allows you to store, review, select and dial telephone numbers of computers that can be called. The software uses wizards, dialog boxes, and other onscreen messages to help you establish a communications connection.

The **file transfer** feature allows you to move one or more files from one computer system to another. For file transfers to work, both the sending and receiving computers must have file transfer software.

Most minicomputers and mainframes are designed to work with terminals that transmit and display data differently than PCs. The **terminal emulation** feature allows a personal computer to act as a specific type of terminal so the personal computer can connect to another, usually larger, computer such as a mainframe. Terminal emulation software performs the necessary conversion of data sent from and received by the personal computer so the computers can communicate.

The **Internet access** feature allows you to use the computer to connect to the Internet to send e-mail, participate in chat rooms, visit World Wide Web sites, and more.

Communications Equipment

A variety of equipment is used to connect computers to each other. The following sections discuss some of the more common types of communications equipment.

Modems

As previously discussed, a computer's digital signals must be converted to analog signals to be transmitted along standard telephone lines. The communications equipment that performs this conversion is a modem. A **modem** not only converts the digital signals of a computer to analog signals, but also converts analog signals back into digital signals that can be used by a computer. The word modem comes from a combination of the words *mo*dulate–to change into a sound or analog signal–and *dem*odulate–to convert an analog signal into a digital signal. Modems are needed at both the sending and receiving ends of a communications channel for data transmission to occur.

An **external modem** (Figure 6-24) is a stand-alone (separate) device that attaches to a computer with a cable and to a telephone outlet with a standard telephone cord. Because external modems are stand-alone devices, they can be moved easily from one computer to another.

Figure 6-24
An external modem connects a computer to a telephone outlet.

An **internal modem** (Figure 6-25) is contained on a circuit board that is installed inside a computer or inserted into an expansion slot. Internal modems generally are less expensive than comparable external modems, but once they are installed, internal modems are not as easy to move.

While some modems can transmit data at rates up to 56,000 bits per second (bps), most personal computers use modems of 28,800 bps. The actual amount of data transmitted by a modem can be higher than these rates through the use of data compression features built into the modem.

inCyber

For details on modems, visit the Discovering Computers Chapter 6 inCyber page (http://www.scsite.com/dc/ch6/incyber.htm) and click Modem.

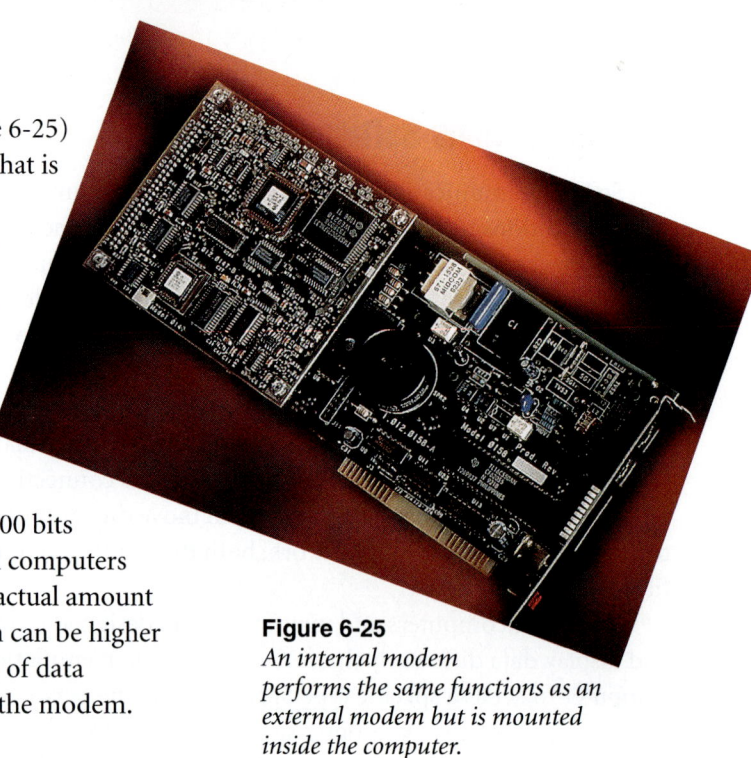

Figure 6-25
An internal modem performs the same functions as an external modem but is mounted inside the computer.

Multiplexers

A **multiplexer**, sometimes referred to as an MUX, combines two or more input signals from several devices into a single stream of data and transmits it over a communications channel (Figure 6-26). The multiplexer at the sending end codes each character with an identifier before combining the data streams. The multiplexer at the receiving end uses these characters to separate the combined data stream into its original parts. By combining the individual data streams into one, a multiplexer increases the efficiency of communications and reduces the cost of using individual communications channels. Multiplexers often are connected to external modems or have internal modems built in.

Figure 6-26
At the sending end, a multiplexer (MUX) combines separate data transmissions into a single data stream. At the receiving end, the multiplexer separates the single stream into its original parts.

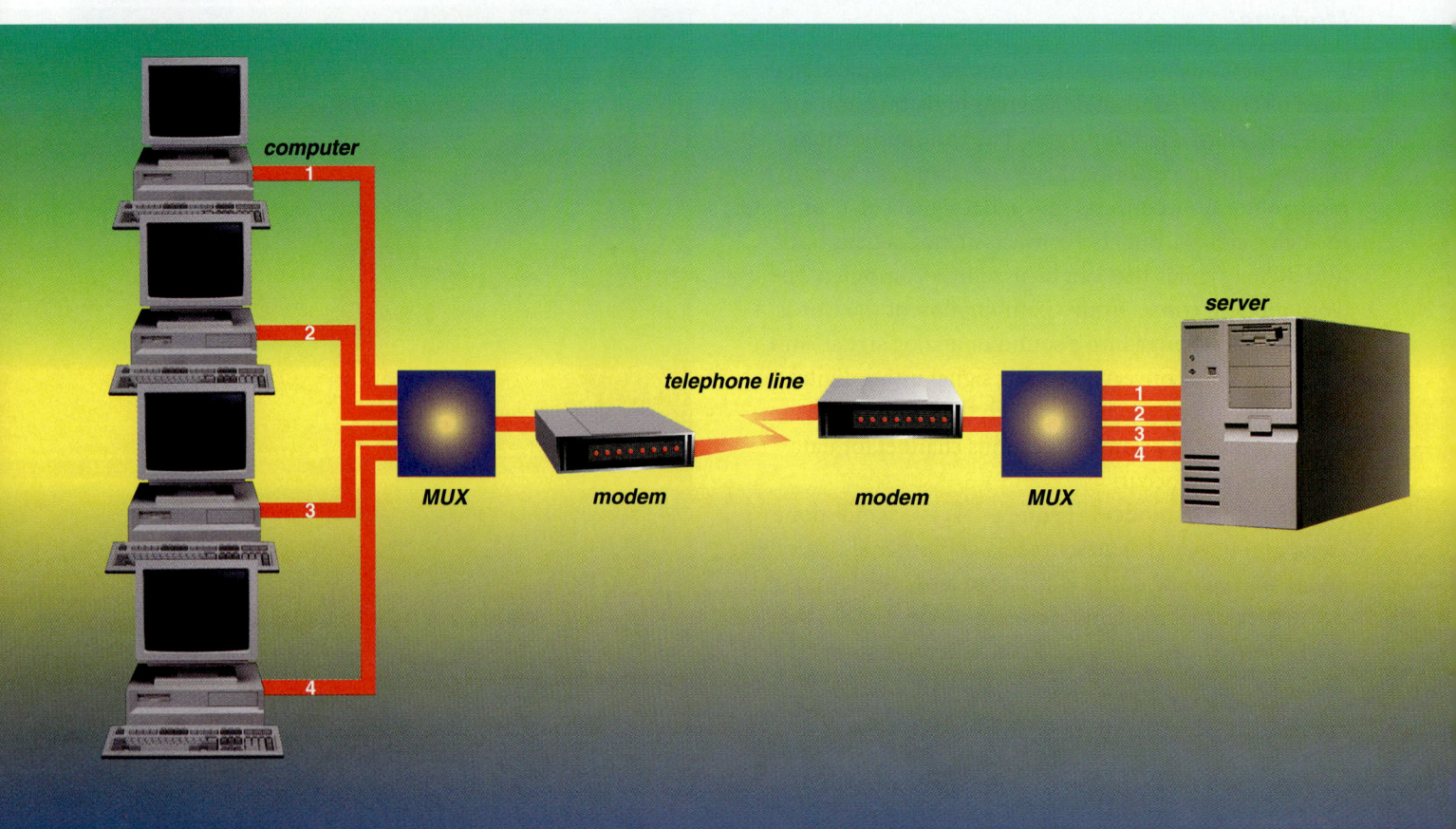

Front-End Processors

A **front-end processor** is a computer dedicated to handling the communications requirements of a larger computer. Relieved of these tasks, the large computer can be dedicated to processing data, while the front-end processor communicates the data. Tasks that a front-end processor handles include **polling** (checking the connected terminals or computers to see if they have data to send); error-checking and correction; and ensuring access security (making sure that a connected device or the user of the connected device is authorized to access the computer).

Network Interface Cards

A **network interface card**, or **NIC** (pronounced *nick*), is a circuit card that fits in an expansion slot of a computer or other device, such as a printer, so the device can be connected to the network (Figure 6-27). Most network interface cards require a cable connection and have connectors on the card for different types of cable. A NIC has circuits that coordinate the transmission and receipt of data and the error-checking of transmitted data.

Figure 6-27
A network interface card.

1. network interface card installs in expansion slot of computer; cards often have connectors for different types of cable; only one type of cable can be attached at a time
2. twisted-pair cable
3. RJ45 modular connector
4. twisted-pair cable attaches to server through a wiring hub
5. coaxial cable
6. BNC twist-lock connector
7. T-connector
8. coaxial cable runs back to server or next computer in network

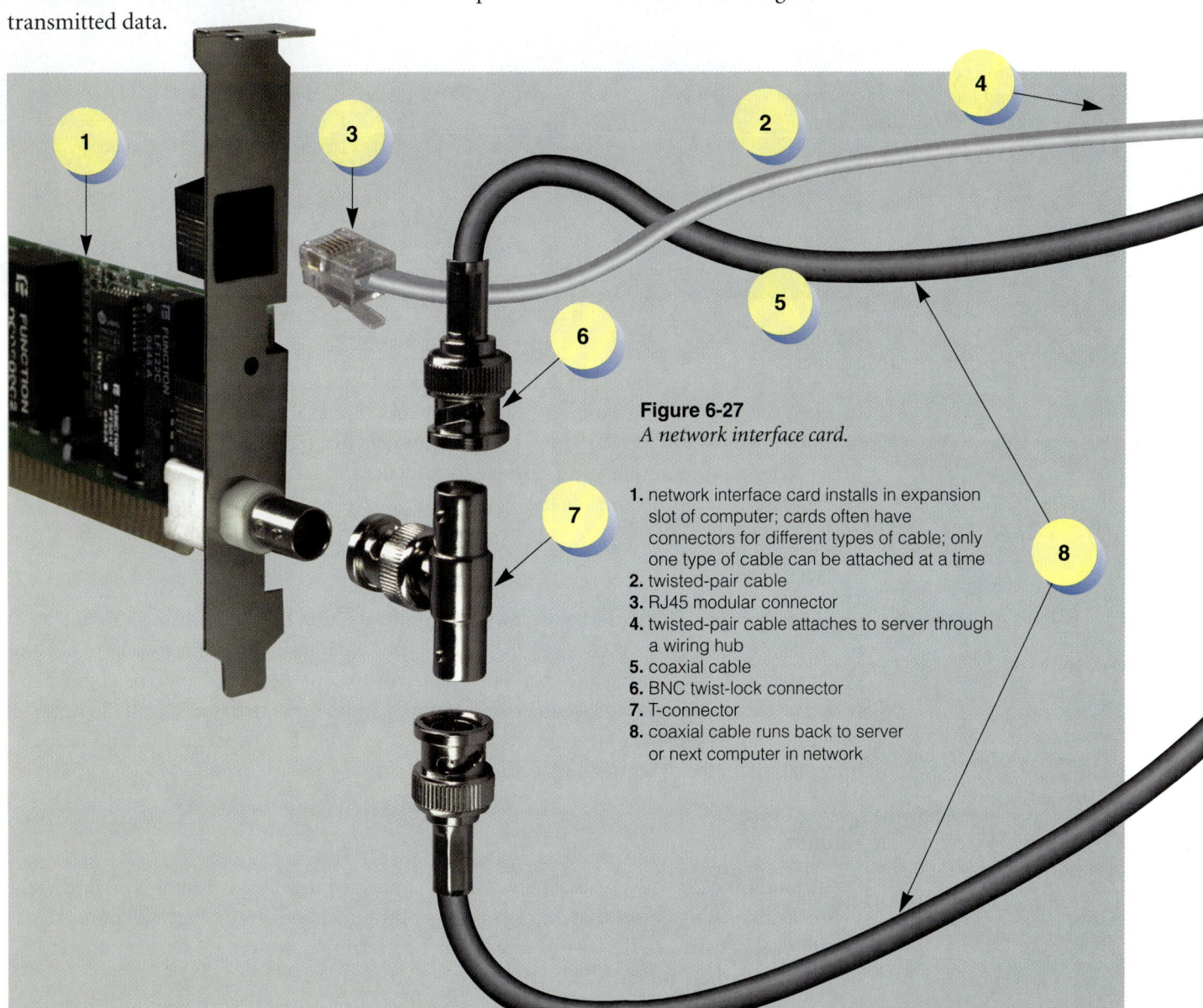

Wiring Hubs

A **wiring hub**, also called a **concentrator** or **multistation access unit** (MAU), allows devices such as computers, printers, and storage devices to be connected to the server (Figure 6-28). The hub acts as the central connecting point for cables that run to the server and each of the devices on a network. Hubs usually contain connectors, called ports, for eight to twelve devices plus the server. A hub that can be connected with another hub to increase the number of devices attached to the server is called a **stackable hub**.

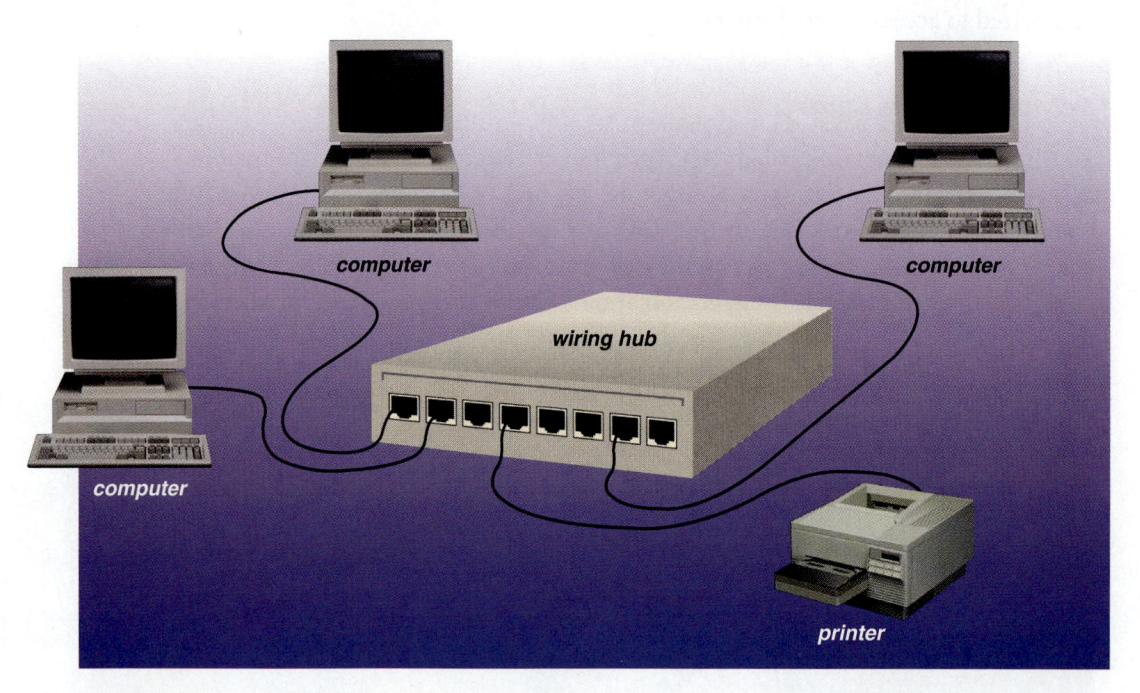

Figure 6-28
A wiring hub acts as a central connecting point for the server and the devices in the network.

Gateways

A **gateway** is a combination of hardware and software that allows users on one network to access the resources on a *different* type of network. For example, a gateway could be used to connect a local area network of personal computers to a mainframe computer network. Many colleges, for example, use a gateway so students and faculty can access the World Wide Web and other networks outside the local region.

Bridges

A **bridge** is a combination of hardware and software that is used to connect *similar* networks. For example, if a company had similar but separate local area networks of personal computers in its accounting and marketing departments, the networks could be connected with a bridge. In this example, using a bridge makes more sense than joining all the personal computers together in one large network, because the individual departments only access information on the other network occasionally.

Routers

A router is used when several networks are connected together. A **router** is an intelligent network connecting device that sends (routes) communications traffic directly to the appropriate network. In the case of a partial network failure, routers are smart enough to determine alternate routes.

Communications Networks

A communications **network** is a collection of terminals, computers, and other equipment that uses communications channels to share data, information, hardware, and software. Networks can be classified as either local area networks or wide area networks.

Local Area Networks (LANs)

A **local area network**, or **LAN**, is a communications network that covers a limited geographic area such as a school computer laboratory, an office, a building, or a group of buildings. The LAN consists of a communications channel that connects a series of computer terminals connected to a central computer or, more commonly, connects a group of personal computers to one another.

LAN Applications Three common applications of local area networks are hardware, software, and information resource sharing.

Hardware resource sharing allows each personal computer on a network to access and use devices that are too costly to provide for each user or cannot be justified for each user because they are used infrequently. For example, suppose a number of personal computers on a network each needed to use a laser printer. A LAN allows you to connect a laser printer to the network, so that whenever a personal computer user on the network needs the laser printer, he or she can access it over the network. Figure 6-29 depicts a simple local area network consisting of four personal computers and a printer linked together by a cable.

Three of the personal computers (computer 1 in the sales and marketing department, computer 2 in the accounting department, and computer 3 in the personnel department) can be used at all times. Computer 4 is used as a **server**, which is a computer dedicated to handling the communications needs of the other computers in the network. The users of this LAN have connected the laser printer to the server so all computers and the server have access to the printer. In small networks, the server computer also can be used to run applications, just like other computers on the network. In large networks, the server usually is dedicated to providing network services such as hardware, software, and information resource sharing.

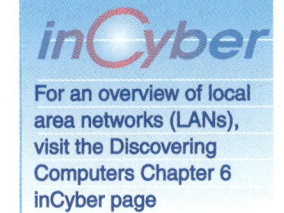

> **inCyber**
>
> For an overview of local area networks (LANs), visit the Discovering Computers Chapter 6 inCyber page (http://www.scsite.com/dc/ch6/incyber.htm) and click LAN.

Local Area Network

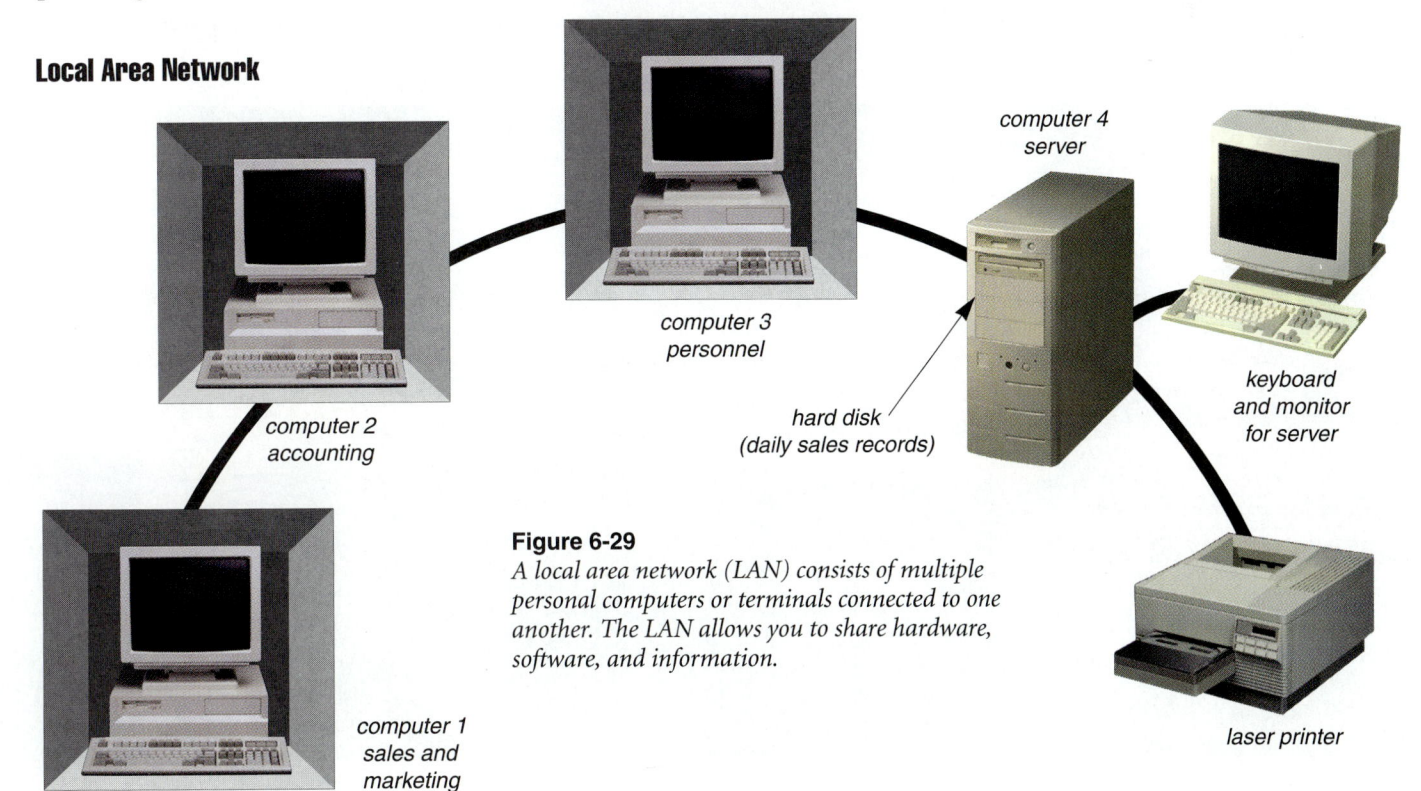

Figure 6-29
A local area network (LAN) consists of multiple personal computers or terminals connected to one another. The LAN allows you to share hardware, software, and information.

Software resource sharing involves storing frequently used software on the hard disk of the server so multiple users can access the software. Sharing the software is more cost-effective than buying and installing the software on each computer. Because sharing software is a common practice for both in-house and commercial software, most software vendors sell network versions of their software. Software vendors issue agreements called **network licenses** or **site licenses**, which allow many users to run the software package. The site license fee usually is based on the number of computers attached to the network and costs less than buying separate copies of the software package for each computer.

Information resource sharing allows anyone using a personal computer on a local area network to access data stored on any other computer in the network. In actual practice, hardware resource sharing and information resource sharing often are combined. For example, in Figure 6-29, the sales records could be stored on the hard disk associated with the server. Anyone needing access to the sales records could use this information resource. The capability of accessing and storing data on shared storage devices is an important feature of many local area networks.

File-Server and Client-Server Networks Information resource sharing usually is provided using either the file-server or client-server method. With the **file-server** method, the server sends an entire file at one time to a requesting computer, which then performs the processing. With the **client-server** method, the server completes some of the processing first and then transmits the data to the requesting computer.

Figure 6-30 illustrates how a server processes a request for information about customers with balances over $1,000, depending on the method used. With the *file-server* method, first you transmit a request for the customer file to the server (1). The server locates the customer file (2) and transmits the entire file to your computer (3). Your computer then selects customers with balances over $1,000 and prepares the report (4). With the *client-server* method, you transmit a request for customers with a balance over $1,000 from your computer (the *client*) to the server (1). The server selects the records of customers with balances over $1,000 (2) and transmits the selected records to your computer (3). Your computer then prepares the report (4). While the client-server method greatly reduces the amount of data sent over a network, it does require a more powerful server system.

---

inCyber

For details on client-server networks, visit the Discovering Computers Chapter 6 inCyber page (http://www.scsite.com/dc/ch6/incyber.htm) and click Client-Server.

Figure 6-30
A request for information about customers with balances over $1,000 would be processed differently by file-server and client-server networks.

FILE-SERVER

1. REQUEST FOR CUSTOMER FILE
3. ENTIRE CUSTOMER FILE TRANSMITTED

4. REQUESTING COMPUTER SELECTS CUSTOMERS WITH BALANCES OVER $1,000 AND PREPARES REPORT

2. SERVER LOCATES AND TRANSMITS ENTIRE CUSTOMER FILE

When a server provides selected information from files stored on the server, and the application software is run on the client system (as described in this example), the server is called a **database server**. If the server computer also runs all or part of the application software, such as a sales order entry program, it is called an **application server**.

Peer-to-Peer Networks A local area network does not have to use a single server computer. A **peer-to-peer network** allows any computer to share the hardware (such as a printer), software, or information located on any other computer in the network. Peer-to-peer networks are appropriate for a small number of users who work primarily on their own computers and need only to use the resources of other computers occasionally.

Network Operating Systems A **network operating system** (NOS) is the system software that makes it possible to implement and control a local area network and allows users to use the files, resources, and other services on that network (such as e-mail). Tasks of the network operating system include:

- **Administration** Adding, deleting, and organizing client users and performing maintenance tasks such as backup.
- **File Management** Locating and transferring files from the server to the client computers.
- **Printer Management** Prioritizing print jobs and reports sent to specific printers on the network.
- **Security** Monitoring and, when necessary, restricting access to network resources.

Different types of networks use different types of network operating systems. Simple peer-to-peer networks need a minimum amount of software to manage their activities. Often, the necessary software is provided by the operating system or by the manufacturer of the hardware used to link the networked systems. Artisoft's LANtastic, Microsoft's Windows 95 and Windows for Workgroups, and Apple's AppleTalk are examples of peer-to-peer network software. Client-server networks, however, need more sophisticated network operating systems to coordinate the number of devices on the network and keep communications running efficiently. The NOS in a client-server system runs on the server computer; the personal computer clients run their own operating systems. Novell's NetWare, Microsoft's Advanced NT Server, and IBM's LAN Server are examples of network operating systems.

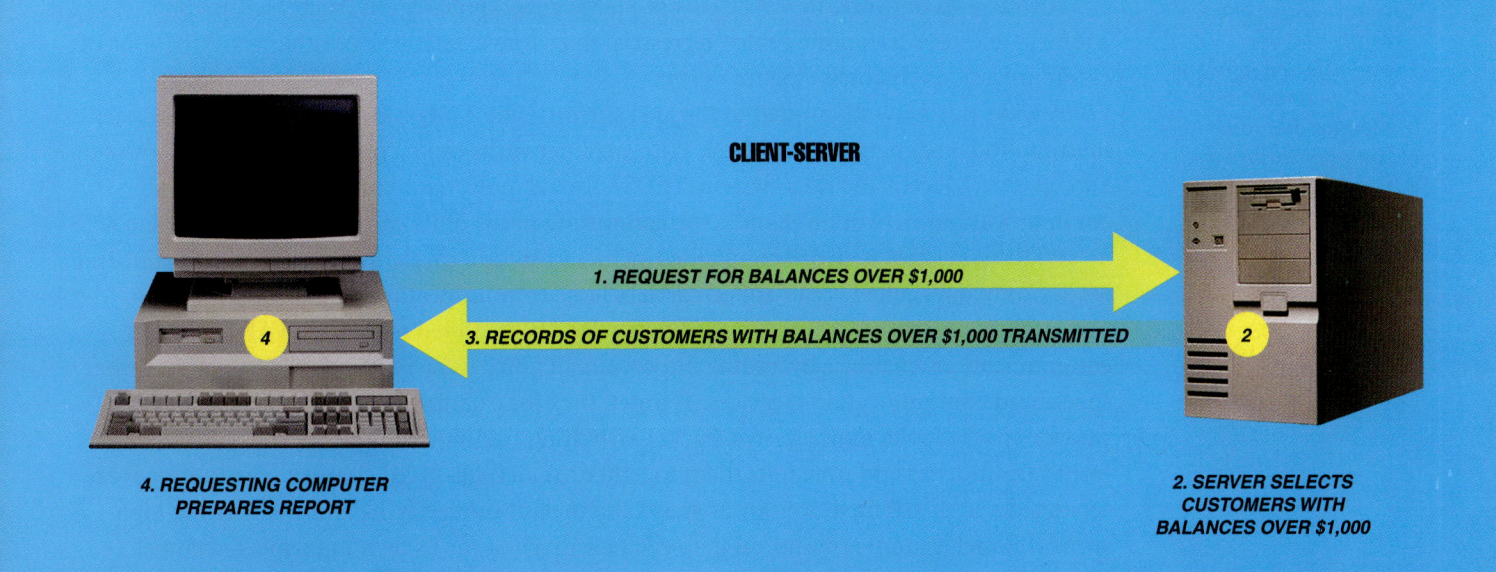

CLIENT-SERVER

1. REQUEST FOR BALANCES OVER $1,000
3. RECORDS OF CUSTOMERS WITH BALANCES OVER $1,000 TRANSMITTED

4. REQUESTING COMPUTER PREPARES REPORT

2. SERVER SELECTS CUSTOMERS WITH BALANCES OVER $1,000

Figure 6-31
The control room for a regional telephone company. Telephone companies use sophisticated software and equipment to monitor and route communications traffic.

Wide Area Networks (WANs)

A **wide area network**, or **WAN**, covers a large geographic region (such as a city or country) and uses telephone cables, terrestrial microwave, satellites, or other combinations of communications channels (Figure 6-31).

A wide area network limited to the area surrounding a city is sometimes referred to as a **metropolitan area network**, or **MAN**. Wide area networks can be privately or publicly owned and operated. Electronic Data Systems (EDS), for example, has built an extensive private communications network to handle the computing needs of its computer services business.

Public wide area network companies include **common carriers** such as AT&T, Sprint, and MCI. Companies called **value-added carriers** lease communications channels from the common carriers to use in value-added networks. **Value-added networks** (VAN) enhance communications channels by adding improvements such as faster data transmission or other specialized communications services. Tymnet, Inc., for example, operates a VAN that provides packet-switching services. **Packet-switching** combines individual packets of data from various users and transmits them together over a high-speed channel. The messages are separated and distributed over lower speed channels at the receiving end. Sharing the high-speed channel is more economical than each user paying for its own high-speed channel.

Network Configurations

The way the equipment is configured in a communications network is called **topology**. A topology is determined by the *logical* connection of the devices in the network–that is, the path the data follows as it is routed from one device to another. The actual *physical* connections, including the cabling, may form a different shape than the one formed by the devices in the network. Any device directly connected to a network, such as a computer or a printer, is referred to as a **node**. Personal computers connected to a network often are referred to as **workstations**. The more common topologies are star, bus, and ring. Combinations of these topologies also are used.

Star Network

A **star network** has a central computer with one or more terminals or smaller computers connected to it, forming a star. A pure star network consists of only point-to-point lines between the central computer and the other computers on the network. Most star networks, such as the one shown in Figure 6-32, are not pure star networks and include both point-to-point lines and multidrop lines.

A star network configuration often is used when the central computer contains all the data required to process input from terminals, such as an airline reservation system.

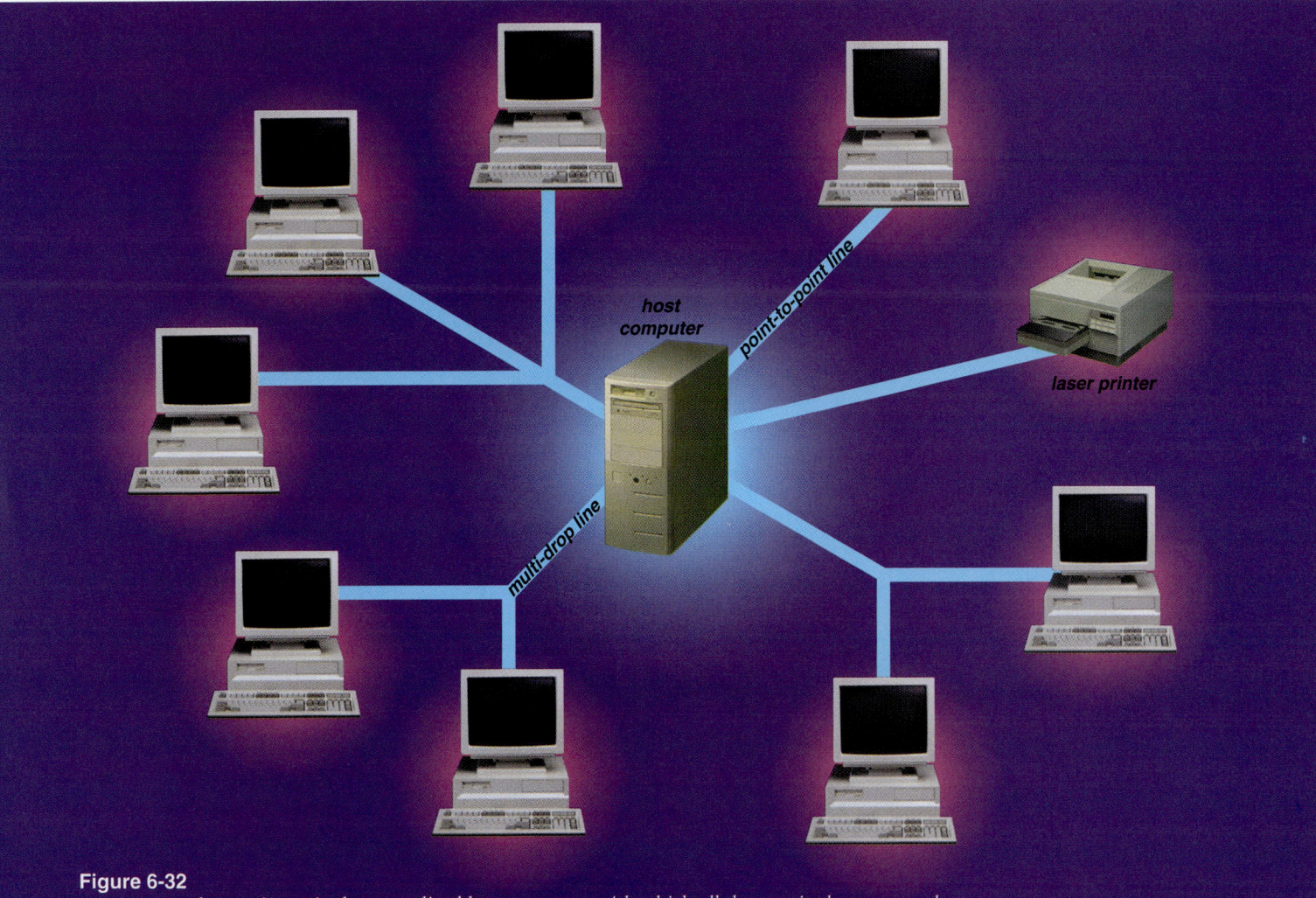

Figure 6-32
A star network contains a single, centralized host computer with which all the terminals or personal computers in the network communicate. Both point-to-point and multidrop lines can be used in a star network.

For example, if seat reservations are being processed on an airline's star network, all the data needed to confirm reservations is contained in the database stored on the central computer. Companies often use star networks to connect terminals to a mainframe or minicomputer that serves as the host computer.

Star networks are relatively efficient and provide close control of the data processed on the network. The major disadvantage of a star network is that the entire network depends on the central computer and its hardware and software. If any of these elements fail, the entire network is disabled. Therefore, in most large star networks, backup computer systems are kept available in case the primary system fails.

Bus Network

In a **bus network**, all the devices or nodes in the network are connected to and share a single data path (Figure 6-33). Bus networks allow data to be transmitted in both directions. Each time data is sent, a destination address is included with the transmission so the data is routed to the appropriate receiving device. A bus network often is physically wired using a single cable running from one device to the next. A bus network also can be wired with a wiring hub at the center so it looks like a star. It still is considered a bus network, however, because a logical bus–a single cable–exists inside the hub. An advantage of a bus network is that devices can be attached or detached from the network at any point without disturbing the rest of the network. In addition, if one computer on the network fails, this does not affect the other users of the network.

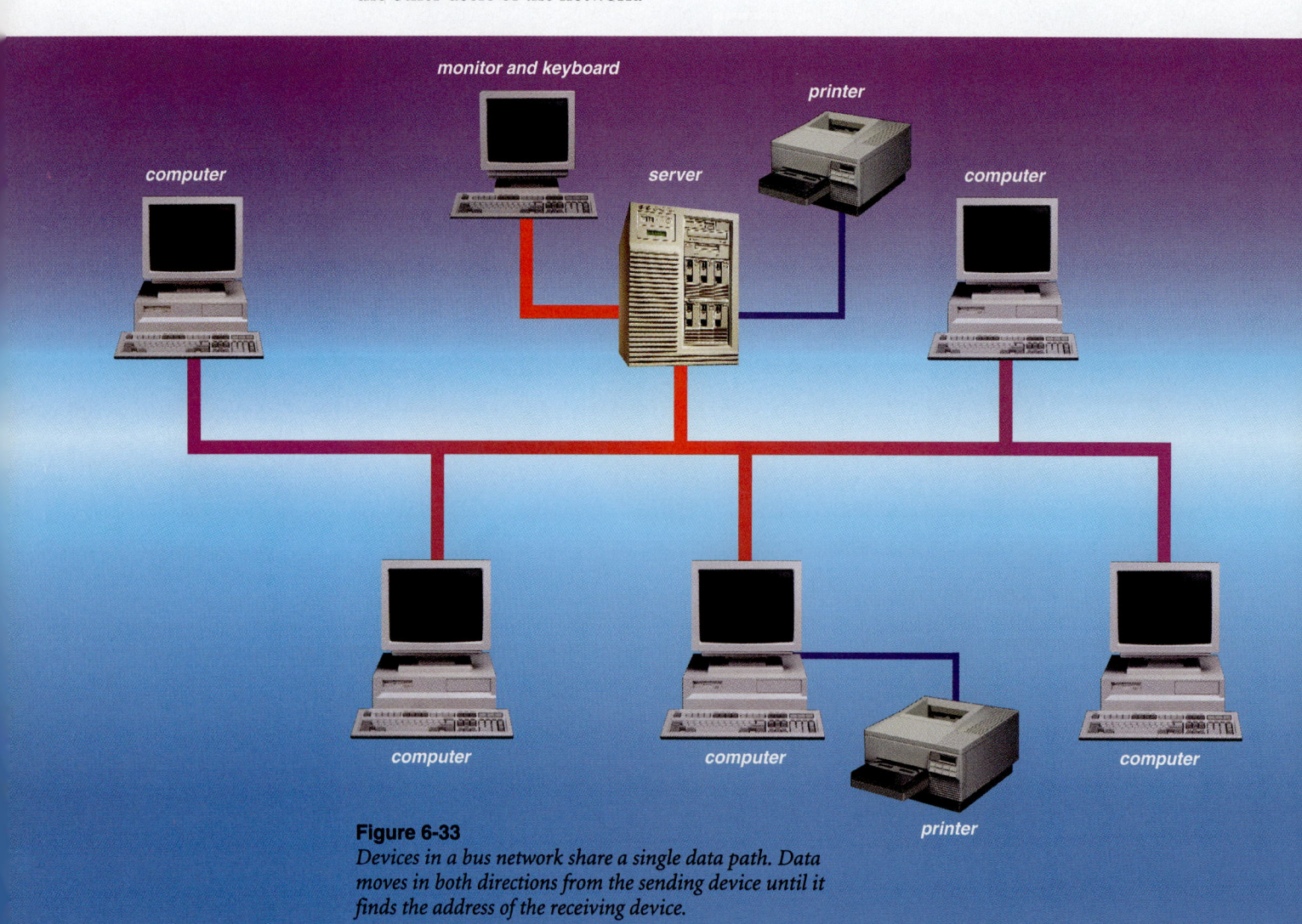

Figure 6-33
Devices in a bus network share a single data path. Data moves in both directions from the sending device until it finds the address of the receiving device.

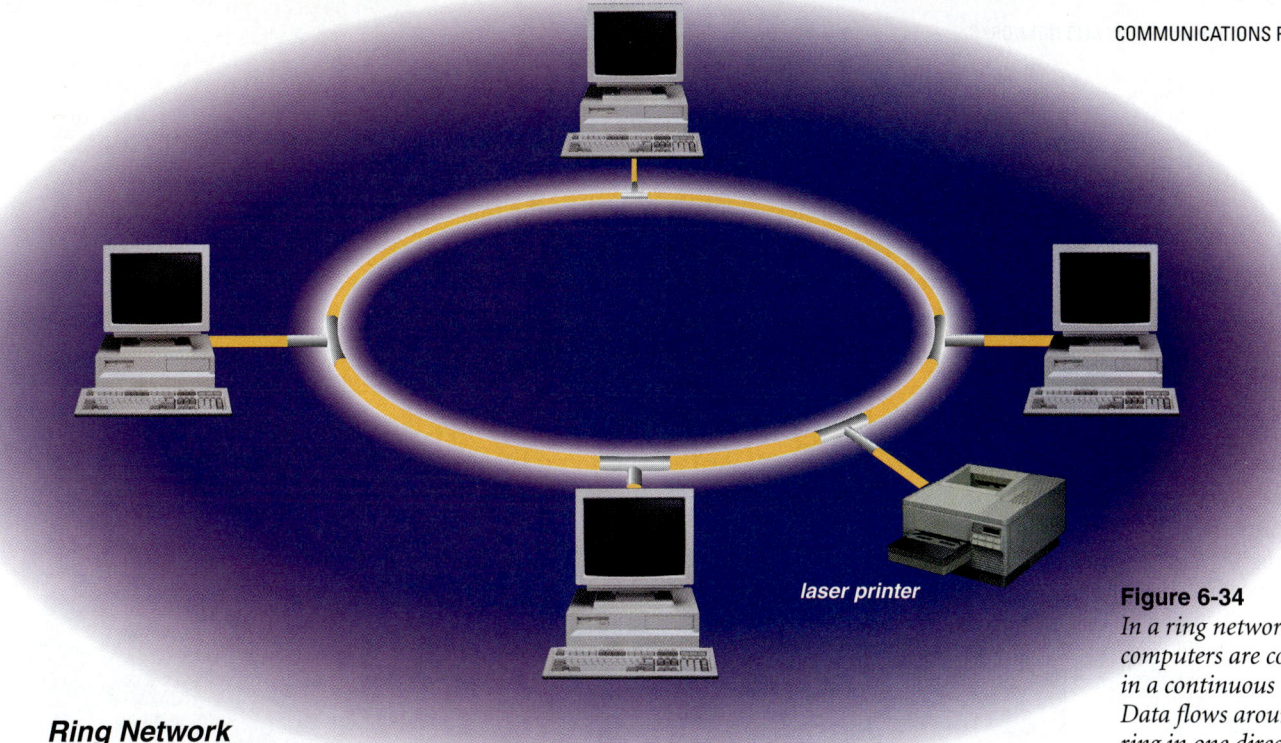

Ring Network

In a **ring network**, all the devices on the network are connected in a continuous loop or ring. Unlike a star network, a ring network does not use a centralized host computer. Rather, a circle of computers communicate with one another (Figure 6-34). Data travels around a ring network in one direction only and passes through each computer. Ring networks sometimes are used to connect large computers in the same area that share data frequently. One disadvantage of a ring network is that if one computer fails, the entire network fails because the data cannot be transmitted past the failed computer.

Figure 6-34
In a ring network, all computers are connected in a continuous loop. Data flows around the ring in one direction only. The actual ring usually exists inside a wiring hub. Separate cables run from the hub ring to the individual devices connected to the network.

Communications Protocols

Communications software is written to work with one or more protocols. A **protocol** is a set of rules and procedures for exchanging information between computers. Protocols define how the communications link is established, how information is transmitted, and how errors are detected and corrected. Using the same protocols, different types and makes of computers can communicate with each other. Over the years, numerous protocols have been developed, some of which can be used together. The table shown in Figure 6-35 lists some of the more widely used protocols. The two most widely used protocols for networks are Ethernet and token ring.

Figure 6-35
A partial list of commonly used communication protocols. Protocols specify the procedures that are used during transmission.

PROTOCOL	DESCRIPTION
Ethernet	Most widely used protocol for LANS.
Token ring	Uses electronic token to avoid transmission conflict by allowing only one device to transmit at a time.
PowerTalk	Links Apple Macintosh computers.
FDDI	Fiber Distributed Data Interface. High-speed fiber-optic protocol.
SNA	System Network Architecture. Primarily used to link large systems.
TCP/IP	Transmission Control Protocol/Internet. Used on the Internet.
X.25	International standard for packet switching.
ATM	Asynchronous Transfer Mode. Protocol developed for transmitting voice, data, and video over any type of media.
Frame Relay	High-speed protocol used to link remote networks.
CDPD	Cellular Digital Packet Data. Protocol used for cellular phones.
IPX	Used on Novell NetWare networks.
Xmodem	PC protocol that uses 128 byte blocks.
Ymodem	PC protocol that uses 1,024 byte blocks.
Zmodem	PC protocol that uses 512 byte blocks.
Kermit	PC protocol that uses variable length blocks.

Ethernet

Ethernet is the most widely used network protocol for LAN networks. Developed in the mid-1970s by Xerox, Ethernet was approved as the first industry standard LAN protocol in 1983. Ethernet is based on a bus topology but can be wired in a star pattern by using a wiring hub. Most Ethernet networks transmit data at 10 Mbps. A higher speed version of Ethernet, called **Fast-Ethernet**, can transmit data at 100 Mbps.

Because Ethernet uses a bus topology, a packet of data can be sent in both directions along the bus whenever a node is ready to transmit. The packet of data, which contains the destination address and the sending address, travels along the network until it arrives at the designated receiving device. If the packet runs into another packet, a **collision** occurs. Ethernet uses a method called **carrier sense multiple access with collision detection (CSMA/CD)** to detect collisions and retransmit the data. This method is illustrated in Figure 6-36.

Figure 6-36
How an Ethernet network transmits data.

1. Computers on an Ethernet bus network monitor the network cable to determine if any workstations are transmitting data. Sometimes, two or more computers try to send data at the same time. In this example, computer A is trying to send data to computer D and computer C is trying to send data to computer B. Each data packet contains the sender's address, the destination address, and the data.

2. When the data packets collide, static is created and a special electronic signal is sent to all computers on the network. The signal indicates a collision has occurred and that data packets should be retransmitted.

3. Each computer waits a random amount of time to retransmit. This usually results in one computer successfully transmitting its data before the other computer starts to retransmit.

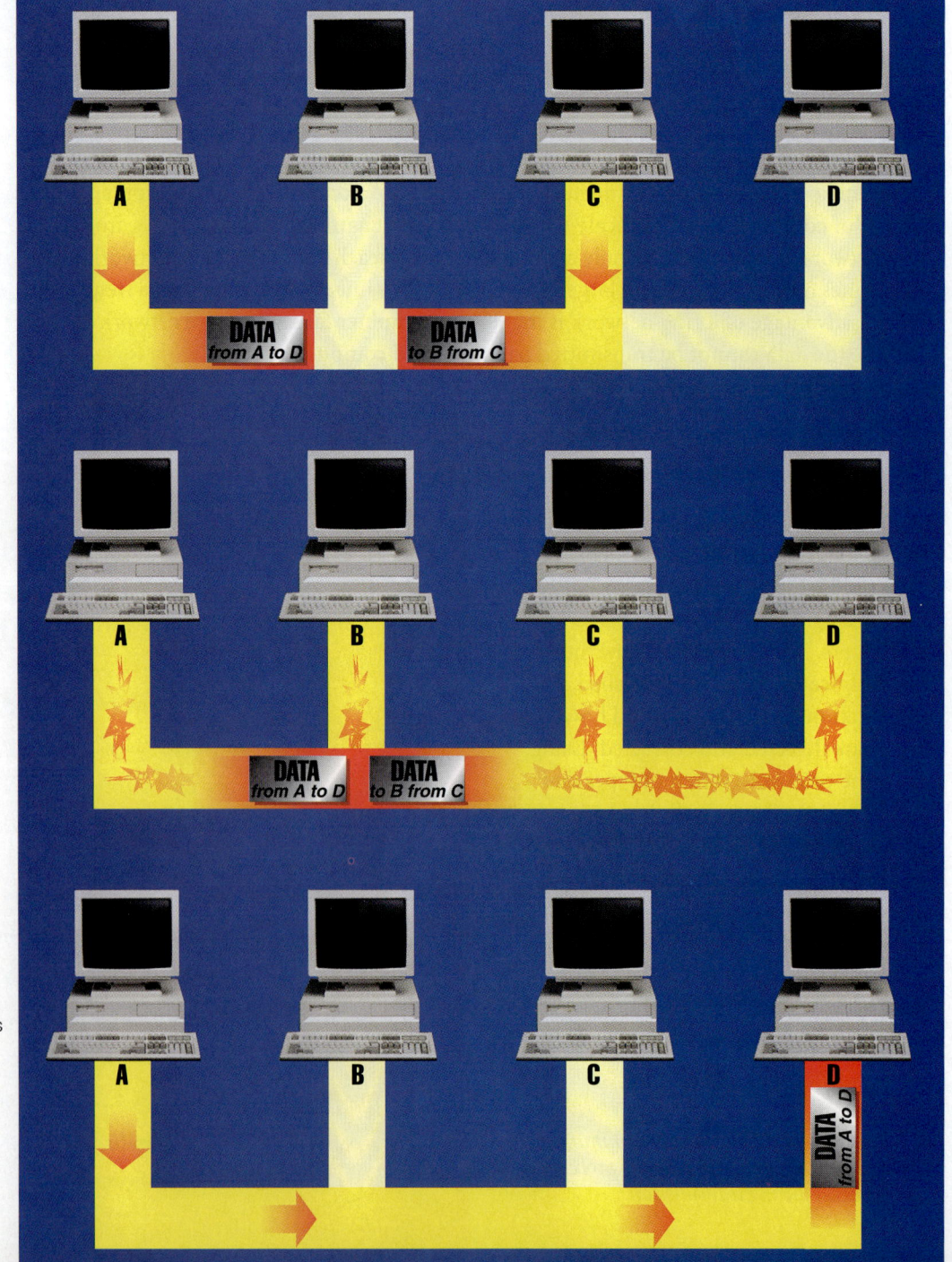

COMMUNICATIONS PROTOCOLS **6.31**

1. To transmit data on a token ring network, an unattached token must be available. A token is a set of bits that is constantly circulating the ring in one direction.

2. If the token is available, a network workstation attaches it to the data packet it wants to transmit. The token is changed so other workstations will know it is not available.

3. Workstation C has to wait to send its data because the token already is attached to another data packet.

4. When the token and data packet reach the workstation D destination, the data packet is replaced with an acknowledgment that says that the packet was received.

5. When the token and the acknowledgment return to workstation A, the token is released and is available to be attached to other data packets waiting to be sent.

Figure 6-37
A logical diagram of how a token ring network transmits data.

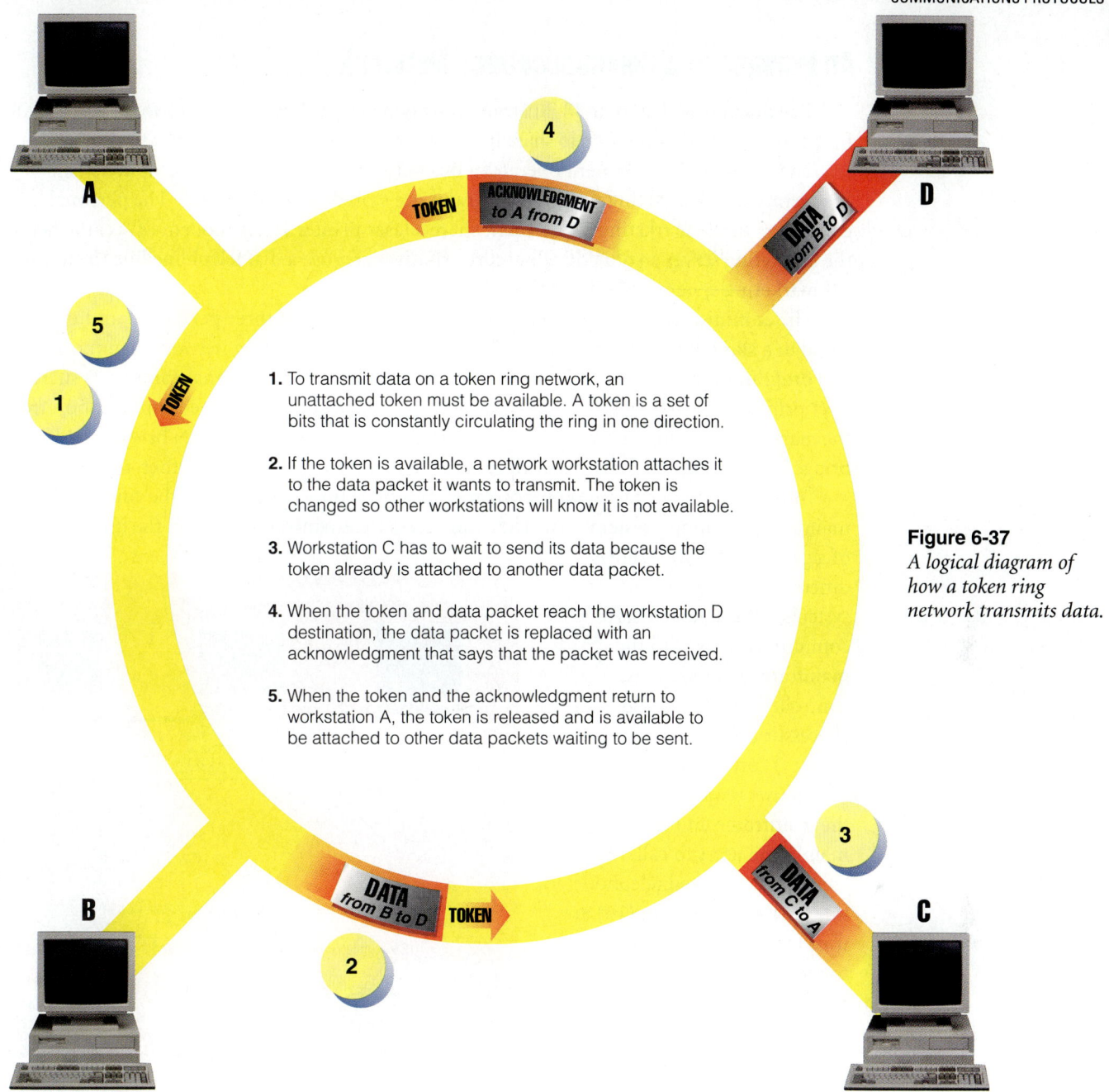

Token Ring

Token ring is the second most widely used protocol for LAN networks. A **token ring network** constantly circulates an electronic signal, called a **token**, around the network (Figure 6-37). Devices on the network that want to send a message take the token and attach it to their data. Once it is attached to data, the token cannot be used by other devices. When data arrives at its destination, the data is replaced with an acknowledgment that the data was received, and the token and the acknowledgment are sent back to the original sending device. When the original sending device receives the token and the acknowledgment, other devices then can use the token to send their data.

The *ring* in token ring applies to the circular sequence in which the computer checks each network node to see if it has data to send. It does not mean that a continuous loop of cable connects all of the nodes. In fact, like Ethernet, token ring networks are wired in a star pattern with separate cables connecting a central wiring hub with each node. Depending on the cabling and equipment used, token ring networks can transfer data at 4 and 16 Mbps. Token ring networks that transfer data at 16 Mbps use two tokens.

An Example of a Communications Network

The diagram in Figure 6-38 illustrates how two personal computer networks and a mainframe computer are connected to share information with each other and with outside sources.

The marketing department operates a bus network of four personal computers (1). Frequently used marketing data and programs are stored in the server (2). The personal computers in the marketing department share a laser printer (3). A modem (4) is attached to the marketing server so outside sales representatives can use a dial telephone line (5) to call the marketing system and obtain product price information.

The administration department operates a bus network of three personal computers (6) wired in a star pattern through a wiring hub. As with the marketing network, common data and programs are stored on a server (7) and the administration personal computers share a laser printer (8). Because the administration department sometimes needs information from the marketing system, the two similar networks are connected with a LAN bridge (9). The bridge allows users on either network to access data or programs on the other network.

Administration department users sometimes need information from the company's mainframe computer system (10). They can access the mainframe through the use of a gateway (11) that allows different types of network systems to be connected. All communications with the mainframe computer are controlled by a front-end processor (12). A dial telephone line (13) connected to a modem (14) allows remote users to call the mainframe and allows mainframe users to call other computers. A leased telephone line (15) and a modem (16) are used for a permanent connection to the computer at the corporate headquarters, several hundred miles away. The leased line can carry the signals of up to four different users. The signals are separated by the use of a multiplexer (17). A gateway (18) connects the front-end processor and mainframe system to a microwave antenna (19) on the roof of the building. The microwave antenna sends and receives data from a computer at the manufacturing plant located two miles away. The front-end processor also controls mainframe computer terminals located throughout the company (20).

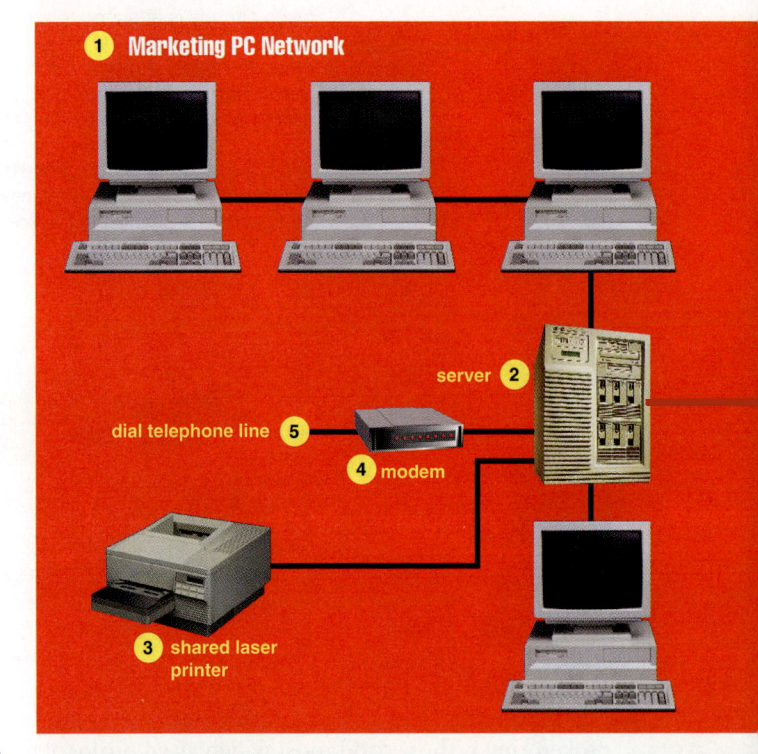

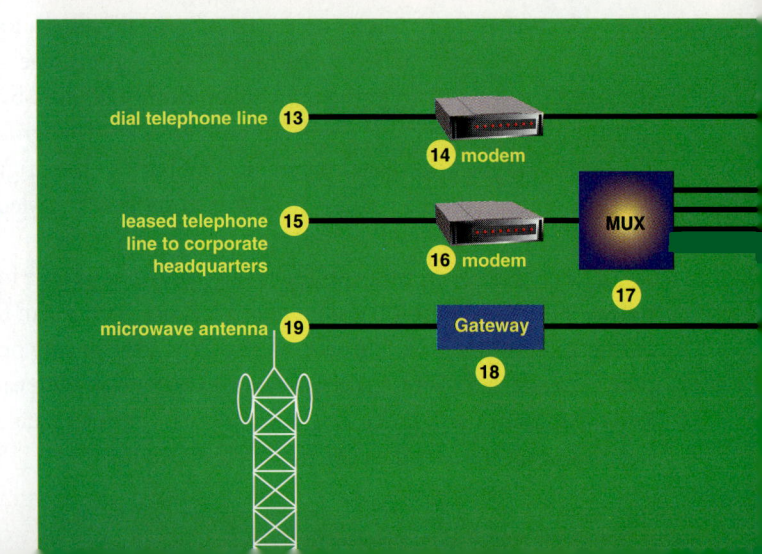

Summary of Communications and Networks

Communications will continue to affect how you work, access and use information, and use computers. Because of communications technology, individuals and organizations no longer are limited to local data resources; they can obtain information from anywhere in the world at electronic speed. Communications technology continues to change, challenging today's businesses to find ways to adapt the technology to make their operations more efficient and to provide better products and services for their customers. Networks are just one way that organizations are using communications technology to meet current business challenges. Today, many companies are focused on **enterprise computing**, which involves connecting all of the computers in an organization into one network, so everyone in the organization (the enterprise) can share hardware, software, information resources, and even processing power. By linking individual computers into networks, organizations not only expand computing resources, but also allow increased communication between workgroups and individuals. For individuals, new communications technology offers increased access to worldwide information and services and provides new opportunities in business and education.

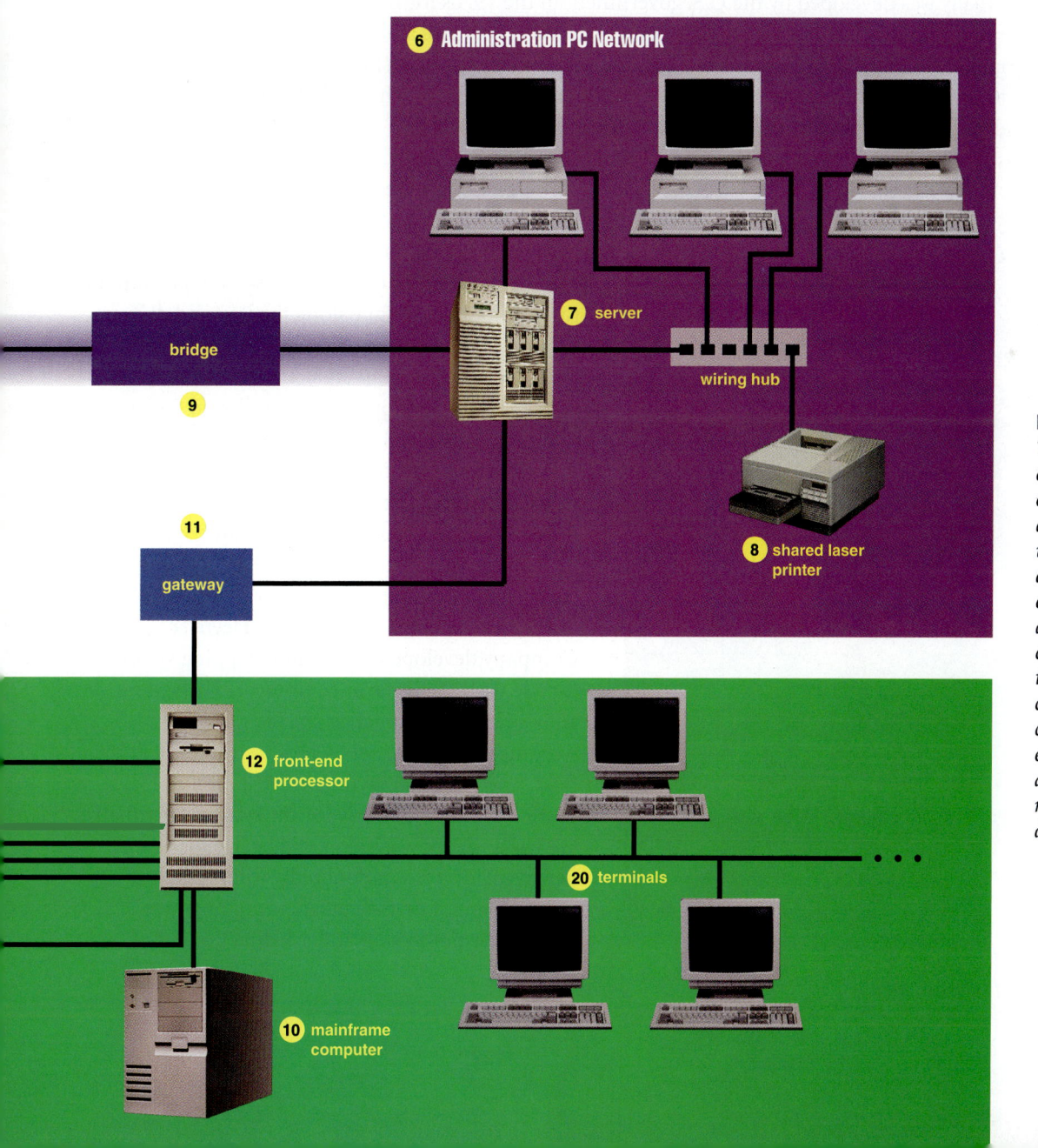

Figure 6-38
The two personal computer networks are connected together with a bridge. A gateway is used to connect the administration personal computer network with a mainframe. All communications with the mainframe are controlled by a separate computer called a front-end processor. Modems are used to connect the networks to leased and dial telephone lines.

COMPUTERS AT WORK

GPS: Tool of the Modern Traveler

In ancient times, mariners learned to use the stars to navigate and determine their position on the globe. Today, travelers have a new constellation to help them find their way; 24 global positioning system (GPS) satellites that circle the earth. The satellites are spread across six, 12,000-mile-high orbits and circle the earth every twelve hours. At any point on the globe, at least five satellites are within range for GPS use. Every thirty seconds, each satellite broadcasts a radio signal giving its precise location over the earth and the time the signal was sent. The time is determined by an onboard atomic clock that is accurate to within one second every 70,000 years. By comparing how long it takes signals from three or more satellites to arrive, a GPS receiver on earth can use the surveying technique of **triangulation** to determine its precise location, including altitude.

The GPS system originally was developed by the U.S. government in the 1970s for military use and was not made available for commercial use until the mid 1980s. Early GPS equipment was expensive and was used primarily in aviation and marine navigation. Hand-held units were available but cost more than $3,000. Today, lower-cost components have enabled GPS technology to be incorporated into many consumer electronic products such as cellular phones and portable computers. Hand-held devices used by hikers are available for less than $200.

Trucking companies were among the first commercial users of GPS systems, usually in combination with separate two-way communications systems. The GPS system locates the truck and the communications system lets the company stay in touch with the driver. Companies can let drivers know about opportunities to pick up more freight along the way and drivers can notify the company if they are delayed or need assistance.

Several developers have combined GPS with mapping software. The latitude and longitude coordinates determined by the GPS receiver are translated into a specific map location that is displayed on a screen. Both Hertz® and Avis® have installed small screens in some of their premium rental cars that can direct a driver to his or her hotel or the nearest bank or restaurant. Deere & Company developed a GPS and mapping system for use with the its farm equipment. The system allows farmers to practice *precision farming*; working their land foot by foot instead of field by field. The potential savings in fertilizer and pesticides more than pay for the system. Eventually, GPS and mapping systems will be installed in all new vehicles. This undoubtedly will reduce the age-old problem of driving partners arguing over whether or not to stop and ask directions.

Figure 6-39

IN THE FUTURE

Anywhere, Anytime Voice and Data Communications

Existing satellite phones are expensive, more than $20,000 each, and require an electronics package the size of a small suitcase. In the near future, satellite communications systems will enable you to talk, or send and receive data, anywhere on earth with a device the size of a cellular phone. To accomplish this goal, several organizations made up of private companies and international government agencies are developing the necessary hardware and software and negotiating with countries for communication rights. Several of these organizations base their plans on using low-earth orbit (LEO) satellites that will circle the earth at an altitude of less than 500 miles. LEO satellites are less expensive to build and put into orbit compared to satellites that are placed in geosynchronous orbits up to 22,300 miles above the earth. Two of the better known organizations planning satellite systems are IRIDIUM, Inc. and Teledesic Corporation.

The IRIDIUM system is a $4 billion project led by the U.S. communications company Motorola. IRIDIUM's plan includes 66 LEO satellites that will provide global wireless telephone service in 1998. Fax, paging, and low-speed (2,400 bps) data transfer capabilities also will be available. IRIDIUM will be a worldwide version of existing cellular phone systems without the patchwork of *no service* areas that now exist.

An even more ambitious $9 billion project is being planned by Teledesic. Two of the principal backers of Teledesic are Bill Gates of Microsoft and cellular phone pioneer Craig McCaw. During a two-year period beginning in 2000, Teledesic plans to orbit 924 LEO satellites; 44 each in 21 polar orbits. The Teledesic satellites will provide high-speed communications up to 2 MB per second. This higher transfer rate will make Teledesic better suited for data communications including much of the international Internet traffic. Unlike traditional satellites that communicate only with ground stations, Teledesic satellites will transmit data from one satellite to another. If necessary, communications traffic will be rerouted to avoid nonfunctioning or overloaded satellites.

In addition to IRIDIUM and Teledesic, nine other groups currently are developing global satellite-based communications systems. Several other organizations plan regional systems to service specific areas such as India and Western Europe. Although it is unlikely that all of these groups will succeed, some will and the ability to phone and be phoned anywhere will be a reality.

Figure 6-40

review

chapter 1 | 2 | 3 | 4 | 5 | 6 | 7 | 8 | 9 | 10 | 11 | 12 | 13 | 14 | I

inCyber | review | terms | yourTurn | hotTopics | outThere | winLabs | webWalk | exercises | news | home

INSTRUCTIONS: *To display this page from the Web, launch your browser and enter the URL, http://www.scsite.com/dc/ch6/review.htm. Click the links for current and additional information.*

1 What Is Communications?

Communications, sometimes called **data communications** or **telecommunications**, refers to the transmission of data and information between two or more computers using a communications channel. Communications technology is necessary for **electronic mail (e-mail)**, **voice mail**, **facsimile (fax)**, **telecommuting**, **videoconferencing**, **groupware**, **electronic data interchange (EDI)**, **global positioning systems (GPSs)**, electronic **bulletin board systems (BBSs)**, **online services**, the **Internet**, and **intranets**.

2 Components of a Communications System

The basic model of a communications system consists of a computer or terminal, communications equipment that sends data, a communications channel, communications equipment that receives data, and another computer. **Communications software** also is required. A **communications channel**, which is the path that data follows as it is transmitted from the sending equipment to the receiving equipment, is made up of one or more transmission media.

3 Transmission Media

Transmission media are the physical materials or other means used to establish a communications channel. Two types of transmission media are physical cabling media and wireless media.

4 Physical Cabling Media

Twisted-pair cable consists of pairs of plastic-coated copper wires that are twisted together. **Coaxial cable** is a high-quality communications line that consists of a copper wire conductor surrounded by three layers: a nonconducting insulator, a woven metal outer conductor, and a plastic outer coating. **Fiber-optic cable** uses smooth, hair-thin strands of glass or plastic to transmit data as pulses of light.

5 Wireless Media

Microwaves are radio waves that can be used to provide high-speed transmission of both voice communication and digital signals. **Wireless transmission** uses carrier-connect radio, infrared light beams, or radio waves to transmit data.

6 Line Configurations

Two major **line configurations** (types of line connections) commonly used in communications are point-to-point lines and multidrop, or multipoint, lines. A **point-to-point line** is a direct line between a sending and receiving device. A point-to-point line may be a **switched line** or a **dedicated line**. A **multidrop**, or **multipoint, line** commonly is used to connect multiple devices along a single line to a main computer, sometimes called a **host computer**.

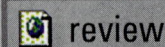

7 Characteristics of Communications Channels

Communications can be categorized by a number of characteristics including the type of signal, transmission mode, transmission direction, and transmission rate. Computer equipment is designed to process data as **digital signals**, or individual electrical pulses. Telephone lines were designed to carry voice transmission in continuous electrical waves called **analog signals**. A modem converts between digital and analog signals. In **asynchronous transmission mode,** data is transmitted in individual bytes at irregular intervals. In **synchronous transmission mode**, large blocks of data are transmitted at regular intervals.

8 Transmission Direction and Transmission Rate

The direction of data transmission is classified in one of three ways. In **simplex transmission**, data flows in one direction only. In **half-duplex transmission**, data can flow in either direction, but only in one direction at a time. In **full-duplex transmission**, data can be sent in both directions simultaneously. The transmission rate of a communications channel is determined by its bandwidth and its speed. **Bandwidth** is the range of frequencies that a communications channel can carry. The speed at which data is transmitted usually is expressed as **bits per second (bps)**.

9 Communications Software

Communications software is separate programs that manage the transmission of data between computers. Communications software has a number of features including **dialing**, **file transfer**, **terminal emulation**, and **Internet access**.

10 Communications Equipment

A **modem** converts digital signals to analog signals, and converts analog signals back into digital signals. A **multiplexer** combines input signals from several devices into a single stream of data and transmits it. After it passes over a communications channel, a multiplexer separates the data stream into its original parts. A **front-end processor** handles the communications requirements of a larger system. A **network interface card** fits in an expansion slot of a computer or other device so the device can be connected to the network. A **wiring hub** allows devices to be connected to the server. A **gateway** allows users on one network to access resources on a *different* type of network. A **bridge** is used to connect *similar* networks. A **router** is an intelligent network connector that sends communications traffic to the appropriate network.

11 Communications Networks

A communications **network** is a collection of terminals, computers, and other equipment that uses communications channels to share data, information, hardware, and software. Networks can be classified as either local area networks or wide area networks.

Local Area Networks (LANs)

12 A **local area network** (**LAN**) is a communications network that covers a limited geographic area. Common applications of local area networks are **hardware resource sharing**, **software resource sharing**, and **information resource sharing**. Information resource sharing usually is provided using either the **file-server method** or the **client-server method**. A **peer-to-peer network** allows any computer on a LAN to share the resources of any other computer on the LAN. A **network operating system** (**NOS**) is the system software that makes it possible to implement and control a LAN.

Wide Area Networks (WANs)

13 A **wide area network** (**WAN**) covers a large geographic region and uses telephone cables, terrestrial microwave, satellites, or other combinations of communications channels. **Common carriers** are public wide area network companies. **Value-added networks** (**VANs**) enhance communications channels leased from common carriers by adding improvements such as faster data transmission or other specialized services.

Network Configurations

14 The way equipment is configured in a communications network is called **topology**. A **star network** topology has a central computer with one or more smaller computers connected to it, forming a star. In a **bus network** topology, all the devices in the network are connected to and share a single data path. In a **ring network** topology, the devices on the network are connected in a continuous loop or ring.

Communications Protocols

15 A **protocol** is a set of rules and procedures for exchanging information between computers. Protocols define how a link is established, how information is transmitted, and how errors are detected and corrected. By using the same protocols, different types and makes of computers can communicate. The two most widely used protocols for networks are **Ethernet** and **token ring**.

6.39 terms

URL: http://www.scsite.com/dc/ch6/terms.htm

chapter 6 terms

1 | 2 | 3 | 4 | 5 | 6 | 7 | 8 | 9 | 10 | 11 | 12 | 13 | 14 | I

inCyber | review | terms | yourTurn | hotTopics | outThere | winLabs | webWalk | exercises | news | home

INSTRUCTIONS: *To display this page from the Web, launch your browser and enter the URL, http://www.scsite.com/dc/ch6/terms.htm. Scroll through the list of terms. Click a term for its definition and a picture. Click the rocket ship for current and additional information about the term.*

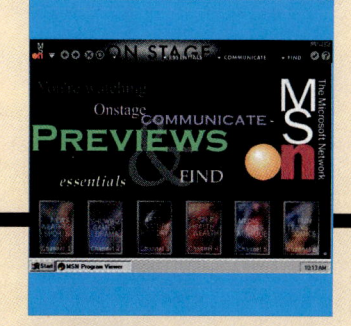

online services

DEFINITION

online services

Online services make information and services such as electronic banking, shopping, news, weather, hotel and airline reservations, investment information, and Internet access available to paying subscribers (**6.6**)

10base2 cable (6.10)
10baseT cable (6.9)

analog signal (6.16)
application server (6.25)
asynchronous transmission mode (6.17)

bandwidth (6.18)
bits per second (bps) (6.18)
bridge (6.22)
bulletin board system (BBS) (6.5)
bus network (6.28)

carrier sense multiple access with collision detection (CSMA/CD) (6.30)
cellular telephone (6.13)
client-server (6.24)
coax (6.9)
coaxial cable (6.9)
collision (6.30)
common carriers (6.26)
communications (6.2)
communications channel (6.8)
communications line (6.8)
communications link (6.8)
communications satellites (6.11)
communications software (6.8), (6.19)
concentrator (6.22)

data communications (6.2)
data link (6.8)
database server (6.25)
dedicated line (6.15)
dialing (6.19)
digital data service (6.17)
digital signal (6.16)

downlink (6.11)

earth stations (6.11)
electronic data interchange (EDI) (6.4)
electronic mail (e-mail) (6.2)
enterprise computing (6.33)
Ethernet (6.30)
external modem (6.19)

facsimile (6.2)
Fast-Ethernet (6.30)
fax (6.2)
fiber-optic cable (6.10)
file-server (6.24)
file transfer (6.19)
front-end processor (6.21)
full-duplex transmission (6.18)

gateway (6.22)
geosynchronous orbit (6.12)
global positioning system (GPS) (6.5)
groupware (6.4)

half-duplex transmission (6.18)
handshake (6.14)
hardware resource sharing (6.23)
host computer (6.15)

information resource sharing (6.24)
information services (6.6)
internal modem (6.20)
Internet (6.7)
Internet access (6.19)
intranets (6.7)
ISDN (integrated services digital network) (6.17)

leased line (6.15)
line configurations (6.14)
local area network (LAN) (6.23)

metropolitan area network (MAN) (6.26)
microwaves (6.11)
modem (6.19)
multidrop line (6.15)
multiplexer (6.20)
multipoint line (6.15)
multistation access unit (MAU) (6.22)

network (6.23)
network interface card (NIC) (6.21)
network licenses (6.24)
network operating system (NOS) (6.25)
node (6.27)

online services (6.6)

packet-switching (6.26)
peer-to-peer network (6.25)
point-to-point line (6.14)
polling (6.21)
private line (6.15)
protocol (6.29)

ring network (6.29)
router (6.22)

shielded twisted-pair (STP) cable (6.9)
simplex transmission (6.18)
site licenses (6.24)
software resource sharing (6.24)

stackable hub (6.22)
star network (6.27)
switched line (6.14)
synchronous transmission mode (6.17)
sys op (6.5)
system operator (6.5)

T1 (6.17)
T3 (6.17)
telecommunications (6.2)
telecommuting (6.2)
terminal emulation (6.19)
terrestrial microwave (6.11)
thinnet (6.10)
token (6.31)
token ring network (6.30)
transmission media (6.9)
twisted-pair cable (6.9)

unshielded twisted-pair (UTP) cable (6.9)
uplink (6.11)

value-added carriers (6.26)
value-added network (VAN) (6.26)
very small aperture terminal (VSAT) (6.12)
videoconferencing (6.3)
voice mail (6.2)

wide area network (WAN) (6.26)
wireless transmission (6.12)
wiring hub (6.22)
workgroup technology (6.4)
workstations (6.27)

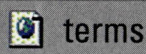

Label the Figure

Instructions: Identify each part of a communication system.

Fill in the Blanks

Instructions: Complete each sentence with the correct term or terms.

1. _____ refers to the transmission of data and information between two or more computers using a channel such as a standard telephone line.
2. One application that relies on communications technology is _____, which is the direct exchange of documents from one business's computer system to another.
3. A(n) _____ is the path that data follows as it is transmitted from the sending equipment to the receiving equipment in a communications system.
4. Three kinds of physical cabling media are _____, which consists of pairs of plastic wires wound together, _____, which is composed of a copper wire conductor surrounded by three layers, and _____, which uses hair-thin strands of glass or plastic to transmit pulses of light.
5. A(n) _____ is a device that attaches to a computer and converts between digital signals and analog signals.

Short Answer

Instructions: Write a brief answer to each of the following questions.

1. How are point-to-point lines different from multidrop lines? How is a switched line different from a dedicated line? What are the advantages and disadvantages of using a switched line? _____
2. How is asynchronous transmission mode different from synchronous transmission mode? What is a parity bit? _____
3. What functions are performed by communications software? What is the purpose of each? _____
4. How are local area networks (LANs) different from wide area networks (WANs)? How is the file-server method of information resource sharing different from the client-server method of information resource sharing? _____
5. Why are communications protocols important? What are the Ethernet and token ring protocols? _____

hotTopics

chapter 6

| 1 | 2 | 3 | 4 | 5 | 6 | 7 | 8 | 9 | 10 | 11 | 12 | 13 | 14 | I |

inCyber | review | terms | yourTurn | hotTopics | outThere | winLabs | webWalk | exercises | news | home

INSTRUCTIONS: *To display this page from the Web, launch your browser and enter the URL, http://www.scsite.com/dc/ch6/hot.htm. Click the links for current and additional information to help you respond to the hotTopics questions.*

1 *A luxury sedan is available with an electronic navigation system that uses* global positioning satellites. To use the system, a driver chooses from lists of destinations by touching a screen on the dashboard. After asking how the driver wants to travel (city streets or highway), a computer shows a map with a suggested route. As the car moves, a computer voice indicates where and when to turn. Of the applications such as the navigation system that rely on communications technology, which would you be most likely to use today? Which would you be most likely to use ten years from now? Which will have the greatest impact on society?

2 *The number of people telecommuting has increased fourfold in the past eight years.* Telecommuting offers several advantages to employees—flexible work schedules, casual dress codes, and no rush-hour traffic. Studies show employers also benefit—less office space is required and telecommuters are 10 to 20 percent more productive than their office-bound brethren. Whether telecommuting is a success, however, appears to depend on three factors: the employee's personality, the employer's willingness to make adjustments, and the nature of the job. What type of personality is necessary to telecommute successfully? What adjustments must be made by employers? Given your personality and the career you plan to pursue, could you be a successful telecommuter? Why?

3 *Many online services and bulletin board systems have taken increased* responsibility for the content of the messages they communicate. But online services and bulletin board systems cover large geographic areas, and standards vary from community to community. Some feel any attempt at control is censorship. Do online services and bulletin board systems have the obligation to decide what is communicated? What role should government take in controlling the type of information transmitted? Why? If you were head of an online service or bulletin board, what standards would you set?

4 *If you have friends or family who live out of town, you (or they) may be paying a substantial* amount to a common carrier for long-distance telephone service. Yet, with a computer, the appropriate software and hardware, and an Internet access provider, you can talk to people anywhere in the world for as long as you want, all for a monthly flat rate (usually around twenty-five dollars). Problems do exist: setting up the equipment can be difficult, conversations are somewhat choppy, and both parties must be online and using the same phone software. Will phone service via the Internet ever replace conventional telephone service? How might common carriers change to accommodate this new mode of communication? Would you be interested in using your computer to call people long distance? Why?

5 *In the course of a usual day, people communicate in different directions. Sometimes they just* listen, sometimes they listen and then respond, and sometimes everyone is able to talk at once. Make a list of interactions you have in a typical day. Classify each communication based on the direction of transmission: those comparable to simplex transmission, those comparable to half-duplex transmission, and those comparable to full-duplex transmission. Explain why you classified each communication as you did. Is there any communication that, by its nature, must have a certain direction of transmission? Would any communication improve if the direction of transmission were different? Why or why not?

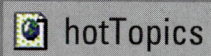

outThere

chapter 1 | 2 | 3 | 4 | 5 | 6 | 7 | 8 | 9 | 10 | 11 | 12 | 13 | 14 | I

inCyber | review | terms | yourTurn | hotTopics | outThere | winLabs | webWalk | exercises | news | home

INSTRUCTIONS: *To display this page from the Web, launch your browser and enter the URL, http://www.scsite.com/dc/ch6/out.htm. Click the links for current and additional information.*

1 *Many schools and offices have a network connecting their computers. These* networks offer advantages that could not be realized if the computers were not joined. Locate a school or office that uses a network and interview someone about how the network works. For what purposes is the network used? What are the advantages of using a network? Does the organization use a single server computer or a peer-to-peer network? What network operating system is used? Why? What network configuration (star, bus, or ring) is used? Why? Is the network connected to another network? If so, how?

2 *As office networks grow increasingly commonplace, network security* has become an important issue. Networks frequently carry sensitive information — research analysis, test data, engineering designs, legal documents, and so on. No organization can afford to leave this type of information vulnerable to hackers, industrial espionage agents, or disgruntled employees. It is estimated that attacks on networks cost companies billions of dollars each year. Visit some Web sites to learn more about network security. How frequent are attacks on networks? What are the results of these attacks? What factors are important in providing network security? How can a network be secured?

3 *Facsimile equipment has become an essential component of even small businesses. Orders,* invoices, and correspondence are faxed routinely between merchants and customers. Fax machines also are becoming increasingly popular in homes. People are faxing notes to friends, letters to magazines, even song requests to radio stations! Because of this, fax machines now are available at a variety of outlets including computer stores, office supply stores, discount stores, and electronics stores. Visit three different types of stores and find similar fax machines in each. Write down the brand name of each machine, the features it offers, the store in which it was found, and the machine's cost. Where would you be most likely to purchase a fax machine? Why?

4 *Choosing a network operating system (NOS) may be one of the more important decisions made* when establishing a network. The network operating system determines the way information, software, and hardware are shared and manipulated. The efficiency and security of a network is to a large extent dependent on the network operating system. Learn about two or more network operating systems by visiting appropriate Web sites. What are the operating system's features? What are its specifications? What hardware is required? With what software is the operating system compatible? Where is the system available? How can it be learned? From what you have discovered, which network operating system do you think is best? Why?

5 *Some experts predict that online information services and the Internet eventually will be as* much a part of our lives as newspapers, magazines, and television. Are all online information services the same? Call the telephone numbers for at least three of the online information service providers listed in Figure 6-6 on page 6.7 to find out how they differ. What services are offered? Is a particular type of computer or user interface required? What is the membership fee? Are other fees charged, such as a minimum monthly charge, hourly access fee, or added cost for certain services? Is Internet access included? How? From the information you learn, in which online service are you most interested? Why?

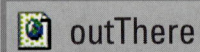

winLabs

chapter 1 | 2 | 3 | 4 | 5 | 6 | 7 | 8 | 9 | 10 | 11 | 12 | 13 | 14 | I

inCyber | review | terms | yourTurn | hotTopics | outThere | winLabs | webWalk | exercises | news | home

INSTRUCTIONS: *To display this page from the Web, launch your browser and enter the URL, http://www.scsite.com/dc/ch6/labs.htm. Click the links for current and additional information.*

1. Shelly Cashman Series Computers of the Future Lab

Follow the instructions in winLabs 1 on page 1.34 to display the Shelly Cashman Series Labs screen. Click Exploring the Computers of the Future. Click the Start Lab button. When the initial screen displays, carefully read the objectives. With your printer turned on, click the Print Questions button. Fill out the top of the Questions sheet and then answer the questions.

2. What is The Microsoft Network

Right-click The Microsoft Network (MSN) icon on the desktop. Click Properties on the shortcut menu. When The Microsoft Network Properties dialog box displays (Figure 6-41), read the information and then answer the following questions: (1) What version of The Microsoft Network are you using? Click the Connection Settings button and then answer the following questions: (1) What is the current service type? (2) What is the telephone number for this service type? (3) What modem, if any, is being used to connect to the MSN? Close the dialog boxes.

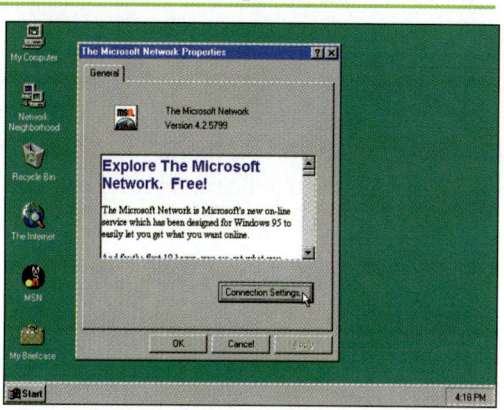

Figure 6-41

3. Understanding Your Modem

Click the Start button on the taskbar, point to Settings on the Start menu, and then click Control Panel on the submenu. Double-click the Modems icon in the Control Panel window. When the Modems Properties dialog box displays, click the General tab. Click the first modem in the list and then click the Properties button. When the modem's dialog box displays, click the General tab (Figure 6-42). Answer the following questions: (1) What is the name of the modem? (2) To which port is the modem connected? (3) What is the maximum speed of the modem? Click the Connection tab and then answer the following questions: (1) What is the number of data bits? (2) What is the parity? (3) What is the number of stop bits? (4) Which call preferences are set on your modem? Close the dialog boxes and Control Panel.

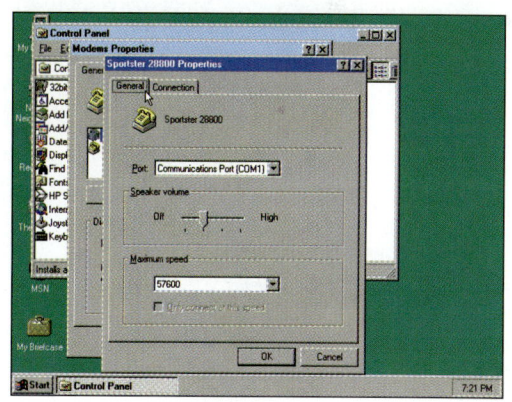

Figure 6-42

4. Using Help to Understand Networks

Click the Start button on the taskbar and then click Help on the Start menu. Click the Contents tab, double-click How To..., and then double-click Use a Network. Double-click Setting up your computer to connect to the network. In the Windows Help window, click the Options button, click Print Topic, and then click the OK button in the Print dialog box. Click the Help Topics button. One at a time, display and print each of the remaining Use a Network topics. Close any open Help window(s). Read the printouts.

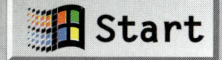

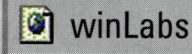

webWalk

chapter 6 | 1 | 2 | 3 | 4 | 5 | 6 | 7 | 8 | 9 | 10 | 11 | 12 | 13 | 14 | I

inCyber | review | terms | yourTurn | hotTopics | outThere | winLabs | webWalk | exercises | news | home

INSTRUCTIONS: *To display this page from the Web, launch your browser and enter the URL, http://www.scsite.com/dc/ch6/walk.htm. Click the exercise link to display the exercise.*

1. Desktop Videoconferencing
Desktop videoconferencing products are applications that can be used on standard desktop computer systems. You can learn more about desktop videoconferencing by completing this exercise.

3. Global Positioning System GPS
GPS is a satellite-based radio navigation system originally employed by the U.S. Department of Defense that now is used to track vehicles and goods and provide accurate position, velocity, and time. To learn more about GPS, complete this exercise.

4. Online Services
Online services, sometimes called information services, provide information and services to paying subscribers. To visit an online service (Figure 6-44), complete this exercise.

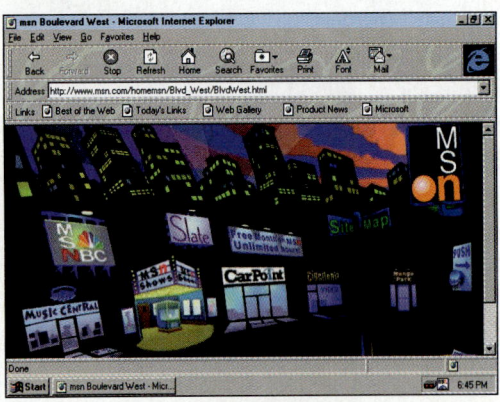

Figure 6-44

7. Real-time auction
Complete this exercise to learn about a Web site that runs a real-time auction in which you can participate.

9. Web Chat
Complete this exercise to enter a Web Chat discussion related to the issues presented in the hotTopics exercise.

2. Groupware
Groupware is software that helps multiple users collaborate on projects and share information (Figure 6-43). Complete this exercise to learn more about groupware.

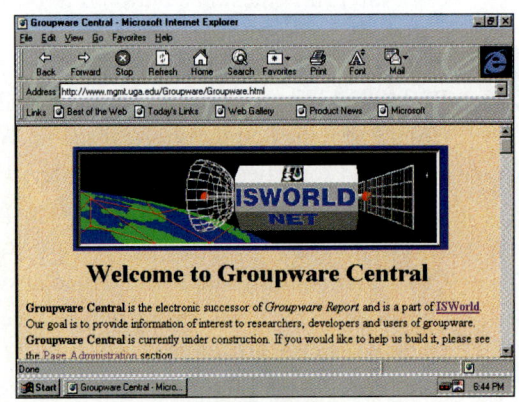

Figure 6-43

5. Information Mining
Complete this exercise to improve your Web research skills by using a Web search engine to find information related to this chapter.

6. Online Investing
Communications technology makes Web services, such as online investing possible. Complete this exercise to learn about a Web site where you can place stock and option orders and manage your portfolio around the clock.

8. Electronic Mail (E-mail)
E-mail allows you to use a computer to transmit messages to and receive messages from other computer users. Complete this exercise to visit a unique web site and send your comments via e-mail.

The Internet and the World Wide Web

OBJECTIVES

After completing this chapter, you will be able to:

- Describe the Internet and how it works
- Describe the World Wide Web portion of the Internet
- Understand how Web documents are linked to one another
- Understand how Web browser software works
- Describe several types of multimedia available on the Web
- Explain how to use a Web search tool to find information
- Describe different ways organizations use intranets and firewalls
- Explain how Internet services such as e-mail, FTP, Gopher, Telnet, Usenet, and Internet Relay Chat help you communicate and access information
- Describe how network computers are used
- Understand how to connect to the Internet and the World Wide Web

CHAPTER 7

The Internet has been described as the fastest growing area of computer technology. The popularity of the World Wide Web, which is the part of the Internet that supports multimedia, has added to this growth. Together, the Internet and the World Wide Web represent one of the more exciting uses of computers today. Already, these highly interactive applications have changed the way people gather information, do research, listen to the radio, take classes, collaborate on projects, and more. Companies and organizations now use the Internet and the World Wide Web to reach customers and vendors and to communicate with employees.

The future will bring even more exciting applications of these technologies. Millions of dollars are being invested in Internet-related hardware and software projects, and new Internet companies are being started everyday. This chapter will explain what the Internet and World Wide Web are, how they work, and how you can use them to communicate and obtain information on an unlimited number of products, services, and subjects.

CHAPTER 7 – THE INTERNET AND THE WORLD WIDE WEB

inCyber

For an overview of the Internet, visit the Discovering Computers Chapter 7 inCyber page (http://www.scsite.com/dc/ch7/incyber.htm) and click Overview.

Figure 7-1
The Internet is a worldwide group of connected networks that allows public access to information and service.

What Is the Internet?

Recall that a network is a group of computers connected by communications equipment and software. When two or more networks are joined together they are called an **internetwork** or **internet** (lowercase i). The term, **the Internet** (uppercase I), is used to describe a worldwide group of connected networks that allow public access to information and services (Figure 7-1).

Some of these networks are local, some are regional, and some are national. Together, these networks create a global network that serves an estimated 40 million users (Figure 7-2). Although each of the networks that makes up the Internet is owned by a public or private organization, no single organization *owns* or controls the Internet. Some say this lack of central control is a strength of the Internet that has allowed it to grow rapidly. Others say the lack of central control is a weakness that will prevent the Internet from handling the increasing volume of users.

Figure 7-2
Internet statistics. All numbers are estimates. Because the Internet is not controlled by any single organization, it is impossible to measure precisely Internet usage or growth.

Internet Statistics

40 million users

200 connected countries

100,000 connected networks

12 million host computers or sites

100,000 Web server computers

Number of users growing at 4% per month

History of the Internet

The Internet began in 1969 as a network of four computers located at the University of California at Los Angeles, the University of California at Santa Barbara, the University of Utah, and the Stanford Research Institute. The initial work was funded by an agency of the U.S. Department of Defense called the **Advanced Research Projects Agency (ARPA)**. The first network thus was called **ARPANET**. The Department of Defense had two major goals for the initial project. The first goal, which was driven by national security concerns, was to develop the hardware and software needed to create a geographically dispersed network that could function even if part of the network was disabled or destroyed. The second goal was to create a way for scientists at different locations to share information and collaborate on military and scientific projects.

Over the years, the total number of computers connected to the original network has grown steadily and, within the last five years, explosively. Within two years of its creation, more than 20 sites were connected to the Internet. Within 10 years, more than 200 sites, including several European sites, were connected; within 20 years, more than 100,000 sites were linked to the original network. Today, experts estimate more than 12 million computers distribute information over the Internet.

In addition to the computer sites linked to the original network, whole networks also were added. One of these networks was operated by the National Science Foundation (NSF) and was called **NSFnet**. The NSFnet included the five United States-based supercomputer centers. NSFnet served as the major U.S. Internet network from 1987 until 1995 when other companies took over responsibility. Figure 7-3 shows a map produced by the NSF that shows the major U.S. Internet connections.

---

inCyber

For the history of the Internet, visit the Discovering Computers Chapter 7 inCyber page (http://www.scsite.com/dc/ch7/incyber.htm) and click History.

Figure 7-3
This map was prepared by the National Science Foundation and shows the major U.S. Internet connections.

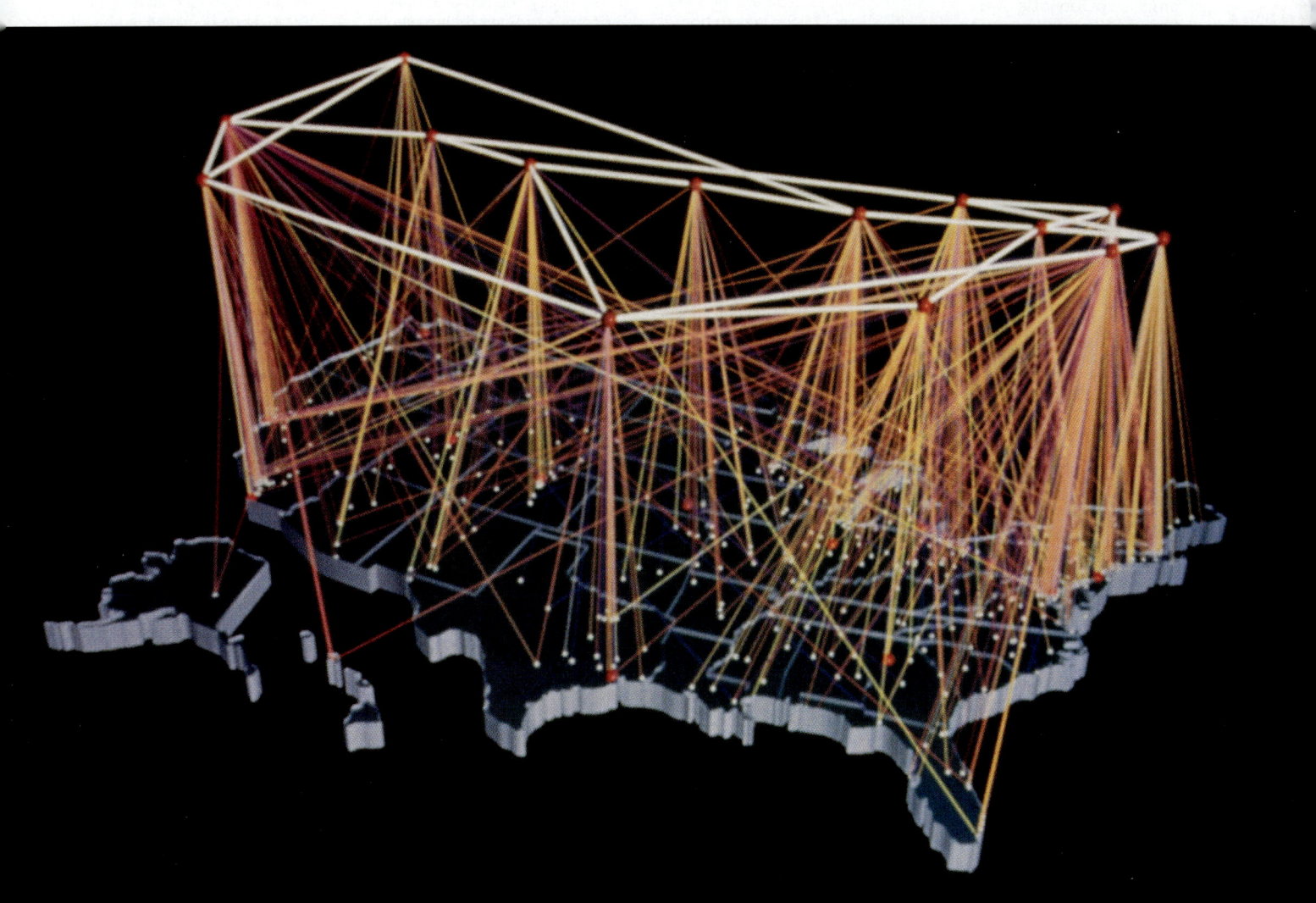

How the Internet Works

As illustrated in Figure 7-4, the Internet operates by taking data, dividing it into separate parts called **packets**, and sending the packets along the best route available to a destination computer. The data might be an e-mail message, a file, a document, or a request for a file. Each packet contains the data and the destination, origin, and sequence information used to reassemble the data at the destination. Although each packet may arrive out of sequence, the receiving computer reassembles the original message. Usually, some data, such as a file or document, is sent back to the computer that sent the original data.

The technique of breaking a message into individual packets, sending the packets along the best route available, and reassembling the data is called *packet switching*. The software used for packet switching on the Internet is a communications protocol named **TCP/IP** (**transmission control protocol/Internet protocol**). As you learned in Chapter 6, a communications protocol specifies the rules, or standards, that are used to transmit data.

The physical part of the Internet includes networks and communications lines owned and operated by many companies. You can connect to these networks in one of several ways.

Figure 7-4
How data is sent over the Internet.

PHASE 1 – Request is sent

1. Individuals connecting from home typically dial in to an Internet service provider (ISP) using a modem over regular telephone lines. Once connected, you can send information or requests over the Internet. You can request a Web page, for example, by typing its Internet address (called a URL).

2. Data sent over the Internet is divided into packets. Each packet has destination and origin information.

3. An Internet service provider (ISP) has a permanent connection to the Internet and provides temporary connections to others for a fee. ISPs use T1 lines leased from local telephone companies to connect to regional host computers.

4. Regional host computers are operated by national Internet service providers. National ISPs consolidate local ISP traffic and provide connections to the Internet backbones, which are the fastest Internet communication lines. If necessary, the regional host computer routes data packets along different paths to their final destinations.

5. National ISPs are connected to one another by metropolitan area exchanges (MAEs), which are facilities where Internet traffic carried by one backbone provider is transferred to another backbone provider.

6. Your request is transferred by another regional host and local ISP to a server, which is any computer directly connected to the Internet that stores and serves data. All of the information on the Internet originates within servers, which are operated by schools, companies, and other organizations. Upon receipt, the server reassembles and interprets the data packets and takes the appropriate action, such as sending a Web page back to your computer.

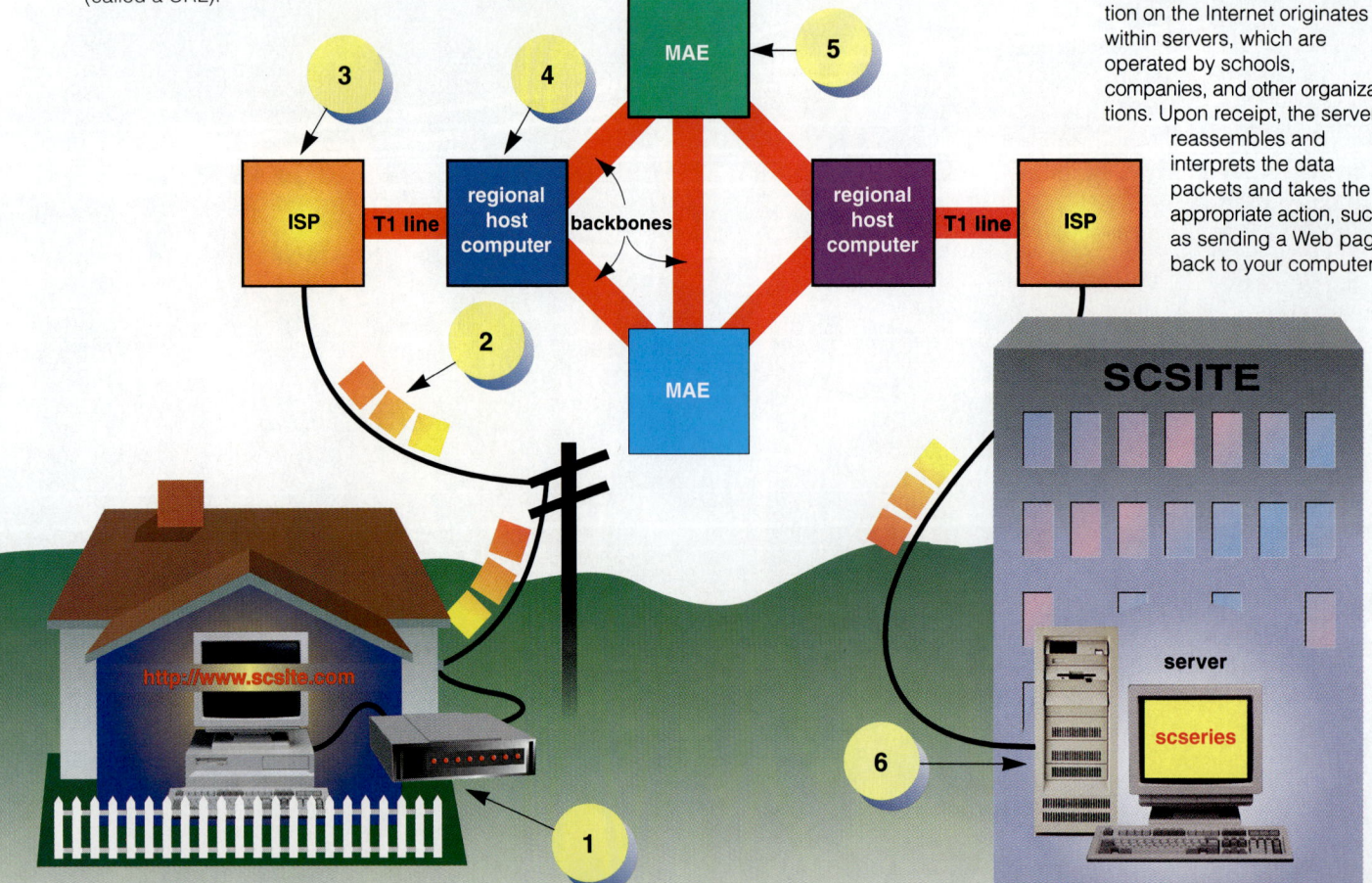

Organizations such as schools and companies often provide Internet access for students and employees. You also can connect through an online service such as America Online. Finally, you might connect to the Internet through an Internet service provider. An **Internet service provider** (ISP) is an organization that has a permanent connection to the Internet and provides temporary connections to others for a fee. Local ISPs connect to regional host computers operated by national Internet service providers.

Regional host computers are connected to the major networks that carry most of the Internet communications traffic by high-speed communications lines called **backbones**. Backbones are like highways that connect major cities across the country. **Metropolitan area exchanges** (MAEs), located in major cities, are used to transfer data packets from one backbone provider to another. MAEs function like highway interchanges. Smaller, slower speed networks extend out from the backbone into regions and local communities like roads and streets. Internet traffic control is provided by routers, located throughout the Internet, which contain network maps. If the most direct path to the destination is overloaded or not operating, routers send the packets along an alternate path. If necessary, each packet can be sent over a different path to the destination.

inCyber

For a list of Internet service providers (ISPs), visit the Discovering Computers Chapter 7 inCyber page (http://www.scsite.com/dc/ch7/incyber.htm) and click ISP.

PHASE 2 – Data is received

1. The server retrieves the requested file, divides it into packets, and sends it back to the local ISP.

2. The local ISP then routes the packets to the national ISP and so on over the Internet, back to your computer. The packets can be routed over the same or a different path than the original request.

3. The requested file displays on your computer screen.

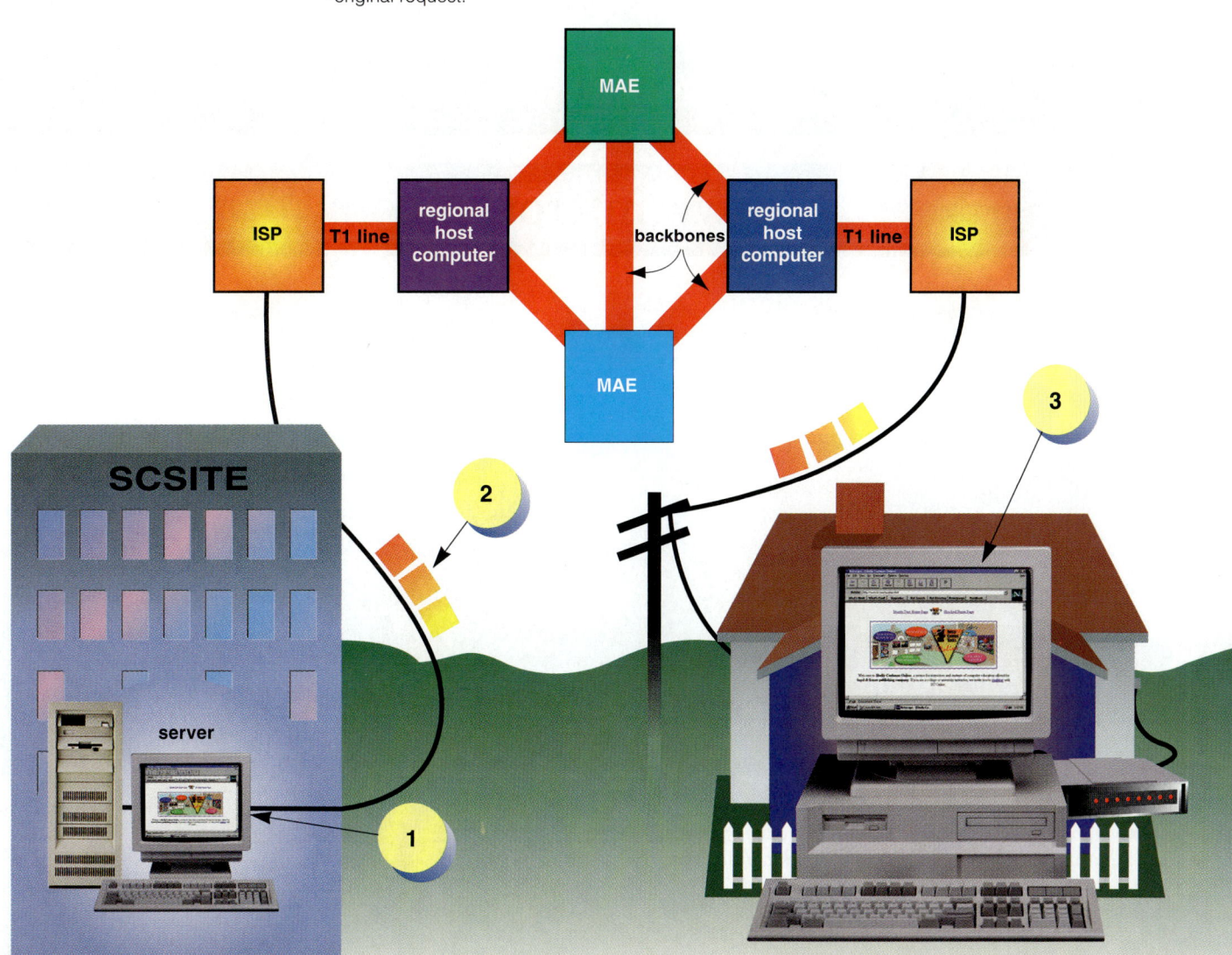

Internet Addresses

Like the postal service, the Internet relies on an addressing system to send data to its destination. Each location on the Internet has a four-part numeric address called an **IP (Internet protocol) address**. The first part of the IP address identifies the geographic region, the second part the company or organization, the third part the computer group, and the fourth and last part, the specific computer.

Because these all-numeric IP addresses are hard to remember and use, the Internet supports the use of a text name that can be substituted for the IP address. The text version of the IP address is called a **domain name**. Figure 7-5 is an example of an IP address and its associated domain name. Like IP addresses, domain names also are separated by periods. For domestic Web sites, the rightmost portion of the domain name contains a domain type abbreviation that identifies the type of organization. For international Web sites, the domain name also includes a country code, such as uk for the United Kingdom or ca for Canada. Figure 7-6 is a list of domain type abbreviations. Domain names are registered in the **domain name system (DNS)** and are stored in Internet computers called domain name servers. **Domain name servers** use the domain name to look up the associated IP address.

Because the rapid growth of the Internet is expected to continue, an expanded IP addressing scheme is being implemented. The new address scheme will increase the number of addresses by a factor of four and will provide added security for data transfers.

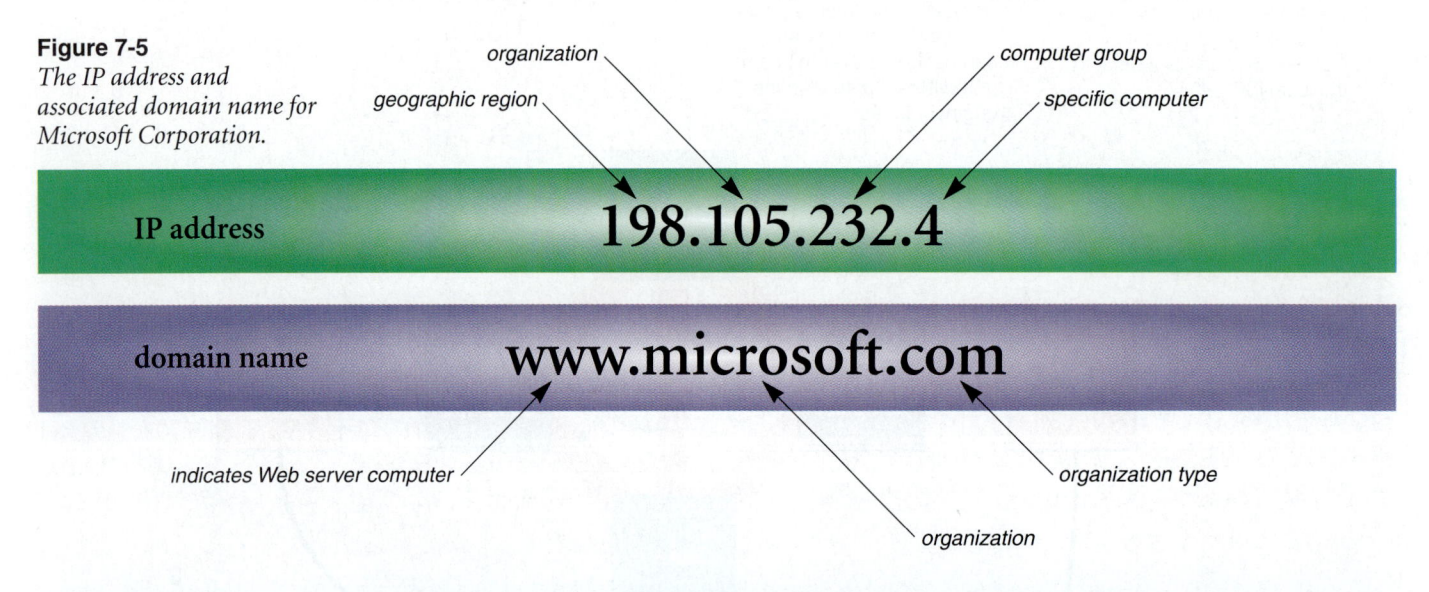

inCyber
For information about registering domain names, visit the Discovering Computers Chapter 7 inCyber page (http://www.scsite.com/dc/ch7/incyber.htm) and click DNS.

Figure 7-5
The IP address and associated domain name for Microsoft Corporation.

IP address: 198.105.232.4
- geographic region
- organization
- computer group
- specific computer

domain name: www.microsoft.com
- indicates Web server computer
- organization
- organization type

Domain Abbreviations

.com	Businesses	.mil	Military
.edu	Colleges and universities	.net	Network and administrative computers
.gov	U.S. government	.org	Miscellaneous organizations
.int	International treaty organizations		

Figure 7-6
Abbreviations used in domain names indicate the organization type. The majority of domain names are registered to businesses.

The World Wide Web (WWW)

In 1991, software was developed in Europe that made the Internet easier to use. Tim Berners-Lee, a programmer working at the European Particle Physics Laboratory (CERN) in Geneva, Switzerland, released a program that allowed you to create a document called a Web page that had built-in links to other related documents. These links, called **hyperlinks**, allowed you to move quickly from one document to another, regardless of whether the documents were located on the same computer or on different computers in different countries. The collection of hyperlinked documents accessible on the Internet has become known as the **World Wide Web**, **WWW**, **W3**, or simply the **Web**. Internet locations that contain hyperlinked documents are called **Web sites**. Multiple Web sites may be on the same computer. For example, many small companies or individuals can have their Web sites located on a single server operated by an Internet service provider.

> **inCyber**
>
> For information about international standards for the World Wide Web (WWW), visit the Discovering Computers Chapter 7 inCyber page (http://www.scsite.com/dc/ch7/incyber.htm) and click WWW.

How a Web Page Works

A **Web page** (Figure 7-7) is a hypertext or hypermedia document residing on an Internet computer that contains text, graphics, video, or sound. A **hypertext** document contains text hyperlinks to other documents. A **hypermedia** document contains text, graphics, video, or sound hyperlinks that connect to other documents.

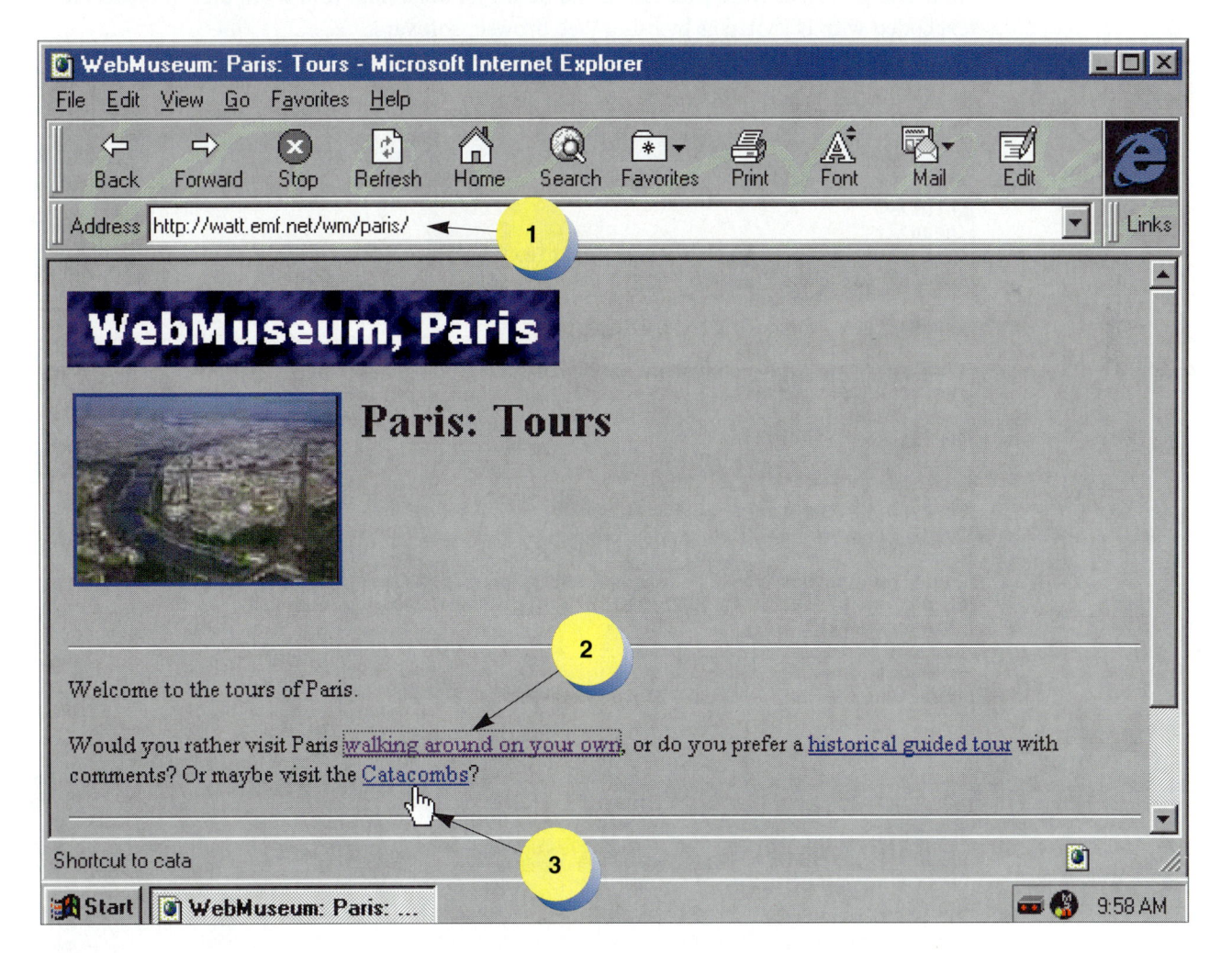

Figure 7-7
An example of a Web page.

1. address of Web page; also called location or URL
2. different color indicates document associated with this hypertext link has been viewed
3. pointer positioned over a hypertext link changes shape to a hand with a pointing finger

Three types of hyperlinks exist. **Target hyperlinks** move from one location in a document to another location in the same document. **Relative hyperlinks** move from one document to another document on the same Internet computer. **Absolute hyperlinks** move to another document on a different Internet computer.

Hypertext and hypermedia allow you to learn in a nonlinear way. Reading a book from cover to cover is a linear way of learning. Branching off and investigating related topics as you encounter them is a nonlinear way of learning. For example, while reading an article on geology, you might want to learn more about mining. Reading about mining might interest you in old mining towns. Reading about old mining towns might inspire you to read about a particular person who made his or her fortune in mining. The ability to branch from one related topic to another in a nonlinear fashion is what makes hyperlinks so powerful and the Internet such an interesting place to explore. Displaying pages from one Web site after another is called **Web surfing** and is like using a remote control to jump from one TV channel to another.

Web pages are created using **hypertext markup language** (HTML), which is a set of special instructions, called **tags**, or **markups**, that specify links to other documents and how the page is displayed. Figure 7-8 shows how the Web page shown in Figure 7-7 looks as text coded with HTML tags. You can generate HTML tags by using Web page authoring software specifically designed for this task or by using Web authoring features included in many applications such as word processing and desktop publishing. Your computer interprets the text coded with HTML tags by using Web browser software.

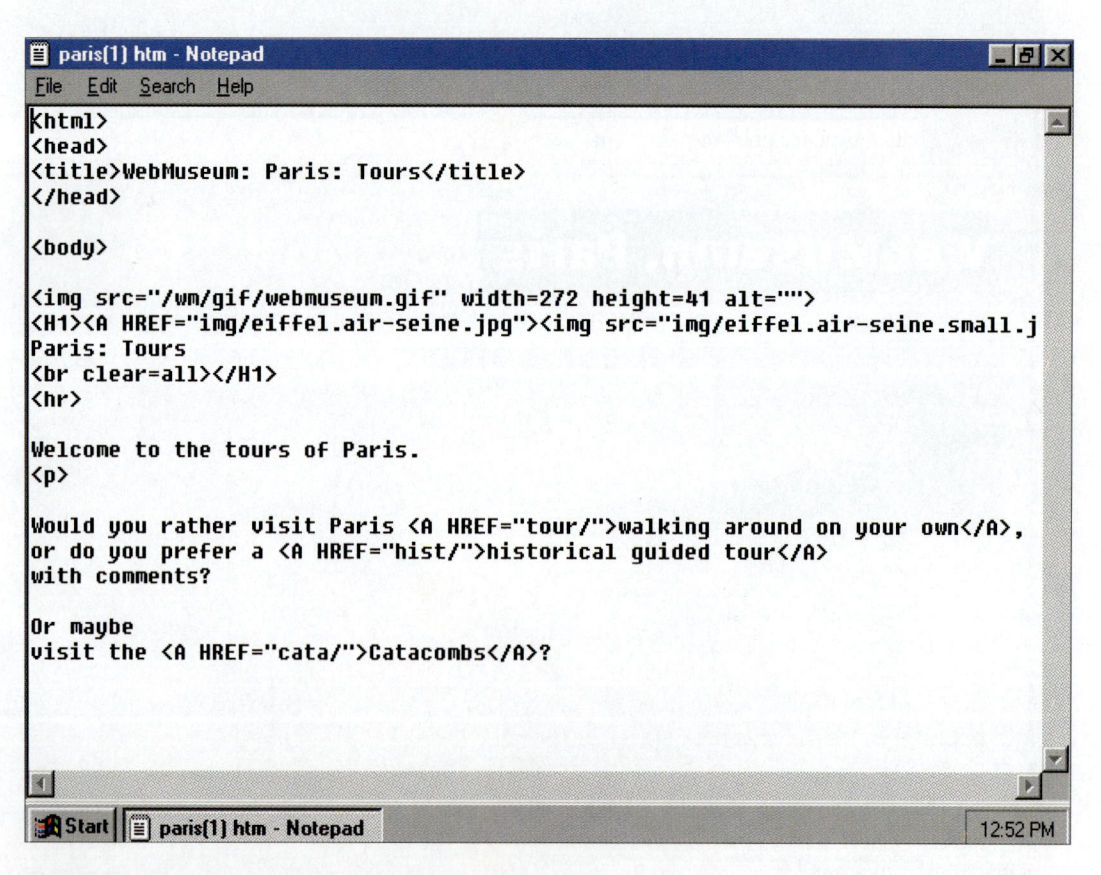

Figure 7-8
This screen shows the HTML text for the Web page in Figure 7-7. Web browser software interprets the HTML instructions inside the angle brackets < > and displays the text, graphics, and hyperlinks accordingly.

THE WORLD WIDE WEB (WWW) **7.9**

Web Browser Software

Web browser software, also called a **Web browser** or simply a **browser**, is a program that interprets and displays Web pages and enables you to link to other Web pages. The first Web browsers used text commands and displayed only text documents. In 1993, however, Marc Andreessen, a student at the University of Illinois, created a graphical Web browser called **Mosaic**. Mosaic displayed documents that included graphics *and* used a graphical interface. The graphical interface, just as it did with other application software programs, made it easier and more enjoyable to view Web documents and contributed to the rapid growth of the Internet. Andreessen later went on to be one of the founders of Netscape, a leading Internet software company that developed the Netscape Navigator Web browser. Figure 7-9 is an example of another Web browser, Microsoft Internet Explorer.

Before you can use a Web browser to view pages on the World Wide Web, your computer has to connect to an Internet computer through an Internet access provider. The Internet connection is established by an Internet communications program. Once the connection to the Internet is established, the browser program is started.

inCyber

For a list of Web browsers, visit the Discovering Computers Chapter 7 inCyber page (http://www.scsite.com/dc/ch7/incyber.htm) and click Browser.

Figure 7-9
Microsoft Internet Explorer Web browser software.

1. Back and Forward buttons – display previously viewed pages
2. Stop button – interrupts transmission
3. Refresh button – reloads current page
4. Home button – returns to designated Home page
5. Search button – displays Web search tool
6. Favorites button – stores locations of favorite Web pages; also called bookmarks
7. Print button – prints all or portion of current page
8. Web address (URL) of current page
9. Links – connections to other sites
10. Address text box – entering a URL in Address text box retrieves that page

When the browser program starts, it retrieves and displays a Web page called a home page. A **home page** is the Web page designated as the page to display each time you launch your browser. Most browsers use the manufacturer's Web page as the default, but you can change your browser's home page at any time. While the term home page often is used to describe the first page at a Web site, technically, the first page at a Web site is called a **welcome page**. A Web site's welcome page often serves as a table of contents for the other pages at the Web site.

The browser retrieves Web pages by using a **Uniform Resource Locator**, or **URL**, which is an address that points to a specific resource on the Internet. URL is pronounced either "you are ell" or "earl," like the man's name. As shown in Figure 7-10, the URL can indicate an Internet site, a specific document at a site, and a location within a document at a site. All Web page URLs begin with **http://**, which stands for **hypertext transfer protocol**, the communications standard used to transfer pages on the Web.

Figure 7-10
Web pages are found and referenced using their address, called a Uniform Resource Locator (URL).

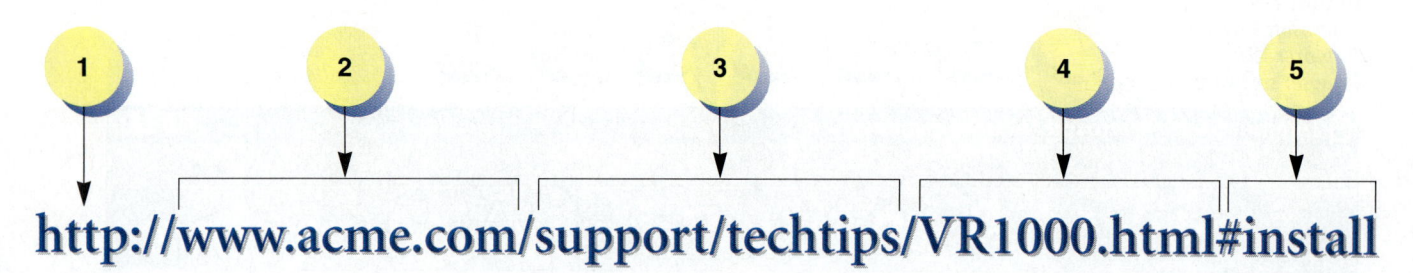

http://www.acme.com/support/techtips/VR1000.html#install

1. protocol – used to transfer data; for Web pages is always http:// (hypertext transfer protocol)
2. domain name – identifies computer that stores Web pages; often, but not always, begins with www
3. directory path – identifies where Web page is stored on computer
4. document name – name of Web page
5. anchor name – reference to a specific part of a long document; always preceded with #

Displaying the Web page on your screen can take anywhere from a few seconds to several minutes, depending on the speed of your connection and the amount of graphics on the Web page. To speed up the display of pages, most Web browsers let you turn off the graphics and display only text.

Browsers display hyperlinks to other documents either as underlined text of a different color or as a graphic. When you position the pointer over a hyperlink, the mouse pointer changes to a small hand with a pointing finger. Some browsers also display the URL of the hyperlinked document at the bottom of the screen. You can display the document by clicking the hyperlink with your pointing device or by typing its URL in the Location text box of the Web browser. To remind you that you have seen a document, some browsers change the color of a text hyperlink after you click it.

Two ways to keep track of Web pages you have viewed are available: a history list and a bookmark list. A **history list** records the pages you have viewed during the time you are connected to the Web (a session). The history list is cleared when you exit your browser program. If you think you might want to return to a page in a future session, you can record its location with a bookmark. A **bookmark** consists of the title of a Web page and the URL of that page. Unlike history lists, bookmark lists, also called *hotlists* or *favorites*, are stored on your computer and can be used in future Web sessions. A bookmark list and a history list both allow you to display a Web page quickly by clicking its name in the list.

Some Web browser programs display only Web pages. Other browsers allow you to use Internet services such as e-mail, file transfers, and others discussed later in this chapter. Two widely used browsers that support these services are Microsoft Internet Explorer and Netscape Navigator.

Multimedia on the Web

Some of the most exciting Web developments involve multimedia, which is the integration of text, graphics, video, animation, and sound. These developments increase the types of information available on the Web, expand the Web's potential uses, and make the Internet a more entertaining place to explore.

To run a multimedia application on the Web, your browser might need an additional program called a plug-in or helper application. **Plug-ins** run multimedia within the browser window; **helper applications** run multimedia in a window separate from the browser. Plug-ins and helper applications can be downloaded from many sites on the Web. Links to these sites often are found with Web multimedia applications. Figure 7-11 is a list of popular plug-ins and helper applications.

A programming language called **Java** is being used to develop much of the multimedia on the Web. Developers use Java to create small programs called **applets** that can be downloaded and run in your browser window. Unlike other programs you download from the Web, applets can be used by any type of computer and are relatively safe from viruses and other tampering. Java is discussed in more detail in the programming chapter.

inCyber

For links to popular plug-ins, visit the Discovering Computers Chapter 7 inCyber page (http://www.scsite.com/dc/ch7/incyber.htm) and click Plug-In.

Multimedia Plug-in and Helper Application Programs

Category	Program Name	Web Site	Comment
Graphics	N/A	N/A	Separate plug-ins usually not required. All browsers display most graphics.
Audio	RealAudio Internet Phone	www.realaudio.com www.vocaltec.com	Streaming audio Internet phone service
Animation	Shockwave	www.macromedia.com	Interactive animation with sound
Video	VivoActive CU-SeeMe	www.vivo.com www.wpine.com	Video viewer Videoconferencing
Virtual Reality	Live3D WebSpace	www.netscape.com www.sd.tgs.com	VRML viewer VRML viewer

Figure 7-11
Plug-in and helper application programs often are required to experience multimedia material on the Web. This table lists popular plug-ins and helper applications and Web sites where they can be obtained.

The following sections discuss multimedia Web developments in the areas of graphics, audio, animation, video, and virtual reality.

Graphics Graphics were the first media used to enhance the text-based Internet. The introduction of graphical browsers enabled illustrations, logos, and other images to be incorporated into Web pages. Today, many Web pages, especially those created by consumer product companies, use colorful graphic designs and images to reinforce their text messages (Figure 7-12). Even prior to the introduction of the Web, the Internet was an excellent source of graphic material. Today, the Web contains thousands of image files on countless subjects that can be downloaded free and used for noncommercial purposes.

Animation Using **animation** on a Web page adds media without greatly increasing download time. Animated graphics can make Web pages more visually interesting or draw attention to important information or links. Text even can be animated to scroll across the page like a ticker used for stocks, news, or sports scores (Figure 7-13). Scrolling text even can contain hyperlinks to a different page. Animation also is used for many Web-based games. Figure 7-14 shows an animated game that was developed with the Java programming language.

Figure 7-12
Many companies use colorful graphics and images on their Web pages.

Figure 7-13
Animation is used to scroll sports news across the screen of this ticker. To learn more about a sports story, you can click the Get Story hyperlink or the scrolling headline itself.

1. sports headlines scroll across the screen

THE WORLD WIDE WEB (WWW) **7.13**

Audio Simple **audio** Web applications consist of individual sound files that must be downloaded before they can be played. More advanced audio Web applications use **streaming audio**, which allows you to hear the sound as it downloads to your computer. Music companies often include audio files on their Web sites to provide samples of the latest hits. Other companies use streaming audio to provide Internet radio channels that broadcast music, interviews, and talk shows (Figure 7-15). Web-based audio also is used for Internet audioconferencing. **Internet audioconferencing**, also called **Internet telephone service** or **Internet telephony**, enables you to talk to other people over the Web. As you speak into a microphone, audioconferencing software and your computer sound card digitize and compress your conversation. Software and equipment at the receiving end reverse the process. Some software allows only one person to speak at a time, but newer packages support two-way simultaneous conversations. Audioconferencing allows you to talk to friends or colleagues for just the cost of your Internet connection. **Internet voice mail** enables you to send and retrieve voice messages.

inCyber

For links to streaming audio, visit the Discovering Computers Chapter 7 inCyber page (http://www.scsite.com/dc/ch7/incyber.htm) and click Streaming Audio.

Figure 7-14
An example of a game developed with the Java programming language.

Figure 7-15
Wine Valley Radio is one of several Internet radio stations. When you click an audio file, such as a conversation or music, an audio control box displays. The control box has start, stop, and volume controls and displays information about the file.

Video Like audio, simple **video** Web applications use individual video files such as movie clips that can be downloaded and played on your computer. Because video files often are large and can take a long time to download, these movie clips usually are quite short. **Streaming video** allows you to view longer or live video images as they are downloaded to your computer. Streaming video also allows you to conduct Internet videoconferences similarly to Internet audioconferences. As you are filmed by a video camera, videoconferencing software and your computer's video board capture, digitize, and compress the images and sounds. This data is divided into packets and sent over the Internet. Equipment and software at the receiving end assemble the packets, decompress the data, and present the image and sound as video. Like traditional videoconferencing, live Internet videoconferences can be choppy and blurry depending on the speed of the slowest communications link.

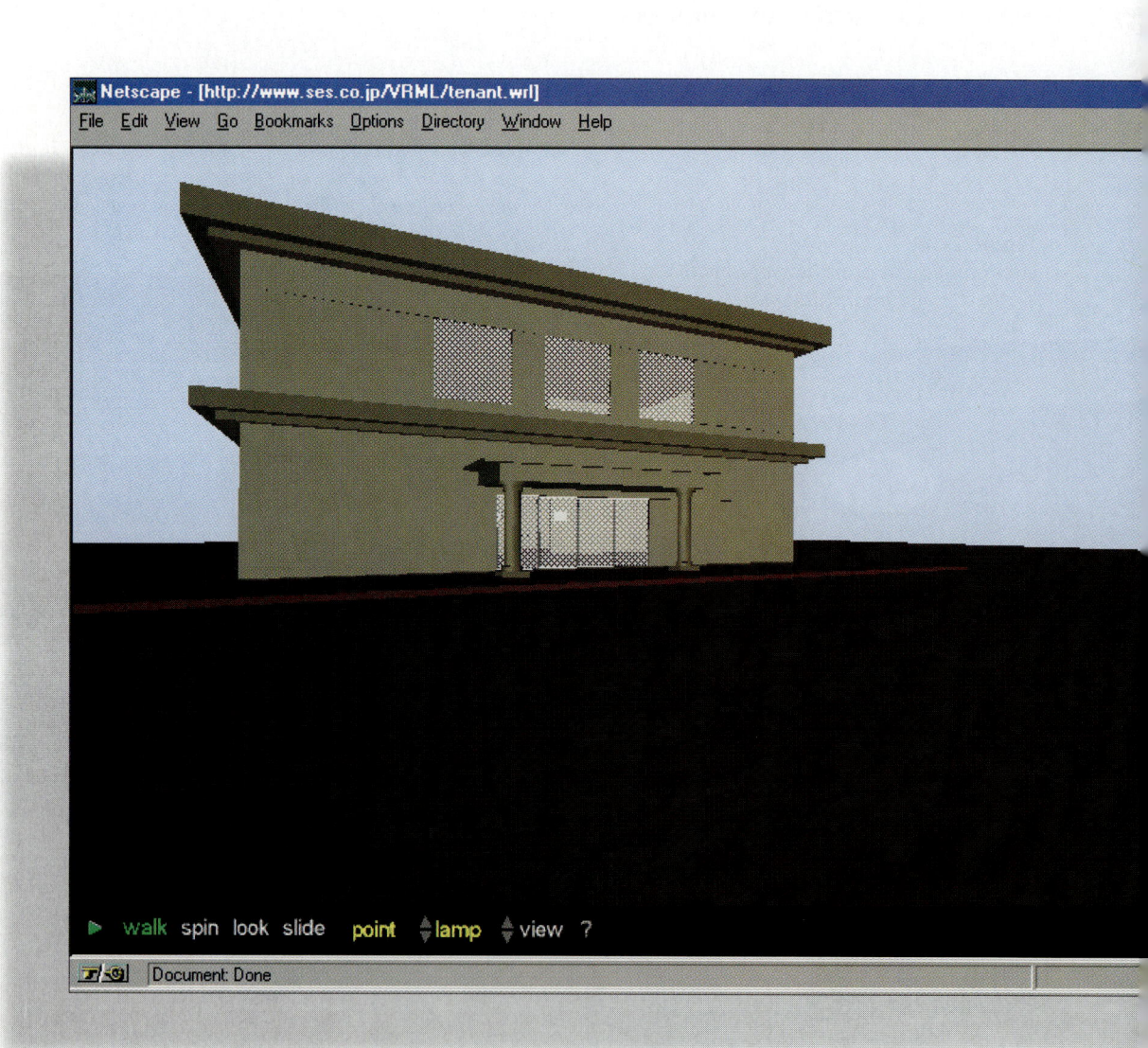

THE WORLD WIDE WEB (WWW)   **7.15**

Virtual Reality   Virtual reality (VR) is the creation of an artificial environment that you can experience. On the Web, VR involves the display of three-dimensional (3-D) images that you can explore and manipulate interactively. Most Web-based VR applications are developed using **VRML (virtual reality modeling language)**. VRML allows a developer to create a collection of 3-D objects, such as a room with furniture. You can walk through such a VR room by moving your pointing device forward, backward, or to the side.

VR often is used for games, but it has many practical applications as well. Architects create VR models of buildings and rooms so they can show their clients how a completed construction project will look before it is built. Figure 7-16 is an example of a building model created with VRML.

inCyber

For links to virtual reality resources, visit the Discovering Computers Chapter 7 inCyber page (http://www.scsite.com/dc/ch7/incyber.htm) and click Virtual Reality.

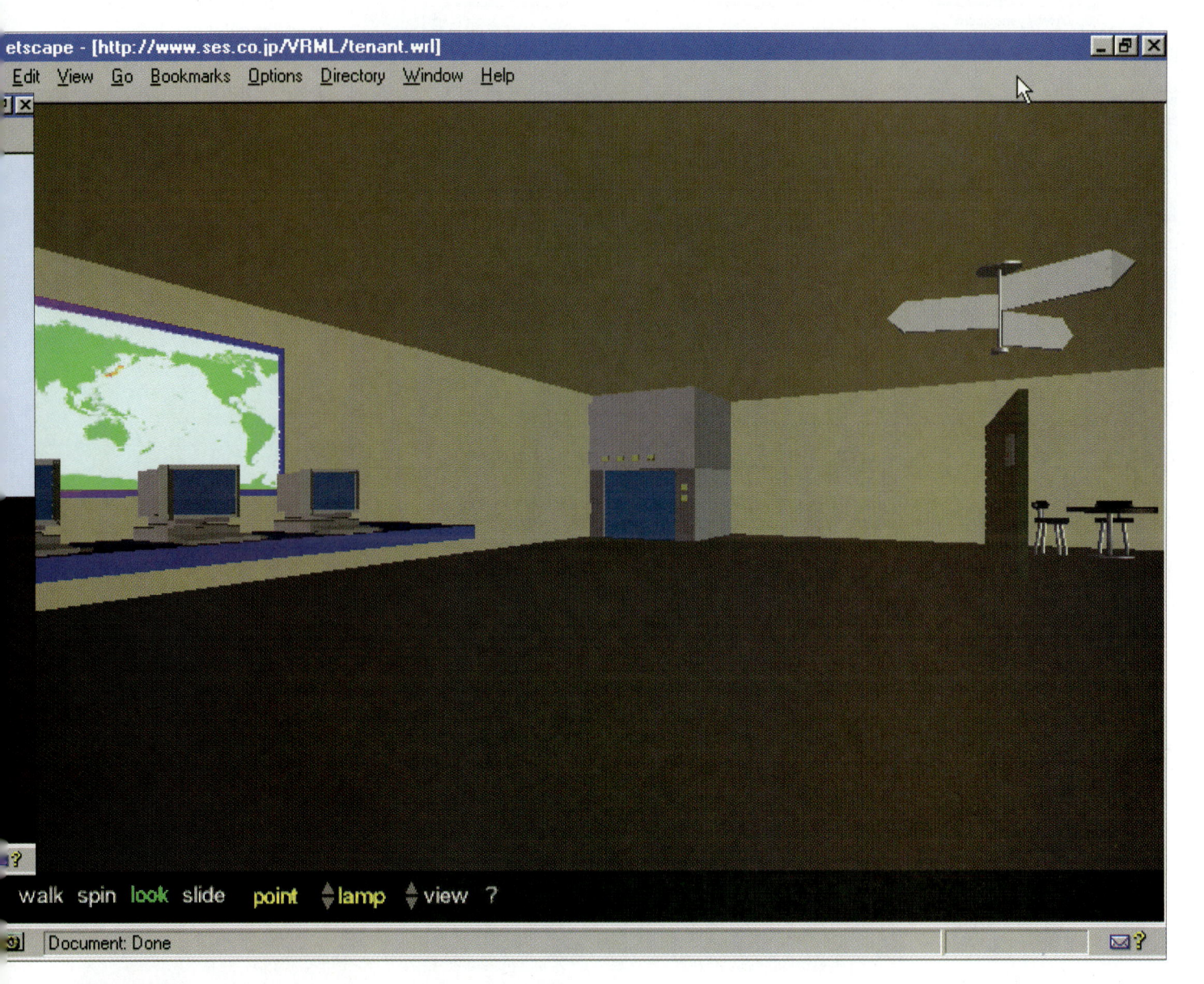

Figure 7-16
These virtual reality images of a building were developed using VRML software. You use your mouse and the controls in the lower-left portion of the screen to walk around or enter the building. As you enter the building, a different image is displayed.

Searching for Information on the Web

Because no single organization controls additions, deletions, and changes to Web sites, no central menu or catalog of Web site content and addresses exists. Several companies, however, maintain organized directories of Web sites and provide search tools to help you find information on specific topics. A **search tool**, also called a **search engine**, is a software program that finds Web sites, Web pages, and Internet files that match one or more keywords that you enter. Some search tools look for simple word matches and others allow for more specific searches on a series of words or an entire phrase. Figure 7-17 is an example of the Yahoo! search tool. Search tools do not actually search the entire Internet — such a search would take an

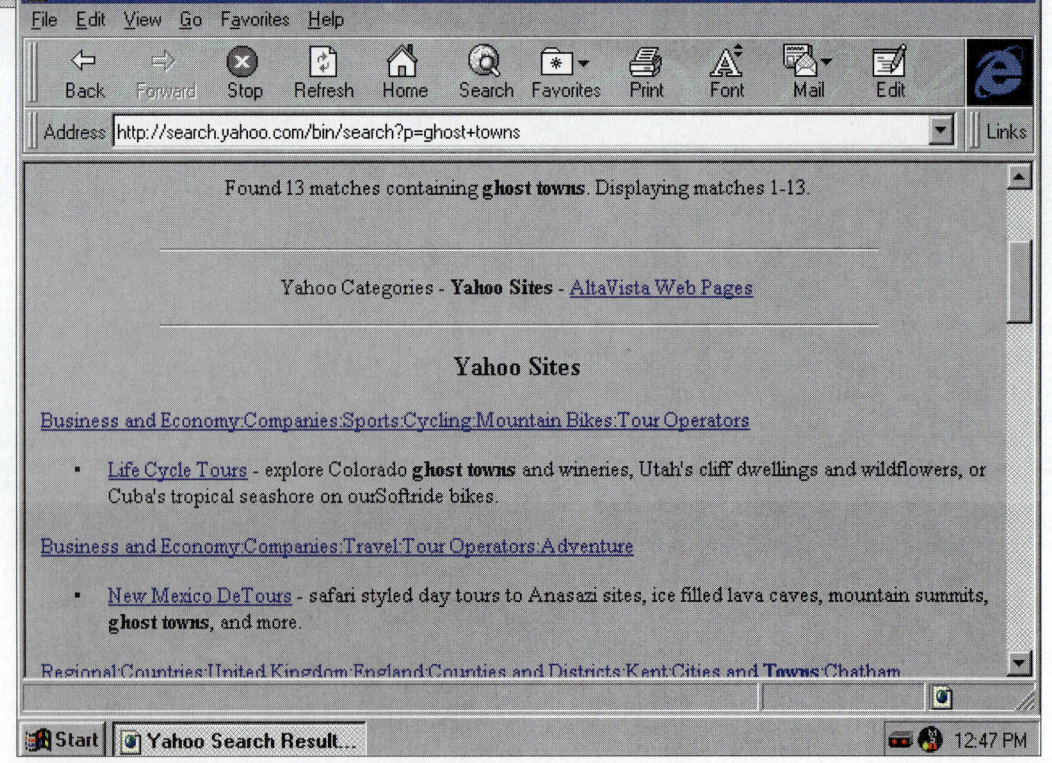

Figure 7-17
Yahoo! combines a search tool and a directory of Web sites. To use the search tool, you enter one or more keywords. The second screen shows that 13 matches were made to the keywords, ghost towns.

inCyber

For links to search tools, visit the Discovering Computers Chapter 7 inCyber page (http://www.scsite.com/dc/ch7/incyber.htm) and click Search Tool.

extremely long time. Instead, they search an index of Internet sites and documents that constantly is updated by the company that provides the search tool. Figure 7-18 lists the Web site addresses of several Internet search tools. Most of these sites also provide directories of Web sites organized in categories such as sports, entertainment, or business.

Web Search Sites

Name	Web Site Location	Comment
Yahoo!	www.yahoo.com	One of the first. Updated daily.
Infoseek	guide-p.infoseek.com	Searches Web or Usenet for words and phrases.
Lycos	www.lycos.com	Comprehensive catalog plus multimedia content searches.
AltaVista	www.altavista.digital.com	Creates indexes from more than 30 million Web pages.
Excite	www.excite.com	Concept-based search tool.
WebCrawler	www.webcrawler.com	Natural language search tool.
Four11	www.Four11.com	Finds user-IDs.
BigBook	www.bigbook.com	Yellow pages for more than 16 million businesses.

Figure 7-18
These search tools and directories can help you find products, services, information, and other Internet users.

Intranets and Firewalls

Recognizing the efficiency and power of the Web, many organizations have applied Web technology to their own internal networks. Internal networks that use Internet and Web technology are called **intranets** (*intra* means inside). Simple intranet applications include electronic publishing of basic organizational information such as telephone directories, event calendars, and employee benefit information. More sophisticated uses of intranets include groupware applications such as project management, group scheduling, and employee conferencing.

Sometimes an organization will allow other organizations to access its internal, private network. For example, a manufacturing company might want to share information with its suppliers, or members of a particular profession such as real estate brokers might decide to share a private network. These are examples of **extranets**, which are private networks that include more than one organization.

While some intranets operate on a LAN at a single location, some intranets and most extranets use many public and private networks to connect remote locations. Anytime a private network connects to a public network, an organization must be concerned about security and unauthorized access to organizational data. To prevent unauthorized access,

---

inCyber

For intranet resources, visit the Discovering Computers Chapter 7 inCyber page (http://www.scsite.com/dc/ch7/incyber.htm) and click Intranet.

organizations implement one or more layers of security called a firewall. A **firewall** is a general term that refers to both hardware and software used to restrict access to data on a network (Figure 7-19). Firewalls are used to deny network access to outsiders and to restrict employees' access to sensitive data such as payroll or personnel records.

A common way to implement a firewall is to place a computer called a **proxy server** between two separate networks. For example, a proxy server might separate an organization's internal network from an Internet network used to share data with remote locations. The proxy server can be programmed to allow access to and from only specific network locations, such as a company office in another state.

A proxy server also makes using the Web more efficient through a process called caching (pronounced cash-ing). **Caching** involves storing a copy of each Web page that is accessed in local storage. When another person requests the same page, the proxy server checks to see if the page has been updated on the Web. If the page has changed, a new file is retrieved from the Web. If the page has not changed, the proxy server retrieves a copy of the page from cache. Retrieving a page from cache is faster than retrieving the page from its original Web location. Caching is similar in concept to cache memory and disk cache explained in earlier chapters.

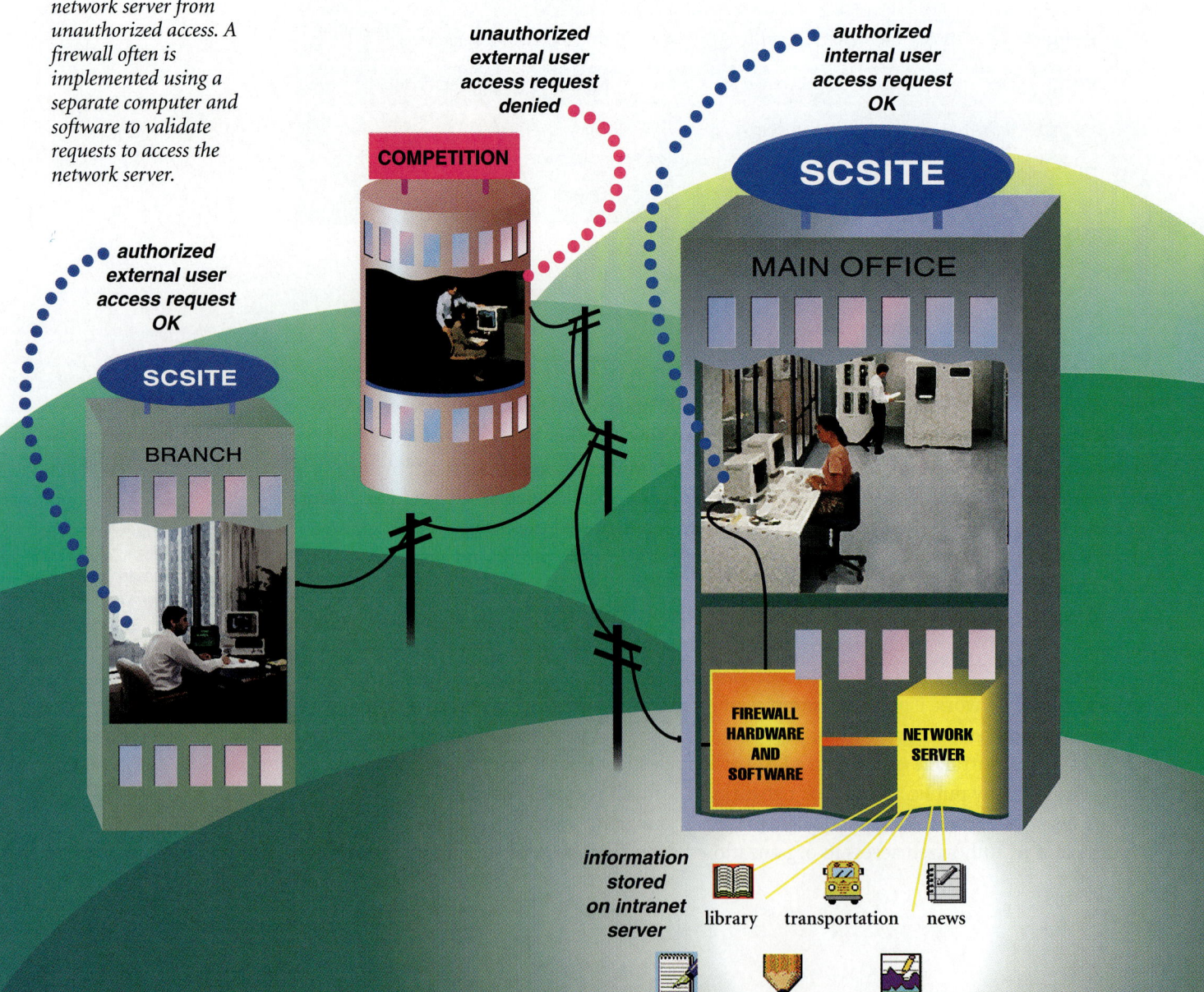

inCyber

For details on the Microsoft Proxy Server, visit the Discovering Computers Chapter 7 inCyber page (http://www.scsite.com/dc/ch7/incyber.htm) and click Proxy Server.

Figure 7-19
Firewall hardware and software protect the network server from unauthorized access. A firewall often is implemented using a separate computer and software to validate requests to access the network server.

Other Internet Services

Although the World Wide Web is the most talked about part of the Internet, many of the Internet services developed prior to the creation of the Web still are used widely. These Internet services include e-mail, FTP, Gopher, Telnet, Usenet, and Internet Relay Chat (IRC).

E-mail

E-mail, the electronic exchange of messages from one person to another, was one of the original features of the Internet. E-mail enabled scientists and researchers working on government-sponsored projects to communicate with their colleagues at other locations. Today, e-mail still is a widely used Internet feature.

Internet e-mail works essentially the same as e-mail on other systems — messages can be created, sent, forwarded, stored, printed, and deleted. To receive e-mail over the Internet, you must have a **mailbox**, which is a file used to collect your messages on an Internet computer. Although your mailbox can be located anywhere on the Internet, it usually is located on the computer that connects you to the Internet, such as the server operated by your Internet service provider (ISP). Most ISPs and online services provide an Internet e-mail program and a mailbox as a standard part of their Internet access services.

An **Internet mailbox address** is a combination of a user name and the domain name that identifies the location of the mailbox computer (Figure 7-20). Your **user name**, or **user-ID**, is a unique combination of characters that identifies you. It must be different from the other user names located on the same mailbox computer. A user name sometimes is limited to eight characters and often is a combination of your first and last names, such as the initial of your first name plus your last name. You also can use a nickname or any combination of characters for your user name, but others may find it harder to remember.

Although no complete listing of Internet e-mail addresses exists, several Internet sites list addresses collected from public sources. These sites also allow you to list your e-mail address voluntarily so others can find it. The site also might ask for other information, such as your high school or college, so others can determine if you are the person they want to reach.

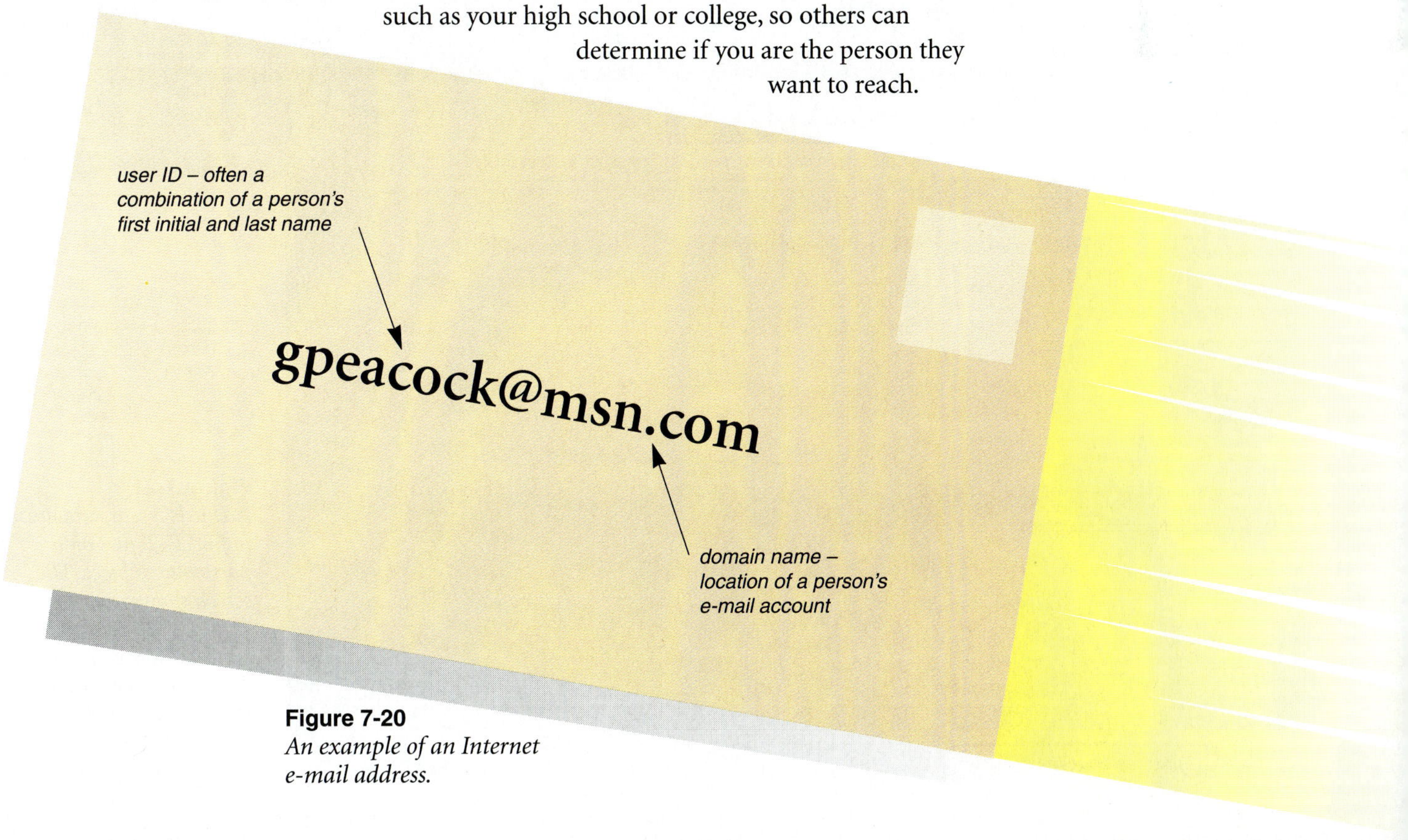

user ID – often a combination of a person's first initial and last name

gpeacock@msn.com

domain name – location of a person's e-mail account

Figure 7-20
An example of an Internet e-mail address.

FTP

FTP (**file transfer protocol**) is an Internet standard that allows you to exchange files with other computers on the Internet. Computers that contain files available for FTP are called **FTP sites** or **FTP servers**.

FTP sites contain a wide variety of file types including text, graphics, audio, video, and program files. Many of these program files can be downloaded at no cost. Others, called **shareware**, are programs you can download and try free but must pay a license fee if you decide to keep them. Some FTP sites limit file transfers to persons who have authorized accounts on the computer. Many FTP computers, however, allow **anonymous FTP**, whereby anyone can log in and transfer some, if not all, available files.

To view or use a FTP file you must first download it to your computer. Many large FTP files are compressed to reduce storage space and download transfer time. Before you use a compressed file you must expand it with a decompression program. Decompression programs usually are available at the FTP site.

Some computers, called **Archie sites** (Figure 7-21), maintain directories of files on the Internet that can be downloaded with FTP. A FTP file search tool called **Archie** can be used to find files on a particular subject. Archie, named after the comic book character, finds files whose names at least partially match a keyword that you enter. An **Archie gateway** is a Web page that provides an easy-to-use interface to the Archie search function.

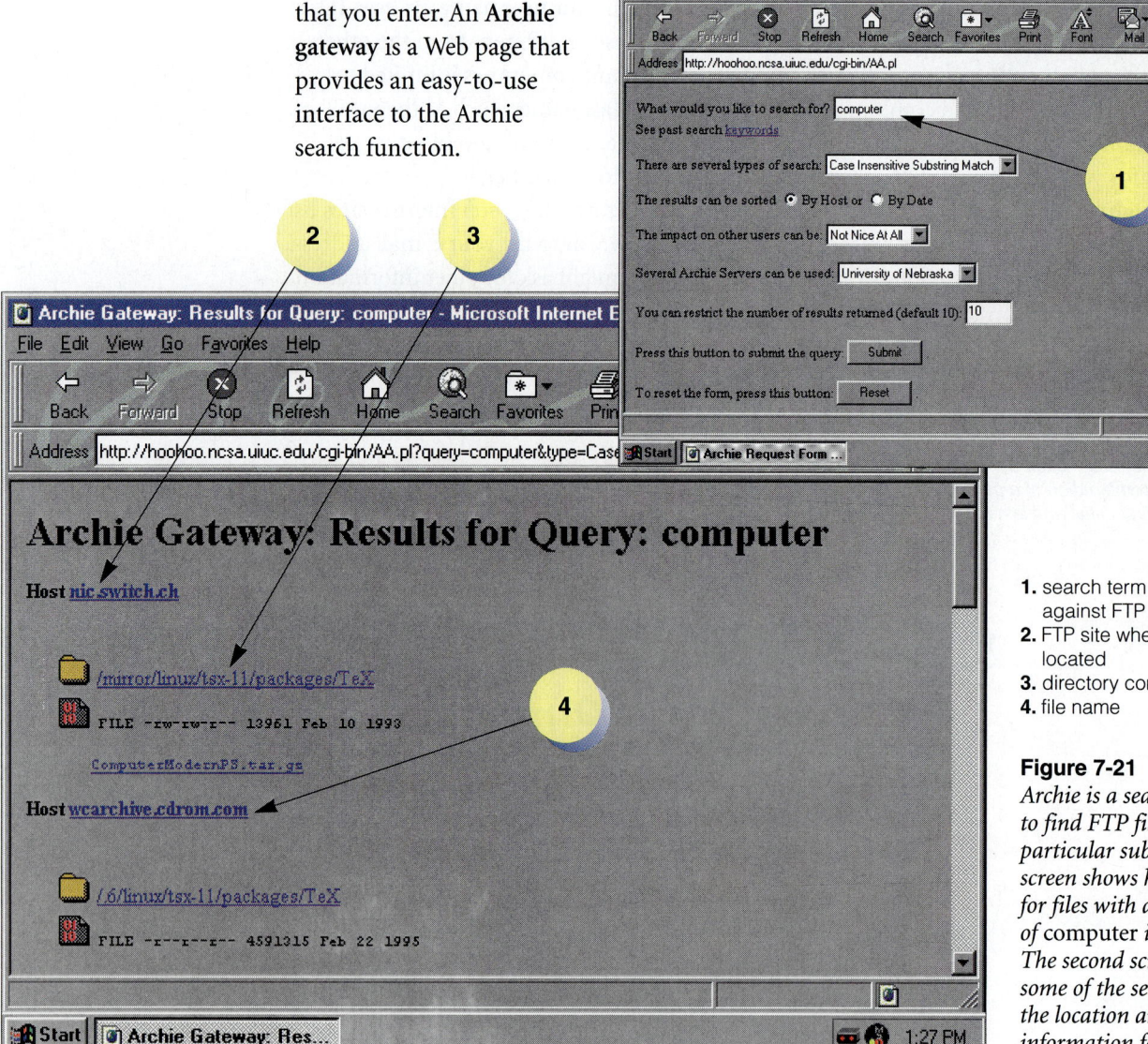

1. search term matched against FTP file names
2. FTP site where file is located
3. directory containing file
4. file name

Figure 7-21
Archie is a search tool used to find FTP files on a particular subject. The first screen shows how a request for files with a search term of computer *is entered. The second screen shows some of the search results; the location and other information for two files.*

Gopher

Before Web-based search tools were developed, Gopher was the primary method used to locate information on the Internet. **Gopher** is a menu-driven program that helps you locate and retrieve files on the Internet. Gopher originally was developed at the University of Minnesota and is named after the school mascot, the Golden Gopher. Internet computers called **Gopher servers** maintain Gopher directories.

Unlike FTP and Archie, Gopher does not require you to know the details of FTP sites and files names. Instead, you browse through Gopher menus, which usually start with a list of topics (Figure 7-22). Choosing an item on the list leads to one or more menus that break down the topic into more specific areas. Eventually, you reach a menu listing individual files you can download. Unlike FTP files, you can view Gopher files before you decide to download. In addition to the menu system, most Gopher servers offer **Veronica** or **Jughead** search programs that search Gopher directories for files on a specific subject. Like Archie, the FTP search tools, Veronica and Jughead, are named after Archie comic book characters.

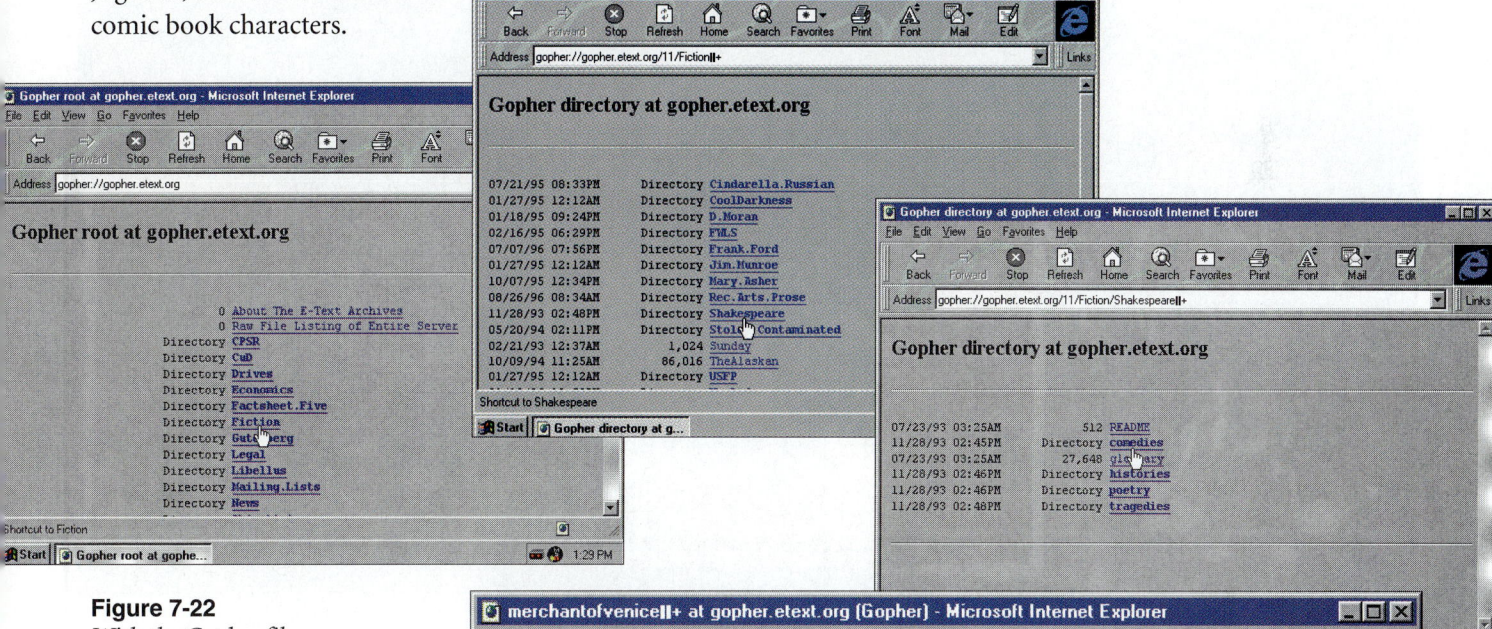

Figure 7-22
With the Gopher file retrieval program, you click a series of menus to narrow in on a subject until you find the document you want. These screens show the search progression from Fiction to Shakespeare to comedies to The Merchant of Venice.

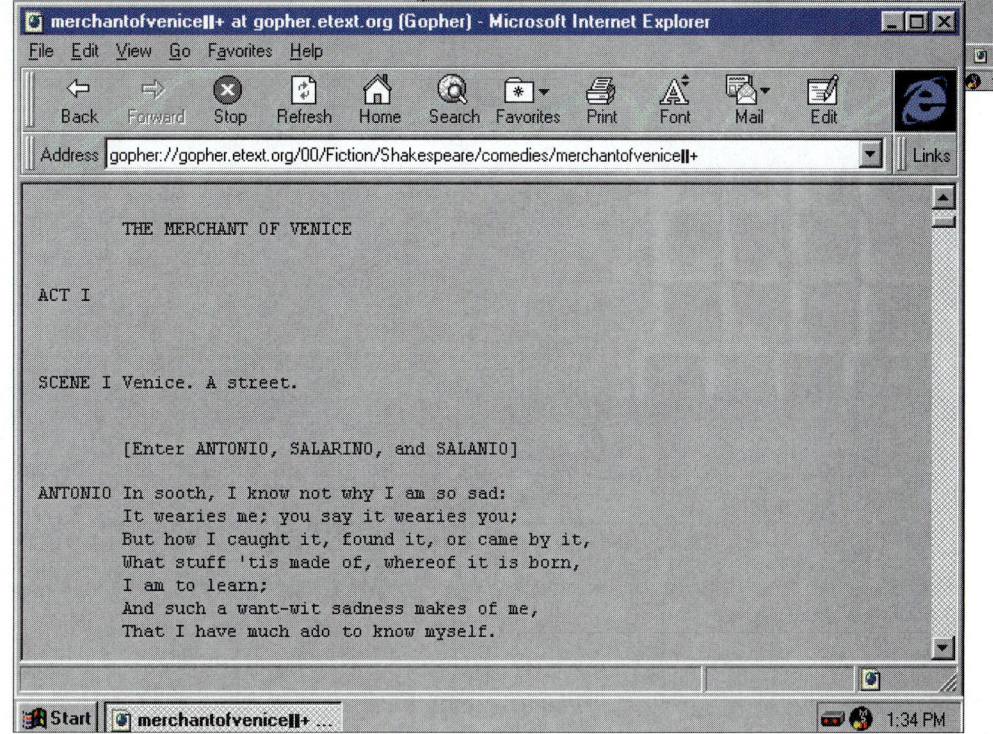

Telnet

Telnet is an Internet protocol that enables you to log into a remote computer on the Internet. Once you make a Telnet connection, you can use the remote computer as if you had a direct, local connection. Telnet often is used to play games on the Internet. One of the more popular types of Internet games is called a MUD. A **MUD** (**multiuser dimension**) is a role-playing game in which you and other participants assume the identity of specific characters. With some MUDs, the computer provides a text description of the characters and situations you encounter as you play the game. Another type of MUD, called a **MOO** (**multiuser object oriented**), allows you to create new characters and game locations, such as a wizard in a castle. Some MOOs have graphics and sound like arcade games. Figure 7-23 is an example of a MOO.

Figure 7-23
An example of a MOO (multiuser object oriented) game that can be played on the Internet using Telnet.

Usenet

Usenet is a collection of news and discussion groups, called **newsgroups**, that are accessed via the Internet. Each of the more than 6,000 newsgroups operates as if it were a bulletin board devoted to a particular subject. Newsgroup subjects are organized in a hierarchical order with a major subject divided into one or more levels of subgroups. Each subgroup is separated by a period. Figure 7-24 shows an example of a Usenet newsgroup discussion.

To participate in a newsgroup, you must use a program called a **newsreader**. The newsreader enables you to access a newsgroup to read a previously entered message, called an **article**, and add an article of your own, called **posting**. A newsreader also keeps track of which articles you have and have not read. Newsgroup members often post articles as a reply to another article — either to answer a question or to comment on material in the original article. These replies often cause the author of the original article, or others, to post additional articles related to the original article. This process can be short-lived or go on indefinitely depending on the nature of the topic and the interest of the participants. The original article and all subsequent related replies are called a **thread**.

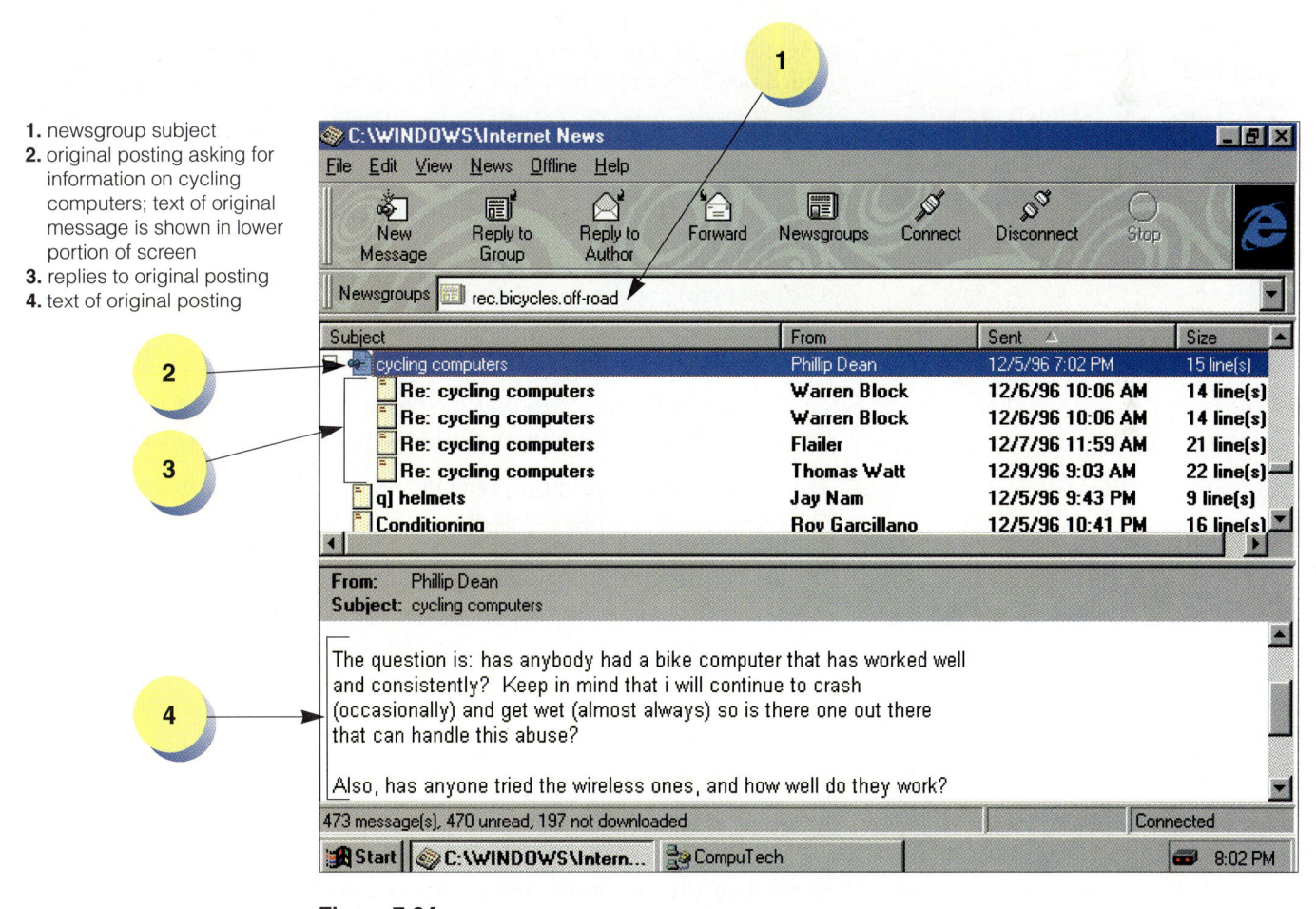

1. newsgroup subject
2. original posting asking for information on cycling computers; text of original message is shown in lower portion of screen
3. replies to original posting
4. text of original posting

Figure 7-24
An example of a Usenet discussion. The top part of the screen shows articles that have been posted in the rec.bicycles.off-road newsgroup. The article posted on 12/5/96 by Phillip Dean, shown in the lower portion of the screen, received several replies.

Some newsgroups are supervised by a **moderator**, who reads each article before it is posted to the newsgroup. If the moderator thinks an article is appropriate for the newsgroup, the moderator posts the article for all members to read. Over time, newsgroup members have developed certain guidelines for posting articles called **netiquette** (short for network etiquette). These guidelines, shown in Figure 7-25, also are appropriate for other communications such as e-mail.

Figure 7-25
Netiquette – guidelines for communicating on a network.

Netiquette (Network Etiquette)

1. Choose your words carefully. Hundreds, maybe thousands, of people may read your article. Say what you mean, keep it brief, and use correct grammar and spelling. Be careful about using sarcasm, humor, or any other language that might be misinterpreted.

2. Read the FAQs. An **FAQ** is a list of frequently asked questions and their answers. FAQs are available for many newsgroups and for other areas on the Internet. For example, most hardware and software companies have FAQ files as part of their support programs. FAQs prevent new users, called **newbies**, and others from asking the same question over and over.

3. Choose a meaningful subject heading. Give the potential reader a good idea of the contents of your article.

4. Do not **SHOUT!** Do not use all capital letters — it is considered the same as shouting.

5. Use acronyms and emoticons to convey meaning quickly. Acronyms such as BTW (by the way) and emoticons such as smileys :) save time and add personality to your message.

6. Control your emotions. Sending an abusive message is called **flaming** and is considered inappropriate and a waste of network resources.

7. Post your article to the appropriate newsgroup. Posting an article (especially one soliciting business) to several inappropriate newsgroups is called **spamming**. It is frowned upon heavily and often results in flames (see 6 above) being sent to the offending person.

Internet Relay Chat (IRC)

Internet Relay Chat, or **IRC**, allows you to join others in real-time conversations on the Internet. To start an IRC session, you must connect to an Internet server using an IRC client program. (Many free IRC clients can be downloaded from the Web.) You then can create or join a conversation group called a **channel** on the Internet server to which you are attached. The channel name should indicate the topic of discussion. The person who creates a channel acts as the **channel operator** and has responsibility for monitoring the conversation and disconnecting anyone who becomes disruptive. Operator status can be shared or transferred to someone else.

You can find IRC channels using the /**list** command. You can participate by using the /**join** command and entering a nickname for yourself. Unless you specify the nickname of another IRC participant, any messages you send go to everyone in the channel. Figure 7-26 is an example of a discussion during an IRC session. Most online services include chat channels as one of their services.

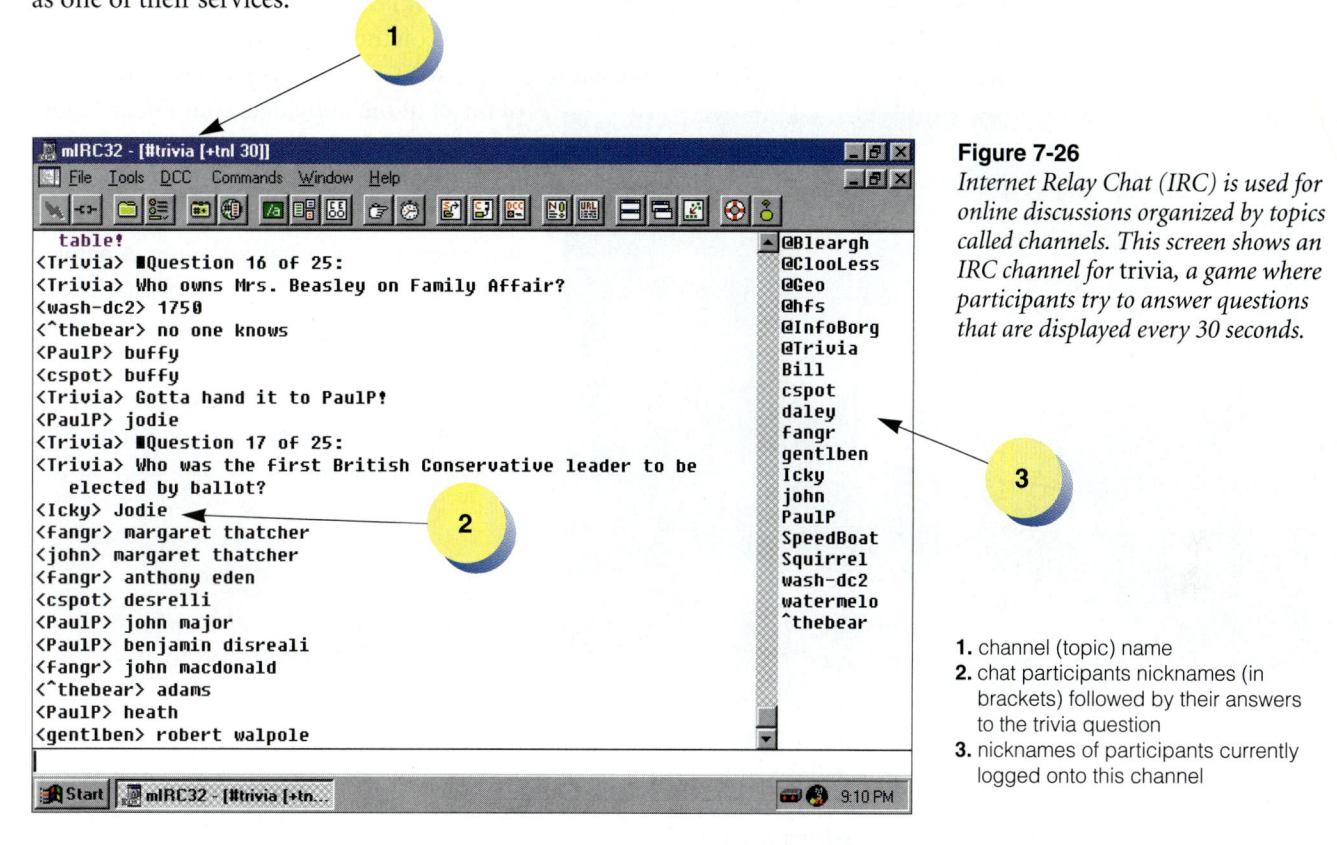

Figure 7-26
Internet Relay Chat (IRC) is used for online discussions organized by topics called channels. This screen shows an IRC channel for trivia, *a game where participants try to answer questions that are displayed every 30 seconds.*

1. channel (topic) name
2. chat participants nicknames (in brackets) followed by their answers to the trivia question
3. nicknames of participants currently logged onto this channel

Network Computers

As a way of reducing the total cost of ownership and the complexity associated with fully configured personal computer systems, many businesses and home users are turning to network computers. A **network computer**, or **NC**, is a computer designed to work while connected to a network, but not as a stand-alone computer. Network computers have limited, if any, built-in storage, because storage is provided by the server to which the network computer is attached. Because they have fewer components and less software than typical PCs, network computers sometimes are referred to as **thin-client** computers. The following sections discuss the types of network computers used in business and the home.

Network Computers for Business

For many business applications, a personal computer has more capability than the application requires. Jobs that primarily involve entering transactions or looking up information in a database, do not need floppy disks, CD-ROMs, or large hard disks. These extra components contribute to both the cost and complexity of the PC and, the more complex a system is, the more expensive it is to maintain. Studies have shown that the average cost to maintain a desktop computer over a three-year life is approximately $8,000 a year. This amount includes the cost of the equipment, software, repairs, training, and support, which usually is provided by someone from the Information Systems department.

Network computers for business reduce these costs in several ways. To begin with, NCs are less expensive to purchase, typically costing $500 to $1,000 compared with $2,000 to $3,000 spent on the average desktop PC. NCs cost less because they have fewer components. NCs have less memory than typical PCs and have no hard, floppy, or CD-ROM disk drives. All storage is done on the server. For software, NCs rely on Java-based applications downloaded from a server. Because all software is stored on the server, software is easier to maintain. A new version of the software has to be upgraded only once, on the server, instead of on all of the individual computers. Figure 7-27 shows a network computer manufactured by Sun Microsystems, Inc.

An alternative to the network computer is the network personal computer. A **network personal computer**, or **netPC**, primarily relies on the server for software and storage but does have a hard disk for storing some data and programs. A netPC can run Java and other programs such as Microsoft Windows applications.

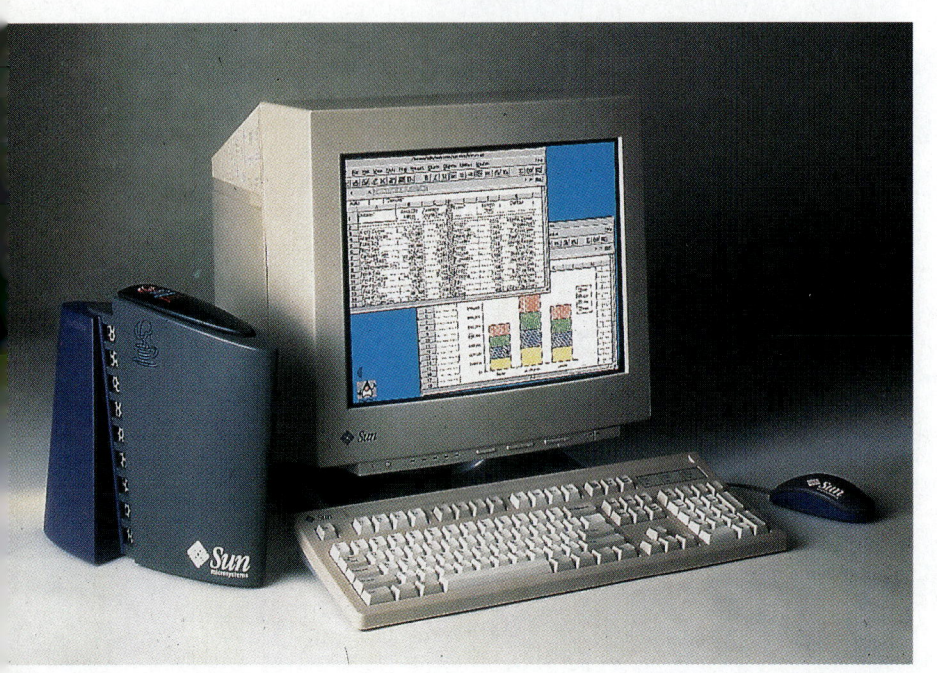

Figure 7-27
JavaStation™, business network computer manufactured by Sun Microsystems, Inc.

Network Computers for the Home

Many potential home computer users do not want the features and components of a personal computer. All they want is the ability to access the information on the Internet they hear about and read about every day. Previously, the only way to access the Internet from home was with a personal computer that new cost at least $1,000 and an average of $2,000. A network computer for the home, sometimes called an **information appliance**, is a device that incorporates Internet access into a device with which you are familiar already, such as a television, a telephone, or a video game console. Instead of costing thousands of dollars, home network computers cost hundreds of dollars, comparable to other mid-range consumer electronics devices. To keep the cost down, manufacturers have eliminated standard computer features, such as any type of disk drive. Instead of a separate monitor, you use your television set. If you want to use the device to enter e-mail, you can use an optional wireless keyboard. One of the more popular home network computers uses a device that looks and acts like a cable TV box (Figure 7-28). This **set-top box** uses your telephone line to connect to an Internet service provider. To navigate Web pages, you use a device that looks like a large TV remote control (Figure 7-29).

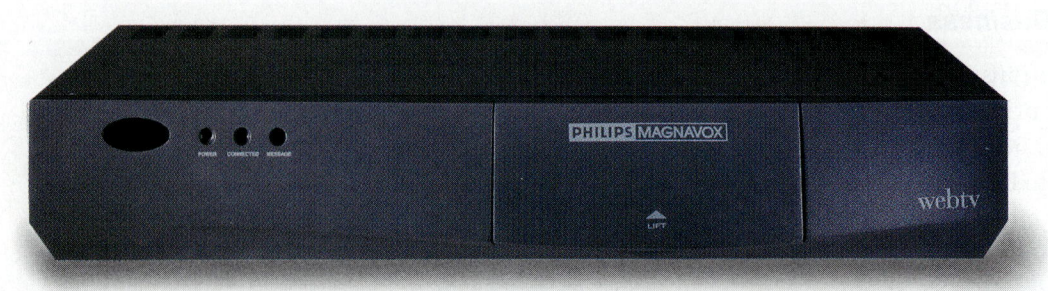

Figure 7-28
One type of home network computer uses a set-top box, similar to a cable TV box.

NETWORK COMPUTERS 7.27

Figure 7-29
This remote control device is used to navigate Web pages on a home network computer.

Summary of Network Computers

Figure 7-30 shows a comparison of the network and personal computer features. In reviewing this table, you should keep in mind that network computers are a quickly evolving category of personal computers. Features and descriptions will likely change over time.

COMPARISON OF NETWORK COMPUTERS AND A PERSONAL COMPUTER

	Home Network Computer	Business Network Computer (NC)	Network Personal Computer (netPC)	Personal Computer
Cost	$200 - $500	$500 - $1,000	$1,000 - $2,000	$2,000 - $3,000
Hardware differences	• set-top box • hand-held remote control • uses TV for monitor	• 8 MB	• 16 MB • small hard disk	• 32 MB • hard, floppy, and CD-ROM disks
What's missing	• hard disk • floppy disk • CD-ROM • keyboard (optional)	• hard disk • floppy disk • CD-ROM	• floppy disk • CD-ROM	• nothing
Software	• Web browser software	• Java-based software downloaded from server	• primarily on server • some software on hard disk • can run Windows	• software applications on hard drive • can download from server • can run Windows
Advantages	• low cost • easy to use • entertainment oriented	• low cost • easy to administer	• lower cost than PC • local storage	• full capabilities
Disadvantages	• unable to run easily productivity software such as wp, ss, db	• no local storage • totally dependent on server • limited software available	• may be more or less computer than needed	• high cost • high maintenance

Figure 7-30
Comparison of different types of network computers and a personal computer.

How to Connect to the Internet and the World Wide Web

The following steps describe how you can connect to the Internet and the World Wide Web.

1. **Determine how you will obtain access to the Internet.** The three more common ways that people connect to the Internet are through their school or work, through an online service, or through an Internet service provider (ISP).

    Through school or work: Most schools and many organizations have direct, high-speed connections to the Internet. Check with the department that operates the computer labs at school or the department that supports the network at work to obtain details about obtaining an Internet account.

    Through an online service: Most online services, such as America Online and CompuServe, offer Internet access as one of their services. If you already use an online service, this is an excellent way to begin using the Internet. Keep a record of the amount of time you spend on the Internet and the effect it has on your online service bill. You may find that it would be less expensive to use an Internet service provider.

    Through an Internet service provider (ISP): As described earlier in the chapter, an Internet service provider (ISP) has a permanent connection to the Internet and provides temporary connections to others for a fee. The most common fee arrangement is a fixed amount, usually about $15 to $30 per month. You may receive a discounted fee if you sign up for an extended period of time, such as a year. The fee usually includes up to a certain number of Internet access hours, say 100 per month. If you use more than this number of hours, you will be charged an additional amount.

    ISPs include many types of organizations, including private companies such as EarthLink and common carriers such as AT&T. Different Internet service providers offer access services to geographic regions of different sizes: some are local or regional, and others serve users nationwide. Figure 7-31 is a list of national Internet service providers. Before choosing an ISP, check the telephone number you will use to connect to the ISP to see if it will be a local or long-distance call. If you live in a medium to large city, most ISPs will provide a local telephone number.

National Internet Service Providers

Name	Telephone	Web Site
AT&T WorldNet℠	800-967-5363	www.att.com/worldnet/wis
EarthLink Network	800-395-8425	www.earthlink.net
network MCI	800-550-0927	www.mci.com
NETCOM	800-538-2551	www.netcom.com
SPRYNET	800-777-9638	www.sprynet.com

Figure 7-31
These companies are national Internet service providers (ISPs). You can find local ISPs in your telephone book yellow pages under Computers-Networks.

If you know existing ISP users, ask them how often they are unable to log on to the network and the level and quality of technical support. Ask to see the ISP's account setup and software installation instructions. The quality, clarity, and content of these instructions will give you an idea of how well the ISP is organized.

Your ISP probably will set up your account using **PPP (point-to-point protocol)**, a widely used version of the Internet communications protocol TCP/IP. Avoid using a **SLIP (serial line Internet protocol)** connection, because SLIP is an older protocol that does not offer the same degree of error checking as PPP.

2. **Obtain the necessary equipment.** You probably already have the equipment necessary to connect to the Internet. At a minimum, you need a computer, a modem, and a telephone line. (If you want to print information, you also will need a printer.) The speed of you computer, modem, and telephone line will affect how rapidly you can access and display information.

   For the computer, any system less than two-years old should suffice. If your system is more than two years old, consult your ISP.

   For the modem, the higher your modem speed the better. Although 14.4 Kbps or 9,600 bps will work, you need a 28.8 Kbps or faster modem to enjoy the features of the Internet. If you do not have a modem, buy the highest speed you can afford. If you have a slower modem, consider replacing it. A slow modem will act as a bottleneck and lead to frustrating delays as Web pages and information download.

   For most users, a normal analog telephone line will be sufficient. You may want to consider adding a second telephone line so your regular telephone line is not tied up while you are online. If you plan to do serious work using the Internet, such as telecommuting, consider installing a digital ISDN line. An ISDN line can transmit data at up to 128 Kbps, which is more than four times faster than a 28.8 Kbps modem. ISDN lines are more costly to install and maintain but can be worth it if you can offset the expense with greater earnings.

3. **Obtain the necessary software.** You need at least two pieces of software to access the Internet and the World Wide Web through an ISP; a communications program and a Web browser program. You also may want software for e-mail, FTP, and other Internet services, although most Web browsers include some or all of these programs. If your browser does not have these functions, your ISP may provide the programs free. Many also can be downloaded from the Internet or purchased from the developers or software retailers. Why would you want to purchase software you can get free? You may need technical support, which is rarely available for free software.

4. **Install the software.** You should be familiar with the ISP's installation instructions if you reviewed them prior to choosing the ISP. Before starting the installation, however, re-read the instructions in full: exceptions or important information sometimes are placed out of sequence in the instructions. Then, follow the instructions for your operating system. Depending on the Internet software, the installation procedure can be simple, using wizards and dialog boxes or complex, requiring changes to confusing system files. If you run into problems, return to installation step one and start over. If the software still does not work, call your ISP for support.

5. **Explore the Internet and the World Wide Web.** The best way to learn how to use the Internet and Web is to log on and explore. Pick a subject and use a search tool to see what is on the Web. Look up your school's home page and see if it describes the place you know. To help you explore, the section following this chapter lists some useful, interesting, and unusual Web sites. Good exploring!

COMPUTERS AT WORK

Doing Business on the World Wide Web

The rapid growth of the World Wide Web is being accelerated by businesses rushing to establish Web sites to promote their products and services. More than 50 percent of the existing Web sites are commercial (as indicated by their .com domain type), and an even higher percentage of new sites are being set up by businesses. These companies recognize that the Web offers a number of unique advantages over traditional ways of doing business. These advantages include:

- Twenty-four-hour access — Your Internet site can be open around the clock. Customers can reach you according to their schedules and time zones, not yours.
- Global presence — Your product message can be read by customers around the world.
- Lower marketing costs — An electronic product brochure or catalog is less expensive to produce than one on paper. In addition, it can be updated quickly.
- Two-way communications — Compliments, complaints, suggestions, and other customer feedback can be recorded and distributed for follow-up.

For retailers, additional advantages include:

- Lower product display and storage costs — Costs associated with displaying a product, such as a showroom or storefront, are eliminated. Storage costs also can be reduced by eliminating the need to store inventory at multiple locations.
- Lower salesperson costs — For many products, customers obtain sufficient information to make a purchase without the assistance of a salesperson. Even if a salesperson is required to close the sale, presales information provided over the Internet increases the salesperson's efficiency.

The volume of product sales over the Web is growing even faster than the number of companies establishing Web sites. For 1996, Forrester Research, Inc. estimated that products in excess of $500 million were sold via online shopping (a combination of Internet and online service providers). By 2000, they estimate that online product sales will be more than $6 billion, which is a twelve-fold increase. It appears that the business and customer rush to the World Wide Web will continue for some time.

Figure 7-32

IN THE FUTURE

The Future of the Internet and the World Wide Web

What is the future of the World Wide Web? Will increasing traffic cause a catastrophic collapse as predicted by some experts, or will the Web continue to evolve as a primary communications channel? Or both? The following are some of the current predictions about the future of the Internet and the World Wide Web:

- Business use of the Web for electronic commerce will be the driving force of the Web's expansion. Businesses will learn how to make money on the Web, and the Web will become self-supporting.
- Within 10 years, the Web will operate at speeds 100 to 1,000 times faster than today.
- Browser capabilities will be incorporated into most software applications. Stand-alone browsers rarely will be used.
- Using the Web will become an integral part of all education.
- By the year 2000, 80 percent of the world's computers will be connected.
- The ability to connect to the Internet will be built into everyday home and office appliances and other devices that use embedded computers, such as automobiles.
- Web search capabilities will be more intelligent and focused.
- Separate proprietary networks for telephone, television, and radio will merge with the Internet. Eventually, a single, integrated network will exist, made up of many different media, that will carry all communications traffic.

To paraphrase the Sun Microsystems, Inc. corporate slogan; the **Internet will be the computer**.

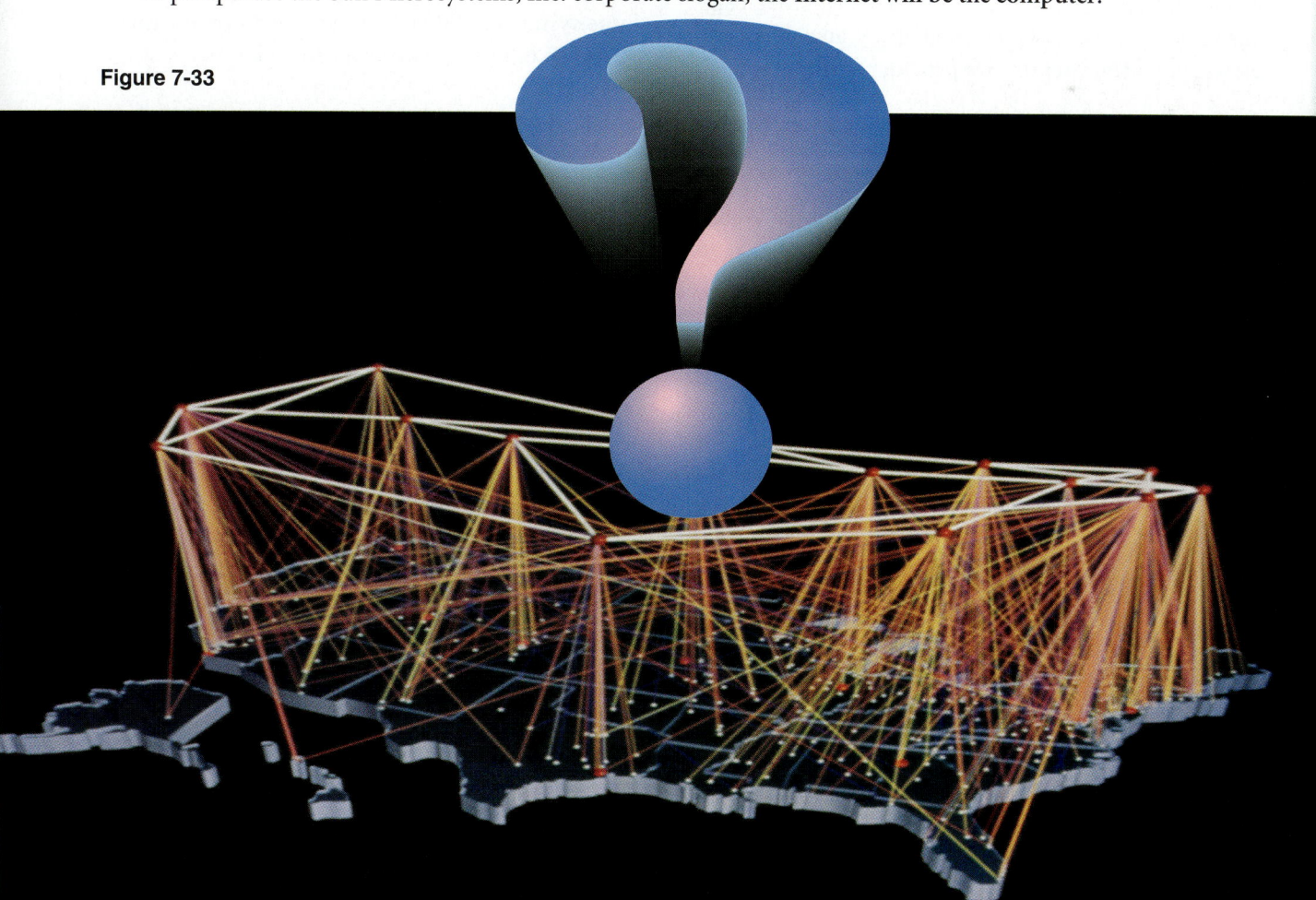

Figure 7-33

review

chapter 1 | 2 | 3 | 4 | 5 | 6 | 7 | 8 | 9 | 10 | 11 | 12 | 13 | 14 | I

inCyber | review | terms | yourTurn | hotTopics | outThere | winLabs | webWalk | exercises | news | home

INSTRUCTIONS: *To display this page from the Web, launch your browser and enter the URL, http://www.scsite.com/dc/ch7/review.htm. Click the links for current and additional information.*

1 The Internet

The term, **the Internet**, is used to describe a worldwide group of connected networks (some local, some regional, and some national) that allows public access to information and services. Together, these networks create a global network that serves approximately 40 million users.

2 How the Internet Works

The Internet operates by dividing data into separate parts, called **packets**, and sending the packets along the best route available to a destination computer. The software used to perform this technique, called *packet switching*, is a communications protocol named **TCP/IP (transmission control protocol/Internet protocol)**. People can connect to the Internet through an organization such as a school or company, an online service, or an **Internet service provider (ISP)**.

3 Internet Addresses

Each location on the Internet has a four-part numeric address called an **IP (Internet protocol) address**. Because IP addresses are difficult to remember and use, the Internet supports a text version, called a **domain name**, that can be substituted for the IP address. Domain names are registered in the **domain name system (DNS)** and are used by **domain name servers** to look up the associated IP address.

4 The World Wide Web

The **World Wide Web (WWW, W3, or the Web)** is a collection of hyperlinked documents accessible on the Internet. **Hyperlinks** can be used to move quickly from one document to another, regardless of whether the documents are located on the same computer or on different computers in different countries. Internet locations that contain hyperlinked documents are called **Web sites**.

5 How a Web Page Works

A **Web page** is a **hypertext** document (document with text hyperlinks) or **hypermedia** document (document with text, graphics, video, or sound hyperlinks) residing on an Internet computer. The three types of hyperlinks are **target hyperlinks** that move from one location in a document to another location in the same document; **relative hyperlinks** that move from one document to another document on the same computer; and **absolute hyperlinks** that move from one document to another document on a different Internet computer. Displaying pages from one Web site after another is called **Web surfing**. Web pages are created using **hypertext markup language (HTML)**, which is a set of special instructions that specify links to other documents and how the page is displayed.

6 Web Browser Software

Web browser software is a program that interprets and displays Web pages and enables you to link to other Web pages. Each time a browser is launched, a **home page** is displayed. The browser retrieves Web pages using a **Uniform Resource Locator (URL)**, which is an address that points to a specific resource on the Internet. Browsers display hyperlinks either as underlined text of a different color or as a graphic. Linked documents can be displayed by clicking the hyperlink or by typing its URL in the Location text box. Two ways to keep track of Web pages that have been viewed are a **history list** and a **bookmark** list.

7 Multimedia on the Web

Some of the more exciting Web developments involve multimedia. To run a multimedia application, a browser may need an additional program called a **plug-in** or **helper application**. A programming language called **Java** is being used to develop much of the multimedia on the Web. Developers use Java to create small programs called applets that can be downloaded and run in a browser window. Multimedia Web developments have been made in the areas of **graphics**, **animation**, **audio**, **video**, and **virtual reality (VR)**.

8 Web Search Tools

A **search tool**, also called a **search engine**, is a software program that finds Web sites, Web pages, and Internet files that match one or more keywords entered. Search tools search an index of Internet sites and documents that is constantly updated.

9 Intranets

Internal networks that use Internet and Web technology are called **intranets**. Intranet applications include electronic publishing and groupware applications. **Extranets** are private networks that include more than one organization. To prevent unauthorized access, organizations implement one or more layers of security called a **firewall**, which refers to both hardware and software used to restrict access to data on a network.

10 Internet Services

Internet services include e-mail, FTP, Gopher, Telnet, Usenet, and Internet Relay Chat (IRC). **E-mail** is the electronic exchange of messages from one person to another. To receive e-mail, you must have a **mailbox**, which is a file used to collect messages on an Internet computer. An **Internet mailbox address** is a combination of a **user name** (a unique combination of characters that identifies you) and the domain name that identifies the location of the mailbox computer.

11 FTP and Gopher

FTP (file transfer protocol) is an Internet standard that allows you to exchange files with other computers on the Internet. Computers that contain files available for FTP are called **FTP sites** or **FTP servers**. An FTP search tool called **Archie** can be used to find files on a particular subject. **Gopher** is a menu-driven program that helps you locate and retrieve files on the Internet. Internet computers called **Gopher servers** maintain Gopher directories. Most Gopher servers offer **Veronica** or **Jughead** search programs.

12 Telnet, Usenet, and Internet Relay Chat (IRC)

Telnet is an Internet protocol used to log into a remote computer on the Internet. **Usenet** is a collection of news and discussion groups, called **newsgroups**. Each newsgroup operates as if it were a bulletin board devoted to a particular subject. **Internet Relay Chat (IRC)** allows you to join in real-time conversations on the Internet.

13 Network Computers

A **network computer** is designed to work while connected to a network, but not as a stand-alone computer. Network computers are also called **thin-client** computers. A **network personal computer**, or **netPC**, relies on the server but does have a hard disk. A **set-top box**, using a phone line, can connect your TV to the Web.

14 Connecting to the Internet

You must perform five steps to connect to the Internet and the World Wide Web. First, determine how you will obtain access to the Internet (through school or work, an online service, or an Internet service provider). Second, obtain the necessary equipment (a computer, a modem, and a telephone line). Third, obtain the necessary software (a communications program and a browser). Fourth, install the software. Fifth, explore the Internet and the World Wide Web.

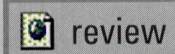

chapter
1 | 2 | 3 | 4 | 5 | 6 | 7 | 8 | 9 | 10 | 11 | 12 | 13 | 14 | I

inCyber | review | terms | yourTurn | hotTopics | outThere | winLabs | webWalk | exercises | news | home

INSTRUCTIONS: *To display this page from the Web, launch your browser and enter the URL, http://www.scsite.com/dc/ch7/terms.htm. Scroll through the list of terms. Click a term for its definition and a picture. Click the rocket ship for current and additional information about the term.*

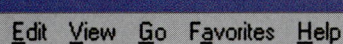

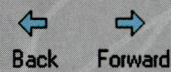

network computer

D E F I N I T I O N

network computer
Relies on the server for software and storage. Does not have a hard disk. **(7.25)**

aboslute hyperlinks (7.8)
Advanced Research Projects
 Agency (ARPA) (7.3)
animation (7.12)
anonymous FTP (7.20)
applets (7.11)
Archie (7.20)
Archie gateway (7.20)
Archie sites (7.20)
ARPANET (7.3)
article (7.23)
audio (7.13)

backbones (7.5)
bookmark (7.11)
browser (7.9)

caching (7.18)
channel (7.25)
channel operator (7.25)

domain name (7.6)
domain name servers (7.6)
domain name system (DNS) (7.6)

e-mail (7.19)
extranets (7.17)

FAQ (7.24)
firewall (7.18)
flaming (7.24)
FTP (file transfer protocol) (7.20)
FTP servers (7.20)
FTP sites (7.20)

Gopher (7.21)
Gopher servers (7.21)
graphics (7.12)

helper application (7.11)
history list (7.11)
home page (7.10)
http:// (7.10)
hyperlinks (7.7)
hypermedia (7.7)
hypertext (7.7
hypertext markup language
 (HTML) (7.8)
hypertext transfer protocol (7.10)

information appliance (7.26)
internet (7.2)
the Internet (7.2)
Internet audioconferencing (7.13)
Internet mailbox address (7.19)
Internet Relay Chat (IRC) (7.25)
Internet service provider (ISP)
 (7.28)
Internet telephone service (7.13)
Internet telephony (7.13)
Internet voice mail (7.13)
internetwork (7.2)
intranet (7.17)
IP (Internet protocol) address
 (7.6)
IRC (7.25)

Java (7.11)
/join (7.25)
Jughead (7.21)

/list (7.25)

mailbox (7.19)
markups (7.8)
metropolitan area exchanges
 (MAEs) (7.5)

moderator (7.24)
MOO (multiuser object oriented)
 (7.22)
Mosaic (7.9)
MUD (multiuser dimension)
 (7.22)

NC (7.25)
netiquette (7.24)
network computer (7.25)
network personal computer (7.26)
net PC (7.26)
newbies (7.24)
newsgroups (7.23)
newsreader (7.23)
NSFnet (7.3)

online service (7.28)

packets (7.4)
plug-in (7.11)
posting (7.23)
PPP (point-to-point protocol)
 (7.29)
proxy server (7.18)

relative hyperlinks (7.8)

search engine (7.16)
search tool (7.16)
set-top box (7.26)
shareware (7.20)
SHOUT! (7.24)
SLIP (serial line Internet protocol)
 (7.29)
spamming (7.24)
streaming audio (7.13)
streaming video (7.14)

tags (7.8)
target hyperlinks (7.8)
TCP/IP (transmission control
 protocol/Internet protocol)
 (7.4)
Telnet (7.22)
thin-client (7.25)
thread (7.23)

Uniform Resource Locator (URL)
 (7.10)
URL (7.10)
Usenet (7.23)
user name (7.19)
user-ID (7.19)

Veronica (7.21)
video (7.14)
virtual reality (VR) (7.15)
VRML (virtual reality modeling
 language) (7.15)

W3 (7.7)
Web (7.7)
Web browser (7.9)
Web browser software (7.9)
Web page (7.7)
Web sites (7.7)
Web surfing (7.8)
welcome page (7.10)
World Wide Web (7.7)
WWW (7.7)

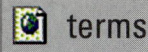

yourTurn

chapter 7

1 | 2 | 3 | 4 | 5 | 6 | 7 | 8 | 9 | 10 | 11 | 12 | 13 | 14 | I

inCyber | review | terms | yourTurn | hotTopics | outThere | winLabs | webWalk | exercises | news | home

INSTRUCTIONS: *To display this page from the Web, launch your browser and enter the URL, http://www.scsite.com/dc/ch7/turn.htm. Click a blank line for the answer. Click the links for current and additional information.*

Label the Figure

1. _____ 2. _____ 3. _____ 4. _____

IP address   198.105.232.4

domain name   www.microsoft.com

5. _____ 6. _____ 7. _____

Instructions: Identify each element of the IP address and associated domain name.

Fill in the Blanks

Instructions: Complete each sentence with the correct term or terms.

1. A(n) _____ is an organization that has a permanent connection to the Internet and provides temporary connections to others for a fee.
2. _____ are Internet locations that contain hyperlinked documents.
3. All Web page URLs begin with _____, which stands for _____, the communications standard used to transfer pages on the Web.
4. A(n) _____ is a type of Internet game in which participants assume the identity of specific characters.
5. IRC channels can be found using the _____ command, and the _____ command is used to participate.

Short Answer

Instructions: Write a brief answer to each of the following questions.

1. What is a hyperlink? How are target hyperlinks, relative hyperlinks, and absolute hyperlinks different? What is hypertext markup language (HTML)? _____
2. How are streaming audio and streaming video similar? How are they different from simple audio and video? For what purposes are they used? _____
3. What is a firewall? How does a proxy server implement a firewall? _____
4. Explain why no central menu or catalog of Web site content and addresses exists. What is a search tool? How does a search tool work? _____
5. What are three different ways to obtain access to the Internet? How is PPP different from SLIP? What type of equipment and software are necessary to access the Internet and the World Wide Web through an ISP? _____

hotTopics

chapter 7

1 | 2 | 3 | 4 | 5 | 6 | 7 | 8 | 9 | 10 | 11 | 12 | 13 | 14 | I

inCyber | review | terms | yourTurn | hotTopics | outThere | winLabs | webWalk | exercises | news | home

INSTRUCTIONS: *To display this page from the Web, launch your browser and enter the URL, http://www.scsite.com/dc/ch7/hot.htm. Click the links for current and additional information to help you respond to the hotTopics questions.*

1 *When Chess Grand Master Gary Kasparov played Big Blue the computer,* IBM created a Web site to follow the chess tournament. It is estimated that at times more than *one million* people saw some of the match online. Experts feel the site was successful because visitors got what they wanted (exciting games with respected analysis), and the event lent itself to the site's design (a view of the chessboard with the capability to interact). Considering these two factors, desirability and appropriateness, what other events could be covered successfully at a Web site? Why? How would you design the Web site? What advantages would coverage at a Web site have over coverage in other media?

2 *An increasing number of doctors is going online as volunteer medical consultants. People* suffering from almost any disease can find relevant support groups, mailing lists, and Web sites. These forums may help reduce feelings of isolation and provide invaluable information. Many doctors, however, still are reluctant to go online. They fear online forums can raise false hopes, repeat unsubstantiated claims, or promote quack remedies. If someone you knew had a serious condition, would you suggest trying the Internet? Why? What cautions would you recommend when exploring a health issue online? How would you advise someone to act on medical information received from the Web?

3 *After hearing a girl had been mistreated by her mother, a student posted a message to Internet* newsgroups urging readers to call the girl's family. The family received several threatening telephone calls. The girl's angry father insisted the allegations were exaggerated and feared the telephone calls could destroy an already vulnerable family. The message's author admitted no wrong doing and claimed people should be free to write what they want on the Internet. While conventional laws regarding libel, slander, and harassment may apply, Internet communications ultimately depend on the writer's sense of responsibility. Are these remedies enough? What, if anything, should be done to guarantee a message's veracity? What obligations do the writers and readers of messages have?

4 *While seeking an explanation for a recently doubled dropout rate, educators at a major* university found that 43 percent of the dropouts disclosed late-night Internet connections, neglecting their studies and failing to attend class. Some colleges have expressed concern about excessive use of the Internet, occasionally called cyberaddiction. Unsure whether this condition is a true addiction or merely a sympton of other problems, colleges have offered a range of solutions, including support groups, turning off computers, and slowing down the machines. Is *cyberaddiction* really a problem? Why? If it is, what can be done? How would you determine if a friend is spending too much time online? What would you do to help?

5 *The freedom and anonymity of the Internet may be both its most appealing and disturbing* characteristics. These features may encourage a woman suffering from ochlophobia (fear of crowds) to discover help in a newsgroup, but these same features allow lawbreakers to send obscene materials, arrange illicit meetings, and swindle unsuspecting readers. What controls should be placed on the Internet? Why? Should people be subject to local ordinances (a California couple recently was prosecuted for violating Tennessee law with pictures downloaded from their bulletin board), or should regulations be global? Why?

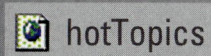

chapter 7 outThere

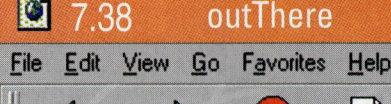

1 | 2 | 3 | 4 | 5 | 6 | 7 | 8 | 9 | 10 | 11 | 12 | 13 | 14 | I

inCyber | review | terms | yourTurn | hotTopics | outThere | winLabs | webWalk | exercises | news | home

INSTRUCTIONS: *To display this page from the Web, launch your browser and enter the URL, http://www.scsite.com/dc/ch7/out.htm. Click the links for current and additional information.*

1 *News and information about a wide range of events are available at various* Web sites. News mavens complain, however, that they are forced to spend too much time surfing the Web trying to track down the material they want. A solution to the complaint is called invited push media, a continuous stream of information that you request be sent to your personal computer. Visit one or more Web sites to find out about a push media application. What is the name of the application? How much does it cost? How does the application work? What type of information is broadcast? How current is it? Does every user get the same information? Would you be interested in downloading a push media application? Why?

2 *Most communities have a number of Internet Service Providers (ISPs) that offer access to the* Internet. Because the monthly rates, the features offered, and the quality of the connection may vary, however, it is wise to do some comparison shopping before signing on with an ISP. Contact at least two ISPs to learn more about each service. What are the rates? Are invoices sent or is a charge automatically billed to a credit card? How many people can use the account? Is disk storage space available for a personal Web page? If so, does the page contain any restrictions? Is the service not accessible at any time? When is technical support available? Try to find users of each ISP and ask them about the quality of the connection. Which ISP do you feel is the better buy? Why?

3 *Eighty percent of the work in preparing a research report is locating the* necessary information. Search tools can help to find relevant information at Web sites, but they fail to cover other possible resources such as magazines, newspapers, and books. To make their inquiries more inclusive, many students are turning to online research services available on the World Wide Web. Visit a Web site to learn more about an online research service. What resources are used by the service? How is using the service similar to using a library? How is it different? Who uses the service? How safe is the service for kids? How much does it cost? Would you use an online research service? Why?

4 *Web browsers are an essential tool when exploring the World Wide Web. If you plan to* spend time on the Internet, it is important to use a browser with which you are comfortable. Visit a software vendor and compare two or more Web browsers. What is the name of each browser? How much does each cost? What types of hardware and software are required? What features are offered by each browser? If possible, try each browser. How are they similar? How are they different? Is one browser easier to use than the other? Why? Which browser does the salesperson recommend? Why? Which would you be more likely to buy? Why?

5 *Not only do teachers suggest that their students use the Internet, more and more teachers are* using the Internet themselves to improve their presentations. Visit one or more Web sites that suggest lesson plans, projects, and activities and look at the available material from a student's point of view. What lesson plans, projects, or activities do you think a student would find most interesting? Why? What suggestions look least promising? Why? What types of teachers would be most likely to benefit from visiting each site? Why? Using the available lesson plans, projects, or activities, how would you teach a lesson in your favorite subject?

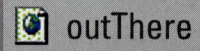

7.39 winLabs

winLabs

inCyber | review | terms | yourTurn | hotTopics | outThere | winLabs | webWalk | exercises | news | home

INSTRUCTIONS: *To display this page from the Web, launch your browser and enter the URL, http://www.scsite.com/dc/ch7/labs.htm. Click the links for current and additional information.*

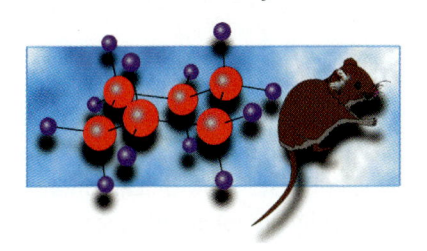

1. Shelly Cashman Series Internet Lab

Follow the instructions in winLabs 1 on page 1.34 to display the Shelly Cashman Series Labs screen. Click Connecting to the Internet. Click the Start Lab button. When the initial screen displays, carefully read the objectives. With your printer turned on, click the Print Questions button. Fill out the top of the Questions sheet and then answer the questions.

2. Shelly Cashman Series World Wide Web Lab

Follow the instructions in winLabs 1 on page 1.34 to display the Shelly Cashman Series Labs screen. Click The World Wide Web. Click the Start Lab button. When the screen displays, read the objectives. With your printer turned on, click the Print Questions button. Fill out the top of the Questions sheet and answer the questions.

3. Understanding Your Internet Properties

Right-click The Internet icon on the desktop. Click Properties on the shortcut menu. When The Internet Properties dialog box displays, click the General tab. Click the question mark button on the title bar and then click Show pictures. Read the information in the pop-up window and then click the pop-up window to close it. Repeat this process for other areas of the dialog box and then answer the following questions: (1) What are three ways to make pages display more quickly? (2) In what color do visited links display? Unvisited links? (3) What is the address bar? Click the Navigation tab and then answer the following questions: (1) What is the Internet address of the start page? (2) How many days of pages display in history? Click the Cancel button.

4. Determining Dial-Up Network Connections

Click the Start button on the taskbar, point to Programs on the Start menu, point to Accessories on the Programs submenu, and then click Dial-Up Networking on the Accessories submenu. When the Dial-Up Networking window displays, right-click a connection in the list (e.g., The Microsoft Network) and then click Connect on the shortcut menu. Write down the User name and the Phone number. Close the dialog box and open window.

5. Using Help to Understand the Internet

Click the Start button on the taskbar and then on the Start menu, click Help. Click the Contents tab, double-click Introducing Windows, and then double-click Welcome to the Information Highway. Double-click An introduction to the Internet (Figure 7-34). In the Windows Help window, click the Options button, click Print Topic, and then click the OK button to print the topic. Click the Help Topics button. Double-click Taking a test drive on the information highway. Print the topic. Close any open window(s).

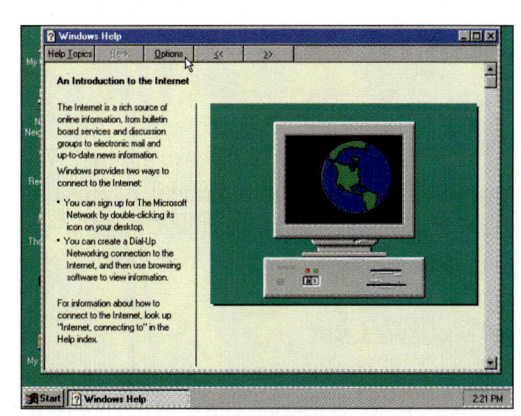

Figure 7-34

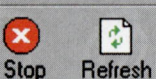

webWalk

chapter 1 | 2 | 3 | 4 | 5 | 6 | 7 | 8 | 9 | 10 | 11 | 12 | 13 | 14 | I

inCyber | review | terms | yourTurn | hotTopics | outThere | winLabs | webWalk | exercises | news | home

INSTRUCTIONS: *To display this page from the Web, launch your browser and enter the URL, http://www.scsite.com/dc/ch7/walk.htm. Click the exercise link to display the exercise.*

1. Web Chat
A chatting application allows Web users to have real-time conversations with each other via the Web (Figure 7-35). To learn more about Web Chatting, complete this exercise.

Figure 7-35

2. Internet Congestion
The expanding population of the Internet is raising concern that the Net will suffer a catastrophic collapse. You can learn more about these concerns by complete this exercise.

3. Real-Time Information
Through the network of computers known as the World Wide Web, complex data can be queried and reported through user-friendly interfaces (Figure 7-36). To visit a Web site where you can access complex, real-time information, complete this exercise.

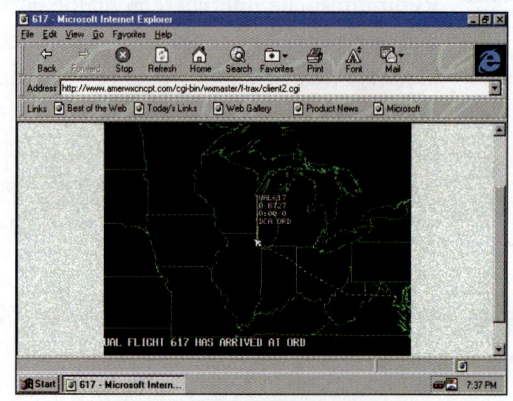

Figure 7-36

4. Web TV
In the near future when you are watching television and an interesting new product is shown, you will be able to click and be connected instantly to the product's Web site. To learn more about Web TV, complete this exercise.

5. Information Mining
Complete this exercise to improve your Web research skills by using a Web search engine to find information related to this chapter.

6. Web Domain Names
A Domain Name such as www.scsite.com that identifies a computer on the web must be registered. Complete this exercise to learn more about how domain names are registered.

7. Interanets
Many organizations have applied Web technology to their own internal networks. Internal networks that use Internet and Web technology are called Intranets. Complete this exercise to learn more about Intranets.

8. Cable Modem
A cable modem is a device that allows high-speed access to the Internet via a cable TVnetwork. Complete this exercise to learn more about cable modems.

9. Web Chat
Complete this exercise to enter a Web Chat discussion related to the issues presented in the hotTopics exercise.

Guide to World Wide Web Sites

The World Wide Web is an exciting and highly dynamic medium. Every day, new Web sites are added, existing ones are changed, and still others cease to exist. Because of this, you may find that a URL listed here has changed or no longer is valid. A continually updated Guide to World Wide Web Sites, which links to the most current versions of these sites, can be found at http://www.scsite.com/dc/ch7/websites.htm.

CATEGORIES

Art	Government and Politics	Reference
Business and Finance	Health and Medicine	Science
Careers and Employment	History	Shopping
Computers and Computing	Humor	Sports
Education	Internet	Travel
Entertainment	Museums	Unclassified!
Environment	News Sources	Weather

7.42 GUIDE TO WORLD WIDE WEB SITES

CATEGORY/SITE NAME	LOCATION (all site locations begin with http://)	COMMENT
Art		
The WebMuseum	sunsite.unc.edu/louvre/net/	Web version of Louvre Museum, Paris
Art Links on the Web	amanda.physics.wisc.edu/outside.html	Links to many art sites
Leonardo da Vinci	www.leonardo.net/museum	Works of the famous Italian artist and thinker
World Art Treasures	sgwww.epfl.ch/BERGER	100,000 slides organized by civilization
The Andy Warhol Museum	www.clpgh.org/warhol	Famous American pop artist
ArtServe	rubens.anu.edu.au	More than 18,000 images
Business and Finance		
Imperative!™	www.tig.com/IBC	How to do business on the web
All Business Network	www.all-biz.com	Links to Web business information
FinanCenter, Inc.	www.financenter.com	Personal finance information
The Wall Street Journal	update.wsj.com	Financial news page
Stock Research Group	www.stockgroup.com	Investment information
PC Quote	www.pcquote.com	Free delayed stock quotes
Careers and Employment		
CareerMosaic®	www.careermosaic.com	Jobs from around the world
E-Span Employment Database	www.espan.com	Searchable job database
CareerMagazine	www.careermag.com	Career articles and information

For an updated list: http://www.scsite.com/dc/ch7/websites.htm

The Andy Warhol Museum

CareerMosaic — November 1996

CareerMosaic J.O.B.S.
Employers A-C D-J K-O P-R S-Z
ResumeCM post or search resumes
CollegeConnection NEW!
Online Job Fairs hire happenings
Career Resource Center chart your career
International Gateway Expanded!
Health Care Connection NEW!

Click here to visit our Online Job Fairs!

GUIDE TO WORLD WIDE WEB SITES **7.43**

CATEGORY/SITE NAME	LOCATION (all site locations begin with http://)	COMMENT
Computers and Computing		
Computer companies	Insert name or initials of most computer companies between www. and .com to find their Web site. Examples: www.ibm.com, www.microsoft.com, www.dell.com.	
The Computer Museum	www.net.org	Exhibits and history of computing
MIT Media Lab	www.media.mit.edu	Information on computer trends
Virtual Computer Library	www.utexas.edu/computer/vcl	Information on computers and computing
Education		
CollegeNET	www.collegenet.com	Searchable database of more than 2,000 colleges and universities
EdLinks	www.marshall.edu/~jmullens/edlinks.html	Links to many educational sites
The Open University	www.open.ac.uk	Independent study courses from U.K.
Entertainment		
Mr. Showbiz	web3.starwave.com/showbiz	Information on latest films
Rock & Roll Hall of Fame	www.rockhall.com	Cleveland museum site
Classics World	www.classicalmus.com	Classical music information
Metaverse	metaverse.com	Music and entertainment news
Playbill On-Line	www.playbill.com	Theater news
Music Boulevard	www.musicblvd.com	Search for and buy all types of music

For an updated list: http://www.scsite.com/dc/ch7/websites.htm

GUIDE TO WORLD WIDE WEB SITES

CATEGORY/SITE NAME	LOCATION (all site locations begin with http://)	COMMENT
Environment		
U.S. Environmental Protection Agency (EPA)	www.epa.gov	U.S. government environmental news
EnviroLink Network	www.envirolink.org	Environmental information
Greenpeace	www.greenpeace.org	Environmental activism
Government and Politics		
U.S. Census Bureau	www.census.gov	Population and other statistics
CIA	www.odci.gov/cia	Political and economic information on countries
The White House	www.whitehouse.gov	Take tour and learn about occupants
FedWorld	www.fedworld.gov	Links to U.S. government sites
The Library of Congress	www.loc.gov	Variety of U.S. government information
Canada Info	www.clo.com/~canadainfo	List of Canadian Web sites
United Kingdom	www.coi.gov.uk/coi	U.K. Central Office of Information
United Nations	www.un.org	Latest UN projects and information
Health and Medicine		
The Interactive Patient	medicus.marshall.edu/medicus.htm	Simulates visit to doctor
Centers for Disease Control and Prevention (CDC)	www.cdc.gov	How to prevent and control disease
Solutions	disability.com	Resource for disability products and services
Women's Medical Health Page	www.best.com/~sirlou/wmhp.html	Articles and links to other sites

For an updated list: http://www.scsite.com/dc/ch7/websites.htm

GUIDE TO WORLD WIDE WEB SITES   7.45

CATEGORY/SITE NAME	LOCATION (all site locations begin with http://)	COMMENT
History		
American Memory	rs6.loc.gov/amhome.html	American history
Virtual Library History Index	history.cc.ukans.edu/history/www-history_main.html	Organized links to history sites / Links to history sites
Historical Text Archive	www.msstate.edu/Archives/History/USA/usa.html	U.S. documents, photos, and database
Humor		
Comedy Central Online	www.comcentral.com	From comedy TV network
The Dilbert Zone	www.unitedmedia.com/comics/dilbert	Humorous insights about working
Calvin & Hobbes Gallery	eus.kub.nl:2080/calvin-hobbes	Comic strip gallery
Late Show Top 10 Archive	www.cbs.com/lateshow/ttlist.html	David Letterman Top 10 lists
Internet		
EFF's Guide to the Internet	www.eff.org/papers/bdgtti/eegtti.html	Comprehensive guide to the Internet
WWW Frequently Asked Questions	www.boutell.com/faq	Common Web questions and answers
Internet Glossary	www.matisse.net/files/glossary.html	Definitions of Internet terms

For an updated list: http://www.scsite.com/dc/ch7/websites.htm

The LIBRARY *of* CONGRESS

AMERICAN MEMORY

Historical Collections for the National Digital Library

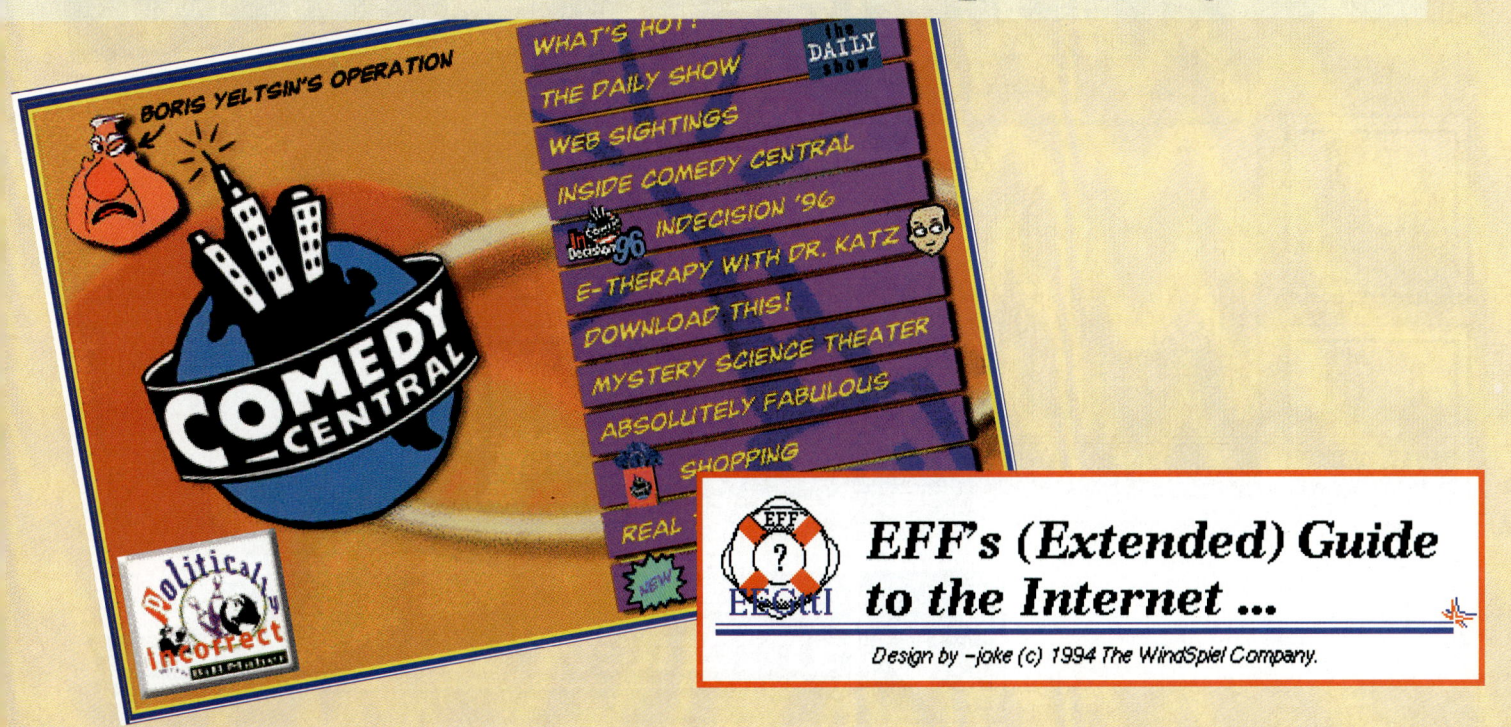

EFF's (Extended) Guide to the Internet ...

Design by –joke (c) 1994 The WindSpiel Company.

GUIDE TO WORLD WIDE WEB SITES

CATEGORY/SITE NAME	LOCATION (all site locations begin with http://)	COMMENT
Museums		
The Smithsonian	www.si.edu	Information and links to Smithsonian museums
U.S. Holocaust Memorial Museum	www.ushmm.org	Dedicated to World War II victims
University of California Museum of Paleontology	ucmp1.berkeley.edu/welcome.html	Great information on dinosaurs and other exhibits
News Sources		
The Electronic Newsstand	www.enews.com	Articles from worldwide publications
Pathfinder	www.pathfinder.com	Excerpts from Time-Warner magazines
Wired News	www.wired.com	*Wired* magazine online and HotWired Network
CNN Interactive	www.cnn.com	CNN all-news network
USA TODAY	www.usatoday.com	Latest U.S. and international news
C/NET	www.cnet.com	Technology news
Reference		
Internet Public Library	ipl.sils.umich.edu	Literature and reference works
The New York Public Library	gopher.nypl.org	Extensive reference and research material
Dictionary Library	math-www.uni-paderborn.de/HTML/Dictionaries.html	Links to many types of dictionaries
Bartlett's Quotations	www.cc.columbia.edu/acis/bartelby/bartlett	Organized, searchable database of famous quotes

For an updated list: http://www.scsite.com/dc/ch7/websites.htm

GUIDE TO WORLD WIDE WEB SITES 7.47

CATEGORY/SITE NAME	LOCATION (all site locations begin with http://)	COMMENT
Science		
The Nine Planets	seds.lpl.arizona.edu/nineplanets/nineplanets/nineplanets.html	Tour the solar system
American Institute of Physics	www.aip.org	Physics research information
Internet Chemistry Index	www.chemie.fu-berlin.de/chemistry/index	List of chemistry information sites
Exploratorium	www.exploratorium.edu	Interactive science exhibits
The NASA Homepage	www.nasa.gov	Information on U.S. space program
Shopping		
BizWeb	www.bizweb.com	Search for products from more than 1,000 companies
CommerceNet	www.commerce.net	Index of products and services
Ventana Online	www.vmedia.com	computer books and software
Internet Book Shop	www.bookshop.co.uk	780,000 titles on more than 2,000 subjects
Internet Shopping Network	www.internet.net	Specialty stores, hot deals, computer products
The Internet Mall™	www.internet-mall.com	Comprehensive list of Web businesses
Consumer World	www.consumerworld.org	Consumer information
Sports		
ESPNET SportsZone	www.espn.com	Latest sports news
NBA Basketball	www.nba.com	Information and links to team sites
NFL Football	www.nfl.com	Information and links to team sites
Sports Illustrated	www.pathfinder.com/si	Leading sports magazine

For an updated list: http://www.scsite.com/dc/ch7/websites.htm

GUIDE TO WORLD WIDE WEB SITES

CATEGORY/SITE NAME	LOCATION (all site locations begin with http://)	COMMENT
Travel		
InfoHub WWW Travel Guide	www.infohub.com	Worldwide travel information
Excite City.Net	www.city.net	Guide to world cities
Virtual Tourist II	wings.buffalo.edu/world/vt2	World map links to information database
TravelWeb℠	www.travelweb.com	Places to stay
Travelocity℠	www.travelocity.com	Online travel agency
Lonely Planet Travel Guides	www.lonelyplanet.com	Budget travel guides and stories
Unclassified!		
Cool Site of the Day	cool.infi.net	Different site each day
Cupid's Network™	www.cupidnet.com/cupid	Links to dating resources
Pizza Hut	www.pizzahut.com	Order pizza online (limited areas)
Weather		
The Weather Channel	www.weather.com	National and local forecasts
INTELLiCAST Guides	www.intellicast.com	International weather and skiing information

For an updated list: http://www.scsite.com/dc/ch7/websites.htm

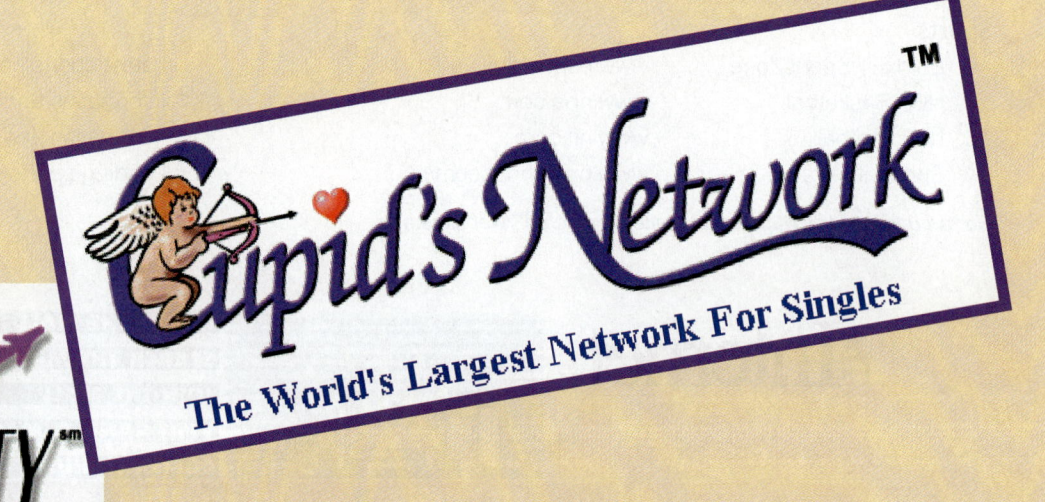

Operating Systems and System Software

OBJECTIVES

After completing this chapter, you will be able to:

- Describe the three major categories of system software

- Define the term operating system

- Describe the functions of an operating system

- Understand what happens when an operating system is loaded

- Explain the difference between proprietary and portable operating systems

- Name and briefly describe the major operating systems that are being used today

- Discuss utilities and language translators

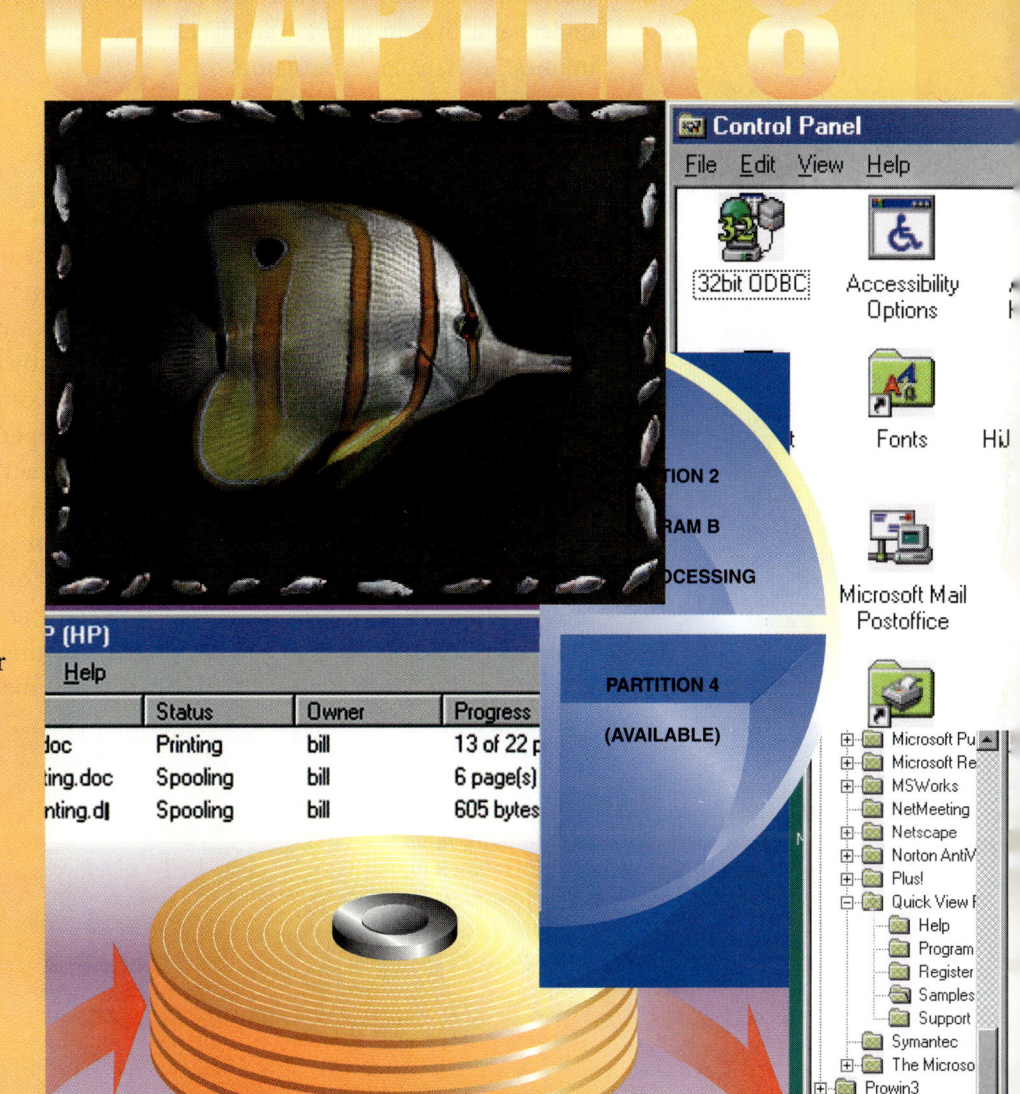

When most people think of software, they think of applications such as word processing, spreadsheet, and database. To run an application on a computer, however, another type of software is needed to serve as an interface between the user, the application, and the hardware. This software consists of programs that are referred to as the operating system. The operating system is just one example of a type of software called system software, which controls the operations of the computer hardware.

This chapter discusses functions performed by system software with a focus on the operating system, its functions, and what happens when the computer loads an operating system. Popular operating systems, utility programs, and language translators also are reviewed.

What Is System Software?

System software consists of all the programs, including the operating system, that are related to controlling the operations of the computer hardware. Some of the functions that system software performs include starting up the computer; loading, executing, and storing application programs; and storing and retrieving files. System software also performs a variety of other functions such as formatting disks, sorting data files, and translating program instructions into binary code that the computer can understand. System software can be classified into three major categories: operating systems, utilities, and language translators.

What Is an Operating System?

An **operating system (OS)** is a set of programs that manages the operations of a computer and functions as an interface between the user, the application programs, and the computer hardware (Figure 8-1). A computer cannot operate without an operating system.

The operating system usually is stored on the computer's hard disk drive. Each time you start the computer, the essential and more frequently used instructions in the operating system are copied from the disk and stored in the computer's memory. This set of essential instructions always resides in memory while you operate the computer and is called the *resident* portion of the operating system. The resident portion of the operating system is called by many different names: the **kernel, supervisor, monitor, executive, master program,** or **control program**. The individual instructions, or commands, contained in the resident portion of the operating system are called **internal commands**. The *nonresident* portion of the operating system consists of the less frequently used instructions, called **external commands**. The nonresident portion of the operating system remains on the disk while you operate the computer, ready to be loaded into memory whenever an external command is needed.

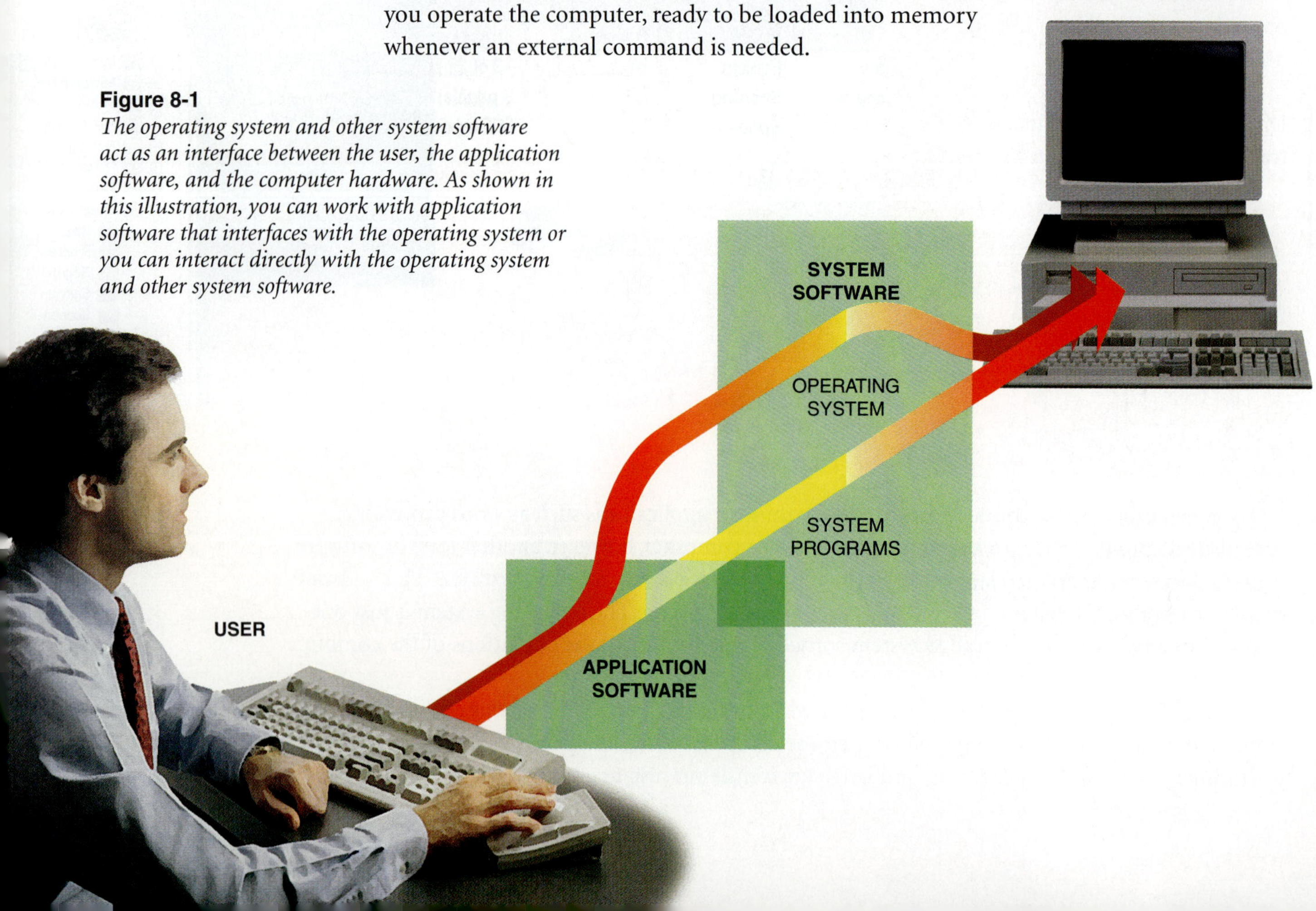

Figure 8-1
The operating system and other system software act as an interface between the user, the application software, and the computer hardware. As shown in this illustration, you can work with application software that interfaces with the operating system or you can interact directly with the operating system and other system software.

WHAT IS AN OPERATING SYSTEM?   8.3

The **user interface** is the feature of the operating system that determines how you interact with the computer. The user interface controls how you enter data and commands (input) and how information is presented on the screen (output). The three types of user interfaces are command-line, menu-driven, and graphical (Figure 8-2). Many operating systems use a combination of these types.

If you are using a **command-line user interface**, you enter keywords (commands) that cause the computer to take a specific action, such as copying a file or sending a file to the printer. The set of commands you use to interact with the computer is called the **command language**.

A **menu-driven user interface** uses menus that present a set of commands or options that causes the computer to take a specific action. You can use the keyboard or a pointing device to select a menu item.

A **graphical user interface** (**GUI**) uses visual clues, such as icons, to help you perform tasks. Icons are small pictures that represent actions, programs, tasks, and other objects, such as documents. An icon of a printer, for example, might represent the Print command. Icons are helpful because they are memorable, use little space on-screen, and can be understood by most people.

Today, many graphical user interfaces incorporate browser-like features, which make them even easier to use. In these browser-like interfaces, icons function like Web hyperlinks, toolbar buttons resemble those used in graphical Web browsers, and multimedia applets can run directly on your screen.

command-line

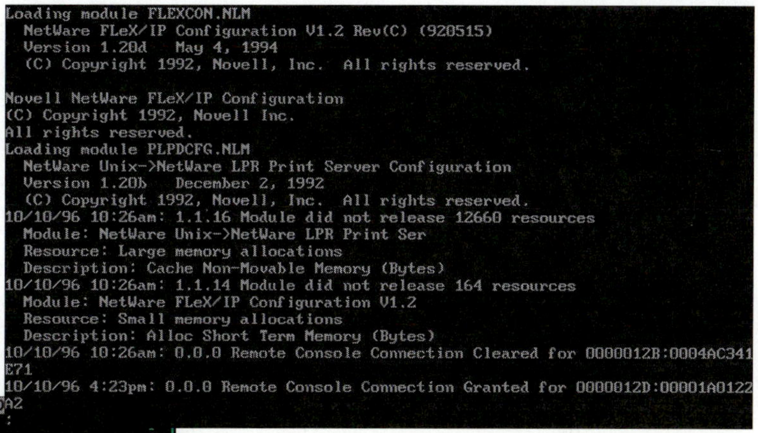

menu-driven

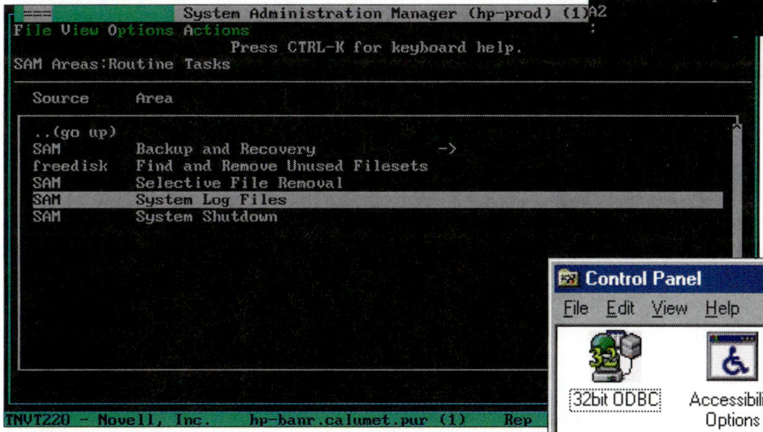

graphical

Figure 8-2
Examples of command-line, menu-driven, and graphical user interfaces. The user interface determines how information is presented on the screen and how you enter data and commands.

Functions of an Operating System

The operating system performs four functions that allow you and the application software to interact with the computer: process management, memory management, input and output management, and system administration.

Process Management

In operating system terms, a **process**, also called a **task**, is a program or part of a program that can be executed (run) separately. Different methods of managing processes include single tasking, multitasking, and multiprocessing (Figure 8-3).

Single Tasking Single tasking operating systems allow only one user to run one program at one time. Single tasking operating systems were the first type of operating systems developed; they still are used on some personal computers today. If you are working on a personal computer with a single tasking operating system, you can load only one application, such as a spreadsheet, into memory. If you want to work on another application, such as word processing, you must exit the spreadsheet application and load the word processing application into memory.

Multitasking Multitasking operating systems allow the computer to work on more than one process or task at a time. Multitasking operating systems used on personal computers usually support a single user running multiple programs at one time. The multitasking operating systems used on larger computers such as servers, minicomputers, and mainframes, usually are **multiuser timesharing** operating systems that allow multiple users to run the same program at one time. A World Wide Web search engine server, for example, would use a multiuser timesharing operating system to allow hundreds of users to enter search requests at one time.

inCyber
For a description of multitasking, visit the Discovering Computers Chapter 8 inCyber page (http://www.scsite.com/dc/ch8/incyber.htm) and click Multitasking.

Operating System Process Management

Single Tasking:	Single user can run one program at a time
Multitasking:	Multiple programs can run
Context switching	User switches back and forth between programs
Cooperative multitasking	Programs switch when they reach a logical break point
Preemptive multitasking	Operating system switches programs based on allocated amount of time and priority
Multiprocessing:	Multiple CPUs
Asymmetric multiprocessing	Tasks assigned to specific CPUs; each CPU has its own memory
Symmetric multiprocessing	Tasks assigned to available CPUs; CPUs share memory

Figure 8-3
Operating systems divide work to be done into processes or tasks. This table summarizes the different methods operating systems use to manage processes.

Multitasking is accomplished in three ways: context switching, cooperative multitasking, and preemptive multitasking.

With **context switching**, multiple processes can be open but only one process is active. A context switch happens when one process relinquishes control of the CPU (stops executing) and another starts. For example, suppose you have two windows open, one with a word processing document and the other with a spreadsheet. As you switch back and forth between these applications, the operating system suspends activity on one task to allow you to work on the other. The operating system saves information about the currently running process so it can restart the process later from exactly where it left off.

With **cooperative multitasking**, multiple processes switch back and forth automatically when they reach logical break points, such as waiting for input. This method of multitasking relies on the processes to relinquish control to other processes. If the processes of one application require substantially more CPU time than those of other applications, problems can arise. Programs must be designed to cooperate in order to work together effectively in this environment.

With **preemptive multitasking**, the operating system prioritizes the processes to be performed and assigns a set amount of CPU time for the execution of each process. Certain processes, such as keyboard input or mouse movement, are given higher priority than other processes, such as sending data to the printer. Every few milliseconds, the CPU evaluates the processes waiting to be executed and chooses the one with the highest priority. This process then is assigned one or more increments of CPU time called a **time slice** (Figure 8-4). When the process finishes its work or the assigned time slice expires, the CPU executes the next highest priority process. If two or more processes have the same priority, such as two users inputting data at the same time, the CPU executes the process that was least recently worked on. Eventually, each process receives a time slice and is executed. Unless the system has a heavy workload, you may not even be aware that your program process was set aside temporarily. Before you notice a delay, the operating system has allocated your program process another time slice and processing continues.

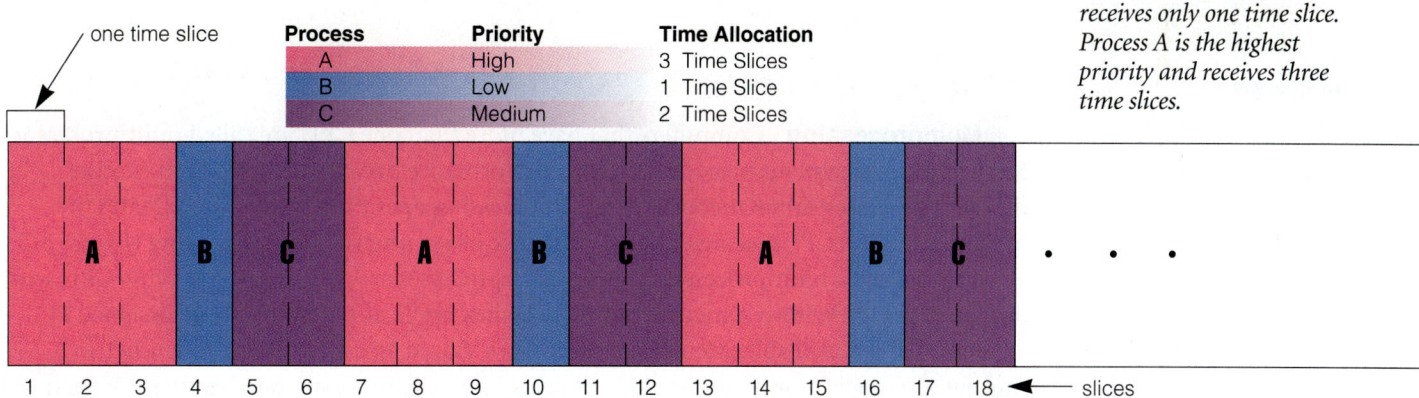

Figure 8-4
A time slice is a brief amount of CPU time given to a process by the operating system. Higher priority (more important) processes receive more consecutive slices than lower priority applications. In this example, process B is the lowest priority, thus it receives only one time slice. Process A is the highest priority and receives three time slices.

Process	Priority	Time Allocation
A	High	3 Time Slices
B	Low	1 Time Slice
C	Medium	2 Time Slices

Some multitasking operating systems permit **multithreading**, which essentially is multitasking within a single program. A **thread** is the smallest amount of program code that can be executed; each thread contains a different action or command. Multithreading allows multiple threads to execute simultaneously within the same program, which frees the program to continue accepting commands (threads). You can continue entering commands without waiting until the previous command is finished processing. Your computer thus seems to run faster.

The terms foreground and background often are used to explain a process's priority in a multitasking operating system. A process is in the **foreground** if it is the currently active process or the process with the highest priority. A process is in the **background** if it has been suspended or has a lower priority.

ASYMMETRIC MULTIPROCESSING

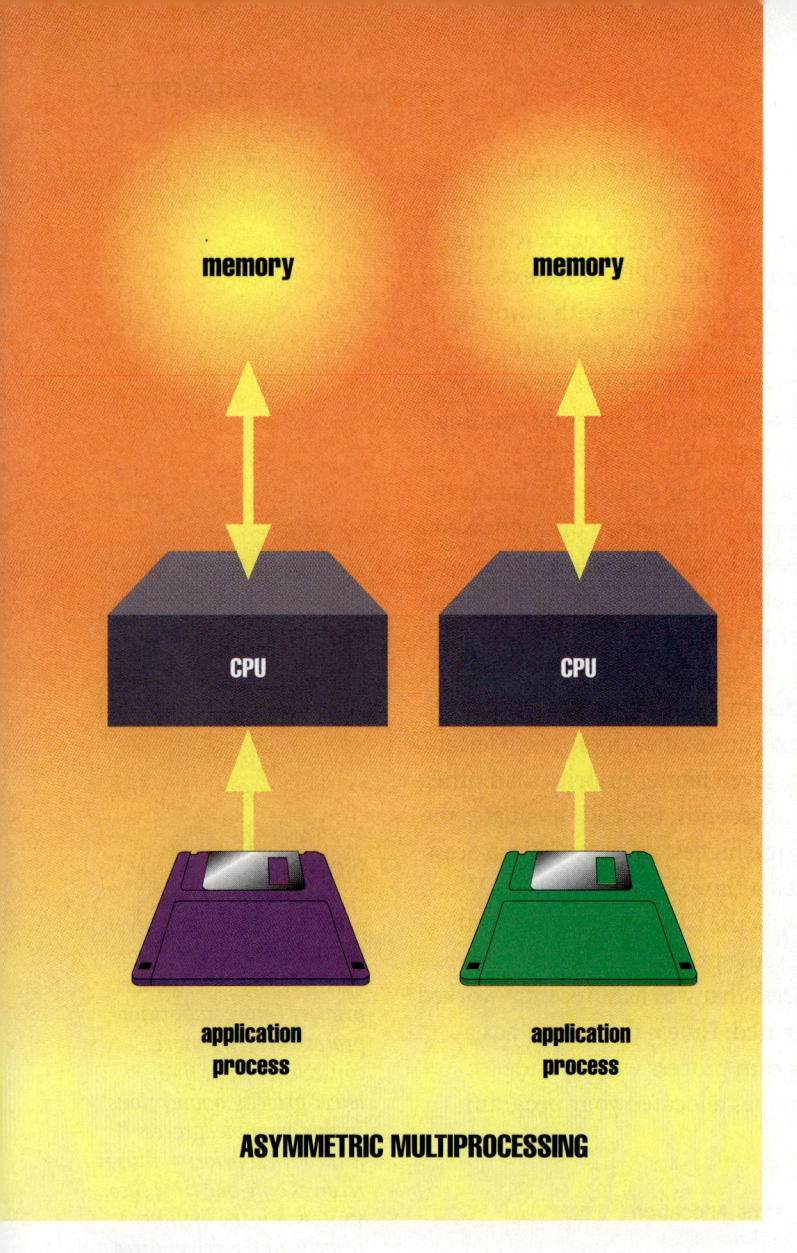

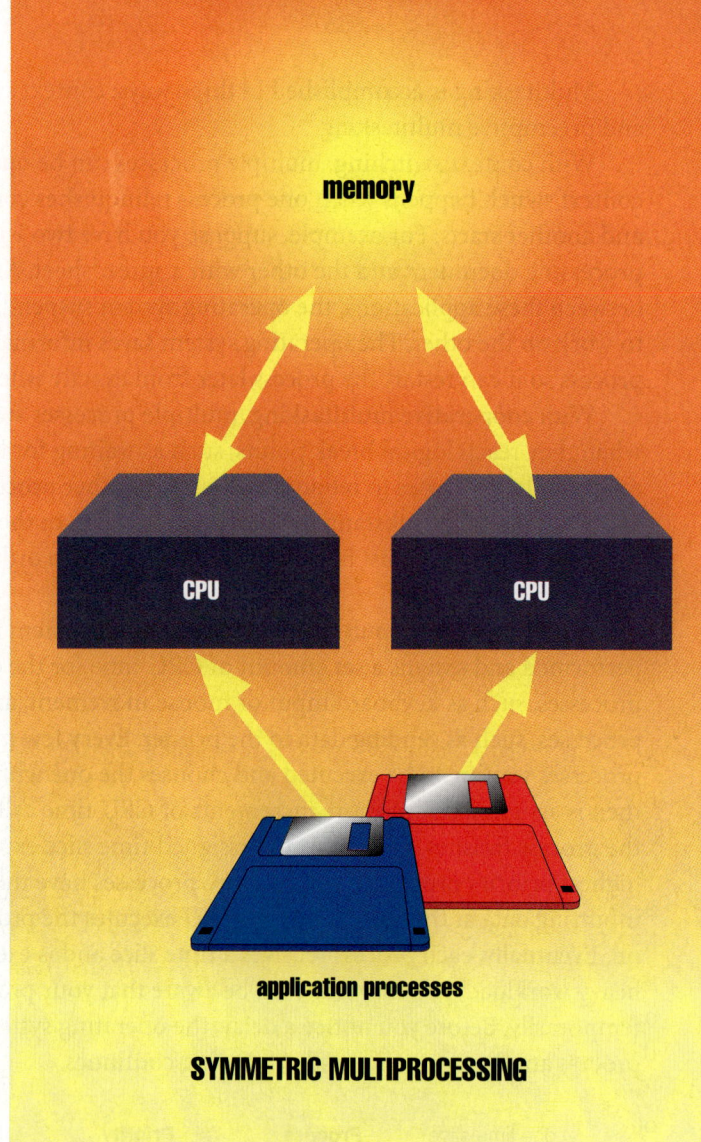

SYMMETRIC MULTIPROCESSING

Figure 8-5
In asymmetric multiprocessing, application processes are assigned to a specific CPU that has its own memory. In symmetric multiprocessing, application processes are assigned to the first available CPU. Memory is shared by all of the CPUs.

Multiprocessing Computers that have more than one CPU are called **multiprocessors**. Multiprocessing systems provide increased performance because the CPUs can execute different processes simultaneously. A **multiprocessing operating system** coordinates the operations of the CPUs, using either asymmetric or symmetric multiprocessing (Figure 8-5). With **asymmetric multiprocessing**, application processes are assigned to a specific CPU with its own memory. With **symmetric multiprocessing**, application processes are assigned to whatever CPU is available. Memory, as needed, is shared among the CPUs. Symmetric multiprocessing is more complex, but achieves a higher processing rate because the operating system has more flexibility in assigning processes to available CPUs.

A unique advantage of multiprocessing systems is that, if one CPU fails, the operating system can shift work to the remaining CPUs. As discussed in Chapter 3, some multiprocessor systems have multiple CPUs designed into a single chip, while others have physically separate CPUs. A system with separate CPUs can serve as a **fault-tolerant computer**; that is, one that can continue to operate even if one of its components fails. Fault-tolerant computers are built with duplicate, or redundant, components such as CPUs, memory, input and output controllers, and disk drives. If any one of these components fail, the system continues to operate using the duplicate component. Fault-tolerant computers are used for airline reservation systems, communications networks, bank teller machines, and other systems that are of critical importance and must be operational at all times.

Memory Management

During processing, some areas of memory are used to store the operating system kernel, application program instructions, and data waiting to be processed. Other areas of memory are used temporarily for calculations, sorting, and other intermediate results. It is the operating system's job to allocate, or assign, each of these items to an area of memory. Data that has just been read into memory from an input device and data that is waiting to be sent to an output device is stored in areas of memory called **buffers**. The operating system assigns the buffers a location in memory and manages the data that is stored in them.

Operating systems also allocate at least some portion of memory for fixed areas called **partitions** (Figure 8-6). Some operating systems allocate all memory for partitions; others allocate only some memory for partitions and use the partitions to store only the kernel and the data held in buffers.

Another way of allocating memory is called virtual memory management, or virtual storage. **Virtual memory management** increases the amount of memory the operating system can use by allocating a set amount of disk space to be used to store items during processing, in addition to the existing memory. The amount of disk space allocated for use as memory is sometimes called the **swap file**.

Virtual memory management is used with multitasking operating systems to maximize the number of programs that can use memory at one time. Without virtual memory management, the operating system loads an entire program into memory during execution. With virtual memory management, the operating system loads only the portion of the program that currently is being used into memory. The most common way operating systems perform virtual memory management is by using a process called paging.

With **paging**, a fixed number of bytes, called a **page**, is transferred from the disk to memory each time data or program instructions are needed. The size of a page, or *frame*, generally ranges from 512 to 4,000 bytes; the exact page size is determined by the operating system. Each time data or instructions are needed, the operating system transfers a page into memory. The operating system continues to bring pages into memory until the

Figure 8-6
Operating systems keep track of programs and their related data by assigning them to a portion of memory called a partition.

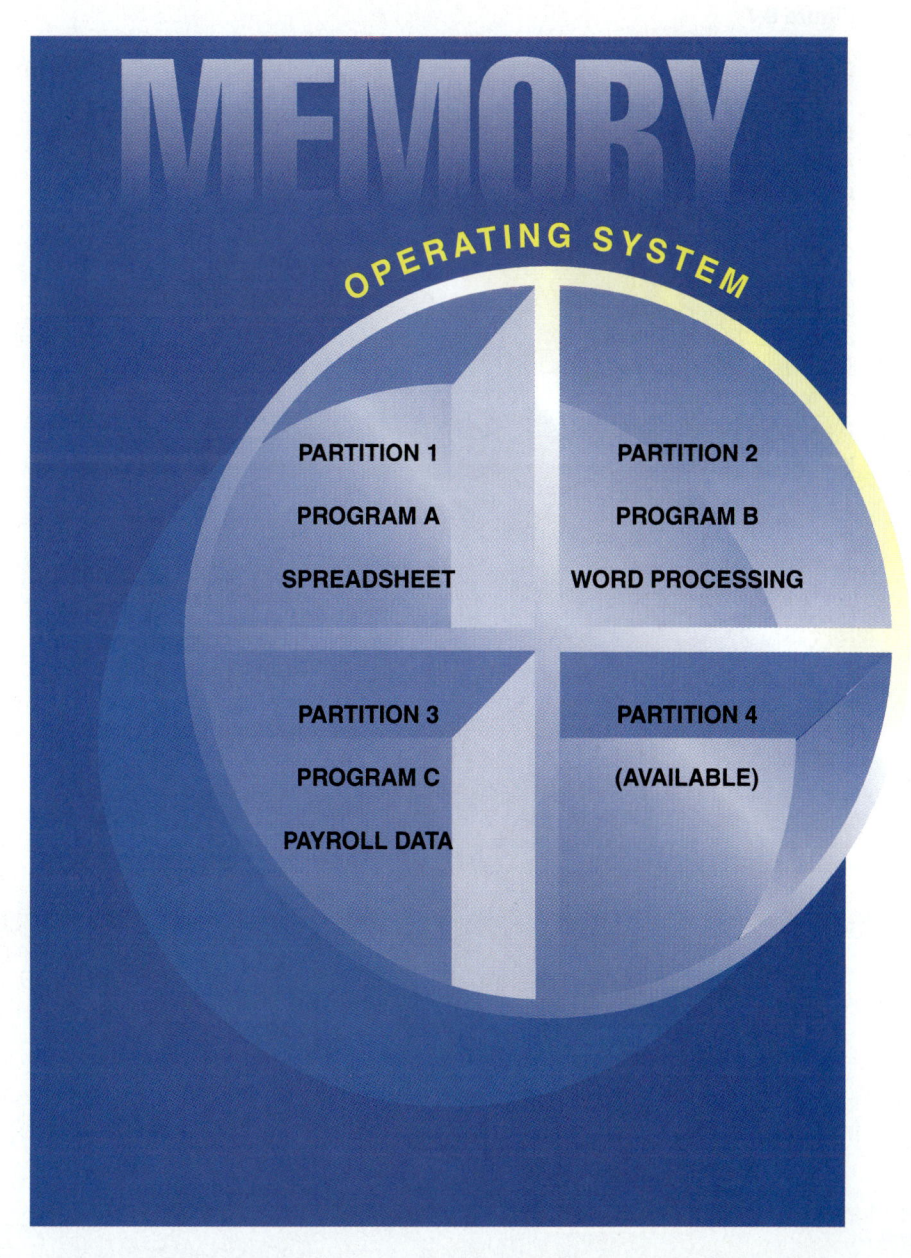

MEMORY

OPERATING SYSTEM

PARTITION 1
PROGRAM A
SPREADSHEET

PARTITION 2
PROGRAM B
WORD PROCESSING

PARTITION 3
PROGRAM C
PAYROLL DATA

PARTITION 4
(AVAILABLE)

area reserved for pages is full. If additional pages are required, the operating system makes room for them by writing one or more of the pages currently in memory back to the disk. This process is referred to as **swapping** (Figure 8-7). The operating system usually swaps the least recently used page back to the disk.

Input and Output Management

At any given time, a computer has to handle many different input and output processes. Two input devices, for example, might be sending data to the computer at the same time that the CPU is sending data to an output or storage device. The operating system is responsible for managing these input and output processes.

The operating system manages these processes differently, depending on the device. If an output device, such as a tape drive, is allocated to a specific user or application, the operating system has to manage input and output requests from only one user or application. If a device such as a disk drive is allocated to multiple users and applications, the operating system has to monitor and prioritize requests from multiple users and applications. The operating system keeps track of disk read and write requests, stores these requests in buffers along with the associated data for write requests, and usually processes them sequentially.

Figure 8-7
With virtual memory management, the operating system expands the amount of memory to include disk space. Data and program instructions are transferred in fixed amounts called pages. Pages are transferred to and from memory and disk as needed. To make room in memory for a new page, the least recently used page is swapped back to the disk or swap file.

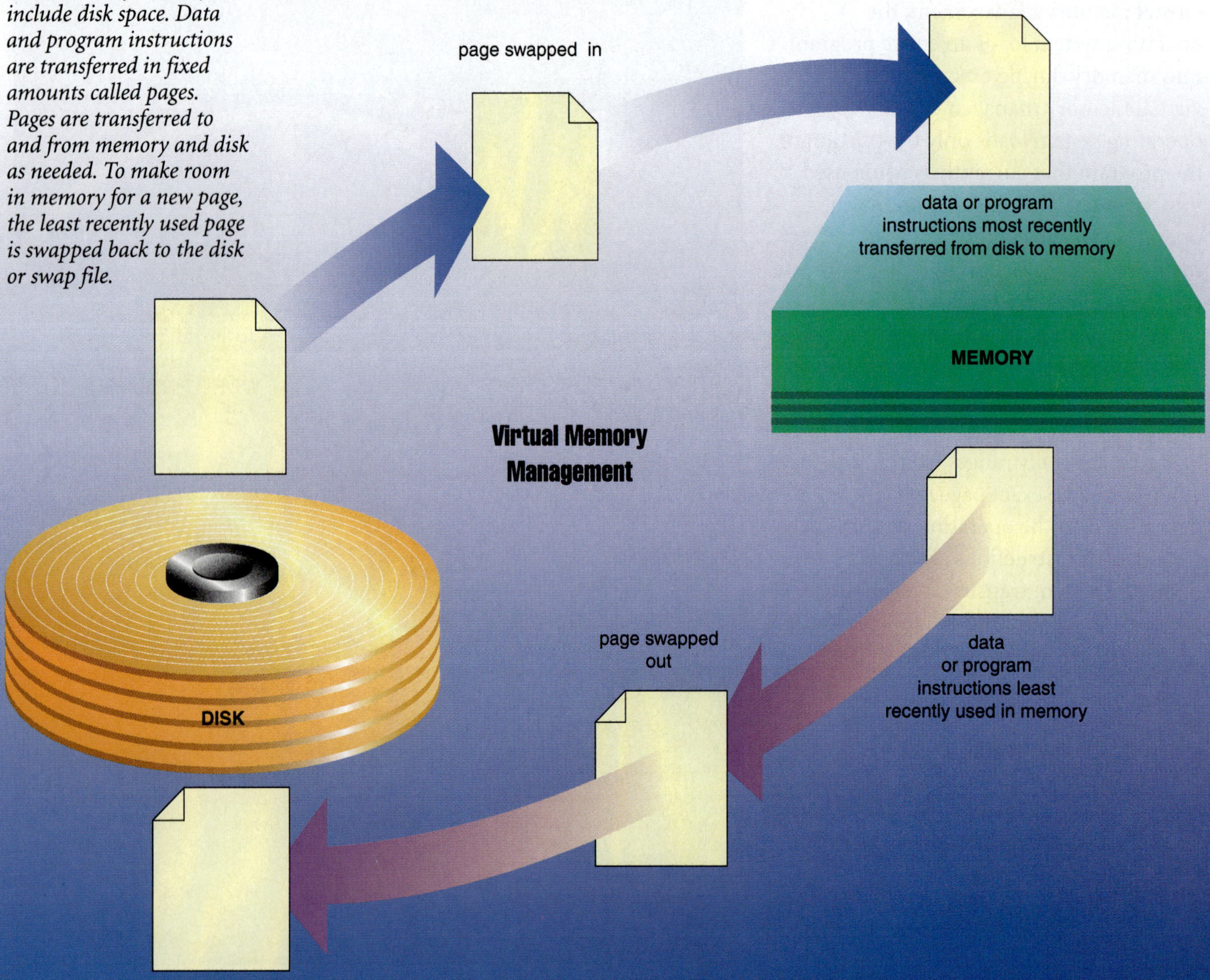

Virtual Memory Management

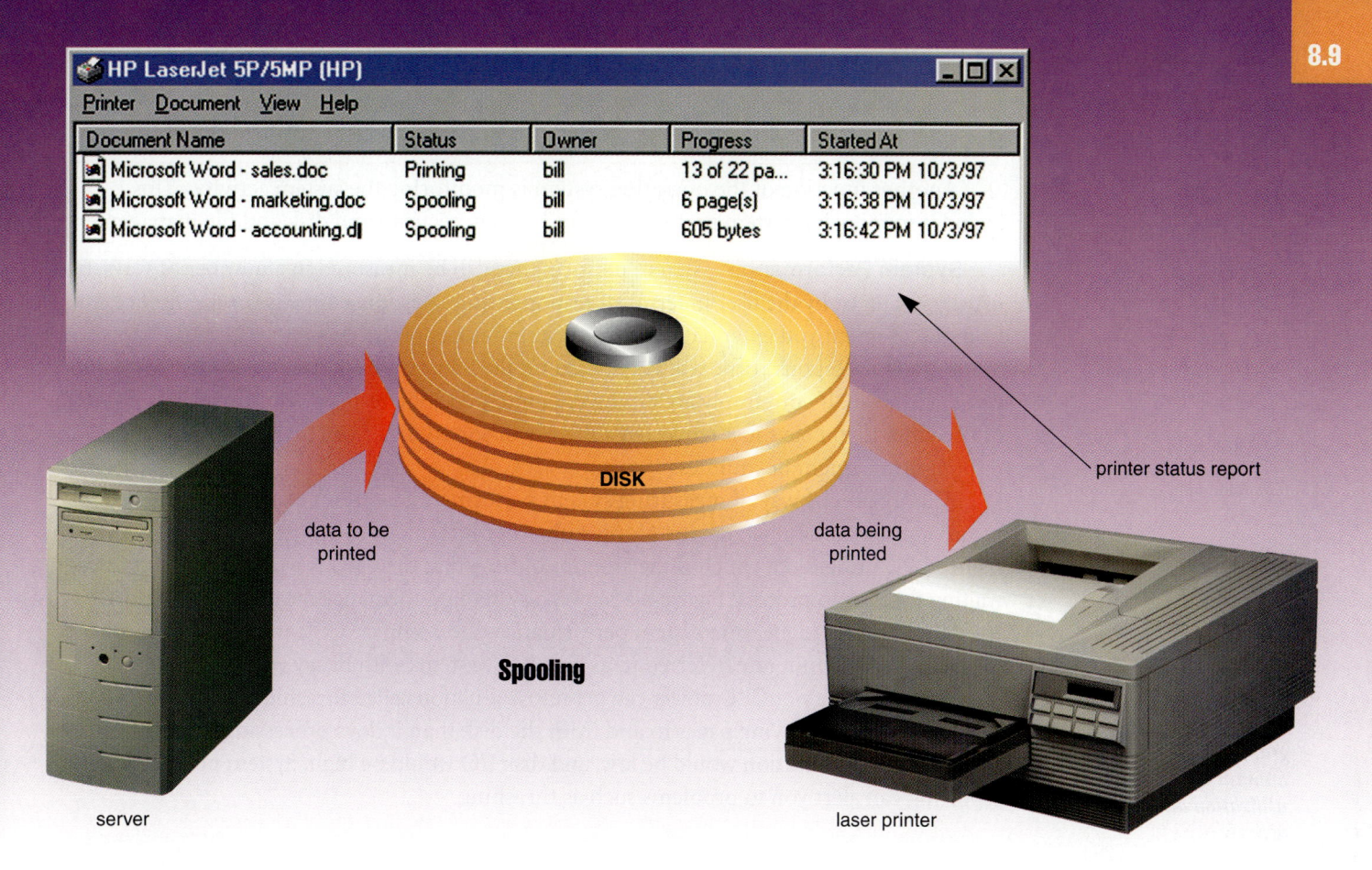

Figure 8-8
Spooling increases both CPU and printer efficiency by writing reports to the disk before they are printed. Writing to the disk is much faster than writing directly to the printer. After the reports are written to the disk, the CPU can begin processing other programs while the report is printing. A printer status report shows the reports in the print spool (the reports waiting to be printed).

Because printers are relatively slow devices compared to other computer system devices, the operating system uses a technique called spooling to increase printer efficiency. With **spooling** (Figure 8-8), a report is first written (saved) to the disk before it is printed. Writing to the disk is much faster than writing to the printer. For example, a report that averages one-half hour of printing time may take only one minute to write to the disk. After the report is written to the disk, the CPU is available to process other programs. The report saved on the disk can be printed at a later time or, on a multitasking operating system, a print program is started. The print program processes the **print spool**, which are the reports on the disk waiting to be printed, while other programs are running. The terms *spool* and *spooling* come from the idea that storing reports temporarily on the disk is like winding thread onto a spool so it can be unwound at a later time.

Because hardware devices use different commands to input and output data, the operating system uses programs called **device drivers** to communicate with each device. The mouse, keyboard, monitor, printer, and other peripheral devices all require separate device drivers. If one of these devices is changed or a new hardware device is added to the system, a new device driver is needed. Installation of new devices is easier if the device and the operating system support Plug and Play technology. With **Plug and Play technology**, the operating system recognizes any new devices and assists in the installation of the device by automatically loading the necessary driver programs and checking for conflicts with other devices. Because they are specific to a hardware device, most device drivers are supplied by the hardware device manufacturer. Some device drivers, especially for common devices such as the mouse, come with the operating system.

inCyber

For reviews of Plug and Play technology, visit the Discovering Computers Chapter 8 inCyber page (http://www.scsite.com/dc/ch8/incyber.htm) and click Plug and Play.

System Administration

Another function of the operating system is monitoring the system activity. This includes monitoring system performance and system security and disk and file management.

System Performance System performance can be measured in a number of ways, but usually is gauged by the user in terms of response time. **Response time** is the amount of time from the moment you enter data until the computer responds.

A system's response time will vary based on the data you have entered or the command you have issued. If you simply are typing data into a file, the response time usually is less than one second. If you have just requested a display of sorted data from several files, however, the response time might be minutes.

A more precise way of measuring system performance is to run a program designed to record and report system activity. Along with other information, these programs usually report **CPU utilization**, which is the amount of time that the CPU is working and not idle, waiting for data to process. Figure 8-9 shows a system performance measurement report.

Another way to measure system performance is to compare CPU utilization with the disk input and output rate, referred to as disk I/O. Systems with heavy workloads and insufficient memory or CPU power can get into a situation called **thrashing**, where the system spends more time moving pages to and from the disk than it does processing data. In this situation, CPU utilization would be low, and disk I/O would be high. System performance reporting can alert you to problems such as thrashing.

Figure 8-9
Most operating systems come with programs that help you monitor system performance. This screen, from the Windows 95 operating system, graphically displays the amount of CPU utilization and disk activity.

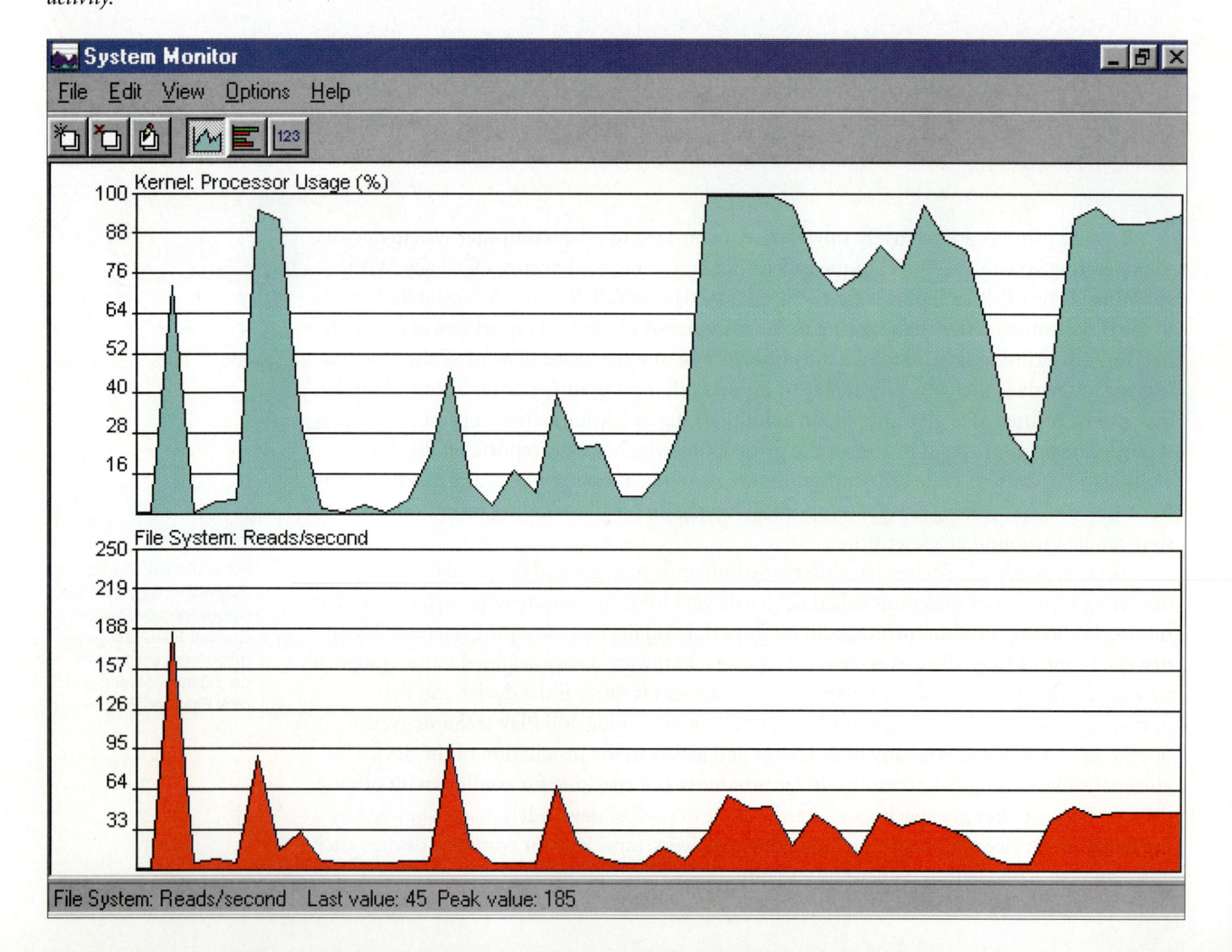

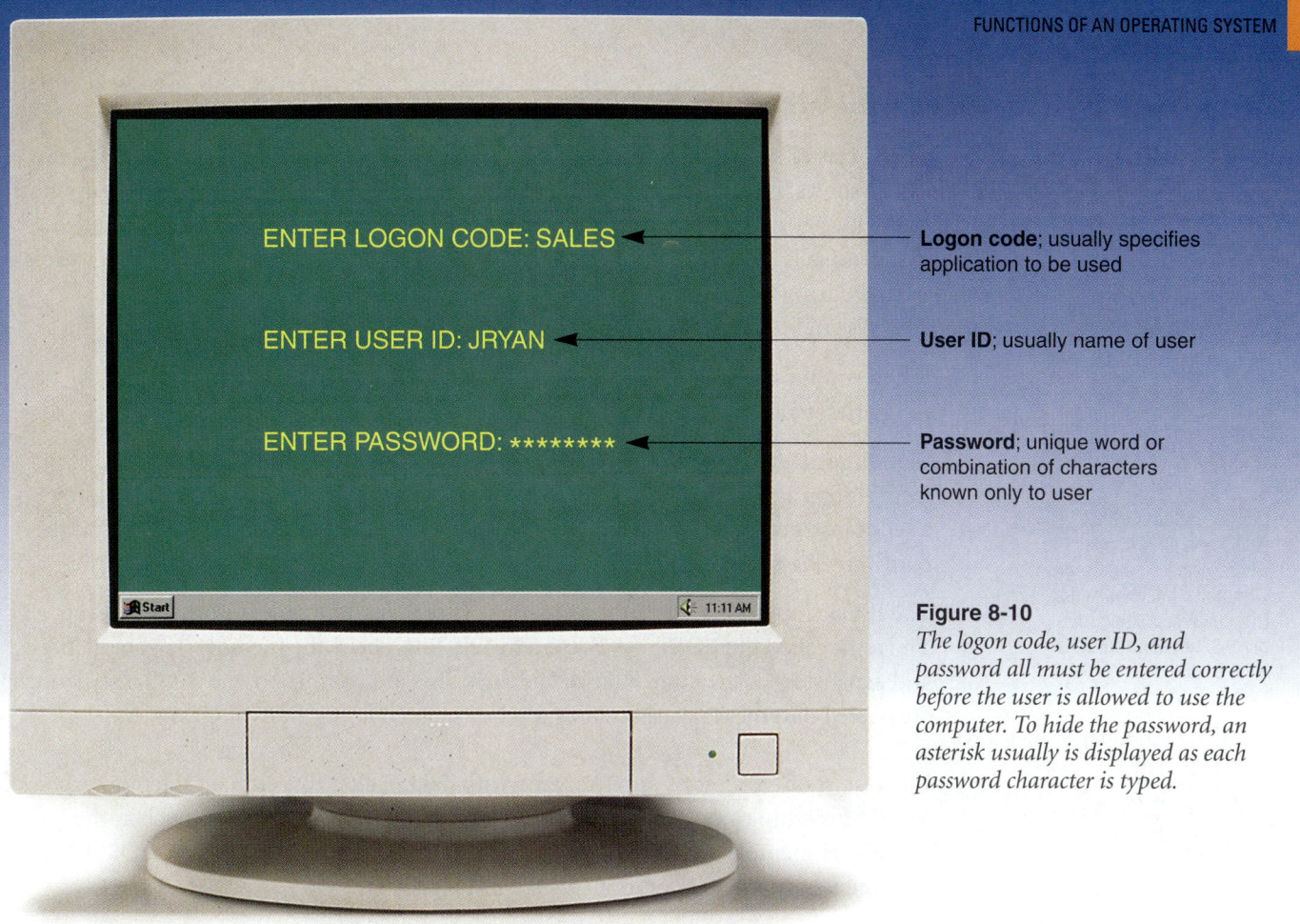

FUNCTIONS OF AN OPERATING SYSTEM **8.11**

ENTER LOGON CODE: SALES ◄──────── **Logon code**; usually specifies application to be used

ENTER USER ID: JRYAN ◄──────── **User ID**; usually name of user

ENTER PASSWORD: ******** ◄──────── **Password**; unique word or combination of characters known only to user

Figure 8-10
The logon code, user ID, and password all must be entered correctly before the user is allowed to use the computer. To hide the password, an asterisk usually is displayed as each password character is typed.

System Security Most multiuser operating systems allow each user to have a logon code, a user ID, and a password. Each is a word or series of characters (Figure 8-10). A **logon code** usually identifies the application that will be used, such as accounting, sales, or manufacturing. A **user ID** identifies the user, such as Jeffrey Ryan or Mary Gonzales. The **password** usually is confidential; often it is known only to you and the computer system administrator. As you enter your password, most systems will hide the actual password characters by displaying a series of asterisks.

Before you are allowed to use a system or an application, you must enter your logon code, user ID, and password correctly. Your entries are compared with entries stored in an authorization file. If they do not match, you are denied access. Both successful and unsuccessful logon attempts often are recorded in a file so management can review who is using or attempting to use the system. These logs also can be used to allocate computer system expenses based on the percentage of system use by an organization's various departments.

Disk and File Management All operating systems contain programs that perform functions related to disk and file management. Some of these functions include formatting hard and floppy disks, listing files stored on the system, deleting files from a disk, copying files from one storage device to another, renaming stored files, and creating folders and directories to organize files.

inCyber
For a list of security tools available on the Internet, visit the Discovering Computers Chapter 8 inCyber page (http://www.scsite.com/dc/ch8/incyber.htm) and click Security System.

Loading an Operating System

The process of loading an operating system into memory is called **booting** the system. Figure 8-11 shows information that is displayed during this process. The actual information displayed will vary depending on the make of the computer and the equipment installed. The boot process is similar for large and small computer systems. The following steps explain what occurs during the boot process on a personal computer using the Windows 95 operating system.

1. When you turn on your computer, the power supply distributes current to the motherboard and the other devices located in the system unit case.

2. The surge of electricity causes the CPU chip to reset itself and look to the BIOS chip for instructions on how to proceed. **BIOS**, which stands for **Basic Input/Output System**, is a set of instructions that provides the interface between the operating system and the hardware devices. The BIOS is stored in a read-only memory (ROM) chip.

3. The BIOS chip begins a set of tests to make sure the equipment is working correctly. The tests, called the **POST**, for **Power On Self Test**, check the memory, keyboard, buses, and expansion cards. After some of the early tests are completed, the BIOS instructions are copied into memory where they can be executed faster than in ROM.

4. The results of POST tests are compared with data in a CMOS chip on the motherboard. The CMOS chip contains key information about system components, such as the amount of memory and number and type of disk drives available. The CMOS chip is updated whenever new components are installed.

5. After the POST tests are completed successfully, the BIOS begins looking for the boot program that will load the operating system. Usually, it first looks in floppy disk drive A.

inCyber

For information about BIOS and CMOS, visit the Discovering Computers Chapter 8 inCyber page (http://www.scsite.com/dc/ch8/incyber.htm) and click BIOS.

BIOS version number and copyright notice

total amount of memory displays after memory test

device detected and tested

message indicating Windows 95 operating system beginning to load

sound card and CD-ROM device drivers loaded

If an operating system disk is not loaded in drive A, the BIOS looks in drive C, which is the drive letter usually given to the first hard disk drive.

6. The boot program is loaded into memory and executed. The boot program then begins loading the resident portion, or kernel, of the operating system into memory.

7. The operating system then loads system configuration information. System configuration information is contained in several files called the registry. The **registry** files contain information on which hardware and software is installed and individual user preferences for mouse speed, passwords, and other user-specific information. In earlier versions of the Windows operating system, hardware and software configuration information was contained in the **CONFIG.SYS** and **AUTOEXEC.BAT** files and other files ending in the letters *ini*.

8. For each hardware device identified in the registry, such as the sound card, a CD-ROM drive, or a scanner, the operating system loads a device driver program. A device driver tells the computer how to communicate with a device.

9. The remainder of the operating system is loaded and the desktop and icons display on the screen. The operating system executes programs in the Start Up folder, which contains a list of programs to start automatically when you start Windows 95.

Figure 8-11
An example of information displayed during the boot process.

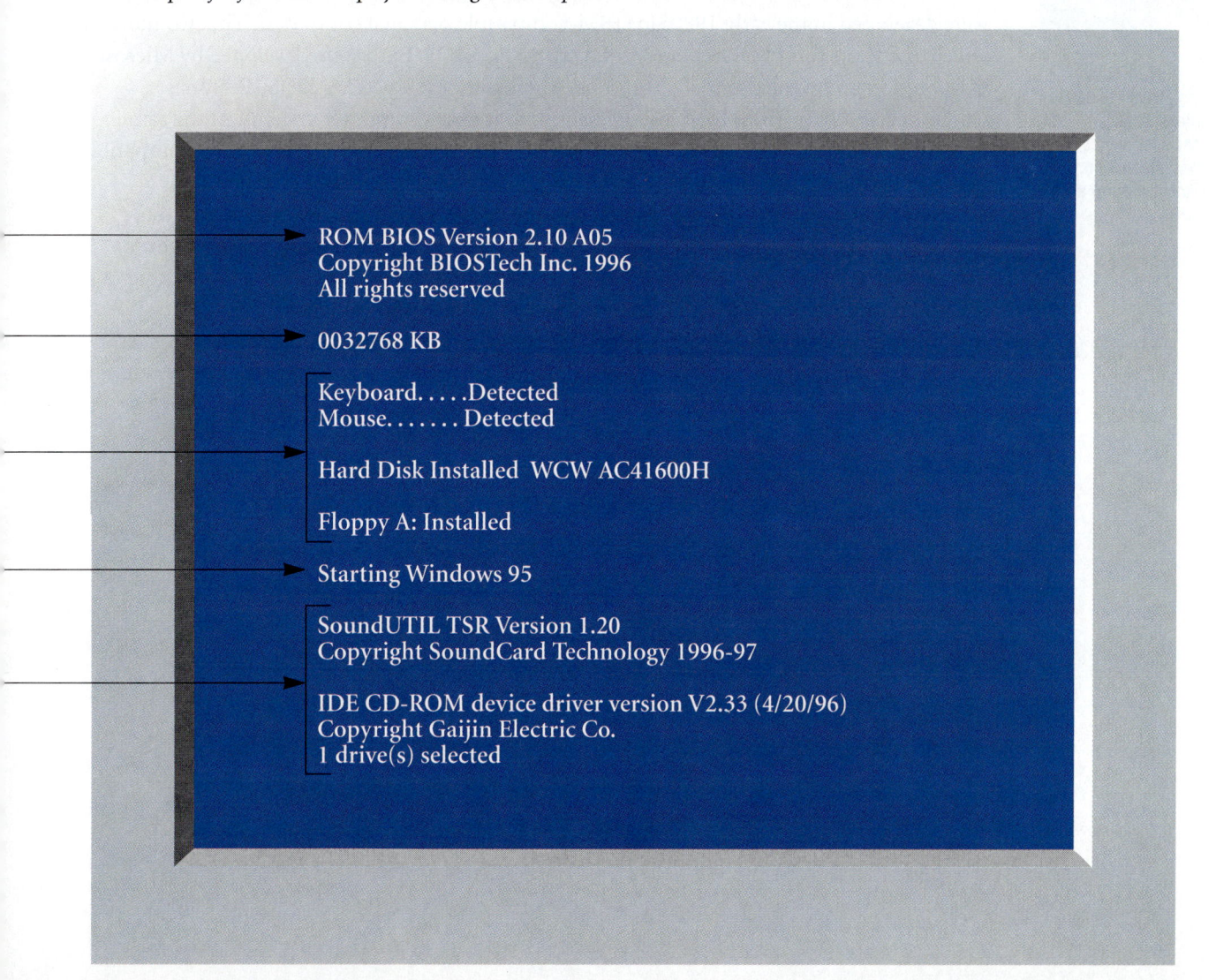

```
ROM BIOS Version 2.10 A05
Copyright BIOSTech Inc. 1996
All rights reserved

0032768 KB

Keyboard.....Detected
Mouse........Detected

Hard Disk Installed  WCW AC41600H

Floppy A: Installed

Starting Windows 95

SoundUTIL TSR Version 1.20
Copyright SoundCard Technology 1996-97

IDE CD-ROM device driver version V2.33 (4/20/96)
Copyright Gaijin Electric Co.
1 drive(s) selected
```

Popular Operating Systems

The first operating systems were developed by manufacturers specifically for the computers in their product line. These operating systems, called **proprietary operating systems**, were limited to a specific vendor or computer model. When manufacturers introduced another computer or model, they often produced an improved and different operating system. Because programs are designed to be used with a particular operating system, users who wanted to switch computer models or vendors had to convert their existing programs to run under the new operating system.

Today, however, the trend is toward **portable operating systems** that will run on many manufacturers' computers. The advantage of portable operating systems is that you can change computer models or vendors, yet retain existing software and data files, which usually represent a sizable investment in time and money.

New versions of an operating system usually will run software written for the previous version of the operating system. If an application written for the old version of the operating system can run under the new version, it is said to be **upward compatible**. If an application written for the new version of an operating system also can run under the previous version, it is said to be **downward compatible**.

The following section discusses some of the more popular operating systems.

DOS

DOS (Disk Operating System) refers to several single tasking operating systems that were developed in the early 1980s for IBM-compatible personal computers. The two more widely used versions of DOS were MS-DOS and PC-DOS. Both were developed by Microsoft Corporation and were essentially the same. Microsoft developed **PC-DOS (Personal Computer DOS)** for IBM; IBM installed and sold it on its computer systems. At the same time, Microsoft marketed and sold **MS-DOS (Microsoft DOS)** to makers of IBM-compatible personal computer systems.

New versions of DOS have been and continue to be developed. Improvements to the later versions of DOS include the capability of running with a command-line or menu-driven user interface and better memory and disk management. Because it does not offer a full graphical user interface and it cannot take full advantage of modern 32-bit microprocessors, DOS no longer is a top-selling operating system. DOS does, however, still have a large installed base of users. An estimated 70 million computers used some version of DOS during its peak.

---

inCyber

For information about DOS, visit the Discovering Computers Chapter 8 inCyber page (http://www.scsite.com/dc/ch8/incyber.htm) and click DOS.

Windows 3.x

Windows 3.x refers to three versions of Microsoft's Windows operating system: Windows 3.0, Windows 3.1, and Windows 3.11. Sometimes, these versions also are referred to as Microsoft Windows or simply Windows (with a capital W). **Windows 3.0** was the first widely used graphical user interface for IBM-compatible personal computers. **Windows 3.1** (Figure 8-12) provided a number of improvements to version 3.0. Windows 3.11, also called **Windows for Workgroups**, is a networking version of Windows 3.1. Although the 3.x versions commonly are referred to as operating systems, actually they are operating environments. An **operating environment** is a graphical user interface that works in combination with an operating system to simplify its use. The operating environment of Windows 3.x, for example, was designed to work with DOS, which is the actual operating system. Common features of an operating environment (such as Windows) include support for mouse usage, icons, and pull-down menus. Windows 3.x also supports cooperative multitasking, so you can have several applications open at the same time.

Closely related to operating environments are operating system shell programs. Like an operating environment, a **shell** acts as an interface between you and the operating system. Operating system shells, however, usually do not support applications windowing or graphics and have only a limited number of utility functions such as file maintenance.

inCyber

For links to resources for Windows 3.x, visit the Discovering Computers Chapter 8 inCyber page (http://www.scsite.com/dc/ch8/incyber.htm) and click Windows 3.x.

Figure 8-12
Microsoft Windows 3.1 is a widely used graphical user interface for IBM-compatible personal computers.

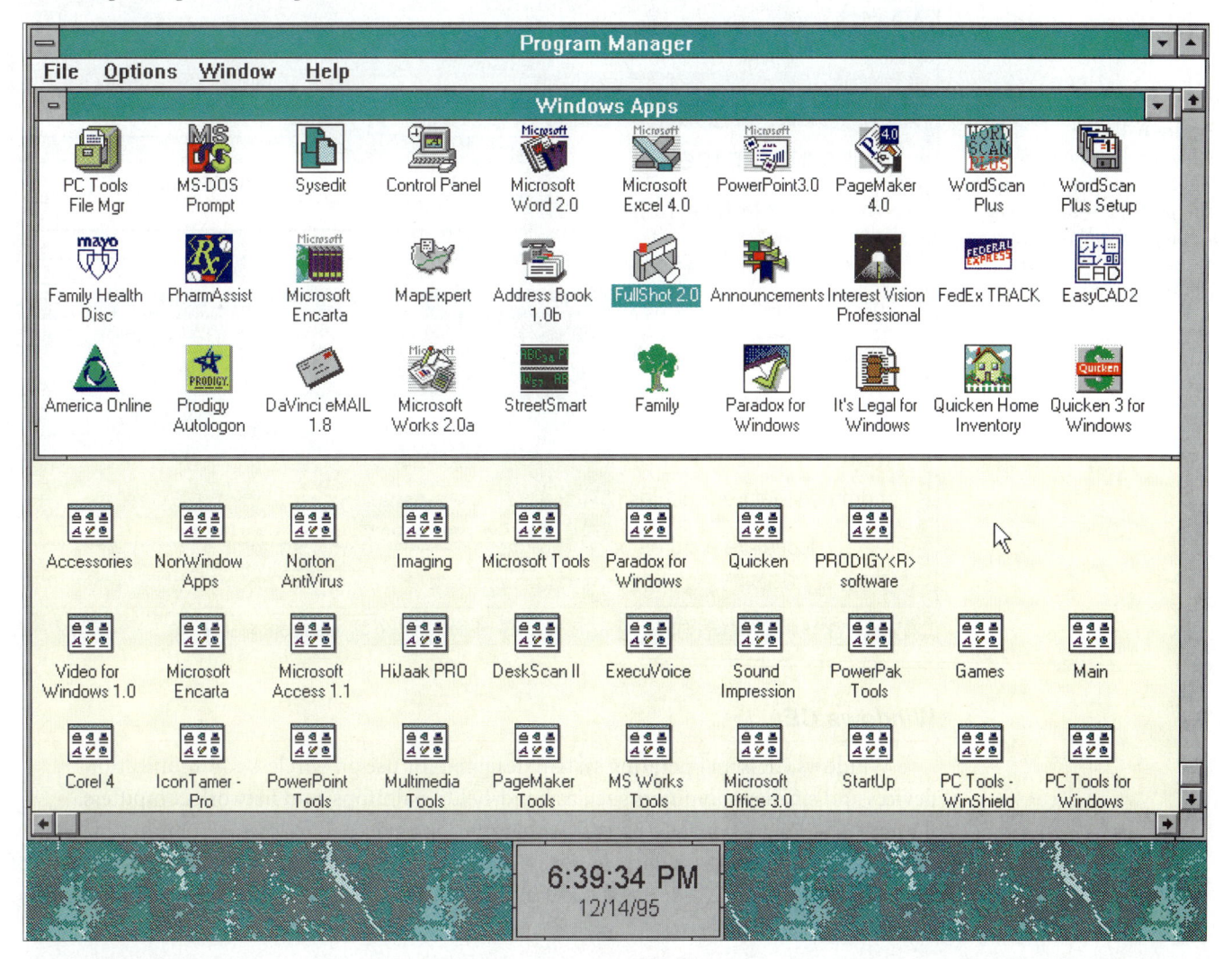

Windows 95 and Beyond

Instead of naming the next major version of its operating system Windows 4.0, Microsoft named it Windows 95, indicating the year it was released. **Windows 95**, also referred to as **Win 95**, is a true operating system and not an operating environment as were the 3.x versions of Windows. Windows 95 thus does not require a separate version of DOS, although some DOS features are included for compatibility. One advantage of Windows 95 is its improved graphical user interface, which makes working with files and programs easier than earlier versions (Figure 8-13). Another advantage is that most programs run faster under Windows 95, because it is written to take advantage of newer 32-bit processors and supports preemptive multitasking. For older, 16-bit programs, Win 95 also supports cooperative multitasking. Windows 95 includes support for peer-to-peer networking and e-mail.

Newer versions of Windows support several different user interfaces, including the traditional Windows interface and new, browser-like interfaces. These new interfaces combine the functionality of Windows with a Web browser and a multimedia Web page. Icons work like hyperlinks; a small window displays television-style news; and an animated ticker provides stock updates, news, or other information. You can display three different files at once in small windows, called **frames**, and move through files by clicking browser-like toolbar buttons. You also can use the interface as a regular Web browser to view Web pages, create Web shortcuts that are updated automatically, and more.

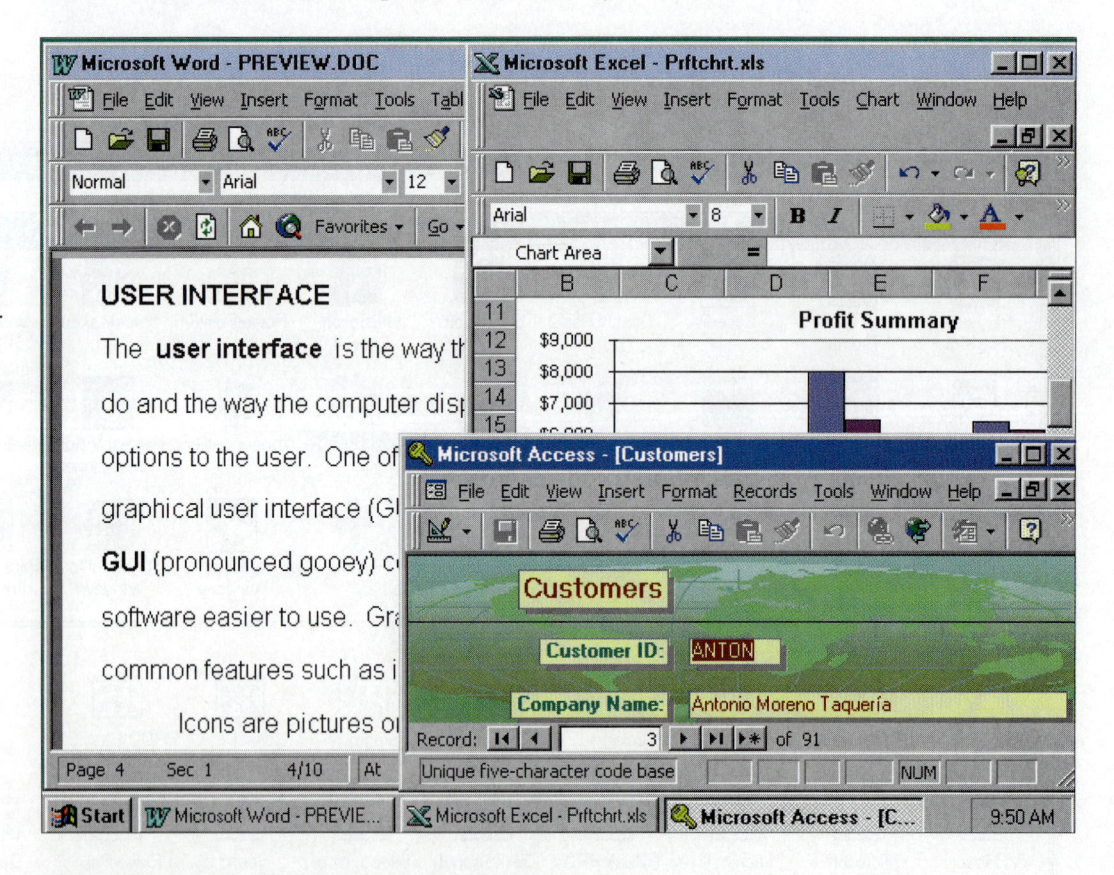

> **inCyber**
>
> For a comprehensive source of Windows 95 tools and information, visit the Discovering Computers Chapter 8 inCyber page (http://www.scsite.com/dc/ch8/incyber.htm) and click Windows 95.

Figure 8-13
Microsoft Windows 95 is a sophisticated graphical user interface operating system that offers built-in peer-to-peer networking and e-mail.

Windows CE

Windows CE is an operating system designed for use on wireless communication devices and smaller computers such as hand-helds, palmtops, and network computers. Because it is designed for use on smaller computing devices, Windows CE requires little memory. On most of these devices, the Windows CE interface incorporates many elements of the Windows graphical user interface. It also has multitasking, multithreading, and e-mail and Internet capabilities.

Windows NT

Microsoft's **Windows NT** (for New Technology), also referred to as **NT**, is a sophisticated graphical user interface operating system designed for client-server networks. Like Windows 95, NT is a complete operating system, not an operating environment. Two versions of NT exist: the Server version for network servers and the Workstation version for computers connected to the network. NT uses a modular design. The central module, called the Executive, contains the kernel and implements virtual memory management, process management, and other basic operating system functions. All other operating system functions are performed by separate modules, which are started by the Executive when they are needed. Other NT features include the following:

- Capability of working with multiple CPUs using symmetric multiprocessing
- Preemptive multitasking and multithreading
- Support of most major networking communications protocols
- System performance measurement
- User and account system security

Windows NT Server also includes tools for developing Internet Web pages and operating a Web page server. Because they are more complex than other versions of Windows, both versions of Windows NT require more disk space, memory, and faster processors.

inCyber

For descriptions of Internet resources for Windows NT, visit the Discovering Computers Chapter 8 inCyber page (http://www.scsite.com/dc/ch8/incyber.htm) and click Windows NT.

Macintosh

The Apple **Macintosh** multitasking operating system was the first commercially successful graphical user interface (Figure 8-14). It was released with Macintosh computers in 1984; since then, it has set the standard for operating system ease of use and has been the model for most of the new graphical user interfaces developed for non-Macintosh systems. For most of its history, the Macintosh operating system was available only on computers manufactured by Apple. In recent years, however, Apple has licensed the operating system to other computer manufacturers. Distinctive features of the latest version of the operating system, called **MacOS**, include built-in networking support, electronic mail, and an extensive step-by-step Help system called Apple Guide.

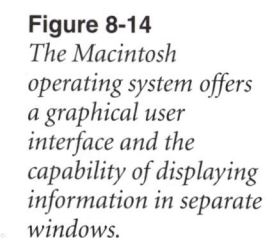

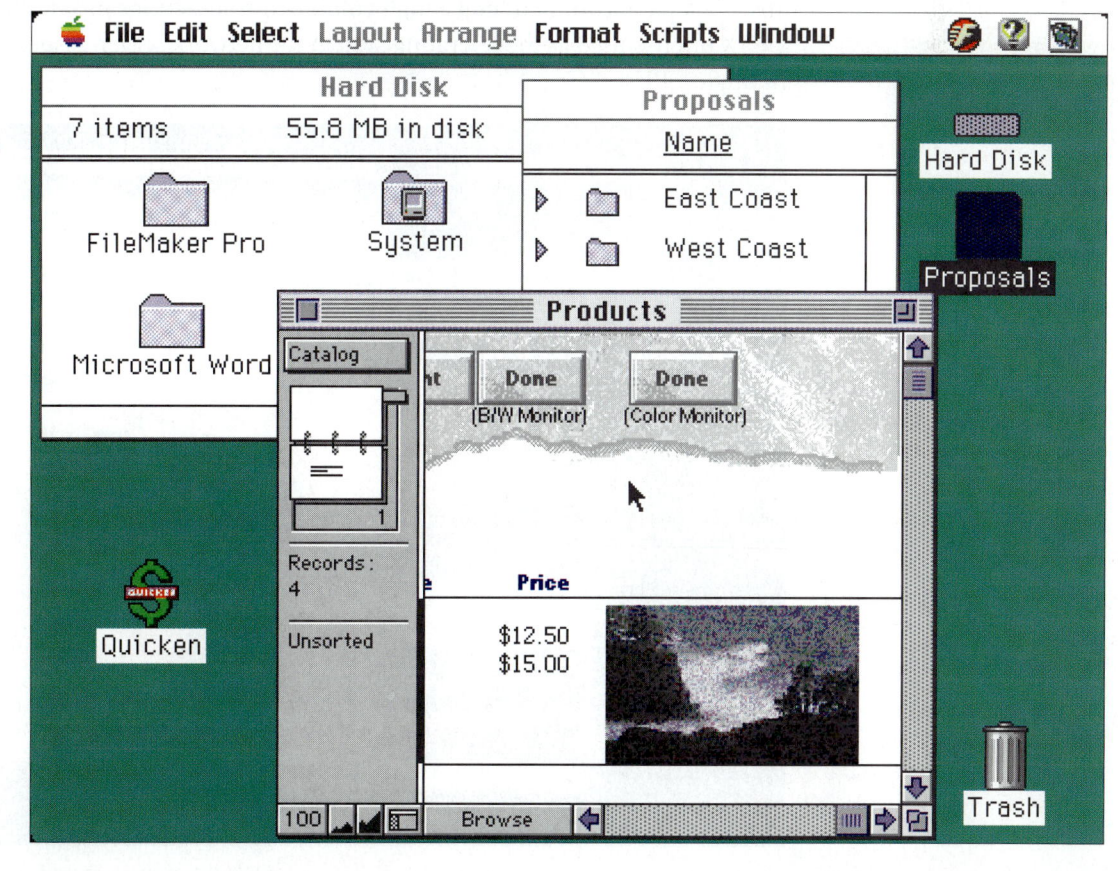

Figure 8-14
The Macintosh operating system offers a graphical user interface and the capability of displaying information in separate windows.

OS/2

OS/2 is IBM's graphical user interface operating system designed to work with 32-bit microprocessors (Figure 8-15). In addition to its capability of running programs written specifically for OS/2, the operating system also can run programs written for DOS and most Windows 3.x programs. The latest version of OS/2, called OS/2 Warp 4, includes the following features:

- Graphical user interface that displays 3-D shadowed icons
- Capability of running Java applets without a Web browser
- Capability of working with multiple CPUs using symmetric multiprocessing
- Preemptive multitasking and multithreading
- Speaker-independent voice recognition that you can use to input data and commands
- Desktop objects that allow you to connect directly to Internet documents and services

Because of IBM's long association with business computing and OS/2's strong networking support, OS/2 has been most widely used by businesses. Like Windows NT, a separate version of OS/2 exists for use on a server.

UNIX

UNIX is a multiuser, multitasking operating system developed in the early 1970s by scientists at Bell Laboratories. Because of federal regulations, Bell Labs (a subsidiary of AT&T) was prohibited from actively promoting UNIX in the commercial marketplace. Bell Labs instead licensed UNIX for a low fee to numerous colleges and universities where it obtained a wide following and was implemented on many different types of computers. After deregulation of the telephone companies in the 1980s, UNIX was licensed to many hardware and software companies. Today, a version of UNIX is available for most computers of all sizes. This widespread availability of UNIX is just one of its advantages. Another advantage is UNIX's capability of handling a high volume of transactions in a multiuser environment. UNIX often is used as the operating system for network servers, especially servers that use multiple CPUs.

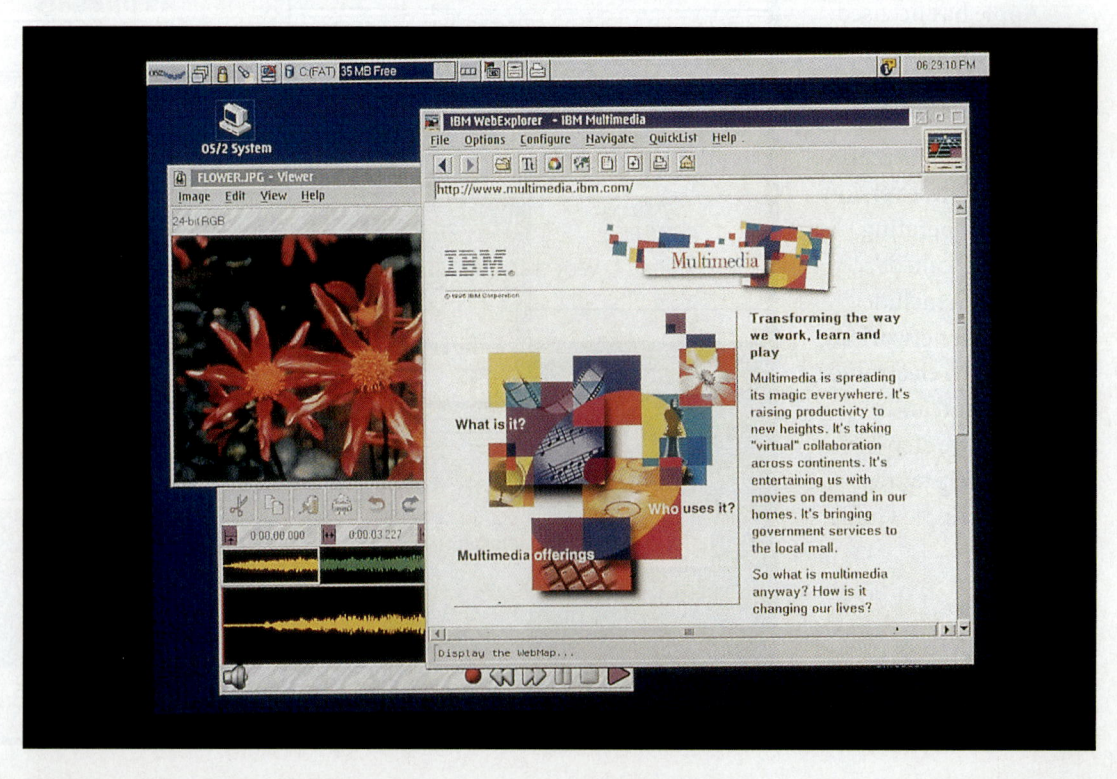

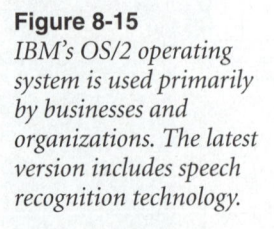

inCyber
For links to OS/2 resources on the Internet, visit the Discovering Computers Chapter 8 inCyber page (http://www.scsite.com/dc/ch8/incyber.htm) and click OS/2.

Figure 8-15
IBM's OS/2 operating system is used primarily by businesses and organizations. The latest version includes speech recognition technology.

UNIX does have some weaknesses, however. UNIX is a command-line operating system and many of its commands are difficult to remember and use. Some versions of UNIX do offer a graphical user environment to help reduce this problem. UNIX also lacks some of the system administration features offered by other operating systems. Finally, several widely used versions of UNIX exist, each of which is slightly different. To move application software from one of these UNIX versions to another, you must convert some programs.

NetWare

NetWare from Novell is a widely used network operating system designed for client-server networks. NetWare has two parts; a server portion that resides on the network server, and a client portion that resides on each client computer connected to the network. The server portion of NetWare allows you to share hardware devices attached to the server (such as a printer), as well as any files or application software stored on the server. The main job of the client portion of NetWare is to communicate with the server. Client computers also have a local operating system, such as Windows.

> **inCyber**
>
> For information on Novell NetWare, visit the Discovering Computers Chapter 8 inCyber page (http://www.scsite.com/dc/ch8/incyber.htm) and click NetWare.

Utilities

Utility programs perform specific tasks related to managing computer resources or files. Most operating systems include many utility programs. These utility programs usually handle frequently performed tasks such as copying and moving files and formatting disks. You also can purchase single, stand-alone utility programs or a package of utility programs designed to work together. These utility programs usually are improvements over the utilities that come with the operating system. A brief description of some of the tasks performed by utility programs follows:

- **File Viewer** The file management programs of some operating systems merely list the names and size of files. To view the contents of a file, you have to start an application program and open the file. Figure 8-16 shows a file viewer utility screen.

Figure 8-16
Quick View Plus is a file viewer utility that lets you quickly see the contents of a file, such as a document or graphic image, without starting an application software package.

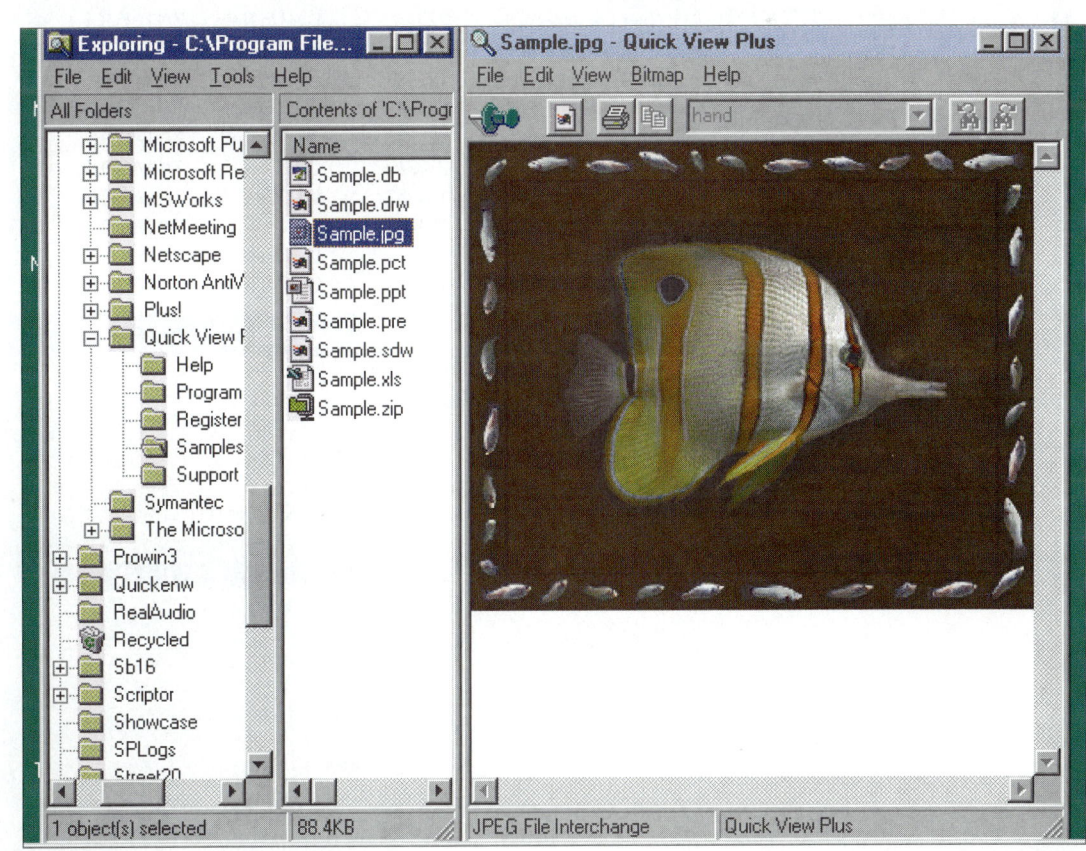

A **file viewer** identifies a file by its name and a three-character extension (the three characters after the period in the file name) and displays the text and graphic contents of a file. You can view the contents of a file without starting the related application.

- **File Conversion** Application software programs create files in many different formats, as identified by the three-character extension after the period in the file name. For example, all Microsoft Word documents have the letters *doc* after the period. **File conversion software** allows you to convert a file from one format to another so the file can be used by another application.

- **File Compression** If you download files frequently or exchange large files with others, you will benefit from **file compression software**, which reduces (compresses) the size of files. Compressed files take less room on a disk (hard drive or floppy) and require less time to download or upload. File compression software also performs decompression routines that can return a compressed file to its original size. More information on data compression can be found in Chapter 5.

- **Backup** **Backup software** allows you to copy files or your entire hard disk on tape or disk cartridges (Figure 8-17). The backup software monitors the copying process and alerts you if you need an additional disk cartridge or tape. Restore programs, which are included with backup software, reverse the process and allow you to reload the copied files to another storage medium.

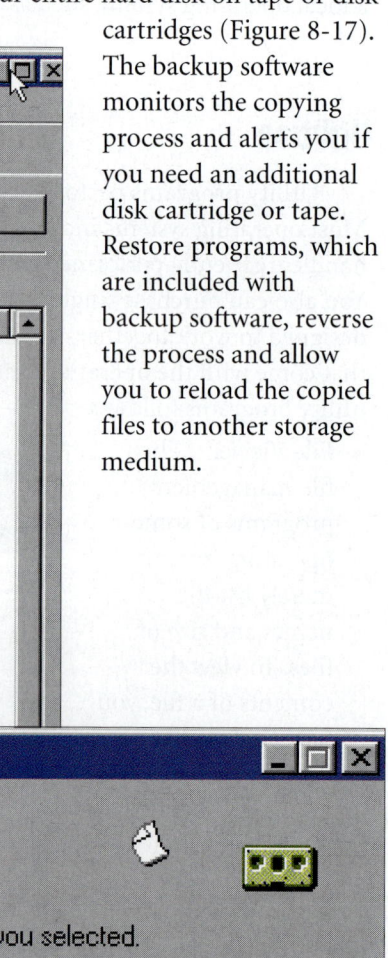

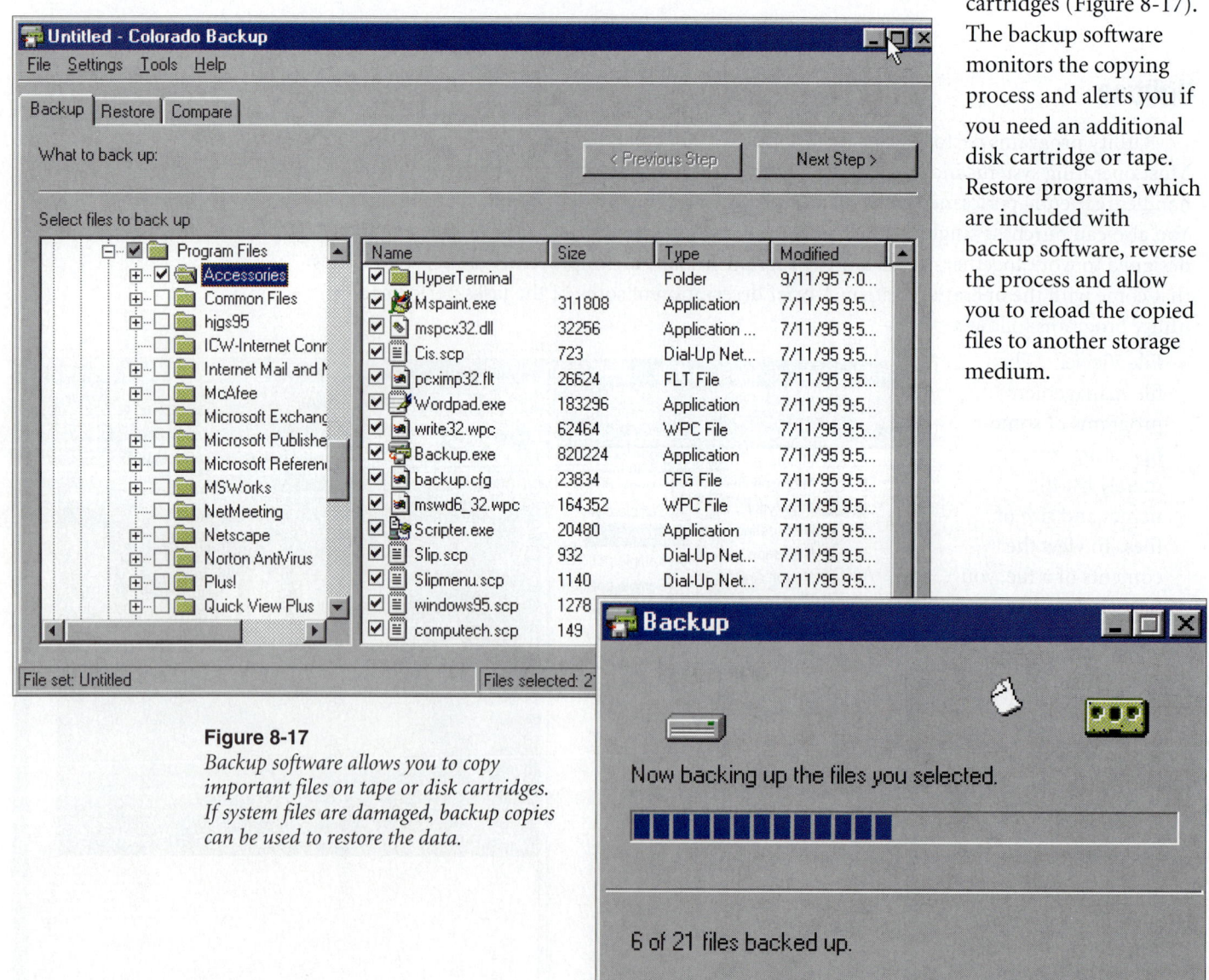

Figure 8-17
Backup software allows you to copy important files on tape or disk cartridges. If system files are damaged, backup copies can be used to restore the data.

- **Diagnostics** Because a computer is a combination of many sophisticated hardware and software components, it is difficult to monitor the operations of every part. A **diagnostic program** helps you determine if the hardware and certain system software programs are installed correctly and functioning properly (Figure 8-18).
- **Uninstaller** When software applications are installed, entries often are made in the system files that are used to help the operating system run the software. If you delete or remove the software application from your computer, these system file entries remain. An **uninstaller** (Figure 8-19) deletes unwanted software and any associated entries in system files.
- **Antivirus** A computer **virus** is a program that copies itself into other programs and spreads through multiple computer systems. Most viruses cause damage to files on the system where the virus is present. **Antivirus programs** prevent, detect, and remove viruses. Viruses and antivirus software also are discussed in Chapter 13, Security, Ethics, and Privacy.

inCyber

For various diagnostic software packages, visit the Discovering Computers Chapter 8 inCyber page (http://www.scsite.com/dc/ch8/incyber.htm) and click Diagnostic Program.

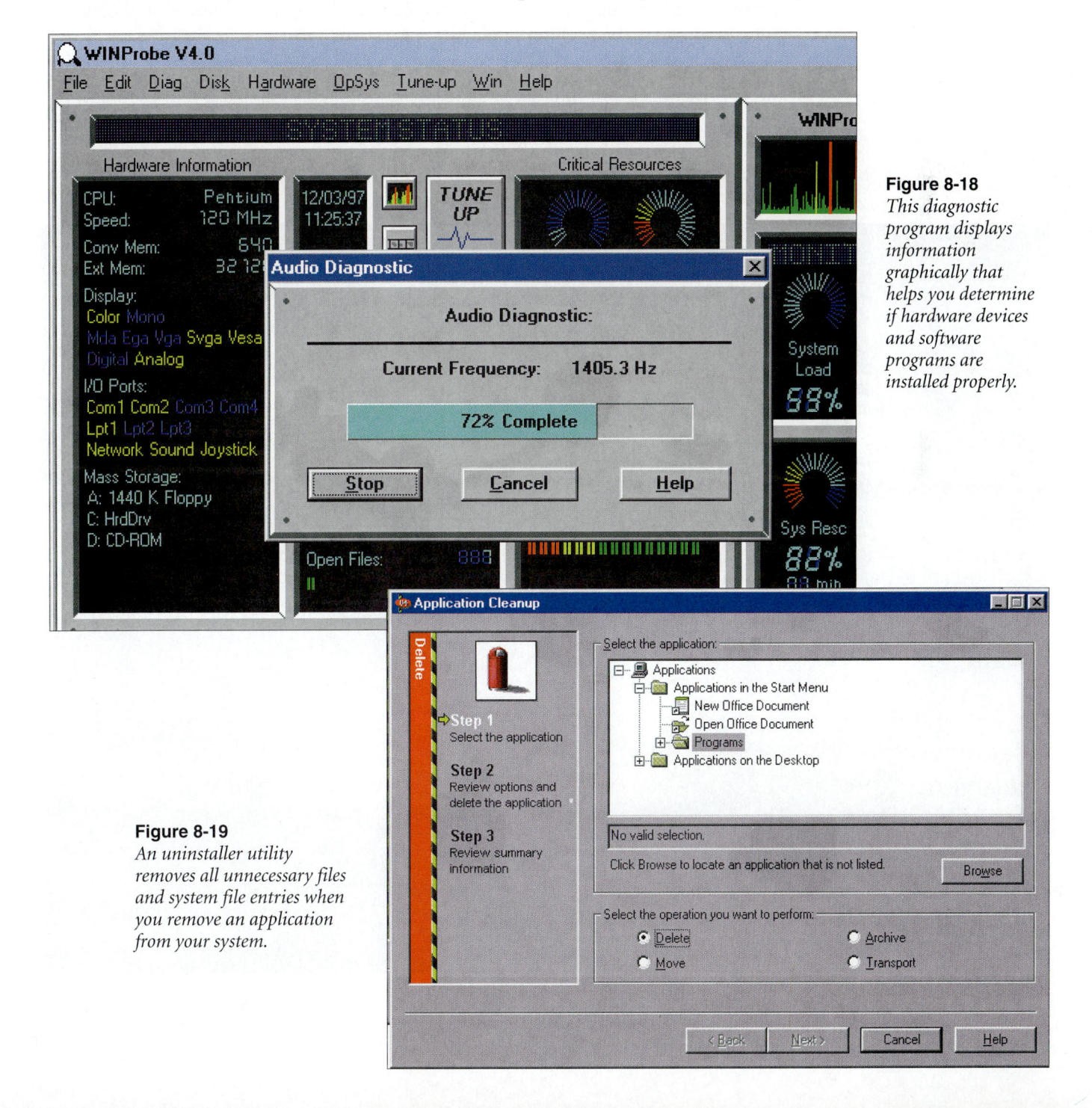

Figure 8-18
This diagnostic program displays information graphically that helps you determine if hardware devices and software programs are installed properly.

Figure 8-19
An uninstaller utility removes all unnecessary files and system file entries when you remove an application from your system.

8.22 CHAPTER 8 – OPERATING SYSTEMS AND SYSTEM SOFTWARE

> **inCyber**
> For files of shareware screen savers, visit the Discovering Computers Chapter 8 inCyber page (http://www.scsite.com/dc/ch8/incyber.htm) and click Screen Saver.

- **Screen Saver** If your computer remains idle for a certain period of time, a **screen saver** automatically displays a moving image on your screen (Figure 8-20). Screen savers originally were developed to prevent a problem called *ghosting*, where a dim image of the current display was etched permanently on the monitor if the display remained on-screen too long. Ghosting is not a problem with today's monitors, but screen savers still are used, primarily for entertainment and security. A screen saver, for instance, prevents someone else from seeing work on your screen if you leave your computer. If you touch any key or your mouse, the screen saver disappears. Screen savers can, however, be set up so that a password is needed to clear it and display the work that was previously on the screen.

- **Desktop Enhancer** A **desktop enhancer** (Figure 8-21) allows you to change the look and organization of your *desktop*, which is the on-screen work area that uses icons and menus to simulate the top of a desk. You can add individual application icons to a taskbar so you can start them quickly or place frequently used applications in separate panels on your desktop. Desktop enhancers also include programs that help you find and manage files more efficiently.

- **Internet Organizer** An **Internet organizer** helps you manage and use your list of favorite Web sites (Figure 8-22). Internet organizers are improved versions of the bookmark or favorites feature included with all Web browser software. Some organizers even will search the Web and report if any of your favorite sites have changed since you last visited them.

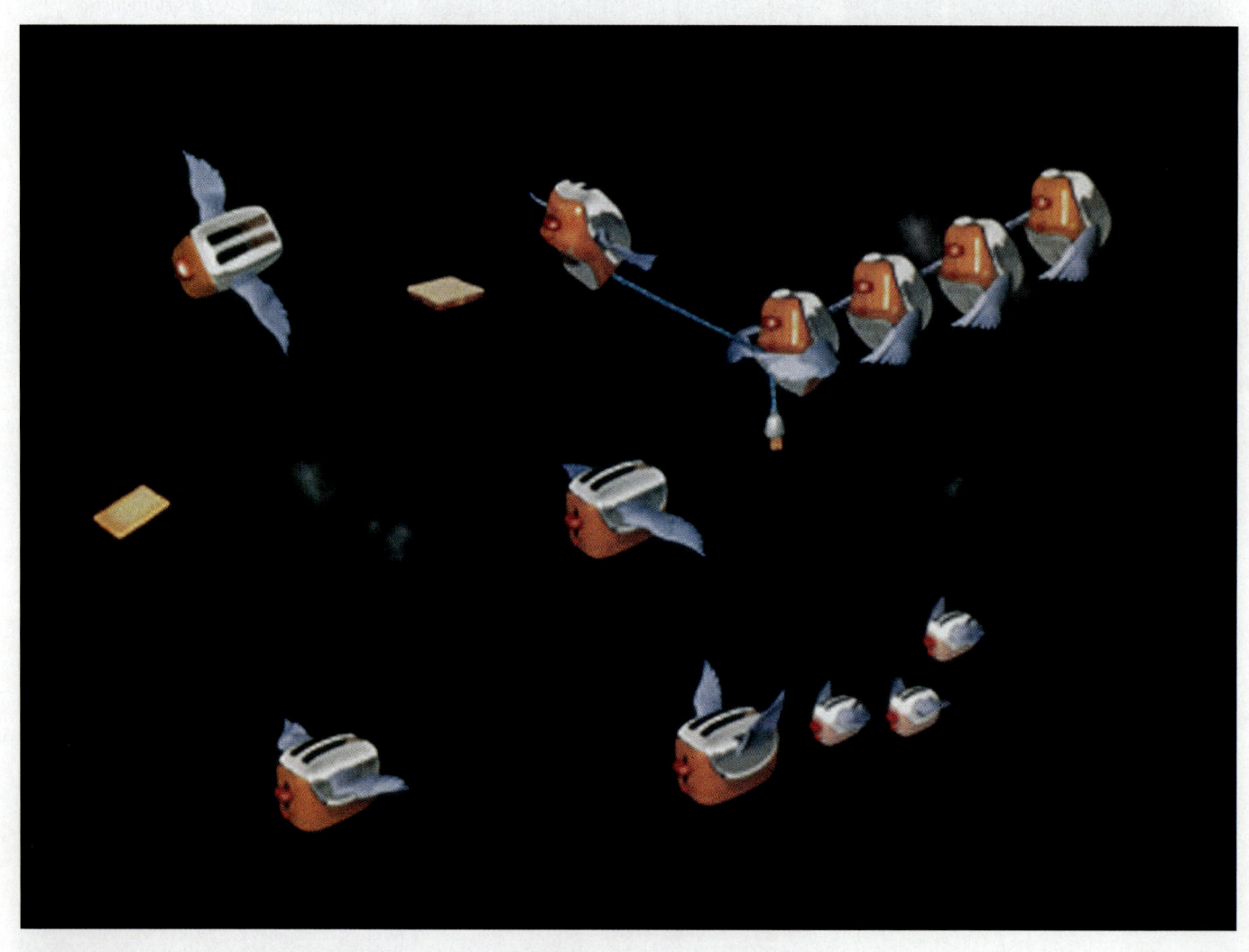

Figure 8-20
If your computer is idle for a while, a screen saver displays a moving image on your monitor. Most screen savers are used for entertainment, but they can be set up to require a password.

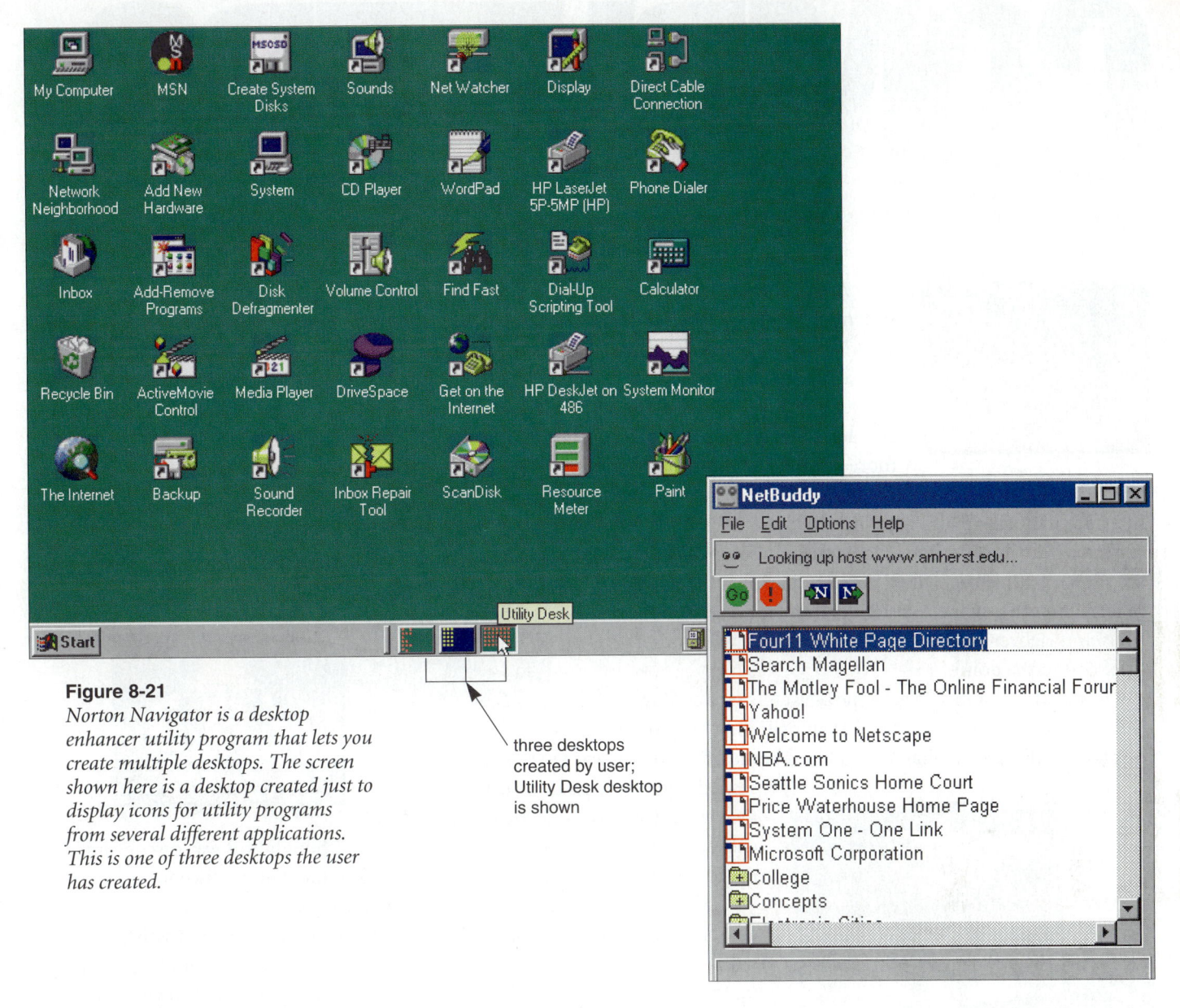

SUMMARY OF OPERATING SYSTEMS AND SYSTEM SOFTWARE   8.23

Figure 8-21
Norton Navigator is a desktop enhancer utility program that lets you create multiple desktops. The screen shown here is a desktop created just to display icons for utility programs from several different applications. This is one of three desktops the user has created.

three desktops created by user; Utility Desk desktop is shown

Figure 8-22
An Internet organizer utility program helps you manage your list of favorite Web sites. The Internet organizer shown on this screen will check your favorite Web pages automatically to see if they have changed.

Language Translators

Special-purpose system software programs called **language translators** are used to convert the programming instructions written by programmers into the binary code that a computer can understand. Language translators are written for specific programming languages and computer systems. Chapter 12, Program Development, explains language translators in more detail.

Summary of Operating Systems and System Software

System software, including the operating system, utilities, and language translators, is an essential part of a computer system. To obtain maximum benefits from your computer system, you should understand all of these well. This is especially true for the latest personal computer operating systems, which include features such as virtual memory management and multitasking. Understanding and being able to use these and other features will allow you to exercise more control over your computer resources.

CHAPTER 8 – OPERATING SYSTEMS AND SYSTEM SOFTWARE

COMPUTERS AT WORK

The Social Interface

Are you tired of reading those plain software and operating system messages in dialog boxes of the same size, shape, and color? With Microsoft's Office 97 Office Assistant, you now have a choice of nine cartoon-like characters, called Assistants, that answer questions, offer tips, and provide Help. The on-screen character makes the message less intimidating, more personal, and hopefully, more fun. These electronic Assistants are a type of **social interface** that use objects with human characteristics to communicate information. Each Assistant, some of which are shown on this page, has a different personality that is reflected in the way the Assistant delivers messages. Some Assistants deliver long, detailed explanations, while others are brief and to the point.

An early version of electronic assistants was used in Microsoft's BoB program. BoB was an operating system interface that displayed a picture of what looked like a home office. If you wanted to schedule something, you clicked the calendar on the wall. If you wanted to write a letter, you clicked the paper and pencil on the desktop. Although BoB was discontinued, the idea of the electronic assistants was incorporated into Office 97.

Eventually, software will make it possible for you to pick your own on-screen assistant, or perhaps have an entire team of electronic assistants with different skills. For example, you might have Albert Einstein help with math, William Shakespeare help with that short story you have to write, and Martha Stewart help with party planning, cooking, gardening, decorating, or practically anything else. Imagine the possibilities if one day soon you are able to choose the likeness of your favorite celebrity as an electronic assistant.

Figure 8-23

IN THE FUTURE: THE NEXT USER INTERFACE   8.25

IN THE FUTURE

The Next User Interface

Using the graphical user interfaces of today, you are able to communicate with a computer using a keyboard and a pointing device. Next-generation operating systems will be more natural and *human-centric*, meaning that they will allow you to interface with the computer using most of the methods you now use to communicate with other humans. These methods include hand gestures, facial expressions, and, of course, spoken words.

The computer will use a video camera to recognize hand gestures and facial expressions. Small cameras already are used by many people for personal videoconferencing and in the future, will be built into most systems just like microphones are built into many systems today. You will train the system to match your gestures and expressions with a limited set of commands. For example, moving your hand one way could indicate forward, a command you could use when reviewing pages of a document. Placing your hand with the palm towards the screen could indicate stop or halt. Nodding your head up and down could indicate yes in response to a dialog box message. Training these systems will be similar to training the simple voice recognition systems that now exist.

Future operating system voice recognition, however, will go beyond today's limited systems. Next-generation operating systems will support continuous speech voice recognition and will use artificial intelligence to determine the meaning of what you are saying. If the computer does not understand something, it will ask you to explain it, just as another person would. When the computer speaks to you, it will be through an on-screen presence that may resemble a person, animal, or other object. IBM and Apple have prototype interfaces that resemble a human head. The head *speaks* to you, asking questions about what you want to do or sharing information about something, such as an error condition. To maintain the consistency of this interface, you respond verbally. To turn off the IBM system, you simply tell the character to go to sleep. The character closes it eyes and droops its head before shutting down the system.

Pen gestures now used with personal digital assistants (PDAs) and pen computers also will be recognized by the operating system. Mousepads also will function as graphics tablets and enable you to input drawings or use a pen stylus instead of a mouse.

All of these operating system and user interface changes are designed to make the computer easier to use, especially for people who still feel uncomfortable using a keyboard. Voice, gesture, and pen input will give everyone more command options and not only make computers easier to use, but also more interesting.

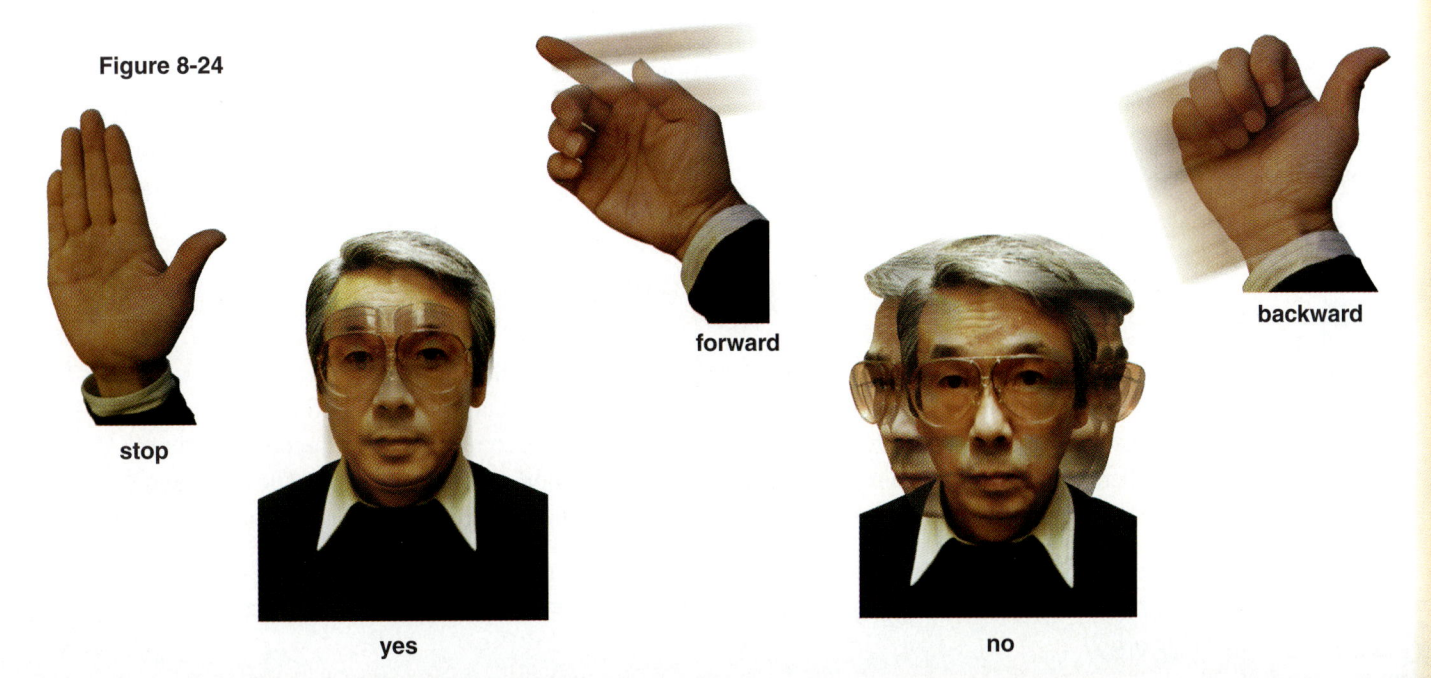

Figure 8-24

stop

forward

yes

no

backward

chapter 8 review

1 | 2 | 3 | 4 | 5 | 6 | 7 | 8 | 9 | 10 | 11 | 12 | 13 | 14 | I

inCyber | review | terms | yourTurn | hotTopics | outThere | winLabs | webWalk | exercises | news | home

INSTRUCTIONS: *To display this page from the Web, launch your browser and enter the URL, http://www.scsite.com/dc/ch8/review.htm. Click the links for current and additional information.*

1 System Software

System **software** consists of the programs, including the operating system, that control the operations of the computer. The three major categories are: operating systems, utilities, and language translators.

2 Operating Systems

An **operating system (OS)** is a set of programs that manages the operations of a computer and functions as an interface among the user, the application programs, and the computer hardware. The **user interface** determines how users interact with the computer. A **graphical user interface (GUI)** uses visual clues to help perform tasks. An operating system performs four functions: process management, memory management, input and output management, and system administration.

3 Process Management

In operating system terms, a **process** is a program or part of a program that can be executed (run) separately. **Single tasking** operating systems allow only one user to run one program at a time. **Multitasking** operating systems allow the computer to work on more than one process at a time.

4 Memory Management

The operating system assigns the operating system **kernel**, application program instructions, data, and intermediate results to areas of memory. Data that has just been read into memory or is waiting to be sent to an output device is stored in areas called **buffers**. At least some portion of memory is allocated for fixed areas called **partitions**, which are used to store the operating system and programs and their related data. **Virtual memory management** increases the amount of memory by using a set amount of disk space to store items during processing, in addition to the existing memory.

5 Input and Output Management

The operating system manages input and output processes differently depending on the device. **Spooling** increases both CPU and printer efficiency. The operating system uses programs called **device drivers** to communicate with each input and output device. With **Plug and Play technology**, the operating system recognizes any new devices and assists in their installation.

6 System Administration

The operating system monitors system performance and system security. System performance usually is gauged by the user in terms of **response time**, which is the amount of time from when data is entered until the system responds. To ensure system security, most multiuser operating systems allow each user to have a **logon code**, a **user ID**, and a **password**. All operating systems contain programs that perform functions related to disk and file management. These functions include formatting disks, listing files, deleting files, copying files, renaming files, and organizing files.

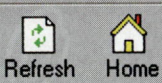

7 Loading an Operating System

Loading an operating system is called **booting**. With the Windows 95 operating system, when the computer is turned on the CPU looks to the BIOS **(Basic Input/Output System)** chip for instructions. The BIOS chip tests the system and then looks for the boot program. The boot program is loaded into memory and begins loading the resident portion of the operating system. The operating system then loads system configuration information. A device driver is loaded for each hardware device. The remainder of the operating system is loaded and the desktop and icons display on the screen.

8 Portable Operating Systems

The trend is toward **portable operating systems** that will run on many manufacturers' computers. Users can change computer models or vendors, yet retain existing software and data files.

9 DOS and Windows 3.X

DOS (Disk Operating System) refers to several single tasking operating systems that were developed for IBM-compatible personal computers. **Windows 3.x** refers to versions of Microsoft's Windows operating system.

10 Windows 95, Windows CE, and Windows NT

Windows 95 is a 32-bit operating system. It has an improved graphical user interface, is written to take advantage of newer 32-bit processors, and supports **preemptive multitasking**. **Windows CE** is an operating system designed for use on wireless communications devices and smaller computers. **Windows NT** is a sophisticated operating system designed for client-server networks.

11 Macintosh, OS/2, UNIX, and Netware

The Apple **Macintosh** multitasking operating system was the first commercially successful graphical user interface. **OS/2** is IBM's graphical user interface operating system designed to work with 32-bit microprocessors. **UNIX** is a multiuser, multitasking operating system available for most computers of all sizes. **NetWare** from Novell is a widely used network operating system designed for client-server networks.

12 Utilities

Utility programs perform specific tasks related to managing computer resources or files. Utility programs include **file viewers**, **file conversion** software, **file compression software**, **backup software**, **diagnostic programs**, **uninstallers**, **antivirus programs**, **screen savers**, **desktop enhancers**, and **Internet organizers**.

13 Language Translators

Special-purpose system software programs called **language translators** convert the programming instructions written by programmers into binary code that a computer can understand.

8 terms

chapter 1 | 2 | 3 | 4 | 5 | 6 | 7 | 8 | 9 | 10 | 11 | 12 | 13 | 14 | I

inCyber | review | terms | yourTurn | hotTopics | outThere | winLabs | webWalk | exercises | news | home

INSTRUCTIONS: *To display this page from the Web, launch your browser and enter the URL, http://www.scsite.com/dc/ch8/terms.htm. Scroll through the list of terms. Click a term for its definition and a picture. Click the rocket ship for current and additional information about the term.*

screen saver

DEFINITION

screen saver
Automatically displays an image on your screen if your computer remains idle for a certain period of time. **(8.22)**

---

antivirus program (8.21)
asymmetric multiprocessing (8.6)
AUTOEXEC.BAT (8.13)

background (8.5)
backup software (8.20)
Basic Input/Output System (8.12)
BIOS (8.12)
booting (8.12)
buffers (8.7)

command language (8.3)
command-line user interface (8.3)
CONFIG.SYS (8.13)
context switching (8.5)
control program (8.2)
cooperative multitasking (8.5)
CPU utilization (8.10)

desktop enhancer (8.22)
device drivers (8.9)
diagnostic program (8.21)
DOS (Disk Operating System) (8.14)
downward compatible (8.14)

executive (8.2)
external commands (8.2)

fault-tolerant computer (8.6)
file compression software (8.20)
file conversion (8.20)
file viewer (8.19)
foreground (8.5)
frames (8.16)

graphical user interface (GUI) (8.3)

internal commands (8.2)
Internet organizer (8.22)

kernel (8.2)

language translators (8.23)
logon code (8.11)

Macintosh (8.17)
MacOS (8.17)
master program (8.2)
menu-driven user interface (8.13)
monitor (8.2)
MS-DOS (Microsoft DOS) (8.14)
multiprocessing operating system (8.6)
multiprocessors (8.6)
multitasking (8.4)
multithreading (8.5)
multiuser timesharing (8.4)

NetWare (8.19)
NT (8.17)

operating environment (8.15)
operating system (OS) (8.2)
OS/2 (8.8)

page (8.7)
paging (8.7)
partitions (8.7)
password (8.11)
PC-DOS (Personal Computer DOS) (8.14)
Plug and Play technology (8.9)
portable operating systems (8.14)
POST (8.12)
Power On Self Test (8.12)
preemptive multitasking (8.5)

print spool (8.9)
process (8.4)
proprietary operating systems (8.14)

registry (8.13)
response time (8.10)

screen saver (8.22)
shell (8.5)
single tasking (8.4)
spooling (8.9)
supervisor (8.2)
swap file (8.7)
swapping (8.8)
symmetric multiprocessing (8.6)
system software (8.2)

task (8.4)
thrashing (8.?)
time slice (8.?)

uninstaller (8.21)
UNIX (8.18)
upward compatible (8.14)
user ID (8.11)
user interface (8.2)
utility programs (8.19)

virtual memory management (8.7)
virus (8.21)

Win 95 (8.16)
Windows 3.0 (8.15)
Windows 3.1 (8.15)
Windows 3.x (8.15)
Windows 95 (8.16)
Windows CE (8.16)
Windows for Workgroups (8.15)
Windows NT (8.17)

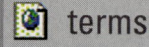

yourTurn

INSTRUCTIONS: *To display this page from the Web, launch your browser and enter the URL, http://www.scsite.com/dc/ch8/turn.htm. Click a blank line for the answer. Click the links for current and additional information.*

Label the Figure

Operating System Process Management

1. _____ — Single user can run one program at a time.

Multitasking:

2. _____

3. _____ — User switches back and forth between programs

4. _____ — Programs switch when they reach a logical breakpoint

5. _____ — Operating system switches programs based on allocated amount of time and priority

Multiprocessing:

6. _____

7. _____ — Tasks assigned to specific CPUs; each CPU has its own memory

8. _____ — Tasks assigned to available CPUs; CPUs share memory

Instructions: Identify the different methods of managing processes.

Fill in the Blanks

Instructions: Complete each sentence with the correct term or terms.

1. _____ can be classified into three major categories: operating systems, utilities, and language translators.
2. A(n) _____ is a set of programs that manages the operations of a computer and functions as an interface among the user, the application program, and the computer hardware.
3. The first operating systems were _____ operating systems limited to a specific vendor or computer model, but the trend today is toward _____ operating systems that will run on many manufacturers' computers.
4. Although commonly referred to as an operating system, the 3.x versions of Windows are actually _____ designed to work with the _____ operating system.
5. Special-purpose system software programs called _____ are used to convert the programming instructions written by programmers into binary code that a computer can understand.

Short Answer

Instructions: Write a brief answer to each of the following questions.

1. What is a user interface? How are command-line user interfaces, menu-driven user interfaces, and graphical user interfaces different? What browser-like features have been incorporated in many graphical user interfaces? _____
2. How are buffers different from partitions? How does virtual memory management increase the amount of memory the operating system can use? What is paging? _____
3. How is an operating system such as Windows 95 loaded into a personal computer? What is the BIOS chip? _____
4. How is Windows 95 similar to earlier versions of Windows? How is it different? What are its advantages? _____
5. What is a utility program? How is file conversion software different from file compression software? What is an Internet organizer? _____

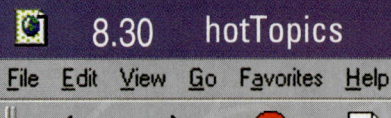

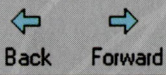

hotTopics

chapter 8

1 | 2 | 3 | 4 | 5 | 6 | 7 | 8 | 9 | 10 | 11 | 12 | 13 | 14 | I

inCyber | review | terms | yourTurn | hotTopics | outThere | winLabs | webWalk | exercises | news | home

INSTRUCTIONS: *To display this page from the Web, launch your browser and enter the URL, http://www.scsite.com/dc/ch8/hot.htm. Click the links for current and additional information to help you respond to the hotTopics questions.*

1 *Most software reviewers agree that Windows 95 is superior to its* predecessors. Users of earlier versions of Windows, however, were slower to embrace the new operating system. A poll of Windows and DOS users conducted three months after the release of Windows 95 found that only 10% thought it extremely likely they would upgrade to Windows 95 within the next six months, 35% believed it possible, and 53% felt it was not likely at all. Why might people be reluctant to adopt new versions of an operating system? What features would be most apt to hasten the acceptance of a new operating system? Why? If you generally were satisfied with a current version of an operating system, how likely would you be to upgrade your system with a new and perhaps superior version? Why?

2 *Steve Wozniak, cofounder of Apple Computer, feels the company erred in initially making* Macintosh a proprietary operating system. The intent was to enhance sales of Apple hardware, but Wozniak now believes the company should have licensed the operating system to other manufacturers for a fee. Imagine you are CEO of Computers and Advanced Technology (CAT), a company that specializes in laptop computers (company slogan: "Life is better with a CAT on your lap"). Your programmers have developed a wonderful new operating system for CAT computers, but they assure you the system can be adapted to work with any personal computers. Would you keep the operating system proprietary, possibly strengthening sales of CAT computers, or would you make the operating system portable and license it to other manufacturers? Why? What factors, if any, might make you change your decision?

3 *New utility programs are being developed constantly to meet user needs. One new program* guards against computer theft by once a week making a silent call to a control center. If the call emanates from an appropriate number, the call is logged. If the computer has been reported stolen, however, the center traces the call to locate the missing computer. What other needs could be addressed by a utility program? What are three specific tasks (not addressed in this chapter) related to managing computer resources or files that all computer users or a specific group of users would like to have performed? What would a utility program do to perform each task? How would the program make a user's computing life easier? If you were to market the program, what would you call it?

4 *Suppose you start a small company. The company uses several different types of personal* computers. You must decide the operating system that will be used with each computer. Keeping in mind the company's purpose, the expertise of personnel, the application software used, and the need for compatibility, which of the operating systems described in this chapter would you choose? Why? Would your choice have been different five years ago? Might it be different five years from now? Why?

5 *Utility programs purchased for an individual personal computer may be different from those* bought for the personal computers on a company's network. Tasks addressed by the utility programs described in this chapter include file viewer, file conversion, file compression, backup, diagnostics, uninstaller, antivirus, screen saver, desktop enhancer, and Internet organizer. Which four utility programs would you be most likely to purchase for your own personal computer? Why? If you were buying four utility programs for a company's personal computers, which would you choose? Why? Compare the two lists. How are they different? How are they similar? Why?

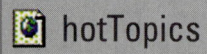

outThere

chapter 8 | 1 | 2 | 3 | 4 | 5 | 6 | 7 | 8 | 9 | 10 | 11 | 12 | 13 | 14 | I

inCyber | review | terms | yourTurn | hotTopics | outThere | winLabs | webWalk | exercises | news | home

INSTRUCTIONS: *To display this page from the Web, launch your browser and enter the URL, http://www.scsite.com/dc/ch8/out.htm. Click the links for current and additional information.*

1 *Transferring the notes taken in class or the term paper scratched out on the bus* to a desktop computer usually involves puzzling over illegible handwriting and typing for hours. Windows CE, which is an operating system available on numerous personal digital assistants, may make life easier. A representative PDA unit comes with a small keyboard, a touch-sensitive screen, and mini Word, Excel, and Schedule+ applications. Weighing less than a pound and running on two AA batteries, it transfers work done to a desktop PC through a simple cable connection. Visit a computer vendor and try a PDA that uses Windows CE. What PDA did you use? How does it work? What are its strengths? What are its weaknesses? Would you consider purchasing the PDA? Why or why not?

2 *Virus protection programs can detect known computer viruses and clean them from a system.* Yet, because new viruses are developed every day, virus protection programs must be updated frequently to handle recently created threats. Fortunately, help is available on the World Wide Web. For a monthly fee, subscribers can download antivirus software that is renewed periodically to deal with the latest viruses. Visit a Web site to learn more about virus protection software. Who provides the software? Who created the software? How is the online virus protection software better than the utility programs available in stores? With what operating systems is the software compatible? How often can it be used? How much does it cost? What other types of utility programs are available?

3 *Just as it is important to get out and kick the tires before deciding on a new car,* it is a good idea to test several operating systems before choosing one for a personal computer. Find two personal computers that use different operating systems. Compare the two operating systems. What is the name of each operating system? What type of interface does each use? What type of operating system (single tasking, context switching, cooperative multitasking, or preemptive multitasking) is each? How does each manage memory, manage input and output, and monitor system activity? What utilities are available? What application software is used with each operating system? Based on what you have learned, which operating system would you choose for your own personal computer? Why?

4 *Operating systems often develop loyal followings. The introduction of Windows 95 led to* renewed controversy concerning the merits of various operating systems, and the debate has been fueled on the World Wide Web by the originators of each operating system. Visit one or more Web pages that compare various operating systems. Who authored the Web page? What operating systems are being compared? How are they compared? According to the Web page, what are the advantages and disadvantages of each operating system? After reviewing the page, are you convinced of the superiority of one operating system? Why or why not?

5 *Bill Gates, a founder of Microsoft Corporation, is the wealthiest man in America.* The $20 billion CEO leads a company that is said to have a greater reach than any organization since the Roman Empire; more than 90 percent of all personal computers have a Microsoft operating system. The story of Bill Gates and Microsoft has been chronicled in several books, including *Hard Drive: Bill Gates and the Making of the Microsoft Empire* (James Wallace), *Accidental Empire: How the Boys of Silicon Valley Make Their Millions and Still Can't Get a Date* (Robert X. Cringely), *Gates* (Stephen Manes), and *The Road Ahead* (Bill Gates). Read one of these books and prepare a brief report. What qualities or factors led to the success of Bill Gates and Microsoft? Why? Will Microsoft's success continue? Why or Why not?

winLabs

INSTRUCTIONS: *To display this page from the Web, launch your browser and enter the URL, http://www.scsite.com/dc/ch8/labs.htm. Click the links for current and additional information.*

1. Shelly Cashman Series System Software Lab

Follow the instructions in winLabs 1 on page 1.34 to display the Shelly Cashman Series Labs screen. Click Evaluating Operating Systems. Click the Start Lab button. When the initial screen displays, carefully read the objectives. With your printer on, click the Print Questions button. Fill out the top of the Questions sheet and then answer the questions.

2. Shelly Cashman Series Ergonomics Lab

Follow the instructions in winLabs 1 on page 1.34 to display the Shelly Cashman Series Labs screen. Click Working at Your Computer. Click the Start Lab button. When the initial screen displays, carefully read the objectives. With your printer on, click the Print Questions button. Fill out the top of the Questions sheet and then answer the questions.

3. Using a Screen Saver

Right-click an empty area on your desktop and then click Properties on the shortcut menu. When the Display Properties dialog box displays, click the Screen Saver tab. To activate or modify a screen saver, click the Screen Saver box arrow and then click Mystify Your Mind or any other selection. Click the Preview button to display the actual screen saver (Figure 8-25). Move the mouse to make the screen saver disappear. Answer the following questions: (1) How many screen savers are available in your Screen Saver list? (2) How many minutes does your system wait before activating a screen saver? Click the Cancel button in the Display Properties dialog box.

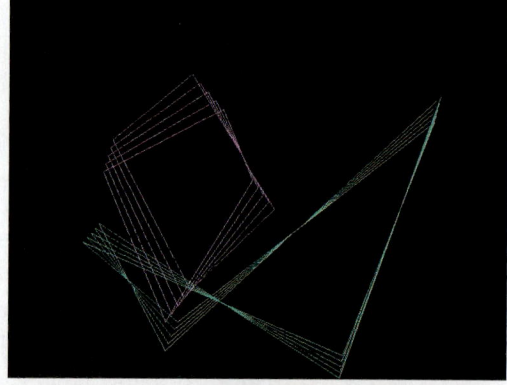

Figure 8-25

4. Changing Desktop Colors

Right-click an empty area on your desktop and then click Properties on the shortcut menu. When the Display Properties dialog box displays, click the Appearance tab. Perform the following tasks: (1) Click the question mark button on the title bar and then click the Scheme box. When the pop-up window displays, right-click it. Click Print Topic on the shortcut menu and then click the OK button in the Print dialog box. Click anywhere to remove the pop-up window. (2) Click the Scheme box arrow and then click Rose to display the color scheme in Figure 8-26. Find a color scheme you like. Click the Cancel button.

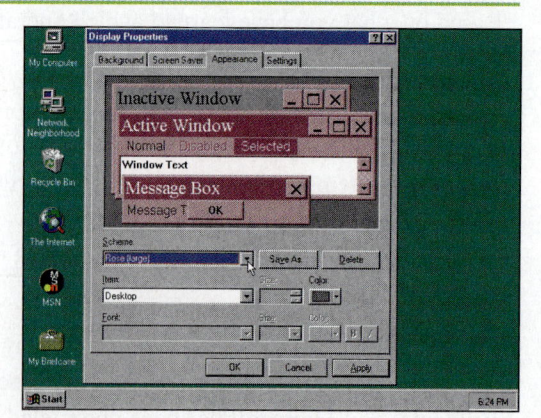

Figure 8-26

5. About Windows 95

Double-click the My Computer icon on the desktop. When the My Computer window displays, click Help on the menu bar and then click About Windows 95. Answer the following questions: (1) To whom is Windows 95 licensed? (2) How much physical memory is available to Windows? Click the OK button. Close My Computer.

webWalk

chapter 8 | 1 | 2 | 3 | 4 | 5 | 6 | 7 | 8 | 9 | 10 | 11 | 12 | 13 | 14 | I

inCyber | review | terms | yourTurn | hotTopics | outThere | winLabs | webWalk | exercises | news | home

INSTRUCTIONS: *To display this page from the Web, launch your browser and enter the URL, http://www.scsite.com/dc/ch8/walk.htm. Click the exercise link to display the exercise.*

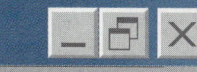

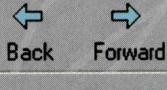

1. Screen Save Utilities
Ghosting is not a problem with today's monitors, but screen savers still are used for entertainment and security. To learn more about screen savers, complete this exercise.

2. File Compression Utilities
If you frequently download files or trade large files with others, you will benefit from file compression software (Figure 8-27). You can learn more about file compression software by completing this exercise.

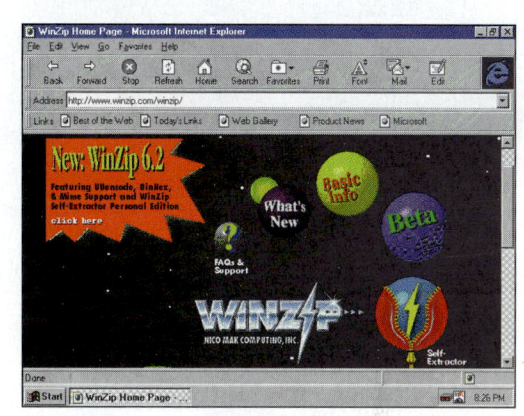

3. Graphical User Interfaces
A graphical user interface (GUI) uses visual clues such as icons to help you perform tasks. You can learn more about GUIs by completing this exercise.

4. All About BIOS
The Basic Input/ Output System (BIOS) is a set of instructions that provides the interface between the operating system and the hardware devices (Figure 8-28). Complete this exercise to learn more about BIOS.

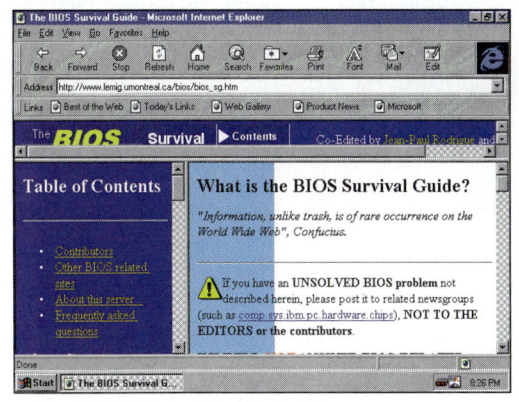

Figure 8-27

5. Information Mining
Complete this exercise to improve your Web research skills by using a Web search engine to find information related to this chapter.

6. Windows CE
Windows CE is an operating system designed for use on wireless communication devices and smaller computers such as hand-helds, palmtops, and network computers. To learn more about Windows CE, complete this exercise.

Figure 8-28

7. Antivirus Utilities
A computer virus is a program that causes damage by copying itself into other programs and spreading through multiple computer systems. Utility programs include virus protection programs that prevent, detect, and remove viruses. Complete this exercise to learn more about computer virus protection.

8. Offline Web Browsing
Offline Web Browsing can save time, money and slow, frustrating Internet connections by organizing scheduled downloads and keeping them updated. Complete this exercise to learn more about offline web browsing.

9. Web Chat
Complete this exercise to enter a Web Chat discussion related to the issues presented in the hotTopics exercise.

How to Purchase, Install, and Maintain a Personal Computer

At some point in time, perhaps during this course, you probably will decide to buy a computer system. It may be your first system or a replacement system. The decision is an important one and will require an investment of both time and money. The following guidelines are presented to help you purchase, install, and maintain your system. The guidelines assume you are purchasing a desktop personal computer, often referred to as a PC. It is further assumed that the computer will be used for home or light business use. Because it is the most widely purchased type of system, some of the guidelines assume an IBM-compatible computer is being purchased. Most of the guidelines, however, may be applied to the purchase of any personal computer including a Macintosh or other non-Windows system. The type of system you purchase should be determined by your software requirements and the need to be compatible with other systems with which you work.

Many of the guidelines also can be applied to purchasing notebook computers. A separate section on notebook computer requirements also is included. A notebook computer may be an appropriate choice if you need computing capability when you travel.

How to Purchase a Computer System

1 **Determine what applications you will use on your computer.** This decision will guide you as to the type and size of computer. Artists and others who work with graphics will need a larger, better quality monitor and additional disk space.

2 **Choose your software first.** Some packages run only on Macintosh computers, others only on a PC. Some packages run only under the Windows operating system. In addition, some software requires more memory and disk space than other packages. Most users will want at least word processing and access to the Internet and World Wide Web. For the most software for the money, consider purchasing an integrated package or a software suite that offers reduced pricing on several applications purchased at the same time. Be sure the software contains the features that are necessary for the work you will be performing.

3 **Be aware of *hidden* costs.** Realize that some additional costs are associated with buying a computer. Such costs might include an additional telephone line or outlet to use a modem, computer furniture, consumable supplies such as floppy disks and paper, floppy disk holders, reference manuals on specific software packages, and special training classes you may want to take. Depending on where you buy your computer, the seller may be willing to include some or all of these in the system purchase price.

4 **Buy equipment that meets the *Energy Star* power consumption guidelines.** These guidelines require that computer systems, monitors, and printers reduce electrical consumption if they have not been used for some period of time, usually several minutes. Equipment meeting the guidelines can display the *Energy Star* logo.

5 **Consider buying from local computer dealers or direct mail companies.** Each has certain advantages. The local dealer can more easily provide hands-on support, if necessary. With a mail-order company, you usually are limited to speaking to someone over the telephone. Mail-order companies usually, but not always, offer the lowest prices. The important thing to do when you are shopping for a system is to make sure you are comparing identical or similar configurations. Local companies can be found in the telephone book. Call first to see if they sell regularly to individual customers; some sell only or primarily to businesses. Telephone numbers for mail-order companies can be found in their advertisements that run in PC periodicals. Most libraries subscribe to several of the major PC magazines. If you call a mail-order firm, ask if it has a catalog that can be sent to you. If you do not buy a system right away, call for another catalog; prices and configurations change frequently.

HOW TO PURCHASE, INSTALL, AND MAINTAIN A PERSONAL COMPUTER

SYSTEM COST COMPARISON WORKSHEET

Category	Field	Desired	#1	#2	#3	#4
Base System	Mfr	–				
	Model					
	Processor	Pentium with MMX				
	Speed	200 MHz				
	Power supply	200 watts				
	Expansion slots	5				
	Local bus video	yes				
	Operating system	Windows				
	Price					
Memory	RAM	32 MB				
	L2 Cache	512 K				
	Price					
Hard Disk	Mfr					
	Size	2.0 GB				
	Price					
Floppy Disk	3 1/2 inch					
Video Graphics	Mfr/Model	64-bit				
	Memory	4 MB				
	Price					
Color Monitor	Mfr/Model					
	Size	17 inch				
	Dot Pitch	0.26 mm				
	Price					
Sound Card	Mfr/Model	16-bit				
	Price					
Speakers	Mfr/Model					
	Number	3 pc				
	Price					
CD-ROM Drive	Mfr/Model					
	Speed	12X				
	Price					
Mouse	Mfr/Model					
	Price					
Fax Modem	Mfr/Model					
	Speed	33.6 Kbps				
	Price					
Printer	Mfr/Model					
	Type	ink jet				
	Speed	6 ppm				
	Price					
Surge Protector	Mfr/Model					
	Price					
Tape Backup	Mfr/Model					
	Price					
UPS	Mfr/Model					
	Price					
Other	Sales Tax					
	Shipping					
	1 YR Warranty	standard				
	1 YR On-Site Svc					
	3 YR On-Site Svc					
	TOTAL					
Software	List free software					

Figure 1
A spreadsheet is an effective way to summarize and compare the prices and equipment offered by different system vendors. List your desired system in the column labeled Desired. Place descriptions on the lines and enter prices in the boxes.

HOW TO PURCHASE A COMPUTER SYSTEM   8.37

6 **Use a spreadsheet, such as the one shown in Figure 1, to compare purchase alternatives.** Use a separate sheet of paper to take notes on each vendor's system and then summarize the information on the spreadsheet.

7 **Consider more than just price.** Do not necessarily buy the lowest cost system. Consider intangibles such as how long the vendor has been in business, its reputation for quality, and reputation for support.

8 **Do some research.** Talk to friends, coworkers, and instructors. Ask what type of system and software they bought and why. Would they recommend their system and the company they bought it from? Are they satisfied with their software? Spend some time at the library or on the Internet reviewing computer periodicals. Most periodicals have frequent articles that rate systems and software on cost, performance, and support issues. Check out the Web sites of different system manufacturers for the latest information on equipment and prices.

9 **Look for free software.** Many system vendors include free software with their systems. Some even let you choose which software you want. Free software only has value, however, if you would have purchased it if it had not come with the computer.

10 **Buy a system compatible with the one you use elsewhere.** If you use a personal computer at work or at some other organization, make sure the computer you buy is compatible. That way, if you need or want to, you can work on projects at home.

11 **Consider purchasing an on-site service agreement.** If you use your system for business or otherwise are unable to be without your computer, consider purchasing an on-site service agreement. Many of the mail-order vendors offer such support through third-party companies. Agreements usually state that a technician will be on-site within 24 hours. Some systems include on-site service for only the first year. It usually is less expensive to extend the service for two or three years when you buy the computer instead of waiting to buy the service agreement later.

12 **Use a credit card to purchase your system.** Many credit cards now have purchase protection benefits that cover you in case of loss or damage to purchased goods. Some also extend the warranty of any products purchased with the card. Paying by credit card also gives you time to install and use the system before you have to pay for it. Finally, if you are dissatisfied with the system and are unable to reach an agreement with the seller, paying by credit card gives you certain rights regarding withholding payment until the dispute is resolved. Check your credit card agreement for specific details.

13 **Avoid buying the smallest system available.** Studies show that many users become dissatisfied because they did not buy a powerful enough system. Plan to buy a system that will last you for at least three years. If you have to buy a smaller system, be sure it can be upgraded with additional memory and devices as your system requirements grow. Consider the following as a minimum recommended system. Each of the components will be discussed separately.

Base System Components

Pentium processor with MMX technology, 200 MHz
200 watt power supply
5 open expansion slots
1 open expansion bay
1 parallel and 2 serial ports
keyboard
512 K level 2 (L2) cache memory
32 MB of RAM
2.0 GB hard disk drive
3 1/2-inch floppy disk drive
64-bit video graphics card with 4 MB memory
17-inch SVGA color monitor
16-bit sound card and speakers
12X CD-ROM drive
mouse or other pointing device
33.6 kbps fax modem
ink-jet or personal laser printer
surge protector
latest version of operating system
FCC Class B approved

Optional Components

color ink-jet printer
multifunction device (printer, scanner, copier, fax machine)
tape backup
cartridge disk drive
ergonomic keyboard
uninterruptable power supply (UPS)

Processor: A Pentium processor with MMX technology with a speed rating of at least 200 megahertz is needed for today's more sophisticated software, even word processing software. Buy a system that can be upgraded to the next generation processor.

Power Supply: 200 watts. If the power supply is too small, it will not be able to support additional expansion cards that you might want to add in the future. The power supply should be UL (Underwriters Laboratory) approved.

Expansion Slots: At least five open slots. Expansion slots are needed for scanners, tape drives, video capture boards, and other equipment you may want to add in the future as your needs change and the price of this equipment becomes lower.

Expansion Bay: At least one open bay. An expansion (drive) bay will let you add another disk drive or a tape drive.

Ports: At least one parallel and two serial ports. The parallel port will be used for your printer. The serial ports can be used for additional printers, external modems, joysticks, a mouse, and certain network connections.

Keyboard: Almost always included with the system. If you can, check out the feel of the keys before you buy. If you like the way another keyboard feels, ask the vendor if you can have it instead. Consider upgrading to an ergonomic keyboard that has built-in wrist rests. Ergonomic keyboards take up more space but are more comfortable and help prevent injuries.

Cache Memory: 512 K of level 2 cache will boost the performance of many applications.

Memory (RAM): 32 megabytes (MB) Each new operating system release recommends (requires) more memory. It is easier and less expensive to obtain the memory when you buy the system than if you wait until later.

Hard Disk: 2.0 gigabytes (GB). Each new software release requires more hard disk space. Even with disk compression programs, disk space is used up quickly. Start with more disk than you ever think you will need.

Floppy Disk Drive: A 3 1/2-inch floppy disk drive is standard on most systems.

Video Graphics Card: A 64-bit local bus video card with 4 MB of memory will provide crisp colors and support full-motion video.

Color Monitor: 17 inch. This is one device where it pays to spend a little more money. A 17-inch super VGA (SVGA) monitor with a dot pitch of 0.26 mm or less will display graphics better than a 15-inch model. For health reasons, make sure you pick a low-radiation model. Also, look for a monitor with an antiglare coating on the screen or consider buying an antiglare filter that mounts on the front of the screen. If you work frequently with graphics, consider a larger 20-inch or 21-inch unit.

Sound Card and Speakers: 16-bit sound card with FM or wavetable synthesis, or both. Powered speakers use batteries to produce a fuller sound. If music is important to you, consider three-piece speakers with a separate subwoofer unit for better bass sounds.

CD-ROM Drive: Much software and almost all multimedia are distributed on CD-ROM. Get at least a 12X speed model.

Pointing Device: Most systems include a mouse as part of the base package. Some people prefer to use a trackball.

Fax Modem: 33.6 kbps. Volumes of information are available on the Internet and from online databases. In addition, many software vendors provide assistance and free software upgrades via their Web sites. For the speed they provide, 33.6 kbps modems are worth the extra money. Facsimile (fax) capability is included in almost all modems. Buy a modem that can be software upgraded. Internal modems cost less but external modems are easier to move to another computer.

Printer: Ink-jet and personal laser printers produce excellent black and white graphic output. Inexpensive color ink-jet printers also are available. If your office space is limited, or you want the additional features, consider a multifunction device that combines a printer, scanner, copier, and fax machine.

Surge Protector: A voltage spike literally can destroy your system. It is low-cost insurance to protect yourself with a surge protector. Do not merely buy a fused multiple plug outlet from the local hardware store. Buy a surge protector designed for computers with a separate protected jack for your telephone (modem) line.

Operating System: Almost all new systems come with an operating system, but it is not always the most current. Make sure the operating system is the one you want and is the latest version.

FCC Class B Approved: The Federal Communications Commission (FCC) provides radio frequency emission standards that computer manufacturers must meet. If a computer does not meet the FCC standards, it could cause interference with radio and television reception. Class B standards apply to computers used in a home. Class A standards apply to a business installation.

Tape Backup: Large hard disks make backing up data on floppy disks impractical. Internal or external tape backup systems are the most common solution. Some portable units, great if you have more than one system, are designed to connect to your printer port. The small tapes can store the equivalent of hundreds of floppy disks.

Cartridge Disk Drive: Removable cartridge disk drives are a fast and portable way to store large amounts of data.

Uninterruptable Power Supply (UPS): A UPS uses batteries to start or keep your system running if the main electrical power is turned off. The length of time they provide depends on the size of the batteries and the electrical requirements of your system but is usually at least 10 minutes. The idea of a UPS is to give you enough time to save your work. Get a UPS that is rated for your size system.

Remember that the types of applications you want to use on your system will guide you as to the type and size of computer that is right for you. The ideal computer system you choose may differ from the general recommendation presented here. Determine your needs and buy the best system your budget will allow.

How to Purchase a Notebook Computer System

Many of the guidelines previously mentioned also apply to the purchase of a notebook computer. The following are some of the considerations unique to notebooks.

1 Carefully determine how you want to use your notebook system. Notebook computers can be divided into three categories: desktop replacement systems, value notebooks, and subnotebooks. *Desktop replacement systems* have all the features and functionality of a full-sized desktop system and are designed for the person who wants only one system or who needs a full-featured system for on-the-road presentations. They include a large hard drive, floppy disk drive, high-speed CD-ROM drive, built-in speakers, PC card slots, and a large (12 inches or larger) active-matrix display. Desktop replacement systems often weigh seven pounds or more and cost between $5,000 and $8,000. *Value notebooks* have lower speed and capacity components than desktop replacement systems but keep most of the functionality. Value notebooks generally weigh between five and seven pounds and cost between $2,500 and $4,000. *Subnotebooks* save weight and size by making the floppy disk drive an optional external device and by having a smaller display screen and keyboard. Subnotebooks generally weigh less than five pounds and cost less than $2,500.

2 If your system frequently will be used to display animation or video or will be used to display information to others, obtain a notebook with an active-matrix screen. Active-matrix screens present a better quality picture that can be seen from the side. Less expensive passive matrix screens sometimes are hard to see in low-light conditions and can be viewed only straight on.

3 If your unit does not have one built-in, consider purchasing a separate CD-ROM drive. Loading software, especially large software suites, is much faster if done from CD-ROM. A separate CD-ROM drive has the advantage of being left behind to save weight.

4 If you will use your system both on the road and at home or in the office, consider a docking station. A docking station usually includes a floppy disk drive, a CD-ROM drive, and a connector for a full-sized monitor and is an alternative to buying a full-sized system when you work at home or in the office.

5 Experiment with different pointing devices and keyboards before you buy. Notebook computer keyboards are not nearly as standardized as keyboards on desktop systems. Some notebooks have wide wrist rests and othershave none. The same is true for pointing devices. Options include pointing sticks, touchpads, and trackballs. One manufacturer offers a small mouse that pulls out from the notebook case. Try them all before you buy.

6 Upgrade memory and disk storage at the time of purchase. As is true with desktop systems, memory and disk upgrades usually are less expensive if done at the time of initial system purchase. Disk storage systems often are custom designed for notebook manufacturers and may not be available two or three years after the notebook was sold.

The following points apply if you plan to travel with your notebook computer.

7 If you are going to use your notebook on an airplane, purchase a second battery. Two batteries should be enough power to work through most flights. If you think you will be working off batteries frequently, choose a system that uses lithium-ion batteries, which last longer than nickel cadmium or nickel hydride batteries.

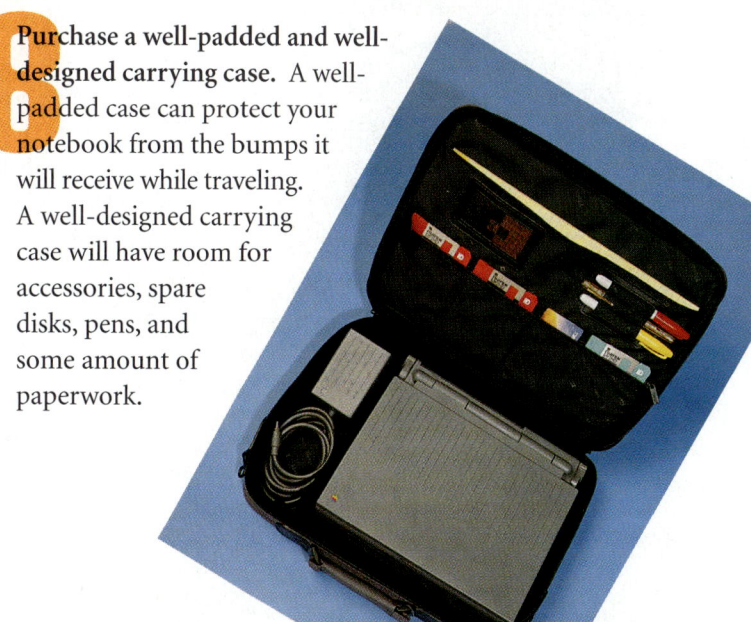

8 Purchase a well-padded and well-designed carrying case. A well-padded case can protect your notebook from the bumps it will receive while traveling. A well-designed carrying case will have room for accessories, spare disks, pens, and some amount of paperwork.

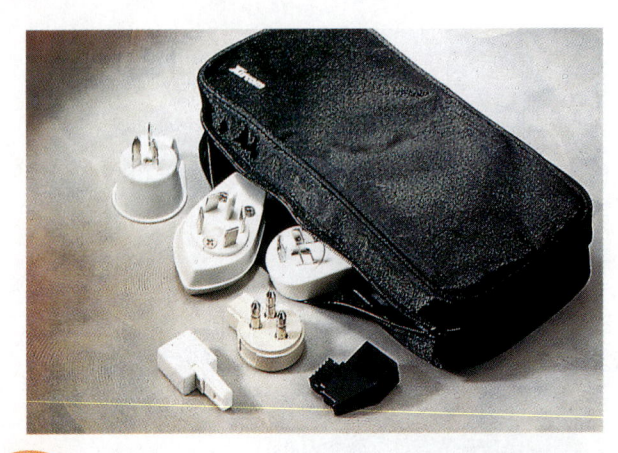

8.40 HOW TO PURCHASE, INSTALL, AND MAINTAIN A PERSONAL COMPUTER

9. If you travel overseas, obtain a set of electrical and telephone outlet adapters. Overseas electrical and telephone connections use different outlets. Several manufacturers sell sets of adapters that will work in most countries.

How to Install a Computer System

1. **Read the installation manuals *before* you start to install your equipment.** Many manufacturers include separate installation instructions with their equipment that contain important information. Take the time to read them.

2. **Allow for adequate workspace around the computer.** A workspace of at least two feet by four feet is recommended.

3. **Install bookshelves.** Bookshelves above and/or to the side of the computer area are useful for keeping manuals and other reference materials handy.

4. **Install your computer in a well-designed work area.** An applied science called ergonomics is devoted to making the equipment people use and surrounding work area safer and more efficient. Ergonomic studies have shown that the height of your chair, keyboard, monitor, and work surface is important and can affect your health. See Figure 2 for specific work area guidelines.

5. **Use a document holder.** To minimize neck and eye strain, obtain a document holder that holds documents at the same height and distance as your computer screen.

6. **Provide adequate lighting.** Use nonglare light bulbs that illuminate your entire work area.

7. **While working at your computer, be aware of health issues.** See Figure 3 for a list of computer user health guidelines.

8. **Have a telephone nearby that can be used while you are sitting at the computer.** Having a telephone near the computer is helpful if you need to call a vendor about a hardware or software problem. Oftentimes, the vendor support person can talk you through the correction while you are on the telephone. To avoid data loss, however, do not place floppy disks on the telephone or near any other electrical or electronic equipment.

9. **Obtain a computer tool set.** Computer tool sets are available from computer dealers, office supply stores, and mail-order companies. These sets will have the right size screwdrivers and other tools to work on your computer. Get one that comes in a zippered carrying case to keep all the tools together.

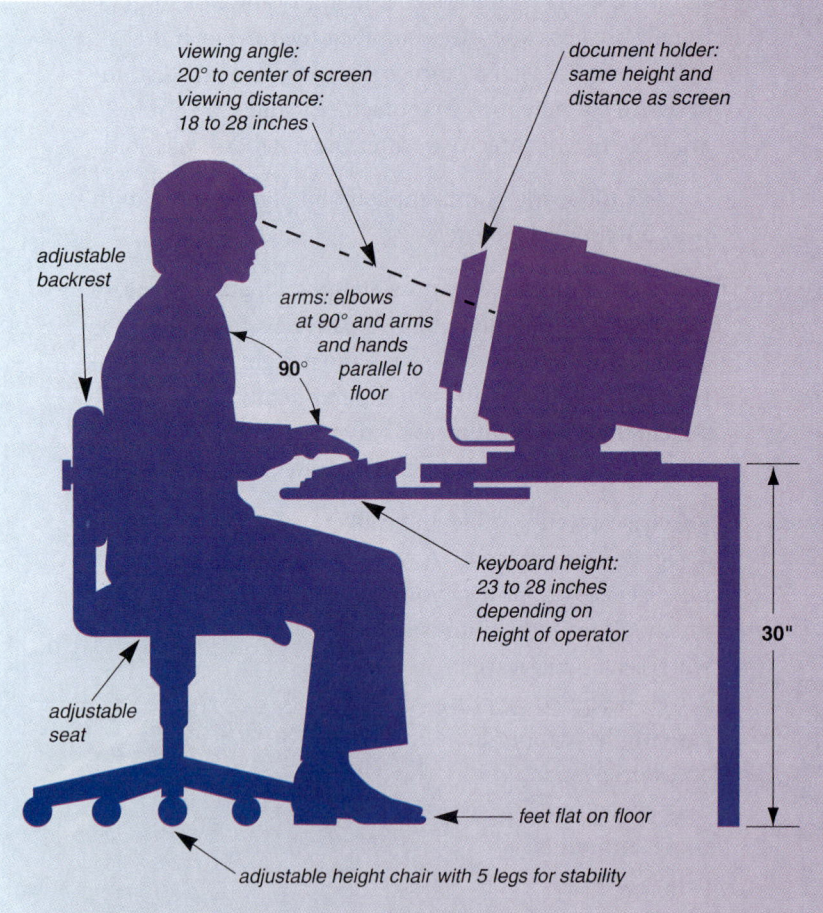

Figure 2
More than anything else, a well-designed work area should be flexible to allow adjustment to the height and build of different individuals. Good lighting and air quality also should be considered.

HOW TO INSTALL A COMPUTER SYSTEM   **8.41**

10. **Save all the paperwork that comes with your system.** Keep it in an accessible place with the paperwork from your other computer-related purchases. To keep different size documents together, consider putting them in a sealable plastic bag.

11. **Record the serial numbers of all your equipment and software.** Write the serial numbers on the outside of the manuals that came with the equipment as well as in a single list that contains the serial numbers of all your equipment and software.

12. **Keep the shipping containers and packing materials for all your equipment.** This material will come in handy if you have to return your equipment for servicing or have to move it to another location.

13. **Look at the inside of your computer.** Before you connect power to your system, remove the computer case cover and visually inspect the internal components. The user manual usually identifies what each component does. Look for any disconnected wires, loose screws or washers, or any other obvious signs of trouble. Be careful not to touch anything inside the case unless you are grounded. Static electricity permanently can damage the chips on the circuit boards. Before you replace the cover, take several photographs of the computer showing the location of the circuit boards. These photos may save you from taking the cover off in the future if you or a vendor has a question about what equipment controller card is installed in what expansion slot. If you feel uncomfortable performing this step by yourself, ask a more experienced computer user to help. If you buy your system from a local dealer, have the dealer perform this step with you before you take possession of your system.

14. **Identify device connectors.** At the back of your system, you will find a number of connectors for the printer, the monitor, the mouse, a telephone line, and so forth. If the manufacturer does not already identify them, use a marking pen to write the purpose of each connector on the back of the computer case.

15. **Complete and send in your equipment and software registration cards right away.** If you already are entered in the vendor's user database, it can save you time when you call with a support question. Being a registered user also makes you eligible for special pricing on software upgrades.

16. **Install your system in an area where the temperature and humidity can be maintained.** Try to maintain a constant temperature between 60 and 80 degrees Fahrenheit when the computer is operating. High temperatures and humidity can damage electronic components. Be careful when using space heaters; their hot, dry air has been known to cause disk problems.

17. **Keep your computer area clean.** Avoid eating and drinking around the computer. Smoking should be avoided also. Cigarette smoke quickly can cause damage to the floppy disk drives and floppy disk surfaces.

18. **Check your home or renters insurance policy.** Some policies have limits on the amount of computer equipment they cover. Other policies do not cover computer equipment at all if it is used for a business (a separate policy is required).

COMPUTER USER HEALTH GUIDELINES

1. Work in a well-designed work area. See Figure 2 on page 8.40 for guidelines.
2. Alternate work activities to prevent physical and mental fatigue. If possible, change the order of your work to provide some variety.
3. Take frequent breaks. Every 15 minutes, look away from the screen to give your eyes a break. At least once per hour, get out of your chair and move around. Every two hours, take at least a 15-minute break.
4. Incorporate hand, arm, and body stretching exercises into your breaks. At lunch, try to get outside and walk.
5. Make sure your computer monitor is designed to minimize electromagnetic radiation (EMR). If it is an older model, consider adding EMR reducing accessories.
6. Try to eliminate or minimize surrounding noise. Noisy environments contribute to stress and tension.
7. If you frequently use the telephone and the computer at the same time, consider using a telephone headset. Cradling the telephone between your head and shoulder can cause muscle strain.
8. Be aware of symptoms of repetitive strain injuries: soreness, pain, numbness, or weakness in neck, shoulders, arms, wrists, and hands. Do not ignore early signs; seek medical advice.

Figure 3
All computer users should follow these guidelines to maintain their health.

How to Maintain Your Computer System

1. **Start a notebook that includes information on your system.** This notebook should be a single source of information about your entire system, both hardware and software. Each time you make a change to your system, adding or removing hardware or software, or when you change system parameters, you should record the change in your notebook. Keep a separate section for user IDs, passwords, and nicknames you use for Web sites and online services. Items you should include in the notebook are the following:
   - Serial numbers of all equipment and software.
   - Vendor support telephone numbers. These numbers often are buried in user manuals. Look up these numbers once and record all of them on a single sheet of paper at the front of your notebook.
   - User IDs, passwords, and nicknames for Web sites and online services.
   - Date and vendor for each equipment and software purchase.
   - Trouble log; a chronological history of any equipment or software problems. This history can be helpful if the problem persists and you have to call for support several times.
   - Notes on discussions with vendor support personnel (can be combined with trouble log).

   See Figure 4 for a suggested outline of notebook contents.

2. **Periodically review disk directories and delete unneeded files.** Files have a way of building up and quickly can use up your disk space. If you think you may need a file in the future, back it up to a floppy disk. Consider using an uninstaller utility program.

3. **Any time you work inside your computer, turn off the power and disconnect the equipment from the power source.** In addition, before you touch anything inside the computer, touch an unpainted metal surface such as the power supply. This will help to discharge any static electricity that could damage internal components.

4. **Reduce the need to clean the inside of your system by keeping the surrounding area dirt and dust free.** Floppy disk cleaners are available but should be used sparingly (some owners never use them unless they experience floppy disk problems). If dust builds up inside the computer, remove it carefully with compressed air and a small vacuum. Do not touch the components with the vacuum.

5. **Backup key files and data.** Use the operating system or a utility program to create an emergency or rescue disk to help you restart your computer if it crashes. Important data files should be copied regularly to disks, tape, or another computer.

6. **Periodically, defragment your hard disk.** Defragmenting your hard disk reorganizes files so they are incontiguous (adjacent) clusters and makes disk operations faster. Always back up your system before you run a defragmentation program.

7. **Protect your system from computer viruses.** Computer viruses are programs designed to *infect* computer systems by copying themselves into other computer files. The virus program spreads when the infected files are used by or copied to another system. Virus programs are dangerous because often they are designed to damage the files of the infected computer. You can protect yourself from viruses by installing an antivirus program on your computer.

8. **Learn to use system diagnostic programs.** If your system did not include diagnostic programs, obtain a set. These programs help you identify and possibly solve problems before you call for technical assistance. Some system manufacturers now include diagnostic programs with their systems and ask that you run the programs before you call for help.

PC OWNER'S NOTEBOOK OUTLINE

1. **Vendors**
   Vendor
   City/State
   Product
   Telephone #
   URL

2. **Internet and online services information**
   Service provider name
   Logon telephone number
   Alternate logon telephone number
   Technical support telephone number
   User ID
   Password

3. **Web site information**
   Web site name
   URL
   User ID
   Password
   Nickname

4. **Serial numbers**
   Product
   Manufacturer
   Serial #

5. **Purchase history**
   Date
   Product
   Manufacturer
   Vendor
   Cost

6. **Software log**
   Date installed/uninstalled

7. **Trouble log**
   Date
   Time
   Problem
   Resolution

8. **Support calls**
   Date
   Time
   Company
   Contact
   Problem
   Comments

9. **Vendor paperwork**

Figure 4
This suggested notebook outline will keep important information about your computer on hand and organized.

Data Management and Databases

OBJECTIVES

After completing this chapter, you will be able to:

- Discuss data management and explain why it is needed
- Describe the hierarchy of data
- Describe sequential files, indexed files, and direct files
- Explain the difference between sequential and random organization and retrieval of records from a file
- Describe the data maintenance procedures for updating data, including adding, changing, and deleting
- Discuss the advantages of a database management system (DBMS)
- Describe hierarchical, network, relational, and object-oriented database systems
- Explain the use of a query language
- Describe the responsibilities of a database administrator
- Explain several guidelines for creating database files
- Discuss personal computer database systems

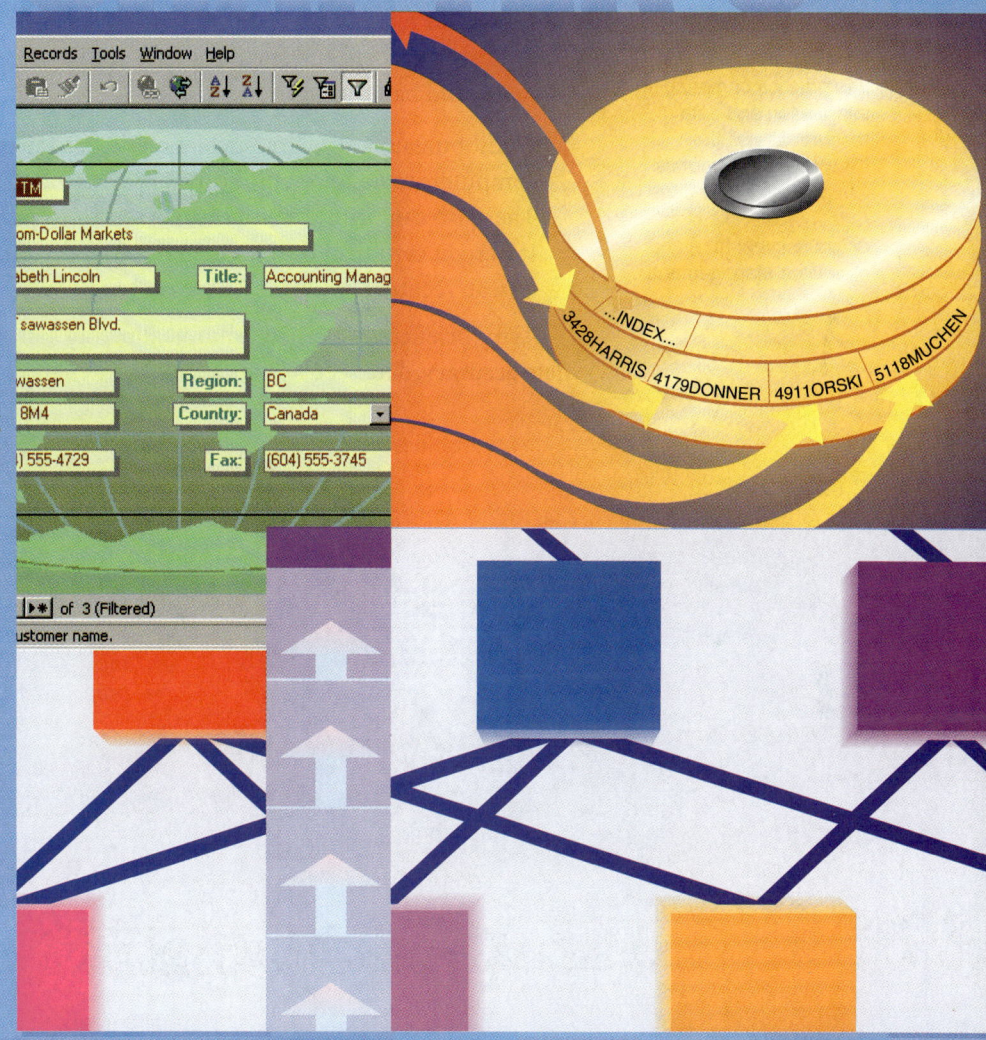

CHAPTER 9

To provide maximum benefit to an organization, data must be managed carefully, organized, and used. The purpose of this chapter is to explain the need for data management, discuss how files on storage devices are organized and maintained, and describe the advantages, organization, and use of databases. Learning this information will help you better understand how data and information are stored and managed on a computer and help you maximize the power of today's databases.

Data Management

Data management refers to the procedures used to acquire, access, and maintain data. The purpose of data management is to ensure that data required for an application will be available in the correct form and at the proper time for processing. Both information systems professionals and users share the responsibility for data management.

To illustrate the need for data management, an example of a credit bureau is used (Figure 9-1). A summary of the application follows.

- A consumer credit bureau acquires data on individuals from numerous sources such as banks and retail stores. The data includes personal data such as driver's license and Social Security numbers and financial data such as income, existing loans, history of paying debts, and bankruptcies.

- Credit bureau customers, such as credit card firms and student loan companies, use computers to access credit bureau records when someone applies for credit or a loan. They also can print a credit history report to place with the person's credit application. If a credit card firm decides to grant an individual credit, this data is added to the credit bureau records.

This brief credit bureau example illustrates three major aspects of data management: data accuracy, data security, and data maintenance.

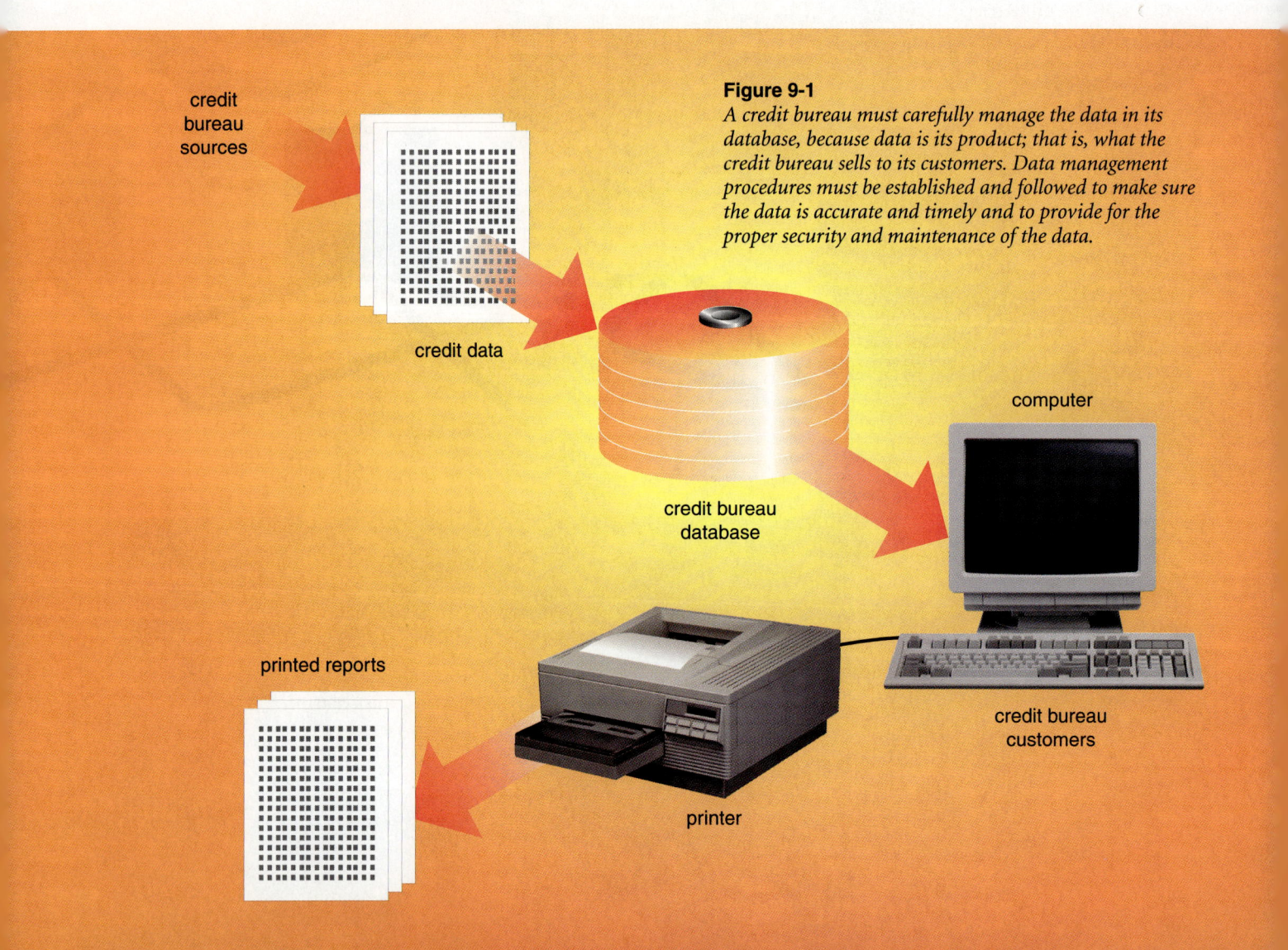

> **inCyber**
>
> For information on the Data Management Association, which furthers the "understanding, development, and practice of managing information and data resources," visit the Discovering Computers Chapter 9 inCyber page (http://www.scsite.com/dc/ch9/incyber.htm) and click Data Management.

Figure 9-1
A credit bureau must carefully manage the data in its database, because data is its product; that is, what the credit bureau sells to its customers. Data management procedures must be established and followed to make sure the data is accurate and timely and to provide for the proper security and maintenance of the data.

Data Accuracy

For you to have confidence in the information provided by a computer system, you first must be confident that the data used to create the information is accurate. **Data accuracy**, sometimes called **data integrity**, means that the source of the data is reliable and the data is reported and entered correctly. For example, if a business incorrectly reports to the credit bureau that an individual did not pay a bill, a customer could be denied credit unjustly. The companies that rely on the credit bureau must be confident that the credit bureau receives accurate data from outside organizations. To generate accurate information, the credit bureau also must be sure to enter all data into the computer correctly. This is called **reliable data entry**.

Accurate data also must be timely. **Timely data** is data that has not lost its usefulness or legitimacy because time has passed. For example, assume that five years ago, an annual income of $30,000 was entered for an individual. Today, that data is not timely because five years have passed and the person may be earning either more or less.

Data Security

Data security involves protecting data to keep it from being misused or lost. For example, because personal credit information is confidential, the credit bureau has systems and procedures that allow only authorized personnel to access the data stored in their records. The credit bureau also performs backup procedures to protect against the loss of data. **Backup** refers to making copies of data files so that if data is lost or destroyed, a timely recovery can be made and processing can continue. Every night, the credit bureau backs up all of its data and stores the copies in a fireproof safe. Backup copies normally are kept in a fireproof safe or in a separate building so that a single disaster, such as a fire, will not destroy both the primary data and the backup copy of the data.

> **inCyber**
> For information on a variety of data security issues, visit the Discovering Computers Chapter 9 inCyber page (http://www.scsite.com/dc/ch9/incyber.htm) and click Data Security.

Data Maintenance

Data maintenance refers to the procedures used to keep data current. Data maintenance, which often is called **updating**, includes procedures for *adding* new data, such as the credit bureau creating a record for a person who has just been granted credit; *changing* existing data, such as posting a change of address to an existing record; and *deleting* obsolete data, such as removing inactive records.

The Hierarchy of Data

Data is organized in a hierarchy in which each higher level is made up of one or more elements from the lower level preceding it. The levels in the hierarchy of data (Figure 9-2) include bit, byte, field, record, file, and database.

- **Bit.** A **bit** is a binary 1 or 0. Usually a bit is combined with other bits to represent data.
- **Byte.** A **byte** is a combination of eight bits. A byte can represent a character such as a letter (A), a number (7), or a symbol (#).
- **Field.** A **field**, sometimes called an **attribute**, is a combination of one or more bytes and is usually the smallest item of meaningful data. For example, three fields can be used for your name; one for your first name, one for your middle name or initial, and one for your last name. Depending on the file system, a field can be either a fixed length and have a specific number of bytes or a variable length and have any number of bytes.

   A **key field** or **key**, is a field that is used to identify the records in a file. Each key field must contain data that is unique to that record. Because they are unique to one item, Social Security numbers, part numbers, or student ID numbers often are used as key fields.
- **Record.** A **record** is a group of related fields. A student record would have individual fields for your first name, last name, middle initial, street address, city, state or province, postal code, telephone number, major, date enrolled, and so on. Records are used to record data about entities. An **entity** is any person, place, thing, or event for which data is collected.
- **File.** A **file** is a collection of related records or data that is stored under a single name. For conventional text and numeric files, such as those used to record business transactions, files consist of many related records. A school's Student file, for example, would consist of thousands of individual student records. Each student record would contain the same fields as the other records.

HIERARCHY OF DATA

Data Element	Can Contain	Example
Database	Related files	Student file, Course file Grades file, Scholarship file
File	Many related records	Amy Lee, 123 Hill Street, ... Tom Sanchez, 1401 Reeder Ct., . . Irving Brown, 1813 Ryan Ave., . . .
Record	Related groups of fields such as a person's name and address data	Amy Lee, 123 Hill Street, Seattle, WA, 99999 206-555-1234
Field	Individual elements of data such as a person's first name	Amy
Byte	One character or other unit of information consisting of eight bits	01000001 (letter A)
Bit	binary digit 0 or 1	Bits can represent any two-state condition, such as on or off, but usually are combined into bytes to represent data.

Figure 9-2

Each level in the hierarchy of data is made up of elements from lower levels.

The term file also refers to other types of files, such as word processing, spreadsheet, or other application or media files, in which data is relatively unstructured. Media files such as graphic, video, or audio files consist mainly of binary data and are referred to as a **BLOB** (**binary large object**). In this chapter, and when discussing database concepts, the term file usually refers to a structured file that is organized in a uniform format.

- **Database.** A **database** is a group of related files. A school's Registration database, for example, might have many individual files related to class scheduling and registration — a Course file, a Section file, a Student file, and so on. Together, all of these files comprise the Registration database. Databases are discussed in more detail later in the chapter.

> **inCyber**
> For details on a binary large object, visit the Discovering Computers Chapter 9 inCyber page (http://www.scsite.com/dc/ch9/incyber.htm) and click BLOB.

Types of File Organization

A file can be organized in one of three ways: sequential, indexed, or direct. Files typically are organized based on the media on which they are stored or the manner in which they are processed. Files stored on tape use sequential organization, while files stored on disks usually use indexed or direct file organization. Advantages and disadvantages exist to using each of the types of file organization.

Sequential File Organization

Sequential file organization means that records are stored sequentially, one after the other. Records stored using sequential file organization normally are stored in ascending or descending order, based on the value in the key field. For example, in Figure 9-3, the file contains student records stored sequentially by student identification number. These records are retrieved one after another in the same sequence in which they are stored.

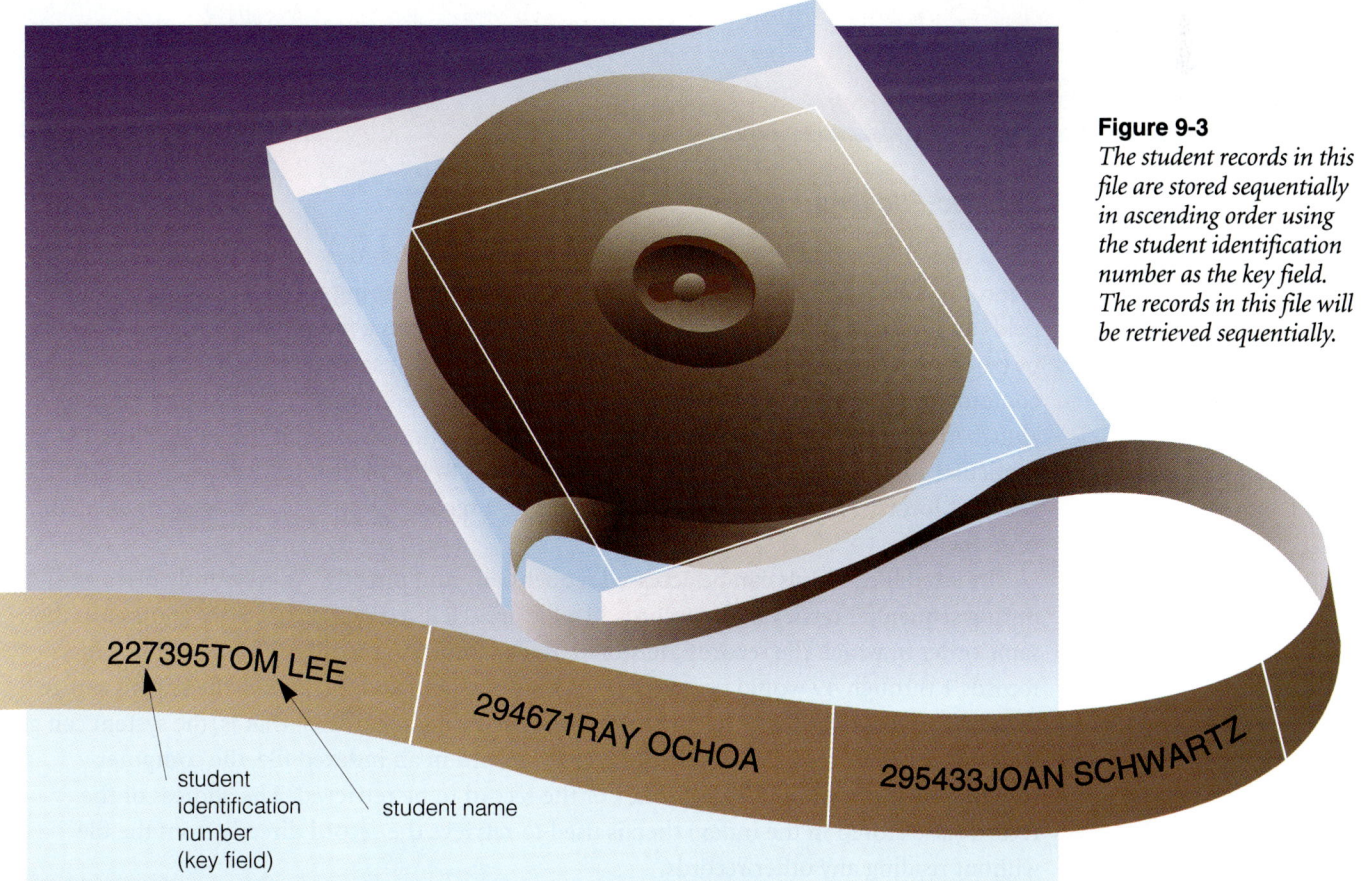

> **inCyber**
> For information on sequential file organization, visit the Discovering Computers Chapter 9 inCyber page (http://www.scsite.com/dc/ch9/incyber.htm) and click Sequential File.

Figure 9-3
The student records in this file are stored sequentially in ascending order using the student identification number as the key field. The records in this file will be retrieved sequentially.

227395TOM LEE
294671RAY OCHOA
295433JOAN SCHWARTZ

student identification number (key field)
student name

Sequential retrieval has a major disadvantage: because records must be retrieved in order, one by one, the computer cannot retrieve a record without reading all preceding records first. Thus, as shown in Figure 9-3, if you want to retrieve the record for Joan Schwartz, the computer first must read the records for Tom Lee and Ray Ochoa. For this reason, you should not use sequential file organization if you will need to access a particular record quickly. Sequential retrieval is appropriate, however, when records usually are processed in order — say, in a weekly payroll application where all employee records are processed sequentially at one time. Another common use of sequential files is for backup files.

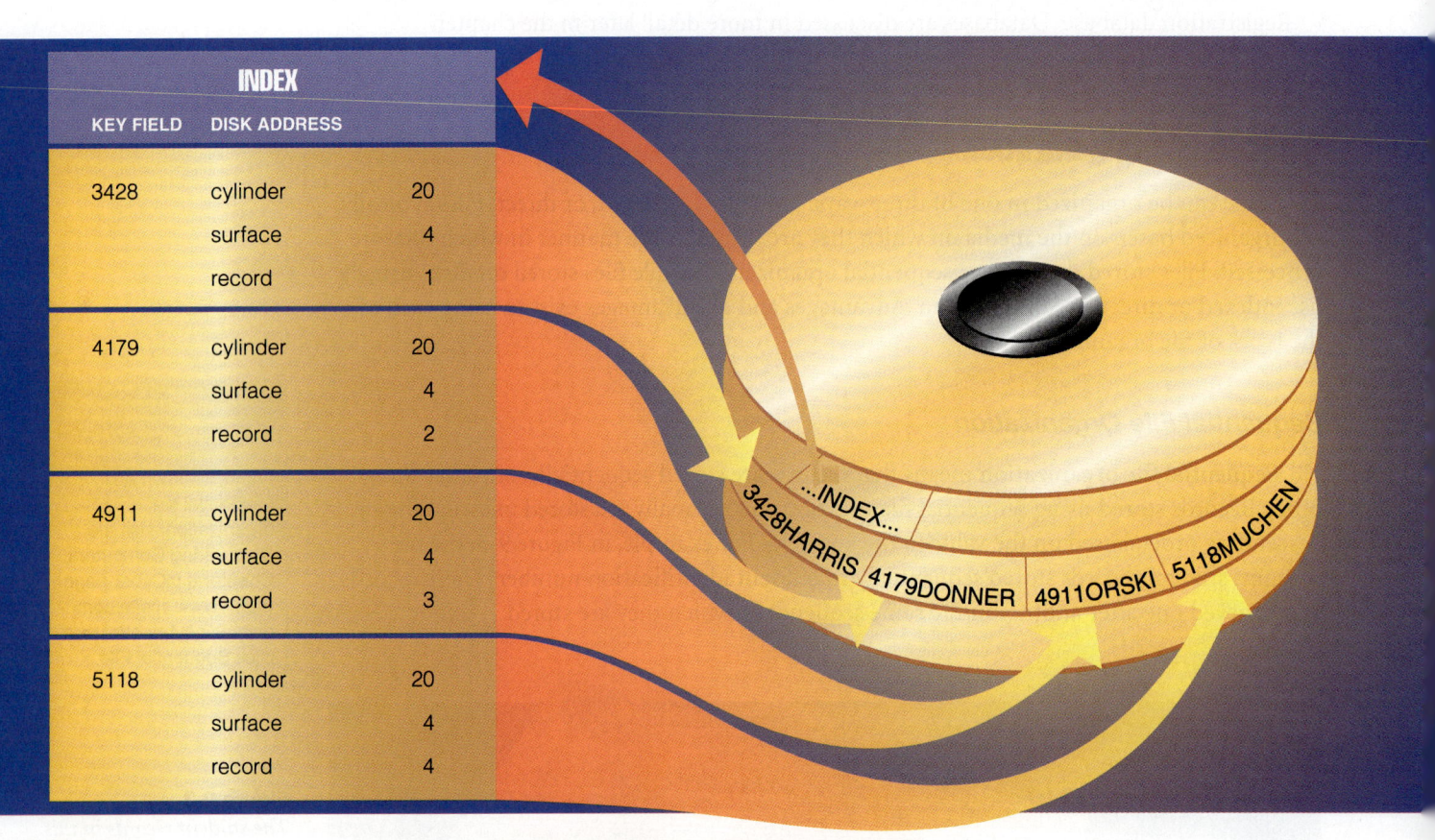

INDEX		
KEY FIELD	DISK ADDRESS	
3428	cylinder	20
	surface	4
	record	1
4179	cylinder	20
	surface	4
	record	2
4911	cylinder	20
	surface	4
	record	3
5118	cylinder	20
	surface	4
	record	4

Figure 9-4
The index in an indexed file contains the record key and the corresponding disk address for each record in the file. Here, the index contains the employee number, which is the key for the employee file and the disk address for the corresponding employee record.

Indexed File Organization

Indexed file organization uses a separate file, called an index, to record the location of a record on a storage device. An **index** consists of a list containing the values of one or more fields and the corresponding disk address for each record in a file (Figure 9-4). The index can be based on a single field, such as the record key field or on several fields, such as a combination of last and first name, which would enable a student file to be accessed in alphabetical order. In the same way that an index for a book points to the page where a particular topic is covered, the index for a file points to the place on a disk where a particular record is located. The index is updated each time a record is added to, changed, or deleted from the file.

Indexed file records can be accessed sequentially and directly. As previously discussed, during sequential retrieval, the records in a file are retrieved one record after another in the same order in which the records are stored. For example, to read the 50th record in a file, records 1 through 49 would be read first. With **direct**, or **random, access**, the system can go directly to a record without having to read the preceding records — that is, the system can go directly to the 50th record. To directly access a record in an indexed file, the computer searches the index until it finds the key of the record to be retrieved. The address of the record (also stored in the index) then is used to retrieve the record directly from the file without reading any other records.

One advantage of indexed files is that each file can have more than one index, each of which can be used to access records quickly in a particular order. For example, an employee file might have three separate indexes, one for employee number, a second for employee name, and a third for Social Security number. Different programs can use the index that enables the program to access the records the fastest. A disadvantage of indexed files is that searching an index for a record in a large file can take a long time. In addition, maintaining one or more indexes adds to the processing time whenever a record is added, changed, or deleted.

Direct File Organization

Direct file organization (sometimes called a *relative* or *random file organization*) uses a record's key value to determine the location on the disk where the record is stored. Suppose, for example, that a file has nine records with key field values ranging from 1 to 9, and that nine locations are available in which to store the records. Using direct file organization, the key field value would specify the relative location where the record was stored. The record with key value of 3 would be placed in relative location 3, the record with key value of 6 would be placed in relative location 6, and so on. These relative locations sometimes are called **buckets**. A bucket can be divided into **slots** to hold more than one record.

Usually, the storage of records in a file is not so simple as in the previous example. Suppose, for example, that an employee file holds a maximum of 100 records, but that the key for each record in the file is a four-digit employee code. In this case, the key cannot be used to specify the location of the record in the file. Record 0003, could be stored in relative location 3 of the 100 storage locations, but where would records 1009 or 3428 be stored? To determine the relative or actual location of the record in the file, an arithmetic formula is used. The process of using a formula to calculate the location of a record is called **hashing**.

One hashing method is the division/remainder method. With this method, the computer divides the key by a prime number close to but not greater than the estimated number of records to be stored in the file. A **prime number** is a number divisible without a remainder only by itself and 1. For example, suppose you have 100 records. The number 97 is the closest prime number to 100 without being greater than 100. The key of the record is then divided by 97 and the remainder from the division operation is the relative location where the record is stored. For example, if the record key is 3428, the relative location where the record will be stored in the file is location 33 (Figure 9-5).

> **inCyber**
>
> For a history of prime numbers and the opportunity to discover the next prime number, visit the Discovering Computers Chapter 9 inCyber page (http://www.scsite.com/dc/ch9/incyber.htm) and click Prime Number.

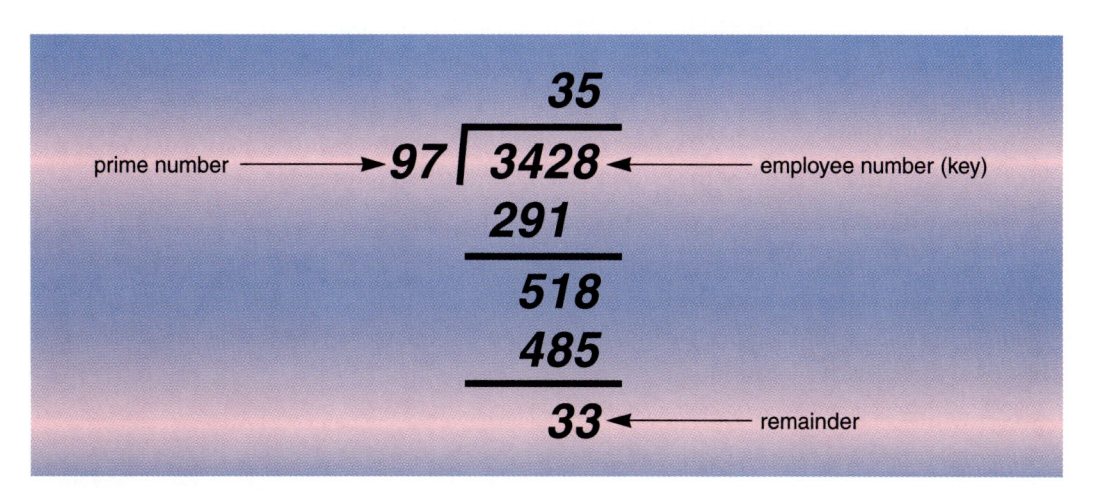

```
                    35
prime number ——▶ 97 ) 3428 ◀—— employee number (key)
                   291
                   ———
                    518
                    485
                   ———
                     33 ◀—— remainder
```

Figure 9-5
When the value 3428 is divided by the prime number 97, the remainder is 33. This remainder is used as the bucket where the record with key 3428 is stored in the direct file.

The hashing techniques used with direct file organization create a problem not found with sequential or indexed files. As previously discussed, every record in a file has a different key that uniquely identifies that record. Sometimes, however, when hashing is used to calculate a storage location, two different keys generate the same location on disk. For example, employee number 3331 generates the same relative location (33) as employee number 3428. When hashing different keys results in the same location, the keys are called **synonyms**. The occurrence of synonyms is called a **collision**. A common way to resolve collisions is to place the record that caused the collision in the next slot in the bucket. If all the slots in the bucket are full, the record is placed in the next available slot in the next available bucket (Figure 9-6).

Figure 9-6
Sometimes the hashing computation produces synonyms, or records, that have the same relative address. In this example, both records have a relative address of 33. When the computer tries to store the second record and finds that location 33 is already full, it stores the second record at the next available location. Here, record 3331 is stored in location 34. In this simple example, only one record is stored per relative location. In practice, multiple records can be stored at each relative location.

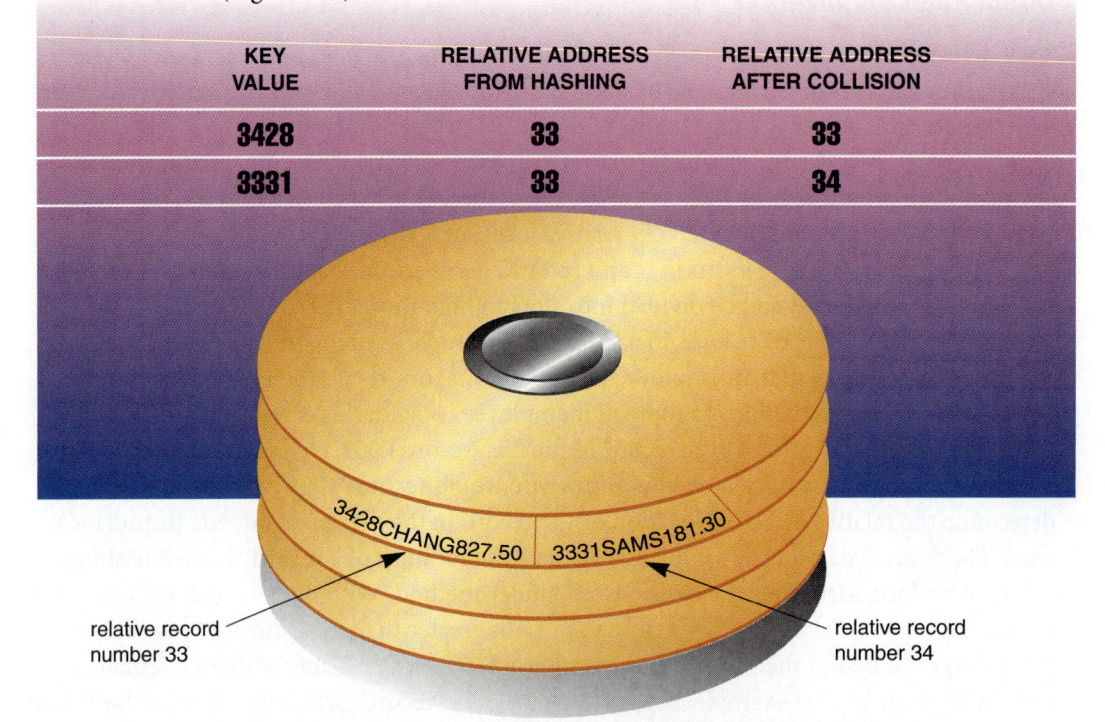

KEY VALUE	RELATIVE ADDRESS FROM HASHING	RELATIVE ADDRESS AFTER COLLISION
3428	33	33
3331	33	34

relative record number 33 — 3428CHANG827.50
relative record number 34 — 3331SAMS181.30

Once a record is stored in its relative location within a direct file, it can be retrieved either directly or sequentially. The method normally used with direct files is direct retrieval. A record is retrieved from a direct file by performing three steps.

1. The program obtains the key of the record to be retrieved. The value of the key, such as an employee number, is entered by the user or is read from another file.
2. The program determines the location of the record to be retrieved by performing the same hashing process as when the record was initially stored. Thus, to retrieve the record with key 3428, the key value would be divided by the prime number 97. The remainder, 33, specifies the location of the bucket where the record is stored.
3. The software directs the computer to bucket 33 to retrieve the record.

Direct files also allow for sequential retrieval. To retrieve a file, the program simply indicates that the record from the first relative location is to be retrieved, followed by the record from the second relative location, and so on. All the records in the file are retrieved based on their relative location in the file.

Summary of File Organization Concepts

Files are organized as sequential, indexed, or direct files. Sequential file organization, which is used with tape storage, requires that records in the file be retrieved sequentially. Indexed and direct file organization, by contrast, is used for disk storage and allows for sequential or direct retrieval.

How Is Data in Files Maintained?

As discussed, data maintenance includes processes needed to keep data current and accurate. Data maintenance, or updating, involves adding records to, changing records in, or deleting records from a file.

Adding Records

Records are added to a file when additional data is needed to make the file current. For example, if a customer opens a new account at a bank, a record containing the data for the new account must be added to the bank's account file. The process that would take place to add this record to the file is shown in Figure 9-7.

1. The bank clerk runs an Account Creation program designed to add new customer account records to the file.
2. The computer program assigns a new account number.
3. The clerk enters personal data about the customer. For purposes of this example, the only personal data entered is the customer name.
4. The clerk enters the initial deposit amount.
5. The program asks the clerk to confirm that the data entered is correct.
6. The program adds the new account record to the file. The location on the disk where the record is written will be determined by the program that manages the disk. In some cases, a new record will be written between other records in the file. In other cases, such as illustrated in Figure 9-7, the new record will be added to the end of the file.

Adding records is a basic part of updating files. When data is stored in a file for later use, records almost always must be added to the keep the data current.

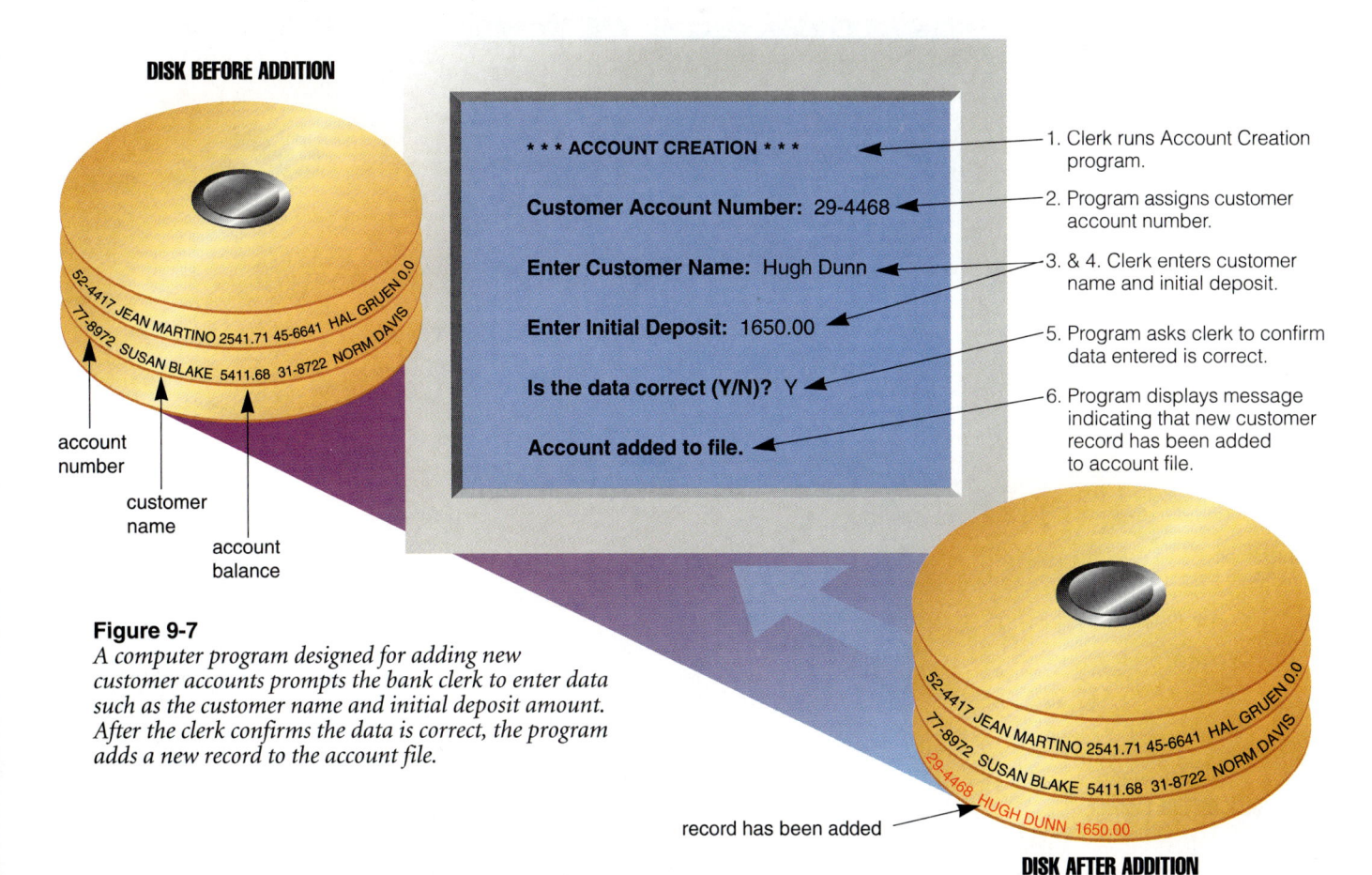

Figure 9-7
A computer program designed for adding new customer accounts prompts the bank clerk to enter data such as the customer name and initial deposit amount. After the clerk confirms the data is correct, the program adds a new record to the account file.

Changing Records

Records in a file are changed for two primary reasons: (1) to correct inaccurate data and (2) to update older data when newer data becomes available.

As an example of the first type of change, assume that a bank clerk enters the customer's last name as Done, instead of Dunn (Figure 9-7). When the customer receives his statement, he notices the error, contacts the bank, and requests that the spelling of his name be corrected. To do this, the clerk would retrieve the record and change Done to Dunn in the last name field. This change corrects the inaccurate data and replaces it with accurate data.

The second and more common reason to change a record is to update data when newer data becomes available. Suppose, for example, that a customer named Jean Martino withdraws $500 (Figure 9-8). The following steps occur to process the withdrawal and update Jean Martino's record.

1. The bank clerk runs an Account Withdrawal program.
2. The bank clerk enters Jean Martino's account number, 52-4417.
3. The program displays Ms. Martino's name and account balance. This information allows the clerk to verify that the correct account number was entered and that sufficient money is available in the account to cover the withdrawal.
4. The clerk enters the withdrawal amount of $500.
5. The program asks the clerk to confirm the transaction.
6. The clerk confirms the transaction, and the account record on the disk is changed. After the change, the record stored on the disk contains the new account balance.

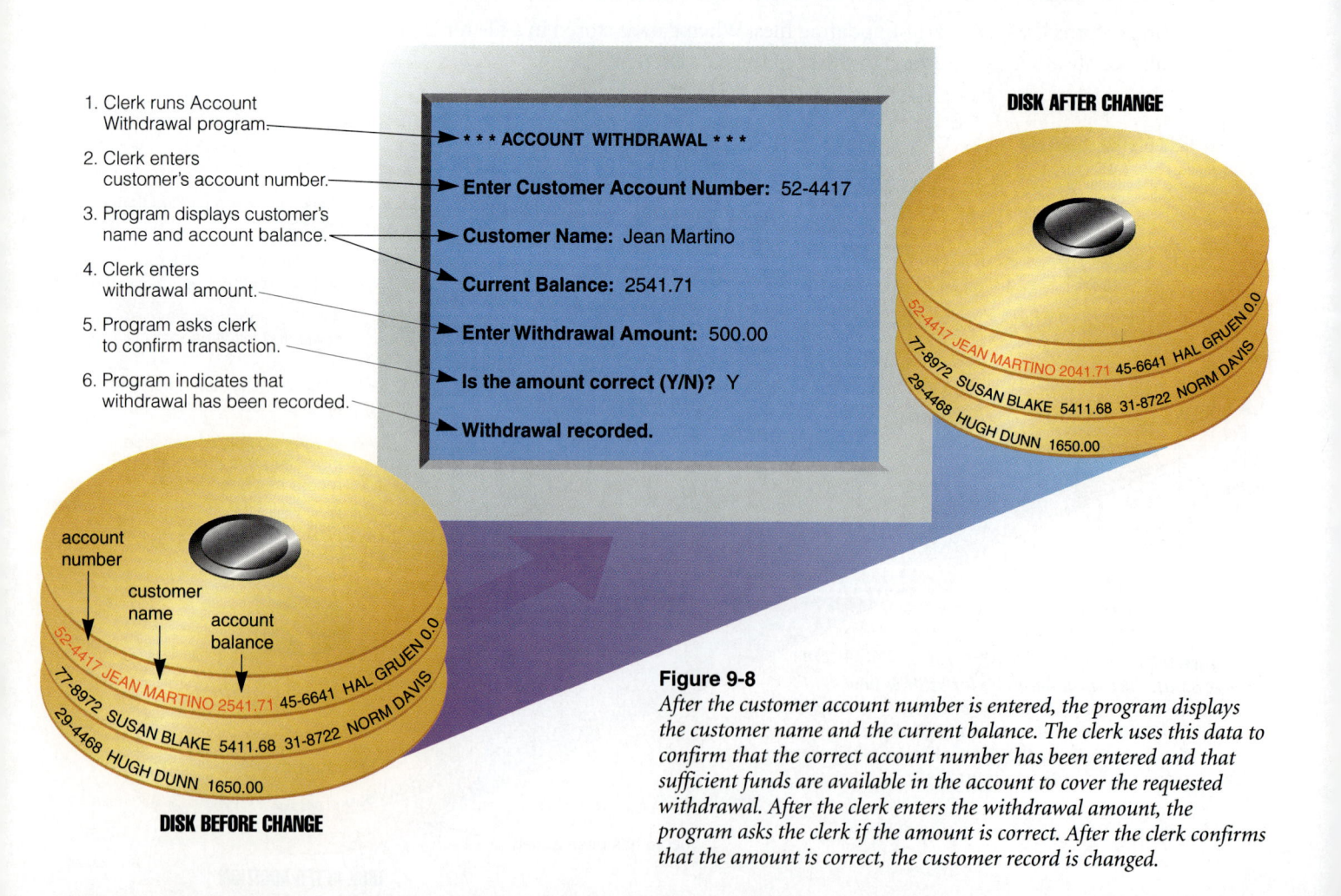

1. Clerk runs Account Withdrawal program.
2. Clerk enters customer's account number.
3. Program displays customer's name and account balance.
4. Clerk enters withdrawal amount.
5. Program asks clerk to confirm transaction.
6. Program indicates that withdrawal has been recorded.

```
* * * ACCOUNT WITHDRAWAL * * *

Enter Customer Account Number: 52-4417

Customer Name: Jean Martino

Current Balance: 2541.71

Enter Withdrawal Amount: 500.00

Is the amount correct (Y/N)? Y

Withdrawal recorded.
```

DISK AFTER CHANGE

52-4417 JEAN MARTINO 2041.71 45-6641 HAL GRUEN 0.0
77-8972 SUSAN BLAKE 5411.68 31-8722 NORM DAVIS
29-4468 HUGH DUNN 1650.00

DISK BEFORE CHANGE

account number
customer name
account balance

52-4417 JEAN MARTINO 2541.71 45-6641 HAL GRUEN 0.0
77-8972 SUSAN BLAKE 5411.68 31-8722 NORM DAVIS
29-4468 HUGH DUNN 1650.00

Figure 9-8
After the customer account number is entered, the program displays the customer name and the current balance. The clerk uses this data to confirm that the correct account number has been entered and that sufficient funds are available in the account to cover the requested withdrawal. After the clerk enters the withdrawal amount, the program asks the clerk if the amount is correct. After the clerk confirms that the amount is correct, the customer record is changed.

Changing records is a routine, yet critical, part of data maintenance. An account record, for instance, might be adjusted several times during a business day for each deposit, each withdrawal, each transfer, and so on. Because data changes often, the ability to change records in a database is needed to keep data accurate and current.

Deleting Records

Records are deleted when they are no longer needed. Figure 9-9 shows the maintenance procedures used to delete a record for Hal Gruen, a customer who has closed his account.

1. The bank clerk runs a Close Customer Account program.
2. The bank clerk enters Hal Gruen's account number, 45-6641.
3. The program displays Hal Gruen's name and account balance.
4. The program asks the clerk to confirm that this is the account to be closed.
5. Upon confirmation, the record is deleted. The actual processing that occurs to delete a record from a file depends on the type of file organization being used and the processing requirements of the application. Sometimes, the record is removed from the file immediately. Other times, as in this example, the record is not removed from the file. Instead, the record is *flagged*, or marked in some manner, so that it will not be processed again. In this example, an asterisk (*) is added at the beginning of the record.
6. The program displays a message indicating that the account has been closed.

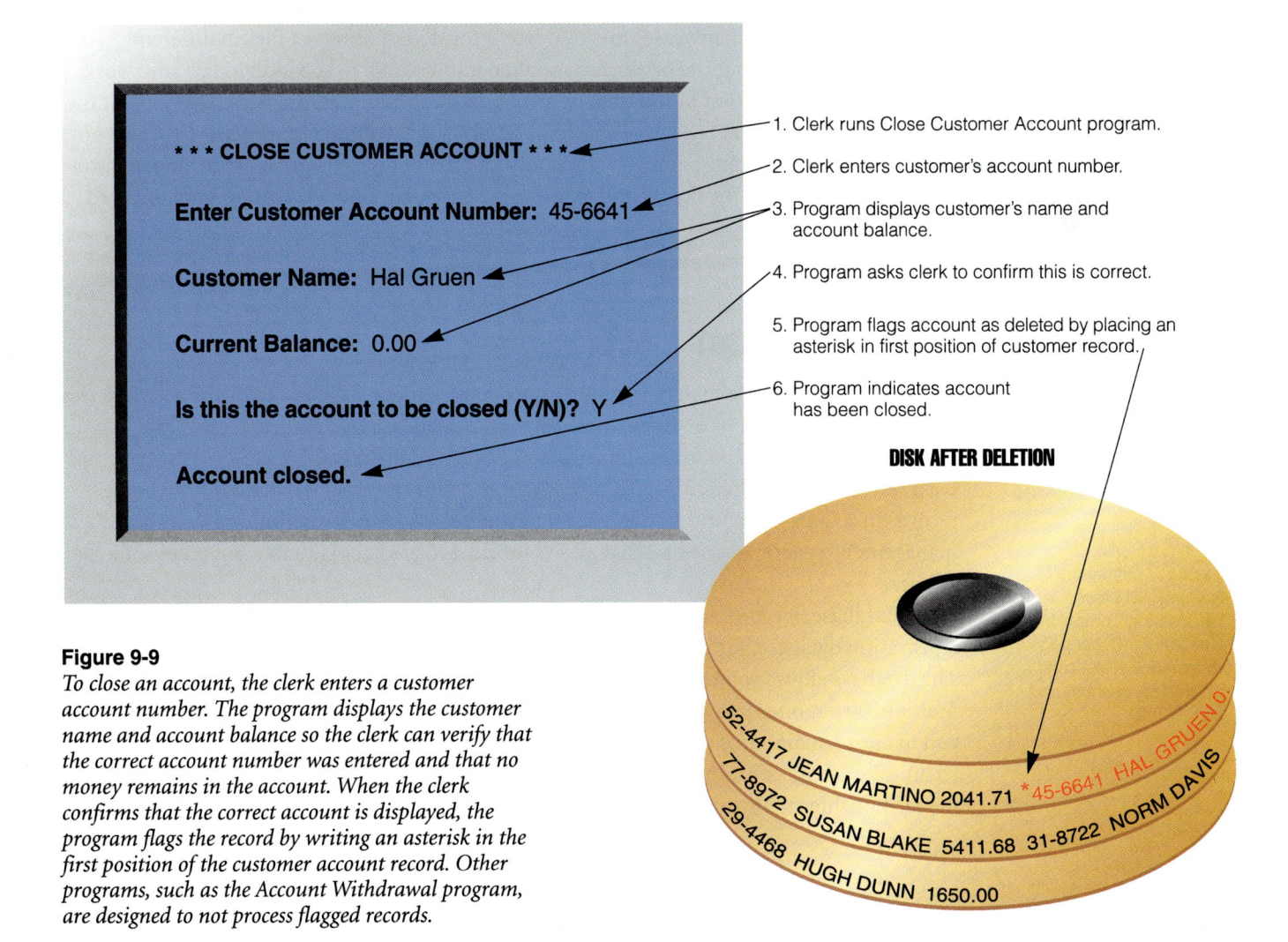

Figure 9-9
To close an account, the clerk enters a customer account number. The program displays the customer name and account balance so the clerk can verify that the correct account number was entered and that no money remains in the account. When the clerk confirms that the correct account is displayed, the program flags the record by writing an asterisk in the first position of the customer account record. Other programs, such as the Account Withdrawal program, are designed to not process flagged records.

* * * CLOSE CUSTOMER ACCOUNT * * *

Enter Customer Account Number: 45-6641

Customer Name: Hal Gruen

Current Balance: 0.00

Is this the account to be closed (Y/N)? Y

Account closed.

1. Clerk runs Close Customer Account program.
2. Clerk enters customer's account number.
3. Program displays customer's name and account balance.
4. Program asks clerk to confirm this is correct.
5. Program flags account as deleted by placing an asterisk in first position of customer record.
6. Program indicates account has been closed.

DISK AFTER DELETION

52-4417 JEAN MARTINO 2041.71 *45-6641 HAL GRUEN 0.
77-8972 SUSAN BLAKE 5411.68 31-8722 NORM DAVIS
29-4468 HUGH DUNN 1650.00

Even though the record is still physically stored on the disk, it effectively is deleted because it will not be retrieved for processing. Flagged records commonly are used in applications where data is no longer active but must be maintained for some period of time. A bank, for example, might flag closed accounts and remove them after one year. Periodically, you should run a utility program that removes flagged records and reorganizes current records. Deleting unneeded records reduces the size of files and creates additional storage space.

Summary of How Data Is Maintained

Data maintenance — the process of updating by adding, changing, and deleting stored data — is essential for generating reliable information. If the data to be processed is inaccurate, the resulting information also will be inaccurate. Basic data maintenance concepts remain the same, regardless of whether the data is stored in a single file or if it is part of a series of files organized in a database.

Databases: A Better Way to Manage and Organize Data

Most organizations realize that next to the skills of their employees, data (and the information it represents) is one of an organization's more valuable assets. They recognize that the information accumulated on sales trends, competitors' products and services, employee skills, and production processes is a valuable resource that would be difficult, if not impossible, to replace.

Unfortunately, in many cases this resource is located in different files in different departments throughout the organization, often known only to the individuals who work with their specific portion of the total information. In these cases, the potential value of the information goes unrealized because it remains unused by other departments that may not know of the data or cannot access it efficiently. In an attempt to organize their information resources and provide for timely and efficient access, many companies have implemented databases.

What Is a Database?

This chapter has discussed previously how data elements (bytes, fields, and records) can be organized in files. A basic file-oriented system is made up of **flat files**, each of which is independent and contains all the information needed to process the records in that one file. Each file contains a different record type — say, student records in a Student file, course records in a Course file, and so on. A **file management system**, sometimes called a flat-file management system, is software that allows the user to create, maintain, and access one file at a time.

A **database**, by contrast, is a collection of related files stored together. A student registration database, for instance, would include the Student file, the Course file, and others. The database allows you to define relationships between these files, so that you can access multiple files at one time. A **database management system (DBMS)** is software that allows you to create, maintain, and report the data and file relationships. Although a flat file technically can be considered a database because it is a collection of data, a flat file lacks the file relationships that truly define a database.

> inCyber
>
> For a description of database management systems, visit the Discovering Computers Chapter 9 inCyber page (http://www.scsite.com/dc/ch9/incyber.htm) and click DBMS.

Why Use a Database?

The following example (Figure 9-10) illustrates some of the advantages of a database system as compared to a file-oriented system. Assume that a business mails catalogs to its customers four times a year. If the business used a file-oriented system, it probably would have a customer file used specifically for the catalog mailing application. This file would contain data about the catalog, as well as customer data such as customer account number, name, and address. Because files used in a file-oriented system are independent of one another, any other applications that require customer information would need to have their own separate customer file or would have the customer data as part of another file. A sales application, an ordering application, and an invoicing application, for example, all might have their own customer files. Duplicating the data in these files not only wastes storage space but also makes data maintenance difficult — each time a customer's data is added, changes, or is deleted, all files containing that data must be updated individually.

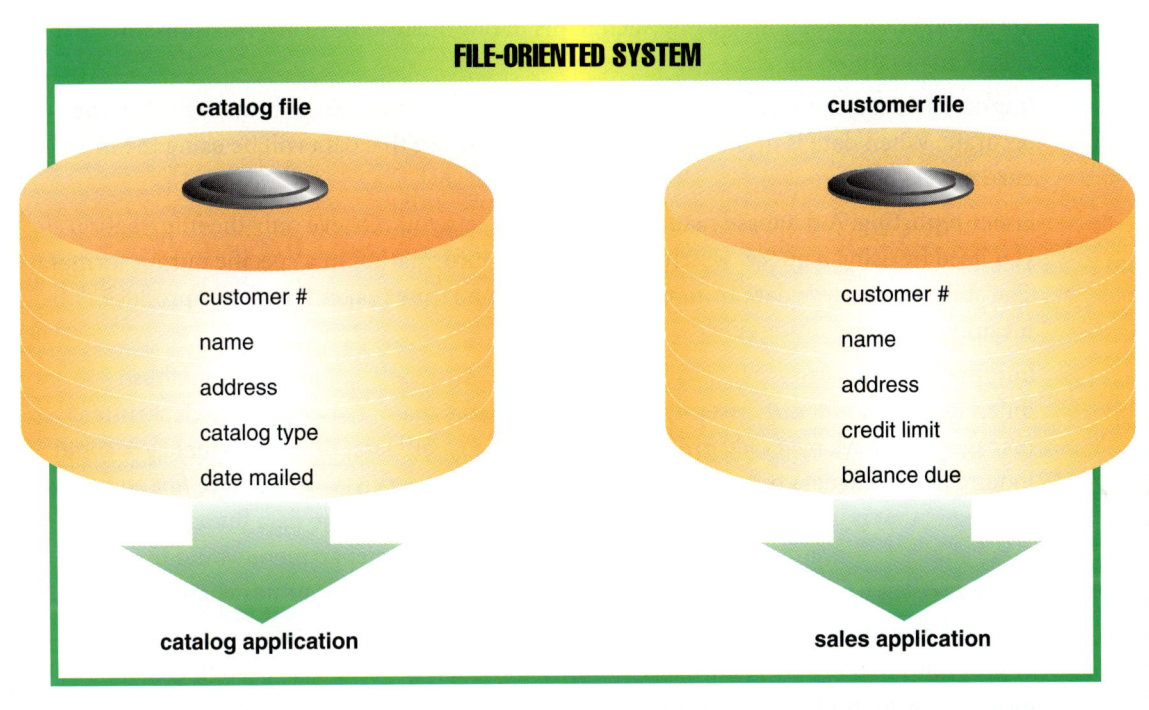

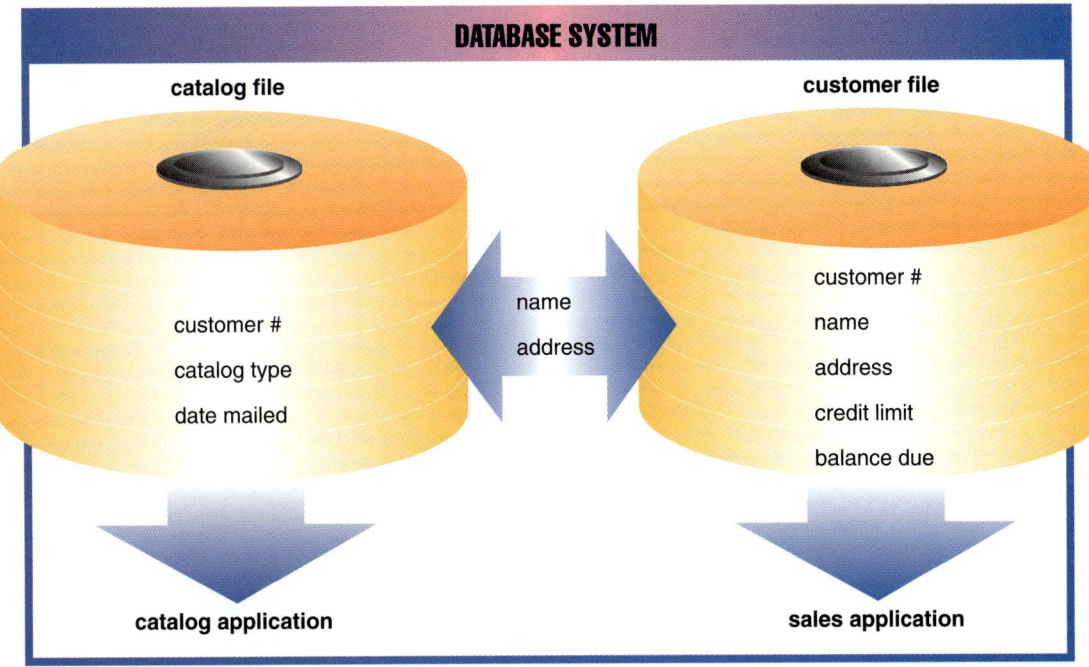

Figure 9-10
In a file-oriented system, each file contains the customer name and address. In the database system, only the customer file contains the name and address. Other files, such as the catalog file, use the customer number to retrieve the customer name and address when it is needed for processing.

By contrast, in a database system, the customer data would be stored by only one of the applications. That is because, in a database system, files are linked through predefined relationships or by common data fields. In this example, the customer account number is used as the common data field that links the catalog file to the customer file. The customer file contains the customer account number, name, and address. The catalog file contains only the customer's account number and the catalog information. When the catalog application software is executed, the customer's name and address are obtained from the customer file. Because the database files are linked, the customer name and address only needs to be stored once. This saves storage space and simplifies data maintenance because updated data only needs to be entered in one file.

As the previous example illustrates, a database system offers a number of advantages over a file-oriented system. These advantages and several others are summarized as follows:

- **Reduced data redundancy.** Redundant, or duplicate, data is reduced greatly in a database system. Frequently used data elements such as names, addresses, and product descriptions are stored in one location. Having such items in one, instead of many, locations lowers the cost of maintaining the data.

- **Improved data accuracy.** Because data is stored only in one place, it is more likely to be accurate. When data is updated, all applications that use this data will be using the most current version.

- **Easier reporting.** A database management system lets you retrieve only the information you need by using a **query**, which is a request for information in a specific output format. The ability to retrieve data from multiple files at one time makes it easier to produce meaningful queries and reports.

- **Improved data security.** Most database management systems allow you to establish different levels of security over information in the database. For example, a department manager may have *read only* privileges on certain payroll data; that is, the manager could inquire about the data but not change it. The payroll supervisor would have *full update* privileges; that is, the supervisor not only could inquire about the data but also could make changes. A nonmanagement employee from another department would have no access privileges to the payroll data and neither could inquire about nor change the data.

- **Reduced development time.** Because data is better organized in a database, development of programs that use this data takes less time and often is easier. The need to create new files is reduced. Instead, new fields are added to existing files.

The following section discusses the ways that databases can be organized.

Types of Database Organization

Databases are organized according to the following types: hierarchical, network, relational, and object-oriented.

Hierarchical Database

In a **hierarchical database** (Figure 9-11), data is organized in a series like a family tree or organization chart (the term *hierarchy* means an organized series). As with a family tree, the hierarchical database has branches made up of parent and child records. Each **parent record** can have multiple child records. Each **child record**, however, can have only one parent. The parent record at the top of the database is referred to as the **root record**. All parent-child relationships are established when the database is created in a separate process that sometimes is called *generating* the database.

After the database is created, access must be made through the established relationships. Data access is sequential in that a search begins at the root record and proceeds down the branch until the requested data is found. This points out two disadvantages of hierarchical databases. First, records located in separate branches of the database cannot be accessed easily at the same time. Second, adding new fields to database records or modifying existing fields, such as adding the four-digit extension to the ZIP code field, requires the redefinition of the entire database. Depending on the size of the database, this redefinition process can take a considerable amount of time. The advantage of a hierarchical database is that, because the data relationships are predefined, access to and updating data is very fast.

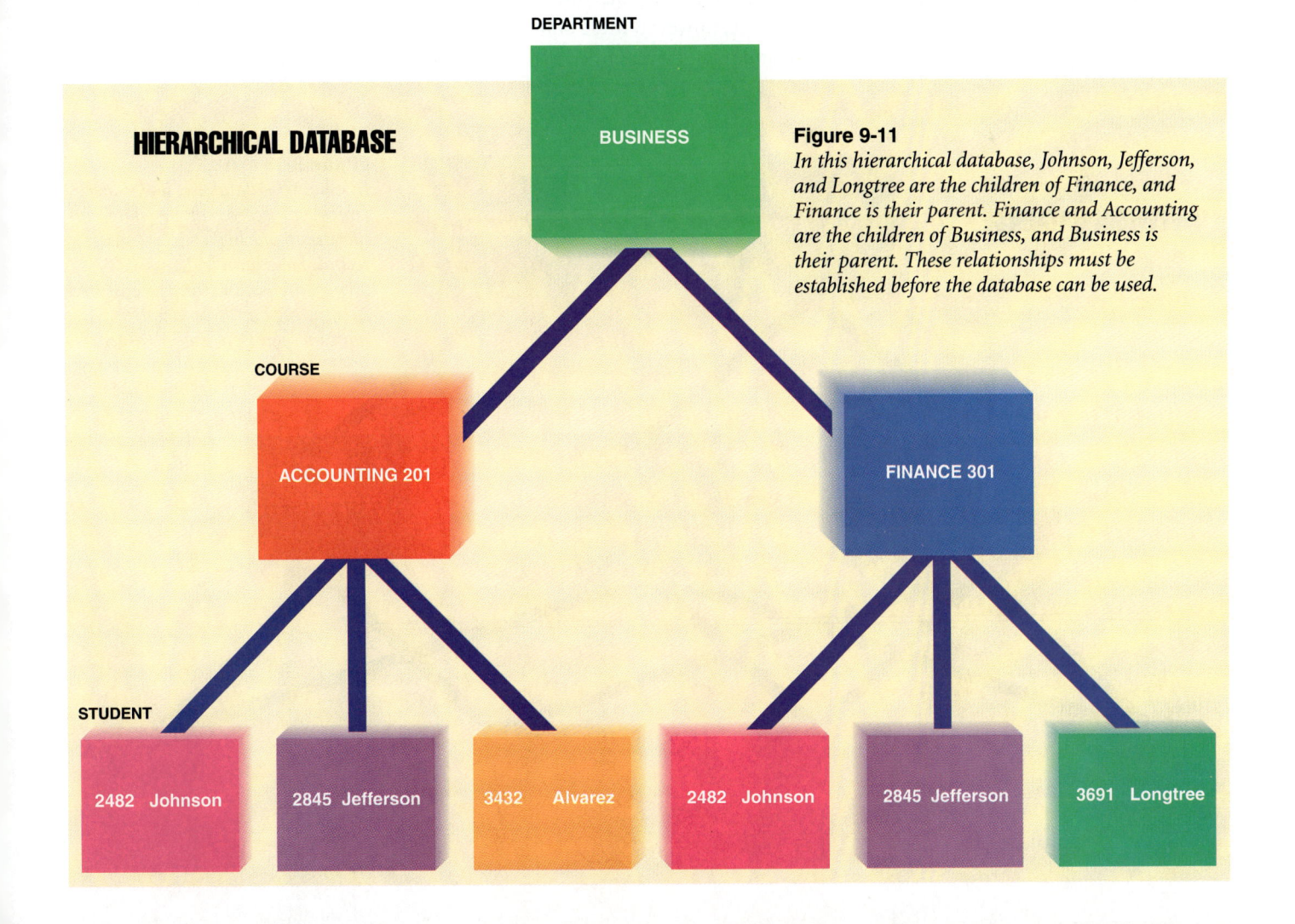

inCyber

For a description of a hierarchical database, visit the Discovering Computers Chapter 9 inCyber page (http://www.scsite.com/dc/ch9/incyber.htm) and click Hierarchical Database.

HIERARCHICAL DATABASE

DEPARTMENT: BUSINESS

COURSE: ACCOUNTING 201, FINANCE 301

STUDENT: 2482 Johnson, 2845 Jefferson, 3432 Alvarez, 2482 Johnson, 2845 Jefferson, 3691 Longtree

Figure 9-11
In this hierarchical database, Johnson, Jefferson, and Longtree are the children of Finance, and Finance is their parent. Finance and Accounting are the children of Business, and Business is their parent. These relationships must be established before the database can be used.

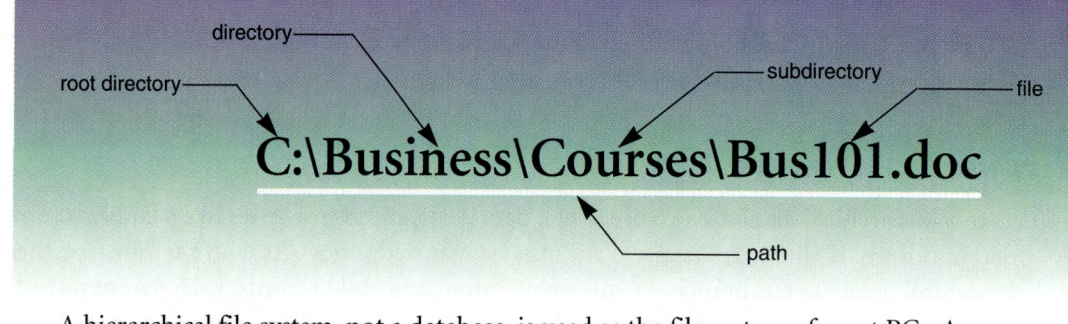

Figure 9-12
Most PCs use a hierarchical file system. Files are stored in directories that may have one or more levels of subdirectories. Some systems call directories and subdirectories folders. The root directory often is a letter indicating a disk drive. The chain of directories from the root to a particular file is called a path.

C:\Business\Courses\Bus101.doc

(root directory, directory, subdirectory, file, path)

inCyber
For an explanation of a network database, visit the Discovering Computers Chapter 9 inCyber page (http://www.scsite.com/dc/ch9/incyber.htm) and click Network Database.

A hierarchical file system, not a database, is used as the file system of most PCs. A **hierarchical file system** has different levels of files that start from a main file called the **root directory**. A lower-level file is called a **subdirectory**, or **folder**. Each subdirectory is a file that contains other subdirectories or one or more data or program files. The chain of directories from the root to a particular file is called a **path**. Figure 9-12 is an example of a hierarchical file path.

Network Database

A **network database** (Figure 9-13) is similar to a hierarchical database except that each child record can have more than one parent. In network database terminology, a child record is referred to as a **member** and a parent record is referred to as an **owner**. Unlike the hierarchical database, the network database is capable of establishing relationships among different branches of the data and thus offers increased access capability for the user. As with the hierarchical database, however, these data relationships must be established prior to the use of the database and must be redefined if fields are added or modified.

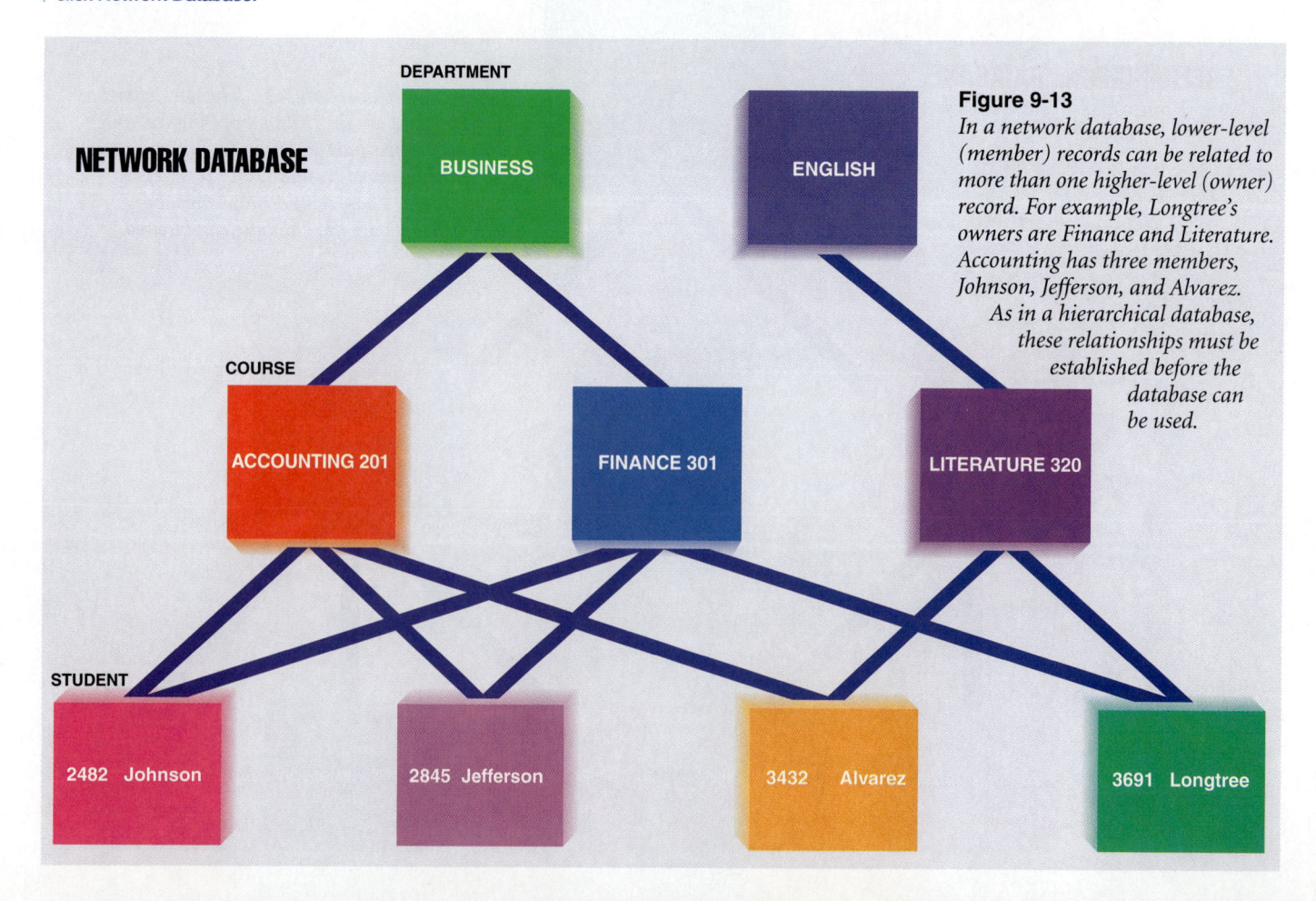

NETWORK DATABASE

DEPARTMENT: BUSINESS, ENGLISH
COURSE: ACCOUNTING 201, FINANCE 301, LITERATURE 320
STUDENT: 2482 Johnson, 2845 Jefferson, 3432 Alvarez, 3691 Longtree

Figure 9-13
In a network database, lower-level (member) records can be related to more than one higher-level (owner) record. For example, Longtree's owners are Finance and Literature. Accounting has three members, Johnson, Jefferson, and Alvarez. As in a hierarchical database, these relationships must be established before the database can be used.

Relational Database

The relational database structure is the most recently developed of the four methods and takes advantage of large-capacity, direct-access storage devices that were not available when the hierarchical and network methods were developed. In a **relational database**, data is organized in **tables** that in database terminology are called **relations**. The tables are further divided into rows called **tuples** and fields called **attributes**. Each table can be thought of as a file and each row as a record. The range of values that a field or attribute can have is called a **domain**. These terms are illustrated with a Student Master Table as shown in Figure 9-14.

Recall that a key advantage of a database is that it allows you to link multiple files. As discussed, you can link multiple files in a hierarchical or a network database, but you must define these relationships when the database is created. With a relational database, you can establish a link between tables (files) at any time, provided the tables have a common field. This field is used to establish the relationship between the tables (Figure 9-15).

Another advantage of a relational database is its capability of adding new fields. To add fields, you simply define them in the appropriate table. With hierarchical and network database systems, the entire database has to be *redefined*; that is existing relationships have to be reestablished to include the new fields. A disadvantage of a relational database is that its more complex software requires more powerful computers to provide acceptable performance.

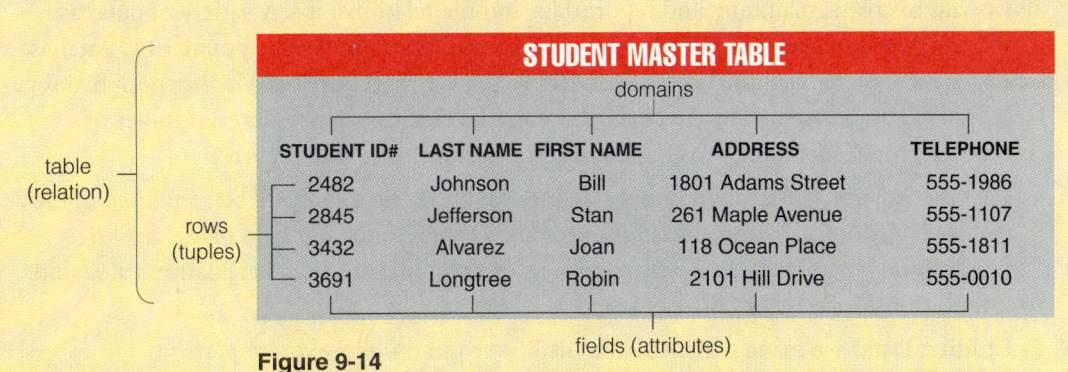

STUDENT MASTER TABLE

table (relation), rows (tuples), domains, fields (attributes)

STUDENT ID#	LAST NAME	FIRST NAME	ADDRESS	TELEPHONE
2482	Johnson	Bill	1801 Adams Street	555-1986
2845	Jefferson	Stan	261 Maple Avenue	555-1107
3432	Alvarez	Joan	118 Ocean Place	555-1811
3691	Longtree	Robin	2101 Hill Drive	555-0010

Figure 9-14
This example shows the terms used with relational databases.

Figure 9-15
In a relational database, files (called tables) do not require predefined relationships as they do with hierarchical or network databases. Instead, common fields are used to link one table to another. For example, Student ID# is used to link the Student Master Table in Figure 9-14 with the Course-Student Table (a). Department ID is used to link the Department Table (b) with the Course-Master Table (c).

a COURSE-STUDENT TABLE

COURSE	STUDENT ID#
ACC201	2482
ACC201	2845
ACC201	3432
FIN301	2482
FIN301	2845
FIN301	3691
LIT320	3432
LIT320	3691

b DEPARTMENT TABLE

DEPARTMENT ID	DEPARTMENT NAME
BUS	Business
ENG	English

c COURSE-MASTER TABLE

COURSE	COURSE NAME	DEPARTMENT ID	UNITS	MAX ENROLLMENT
ACC201	Advanced Accounting	BUS	4	50
FIN301	Investments	BUS	2	30
LIT320	Modern Literature	ENG	3	20

Object-Oriented Database

In recent years, another type of database structure has been developed based on object-oriented technology. An **object-oriented database** keeps track of objects, which are entities that contain both data and the action that can be taken on the data. For example, a non-object-oriented database employee record would contain data only about the employee, such as employee number, name, address, department, pay rate, and so on. An object-oriented database employee record would contain all of this data, as well as instructions on how to display or print the employee record and how to calculate the employee's pay. Object-oriented databases also are designed to store unstructured data such as photographs, video, and audio clips. A bank, for example, might scan and store images of checks in an object-oriented database and send these to customers with their monthly statements. Some relational databases also can store unstructured data. An employee database, for example, might include a photograph with each employee record. Object-oriented technology is discussed in more detail in Chapter 12.

inCyber

For information about the issues relevant to object-oriented databases, visit the Discovering Computers Chapter 9 inCyber page (http://www.scsite.com/dc/ch9/incyber.htm) and click Object-Oriented Database.

Database Management Systems

As previously discussed, a database management system (DBMS) is the software that allows you to create, maintain, and report data and file relationships. A variety of database management systems are available for personal computers. Some of the popular PC database management systems include Access, Paradox, Approach, and FoxPro. Whether designed for large systems or personal computers, database management systems share a number of common features, including those listed below and summarized in Figure 9-16.

- **Data dictionary.** The **data dictionary** defines each data field that will be contained in the database files. Information stored in the data dictionary includes field name, field size, description, type of data (e.g., text, numeric, or date), default value, validation rules, and the relationship to other data elements.

- **Utilities.** Database management system **utility programs** allow you to perform a number of maintenance tasks including creating files and dictionaries, monitoring performance, copying data, and deleting unwanted records.

- **Security.** Most database management systems allow you to specify different levels of user **access privileges** for each data field in the database. Access privileges can be established for each user for each type of access (retrieve, update, and delete) to each data field. When defining access privileges, remember that data in a database is subject more to unauthorized access than a file-oriented system because this single source of data is used by many people.

- **Replication.** Sometimes data needs to be stored in two or more locations. For example, suppose that a product database is maintained and stored at a company's main office and that a copy is stored at each branch office. To keep the branch office databases up to date, data must be distributed to the branch office computers. The process of distributing data to other computers is called **replication**. Most database software packages designed for networks have several ways of performing replication, including instant updates for time-sensitive data and periodic updates for less critical data.
- **Recovery.** More sophisticated database management systems keep a log that tracks what a record looked like before and after a change is made (called the before and after *image*). This log is used to restore the database in the event of a hardware or software malfunction. Using **forward recovery**, also called **rollforward**, the log is used to reenter transactions automatically from the last time the system was backed up. Using **backward recovery**, also called **rollback**, the log is used to reverse transactions that took place during a certain period of time, such as an hour. The transactions for this period of time then have to be reentered.
- **Query language.** The **query language** is one of the more valuable features of a database management system. It allows you to retrieve information from the database based on the criteria and in the format you specify.

FEATURE	DESCRIPTION
Data Dictionary	Defines data files and fields
Utility Program	Creates files and dictionaries, monitors performance, copies data, and deletes unwanted records
Security	Controls different levels of access to a database
Replication	Distributes data to other computers
Recovery	Helps restore database after an equipment or software malfunction
Query Language	Creates views and specifies report content and format

Figure 9-16
Summary of common database management system features.

Query Languages: Access to the Database

A **query language** is a simple English-like language that allows you to specify the data you want to see on a report or screen display. Although each query language has its own grammar, syntax, and vocabulary, these languages generally can be learned in a short time by persons without a programming background.

Most database management systems include a feature called query-by-example. **Query-by-example** (QBE) helps you construct a query by displaying a list of the fields that are available in the files from which the query will be made. In addition, you can specify selection criteria to limit the number of records displayed. Figure 9-17 shows one type of query-by-example screen from the Microsoft Access database.

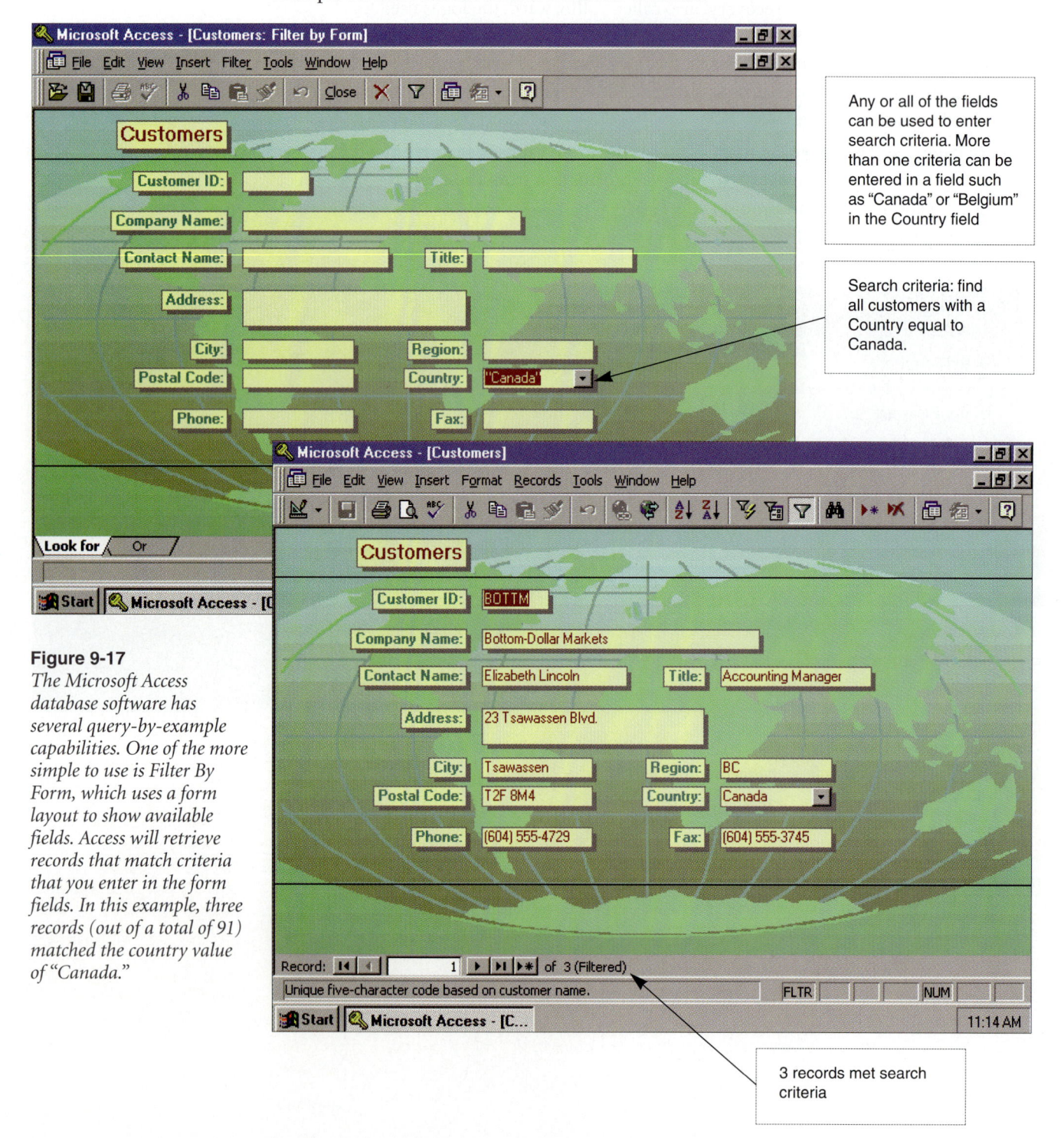

Any or all of the fields can be used to enter search criteria. More than one criteria can be entered in a field such as "Canada" or "Belgium" in the Country field

Search criteria: find all customers with a Country equal to Canada.

Figure 9-17
The Microsoft Access database software has several query-by-example capabilities. One of the more simple to use is Filter By Form, which uses a form layout to show available fields. Access will retrieve records that match criteria that you enter in the form fields. In this example, three records (out of a total of 91) matched the country value of "Canada."

3 records met search criteria

Querying a Relational Database

You can query a database to manipulate the data from one or more files to create a unique **view**, or subset, of the total data. Relational operators are used to specify search criteria and perform these manipulations. Select, project, and join are three **relational operations** that are used to query a relational database (Figure 9-18).

The **select relational operation** selects certain records (rows or tuples) based on criteria you enter. In the example, you instruct the database to select records from the sales order file that contain part number C-143. Selection criteria can be applied to more than one field and can include tests to determine if a field is greater than, less than, equal to, or not equal to a value you specify. Connectors such as AND and OR also can be used.

The **project relational operation** specifies the fields (attributes) that appear on the query output. In the example, you want to see the names of the customers who placed orders for part number C-143.

The **join relational operation** is used to combine two files (relations or tables). In the example, the customer number, a field contained in each file, is used to join the two files. After the query is executed, most query languages allow you to give the query a unique name and save it for future use.

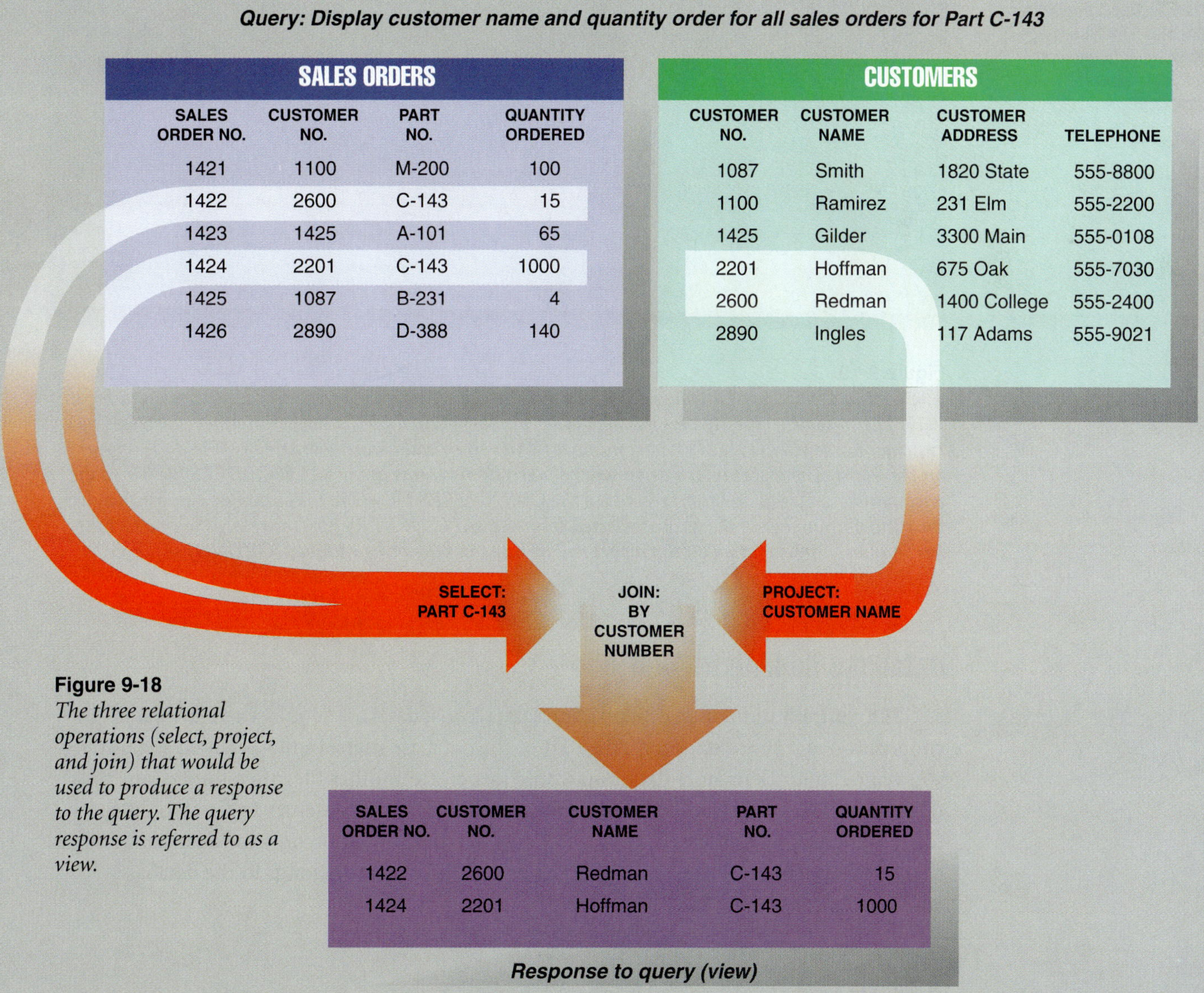

Query: Display customer name and quantity order for all sales orders for Part C-143

SALES ORDERS

SALES ORDER NO.	CUSTOMER NO.	PART NO.	QUANTITY ORDERED
1421	1100	M-200	100
1422	2600	C-143	15
1423	1425	A-101	65
1424	2201	C-143	1000
1425	1087	B-231	4
1426	2890	D-388	140

CUSTOMERS

CUSTOMER NO.	CUSTOMER NAME	CUSTOMER ADDRESS	TELEPHONE
1087	Smith	1820 State	555-8800
1100	Ramirez	231 Elm	555-2200
1425	Gilder	3300 Main	555-0108
2201	Hoffman	675 Oak	555-7030
2600	Redman	1400 College	555-2400
2890	Ingles	117 Adams	555-9021

SELECT: PART C-143   **JOIN:** BY CUSTOMER NUMBER   **PROJECT:** CUSTOMER NAME

Figure 9-18
The three relational operations (select, project, and join) that would be used to produce a response to the query. The query response is referred to as a view.

SALES ORDER NO.	CUSTOMER NO.	CUSTOMER NAME	PART NO.	QUANTITY ORDERED
1422	2600	Redman	C-143	15
1424	2201	Hoffman	C-143	1000

Response to query (view)

Structured Query Language

One of the more widely used query languages is **Structured Query Language**, often referred to as **SQL** (sometimes pronounced *see-qwell*). Originally developed for large systems, SQL is now available in most database products. Figure 9-19 shows an example of the SQL statements that would be used to create the view shown in Figure 9-18.

As with large system packages, many personal computer database system vendors have developed or modified existing packages to support Structured Query Language (SQL). You can use one of these PC packages to query a mainframe database that supports SQL.

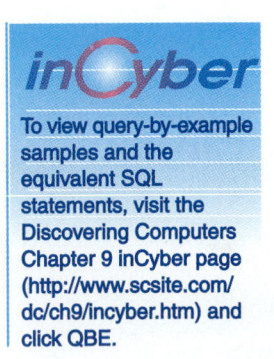

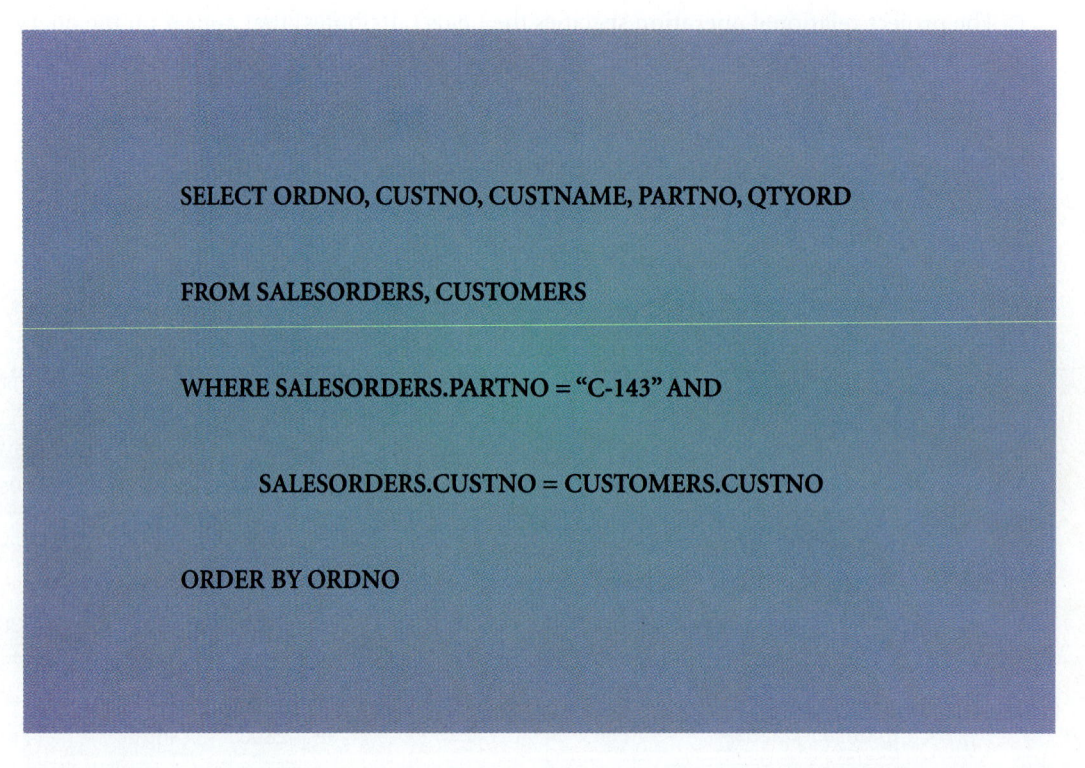

> **inCyber**
> To view query-by-example samples and the equivalent SQL statements, visit the Discovering Computers Chapter 9 inCyber page (http://www.scsite.com/dc/ch9/incyber.htm) and click QBE.

```
SELECT ORDNO, CUSTNO, CUSTNAME, PARTNO, QTYORD

FROM SALESORDERS, CUSTOMERS

WHERE SALESORDERS.PARTNO = "C-143" AND

      SALESORDERS.CUSTNO = CUSTOMERS.CUSTNO

ORDER BY ORDNO
```

Figure 9-19
These Structured Query Language (SQL) statements will generate the response (view) shown in Figure 9-18. The statements specify that the sales order number (ORDNO), customer number (CUSTNO), customer name (CUSTNAME), part number (PARTNO), and quantity ordered (QTYORD) appear on the report. The report information will be taken from records in the SALESORDERS file where the part number is C-143 and from records in the CUSTOMERS file where the customer number matches the customer number in the records selected from the SALESORDERS file (the records with a C-143 part number). Information on the report will be listed in sales order number (ORDNO) sequence.

Database Administration

The centralization of an organization's data into a database requires a great deal of cooperation and coordination on the part of the database users. In file-oriented systems, if you wanted to track or store data, you would just create another file, often duplicating data that already was being tracked by someone else. In a database system, you first would check to see if some or all of the data is already in the database or, if not, how the data can be added to the system. The role of coordinating the use of the database belongs to the database administrator.

The Role of the Database Administrator

The **database administrator**, or **DBA**, is the person responsible for managing all database activities (Figure 9-20). In small organizations, this person usually has responsibilities in addition to database administration, such as the overall management of the computer resources. In medium and large organizations, database administration is a full-time job for one or more people. The job of the DBA usually includes the following responsibilities:

- **Database design**. The DBA determines the design of the database and specifies where to add additional data fields, files, and records when they are needed.
- **User coordination**. The DBA is responsible for letting users know what data is available in the database and how the users can retrieve it. The DBA also reviews user requests for additions to the database and helps establish priorities for their implementation.

For details on a database administrator's job responsibilities, visit the Discovering Computers Chapter 9 inCyber page (http://www.scsite.com/dc/ch9/incyber.htm) and click DBA.

Figure 9-20
The database administrator (DBA) plays a key role in managing a company's data. The DBA should possess good technical and management skills.

- **Performance monitoring.** The performance of the database, usually measured in terms of response time to a user request, can be affected by a number of factors such as file sizes and the types and frequency of inquiries during the day. Most database management systems have utility programs that enable the DBA to monitor these factors and make adjustments to provide for more efficient database use.
- **System security.** The DBA is responsible for establishing and monitoring system access privileges to prevent the unauthorized use of an organization's data.
- **Data distribution.** If an organization's data is stored on two or more servers, the DBA establishes procedures to distribute the data on a timely basis.
- **Backup and recovery.** The centralization of data in a database makes an organization particularly vulnerable to a computer system failure. The DBA often is responsible for minimizing this risk, by making sure that all data is regularly backed up and preparing (and periodically testing) contingency plans for a prolonged equipment or software malfunction.

In addition to the DBA, the user also has a role in database administration.

The Role of the User in a Database System

One of the user's first responsibilities is to become familiar with the data in the existing database. First-time database users often are amazed at the wealth of information available to help them perform their jobs more effectively.

Another responsibility of the user, in organizations of any size, is to play an active part in the specification of additions to the database. The maintenance of an organization's database is an ongoing task that must be measured constantly against the overall goals of the organization. Therefore, users must participate in designing the database that will be used to help them achieve those goals and measure their progress.

Guidelines for Designing Database Files

Carefully designed database files can make it easy for a user to query a database and create reports. For relational database files, a process called **normalization** is used to organize data into the most efficient and logical file relationships. For flat files, formal rules do not exist, but the common sense guidelines shown in Figure 9-21 can be applied to both relational and flat files. These guidelines apply to databases of all sizes.

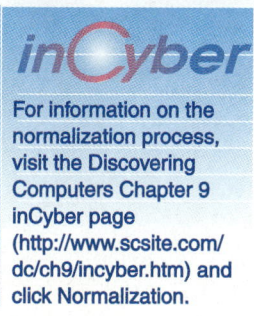

> **inCyber**
>
> For information on the normalization process, visit the Discovering Computers Chapter 9 inCyber page (http://www.scsite.com/dc/ch9/incyber.htm) and click Normalization.

DATABASE FILE GUIDELINES

Design your file on paper first.

Write down everything you want to keep track of in the database. Organize the data into logical groups. Large groups of data should be separate files.

Include a unique key field.

Database systems need a unique field to identify each record. If one is not specified, database systems usually assign a sequential number to each record. That may be fine for a list of personal friends, but it is not efficient for large files or files that are frequently accessed. For some data, the choice is obvious such as the Social Security number for an employee file. If a unique field has to be established, avoid creating one that has built-in *significance* such as a combination of customer's address and name (e.g., 1813WILL). Significant key fields make sense at first but eventually break down when duplicates are encountered.

Use separate fields for logically distinct items.

If an item will ever need to be referred to separately, it should be stored in a separate field. A person's name is a good example. To be thorough, you need at least six fields: Salutation (Mr., Mrs., Ms.), First Name, Middle Name or Initial, Last Name, Suffix (Jr.), and Nickname.

Do not create fields for information that can be derived from entries in other fields.

For example, in an employee file, do not include a field for age. Instead, store the employee's birth date. That way, the employee's age always can be calculated accurately.

Allow enough space for each field.

Think about the type of data that will be stored and allow sufficient but not unnecessary space. If foreign names and addresses are going to be stored, allow extra room. Numeric fields should be equal to the largest total that may be displayed or printed from the data.

Set default values for frequently entered data.

Some database programs let you set a field value for use during data entry. Unless you override it, the value is entered as part of the record. An example would be a state code in a name and address file. If most of the entries in a name and address file will be from the same state, say Oregon, a default value of OR can be assigned to the state code. The value OR will be displayed automatically during data entry. If the new entry is from Oregon, the state code does not have to be entered. If the new entry is not from Oregon, the user enters the correct two-letter state code.

Figure 9-21
Guidelines for creating database files.

Summary of Data Management and Databases

Understanding the data management, file, and database concepts that are presented in this chapter gives you a knowledge of how data is stored and managed on a computer. This information will be useful to you, whether you are a home computer user who wants to store personal data on floppy disks or a hard drive, or a computer user accessing the database of the company where you are employed.

COMPUTERS AT WORK

Data Warehouses and Data Mining

To provide the information decision makers need, many organizations have created a **data warehouse**, which is a database that collects and organizes data from different sources. The sources always include internal operational data such as sales and customer records and also may include relevant external data such as interest rates, published industry statistics, and news articles on specific topics. The goal of a data warehouse is to provide meaningful data that decision makers can use by themselves. This involves careful planning and the participation of the decision makers to determine what data should be stored in the data warehouse. Understandably, the contents of the data warehouse change over time as new requirements are identified. Sometimes a data warehouse becomes so large that a subset of data is copied to a **data mart**, a separate database designed for a specific group of users, such as the marketing department.

To access a data warehouse, most systems support a query language such as SQL. For infrequent users, managed-query capabilities exist to help them build an information request. A more sophisticated approach to obtaining information is to use data mining. **Data mining** uses methods such as statistical analysis and rule-based reasoning to search for patterns in data. Retailers use data mining tools to look for buying trends. Wal-Mart, for example, analyzes 20 million point-of-sale transactions each day to look for products that are selling faster or slower than expected. Besides analyzing past events, data mining also is used to predict events. One bank, for example, analyzed customers who had closed their accounts and developed a list of customer characteristics such as age, income, and occupation. The bank then matched this profile against their existing customers and identified the ones most likely to leave. The bank targeted these customers with specific promotions that resulted in a decreased number of closed accounts.

Data warehouses put meaningful data closer to the people who can use it to make decisions. Data mining gives those decision makers the tools necessary to convert the data into information.

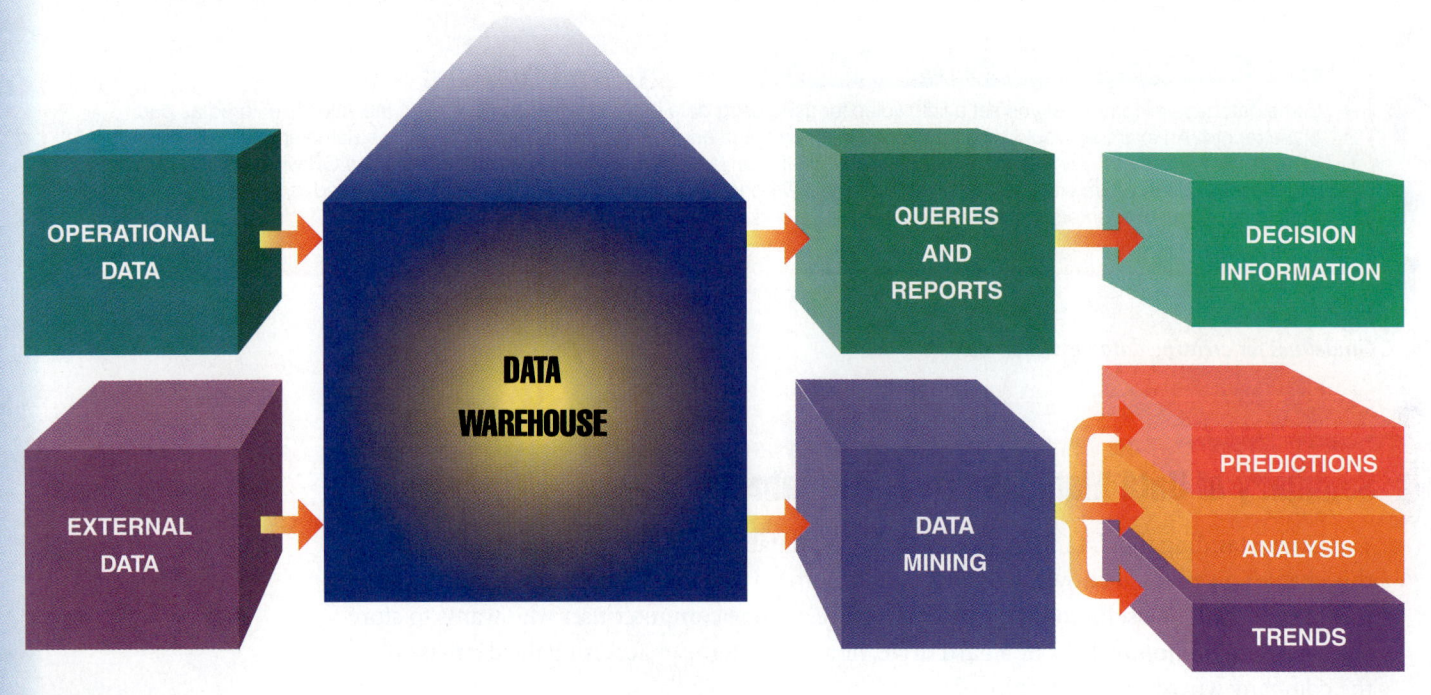

Figure 9-22

IN THE FUTURE

Storing All Types of Data

Most databases used today are designed to store text; the words and numbers used to represent the majority of data. Text fits well into the tables used by relational database systems and can be easily sorted, compared, and retrieved by database query languages such as SQL. In the future, however, databases will have the capability of storing, comparing, and retrieving all types of data, including multimedia data elements such as sound, graphics, photographic images, and video. Multimedia data elements usually are much larger than simpler text data items and are more difficult to compare with one another because of the complexity of their data.

One way to handle these complex data types may be through the use of object oriented databases. Object-oriented databases store all data types as objects. This includes items that contain the data as well as information about the data, such as how an item should be displayed, if the item is text or an image, or played, and if it is an audio or video data item. Although they have existed for several years, object-oriented databases are not yet widely used. One reason is that a standardized query language such as SQL does not exist for object-oriented databases. Another reason is that the majority of data stored by individuals and organizations records transactions that easily can be represented by text and, therefore, the need to store complex data elements still is relatively low. Combining text and multimedia data elements, however, will offer several advantages. For example, consider a music database that includes the actual music for each item, or an employee file that includes a photograph of the person, or an inventory parts file that includes a video of how to install the part. These are just some of the applications that are being developed today. In the future, even more complex data types may be added to the database. Think of the possibilities if a database could store data for taste, touch, and smell!

Figure 9-23

chapter 9 review

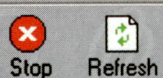

1 | 2 | 3 | 4 | 5 | 6 | 7 | 8 | 9 | 10 | 11 | 12 | 13 | 14 | I

inCyber | review | terms | yourTurn | hotTopics | outThere | winLabs | webWalk | exercises | news | home

INSTRUCTIONS: *To display this page from the Web, launch your browser and enter the URL, http://www.scsite.com/dc/ch9/review.htm. Click the links for current and additional information.*

1 Data Management

Data management refers to the procedures used to acquire, access, and maintain data. Three major aspects of data management are data accuracy, data security, and data maintenance. **Data accuracy (data integrity)** means that the source of the data is reliable and the data is reported and entered correctly. **Data security** involves protecting data to keep it from being misused or lost. **Data maintenance** refers to the procedures used to keep data current.

2 The Hierarchy of Data

Data is organized in a hierarchy in which each higher level is made up of one or more elements from the lower level preceding it. A **bit** is a binary digit that usually is combined with other bits to represent data. A **byte** is a combination of eight bits that can represent a character. A **field** is a combination of one or more bytes and usually is the smallest item of meaningful data. A **record** is a group of related fields. A **file** is a collection of related records or data that is stored under a single name. A **database** is a group of related files.

3 Sequential File Organization

Files typically are organized based on the media on which they are stored or the manner in which they are processed. **Sequential file organization**, which is used with files stored on tape, means that records are stored sequentially, one after the other. Records are retrieved in the same order in which they are stored; the computer cannot retrieve a record without reading all the preceding records first.

4 Indexed File Organization

Indexed file organization uses a separate file, called an index, to record the location of a record on a storage device. An **index** consists of a list containing the values of one or more fields and the corresponding disk address for each record. Indexed files can be accessed sequentially and directly. With **direct**, or **random**, **access**, the system can go directly to a record without having to read the preceding records.

5 Direct File Organization

Direct file organization uses a record's key value to determine the location on the disk where the record is stored. In a process called **hashing**, a formula is used to calculate the location of a record. Once a record is stored in its relative location within a direct file, it can be retrieved either directly or sequentially.

6 Data Maintenance

Data maintenance includes processes needed to keep data current and accurate. Records are added when additional data is needed to make the file current. Records are changed to correct inaccurate data and to update older data. Records are deleted when they are no longer needed.

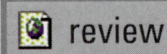

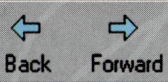

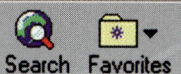

7 Database Management Systems

A basic file-oriented system is made up of **flat files**, each of which is independent and contains all the information needed to process the records in that one file. A **database management system (DBMS)** is software that allows data and file relationships to be created, maintained, and reported. A database management system offers a number of advantages over a file-oriented system including reduced data redundancy (duplication), increased data accuracy, easier reporting, improved data security, and reduced development time. Databases are organized according to the following four types: hierarchical, network, relational, and object-oriented.

8 Hierarchical and Network Databases

In a **hierarchical database**, data is organized in a series like a family tree. Each **parent record** can have multiple child records, but each **child record** can have only one parent. All parent-child relationships are established when the database is created in a separate process that sometimes called is *generating* the database. A **network database** is similar to a hierarchical database except that each child record can have more than one parent. A child record is referred to as a **member**, and a parent record is referred to as an **owner**. Relationships can be established among different branches of the data, offering increased access capability for the user. Like a hierarchical database, however, data relationships must be established prior to the use of the database and must be redefined if fields are added or modified.

9 Relational and Object-Oriented Databases

In a **relational database**, data is organized in **tables** that are called **relations**. The tables are further divided into rows (called **tuples**) and fields (called **attributes**). The range of values that an attribute can have is called a **domain**. With a relational database, links between tables (files) can be established at any time, provided the tables have a common field. An **object-oriented database** keeps track of objects, which are entities that contain both data and the action that can be taken on the data. Object-oriented databases also are designed to store unstructured data such as photographs, video, and audio clips.

10 PC Database Management Systems

Popular PC database management systems include Access, Paradox, Approach, and FoxPro. Database management systems share a number of common features including a data dictionary, utilities, security, replication, recovery, and a query language.

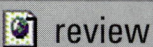

11 Query Languages

A **query language** is a simple English-like language that can be used to specify the data seen on a report or screen display. **Query-by-example (QBE)** helps to construct a query by displaying a list of fields available in the files from which the query will be made. Three **relational operations** are used to query a relational database. The **select relational operation** picks certain records based on designated criteria. The **project relational operation** specifies fields that will appear on the query output. The **join relational operation** combines two files. One of the more widely used query languages is **Structured Query Language (SQL)**.

12 Database Administration

The **database administrator (DBA)** is the person responsible for managing all database activities. The job of the DBA usually includes database design, user coordination, performance monitoring, system security, data distribution, and backup and recovery.

13 Guidelines for Creating Database Files

Carefully designed database files make it easier for a user to query a database and create reports. A process called **normalization** is used to organize the data in relational database files into the most efficient and logical file relationships. The following guidelines can be applied to both relational and flat files: design the file on paper first, include a unique key field, use separate fields for logically distinct items, do not create fields for information that can be derived from entries in other fields, allow enough space for each field, and set default values for frequently entered data.

9 terms

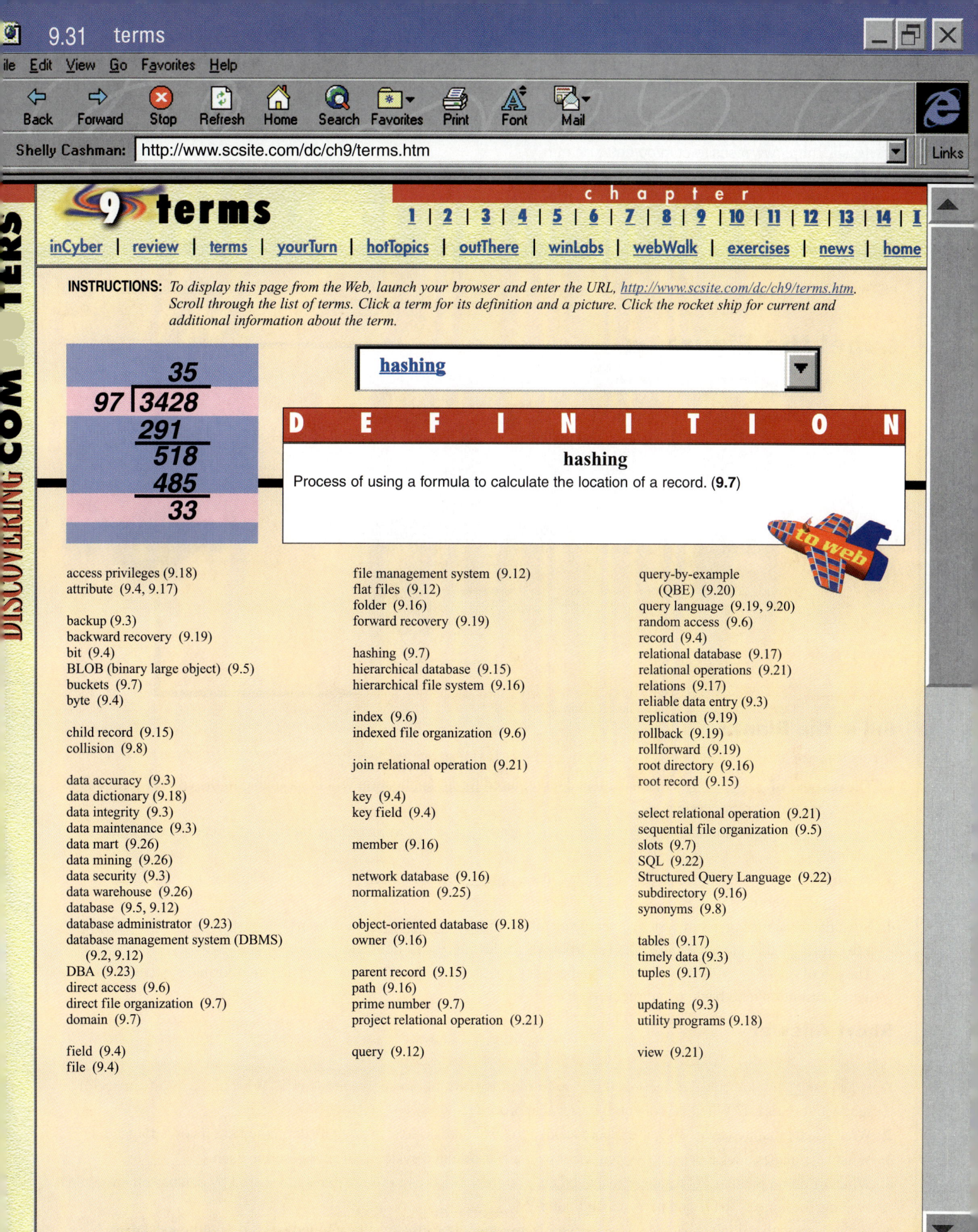

chapter 1 | 2 | 3 | 4 | 5 | 6 | 7 | 8 | 9 | 10 | 11 | 12 | 13 | 14 | I

inCyber | review | terms | yourTurn | hotTopics | outThere | winLabs | webWalk | exercises | news | home

INSTRUCTIONS: *To display this page from the Web, launch your browser and enter the URL, http://www.scsite.com/dc/ch9/terms.htm. Scroll through the list of terms. Click a term for its definition and a picture. Click the rocket ship for current and additional information about the term.*

hashing

DEFINITION

hashing
Process of using a formula to calculate the location of a record. (9.7)

access privileges (9.18)
attribute (9.4, 9.17)

backup (9.3)
backward recovery (9.19)
bit (9.4)
BLOB (binary large object) (9.5)
buckets (9.7)
byte (9.4)

child record (9.15)
collision (9.8)

data accuracy (9.3)
data dictionary (9.18)
data integrity (9.3)
data maintenance (9.3)
data mart (9.26)
data mining (9.26)
data security (9.3)
data warehouse (9.26)
database (9.5, 9.12)
database administrator (9.23)
database management system (DBMS) (9.2, 9.12)
DBA (9.23)
direct access (9.6)
direct file organization (9.7)
domain (9.7)

field (9.4)
file (9.4)

file management system (9.12)
flat files (9.12)
folder (9.16)
forward recovery (9.19)

hashing (9.7)
hierarchical database (9.15)
hierarchical file system (9.16)

index (9.6)
indexed file organization (9.6)

join relational operation (9.21)

key (9.4)
key field (9.4)

member (9.16)

network database (9.16)
normalization (9.25)

object-oriented database (9.18)
owner (9.16)

parent record (9.15)
path (9.16)
prime number (9.7)
project relational operation (9.21)

query (9.12)

query-by-example (QBE) (9.20)
query language (9.19, 9.20)
random access (9.6)
record (9.4)
relational database (9.17)
relational operations (9.21)
relations (9.17)
reliable data entry (9.3)
replication (9.19)
rollback (9.19)
rollforward (9.19)
root directory (9.16)
root record (9.15)

select relational operation (9.21)
sequential file organization (9.5)
slots (9.7)
SQL (9.22)
Structured Query Language (9.22)
subdirectory (9.16)
synonyms (9.8)

tables (9.17)
timely data (9.3)
tuples (9.17)

updating (9.3)
utility programs (9.18)

view (9.21)

yourTurn

chapter 1 | 2 | 3 | 4 | 5 | 6 | 7 | 8 | 9 | 10 | 11 | 12 | 13 | 14 | I

inCyber | review | terms | yourTurn | hotTopics | outThere | winLabs | webWalk | exercises | news | home

INSTRUCTIONS: *To display this page from the Web, launch your browser and enter the URL, http://www.scsite.com/dc/ch9/turn.htm. Click a blank line for the answer. Click the links for current and additional information.*

Label the Figure

HIERARCHY OF DATA

Data Element	Can Contain	Example
1. _____	Related files	Student file, Course file Grades file, Scholarship file
2. _____	3. _____	Amy Lee, 123 Hill Street, ... Tom Sanchez, 1401 Reeder Ct., . . Irving Brown, 1813 Ryan Ave., . . .
4. _____	Related groups of fields such as a person's name and address data	Amy Lee, 123 Hill Street, Seattle, WA, 99999 206-555-1234
5. _____	6. _____	Amy
7. _____	One character or other unit of information consisting of eight bits	01000001 (letter A)
8. _____	9. _____	Bits can represent any two-state condition, such as on or off, but usually are combined into bytes to represent data.

Instructions: Identify each element in the hierarchy of data.

Fill in the Blanks

Instructions: Complete each sentence with the correct term or terms.

1. The purpose of _____ is to ensure that data required for an application will be available in the correct form and at the proper time for processing.
2. _____ organization uses a separate file, called a(n) _____, to record the location of a record on a storage device.
3. In a(n) _____ database, data is organized like a family tree, with each _____ record having only one _____ record.
4. Most database management systems include a feature called _____, which helps to construct a query by displaying a list of fields that are available in the file from which the query will be made.
5. The job of _____ usually includes database design, user coordination, performance monitoring, system security, data distribution, and backup and recovery.

Short Answer

Instructions: Write a brief answer to each of the following questions.

1. How is sequential retrieval of records different from direct or random access to records? What is the disadvantage of sequential retrieval? When is sequential retrieval appropriate? _____
2. What is data maintenance? Why are records added to, changed, or deleted from a file? When are records flagged? _____
3. What advantages does a database system offer over a file-oriented system? Briefly describe each. _____
4. What are some popular PC database management systems? What common features are shared by database management systems for large systems and personal computers? _____
5. What is normalization? What are some common-sense guidelines that can be applied when designing a database? _____

_9.33_ **hotTopics**

9 hotTopics

chapter 1 | 2 | 3 | 4 | 5 | 6 | 7 | 8 | 9 | 10 | 11 | 12 | 13 | 14 | I

inCyber | review | terms | yourTurn | hotTopics | outThere | winLabs | webWalk | exercises | news | home

INSTRUCTIONS: *To display this page from the Web, launch your browser and enter the URL, http://www.scsite.com/dc/ch9/hot.htm. Click the links for current and additional information to help you respond to the hotTopics questions.*

1. *The United States Supreme Court decision in Feist v. Rural Telephone* removed much of the protection corporate databases previously had enjoyed. This decision held that despite the effort involved in compiling a database, the database creators did not deserve copyright protection in the same manner as a book. Why do you think the court decided as it did? How is a book different from a database? Was the Supreme Court's decision right? Why? What effect will the Supreme Court's decision have on corporate databases?

2. *Most corporations have personnel databases containing data on an employee's position, salary,* employment history, attendance, and job performance. Employee databases also may include a picture, personal information (health, family, interests, and so on) and supervisors' opinions. Because they are a key factor in determining promotion, some people feel private or unsubstantiated information has no place in a personnel file. A picture could lead to discrimination based on age, gender, race, or other factors. What kind of information can legitimately be included in a personnel database? Why? What kind of information should not be included? Why? What circumstances, if any, might alter the type of information that should be included in a personnel database?

3. *To reduce data redundancy, improve data accuracy, make reporting easier,* increase data security, and lessen development time, most schools use a database management system to handle student records. Imagine if, however, a school chose to use a file management system instead. Personal data might be kept in a central office file; financial data in the business office file; data on credits earned in the academic affairs office files; and data on grades received in each individual instructor's files. How would such a system affect life as a student? What would be the disadvantages of a file management system? What advantages might a file management system have over a database management system?

4. *Database administrators frequently start at a salary of more than $50,000 per year, and senior* DBAs can earn more than $100,000 annually. Database administrators typically have taken courses in computer science, programming or systems analysis, and business. DBAs must be aware of new technologies, able to resolve conflicts, curious and tenacious, and interested in a wide range of subjects. Create a resume you could use in applying for a job as a database administrator. Include applicable courses you have taken and those you plan to take. Describe relevant work experiences. Give examples of situations where you demonstrated some of the qualities required of a database administrator.

5. *Data security is part of data management. One aspect of data security involves limiting access* and update privileges to select individuals. Some people may be allowed to see only specific data. Other people may be allowed to see and change certain data. Another group may be granted complete access and update privileges. Consider a student file. In addition to a student's name, address, and grades, this file may contain information on a student's gender, ethnicity, family, financial status, health, extracurricular activities, disciplinary record, and so on. Using this file as an example, list what data each of the following should be able to access: the student, other students, faculty, administrators, potential employers, and other outside organizations. Which groups should have update privileges? What data should they be able to update? Explain your answers.

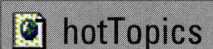

outThere

chapter 9 | 1 | 2 | 3 | 4 | 5 | 6 | 7 | 8 | 9 | 10 | 11 | 12 | 13 | 14 | I

inCyber | review | terms | yourTurn | hotTopics | outThere | winLabs | webWalk | exercises | news | home

INSTRUCTIONS: *To display this page from the Web, launch your browser and enter the URL, http://www.scsite.com/dc/ch9/out.htm. Click the links for current and additional information.*

1 *Automobile dealers frequently use databases that contain information both* about cars on their own lots and cars in the inventories of other dealers that sell the same make. Salespeople use these databases to find a car that meets a customer's requirements. If the car is in another dealer's inventory, the salesperson makes a dealer trade by exchanging a car in stock for the desired car. Visit an automobile dealership that uses a computerized database and ask a salesperson for a demonstration. How many dealers are represented in the database? How is the database used? What criteria can be employed when querying the database? How often is the database updated? What are the advantages and disadvantages offered by using the database?

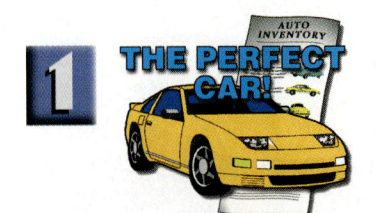

2 *Apartment hunting is a daunting task, especially if the search has to be made in a new city.* The chore has been simplified, however, by a database on the Web that has more than 1,000,000 listings. It is queried by specifying an area, a price range, and the number of bedrooms. Apartments also can be sorted by their features (swimming pool, dishwasher, garage, and so on). Listings provide descriptions of apartments that meet the user's criteria and include a floor plan, photographs, and map. For some locations, users can download a 360 degree view, allowing them to walk around the apartment. Visit the real-estate Web site and try searching for an apartment. Step by step, how does the process work? What are the advantages of apartment hunting online? What are the disadvantages?

3 *Most libraries use computerized databases to keep track of their collections. These databases* are used to determine if the library owns a certain book, where the book can be found, and whether the book is available. It is possible to search for books by title, author, or subject matter. Many databases contain not only books on the library's own shelves, but also titles in related libraries. Visit a public or school library that uses a database. Interview a librarian to find out more about how the database is used. How many books are represented? What type of information does the database contain? How is the database searched? How frequently is it updated? What are the benefits of using a database? What are the drawbacks?

4 *Reviews of movies on a video store's new release shelf are fairly easy to find, but critiques of* other movies in stock may be less accessible. To help film buffs, information on more than 85,000 movie titles is available from a database on the World Wide Web. The Internet Movie Database Ltd. can be searched using a movie's title, cast members, year produced, characters, genre, awards, or other criteria. Each movie's page offers a brief description and rating and includes links to such items as stars, summary, reviews, and recommendations. Visit the movie database Web site and search for several movies. What search criteria was used? How many movies were found? How complete was the information provided? Who would benefit most from using the movie database? Why?

5 *The National Crime Information Center (NCIC), which is the FBI's index of* documented criminal justice information, provides law enforcement personnel with data on wanted or missing persons and stolen property. Law officers can access the NCIC database 24 hours a day, 365 days a year when conducting their own investigations. Visit a local police department to learn about the role computerized databases play in law enforcement. What databases does the department access? What information do the databases contain? How are they used? How are they searched? How often are they updated? In what ways does a database contribute to law enforcement? What are the advantages and disadvantages of using a computerized database?

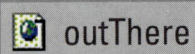

winLabs

chapter 1 | 2 | 3 | 4 | 5 | 6 | 7 | 8 | 9 | 10 | 11 | 12 | 13 | 14 | I

inCyber | review | terms | yourTurn | hotTopics | outThere | winLabs | webWalk | exercises | news | home

INSTRUCTIONS: *To display this page from the Web, launch your browser and enter the URL, http://www.scsite.com/dc/ch9/labs.htm. Click the links for current and additional information.*

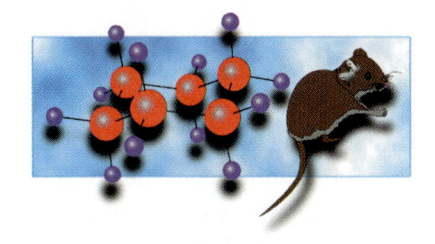

1. Shelly Cashman Series Database Lab

Follow the instructions in winLabs 1 on page 1.34 to display the Shelly Cashman Series Labs screen. Click Designing a Database. Click the Start Lab button. When the initial screen displays, carefully read the objectives. With your printer on, click the Print Questions button. Fill out the top of the Questions sheet and then answer the questions.

2. Working with Folders

Right-click the My Computer icon on the desktop and then click Explore on the shortcut menu to open Windows Explorer. Maximize the Exploring window. Click View on the menu bar and then click Large Icons.

Insert your Student Floppy Disk into drive A. If necessary, drag the vertical scroll box to the top of the scroll bar in the All Folders area. Click the My Computer icon in the All Folders area and then double-click the 3fi Floppy [A:] icon in the Contents area to display the contents of drive A. Click the 3fi Floppy [A:] icon in the All Folders window to select it.

Click File on the menu bar, point to New, and then click Folder on the submenu. When the new folder displays in the Contents area, type `winlabs` and then press ENTER. Click the plus sign next to the 3fi Floppy [A:] icon in the All Folders area to display the winlabs folder in the All Folders area. Click View on the menu bar, point to Arrange Icons, and then click by Name (Figure 9-24).

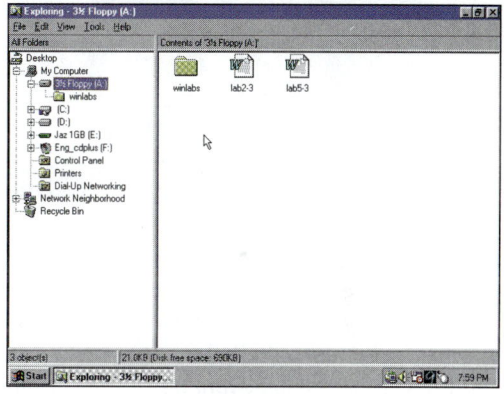

Figure 9-24

Click the winlabs folder in the All Folders area to display its contents. What are the contents of this folder? Click the 3fi Floppy [A:] icon in the All Folders area. What are the contents of this folder?

3. Working with Files in Folders

You must complete winLabs 2 before proceeding with this Lab. Open Windows Explorer as discussed in winLabs 2 and then maximize it. Display the contents of drive A as discussed in winLabs 2 (see Figure 9-24).

Click the 3fi Floppy [A:] icon in the All Folders area, if necessary, and then click the first file in the Contents area (lab2-3). While holding down the CTRL key, click the second file (lab5-3) and then release the CTRL key. Right-drag the selected files to the winlabs folder. When the winlabs folder is highlighted, release the right mouse button (Figure 9-25). Click Move Here on the shortcut menu. Double-click the winlabs folder in the Contents area. How many files are in the winlabs folder? Click the 3fi Floppy [A:] icon in the All Folders area. What displays in the Contents area? Close Windows Explorer.

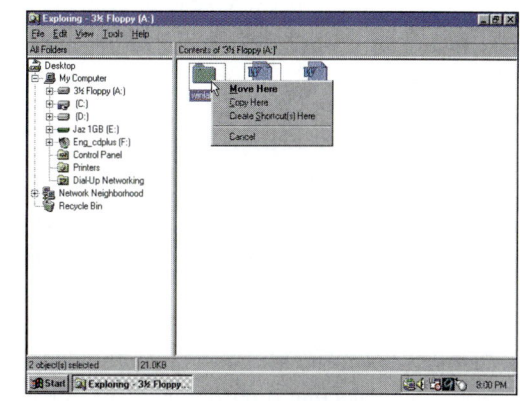

Figure 9-25

webWalk

chapter 9 | 1 | 2 | 3 | 4 | 5 | 6 | 7 | 8 | 9 | 10 | 11 | 12 | 13 | 14 | I

inCyber | review | terms | yourTurn | hotTopics | outThere | winLabs | webWalk | exercises | news | home

INSTRUCTIONS: *To display this page from the Web, launch your browser and enter the URL, http://www.scsite.com/dc/ch9/walk.htm. Click the exercise link to display the exercise.*

1. Art Imagebase
Database fields can contain graphic information as well as text. To visit the largest searchable art imagebase in the world (Figure 9-26), complete this exercise.

Figure 9-26

4. Timely Data
Accurate data also must be timely. Timely data is data that has not lost its usefulness because time has passed. To see how one package shipper makes time-critical information available over the Web, complete this exercise.

5. Information Mining
Complete this exercise to improve your Web research skills by using a Web search engine to find information related to this chapter.

6. Query-By-Example
Most database management systems include a feature called query-by-example (QBE). QBE helps you construct a query by displaying a list of fields that are available. To see a Web-based implementation of query-by-example, complete this exercise.

8. Online Stores
Web sites that offer products for sale over the Internet must provide database search capability as well as online order entry. Complete this exercise to learn more about database query and order entry in a large online music store.

2. Data Integrity
Data accuracy, sometimes called data integrity, means the source of the data is reliable and the data is reported and entered correctly. To see one example of how critical data accuracy can be to a business, complete this exercise.

3. Database Queries
You can query a database to manipulate the data to create a unique subset of the total data. Relational operators are used to specify search criteria and perform these manipulations. For an example of how relational operators are used (Figure 9-27), complete this exercise.

Figure 9-27

7. Database Navigation
Web-based databases must provide a system for users to navigate the Web site as well as query the database. Complete this exercise to learn how a Web site makes its collection of images available over the World Wide Web.

9. Web Chat
Complete this exercise to enter a Web Chat discussion related to the issues presented in the hotTopics exercise.

Information Systems

CHAPTER 10

OBJECTIVES

After completing this chapter, you will be able to:

- Define the term information system and identify the six elements of an information system

- Describe why information is important to an organization

- Explain how managers use information by describing the four managerial tasks

- Discuss the different levels in an organization and how the information requirements differ for each level

- Describe the different functional areas found in an organization

- Explain the qualities that all information should have

- Describe the different types of information systems and the trend toward integration

- Explain how personal computers are used in management information systems

An **information system** is a collection of elements that provides accurate, timely, and useful information. As discussed in Chapter 1, all information systems that use a computer are comprised of the six elements: hardware, software, accurate data, trained information systems personnel, knowledgeable users, and documented procedures. Each element contributes to a successful information system and, conversely, a weakness in any of these elements can cause an information system to fail. Whether you create, use, or change any type of information system, you should consider all six elements to ensure a successful outcome to your activities.

Why Is Information Important to an Organization?

Having accurate information on products, employees, operations, and competitors is crucial to an organization's current and future success. Most organizations realize that the information they obtain from internal and external sources is a vital asset. Like more tangible assets such as buildings and equipment, an organization's information has both a present and future value and has costs associated with its acquisition, maintenance, and storage. These costs are not trivial. Today, most organizations spend more on information technology than they spend on production equipment.

Companies are willing to make the investment in information technology because information is no longer thought of as a by-product of doing business, but rather as a key ingredient in both short- and long-range decision making. Just as many companies have long had product strategies, some companies now are developing *information strategies* that specify the types of information they want available for decision making (Figure 10-1).

Several factors contribute to the need for timely and accurate information. Among these factors are expanded markets, increased competition, shorter product life cycles, government regulation, and increased cost pressure.

Expanded markets means that to be successful today, many businesses must sell their products and services in as many markets as possible. Often, this means international as well as national distribution. The automotive industry is an example of this trend. The number of automobile producers has decreased, and the surviving companies are distributing their

---

inCyber

For details on how an organization has implemented an information system, visit the Discovering Computers Chapter 10 inCyber page (http://www.scsite.com/dc/ch10/incyber.htm) and click Information System.

Critical Questions to Answer During Information Strategy Development

1. **What internal and external factors will affect the future success of the organization?**

   Examples: interest rates, labor costs, raw material prices, government regulation, consumer trends, competive products.

2. **What sources of information are available to monitor these factors?**

   Examples: Newspapers, trade journals, government studies, private research, World Wide Web.

3. **How often should each of these factors be monitored? Daily, weekly, monthly, quarterly, annually?**

4. **What form should reports on these factors take? Written, oral, statistical, graphic, on-site visits?**

5. **Who should receive these reports?**

Figure 10-1
Questions an organization must answer when developing an information strategy.

products in new markets worldwide. When companies expand their markets into a larger number of potential selling areas, they must have information about these markets. For some businesses, the World Wide Web has proven to be an effective two-way information channel that allows them to reach customers in previously untapped markets.

Increased competition means that competing companies are stronger financially, better organized, have unique products or services, or some other business advantage. To compete successfully, it is important for an organization to have current information on competitors' products and services, sales and marketing strategies, and more. Many companies now maintain large databases that include information on competitive product features, prices, and methods of distribution. For consumer product companies, this information often includes sales and percent of the total market. Companies can use this information to measure the success of a new advertising campaign. A business can test a campaign in a limited geographic area (such as a city) to see the effect on sales before using the advertising nationwide.

Shorter product life cycles means that companies have less time to perfect a product. This means that before they introduce new or modified products, they must have accurate information about the product requirements of potential customers. This has led to the increased use of test marketing. Company managers then use the results of tests to decide on advertising, packaging, and product features. Shorter product life cycles also require companies to begin work on the next generation of products earlier. To do this, managers must have information about existing product features that customers want changed and new features that they want added. Many companies use the Internet as one way to gather this type of customer feedback.

Government regulation also has contributed to the need for more information. One good example of this is in human resources management. To comply with equal employment opportunity (EEO) guidelines and laws, organizations must keep detailed records on employee testing, hiring, and promotion practices. The employee database, once used almost exclusively for payroll purposes, now has been expanded to include valuable information on employee skill and education levels, as well as the results of performance reviews. With this information, companies can document their compliance with government regulations and guidelines.

Increased cost pressure means that organizations must reduce product and service costs to remain competitive and stay in business. If an organization cannot increase prices or sales volume, due to competition or other factors, lower costs are the only way the organization can increase or maintain the profit margins necessary to invest in the future. As a goal, many organizations strive to be the lowest cost supplier in their industry. To lower costs, organizations must have accurate product cost information.

How Do Managers Use Information?

All employees in an organization need information to perform their jobs effectively; but the primary users of information are managers. **Managers** of an organization are the men and women responsible for directing the use of resources such as people, money, materials, and information so the organization can operate efficiently and prosper. Managers work toward this goal by performing the four management tasks of planning, organizing, leading, and controlling.

1. **Planning** involves establishing goals and objectives and establishing the strategies or tactics needed to meet these goals and objectives. The planning activities of a vice president of sales, for example, might include preparing a three- to five-year plan that includes strategies on how to enter new markets or increase existing market share. A regional sales manager, in turn, would establish specific policies and procedures to implement the strategies — say, targeted advertising campaigns to new markets or a new Web site with an online catalog. In anticipation of the increased sales volume, a purchasing supervisor might plan a specific inventory quantity to be maintained for a part.

2. **Organizing** includes identifying and bringing together the resources necessary to achieve the plans of an organization. Resources include people, money, materials (facilities, equipment, raw materials), and information. Organizing also involves establishing the management structure of an organization such as the departments and reporting relationships. For example, to introduce a product into new markets, a company might budget money for market research and organize a sales group to focus on the new markets.

3. **Leading**, sometimes referred to as **directing**, involves instructing and authorizing others to perform the necessary work. To lead effectively, managers must be able to communicate what needs to be done and motivate people to do the work. Leadership often takes place at daily or weekly meetings where managers meet with their employees to discuss job priorities.

4. **Controlling** involves measuring performance and, if necessary, taking corrective action. Daily production reports are a control device that gives managers the information they need to make any necessary adjustments in production rate or product mix.

Figure 10-2 shows how the four management tasks usually are performed in a sequence that becomes a recurring cycle. Actual performance is measured against a previously established plan as part of the control task; often this results in a revised plan. The revised plan may result in additional organizational and leadership activities. Performance then is measured against the revised plan, and the cycle repeats itself. The four tasks are related and a change in one task usually affects one or more of the other tasks.

All managers perform these management tasks. Their level in the organization and their assigned functional area influences the information they need to perform the tasks.

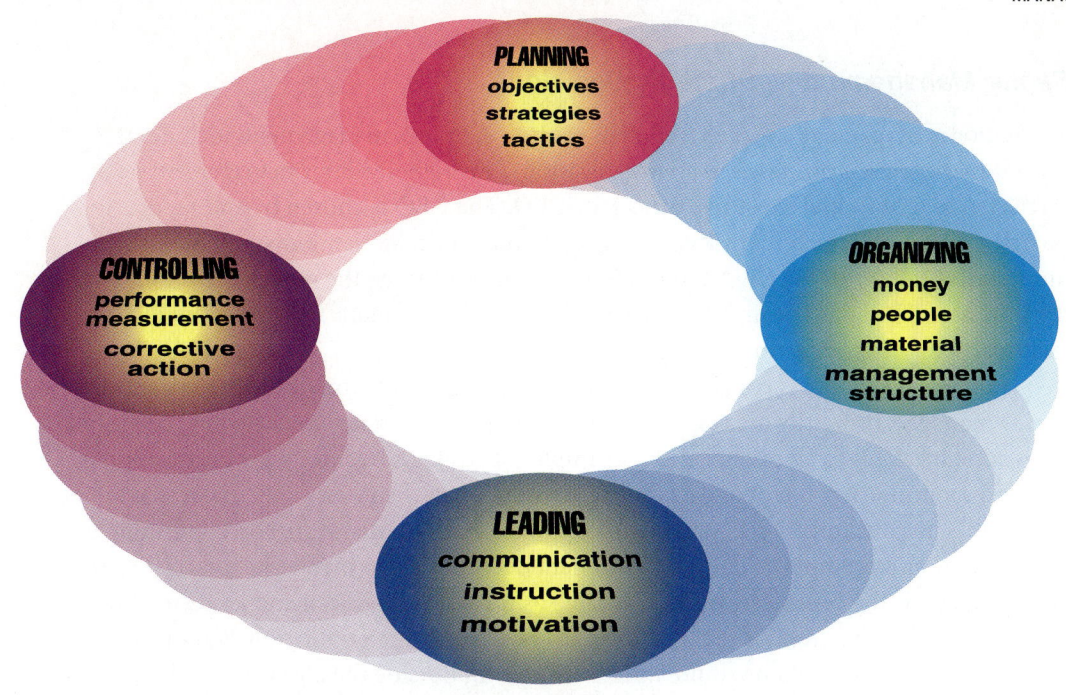

Figure 10-2
The four tasks performed by management are planning, organizing, leading, and controlling. These tasks are part of a recurring cycle; actions connected with any one task usually affect one or more of the other tasks.

Management Levels in an Organization

Management usually is classified into three levels; senior management, middle management, and operational management. The names for these levels can vary. As shown in Figure 10-3, these three levels of management are above a fourth level of the organization consisting of the production, clerical, and nonmanagement staff. Together, these four levels make up the entire organization. The following sections discuss these levels and their different information requirements.

inCyber

For a listing of job opportunities in various levels of management, visit the Discovering Computers Chapter 10 inCyber page (http://www.scsite.com/dc/ch10/incyber.htm) and click Management Levels.

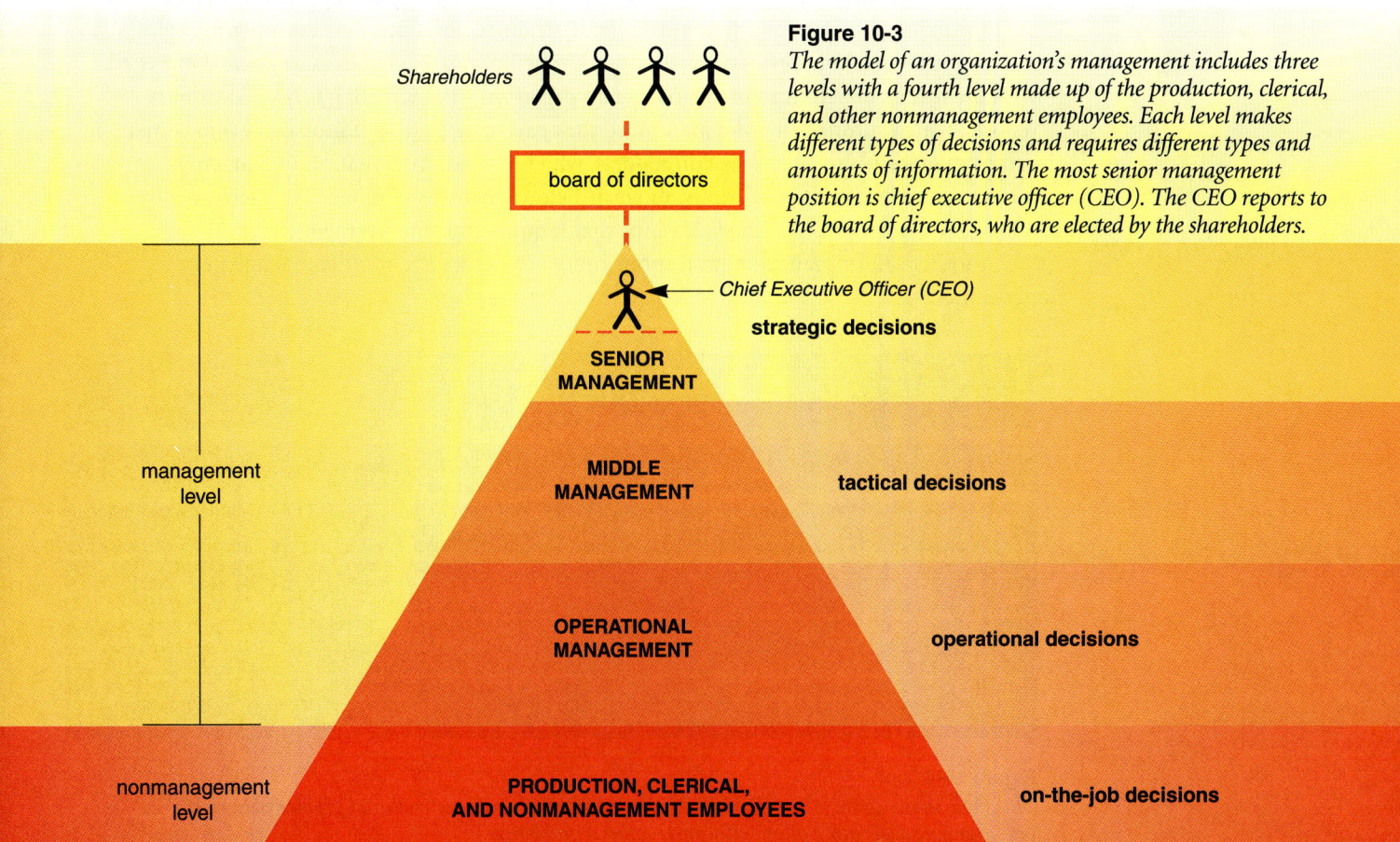

Figure 10-3
The model of an organization's management includes three levels with a fourth level made up of the production, clerical, and other nonmanagement employees. Each level makes different types of decisions and requires different types and amounts of information. The most senior management position is chief executive officer (CEO). The CEO reports to the board of directors, who are elected by the shareholders.

Senior Management — Strategic Decisions

Senior management, also referred to as executive, or top, management, includes the highest management positions in an organization. The highest senior management position is referred to as the **chief executive officer**, or **CEO**. The CEO is chosen by and reports to the **board of directors**, which is an advisory group that includes nonemployee members who meet periodically with the CEO and other officers to determine the overall direction of the organization. The board of directors is elected by the shareholders, who are individuals who own shares of the corporation's stock.

Senior management is concerned with the long-range direction of the organization. Senior managers primarily are responsible for **strategic decisions** that deal with the overall goals and objectives of an organization. Examples of strategic decisions are the decision to add or discontinue a product line or to diversify into a new business. The time frame for such decisions is usually long-range, starting one or more years in the future and continuing for several years or indefinitely. Senior management decisions often involve factors that cannot be controlled by the organization directly, such as the changing social and economic trends. An example of such a trend is the increasing average age of the population. Senior management decisions often require information from outside the company, such as industry statistics, consumer surveys, or broad economic indicators such as the change in personal income or the number of new houses being built.

The problems faced by senior management often are described as *unstructured*. **Unstructured problems** rely on intuition and judgment and often do not have a clear method for their solution. Lower levels of management tend to deal more with **structured problems** that are more routine, involve specific facts, and have an established method of being resolved. Figure 10-4 shows some of the characteristics of unstructured and structured problems.

Senior management also is responsible for monitoring current operations to ensure they are meeting the objectives of previously made strategic decisions. For example, are sales of a new product meeting previously forecasted levels? Because senior managers are concerned with the results of activities in all areas of an organization, they often rely on summary reports, which summarize information, so they can review all operations in a timely manner. Senior managers also use exception reports, which present information on current operations only if it is significantly above or below what was planned. This helps senior managers to focus on only the variations that require their involvement.

Another senior management responsibility is to supervise middle management personnel.

---

inCyber

For details on Bill Gates, CEO of Microsoft Corporation, visit the Discovering Computers Chapter 10 inCyber page (http://www.scsite.com/dc/ch10/incyber.htm) and click CEO.

Characteristic	Structured Problem	Unstructured Problem
Level of detail	detail	summary
Time frame	current or past	future
Focus	functional	cross-functional
Information requirements	internal	external
Results	near-term, measurable	long-term, hard to measure

Figure 10-4
This table shows some of the characteristics of structured and unstructured problems. Senior management deals more often with unstructured problems.

Middle Management — Tactical Decisions

Middle management is responsible for implementing the strategic decisions of senior management. To do this, middle managers make **tactical decisions** that implement specific programs and plans necessary to accomplish the stated objectives. For example, if senior management makes the strategic decision to develop a new product line, a middle manager might make the tactical decision on how best to advertise and promote the company's new products. Tactical decisions usually involve a shorter time frame than strategic decisions but often cover an entire year. Although middle managers are interested in external events that affect their work, they generally are more concerned with the internal operations of the organization and, therefore, rely on information generated by the organization. Like senior management, middle management uses summary and exception reports, although not to the same extent. Sometimes, middle management also reviews the information in detail reports to understand performance variances.

Middle management also is responsible for supervising operational management.

Operational Management — Operational Decisions

Operational management supervises the production, clerical, and nonmanagement staff of an organization. In performing their duties, operational managers make **operational decisions** that usually involve an immediate action such as accepting or rejecting an inventory delivery or approving a purchase order. The operational decisions should be consistent with and support the tactical decisions made by middle management. The time frame of operational decisions usually is very short, such as a day, a week, or a month. Operational managers directly supervise the production and support of an organization's product or service; thus, they need detail reports with specific information on what was produced. Summary and exception reports, long an important tool for senior- and middle-level managers, increasingly are being used by operational managers. Two reasons exist for this change. First, upper levels of management are allowing lower levels of management to make more decisions. Second, decentralized network computer systems have made the information necessary to make these decisions more easily available.

Nonmanagement Employees — On-the-Job Decisions

Nonmanagement employees, who include production, clerical, and staff personnel, also need frequent information to perform their jobs. New, flexible manufacturing systems, for example, have increased the need for information to be available to the production worker. Instead of working at the same task all the time, production workers often work as a group on related tasks. Some manufacturing plants even allow a group of workers to move with the product from the beginning of the production process to the end. Both approaches require production workers to understand more about the production process than ever before. Often, workers obtain needed information through production-floor terminals that allow them to inquire about the next production process or tool required. Some systems tell the workers what job they should work on next.

Clerical and nonproduction workers also have more information available to them than in the past. For example, documentation of administrative policies and procedures often are available online for immediate access in a corporate database on an intranet. As previously mentioned, all of these changes are part of a trend toward giving lower level, nonmanagement employees the information they need to make decisions previously made by managers.

---

inCyber

To learn about operational management services, visit the Discovering Computers Chapter 10 inCyber page (http://www.scsite.com/dc/ch10/incyber.htm) and click Operational Management.

Functional Areas in an Organization

Most organizations are divided into functional areas that deal with related types of activities. Four functional areas that most organizations share are operations, sales and marketing, finance, and human resources. Many organizations also have a fifth area, information systems, that provides information support for the entire organization (Figure 10-5). Each functional area usually is managed by a senior-level manager such as a vice president and has different levels of managers as shown in Figure 10-6.

- **Operations** carries out the primary activity of an organization. For a manufacturer, operations includes designing, making, and distributing products. Organizations that make products requiring a substantial amount of design often have a separate functional area for engineering.

- **Sales and marketing** sell and promote an organization's product or service. Sales is responsible for obtaining a customer's commitment to purchase a product or service. Marketing is responsible for creating an awareness of and a desire for the product or service. Organizations that require a substantial amount of promotion, such as automobiles or other consumer goods, often have a separate functional area for marketing.

- **Finance** includes all activities related to recording the monetary transactions of an organization. These transactions include sales, expenses, purchasing assets, and borrowing money. Many organizations include information systems activities in the finance area. Other organizations, however, recognize that information systems activities support the entire organization and have information systems as a separate functional area.

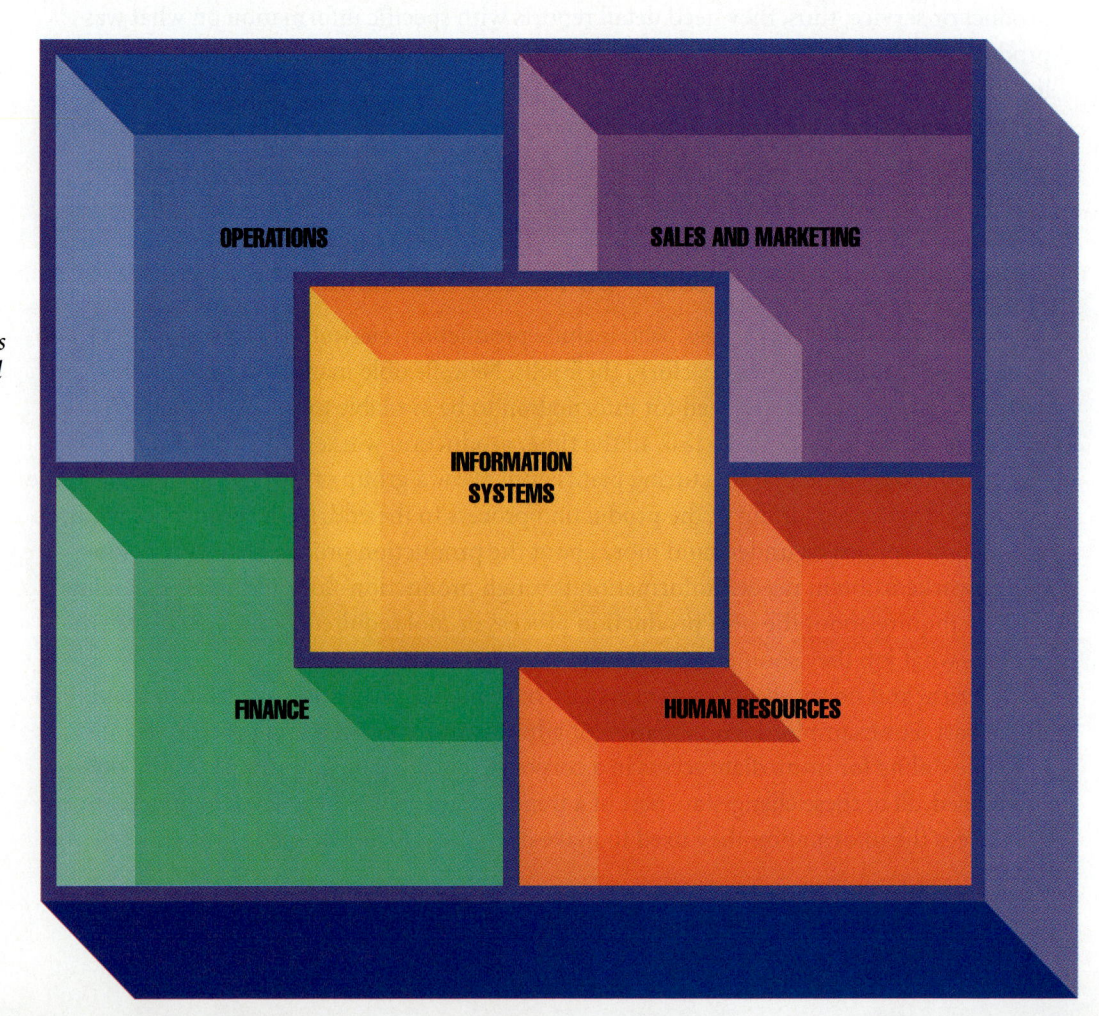

Figure 10-5
Most organizations are divided into functional areas such as operations, sales and marketing, finance, human resources, and information systems.

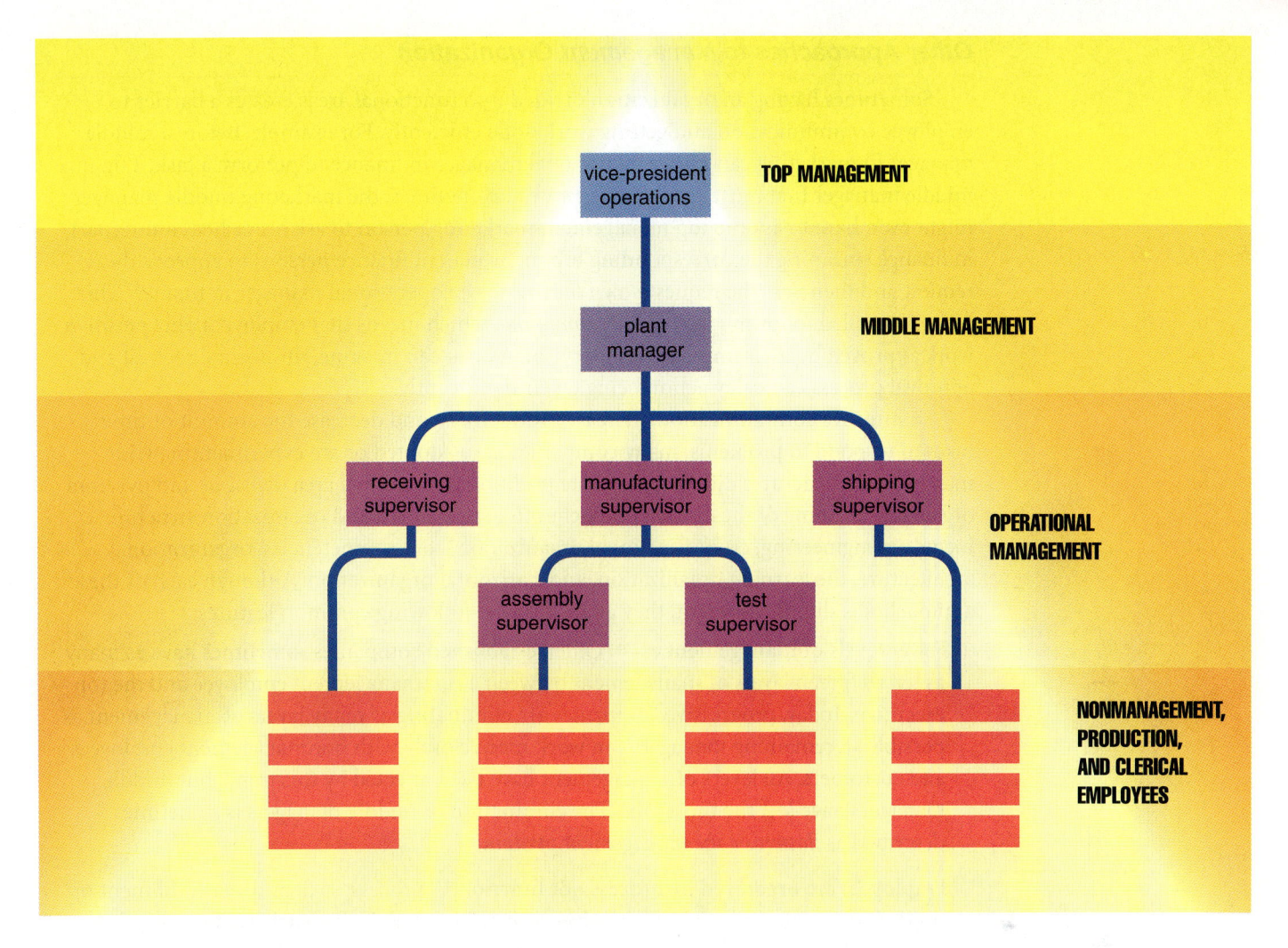

Figure 10-6
As shown in this organization chart for the operations area, functional groups usually have employees at each level of the organization. Within a level, two or more layers of management sometimes exist as shown above in the operational management level.

- **Human resources** manages the people who work for the organization. Human resources makes sure employees are evaluated fairly and consistently and receive the training and guidance they need to continue their careers. Human resources consults with senior management on pay, benefit, and employee development programs.

- **Information Systems** provides support for the entire organization by managing the organization's information and information systems. Information systems managers are responsible for acquiring, maintaining, and controlling all aspects of information technology, including day-to-day operations, building new information systems, and providing technical support for users.

Other Approaches to Management Organization

Sometimes having an organization divided into functional areas creates a barrier to employee communication and getting work done efficiently. For example, before a middle manager in marketing can ask an operational manager in finance to perform a task, a finance middle manager first must approve the request. Sometimes, the marketing middle manager might even have to ask the top management marketing person to ask his or her counterpart in finance (meaning the corresponding top management finance person) to approve the request and then pass the request *down the line* to the operational manager in finance. This process is called following the *chain of command*, which means that employees only perform work approved by their immediate supervisor. As you can imagine, this formal request and approval process can delay action being taken significantly.

To improve communication, increase productivity, and decrease the amount of time it takes to respond to problems, many companies have adopted or are experimenting with management structures different from the traditional functional area divisions and pyramid organization. Some of these new approaches to management and organization structure include reengineering, cross-functional organization, core competencies, organizational architecture, the learning organization, and horizontal organization. Although each of these approaches is slightly different, they all include the following common features:

- **Fewer levels of management exist.** Older, established companies sometimes have as many as ten to fifteen layers of management between a nonmanagement employee and the top executive. Today, progressive companies are eliminating as many layers of management as possible so remaining managers can work more closely with nonmanagement employees and customers. All layers of management have been affected by this trend, but middle managers have lost the most jobs. The elimination of middle managers is sometimes described as *flattening the management pyramid*.

- **Employees are organized by process not function.** A process, such as order fulfillment or product development, typically involves several functional areas such as sales, manufacturing, engineering, and finance. Some companies now place all employees involved with a process into a single group dedicated to carrying out the process tasks efficiently. The person responsible for managing the process group is called the *process owner*.

- **Self-managed teams are used wherever possible.** Although they have long been used for one-time projects, teams of employees with different functional backgrounds now are being given ongoing responsibilities and being told to manage themselves. An important requirement for this approach is to give the team a well-defined purpose and measurable performance goals.

- **Employees continuously must learn new skills.** Technology and competition both have increased the rate of change in most organizations. To keep up with this change, employees must learn new skills. Few employees, if any, will perform the same job throughout their career. Many organizations recognize this trend and provide or encourage all employees to participate in continuing education programs.

The impact of these new management methods and structures on information and information systems needs has been significant. Task and process teams often require information that previously was prepared by separate functional departments. Having fewer levels of management requires managers to rely more on exception reports to help them allocate their limited time to the most important areas. With the increasing pressure to reduce costs, information systems managers have been encouraged to **downsize** operations by moving applications from mainframe and minicomputer systems to networks of personal computers. A related term, **rightsize**, means to match an organization's information processing requirements with an appropriate mix of computer systems. Some companies have eliminated their in-house information systems department altogether. In a process called **outsourcing**, companies hire outside firms to provide information systems support for a contracted fee.

Whatever form of organization companies adopt, they realize that they must develop an *information architecture* that matches their *organization architecture*. **Information architecture** refers to the way an organization provides information to different organization levels or groups.

Now that the importance of information to an organization and how various levels use it has been discussed, the characteristics, or qualities, that all information should have will be explained.

> To learn about outsourcing issues, visit the Discovering Computers Chapter 10 inCyber page (http://www.scsite.com/dc/ch10/incyber.htm) and click Outsourcing.

Qualities of Valuable Information

As previously mentioned, the purpose of processing data is to create information. Just as data should have certain characteristics to be valuable, so too should information. These characteristics, or qualities, of valuable information (Figure 10-7) include being accurate, verifiable, timely, organized, meaningful, useful, and cost effective.

- **Accurate** means that information is correct. Inaccurate information often is worse than no information at all. Accuracy is also a characteristic of data. Although accurate data does not guarantee accurate information, it is impossible to produce accurate information from erroneous data. This often is referred to as *GIGO*, which stands for *garbage in, garbage out*; it means that, if you input erroneous data (garbage in), you will output inaccurate information (garbage out).

QUALITIES OF VALUABLE INFORMATION	
ACCURATE	Is correct
VERIFIABLE	Can be confirmed
TIMELY	Is of an age relevant to the use
ORGANIZED	Is arranged to meet requirements
MEANINGFUL	Is relevant to user
USEFUL	Results in decision being made or action being taken
COST EFFECTIVE	Costs less to produce than its value

Figure 10-7
The qualities of valuable information are characteristics that all information should have, whether or not it is produced by a computer.

- **Verifiable** means that you can confirm information. For example, before relying on the totals listed in a summary report, an accountant wants to know that these amounts are supported by details of the transactions. The accountant can verify the accuracy of the report totals by adding up the supporting detail records for some of the totals and comparing the results to the report.

- **Timely** means that the age of the information is suited to the use of the information. Although most information loses its value with time, some information, such as trends, becomes more valuable as time passes and more information is obtained. For example, up-to-the-minute information may be required for some decisions, such as reordering a key part, while older information may be appropriate for other decisions, such as determining which employees took vacations in a prior month. The point to remember is that the timeliness must be appropriate for any decisions that will be made based on the information.

- **Organized** means that the information is arranged to suit your requirements. For example, a sales manager that assigns territories on a geographic basis would need prospective customer lists sorted by postal code and not by prospective customer name.

- **Meaningful** information is relevant to the person who receives it. Certain information is meaningful only to specific individuals or groups within an organization. You should eliminate extraneous and unnecessary information and always consider the audience when you are accumulating or reporting information.

- **Useful** information results in an action being taken or specifically not being taken, depending on the situation. Often, the usefulness of information is improved through exception reporting, which focuses only on the information that exceeds certain limits. For example, an inventory report showing items whose balance on hand is less than a predetermined minimum quantity allows an inventory manager to make reorder decisions far faster then if he or she had to review the entire inventory report to find such items.

- **Cost-effective** information costs less to produce than the value of the information. Many organizations periodically review the information they produce in reports to determine if the reports maintain the qualities of information just described. The cost of producing these reports can, therefore, still be justified or possibly reduced. Sometimes the value of information is hard to determine. If it cannot be determined, perhaps the information should be produced only as people require it, instead of on a regular basis.

Although the qualities of information have been discussed in conjunction with computers and information systems, these qualities apply to all information regardless of how it is produced. Knowing these qualities will help you evaluate the information you receive and provide every day, whether or not it is generated by computers or information systems.

Types of Information Systems

Information systems generally are classified into five categories: (1) office systems; (2) transaction processing systems; (3) management information systems; (4) decision support systems; and (5) expert systems.

Office Systems

Office systems include software applications for administrative tasks that occur throughout the organization. These applications, sometimes referred to as *productivity software*, include word processing, desktop publishing, spreadsheet, database, presentation graphics, Web browsers, e-mail, personal information management, project management, and groupware, many of which were discussed in Chapter 2. Other office systems involve communications technology such as voice mail, facsimile (fax), videoconferencing, and electronic data interchange (EDI). These applications were discussed in Chapter 6.

Transaction Processing Systems

Transaction processing systems (TPS) process data generated by the day-to-day transactions of an organization (Figure 10-8). Examples of TPS are billing systems, inventory control systems, accounts payable systems, and order entry systems.

inCyber

For information on how a company uses a transaction processing system (TPS), visit the Discovering Computers Chapter 10 inCyber page (http://www.scsite.com/dc/ch10/incyber.htm) and click TPS.

Figure 10-8
Transaction processing systems (TPS) process the day-to-day transactions of an organization.

When computers first were used for processing business applications, the information systems developed were primarily TPS. Usually, the purpose was to computerize an existing manual system. Computerizing these systems often resulted in faster processing, reduced clerical costs, and improved customer service. The first TPS were usually batch processing systems. In **batch processing**, transaction data is collected and, at a later time, all transactions are processed together as a group. As computers became more powerful, online transaction processing systems were developed. With **online transaction processing** (OLTP), transactions are processed as they are entered. All related records are updated at the same time. Today, most TPS use online transaction processing. Some processing tasks, however, such as calculating payroll checks or printing invoices, are performed most efficiently on a batch basis and thus continue to be batch processed.

Although TPS were designed originally to process daily transactions, the systems were modified over time to provide summary, exception, and trend reporting useful to management. Today, a TPS often is a part of a management information system.

Management Information Systems

Management information systems evolved as managers realized that computer processing could be used for more than just day-to-day transaction processing and that the computer's capability of performing rapid calculations and data comparisons could be used to produce meaningful information for management. **Management information systems** (MIS) refer to computer-based systems that generate the timely and accurate information needed for managing an organization. Frequently, a management information system is integrated with a transaction processing system. For example, to process a sales order, the transaction processing system records the sale, updates the customer's account balance, and makes a deduction from the inventory. In the related management information system, reports are produced that show slow or fast selling products, customers with past due account balances, and inventory items that need reordering. In the management information system, the focus is on the information that management needs to do its job (Figure 10-9).

---

inCyber

For details on how a management information system is used in the health-care industry, visit the Discovering Computers Chapter 10 inCyber page (http://www.scsite.com/dc/ch10/incyber.htm) and click MIS.

Figure 10-9
Management information systems focus on the summary information and exceptions that managers use to perform their jobs.

TYPES OF INFORMATION SYSTEMS **10.15**

A special type of management information system is the executive information system. **Executive information systems (EIS)** are management information systems that have been designed for the information needs of senior management. Companywide management information systems usually address the information needs of all levels of management. EIS originally were designed for senior managers who were not as familiar with computers as other levels of management, and thus, use a touch screen to make them easy to use. One leading system uses a remote control device similar to those used to control a television set. Another distinguishing characteristic of an EIS is the graphic presentation of processing options and the resulting information (Figure 10-10). Again, this is designed to make the system easier to use.

Because executives focus on strategic issues, EIS often have access to external databases such as the Dow Jones News/Retrieval service or other sources of information available on the Internet. Such external sources of information can provide current information on interest rates, commodity prices, and other leading economic indicators.

EIS are difficult to implement because the systems must meet the specific needs of the individual executives who will use the system. For example, many executives prefer to have information presented in a particular sequence with the option of seeing different levels of supporting detail information such as cost data on a spreadsheet. The desired sequence and level of detail varies for each executive. EIS must be tailored to the executives' requirements or the executives will continue to manage with information they have obtained through previously established methods.

inCyber

For a look at the features of the Dow Jones Business Information Services, visit the Discovering Computers Chapter 10 inCyber page (http://www.scsite.com/dc/ch10/incyber.htm) and click Dow Jones.

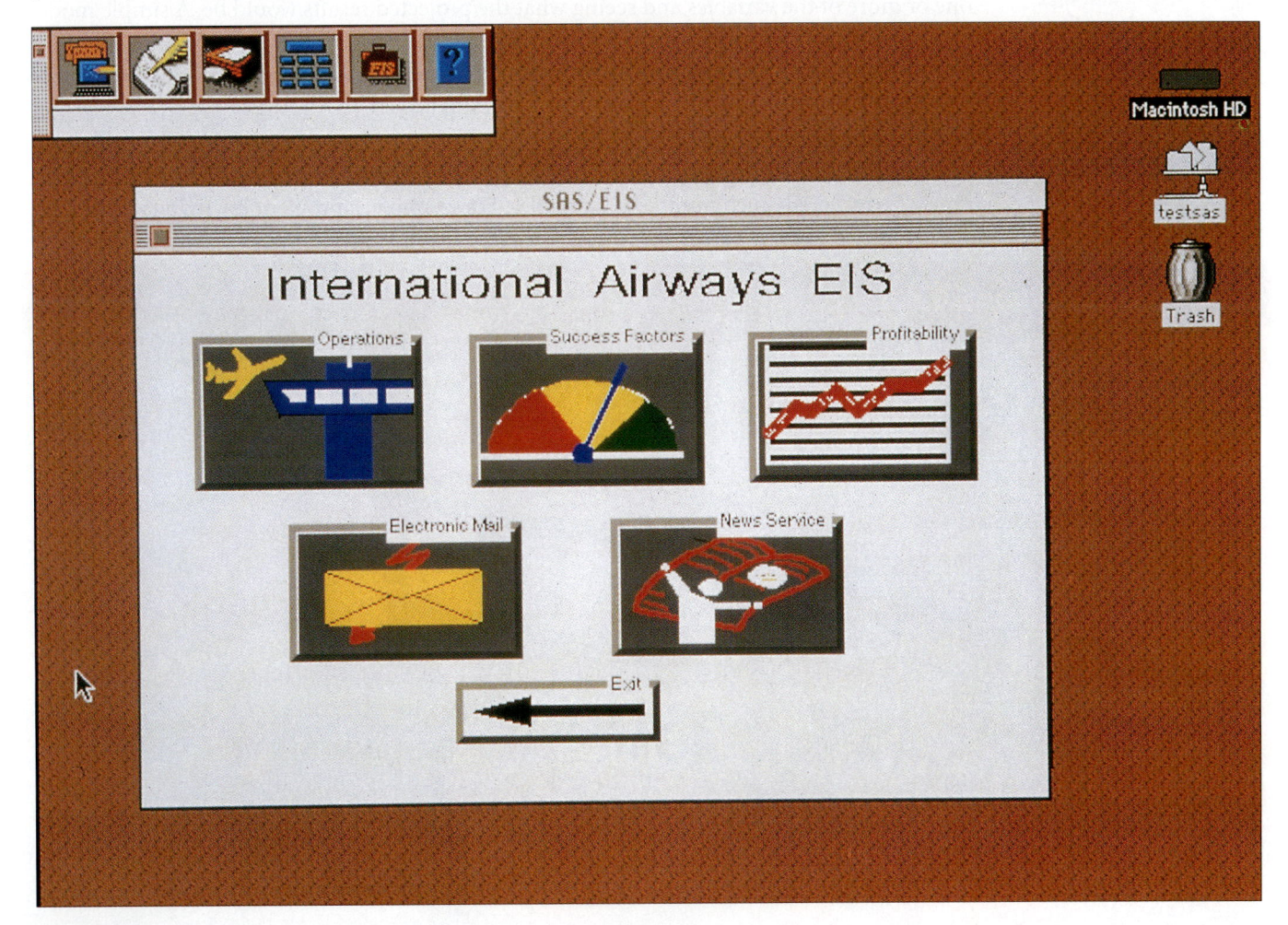

Figure 10-10
Executive information systems (EIS) present senior management with summarized information in a graphic format.

Decision Support Systems

Frequently, management needs information that is not provided routinely by transaction processing or management information systems. A vice president of finance, for example, may want to know how company profits would be affected if interest rates on borrowed money increased and raw material prices decreased. Decision support systems have been developed to provide this information.

Decision support systems (DSS) are systems designed to help someone reach a decision by summarizing or comparing data from internal or external sources or both. Internal sources include data from an organization's database such as sales, manufacturing, or financial data. Data from external sources could include information on interest rates, population trends, new housing construction, or raw material pricing. Using a DSS, managers can manipulate the data to help with decisions. Frito Lay, for example, collects and reports sales data on its own and competitor products every day (Figure 10-11). The information is part of a DSS that allows Frito Lay to analyze important trends in days or weeks instead of the months that it used to take.

Some decision support systems include query languages, statistical analysis capabilities, spreadsheets, and graphics that help the user evaluate the decision data. Such decision support systems sometimes are referred to as **online analytical processing (OLAP) systems**. Some decision support systems also include capabilities that allow you to create a model of the variables affecting a decision. With a **model**, you can ask *what-if* questions by changing one or more of the variables and seeing what the projected results would be. A simple model for determining the best product price would include factors for the expected sales volume at each price level. Many people use electronic spreadsheets for decision support to complete simple modeling tasks.

DSS sometimes are combined with executive information systems (EIS). Generally speaking, DSS are more analytical and are designed to work on unstructured problems that do not have a predefined number of variables. For example, a problem involving how to

---

inCyber

For details on the development of a decision support system, visit the Discovering Computers Chapter 10 inCyber page (http://www.scsite.com/dc/ch10/incyber.htm) and click DSS.

Figure 10-11
Frito Lay, a major producer of snack foods, has developed a decision support system that uses sales information collected daily on hand-held terminals by more than 10,000 salespeople. The system helps Frito Lay spot sales trends in days or weeks instead of the months it used to take.

TYPES OF INFORMATION SYSTEMS **10.17**

finance a company's growth would involve estimates of sales, income, depreciation, interest rates, and other variables that would best be handled by a DSS. EIS are oriented primarily toward collecting and presenting meaningful information from a variety of sources.

Expert Systems

Expert systems, sometimes called **knowledge systems**, are computerized systems that simulate the human experts' reasoning and decision-making processes. Expert systems are made up of the combined subject knowledge of the human experts, called the **knowledge base**, and the **inference rules** that determine how the knowledge is used to reach decisions. Because it contains the knowledge and reasoning of the experts, the computer also becomes an *expert* on the subject. Although they may appear to *think*, the current expert systems actually operate within narrow preprogrammed limits and cannot make decisions based on common sense or on information outside of their knowledge base. An example of how a simple expert system uses rules to identify an animal is shown in Figure 10-12.

inCyber

For information on knowledge system development, visit the Discovering Computers Chapter 10 inCyber page (http://www.scsite.com/dc/ch10/incyber.htm) and click Knowledge System.

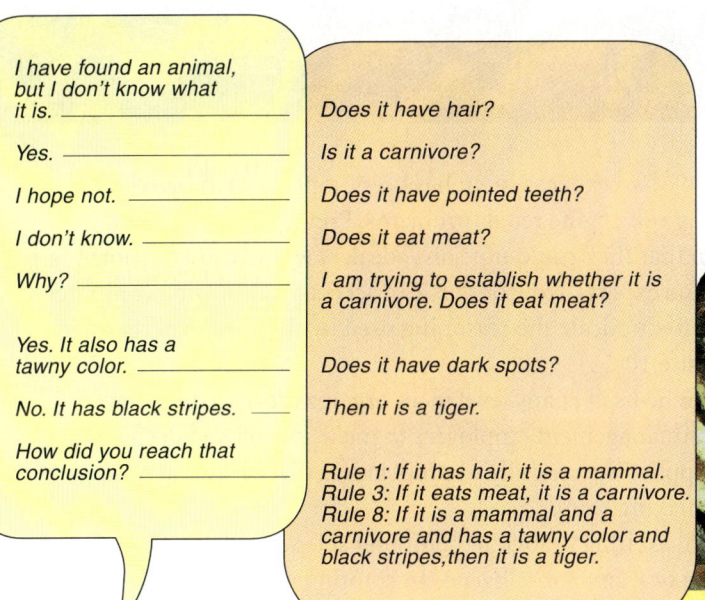

Figure 10-12
A simulated dialogue between a user and a simple expert system is designed to identify an animal based on observations about the animal provided by the user. Notice how answers to certain questions result in other questions that narrow the possible conclusions. Once a conclusion is reached, the expert system can display or print the rules upon which the conclusion was based.

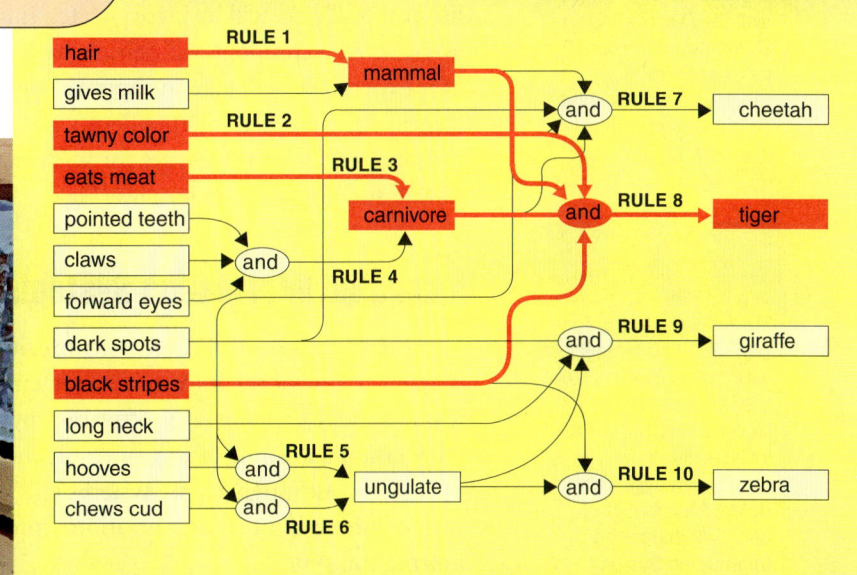

I have found an animal, but I don't know what it is.

Yes.

I hope not.

I don't know.

Why?

Yes. It also has a tawny color.

No. It has black stripes.

How did you reach that conclusion?

Does it have hair?

Is it a carnivore?

Does it have pointed teeth?

Does it eat meat?

I am trying to establish whether it is a carnivore. Does it eat meat?

Does it have dark spots?

Then it is a tiger.

Rule 1: If it has hair, it is a mammal.
Rule 3: If it eats meat, it is a carnivore.
Rule 8: If it is a mammal and a carnivore and has a tawny color and black stripes, then it is a tiger.

Figure 10-13
Ford Motor Company has developed an expert system that incorporates the knowledge of its engine repair experts. Instead of calling the individuals, Ford dealers now can access the expert system when they are trying to diagnose engine problems.

A more practical application of an expert system has been implemented by Ford Motor Company to help its dealers diagnose engine repair problems. Previously, when they encountered an engine problem that they could not solve, dealers would call Dearborn, Michigan to talk with Ford engine experts. Now dealers can access a nationwide computer system that Ford has developed to duplicate the reasoning used by the Ford experts when troubleshooting a problem (Figure 10-13).

Although expert systems can be used at any level in an organization, to date they primarily have been used by nonmanagement employees to make job-related decisions. Expert systems also have been applied successfully to problems as diverse as diagnosing illnesses, searching for oil, and making soup.

Expert systems are part of an exciting branch of computer science called **artificial intelligence** (**AI**), the application of human intelligence to computer systems. Experts predict that eventually, AI will be incorporated into most computer systems and many individual products. AI technology will sense what you are doing and, based on logical assumptions and prior experience, will take the appropriate action to complete the task. AI technology is used in **agent software** that independently carries out tasks on your behalf. Some people use agent software to search the Internet for information that matches their preferences on a particular subject, such as music or movies (Figure 10-14).

Integrated Information Systems

With today's sophisticated software, it can be difficult to classify a system as belonging uniquely to one of the information system types that have been discussed. For example, much of today's application software provides both transaction and management information and some of the more advanced software even includes some decision support capabilities. Although expert systems still operate primarily as separate systems, the trend is clear: combine all of an organization's information needs into a single, integrated information system.

---

inCyber

For files, programs, and publications regarding artificial intelligence (AI), visit the Discovering Computers Chapter 10 inCyber page (http://www.scsite.com/dc/ch10/incyber.htm) and click AI.

inCyber

For a description of the attributes of an integrated information system, visit the Discovering Computers Chapter 10 inCyber page (http://www.scsite.com/dc/ch10/incyber.htm) and click Integrated Information System.

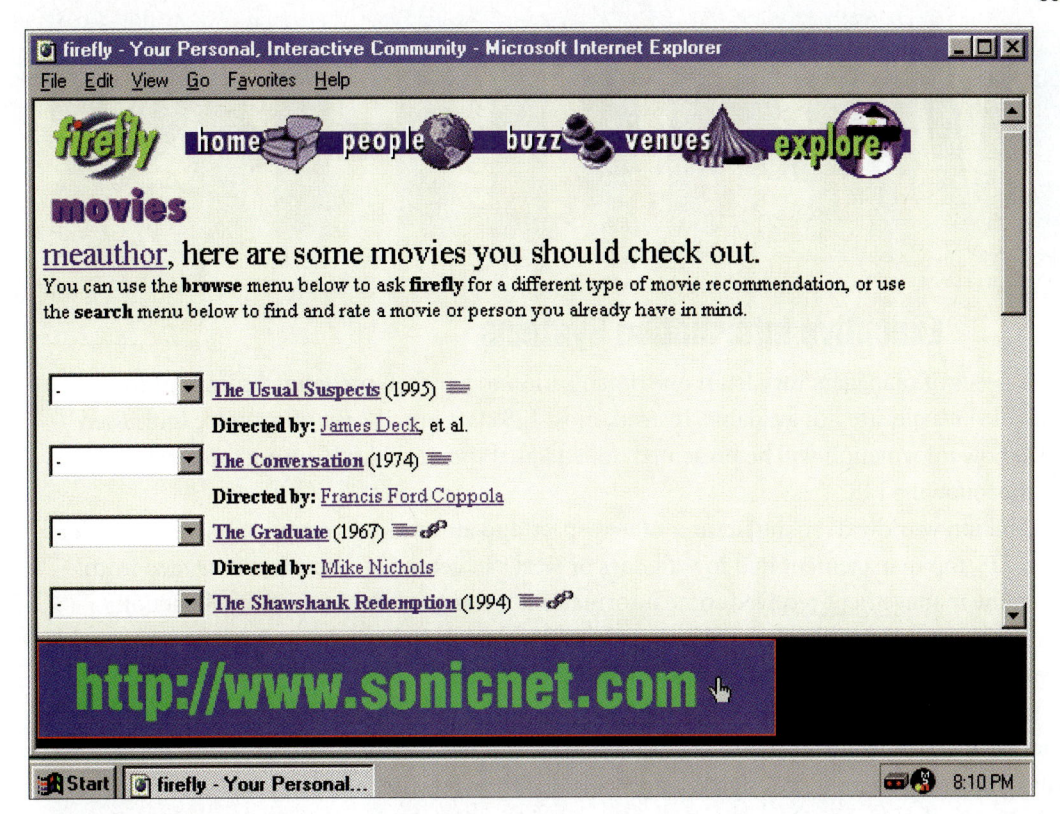

Figure 10-14
Firefly is a World Wide Web software agent program that recommends movies and music. Ratings of movies and music you enter are matched against ratings of other Firefly users. Recommendations are based on favorable ratings of others who have similar preferences.

The Role of Personal Computers in Information Systems

Personal computers play a significant role in modern information systems. As organizations move toward decentralized decision making, networked personal computers give managers access to information they need to make decisions. Nonmanagement employees also benefit by having information available through networked personal computers on their desks or in the production area. For many applications, personal computers are more cost effective than larger systems. One study estimated that the cost to process a million transactions on a mainframe is fifty times more expensive than on a personal computer. Flexibility is another advantage of personal computers; personal computers can be added more quickly to an existing system than the corresponding amount of equipment that would be needed with larger systems. Many professionals believe that the ideal information system involves a network of personal computers attached to a server that stores the common information that many users access. This centralized data and decentralized computing arrangement allow users and organizations the most flexibility over controlling their information resources. For these reasons, many organizations use this computing arrangement.

Summary of Information Systems

Numerous factors have combined to make information an increasingly important asset for most organizations. Organizations manage this valuable asset through the use of information systems, which provide the information necessary to manage the activities of the organization. Information systems provide different types of information based on the users' needs, which often are related to the users' levels in the organization. New approaches to management and ongoing changes in organizational structures will continue to require corresponding changes in information systems.

The trend of information systems is to combine and integrate office, transaction processing, management information, decision support, and expert systems that previously operated independently.

COMPUTERS AT WORK

Executive Information Systems

Because the information needs of managers vary from one organization to another, predefined solutions for executive information systems (EIS) usually are not available. Instead, most EIS start out as a set of software tools used by managers to define what and how information will be presented. AlliedSignal Inc. and Hertz®, using tools provided by Comshare, Inc., developed the following EIS.

AlliedSignal Inc. is a $12 billion worldwide manufacturer of aerospace and automotive components and specialty materials. Before developing an EIS, top management had to wait days or weeks to get the information it needed from various operating units. By the time management received some information, it was too late to take effective action. After consulting with 150 managers at 15 sites, AlliedSignal developed an EIS to track 29 key measures of the company's performance, including figures for sales and income, and on-time shipments. Using Comshare's Commander Decision™ software, the prototype for this system was developed in just 30 days and the entire EIS was operational three months later. Since then, the system has been expanded from 150 to 500 users and several new performance measures have been added. Most of the performance measures are updated nightly and available for review the following day.

Hertz® is an international car and truck rental corporation with rental locations in thousands of airports and city locations. Because vehicle rentals are extremely price-sensitive, it is important for Hertz management to know what its competitors are charging and to adjust its rates accordingly. The data required for these decisions is staggering; literally millions of prices for different combinations of vehicle categories and rental markets. Hertz knew that this data had to be reviewed on an exception basis; looking only at competitors prices that varied significantly from Hertz rates. To do this, Hertz developed an EIS that uses intelligent agent software from Comshare to identify situations that need management attention. The intelligent agent software, called Detect and Alert®, gathers and analyzes the price information automatically and presents only cases that exceed limits established by management. This way, exceptions are kept to a minimum and can be reviewed by a small staff. The exception criteria can be changed easily if management decides to focus on a particular area.

AlliedSignal and Hertz are two examples of major corporations that are using EIS to help managers obtain the information they need to make decisions on a timely basis. With flexible EIS software tools, they can continue to refine their systems as business conditions change.

Figure 10-15

IN THE FUTURE

The Cyber Corporation

In recent years, the term used to describe the organization of the future was the **virtual corporation**, which is an alliance of individual companies that temporarily join together to offer goods and services. Virtual corporations form quickly and stay together only as long as the business opportunity remains profitable. Today, business futurists are talking about the **cyber corporation**, or **cybercorp**, which is a virtual corporation that uses the Internet and other networks to conduct much of its business.

In a virtual corporation, the capabilities of one company are increased by adding the capabilities of one or more other companies. Each virtual partner contributes its **core competencies** — what it does best. One company may be responsible for product design, another for manufacturing, and a third for sales. The initial idea for a product may come from another company. This partnering approach has been used in the past for one-time projects such as motion pictures and construction projects and now is being applied to consumer products and services, as well.

To communicate with one another, cybercorp partners need **interenterprise information systems** that enable them to share all relevant information on a timely basis. The networks and software applications necessary to handle this information flow must be established quickly with the thought that they may exist for only as long as the joint product or service is in demand. Initially, many cybercorp networks will use the Internet and Web sites to communicate. Later, if speed, security, and other factors require it, private intranets will be established. Besides linking the cybercorp partners, the network must reach out to existing and potential customers. The cybercorp will use public and private networks for all forms of customer contact; including advertising, order taking, and customer service. Some products such as software and traditionally printed products such as newspapers, magazines, and research reports, even will be delivered over the network. The cost savings for printed materials will be tremendous.

Many legal and organizational challenges will have to be worked out before cybercorps can operate as well as predicted by management theorists. When they are in operation, it will be the information networks that hold them together. In fact, it may be that information is the only inventory that a cybercorp owns.

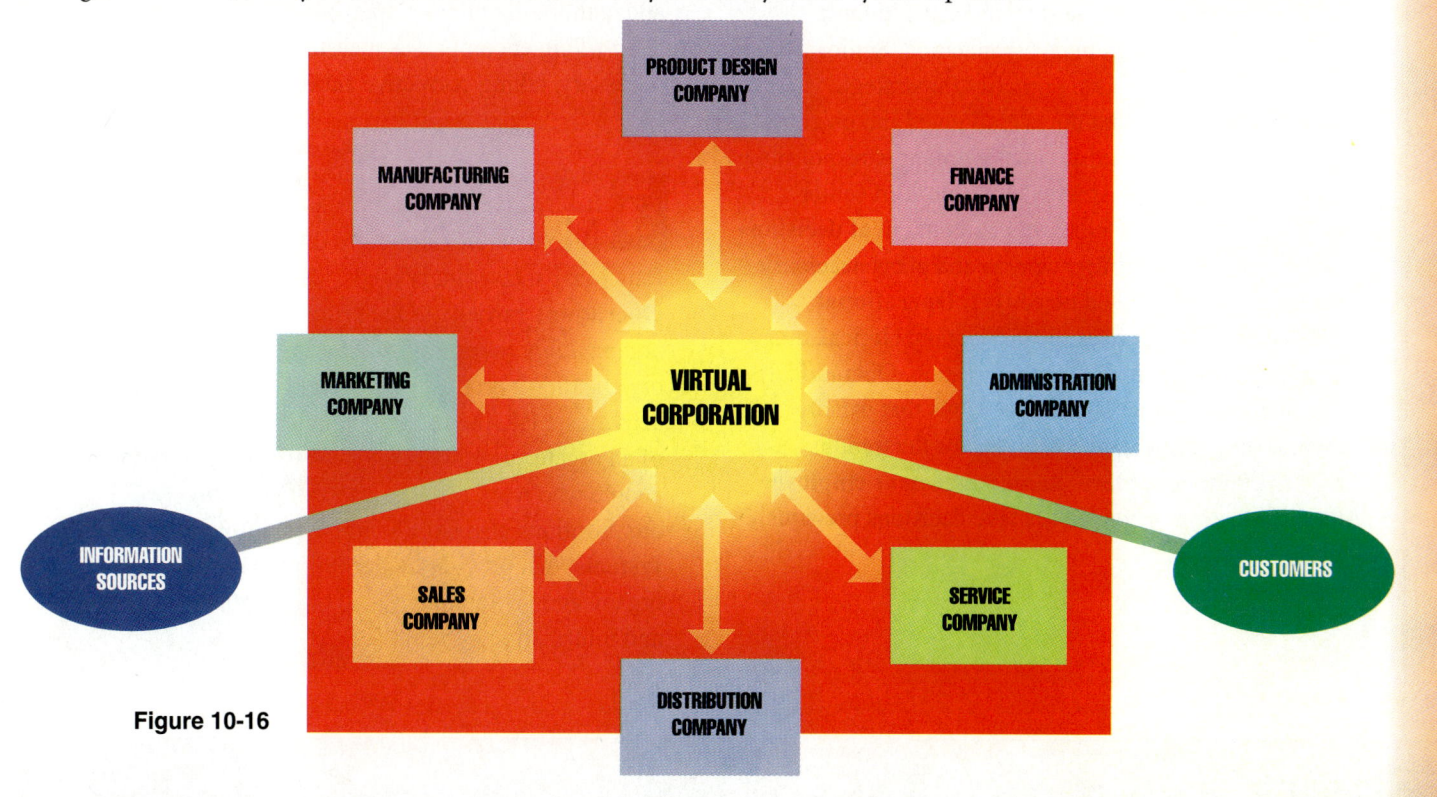

Figure 10-16

chapter 10 review

1 | 2 | 3 | 4 | 5 | 6 | 7 | 8 | 9 | 10 | 11 | 12 | 13 | 14 | I

inCyber | review | terms | yourTurn | hotTopics | outThere | winLabs | webWalk | exercises | news | home

INSTRUCTIONS: *To display this page from the Web, launch your browser and enter the URL, http://www.scsite.com/dc/ch10/review.htm. Click the links for current and additional information.*

1 Information Systems

An **information system** is a collection of elements that provides accurate, timely, and useful information. All information systems that use a computer are comprised of six elements: hardware, software, accurate data, trained information systems personnel, knowledgeable users, and documented procedures.

2 Why Information is Important

Accurate information is crucial to an organization's current and future success. Information is a key ingredient in both short- and long-term decision making. Among factors that contribute to the need for timely and accurate information are expanded markets, increased competition, shorter product life cycles, government regulation, and increased cost pressure.

3 How Managers Use Information

Managers of an organization are the women and men responsible for directing the use of resources such as people, money, materials, and information so the organization can operate efficiently and prosper. Managers work toward this goal by performing four management tasks. *Planning* involves establishing goals and objectives and determining the strategies or tactics needed to meet them. *Organizing* includes identifying and bringing together the resources necessary to achieve the plans of an organization. *Leading* entails instructing and authorizing others to perform the necessary work. *Controlling* encompasses measuring performance and, if necessary, taking corrective action.

4 Management Levels

Management usually is classified into three levels. **Senior management** includes the highest management positions in an organization. Senior managers are responsible primarily for strategic decisions that deal with the overall goals and objectives of an organization. **Middle management** is responsible for implementing the **strategic decisions** of senior management. Middle managers make **tactical decisions** that implement specific programs and plans necessary to accomplish the stated objectives. **Operational management** supervises the production, clerical, and nonmanagement staff of an organization. Operational managers make **operational decisions** that usually involve an intermediate action. Today, the trend is toward giving lower level **nonmanagement employees** the information they need to make decisions previously made by managers.

5 Functional Areas

Most organizations are divided into four functional areas with related types of activities. **Operations** carries out the primary activity of an organization. **Sales and marketing** sell an organization's product or service. **Finance** includes all activities related to recording the monetary transactions of an organization. **Human resources** manages the people who work for an organization. Many organizations also have a fifth area, **information systems**, that provides support for the entire organization by managing the organization's information and information systems.

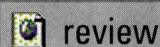

6 Other Approaches to Management Organization

Many companies have adopted or are experimenting with structures different from the traditional functional organization. These approaches include fewer levels of management, employees organized by process not function, use of self-managed teams wherever possible, and employees continuously learning new skills. Whatever form of organization companies adopt, they must develop an **information architecture** (the way information is provided to different levels or groups) that matches their *organization architecture*.

7 Qualities of Information

The qualities, or characteristics, of valuable information include being accurate, verifiable, timely, organized, meaningful, useful, and cost effective. **Accurate** information is correct. **Verifiable** information can be confirmed. **Timely** information has an age appropriate to its use. **Organized** information is arranged to suit requirements. **Meaningful** information is relevant to the person who receives it. **Useful** information results in an action being taken or not taken. **Cost effective** information has a value greater than its price.

8 Types of Information Systems

Information systems generally are classified into five categories: office systems, transaction processing systems, management information systems, decision support systems, and expert systems. **Office systems** include software applications for administrative tasks that occur throughout the organization. These applications are sometimes referred to as *productivity software*.

9 Transaction Processing Systems

Transaction processing systems (TPS) process data generated by the day-to-day transactions of an organization. The first TPS were usually **batch processing** systems in which transaction data was collected and, at a later time, processed together as a group. Today, most TPS use **online transaction processing (OLTP)**, processing transactions as they are entered. Over time, TPS have been modified to provide summaries, trends, and exception data useful to management. TPS often are a part of management information systems.

10 Management Information Systems

A **management information system (MIS)** refers to a computer-based system that generates timely and accurate information for managing an organization. The focus is on the information that management needs to do its job. A special type of MIS is the **executive information system (EIS)**, which is designed for the information needs of senior management.

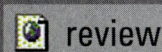

11. Decision Support System

A **decision support system (DSS)** is a system designed to help someone reach a decision by summarizing or comparing data from either or both internal and external sources. DSS that include query languages, statistical analytical capabilities, spreadsheets, and graphics to help the user evaluate the decision data sometimes are referred to as **online analytical processing (OLAP) systems**. More advanced systems also include capabilities that allow users to create a **model** of variables affecting a decision.

12. Expert Systems

An **expert system** is a computerized system that simulates a human experts' reasoning and decision-making processes. Expert systems are made up of the combined subject knowledge of human experts, called the **knowledge base**, and the **inference rules** that determine how the knowledge is used to reach decisions. Expert systems are part of a branch of computer science called **artificial intelligence** (**AI**).

13. Integrated Information Systems

With today's sophisticated software, it can be difficult to classify a system as belonging uniquely to one of the information system types. Although expert systems still operate primarily as separate systems, the trend is clear: combine all of an organization's information needs into a single, integrated information system.

14. Personal Computers in Information Systems

As organizations move toward decentralized decision making, both managers and nonmanagement employees benefit by having information available through networked personal computers. Many professionals believe the ideal information system involves a network of personal computers attached to a server that stores common information many users access. This centralized data and decentralized computing arrangement allows users and organizations the most flexibility over controlling their information resources.

10 terms

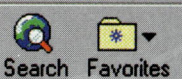

chapter 1 | 2 | 3 | 4 | 5 | 6 | 7 | 8 | 9 | 10 | 11 | 12 | 13 | 14 | I

inCyber | review | terms | yourTurn | hotTopics | outThere | winLabs | webWalk | exercises | news | home

INSTRUCTIONS: *To display this page from the Web, launch your browser and enter the URL, http://www.scsite.com/dc/ch10/terms.htm. Scroll through the list of terms. Click a term for its definition and a picture. Click the rocket ship for current and additional information about the term.*

decision support system (DSS)

DEFINITION

decision support system (DSS)
A system designed to help someone reach a decision by summarizing or comparing data from internal or external sources or both. (**10.16**)

accurate (10.11)
agent software (10.18)
artificial intelligence (AI) (10.18)

batch processing (10.14)
board of directors (10.6)

chief executive officer (CEO) (10.6)
controlling (10.4)
cost effective (10.12)

decision support system (DSS) (10.16)
directing (10.4)
downsize (10.11)

executive information system (EIS) (10.15)
expert systems (10.17)

finance (10.8)

human resources (10.9)

inference rules (10.17)

information architecture (10.11)
information system (10.6, 10.9)

knowledge base (10.17)
knowledge system (10.17)

leading (10.4)

management information system (MIS) (10.14)
managers (10.4)
meaningful (10.12)
middle management (10.7)
model (10.16)

nonmanagement employees (10.7)

office systems (10.13)
online analytical processing (OLAP) systems (10.16)
online transaction processing (OLTP) (10.14)
operational decisions (10.7)
operational management (10.7)

operations (10.8)
organized (10.12)
organizing (10.11)
outsourcing (10.11)

planning (10.4)

rightsize (10.11)

sales and marketing (10.8)
senior management (10.6)
strategic decisions (10.6)
structured problems (10.6)

tactical decisions (10.7)
timely (10.12)
transaction processing system (TPS) (10.13)

unstructured problems (10.6)
useful (10.12)

verifiable (10.12

chapter 10 yourTurn

1 | 2 | 3 | 4 | 5 | 6 | 7 | 8 | 9 | 10 | 11 | 12 | 13 | 14 | I

inCyber | review | terms | yourTurn | hotTopics | outThere | winLabs | webWalk | exercises | news | home

INSTRUCTIONS: *To display this page from the Web, launch your browser and enter the URL, http://www.scsite.com/dc/ch10/turn.htm. Click a blank line for the answer. Click the links for current and additional information.*

Label the Figure

1. _____ objectives strategies tactics

2. _____ money people material management structure

3. _____ communication instruction motivation

4. _____ performance measurement corrective action

Instructions: Identify the four tasks performed by management.

Fill in the Blanks

Instructions: Complete each sentence with the correct term or terms.

1. All _____ that use a computer are comprised of six elements: hardware, software, accurate data, trained information systems personnel, knowledgeable users, and documented procedures.
2. _____ of an organization are the women and men responsible for directing the use of resources such as people, money, materials, and _____ so the organization can operate efficiently and prosper.
3. _____ management makes _____ decisions that implement specific programs and plans.
4. _____ is the functional area that manages the people who work for an organization.
5. Terms used to describe the qualities of information include: _____, _____, _____, _____, _____, _____, and _____.

Short Answer

Instructions: Write a brief answer to each of the following questions.

1. Why is information important to an organization? What factors have contributed to the need for timely and accurate information? _____
2. How are unstructured problems different from structured problems? What are the characteristics of each type of problem? What levels of management tend to deal with each type of problem? _____
3. What are the functional areas that most organizations share? What are the responsibilities of each? _____
4. What are the five categories into which information systems generally are classified? How are they different? _____
5. How are personal computers used in management information systems? According to many professionals, what does the ideal information system involve? Why? _____

10 hotTopics

chapter 1 | 2 | 3 | 4 | 5 | 6 | 7 | 8 | 9 | 10 | 11 | 12 | 13 | 14 | I

inCyber | review | terms | yourTurn | hotTopics | outThere | winLabs | webWalk | exercises | news | home

INSTRUCTIONS: *To display this page from the Web, launch your browser and enter the URL, http://www.scsite.com/dc/ch10/hot.htm. Click the links for current and additional information to help you respond to the hotTopics questions.*

1 *The cost of health care in the United States is more than $800 billion and* growing at about 13 percent annually. Some people feel that information technology can slow the debilitating increase in health-care costs. One of the country's largest health maintenance organizations uses computerized systems that maintain medical records, order and report the results of lab tests, send prescriptions, and even help doctors make diagnoses. How would these systems lower health-care costs? What effect might they have on the quality of health care? What disadvantages, if any, could result from applying information technology to health care?

2 *Some studies indicate that the use of computerized information systems has resulted in* only a marginal increase in productivity. According to one survey of companies that introduced new office systems, approximately 40 percent failed to meet their goals. Analysts suggest it is not the systems that are at fault, but the way they are being used. Workers spend too much time on relatively unimportant tasks (such as sorting irrelevant information, polishing memos, or surfing the Web). Some analysts maintain that computers simply have caused organizations to set their goals unrealistically high. Why else might a company fail to reach its goals? What factors are most important? Why? What steps could a manager take to enhance productivity?

3 *Compared to humans, expert systems are inexpensive to use, easy to duplicate, and impossible* to tire. Developing an effective expert system, however, poses several problems. Because expert systems demand a large database, a powerful control program is required to resolve conflicts and produce timely conclusions. Human experts who supply the knowledge base are expensive and may be unwilling or unable to furnish inference rules in a suitable form. Incorporating a human expert's experience and intuitive knowledge into an expert system can be almost impossible. Keeping these difficulties in mind, in what areas could expert systems be used effectively? In what fields should they be avoided? Why? How could the issues involved in creating an expert system be addressed?

4 *While 50 years ago, managers had too little information, today they may have too much.* Managers can be overwhelmed by the data available from information systems, online public business databases (currently more than 5,000 exist), and improved communications. Some consultants believe the flood of facts has added to managerial stress, forcing managers to spend more time sifting information than making crucial business decisions. Can there ever be too much information? Why or why not? How could too much information adversely affect decision making? What can be done about an information glut?

5 *The quality of education has become a major concern in the United States. Critics point to* declining test scores, rising drop-out rates, and unready graduates as symptomatic of an ailing educational system. Some reformers believe the remedy is to run schools on a more businesslike basis. School personnel would be organized in traditional management levels, perform conventional managerial tasks, and use suitable management tools to produce a quality product — an educated student. Using an elementary school, high school, or college as a sample organization, identify school personnel that might be categorized at each management level. Justify the classification based on the kind of decisions made by the personnel and the information they require. What type of information system would be used at each level? Why? Would another approach to management organization be more appropriate? Why or why not?

chapter 10 outThere

| 1 | 2 | 3 | 4 | 5 | 6 | 7 | 8 | 9 | 10 | 11 | 12 | 13 | 14 | I

inCyber | review | terms | yourTurn | hotTopics | outThere | winLabs | webWalk | exercises | news | home

INSTRUCTIONS: *To display this page from the Web, launch your browser and enter the URL, http://www.scsite.com/dc/ch10/out.htm. Click the links for current and additional information.*

1 *Expert systems occasionally have been a source of controversy. A British doctor* created a medical uproar with an expert system that determines whether a patient is likely to live or die. The program assesses a patient's chances based on his or her condition and medical history. Supporters maintain that by withdrawing treatment from those who are hopelessly ill, patients can be spared prolonged suffering and resources can be put to better use. Using library materials and Internet resources, prepare a report on this or another controversial expert system. For what purpose is the expert system used? What advantages does it offer? Why is the system controversial? Is your overall reaction to the expert system positive or negative? Why?

2 *A company's database typically contains information on current and past customers, their* orders, and their billing status. Some organizations believe these databases also have a greater, although less obvious, value to a company—the potential to foresee trends and predict customer behavior. A growing technology called data mining combines several techniques to analyze large amounts of data and determine patterns that can be used to anticipate future tendencies. Visit some Web sites to learn more about this new technology. What benefits does it offer? How did data mining evolve? What tools and techniques are used? What is the future of data mining?

3 *A recent development in information systems is communication and data-sharing among* different organizations. An interorganizational information system (IOIS) is a technological or social system used to help in the collection, analysis, and relay of information among organizations. Some companies already are using electronic data interchange, which is a procedure that facilitates the exchange of data from one organization's computer to another's. Using recent computer magazines and the Web, prepare a report on interorganizational information systems. How might these systems be used? What tools will be needed to manage these systems? What are the possible benefits of interorganizational systems? What are the potential disadvantages?

4 *Developing even the most basic expert system can be a daunting task. Not only is a* comprehensive knowledge base required, it also is necessary to create and organize the inference rules that are used to make a decision. An interesting exercise in creating an expert system is available on the World Wide Web. The site provides the knowledge base and asks you to compose inference rules that reflect the human authority's expertise. Visit the Web site and try creating the expert system. Draw a diagram to represent the problem. Write a set of rules that incorporate the expert's knowledge. Organize and edit the rules so that they result in effective decision making, and then run the expert system to make sure it works. What is the most difficult part of developing an expert system?

5 *The type of information system employed and the purpose for which it is used depends on an* individual's level in an organization. Interview a manager and a nonmanagement employee at a local company. Find out the level of management by determining the kinds of decisions the manager makes and what information he or she uses to reach those decisions. What type of information systems do the manager and nonmanagement employee use? How are the systems used? In what way do the information systems influence their decisions? Is any information necessary that is not provided by the systems? What? Could the information be provided by an information system? How were the manager and nonmanagement employee's jobs different before the information systems were introduced? Are their jobs easier or more difficult as a result of the information systems? Why?

10 winLabs

chapter 1 | 2 | 3 | 4 | 5 | 6 | 7 | 8 | 9 | 10 | 11 | 12 | 13 | 14 | I

inCyber | review | terms | yourTurn | hotTopics | outThere | winLabs | webWalk | exercises | news | home

INSTRUCTIONS: *To display this page from the Web, launch your browser and enter the URL, http://www.scsite.com/dc/ch10/labs.htm. Click the links for current and additional information.*

1 *Movie* Box Office Simulation

Insert your Student Floppy Disk in drive A or see your instructor for the location of the Movie Box Office program. Click the Start button on the taskbar and then click Run on the Start menu. In the Open text box, type the path and file name of the program. For example, type `a:movie.exe` and then press ENTER. The first customer wishes to purchase two tickets to a matinee performance of *The Client* (Figure 10-17). Notice the amount due and then click the ENTER button. Enter the following transactions and write down the amount due for each transaction: (1) *The Abyss*, no matinee, 3 tickets; (2) *Forrest Gump*, matinee, 1 ticket; (3) *Beverly Hills Cop*, matinee, 2 tickets.

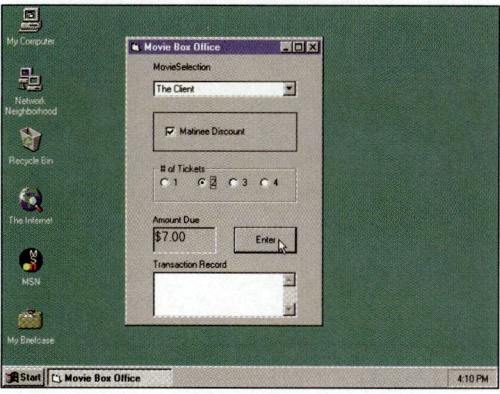

Figure 10-17

2 Changing Desktop Patterns and *Wallpaper*

Right-click an empty area on your desktop and then click Properties on the shortcut menu. Click the Background tab. Click Plaid or another choice in the Pattern area, and then click the Apply button. The desktop displays the selected pattern. Click Squares or another choice in the Wallpaper area, and then click the Apply button. The desktop displays the Squares wallpaper. If you select wallpaper, it overrides any patterns selected. Practice selecting various wallpaper. Turn off the patterns and wallpaper by selecting [None] in each list in the Display Properties dialog box and then click the OK button.

3 Working with Pictures

Bring a picture no smaller than 3½" x 5" to class. Ask your instructor for assistance in scanning the picture to create a digital version on your Student Floppy Disk using your name as the file name. Double-click the My Computer icon, double-click the 3½ floppy [A:] icon, and then double-click your file icon. The Paint window should display your scanned picture (Figure 10-18). To print the picture, click File on the menu bar, click Print, and then click the OK button. Close Paint.

Figure 10-18

4 More About Using Help

Click the Start button on the taskbar and then click Help on the Start menu. When the Help Topics: Windows Help dialog box displays, click the Index tab. Type `recycle bin` in the text box and then double-click emptying. When the Windows Help window displays, click the Options button, click Print Topic, and then click the OK button to print its contents. Close the Help window.

10 webWalk

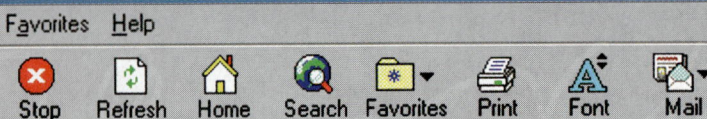

chapter 1 | 2 | 3 | 4 | 5 | 6 | 7 | 8 | 9 | 10 | 11 | 12 | 13 | 14 | I

inCyber | review | terms | yourTurn | hotTopics | outThere | winLabs | webWalk | exercises | news | home

INSTRUCTIONS: *To display this page from the Web, launch your browser and enter the URL, http://www.scsite.com/dc/ch10/walk.htm. Click the exercise link to display the exercise.*

1. Decision Support System
A decision support system (DSS) is a system designed to help someone reach a decision by summarizing or comparing data from internal or external sources, or both. Complete this exercise to work with a DSS available on the Web.

2. Agent Software
Artificial intelligence technology is used in agent software that independently carries out tasks on your behalf. To learn more about a Web-based application of an intelligent agent (Figure 10-19), complete this exercise.

3. Integrated Information Systems
It can be difficult to classify a system as belonging uniquely to one particular information system type. You can learn about a space exploration information system that integrates all of the information system types discussed by completing this exercise.

4. Expert Systems
Expert systems are computer systems that simulate human experts reasoning and decision making processes. To experience working with a Web-based expert system (Figure 10-20), complete this exercise.

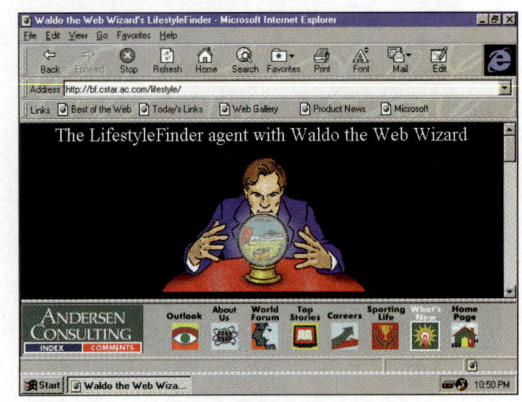

Figure 10-19

5. Information Mining
Complete this exercise to improve your Web research skills by using a Web search engine to find information related to this chapter.

6. Office Systems
Office systems include software applications for administrative tasks as well as communications technology that occur throughout the organization. Complete this exercise to learn more about advanced office systems.

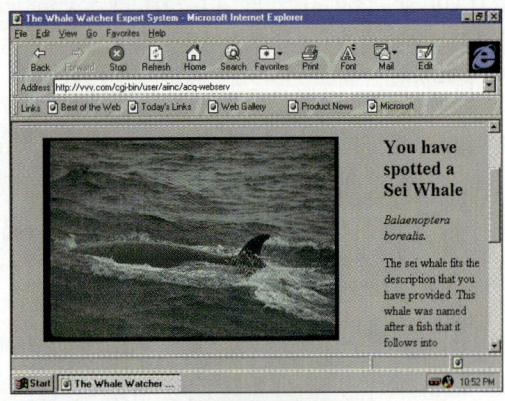

Figure 10-20

7. Qualities of Information
The qualities of valuable information are characteristics that all information should have, whether or not it is produced by a computer. Complete this exercise to visit a unique Web site and learn more about the qualities that make information valuable.

8. Executive Information Systems
Executive Information Systems (EIS) are management information systems that have been structured for the special information needs of senior management. To learn more about Executive Information Systems, complete this exercise.

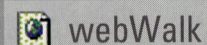

9. Web Chat
Complete this exercise to enter a Web Chat discussion related to the issues presented in the hotTopics exercise.

Information Systems Development

OBJECTIVES

After completing this chapter, you will be able to:

- Explain the phases in the system development life cycle
- Identify the guidelines for system development
- Discuss the importance of project management, feasibility assessment, data and information gathering techniques, and documentation
- Identify items that initiate the system development life cycle
- Describe how structured tools, such as entity-relationship diagrams and data flow diagrams, are used in the analysis and design phases
- Discuss the importance of the project dictionary
- Differentiate between commercial application software and custom software
- Identify program development as part of the system development life cycle
- Discuss several techniques used to convert to a new system
- Describe methods used to support an information system

CHAPTER 11

A system is a set of components that interact to achieve a common goal. The components of an information system include hardware, software, data, people, and procedures. The goal of an information system is to provide users with useful, timely, and accurate information so they can make effective decisions. The kinds and types of information users need often change over time. This may be due to changes within the organization (internal changes) such as new product development, a change in management, or a new payroll plan. Or, these changes may result from external forces, such as competition or government regulations. When the information requirements change, the information system must meet the new requirements. In some cases, the current information system is modified; in other cases, an entirely new information system is developed. As a computer user, you may someday participate in the modification of an existing system or the development of a new system. Information system development is broken down into phases, referred to collectively as the system development life cycle. This chapter discusses and illustrates each phase of this process by using a case study about North Harbor State Bank.

What Is the System Development Life Cycle?

The **system development life cycle (SDLC)** is an organized set of activities used to guide those involved through the development of an information system. Much like a recipe assists a cook through the steps in preparing a meal, the SDLC guides those involved through system development. Some activities in SDLC may be performed at the same time and others are sequential. Depending on the type and complexity of the information system being developed, the duration of the individual activities varies from one system to the next; in some cases, an activity may be skipped entirely. The many activities of the SDLC are grouped into five larger categories called **phases**.

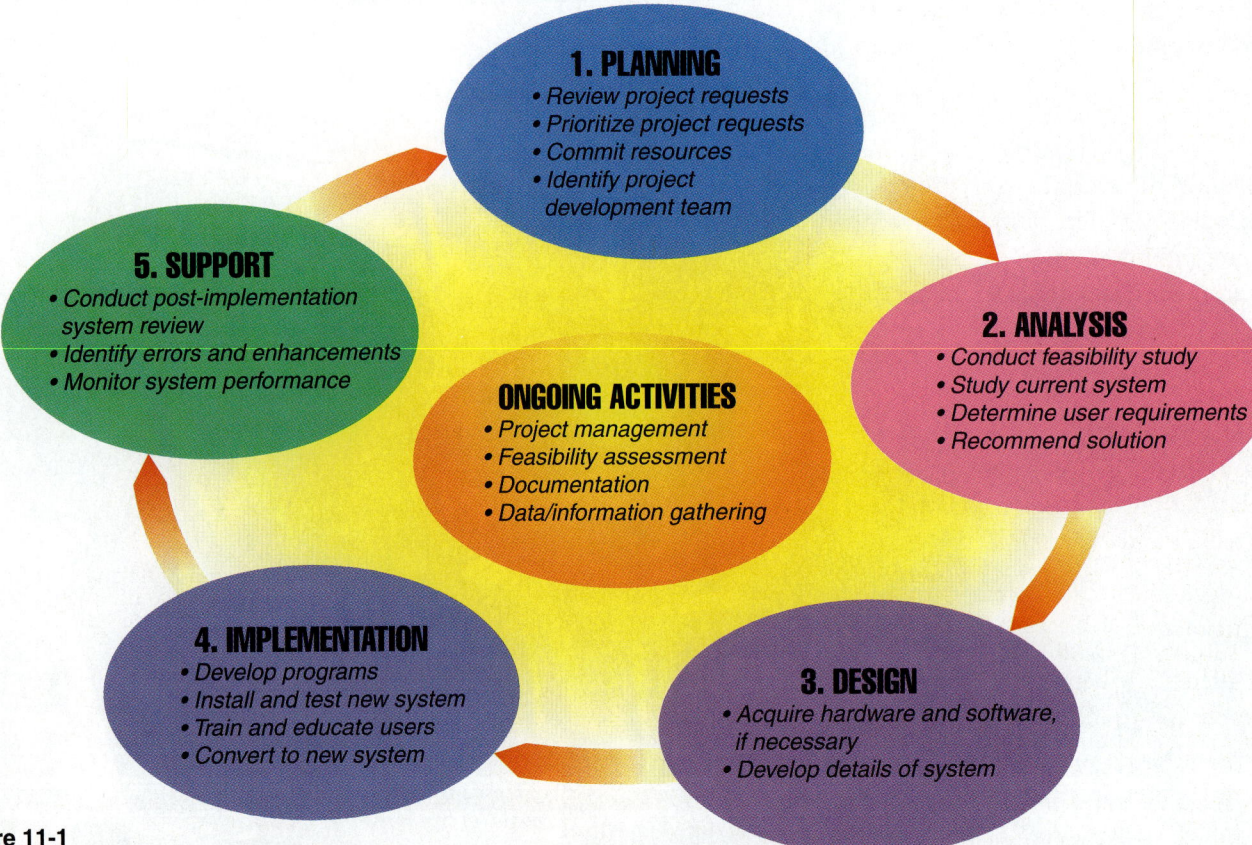

1. PLANNING
- Review project requests
- Prioritize project requests
- Commit resources
- Identify project development team

2. ANALYSIS
- Conduct feasibility study
- Study current system
- Determine user requirements
- Recommend solution

3. DESIGN
- Acquire hardware and software, if necessary
- Develop details of system

4. IMPLEMENTATION
- Develop programs
- Install and test new system
- Train and educate users
- Convert to new system

5. SUPPORT
- Conduct post-implementation system review
- Identify errors and enhancements
- Monitor system performance

ONGOING ACTIVITIES
- Project management
- Feasibility assessment
- Documentation
- Data/information gathering

Figure 11-1
The system development life cycle consists of five phases that form a loop. The planning phase just recently has been recognized as a critical part of the life cycle; thus, some life cycles may not yet include it.

Phases in the System Development Life Cycle

The system development life cycle can be grouped into five major phases:

1. Planning
2. Analysis
3. Design
4. Implementation
5. Support

As depicted in Figure 11-1, the phases in the SDLC form a loop; that is, information system development is an ongoing process for an organization. Notice that a loop is formed because the support phase points back to the planning phase. This connection occurs when the information requirements of users change, which means the information system must be changed to meet these new requirements. Thus, the planning phase for a new system begins and the system development life cycle begins again.

Before continuing with an explanation of the individual phases of the SDLC, some general guidelines for system development are discussed. Then, participants of the various phases of the life cycle will be identified. Also addressed are the ongoing activities that occur throughout the entire system development life cycle.

Guidelines for System Development

The development of an information system should follow three general guidelines: (1) use a phased approach, (2) involve the users, and (3) develop standards.

First, the system development life cycle should be grouped into phases, each of which contains activities or tasks. Using a phased approach involves defining the phases of the SDLC and determining what activities and tasks will occur in each phase. Many SDLCs contain the five major phases outlined in Figure 11-1, while others have more or fewer phases. Regardless, all life cycles perform the same activities. For example, some SDLCs place the develop programs activity in an entirely separate phase called Construction or Development. Other differences between SDLCs are the terminology, the order of activities, the level of detail, and so on, within each phase.

Second, users must be involved throughout the entire development process. **Users** include anyone for whom the system is being built; customers, data entry clerks, accountants, sales managers, and owners are all examples of users. System developers must remember that the final system ultimately is delivered to the user. If the system is to be successful, the user must have input in all stages of development.

Third, standards for the development of the information system should be defined and written. Having standards helps multiple people working on the same development project produce consistent results. For example, one developer might refer to a part number in a database as a Part Id, while another calls it a part identification number, and still others call it a part number, part no., part #, part code, and so on. A system created in this way would be so confusing that is could never function correctly! If standards are defined and agreed upon throughout the project, then one term, such as part number, can be used by everyone involved.

Who Participates in the System Development Life Cycle?

Any person who will be affected by the proposed system should participate in its development. Participants can be categorized as users and information systems personnel, which includes analysts and programmers. Systems analysts are the liaison between the users and the programmers; they convert user requests into technical specifications. Throughout the entire life cycle, systems analysts prepare many reports, drawings, and diagrams. They also meet with users, vendors, other analysts, and programmers to discuss various aspects of the project (Figure 11-2). Not only must systems analysts be familiar with business operations and computer programming techniques, they also must have excellent communication and interpersonal skills.

Figure 11-2
User involvement throughout the entire system development life cycle is crucial to a project's success. The systems analyst often uses diagrams to explain various aspects of the system to users.

CHAPTER 11 – INFORMATION SYSTEMS DEVELOPMENT

For each system development project, the organization usually forms and assigns a **project team** to work on the project from beginning to end. The project team is composed of both users and information system personnel, including a systems analyst. One member of the team, designated as the project leader, manages and controls the activities of the project team members.

Project Management

Project management is the process of planning, scheduling, and then controlling the individual activities during the system development life cycle. The goal of project management is to deliver an acceptable system to the user in an agreed-upon time frame, while maintaining costs.

To effectively plan and schedule a project, the project leader must identify these items:

- The **scope** of the project; that is, the range or extent of the project
- Activities to be completed
- Time estimates for each activity
- Cost estimates for each activity
- The order in which activities must occur
- Activities that may be performed concurrently

Once identified, these items usually are recorded by the project leader in a **project plan**. A popular tool used to plan and schedule the time relationships between project activities is called a Gantt chart (Figure 11-3). A **Gantt chart**, developed by Henry L. Gantt, is a bar chart, with each bar representing a project phase or activity. The left side, or vertical axis, displays the list of activities to be completed; and a horizontal axis across the top or bottom of the chart shows time.

Time estimates assigned to activities should be realistic; otherwise, the success of a project is in jeopardy from the beginning. If project members do not believe the schedule is reasonable, they may not participate to the full extent of their abilities, which could lead to missed deadlines and delivery dates.

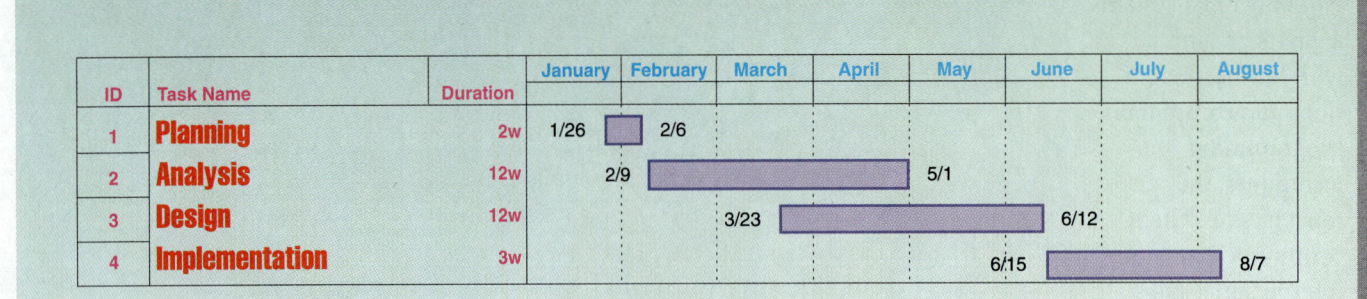

---

inCyber

For details on the project management process, visit the Discovering Computers Chapter 11 inCyber page (http://www.scsite.com/dc/ch11/incyber.htm) and click Project Management.

ID	Task Name	Duration	January	February	March	April	May	June	July	August
1	Planning	2w	1/26 — 2/6							
2	Analysis	12w		2/9 ——————————————— 5/1						
3	Design	12w			3/23 ——————————————— 6/12					
4	Implementation	3w						6/15 ———— 8/7		

Figure 11-3
Project management software assists managers in planning, scheduling, and controlling a project's activities. Microsoft Project provides a facility for drawing Gantt charts, which are an effective way of showing the time relationships of the project activities.

Once a project begins, the project must be monitored and controlled. Some activities will take less time than originally planned and others will take longer. It is possible the project manager may realize that due to excessive time devoted to a particular activity, the original expected delivery date of a project will not be met. In these cases, the scheduled completion date may be extended or the scope of the system development may be reduced, which results in a less comprehensive system being delivered at the original scheduled completion date. In either case, the original project plan must be revised and presented to users for approval.

One aspect of managing projects is making sure each **deliverable** — a tangible item, such as a chart, diagram, report, or program file — is transmitted on time and according to plan. Project management software, such as Microsoft Project, enables managers to effectively and efficiently plan, schedule, and control development projects (Figure 11-3).

> **inCyber**
> To view Gantt charts, visit the Discovering Computers Chapter 11 inCyber page (http://www.scsite.com/dc/ch11/incyber.htm) and click Gantt Chart.

Feasibility Assessment

Feasibility is a measure of how suitable the development of a system will be to the organization. A project determined feasible at one point may become infeasible at a later point in the life cycle. Thus, feasibility must be reassessed frequently during the project development.

Feasibility generally is tested using three criteria. **Operational feasibility** measures how well the final system will work in the organization. In other words, operational feasibility addresses these questions: Will the users like the new system? Will they use it? Will it meet their requirements? Will it cause any changes to their work environment? **Technical feasibility** measures whether the organization has or can obtain the hardware, software, and people needed to deliver and then support the final system. For most system projects, the technology exists; the challenge is obtaining funds to pay for such resources, which is addressed in **economic feasibility**. Economic, or *cost/benefit*, feasibility measures whether the lifetime benefits of the proposed system will exceed the lifetime costs. Many financial techniques, such as return on investment and payback analysis, are used to perform this cost/benefit analysis. Often, the systems analyst is unfamiliar with these financial techniques so he or she requests the assistance of a financial analyst (Figure 11-4) to assess economic feasibility.

Figure 11-4
Often the systems analyst requests the expertise of a financial analyst to assist with dollar figures for the cost/benefit section of a feasibility report to determine if the proposed system is financially feasible.

Documentation

During the entire system development life cycle, much documentation is produced by project team members. **Documentation** is the compilation and summarization of data and information; it includes reports, diagrams, programs, or any other deliverable generated during the project. The entire collection of documentation for a single project is stored in a **project notebook**. The project notebook might be a simple one, such as a large three-ring binder, or it may be more sophisticated, such as an automated project notebook that can be created and stored using a computerized analysis and design software package. An automated project notebook is called a **project dictionary** or **repository**.

Well-written, thorough documentation makes it easier for everyone involved to understand all aspects of project development — from economic decisions to system features to security considerations. Documentation should be an ongoing part of the system development life cycle. Too often, documentation is put off because project team members consider it an unimportant or unproductive part of system development. In these cases, documentation is pushed to the end of the entire project or not done at all. Without complete and accurate documentation, users and system personnel may not know how to use, operate, or support the system. Having quality documentation also makes it easier to modify the system to meet changing information requirements.

Data and Information Gathering Techniques

Throughout the SDLC, the project team gathers data and information. Accurate and timely data and information is needed for many reasons — to keep a project on schedule, to assess feasibility, to ensure that the system is meeting requirements, and so on. Several methods are used during the system development process to gather data and information: (1) reviewing current system documentation, (2) observation, (3) questionnaires, and (4) interviews.

By reviewing current system documentation, such as a company's organization chart, memos, and meeting minutes, you can learn the history of a project and also about business operations, weaknesses and strengths, and so on. To learn exactly how a system functions or an operation is performed, you can observe an employee or machine. To obtain data and information from a large number of people, you could send a questionnaire.

The most important data and information gathering technique is the interview, because it enables you to clarify responses and probe for feedback from users individually. An interview can be unstructured or structured. An **unstructured interview** relies on the interviewee (the user) to direct the conversation based on a general goal. In a **structured interview**, the interviewer (the systems analyst) directs the conversation by following a specific set of topics and asking predefined questions. Structured interviews tend to be more successful for the systems analyst.

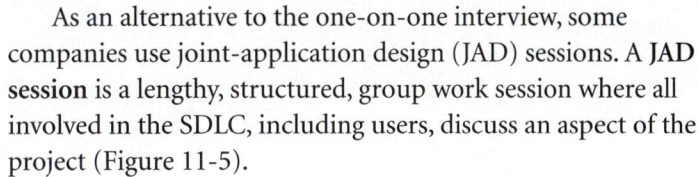

As an alternative to the one-on-one interview, some companies use joint-application design (JAD) sessions. A **JAD session** is a lengthy, structured, group work session where all involved in the SDLC, including users, discuss an aspect of the project (Figure 11-5).

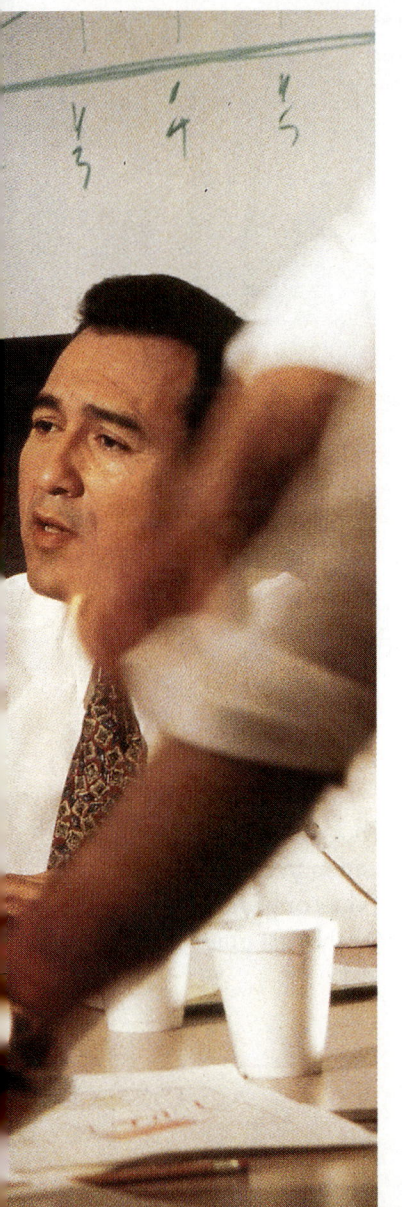

What Initiates the System Development Life Cycle?

A new or modified information system may be requested for a variety of reasons, some external and some internal. An external reason would be that an order has been issued by management or some other governing body, that insists you make a change to a system. For example, a worldwide recording studio might require all offices to use the same e-mail system. Competition is another external reason for systems development. For example, once one bank offers Internet access to account information, others will have to follow suit — or run the risk of losing customers.

As previously indicated, another reason for changing an information system is a change in information requirements. For example, if a school wanted to provide students with the ability to register for classes using the telephone, the school would have to modify the existing registration system to include this enhancement. The most obvious reason for system development is a problem with the existing system. For example, the stock-on-hand on a report may not match the actual stock-on-hand in the warehouse.

Figure 11-5
During a JAD session, the systems analyst is the moderator, or leader, of the discussion. Another member, called the scribe, records facts and action items assigned during the discussion.

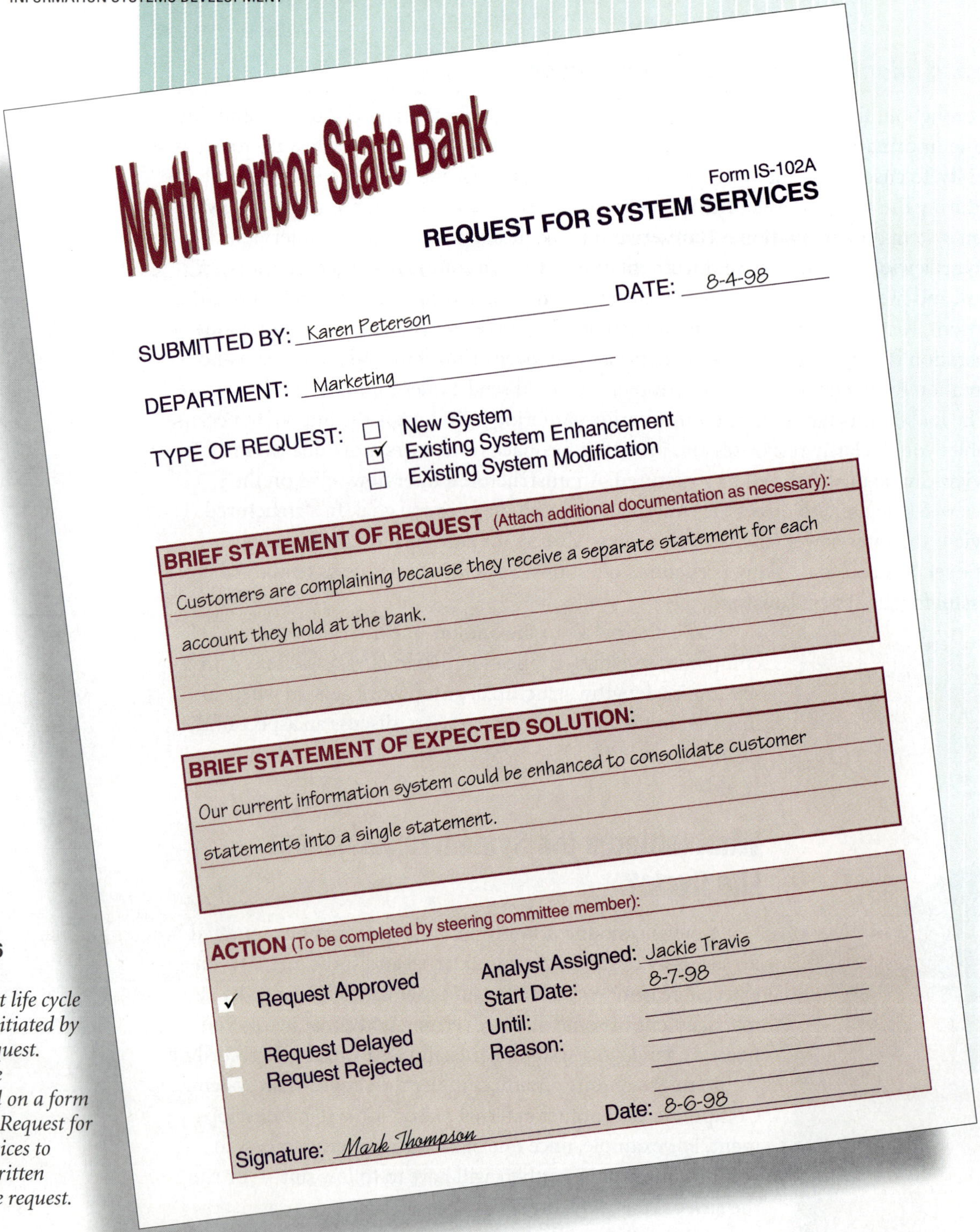

11.8 CHAPTER 11 – INFORMATION SYSTEMS DEVELOPMENT

North Harbor State Bank

Form IS-102A

REQUEST FOR SYSTEM SERVICES

DATE: 8-4-98

SUBMITTED BY: Karen Peterson

DEPARTMENT: Marketing

TYPE OF REQUEST:
- ☐ New System
- ☑ Existing System Enhancement
- ☐ Existing System Modification

BRIEF STATEMENT OF REQUEST (Attach additional documentation as necessary):

Customers are complaining because they receive a separate statement for each account they hold at the bank.

BRIEF STATEMENT OF EXPECTED SOLUTION:

Our current information system could be enhanced to consolidate customer statements into a single statement.

ACTION (To be completed by steering committee member):

- ✓ Request Approved
- ☐ Request Delayed
- ☐ Request Rejected

Analyst Assigned: Jackie Travis
Start Date: 8-7-98
Until:
Reason:

Signature: Mark Thompson   Date: 8-6-98

Figure 11-6
The system development life cycle usually is initiated by a project request. Requests are documented on a form such as this Request for System Services to provide a written record of the request.

The initial request for a new or modified system may be verbal, but eventually it is written on a standard form that becomes the first item of documentation in the project notebook (Figure 11-6). It is important that a request for system services or project request be completed so that all requests are organized in a similar format for the first phase of the system development life cycle: planning.

North Harbor State Bank – A Case Study

To help you better understand real-world applications of the system development life cycle, a case study is presented following the discussion of each phase. So that you easily can identify the case study in this chapter, it is shaded in the color teal. Although the case is based on a fictitious bank, it is designed to be as realistic as possible. The following paragraphs present a background on North Harbor State Bank.

North Harbor State Bank, founded in 1902, is the tenth largest bank in the Chicagoland area with more than $84 million in assets and $39 million in equity capital. In addition to the main office downtown, North Harbor has 22 branches in the suburbs. North Harbor's primary line of business is personal banking — serving individuals and families. Services provided to customers include checking and savings accounts, home mortgages, personal loans, retirement accounts, bank cards, check cards, ATM cards, and an automated 24-hour telephone banking system.

North Harbor tries to keep its computer hardware and software capabilities up-to-date so it can continue to provide the best possible service to its customers. Practically every system at North Harbor State Bank is computerized. To maintain its competitive edge, North Harbor recently put a home page on the Internet (Figure 11-7). This Web page provides customers with 24-hour access to the bank's information. Eventually, North Harbor plans to provide customers with the ability to make transactions, such as account transfers, through this Web page.

In last month's statements, Karen Peterson, vice president of marketing, included a customer satisfaction survey. After tabulating the results, Karen was pleased to learn that customers still are extremely satisfied with the wide variety of services provided by North Harbor. The one comment that recurred continually came from customers that have many accounts at North Harbor and receive several statements each month. For example, one customer wrote, "I have checking, savings, automobile loan, home mortgage, and retirement accounts with North Harbor, and I receive five separate statements each month. Although I am extremely satisfied with services on each of these accounts, I would prefer receiving a single monthly statement with all accounts consolidated. A consolidated statement would enable me to manage my personal finances more efficiently."

After Karen discusses this suggestion with other vice presidents, she decides that consolidating the monthly statements not only would make North Harbor customers happier, but it also could save North Harbor a great deal of time and money. Thus, Karen fills out a Request for System Services form (Figure 11-6) and submits it to Mark Thompson, chair of North Harbor's steering committee.

Figure 11-7
To help you better understand real-world applications of the SDLC, a case study is presented throughout this chapter about North Harbor State Bank. North Harbor tries to keep its computer hardware and software capabilities up-to-date so it can continue to provide the best possible service to its customers. To maintain its competitive edge, North Harbor recently put a home page on the Internet. Many systems analysts assist companies with developing home pages, such as this, on the World Wide Web.

Planning Phase

The **planning phase** for a project begins when the steering committee receives a project request. The **steering committee** is a decision-making body for an organization; it usually consists of five to nine people, including a mix of vice presidents, managers, users, and information system personnel. During the planning phase, four major activities are performed: (1) review the project requests, (2) prioritize the project requests, (3) commit resources such as money, people, and equipment to approved projects, and (4) identify a project development team for each approved project.

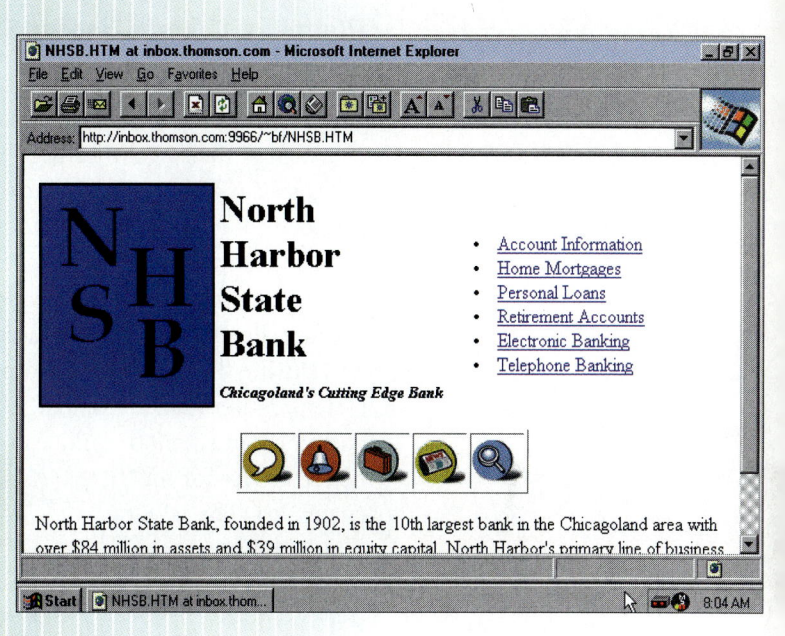

Any project requests imposed by management or some other governing body are given the highest priority and immediate attention. The remaining project requests are evaluated by the steering committee based on their value to the organization. Some projects are rejected, and others are approved. Of the approved projects, it is possible that only a few will begin immediately. Others will have to wait for additional funds or resources to become available.

Planning at North Harbor State Bank

After receiving the completed project request (Figure 11-6 on page 11.8), Mark Thompson distributes it to all members of the steering committee so they are prepared to discuss it at their next meeting. The steering committee members of North Harbor are as follows: Mark Thompson, controller and chair of steering committee; Julie Weldon, vice president of lending; Rita Ortiz, head cashier; Jim Davidson, teller; Jackie Travis, senior systems analyst; and Bob Kramer, vice president of information systems. Mark also invites Karen Peterson to the next steering committee meeting to answer any additional questions because she originated the request.

During the meeting, the committee decides the request identifies an enhancement to the system, rather than a problem. They feel that the nature of the enhancement (to consolidate customer statements) could lead to considerable savings for the bank, as well as provide better service for the customers. The request is approved. Mark indicates that the bank has adequate funds in its budget to begin the project immediately. Thus, a system development project team is assembled and Jackie Travis, senior systems analyst, is assigned as the team leader for the Consolidated Statement Project. Jackie and her team immediately begin the next phase: analysis.

North Harbor State Bank

MEMORANDUM

To: Steering Committee
From: Jackie Travis, Project Leader
Date: August 17, 1998
Subject: Feasibility Study of Consolidated Statement Project

Below is the feasibility study in response to the request for consolidated statements. Your approval is necessary before the next phase of the project will begin.

Introduction

The purpose of this feasibility report is to determine whether it is beneficial for North Harbor to continue studying the Consolidated Statement Project. Customers have indicated a desire to receive a single monthly statement, rather than one for each separate account they hold at our bank. This project would affect every department that issues and maintains accounts: checking and savings, home mortgages, personal loans, retirement accounts, bank cards, check cards, ATM cards, and 24-hour telephone service.

Existing System

Background

North Harbor has tried to remain current with its computer hardware and software capabilities so it could continue to provide the best possible service to its customers. To maintain its competitive edge, a customer satisfaction survey was sent in recent monthly statements. An analysis of the results indicated that customers were, for the most part, extremely satisfied with North Harbor's products and services – with one major exception. Customers with multiple accounts would prefer receiving one monthly statement with all accounts consolidated.

Problems

The following problems have been identified with North Harbor's current information system:

- Customers with multiple accounts are beginning to complain about the volume of paperwork they receive from the bank.
- Nonconsolidated statements lead to non-uniformity of customer records; thus, looking up information about a customer often is confusing.
- Employees are duplicating efforts by sending multiple statements to the same address, and temporary clerks often are hired to assist in this activity.
- Resources are wasted including employee time, equipment usage, and supplies.

Analysis Phase

The **analysis phase** is divided into two major tasks: the feasibility study and detailed analysis. The feasibility study contains one activity: (1) conduct a preliminary investigation. Detailed analysis contains three additional activities: (2) study how the current system works, (3) determine the user's wants, needs, and requirements, and (4) recommend a solution.

The Feasibility Study

The purpose of the **feasibility study**, or **preliminary investigation**, is to determine whether or not the problem or enhancement identified in a project request is worth pursuing. Should the company continue committing resources to this project? To answer this question, the systems analyst performs a very general investigation and then compiles his or her findings in a report also called a feasibility study, or feasibility report (Figure 11-8).

The most important aspect of this preliminary investigation is an accurate problem definition; that is, the identification of the true nature of the problem. The perceived problem or enhancement identified on the project request may or may not be the actual problem. For example, suppose a project request indicates that the customers of a bank complain it takes too long for the Loan department to approve or reject their loan applications. An investigation might reveal that the Loan department has to request the customers' savings and checking account information from the other departments in the bank, and the responses from the other departments can take up to 24 hours. The preliminary investigation determines the real problem is that the customers' information is not easily accessible and available to the loan officers.

The preliminary investigation begins with an interview of the user who submitted the project request. Depending on the nature of the request, other users may be interviewed as well. For example, a request might involve data or a process affecting more than one department. In the bank case, managers of the lending, savings, and checking departments would be interviewed. The preliminary investigation is quite short when compared to the remainder of the project, usually just a few days. Upon completion of the preliminary investigation, the systems analyst writes the feasibility study report that presents his or her findings and a recommendation to the steering committee.

The feasibility study report (Figure 11-8) contains these major sections: introduction, existing system, benefits of a new system, feasibility of a new system, and the recommendation.

inCyber

To view an actual feasibility study, visit the Discovering Computers Chapter 11 inCyber page (http://www.scsite.com/dc/ch11/incyber.htm) and click Feasibility Study.

Figure 11-8
Because they write so many reports, a systems analyst's written communication skills must be excellent. A feasibility report is shown in this figure. To be effective, a report must be prepared professionally and well organized. This report was prepared using a professional report template provided with a popular word processing package.

FEASIBILITY STUDY
Page 2

Benefits of a New System

The following benefits could be realized if a new consolidated statement system were developed:

- Customers would be more satisfied, leading to long-term relations.
- Supplies expenses would be reduced by 20%.
- Through a more efficient use of employees' time, the bank could realize a 10% reduction in temporary clerks.
- Printers would last 40% longer, due to a much lower usage rate.

Feasibility of a New System

Operational

A new system will decrease the amount of equipment usage and paperwork. Individual and consolidated account information will be available in an easily accessible form with summaries provided to management. Employees will have time to complete meaningful job duties, alleviating the need to hire some temporary clerks. Customers will be more satisfied with the bank's services.

Technical

North Harbor has the hardware necessary for the consolidated statements. It, however, must either acquire the software or build it in-house.

Economic

A detailed summary of the costs and benefits, including all assumptions, is attached. Depending on whether a commercial software package can be acquired or the system needs to be developed by our own staff, the potential costs of the proposed solution could range from $5,000 to $25,000. The estimated savings in supplies and postage alone will exceed $20,000.

If you have any questions on the attached detailed cost/benefit summary or require further information, please contact me.

Recommendation

Based on the findings presented in this report, we recommend to continue studying the Consolidated Statement Project.

The introduction identifies and states the purpose of the report, the problem, and the scope of the project. The existing system section outlines the background of the request and the problems and limitations of the current system. The benefits section addresses the benefits that could be realized from the proposed solution. The feasibility section assesses operational, technical, and economic feasibility of the proposed solution. The recommendation section of the feasibility study addresses whether or not to continue with further study of the problem or enhancement.

In some cases, as a result of the preliminary investigation, the company decides to end the project based on cost; in other words, the project is infeasible so it is dropped. If, however, the recommendation is to continue, and the steering committee approves this recommendation, then detailed analysis begins.

Feasibility Study at North Harbor State Bank

Jackie Travis, senior systems analyst assigned to this project, meets with Karen Peterson to discuss her project request. During the interview, Jackie reviews the questionnaires sent to customers and discovers that the request to consolidate statements was made by many of the customers with multiple accounts at North Harbor. Jackie also interviews John Williams, vice president of operations, to obtain a general understanding of how the checking and savings statements are prepared and distributed. When asked for his perspective on consolidating statements at the bank, John thinks it is a great idea. Jackie's final interview is with Mark Thompson, controller, to obtain some general cost and benefit figures for the feasibility study.

After preparing the feasibility study (Figure 11-8 on the previous page), Jackie submits it to the steering committee for its review and approval. Jackie's recommendation is to continue into the detailed analysis phase for this project. The steering committee agrees. Jackie and her team begin detailed analysis.

Detailed Analysis

Detailed analysis involves three major activities: (1) study the current system in depth so you thoroughly understand the current operations, uncover all possible problems and enhancements, and determine the causes and effects of these problems or enhancements, (2) identify the users' wants, needs, and requirements for the proposed system, and (3) present alternative solutions to the problem and then recommend a proposed solution. Detailed analysis sometimes is called **logical design** because you develop the proposed solution with regard to any specific hardware or software, and no attempt is made to identify which procedures should be automated and which should be manual.

During detailed analysis, all of the data and information gathering techniques are used: interviews, observation, reviewing documentation, and questionnaires. While obtaining data and information, the systems analyst must use a questioning approach with a problem-solving attitude. Often systems analysts find that operations are being performed not because they are efficient or effective, but because they always have been performed that way.

An important benefit from studying the current system and determining user requirements is that these activities build valuable relationships between the systems analyst and users. The systems analyst has much more credibility with users if he or she understands how the users currently perform their job responsibilities (Figure 11-9) and respects their concerns. This point may seem obvious, but many systems are created or modified without these activities, or even worse, without user participation.

Figure 11-9 ▶
The systems analyst should meet with users and observe their daily activities. These meetings build valuable relation-ships, as well as give the analyst an opportunity to see users in action.

Structured Analysis and Design Tools

The systems analyst collects vast amounts of data and information as he or she studies the current system and identifies user requirements. One of the difficulties in analyzing any system is documenting the findings in a way that can be understood by users, programmers, and other systems analysts. **Structured analysis and design** addresses this problem by using graphics to present the findings. Structured analysis and design uses tools such as entity-relationship diagrams, data flow diagrams, and the project dictionary to document specifications of an information system in the project notebook.

inCyber

For an explanation of structured analysis and design, visit the Discovering Computers Chapter 11 inCyber page (http://www.scsite.com/dc/ch11/incyber.htm) and click Structured Analysis.

Entity-Relationship Diagrams One of the more difficult tasks in the analysis phase is to organize and document all of the data and information needed by an organization. For example, a bank might need to store data about many objects, such as accounts, transactions, statements, customers, departments, and so on. Each object about which data is stored, is called an **entity**. An **entity-relationship diagram (ERD)** is a tool used to represent graphically the associations between entities in the project (Figure 11-10).

On the ERD, entity names usually are described with a noun and written in all capital letters. Relationships describe the association between two entities. The relationship between the CUSTOMER and TRANSACTION entities in Figure 11-10 is read as follows: A CUSTOMER initiates one or more TRANSACTIONs, and a TRANSACTION is initiated by one CUSTOMER.

Because they are visual, ERDs particularly are useful for reviewing the existing or proposed entities with the user (Figure 11-10). Once the ERD is approved by users, all data items associated with an entity are identified. For example, an entity called CUSTOMER might have these data items: Account Number, First Name, Middle Name, Last Name, Address, City, State, Zip Code, Telephone Number, Checking Balance, Savings Balance, and so on.

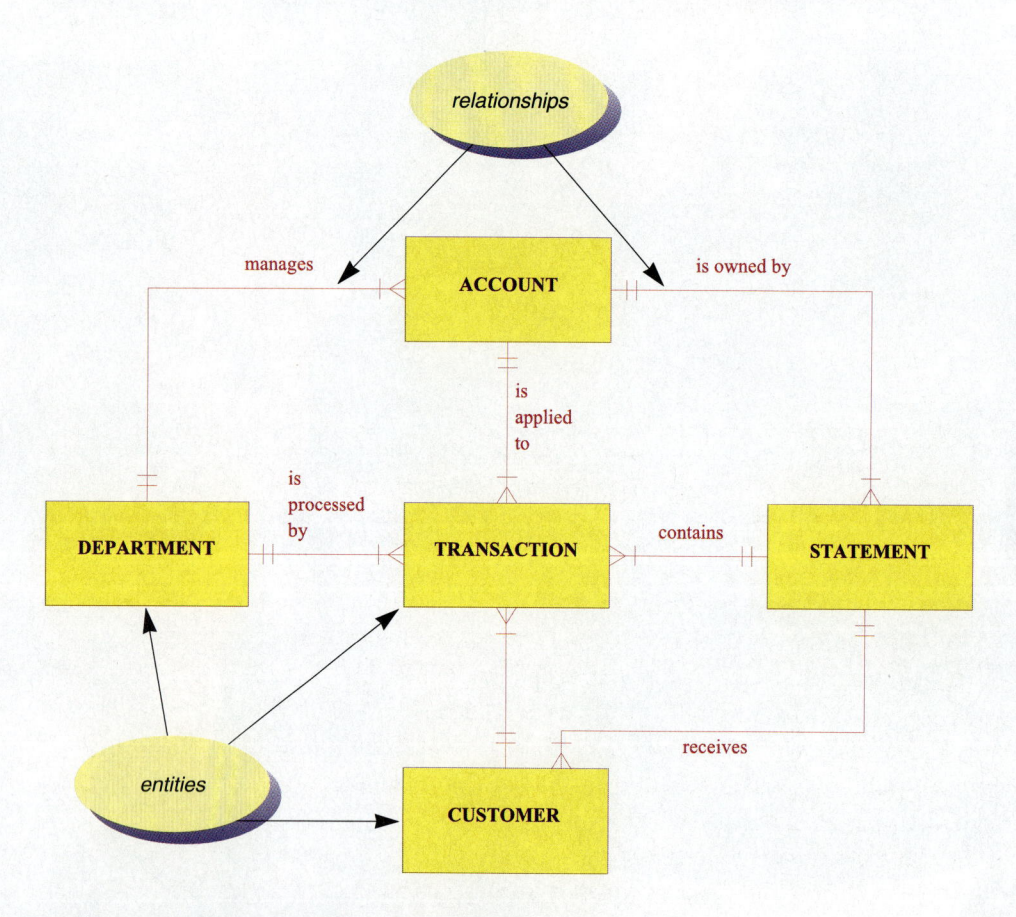

Figure 11-10
Entity-relationship diagrams (ERDs) are used to represent graphically the association between entities in a project. In this ERD, the TRANSACTION entity has a relationship with every other entity in the diagram (represented by the lines). Thus, the TRANSACTION entity is the central entity in the system.

ANALYSIS PHASE **11.15**

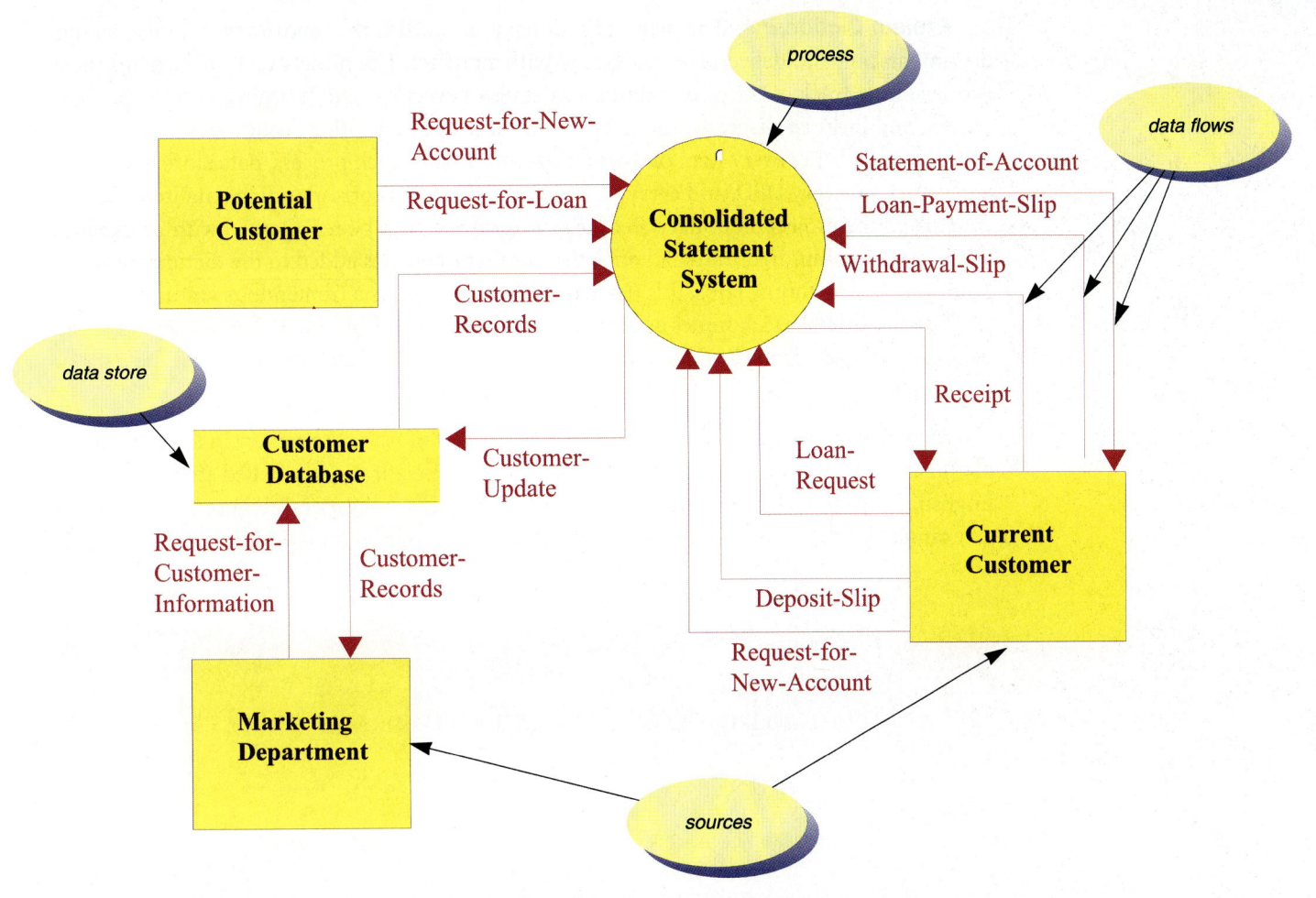

Figure 11-11
Data flow diagrams (DFDs) are used to represent graphically the flow of data through a system. This figure, called the context diagram, shows only one process — the Consolidated Statement System being studied. Data stores or files, such as the customer database, are written inside two parallel lines. Data sources both send and receive data to and from the system.

Data Flow Diagrams Another monumental task of analysis is to organize and document the *flow of data* within an organization. A **data flow diagram** (DFD) is a tool used to represent graphically the flow of data of a system. The key components of a DFD (Figure 11-11) are the data flows, the processes, the data stores, and the sources. A **data flow**, represented by a line with an arrow, shows the input or output of data or information in to or out from a process. A **process**, which transforms an input data flow into an output data flow, is drawn as a circle. A **data store**, shown as two parallel lines, represents a holding place for data and information, such as a filing cabinet, a checkbook register, or an electronic file or database in a computer system. A **source** (or *agent*), drawn as a square, identifies an entity outside the system that sends data into the system or receives information from the system.

Because these also are visual, DFDs are useful for reviewing the existing or proposed system with the user. DFDs are prepared on a level-by-level basis. The top level DFD, called a **context diagram**, identifies only the major process; that is, the system being studied. Lower-level DFDs add detail and definition to the higher levels — much like *zooming in* on a computer screen. For example, in Figure 11-11, the Consolidated Statement System process would be split into its subprocesses of checking, savings, loans, and so on.

---

inCyber

For information about data flow diagrams (DFD), visit the Discovering Computers Chapter 11 inCyber page (http://www.scsite.com/dc/ch11/incyber.htm) and click DFD.

Project Dictionary The **project dictionary**, also called the **repository**, contains all the documentation and deliverables associated with a project. The project dictionary helps those involved keep track of the huge amount of details in every system. It begins with the project request and includes diagrams such as the ERD and DFDs. Another section of the project dictionary describes every item on these diagrams; that is, each process, data store, data flow, and source on every DFD, and every entity on the ERD and corresponding data items have an entry in the project dictionary. Because some systems can be represented with 25 or more DFDs and have hundreds of data items, the number of entries added to the dictionary at this point can be enormous. Thus, this particular activity requires a tremendous amount of time.

Several different techniques exist to describe the entries from the DFDs and ERDs in the project dictionary. Some of these include structured English, decision tables, and the data dictionary.

Structured English Each process on every DFD must have an entry in the project dictionary. One technique used to write these process specifications is called **structured English**, which is a style of writing that describes the steps in a process. Figure 11-12 shows an example of structured English describing the process of making a withdrawal.

STRUCTURED ENGLISH for MAKING A WITHDRAWAL PROCESS

For each customer making a withdrawal, perform the following steps:

    Obtain Withdrawal-Slip from customer

    Recalculate Amount-of-Withdrawal on Withdrawal-Slip

    If Amount-of-Withdrawal is less than $3,000 then:

        Obtain one form of identification from customer

    Otherwise (Amount-of-Withdrawal is greater than or equal to $3,000) then:

        Ask for two forms of identification from customer (one must be photo)

        Ask customer for desired denomination of bills

    Enter Amount-of-Withdrawal into system

    Print receipt

    Issue cash and receipt

Figure 11-12
Structured English is a technique used to describe a process in the dictionary. This structured English example describes the process for making a withdrawal at North Harbor State Bank.

	Rules							
	1	2	3	4	5	6	7	8
Conditions:								
1. Account Type: (Silver or Gold)	S	G	S	G	S	G	S	G
2. Balance less than $200 during month?	Y	Y	N	N	Y	Y	N	N
3. Average daily balance less than $500 during month?	Y	Y	Y	Y	N	N	N	N
Actions:								
1. No Interest Earned	X							
2. 3½% Interest		X	X		X			
3. 5¼% Interest				X		X	X	
4. 6½% Interest								X

Figure 11-13
Decision tables are a technique used to describe a policy in the dictionary. Policies usually have multiple conditions leading to an action. This decision table describes the policy for computing interest on a checking account at North Harbor State Bank. For example, if the account is a gold account, the balance was more than $200 all month, and the average daily balance was more than $500 all month, then the interest rate used in the computation should be 6½%.

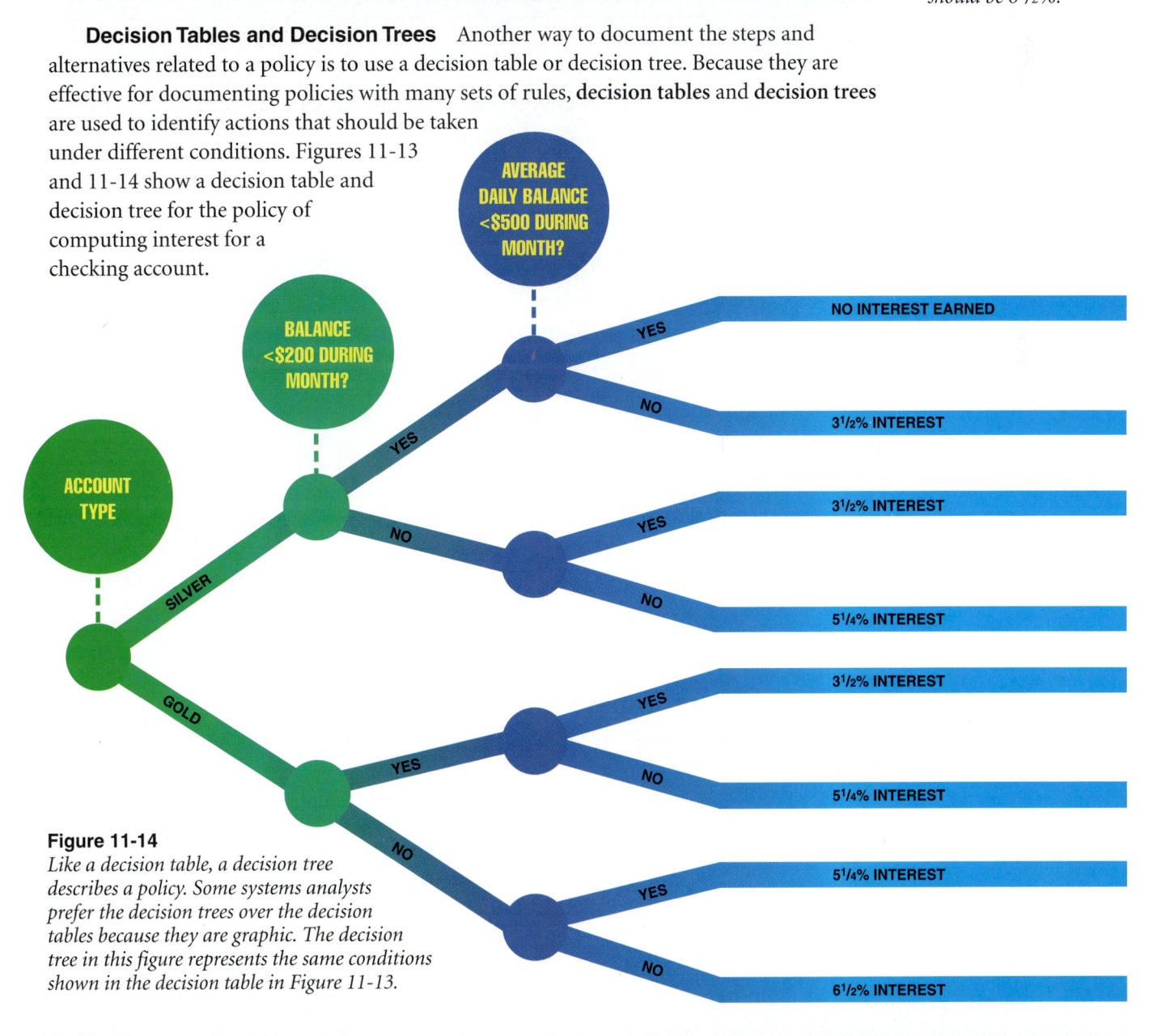

Decision Tables and Decision Trees Another way to document the steps and alternatives related to a policy is to use a decision table or decision tree. Because they are effective for documenting policies with many sets of rules, **decision tables** and **decision trees** are used to identify actions that should be taken under different conditions. Figures 11-13 and 11-14 show a decision table and decision tree for the policy of computing interest for a checking account.

Figure 11-14
Like a decision table, a decision tree describes a policy. Some systems analysts prefer the decision trees over the decision tables because they are graphic. The decision tree in this figure represents the same conditions shown in the decision table in Figure 11-13.

Data Dictionary   Each data item has an entry in the **data dictionary** section (Figure 11-15) of the project dictionary. In addition to the data item's name and description, the data dictionary includes information about the characteristics of each data item such as length, type (alphabetic, numeric, date, and so on), and any validation rules. **Validation rules** include valid codes, ranges, or values for the data item; for example, a State Code data item would have a validation rule indicating that only the current fifty states (CA, IL, WI, and so on) are valid. These validation rules later are translated into actual program code or configured in the purchased software. The data dictionary is created by the systems analyst in detailed analysis and used in all subsequent phases of the system development life cycle.

For more information on data dictionaries, visit the Discovering Computers Chapter 11 inCyber page (http://www.scsite.com/dc/ch11/incyber.htm) and click Data Dictionary.

```
Date: 10/2/98                    Project:    NHSB                         Page:   1
Time: 3:33 PM
                                    Single Entry Listing
                                    Entity Relationship
_____
Account Number                                     Data Element

     Description:

          Unique identification number assigned to each account at the bank

     Alias:

          Account Identification Number

     Values & Meanings:

          7 digits in the form 9999-999

     Data element attributes

          Storage Type:   Number
          Length:         7
          Picture:        9999-999
          Display Format: 9999-999
          Allow Null:     No

     Notes:

          Required element; may not be blank; may not be duplicated

     Location:

              Class -->              CUSTOMER

     Date Last Altered: 10/2/98            Date Created:10/2/98
     --------------------------------------------------------------------
```

Figure 11-15
The data dictionary records information about each of the data items that make up the data flows and entities in the system.

The Build-or-Buy Decision

After the systems analyst has studied the current system and determined all user requirements, he or she prepares a report that presents alternative solutions for the project. This report, often called the **system proposal**, assesses the feasibility of each alternative solution and then recommends the most feasible solution for implementation. Thus, feasibility is reassessed again at this point in the SDLC, especially financial feasibility. If the steering committee approves the recommended solution or one of the alternate solutions, the project enters the design phase.

When the steering committee discusses the system proposal and decides which alternative to implement, it usually is facing a **build-or-buy decision**. That is, the organization is deciding whether to buy a commercial software package from an outside source or build the entire system from scratch.

What Is Commercial Application Software?

Commercial application software is already developed software available for purchase. This prewritten software is available for computers of all sizes. You probably are familiar with the numerous application packages available for personal computers, such as word processors, spreadsheets, and databases.

Vendors offer two types of commercial application software: horizontal and vertical. Products such as word processors, spreadsheets, and accounting packages can be used by many different types of organizations, are **horizontal application software.** If an organization has a unique way of doing business, however, then it requires a package specifically for that job. Software developed for a specific industry is called **vertical application software** and includes industries such as real estate, libraries, and property management. Each of these industries has unique information processing requirements.

Horizontal application packages tend to be widely available because they can be used by a greater number of organizations; thus, they usually are less expensive than vertical application packages. You can search the Internet for names and vendors of vertical and horizontal packages simply by entering your requirement as the search criteria (Figure 11-16). Other sources for names and vendors include computer magazines and **trade publications**, which are magazines written for specific businesses or industries. Companies and individuals who have written software for these industries often advertise in trade publications.

> **inCyber**
>
> For an explanation of commercial application software, visit the Discovering Computers Chapter 11 inCyber page (http://www.scsite.com/dc/ch11/incyber.htm) and click Commercial Application.

Figure 11-16
Yahoo! or any other search engine on the Internet can be used to locate vendors of application software packages. This search of accounting software returned more than 460 matches.

What Is Custom Software?

With so many software application packages available commercially, why would an organization choose to build its own applications? The most common reason is the organization's software requirements are so unique that it is unable to locate a package that meets all its needs. In this case, the organization can choose to develop the software in-house using its own information system personnel or have it developed by an outside source specifically for them. Application software developed by the user or at the user's request is called **custom software**.

The main advantage of custom software is that it matches the organization's requirements exactly. The main disadvantages are that usually it is more expensive than commercial application software and takes longer to design and implement.

Detailed Analysis at North Harbor State Bank

Jackie and her team begin performing the activities in the detailed analysis phase of the Consolidated Statement Project. As part of the study and requirements activities, they use several of the data and information gathering techniques available to them: interviewing several people throughout the bank, observing the preparation and distribution of the statements, and reviewing the questionnaires and monthly statements. They prepare many documents to record their findings including an entity-relationship diagram (see Figure 11-10 on page 11.14), a data flow diagram (see Figure 11-11 on page 11.15), a process specification using structured English (see Figure 11-12 on page 11.16), a process specification using a decision table (see Figure 11-13 on page 11.17), and a data dictionary entry for the account number data item (see Figure 11-15 on page 11.18).

After studying the existing system and obtaining user requirements for two months, Jackie discusses her findings with her supervisor, Bob Kramer. Based on Jackie's findings, Bob writes a system proposal for the steering committee to review. The report assesses the feasibility of "build-versus-buy" scenarios; that is, should North Harbor buy a commercial software package or should they build a consolidated system from scratch?

Bob recommends the analysis team attempt to find a suitable commercial software package that will meet the users' requirements and run on North Harbor's current hardware. The steering committee agrees with Bob's request, but adds that if a commercial software package of this nature does not exist, then a custom consolidated system will be built. Jackie and her team begin the design phase of the project.

---

inCyber

For examples of custom software applications, visit the Discovering Computers Chapter 11 inCyber page (http://www.scsite.com/dc/ch11/incyber.htm) and click Custom Software.

Figure 11-17 ▶
The systems analyst can save much time by researching through the Internet. Many trade journals and magazines, such as PC Magazine, Byte, *and* PC World, *are online on the Web.*

Design Phase

The **design phase** consists of two major activities: (1) if necessary, acquire essential hardware and software and (2) design all of the details of the system to be implemented. These two activities often are performed concurrently rather than sequentially.

Acquiring Essential Hardware and Software

Once a solution has been approved by the steering committee, you begin the tasks to acquire essential hardware and software to meet the requirements of the proposed solution. It is possible that this activity in design may be skipped, if no new hardware or software is required. If it is necessary, the selection of appropriate products is crucial for the success of the system. Four major tasks are performed in this activity: (1) identify technical specifications, (2) solicit vendor proposals, (3) test and evaluate vendor proposals, and (4) make a decision.

Identifying Technical Specifications

The first step in acquiring essential hardware and software is to identify all the hardware and software requirements with respect to functionality, features, and performance. To obtain this criteria, the systems analyst must do a lot of research by visiting a library, researching on the Internet, talking with other analysts, and so on. Many trade journals, newspapers, and magazines are now online on the Web (Figure 11-17), allowing the analyst to locate information more quickly and easily than in the past.

inCyber

For an example of an interactive request for quotation, visit the Discovering Computers Chapter 11 inCyber page (http://www.scsite.com/dc/ch11/incyber.htm) and click RFQ.

Once the requirements have been collected, the systems analyst summarizes the hardware and software requirements in either a request for proposal or a request for quotation to send to prospective vendors. You use a **request for quotation** (**RFQ**) when you know which product(s) you want, and the vendor is instructed to quote a price for the specified product(s). You use a **request for proposal** (**RFP**) when you want the vendor to select the product(s) that meets your requirements and then quote the price(s). Just as the depth of an application system varies, so does the length of an RFP or RFQ; some can be as short as a couple of pages, with others consisting of more than one hundred pages. Some companies prefer to use a **request for information** (**RFI**), which is a less formal method using a standard form to request information about a product or service.

Soliciting Vendor Proposals

With either an RFP or RFQ in hand, you are ready to send it to potential vendors. Many hardware and software vendors make their product catalogs available on the Internet so you have up-to-date and easy access to products, prices, technical specifications, and ordering information (Figure 11-18). If you are unable to locate a vendor on the Internet, you could visit a local computer store for smaller systems or contact computer manufacturers for larger systems.

A **value-added reseller** (**VAR**) is another source for hardware and software products. VARs have resale agreements with one or more computer manufacturers and take full responsibility for equipment, software, installation, and training.

Figure 11-18
Many hardware and software vendors are putting their product and services catalogs on the Internet. This figure shows the table of contents page for IBM's Desktop Software Catalog.

Figure 11-19
When searching for hardware and software vendors, the Internet is an excellent resource. Many VARs advertise on the Internet. This figure shows the home page for Global Data Center Inc., which provides complete systems.

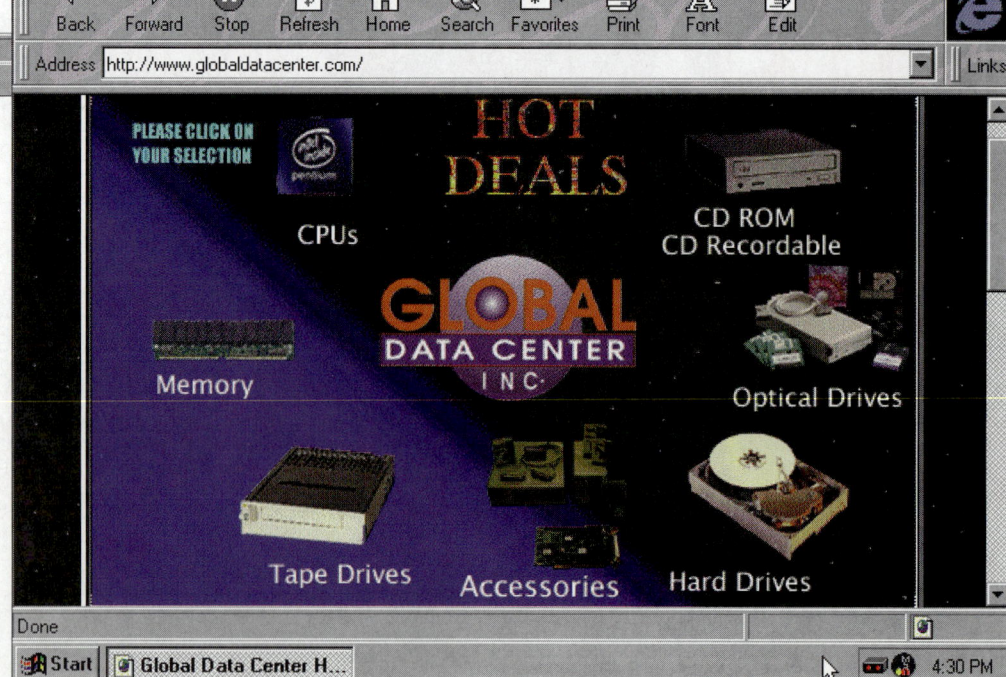

Sometimes, they even provide equipment maintenance. Some VARs offer one product or service, while others provide complete systems (Figure 11-19). The advantage of a full-scale VAR is that you only have to deal with a single company for an entire system.

Another means of identifying software suppliers is to hire a computer consultant to assist you with this task. Although consultant's fees may be high, it may be worth the expert advice. Many consultants specialize in assisting organizations of all sizes with the task of identifying and installing software packages. For a good consultant reference, contact a professional organization in your industry or a local university.

Testing and Evaluating Vendor Proposals

After you send RFPs and RFQs to potential vendors, you will begin receiving proposals and quotations. The most difficult task is to evaluate the proposals and then select the best one. A popular technique is to establish a scoring system that you can use to rate each proposal. Try to be as objective as possible while rating each proposal.

During this task, many information gathering techniques are used. You should obtain user references from the software vendors and, talk to current users of the software for their opinions, and ask the vendor for a demonstration of the product(s) specified (Figure 11-20). You may, however, prefer to test the software yourself. In this case, the vendor could supply you with a demonstration copy of the software to test on your equipment or set up a hardware and software configuration at its site so you can be sure it will meet your needs.

Figure 11-20
You should ask to see a demonstration of any program you are considering purchasing. During or after the demonstration, you should rate how well the package meets your requirements.

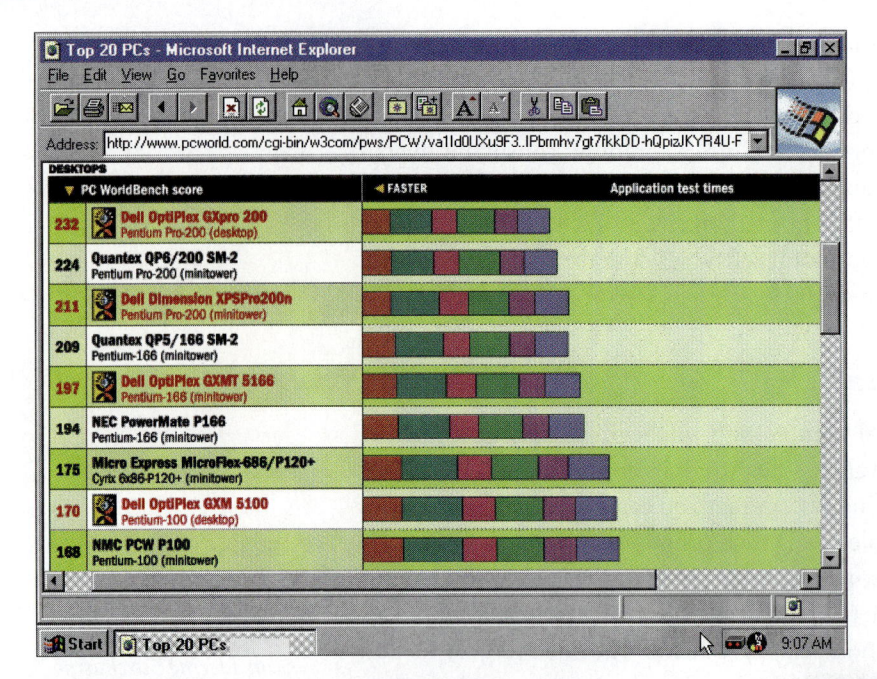

If you are concerned about whether the software can handle a certain transaction volume efficiently, you may want to perform a benchmark test. A **benchmark test** measures the time it takes to process a set number of transactions. For example, a benchmark test could consist of measuring the time it takes a payroll package to print 50 paychecks. Comparing the time it takes different accounting packages to print the same 50 paychecks is one way of measuring the package's relative performance. Many computer magazines perform benchmark tests while reviewing hardware and software and then publish these results for consumers to review (Figure 11-21).

Figure 11-21
Many publications, both online and hard copy, regularly evaluate software and hardware. This benchmark test from PC World Online tested desktop computers. The test included developing documents in Word 7 for Windows 95, Excel 7 for Windows 95, Picture Publishers 6 for Windows 95, Paradox 5 for Windows, WordPerfect 6.1 for Windows, and Lotus 1-2-3 Release 5 for Windows.

Making a Decision

Having rated the proposals, the systems analyst presents a recommendation to the steering committee. The recommendation could be to award a contract to a vendor or to not make any purchases at this time. When you purchase hardware, you usually own it; however, when you purchase software, you do not. With software, you purchase a software license (Figure 11-22), which is the right to use the software under certain terms and conditions. Most license agreements state that the software may not be used on more than one computer or by more than one user. Other license restrictions include copying the software, modifying it, or translating it to another language. These restrictions are designed to protect the rights of the software developer, who does not want someone else to benefit unfairly from the developer's work.

Figure 11-22
A software license grants the purchaser the right to use the software but does not include ownership rights.

Software Acquisition at North Harbor State Bank

Based on the direction of the steering committee, Jackie and her team prepare a requirements list from the information obtained during analysis. Because no new hardware is required, the list includes only software. Then, they prepare an RFP and submit it to fifteen vendors: nine through the Internet and six local computer stores. Fourteen vendors send a response within the three-week deadline set by North Harbor.

Of the fourteen replies, North Harbor selects two to evaluate. They eliminate the other twelve because these vendors did not offer adequate support for the software once it was installed. The project team asks for demonstration copies of the software from the remaining two vendors. In addition, they contact three current users of each package for their opinions. After evaluating these two software packages, the team is disappointed because both require substantial modifications to meet North Harbor's technique of processing statements.

Jackie summarizes her team's findings in a report to the steering committee. North Harbor now faces a build decision. That is, should they develop the software themselves or have a third party develop the software? After discussing the alternatives, the steering committee authorizes the information systems department to begin development of custom software for the Consolidated Statement Project. As a courtesy and to maintain good working relationships, Jackie sends a letter to all fourteen vendors informing them of North Harbor's decision.

Detailed Design

Once the data and process requirements have been identified, the next step is to develop **detailed design specifications** for the components in the proposed solution. Whereas detailed analysis sometimes is referred to as logical design, detailed design sometimes is called **physical design** because it specifies hardware and software for automated procedures. The activities to be performed include developing designs for the databases, inputs, outputs, and programs. Depending on whether commercial application software is being purchased or custom software is being developed, the length and complexity of each of these activities may vary.

Database Design Data is the central resource in an information system. Thus, it is crucial that the content of the data dictionary be current, consistent, and correct. During database design, the systems analyst builds the data dictionary information developed during the analysis phase so it represents accurately the data requirements of the organization. The systems analyst works closely with the database administrator to identify those data elements that currently exist within the organization and those that must be developed.

With relational database systems, the structure of each table in the system must be defined, as well as relationships between the tables. Table structure definitions include details of records and fields within the records. Another issue that must be addressed is user access rights; that is, the analyst must define which data elements each user can access, when they can access the data elements, what actions can they perform on the data elements, and under what circumstances they can access the elements (Figure 11-23). Users with similar items, actions, or constraints would be grouped into a class, which then would be implemented for the security of the database. The systems analyst also must consider the volume of database activity. For example, large, frequently accessed tables may require a separate index file so that inquiries are processed in an acceptable time frame.

> **inCyber**
>
> For a description of data security resources, visit the Discovering Computers Chapter 11 inCyber page (http://www.scsite.com/dc/ch11/incyber.htm) and click Data Security.

USER NAME	ITEM	ACTION	CONSTRAINT
Jane Smith	Customer Balance	Inquiry	None
Jane Smith	Customer Balance	Modify	Balance < $5000
Jane Smith	Customer Balance	Delete	Not Allowed
Tom Greason	Customer Balance	Inquiry, Modify, Delete	None
Rita Waldon	Pay Rate	Inquiry	Pay Rate < $40
Rita Waldon	Pay Rate	Modify, Delete	Not Allowed
Tom Greason	Pay Rate	Inquiry, Modify, Delete	Always
Bob Travers	Customer Address	Inquiry, Modify, Delete	None

Figure 11-23
Data security is an important issue that the systems analyst must address. This figure shows a popular model for data security.

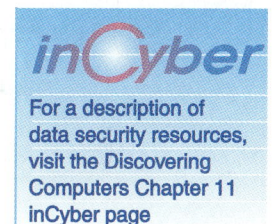

Input and Output Design Because users ultimately will be working with the inputs and outputs, it is crucial to involve users during input and output design. During this activity, the systems analyst carefully designs every menu, screen, and report specified in the requirements. Usually, the outputs are designed first because they drive the requirements for the inputs. Two types of layouts should be developed for each input and output: a mockup and a layout chart. A **mockup** is a sample of the input or output containing actual data (Figure 11-24); mockups are shown to users for their approval.

Once approved, a **layout chart** is developed for the programmer; layout charts are more technical and contain programming-like notations for the data items (Figure 11-25).

Other issues that must be addressed during input and output design are the types of media to use (paper, video, audio); formats (graphic or narrative); and data entry validation techniques, which include making sure the inputted data is correct (for example, a pay rate cannot be less than 0).

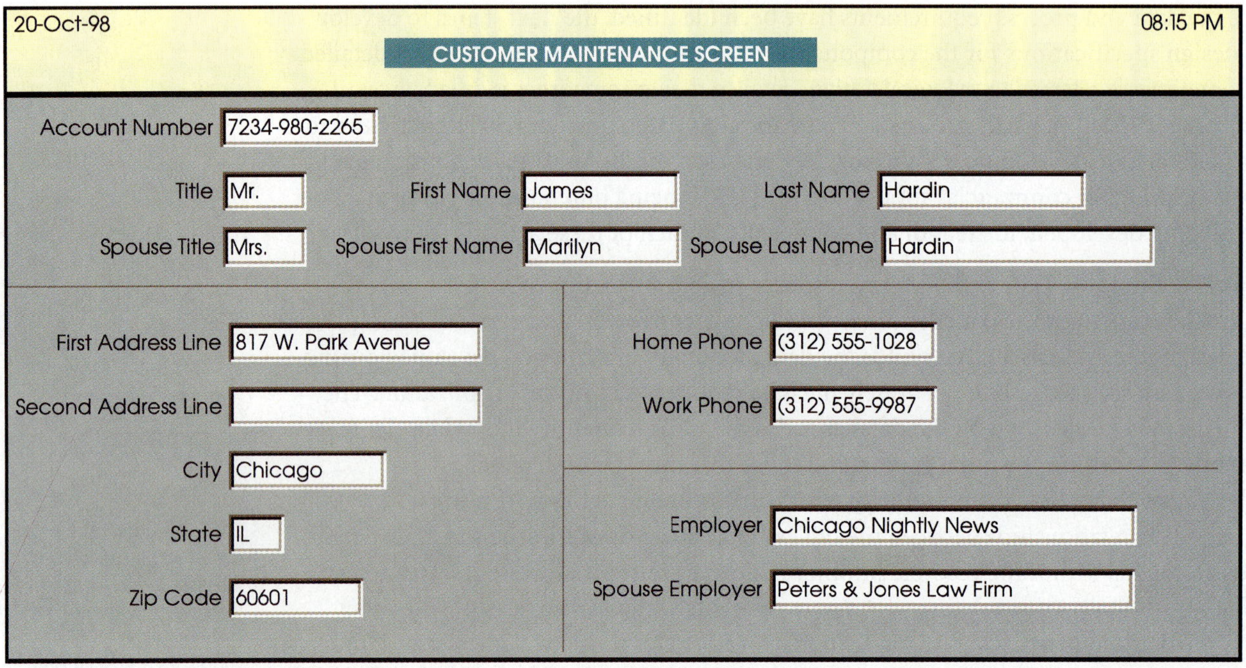

Figure 11-24
Users must give their approval on all inputs and outputs. This input screen is a mockup (containing actual data) for the user to review.

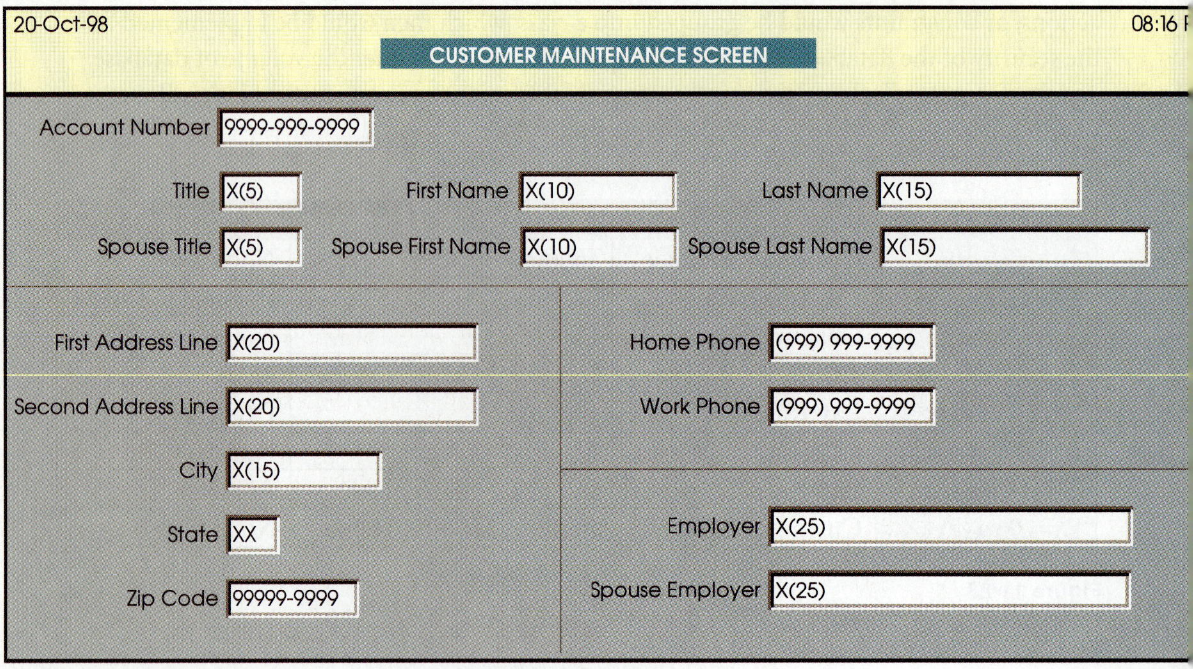

Figure 11-25
Once users approve a mockup, the layout chart (with technical specifications) is given to the programmer. This layout chart is for the mockup in Figure 11-24.

DESIGN PHASE   11.27

Program Design   During program design, the systems analyst identifies the processing requirements, or the **logic**, for each program in the system. To accomplish this, the analyst uses top-down and structured programming tools, which are discussed in the next chapter.

Once the processing requirements are developed, the **program specification package** is prepared so that these requirements can be communicated clearly to the programmer. The program specification package contains the relationship between each program in a process, as well as the input, output, processing, and database specifications. Relationships among programs in a process often are documented with system flowcharts (Figure 11-26). A **system flowchart** shows a major process (each of which may require one or more programs), the timing of the process, the outputs generated (including their distribution and media), database tables required, and the types of input devices (such as, terminals) that will provide data to the system. A system flowchart is very different from a data flow diagram. A DFD shows the flow of data through the system; whereas, a system flowchart shows methods and procedures.

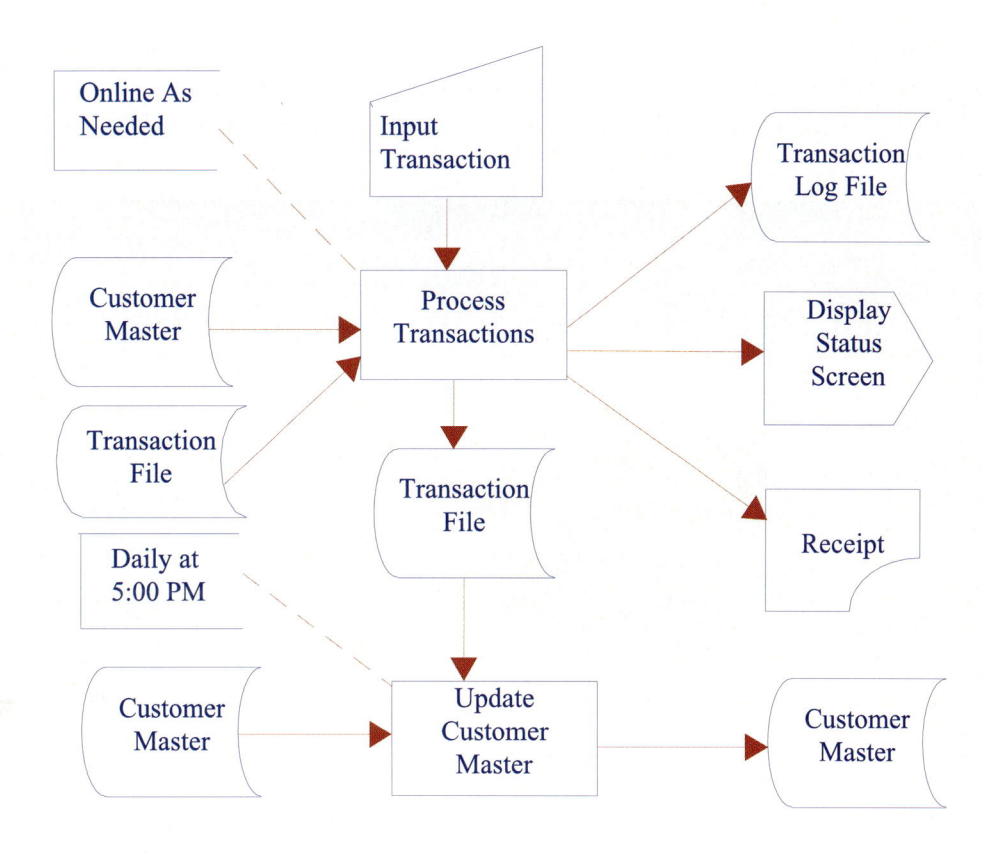

Figure 11-26
The system flowchart graphically shows the hardware and software used to process data. This system flowchart describes the process of a transaction being entered, such as a customer making a deposit or a withdrawal. This chart contains five symbols with these meanings: rectangle with a slanted top — data entry; rectangle — program; rectangle with curved edges — file; rectangle with cut corner — hard copy; rectangle with no right side — comment. Comments are connected to the chart with dotted lines because they represent timing, not data flow.

Prototyping

Many systems analysts today are using a prototyping approach to perform detailed analysis activities. The process of developing software with prototypes sometimes is called **rapid application development (RAD)**. A **prototype** is a working model of the proposed system. That is, the analyst actually builds a functional form of the solution during design. The main advantage of a prototype is that users can work with the system before it is completed — to make sure it meets their needs. The Customer Maintenance Screen in Figure 11-24 on page 11.26 actually is a prototype created in Microsoft Access. Once a prototype is approved, the solution is implemented more quickly than without a prototype. In many cases, prototyped systems do not require a programmer for implementation; the analyst can convert the working model to the actual solution. That is, these systems are developed rapidly.

Some organizations use prototyping during design, while others begin earlier during analysis or even planning. Beginning a prototype in the planning or analysis phase might lead to problems. When the development team sees a working model so early in the life cycle, they tend to skip critical analysis and design steps and overlook key features in the proposed solution. A common pitfall of a prototype is that it is documented inadequately, or worse, not documented at all. Prototyping can be an effective tool if the development team and the users discipline themselves to follow all activities within the life cycle; prototyping should not eliminate or replace activities — just improve the quality of these activities.

CASE Tools

Many systems analysts now use computer software specifically designed to assist in the system development life cycle process. **Computer-aided software engineering (CASE)** products are computer-based tools designed to support one or more phases of the SDLC. This technology is intended to increase the efficiency and productivity of the project team.

Some CASE tools exist separately; that is, one software package is a dictionary while another enables you to generate drawings. The most effective tools, however, are those developed as an integrated product (Figure 11-27), sometimes called I-CASE or a CASE workbench.

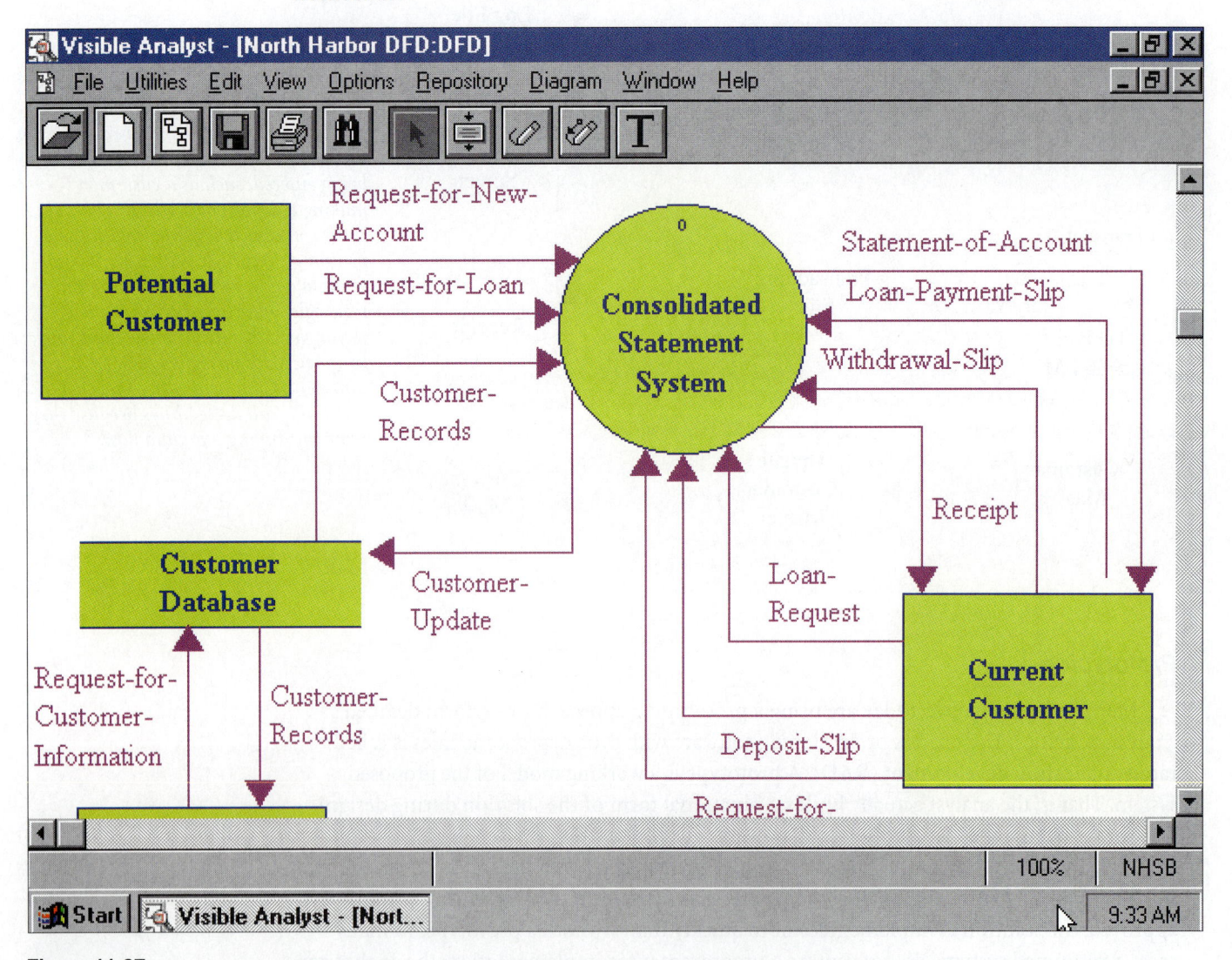

Figure 11-27
Integrated computer-aided software engineering (I-CASE) packages assist analysts in the development of an information system. Visible Analyst Workbench (VAW) by Visible Systems Corporation enables analysts to create structured diagrams (ERDs and DFDs), as well as build the project dictionary. Figures 11-10, 11-11, 11-15, and 11-26 all were created using VAW.

I-CASE products include the following capabilities.

- Project repository facility that stores diagrams, specifications, descriptions, programs, and any other deliverable generated during the life cycle activities
- Graphics facility that enables the drawing of diagrams, such as DFDs and ERDs
- Prototyping facility used to create models of the proposed system
- Quality assurance facility to analyze deliverables, such as graphs and the data dictionary for accuracy
- Code generators that create actual computer programs from design specifications
- Housekeeping facility that establishes user accounts and provides backup and recovery functions

CASE tools are designed to support a wide variety of system development life cycles. Depending on the one your organization adopts and follows, you can customize the tools so all deliverables, such as DFDs and ERDs, are standardized.

Quality Review Techniques

Before you submit the detailed design specifications to the programming team, the specifications should be reviewed by users, the senior systems analyst, and other members of the project team. One common review technique is a **structured walkthrough**, which is a step-by-step review of any deliverable. Deliverables that may be walked through include the reports, diagrams, mockups, layout charts, and dictionary entries. The purpose of a walkthrough is to identify errors in the deliverable being reviewed. If any errors are identified, they must be corrected by the information system personnel before anyone continues with activities in the life cycle. Structured walkthroughs are used throughout the entire SDLC to review a variety of deliverables.

As at the end of other phases in the life cycle, a feasibility assessment once again is performed to determine if it still is beneficial to implement the proposed solution. It does not happen often, but some projects are terminated at this point because they become infeasible. Although you may feel that much time and money has been wasted, it is less costly in the long run to terminate the project than to implement an inadequate or incorrect solution. If the steering committee decides the project still is feasible, the project enters the implementation phase.

Detailed Design at North Harbor State Bank

As approved by the steering committee, Jackie and her team begin designing the consolidated statement system for North Harbor State Bank. After studying existing statements and interviewing more users and customers, the team is able to design modifications to the database, input screens, the new consolidated statement, and the associated programs. They prepare several documents including a mockup (see Figure 11-24 on page 11.26), a layout chart (see Figure 11-25 on page 11.26), and a system flowchart (see Figure 11-26 on page 11.27).

After completing the detailed design, Jackie meets with several users and the information system personnel to walkthrough her deliverables. They locate two errors, which she corrects prior to presenting the design specifications to the steering committee. The committee agrees with the design solution and consents to implement it.

---

inCyber

For information on the Visible Analyst Workbench (VAW), visit the Discovering Computers Chapter 11 inCyber page (http://www.scsite.com/dc/ch11/incyber.htm) and click VAW.

Implementation Phase

Once the design has been completed, the project enters the **implementation phase**. The purpose of implementation is to construct, or build, the new system and then deliver it to the users. Four major activities are performed in this phase: (1) develop programs, (2) install and test the new system, (3) train and educate users, and (4) convert to the new system. Each of these activities is discussed in the following sections.

Develop Programs

Once the program specification package is delivered to the programmers, the process of developing programs or software begins. Just as the system development life cycle follows an organized set of activities, so does program development. The **program development life cycle (PDLC)** follows these six steps: (1) analyze the problem, (2) design the program, (3) code the program, (4) test the program, (5) formalize the solution, and (6) maintain the program. Chapter 12 explains the program development life cycle in depth. The important concept to understand now is that the PDLC is a part of the implementation phase, which is part of the SDLC.

For a summary of the phases and activities associated with a company's program development life cycle (PDLC) process, visit the Discovering Computers Chapter 11 inCyber page (http://www.scsite.com/dc/ch11/incyber.htm) and click PDLC.

Install and Test the New System

If new hardware was acquired, the hardware must be installed and tested at this point. Both commercial software application packages and custom software programs then have to be installed on the hardware. It is extremely important that the hardware and software be tested thoroughly. Just as you test individual programs, you also should test that all the programs work together in the system. It is better to find errors at this point so you can correct them before putting the system into production; that is, delivering it to the users.

Three types of tests are performed during this activity:

- **System Test** Checks all programs in an application
- **Integration Test** Checks application to be sure it works with other applications
- **Acceptance Test** Performed by end-users, checks that new system works with actual data

Train and Educate Users

For a system to be effective, users must be trained properly on its functionality. They must be trained on how to use both the hardware and the software. Training involves showing users exactly how they will use the new system. This type of training could include classroom-style lectures (Figure 11-28) or one-on-one sessions. Whichever technique is used, it should include hands-on sessions using realistic sample data on the equipment the users will have. Well-designed user manuals also should be provided to users for reference.

Education is the process of learning new principles or theories that help users understand the system. For example, many companies use total quality management (TQM) to maintain quality in a system. In this case, employees need to be educated on the concepts and practices of TQM.

Convert to the New System

The final activity in implementation is to change to the new system from the old system. This conversion can take place using one or more of the following strategies: direct, parallel, phased, or pilot (Figure 11-29).

With **direct conversion**, the user stops using the old system one day and begins using the new system the next. The advantage of this strategy is it requires no transition costs and is fast, which explains why some analysts call it an *abrupt cutover*. The disadvantage is it is extremely risky and can disrupt operations seriously if the new system does not work correctly the first time.

Figure 11-28
Users must be trained properly on the new system. Training could be one-on-one sessions or classroom-style lectures.

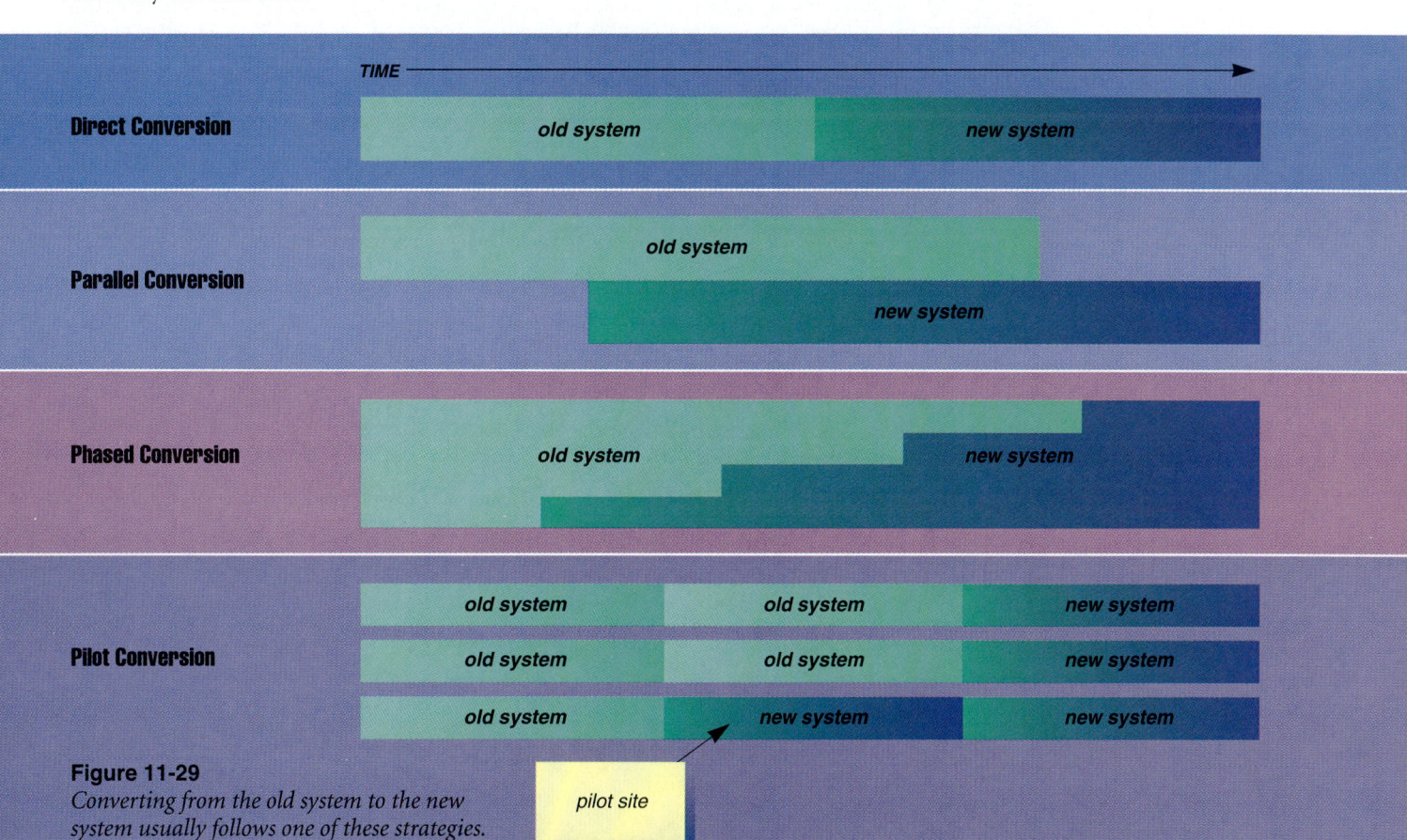

Figure 11-29
Converting from the old system to the new system usually follows one of these strategies.

Parallel conversion consists of running the old system alongside the new system. Results from both systems are compared, and if they agree, the old system either is terminated abruptly or is phased out. The advantage of this strategy is that any problems with the new system can be solved before the old system is terminated. The disadvantage is that it is costly to operate two systems simultaneously.

Phased conversion is used with larger systems that can be broken down into individual sites that can be implemented separately at different times. Each individual site uses either a direct or parallel conversion. An example of a phased conversion could be for an accounting system, with the accounts receivable, accounts payable, general ledger, and payroll sites all implemented separately in phases.

With a **pilot conversion**, the new system is used by only one location in the organization so it can be tested. Once the pilot site approves the new system, other sites convert using one of the aforementioned conversion strategies.

At the beginning of the conversion, existing data must be made ready for the new system. Converting existing manual and computer-based files so they can be used by a new system is called **data conversion**.

Implementation at North Harbor State Bank

Upon receiving the program specification package, Adam Jacobs and two other programmers work together to develop the code for the design. Jackie works closely with the three programmers to answer questions about the design and to check the progress of their work. When the programming team completes its work, the custom software is given to Jackie for testing.

Jackie arranges several training classes for the employees of North Harbor State Bank. She also prepares a detailed user guide for each employee that has access to the system. Jackie wants to be sure that everyone is prepared thoroughly for the new system.

Jackie consults her boss, Bob Kramer, for his opinion on the conversion. He suggests that the main office in Chicago be a pilot site that uses the new system for one month. The pilot site will use a parallel conversion because it is the safest way to implement the new system. If, after a month, the main office approves the system, the other branches would use a direct conversion to move to the new system.

Support Phase

The purpose of the **support phase** is to provide continuous assistance for a system and its users after it is implemented. Four major activities are performed in the support phase: (1) conduct a post-implementation system review, (2) identify errors, (3) identify enhancements, and (4) monitor performance.

One of the first activities performed in the support phase is the **post-implementation system review**, which is a meeting with users to determine if the system is performing according to their expectations. If it is not, you must determine what must be done to satisfy the users — which means you begin planning all over again. Thus, the loop forms in the system development life cycle.

Sometimes, users identify errors in the system; that is, it does not produce correct results. These errors are caused from problems with design (logic) or programming (syntax). Often these errors are minor. For example, the total of a column might be incorrect on a customer statement. Other times, however, the error requires more serious investigation by the systems analyst before a correction can be determined — back to the planning phase again.

In some cases, users would like the system to do more; that is, they have additional requirements. System enhancement involves modifying or expanding an existing application system — back to the planning phase again.

Performance monitoring is another activity that the systems analyst performs during the support phase. The purpose is to determine if the system is inefficient at any point and if the inefficiency is causing a problem. For example, is the time it takes to print a customer statement reasonable? If not, the analyst must investigate solutions to make the system response times more acceptable — back to the planning phase again.

Support at North Harbor State Bank

During the post-implementation system review, Jackie learns that the customers of North Harbor State Bank are extremely satisfied with the new consolidated statements. Management is very happy because the consolidation project has saved the bank a huge amount of money.

Six months after the new consolidated statement system has been in operation, Karen Peterson sends another customer satisfaction survey to determine if the customers have any other wants or needs of North Harbor. When Karen tabulates the survey results, she is delighted to learn that not a single customer who responded is dissatisfied! Karen passes the good news on to the steering committee.

Summary of the System Development Life Cycle

Although the system development life cycle is an organized set of activities, it takes a skilled systems analyst to coordinate a development project effectively and efficiently. Many of the activities overlap and many are performed simultaneously. Structured development tools, prototyping, and CASE technology all have made the SDLC a more efficient process, but the success of any project depends on effective communication and a strong commitment of the involved parties. The understanding you have gained from this chapter will help you participate in information system development projects and give you an appreciation for the importance of each of its phases.

COMPUTERS AT WORK

System Development Methodologies — What Are the Differences?

Just as many models and makes of cars are on the market, many different SDLCs also exist. As each car manufacturer feels its automobile is the best, each author of an SDLC feels his or her process for building a system is the best. When someone writes his or her own comprehensive version of the entire system development life cycle, it often is called a system development **methodology**.

Some methodologies are published in textbooks for use in the classroom. Noted structured systems analysis and design authors include Chris Gane and Trish Sarson, James Martin, and Ed Yourdon. Other methodologies are sold by vendors. That is, a methodology vendor develops and writes all the phases, activities, and tools required for its SDLC, packages it, and then sells it in the form of instruction guides, software, training, course materials, and consulting. One popular commercial methodology is called **STRADIS** by Structured Solutions, Inc. In the job market, some companies seek systems analysts with experience in structured methodologies in general; while others require specific commercial methodology experience.

So what are the differences among the various published and commercial methodologies? Not much, really. Many contain the five major phases discussed in this chapter: planning, analysis, design, implementation, and support, while others have more or fewer phases. Regardless of phase names, they all contain the same basic activities and tasks. Other differences lie mostly in the terminology used. For example, this chapter used the term feasibility study; whereas, STRADIS uses initial study report or ISR. Another difference may be in the placement of certain activities. For example, this chapter positioned the creation of the system proposal at the end of analysis; while others position it at the beginning of design.

Whether you are versed in published or commercial methodologies is not the real issue. What is important is that you understand that any system development project must be disciplined and organized to be successful.

Figure 11-30

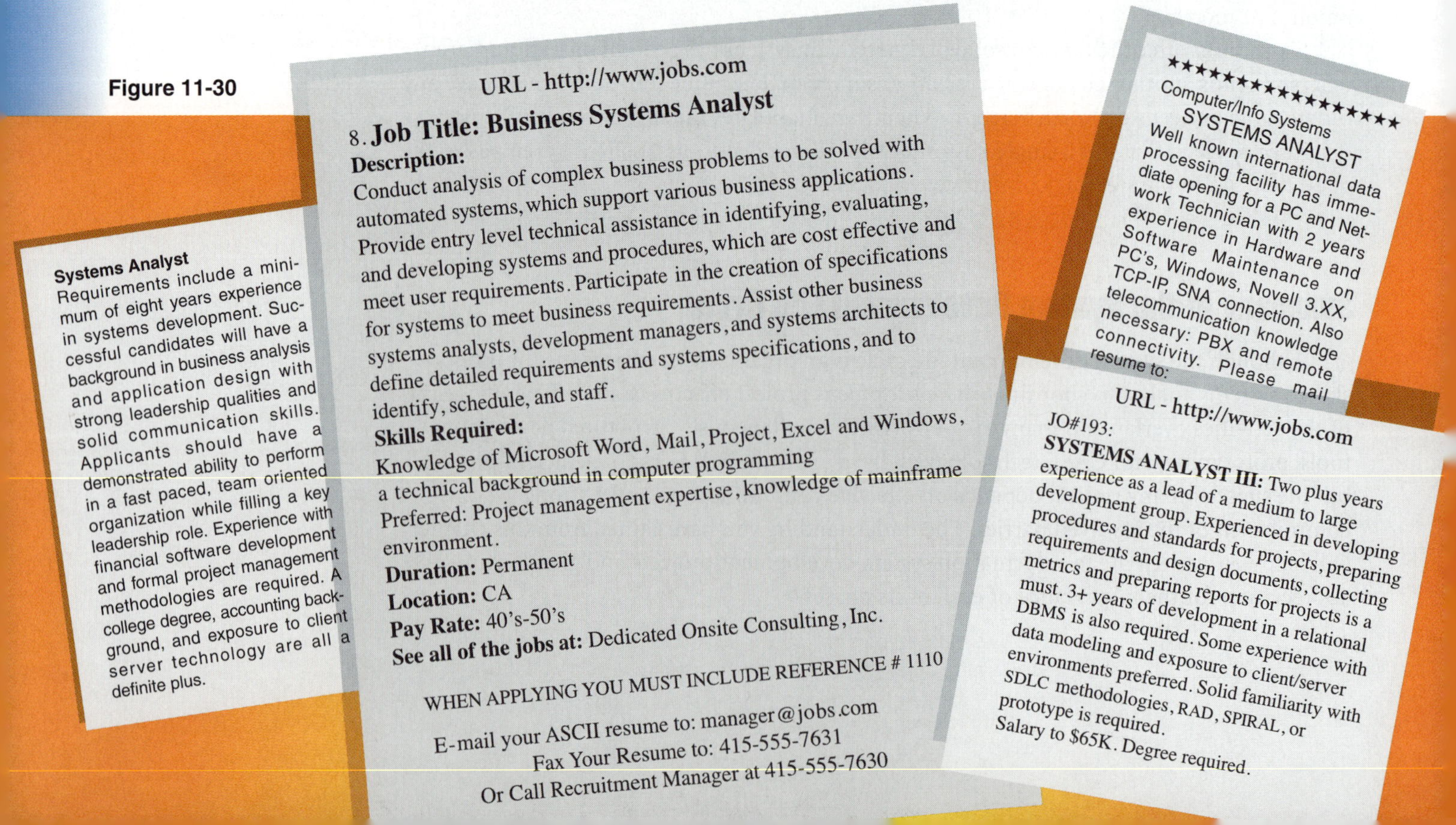

Systems Analyst
Requirements include a minimum of eight years experience in systems development. Successful candidates will have a background in business analysis and application design with strong leadership qualities and solid communication skills. Applicants should have a demonstrated ability to perform in a fast paced, team oriented organization while filling a key leadership role. Experience with financial software development and formal project management methodologies are required. A college degree, accounting background, and exposure to client server technology are all a definite plus.

URL - http://www.jobs.com

8. Job Title: Business Systems Analyst

Description:
Conduct analysis of complex business problems to be solved with automated systems, which support various business applications. Provide entry level technical assistance in identifying, evaluating, and developing systems and procedures, which are cost effective and meet user requirements. Participate in the creation of specifications for systems to meet business requirements. Assist other business systems analysts, development managers, and systems architects to define detailed requirements and systems specifications, and to identify, schedule, and staff.

Skills Required:
Knowledge of Microsoft Word, Mail, Project, Excel and Windows, a technical background in computer programming
Preferred: Project management expertise, knowledge of mainframe environment.
Duration: Permanent
Location: CA
Pay Rate: 40's-50's
See all of the jobs at: Dedicated Onsite Consulting, Inc.

WHEN APPLYING YOU MUST INCLUDE REFERENCE # 1110

E-mail your ASCII resume to: manager@jobs.com
Fax Your Resume to: 415-555-7631
Or Call Recruitment Manager at 415-555-7630

****
Computer/Info Systems
SYSTEMS ANALYST
Well known international data processing facility has immediate opening for a PC and Network Technician with 2 years experience in Hardware and Software Maintenance on PC's, Windows, Novell 3.XX, TCP-IP, SNA connection. Also telecommunication knowledge necessary: PBX and remote connectivity. Please mail resume to:

URL - http://www.jobs.com
JO#193:
SYSTEMS ANALYST III: Two plus years experience as a lead of a medium to large development group. Experienced in developing procedures and standards for projects, preparing requirements and design documents, collecting metrics and preparing reports for projects is a must. 3+ years of development in a relational DBMS is also required. Some experience with data modeling and exposure to client/server environments preferred. Solid familiarity with SDLC methodologies, RAD, SPIRAL, or prototype is required.
Salary to $65K. Degree required.

IN THE FUTURE

The Virtual Classroom

Figure 11-31

Imagine that you are ready to train all company employees on a new system, but you have a dilemma. The employees are located at plants and branches throughout the state, country, or even the world. You could send user manuals to each employee, but you know face-to-face training is the most effective. You could have them all fly-in to a week-long training session, but your company has a training budget that cannot accommodate airfare, hotels, meals, and lost productivity for 6,000 people. How then are you going to train the company's workforce on the functionality of the new system at a reasonable cost? The answer could be distance learning.

Distance learning is the delivery of education at one location while the learning takes place at other locations. Several major universities, such as Purdue and MIT, already offer distance learning classes. Although some corporations such as Hewlett-Packard already have started saving millions of dollars by using distance learning to train employees, most just are beginning to investigate the possibility because the technology is so new.

For corporate training, the most convenient form of distance learning is the **desktop video classroom**, where each employee sits at a computer in his or her office or home to attend class. This type of long-distance learning is accomplished via a telephone, a telephone network, two-way video, two-way computer hookups, a videoconference board, camera, headset, and videoconference software. Through the desktop video classroom, the employee sees full color and full motion with live audio and video communication, all through the Windows 95 interface. This technology enables the employee and instructor to work together as if they were side by side — in a virtual classroom.

With the cost of each individual desktop video configuration exceeding $5,000, companies may wait for prices to drop. And, like all other technology, prices will no doubt become more reasonable. If you computed costs of airfare, hotel, food, and lost productivity of each employee in a class, reasonably priced desktop video solutions are definitely a distance learning solution not too far in the distance.

11 review

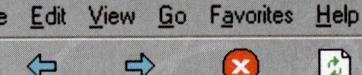

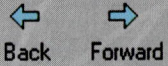

chapter | 1 | 2 | 3 | 4 | 5 | 6 | 7 | 8 | 9 | 10 | 11 | 12 | 13 | 14 | I

inCyber | review | terms | yourTurn | hotTopics | outThere | winLabs | webWalk | exercises | news | home

INSTRUCTIONS: *To display this page from the Web, launch your browser and enter the URL, http://www.scsite.com/dc/ch11/review.htm. Click the links for current and additional information.*

1 System Development Life Cycle

The **system development life cycle (SDLC)** is an organized set of activities used to guide those involved through the development of an information system. The many activities of the SDLC can be grouped into five major **phases**: (1) planning, (2) analysis, (3) design, (4) implementation, and (5) support. Certain ongoing activities occur throughout the entire SDLC.

2 Guidelines for Systems Development

Development of an information system should follow three general guidelines. A phased approach should be used to define the phases of the SDLC and determine what activities and tasks will occur in each phase. Users must be involved throughout the entire development process. Finally, standards for the development of the information system should be defined and written.

3 Project Management

Project management is the process of planning, scheduling, and controlling the individual activities during the SDLC. One aspect of project management is making sure each **deliverable**—tangible item—is transmitted on time and according to plan. **Feasibility** assessment is a measure of how suitable the development of a system will be to the organization. **Documentation** is the compilation and summarization of data and information in a **project notebook**. A **project team**, composed of users and information systems personnel, gathers data and information throughout the SDLC.

4 Initiating the System Development Life Cycle

A new or modified information system may be requested for a variety of reasons, some external and some internal. External reasons include orders from a governing body or competitive developments. Internal reasons might be a change in system requirements or response to a problem. The initial request eventually is written on a standard form that becomes the first item of documentation in the project notebook.

5 Planning Phase

The **planning phase** for a project begins when the steering committee receives a project request. During the planning phase, four major activities are performed: review project requests, prioritize project requests, commit resources to approved projects, and identify a project development team for each approved project.

6 Analysis Phase

The **analysis phase** is divided into the feasibility study and detailed analysis. The **feasibility study** determines whether or not the problem or enhancement identified in a project request is worth pursuing. **Detailed analysis** involves studying the current system in depth, identifying the user's wants and needs, and recommending a solution. Detailed analysis sometimes is called **logical design** because the proposed solution is developed without regard to specific hardware or software.

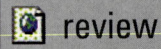

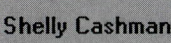

7 Structured Analysis and Design Tools

Structured analysis and design uses graphics to present findings in a way that can be understood by users, programmers, and other systems analysts. An **entity relationship diagram (ERD)** is a tool used to represent graphically associations between **entities** (objects about which data is stored) in the project. A **data flow diagram (DFD)** is a tool used to represent graphically the flow of data in a system.

8 Project Dictionary

The **project dictionary** contains all the documentation and deliverables associated with a project. A style of writing called **structured English** is used to describe the steps in a process. **Decision tables** and **decision trees** are used to identify actions that should be taken under different conditions. The **data dictionary** section of the **project dictionary** includes each data item's name, description, and characteristics. **Validation rules** indicate valid codes, ranges, or values for a data item.

9 Build-or-Buy Decision

A **system proposal** assesses the feasibility of alternative solutions and then recommends the most practicable solution for implementation. The steering committee usually faces a **build-or-buy decision**; that is, whether to build **custom software** (software developed from scratch by the user or at the user's request) or to buy **commercial application software** (already developed software available for purchase).

10 Design Phase

The **design phase** consists of acquiring the essential hardware and software and designing all of the details of the system to be implemented. Acquiring essential hardware and software involves identifying technical specifications, soliciting vendor proposals, testing and evaluating vendor proposals, and making a decision. Once the data and process requirements have been identified, **detailed design specifications** are developed for the components of the proposed solution. Detailed design, sometimes called **physical design**, specifies the hardware and software for automated procedures. Designs are developed for the databases, inputs, outputs, and programs.

11 Prototyping and Case Tools

Many systems analysts use a prototyping approach to perform detailed analysis activities. A **prototype** is a working model of the proposed system that allows users to work with the system before it is completed to make sure it meets their needs. **Computer-aided software engineering (CASE)** products are computer-based tools designed to support one or more phases of the SDLC. Step-by-step reviews called **structured walkthroughs** are used throughout the SDLC to identify errors.

chapter 11 review

inCyber | review | terms | yourTurn | hotTopics | outThere | winLabs | webWalk | exercises | news | home

12 Implementation Phase
The purpose of the **implementation phase** is to construct the new system and deliver it to the users. Program development follows six steps called the **program development life cycle (PDLC)**. Once the program is developed, the new system is installed and tested. Three types of tests are performed: **system test**, **integration test**, and **acceptance test**. Users must be trained properly on the system's functionality and educated in the new principles or theories that help them understand the system. The final activity in the implementation phase is to convert to the new system from the old one.

13 Conversion
Conversion can take place using one or more strategies. With direct conversion, the user stops using the old system one day and begins using the new system the next. **Parallel conversion** consists of running the old system alongside the new system. If the results agree, the old system is terminated or phased out. **Phased conversion** is used with large systems that can be broken down into individual sites and implemented separately at different times. With a **pilot conversion**, the new system is used by only one location in the organization so it can be tested.

14 Support Phase
The purpose of the **support phase** is to provide continuous assistance for a system and its users after it is implemented. During the support phase, a **post implementation review** is conducted to determine if the new system is performing according to users' expectations. Errors and potential system enhancements are identified. Performance is monitored to determine if the system is inefficient at any point and if the inefficiency is causing a problem.

11 terms

chapter 1 | 2 | 3 | 4 | 5 | 6 | 7 | 8 | 9 | 10 | 11 | 12 | 13 | 14 | I

inCyber | review | terms | yourTurn | hotTopics | outThere | winLabs | webWalk | exercises | news | home

INSTRUCTIONS: *To display this page from the Web, launch your browser and enter the URL, http://www.scsite.com/dc/ch11/terms.htm. Scroll through the list of terms. Click a term for its definition and a picture. Click the rocket ship for current and additional information about the term.*

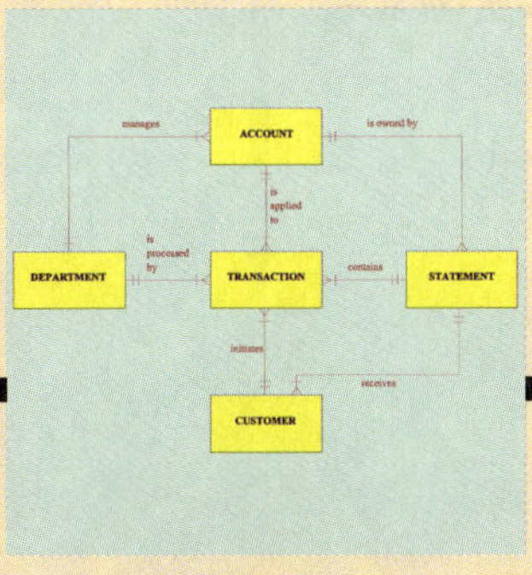

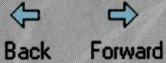

entity-relationship diagram (ERD)

DEFINITION

entity-relationship diagram (ERD)
A tool used to represent the associations between entities in the project graphically. (**11.14**)

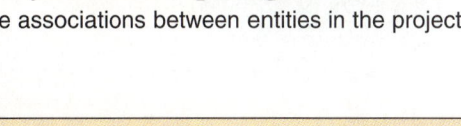

---

acceptance test (11.30)
analysis phase (11.11)

benchmark test (11.24)
build-or-buy decision (11.19)

commercial application software (11.19)
computer-aided software engineering (CASE) (11.28)
context diagram (11.15)
custom software (11.20)

data conversion (11.32)
data dictionary (11.18)
data flow (11.15)
data flow diagram (DFD) (11.15)
data store (11.15)
decision tables (11.17)
decision trees (11.17)
deliverable (11.5)
design phase (11.21)
desktop video classroom (11.35)
detailed analysis (11.12)
detailed design specifications (11.24)
direct conversion (11.31)
distance learning (11.36)
documentation (11.6)

economic feasibility (11.5)
entity (11.14)
entity-relationship diagram (ERD) (11.14)

feasibility (11.5)
feasibility study (11.11)

Gantt chart (11.4)

horizontal application software (11.19)

implementation phase (11.30)
integration test (11.30)

JAD session (11.7)

layout chart (11.24)
logic (11.27)
logical design (11.12)

methodology (11.12)
mockup (11.24)

operational feasibility (11.5)

parallel conversion (11.32)
phased conversion (11.32)
phases (11.2)
physical design (11.24)
pilot conversion (11.32)
planning phase (11.9)
post-implementation system review (11.33)
preliminary investigation (11.11)
process (11.15)
program development life cycle (PDLC) (11.30)
program specification package (11.27)
project dictionary (11.6, 11.16)
project management (11.4)
project notebook (11.6)

project plan (11.4)
project team (11.4)
prototype (11.27)

rapid application development (RAD) (11.27)
repository (11.6, 11.16)
request for information (RFI) (11.22)
request for proposal (RFP) (11.22)
request for quotation (RFQ) (11.22)

scope (11.4)
source (11.15)
steering committee (11.9)
STRADIS (11.34)
structured analysis and design (11.13)
structured English (11.16)
structured interview (11.7)
structured walkthrough (11.29)
support phase (11.33)
system development life cycle (SDLC) (11.2)
system flowchart (11.27)
system proposal (11.19)
system test (11.30)

technical feasibility (11.5)
trade publications (11.19)

unstructured interview (11.7)
users (11.3)

validation rules (11.18)
value-added reseller (VAR) (11.22)
vertical application software (11.19)

11 yourTurn

chapter 1 | 2 | 3 | 4 | 5 | 6 | 7 | 8 | 9 | 10 | 11 | 12 | 13 | 14 | I

inCyber | review | terms | yourTurn | hotTopics | outThere | winLabs | webWalk | exercises | news | home

INSTRUCTIONS: *To display this page from the Web, launch your browser and enter the URL, http://www.scsite.com/dc/ch11/turn.htm. Click a blank line for the answer. Click the links for current and additional information.*

Label the Figure

1. _____
   - Review project requests
   - Prioritize project requests
   - Commit resources
   - Identify project development team

2. _____
   - Conduct feasibility study
   - Study current system
   - Determine user requirements
   - Recommend solution

3. _____
   - Acquire hardware and software, if necessary
   - Develop details of system

4. _____
   - Develop programs
   - Install and test new system
   - Train and educate users
   - Convert to new system

5. _____
   - Conduct post-implementation system review
   - Identify errors and enhancements
   - Monitor system performance

(center)
- Project management
- Feasibility assessment
- Documentation
- Data/information gathering

Instructions: Identify the phases in the system development life cycle.

Fill in the Blanks

Instructions: Complete each sentence with the correct term or terms.

1. A popular project management tool used to plan and schedule time relationships is a(n) _____, in which each bar represents a project phase or activity.
2. Structured analysis and design uses graphics tools such as the _____ to represent associations between entities.
3. The _____, which contains all the documentation and deliverables associated with a project, helps keep track of the huge amount of details in every system.
4. The _____, which is part of the SDLC, follows six steps: analyze the problem, design the program, code the program, test the program, formalize the solution, and maintain the program.
5. Conversion to a new system can take place using one or more of the following strategies: _____, _____, _____, or _____.

Short Answer

Instructions: Write a brief answer to each of the following questions.

1. What are three general guidelines for the development of an information system? How do standards help? _____
2. What methods are used during the system development process to gather data and information? How is an unstructured interview different from a structured interview? What is a JAD session? _____
3. What initiates the system development life cycle? Why is it important that a request for system services or a project request be completed on a standard form? _____
4. What is the build-or-buy decision? What are the advantages and disadvantages of custom software? _____
5. What is the purpose of the support phase? What activities are performed to support an information system? _____

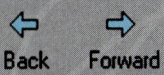

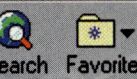

hotTopics chapter 11

1 | 2 | 3 | 4 | 5 | 6 | 7 | 8 | 9 | 10 | 11 | 12 | 13 | 14 | I

inCyber | review | terms | yourTurn | hotTopics | outThere | winLabs | webWalk | exercises | news | home

INSTRUCTIONS: *To display this page from the Web, launch your browser and enter the URL, http://www.scsite.com/dc/ch11/hot.htm. Click the links for current and additional information to help you respond to the hotTopics questions.*

1 *Eighteen months after a new $5 million information system was supposed to be* in full operation, workers for a county in New York were grumbling that the system was plagued with errors. The head of the county's Civil Service Employees Association reported that complaints were coming in from virtually all departments. During system development, problems are easier and less expensive to remedy at some phases in the system development life cycle than at others. When would it be easiest and least expensive to identify and solve problems? Why? At what phase would it be most difficult and most expensive? Why?

2 *Entity-relationship diagrams, data flow diagrams, decision tables and decision trees, and system* flow charts frequently are used when developing information systems. These tools help clarify relationships among objects, data flow, decision alternatives, and hardware and software requirements. Prepare two or more of the following to represent graphically one aspect of class registration at the beginning of a semester.
- An entity-relationship diagram symbolizing associations between entities when you register.
- A data flow diagram illustrating the flow of information through your school's computer system during registration.
- A decision table or decision tree showing whether or not you will register for a class given at least two conditions.
- A system flowchart documenting the data you enter, processes you perform, files you use, and reports you produce.

3 *People often go through phases similar to the SDLC when faced with reasons to make a major* change. Think of an important adjustment that you made in your life. What change did you make? Would you consider the reason for the change internal or external? Why? List in the order in which they were taken all of the steps you followed as you made the alteration. Using the system development life cycle as a guide, in which phase would you place each step that you took? Why? Which phase do you think was most crucial in solving your problem? Why? Which phase do you think was least important? Why?

4 *Imagine you are the head of the information systems department for a small manufacturing* firm. Several department managers have contacted your office complaining that the current information system is outdated and no longer meets their needs. You have organized a committee to investigate the problem. At your first meeting, George, a department manager, suggests that a representative from Colonial Computing, the vendor that supplied the current computer system, be made a part of the system development team. Martha, another department manager, strongly disagrees. In fact, she maintains that if it is necessary to acquire a new system, your firm should consider using several different vendors instead of a single supplier. What are the strengths and weaknesses of the suggestions made by each department manager? As head of the committee, how would you resolve the conflict?

5 *Occasionally, organizations hire outside consultants to find sources of commercial application* software. Using information furnished by the organization, these consultants identify potential vendors, solicit offers, evaluate proposals, and make recommendations. Although some organizations feel these consultants have saved them considerable sums of money, others insist they would have been better off not hiring a consultant. Under what circumstances do you think a company should hire a consultant? Would a consultant be more valuable to a company looking for horizontal application software or vertical application software? Why? What advantages, if any, might a consultant have in locating software suppliers, choosing appropriate software packages, and helping implement those packages? To be most effective, what level of cooperation would a consultant need from the organization?

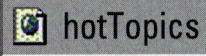

11 outThere

chapter | 1 | 2 | 3 | 4 | 5 | 6 | 7 | 8 | 9 | 10 | 11 | 12 | 13 | 14 | I

inCyber | review | terms | yourTurn | hotTopics | outThere | winLabs | webWalk | exercises | news | home

INSTRUCTIONS: To display this page from the Web, launch your browser and enter the URL, http://www.scsite.com/dc/ch11/out.htm. Click the links for current and additional information.

1. *In 1996, the median salary for systems analysts was $55,000. Top systems* analysts were making as much as $90,000. Some authorities believe that soon all types of businesses, large and small, will need systems analysts to monitor the information systems essential to modern companies. It is expected that more than 20,000 systems analyst positions will be added by the year 2000. By using want ads from newspapers, computer publications, or trade journals, and possibly calling some prospective employers, find out what qualities employers are looking for in a systems analyst. What type of education is required? What experience is expected? What achievements seem to make applicants more suitable?

2. *Although information systems is a functional area in many organizations, some companies* turn to outside consultants to meet their developmental needs. These consultants offer expertise, experience with tools from numerous software manufacturers, access to talented developers, proven project management techniques, and a library of reusable code that can provide a basis for custom software. Visit an information system development Web site. What types of projects have been developed? What services are provided? What tools and technology are used? How are clients supported? When might a company decide to use an information systems development consultant instead of developing a system in-house?

3. *Is the system development life cycle always the best method of creating solutions to information* system problems? Some analysts feel that prototyping results in greater user satisfaction and an increased likelihood that users will be able to work with the final system. Interview a systems analyst at a company, or from the information systems department in your school, about his or her opinion of the system development life cycle versus prototyping. What is the best approach to developing information systems? What are the advantages and disadvantages of the SDLC? What are the advantages and disadvantages of prototyping? Under what circumstances would he or she choose to use each approach? Why?

4. *Modern computer-aided software engineering (CASE) products make it easier for companies to* develop their own information systems. These user-friendly tools are designed for a wide range of people. Suppliers of CASE products offer software and systems engineering tools, software training, and education and training in software engineering. Visit the Web site of one or more CASE tool suppliers. What tools are offered? How are they used? What classes or other types of support are provided? How much do the tools cost? What are the operating system and hardware requirements? If possible, download a demonstration of a CASE product. For what purpose is the tool used? How does it enhance the system development process?

5. *Identify a problem that could be solved using a personal computer and commercial application* software. Write a request for proposal (RFP) for the software. The RFP should be a checklist indicating the features necessary in the application software. Keep in mind the data that will be processed, the output required, and the people who will use the software. Visit a software vendor and, using your RFP, find at least two software packages that meet most of your requirements. Evaluate the software by scoring each package against your list of requirements, talking to people who use the software (if possible), and trying the software yourself. On the basis of your evaluation, which software package would you choose? Why? Would it be necessary to customize the software? How?

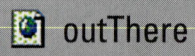

11 winLabs

chapter 1 | 2 | 3 | 4 | 5 | 6 | 7 | 8 | 9 | 10 | 11 | 12 | 13 | 14 | I

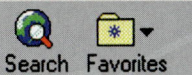

inCyber | review | terms | yourTurn | hotTopics | outThere | winLabs | webWalk | exercises | news | home

INSTRUCTIONS: *To display this page from the Web, launch your browser and enter the URL, http://www.scsite.com/dc/ch11/labs.htm. Click the links for current and additional information.*

Traffic Sign Tutorial

Insert your Student Floppy Disk into drive A or see your instructor for the location of the Traffic Sign Tutorial program. Click the Start button on the taskbar and then click Run on the Start menu. In the Open text box, type the path and file name of the traffic.exe program and then press ENTER to display the Traffic Sign Tutorial window (Figure 11-32). Drag the signs to their correct containers.

Click Options on the menu bar and then click Clear to reset the tutorial. Click Options on the menu bar and then click Show. Click Options on the menu bar and then click Clear. Click Options on the menu bar and then click Quiz. Answer the quiz questions.

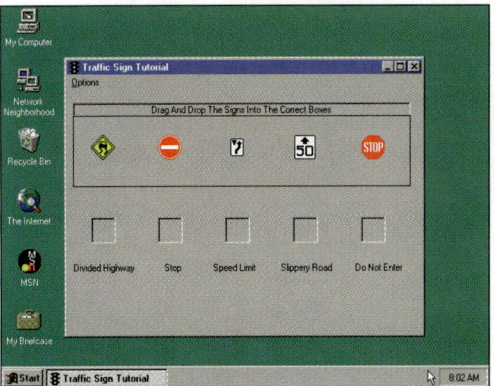

Figure 11-32

Creating a Drawing

Click the Start button on the taskbar; point to Programs on the Start menu; point to Accessories on the Programs submenu; and then click Paint on the Accessories submenu. Maximize Paint. Change the background color to bright pink by right-clicking the color bright pink in the color box at the bottom of the Paint window, clicking File on the menu bar, and then clicking New. Click the Brush tool in the tool box at the left edge of the Paint window. Change the foreground color to light yellow by clicking the color light yellow in the color box.

Move the mouse pointer into the bright pink window. Use the mouse to write your name in cursive (Figure 11-33). If you make a mistake, click Edit on the menu bar and then click Undo to erase your last draw. Click File on the menu bar and then click Save. Type `a:lab11-2` in the File name text box. Click the Save button. Click File on the menu bar and then click Print. Click the OK button. Close Paint.

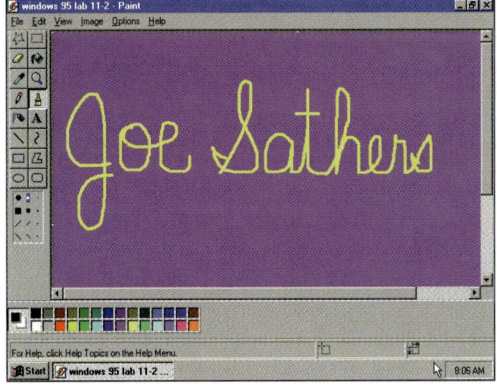

Figure 11-33

Capturing Screen Images

Click the Start button on the taskbar; point to Programs on the Start menu; and then point to Accessories on the Programs submenu. Press the PRINT SCREEN key. Click WordPad on the Accessories submenu. In WordPad, type `Below is a Windows 95 Screen Shot:` and then press ENTER twice. Click Edit on the menu bar and then click Paste. Practice using the scroll bar to scroll through the document. Click the Print button on the toolbar to print the file. Close WordPad. Do not save the file.

Using Paint's Help

Open Paint as described in winLabs 2. Click Help on Paint's menu bar. Click Help Topics. When the Help Topics: Paint Help dialog box displays, click the Contents tab. Double-click the Drawing Lines and Shapes book. Display and read each of the topics. Answer the following questions: (1) How do you draw a straight line? (2) How do you draw a circle? Close all open windows.

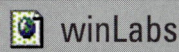

11 webWalk

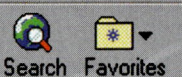

chapter | 1 | 2 | 3 | 4 | 5 | 6 | 7 | 8 | 9 | 10 | 11 | 12 | 13 | 14 | I

inCyber | review | terms | yourTurn | hotTopics | outThere | winLabs | webWalk | exercises | news | home

INSTRUCTIONS: *To display this page from the Web, launch your browser and enter the URL, http://www.scsite.com/dc/ch11/walk.htm. Click the exercise link to display the exercise.*

1. System Development Life Cycle (SDLC)
The core of the SDLC is based on a standard approach to problem solving. To learn about different approaches to the system development life cycle, complete this exercise.

3. Value-Added Resellers (VARs)
A value-added reseller is a source for hardware and software. VARs have resale agreements with computer manufacturers and take full responsibility for equipment, software, installation, and training. You can learn more about the services offered by a VAR by completing this exercise.

4. Computer-Aided Software Engineering (CASE)
One of the more difficult tasks in the analysis phase is to organize all of the data and information needed by an organization and document the flow of data within an organization. To learn more about one of the many CASE products available to facilitate this process (Figure 11-35), complete this exercise.

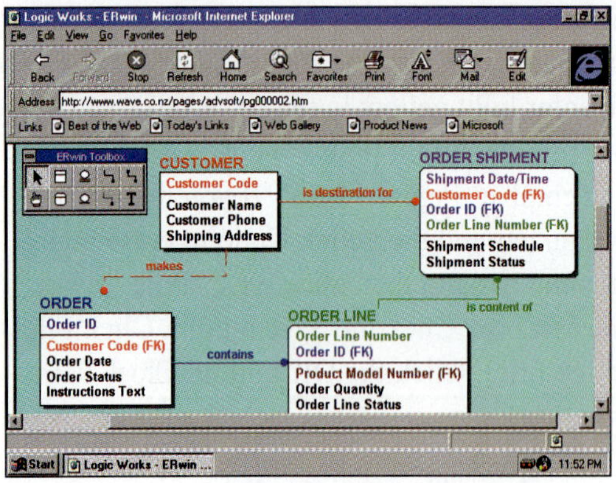

Figure 11-35

2. Online Magazines
Many trade journals and magazines are online on the Web (Figure 11-34). You can learn more about online computer trade magazines by completing this exercise.

Figure 11-34

5. Information Mining
Complete this exercise to improve your Web research skills by using a Web search engine to find information related to this chapter.

6. Rapid Application Development (RAD)
Rapid Application Development (RAD) is a software development approach that attempts to decrease the amount of time it takes to develop a new application. Learn more about RAD by completing this exercise.

7. Software Quality
Quality Control (QC) and Quality Assurance (QA) are important in all phases of the SDLC. Complete this exercise to learn more about Software Quality.

8. Project Management Software
Project management software assists managers in planning, scheduling, and controlling a project's activities. Complete this exercise to learn more about project management software.

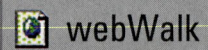

9. Web Chat
Complete this exercise to enter a Web Chat discussion related to the issues presented in the hotTopics exercise.

Program Development and Programming Languages

CHAPTER 12

OBJECTIVES

After completing this chapter, you will be able to:

- Define the term computer program
- Explain the six steps in the program development life cycle
- Describe top-down program design
- Explain structured program design and the three basic control structures
- Define the term programming language
- Explain the differences among the categories of programming languages
- Discuss the object-oriented approach to program development
- Identify programming languages commonly used today
- Discuss application generators, macros, and RAD tools
- Discuss how HTML is used to create a Web page
- Identify various uses of a script and popular scripting languages

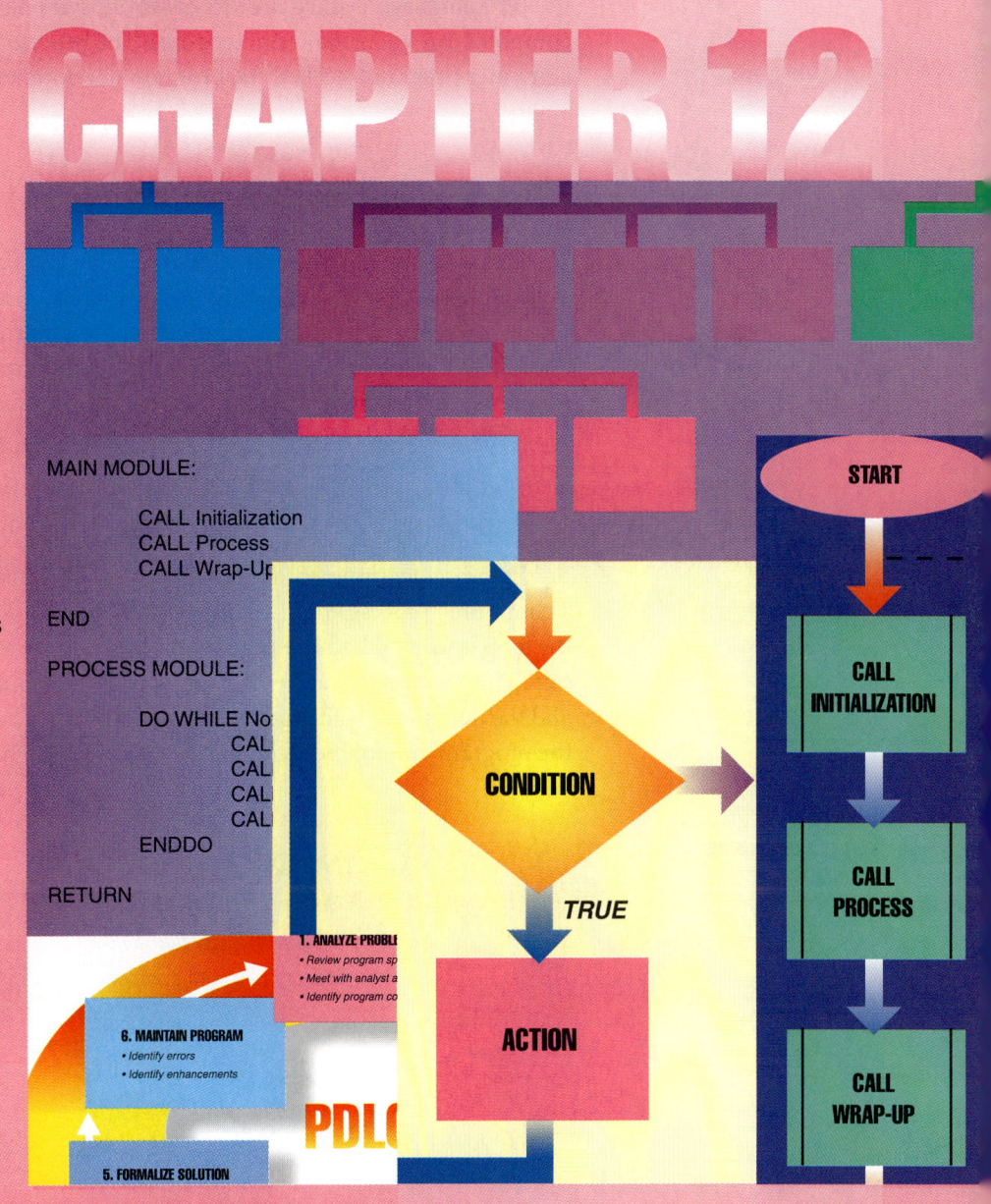

The system development life cycle consists of five phases, one of which is implementation. A major part of the implementation phase is writing and testing computer programs that process data into useful information. During implementation, a key role of the programmer — the person who writes computer programs — is to translate the design specifications developed in the previous phases of the system development life cycle into a program that produces information that meets the requirements of users.

Although you may never write a computer program yourself, you someday may request information that requires that a program be written or modified; thus, you should understand how programs are developed. Program development is broken down into six steps, which are collectively referred to as the program development life cycle. This chapter discusses each step of the program development life cycle and presents the tools used to make this process efficient. This chapter also explains the different programming languages used to write computer programs.

What Is a Computer Program?

A **computer program** is a step-by-step set of instructions that directs a computer to perform the tasks necessary to process data into information. These instructions can be written, or *coded*, by a computer programmer in a variety of **programming languages**, which are sets of words, symbols, and codes used to create instructions a computer can understand or recognize. The process that programmers use to build a computer program is called the program development life cycle.

The Program Development Life Cycle

The **program development life cycle** (PDLC) is an outline of each of the steps used to build computer programs. Similar to the way the system development life cycle guides the systems analyst through the development of an information system, the program development life cycle is a tool used to guide computer programmers through the development of a program. The program development life cycle consists of six steps (Figure 12-1).

1. Analyze Problem
2. Design Program
3. Code Program
4. Test Program
5. Formalize Solution
6. Maintain Program

Program development is an ongoing process within an information system. Because it is a continuing process, the steps in the PDLC form a loop, as shown in Figure 12-1. Notice that the loop is formed because the Maintain Program step connects back to the Analyze Problem step. This connection occurs when errors in or improvements to the program are identified, and the decision is made to modify the program. The Analyze Problem step thus begins, and the program development life cycle starts over.

Figure 12-1
The program development life cycle consists of six steps that form a loop.

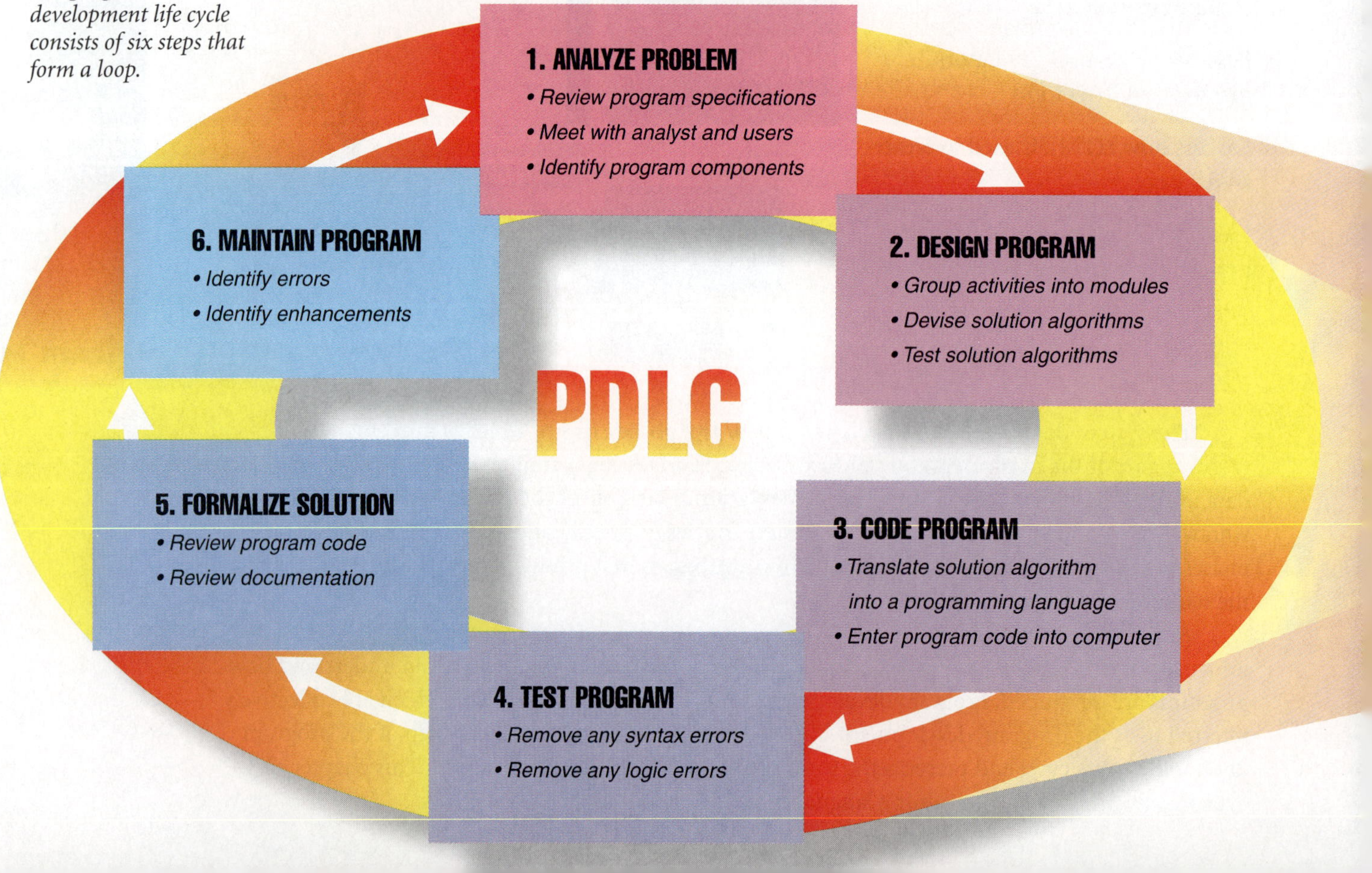

1. ANALYZE PROBLEM
- Review program specifications
- Meet with analyst and users
- Identify program components

2. DESIGN PROGRAM
- Group activities into modules
- Devise solution algorithms
- Test solution algorithms

3. CODE PROGRAM
- Translate solution algorithm into a programming language
- Enter program code into computer

4. TEST PROGRAM
- Remove any syntax errors
- Remove any logic errors

5. FORMALIZE SOLUTION
- Review program code
- Review documentation

6. MAINTAIN PROGRAM
- Identify errors
- Identify enhancements

PDLC

What Initiates the Program Development Life Cycle?

Requests for a new or modified program usually occur at the end of the analysis phase of the system development life cycle (SDLC). Recall from Chapter 11 that the SDLC consists of five major phases: planning, analysis, design, implementation, and support. At the end of the analysis phase, the company faces a build-or-buy decision; that is, should they buy a commercial software package from an outside source or build custom software specifically designed to meet their needs? If the company decides to build custom software, they then must decide whether to have the software developed by an outside source or to develop the software in-house. If the company chooses to develop the software in-house, the design phase of the SDLC focuses on developing a detailed set of system and program requirements for the programmer(s). These detailed design specifications, called the **program specification package**, communicate the input, output, processing, and data requirements of each program to the programmer.

Preparing the program specification package is the last step in the design phase of the SDLC. Once the programmer receives the program specification package, the implementation phase begins, with the programmer analyzing the problem to be solved by the program(s). The program development life cycle thus begins at the start of the implementation phase. All of the steps of the PDLC are completed within the implementation phase of the system development life cycle (Figure 12-2).

The scope of the program specification package largely determines the number of programmers working on a program. If the specifications have a large scope, a **programming team** usually is assigned to develop the program(s). If the specifications are fairly simple, a single programmer might complete all of the development tasks. Whether a single programmer or a programming team, all of the programmers involved must interact with members of the system development project team (including the systems analyst and the users) throughout the program development life cycle. By following the steps in the PDLC, the programmers create programs that are correct (produce accurate information) and maintainable (easy to modify). Involving the project team leads to programs that meet user requirements.

inCyber

For an explanation of the system development life cycle, visit the Discovering Computers Chapter 12 inCyber page (http://www.scsite.com/dc/ch12/incyber.htm) and click SDLC.

Figure 12-2
The program development life cycle is part of the implementation phase of the system development life cycle.

Step 1 – Analyze Problem

The first step in the program development life cycle is to analyze the problem to be solved by the program, so that you can begin to develop an appropriate solution. This step consists of three major tasks: (1) review the program specifications package, (2) meet with the systems analyst and users, and (3) identify the program's input, output, and processing components.

First, you must review the program specification package that contains input, output, processing, and data requirements. Within the program specification package, these requirements are presented as a variety of tangible deliverables, such as charts, diagrams, reports, or files. Screen and report layout charts, for example, are used to document input and output requirements. System flowcharts, structured English, decision tables, and decision trees document program design (processing) requirements. The data dictionary identifies the data requirements of the program. Thoroughly reviewing these deliverables helps the programmer understand the nature of the program and its requirements.

In addition to reviewing the deliverables, the programmer meets with the systems analyst and the users to understand the purpose of the program from the users' perspective. Recall from Chapter 11 that a guideline of system development is to involve users throughout the entire development process.

If, after reviewing the program specifications package and meeting with the systems analyst and users, the programmer thinks some aspect of the design specifications should be changed, he or she discusses the change with the systems analyst and the users. If everyone agrees on the change, the design specifications are modified. A programmer should never make any change without both the systems analyst's and users' approval.

Once design specifications are agreed upon, the programmer must define the input, processing, and output (IPO) requirements of the program. To collect and better define these requirements, many programmers use a tool called a *defining diagram*, or IPO chart (Figure 12-3). An **IPO chart** identifies the inputs to the program, the outputs to be generated, and the processing steps required to transform the inputs into the outputs. As with the program specification package, you should review the contents of the IPO chart with the systems analyst and the users to ensure that you completely understand *what* the program is to accomplish. Once the problem analysis is complete, the programmer begins designing a program to solve the problem.

Figure 12-3
IPO (Input Process Output) charts are a tool used to assist the programmer in analyzing the program.

INPUT	PROCESSING	OUTPUT
Unit price	Read unit price, quantity purchased, discount code	Net amount due
Quantity purchased	Calculate gross amount due	
Discount code	If discount applies, calculate discount amount	
	Calculate net amount due	
	Print net amount due	

Step 2 – Design Program

Designing the program involves three tasks: (1) group the program activities into modules, (2) devise a solution algorithm for each module, and (3) test the solution algorithms. The first task is called top-down design, which continues to focus on *what* must be done (the requirements). The remaining two tasks — part of a process called structured design — determine *how* to build the program based on the requirements.

Top-Down Design

The objective of **top-down design** is to take the original set of program specifications and break it down into smaller, more manageable components, each of which is easier to solve than the original one. With top-down design, the programmer uses a telescopic approach to view the program; that is, you begin with the big picture and then *zoom in* on the details.

The first step of top-down design is identifying the major activity of the program, sometimes called the *main routine*. Next, you decompose (or break down) the main routine into smaller sections, which often are called *subroutines* because they are subordinate to the main routine. Then, you look at each subroutine and decide if it can be decomposed further. You continue decomposing subroutines until each one performs a single function. A section of a program dedicated to performing a single function is called a **module**. Each subroutine is a module; the main routine often is called the main module.

A **hierarchy chart**, also called *structure chart,* or *top-down chart,* or *visual table of contents,* is a tool used to represent these program modules graphically (Figure 12-4). Each module is represented by a rectangle labeled with the module name. The main module is located at the top. All other modules are below the main module, connected by lines that indicate their relationships. In Figure 12-4, for example, the initialization, process, and wrap-up modules are subordinate to the main module.

Programs developed using the top-down approach benefit from the simplicity of their design — they usually are reliable and easy to read and maintain. For these reasons, many computer professionals and programmers recommend the top-down approach to program design.

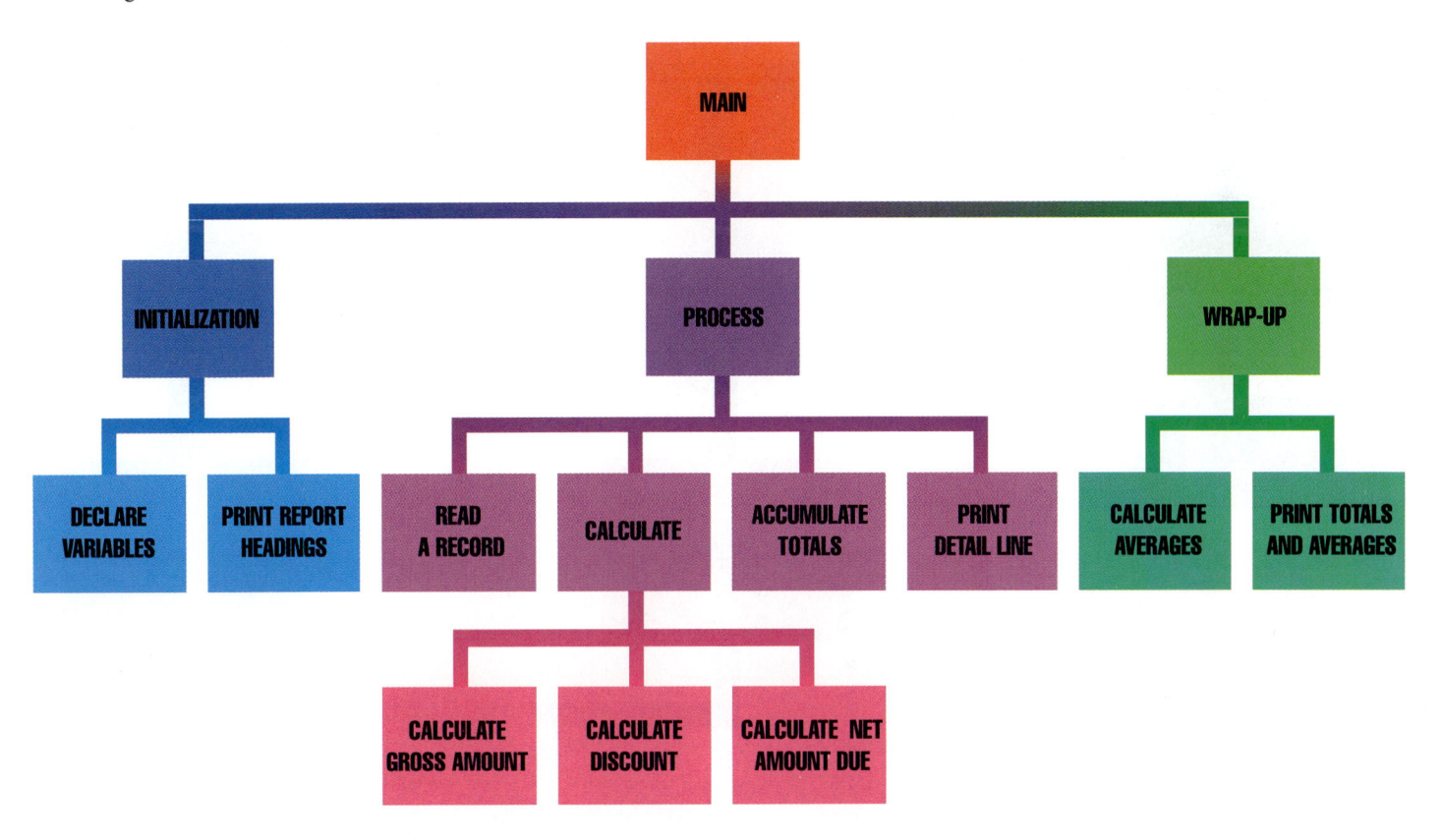

Figure 12-4
The hierarchy chart is a tool used by the programmer during top-down design. On the hierarchy chart, the program modules are drawn as rectangles. All modules are subordinate to the main module.

Structured Design

Once the programmer has identified the modules for a program (the *what*), the next step is to identify the logical order of the procedures required to accomplish the function described in each module (the *how*). A graphic or written description of the step-by-step procedures for a module is called the **solution algorithm** or **program logic**. Determining the logic for a program usually is the most challenging task for the programmer. It requires an understanding of structured design concepts as well as creativity. Thus, designing the solution algorithm is both an art and a skill.

Structured design is a methodology in which all program logic is constructed from a combination of three control structures or constructs. A **control structure** is a series of instructions that control the logical order in which the program instructions are executed. Each module in a program usually contains more than one control structure. The three basic control structures used in structured design are sequence, selection, and repetition.

Sequence Control Structure The **sequence control structure** is used to show a single action or one action followed sequentially by another, as shown in Figure 12-5. Actions can be inputs, processes, and outputs. Examples of actions might include reading a record, calculating averages and totals, and printing totals.

Selection Control Structure The **selection control structure** is used to tell the program which action to take, based on a certain condition. When the condition is evaluated, its result is either true or false. In Figure 12-6, the condition is represented by a diamond symbol. If the result of the condition is true, then one action is performed; if it is false, a different (or possibly no) action is performed.

inCyber
For an explanation of a structured design application, visit the Discovering Computers Chapter 12 inCyber page (http://www.scsite.com/dc/ch12/incyber.htm) and click Structured Design.

Figure 12-5
The sequence control structure is used to show a single action or one action followed by another.

Figure 12-6
One form of the selection control structure is the if-then-else, which is used to direct the program toward one course of action or another based on the evaluation of a condition.

For example, the selection control structure can be used to determine if an employee should receive overtime pay. Suppose the condition is, Is Hours Worked greater than 40? If the response is yes (true), then the action would calculate straight-time pay and overtime pay. If the response is no (false), then the action would calculate only straight-time pay. For this reason, this form of the selection control structure sometimes is called an **if-then-else control structure**.

When the condition in an if-then-else is evaluated, it yields one of two possibilities: true or false. The **case control structure** is a variation of the selection control structure; it is used when a condition can yield one of three or more possibilities (Figure 12-7). The size of a soft drink, for example, might be one of four possibilities: small, medium, large, or extra large. A case control structure would be used to determine the price based on the size purchased.

Repetition Control Structure The **repetition control structure**, also called the *looping*, or *iteration*, control structure, is used when a set of actions are to be performed repeatedly as long as a certain condition is met. Two forms of the repetition control structure exist: do-while and do-until.

> **inCyber**
> For an explanation of case control structure, visit the Discovering Computers Chapter 12 inCyber page (http://www.scsite.com/dc/ch12/incyber.htm) and click Case.

CASE CONTROL STRUCTURE

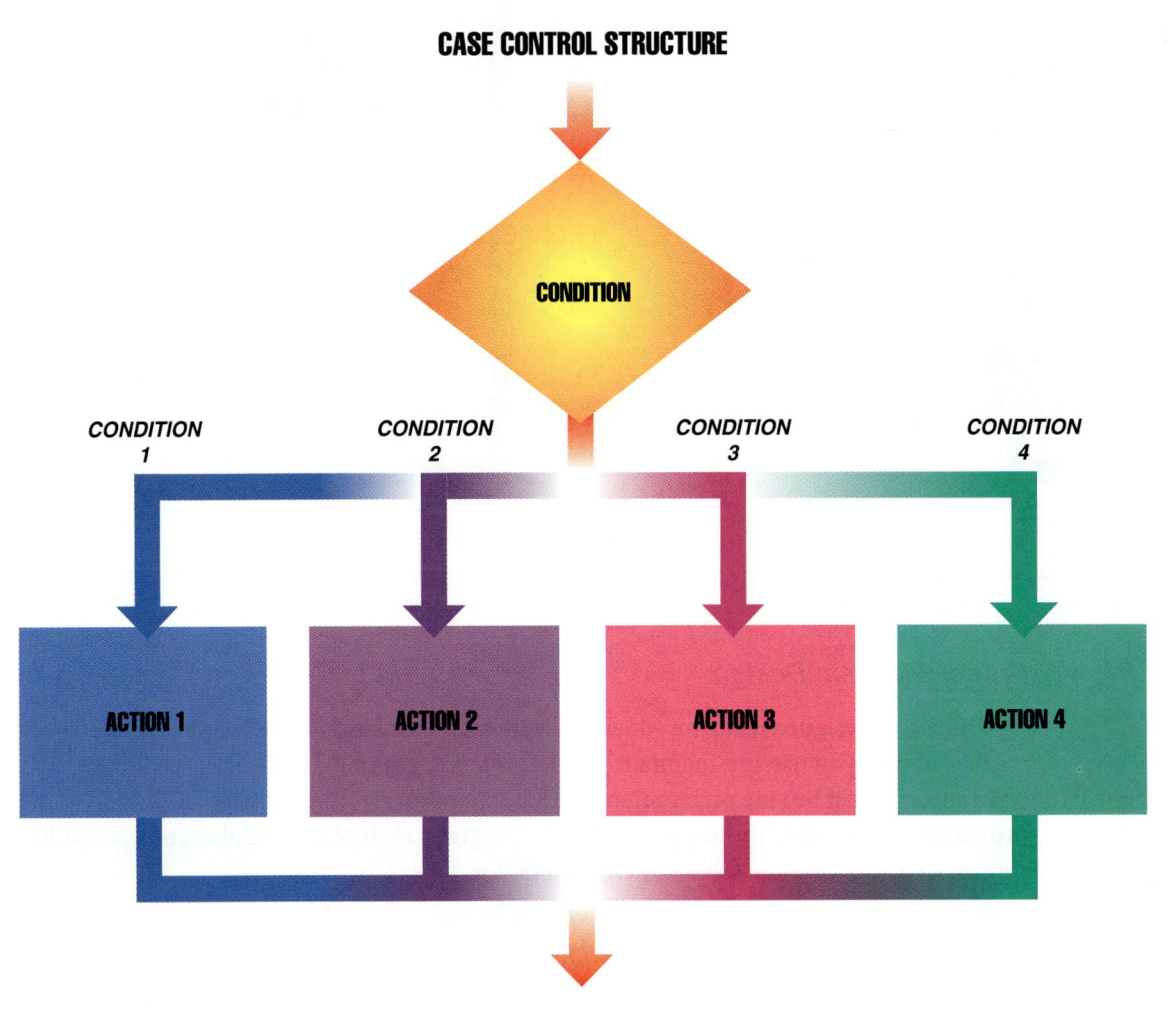

Figure 12-7
Another form of the selection control structure is the case, which allows for more than two alternatives when the condition is evaluated.

The **do-while control structure** repeats as long as a condition is true (Figure 12-8). The do-while control structure tests the condition at the *beginning* of the loop and, if the result of the condition is true, the action(s) inside the loop is executed. Then, the program *loops* back and tests the condition again. If the result of the condition is still true, the action(s) inside the loop is executed again. This looping process continues until the condition being tested becomes false. At that time, the program exits the loop and moves to another set of actions in the algorithm. The do-while control structure is used frequently to process all records in a file. For example, a payroll program using a do-while control structure would loop once for each employee and terminate looping when the last employee's payroll has been processed.

The do-until control structure is similar to the do-while, but it has two major differences. First, the **do-until control structure** tests the condition at the *end* of the loop (Figure 12-9). This means that the action(s) in a do-until control structure always will execute at least once. A do-while control structure, by contrast, might never execute at all, if the condition is false the first time it is tested. Second, where the do-while exits when the condition is false, the do-until control structure exits the loop when the condition is true.

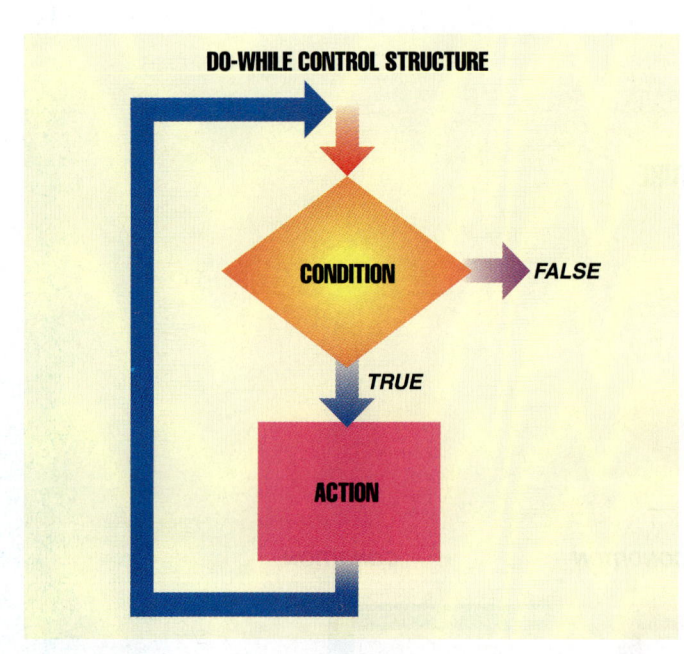

Figure 12-8
One form of the repetition control structure is the do-while, which tests the condition at the beginning of the loop.

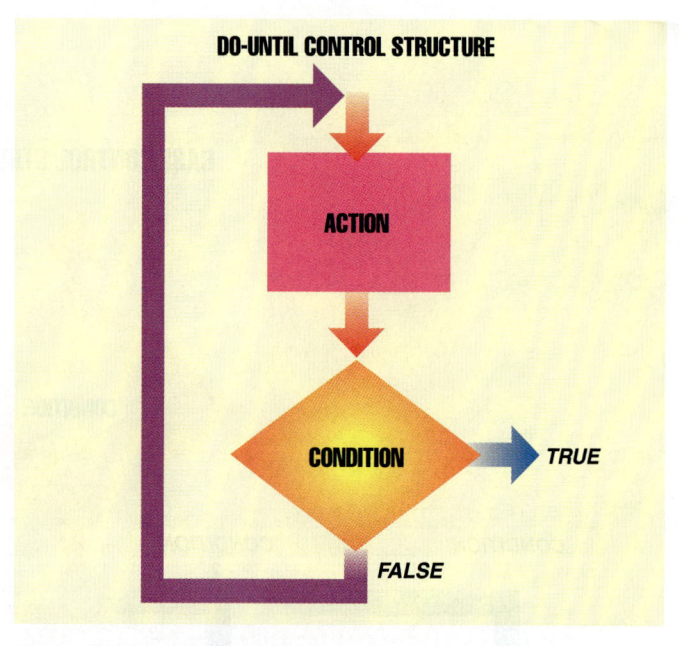

Figure 12-9
Another form of the repetition control structure is the do-until, which tests the condition at the end of the loop.

Proper Program Design

Programs designed using top-down and structured techniques are simple, yet effective, reliable, and easy to use and maintain. While designing programs using these techniques, a programmer must be sure each program adheres to proper program design. A **proper program** is constructed in such a way that the program, each of its modules, and each of its control structures has the following characteristics:

1. No dead code
2. No infinite loops
3. One entry point
4. One exit point

Dead code is code that never is executed in a program. Sometimes when a programmer writes a program, he or she writes a section of code, and then decides not to use the code, but leaves the *dead code* in the program. Dead code serves no purpose and, thus, should not exist. An **infinite loop** is a set of instructions that repeats indefinitely, or forever. Properly designed business programs should not contain infinite loops.

An **entry point** is the location where a program, a module, or a control structure begins, and an **exit point** is where it ends. Figure 12-10 shows the entry and exit points of a module with multiple control structures: an if-then-else control structure within a do-while control structure. The entry point of the do-while control structure is just prior to the first condition, and the exit point occurs when the result of this condition is false. The entry point of the if-then-else control structure occurs just prior to the second condition, and the exit point occurs just after one of the two actions is executed.

Prior to the introduction of structured design concepts, many programs had multiple entry and exit points, which made them awkward to read and difficult to maintain. Because these poorly designed programs frequently jumped from one section of code to another, they often were called *spaghetti code*. That is, if you drew a line connecting all of the jumps together, the resulting line would look like a bowl of spaghetti! If you restrict program logic to the three basic control structures, however, your algorithms naturally will follow the single entry and single exit point rules.

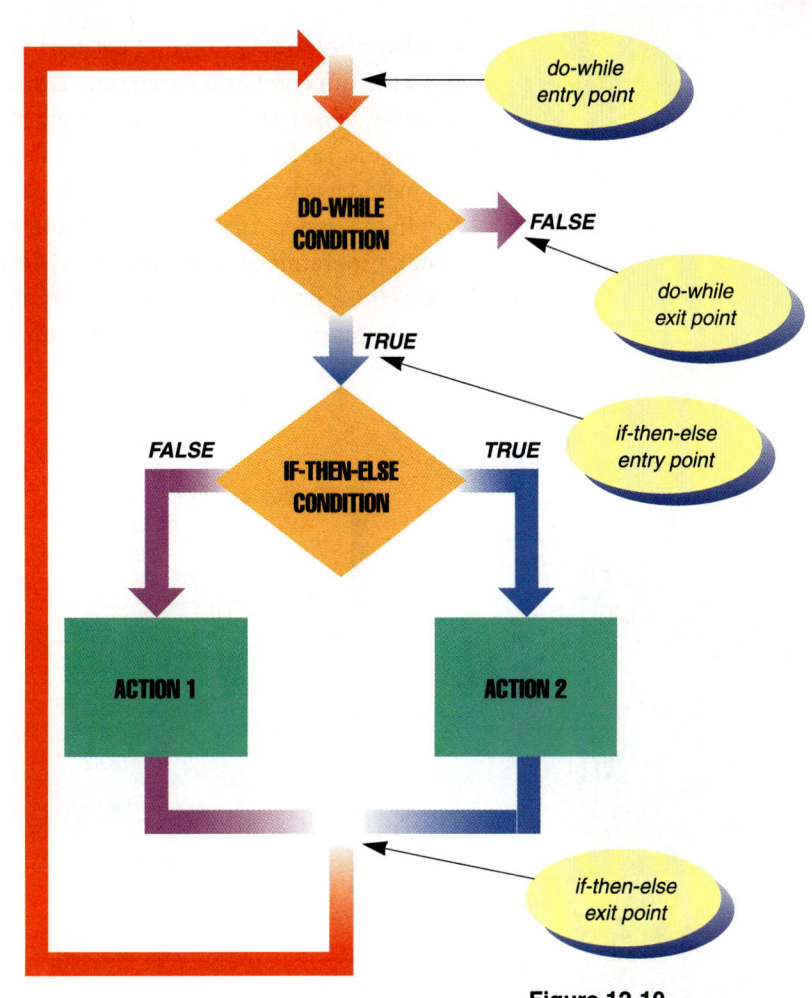

Figure 12-10
Program modules often have control structures nested inside one another, each of which should have one entry point and one exit point. In this example, an if-then-else is nested inside a do-while. The entry and exit points adhere to proper program design.

Design Tools

To help develop the logic for a solution algorithm, programmers use design tools. Three commonly used design tools are program flowcharts, Nassi-Schneiderman charts, and pseudocode.

Program Flowchart A **program flowchart** is a design tool used to show graphically the logic in a solution algorithm. The American National Standards Institute (ANSI) published a set of standards for program flowcharts in the early 1960s. These standards, still used today, specify symbols used to represent various operations in a program's logic (Figure 12-11).

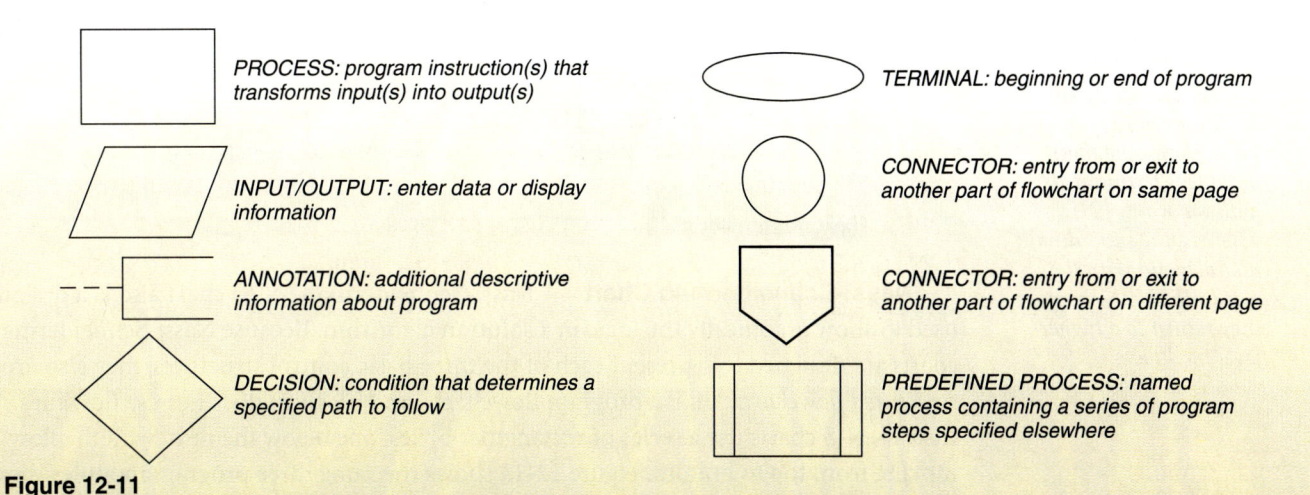

Figure 12-11
Standard symbols used to create program flowcharts.

Most symbols on a program flowchart are connected by *flowlines*, which are solid lines that show the direction of the program. Dotted lines are used to connect annotation or comment symbols, which explain or clarify logic in the algorithm.

Figure 12-12 shows the program flowchart for three modules of the program shown in the hierarchy chart in Figure 12-4 on page 12.5.

In the past, programmers used a template to trace the symbols for a flowchart on paper. Today, programmers use commercial flowcharting software to develop flowcharts, which makes these flowcharts easy to modify and update. Today's flowcharts also use structured design constructs, which early program flowcharts did not use.

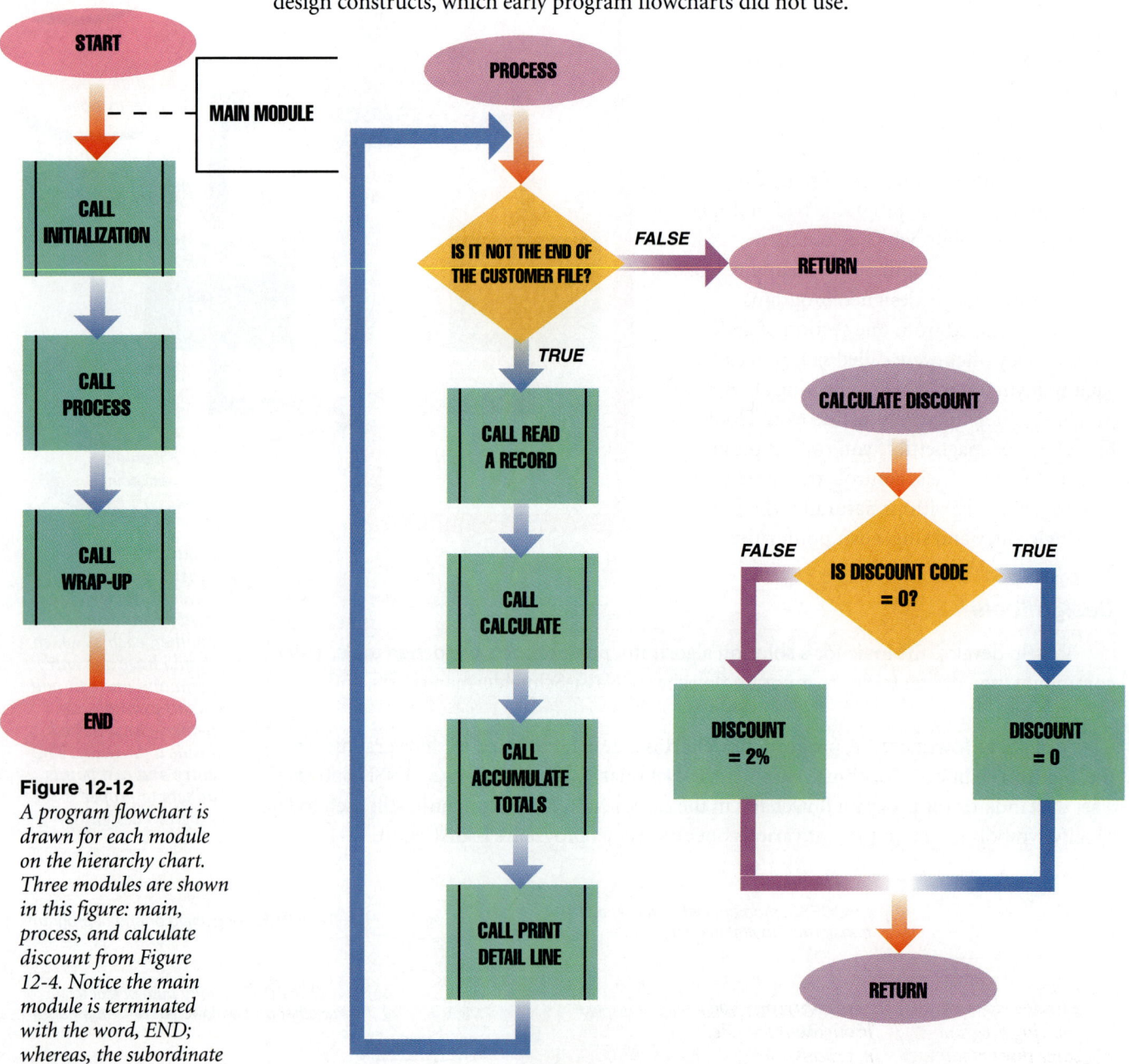

Figure 12-12
A program flowchart is drawn for each module on the hierarchy chart. Three modules are shown in this figure: main, process, and calculate discount from Figure 12-4. Notice the main module is terminated with the word, END; whereas, the subordinate modules end with the word, RETURN, because they return to a higher-level module.

Nassi-Schneiderman Chart A Nassi-Schneiderman (N-S) chart also is a design tool used to show graphically the logic in a solution algorithm. Because Nassi-Schneiderman charts are designed to represent each of the three basic control structures, they also are called *structured flowcharts*. Unlike program flowcharts, an N-S chart does not use flowlines. Instead, N-S charts use a series of rectangular boxes, one below the next, with the flow always moving from top to bottom. Figure 12-13 shows the same three program modules shown in Figure 12-12 in the form of an N-S chart.

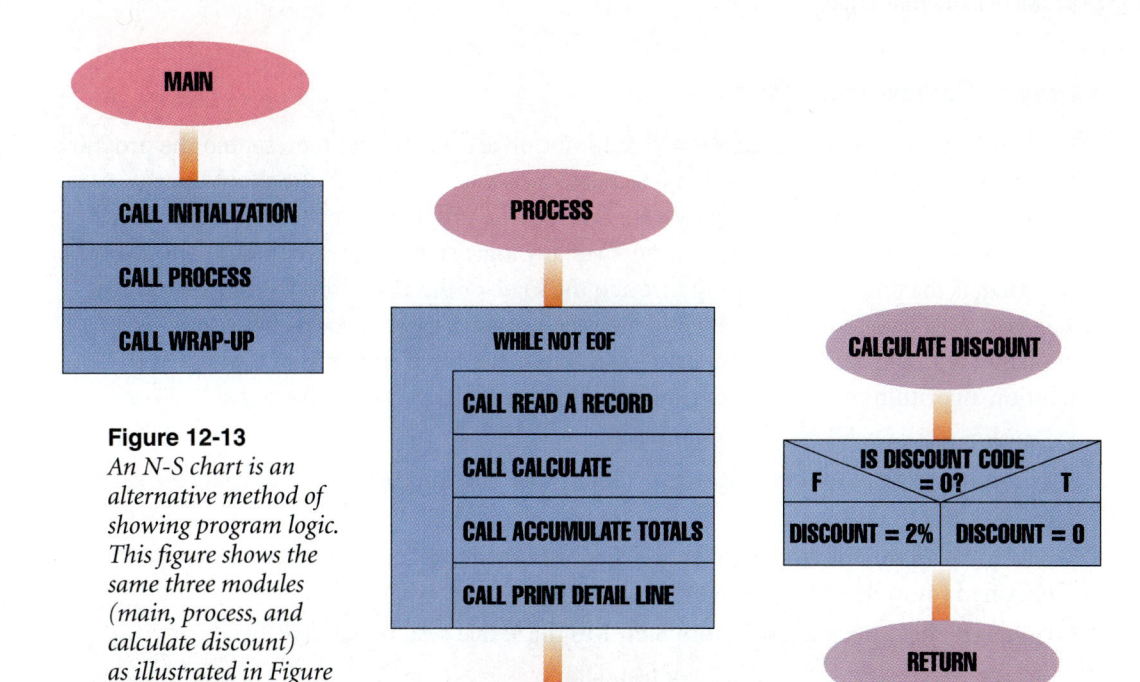

MAIN

| CALL INITIALIZATION |
| CALL PROCESS |
| CALL WRAP-UP |

Figure 12-13
An N-S chart is an alternative method of showing program logic. This figure shows the same three modules (main, process, and calculate discount) as illustrated in Figure 12-12 with program flowcharts.

PROCESS

| WHILE NOT EOF |
| CALL READ A RECORD |
| CALL CALCULATE |
| CALL ACCUMULATE TOTALS |
| CALL PRINT DETAIL LINE |

RETURN

CALCULATE DISCOUNT

| IS DISCOUNT CODE = 0? |
| F | T |
| DISCOUNT = 2% | DISCOUNT = 0 |

RETURN

Pseudocode Some programmers prefer to explain the logic in a solution algorithm with a more English-like technique (rather than a graphical flowcharting technique). A design tool called **pseudocode** uses an abbreviated form of English to outline program logic. The three basic control structures are represented through indentation: the beginning and end of the module are placed at the left margin, and the actions within the module are indented. This allows you to identify clearly the actions within a module. The actions within a control structure in a module also are indented, so that the beginning and end of the control structure can be clearly identified. Figure 12-14 shows the pseudocode for the same three program modules as in Figures 12-12 and 12-13.

```
MAIN MODULE:

        CALL Initialization
        CALL Process
        CALL Wrap-Up
END

PROCESS MODULE:

        DO WHILE Not EOF
                CALL Read A Record
                CALL Calculate
                CALL Accumulate Totals
                ALL Print Detail Line
        ENDDO
RETURN

CALCULATE DISCOUNT MODULE:

        IF Discount Code = 0 THEN
                Discount = 0
        ELSE
                Discount = .02
        ENDIF
RETURN
```

Figure 12-14
Pseudocode is yet another alternative method of showing program logic. This figure shows the same three modules (main, process, and calculate discount) as illustrated in Figure 12-12 with program flowcharts and Figure 12-13 with N-S charts.

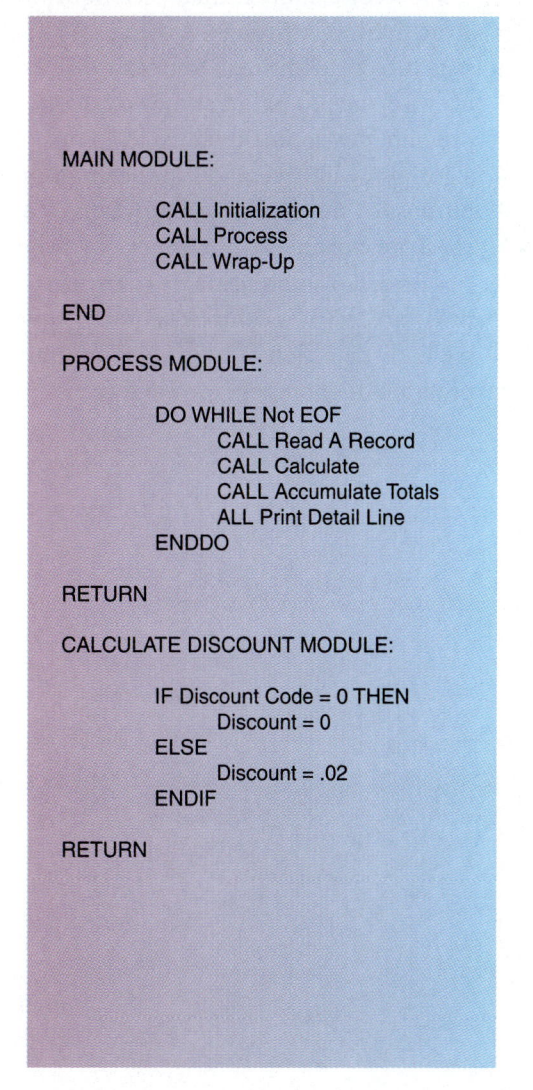

Quality Review Techniques

Once a programmer has developed the solution algorithm and represented the program logic using a program flowchart, an N-S chart, or pseudocode, he or she should perform a quality review of the program. During this review, the programmer checks the solution algorithm for correctness and tries to uncover any logic errors. One technique, called **desk checking**, is the process of stepping through the logic of the algorithm with test data. **Test data** is sample data that simulates valid data the program might process when it is implemented. The desk check can be performed by the programmer that developed the solution algorithm or another programmer. Desk checking involves five steps.

1. Develop sets of valid test data (inputs).
2. Without using the solution algorithm, determine the expected result (output) for each set of data.
3. Step through the solution algorithm using one set of test data. Write down the actual result obtained (output) using the solution algorithm.
4. Compare the expected result from Step 2 to the actual result from Step 3.
5. Repeat Steps 3 and 4 for each set of test data.

If the expected result and actual result do not match for each set of the data, the program has a **logic error**. You must review the logic of the solution algorithm to determine the source of the logic error and then correct it.

A second, more formal, technique for checking the solution algorithm is called a **structured walkthrough**. As discussed in Chapter 11, a systems analyst commonly uses a structured walkthrough to review deliverables during the system development life cycle; likewise, the programmer may request a walkthrough of a solution algorithm during the program development life cycle. In this case, the programmer explains the logic of the algorithm while members of the programming team step through the program logic. The purpose of this type of walkthrough is to identify any errors in the program logic and to check for possible improvements in program design.

Errors or improvements discovered during program design can be corrected easily. Once program design is complete and the programmer begins coding, errors are more difficult to fix. Early detection of errors and program design improvements thus reduces the overall program development time and cost.

Step 3 – Code Program

Coding a program involves two steps: (1) translate the solution algorithm into a programming language and (2) enter the programming language code into the computer. As previously mentioned, many different programming languages exist. Each of these has a particular set of grammar or rules that specify how the instructions in a solution algorithm are to be written, called **syntax**. An instruction to add three numbers, for example, is written differently in each programming language, according to its syntax. Fortunately, many of the commonly used programming languages follow a set of **code standards** developed by the American National Standards Institute (ANSI). Following these code standards ensures that the final program will run on many different types of computers, as well as many different operating systems.

As you enter the program into the computer, you should take time to document the program code thoroughly. In addition to any external program documentation such as flowcharts or N-S charts, a program also has its own documentation, called *comments* or *remarks*. A program should include both global and internal comments (Figure 12-15). Global comments are positioned at the top of the program to identify the program, its author, and the date written and to explain the program's purpose. Internal comments are written throughout the body of the program to explain the purpose of the code statements within the program. Programs that are documented thoroughly are much easier to maintain at a later date.

Step 4 – Test Program

Once the solution algorithm has been coded, the next step is to **test** the program. Thorough testing is very important, because once the program is put into use, many users will rely on the program and its output to support daily activities and decisions. The goal of program testing is to ensure that the program runs correctly and is error-free. Errors uncovered during this step usually are one of two types: (1) syntax errors or (2) logic errors.

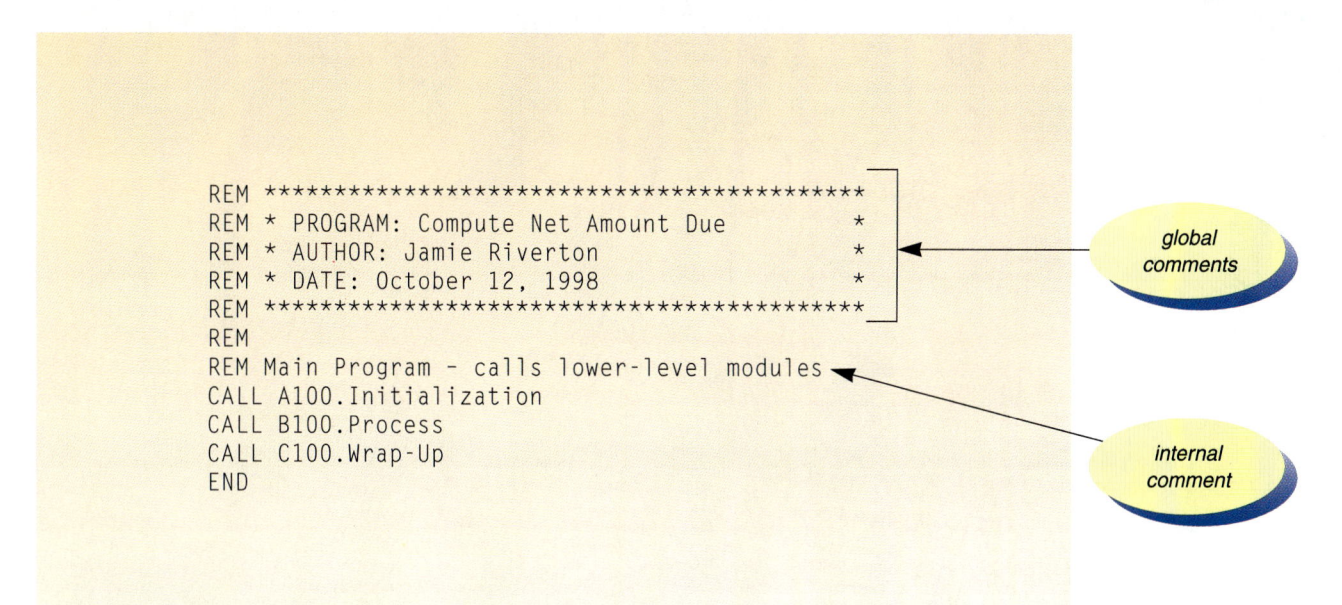

```
REM *********************************************
REM * PROGRAM: Compute Net Amount Due           *
REM * AUTHOR: Jamie Riverton                    *
REM * DATE: October 12, 1998                    *
REM *********************************************
REM
REM Main Program - calls lower-level modules
CALL A100.Initialization
CALL B100.Process
CALL C100.Wrap-Up
END
```

global comments — (top block of REM statements)

internal comment — (REM Main Program - calls lower-level modules)

Figure 12-15
Thorough documentation leads to maintainable programs. A program should contain global comments (at the top of the program) and internal comments (throughout the body of the program). In this QuickBASIC program, comments are identified by the letters, REM, which are an abbreviation for REMARK.

A **syntax error** occurs when the code violates the syntax, or grammar, of the programming language. For this reason, syntax errors sometimes are referred to as programming grammar errors. Misspelling a command, leaving out required punctuation, or typing command words out of order all will cause syntax errors. Syntax errors often are discovered the first time the computer executes the program code. When a syntax error is located, a message either immediately displays on the screen or is written to a log file. Either way, the programmer must review and correct all syntax errors.

The procedure for testing for **logic errors** at this step is similar to the desk checking techniques used in the Design Program step. First, test data must be developed. Unlike the Design Program step, in which the programmer develops the test data, the systems analyst usually develops the test data in the Test Program step. This ensures that the test data is unbiased. The test data should include both valid (correct) and invalid (incorrect) input data. When valid test data is input, the program should output the correct result. If the expected result and actual result do not match, the program has a logic error. You must review the logic of the program code to determine the source of the logic error and then correct it.

Another purpose of using test data is to try to *crash* the system; that is, try to make it fail. For example, if the pay rate for employees cannot exceed $55 per hour, then the test data should use some valid pay rates, such as $25 and $10.50, as well as some invalid ones, such as $-32.00 and $72.50. When you input an invalid pay rate, the program should display an error message and allow you to re-enter the pay rate. If, however, the program accepts the invalid pay rates, a logic error has occurred.

Figure 12-16
In 1945, the cause of the temporary failure of the world's first electro-mechanical computer, the Mark 1, was traced to a dead moth (shown taped to the log book) caught in the electrical components. Some say this event is the origin of the term, bug, meaning computer error.

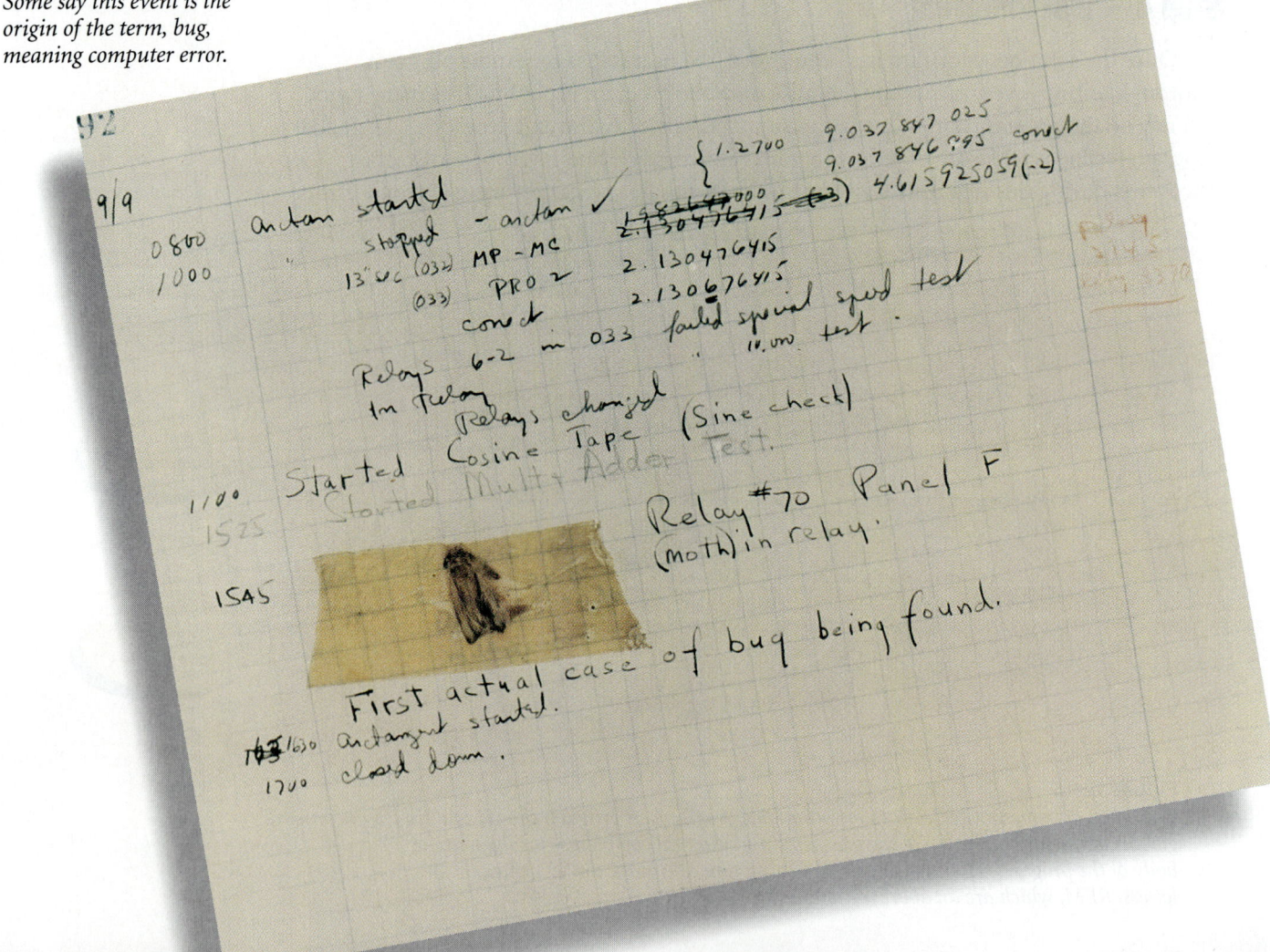

The process of locating and correcting syntax and logic errors in a program is called **debugging** the program. The errors themselves are referred to as **bugs**; thus, removing the errors is *debugging*. A popular story is that the term, bug, originated when the failure of one of the first computers was traced to a moth (a bug) lodged in the computer's electronic components (Figure 12-16). Most programming languages include a **debug utility** or **debugger**. A debugger allows you to identify syntax errors and to find logic errors by examining program values (such as the result of a calculation) while the program runs in slow motion.

If a program has been well designed during the Design Program step, then testing should not require much time. If the programmer did not test the solution algorithm thoroughly during design, however, then many logic errors may exist and testing will take longer. As a general rule, the more time and effort the programmer spends in analyzing and designing the solution algorithm, the less time he or she will spend debugging the program.

Step 5 – Formalize Solution

In **formalizing the solution**, the programmer performs two activities: (1) review the program code and (2) review all the documentation.

First, you want to review the program for any dead code and remove it. After you remove any dead code, you should run the program one final time to be sure it still works.

After reviewing the program code, the programmer gives the program and all of the documentation to the systems analyst. The documentation includes the following: a hierarchy chart; a solution algorithm in the form of an N-S chart, a program flowchart, or pseudocode; test data; and program code listings containing global and internal comments. You should review each of these documents to be sure they are complete and accurate.

Documentation becomes especially valuable if changes must be made to the program at a later date. For example, one year later, a new programmer might have to update the program. Proper documentation substantially reduces the amount of time the new programmer spends learning about the program, so he or she can make changes more effectively and efficiently.

Step 6 – Maintain Program

Maintaining a program involves two activities: (1) correct errors and (2) add enhancements. Once a program is implemented, or placed into production, users use the program to process real, or *live*, transactions. During the course of its use, a program will require maintenance. One type of maintenance occurs when users find syntax or logic errors. If the solution algorithm and program code were tested thoroughly in the previous steps, the number of errors found during production should be very small.

A more common type of maintenance occurs when a user would like the program to have different features or functionality. Program enhancement involves modifying or expanding the existing program.

When an error or an enhancement is identified, the user usually notifies the systems analyst, who in turn contacts and meets with the programmer. Sometimes, this is the same programmer that wrote the original program; other times, that programmer is unavailable, and a new programmer meets with the systems analyst. During the initial meeting, the systems analyst and the programmer begin *analyzing the problem or enhancement*, which is Step 1 in the program development life cycle. The program development life cycle thus completes its loop and the program development life cycle begins again.

Summary of the Program Development Life Cycle

The key to developing high-quality programs for an information system is to follow the steps in the program development life cycle and to complete the activities within each step. The program specification package, for example, should be understood completely before design begins. Programmers should use the top-down approach to program design; and the program code itself should be structured; that is, it should use the three basic control structures. Finally, the program should be tested thoroughly and documented completely. If each of the steps in the program development life cycle is followed carefully and thoroughly, the resulting programs will be correct, readable, and easy to maintain.

What Is a Programming Language?

A **programming language** is a set of words, symbols, and codes that enables the programmer to communicate the solution algorithm to the computer. Just as humans understand a variety of spoken languages (English, Spanish, French, and so on), computers recognize a variety of programming languages. A computer programmer can select from a variety of programming languages to code a solution algorithm.

Categories of Programming Languages

Several hundred programming languages exist, each with its own language rules or syntax. Some languages were developed for specific computers; others were developed for specific uses, such as scientific or business applications. As previously noted, the American National Standards Institute (ANSI) has standardized some of these languages. Programs written in an ANSI-standard language can run on many different types of computers, as well as many different operating systems.

Programming languages are classified in five major categories: machine languages, assembly languages, third-generation languages, fourth-generation languages, and natural languages. Machine and assembly languages are referred to as low-level languages; third-generation, fourth-generation, and natural languages are called high-level languages. A **low-level language** is machine-dependent; that is, it is written to run on one particular computer. A **high-level language** is machine-independent, which means high-level language code can run on many different types of computers.

---

inCyber

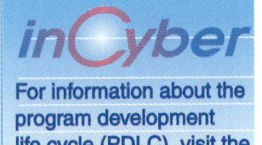

For information about the program development life cycle (PDLC), visit the Discovering Computers Chapter 12 inCyber page (http://www.scsite.com/dc/ch12/incyber.htm) and click Program Development.

Machine Languages

The only language that the computer directly understands is **machine language**, which also is called the first-generation language. Machine language instructions use a series of binary digits (1s and 0s) that correspond to the on and off electrical states of a computer (Figure 12-17). Because the computer understands machine language directly, these programs do not require translation. One disadvantage of machine language programs is that, while they run efficiently on the computer for which they were developed, machine language programs run *only* on the machine for which they were developed; that is, they are **machine-dependent**. Second, as you might imagine, coding in the 1s and 0s of machine language can be tedious and time-consuming.

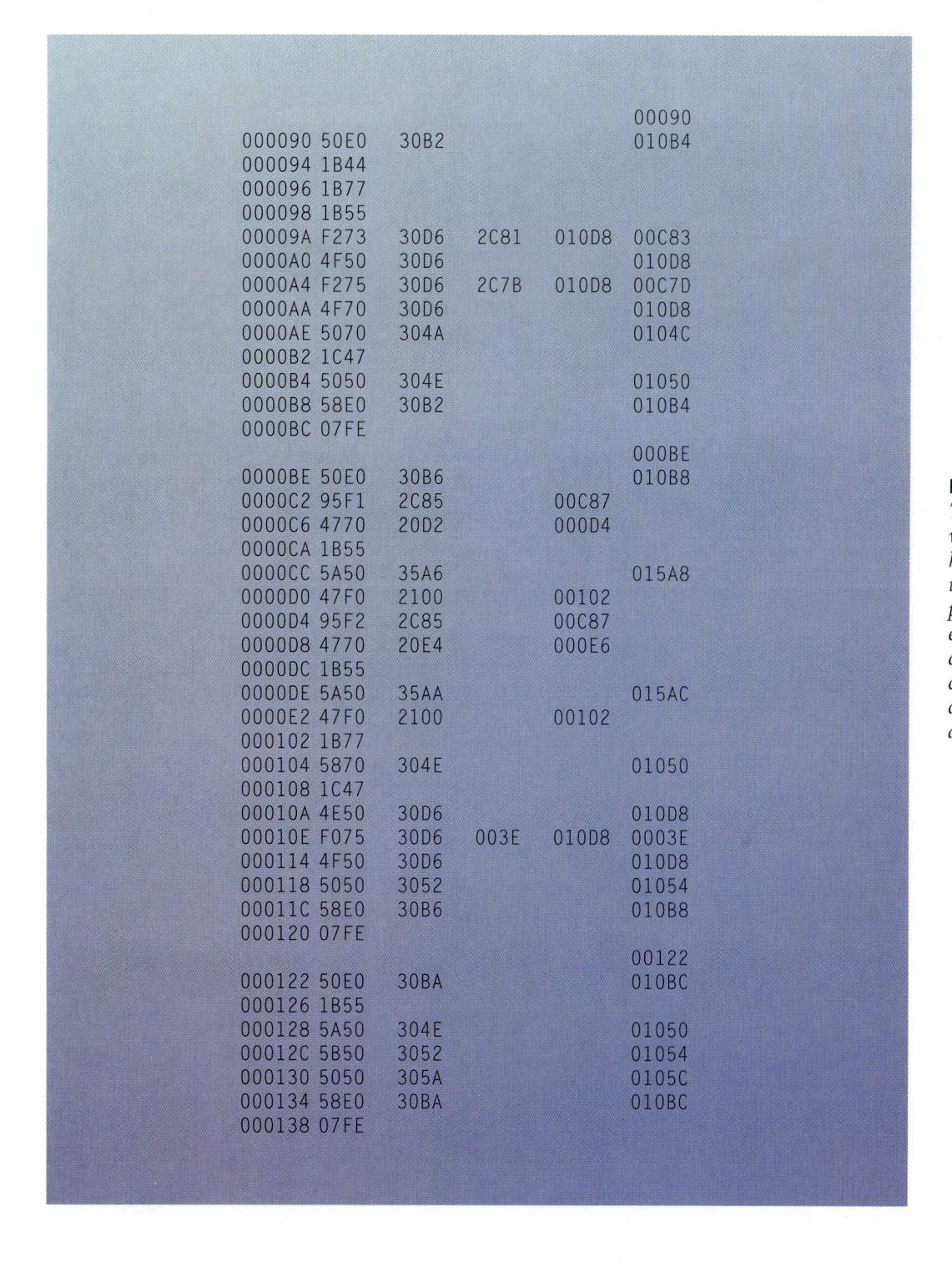

```
                                              00090
000090 50E0    30B2                           010B4
000094 1B44
000096 1B77
000098 1B55
00009A F273    30D6    2C81    010D8   00C83
0000A0 4F50    30D6                    010D8
0000A4 F275    30D6    2C7B    010D8   00C7D
0000AA 4F70    30D6                    010D8
0000AE 5070    304A                    0104C
0000B2 1C47
0000B4 5050    304E                    01050
0000B8 58E0    30B2                    010B4
0000BC 07FE
                                              000BE
0000BE 50E0    30B6                           010B8
0000C2 95F1    2C85            00C87
0000C6 4770    20D2            000D4
0000CA 1B55
0000CC 5A50    35A6                    015A8
0000D0 47F0    2100            00102
0000D4 95F2    2C85            00C87
0000D8 4770    20E4            000E6
0000DC 1B55
0000DE 5A50    35AA                    015AC
0000E2 47F0    2100            00102
000102 1B77
000104 5870    304E                    01050
000108 1C47
00010A 4E50    30D6                    010D8
00010E F075    30D6    003E    010D8   0003E
000114 4F50    30D6                    010D8
000118 5050    3052                    01054
00011C 58E0    30B6                    010B8
000120 07FE
                                              00122
000122 50E0    30BA                           010BC
000126 1B55
000128 5A50    304E                    01050
00012C 5B50    3052                    01054
000130 5050    305A                    0105C
000134 58E0    30BA                    010BC
000138 07FE
```

Figure 12-17
The machine language version (printed in hexadecimal) of these three modules in the program designed earlier in Figure 12-4: calculate gross amount, calculate discount, and calculate net amount due.

```
*            THIS MODULE CALCULATES THE GROSS PAYMENT
CALGROSS  EQU   *
          ST    14,SAVEGROS
          SR    4,4
          SR    7,7
          SR    5,5
          PACK  DOUBLE,QTYIN
          CVB   5,DOUBLE
          PACK  DOUBLE,PRICEIN
          CVB   7,DOUBLE
          ST    7,PRICE
          MR    4,7
          ST    5,GROSS
          L     14,SAVEGROS
          BR    14
*            THIS MODULE CALCULATES THE DISCOUNT
CALCDISC  EQU   *
          ST    14,SAVDISC
TEST1     CLI   CODEIN,C'1'
          BNE   TEST2
          SR    5,5
          A     5,=F'0'
          B     AROUND
TEST2     CLI   CODEIN,C'2'
          SR    5,5
          A     5,=F'2'
AROUND    SR    7,7
          L     7,GROSS
          MR    4,7
          CVD   5,DOUBLE
          SRP   DOUBLE,62,5
          CVB   5,DOUBLE
          ST    5,DISC
          L     14,SAVEDISC
          BR    14
*            THIS MODULE CALCULATES THE NET PAYMENT
CALCNET   EQU   *
          ST    14,SAVENET
          SR    5,5
          A     5,GROSS
          S     5,DISC
          ST    5,NET
          L     14,SAVENET
          BR    14
```

Figure 12-18

The assembly language version of machine language shown in Figure 12-17.

Assembly Languages

Because machine language programs were so difficult to write, a second generation of programming languages, called assembly languages, evolved. **Assembly language** instructions are written as symbols and codes (Figure 12-18); assembly language thus is referred to as a **symbolic programming language**. As with machine languages, assembly languages often are difficult to learn and are machine-dependent. Assembly languages do have several advantages over machine languages. Instead of using a series of bits, the programmer uses meaningful abbreviations for program instructions, called **symbolic instruction codes**, or **mnemonics**. For example, the programmer writes A for addition, C for compare, L for load, M for multiply, and so on. Another advantage of assembly languages is that the programmer can refer to storage locations with **symbolic addresses**. For example, instead of using the actual numeric storage address of a unit price, the programmer can use the symbolic name PRICE.

One disadvantage of an assembly language program is that it must be translated to machine language before the computer can understand it. The program containing the assembly language code is called a **source program**. The computer cannot understand or execute this source program until it is translated. A program called an **assembler** is used to convert the assembly language source program into machine language that the computer can understand.

One assembly language instruction usually translates into one machine language instruction. In some cases, however, the assembly language includes **macros**, which generate more than one machine language instruction for a single assembly language instruction. Macros save the programmer time during program development, because one machine language instruction can trigger several actions.

Third-Generation Languages

The disadvantages of low-level machine and assembly languages led to the development of high-level languages in the late 1950s and 1960s. Unlike low-level languages, high-level languages make it easy for programmers to develop and maintain programs. In addition to being easy for programmers to learn and use, high-level languages are **machine-independent**, meaning they run on many different types of computers. Three categories of high-level languages exist: third-generation languages, fourth-generation languages, and natural languages.

A **third-generation language** (3GL) instruction is written as a series of English-like words. For example, the programmer writes ADD for addition or PRINT to print. Many third-generation languages also use arithmetic operators such as * for multiplication, + for addition, and so on. These English-like words and arithmetic notations simplify the program development process for the programmer.

Third-generation languages require that the program instructions tell the computer *what* is to be accomplished and *how* to do it; thus, 3GLs often are called **procedural languages**. With most 3GLs, these procedures are developed using both the top-down approach (modules) and structured constructs (sequence, selection, and repetition) within each module.

Like an assembly language program, the actual 3GL code is called the source program and must be translated to machine language before the computer can understand it. This translation process can be very complex, because one 3GL source program instruction translates into many machine language instructions. For third-generation languages, the translation is performed using one of two types of programs: a compiler or an interpreter.

A **compiler** converts the entire source program into machine language at one time. The machine language version that results from compiling the 3GL is called the **object code** or **object program**. The object code is stored on disk for execution at a later time.

While it is compiling the source program into object code, the compiler checks the source program's syntax and verifies that the data to be used in calculations or comparisons is defined properly in the program. The compiler then produces a program listing, which contains the source code and a list of program statements that violate the program language rules or syntax. This listing helps the programmer make necessary changes to the source code and debug the program. Figure 12-19 illustrates the compilation process.

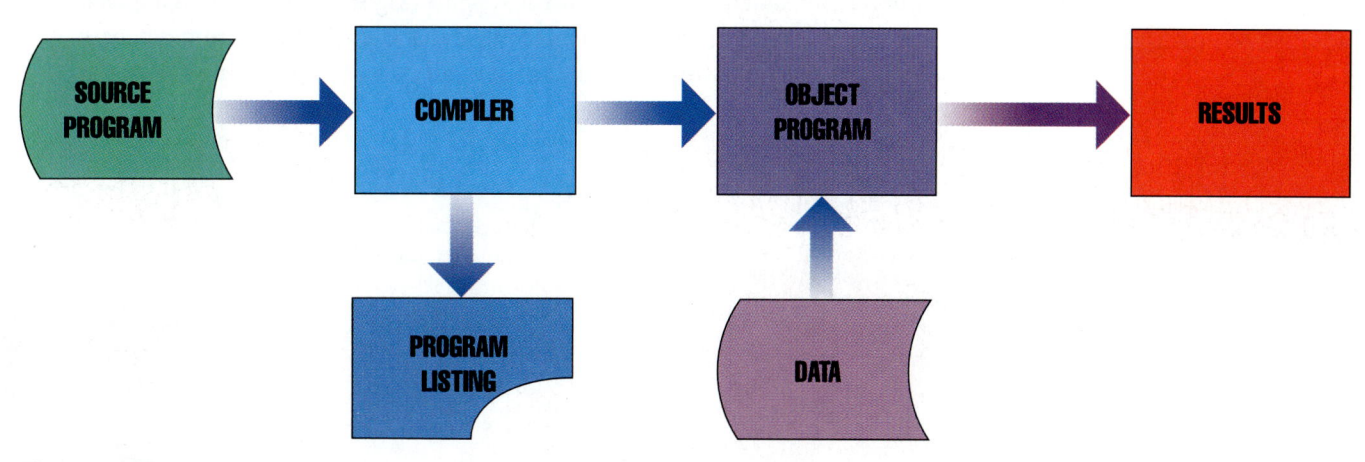

Figure 12-19
When a compiler is used, the entire source program is converted into a machine language object program. If the compiler encounters any errors, it records them in the program listing file, which the programmer may print when the entire compilation is complete. When the user wants to run the program, the object program is loaded into the memory of the computer and the program instructions begin executing.

While a compiler translates an entire program, an **interpreter** translates one program code statement at a time. That is, an interpreter reads a code statement, converts it to one or more machine language instructions, and then executes the machine language instructions — all before moving to the next code statement in the program. Each time you run the source program, it is interpreted into machine language, statement by statement, and then executed. No object program is produced. Figure 12-20 illustrates the interpretation process. One advantage of an interpreter is that it immediately displays feedback when it finds a code statement error. The programmer can correct any errors — that is, debug the code — before the interpreter evaluates the next line. The disadvantage is that interpreted programs do not run as fast as compiled programs because the program must be translated to machine language each time it is executed.

Many programming languages include both an interpreter and a compiler. The programmer uses the interpreter while debugging the program statement by statement, and then compiles the program when it is ready to be delivered to the users.

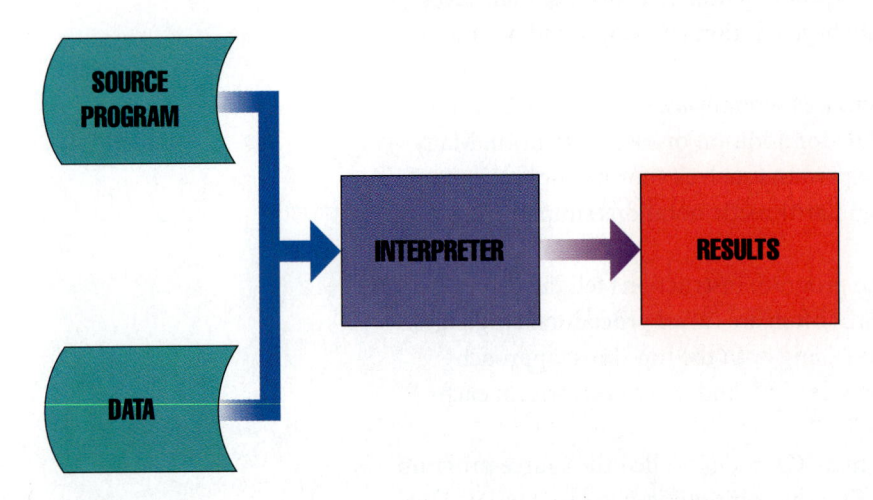

Figure 12-20
When an interpreter is used, one line of the source program at a time is converted into machine language and then immediately executed by the computer. If the interpreter encounters an error while converting a line of code, an error message immediately displays on the screen and the interpretation stops.

Fourth-Generation Languages

Like a 3GL, a **fourth-generation language** (4GL) uses English-like statements. A 4GL, however, is a **nonprocedural language**, which means the programmer has only to specify *what* is to be accomplished without explaining *how*. Consequently, coding programs in a 4GL requires much less time and effort on the part of the programmer. In fact, 4GLs are so easy to work with that users with very little programming background can develop programs using a fourth-generation language.

Many 4GLs work in conjunction with a database and its project dictionary or repository. These powerful languages allow database administrators to define the database and its structure, help programmers maintain the contents of the database tables, and let users query the database. SQL (Structured Query Language), for example, is a popular ANSI-standard 4GL used with relational database management systems (Figure 12-21). SQL is a **query language** that allows users and programmers to retrieve and display data from database tables. For example, one query might request a list of all customers receiving a discount.

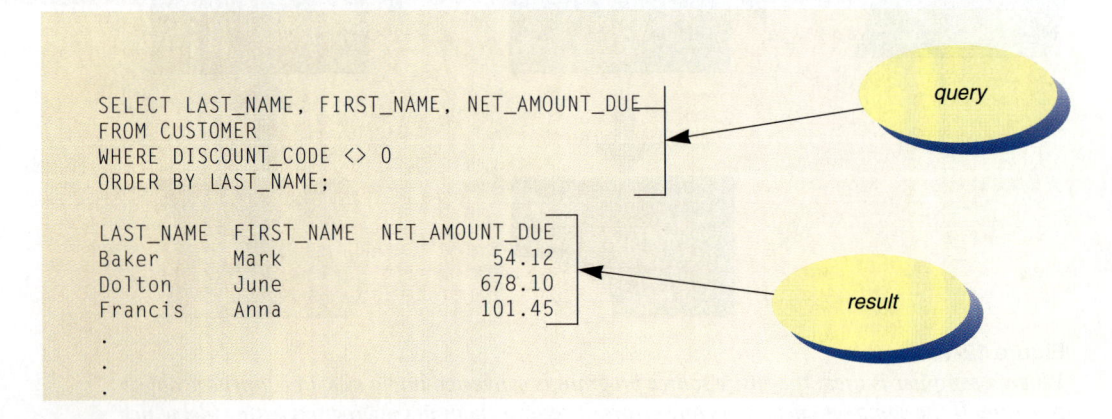

```
SELECT LAST_NAME, FIRST_NAME, NET_AMOUNT_DUE
FROM CUSTOMER
WHERE DISCOUNT_CODE <> 0
ORDER BY LAST_NAME;

LAST_NAME  FIRST_NAME  NET_AMOUNT_DUE
Baker      Mark                 54.12
Dolton     June                678.10
Francis    Anna                101.45
   .
   .
   .
```

Figure 12-21
SQL is a fourth-generation language that can be used to query database tables. This query produces an alphabetical list of those customers who receive a discount; that is, their discount code is not equal to zero.

Some database management systems (DBMSs) provide a software tool called a report generator. Like SQL, a **report generator**, or **report writer**, allows you to access and display data; in fact, it works behind the scenes to build a 4GL query for you. A report generator also allows you to format the query results professionally for display or hard copy output. Report generators usually are menu-driven tools with graphical interfaces, which makes them very easy to use.

The emergence of software and program development tools such as query languages and report writers has **empowered** users — that is, these tools have given users the ability to write simple programs and satisfy information processing requests on their own. In the past, for example, database queries and reports were generated by information systems personnel. Now, using these types of tools, users can build queries, access data, and display and format reports themselves. More program development tools are discussed later in the chapter.

Natural Languages

Whereas a fourth-generation language program must follow a specific set of rules and syntax, a natural language program does not. A **natural language**, sometimes called a fifth-generation language, is a type of query language that allows the user to enter requests that resemble human speech. For example, an SQL query to obtain a list of GPAs that exceed 3.5 might be written as SELECT LAST_NAME, FIRST_NAME FROM STUDENT WHERE GPA > 3.5. A natural language version of that same query might be written as TELL ME THE NAMES OF STUDENTS WITH GPA OVER 3.5.

Natural languages often are associated with expert systems and artificial intelligence. These systems are popular in the medical field, but are not widely used in business applications.

inCyber
To see how a natural language system works, visit the Discovering Computers Chapter 12 inCyber page (http://www.scsite.com/dc/ch12/incyber.htm) and click Natural Language.

Object-Oriented Program Development

As discussed, the introduction of structured program design and its three basic constructs largely solved the problem of spaghetti code. Structured program design does not, however, provide a way to keep the data and the program (or procedure) together. Each program, therefore, has to define how the data will be used for that particular program. This can result in redundant programming code that must be changed every time the structure of the data is changed, such as when a new field is added to a table in a database.

A newer approach to developing software, called the object-oriented approach, eliminates this problem. With the **object-oriented** approach, the programmer packages the data and the program (or procedure) into a single unit called an **object**. The procedures in the object are called **operations**, or **methods**, and the data elements are called **attributes**, or **variables**.

The concept of packaging methods and attributes into a single object is called **encapsulation**; that is, the details of the object are encapsulated, or *hidden* from the user. The user knows the method that can be requested of the object but does not know the specifics of how the method is performed. For example, while you know how to accelerate your car, you might not know the mechanics of how the car actually speeds up when you push the gas pedal. Thus, the details of your car are encapsulated, or hidden from you. Because encapsulation hides details of the object, it is sometimes called *information hiding*.

An object may be part of a larger category of objects, called a **class**. Every object in a class shares similar methods and attributes as the original object. Each class can have one or more lower levels called **subclasses** (Figure 12-22). For example, fire truck, delivery truck, and dump truck are all subclasses of the higher-level class, truck. The higher-level class is called a **superclass**. Each subclass inherits the methods and attributes of the objects in its superclass. For example, all trucks have clearance lights (which would be an attribute in the truck object), but only fire trucks have fire hoses. This concept of lower levels inheriting methods and attributes of higher levels is called **inheritance**.

A specific occurrence of an object or object class is called an **object instance**. For example, Engine 12 sitting in the fire station in your town is an instance of the fire truck object.

To make an object do something, you send it a message. A **message** tells the object what to do; that is, it indicates the name of the method to be used. For example, turn right might be a method of the truck object.

A major benefit of the object-oriented approach is the ability to reuse and modify existing objects. For example, if a program had to track the movement of six fire trucks, a programmer could reuse the fire truck object over and over again. Thus, the object-oriented approach to program development saves programming time. When using this approach, however, the development team must use different analysis, design, and programming techniques and tools than those used in structured program development.

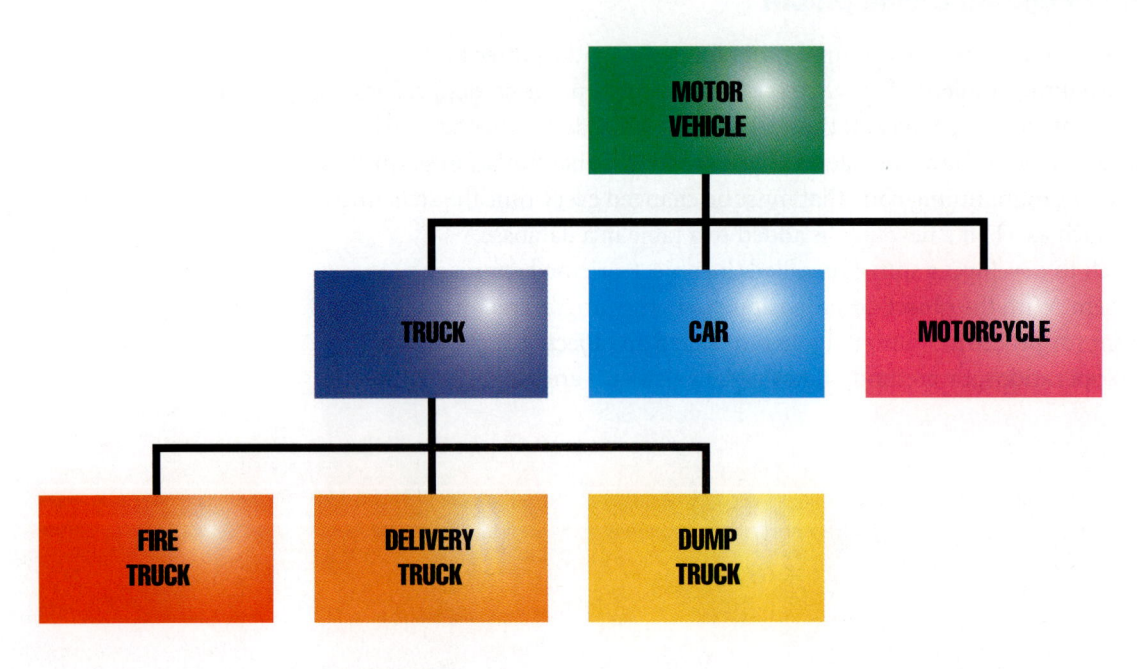

Figure 12-22
A generalization hierarchy is an object-oriented analysis tool used to show the relationship between classes of an object. In this figure, truck has three subclasses. A subclass inherits (or acquires) the attributes and methods of its higher class.

Object-Oriented Programming

If the object-oriented approach to program development is used, then the programming language used to implement the design model is an **object-oriented programming** (OOP) **language**.

One feature of an OOP language is that it is event-driven. An **event** is simply the OOP term for message. An event-driven program is designed to check for and respond to a set of messages or events. An event could be pressing a key on the keyboard, clicking the mouse, or typing a value into a text box. Some programming languages are only event-driven, while others are complete object-oriented languages. The next section covers specific examples of these and other programming languages in more detail.

inCyber

For links to object-oriented information, visit the Discovering Computers Chapter 12 inCyber page (http://www.scsite.com/dc/ch12/incyber.htm) and click OOP.

Popular Programming Languages

Although hundreds of programming languages have been developed, only a few are used widely enough today to be recognized as industry standards. Most of these are high-level languages that can be used on a variety of computers. This section discusses the commonly used programming languages, their origins, and their primary purpose.

To illustrate the similarities and differences of these languages, the program code for each language is shown. The code solves the same basic problem shown in the machine language in Figure 12-17 on page 12.17 and in the assembly language in Figure 12-18 on page 12.18. Using the same problem in each — computing the net amount due from a customer — allows you to compare languages solving the same problem. To compute the net amount due, you first multiply the quantity purchased by the unit price to obtain the gross price. Then, you compute the discount as follows: customers with a code of 0 receive no discount; all others receive a 2% discount. Finally, you subtract the discount from the gross price to determine the net amount due from the customer.

BASIC

Beginner's All-purpose Symbolic Instruction Code, or **BASIC**, was developed in the mid-1960s by John Kemeny and Thomas Kurtz at Dartmouth College. BASIC was designed to be a simple, interactive problem-solving language (Figure 12-23). Because it is so easy to learn and use, BASIC originally was intended as, and often is still, the introductory programming course for students. Today, BASIC is widely used on both personal computers and minicomputers to develop business applications. Many versions of BASIC exist, including MS-BASIC and QuickBASIC (or QBasic).

```
REM COMPUTE GROSS AMOUNT DUE
Gross.Amount = Unit.Price * Quantity.Purchased

REM COMPUTE NET AMOUNT DUE
IF Discount.Code = 0 THEN
    Net.Amount.Due = Gross.Amount
ELSE
    Discount.Amount = .02 * Gross.Amount
    Net.Amount.Due = Gross.Amount - Discount.Amount
END IF

REM PRINT NET AMOUNT DUE
PRINT USING "The net amount due is $###,###.##"; Net.Amount.Due
```

Figure 12-23
This figure shows an excerpt from a BASIC program. The code shows the computations for gross amount, discount amount, and net amount due; the decision to evaluate the discount value; and the output of the net amount due.

Visual Basic

Developed by Microsoft Corporation in the early 1990s, **Visual Basic** is a Windows application designed to assist programmers in developing other event-driven Windows applications. The first step in building a Visual Basic application is to design the graphical user interface (Figure 12-24a) using Visual Basic objects. Visual Basic objects, or *controls*, include items such as command buttons, text boxes, and labels.

Next, you write any code needed to define program events (Figure 12-24b). An event in Visual Basic can be the result of an action initiated by a user; for example, when a user clicks an object on the Visual Basic screen, the Click event is executed. Visual Basic events also can be created using code statements written in Visual Basic's own programming language. Visual Basic's programming language is very similar to BASIC and is easy to learn and use. Once you have completed these steps, you can generate the final application (Figure 12-24c). Because it is so easy to use, even novice programmers can create professional Windows-based GUI applications using Visual Basic.

inCyber

For more information on Visual Basic, visit the Discovering Computers Chapter 12 inCyber page (http://www.scsite.com/dc/ch12/incyber.htm) and click Visual Basic.

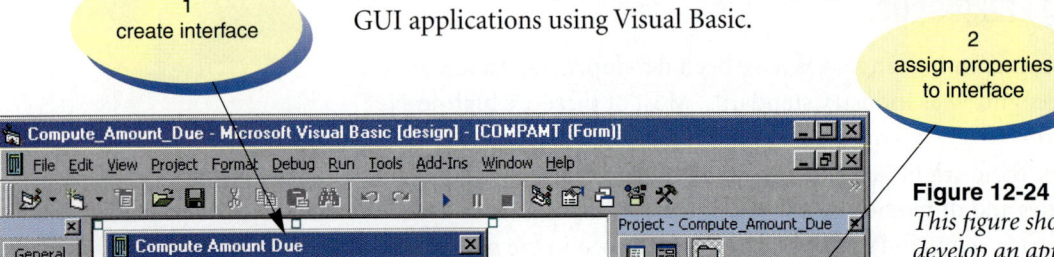

1 — create interface
2 — assign properties to interface
3 — write code and assign it to COMPUTE button

Figure 12-24
This figure shows how Visual Basic is used to develop an application. The first screen shows how the programmer designs the user interface. Unit Price and Quantity Purchased will be entered by the user. If appropriate, the Apply Discount check box will be selected; and finally, the COMPUTE button will be clicked to display the Total Due. The second screen shows the program code associated with the COMPUTE button. The code shows the computations for gross amount, discount amount, and net amount due; the decision to evaluate the discount value; and the output of the net amount due. The third screen shows the finished application with values entered and the resulting Total Due displaying.

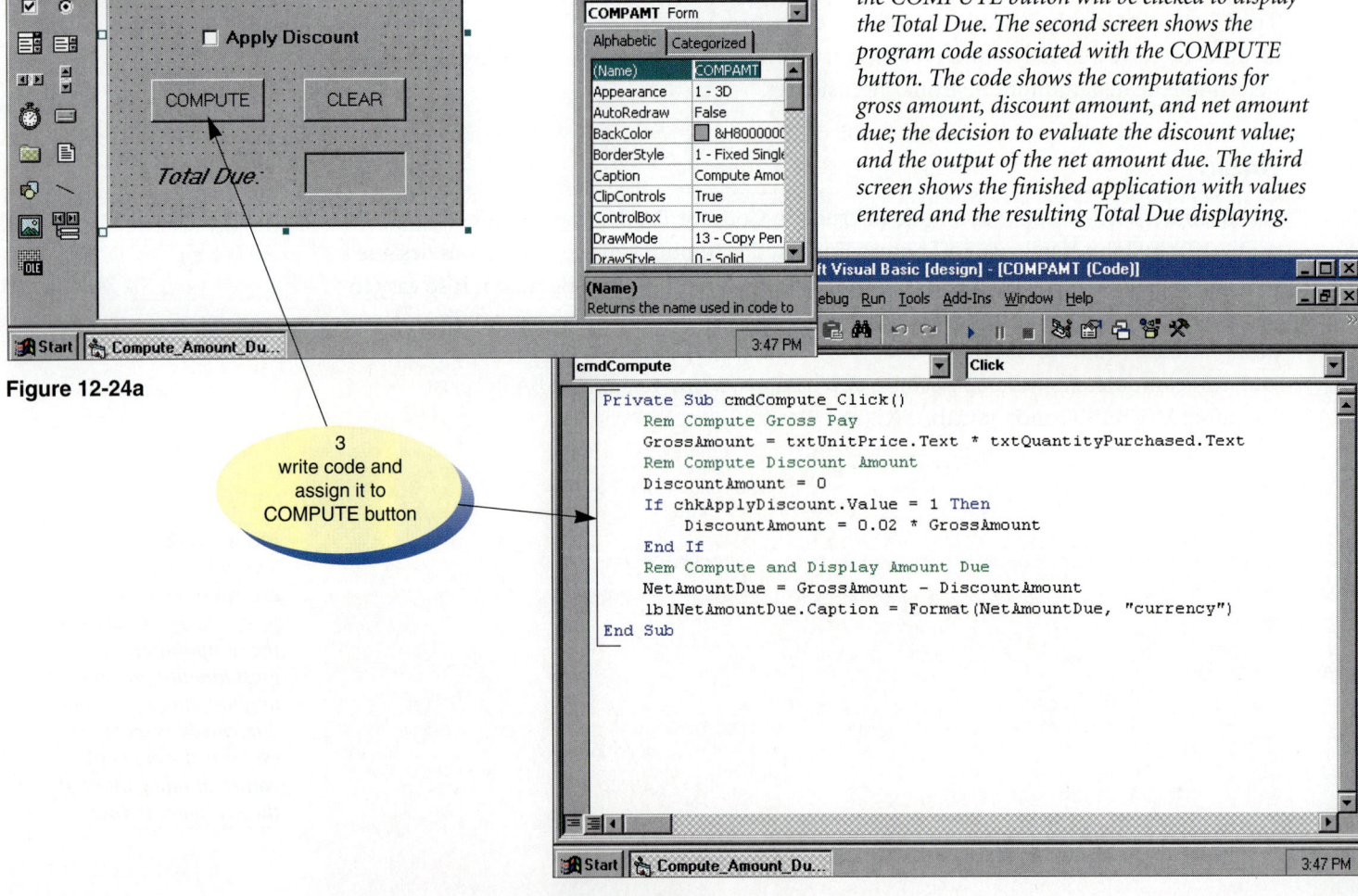

Figure 12-24a

Figure 12-24b

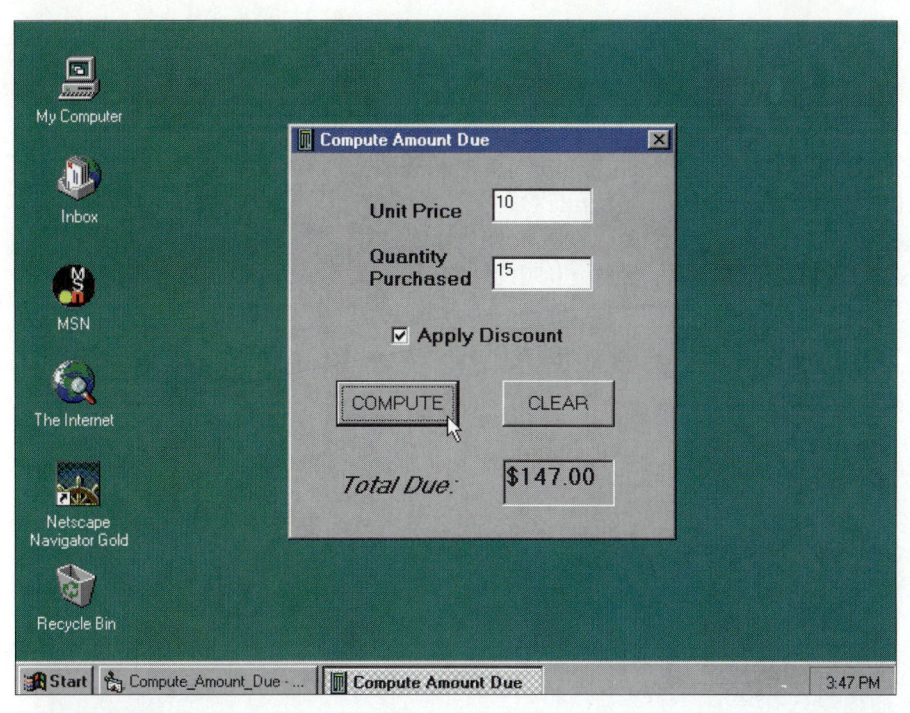

Figure 12-24c

COBOL

COBOL (COmmon Business Oriented Language) was developed in the early 1960s as a result of a joint effort between the U.S. government, businesses, and major universities. Naval officer Grace Hopper, a pioneer in computer programming, was a prime developer of the COBOL language.

COBOL is one of the more widely used programming languages for business applications. Although COBOL programs often are lengthy, their English-like statements make them easy to read, write, and maintain (Figure 12-25). While COBOL especially is useful for processing transactions on mainframes, COBOL is used on hardware platforms ranging from mainframes to personal computers. The most popular personal computer COBOL program is Micro Focus Personal COBOL.

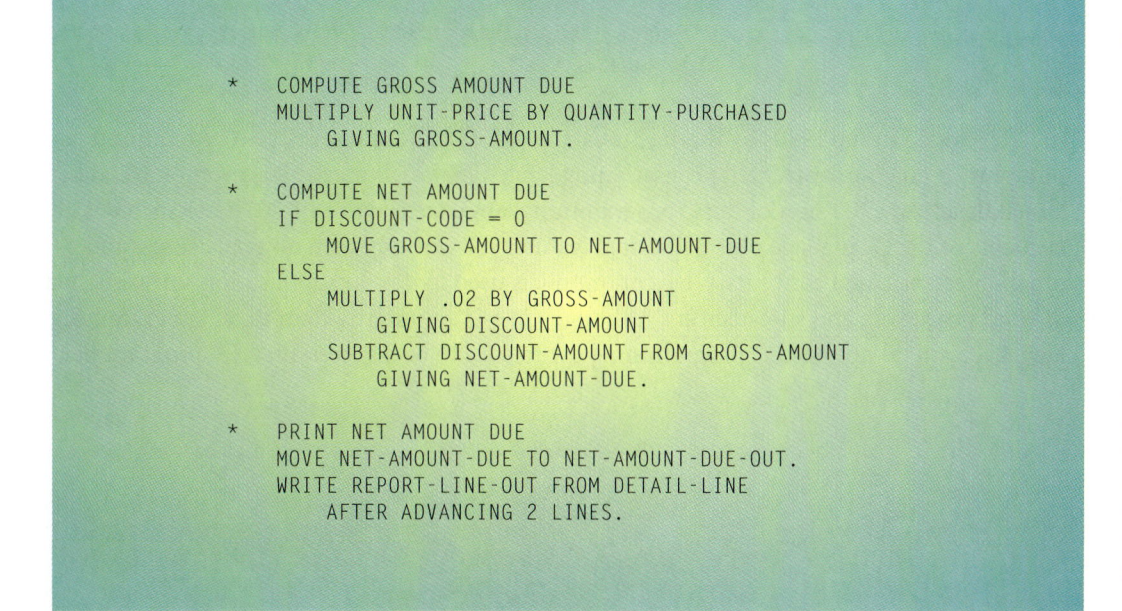

inCyber

For a biography of Grace Hopper, visit the Discovering Computers Chapter 12 inCyber page (http://www.scsite.com/dc/ch12/incyber.htm) and click Hopper.

```
*       COMPUTE GROSS AMOUNT DUE
        MULTIPLY UNIT-PRICE BY QUANTITY-PURCHASED
            GIVING GROSS-AMOUNT.

*       COMPUTE NET AMOUNT DUE
        IF DISCOUNT-CODE = 0
            MOVE GROSS-AMOUNT TO NET-AMOUNT-DUE
        ELSE
            MULTIPLY .02 BY GROSS-AMOUNT
                GIVING DISCOUNT-AMOUNT
            SUBTRACT DISCOUNT-AMOUNT FROM GROSS-AMOUNT
                GIVING NET-AMOUNT-DUE.

*       PRINT NET AMOUNT DUE
        MOVE NET-AMOUNT-DUE TO NET-AMOUNT-DUE-OUT.
        WRITE REPORT-LINE-OUT FROM DETAIL-LINE
            AFTER ADVANCING 2 LINES.
```

Figure 12-25
This figure shows an excerpt from a COBOL program. The code shows the computations for gross amount, discount amount, and net amount due; the decision to evaluate the discount value; and the output of the net amount due. Notice how much more wordy this program is compared to the BASIC program in Figure 12-23. It is, however, much more readable than the BASIC program.

C

The C programming language, developed in the early 1970s by Dennis Ritchie at Bell Laboratories, originally was designed as a language to write system software. Today, C is used to develop a wide variety of software, including operating systems and application software such as word processors and spreadsheets. While C is a powerful programming language that requires professional programming skills, its expanded use has allowed it to be categorized as a general-purpose language that is effective for both business and scientific applications (Figure 12-26). C runs on practically any hardware and software platform, but most often is used with the UNIX operating system. In fact, most of the UNIX operating system is written in C.

```
/* Compute Gross Amount Due                                    */
gross = price * qty_purch;

/* Compute Net Amount Due                                      */
if (disc_code == 0)
    net = gross;
else
    {
    disc_amt = .02 * gross;
    net = gross - disc_amt;
    }

/* Print Net Amount Due                                        */
printf("The net amount due is %d\n", net);
```

Figure 12-26
This figure shows an excerpt from a C program. The code shows the computations for gross amount, discount amount, and net amount due; the decision to evaluate the discount value; and the output of the net amount due.

C++

Developed in the 1980s by Bjarne Sroustrup at Bell Laboratories, C++ (pronounced C plus plus) is an object-oriented programming language, which means it is event-driven like Visual Basic. An extension of the C programming language (Figure 12-26), C++ includes all elements of the C language plus additional features for working with objects, classes, and other object-oriented concepts. C++ commonly is used to develop application software, such as word processors and spreadsheets. Although C++ is an outgrowth of the C programming language, you do not need C programming experience to be a successful C++ programmer.

FORTRAN

FORTRAN, which stands for **FOR**mula **TRAN**slator, was one of the first high-level programming languages. Developed in the late 1950s by a team of IBM programmers led by John Backus, FORTRAN was designed for scientific applications (Figure 12-27). Because the FORTRAN language is designed to handle complex mathematical and logical expressions, it is used most often by scientists, engineers, and mathematicians.

```
C       COMPUTE GROSS AMOUNT DUE
        GROSS = PRICE * QTY

C       COMPUTE NET AMOUNT DUE
        IF (CODE .EQ. 0) THEN
            NET = GROSS
        ELSE
            DISC = .02 * GROSS
            NET = GROSS - DISC
        ENDIF

C       PRINT NET AMOUNT DUE
        WRITE(CRTOUT,*) 'THE NET AMOUNT DUE IS $', NET
```

Figure 12-27
This figure shows an excerpt from a FORTRAN program. The code shows the computations for gross amount, discount amount, and net amount due; the decision to evaluate the discount value; and the output of the net amount due.

Pascal

In the late 1960s, a Swiss scientist named Niklaus Wirth created the **Pascal** programming language for the purpose of teaching structured programming concepts to students (Figure 12-28). He named the programming language in honor of the seventeenth-century French mathematician Blaise Pascal, who developed one of the earliest calculating machines. Today, the Pascal programming language is used on both personal computers and minicomputers to develop scientific applications. An object-oriented version of Pascal, called Turbo Pascal, has been developed by Borland Corporation.

```
(* COMPUTE GROSS AMOUNT DUE *)
GROSSAMOUNT := UNITPRICE * QUANTITYPURCHASED

(* COMPUTE NET AMOUNT DUE *)
IF DISCOUNTCODE = 0 THEN
    NETAMOUNTDUE := GROSSAMOUNT
ELSE
    BEGIN
        DISCOUNTAMOUNT := 02 * GROSSAMOUNT;
        NETAMOUNTDUE := GROSSAMOUNT - DISCOUNTAMOUNT
    END
END IF

(* PRINT NET AMOUNT DUE *)
WRITELN ('THE NET AMOUNT DUE IS $', NETAMOUNTDUE:7:2)
```

Figure 12-28
This figure shows an excerpt from a Pascal program. The code shows the computations for gross amount, discount amount, and net amount due; the decision to evaluate the discount value; and the output of the net amount due.

Ada

Derived from the Pascal programming language, **Ada** was developed in the late 1970s by the U.S. Department of Defense, which requires Ada to be used for all U.S. government military projects. The Department of Defense named the programming language after Augusta Ada Lovelace Byron, the Countess of Lovelace, who is thought to be the first female computer programmer. Ada originally was designed to meet the needs of embedded computer systems, which are computer systems that act as a control mechanism inside other computer systems (Figure 12-29). The Ada language, however, also can be used for business applications.

Figure 12-29
This figure shows an excerpt from an Ada program. The code shows the computations for gross amount, discount amount, and net amount due; the decision to evaluate the discount value; and the output of the net amount due.

```
-- COMPUTE GROSS AMOUNT DUE
GROSS_AMOUNT := UNIT_PRICE * QUANTITY_PURCHASED;

-- COMPUTE NET AMOUNT DUE
if DISCOUNT_CODE = 0 then
      NET_AMOUNT_DUE := GROSS_AMOUNT;
else
      DISCOUNT_AMOUNT := 02 * GROSS_AMOUNT;
      NET_AMOUNT_DUE := GROSS_AMOUNT - DISCOUNT_AMOUNT;
end if;

-- PRINT NET AMOUNT DUE
PUT ("THE NET AMOUNT DUE IS $");
PUT (NET_AMOUNT_DUE,7,2);
```

RPG

RPG, which stands for **Report Program Generator**, was introduced by IBM in the early 1960s to assist businesses in generating reports (Figure 12-30). Today, it also is used for complex computations and complicated file updating. Because RPG is a nonprocedural language, many advocates of RPG (and other report generators) claim it paved the way for 4GLs. Although a version with limited functionality is available for the personal computer, RPG primarily is used for application development on IBM midrange computer systems, such as the AS/400.

Figure 12-30
This figure shows an excerpt from an RPG program. The code shows the computations for gross amount, discount amount, and net amount due; the decision to evaluate the discount value; and the output of the net amount due.

```
C* COMPUTE GROSS AMOUNT DUE
C          PRICE    MULT QTY        GROSS   72
C*
C* COMPUTE NET AMOUNT DUE
C          CODE     IFEQ 0
C                   Z-ADDNET         GROSS   72
C                   ELSE
C          GROSS    MULT .02        DISC    52
C          GROSS    SUB  DISC       NET     72
C                   ENDIF
C
C* PRINT NET AMOUNT DUE
C                   EXCPTDETAIL
C*
O* OUTPUT SPECIFICATIONS
OQPRINT  E 2         DETAIL
O                                23 'THE NET AMOUNT DUE IS $'
O                       NET  J   34
```

Other Programming Languages

In addition to the commonly used programming languages just discussed, a number of other languages sometimes are used. Figure 12-31 lists some of these languages and their primary uses.

How to Select a Programming Language

Although each programming language has its own unique characteristics, selecting a language for a programming task can be a difficult decision. You should consider the following factors.

1. *The programming standards of the organization* — many organizations have programming standards that specify a particular language to be used for all applications.
2. *The need to interface with other programs* — if a program is going to work with other programs, it should be written in the same language as the other programs or a language compatible with the other programs.
3. *The suitability of the language to the application* — most languages are designed to work with particular applications, such as business applications, scientific applications, and so on.
4. *The need for portability to other systems* — if an application is to run on multiple hardware and software platforms, a language common to these systems should be selected.

Language	Description
ALGOL	ALGOrithmic Language, the first structured procedural language
APL	A Programming Language, a scientific language designed to manipulate tables of numbers
FORTH	Similar to C, used for device control applications
HYPERTALK	An object-oriented programming language developed by Apple to manipulate cards that can contain text, graphics, and sound
LISP	LISt Processing, a language used for artificial intelligence applications
LOGO	An educational tool used to teach programming and problem-solving to children
MODULA-2	A successor to Pascal used for developing systems software
PILOT	Programmed Inquiry Learning Or Teaching, used to write computer-aided instruction programs
PL/I	Programming Language One, a business and scientific language that combines many features of FORTRAN and COBOL
PROLOG	PROgramming LOGic, used for development of expert systems
SMALLTALK	Object-oriented programming language

Figure 12-31
Other programming languages.

Program Development Tools

The power of program development tools, or software tools, was noted earlier in this chapter in the discussion of query languages and report writers. **Program development tools** not only meet the complex processing requirements of programmers, but they also empower users because they are so easy to learn and use. This empowerment of users has allowed programmers to focus their development efforts on larger information systems projects, while empowered users create their own applications or simple programs within applications.

Application Generators

An **application generator**, or **program generator**, is a program that allows an application to be built without writing extensive code in a programming language. For this reason, programmers using an application generator to create an application can be more productive in a shorter time frame. In fact, many users unfamiliar with programming concepts can build applications with an application generator. As with 4GLs, then, application generators empower users with the capability of creating applications on their own.

When using an application generator, the developer (a programmer or user) works with menu-driven tools that have easy-to-use graphical interfaces. Some application generators create source code; others simply create object code. Although application generators are available as stand-alone programs, most often, you see them bundled with, or as a part of, a database management system. Common tools included with an application generator include report writers, form builders, and menu generators.

As discussed earlier, a report writer or report generator is a software tool that enables a developer to format data professionally for display or hard copy. With a report writer, you easily can include page numbers, dates, subtotals, totals, numeric formatting (such as dollars and cents), and column headings.

A **form builder**, or **screen painter**, allows the developer to design an input or output form on the computer screen. With a form builder, the developer simply types titles and headings directly on the screen and then describes the data elements to be used, usually by clicking at the location where the desired data element should display (Figure 12-32). The data elements are already defined in the data dictionary; thus, the format specifications such as length, type, and validation, are already defined. When the developer clicks the screen, the form builder simply accesses the dictionary for the format specifications of the data elements.

A **menu generator** allows the developer to create a menu, or list of choices, for the application options. For example, if you create three reports and two forms for an application, your menu would contain at least six options: one for each report, one for each form, and one to exit, or quit, the application.

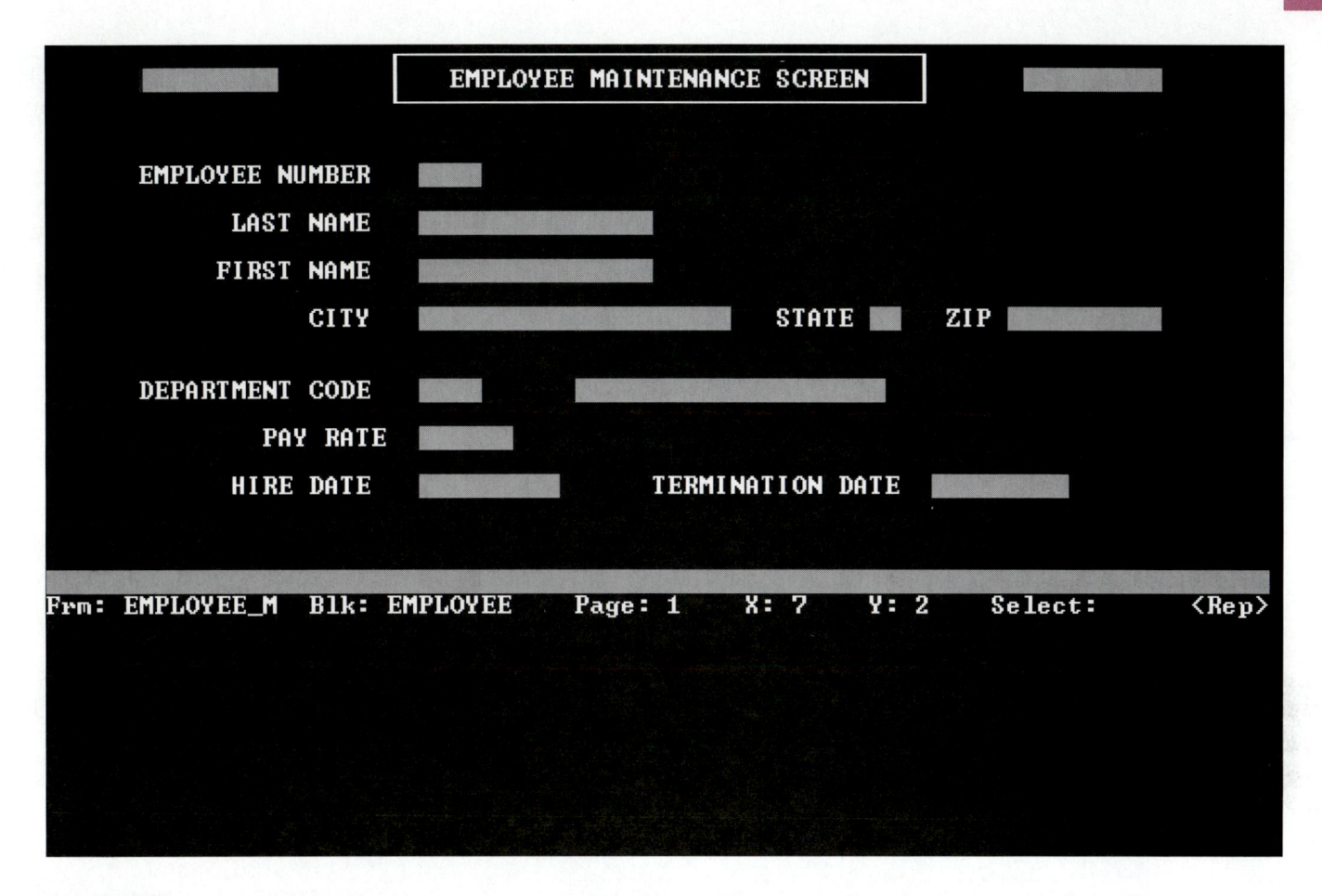

PROGRAM DEVELOPMENT TOOLS **12.31**

```
                    EMPLOYEE MAINTENANCE SCREEN

        EMPLOYEE NUMBER   ▓▓▓
             LAST NAME    ▓▓▓▓▓▓▓▓▓▓▓▓▓▓▓
            FIRST NAME    ▓▓▓▓▓▓▓▓▓▓▓▓▓▓▓
                  CITY    ▓▓▓▓▓▓▓▓▓▓▓▓▓▓▓▓▓▓▓   STATE ▓▓   ZIP ▓▓▓▓▓▓▓▓

        DEPARTMENT CODE   ▓▓▓▓   ▓▓▓▓▓▓▓▓▓▓▓▓▓▓▓▓
              PAY RATE    ▓▓▓▓▓
             HIRE DATE    ▓▓▓▓▓▓      TERMINATION DATE ▓▓▓▓▓▓▓


Frm: EMPLOYEE_M   Blk: EMPLOYEE    Page: 1    X: 7    Y: 2    Select:       <Rep>
```

Figure 12-32
With a form builder, the developer paints the screen to represent the input or output screen. In this figure, SQL*Forms by Oracle Corporation is used to create an Employee Maintenance Screen.

Macros

Empowered users also can create simple programs within applications by writing macros. A **macro** is a series of statements that instructs an application how to complete a task. Macros are used to automate routine, repetitive, or difficult tasks in an application such as word processing, spreadsheets, or databases. You usually can create a macro in one of two ways: (1) record the macro or (2) write the macro.

If you want to automate a routine or repetitive task, such as formatting or editing, you would **record a macro**. A macro recorder is similar to a movie camera, in that it records all actions you perform until you turn it off. To record a macro, you begin the macro recorder in the application and then record a series of actions. Once the macro is recorded, you can run it any time you want to perform that same set of actions. For example, you could record the actions required to format a number as a subscript, and then run the Format Number As Subscript macro repeatedly to change a selected number in a document to a subscript.

---

inCyber

For a variety of Excel macros, visit the Discovering Computers Chapter 12 inCyber page (http://www.scsite.com/dc/ch12/incyber.htm) and click Macro.

CHAPTER 12 – PROGRAM DEVELOPMENT AND PROGRAMMING LANGUAGES

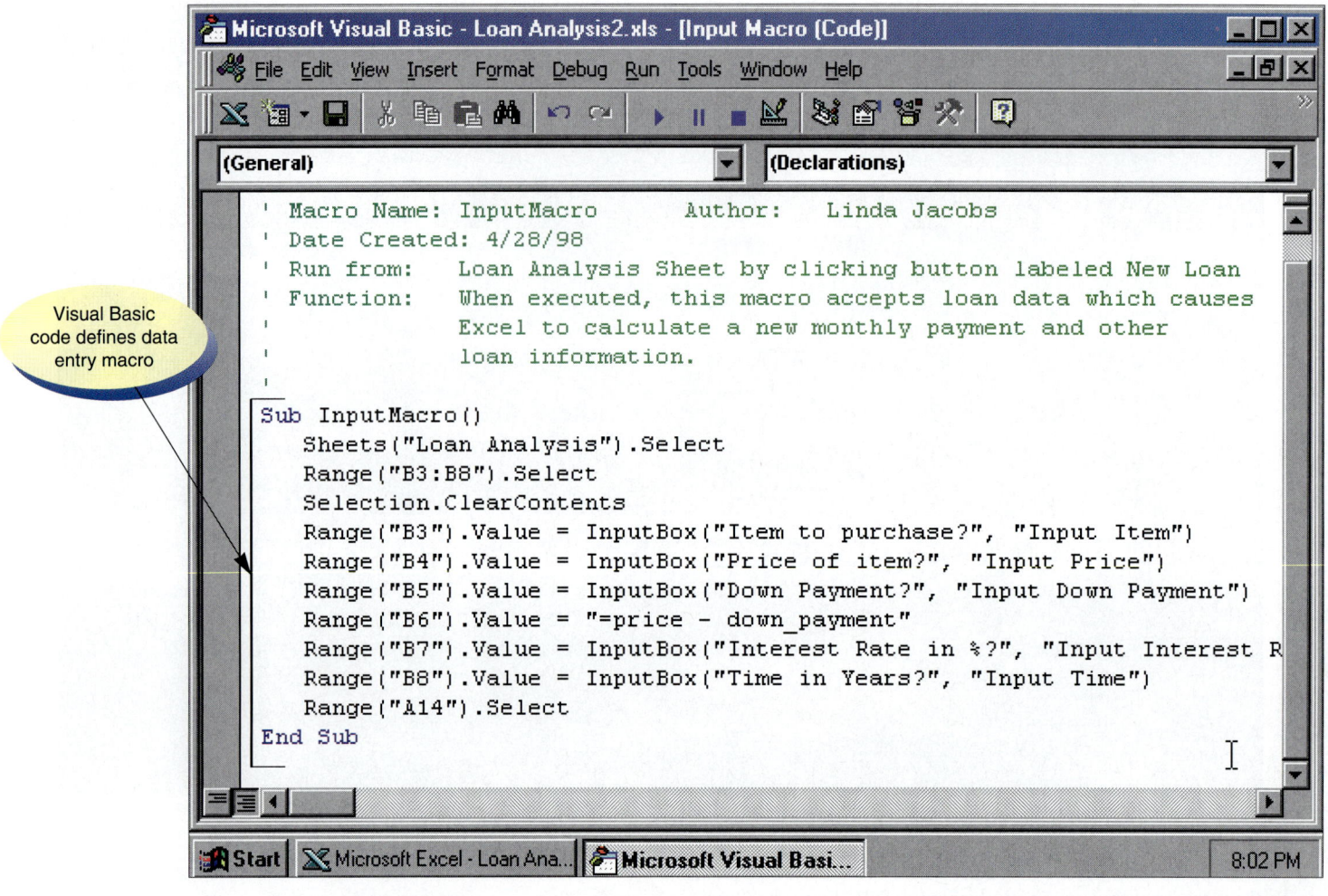

Visual Basic code defines data entry macro

```
' Macro Name: InputMacro       Author:     Linda Jacobs
' Date Created: 4/28/98
' Run from:      Loan Analysis Sheet by clicking button labeled New Loan
' Function:      When executed, this macro accepts loan data which causes
'                Excel to calculate a new monthly payment and other
'                loan information.
'
Sub InputMacro()
    Sheets("Loan Analysis").Select
    Range("B3:B8").Select
    Selection.ClearContents
    Range("B3").Value = InputBox("Item to purchase?", "Input Item")
    Range("B4").Value = InputBox("Price of item?", "Input Price")
    Range("B5").Value = InputBox("Down Payment?", "Input Down Payment")
    Range("B6").Value = "=price - down_payment"
    Range("B7").Value = InputBox("Interest Rate in %?", "Input Interest R
    Range("B8").Value = InputBox("Time in Years?", "Input Time")
    Range("A14").Select
End Sub
```

Figure 12-33   **Figure 12-33a**

The first screen shows a Visual Basic macro used to automate a loan data entry into a worksheet. After a macro is written, the user clicks the New Loan button to launch the macro. The second screen shows the macro guiding the user through the data entry process.

If you are familiar with programming techniques, you can write your own macros instead of recording them. Many applications use Visual Basic or a similar language as their macro programming language. Macros written in Visual Basic code use the three basic structured programming constructs within modules as well as objects, classes, and other object-oriented concepts. The objects in a Visual Basic macro, however, apply only to the specific application for which the macro was developed. For example, in a spreadsheet, an object might be a cell, a range of cells, a chart, or the worksheet.

The macro in Figure 12-33a shows an Excel macro used to automate the data entry process for a loan. Figure 12-33b shows the dialog box generated from the macro that prompts the user to enter the name of the item being purchased.

RAD Tools: Visual Basic, Delphi, and PowerBuilder

Rapid application development (**RAD**) is the process of developing software through prototyping. The idea behind **prototyping** is to create a model, or *prototype*, that meets the users' requirements as closely as possible. This way, a minimum amount of work is required to convert the prototype into an implemented solution; thus, the application is developed rapidly.

Figure 12-33b

- dialog boxes guide you through data entry process
- New Loan button launches macro

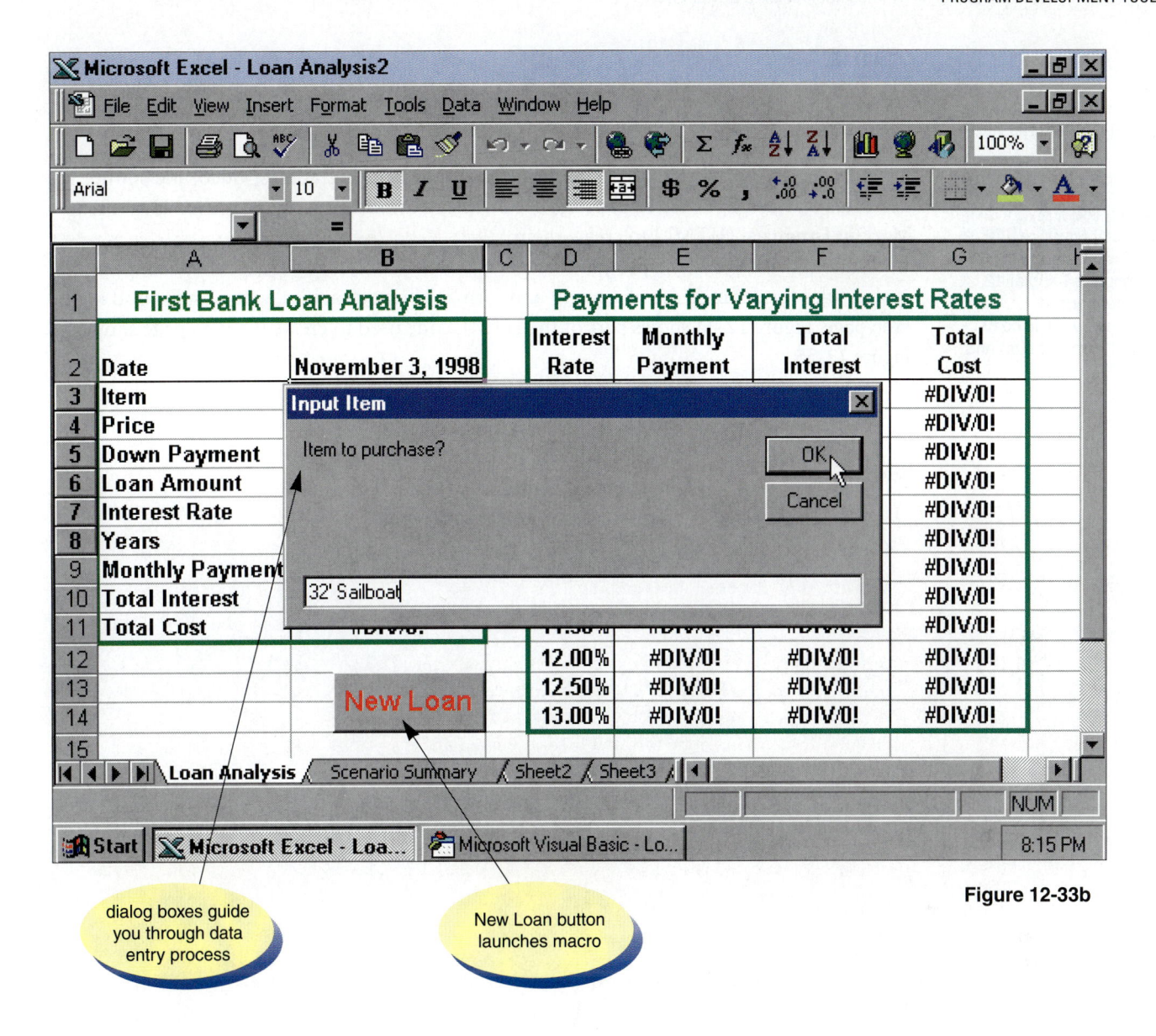

Rapid application development requires the use of RAD tools, which allow you to develop easy-to-maintain, component-based applications. A **component** is simply another term for object. Thus, a RAD tool must include an object-oriented programming language. Three popular RAD tools are Visual Basic, Delphi, and PowerBuilder.

Visual Basic Microsoft's **Visual Basic** was one of the first programming environments to allow developers to drag-and-drop objects to build Windows applications. The ease of use of Visual Basic's event-driven programming makes it a popular RAD tool.

Delphi Borland's **Delphi** is another popular RAD tool. This powerful tool offers a drag-and-drop visual-programming environment. Whereas Visual Basic uses only an event-driven language, Delphi uses Object Pascal, which provides full object-oriented capabilities. Because it has more functionality and features than Visual Basic, Delphi is slightly more complicated to learn and use.

PowerBuilder Another RAD tool, called **PowerBuilder**, uses a proprietary language to help with rapid application development. This language, called PowerScript, is similar to BASIC and C. Although PowerBuilder is not completely object-oriented like Delphi, it can be used to create powerful applications. PowerBuilder is very difficult to learn.

inCyber

For information on Borland's Delphi, visit the Discovering Computers Chapter 12 inCyber page (http://www.scsite.com/dc/ch12/incyber.htm) and click Delphi.

HTML

For a guide to HyperText Markup Language, visit the Discovering Computers Chapter 12 inCyber page (http://www.scsite.com/dc/ch12/incyber.htm) and click HTML.

Recall that the collection of linked documents accessible on the Internet has become known as the World Wide Web, or simply, the Web. Each linked document on the Web, called a Web page, is a hyperlinked document that can contain text, graphics, video, and sound. The designers of Web pages, called authors, use a special formatting language called **HyperText Markup Language (HTML)** to create them.

Although not actually a programming language, HTML is a language that has specific syntax rules for defining the placement and format of text, graphics, video, and sound on a Web page. Figure 12-34 shows part of the HTML code used to create the Web page shown in Figure 12-35.

```
<HTML>

<HEAD>

<TITLE>Shelly Cashman Online</TITLE>

</HEAD><BODY BGCOLOR="FFFFFF">

<center>
<table>
<tr><td align=middle>
<A HREF="/bf/sindex.html">Mostly Text Home Page</A></td>
<td align=middle><A HREF="/bf/scwnew.html"><IMG BORDER=0
SRC="/bf/IMAGES/wnewbut.gif" ALT="[What's New]"></A></td>
<td align=middle><A HREF="/bf/scshock.html">Shocked Home Page</A></td></tr></table>

</center><P>

</center><P>

<MAP NAME="schead">

<AREA SHAPE="poly" HREF="/bf/teachres.html" COORDS="13,59 29,44 55,39 78,40 96,44
108,52 111,59 111,63 106,70 93,76 78,83 64,84 38,78 22,76 16,68 13,58 12,56 15,68">

<AREA SHAPE="poly" HREF="/bf/communit.html" COORDS="150,40 167,26 189,20 203,20
216,22 235,26 246,34 249,39 249,43 247,48 240,54 225,63 211,63 196,63 182,62 172,58
160,52 152,44 155,35">

<AREA SHAPE="poly" HREF="/bf/serinfo.html" COORDS="112,168 106,158 108,153 115,148
126,143 141,139 152,137 161,136 182,138 199,144 207,145 215,154 218,162 213,167
204,175 181,180 163,180 144,180 122,174 112,167">

<AREA SHAPE="poly" HREF="/bf/scstudnt.html" COORDS="410,150 428,135 450,132 471,132
494,138 503,144 507,149 507,157 500,166 488,170 474,175 448,175 426,168 413,160
410,149">

</MAP>
```

Figure 12-34
HyperText Markup Language (HTML) is used to create Web pages. This figure shows part of the HTML code used to generate a portion of the Web page shown in Figure 12-35.

You can write HTML code using any text editor or standard word processing software package. You must save the code as an ASCII file with an .htm extension, however, rather than as a formatted word processing document. You also can use an HTML editor to create a Web page. Two basic types of HTML editors exist: stand-alone and add-on. A **stand-alone HTML editor** is a complete editing software package in itself; that is, it does not require any other program to create the Web page. An **add-on HTML editor** is an editing software tool that requires an existing software package, such as a word processor. One advantage of an add-on HTML editor is that the functionality of the existing software and the add-on tool usually are quite similar, so you can learn to use the editing tool very quickly.

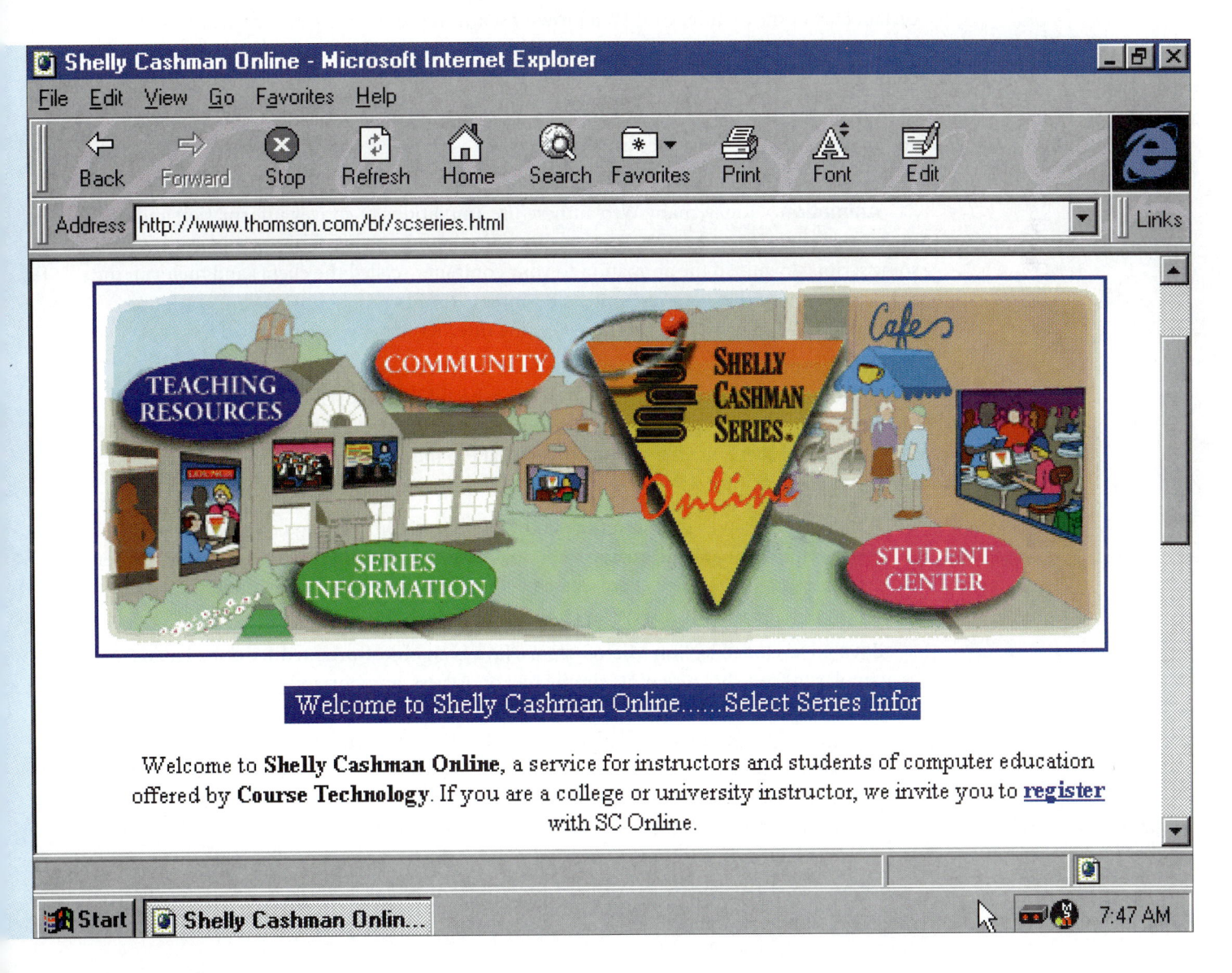

Figure 12-35
Web page created from part of the HTML code in Figure 12-34.

Script and Scripting Languages: Java and PERL

A **script** is a short program that acts as a link between your Web browser and the Internet server. For example, every time you use a search engine such as Yahoo! or Lycos to search for Web sites, you are accessing a script that allows you to interface with the search engine. Scripts are written for three reasons: (1) to send information from your computer to the Internet server, (2) to add multimedia capabilities of your Web browser, and (3) to shift the computational work from the Internet server to your computer. The following paragraphs explain a variety of scripts currently on the Internet.

Imagemap One common use of a script is to create an imagemap. Many Web pages contain **imagemaps**, which are pictures that point to a URL (Uniform Resource Locator). Imagemaps are used in place of, or in addition to, plain text hyperlinks. When you click a certain part of the picture, your Web browser sends the coordinates of the clicked location to the Web server, which in turn locates the corresponding URL and sends the Web page to your computer.

Counter You may have accessed a Web site that informed you what number visitor you were to the site. These sites use a script called a **counter** to keep track of the number of visitors.

Animation Today, many Web authors use animations to convey information and to make their pages more creative. Because animation requires a lot of processing overhead, some scripts download the animation to your computer (called the client) and then run the animation script using your computer's resources. Running the script on your computer is faster and more efficient that running it on the Internet server.

Processing Form Scripts often are used in processing forms. A **processing form** is used to collect data from visitors to a Web site, who fill in blank fields and then click a submit or send button (Figure 12-36). When you click the submit or send button on the processing form, the script is executed. It transmits your data to the server, processes it, and then, if appropriate, sends information back to your Web browser via the server.

Although you can write a script in almost any programming language, the more common scripting languages are C, C++, Java, and PERL. C and C++ were discussed earlier in the chapter. Java and PERL are discussed below. Before writing a script, however, you should check to be sure your server is configured to allow its use.

Java Developed by Sun MicroSystems, **Java** is an object-oriented scripting language, very similar to C++. Because of its simplicity, robustness, and portability, many script programmers think that Java will be the scripting language of the future.

A simpler version of Java, called JavaScript, has been created by Netscape. **JavaScript** can be embedded directly into the HTML of the Web page; the script runs directly in your Web browser. This kind of script is called an **applet**. The advantage of JavaScript applets is that most browsers can execute these scripts directly on your computer without having to call the server, which results in faster responses and reduces the load on the Web server.

PERL Developed by Larry Wall, **PERL** stands for Practical Extraction and Reporting Language. Although originally designed as a procedural language like C, the latest release of PERL is object-oriented like Java.

---

inCyber

For a guide to writing programs using the Java language, visit the Discovering Computers Chapter 12 inCyber page (http://www.scsite.com/dc/ch12/incyber.htm) and click Java.

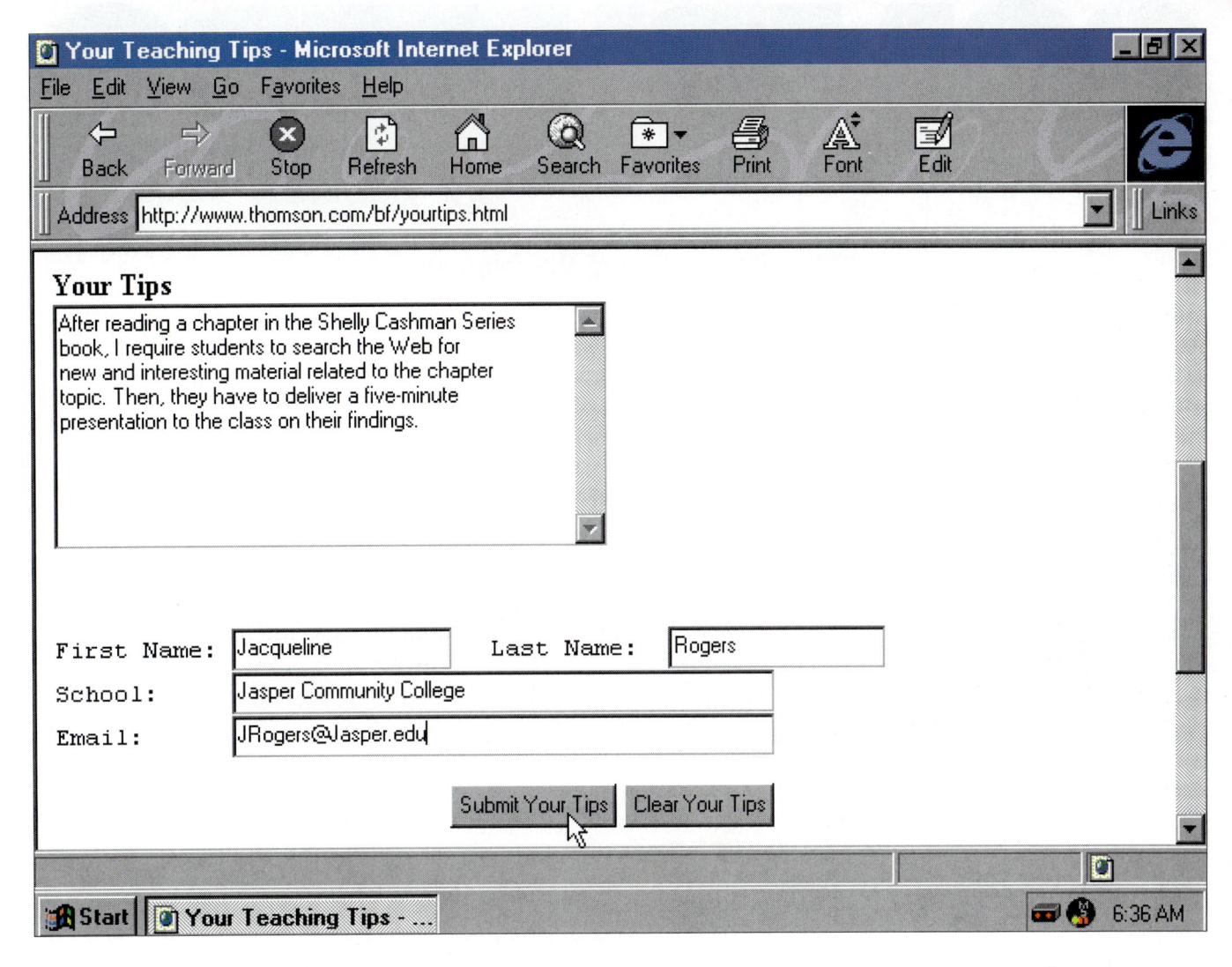

Figure 12-36
One popular use of a script is to create a processing form. This figure shows a Shelly Cashman Online processing form asking for an instructor's teaching tips.

Summary of Program Development and Programming Languages

Because of their large installed base, procedural languages such as COBOL will continue to be used for many years. A trend does exist, however, toward using nonprocedural languages, natural languages, and object-oriented languages to create programs. As users empower themselves and create programs with program development tools such as application generators, macros, and RAD tools, programmers will be able to focus more time and energy on larger information system development projects. Finally, as more and more companies and individuals link to the Internet, the demand for experts in the area of HTML and scripting will continue to grow.

Your knowledge of the program development life cycle and programming languages will help you understand how the computer converts data into information and help you obtain better results if you participate directly in the programming process.

COMPUTERS AT WORK

COBOL: Conversion of the Century

Due to the emergence of 4GLs, natural languages, object-oriented languages, and application generators, many computer professionals have predicted that COBOL's popularity eventually would decline. Yet, it has not. In fact, COBOL programmers are in more demand today than they possibly ever have been. Why? Because of the *millennium bug*.

When the clock strikes midnight on New Year's Eve, 1999, many people around the world will celebrate the arrival of the new century. Many businesses, however, will not be celebrating. The arrival of the year 2000 is going to wreak havoc on millions of computer systems. The problem will arise because most current hardware and software represents a year as two digits; e.g., 96, 97, 98, 99. When 2000 arrives, these two digits will read 00, which the computer likely will interpret as 1900. If left as is, these computer systems will, at the very least, stop working correctly. For example, problems such as negative ages could lead to a newborn baby receiving a Social Security check. Coined *The Year 2000 Problem or millennium bug*, this problem will have an estimated half of the current supply of programmers very busy by the year 1999.

With more than 70 billion lines of COBOL code used in current applications around the world, COBOL programmers are in hot demand. Corporations need COBOL programmers to rewrite programs to deal with the millennium bug. Although time-consuming, fixing the problem is not difficult. The hurdle lies in the search for experienced COBOL programmers! Many have retired or moved on to the more trendy development tools. To entice COBOL programmers, companies are going to have to pay the price. Some experts predict that current salaries of COBOL programmers will double. That is enough to make many programmers catch the COBOL bug!

Figure 12-37

IN THE FUTURE: VERBAL PROGRAM DEVELOPMENT 12.39

IN THE FUTURE

Verbal Program Development

Imagine this scenario: You sit in front of the computer and say, "Customers with a discount code other than 0 should receive a 2% discount." Immediately, the computer converts your English statement to the necessary IF statement to handle this logic and then writes the logic in the programming language you specify. Is this possible?

Voice recognition technology (VRT) has been around for more than fifty years in a variety of forms. Some VRT software is speaker-dependent and some is not. Speaker-dependent software requires the computer to make a profile of your voice, which involves extensive exercises with the computer. Speaker-independent software, conversely, does not require a voice profile; you can begin using this software upon installation.

VRT also can be categorized as discrete speech input, continuous speech input, and natural speech input. **Discrete speech input** requires that you pause between spoken words so the computer can recognize the beginning and ending of words. **Continuous speech input** limits your spoken vocabulary to words stored in the computer system. **Natural speech input** places no limitations on your speech; that is, you talk to the computer, and it understands what you are saying. Unfortunately, natural speech input software is not yet available.

Currently, several voice-aware software products are available. **Voice-aware** programs allow you to dictate the programming language syntax to create the program, as well as to dictate the buttons you wish to click as you run the program. The ultimate goal is to have the computer interpret a programmer's spoken word into the correct programming language syntax. Some claim that natural speech input software will be available by the early part of the twenty-first century!

Figure 12-38

. . . Customers with a discount code other than zero should receive . . .

```
REM COMPUTE GROSS AMOUNT DUE
   Gross.Amount = Unit.Price * Quantity.Purch
REM COMPUTE NET AMOUNT DUE
   IF Discount.Code = 0 THEN
      Net.Amount.Due = Gross.Amount
   ELSE
      Discount.Amount = .02 * Gross.Amount
      Net.Amount.Due = Gross.Amount - Discount.A
   END IF
REM PRINT NET AMOUNT DUE
```

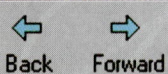

chapter 12 review

1 | 2 | 3 | 4 | 5 | 6 | 7 | 8 | 9 | 10 | 11 | 12 | 13 | 14 | I

inCyber | review | terms | yourTurn | hotTopics | outThere | winLabs | webWalk | exercises | news | home

INSTRUCTIONS: *To display this page from the Web, launch your browser and enter the URL, http://www.scsite.com/dc/ch12/review.htm. Click the links for current and additional information.*

1 Program Development Life Cycle

A **computer program** is a step-by-step set of instructions that directs a computer to perform tasks. The **program development life cycle (PDLC)** is an outline of the six steps used to build computer programs. A **program specifications package** communicates the input, output, processing, and data requirements of each program.

2 Analyze Problem and Design Program

Analyzing the problem consists of reviewing the program specifications package and identifying the program's components. Designing the program involves grouping the program activities in modules, devising a solution for each module, and testing the solution algorithm.

3 Top-Down Design

The objective of **top-down design** is to take the original set of program specifications and break it down into smaller, more manageable components (subroutines). Each subroutine that performs a single function is called a **module**.

4 Structured Design

Program logic is a description of the step-by-step procedures for a module. **Structured design** is a methodology in which all program logic is constructed from a combination of three **control structures**: the **sequence control structure**, the **selection control structure**, and the **repetition control structure**.

5 Proper Program Design

A **proper program** is designed in such a way that the program, each of its modules, and each of the control structures has no **dead code**, no **infinite loops**, one **entry point**, and one **exit point**.

6 Code Program and Test Program

Coding a program involves translating the solution algorithm into a programming language. **Testing** ensures a program runs correctly. **Syntax errors** occur when the code violates the rules of the programming language. **Logic errors** are present when the expected result and the actual result do not match. Errors in a program are referred to as **bugs**. The process of locating and correcting errors is called **debugging** the program.

7 Formalize Solution and Maintain Program

In **formalizing the solution**, the programmer removes any dead code. Documentation allows a programmer to make changes effectively and efficiently. **Maintaining** a program involves correcting errors and adding enhancements.

12 review

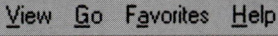

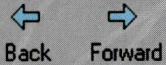

chapter
1 | 2 | 3 | 4 | 5 | 6 | 7 | 8 | 9 | 10 | 11 | 12 | 13 | 14 | I

inCyber | review | terms | yourTurn | hotTopics | outThere | winLabs | webWalk | exercises | news | home

8 Categories of Programming Languages

A **programming language** is a set of words, symbols, and codes that enables the programmer to communicate the solution algorithm to the computer. Programming languages are classified in five major catagories: machine languages, assembly languages, third generation languages, fourth generation languages, and natural languages.

9 Low-Level Languages

Machine language uses binary digits that correspond to the on and off electrical states of a computer. **Assembly language** is written as symbols and codes. Machine and assembly languages are referred to as **low-level languages** because they are **machine dependent**.

10 High-Level Languages

Third generation language (3GL) instructions are written as a series of English-like words. **Fourth generation language (4GL)** uses English-like statements but is a **nonprocedural language**, meaning the programmer has to specify *what* is to be accomplished without explaining *how*. **Natural language** allows the user to enter requests that resemble human speech. Third generation, fourth generation, and natural languages are called **high-level languages** because they are **machine independent**.

11 Object-Oriented Programming

The **object-oriented** approach eliminates redundant code by packaging the data and the program (or procedure) into a single unit called an **object**, which can be reused and modified.

12 Popular Programming Languages

BASIC is a simple, interactive problem-solving programming language. **Visual Basic** is a Windows application that assists programmers in developing event-driven applications. **COBOL** is used for business applications. The **C** programming language is used to develop a variety of system software and application software. **C++** is an object-oriented extension of C. **Pascal** was created to teach structured programming concepts. **Ada** is used for U.S. government military projects. **RPG** assists businesses in generating reports.

13 Program Development Tools

Program development tools meet the complex processing requirements of programmers. A **macro** is a series of statements that instructs an application how to complete a task. **Rapid application development (RAD)** is the process of developing software through **prototyping**.

14 HTML

Designers of Web pages use a language called **HyperText Markup Language** (**HTML**) to create them. HTML code can be written using any text editor. A **script** is a short program that acts as a link between a Web browser and an Internet server. The more common scripting languages are C, C++, **Java**, and **PERL**.

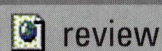

chapter 12 terms

| 1 | 2 | 3 | 4 | 5 | 6 | 7 | 8 | 9 | 10 | 11 | 12 | 13 | 14 | I |

inCyber | review | terms | yourTurn | hotTopics | outThere | winLabs | webWalk | exercises | news | home

INSTRUCTIONS: *To display this page from the Web, launch your browser and enter the URL, http://www.scsite.com/dc/ch12/terms.htm. Scroll through the list of terms. Click a term for its definition and a picture. Click the rocket ship for current and additional information about the term.*

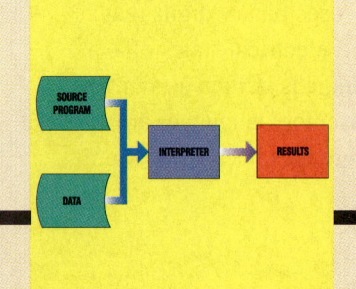

interpreter

DEFINITION

interpreter
Translates one program code statement at a time versus translating an entire program. (**12.20**)

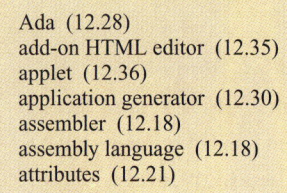

Ada (12.28)
add-on HTML editor (12.35)
applet (12.36)
application generator (12.30)
assembler (12.18)
assembly language (12.18)
attributes (12.21)

BASIC (12.23)
bugs (12.15)

C (12.26)
C++ (12.26)
case control structure (12.7)
class (12.22)
COBOL (12.25)
code standards (12.13)
coding (12.13)
compiler (12.19)
component (12.33)
computer program (12.2)
continuous speech input (12.39)
control structure (12.6)
counter (12.36)

dead code (12.8)
debug utility (12.15)
debugger (12.15)
debugging (12.15)
Delphi (12.33)
desk checking (12.12)
discreet speech input (12.39)
do-until control structure (12.8)
do-while control structure (12.8)

empowered (12.21)
encapsulation (12.22)
entry point (12.9)

event (12.23)
exit point (12.9)

form builder (12.30)
formalizing the solution (12.15)
FORTRAN (12.27)
fourth-generation language (4GL) (12.20)

hierarchy chart (12.5)
high-level language (12.16)
HyperText Markup Language (HTML) (12.34)

if-then-else control structure (12.7)
imagemaps (12.36)
infinite loop (12.8)
inheritance (12.22)
interpreter (12.20)
IPO chart (12.4)

Java (12.36)
JavaScript (12.36)

logic error (12.12)
logic errors (12.14)
low-level language (12.16)

machine language (12.17)
machine-dependent (12.17)
machine-independent (12.19)
macro (12.18, 12.30)
maintaining (12.15)
menu generator (12.30)
message (12.22)
methods (12.21)
mnemonics (12.18)
module (12.5)

Nassi-Schneiderman (N-S) chart (12.10)
natural language (12.21)
natural speech input (12.39)
nonprocedural language (12.20)

object (12.21)
object code (12.19)
object instance (12.22)
object program (12.19)
object-oriented (12.21)
object-oriented programming (OOP) language (12.23)
operations (12.21)

Pascal (12.27)
PERL (12.36)
PowerBuilder (12.33)
procedural languages (12.19)
processing form (12.36)
program development life cycle (PDLC) (12.2)
program development tools (12.30)
program flowchart (12.9)
program generator (12.30)
program logic (12.6)
program specification package (12.3)
programming language (12.2, 12.16)
programming team (12.3)
proper program (12.8)
prototyping (12.32)
pseudocode (12.11)

query language (12.20)

rapid application development (RAD) (12.32)

record a macro (12.31)
repetition control structure (12.7)
report generator (12.21)
report writer (12.21)
RPG (12.28)

screen painter (12.30)
script (12.36)
selection control structure (12.6)
sequence control structure (12.6)
solution algorithm (12.6)
source program (12.18)
stand-alone HTML editor (12.35)
structured design (12.6)
structured walkthrough (12.12)
subclasses (12.22)
superclass (12.22)
symbolic addresses (12.18)
symbolic instruction codes (12.18)
symbolic programming language (12.18)
syntax (12.13)
syntax error (12.14)

test (12.13)
test data (12.12)
third-generation language (3GL) (12.19)
top-down design (12.5)

variables (12.21)
Visual Basic (12.24, 12.33)
voice-aware (12.39)

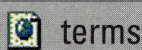

12 yourTurn

chapter 1 | 2 | 3 | 4 | 5 | 6 | 7 | 8 | 9 | 10 | 11 | 12 | 13 | 14 | I

inCyber | review | terms | yourTurn | hotTopics | outThere | winLabs | webWalk | exercises | news | home

INSTRUCTIONS: To display this page from the Web, launch your browser and enter the URL, http://www.scsite.com/dc/ch12/turn.htm. Click a blank line for the answer. Click the links for current and additional information.

Label the Figure

1. _____
   - Review program specifications
   - Meet with analyst and users
   - Identify program components

2. _____
   - Group activities into modules
   - Devise solution algorithms
   - Test solution algorithms

3. _____
   - Translate solution algorithm into a programming language
   - Enter program code into computer

4. _____
   - Remove any syntax errors
   - Remove any logic errors

5. _____
   - Review program code
   - Review documentation

6. _____
   - Identify errors
   - Identify enhancements

PDLC

Instructions: Identify each step in the program development life cycle.

Fill in the Blanks

Instructions: Complete each sentence with the correct term or terms.

1. A(n) _____ is a step-by-step set of instructions that directs a computer to perform the tasks.
2. A(n) _____ is a set of words, symbols, and codes that enable a programmer to communicate a solution algorithm.
3. _____ languages and _____ languages are referred to as _____ languages because they are machine-dependent; that is, written to run on one particular computer.
4. _____, a Windows application designed to assist programmers in developing event-driven applications, is very similar to the _____ programming language.
5. Common tools included with a(n) _____ include report writers, form builders, and menu generators.

Short Answer

Instructions: Write a brief answer to each of the following questions.

1. What is top-down design? How is a hierarchy chart used? Why do computer professionals and programmers recommend the top-down approach to program design? _____
2. What is structured design? Describe the three basic control structures used in structured design. How is the do-while control structure different from the do-until control structure? _____
3. What is the object-oriented approach to program development? How does inheritance affect objects? What is a major benefit of the object-oriented approach? _____
4. What is HyperText Markup Language (HTML)? Define a stand-alone HTML editor and an add-on HTML editor. _____
5. Why are scripts written? What is Java? Why do JavaScript applets result in faster responses? _____

hotTopics

chapter 12

1 | 2 | 3 | 4 | 5 | 6 | 7 | 8 | 9 | 10 | 11 | 12 | 13 | 14 | I

inCyber | review | terms | yourTurn | hotTopics | outThere | winLabs | webWalk | exercises | news | home

INSTRUCTIONS: *To display this page from the Web, launch your browser and enter the URL, http://www.scsite.com/dc/ch12/hot.htm. Click the links for current and additional information to help you respond to the hotTopics questions.*

1 *The consequences of bugs in computer programs can be staggering. One* mistake in the code controlling a Canadian nuclear facility caused more than 3,000 gallons of radioactive water to be spilled. A bug in AT&T's long distance switching software cost the company $60 million. Despite sophisticated debugging utilities, experts estimate that one in every 5,000 lines of code contains an error. Given that many programs contain hundreds of thousands, even millions, of code lines, is it possible to remove all bugs? Why or why not? What can be done to reduce the number of software bugs? If software bugs are inevitable, or at least to be expected, what steps can people relying on computer programs take to deal with them?

2 *Like a road map, flowcharts trace the course from a starting point to a destination. With this* design tool, programmers can write solution algorithms that place tasks in the correct logical sequence. A thorough flowchart can be difficult to develop, however. Using structured design constructs and the flowchart symbols shown in Figure 12-11, prepare a program flowchart showing the logical steps in performing a common task such as balancing a check book, changing the oil in a car, or shopping for groceries. Include any necessary annotations and a separate sheet describing any predefined processes. Be as detailed and accurate as possible. When you are finished, ask a classmate to check the logic of the flowchart by desk checking or performing a structured walk-through.

3 *When computers were first introduced in schools, programming was routinely taught to* students at the college, high school, and even elementary school levels. Yet, as time passed, the emphasis turned toward learning to use application software. Some educators feel programming still should be an integral part of computer education. They point out that many applications include a programming language. Instructors claim that programming even improves logical and critical thinking skills. How important is it to learn programming? Why? Who should be taught computer programming? Should programming in some form be a part of computer education? Why?

4 *Computer programmers have an unenviable image. Often perceived as "nerds,"* they are frequently pictured as socially awkward introverts with thick glasses and plastic pocket protectors. In reality, programmers are like other highly talented white-collar workers. One programmer describes her job as being a combination of engineer and artist. What do you think she meant by this? Is computer programming a science, a skill, a craft, or an art? Why? Programmers in small organizations generally are responsible for all five steps in program development, while those in large organizations often divide up program development. If you were a programmer, would you prefer to work in a small or a large organization? Why? If you did work in a large company, in what steps of program development would you be most interested? Why?

5 *Although machine language is considered a low-level language, this does not mean that* machine language programs are easy to write. In fact, machine language programs tend to be difficult to code, impossible to abridge, and prone to error. Machine language programs, however, execute very quickly, saving crucial seconds and providing a competitive advantage in some applications. Each category of programming language is suitable for some applications. Using the five categories into which programming languages can be classified, describe an application that would be ideal for a language in each category. Explain why a language in that category would be an appropriate choice for the applications. If possible, tell what specific programming language should be used.

chapter 12 outThere

1 | 2 | 3 | 4 | 5 | 6 | 7 | 8 | 9 | 10 | 11 | 12 | 13 | 14 | I

inCyber | review | terms | yourTurn | hotTopics | outThere | winLabs | webWalk | exercises | news | home

INSTRUCTIONS: *To display this page from the Web, launch your browser and enter the URL, http://www.scsite.com/dc/ch12/out.htm. Click the links for current and additional information.*

1 *Some application packages come with programming languages (sometimes called macro languages) that can be used to write* programs within the application. *For example, Microsoft Excel, a spreadsheet program, includes Visual Basic. Visit a software vendor and find an application package that contains a programming language. What is the name of the application? What is the name of the associated programming language? For what purpose is the language used?* If possible, ask to see a demonstration of the programming language. Does it appear difficult to use? Why? How does the programming language enhance the application? Would the programming language be a significant factor in your decision whether or not to purchase the package? Why?

2 *Programming languages can be classified in several ways. They can be labeled procedural* (concerned with *how* something is done) or nonprocedural (concerned with *what* is to be done). They might be described as business-oriented (capable of handling large data files) or scientific-oriented (capable of performing sophisticated calculations). They could be characterized as general-purpose (designed to solve various types of problems) or special-purpose (designed to deal with a specific type of problem or application). Using library or Internet resources, prepare a report on one of the programming languages listed in Figure 12-31. Describe the history, intent, and use of the language. Then, categorize the language according to the classifications suggested above. Explain why you classified the language as you did.

3 *Choosing a programming language is one of the more important decisions an organization has* to make when developing custom software. A poor choice can be a costly mistake, resulting in a program that is difficult to maintain, incompatible with other software, and unproductive when used. Visit a local organization and interview someone in the information systems department about recently developed custom software. What type of application was developed? What programming language was used? Why? Which of the considerations that were outlined in this chapter for selecting a programming language was most important? Why? Which was least important? Why? In hindsight, was the best language chosen? If not, what programming language would have been better?

4 *Unlike the names of other programming languages,* Java *is not an acronym.* Originally, the language was called Oak, but developers sought a name that evoked the speed, liveliness, and interactivity of this new programming language. The name Java — a reminder of the hot, aromatic beverage that is a programmer's frequent companion — was a natural choice. Find out more about Java on the World Wide Web. How was Java developed? How are Java applications (applets) different from other applications? Who is using Java? How? What are the advantages of Java? What are the disadvantages? What is JavaSoft?

5 *At one time, computer programs consisting of 3,000 lines of code were thought to be long.* Today, programs used in automobile transmissions have almost 20,000 lines of code, word processing programs can be more than 50,000 lines, and programs used by telephone companies are two million lines long! In the future, some experts see such trends as continued movement towards natural languages and greater participation in programming by computer users. Using computer magazines and library or Web resources, prepare a report on what programming will be like in ten years. How will programming be different from what it is today? Who will be doing the programming? How will they be doing it? What effect might developments in computer hardware have on programming?

12 winLabs — chapter 1 | 2 | 3 | 4 | 5 | 6 | 7 | 8 | 9 | 10 | 11 | 12 | 13 | 14 | I

inCyber | review | terms | yourTurn | hotTopics | outThere | winLabs | webWalk | exercises | news | home

INSTRUCTIONS: *To display this page from the Web, launch your browser and enter the URL, http://www.scsite.com/dc/ch12/labs.htm. Click the links for current and additional information.*

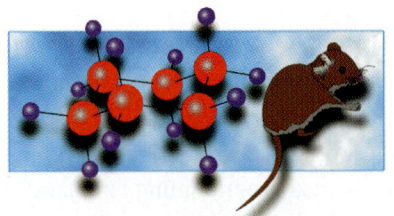

1 Shelly Cashman Series Programming Language Lab
Follow the instructions in winLabs 1 on page 1.34 to display the Shelly Cashman Series Labs screen. Click Choosing a Programming Language. Click the Start Lab button. When the initial screen displays, carefully read the objectives. With your printer turned on, click the Print Questions button. Fill out the top of the Questions sheet and then answer the questions.

2 Adjusting Keyboard Speed
Click the Start button on the taskbar, point to Settings on the Start menu, and then click Control Panel on the Settings submenu. Double-click the Keyboard icon in the Control Panel window. When the Keyboard Properties dialog box displays, click the Speed tab (Figure 12-39). Use the question mark button to answer the following two questions: (1) What is repeat delay? (2) What is repeat rate? Click the General tab. What type of keyboard is connected to your system? Click the Cancel button.

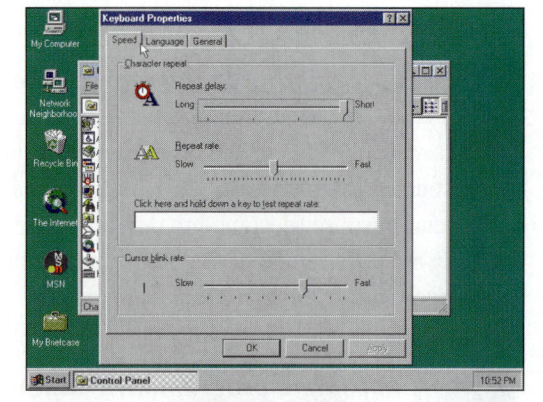

Figure 12-39

3 Searching for Executable Files
Click the Start button on the taskbar, point to Find on the Start menu, and then click Files or Folders on the Find submenu. In the Find dialog box, click the Name & Location tab, click View on the menu bar, and then click Details. Type `*.exe` in the Named text box. Type `c:\` in the Look in text box. Select Include subfolders. Click the Find Now button. Sort the files alphabetically by name by clicking the Name column heading (Figure 12-40). Scroll through the list of files and find the filename, Notepad. In what folder is Notepad located. How large is the file, in bytes?

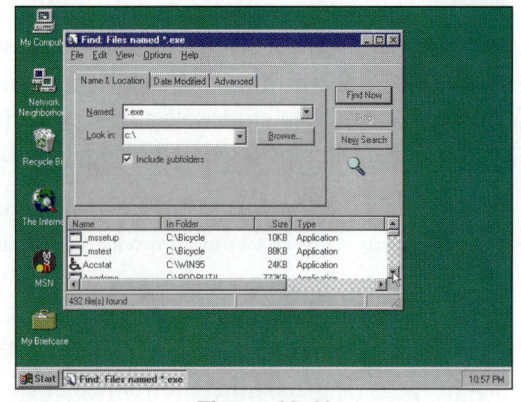

Figure 12-40

4 Accessing the MS-DOS Prompt
Click the Start button on the taskbar, point to Programs on the Start menu, and then click MS-DOS Prompt on the Programs submenu. When the MS-DOS Prompt window displays, type `ver` and then press ENTER. Write down the operating system installed on your computer. Type `cls` and then press ENTER. Type `vol` and then press ENTER. Write down the volume label and serial number for the current drive. Click the Full Screen button. Type `exit` and then press ENTER.

5 Using Help
Click the Start button on the taskbar and then click Help on the Start menu. When the Help Topics: Windows Help window displays, click the Find tab. Type `programs` in the text box. Double-click Adding a new submenu to the Programs menu. Print the topic. Close Help.

webWalk

chapter 1 | 2 | 3 | 4 | 5 | 6 | 7 | 8 | 9 | 10 | 11 | 12 | 13 | 14 | I

inCyber | review | terms | yourTurn | hotTopics | outThere | winLabs | webWalk | exercises | news | home

INSTRUCTIONS: *To display this page from the Web, launch your browser and enter the URL, http://www.scsite.com/dc/ch12/walk.htm. Click the exercise link to display the exercise.*

1. Object-Oriented Program Development
The object-oriented approach to developing software eliminates the problem of each program defining how the data is used for that particular program. To learn more about object-oriented design and development, complete this exercise.

3. HyperText Markup Language (HTML)
The designers of Web pages use a special formatting language called HTML to create the pages. Complete this exercise to learn more about HTML.

4. Image Maps
One common use of a script is to create an image map (Figure 12-42). When you click a certain part of the picture, the Web browser sends the coordinates of the clicked location to the Web server, which in turn locates the corresponding URL and sends the web page to your computer. To work with image maps on Web pages, complete this exercise.

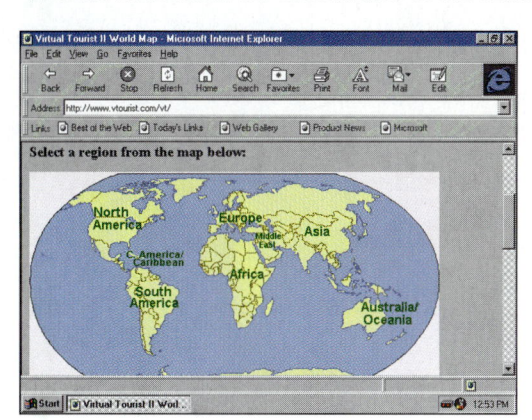

Figure 12-42

7. Visual Basic
Visual Basic is a Windows application that serves as a development environment for programmers to create event-driven, GUI applications for the Windows operating system. Complete this exercise to learn more about Visual Basic.

9. Web Chat
Complete this exercise to enter a Web Chat discussion related to the issues presented in the hotTopics exercise.

2. Application Generators
When using an application generator, the developer works with menu-driven tools that have easy to use graphical interfaces. To use an application generator that produces Web pages (Figure 12-41), complete this exercise.

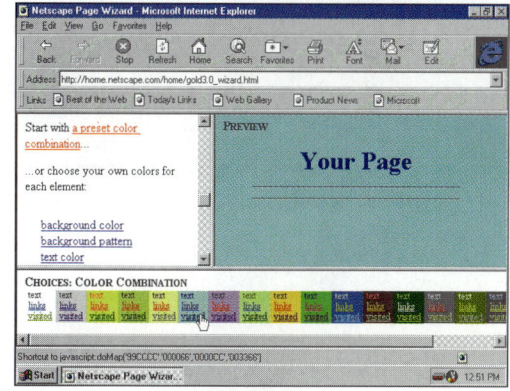

Figure 12-41

5. Information Mining
Complete this exercise to improve your Web research skills by using a Web search engine to find information related to this chapter.

6. Java
Java is described by its creators as a "simple, object-oriented, distributed, interpreted, robust, secure, architecture neutral, portable, high-performance, multithreaded, buzzword-compliant, general-purpose programming language." Complete this exercise to learn more about Java.

8. Verbal Program Development
Voice-aware programs allow you to dictate the programming language syntax to create a program, as well as dictate the buttons you wish to click as you run the program. To learn more about voice-aware programs, complete this exercise.

Careers in the Information Age

After reading the chapters in this book, you may be interested enough in computers to consider a career in the information processing industry. The information processing industry is growing rapidly and offers many rewarding jobs via typical job-searching methods, as well as career-oriented sites on the World Wide Web (Figure 1). This section discusses the types of positions available, how much they currently pay, and how to prepare for a job.

Figure 1
Information on computer-related jobs is available at many sites on the World Wide Web.

The Information Processing Industry

The **information processing industry** is one of the larger industries in the world with annual sales of nearly $300 billion. Approximately one-half of this total is related to equipment sales and the other half comes from software and service sales. Job opportunities in the industry are found primarily in three areas: the companies that manufacture computer-related equipment; the companies that develop software; and the companies that hire information processing professionals to work with these products. As in any major industry, many service companies also exist that support each of these three areas. Examples are companies that sell computer supplies and companies that consult on communications networks.

THE INFORMATION PROCESSING INDUSTRY   12.49

The Computer Software Industry

The **computer software industry** includes all the developers and distributors of applications and system software. Thousands of companies provide a wide range of software from operating systems to complete business systems. Software is a huge industry with annual sales exceeding $100 billion. Leading companies include Microsoft, Oracle, Computer Associates, Novell, and Lotus. Most software companies specialize in one particular type of software product such as business application software or productivity tools such as word processing or spreadsheets; however, the larger companies have multiple products.

Information Processing Professionals

Information processing professionals are the people who put the equipment and software to work to produce information for the end user (Figure 3). These people include programmers and systems analysts who are hired by companies to work in an information systems department. These and other positions available in the information processing industry are discussed in the next section.

Figure 2
A notebook computer is carefully assembled.

The Computer Equipment Industry

The **computer equipment**, or **hardware**, **industry** includes all manufacturers and distributors of computers and computer-related equipment such as disk and tape drives, monitors, printers, and communications equipment (Figure 2).

The five larger minicomputer and mainframe manufacturers in the United States — IBM, Hewlett-Packard, Digital, UNISYS, and NCR — are huge organizations with tens of thousands of employees worldwide. The largest computer company, IBM, has annual sales of more than $70 billion. Major personal computer manufacturers include Compaq, Packard Bell, Apple, IBM, Hewlett-Packard, and Gateway2000. In addition to the major companies, the computer equipment industry also is known for the many new start-up companies that appear each year. These new companies take advantage of rapid changes in equipment technology, such as wireless communications, networking, multimedia, and fiber optics, to create new products and new job opportunities. Besides the companies that make end user equipment, thousands of companies make components that most users never see. These companies manufacture chips (processor, memory, and special-purpose), power supplies, wiring, and the hundreds of other parts that go into computer equipment.

Figure 3
Computer professionals must be able to understand the end user's point of view and often meet with the user to review his or her information processing requirements.

What Are the Career Opportunities in Information Processing?

The use of computers in so many aspects of life has created thousands of new jobs. Because of rapid changes in technology, many of the current jobs did not even exist ten years ago. The following section describes some of the current career opportunities.

Working in an Information Systems Department

The people in the information systems department work together as a team to meet the information demands of their organizations. Several job positions already have been discussed, including database administrator (Chapter 9), systems analysts (Chapter 11), and programmers (Chapter 12). In addition to these jobs, many other positions exist. These positions can be divided into four main groups:

1. Operations
2. System development
3. Technical services
4. End user computing

The chart in Figure 4 shows some of the management and nonmanagement positions in each of these groups that are described in the following section.

Operations The **operations group** is responsible for operating the centralized (computer center) equipment and network administration including both data and voice communications. The **computer operator** performs equipment-related activities such as monitoring performance, running jobs, and backup and restore. A **communications specialist** evaluates, installs, and monitors data and/or voice communications equipment and software and is responsible for connections to the Internet and other wide area networks. A **network**, or **LAN, specialist** installs and maintains local area networks. A **control clerk** accounts for all input and output processed by the computer center. A **data entry operator** uses a data entry device, such as a terminal or PC, to transcribe data from source documents into a computer. The **data librarian** maintains the collection of production and backup tapes and disks.

System Development The **system development group** is responsible for analyzing, designing, developing, and implementing new information systems and main-taining and improving existing systems. The **systems analyst** works closely with users to analyze their requirements and design an information system solution. The **application programmer** converts the system design into the appropriate computer language. The **Internet specialist**, also called a **Webmaster**, is responsible for creating, or helping users to create, Web pages and for maintaining an organization's Web site. The **technical writer** works with the analyst, programmer, and user to create program and system documentation and user manuals.

GROUP	MANAGEMENT	NONMANAGEMENT
Operations	Computer Operations Manager Network Administration Manager Voice Communications Manager	Computer Operator Communications Specialist Network (LAN) Specialist Control Clerk Data Entry Operator Data Librarian
System Development	System Development Manager Programming Manager Project Manager	Systems Analyst Application Programmer Internet Specialist (Webmaster) Technical Writer
Technical Services	Technical Support Manager Database Administrator System Software Manager Quality Assurance Manager	Technical Evaluator Database Analyst System Programmer Quality Assurance Specialist
End User Computing	End User Computing Manager Information Center Manager Office Automation Manager Training Manager	PC Support Specialist Information Center Specialist Office Automation Specialist Trainer EIS Specialist

Figure 4
This table shows some of the management and nonmanagement jobs available within an information systems department.

Technical Services The **technical services group** is responsible for the evaluation and integration of new technologies, the administration of the organization's data resources, and support of the central computer operating system or servers. A **technical evaluator** researches new technologies, such as wireless communications, and recommends how such technologies can be used by the organization. The **database analyst** is familiar with the organization's database structure and assists systems analysts and programmers in developing or modifying applications that use the database. The **system programmer** installs and maintains operating system software and provides technical support to other staff. The **quality assurance specialist** reviews programs and documentation to make sure they meet the organization's standards.

End User Computing The **end user computing group** is responsible for assisting end users in working with existing systems and in using productivity software and query languages to obtain the information necessary to perform their jobs. The **PC support specialist** installs and supports personal computer equipment and software, including Web browsers. The **information center specialist** assists users in obtaining information from an organization's existing database and putting it in a form they can use, such as presentation graphics. The **office automation specialist** assists users in implementing both computerized and noncomputerized office automation technologies. A **trainer** develops education and training materials to teach users how to use existing and new applications. The **executive information system (EIS) specialist** works with senior management to develop reports and systems to meet its information requirements.

As you can see, an information systems department provides career opportunities for people with a variety of skills and talents. Other information industry jobs are found in the areas of sales, service and repair, education and training, and consulting.

Sales

Sales representatives must have a general understanding of computers and a specific knowledge of the product they are selling. Strong interpersonal, or people, skills are important, including listening ability and strong oral and written communication skills. Sales representatives usually are paid based on the amount of product they sell, and top sales representatives often are the most highly compensated employees in a computer company.

Some sales representatives work directly for equipment and software manufacturers and others work for resellers. Many personal computer products are sold through dealers (Figure 5). Some dealers, such as Egghead Discount Software, specialize in selling the more popular software products.

Figure 5
Computer retailers need sales people who understand personal computers and have good people skills.

Service and Repair

Being a **service and repair technician** is a challenging job for individuals who like to troubleshoot and solve problems and have a strong background in electronics (Figure 6). In the early days of computers, repairs often

Figure 6
Computer service and repair requires a knowledge of electronics.

were made at the site of the computer equipment. Today, however, malfunctioning components, such as circuit boards, usually are replaced and taken back to the service technician's office or sent to a special facility for repair. Many equipment manufacturers include special diagnostic software with their computer equipment that helps the service technician identify the problem. Using a modem, some computer systems can telephone another computer automatically at the service technician's office and leave a message that a malfunction has been detected.

Education and Training

The increased sophistication and complexity of today's computer products has opened wide opportunities in computer education and training (Figure 7). Qualified instructors are needed in schools, colleges, universities, and private industry. In fact, the high demand for instructors has created a shortage at the university level, where many educators have been lured into private industry because of higher pay. This shortage probably will not be filled in the near future; the supply of Ph.D.s, usually required at the university level, is not keeping up with the demand.

Figure 7
A high demand exists in schools and industry for qualified instructors who can teach information processing subjects.

Consulting

After building experience in one or more areas, some individuals become consultants, people who draw upon their experiences to give advice to others. Consultants not only must have strong technical skills in their area of expertise, but also must have the people skills to communicate their suggestions effectively to their clients. Qualified consultants are in high demand for such tasks as computer system selection, system design, and communications network design and installation.

Compensation and Growth Trends for Information Processing Careers

Compensation is a function of experience and demand for a particular skill. **Demand** is influenced by geographic location, with metropolitan areas usually having higher pay than rural areas. Figure 8 shows the result of a salary survey of more than 95,000 computer professionals across the United States and Canada.

As shown in Figure 9, some industries pay higher than others for the same job. According to the survey, the communications, utility, and financial service (e.g., banking and insurance) industries pay the highest salaries. These industries have many challenging applications and pay the highest rate to obtain the most highly qualified employees.

According to the U. S. Bureau of Labor Statistics, the fastest growing computer career positions through the year 2005 will be systems analyst, programmer, and computer repair technician (Figure 10).

Figure 8
Salary levels (in thousands of dollars) for different computer industry positions. (Source: Source EDP, 1996 Computer Salary Survey)

SYSTEM DEVELOPMENT	Median Salary ($000)
Mainframe	
Junior Programmer	34
Programmer/Analyst	41
Senior Programmer/Analyst	49
Midrange	
Junior Programmer	33
Programmer/Analyst	40
Senior Programmer/Analyst	50
Client/Server	
Junior Programmer	35
Programmer/Analyst	43
Senior Programmer/Analyst	52
GUI	
Junior Programmer	34
Programmer/Analyst	42
Senior Programmer/Analyst	50

COMPENSATION AND GROWTH TRENDS FOR INFORMATION PROCESSING CAREERS

	Median Salary ($000)
Software Engineer	
Junior Software Engineer	37
Software Engineer	45
Senior Software Engineer	55

BUSINESS SYSTEMS

Systems Analyst	50
Consultant	59
EDI Analyst	47

SPECIALISTS

Database Management	
Database Analyst	54
Database Administrator	59
LAN Administrator	43
Network Engineer	48
PC Specialists	
PC Software Specialist	36
PC Analyst	45
System Administrator/Manager	48
WAN Administration	
Voice Analyst	48
Data Communications Analyst	55
WAN Administrator	47
System Programmer	54
EDP Auditing	
EDP Auditor	42
Senior EDP Auditor	53
Technical Writing	
Writer	34
Editor	44
System Architect	49

MANAGEMENT

MIS Director/CIO	
Small/Medium Shop	66
Large Shop	97
Manager of Business Applications	72
Applications Development	74
Technical Services	70
VP/Manager of Systems Engineering	76
VP/Manager of Customer Support	67
Project Manager	63
Project Leader	54

SALES

Account Representative	69
Pre/Post Sales Support Representative	52
Management	86

DATA CENTER

Data Center Manager	58
Operations Support	
Technician	29
Senior Technician	38
Communications/Network	
Operator	33
Senior Operator	44

PROGRAMMER	Salary	% of Average
Transportation/Utilities	$41,894	115.1%
Financial Services	41,252	113.3%
Information Services	38,924	106.9%
Medical/Legal Services	36,514	100.3%
Construction/Mining/Agriculture	36,000	98.9%
Government	35,740	98.2%
Manufacturing	35,503	97.5%
Retail	35,143	96.5%
Other Services	33,187	91.2%
Education	29,840	82.0%
Average	$36,400	100.0%

Figure 9
Some industries tend to pay more for the same job position. This table shows the average 1996 salary for a programmer. (Source: Datamation *Magazine 1996 Salary Survey)*

PROJECTED GROWTH 1992 - 2005
(thousands of jobs)

	1992	2005	Change	% Change
Systems Analyst	455	956	501	110%
Programmer	555	723	168	30%
Computer Repair Technician	83	120	37	45%

Figure 10
Projected growth rates for computer-related careers as compiled by the U.S. Bureau of Labor Statistics.

Preparing for a Career in Information Processing

To prepare for a career in the information processing industry, individuals must decide in which computer field they are interested and obtain education in that field. This section discusses the three major computer fields and some of the opportunities for obtaining education in those fields.

What Are the Fields in the Information Processing Industry?

While this book has focused primarily on the use of computers in business, three broad fields in the information processing industry actually exist: computer information systems; computer science; and computer engineering. **Computer information systems (CIS)** refers to the use of computers to provide the information needed to operate businesses and other organizations. The field of **computer science** includes the technical aspects of computers such as hardware operation and system software. **Computer engineering** deals with the design and manufacturing of electronic computer components and computer hardware. Each field provides unique career opportunities and has specialized requirements.

Obtaining Education for Information Processing Careers

Trade schools, technical schools, community colleges, colleges, and universities all offer formal education and certification or degree programs in computer information systems, computer science, and computer engineering. Usually, schools have separate programs for each area.

With the wide variety of career opportunities that exist in information processing, it is difficult to make anything other than broad general statements when discussing degree requirements for employment in the industry. As in most other industries, the more advanced degree an individual has in a chosen field, the better that individual's chances are for success. While not having a degree may limit a person's opportunities for securing a top position, it neither will prevent entry nor preclude success in an information processing career.

Career Development in the Information Processing Industry

For individuals employed in the information processing industry, several means are available for developing skills and increasing recognition among peers. These include professional organizations, certification, and professional growth and continuing education activities. Numerous publications also can help an individual keep up with changes in the information processing industry.

Professional Organizations

Computer-related organizations have been formed by people who have common interests and a desire to share their knowledge. Two of the organizations that have been influential in the industry include the Association for Computing Machinery (ACM) and the Data Processing Management Association (DPMA). The **Association for Computing Machinery (ACM)** is composed of people interested in computer science and computer science education. A large number of college and university computer educators are members. The **Data Processing Management Association (DPMA)** is a professional association of programmers, systems analysts, and information processing managers. Both ACM and DPMA offer the following benefits.

- Chapters throughout the United States and in several foreign countries
- Monthly meetings
- Workshops, seminars, and conventions
- Journals and articles
- Special-interest groups (SIGs)
- Continuing education material
- Student chapters

Attending professional meetings provides an excellent opportunity for students to learn about the information processing industry and to meet and talk with professionals in the field.

In addition to these and other professional organizations, user groups exist for most makes of computers. A **user group** is a group of people with common computer equipment or software interests that meets regularly to share information. Most metropolitan areas have one or more local computer societies that meet monthly to discuss topics of common interest about personal computers. For anyone employed or simply interested in the computer industry, these groups can be an effective and rewarding way to learn and continue career development.

Certification

Many professions offer certification programs as a way of encouraging and recognizing the efforts of their members to attain a level of knowledge about their professions. Many computer industry companies such as Novell, Microsoft, and IBM offer certification programs on their hardware and software products. Although no states presently require that computer professionals be certified or licensed, it has been proposed by some groups.

The **Institute for the Certification of Computer Professionals** (ICCP) administers the most widely recognized certification program in the information processing industry. The Institute is sponsored and supported by several professional organizations including ACM and DPMA. Prior to 1994, the ICCP offered four different certification designations. The best known of these was the Certified Data Processor, or CDP. Other designations were Certified Computer Programmer (CCP) and Certified Systems Professional (CSP). Starting in 1994, all three designations were combined under one standard title, **Certified Computing Professional** (CCP). A separate designation, **Associate Computing Professional** (ACP) exists for entry-level personnel. To become certified, a CCP candidate must pass a core examination and any two specialty examinations. ACP candidates must pass the core examination and at least one computer language test. Figure 11 summarizes the requirements for the certifications.

CERTIFIED COMPUTING PROFESSIONAL (CCP) → **CORE EXAMINATION** ← **ASSOCIATE COMPUTING PROFESSIONAL (ACP)**

CORE EXAMINATION		
Human and Organization Framework	Data and Information	Technology
System Concepts	System Development	Associated Disciplines

any two of the following

CCP EXAMINATIONS

Procedural Programming	System Security
System Development	Software Engineering
Business Information Systems	System Programming
Communications	Data Resource Management
Microcomputing and Networks	Office Information Systems
Management	

CCP CERTIFICATION

any one of the following

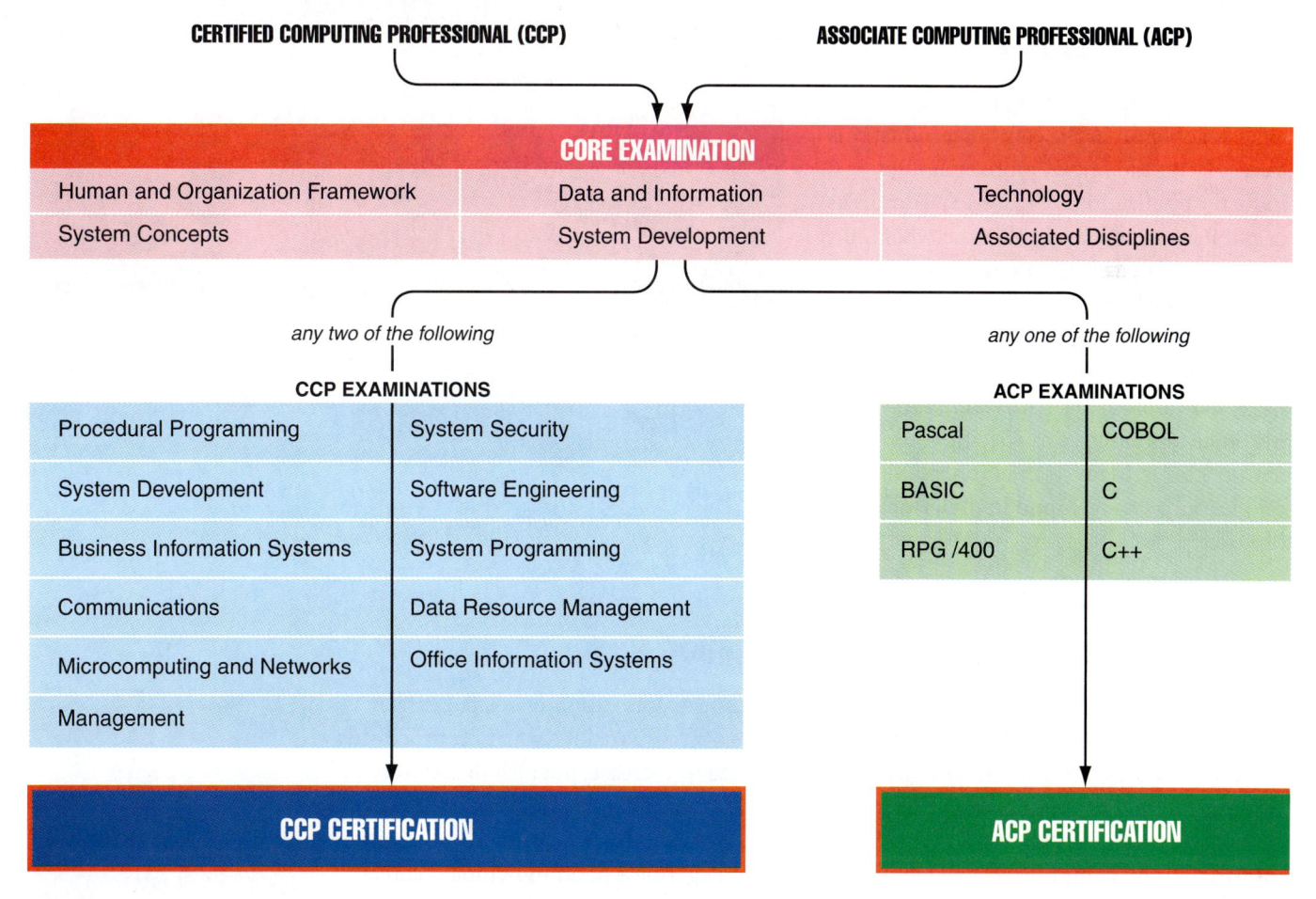

ACP EXAMINATIONS

Pascal	COBOL
BASIC	C
RPG /400	C++

ACP CERTIFICATION

Figure 11
The Institute for the Certification of Computer Professionals (ICCP) offers two certification programs. This chart summarizes the examination requirements for each program.

Professional Growth and Continuing Education

Because of rapid changes in technology, staying aware of new products and services in the information processing industry can be a challenging task. One way of keeping up is by participating in professional growth and continuing education activities. This broad category includes events such as workshops, seminars, conferences, conventions, and trade shows that provide both general and specific information on equipment, software, services, and issues affecting the industry, such as computer security. Workshops and seminars usually consist of one or two days, while conferences, conventions, and trade shows often continue a week. The largest trade show in the United States, **COMDEX**, brings together more than 2,000 vendors to display their newest products and services to more than 225,000 attendees (Figure 12).

Figure 12
COMDEX is one of the larger computer product trade shows in the world. More than 2,000 vendors display their newest products and services to more than 225,000 attendees.

Computer Publications

Another way of keeping informed about what is going on in the computer industry is to regularly read one or more computer industry publications (Figure 13). Hundreds of publications are available from which to choose. Some publications, such as *PC Week*, *Computerworld*, and *InfoWorld*, and are like newspapers and cover a wide range of issues. Other publications are oriented toward a particular topic area such as communications, personal computers, or a specific equipment manufacturer. Many of the more popular publications can be found in public or school libraries.

Figure 13
Numerous computer industry publications are available at bookstores, libraries, or by subscription.

Summary of Computer Career Opportunities

With the increased use of computers, the prospects for computer-related career opportunities are excellent. Not only are the numbers of traditional information processing jobs, such as programmer and systems analyst, expected to increase, but also the continued computerization of existing occupations will create additional job opportunities. The many career sites located on the World Wide Web (Figure 1 on page 12.48) have made obtaining information on computer related job openings easier. Regardless of an individual's career choice, a basic understanding of computers should be an essential part of any employee's job skills.

Security, Privacy, and Ethics

OBJECTIVES

After completing this chapter, you will be able to:

- Identify the different types of security risks that can threaten computer systems

- Describe different ways computer systems can be safeguarded

- Describe how a computer virus works and the steps that can be taken to prevent viruses

- Explain why computer backup is important and how it is accomplished

- Discuss the steps in a disaster recovery plan

- Discuss issues relating to information privacy

- Discuss ethical issues with respect to the information age

- Specify security, privacy, and ethics issues that relate to the Internet

CHAPTER 13

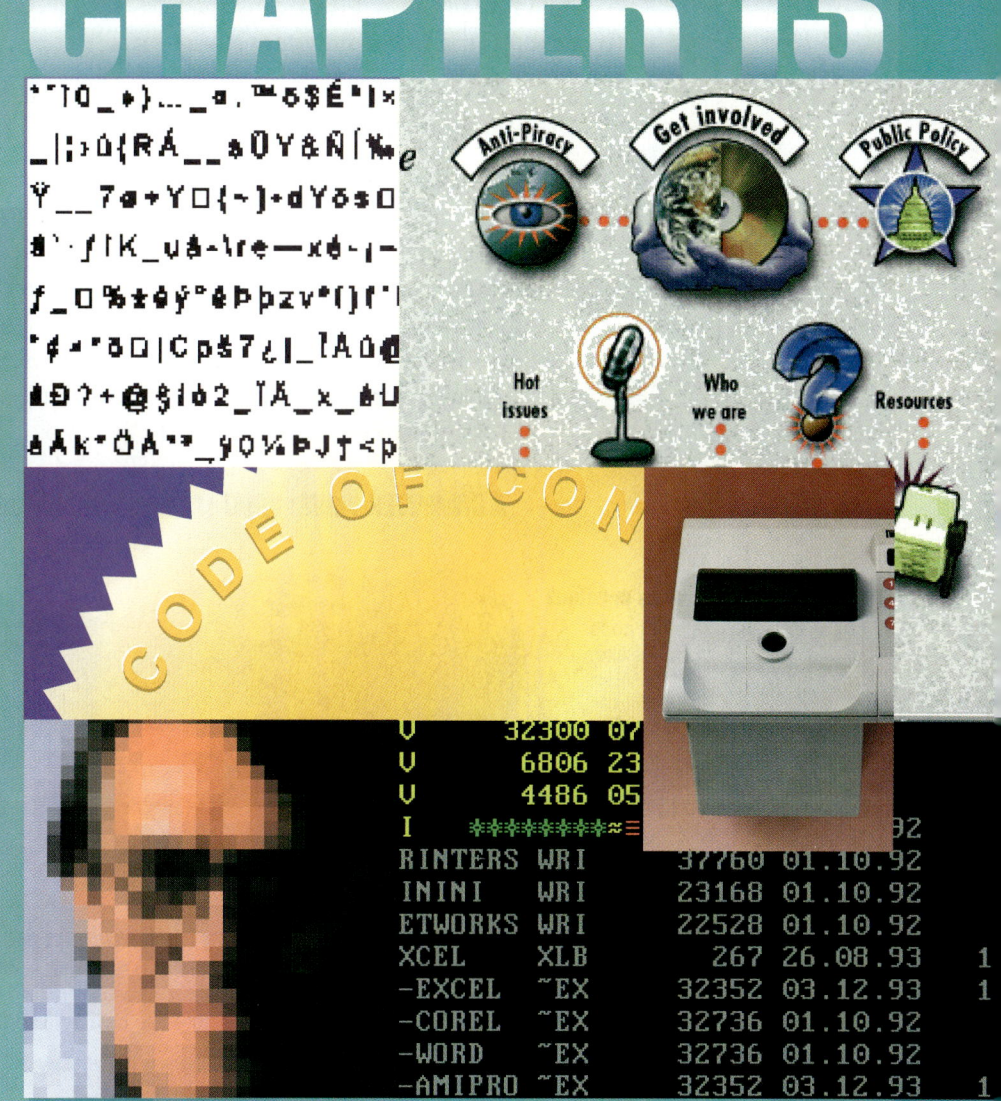

Because people and organizations depend on computers every day for a variety of significant tasks, it is important to make sure the systems they use are protected from loss, damage, and misuse. This chapter identifies some potential risks to computer systems and software and the safeguards that can be taken to minimize these risks. Information privacy also is discussed, including the current laws that are designed to keep certain data confidential. In addition, the chapter reviews concerns about the ethical use of computer systems and which activities are right, wrong, or even criminal. Finally, the security, privacy, and ethics issues that relate to the Internet are covered.

Computer Security: Risks and Safeguards

A **computer security risk** is defined as any event or action that could cause a loss of or damage to computer equipment, software, data and information, or processing capability. Some of these risks, such as viruses, unauthorized access and use, and information theft, involve deliberate acts that are against the law. Any illegal act involving a computer generally is referred to as a **computer crime**. The following section describes some of the more common computer security risks and what can be done to minimize or prevent their consequences. This section concludes with a discussion of how to develop an overall computer security plan.

Computer Viruses

A **computer virus** is a potentially damaging computer program designed to *infect* other software or files by attaching itself to the software or files with which it comes in contact. Virus programs often are designed to damage computer systems by destroying or corrupting data. If an infected file is transferred to or accessed by another computer system, the virus will spread to the other system. Figure 13-1 shows how a virus can spread from one system to another. Viruses have become a serious problem in recent years. Currently, more than 9,000 known virus programs exist, and the increased use of networks has made the spread of these viruses easier than ever.

inCyber

For comprehensive details on computer virus prevention, recognition, and removal, visit the Discovering Computers Chapter 13 inCyber page (http://www.scsite.com/dc/ch13/incyber.htm) and click Computer Virus.

A COMPUTER VIRUS: WHAT IT IS AND HOW IT SPREADS

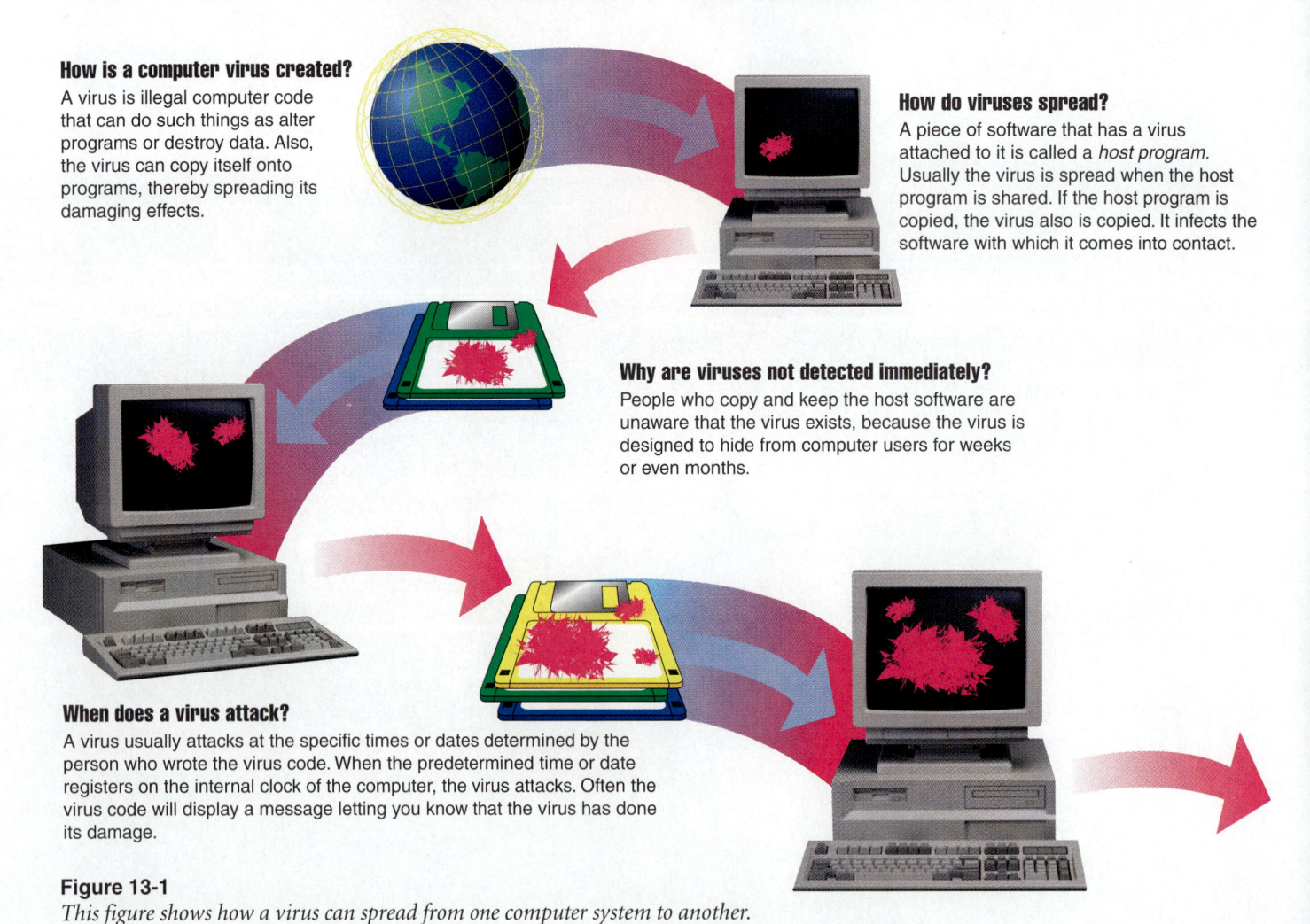

How is a computer virus created?
A virus is illegal computer code that can do such things as alter programs or destroy data. Also, the virus can copy itself onto programs, thereby spreading its damaging effects.

How do viruses spread?
A piece of software that has a virus attached to it is called a *host program*. Usually the virus is spread when the host program is shared. If the host program is copied, the virus also is copied. It infects the software with which it comes into contact.

Why are viruses not detected immediately?
People who copy and keep the host software are unaware that the virus exists, because the virus is designed to hide from computer users for weeks or even months.

When does a virus attack?
A virus usually attacks at the specific times or dates determined by the person who wrote the virus code. When the predetermined time or date registers on the internal clock of the computer, the virus attacks. Often the virus code will display a message letting you know that the virus has done its damage.

Figure 13-1
This figure shows how a virus can spread from one computer system to another.

Although numerous variations are present, four main types of viruses exist: boot sector viruses, file viruses, Trojan horse viruses, and macro viruses. A **boot sector virus** replaces the boot program that is used to start the computer system with a modified, infected version of the boot program. When the infected boot program is run, it loads the virus into the computer's memory. Once a virus is in memory, it spreads to any floppy disk inserted into the computer. A **file virus** inserts virus code into program files. The virus then spreads to any program that accesses the infected program. A **Trojan horse virus** (named after the Greek myth) is a virus that hides within or is designed to look like a legitimate program. A **macro virus** uses the macro language of an application, such as word processing, to hide virus code. When a document with an infected macro is opened, the macro virus is loaded into memory. Certain actions, such as saving the document, activate the virus. Macro viruses often are made part of templates so that any document created using the template is infected.

Some viruses are harmless pranks that simply freeze a computer system temporarily and display sounds or messages. For example, when the Green Caterpillar virus is triggered, it displays what looks like a green caterpillar on your screen (Figure 13-2). Other viruses contain logic bombs or time bombs. A **logic bomb** is a program that is activated when a certain condition is detected. One disgruntled worker, for example, planted a logic bomb that began destroying files when his name was added to a list of terminated employees. A **time bomb** is a type of logic bomb that is activated on a particular date. A well-known time bomb is the Michelangelo virus, which destroys data on your hard disk on March 6, Michelangelo's birthday.

Another type of malicious program is a worm. Although it often is called a virus, a worm, unlike a virus, does not attach itself to another program. Instead, a **worm** program is designed to copy itself repeatedly in memory or on a disk drive until no memory or disk space remains. When no memory or disk space remains, the computer stops working. Some worm programs are designed to copy themselves to other computers on a network.

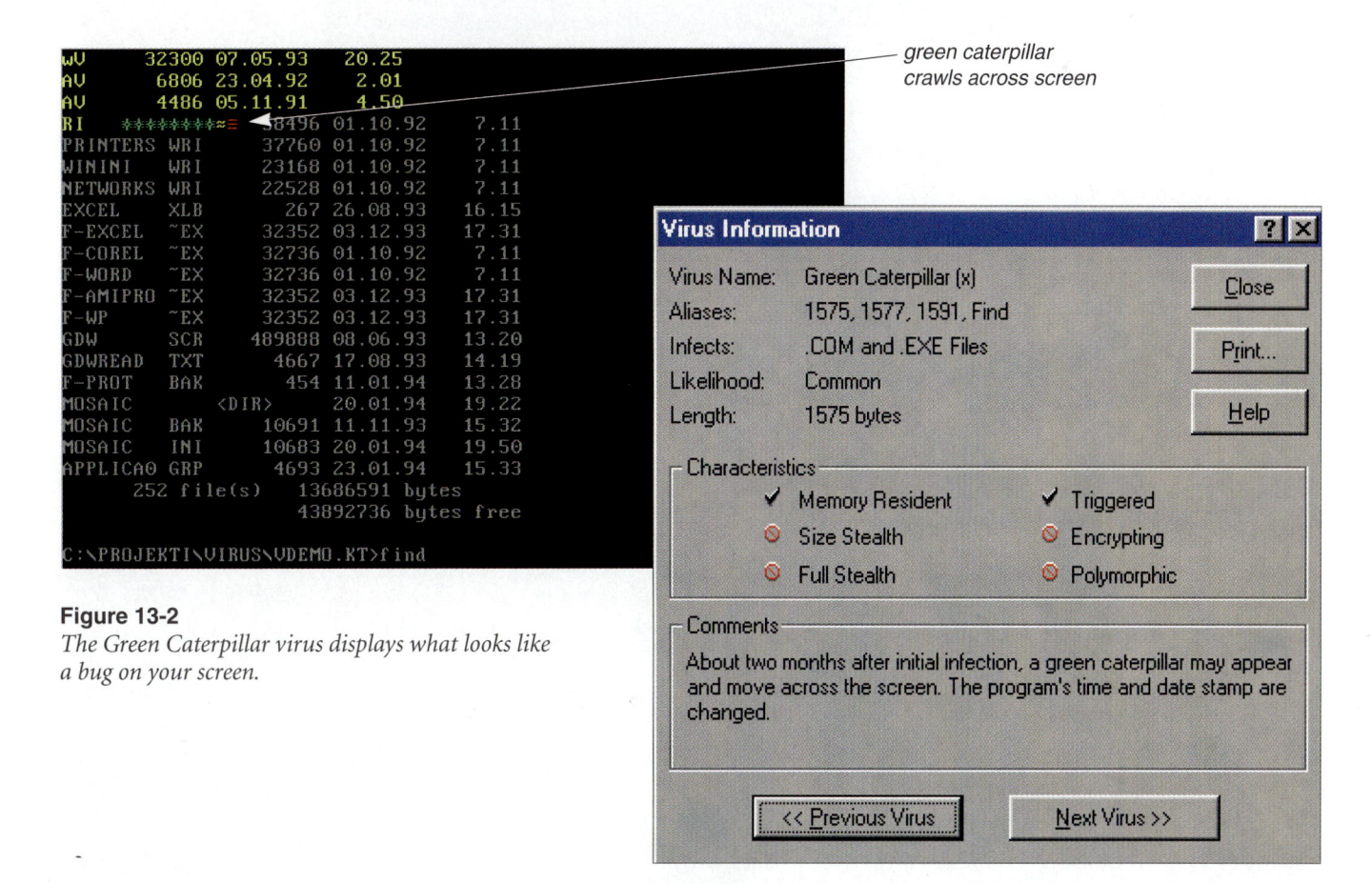

Figure 13-2
The Green Caterpillar virus displays what looks like a bug on your screen.

Virus Detection and Removal

To protect against computer viruses, **antivirus programs**, called **vaccines**, have been developed. Antivirus programs work by looking for programs that attempt to modify the boot program, the operating system, and other programs that normally are read from but not written to (Figure 13-3). Antivirus programs also look for specific patterns of known virus code called a **virus signature**, which they compare to a virus signature file. Virus signature files need to be updated frequently to include newly discovered viruses, so an antivirus program can protect against viruses written after the antivirus program was released. Even with an updated virus signature file, antivirus programs have difficulty detecting viruses such as the polymorphic virus. A **polymorphic virus** is designed to modify its program code each time it attaches itself to another program or file. Because its code never looks the same, a polymorphic virus cannot be detected with a virus signature.

Another way vaccine programs prevent viruses is by *inoculating* existing program files. When a program file is **inoculated**, information such as the file size and file creation date is recorded in a separate inoculation file. Using this information, the vaccine program can tell if a virus program has tampered with the program file. Some sophisticated virus programs, however, take steps to avoid detection. A virus might infect a program, for example, and yet still report the size and creation date of the original, uninfected program. A virus that uses methods to avoid detection sometimes is called a **stealth virus**.

inCyber

For a collection of antivirus protection programs, visit the Discovering Computers Chapter 13 inCyber page (http://www.scsite.com/dc/ch13/incyber.htm) and click Antivirus Programs.

Figure 13-3
Antivirus programs check disk drives and memory for computer viruses. The top screen allows you to select the drives to be scanned. The middle screen displays the status during the scan, and the bottom screen shows the results.

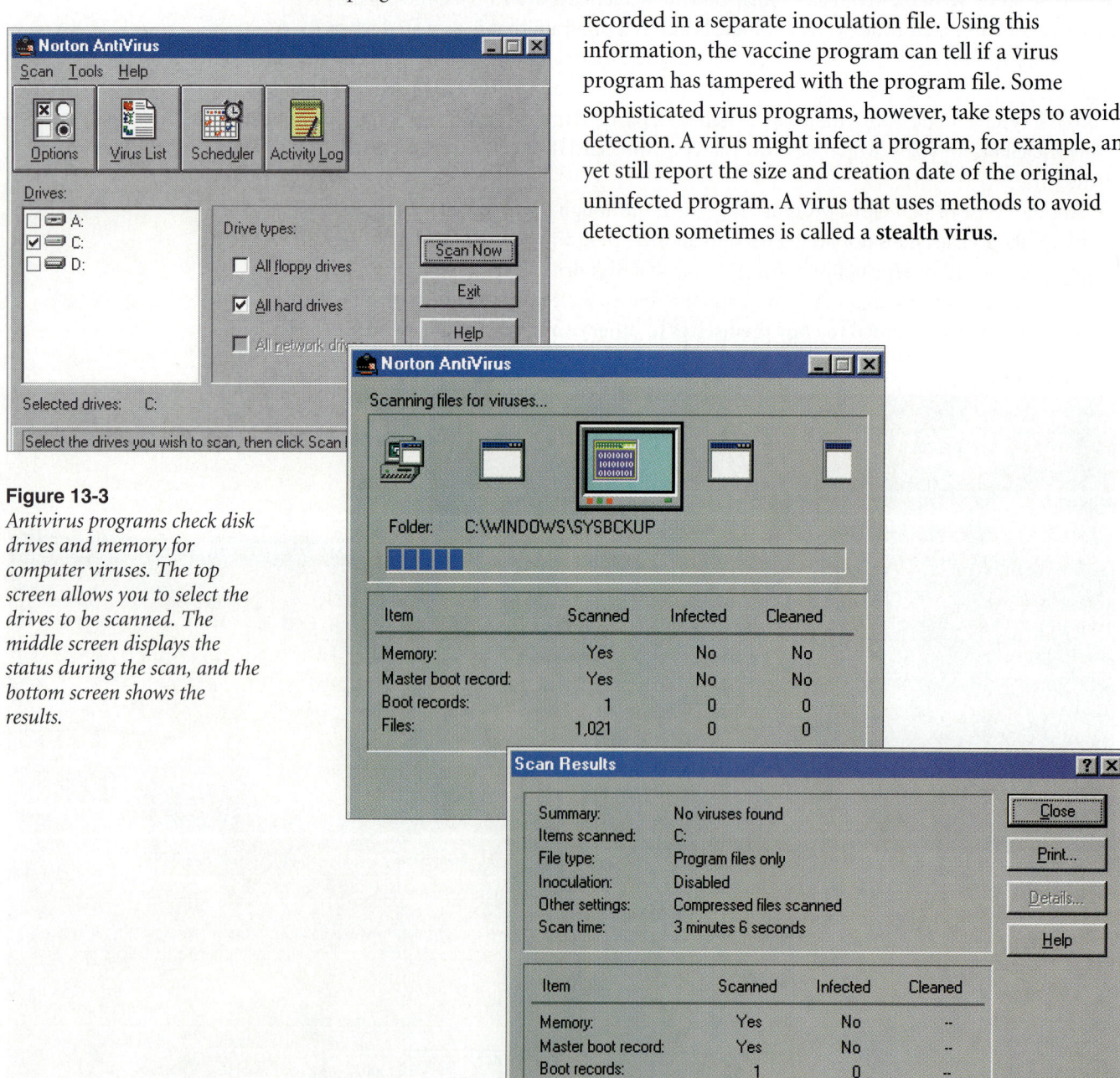

Besides detecting viruses and inoculating against them, antivirus programs also have utilities to remove or repair infected programs and files. If the virus has infected the boot program, however, the antivirus program first will require you to restart the computer with a floppy disk called a rescue disk. The **rescue disk** contains an uninfected copy of certain operating system commands and essential information about the computer that enables the computer to restart correctly. Once the computer has been restarted *cleanly*, the repair and removal programs can be run. Sometimes damaged files cannot be repaired and must be replaced with uninfected backup copies, which are discussed later in this chapter.

To protect against being infected by a computer virus, experts recommend the following:

- Install virus protection software on every system on which you work. The cost of antivirus software is much less than the cost of rebuilding damaged files. As a result, most businesses and large organizations have adopted this policy.

- Before using any floppy disk, use a virus scan program to check for viruses. This holds true even for shrink-wrapped software from major developers. Even commercial software has been infected and distributed to unsuspecting users.

- Check all downloaded programs for viruses. Viruses often are first placed in seemingly innocent programs so they will affect a large number of users.

Companies and individuals who need help with virus-infected PCs can contact the National Computer Security Association (NCSA) at 900-555-NCSA (6272) for low-cost assistance.

Unauthorized Access and Use

Unauthorized access is the use of a computer system without permission; in other words, computer trespassing. Individuals who try to access computer systems illegally are called **crackers**. The term **hacker**, although originally a positive term, also has become associated with people who try to break into computer systems. Crackers and hackers typically break into systems by connecting to the system via a modem and logging in as a user. Some intruders do no damage; they merely wander around the accessed system before logging off. Other intruders leave some evidence of their presence either by leaving a message or deliberately altering data.

Unauthorized use is the use of a computer system or computer data for unapproved or possibly illegal activities. Unauthorized use may range from an employee using a computer to keep his or her child's soccer league scores to someone gaining access to a bank system and completing an unauthorized transfer.

The key to preventing both unauthorized access and unauthorized use of computers is by implementing **access controls**, which are security measures that define who can access a computer, when they can access it, and what actions they can take while accessing this computer. Many commercial software packages are designed to implement these types of access controls through a two-phase process called identification and authentication. **Identification** verifies that you are a valid user, and **authentication** verifies that you are who you claim to be. Three methods of authentication exist: remembered information, possessed objects, and biometric devices.

---

inCyber

For a description of the National Computer Security Association (NCSA), visit the Discovering Computers Chapter 13 inCyber page (http://www.scsite.com/dc/ch13/incyber.htm) and click NCSA.

inCyber

To learn about terms in a hacker's vocabulary, visit the Discovering Computers Chapter 13 inCyber page (http://www.scsite.com/dc/ch13/incyber.htm) and click Hacker.

Remembered Information With **remembered information authentication**, you are required to enter a word or series of characters that matches an entry in a security file in the computer. As discussed in Chapter 8, most multiuser operating systems provide for a logon code, a user ID, and a password (all forms of remembered information) that all must be entered correctly before you are allowed to use an application program. The logon code, user ID, and password must match entries in an authorization file.

You usually select your own password by choosing a word or series of characters that will be easy to remember. If your password is too simple or obvious, however, such as your initials or birthday, others may guess it easily. As shown in Figure 13-4, each character added to a password significantly increases the number of possible combinations and the length of time it would take for someone to guess the password. Some techniques you can follow to create passwords are:

- Choose names of obscure places in other countries
- Join two words together
- Mix initials and dates together
- Add one or more numbers at the beginning, middle, or end of a word
- Choose words from other languages
- Choose family names far back in your genealogy
- Add letters to or subtract letters from an existing word

Generally, the more creative you are when assigning a password, the harder it is for someone to figure out.

Many software programs have certain guidelines you must follow when you create your password. Many, for example, require passwords to have a minimum length of six characters and use a mixture of numbers and letters. Suppose a software package requires a password with a length between six and ten characters, two of which must be numeric. Following these guidelines, the password MIKE1 is invalid (it is too short), but MIKE0402 is valid. This password also is easy for the user to remember—MIKE is the user's son's name and April 2 is Mike's birthday (04/02)—but not so simple that it will be guessed easily.

Figure 13-4
This table shows the effect of increasing the length of a password made up of letters and numbers. The longer the password, the more effort required to discover it. Long passwords, however, are more difficult for users to remember.

PASSWORD PROTECTION

NUMBER OF CHARACTERS	POSSIBLE COMBINATIONS	Average Time to Discover HUMAN	COMPUTER
1	36	3 minutes	.000018 second
2	1,300	2 hours	.00065 second
3	47,000	3 days	.02 second
4	1,700,000	3 months	1 second
5	60,000,000	10 years	30 seconds
10	3,700,000,000,000,000	580 million years	59 years

- Possible characters include the letters A-Z and numbers 0-9
- Human discovery assumes one try every 10 seconds
- Computer discovery assumes one million tries per second
- Average time assumes password would be discovered in approximately half the time it would take to try all possible combinations

COMPUTER SECURITY: RISKS AND SAFEGUARDS   **13.7**

Even long and creative passwords do not provide complete protection against unauthorized access. Unauthorized **sniffer** programs can copy passwords as they are entered. The copied passwords later are retrieved by unauthorized users and used to logon to the computer. Because the password used is valid, the unauthorized access is difficult to detect.

A variation of remembered information authentication is called dialog authentication. With **dialog authentication**, the user is asked to enter one of several possible items of personal information, such as a spouse's first name, a birth date, or a mother's maiden name, which is chosen randomly from information on file. Like a password, if the dialog response does not match the information on file, access is denied.

Possessed Objects   A **possessed object** is any item that you must carry to gain access to a computer facility. Examples of possessed objects are badges, cards, and keys. Possessed objects often are used in conjunction with personal identification numbers. A **personal identification number (PIN)** is a numeric password, either assigned by an organization or selected by you. Like the PIN you must enter when using an automated teller machine (ATM) card, a PIN used with a possessed object provides an additional level of security.

Biometric Devices   A **biometric device** is one that verifies personal characteristics such as fingerprints, hand size, signature and typing patterns, and retinal (eye) and voice patterns to authenticate the person requesting access. A biometric device translates a personal characteristic into a digital code that is compared to a digital code stored in the computer. If the digital code in the computer does not match the code, access is denied.

Many types of biometric security devices are currently in use. Fingerprint or thumbprint scanners, for example, are used to verify fingerprints (Figure 13-5). The shape, size, and other characteristics of a person's hand also can be measured using hand geometry systems.

inCyber

For a comprehensive list of resources concerning biometric devicesd, visit the Discovering Computers Chapter 13 inCyber page (http://www.scsite.com/dc/ch13/incyber.htm) and click Biometric.

Figure 13-5
A user's identity can be verified by his or her fingerprint with a fingerprint scanner.

Biometric pens measure the pressure exerted and the motion used to write signatures (Figure 13-6), while keystroke analysis devices measure typing patterns and rhythms. Retinal scanners (Figure 13-7) even can be used to read patterns in the tiny blood vessels in the back of the eye, which are as unique as a fingerprint. Finally, biometric devices can verify a person's voice by digitizing spoken words and comparing them against previously recorded digital patterns.

Biometric security devices are gaining popularity because they are a virtually foolproof method of authentication. Unlike passwords and possessed objects, which can be copied, duplicated, or lost, personal characteristics are unique and cannot be forgotten or misplaced. Biometric devices do have some disadvantages. For example, if you cut your finger, a fingerprint scanner may reject you. If you are nervous, a voice, signature, or typing pattern may not match the one on file. Biometric devices also are more expensive than other authentication techniques and thus are used primarily by government security organizations, the military, and financial institutions that deal with highly sensitive data.

An access control method sometimes used to authenticate remote users is a callback system. With a **callback system**, you can be connected to the computer system only after the computer calls you back at a previously established telephone number. To initiate the callback system, you call the computer and enter a logon code, user ID, and password. If these entries are valid, the computer instructs you to hang up and then calls you back at the previously established number. This method provides an additional layer of security to remembered information; even if a person steals or guesses a logon code, user ID, and password, that person also must be at the authorized telephone number to access the system. Callback systems function only for users who regularly work at the same remote location, such as from home or a branch office.

Figure 13-6
A biometric pen device measures the characteristics of a person's signature.

Because they require the user to be at a certain location, callback systems do not work well for employees who travel and need to access the computer from different locations and telephone numbers.

Figure 13-7
This retinal scanner identifies a user by reading the tiny blood vessel patterns in the back of the eye.

The authentication technique an organization uses should correspond to the degree of risk associated with the unauthorized access. In addition, an organization should review regularly the levels of authorization for users to determine if the levels still are appropriate. No matter what type of identification and authentication is used, the computer system should record both successful and unsuccessful access attempts. Unsuccessful access attempts should be investigated immediately to make sure they were not attempted security breaks. Successful access should be reviewed for irregularities, such as use of the system after normal working hours or from remote terminals. Records of system usage also can be used to allocate information processing expenses based on the percentage of system use by various departments.

In addition, organizations should have written policies regarding the use of computers by employees for personal reasons. Some organizations prohibit such use entirely. Others permit personal use on the employee's own time, before or after work. Most organizations have informal policies, which are decided on a case-by-case basis. Whatever the policy, it should be documented and made clear to employees.

Hardware Theft

In the case of desktop and larger computer systems in a home or office, hardware theft generally is not a problem. While physical access controls such as locked doors and windows usually are adequate to protect the equipment, many offices and some homeowners also install alarm systems for additional security. School computer labs and other areas with a large number of semifrequent users often install additional physical security devices such as cables that lock the equipment to a desk or floor (Figure 13-8).

With portable equipment such as notebook computers or personal digital assistants (PDAs), hardware theft poses a more serious risk. High-end notebook computers, some of which cost more than $5,000, are particularly at risk; their size and weight make them easy to steal and their value makes them tempting targets for thieves.

Common sense and a constant awareness of the risk are the best preventive measures against theft of portable computing devices. Such devices should not be left out in the open, such as on the seat of a car, or be left unattended in a public place, such as an airport or a restaurant. Physical devices such as cables that temporarily can lock a portable to a desk or table also can be used. Finally, all information stored on portable computing devices should be backed up regularly.

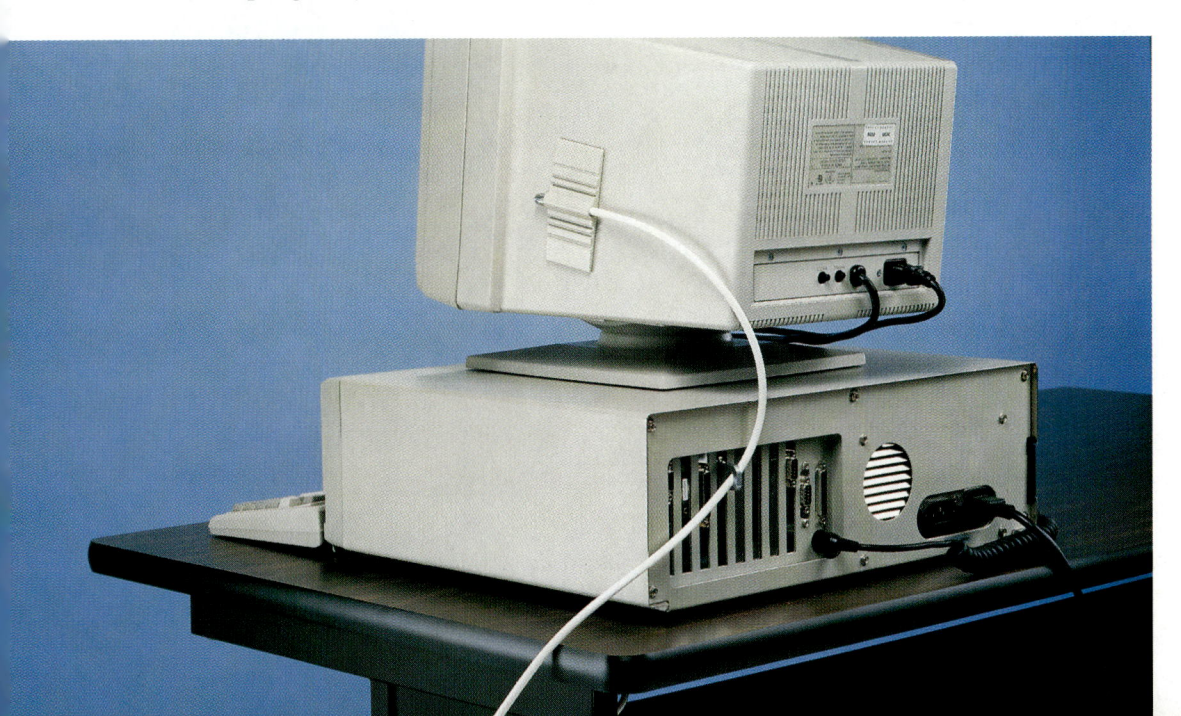

Figure 13-8
Cable locking devices can be used to prevent the theft of desktop and portable computer equipment.

Software Theft

Software theft can take the form of physically stealing a CD-ROM or floppy disk, but most likely the theft involves software piracy. **Software piracy** is the unauthorized and illegal copying of copyrighted software. Even after you have purchased a software package, you do not have the right to copy, loan, rent, or in any way distribute the software. Doing so not only is a violation of copyright law, it also is a federal crime. Despite this, experts estimate that, for every authorized copy of software in use, at least one unauthorized copy is made. One study reported that software piracy resulted in worldwide losses of more than $15 billion per year.

Software piracy continues for several reasons. In some countries, legal protection for software does not exist; while in others, laws rarely are enforced. In addition, many buyers believe they have the right to copy the software for which they have paid hundreds, even thousands of dollars—particularly when it is on an inexpensive floppy disk or CD-ROM. Finally, particularly in the case of floppy disks, software piracy is a simple crime to commit.

Software companies, by contrast, take illegal copying seriously, and in some cases, offenders have been prosecuted to the fullest extent of the law. Penalties can include fines up to $250,000 and up to five years in jail. Many organizations and businesses have written policies prohibiting the copying and use of copyrighted software. Some of these organizations enforce the policy by periodically checking to make sure that all software is properly licensed. To promote a better understanding of piracy problems and, if necessary, to take legal action, a number of major U.S. software companies formed the **Business Software Alliance** (BSA). BSA operates a Web site (Figure 13-9) and antipiracy hotlines in the United States and 53 countries.

To reduce software costs for organizations with large numbers of users, software vendors often offer special discount pricing or site licensing. With discount pricing, the more copies of a program an organization purchases, the greater the discount. Purchasing a software

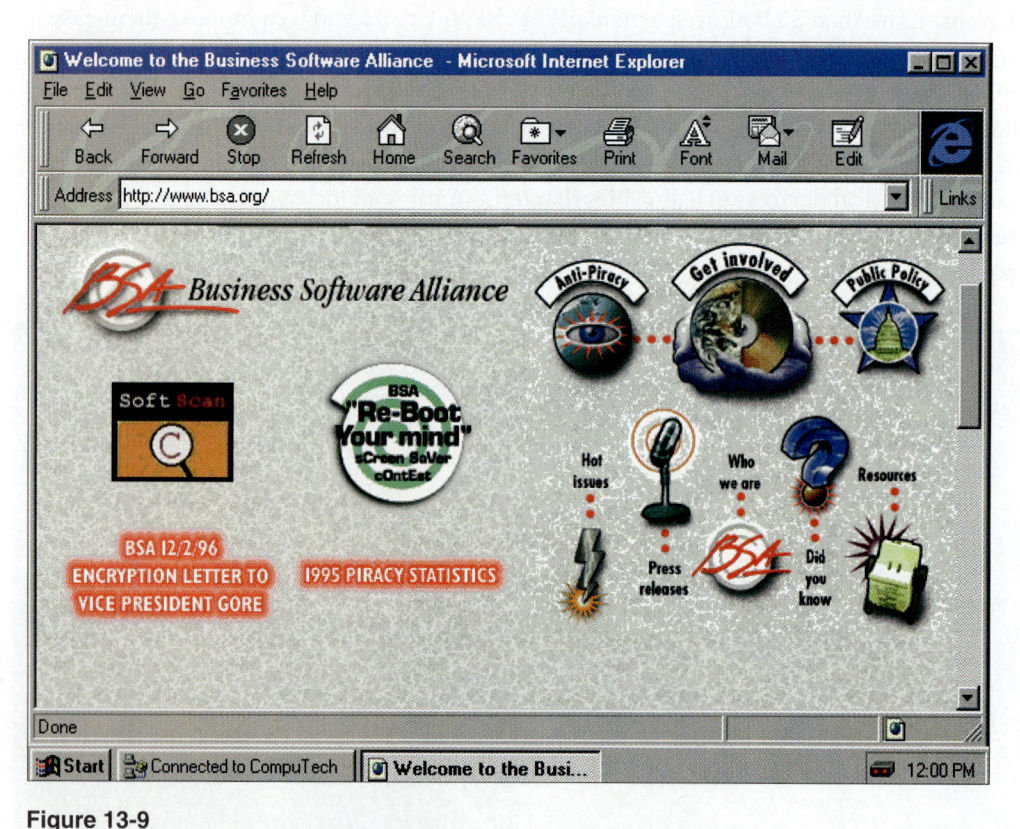

> **inCyber**
>
> For information on the Business Software Alliance (BSA), visit the Discovering Computers Chapter 13 inCyber page (http://www.scsite.com/dc/ch13/incyber.htm) and click BSA.

Figure 13-9
The Business Software Alliance (BSA) Web site provides the latest information about software piracy. BSA fights against software piracy by conducting educational programs and operating antipiracy hotlines in the United States and 53 other countries.

site license gives an organization the right to install the software on multiple computers at a single site. Site license fees usually are lower than the cost of purchasing individual copies of the software package for each computer. Network versions of many software packages also are available. These packages allow network users to share a single copy of the software that resides on the network server. Network software site licenses can be priced based on a fixed fee for an unlimited number of users, a maximum number of users, or on a per-user basis.

Information Theft

The deliberate theft of information from a computer system may occur for several reasons. Organizations may steal or buy stolen information to learn about a competitor. Credit card and telephone charge card numbers may be stolen to be used for purchases or charges. Both types of numbers frequently are stored in an accounting or administrative department file on the computer; once the system is accessed, any or all of these numbers can be stolen.

Most organizations prevent information theft by implementing the user identification and authentication controls discussed in the previous section of this chapter on Unauthorized Access and Use. These controls, however, work best to prevent the theft of information that resides on computers located on an organization's premises. Information transmitted over networks offers a higher degree of risk because it can be intercepted. Portable computing devices that contain sensitive company information generally do not have the same level of access controls and, therefore, also carry a higher risk of information theft.

One way to protect sensitive data is to use encryption. **Encryption** is the process of converting readable data, called **plaintext**, into unreadable characters, called **ciphertext**. Encryption involves applying a formula that uses a code, called an **encryption key**, to convert the plaintext to ciphertext. The same encryption key also is used by the person who receives the ciphertext message to decrypt (or decipher) the data back into the original plaintext. A more secure way of encrypting data, called **public key encryption**, uses two encryption keys (Figure 13-10). With public key encryption, you use encryption software to generate two

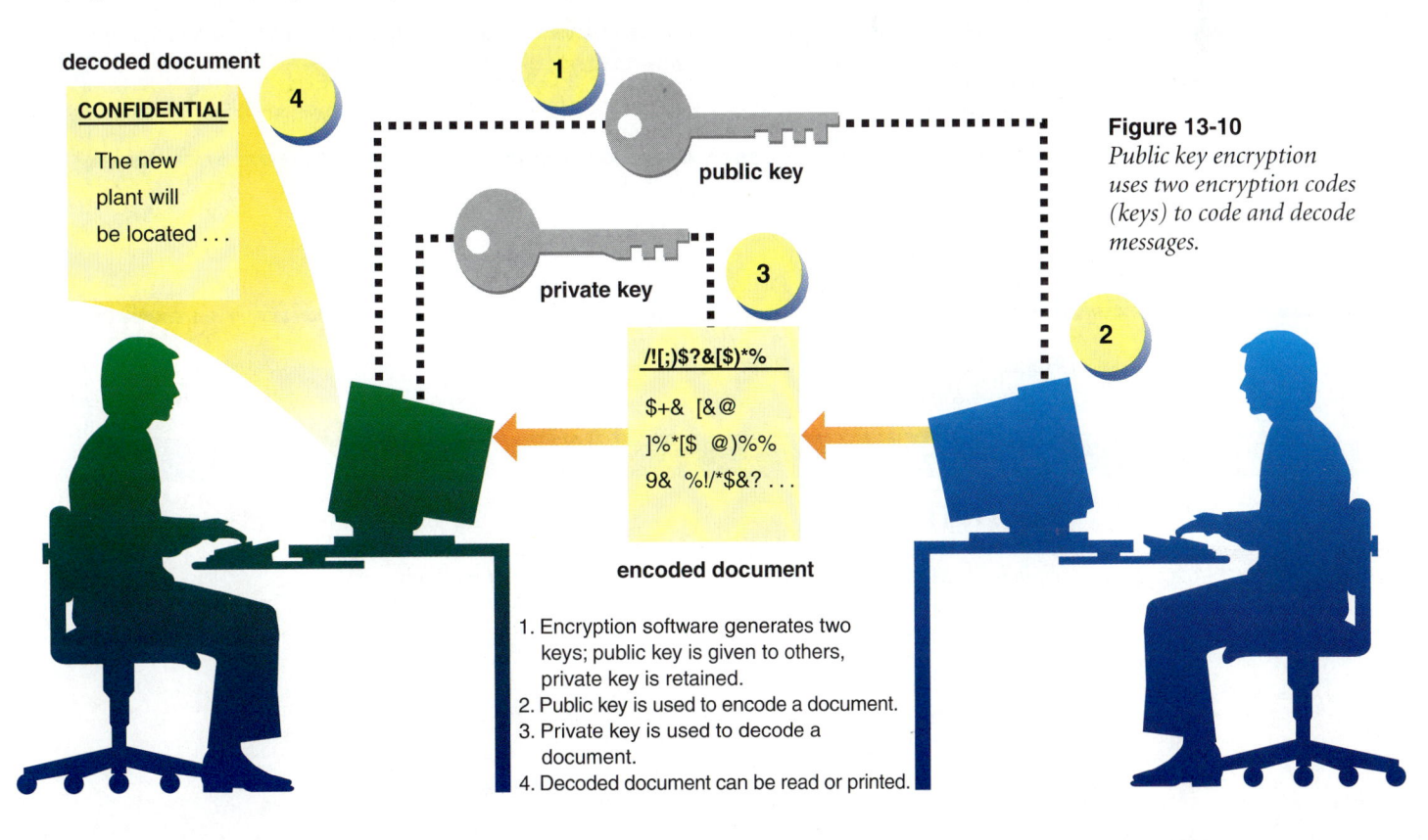

Figure 13-10
Public key encryption uses two encryption codes (keys) to code and decode messages.

1. Encryption software generates two keys; public key is given to others, private key is retained.
2. Public key is used to encode a document.
3. Private key is used to decode a document.
4. Decoded document can be read or printed.

For details on the data encryption standard (DES), visit the Discovering Computers Chapter 13 inCyber page (http://www.scsite.com/dc/ch13/incyber.htm) and click DES.

keys, a public key and a private key. You keep the private key and give the public key to another person. That person uses the public key to encrypt a message that can be read only with your private key. When you receive the message, you use your private key to decipher it.

Many data encryption methods exist; some examples of simple encryption methods are shown in Figure 13-11. Encryption methods often will use more than one of these techniques, such as a combination of transposition and substitution. While most organizations use available software packages for encryption, some develop their own encryption methods. An encryption method widely used by the U.S. government is the **data encryption standard** (**DES**). Figure 13-12 shows how the Gettysburg Address appears after encryption using DES.

Since 1993, the U.S. government has proposed several ideas for developing a standard for voice and data encryption that would enable government agencies, such as the National Security Agency (NSA) and the Federal Bureau of Investigation (FBI), to monitor private communications. An early government proposal called for the use of an encryption formula implemented in a tamper-resistant microprocessor called the **Clipper chip**. Widespread opposition to this hardware approach caused the idea to be abandoned. In its place, the government proposed a key escrow plan, similar to the public key encryption method. The government's **key escrow** plan proposed using independent escrow organizations that would have custody of private keys that could decode encrypted messages. If necessary, authorized government agencies could obtain the necessary key. This plan also has been opposed and has not yet been implemented.

ENCRYPTION METHODS

NAME	METHOD	PLAINTEXT	CIPHERTEXT	EXPLANATION
Transposition	Switch the order of characters	COMPUTER	OCPMTURE	Adjacent characters swapped
Substitution	Replace characters with others	PRINTER	EOJLZRO	Each letter replaced with another
Expansion	Insert characters between existing characters	TAPE	TYAYPYEY	Letter Y inserted after each character
Compaction	Remove characters and store elseware	HARDWARE	HADWRE	Every third letter removed (R and A)

Figure 13-11
This table shows four methods of encryption; or translating plaintext into ciphertext. Most encryption programs use a combination of methods.

COMPUTER SECURITY: RISKS AND SAFEGUARDS **13.13**

The Gettysburg Address

Four score and seven years ago our fathers brought forth on this continent, a new nation, conceived in liberty, and dedicated to the proposition that all men are created equal.

Now we are engaged in a great civil war, testing whether that nation or any nation so conceived and so dedicated, can long endure. We are met on a great battle field of that war. We have come to dedicate a portion of that field as a final resting place for those who here gave their lives that the nation might live. It is altogether fitting and proper that we should do this.

Figure 13-12
This figure shows the first two paragraphs of the Gettysburg Address in plaintext and ciphertext. It was encrypted using a software package that employs the DES encryption formula.

System Failure

Theft is not the only cause of hardware, software, data, or information loss. Any of these also can occur during a **system failure**, which is the prolonged malfunction of a computer system. System failures are caused by natural disasters such as fires, floods, or storms or by events such as electrical power problems.

One of the more common causes of system failures is electrical power variations. Electrical power variations can cause loss of data or loss of equipment. If the computer equipment is connected to a network, multiple systems can be damaged with a single power disturbance. Electrical disturbances include noise, undervoltages, and overvoltages.

Noise is any unwanted signal, usually varying quickly, that is mixed with the normal voltage entering the computer. Noise is caused by external devices such as fluorescent lighting, radios, and televisions, as well as from components within the computer itself. While noise generally is not a risk to hardware, software, or data, computer power supplies are designed to filter out noise.

An **undervoltage** occurs when the electrical supply drops. In North America, electricity normally flows from the wall plug at approximately 120 volts. Any significant drop below 120 volts is considered an undervoltage. A **brownout** is a prolonged undervoltage; a **blackout** is a complete power failure. Undervoltages can cause data loss but generally do not cause equipment damage.

An **overvoltage**, or **power surge**, occurs when the incoming electrical power increases significantly above the normal 120 volts. A momentary overvoltage, called a **spike**, occurs when the power increase lasts for less than one millisecond (one thousandth of a second). Spikes are caused by uncontrollable disturbances such as lightning bolts or controllable disturbances such as turning on a piece of equipment that is on the same electrical circuit. Overvoltages can cause immediate and permanent damage to hardware.

inCyber

To learn about the consequences of a system failure, visit the Discovering Computers Chapter 13 inCyber page (http://www.scsite.com/dc/ch13/incyber.htm) and click System Failure.

Figure 13-13
Circuits inside a surge protector safeguard against overvoltages.

inCyber
For details on how surge protectors work and how to select one for your needs, visit the Discovering Computers Chapter 13 inCyber page (http://www.scsite.com/dc/ch13/incyber.htm) and click Surge Protector.

To protect against overvoltages, surge protectors are used. A **surge protector**, also called a **surge suppressor**, uses special electrical components to smooth out minor voltage errors, provide a stable current flow, and keep an overvoltage from reaching the computer equipment (Figure 13-13). Small overvoltages are absorbed by the surge protector without damage. Large overvoltages, such as those caused by a lightning strike, will cause the surge protector to fail in order to protect the computer equipment. Surge protectors are not 100 percent effective; large power surges can bypass the protector and repeated small overvoltages can weaken a surge protector permanently. Some experts recommend replacing surge protectors every two to three years.

For additional electrical protection, many users connect an uninterruptable power supply to the computer. An **uninterruptable power supply (UPS)** is a device that contains surge protection circuits and one or more batteries that can provide power during a temporary or permanent loss of power (Figure 13-14). The amount of time a UPS allows you to continue working depends on the electrical requirements of the computer system and the size of the batteries in the UPS. A UPS for a personal computer should provide from ten to thirty minutes of use in the case of a total power loss. This should be enough time to save current work and shut down the computer properly.

Figure 13-14
If power fails, an uninterruptable power supply (UPS) uses batteries to provide electricity for a limited amount of time.

Backup Procedures

To prevent against data loss caused by a system failure, computer users should have backup procedures. A **backup** is a copy of information stored on a computer. To *back up* a file means to make a copy. **Backup procedures** specify a regular plan of copying and storing key data and program files. In the case of a system failure or the discovery of corrupted files, backup copies are used to **restore** the files (reload the files on the computer). Backup copies normally are kept in fireproof safes or vaults, or **offsite** in a building different from the computer site. Offsite storage is used so that a single disaster, such as a fire, will not destroy both the primary and the backup copy of the data.

An organization or individual can perform three types of backup: full, differential, or incremental. A **full backup** duplicates all of the files in the computer. Because all program and data files are copied, a full backup provides the best protection against data loss. A full backup can take a long time, however, and thus, often is used in conjunction with differential and incremental backups. A **differential backup** duplicates only the files that have changed *since the last full backup*. An **incremental backup** duplicates only the files that have changed since the last full or *incremental backup*. The key difference between a differential backup and an incremental backup is the number of backup files and the time required for backup. With a differential backup, you always have two backups; the full backup and the differential backup of all changes since the last full backup. With incremental backups, you may have several incremental backup copies. The first incremental backup contains copies of files that have changed since the last full backup. Subsequent incremental backups contain copies of files that have changed since the previous incremental backup. For files that contain many changes and comprise a large portion of the total data, incremental backup usually is fastest. If files contain only a few changes, differential backups may be appropriate. Figure 13-15 outlines the advantages and disadvantages of each type of backup.

TYPE OF BACKUP	ADVANTAGES	DISADVANTAGES
Full	Fastest recovery method. All files are saved.	Longest backup time.
Differential	Fast backup method. Requires minimal space to backup.	Recovery is time consuming because need last full backup plus the differential backup.
Incremental	Fastest backup method. Requires minimal space to backup. Only most recent changes saved.	Recovery is most time consuming because need last full backup and all incremental backups since last full backup.

Figure 13-15
The advantages and disadvantages of different backup methods

Generally, an organization develops a policy and procedures in which a full backup is performed at regular intervals, such as at the end of each week and at the end of the month. Between full backups, differential or incremental backups are performed. Figure 13-16 shows an approach for backing up a system for one month. This combination of full and incremental backups provides an efficient way of protecting data and provides several restore starting points if a problem with incorrect data is found. Whatever backup procedures an organization adopts, they should be clearly stated, documented in writing, and followed consistently.

Sometimes, a **three-generation backup policy** is used in which important individual files are backed up separately. The oldest copy of the file is called the **grandfather**. The second oldest copy of the file is called the **father**. The most recent copy of the file is called the **son**.

Backup and restore programs are available from many sources including most developers of antivirus programs and utility software. Backup and restore programs also are included with most operating systems and with backup devices such as cartridge tape or cartridge disk drives.

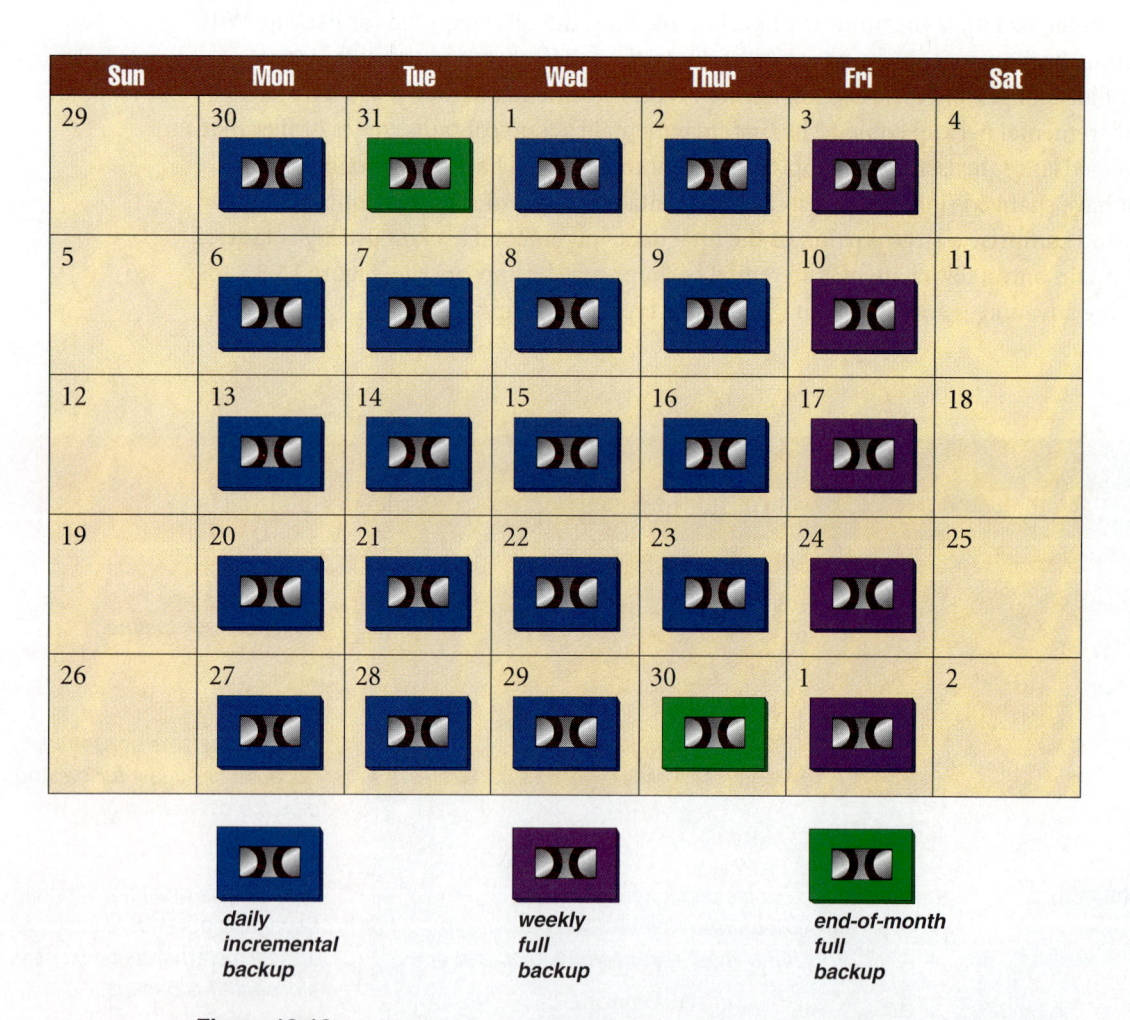

Figure 13-16

This calendar shows a backup strategy for a month. The tapes used for Monday, Tuesday, Wednesday, and Thursday would be the same each week. The tapes used for the Friday backups would be used again the following month. A new tape would be used each month for the end-of-month backup. End-of-month backup tapes usually are kept for at least one year. Some companies always end the month on the Friday closest to the last calendar day of the month. This gives them the weekend to perform the more time-consuming end-of-month backup.

Disaster Recovery Plan

Because the prolonged loss of computing capability can seriously damage an organization's ability to function, a disaster recovery plan should be developed. A **disaster recovery plan** is a written plan describing the steps an organization would take to restore computer operations in the event of a disaster. A disaster recovery plan contains four major components: the emergency plan, the backup plan, the recovery plan, and the test plan (Figure 13-17).

The Emergency Plan An **emergency plan** specifies the steps to be taken immediately after a disaster strikes. The emergency plan usually is organized by type of disaster, such as fire, flood, or earthquake. Depending on the nature and extent of the disaster, some emergency procedures will differ. All emergency plans should contain the following information:

1. Names and telephone numbers of people and organizations to be notified (e.g., management, fire department, police department)
2. Procedures to be followed with the computer equipment (e.g., equipment shutdown, power shutoff, file removal)
3. Employee evacuation procedures
4. Return procedures; that is, who can reenter the facility and what actions they are to perform

> **inCyber**
> For details on the necessity of having a disaster recovery plan, visit the Discovering Computers Chapter 13 inCyber page (http://www.scsite.com/dc/ch13/incyber.htm) and click Disaster Recovery Plan.

PARTS OF A DISASTER RECOVERY PLAN

Emergency Plan
Evacuation plans and list of people to notify

Backup Plan
Identity and location of backup resources

Recovery Plan
Specific steps and time plan to resume computer operations

Test Plan
Simulates diasters to find weaknesses in overall plan

Figure 13-17
Summary of the four parts of a disaster recovery plan.

The Backup Plan Once the procedures in the emergency plan have been executed, the next step is to follow the backup plan. The **backup plan** specifies how an organization will use backup files and equipment to resume information processing. Because an organization's normal location may be destroyed or unusable, the backup plan should include an alternate computer facility. The backup plan identifies these items:

1. The location of backup data, supplies, and equipment
2. The personnel responsible for gathering backup resources and transporting them to the alternate computer facility
3. A schedule indicating the order and approximate time each application should be up and running

For a backup plan to be successful, it is crucial that all critical resources are backed up; that is, hardware, software, data, facilities, supplies, and documentation. Because personnel could be injured in a disaster, it also is crucial that additional people, including possibly nonemployees, are trained in the backup and recovery procedures.

The location of the alternate computer facility also is important. It should be close enough to be convenient, yet not too close that a single disaster, such as an earthquake, could destroy both the main and alternate computer facilities. Two types of alternate computer facilities exist: a hot site and a cold site. A **hot site** is an alternate computer facility that has compatible computer resources; that is, it already has installed the necessary hardware, software, and communications equipment. Because installing and maintaining a hot site is quite expensive, many organizations instead use a cold site as their alternate computer facility. A **cold site** is an empty facility that can accommodate the necessary computer resources. A cold site requires immediate installation of computer equipment and software in case of disaster. An alternative to maintaining a hot or cold site is to enter into a **reciprocal backup relationship** with another firm; that is, in case of disaster, one firm provides space and sometimes equipment to the other.

The Recovery Plan The **recovery plan** specifies the actions to be taken to restore full information processing operations. Like the emergency plan, the recovery plan differs for each type of disaster. To prepare for disaster recovery, planning committees should be established, with each one responsible for different forms of recovery. For example, one committee could be in charge of hardware replacement, while another could be responsible for software replacement.

The Test Plan To provide assurance that the disaster plan is complete, it should be tested. A **disaster recovery test plan** contains information for simulating different levels of disasters and recording an organization's ability to recover. In a simulation, all personnel would be required to follow the steps outlined in the disaster recovery plan. Any needed recovery actions that are *not* specified in the plan should be added. Although simulations can be scheduled, the best test of the plan is to simulate a disaster without advance notice.

Developing a Computer Security Plan

The individual risks and safeguards previously mentioned and the disaster recovery plan all should be incorporated into an overall computer security plan. A **computer security plan** summarizes in writing all of the safeguards that are in place to protect an organization's information assets. A computer security plan should do the following:

- Identify all information assets of an organization including equipment, software, documentation, procedures, people, data, facilities, and supplies.
- Identify all security risks that may cause an information asset loss. Risks should be ranked from most likely to occur to least likely to occur. An estimated value should be placed on each risk including the value of lost business. For example, what is the estimated loss if customers cannot place orders for one hour, one day, or one week?
- For each risk, identify the safeguards that exist to detect, prevent, and recover from a loss.

The computer security plan should be updated annually or more frequently for major changes in information assets, such as the addition of a new computer or the implementation of a new application. In developing the plan, you should keep in mind that some degree of risk is unavoidable. The more secure a system is, the more difficult it is for everyone to use. The goal of a computer security plan is to match an appropriate level of safeguards against the identified risks. Fortunately, most organizations will never experience a major information system disaster. Because many organizations and individuals rely heavily on computers, however, disaster recovery must be planned for.

Information Privacy

Information privacy refers to the right of individuals and organizations to deny or restrict the collection and use of information about them. In the past, information privacy was easier to maintain because information tended to be kept in separate locations; individual stores had their own credit files, government agencies had separate records, doctors had separate files, and so on. It is now, however, technically and economically feasible to store large amounts of related data about individuals in one database. Computers also can be used to monitor employee activities. As a result, many have concerns about how the unauthorized collection and use of data and monitoring affects their privacy.

Unauthorized Collection and Use of Information

Many individuals are surprised to learn that information provided for magazine subscriptions, product warranty registration cards, contest entry forms, and other separate documents often is sold to national marketing organizations. By combining this acquired data with other information obtained from public sources such as driver's license and vehicle registration information, national marketing organizations can create an electronic profile of an individual. This electronic profile then is sold to organizations that want to send information on their products, services, or causes to a specific group of individuals, such as all sports car owners, over 40 years of age, living in the southeastern United States, for example. Direct marketing supporters say that using information in this way lowers overall selling costs, which, in turn, lowers product prices. Critics contend that the combined information in electronic profiles can reveal more about individuals than anyone has a right to know; they claim that, at a minimum, individuals should be informed that the information they furnish may be provided to others and have the right to deny such use.

The concern about privacy has led to federal and state laws regarding the storage and disclosure of personal data (Figure 13-18). Common points in some of these laws include the following:

1. Information collected and stored about individuals should be limited to what is necessary to carry out the function of the business or government agency collecting the data.

2. Once collected, provisions should be made to restrict access to the data to those employees within the organization who need access to it to perform their job duties.

3. Personal information should be released outside the organization collecting the data only when the person has agreed to its disclosure.

4. When information is collected about an individual, the individual should know that the data is being collected and have the opportunity to determine the accuracy of the data.

---

inCyber

For extensive information on a variety of issues related to information privacy, ethics, and the law, visit the Discovering Computers Chapter 13 inCyber page (http://www.scsite.com/dc/ch13/incyber.htm) and click Information Privacy.

DATE	LAW	PURPOSE
1996	National Information Infrastructure Protection Act	Penalties for theft of information across state lines, threats against networks, and computer system trespassing.
1994	Computer Abuse Amendments Act	Amends 1984 act to outlaw transmission of harmful computer code such as viruses.
1992	Cable Act	Extends privacy of Cable Communications Policy Act of 1984 to include cellular and other wireless services.
1991	Telephone Consumer Protection Act	Restricts activities of telemarketers.
1988	Computer Matching and Privacy Protection Act	Regulates the use of government data to determine the eligibility of individuals for federal benefits.
1988	Video Privacy Protection Act	Forbids retailers from releasing or selling video-rental records without customer consent or a court order.
1986	Electronic Communications Privacy Act (ECPA)	Provides the same right of privacy protection for the postal delivery service and telephone companies to the new forms of electronic communications, such as voice mail, e-mail, and cellular telephones.
1984	Cable Communications Policy Act	Regulates disclosure of cable TV subscriber records.
1984	Computer Fraud and Abuse Act	Outlaws unauthorized access of federal government computers.
1978	Right to Financial Privacy Act	Strictly outlines procedures federal agencies must follow when looking at customer records in banks.
1974	Privacy Act	Forbids federal agencies from allowing information to be used for a reason other than which it was collected.
1974	Family Educational Rights and Privacy Act	Gives students and parents access to school records and limits disclosure of records to unauthorized parties.
1970	Fair Credit Reporting Act	Prohibts credit reporting agencies from releasing credit information to unauthorized people and allows consumers to review their credit records.

Figure 13-18
Summary of the major U.S. government laws concerning privacy.

Several federal laws deal specifically with computers. The 1986 Electronic Communications Privacy Act (ECPA) provides the same protection that covers mail and telephone communications to electronic communications such as voice mail. The 1988 Computer Matching and Privacy Protection Act regulates the use of government data to determine the eligibility of individuals for federal benefits. The 1984 and 1994 Computer Fraud and Abuse Acts outlaw unauthorized access to federal government computers and the transmission of harmful computer code such as viruses. One law with an apparent legal loophole is in the Fair Credit Reporting Act. Although the act limits the rights of others viewing a credit report to those with a *legitimate business need*, a legitimate business need is not defined. The result is that just about anyone can say they have a legitimate business need and gain access to someone's credit report. Credit reports contain much more than just balance and payment information on mortgages and credit cards. The largest credit bureaus maintain information on family income, number of dependents, employment history, bank balances, driving records, lawsuits, and Social Security numbers. In total, these credit bureaus have more than 400 million records on more than 160 million people. Some credit bureaus sell combinations of the data they have stored in their databases to direct marketing organizations. Because of continuing complaints about credit report errors and the invasion of privacy, the U.S. Congress is considering a major revision of the Fair Credit Reporting Act.

Employee Monitoring

Employee monitoring involves the use of computers to observe, record, and review an individual's use of a computer, including communications such as e-mail, keyboard activity (used to measure productivity), and Internet sites visited. A frequently discussed issue is whether or not an employer has the right to read employee e-mail messages. Actual policies vary widely with some organizations declaring that e-mail messages will be reviewed regularly and others stating that e-mail is considered private. Most organizations, estimated in one study to be approximately 75 percent, do not have formal e-mail policies, which, in effect, means that e-mail can be read without employee notification.

At present, no laws exist relating to e-mail. The 1986 Electronic Communications Privacy Act does not cover communications within an organization. Because many believe that such internal communications should be private, several lawsuits have been files against employers. In response to the issue of workplace privacy, the U.S. Congress proposed the Privacy for Consumers and Workers Act, which states that employers must notify employees if they are monitoring electronic communications. Supporters of the legislation hope that it also will restrict the types and amount of monitoring that employers can conduct legally.

Ethics and the Information Age

As with any powerful technology, computers can be used for both good and bad actions. The standards that determine whether an action is good or bad are called ethics. **Computer ethics** are the moral guidelines that govern the use of computers and information systems. Five areas of computer ethics that are discussed frequently are unauthorized use of computer systems, software theft (piracy), information privacy, information accuracy, and codes of ethical conduct. Unauthorized use, software piracy, and information privacy were discussed earlier in this chapter. The following section deals with the accuracy of computer information and codes of conduct.

Information Accuracy

Organizations have been concerned constantly about the accuracy of computer input. Inaccurate input, sometimes called **dirty data**, can result in erroneous information and incorrect decisions based on that information. Information accuracy today is even more of an issue because many users access information maintained by other organizations, such as on the Internet. Sometimes, the organization providing access to the information did not create the information. An example is the airline flight schedules available from several online service providers. The question that arises is, who is responsible for the accuracy of the information? Does the responsibility rest solely with the original creator of the information or does the service that passes along the information also have some responsibility to verify its accuracy? Legally, these questions have not been resolved.

In addition to concerns about the accuracy of computer input, some people have raised questions about the ethics of using computers to alter output, primarily graphic output such as retouched photographs. Using graphics equipment and software, photographs can be digitized and edited to add, change, or remove images (Figure 13-19). One group that is opposed to any manipulation of an image is the National Press Photographers Association.

Figure 13-19
A digitally altered photograph shows sports star Michael Jordan (born 1963) meeting famous scientist Albert Einstein (who died in 1955).

It believes that allowing even the slightest alteration eventually could lead to deliberately misleading photographs. Others believe that digital photograph retouching is acceptable as long as the significant content or meaning of the photograph is not changed. Digital retouching is another area where legal precedents have not yet been established.

Codes of Conduct

Recognizing that individuals and organizations need specific standards for the ethical use of computers and information systems, a number of computer-related organizations have established **codes of conduct**, which are written guidelines that help determine whether a specific computer action is ethical or unethical (Figure 13-20). Many businesses have adopted similar codes of conduct and made them known to their employees. One of the problems with ethical issues in business is that some people believe that ethical decisions are the responsibility of management, not employees. This often is true in service departments, such as information systems or accounting, whose organizational function can be interpreted as providing whatever information or service management wants. Establishing codes of conduct that apply to an entire organization can help all employees, including management, make ethical decisions by providing a standard against which they can measure their actions.

CODE OF CONDUCT

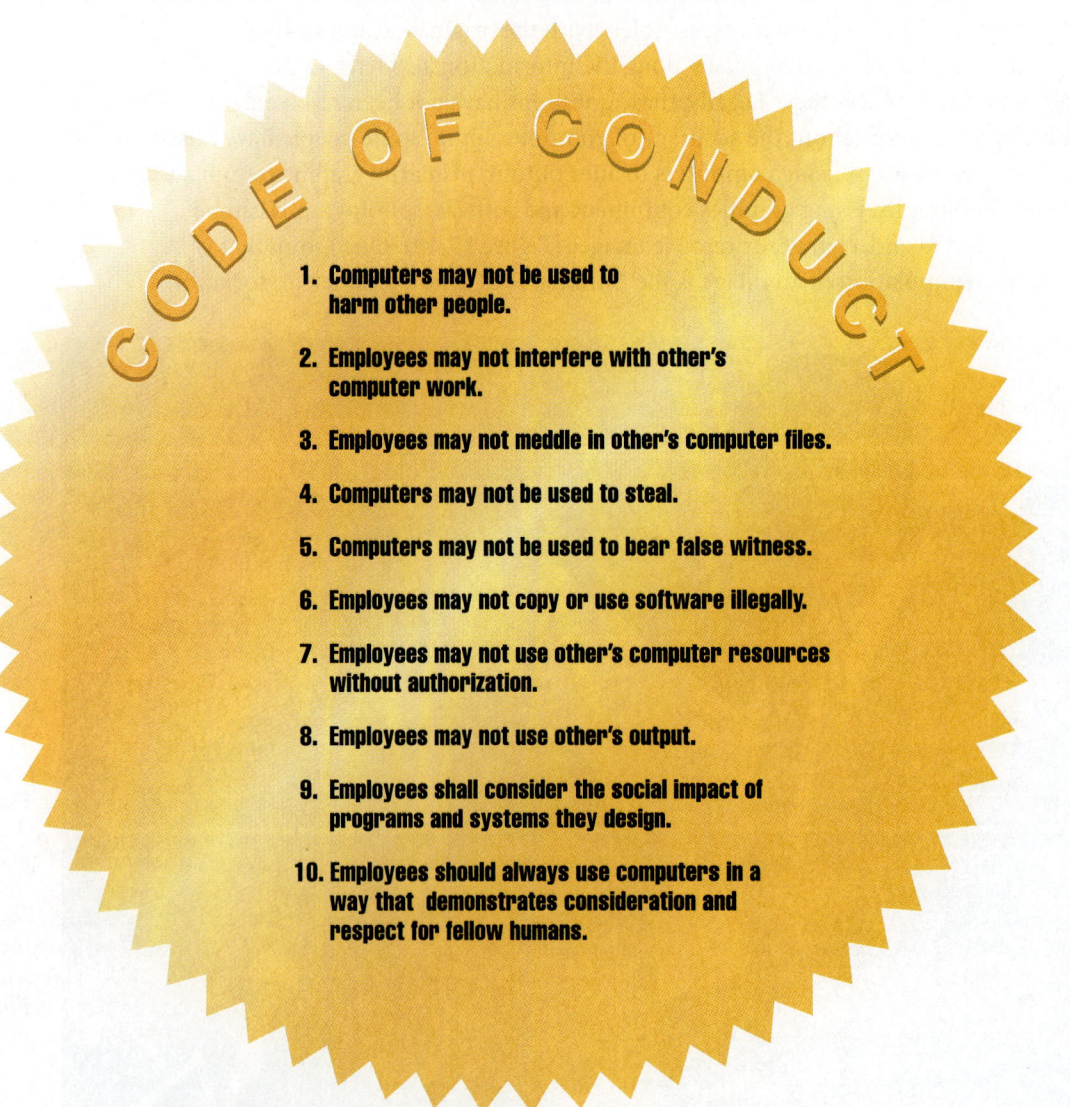

1. Computers may not be used to harm other people.
2. Employees may not interfere with other's computer work.
3. Employees may not meddle in other's computer files.
4. Computers may not be used to steal.
5. Computers may not be used to bear false witness.
6. Employees may not copy or use software illegally.
7. Employees may not use other's computer resources without authorization.
8. Employees may not use other's output.
9. Employees shall consider the social impact of programs and systems they design.
10. Employees should always use computers in a way that demonstrates consideration and respect for fellow humans.

Figure 13-20
An example of a code of conduct that an employer may distribute to employees.

Internet Security, Privacy, and Ethics Issues

The widespread use of the Internet has raised several issues regarding security, privacy, and ethics. These issues are discussed in the following sections.

Internet Security and Privacy

As previously mentioned, information transmitted over networks has a higher degree of security risk than information kept on the organization's premises. On a vast network such as the Internet with no central administrator, the risk is even greater; every computer along the route your data takes can look at what is being sent or received. Fortunately, most Web browser software has several methods to keep data secure and private (Figure 13-21).

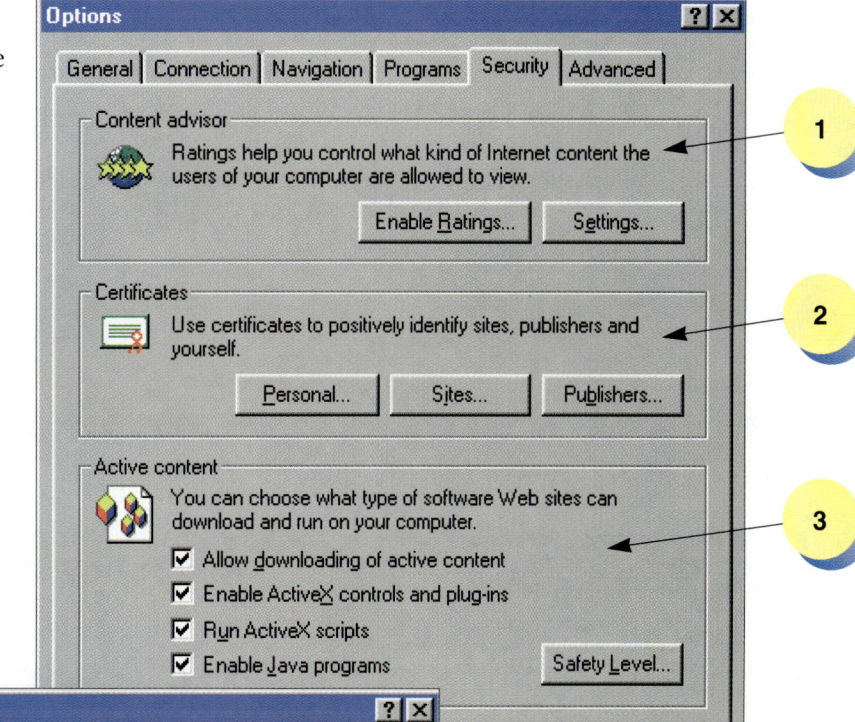

Figure 13-21
Most Web browser programs allow you to establish different levels of security over Internet and Web communications. These options are available with Microsoft's Internet Explorer browser.

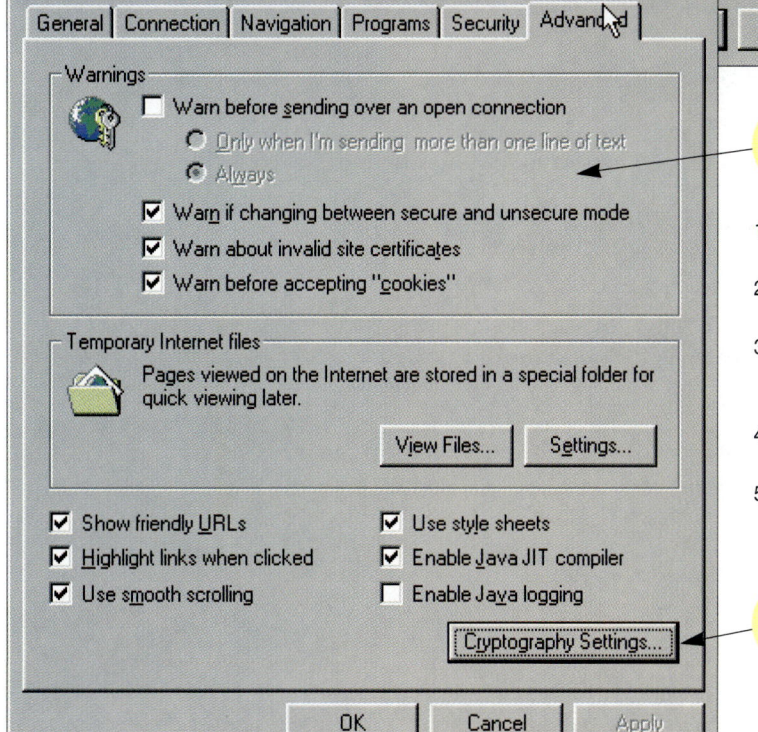

1. Content advisor uses a rating system to set limits on the kinds of material that can be viewed.
2. Certificates authenticate individuals, Web sites, and software publishers.
3. Active content lets you control the downloading of programs that run on your computer while you are visiting Web sites.
4. Warnings let you know about possible security problems, such as *cookies*.
5. Cryptography lets you establish the encryption protocols used when transmitting and receiving data.

To provide secure data transmission, many Web browsers use **encryption**. One of the most popular Internet encryption methods is **Secure Socket Layer (SSL)**. SSL provides two-way encryption along the entire route data takes to and from your computer. Another way of providing security is with certificates. **Certificates**, also called **digital IDs** or **digital signatures**, are an encrypted code that identifies a person, Web site, or company. Using certificates for authentication ensures that an impostor is not participating in an Internet transaction.

The unauthorized collection and use of information is another issue raised by the Internet. Many companies use a Web-based technology called cookies to gather information about you and your Web browsing habits. A **cookie** is a file that a Web server stores on your computer when you visit a Web site. The Web server retrieves the cookie file each time you revisit that site. Cookies sometimes are used only to record your viewing preferences, such as whether or not you want animated graphics to display. Cookies can be used, however, to record what pages you view and what purchases you make. Used in this way, cookies create a profile of your viewing and buying habits. This profile later can be read by the Web site that placed the cookie on your system. If you have the cookie warning feature turned on, you will see a message such as the one shown in Figure 13-22. After being alerted by the message, you can choose to accept or reject the cookie.

inCyber

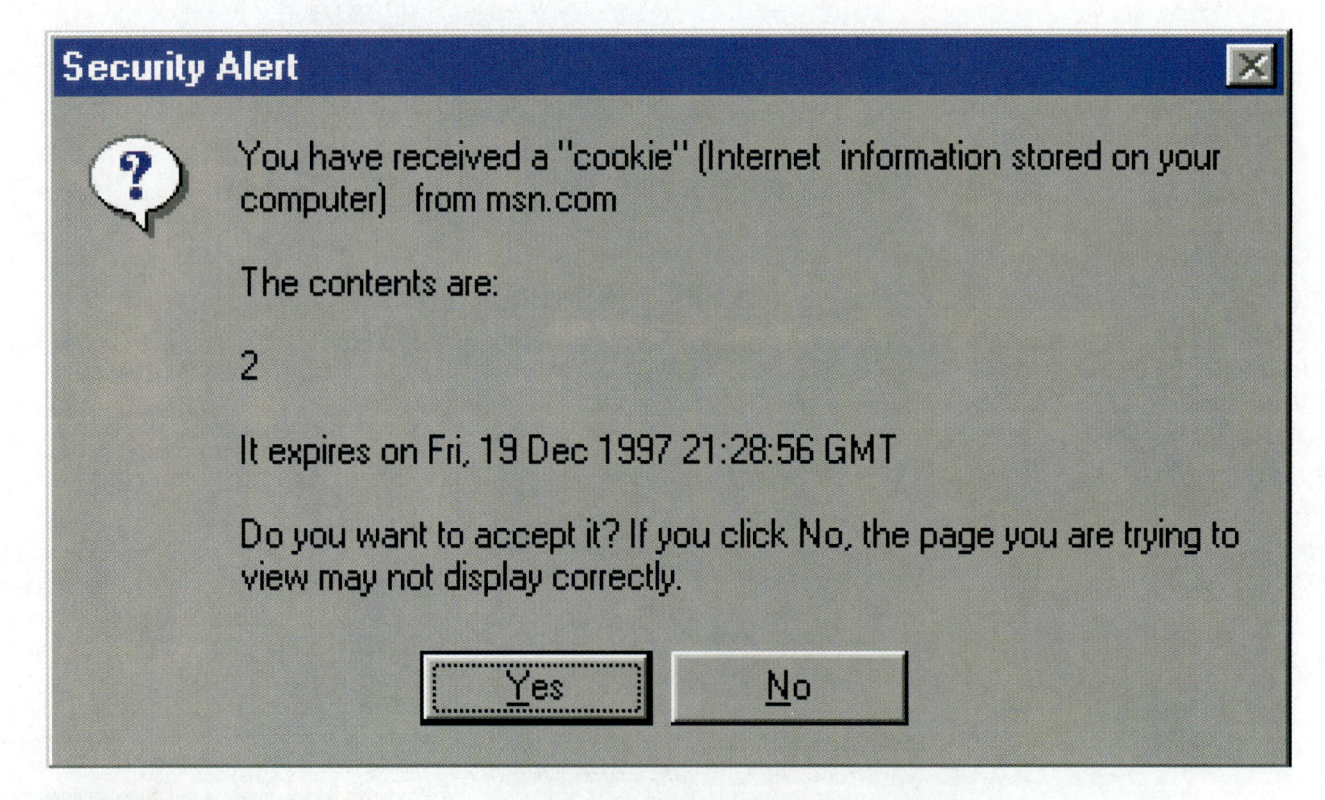

For details of how cookie files are used, visit the Discovering Computers Chapter 13 inCyber page (http://www.scsite.com/dc/ch13/incyber.htm) and click Cookie.

Figure 13-22
A cookie is a file that a Web server stores on your computer. If you tell the Web browser to warn you, you can decide to accept or reject the cookie.

Objectionable Materials on the Internet

The most discussed ethical issue concerning the Internet is the availability of objectionable material, such as racist literature and obscene pictures. Some believe that such materials should be banned, while others believe that the materials should be restricted and unavailable to minors. Opponents argue that banning any materials violates constitutional guarantees of free speech. Responding to pressure for restrictions, in February 1996, President Clinton signed the **Communications Decency Act**, which made it a criminal offense to distribute *indecent or patently offensive material* online. The law was appealed immediately and, in June 1996, it was declared unconstitutional.

One approach to restricting access to certain material is a rating system similar to those used for videos. If content at the Web site goes beyond the rating limitations set in the Web browser software (Figure 13-23), you are not allowed access to the site. Concerned parents can set the rating limitations and prevent them from being changed by using a password.

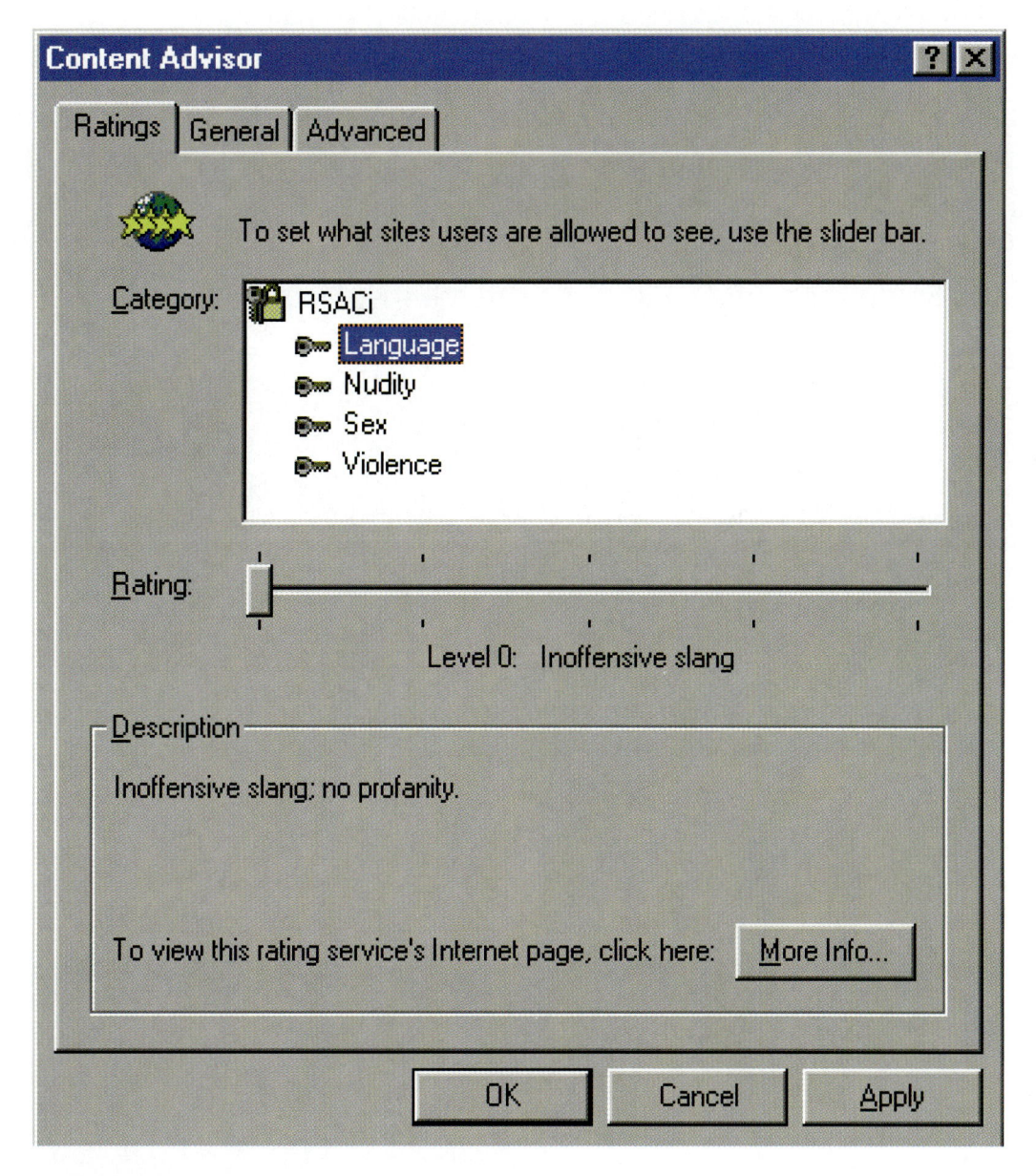

Figure 13-23
The Microsoft Internet Explorer Web browser allows you to set limits on the types of material that can be viewed.

Summary of Security, Privacy, and Ethics

The livelihood of many organizations and individuals depends on the computer systems and networks they use every day. This increased reliance on computer systems and information sent over networks makes it essential to take steps to protect the systems and information from known risks. At the same time, organizations and individuals also have an obligation to use computer systems responsibly and not abuse the power computer systems provide. This responsibility presents constant challenges, which sometimes weigh the rights of the individual against increased efficiency and productivity.

The computer must be thought of as a tool whose effectiveness is determined by the knowledge, skill, experience, and ethics of the user. To test your knowledge, answer the ethics questionnaire in Figure 13-24. The computer knowledge you have acquired should help you be better able to participate in decisions on how to use computerized information systems efficiently *and* ethically.

COMPUTER ETHICS

	Ethical	Unethical	Crime

1. An employee uses his computer at work to send e-mail to his relatives. ☐ ☐ ☐

2. An employee uses the Web to access an all-sports news site. So he can periodically check the news, he leaves the Web connection running in the background all day. ☐ ☐ ☐

3. An employee installs a new upgraded version of a word processing program on his office computer. Because no one will be using the old version of the program, the employee takes it home to use on his personal computer so his children can use it to write school papers. ☐ ☐ ☐

4. While reviewing her employees e-mail messages, a department manager discovers that one of her employees is using the e-mail system to operate a weekly football betting pool. ☐ ☐ ☐

   employee ☐ ☐ ☐
   manager ☐ ☐ ☐

5. A company hires a consultant to develop a custom program. After completing the program, the consultant tries to license the program to other companies. ☐ ☐ ☐

6. While reviewing a list of available programs at a Web site, a user notices the name of a program that is similar to a popular spreadsheet package. After downloading the program, the user discovers that the program appears to be a test version of a popular spreadsheet program that sells for $200 in computer stores. The user keeps and uses the program. ☐ ☐ ☐

7. A programmer is asked to write a program that she knows will generate inaccurate financial information. When she questions her manager about the program, she is told to write the program or risk losing her job. She writes the program. ☐ ☐ ☐

   programmer ☐ ☐ ☐
   manager ☐ ☐ ☐

8. As a practical joke, an employee enters a program on the company computer. Each time an employee uses a floppy disk on the company network, the program is copied to the floppy disk. The first time the floppy disk is used after January 1, a "Happy New Year" message is displayed. ☐ ☐ ☐

9. A newspaper uses photo retouching software to remove a billboard advertisement for a competitive newspaper from the background of a front page photo. ☐ ☐ ☐

10. A company occasionally uses software to monitor the productivity of its staff. It only uses the software to monitor an employee thought to be repeatedly goofing off. ☐ ☐ ☐

Figure 13-24
Indicate whether you think the described situation is ethical, unethical, or a crime. Discuss your answers with your instructor and other students.

COMPUTERS AT WORK

Active Badges

Are you concerned about the number of telephone calls you have missed because you were away from your desk? Do you become frustrated by not being able to find a co-worker you know is in the building? These and similar employee location problems are being solved by the **Active Badge system** developed by Olivetti Research Ltd of Cambridge, England.

The active badge contains a small transmitter and is worn on the outside of clothing. Every fifteen seconds, the badge emits an infrared signal that is picked up by sensors in offices and hallways. Infrared signals are used because they do not penetrate walls and, therefore, can be traced to a specific location. The sensors are connected to a computer that updates a database of locations and users. The computer used for the sensors is connected to an organization's main computer or computer network so users can display location information.

If a user is in a meeting or otherwise does not want to be disturbed, he or she can press a button on the badge twice. This results in a *busy* message on the location display. The busy status remains until the user changes locations. If a user does not want to be located at all, he or she can place the badge in a pocket, purse, or drawer. The badges have a light sensor that shuts them off in the dark.

Advanced versions of the devices, called authentication badges, currently are under development. Authentication badges contain small microprocessors that can be programmed. One anticipated use of authentication badges is as security devices that will let authorized users enter restricted areas.

Similar technology is installed in the 40,000 square foot home of Microsoft founder Bill Gates. When visitors enter the home, they are issued badges that are used to control lights, temperature, music, and video displays as guests move from room to room.

Active badges are just one type of device called a Portable Interactive Computing Object (PiCO). Olivetti has plans for an entire family of smart PiCO devices that can be attached to persons or things. Olivetti believes the increased productivity of the devices will more than offset any concerns about privacy.

Figure 13-25

As of: 01:43 p.m. June 22, 1998

Name	Extension	Position	Seen	Status
P Ainsworth	343	lab	static	
F Bolduc	410		June 15, 5:15 p.m.	on vacation
M Charles	316	room 316	static	with Ryan
D Clarke	218	east corridor	moving	
L Gannon	232	room 232	11:45 a.m.	unknown
G Harvee	340	cafeteria	static	
B Herringbone	210	conference room	static	BUSY
A Jackson	0	reception	static	
B Nicely	398	stockroom	moving	
F Peacock	308	computer room	static	
J Quasley	215	conference room	static	BUSY
J Ryan	204	room 316	static	with Charles
V Sutherland	653	room 653	static	
T Turner	415	room 415	12:30 p.m.	unknown
C Uleke	235		June 19, 7:04 p.m.	out
T Walkman	100	conference room	static	BUSY

IN THE FUTURE

Taking People at Face Value

Someday soon, computerized security systems may identify you the same way friends and associates do, by recognizing your face. Developers claim that **computerized facial recognition** (CFR) is as accurate as fingerprints and is less likely to make the person being identified nervous or uncomfortable.

Recent advances in CFR have reduced greatly the amount of data stored for each face and the amount of time it takes to analyze and match a live image, called a target image. One approach converts the target image into a series of light and dark areas. Distinctive areas of the target image are compared against a set of reference data based on all the faces in the database. The reference data serves as the equivalent of an *average face*. Comparing the target image against the average face reference data takes less than a second and is much faster than older systems that compared a target image against all images in the database. Differences between the target image and the reference data are calculated and converted to a numerical value. The numerical value then is used to find the closest match in the database.

One likely use of CFR will be at automated teller machines. Your facial image could be stored on your ATM card along with your account information. State motor vehicle departments could use digitized facial images to identify people who claim to have lost their drivers licenses and help eliminate false IDs. Government benefit programs could use CFR to verify a recipient's identification. These are just some of the possible applications.

Unlike humans, a computer with CFR will never say, "I recognize your face, but I cannot remember your name."

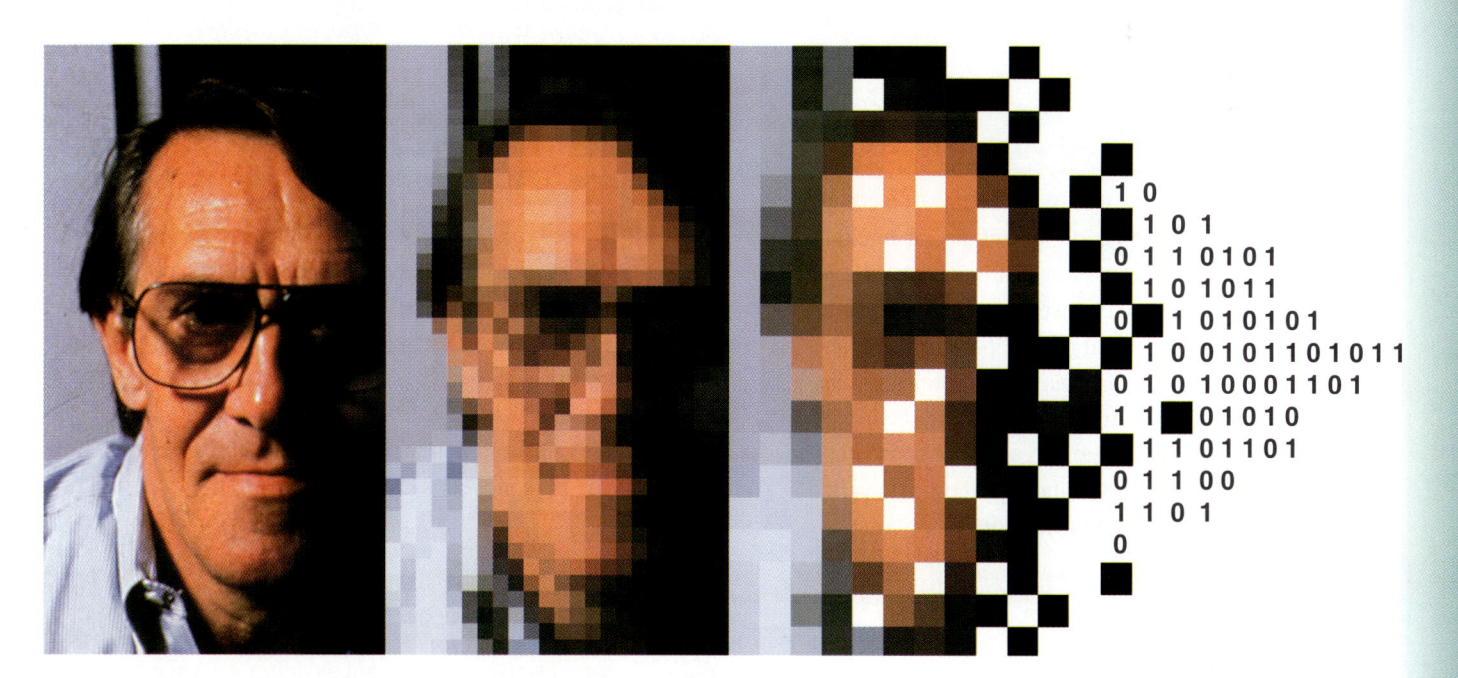

Figure 13-26

inCyber | review | terms | yourTurn | hotTopics | outThere | winLabs | webWalk | exercises | news | home

INSTRUCTIONS: *To display this page from the Web, launch your browser and enter the URL, http://www.scsite.com/dc/ch13/review.htm. Click the links for current and additional information.*

1 Computer Security Risks

A **computer security risk** is any event or action that could cause a loss to computer equipment, software, information, or processing capability. Security risks include computer viruses, unauthorized access and use, theft, and system failure. Any illegal act involving a computer generally is referred to as a **computer crime**.

2 Computer Viruses

A **computer virus** is a potentially damaging computer program designed to infect other software. Virus programs often are intended to damage computer systems by destroying or corrupting data. A **boot sector virus** replaces the program used to start the system with a modified version of the program. A **file virus** inserts virus code into program files. A **Trojan horse virus** hides within or is designed to look like a legitimate program. A **macro virus** uses the macro language of an application to hide virus code.

3 Virus Detection and Removal

Antivirus programs, called **vaccines**, have been developed to protect against computer viruses. Vaccines look for specific patterns of virus code called a **virus signature**. Antivirus programs have utilities to remove or repair infected programs and files. A **rescue disk** is a floppy disk that contains an uninfected copy of certain operating system commands and essential information that enables the computer to restart correctly.

4 Unauthorized Access and Use

Unauthorized access is the use of a computer system without permission. **Crackers**, or **hackers**, are people who try to access computer systems illegally. **Unauthorized use** is the use of a computer system or computer data for illegal or unapproved activities. Unauthorized access and use can be prevented by establishing **access controls**, which are security measures that define who can access a computer. Access controls are implemented through a process called **identification** and **authentication**.

5 Methods of Authentication

Three methods of authentication are remembered information, possessed objects, and biometric devices. A **remembered information authentication** requires users to enter a word or series of characters that match an entry in a security file. A **possessed object** is any item that a user must carry to gain access to a computer facility. A **biometric device** authenticates a user by verifying personal characteristics.

6 Theft

Portable computer equipment can pose serious theft risks. Common sense and constant awareness are the best preventive measures. Software theft usually involves **software piracy**, which is the unauthorized and illegal copying of copyrighted software. Copying, lending, renting, or distributing copyrighted software is a federal crime. Information theft often can be prevented by identification and authentication controls. Sensitive data sent over networks can be protected by **encryption**, which is the process of converting between data into unreadable characters.

7 System Failure

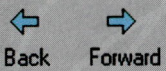

A **system failure** is a prolonged malfunction of a computer system. A common reason for system failures is electrical power variation, which can result in loss of data or immediate and permanent damage to hardware. An **undervoltage** occurs when the electrical supply drops. An **overvoltage**, or **power spike**, occurs when the incoming electrical power increases significantly above the normal 120 volts. A **surge protector**, also called a **surge suppresser**, and an **uninterruptable power supply (UPS)** help protect against electrical power variations.

8 Backup Procedures

To prevent data loss caused by system failure, computer users should have backup procedures. **Backup procedures** specify a regular plan of copying and storing key data and program files. In case of system failure or the discovery of corrupted files, backup copies are used to **restore** (reload) the files. A **full backup** duplicates all files in the computer. A **differential backup** duplicates only the files that have changed *since the last full backup*. An **incremental backup** duplicates only the files that have changed since the last full or incremental backup.

9 Disaster Recovery Plan

A **disaster recovery plan** describes the steps an organization would take to restore computer operations in the event of a disaster. A disaster recovery plan has four major components. The **emergency plan** specifies the steps to be taken immediately after a disaster strikes. The **backup plan** specifies how an organization will use backup files and equipment to resume information processing. The **recovery plan** specifies the actions to be taken to restore full information processing operations. The disaster recovery **test plan** contains information for simulating different levels of disaster and an organization's ability to recover.

10 Computer Security Plan

A **computer security plan** summarizes the safeguards that are in place to protect an organization's information assets. A computer security plan should identify all information assets, identify security risks that may cause an information asset loss, and identify safeguards that exist to detect, prevent, and recover from a loss.

11 Information Privacy

Information privacy refers to the rights of individuals and organizations to deny or restrict the collection and use of information about them. Two issues related to information privacy are unauthorized collection and use of information and employee monitoring. Unauthorized collection and use of information occurs when data about an individual is gathered without the individual's knowledge or permission. **Employee monitoring** involves the use of computers to observe, record, and review an individual's use of a computer, including communications (such as e-mail), keyboard activity, and Internet sites visited.

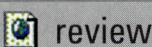

12 Ethics and the Information Age

Computer ethics are moral guidelines that govern the use of computers and information systems. One area of computer ethics is information accuracy. Erroneous information can result from inaccurate input, sometimes called **dirty data**. Legally, questions regarding responsibility for information accuracy have not been resolved. The ethics of using computers to alter output, such as digital photograph retouching, also has been questioned. This is another area where legal precedents have not been established. Recognizing that individuals and organizations need specific standards for ethical use of computers and information systems, a number of computer-related organizations have established **codes of conduct**, which are written guidelines that help determine whether a specific computer action is ethical or unethical.

13 Internet Security, Privacy, and Ethics

A popular method used to keep data secure and private on the Internet is **Secure Socket Layer (SSL)**, which provides two-way encryption along the entire route that data travels. **Certificates**, which are encrypted identifying codes, offer assurance that an imposter is not participating in an Internet transaction. **Cookies**, which are files that can store information about an individual's viewing preferences and buying habits, are a Web-based technology that has raised concerns about the unauthorized collection and use of information. The most discussed ethical issue concerning the Internet is the availability of objectionable material. One approach to restricting access to certain material is a rating system similar to that used for videos.

13.35 terms

chapter
1 | 2 | 3 | 4 | 5 | 6 | 7 | 8 | 9 | 10 | 11 | 12 | 13 | 14 | I

inCyber | review | terms | yourTurn | hotTopics | outThere | winLabs | webWalk | exercises | news | home

INSTRUCTIONS: *To display this page from the Web, launch your browser and enter the URL, http://www.scsite.com/dc/ch13/terms.htm. Scroll through the list of terms. Click a term for its definition and a picture. Click the rocket ship for current and additional information about the term.*

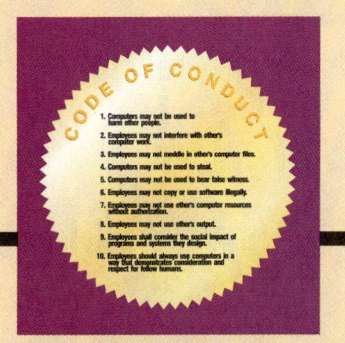

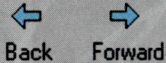

codes of conduct

DEFINITION
codes of conduct
Written guidelines that help determine whether a specific computer action is ethical or unethical. **(13.24)**

access controls (13.5)
Active Badge system (13.30)
antivirus programs (13.4)
authentication (13.5)

backup (13.15)
backup plan (13.18)
backup procedures (13.15)
biometric device (13.7)
blackout (13.13)
boot sector virus (13.3)
brownout (13.13)
Business Software Alliance (BSA) (13.10)

callback system (13.8)
certificates (13.26)
ciphertext (13.11)
Clipper chip (13.12)
codes of conduct (13.24)
cold site (13.18)
Communications Decency Act (13.27)
computer crime (13.2)
computer ethics (13.23)
computer security plan (13.19)
computer security risk (13.2)
computer virus (13.2)
computerized facial recognition (CFR) (13.31)
cookie (13.26)
crackers (13.5)

data encryption standard (DES) (13.12)
dialog authentication (13.7)
differential backup (13.15)
digital IDs (13.26)
digital signatures (13.26)

dirty data (13.23)
disaster recovery test plan (13.18)

emergency plan (13.17)
employee monitoring (13.22)
encryption (13.11, 13.26)
encryption key (13.11)

father (13.16)
file virus (13.3)
full backup (13.15)

grandfather (13.16)

hacker (13.5)
hot site (13.18)

identification (13.5)
incremental backup (13.15)
information privacy (13.20)
inoculated (13.4)

key escrow (13.12)

logic bomb (13.3)

macro virus (13.3)

noise (13.13)

offsite (13.15)
overvoltage (13.13)

personal identification number (PIN) (13.7)
plaintext (13.11)
polymorphic virus (13.4)

possessed object (13.7)
power surge (13.13)
public key encryption (13.11)

reciprocal backup relationships (13.18)
recovery plan (13.17, 13.18)
remembered information authentication (13.6)
rescue disk (13.5)
restore (13.15)

Secure Socket Layer (SSL) (13.26)
site license (13.11)
sniffer (13.7)
software piracy (13.10)
son (13.16)
spike (13.13)
stealth virus (13.4)
surge protector (13.14)
surge suppresser (13.14)
system failure (13.13)

three-generation backup policy (13.16)
time bomb (13.3)
Trojan horse virus (13.3)

unauthorized access (13.5)
unauthorized use (13.5)
undervoltage (13.13)
uninterruptable power supply (UPS) (13.14)

vaccines (13.4)
virus signature (13.4)

worm (13.3)

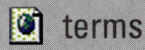

yourTurn

chapter 13

1 | 2 | 3 | 4 | 5 | 6 | 7 | 8 | 9 | 10 | 11 | 12 | 13 | 14 | I

inCyber | review | terms | yourTurn | hotTopics | outThere | winLabs | webWalk | exercises | news | home

INSTRUCTIONS: *To display this page from the Web, launch your browser and enter the URL, http://www.scsite.com/dc/ch13/turn.htm. Click a blank line for the answer. Click the links for current and additional information.*

Label the Figure

PARTS OF A DISASTER RECOVERY PLAN

1. _____
   Evacuation plans and list of people to notify

2. _____
   Identity and location of backup resources

3. _____
   Specific steps and time plan to resume computer operations

4. _____
   Simulates disasters to find weaknesses in overall plan

Instructions: Identify each part of a disaster recovery plan.

Fill in the Blanks

Instructions: Complete each sentence with the correct term or terms.

1. A(n) _____ is a potentially damaging computer program designed to infect other software.
2. A(n) _____ uses special electrical components to keep an overvoltage, or _____, from reaching computer equipment.
3. When a three generation backup policy is used, the oldest copy of the file is the _____, the second oldest copy is the _____, and the most recent copy of the file is called the _____.
4. _____ involves the use of computers to observe, record, and review an individual's use of a computer, including communications, keyboard activity, and Internet sites visited.
5. A(n) _____ is a file that a Web server stores on an individual's computer when a Web site is visited.

Short Answer

Instructions: Write a brief answer to each of the following questions.

1. What is a computer security risk? What are different types of security risks that can threaten computer systems? What is a computer crime? _____
2. Why is a polymorphic virus difficult to detect? How does inoculating program files prevent viruses? What do experts recommend to help protect against being infected by a computer virus? _____
3. Why is computer backup important? How are a full backup, differential backup, and incremental backup different? Why are backup copies normally kept offsite? _____
4. What is a computer security plan? What is the goal of a computer security plan? _____
5. How do Web browser programs allow users to establish different levels of security over Internet communications? What is Secure Socket Layer (SSL)? What are certificates? _____

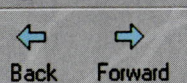

13 hotTopics   chapter 1 | 2 | 3 | 4 | 5 | 6 | 7 | 8 | 9 | 10 | 11 | 12 | 13 | 14 |

inCyber | review | terms | yourTurn | hotTopics | outThere | winLabs | webWalk | exercises | news | home

INSTRUCTIONS: *To display this page from the Web, launch your browser and enter the URL, http://www.scsite.com/dc/ch13/hot.htm. Click the links for current and additional information to help you respond to the hotTopics questions.*

1 *A recently enacted policy in New York state allows licensing and* disciplinary records of professionals in 38 fields to be accessed via the Internet. The Web site includes information on license status, educational background, and any conduct that led to disciplinary action for more than 600,000 people. The policy is intended to help people choose a professional; but critics fear the information may be inaccurate, and any defense or explanation for alleged misconduct may be ignored. Should professional licensing and disciplinary records be easily available? Why? What professionals, and what type of information, should be available to public scrutiny? How could concerns about information accuracy and professional explanations be addressed?

2 *Studies show millions of employees use their office computers to surf the Internet, play games,* and send personal messages. An audit found workers at some organizations average 90 minutes a day of wasted time. In response, some managers have turned to software programs that monitor Internet activities, erase games from office PCs, and measure efficiency. Some employees find the software dehumanizing and feel people should be free to surf the net or play a game on their lunch hour. What limits, if any, should be placed on employee use of office computers? How closely should employers be able to monitor their workers? Why?

3 *Under pressure from German prosecutors, an online service blocked four million subscribers* from reaching allegedly indecent sites on the Internet. Because the service was unable to keep only German users from certain material, all subscribers were banned. Eventually, parental filters were installed and access was restored. Numerous conflicts have arisen pitting the global nature of the Internet against local standards of decency. What should online services, Internet providers, or the government do to reconcile the Internet with local community standards? Some services suggest an industry wide rating system? Should a rating system be employed? Why?

4 *Employees often are guided by an organization's code of conduct when making judgments* about computer ethics, but students usually must make their own decisions. One site on the Web offers an archive of term papers gathered from college fraternities. Students can download a paper, make any necessary changes, print out a copy, and then turn it in as their own. Other sites offer translations, calculations, or studies. How can instructors keep students from claiming the work of others? How is using the Web for research different from using it to copy someone's work? What should be the consequences for plagiarizing from a Web site? What legitimate reasons might students have for obtaining a term paper from the Web?

5 *In 1990, Lotus Development Corporation created a database of consumer information called* Marketplace that it planned to sell to small and medium businesses. After thousands of consumers asked that their names be removed from the database, Lotus withdrew the product. Nevertheless, other databases are routinely bought and sold. Although certain benefits are gained from shared databases, the problem with selling them is twofold: accuracy and privacy. A study of 1,500 reports from three large credit bureaus discovered mistakes in 43 percent of the files, and it is generally agreed that some personal information should not be made public. What measures can be taken to solve these problems? What restrictions should be placed on selling or sharing databases? Should some databases not be shared under any circumstances? Why?

chapter 13 outThere

1 | 2 | 3 | 4 | 5 | 6 | 7 | 8 | 9 | 10 | 11 | 12 | 13 | 14 | I

inCyber | review | terms | yourTurn | hotTopics | outThere | winLabs | webWalk | exercises | news | home

INSTRUCTIONS: *To display this page from the Web, launch your browser and enter the URL, http://www.scsite.com/dc/ch13/out.htm. Click the links for current and additional information.*

1 *By the year 2000, laptop computers are expected to account for more than* 35% of personal computer sales. With the growing number of laptop users has come increasing concern about the vulnerability of portable PCs. An insurer of personal computers reported claims for almost $1 billion worth of equipment in 1995. Among incidents reported were accidental damage (238,000 cases), theft (208,000 cases), power surges (38,000 cases), and loss during transit (19,000 cases). Visit a computer vendor and make a list of products that help safeguard portable PCs. What is the purpose of each product? How much does it cost? How is it used? If you could purchase only one item to protect your portable PC, what would you buy? Why?

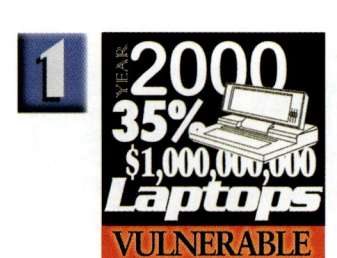

2 *One security expert estimates that by the year 2000 more than 8,500,000 virus* strains will be in existence for personal computers. Viruses have destroyed bank accounts, demolished hospital records, and devastated programs in thousands of PCs. In response to this challenge, several software developers are marketing antivirus programs on the Web. Visit the Web site of one of these developers. How many antivirus programs does the developer offer? For what operating systems are they designed? What viruses are detected? How current are the programs? How much do they cost?

3 *In many organizations, a computer security officer is responsible for protecting the privacy of an* organization's records and for helping prosecute people who illegally access an organization's computers. Computer security officers can have a wide range of backgrounds — programmers, police officers, even hackers. Interview a computer security consultant or a security officer at a local organization. What are the gravest security threats? How should these threats be handled? Does a code of conduct regarding computer use exist? If so, what is it and to whom does it apply? What should be done with violators?

4 *In 1995, software piracy cost developers more than $15 billion. The software industry lost more* than $28,900 every minute due to software theft. Rates of software piracy vary. North America's 27% average was the lowest rate of piracy, while Eastern Europe's 83% average was the highest. Computer users have mixed feelings about software piracy. In a recent survey, 78% of respondents agreed that software should not be copied illegally, but 47% admitted they had done it. Visit the Business Software Alliance (BSA) Web site. How does software piracy negatively impact consumers? What are some hot issues regarding software piracy? What is BSA's public policy? What is the BSA software scanner? How does BSA deal with violators of software copyright law?

5 *A twenty-year-old Missouri hacker recently confessed that he had broken into the computer* systems of two major corporations, collecting passwords and changing files. Prosecutors connected the hacker to the Internet Liberation Front, a group of hackers who oppose the commercialization of cyberspace. What motivates hackers? Are they idealistic heroes, intellectual adventurers, malicious busybodies, or high-tech thieves? Are their motivations different from those who create computer viruses? Should hackers be deterred? Prepare a report on a hacker-related book to answer these, and some of your own, questions about hackers. Suggested titles include: *Cyberpunk—Outlaws and Hackers on the Computer Frontier* (Katie Hafner and John Markoff), *Hackers: Heroes of the Computer Revolution* (Steven Levy), and *The Hacker Crackdown: Law and Disorder on the Electronic Frontier* (Bruce Sterling).

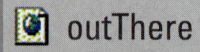

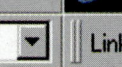

INSTRUCTIONS: *To display this page from the Web, launch your browser and enter the URL, http://www.scsite.com/dc/ch13/labs.htm. Click the links for current and additional information.*

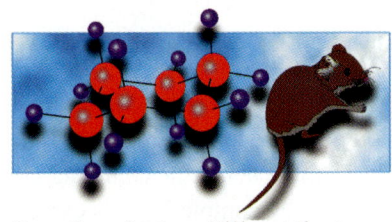

Shelly Cashman Series Antivirus Lab

Follow the instructions in winLabs 1 on page 1.34 to display the Shelly Cashman Series Labs screen. Click Keeping Your Computer Virus Free. Click the Start Lab button. When the initial screen displays, carefully read the objectives. With your printer on, click the Print Questions button. Fill out the top of the Questions sheet and then answer the questions.

Understanding Backup

Click the Start button on the taskbar, point to Programs on the Start menu, point to Accessories on the Programs submenu, point to System Tools on the Accessories submenu, and then click Backup on the System Tools submenu. If a Welcome screen displays, click the OK button. If a Microsoft Backup screen displays, click the OK button. When the Untitled - Microsoft Backup window displays, maximize it and then click the Backup tab. Click Help on the menu bar and then click Help Topics. Double-click Backing Up, Restoring, and Comparing Files and then double-click Backing up your entire system. Print the Help topic. Close Help.

Click the box to the left of the [C:] icon in the Select files to backup area. Look at the bottom right corner of the window. How many files will be backed up? How many kilobytes are in these files? Close Microsoft Backup.

Scanning a Disk

Click the Start button on the taskbar, point to Programs on the Start menu, point to Accessories on the Programs submenu, point to System Tools on the Accessories submenu, and then click ScanDisk on the System Tools submenu. Click the Advanced button in the ScanDisk window. When the ScanDisk Advanced Options dialog box displays, click Always in the Display summary area and then click the OK button.

Insert your Student Floppy Disk into drive A. Click 3½ Floppy [A:] in the Select the drive(s) you want to check for errors area. Click Thorough in the Type of test area (Figure 13-27). Click the Start button. When the ScanDisk Results dialog box displays, answer these questions: (1) What errors, if any, were detected? (2) In bytes, what is your total disk space? (3) How many folders are on the floppy disk? (4) How many user files are on the floppy disk? Click the Close button. Close ScanDisk.

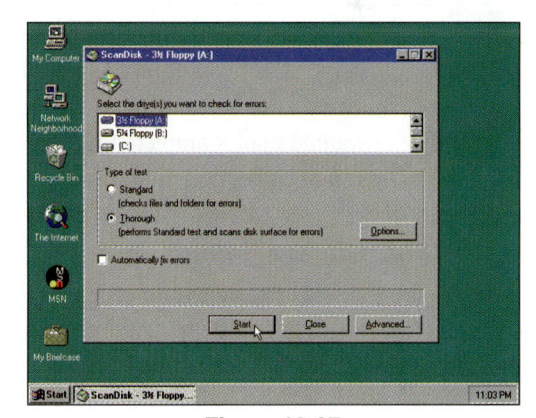

Figure 13-27

Checking System Resources

Click the Start button on the taskbar, point to taskbar, point to Programs on the Start menu, point to Accessories on the Programs submenu, point to System Tools on the Accessories submenu, and then click Resource Meter on the System Tools submenu. If a Resource Meter dialog box displays, click the OK button. Double-click the resource meter icon that displays to the left of the time on the taskbar. What percentage of system resources is free? What percentage of user resources is free? Click the OK button. Right-click the resource meter icon on the taskbar and then click Exit on the shortcut menu.

chapter 13 webWalk

1 | 2 | 3 | 4 | 5 | 6 | 7 | 8 | 9 | 10 | 11 | 12 | 13 | 14 | I

inCyber | review | terms | yourTurn | hotTopics | outThere | winLabs | webWalk | exercises | news | home

INSTRUCTIONS: *To display this page from the Web, launch your browser and enter the URL, http://www.scsite.com/dc/ch13/walk.htm. Click the exercise link to display the exercise.*

1. Web Copyrights
Many of the currently available Web browsers and editors make it easy for you to copy elements from other Web pages for your own use. Having this ability however, does not necessarily make it legal. To learn more about copyright law and the Web (Figure 13-28), complete this exercise.

Figure 13-28

2. Computer Crime
Many computer crimes fall under the jurisdiction of the Federal Bureau of Investigation. You can learn more about the computer crimes the FBI investigates by completing this exercise.

3. Cyberbanking Security
Many people are reluctant to use Web-based online banking services because they lack confidence in the security of their transactions. To learn more about one bank's Web security features (Figure 13-29), complete this exercise.

Figure 13-29

4. Junk Mail and Privacy
Chances are your mailbox is overflowing with catalogs, sales ads, and prize offers you never requested. If you prefer not to have your name and address exchanged for marketing purposes, or are tired of unwanted mail, complete this exercise to learn steps you can take to be removed from mailing lists.

5. Information Mining
Complete this exercise to improve your Web research skills by using a Web search engine to find information related to this chapter.

6. Software Piracy
The Business Software Alliance (BSA) Web site provides the latest information about software piracy. BSA fights against software piracy by conducting educational programs and by operating antipiracy hotlines. To learn more, complete this exercise.

7. Internet Filtering Software
Internet filtering software is used to manage Internet access, limit the time spent online, and block access to sites. Complete this exercise to learn more about Internet filtering software.

8. Encryption
Encryption is the process of converting readable data called plaintext into unreadable characters called ciphertext. To learn more about encryption, complete this exercise.

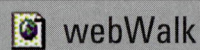

9. Web Chat
Complete this exercise to enter a Web Chat discussion related to the issues presented in the hotTopics exercise.

Multimedia

CHAPTER 14

OBJECTIVES

After completing this chapter, you will be able to:

- Define multimedia
- Describe types of media used in multimedia applications
- List and describe the different uses of multimedia applications
- List and describe the different types of multimedia equipment
- Explain how a multimedia application is developed
- Describe several multimedia authoring software packages

Today, multimedia is playing an increasingly important role in business, industry, entertainment, and education by changing the way computers are used. Multimedia combines text, graphics, audio, video, and other media elements into one application. Unlike television, which also combines the same elements, many multimedia applications are interactive; that is, they allow you to choose what material will be presented and in what sequence. This interactivity, which is one of the key features of multimedia, makes it well-suited for numerous uses such as video games, flight simulators, virtual reality, electronic magazines, educational and training tutorials and more. Multimedia authoring software provides the tools needed to combine media elements and build these types of finished multimedia applications.

This chapter will introduce you to multimedia and describe the various media components that can be used in a multimedia application. After learning about the different types and uses of multimedia applications, you will learn about the equipment needed to create these applications. Finally, you will learn how multimedia applications are developed and about the authoring software packages used to build them.

What Is Multimedia?

Multimedia refers to any computer-based presentation software or application that integrates at least two or more of these elements: text, color, graphics, animation, audio, and video. **Interactive multimedia** is a multimedia application that accepts input from the user by means of the keyboard or a pointing device such as a mouse and performs some action in response. Most interactive multimedia applications let you move through the materials at your own pace, completing certain tasks and receiving feedback as you progress. The multimedia learning software shown in Figure 14-1, for example, supports self-paced review of computer hardware concepts.

The addition of animation, audio, and video to programs and the increased availability of multimedia hardware are making computers more fun to use than ever. This section will give you an introduction to the many media elements used in multimedia.

Text

Text is the fundamental component in many multimedia programs. Multimedia applications not only use ordinary text to convey basic information, they also use a variety of textual effects to emphasize and clarify information. For example, certain words or phrases can be emphasized by changing the font size or style; different colors can be used for different blocks of text on a screen. Figure 14-1 illustrates an effective use of text color in a multimedia application. Notice how the correct answer and feedback display in red. Multimedia applications also use text-based menus with buttons (Figure 14-2) to allow you to display information quickly on a certain topic.

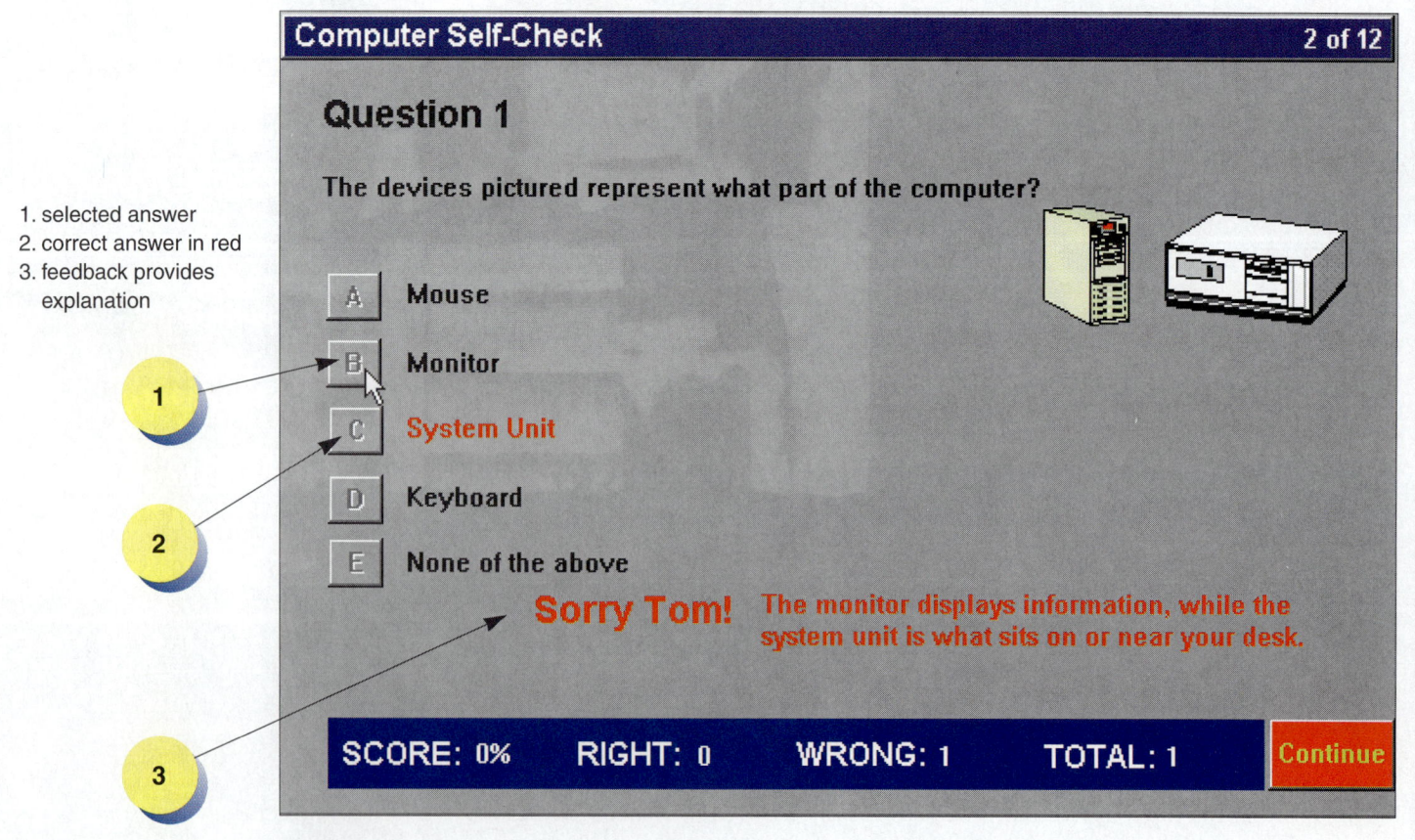

> **inCyber**
> For a view of MTV's interactive multimedia site, visit the Discovering Computers Chapter 14 inCyber page (http://www.scsite.com/dc/ch14/incyber.htm) and click Multimedia.

1. selected answer
2. correct answer in red
3. feedback provides explanation

Figure 14-1
In this interactive multimedia computer concepts tutorial, the user has selected answer B (Monitor). Immediate feedback is provided, showing the correct answer and giving an explanation. A running score also is given.

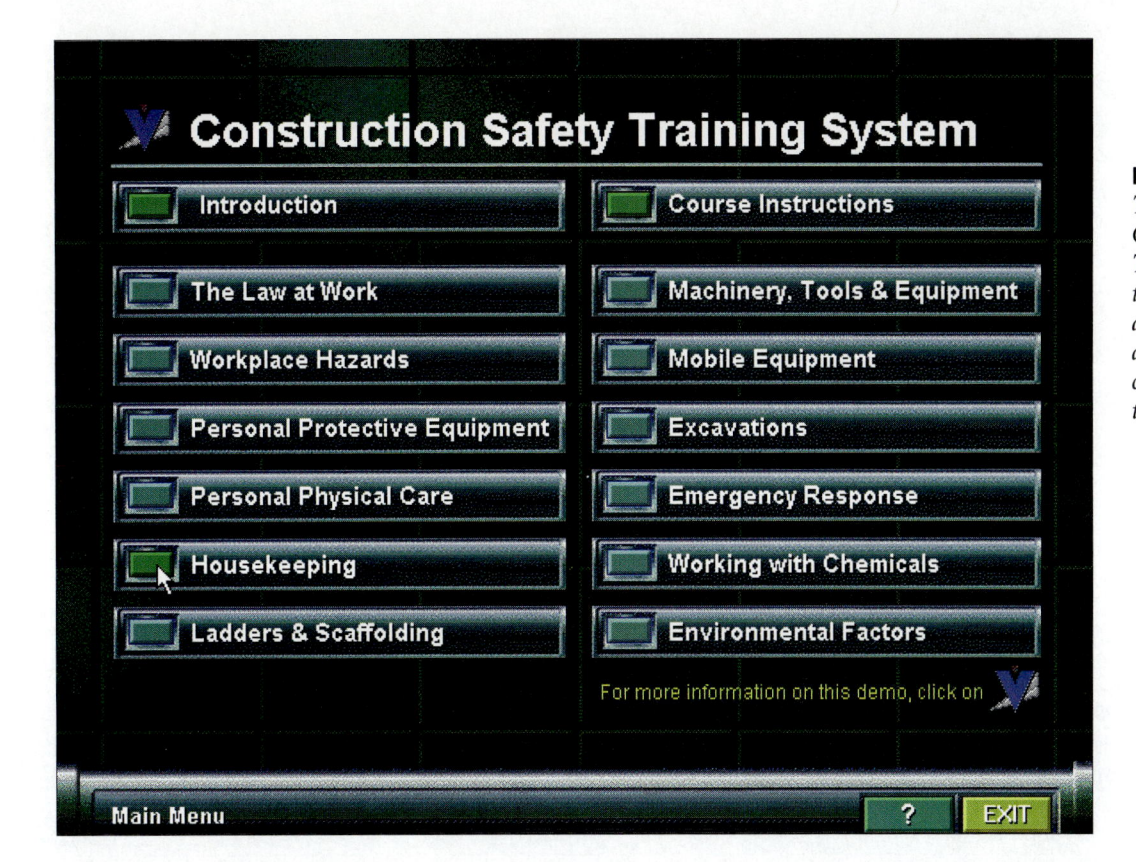

Figure 14-2
The main menu for this Construction Safety Training System provides text and buttons that allow you to go quickly to a particular topic. In this case, the user has selected the topic, Housekeeping.

Interactive Links

You interact with a multimedia application using a mouse or other pointing device to click **interactive links**, called *hyperlinks*. These hyperlinks, which work much like hyperlinks found on the Web, can be text-based hypertext links, known as **hotwords**. Multimedia applications also contain hypermedia links that use graphics, animation, or other clickable objects. Hyperlinks allow you to access information quickly in a nonlinear fashion. For example, you can click a hotword to display additional information, such as a definition or a related topic (Figure 14-3).

Figure 14-3
This screen on the Whales CD-ROM from the Discovery Channel contains text with several hotwords. The definition for the word, crustaceans, is displayed when you click that word in the text on the screen.

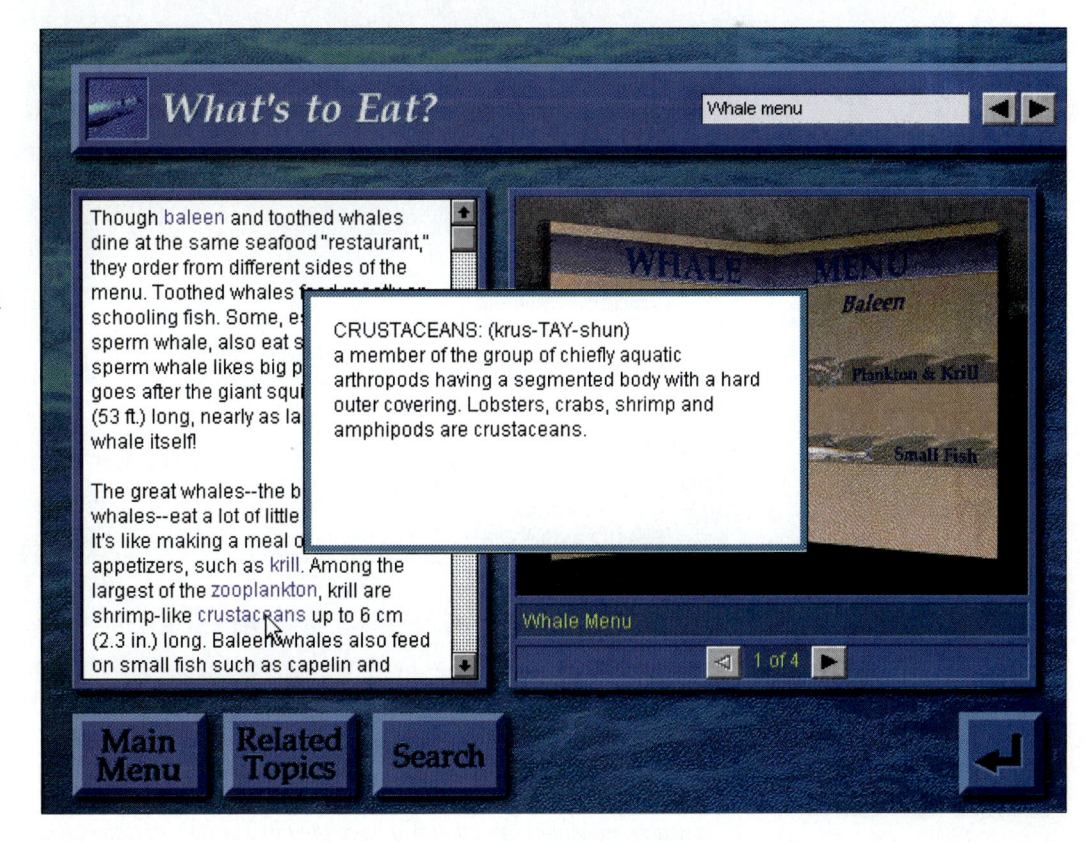

Still Graphic Images

Still graphic images are graphics that contain no movement, such as photographs or drawings. The term **graphic** typically refers to a still graphic image. The graphics used in multimedia applications are obtained in several ways. You can buy a clip art collection, which is a set of previously created art grouped by themes, or you can create your own graphics using a drawing software package. Many presentation graphics and multimedia authoring packages even provide their own drawing tools for creating graphics (Figure 14-4). If you want to obtain photographs for use in a multimedia application, you can use a color scanner to digitize photos, take photographs using a digital camera, or even buy them in a photo collection on a CD-ROM.

Graphics play an important role in multimedia because people are more visually oriented than ever. Television, movies, and highly visual magazines, for example, are a key source of information for many. The popularity of graphical user interfaces such as Windows and graphical Web browsers also demonstrate the importance of graphics in the computer environment.

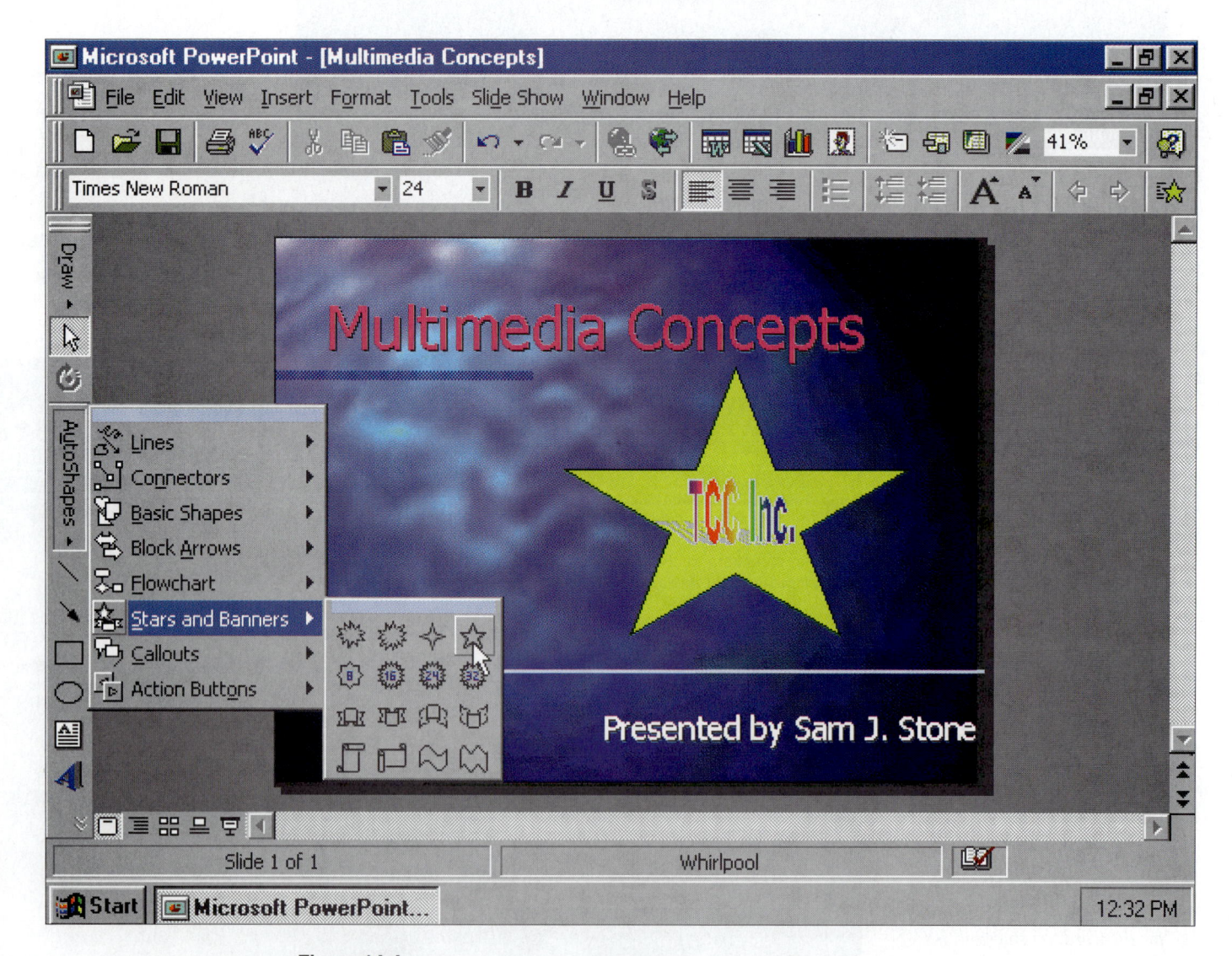

Figure 14-4
Using Microsoft PowerPoint's AutoShapes Drawing palette allows you to draw a star or other shapes to include in a multimedia presentation. This type of graphic image is a resizable, movable object that can be colored in a variety of different ways.

Animation

Animation refers to moving graphic images. Animations range in scope from the simple motion of a basic graphic image to the complex movement of very detailed images. Animations can be used in multimedia applications to convey information more vividly than just text and graphics. An animation showing an engine piston valve opening and closing as it moves up and down provides a far better understanding of how an internal combustion engine works than just a written explanation. Commercial software packages such as Autodesk Animator allow programmers to create very detailed and highly dynamic animations that can be used by most popular multimedia authoring software packages (Figure 14-5).

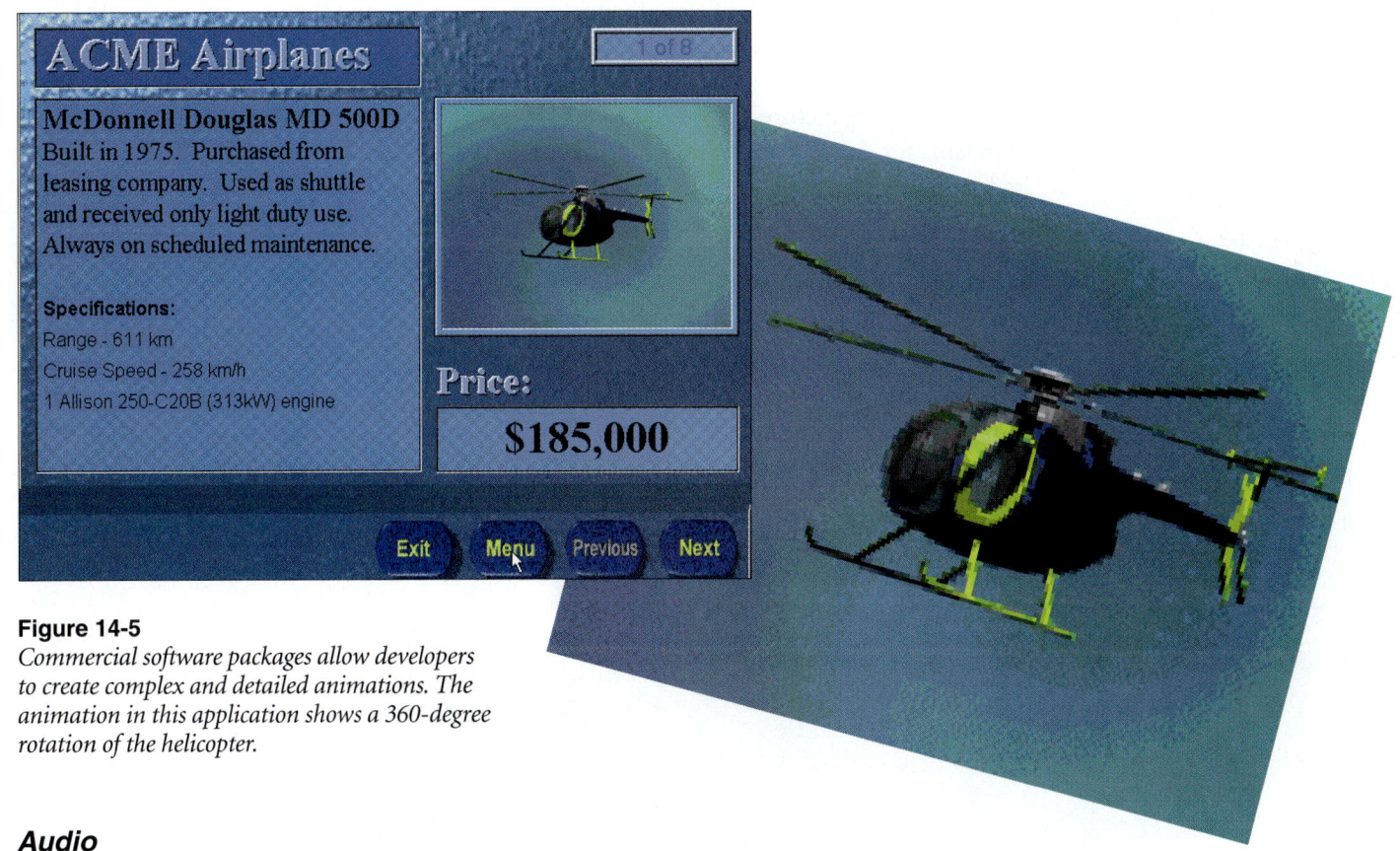

inCyber

For a look at animated movies and icons on the Web, visit the Discovering Computers Chapter 14 inCyber page (http://www.scsite.com/dc/ch14/incyber.htm) and click Animation.

Figure 14-5
Commercial software packages allow developers to create complex and detailed animations. The animation in this application shows a 360-degree rotation of the helicopter.

Audio

Audio is sound that has been digitized and stored in some form for replay. The audio used in multimedia applications can be obtained in several ways. Sounds can be captured digitally using a microphone, CD-ROM, radio, or any other device that can transmit sound into the hardware that is installed in a personal computer. Audio also can be played from a synthesizer, keyboard, or other musical device connected to the computer using a MIDI port.

As with animation, integrating audio into a multimedia application allows you to provide information not possible through any other method of communication in a computer environment. The sound of the beating of a human heart, a native French speaker reciting vocabulary, or a passage from a symphony all are things that cannot be conveyed well without the use of sound. Using audio in a multimedia application to supplement text and graphics can enhance understanding. An actor's narration added to the text of a Shakespearean play, for example, can enhance your understanding of the passage.

Video

Today, more and more multimedia applications integrate video. **Video** is comprised of photographic images that display at speeds of 15 to 30 frames per second and provide the appearance of motion in real-time. To use video in multimedia applications, you must *digitize* it, possibly using digital video production software. You also can use digital video production software to edit and add video to multimedia applications.

Incorporating video into a multimedia application presents a challenge for multimedia developers, however, because video files are so large: a single second of uncompressed video running at the speed of a movie requires 30 MB of storage space. One way to reduce the size of the files is video compression. **Video compression** works by taking advantage of the fact that only a small portion of the image changes from frame to frame. Thus, a video compression program might store the first reference frame and then, assuming that the following frames will be almost identical to it, store only the changes from one frame to the next (Figure 14-6). The video then is decompressed before it is viewed.

The Moving Pictures Experts Group, or **MPEG** (pronounced *em-peg*), has developed standards for video compression and decompression. MPEG compression methods can reduce the size of video files up to 95 percent, while retaining near-television quality. This and other improvements in video technology have allowed video to play a more important role in multimedia applications.

inCyber

For a description of MPEG resources, visit the Discovering Computers Chapter 14 inCyber page (http://www.scsite.com/dc/ch14/incyber.htm) and click MPEG.

Figure 14-6
In many video clips, only a small portion of the image changes from frame to frame. In a clip of a person talking, for example, the facial expressions will change, but the background remains constant. A video compression program will store a first reference frame and then store only the changes from one frame to the next.

Multimedia Applications

Multimedia is used in a wide variety of applications for many different areas. **Multimedia applications** are used by instructors for classroom presentations, by marketers in interactive advertisements, and by businesses for job training. Another important use of interactive multimedia is to create **simulations**, which are computer-based models of real-life situations. Computer simulations can replace costly and sometimes hazardous demonstrations and training in areas such as chemistry, biology, medicine, and flight.

The following sections provide a more detailed look at different types of multimedia applications, such as computer-based training, special education, electronic books and references, how-to guides, and magazines. The sections also address the use of multimedia for entertainment, virtual reality, information kiosks, and electronic marketing and sales, as well as its importance on the World Wide Web.

Computer-Based Training

Computer-based training (CBT) is the use of computer-aided instruction to teach specific skills. CBT is used in business and industry, sports, and education for employee or student training. Many companies are using CBT to train new employees and to update the job skills of current ones. Airlines, for example, use multimedia simulations to train employees for emergency situations (Figure 14-7), while sports athletes use multimedia computer-based training to practice baseball, football, soccer, tennis, and golf skills.

CBT allows flexible, on-the-spot training. Training stations can be set up in corporate training labs or right at employees' workstations, so they can update their job skills without leaving the workplace — or even their desks. Interactive training software called **courseware** also can be distributed on CD-ROM or shared over a network.

> **inCyber**
> For information about companies that have used interactive computer-based training, visit the Discovering Computers Chapter 14 inCyber page (http://www.scsite.com/dc/ch14/incyber.htm) and click CBT.

Figure 14-7
At the American Airlines Learning Center, instructors use a computer-based training (CBT) program called WorldTutor for employee training. Using WorldTutor has reduced training time and cost dramatically.

Computer-based training provides a unique learning experience because learners can receive instant feedback — say, positive feedback for correct responses, additional information for incorrect answers, and immediate scoring and results. Testing and self-diagnostic features allow you to verify that information has been learned. Some of the many other advantages of CBT over traditional training include:

- Self-paced study — Students can progress at their own pace, skipping strong areas to focus on areas of weakness. The multimedia content appeals to many types of learners.
- Reduced training time — Self-paced instruction encourages students to take the most efficient path to content mastery.
- One-on-one interaction — Trainers can spend more time with trainees, because computers handle test delivery and grading.
- Reduced training costs — Reduction in training time and elimination of travel reduces costs.
- Unique instructional experience — Simulations allow students to learn skills in hazardous, emergency, or other real-world situations. The same information can be conveyed in different ways.

For these reasons, multimedia applications not only are used in business, but also in education. They make the learning process more interesting, allow students to perform experiments in a risk-free environment, and provide instant feedback and testing (Figure 14-8). Multimedia applications also appeal to different learning styles and provide a new type of learning experience. A student using a multimedia study guide, for example, could listen to a speaker reciting French vocabulary to help with the pronunciation of difficult words.

Special Education

Multimedia applications are used for the education and training of both the physically impaired and learning disabled. The use of graphics and large font sizes can aid individuals with a visual impairment; the totally visually impaired benefit from the audio capabilities of multimedia applications. Similarly, the visual materials in a multimedia application make learning easier for the hearing impaired. The ability to work at one's own pace is a major benefit for the learning disabled. Being able to practice and review at their own pace aids people with learning disabilities, by alleviating the pressure to keep up with their peers.

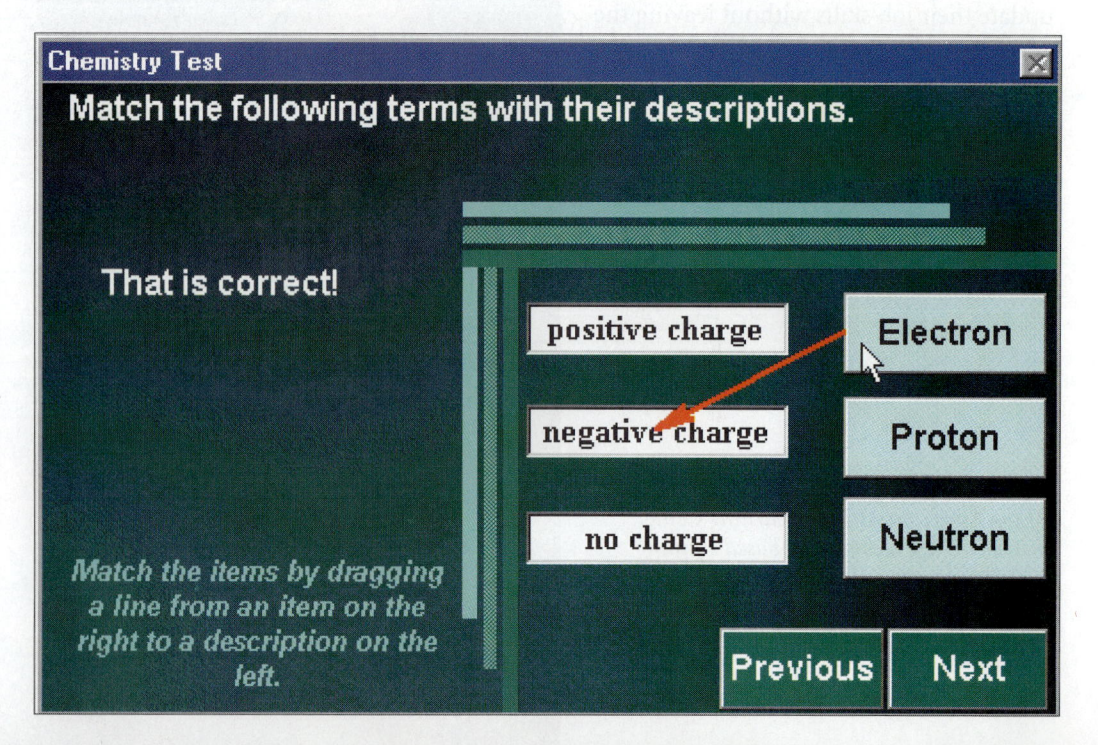

Figure 14-8
This interactive chemistry test contains a series of matching, multiple-choice, true/false, and fill-in-the-blank questions. Feedback is provided for both correct and incorrect answers, and a score is calculated at the end of the test.

Electronic Books and References

Electronic books are digitized texts that use hyperlinks to give the user instantaneous access to information. These texts contain **hotwords** that serve as hyperlinks. You can click a hotword to display a definition, play a sound, show a graphic, or play a video sequence. You typically turn pages of an electronic book by clicking icons (Figure 14-9). A table of contents, glossary, and index also are available at the click of a button.

Another popular type of electronic book includes **electronic reference** texts, such as multimedia encyclopedias on CD-ROMs. Like electronic books, multimedia electronic reference texts use text, graphics, sound, animation, and video to explain a topic or provide additional information. The multimedia encyclopedia, Microsoft Encarta, for example, includes the complete text of a multivolume encyclopedia, new articles on history, modern culture, computers, photos, animations, and detailed illustrations. This information can be accessed by using menus that allow you to select from a list of topics.

inCyber

To read a passage from an electronic book, visit the Discovering Computers Chapter 14 inCyber page (http://www.scsite.com/dc/ch14/incyber.htm) and click Electronic Book.

Figure 14-9
The complete text of The Road Ahead *by Bill Gates is contained on a CD-ROM. In addition to the text, the CD-ROM includes numerous hyperlinks, audio and visual clips showing future technologies, and more. This figure shows a page from the CD-ROM version of the book.*

1. hyperlinks to additional information (hotwords)
2. to table of contents
3. to previous page
4. to next page
5. to index

Health and medicine are two areas where multimedia reference texts are playing an important role. Instead of using volumes of books, health clinics rely on reference CD-ROMs for information, illustrations, animations, and photographs on hundreds of health and first aid topics (Figure 14-10). The reference CD-ROM called *A.D.A.M.* (Animated Dissection of Anatomy for Medicine) is used by medical students to learn about the body and by practicing physicians to communicate information to their patients.

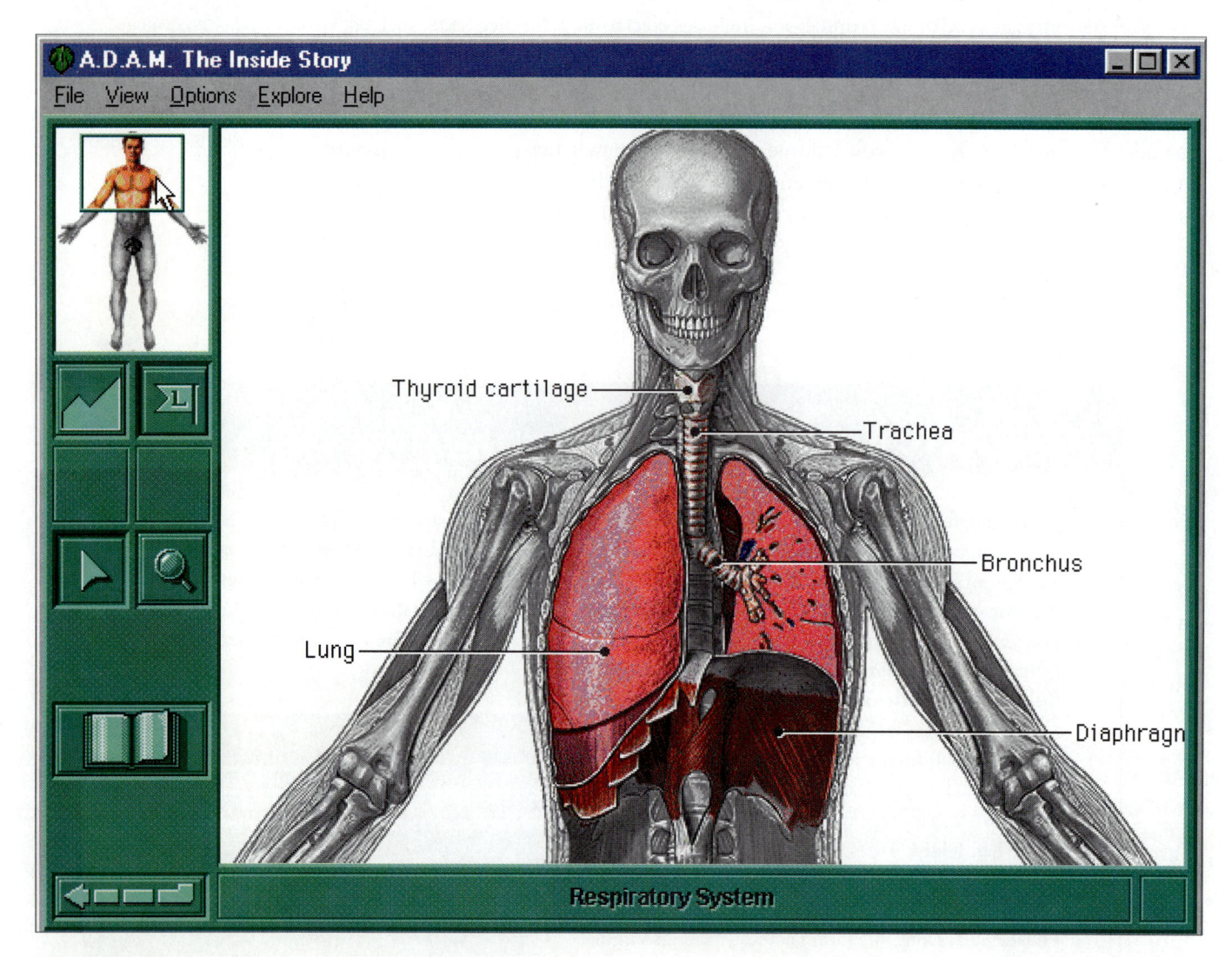

Figure 14-10
Interactive CD-ROMs such as A.D.A.M. can be used to study the respiratory system and other systems of the body.

How-To Guides

A tremendous number of interactive multimedia applications are available today to help individuals in their daily lives. These applications fall into the broad category of **how-to-guides**, which are products that allow you to plan, learn practical new skills, and have fun in the process. How-to guides can be used to help you buy a home or a car, design a garden, plan a vacation, repair your home, car, or computer, and more. Similar to the computer-based training applications used by businesses, how-to guides allow you to train, become more productive, and try out your skills in a risk-free environment. The skills you learn with a how-to guide, however, usually apply to making your life (not just your job) more productive.

One multimedia landscaping how-to guide, for example, allows you to place trees, shrubs and flowers, and then add features such as pathways, fences, and retaining walls to complete the design (Figure 14-11). Another gardening how-to guide allows you to explore a database of plants with color photographs and the growth attributes of each.

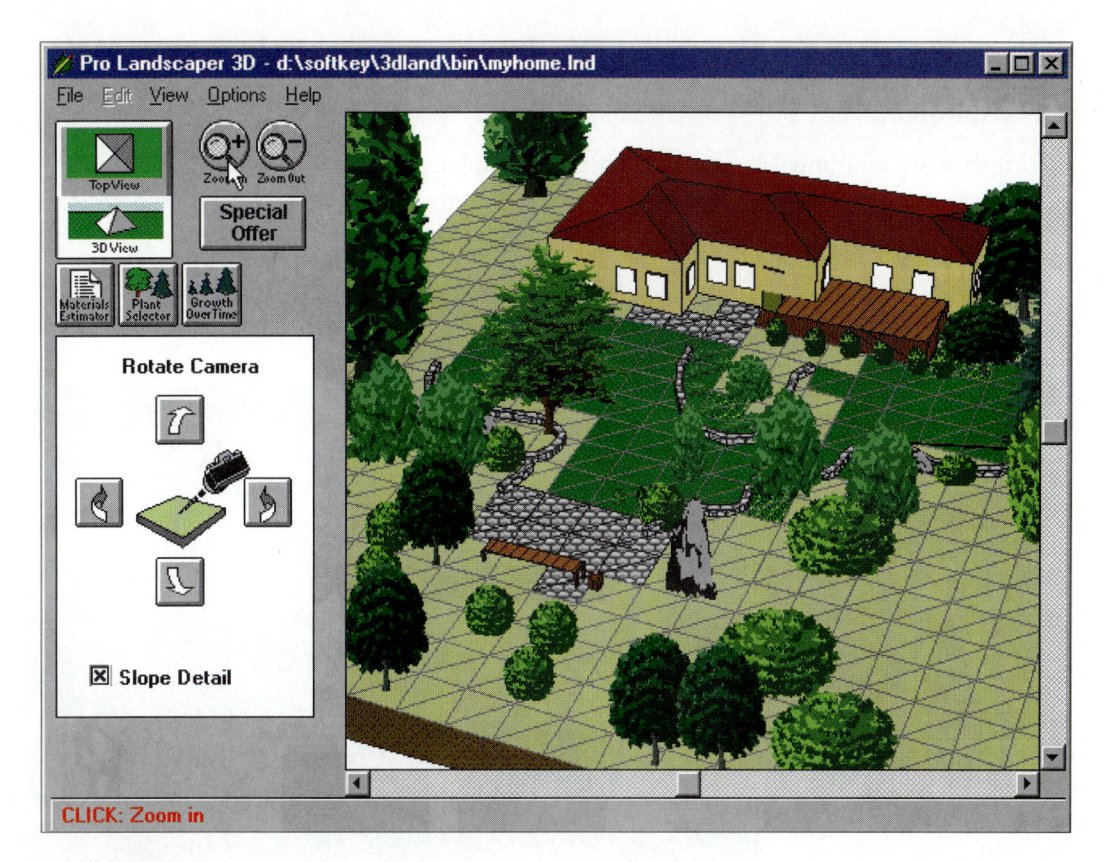

Figure 14-11
A 3-D view of a house with plants, trees, patio, and garden area.

inCyber

For links to multimedia magazines, newspapers, and books, visit the Discovering Computers Chapter 14 inCyber page (http://www.scsite.com/dc/ch14/incyber.htm) and click Magazines.

Magazines

Several multimedia magazines now are available and more are being created each month. **Multimedia magazines** often have the familiar appearance of a print-based magazine and include regular sections and articles, such as departments, editorials, and more. Unlike printed publications, multimedia magazines use many types of media to convey information. Audio and video clips can be included to showcase recent album releases or movies; animations can depict weather patterns or election results. The magazine, **NautilusCD**, for instance, has the appearance of a printed publication but presents the content with multimedia articles that contain sound, images, movies, demos, and more (Figure 14-12). Multimedia magazines usually are distributed using CD-ROMs or the World Wide Web.

Figure 14-12
The contents screen for this issue of the NautilusCD multimedia magazine shows the different departments, such as Entertainment, Education, and ComputerWare.

Entertainment

Interactive multimedia computer games use graphics, sound, and video to create a realistic and entertaining game situation. Often the game simulates a real or fictitious world, in which you play the role of a character and have direct control of what happens in the game. Other new multimedia products provide **edutainment**, which is an experience meant to be both educational and entertaining (Figure 14-13). These CD-ROMs often are used to teach children in a fun and appealing way.

Interactive CD-ROMs also are being used by the music industry. For example, you can purchase interactive CD-ROMs that let you play musical instruments along with your favorite rock musician, read about the musician's life and interests, and even create your own version of popular songs. Like interactive games, these applications give you a character role and put you in control of the application.

inCyber

For a comprehensive list of virtual reality sites, visit the Discovering Computers Chapter 14 inCyber page (http://www.scsite.com/dc/ch14/incyber.htm) and click Virtual Reality.

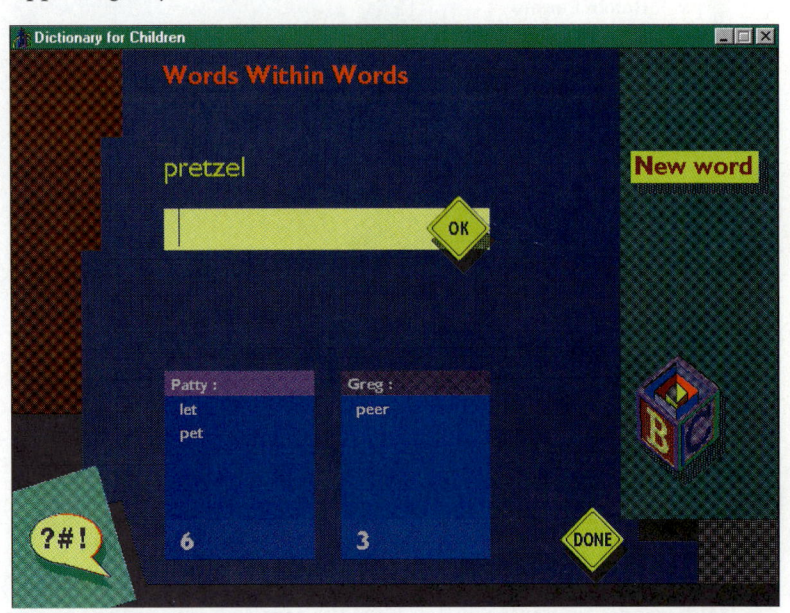

Figure 14-13
Interactive multimedia computer games use graphics, sound, and video to create an entertaining game experience.

Virtual Reality

Another application of multimedia is **virtual reality** (**VR**), which is the use of a computer to create an artificial environment that you can experience by interactively exploring and manipulating the environment. In its simplest form, VR software displays what appears to be a three-dimensional view of a place that can be explored by the user, such as a landscape or a building. Architects are using this type of software to show clients what proposed construction or remodeling will look like (Figure 14-14).

In more advanced forms, VR software requires you to wear specialized headgear, body suits, and gloves to enhance the experience of the artificial environment (Figure 14-15). The headgear displays the artificial environment in front of both of your eyes. The body suit and the gloves sense your motion and direction, allowing you to move through and pick up and hold items displayed in the virtual environment. Eventually, experts predict, the body suits will provide tactile feedback so you can experience the touch and feel of the virtual world.

Your first encounter with VR likely will be through a three-dimensional electronic game. In such games, special visors allow you to *see* the computer-generated environment. As you walk around the game's electronic landscape, sensors in the surrounding game machine record your movements and change your view of the landscape accordingly. You also might use a Web-based VR application developed using virtual reality modeling language (VRML).

Figure 14-14
One of the first practical applications of virtual reality software was in the architectural profession. Architects use VR software to create a model of the project on which they are working. Clients then can walk through the virtual project and specify design changes before the project is built.

Companies are beginning to use VR for more practical, commercial applications, as well. Office furniture companies, for example, have created virtual showrooms in which customers wander among and inspect available products. Automobile and airplane manufacturers are using virtual prototypes to test new models and shorten product design time. Telecommunications firms and others even are using PC-based VR applications for employee training. As computing power and the use of the Web increase, practical applications of VR will continue to emerge.

Figure 14-15
A virtual reality body suit allows the VR software to interpret the body movements of the wearer. The software then manipulates the image in the virtual environment, which is displayed in the headset.

Information Kiosks

An **information kiosk** is a computerized information or reference center that allows you to select various options to find specific information or simply browse through choices. A typical information kiosk is a self-service structure equipped with PC hardware and software; kiosks often use touch screen monitors or keyboards for input devices. All of the data and information needed for the application is stored directly on the computer.

Information kiosks often are used to provide information in public places where visitors or customers have common questions. Locations such as shopping centers, hotels, and airports, for example, use kiosks to provide information on available services, product locations, maps, and other information (Figure 14-16). Museums and libraries use kiosks to allow visitors to find the location of a specific exhibit or text.

Information kiosks also are used for interactive multimedia marketing. Using a kiosk allows you to try options and explore scenarios as you shop for a product or service. For example, you might be able to try different color combinations or take short quizzes to determine which product suits you best. Once customers are involved with the product, they are more likely to purchase it.

inCyber

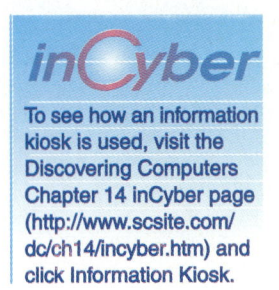

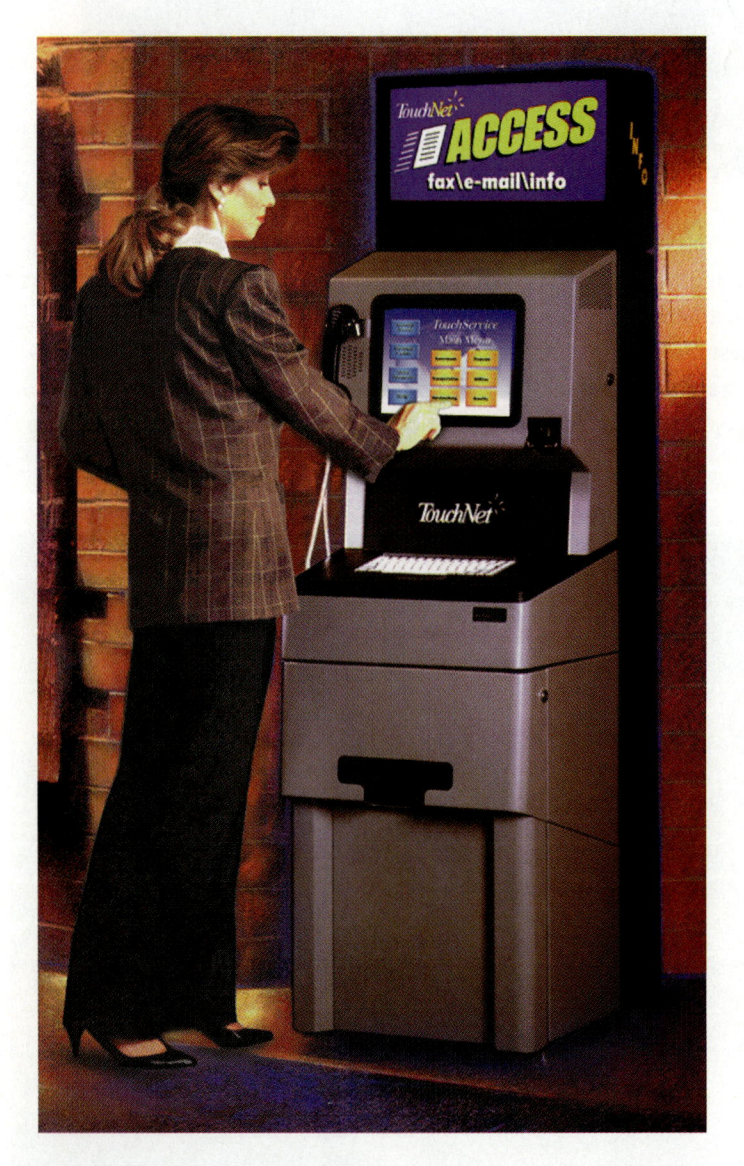

To see how an information kiosk is used, visit the Discovering Computers Chapter 14 inCyber page (http://www.scsite.com/dc/ch14/incyber.htm) and click Information Kiosk.

Figure 14-16
Using information kiosks in airports, travelers can check on hotel location and availability, confirm car rentals, read about local attractions, and more. Some kiosks even print out local maps and directions to specific sites.

Electronic Marketing and Sales

Multimedia is used extensively by many businesses and industries to advertise and sell products and create marketing presentations. Multimedia authoring software, for instance, has made television commercials with unique media effects easier and less expensive to produce. Sales representatives also use multimedia in marketing presentations created using presentation graphics programs (Figure 14-17). Overhead projection systems can be used to give these presentations to both small and large audiences.

Figure 14-17
This Microsoft PowerPoint presentation shows how a travel agency uses multimedia to present information about one of its Caribbean cruises. The use of color and graphics for this part of the presentation is highly effective.

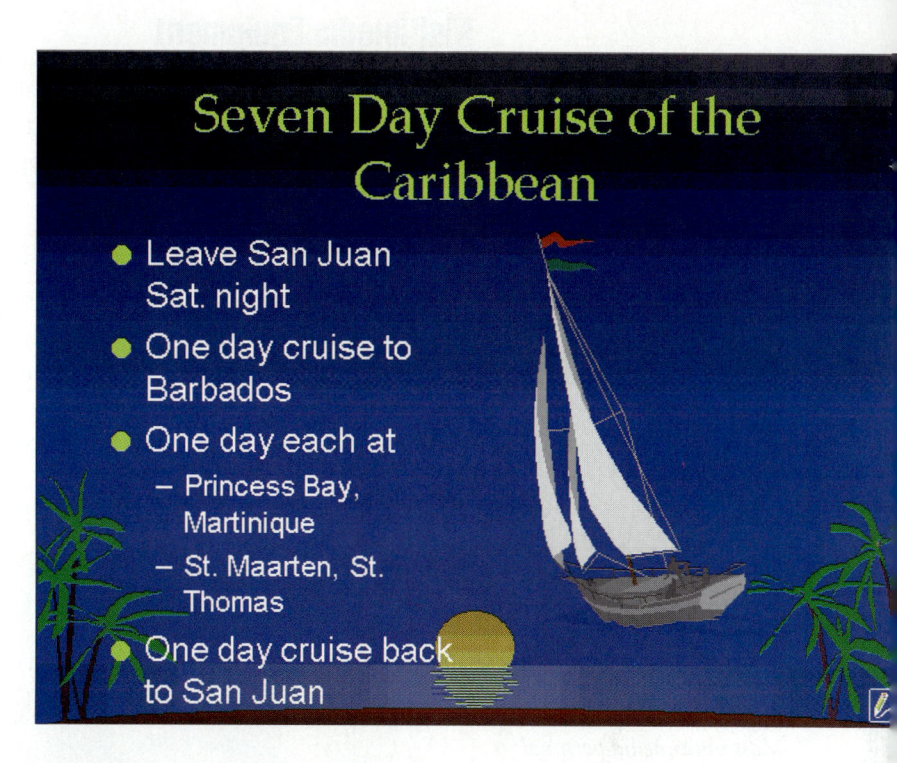

The Internet and the World Wide Web Applications

Multimedia applications also are playing an important role on the World Wide Web, which is the portion of the Internet that supports multimedia. The Web uses many types of media to deliver information and enhance the Web experience (Figure 14-18). Graphics and animations are used to reinforce Web page content and deliver constantly updated information, and audio and video clips are used for online radio stations, movie previews, and games. Hypertext and hypermedia make it easier to navigate through this vast information resource. Multimedia makes up much of the information on the Web today. Many of the applications previously discussed can be delivered over the Web — games, magazines, virtual reality, and more.

New multimedia authoring software packages include tools for creating and delivering multimedia applications on the Internet and the World Wide Web. Some of these authoring software packages allow you to create applications in the Windows environment and then convert them to HTML and Java for use on the Web.

Figure 14-18
A NASA Web server offers textual and graphical information about the Mission to Saturn. By clicking the thumbnail picture, you can obtain a larger, more detailed image of Saturn and its rings.

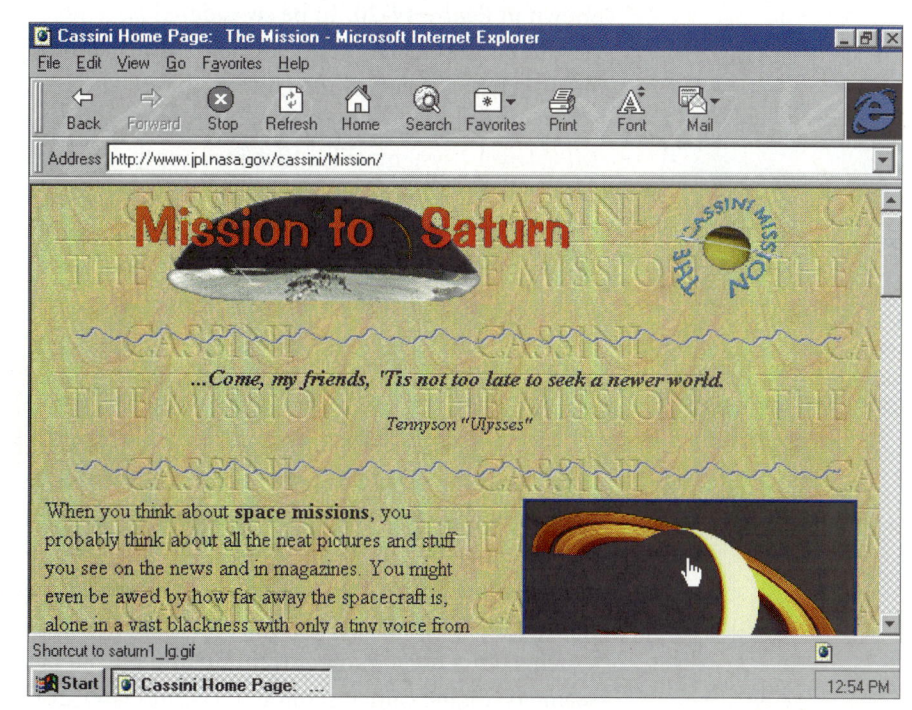

Multimedia Equipment

Equipment selection is an important process in both the development and delivery of multimedia products. This section describes the different equipment needed to develop and display a multimedia presentation or application.

Multimedia Personal Computer

A **multimedia personal computer** is a computer system that uses specific hardware and software components to input, process, and output the various types of media. Multimedia personal computers (Figure 14-19) often are referred to by their **MPC level**, or **specification**, which is a set of multimedia hardware and software standards developed by the Multimedia PC Marketing Council and several major computer manufacturers.

Figure 14-19
Most multimedia personal computers are equipped with devices such as a microphone, a CD-ROM drive, speakers, and a high-resolution monitor.

Two different levels of MPC standards and the year in which they were developed are shown in Figure 14-20. To be considered an MPC Level 3 or Level 2 system, a system must have all of the elements and components listed in Figure 14-20, all of which must meet the full functional specifications outlined.

The level of multimedia personal computer you need depends on your intended use. An MPC Level 2 system will suffice for simply running multimedia applications, although an MPC Level 3 system will provide better video playback and response time. For authoring multimedia applications, you need at least an MPC Level 3 system. You even should consider adding a faster processor, more memory, and more hard disk storage capacity — a system with a 200 MHz Pentium processor with MMX™ technology, 32 MB RAM, and 3 to 5 GB hard disk is recommended. **MMX™ technology** is an extension to the Pentium processor instruction set that yields a 50 to 100% improvement in the clarity and speed of audio, video, and speech.

Media devices in the multimedia personal computer, such as the sound card and CD-ROM drive, need instructions for their control. **Multimedia extensions** are system software that operate in the background of a Windows application and are responsible for the playing or displaying of media.

In addition to these required components, many other devices and components are used in multimedia computer systems. Along with the audio and video components, multimedia systems often use a number of input and output devices such as overhead projection systems, scanners, digital cameras, photo CDs, and laser disks.

---

inCyber

For an explanation of MMX™ technology, visit the Discovering Computers Chapter 14 inCyber page (http://www.scsite.com/dc/ch14/incyber.htm) and click MMX™ Technology.

MULTIMEDIA EQUIPMENT 14.17

	MPC Level 2 Specifications	**MPC Level 3** Specifications
Date introduced	May 1993	June 1995
CPU	25 MHz 486SX	75 MHz Pentium
RAM	At least 4 megabytes of RAM (8 megabytes recommended)	8 megabytes of RAM
Magnetic storage	Floppy disk drive, hard drive (160 MB minimum)	Floppy disk drive, hard drive (540 MB minimum)
Optical storage	Double-speed (2x)	Quad-speed (4X)
Audio	16-bit	16-bit wavetable, MIDI playback
Video display	At least 640 x 480 with 65,536 (64K) colors	At least 640 x 480 with 65,536 (64K) colors; MPEG-1 (full-screen video)
Input	101-key keyboard (or functional equivalent), two-button mouse	101-key keyboard (or functional equivalent), two-button mouse
I/O	Serial port, parallel port, MIDI I/O port, joystick port	Serial port, parallel port, MIDI I/O port, joystick port
System software	Compatibility with Windows 3.1/ Windows 3.0 plus multimedia extensions	Compatibility with Windows 3.1/ Windows 3.0 plus multimedia extensions

Figure 14-20
This table compares Level 2 and Level 3 MPC standards.

Sound Card A **sound card** is a circuit board that houses processors used to provide both audio input and output (Figure 14-21). The typical sound card has three primary subsystems: an audio digitizer, a wavetable synthesizer, and a mixer. The audio digitizer is a pair of analog-to-digital and digital-to-analog converters. The wavetable synthesizer has the capability of producing sounds. The mixer combines these two signals along with mixing audio from a CD-ROM. The sound card can be used to record most any audio signal. The sound card has two jacks for input. One jack is used for input from a microphone, while the other is used to accept input from a radio, stereo, tape player, external CD player, or any other audio source. The remaining jack connects devices such as speakers, headphones, or a stereo sound system that are used for the final playback of the sound.

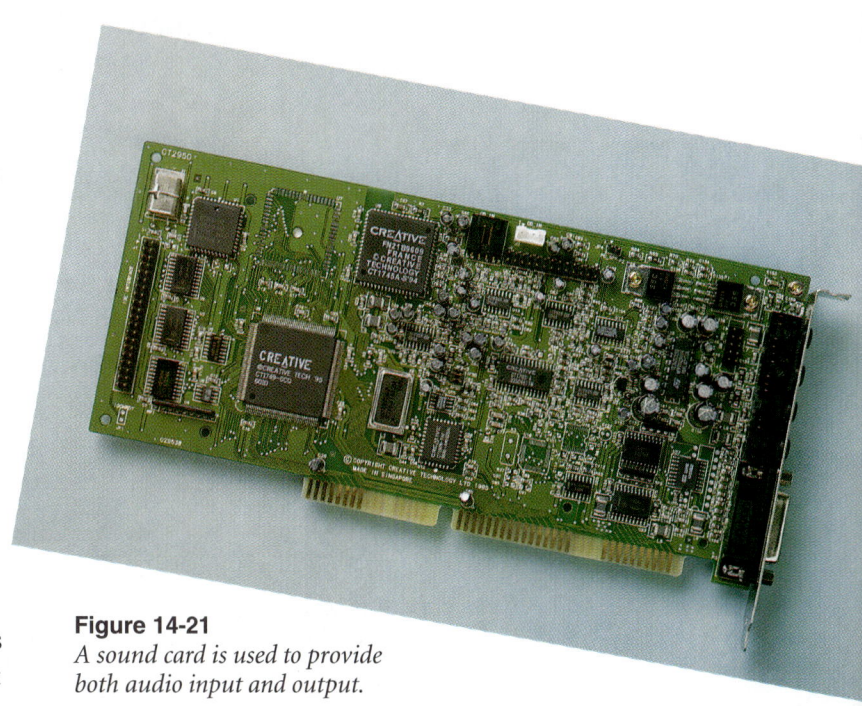

Figure 14-21
A sound card is used to provide both audio input and output.

CD-ROM Drive As discussed in Chapter 5, a **CD-ROM** is an optical storage medium that can hold almost 650 MB of data. The CD-ROM's large storage capacity makes it an excellent medium for storing and distributing multimedia applications that contain many large graphics, audio, and video files.

Today, most computer systems include a CD-ROM drive as standard equipment. When you are buying a system, the most important consideration for a CD-ROM drive for a multimedia personal computer is speed. The faster the transfer rate of the CD-ROM, the better the video playback will be. CD-ROM drives with slower transfer rates tend to output poor quality video, in which the audio and video is not fully integrated. Today, most of the CD-ROM drives being sold are quad-speed or higher, thus providing smoother playback of video files containing audio and video.

Most CD-ROM drives sold today also are internal; that is, they are installed inside the system unit of the personal computer. Most of these CD-ROM drives also have headphone plugs in the face of the drive and connectors that allow the CD-ROM to be connected directly to the sound card. By connecting the CD-ROM to the sound card and then connecting the sound card to a stereo system or speakers, you can obtain high-quality audio output.

Speakers Small stereo **speakers**, such as those shown in Figure 14-19 on page 14.16, provide an easy and inexpensive way to play audio on a multimedia personal computer. For presentations, you might want to invest in amplified speakers or even a stereo system, which can be connected directly to the sound card.

Video Display The **video display** is an important part of a multimedia personal computer system. When choosing a display for your multimedia personal computer, you must evaluate both the monitor and the display adapter, which generates the output required to display text and graphics on a monitor. To effectively display multimedia applications, your system should have at least a standard VGA monitor and display adapter. Adding memory to your display adapter will extend the graphics display to allow a VGA monitor to

Figure 14-22
An LCD projector panel, such as this InFocus color LCD panel, can be used with a laptop and overhead projector to deliver an effective multimedia presentation.

display 640 x 480 resolution, with 65,536 colors. A Super VGA (SVGA) monitor and adapter will provide higher resolution and better color display. SVGA monitors are standard on most computer systems sold today.

Overhead Projection Systems

For individual presentations or presentations to small groups, a large SVGA monitor often is appropriate. For larger group presentations, a large-screen TV monitor might be needed. Connecting the multimedia computer to the monitor requires an **NTSC converter**, which converts the digital signal to an analog signal that can be displayed on the television monitor. **NTSC** stands for National Television System Committee, which is the organization that sets the standards for most video and broadcast television equipment.

For presenting to even larger groups, an **overhead projection system** often is used. One such system uses an **LCD projector panel** (Figure 14-22), which is a flat-screen panel that is placed on top of an overhead projector. The computer is connected to the LCD projector panel, which then projects the images onto a screen by using the overhead projector as a light source. You can view the presentation on the computer monitor and the projection screen at the same time.

Another type of projection system is a **video projector** (Figure 14-23), which is connected directly to a computer with a cable and uses its own light source to display a multimedia application or presentation onto a screen. Some projectors can display SVGA output directly from the computer; others require an NTSC converter. Many of these video projectors have audio capabilities, as well.

inCyber

For information on LCD projector panels, visit the Discovering Computers Chapter 14 inCyber page (http://www.scsite.com/dc/ch14/incyber.htm) and click LCD Projector Panel.

Figure 14-23
A video projector uses its own light source to display a multimedia application or presentation onto a screen. Many projectors have audio output capabilities as well.

Video Capture Card

A **video capture card** is an expansion card, or adapter, that plugs into the computer's expansion slot and enables you to connect a video camera or videocassette recorder to a computer and manipulate the video input. Video capture software used with the card compresses the video data so the video files are small enough to be stored on a hard disk. Many manufacturers of video capture cards are using Intel's proprietary **digital video interleave**, or **DVI**, compression technology for their video compression. As with MPEG compression, DVI compression is capable of reducing the size of the file while maintaining the image quality. Unlike early versions of MPEG, DVI creates video files that can be replayed using only software; no other adapters or hardware are needed. Early versions of MPEG required additional hardware, but today several software-only MPEG technologies exists.

Scanners, Digital Cameras, and Photo CDs

Multimedia developers can add color images and photos to multimedia applications using color scanners, digital cameras, and photo CDs. A **color scanner** is used to convert images into a digitized format for use in multimedia applications (Figure 14-24). More expensive scanners can produce images at a resolution as high as 1,200 dpi (dots per inch) in 16.7 million colors. Less-expensive scanners can produce good graphic images at a resolution of 600 dpi and 256 colors. The basic software that comes with scanners (Figure 14-25) allows scanned images to be saved in many different file formats. If a wider variety of image editing possibilities are needed, more sophisticated software packages are available. Many times, the quality of a photograph can be improved using this software.

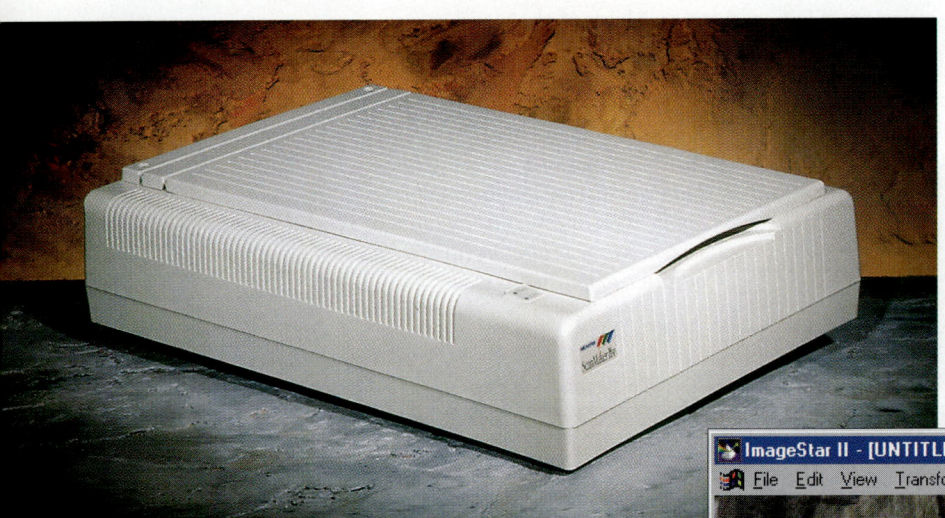

inCyber
For details on low-cost scanners, visit the Discovering Computers Chapter 14 inCyber page (http://www.scsite.com/dc/ch14/incyber.htm) and click Scanners.

Figure 14-24
A color scanner can convert images into digitized format for multimedia applications.

Figure 14-25
The basic software that comes with scanners allows scanned images to be saved in many different file formats.

MULTIMEDIA EQUIPMENT **14.21**

Figure 14-26
An easy and effective way to obtain digitized color photographs is by using a digital camera. Once the photographs are input into a computer, they can be incorporated into a multimedia application.

Another easy and effective way to obtain color photographs for a multimedia application is by using a digital camera (Figure 14-26). As discussed in Chapter 3, **digital cameras** work much like regular cameras, except they use a small reusable disk or internal memory to store digital photographs. These photographs then are input into a computer using the appropriate hardware and software. You then can incorporate them into a multimedia application.

A relatively new way of obtaining and storing digital images is the **Photo CD system** (Figure 14-27). The Photo CD system uses write-once compact disks to store photographic images that can be integrated into multimedia applications. The photos can be taken by any 35mm camera; when the film is developed, the images are transferred to a Photo CD master disk that holds about 100 images. Photos stored on a Photo CD can be read by practically any computer equipped with a CD-ROM drive. They also can be viewed on a television using a Photo CD player.

Figure 14-27
Photo CDs are write-once compact disks that can store about 100 photographic images. Photos on the CD can be taken by any 35mm camera; the images are transferred to the Photo CD master disk when the film is developed.

Laser Disks

Laser disks and laser disk players are part of a read-only video disk system based upon the same optical disk technology used for CD-ROMs. Laser disks and laser disk players provide high-quality display of audio and video (Figure 14-28).

One common format used for recording information on a laser disk is called CAV. **CAV** stands for **constant angular velocity** and refers to the way information is accessed from the disk. Using the CAV format allows you to display single frames of video sequence or play a clip slowly, frame by frame. A double-sided CAV laser disk holds up to 60 minutes of high-quality audio and video. Another laser disk format, called **CLV**, for **constant linear velocity**, can store more information than CAV disks, but is not as well-suited to showing single frames.

Giving a multimedia presentation using a laser disk player requires several key pieces of hardware and software. First, the laser disk player is connected to the computer via the serial port. **MCI (media control interface) commands** are used to send instructions from the computer to the laser disk player. Today, many laser disk players come with software that includes MCI commands built into buttons that can be used to play, pause, and move forward and backward on the disk.

Finally, to show the video from a laser disk player, a separate monitor or projector is needed (the computer monitor is needed to display MCI commands or the laser disk controls).

Video Overlay Cards

An alternative to using two separate monitors with a laser disk is to use a **video overlay card**. Once a video overlay card is installed in the computer, the computer monitor can display the button controls or MCI commands in one window and display the video from the laser disk in an overlay window. The laser disk audio is connected directly to a stereo sound system or the computer's sound card. Such a system allows for an impressive multimedia presentation but is quite expensive. In addition, finding a compatible laser disk player, overlay card, software, and computer often is difficult. Another disadvantage of this system is that presentations must be developed specifically for the systems on which they are played.

Figure 14-28
Laser disk systems use speakers, a monitor or video projector, software, an overlay board, and other devices to provide high-quality multimedia display.

Developing Multimedia Applications

As with all program development, **developing multimedia applications** follows a standard process with several phases. While some of the terminology is different, the basic activities completed within each phase closely follow those of the program development life cycle presented in Chapter 12. Figure 14-29 lists some basic guidelines that apply to the various phases of the multimedia application development process. The next sections will focus on a few of these phases — analysis, design, and production — as well as introducing you to several popular multimedia authoring software packages.

> **inCyber**
>
> For an extensive list of multimedia development resources, visit the Discovering Computers Chapter 14 inCyber page (http://www.scsite.com/dc/ch14/incyber.htm) and click Multimedia.

Factor	Activity
Know your audience	Include a self-assessment test to gauge learner needs.
Give the user control	Provide a means for the user to navigate his or her own course.
Use icons with clear meaning	Use left and right arrows for sequential pages, a stop sign for exit, and so on.
Immerse the user	Recreate the tasks users have to perform.
Require interaction	Ask questions and provide feedback.
Review concepts	Use self-building exercises.
Engage the user	Make the program attractive and appealing to the eye and ear.
Test the program	Test on the target platform with a target audience.

Figure 14-29
Multimedia development guidelines.

Analysis

Careful planning during the **analysis** phase leads to success in a multimedia project. The first step is to have all of the individuals involved in the project get together to determine the objectives and requirements for the application and specify the key elements needed for the actual production. For larger projects with specific learning objectives, analysis particularly is important. For example, if you are building a multimedia training program, you must determine basic content needs, testing and scoring features, number of users it should support, and so on. Larger projects, such as commercial CD-ROM products, usually involve a project team, including a producer, an art director, an interface designer, a content designer, and the main programmer. For smaller multimedia projects, the developer can play a variety of different roles, which may include content development, interface design, and programming.

Design

Once basic requirements have been determined, **design** begins. Careful planning equally is critical during the design phase of a multimedia project. Throughout design, an important tool for the project team is a *flowchart*, or map, which includes all of the various media elements in the application and serves as a blueprint to which the project team or individual developer can refer. Another important tool used during the design phase of a multimedia project is the project script. The **project script** provides more detailed information to supplement the flowchart and provides a written record of how the various media elements will be used in the production.

Another important part of designing an effective multimedia application is the process of screen design. The colors and layout used for individual screens greatly influence the overall effect of the finished product. Simple screens with consistent backgrounds and a few bright colors, for example, usually are clearer and less distracting to a reader. Other basic screen design principles to remember are shown in Figure 14-30.

Design Element	Explanation
Alignment	Use left-alignment to provide a more natural reading flow.
Balance	Avoid centering objects on the page. Place a graphic off to one side and text on the other.
Brevity	Use short, concise phrases.
Color	Keep the number of colors to a minimum, and use light text on a dark, consistent background.
Emphasis	Emphasize key concepts by using media elements such as video, audio, and graphics.
Font size	Use a font size big enough for your audience to read.
Formatting	Use appropriate formatting, such as bold formatting of keywords, to ensure your message is clear.
Navigation	Place navigation buttons at the bottom of the screen.
Number of ideas	Present only a few ideas per page.

Figure 14-30
This table details effective screen design principles.

Production

Multimedia **production** is the actual process of creating the various media elements used in the multimedia application and putting them together using a multimedia authoring software program. Original graphics and animations are created by artists using the various computerized drawing packages, while photographs are obtained by scanning images or using a digital camera or Photo CD. Digital video and audio are obtained by recording clips using recording devices and a video capture or sound card. When all of the media elements have been obtained, authoring begins. During **authoring**, the programmer or developer uses a multimedia authoring software package such as ToolBook, Authorware, or Director to combine these elements together. Finally, the developer tests the program to make sure it performs the way it was designed.

Multimedia Authoring Software

The development of an interactive multimedia application involves the use of multimedia authoring software. **Multimedia authoring software** allows you to combine text, graphics, animation, audio, and video into a finished application. Authoring programs also allow you to design the screen on which the material is presented to create *interactivity*; that is, to create places in the program that respond to user input. Once various media elements are added to the program, you use the multimedia authoring software to assign relationships and actions to elements. The programs also help you create a structure that lets the user navigate through the material presented.

One of the more important activities of the production phase of multimedia development — even, perhaps, in the whole development process — is the selection of the multimedia authoring software package. The following are important factors to consider when selecting a multimedia authoring software package:

- Quality of application developed
- Ease of use and documentation
- Responsiveness of vendor's service and technical support
- Compatibility with other applications
- Ease of programming
- Functionality
- System requirements both for user and developer

Most of today's popular authoring packages share similar features and are capable of creating similar applications. The major differences exist in the ease of use for development. This section will provide a closer look at three popular multimedia authoring packages: Toolbook, Authorware, and Director.

ToolBook   ToolBook, from Asymetrix Corporation, is one of the more widely used multimedia authoring software packages. **ToolBook** uses a graphical user interface and an object-oriented approach so you can design your applications using basic objects such as buttons, fields, graphics, backgrounds, and pages (Figure 14-31).

ToolBook uses a familiar book metaphor to help you build a multimedia application. The program or application that you build is called a **book**, and each screen is called a **page**. You begin building an application by creating a series of pages. Next, objects such as text fields, buttons, and graphics are added to each page.

As discussed in Chapter 12, each object can have a set of properties that defines the object's behavior. A Next Button object, for example, might move to the next page of the book. You can change an object's properties by writing a script in **OpenScript**, which is the ToolBook programming language.

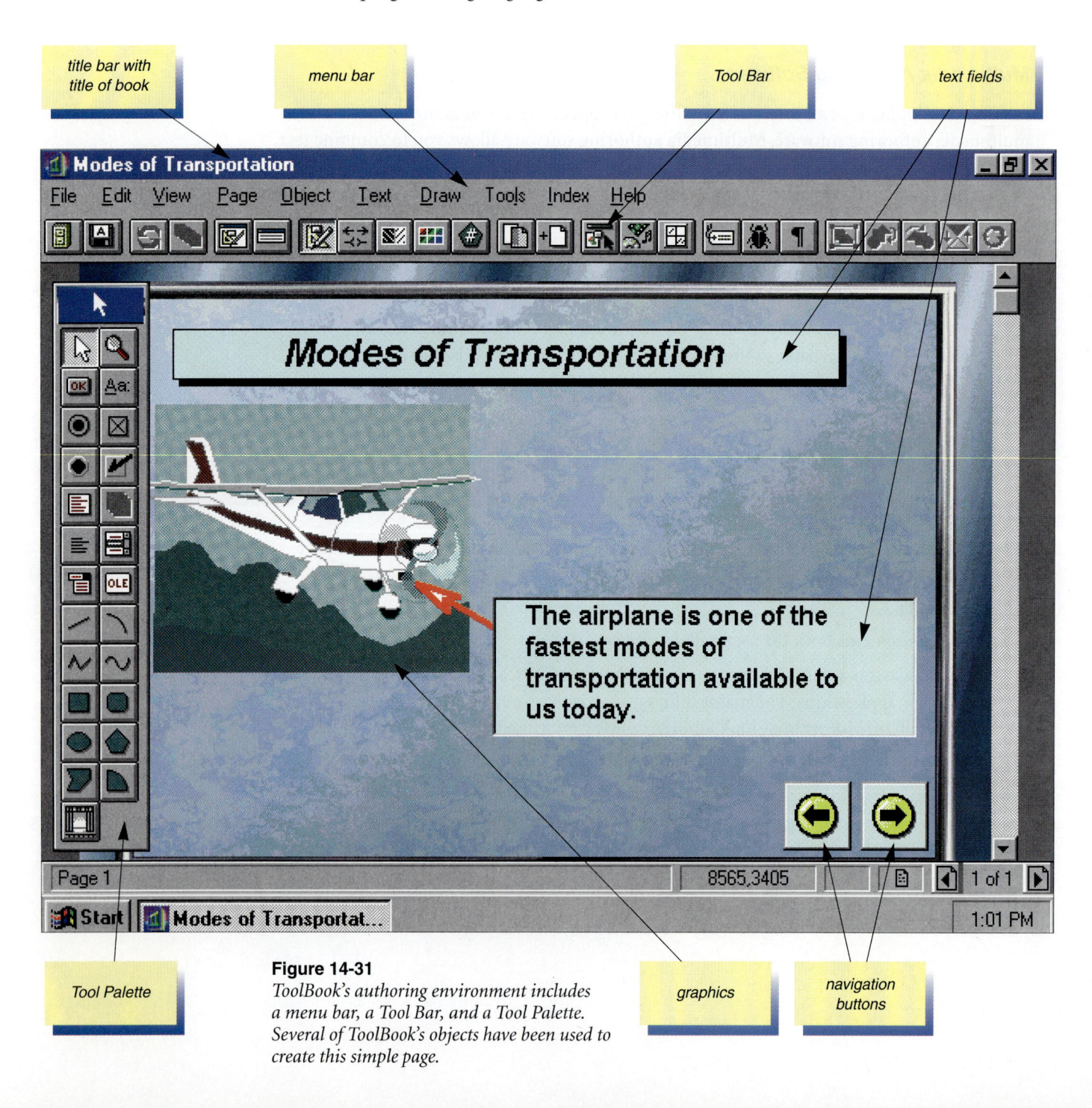

Figure 14-31
ToolBook's authoring environment includes a menu bar, a Tool Bar, and a Tool Palette. Several of ToolBook's objects have been used to create this simple page.

Instead of writing scripts to define objects and their behaviors, you can use ToolBook objects called widgets. **Widgets** are graphical objects that are *pre-scripted*, or contain properties that give them a certain behavior. ToolBook provides a number of widgets in a **Widget Catalog**; you can drag a widget directly from the Widget Catalog onto a page, and the widget will behave according to its pre-scripted behaviors or assigned properties. A Save Button widget, for example, will allow the user to save his or her work when running the multimedia application.

Widgets eliminate much of the programming involved in developing multimedia applications. Using widgets, you easily can define page navigation and add media components such as animation, audio, and video. Widgets also assist in adding questions, feedback, and scoring capabilities to multimedia applications (Figure 14-32). Several types of widgets available with ToolBook are shown in Figure 14-33. ToolBook also provides basic layout templates for tests, glossaries, Internet applications, and more.

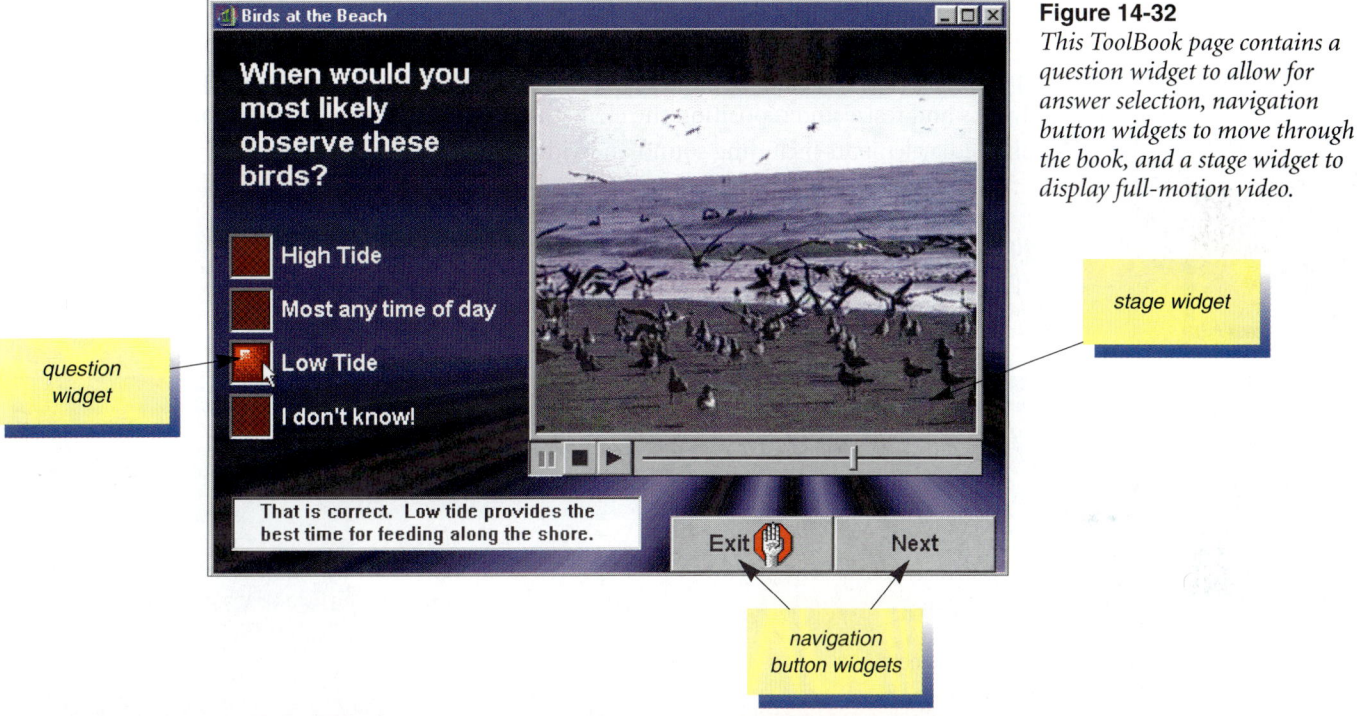

Figure 14-32
This ToolBook page contains a question widget to allow for answer selection, navigation button widgets to move through the book, and a stage widget to display full-motion video.

Widget Category	Examples
Action buttons	Cancel, Done, Exit and Save, Run an Application, and Student Notes
Media clip controls	Audio and Video Players, Video Stage and Controls, and Volume Control
Navigation buttons	Basic Buttons, Full Button Sets, Go to Page Buttons, Jump to URL, Next and Previous, Page Names, and Page Number
Questions	Arrange Objects, Drag Objects, Drop Targets, Fill-in-the-Blank, Match Items (buttons and fields), Multiple Choice (buttons, fields, and objects), Order Text, Rating by Multiple Choice, Select Text, Sliders, and True/False
Response checking	Check Response on a Page, Check all Responses on Page, and Check all Responses in Book

Figure 14-33
ToolBook provides several types of widgets to help the developer during multimedia authoring.

ToolBook also can be used to convert a multimedia application into HTML and Java. The multimedia application then can be distributed over the Internet. One of the more exciting uses of multimedia on the Internet is **distributed learning** or **distance learning**, in which students and employees at remote locations take training courses and other classes via the World Wide Web.

Authorware Authorware Professional, from Macromedia Inc., is another multimedia authoring software package that provides the tools developers need to build interactive multimedia training and educational programs.

Authorware uses a flowchart metaphor to help you build a multimedia application. You drag icons from a fixed set of icons, called a **toolbox**, into a **flow line**, which graphically represents the flow, or sequence, of action in the application (Figure 14-34). Each icon in the toolbox represents a specific programming task; the flow line can be expanded to include more icons or content without programming. Figure 14-35 shows an application developed in Authorware.

Authorware also has a graphic toolbox that contains various display elements. This graphic toolbox contains buttons that allow you to draw lines, circles, rectangles, and polygons and resize and reposition the elements. Authorware also simplifies adding various multimedia elements including sound and video.

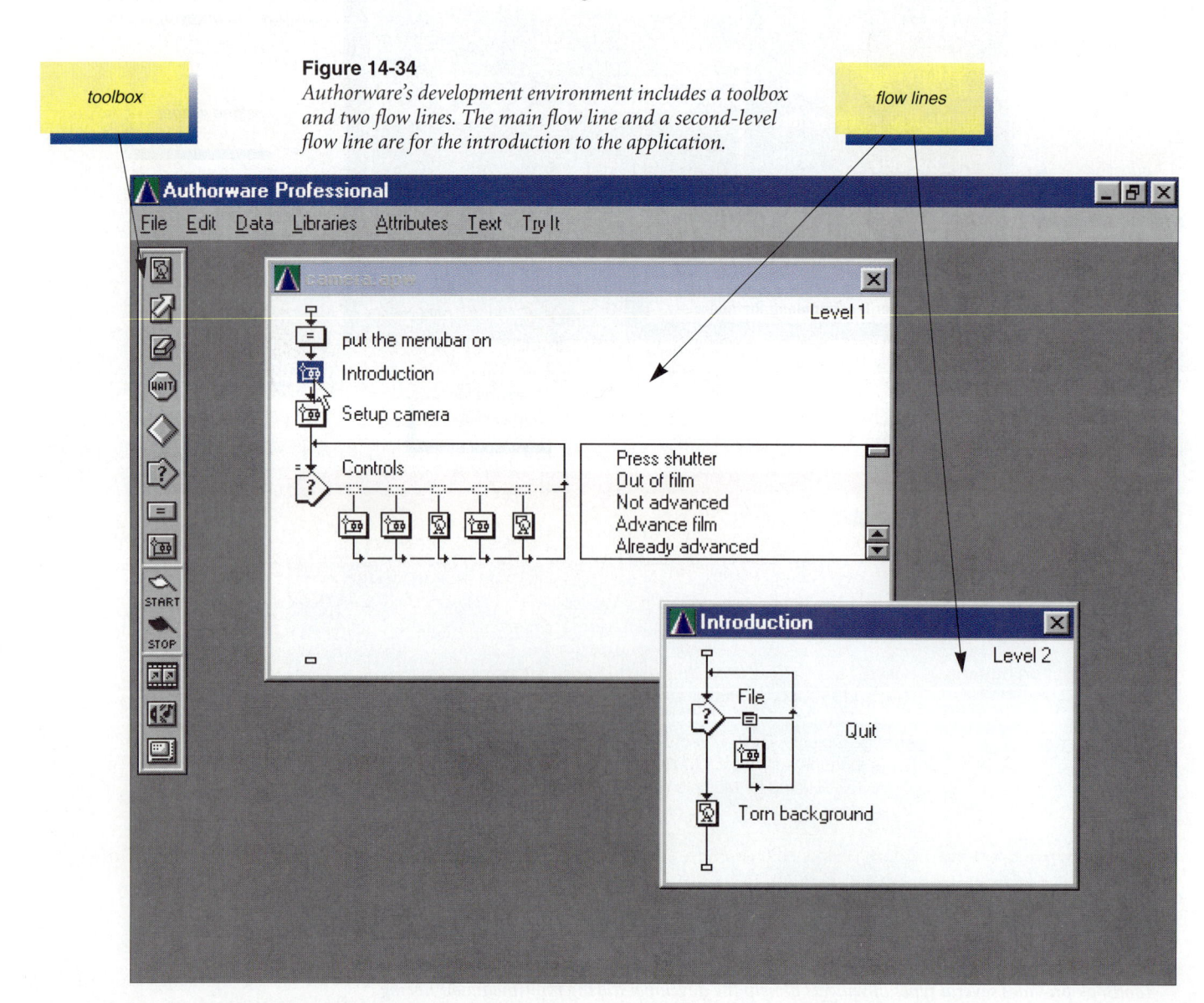

Figure 14-34
Authorware's development environment includes a toolbox and two flow lines. The main flow line and a second-level flow line are for the introduction to the application.

DEVELOPING MULTIMEDIA APPLICATIONS **14.29**

Authorware offers a powerful authoring environment for the development of interactive multimedia magazines, catalogs, reference titles for CD-ROMs, and applications for information kiosks. Authorware applications also can be designed for and distributed over the Web. These applications can be viewed using a Web browser plug-in called **Shockwave** (Figure 14-36).

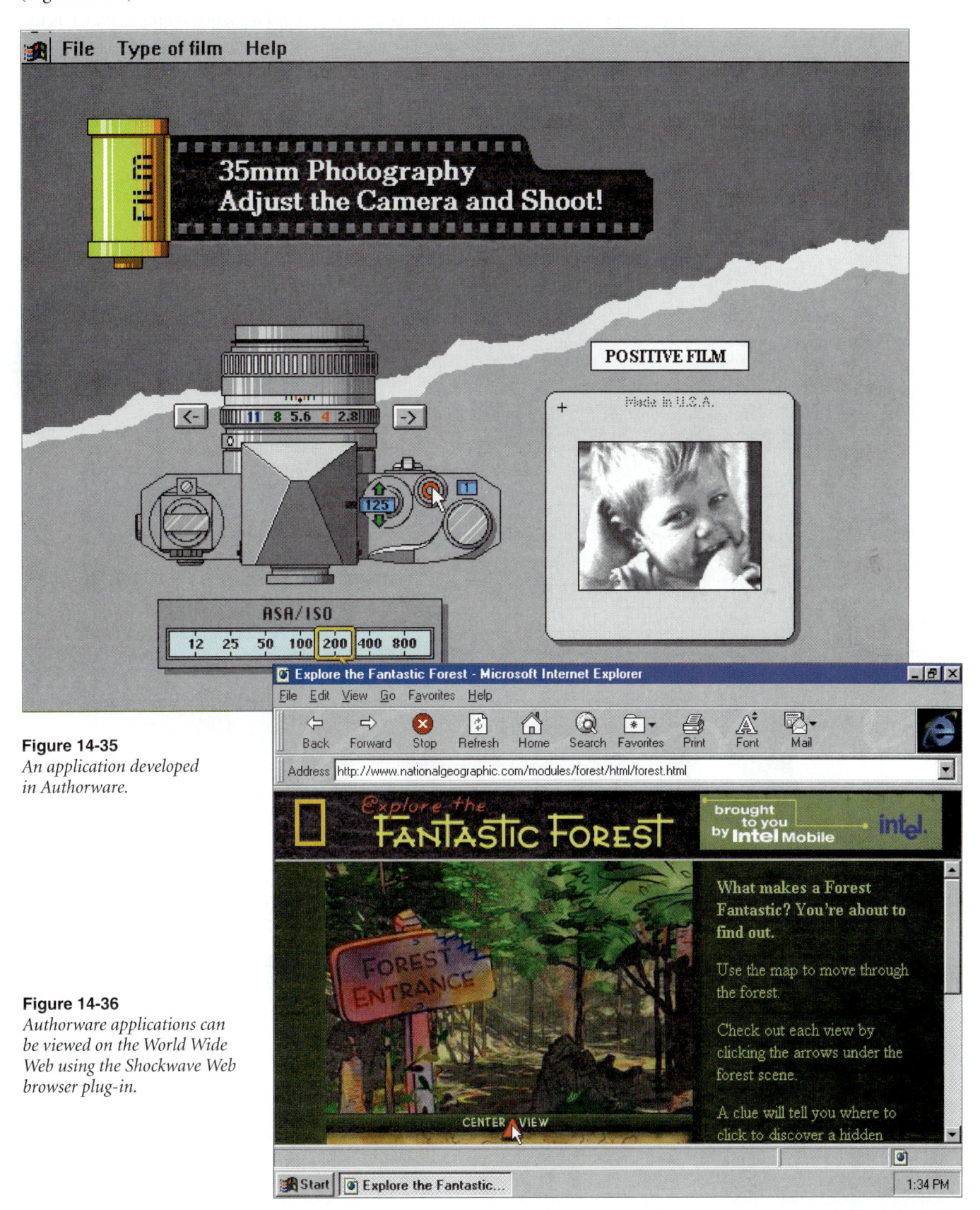

Figure 14-35
An application developed in Authorware.

Figure 14-36
Authorware applications can be viewed on the World Wide Web using the Shockwave Web browser plug-in.

Director Director, from Macromedia Inc., is a popular multimedia authoring program with powerful features that allow you to create highly interactive multimedia applications. Director uses the metaphor of a theater or movie production to help you build a multimedia application. Three integrated windows — Cast, Score, and Paint — are used to create and sequence text and other media elements. The **Cast window** serves as a database of various media, such as text, graphics, animations, audio, and video. The **Score Window**, which is the heart of Director, lets you create and edit animations, synchronize the various media elements such as audio and video, and precisely control transitions, colors, and the speed or tempo of the application (Figure 14-37). The **Paint window** contains a complete drawing and painting program for creating and editing graphics and adding animation effects. Director's programming language, **Lingo**, also can be used to add interactivity to a multimedia application.

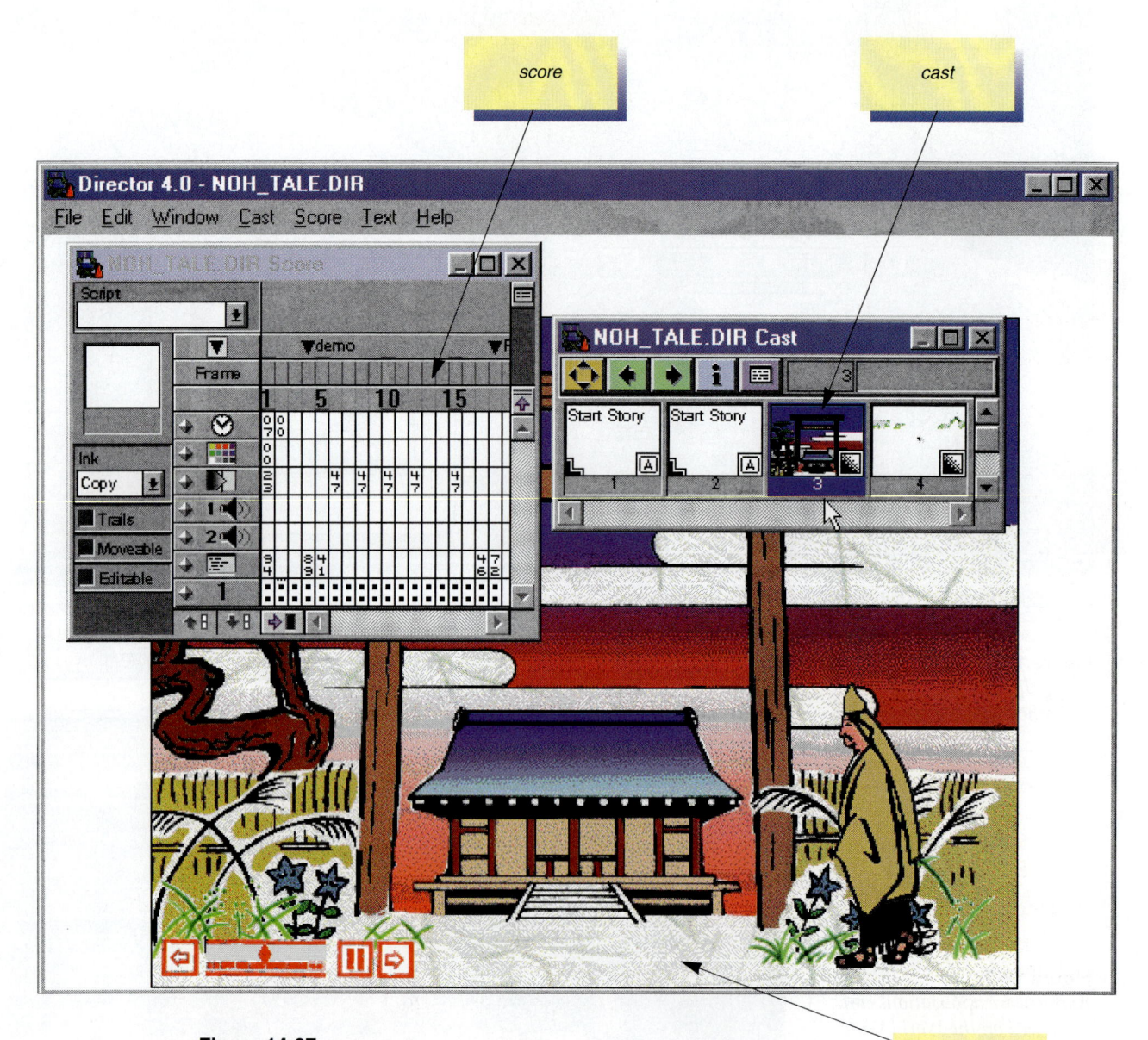

Figure 14-37
Director's development environment showing the Score and Cast for this particular part of the application.

Director's powerful features make it well-suited for developing electronic presentations, CD-ROMs for education and entertainment, simulations, and more. As with Authorware, applications developed in Director can be viewed on the Web using the Shockwave browser plug-in.

Figure 14-38 provides a comparison of the three multimedia authoring software packages just discussed. The benefits and features of each package are suitable for producing creative multimedia applications.

Comparisons of Multimedia Authoring Software

Software	Metaphor Used	Key Features	Uses
ToolBook	Book	Object-oriented approach; uses widgets (pre-scripted objects); can convert to HTML and Java	CBT, kiosks, electronic books and references, Internet applications
Authorware	Flowchart	Toolbox of icons for building flow line; graphic toolbox for drawing; applications can be viewed on Web using Shockwave plug-in	Interactive multimedia magazines, catalogs, reference titles, kiosks
Director	Theater or movie production	Cast, Score, and Paint windows for creating and sequencing text and media elements; applications can be viewed on Web using Shockwave plug-in	Electronic presentations, CD-ROMs for education and entertainment, simulations

Figure 14-38
This table compares the features and uses of multimedia authoring software.

Summary of Multimedia

This chapter examined the field of multimedia and introduced you to the different elements used in multimedia applications. After discussing a variety of different uses of multimedia applications, the chapter covered the components of a multimedia personal computer, with a focus on the hardware needed to develop and deliver a multimedia application. Finally, you learned how a multimedia application is developed and were presented a look at three multimedia authoring software packages: ToolBook, Authorware, and Director. With this knowledge, you will be able to understand better the key elements of multimedia, explain how it is shaping present and future uses of computers, and describe how these exciting and innovative multimedia applications are produced.

14.32 CHAPTER 14 – MULTIMEDIA

COMPUTERS AT WORK

Multimedia Marketing Hits the Slopes

Figure 14-39b

Figure 14-39a

Figure 14-39c

Figure 14-39d

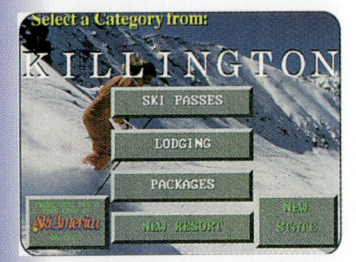

Figure 14-39e

Figure 14-39f

Headed for the ski resort? Think about how great it would be if, instead of waiting in line for a lift ticket, you could head straight onto the slopes. Well, thanks to one innovative, customer-driven company, those dreaded lift ticket lines may be a thing of the past. Ski America Interactive Multimedia Marketing Systems offers convenient, user-friendly information kiosks that provide an extraordinary array of ski travel-related services — from ski lift tickets and lodgings to vacation arrangements and more.

Ski America was the first to offer a transaction-based interactive multimedia marketing system for ski shops. The following steps show how a skier can use this kiosk to purchase ski tickets.

- Skier touches the screen to move through the Automated Ticketing Machine (Figure 14-39a)
- Skier is given a choice for the purchase of a gift certificate (Figure 14-39b)
- Skier chooses the state of interest, Vermont in this case (Figure 14-39c)
- Skier then chooses the ski resort, Killington in this case (Figure 14-39d)
- Skier then chooses lift tickets, lodging package, or special offerings (Figure 14-39e)
- Skier further targets selection for type of passes (Figure 14-39f)
- Skier obtains a verification list (Figure 14-39g)
- Skier then completes the transaction with a credit card and receives vouchers for the items purchased (Figure 14-39h)

Ski America has developed an open marketing system that makes using their kiosks a real growth opportunity for ski shops, ski areas and resorts, travel services, and ski product manufacturers who are focused on raising the convenience level for their customers. Stores using Ski America's interactive multimedia marketing system hope to increase store traffic, increase the frequency of store visits, and increase retail sales. Customers using Ski America's interactive multimedia marketing system simply hope to reduce the long wait in the lift lines.

Figure 14-39g

Figure 14-39h

IN THE FUTURE

Hybrid CD-ROMs: CD-ROMs Will Never Be the Same

When you put a CD-ROM into your CD-ROM drive, you expect it to be the same every time, right? Sure, it is static, but it holds hundreds of megabytes of information and is fast and reliable. With the popularity of the Internet, you just may want to connect to the World Wide Web. It's an exciting, dynamic source of up-to-date information, but sometimes can be slow. Now, with the hybrid CD-ROM, you can have the best of both worlds.

A **hybrid CD-ROM** combines a CD-ROM application on a local system with an Internet application on the World Wide Web (Figure 14-40). With a hybrid CD-ROM, the static portion of the application resides on a CD-ROM, and the time-sensitive portions of the application can be delivered *live* from any Web server. Any type of media can be linked to the Web, but, because of the limited delivery bandwidth currently available at many sites, large media files usually reside on a CD-ROM, while text and small images are updated via the Internet. The same multimedia authoring software used to create traditional multimedia CD-ROMs — ToolBook, Director, and others — can be used to create these exciting hybrid CD-ROMs.

Then what do you do with a hybrid CD-ROM? Consider Compton's Encyclopedia, which allows readers to download updated entries from America Online. Imagine if this book were a hybrid CD-ROM: every day, the pages could provide new information about processor speeds, software tools, or the rapidly changing Internet. Over time, uses of hybrid CD-ROMs will range from games in which you compete over networks to ever-current magazines and textbooks to electronic catalogs with the latest prices and products where orders are accepted online.

Hybrid CD-ROMs continue to grow in popularity. More and more titles that include online communications, links to expanded content, and network game play are being produced, and the technology is moving out of the corporate market and into the consumer mainstream. At year end 1995, just 311 hybrid CD-ROM titles were in print worldwide. By 2000, more than 25,000 hybrid CD titles are expected to be on the market, meaning your CD-ROMs may never be the same again!

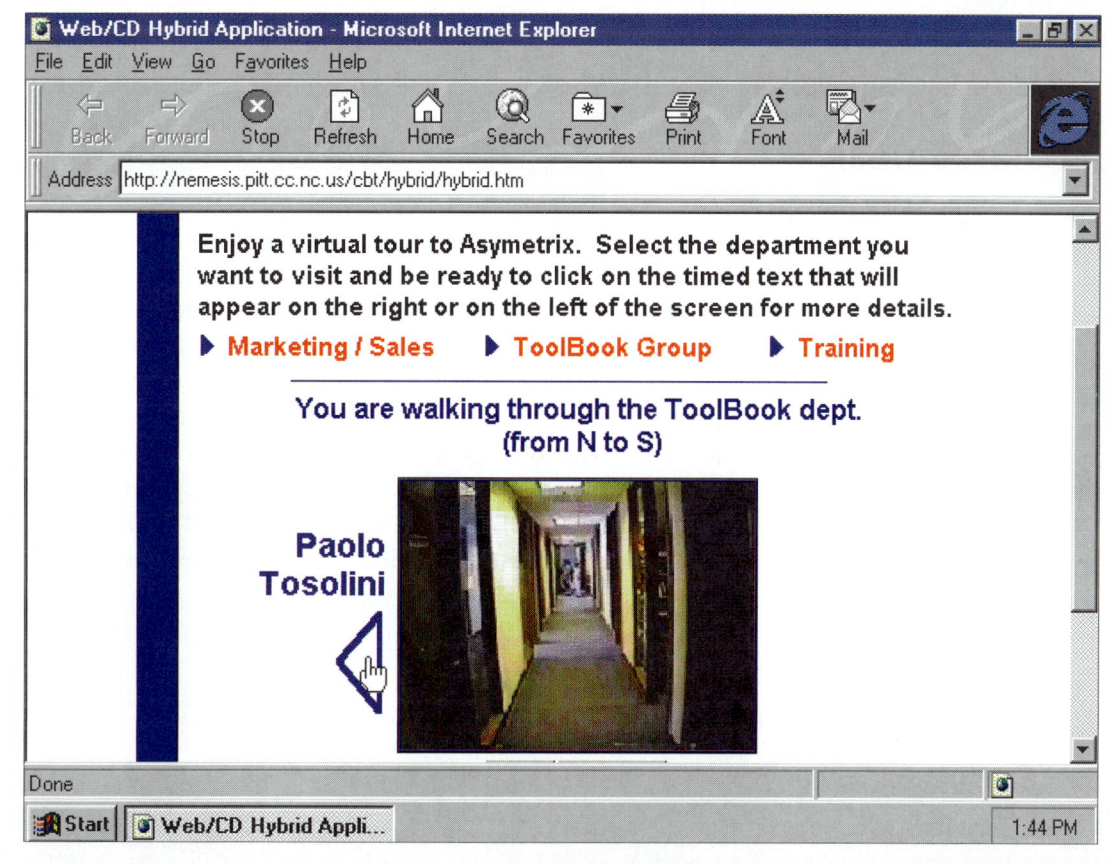

Figure 14-40

14 review

chapter 1 | 2 | 3 | 4 | 5 | 6 | 7 | 8 | 9 | 10 | 11 | 12 | 13 | 14 | I

inCyber | review | terms | yourTurn | hotTopics | outThere | winLabs | webWalk | exercises | news | home

INSTRUCTIONS: *To display this page from the Web, launch your browser and enter the URL, http://www.scsite.com/dc/ch14/review.htm. Click the links for current and additional information.*

1 What is Multimedia?
Multimedia refers to any computer-based presentation software or application that integrates at least two or more of these elements: text, color, graphics, animation, audio, and video. **Interactive multimedia** accepts input from the user by means of the keyboard or a pointing device.

2 Media Elements
Text is the fundamental component in many multimedia programs. A pointing device is used to interact with a multimedia application by clicking **interactive links**, called *hyperlinks*, that allow information to be accessed quickly in a nonlinear fashion. **Still graphic images** are graphics that contain no movement, such as photographs or drawings. **Animation** refers to moving graphic images that can transmit information more vividly than text and graphics. **Audio** is sound that has been digitized and stored in some form for replay. **Video** is comprised of photographic images that provide the appearance of motion in real-time.

3 Multimedia Applications
Multimedia applications are used by instructors for classroom presentations, by marketers in interactive advertisements, and by businesses for job training. Another use of interactive multimedia is to create **simulations**, which are computer-based models of real-life situations. Multimedia applications include computer-based training, special education, electronic books and references, how-to guides, and magazines. Multimedia also is used in entertainment, virtual reality, information kiosks, electronic marketing and sales, and on the World Wide Web.

4 Computer-Based Training
Computer-based training (CBT) is the use of computer-aided instruction to teach specific skills. CBT offers a unique learning experience because learners can receive instant feedback. Multimedia applications appeal to different learning styles and provide a new type of experience. Multimedia applications also are used for education and training for both the physically impaired and the learning disabled.

5 Electronic Books
Electronic books are digitized text that use hyperlinks to give the user instantaneous access to information. These texts contain **hotwords** that can be clicked to display a definition, play a sound, show a graphic, or play a video sequence. **Electronic reference** texts such as multimedia encyclopedias are a popular type of electronic book on CD-ROMs. **How-to-guides** are a broad category of multimedia applications that help individuals in their daily lives. **Multimedia magazines** often have the familiar appearance of a print-based magazine but use many types of media to convey information.

6 Entertainment

Interactive multimedia computer games use graphics, sound, and video to create a realistic and entertaining game situation. Some multimedia products provide **edutainment**, which is an experience meant to be both educational and entertaining. **Virtual reality (VR)** is the use of a computer to create an artificial environment that can be experienced by interactively exploring and manipulating the environment. VR is used for three-dimensional games, commercial applications, and employee training.

7 Information Kiosks and Electronic Marketing

An **information kiosk** is a computerized information or reference center that allows people to find specific information or simply browse through choices. Information kiosks often are used to provide information in public places and for interactive multimedia marketing. Many businesses and industries use multimedia to advertise products or create marketing presentations. Multimedia authoring software makes television commercials with unique media effects easier to produce. Presentation graphics programs are used to develop marketing presentations.

8 Internet and World Wide Web Applications

The World Wide Web, which is the portion of the Internet that supports multimedia, uses many types of media to deliver information and enhance the Web experience. Graphics and animation reinforce Web page content. Audio and video clips are used for online radio stations, movie reviews, and games. Hypertext and hypermedia make it easier to navigate through the maze of information.

9 Multimedia Personal Computer

A **multimedia personal computer** is a computer system that uses specific hardware and software components to input, process, and output the various types of media. Multimedia personal computers often are referred to by a set of multimedia hardware and software standards called their **MPC level**, or **specifications**. Media devices in the multimedia personal computer include a **sound card**, **CD-ROM** drive, **speakers**, and **video display**. Along with audio and video components, multimedia systems often use a number of input and output devices such as **overhead projection systems**, **video projectors**, **video capture cards**, scanners, digital cameras, **Photo CD systems**, laser disks, and **video overlay cards**.

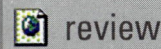

10. Developing Multimedia Applications

Developing multimedia applications follows a standard process with several phases. During the **analysis** phase, objectives and requirements for the application are established, and the key elements needed for the actual production are specified. In the **design** phase, a *flowchart* maps the various media elements in the application and serves as a blueprint for the developer. A **project script** provides more detailed information and offers a written record of how media elements will be used in the production. Multimedia **production** is the phase in which the various media elements are created and put together. The programmer or developer uses a multimedia authoring software package to combine elements of the multimedia application.

11. Multimedia Authoring Software

Multimedia authoring software allows text, graphics, animation, audio, and video to be combined into a finished production. The screen on which material is presented can be designed to create *interactivity*; that is, with places in the program that respond to user input. Three popular multimedia authoring packages are ToolBook, Authorware, and Director.

12. ToolBook

ToolBook uses a graphical user interface and an object-oriented approach to design applications with basic objects such as buttons, fields, graphics, backgrounds, and pages. ToolBook employs a **book** metaphor to help build a multimedia application. An object's properties can be changed by writing a script in **OpenScript**, which is the ToolBook programming language. Pre-scripted graphical objects called **widgets** contain properties that give them certain behaviors, eliminating much of the programming involved in developing multimedia applications.

13. Authorware

Authorware uses a flowchart metaphor to help build a multimedia application. Icons are dragged from a fixed set of icons, called a **toolbox**, into a **flow line** that graphically represents the sequence of action in the application. Each icon represents a specific programming task. Authorware simplifies adding various multimedia components and has a graphic toolbox that contains different display elements. Authorware applications can be viewed using a Web browser plug-in called **Shockwave**.

14. Director

Director is a popular multimedia authoring program with powerful features that can be used to create highly interactive multimedia applications. Director uses the metaphor of a theater or movie production to help build multimedia applications. Three integrated windows—the **Cast window**, the **Score window**, and the **Paint window**—are used to create and sequence text and other media elements. Director's programming language, **Lingo**, also can be used to add interactivity to a multimedia application.

14 terms

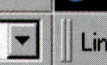

chapter 1 | 2 | 3 | 4 | 5 | 6 | 7 | 8 | 9 | 10 | 11 | 12 | 13 | 14 | I

inCyber | review | terms | yourTurn | hotTopics | outThere | winLabs | webWalk | exercises | news | home

INSTRUCTIONS: *To display this page from the Web, launch your browser and enter the URL, http://www.scsite.com/dc/ch14/terms.htm. Scroll through the list of terms. Click a term for its definition and a picture. Click the rocket ship for current and additional information about the term.*

Director

DEFINITION

Director
A popular multimedia authoring program with powerful features that allow you to create highly interactive multimedia applications. (**14.30**)

---

analysis (14.23)
animation (14.5)
audio (14.5)
authoring (14.25)
Authorware (14.28)

book (14.26)

Cast window (14.30)
CAV (constant angular velocity) (14.22)
CD-ROM (14.18)
CLV (constant linear velocity) (14.22)
color scanner (14.20)
computer-based training (CBT) (14.7)
courseware (14.7)

design (14.24)
developing multimedia applications (14.23)
digital camera (14.21)
digital video interleave (DVI) (14.20)
Director (14.30)
distance learning (14.28)
distributed learning (14.28)

edutainment (14.12)
electronic books (14.9)
electronic reference (14.9)

flow line (14.28)

graphic (14.4)

hotwords (14.3, 14.9)
how-to-guides (14.10)
hybrid CD-ROM (14.33)

information kiosk (14.14)
interactive links (14.3)
interactive multimedia (14.2)

LCD projector panel (14.19)
Lingo (14.30)

MCI (media control interface) commands (14.22)
MMX™ technology (14.16)
MPC level (14.16)
MPEG (Moving Pictures Experts Group) (14.6)
multimedia (14.2)
multimedia applications (14.7)
multimedia authoring software (14.25)
multimedia extensions (14.16)
multimedia magazines (14.11)
multimedia personal computer (14.16)

NautilusCD (14.11)
NTSC (National Television System Committee) (14.19)
NTSC converter (14.19)

OpenScript (14.26)
overhead projection system (14.19)

page (14.26)
Paint window (14.30)
Photo CD system (14.26)
production (14.25)
project script (14.24)

Score window (14.30)
Shockwave (14.29)
simulations (14.7)
sound card (14.17)
speakers (14.18)
specifications (14.16)
still graphic images (14.4)

text (14.2)
ToolBook (14.26)
toolbox (14.28)

video (14.6)
video capture card (14.20)
video compression (14.6)
video display (14.18)
video overlay card (14.22)
video projector (14.19)
virtual reality (VR) (14.12)

Widget Catalog (14.27)
widgets (14.27)

yourTurn

chapter 1 | 2 | 3 | 4 | 5 | 6 | 7 | 8 | 9 | 10 | 11 | 12 | 13 | 14 | I

inCyber | review | terms | yourTurn | hotTopics | outThere | winLabs | webWalk | exercises | news | home

INSTRUCTIONS: *To display this page from the Web, launch your browser and enter the URL, http://www.scsite.com/dc/ch14/turn.htm. Click a blank line for the answer. Click the links for current and additional information.*

Label the Figure

	MPC Level 2 Specifications	MPC Level 3 Specifications
Date Introduced	May 1993	June 1995
CPU	1._____	2._____
RAM	3._____	4._____
Magnetic storage	5._____	6._____
Optical storage	7._____	8._____
Audio	9._____	10._____
Video display	11._____	12._____
Input	101-key keyboard (or functional equivalent), two-button mouse	101-key keyboard (or functional equivalent), two-button mouse
I/O	Serial port, parallel port, MIDI I/O port, joystick port	Serial port, parallel port, MIDI I/O port, joystick port
System software	Compatibility with Windows 3.1/Windows 3.0 plus multimedia extensions	Compatibility with Windows 3.1/Windows 3.0 plus multimedia extensions

Instructions: Complete this table comparing Level 2 and Level 3 MPC standards.

Fill in the Blanks

Instructions: Complete each sentence with the correct term or terms.

1. _____ refers to any computer-based presentation software or application that integrates at least two or more of these elements: text, color, graphics, animation, audio, and video.
2. A mouse is used to interact with a multimedia application by clicking interactive links called _____.
3. A(n) _____, which is a flat-screen panel placed on top of an overhead projector, is a type of _____ that is often used for presenting to large groups.
4. In the _____ phase of developing multimedia applications, the _____ offers more detailed information to supplement the flowchart and provides a written record of how various media elements will be used in the production.
5. Students at remote locations taking courses via the World Wide Web are using _____.

Short Answer

Instructions: Write a brief answer to each of the following questions.

1. Why does incorporating video into a multimedia application present a challenge for developers? What is video compression? How has MPEG helped video play a more important role in multimedia applications? _____
2. What is computer-based training (CBT)? What advantages does CBT offer over traditional training? _____
3. Why are CD-ROMs an excellent medium for storing and distributing multimedia applications? When buying a computer system, what is the most important consideration for a CD-ROM drive? Why? _____
4. What are important features to look for when selecting a multimedia authoring package? _____
5. What metaphor does Director use to help build a multimedia application? How are the Cast window, Score window, and Paint window different? For what types of multimedia applications is Director well-suited? _____

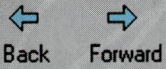

hotTopics

chapter 1 | 2 | 3 | 4 | 5 | 6 | 7 | 8 | 9 | 10 | 11 | 12 | 13 | 14 | I

inCyber | review | terms | yourTurn | hotTopics | outThere | winLabs | webWalk | exercises | news | home

INSTRUCTIONS: *To display this page from the Web, launch your browser and enter the URL, http://www.scsite.com/dc/ch14/hot.htm. Click the links for current and additional information to help you respond to the hotTopics questions.*

1. *Most people remember dissecting a frog in high school biology class—the* odor of formaldehyde, the nervous laughter, the unsuspecting classmate who finds a webbed foot in his lunch bag. For many students, conventional dissections are being replaced by multimedia applications. Students use computers to view color graphics of a frog's anatomy, video of biological systems, and interactive quizzes that cheer ("ribbit") correct answers. Although these CD-ROM programs are supported by animal rights activists and squeamish students, many biology teachers believe there is no substitute for genuine dissection. Can multimedia applications replace hands-on experiences? Why or why not? Who should make the choice between multimedia programs and traditional dissection? Why? On what basis should the choice be made?

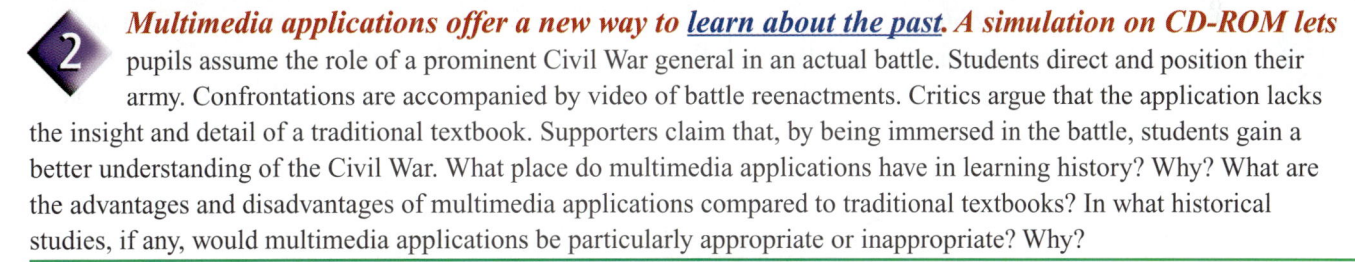

2. *Multimedia applications offer a new way to learn about the past. A simulation on CD-ROM lets* pupils assume the role of a prominent Civil War general in an actual battle. Students direct and position their army. Confrontations are accompanied by video of battle reenactments. Critics argue that the application lacks the insight and detail of a traditional textbook. Supporters claim that, by being immersed in the battle, students gain a better understanding of the Civil War. What place do multimedia applications have in learning history? Why? What are the advantages and disadvantages of multimedia applications compared to traditional textbooks? In what historical studies, if any, would multimedia applications be particularly appropriate or inappropriate? Why?

3. *Technology and the arts are sometimes uncomfortable companions. A recently developed* multimedia application on CD-ROM, however, uses computer technology to examine one of the world's more recognizable art treasures. Users are encouraged to reexamine Vincent van Gogh's *Starry Night* and to see the painting as a meticulous reproduction of a particular night sky. An art historian explains that the visual data from which the work was created is so precise it is possible to identify the time, place, and artist's orientation. In what other ways can multimedia applications enhance experiencing art? What type of art is most amenable to multimedia treatment? Why?

4. *One of the more popular multimedia how-to-guides is the "Complete* Do-It-Yourself Guide" from Reader's Digest. This CD-ROM offers tips on a wide range of household projects. Step-by-step instructions are provided for hundreds of home-repair tasks, from caulking windows to splicing wires. A feature called The Estimator estimates the cost of a project. Who would be most likely to use the Reader's Digest guide? Why? What advantages does a multimedia how-to-guide offer over traditional how-to-guidebooks? What are the disadvantages? In what other areas could multimedia how-to-guides be used? Why?

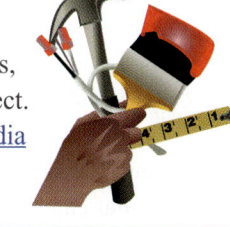

5. *Many sports are replicated in authentic, real-life multimedia applications. A new football* simulation employed twenty-two players for four weeks filming possible game situations. Users see the field from the quarterback's perspective with charging linemen, a player-strewn field, and coaches shouting from the sidelines. Participants can choose from 900 plays, audibilize at the line of scrimmage, and even resort to a hurry-up offense. Some people feel multimedia applications steal the real value from a sports experience. Instead of developing the physical fitness, camaraderie, and sportsmanship inherent in sports, multimedia devotees just learn how to press a button on the mouse. Do multimedia applications ignore the real value of sports? Why? When are multimedia sports applications appropriate? Could multimedia sports applications be a legitimate part of a physical education course? Why?

14 outThere

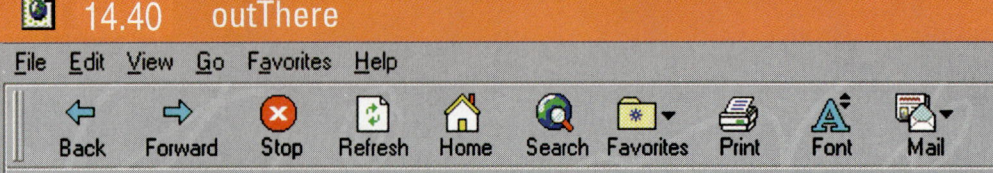

chapter
1 | 2 | 3 | 4 | 5 | 6 | 7 | 8 | 9 | 10 | 11 | 12 | 13 | 14 | I

inCyber | review | terms | yourTurn | hotTopics | outThere | winLabs | webWalk | exercises | news | home

INSTRUCTIONS: To display this page from the Web, launch your browser and enter the URL, http://www.scsite.com/dc/ch14/out.htm. Click the links for current and additional information.

1. *Many elementary schools are using multimedia simulations to help students* better understand the past or gain a greater appreciation of other cultures. In a multimedia application called Oregon Trail, students learn about westward expansion by making many of the same decisions and "experiencing" some of the same hardships that settlers faced in the nineteenth century. In an application called Amazon Trail, students learn about the flora, fauna, and cultures of the Amazon rain forest by making a simulated canoe trip down the Amazon River. Visit a school that uses multimedia simulation. What application is used? At what grade level? How is the application used? What supplemental materials are used? How do students and teachers feel about using the application? How does computer-aided instruction compare with traditional approaches to learning?

2. *When most people decide to take a vacation, one of their first stops is a travel agent. They take* home brochures, study the pictures and data, and then return to make travel arrangements. A new site makes it possible to plan a vacation via the World Wide Web. Select a geographic region, and a multimedia application provides information, pictures, maps, and even videos of different locales. After choosing a destination, you can view comprehensive flight schedules and book airline tickets online. Visit the travel Web page and use it to plan a dream vacation. How does multimedia enhance the site? What development guidelines (Figure 14-29) and design principles (Figure 14-30) described in this chapter are illustrated on the Web site? How could the travel Web page be improved?

3. *Multimedia reference books are becoming a popular alternative to printed reference books.* Multimedia encyclopedias have easy-to-use indexes, provide links to related topics, and sometimes offer audio or video enhancements. Most electronic reference books are updated more frequently than printed resources. Many people feel, however, that printed reference books still supply more in-depth information than multimedia applications. Choose a topic in which you are interested. Research the topic using both a multimedia reference book and a printed reference book. What was the name of each reference? Which reference was easier to use? Why? What information was provided by both references? What information was provided by one reference but not the other? When would you be most likely to use a multimedia reference? When would you use a printed reference? Why?

4. *No sports championship is better represented on the World Wide Web than the World Series.* Information is provided for as far back as 1903 on key games, plays, players, and managers. Icons provide close-up views of memorabilia, and hyperlinks connect to video of former stars and audio of memorable radio moments (such as the call of Willie Mays' spectacular catch in 1954). Visit a World Series site or another site dealing with sports championships. How does multimedia enhance the site? What development guidelines and design principles are illustrated in the Web site? How could the site be improved?

5. *When the multimedia game Myst was released in 1993, it quickly became the most popular* CD-ROM game in history. The innovative interactive drama earned more than $100 million and was played by 2.5 million people. The game's success has been attributed to a user-friendly interface, photorealistic graphics, and an imaginative story line. What makes a multimedia game a success? Visit a software vendor and try one or more multimedia games. What is the name of the game? How is it played? What multimedia elements are used? What are the best features of the game? What are the game's weaknesses? Would you recommend this game? Why?

14 winLabs

chapter 1 | 2 | 3 | 4 | 5 | 6 | 7 | 8 | 9 | 10 | 11 | 12 | 13 | 14 | I

inCyber | review | terms | yourTurn | hotTopics | outThere | winLabs | webWalk | exercises | news | home

INSTRUCTIONS: *To display this page from the Web, launch your browser and enter the URL, http://www.scsite.com/dc/ch14/labs.htm. Click the links for current and additional information.*

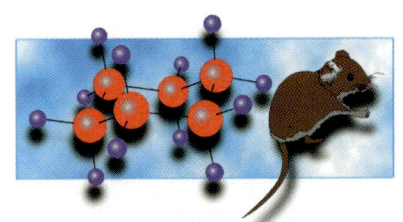

1 Shelly Cashman Series Multimedia Lab
Follow the instructions in winLabs 1 on page 1.34 to display the Shelly Cashman Series Labs screen. Click Understanding Multimedia. Click the Start Lab button. When the initial screen displays, carefully read the objectives. With your printer turned on, click the Print Questions button. Fill out the top of the Questions sheet and then answer the questions.

2 Playing Audio Compact Disks
Click the Start button on the taskbar, point to Programs on the Start menu, point to Accessories on the Programs submenu, point to Multimedia on the Accessories submenu, and then click CD Player on the Multimedia submenu. When the CD Player window displays (Figure 14-41), click Help on the menu bar and then click Help Topics. Double-click the Playing CDs topic. Print the Playing a CD topic. Close any open Help window(s). Answer these questions: (1) How to you play a CD? (2) How do you stop a CD? (3) How do you eject a CD from the drive? If your system has a CD-ROM drive and a sound card, insert a CD into the CD-ROM drive and then play it. Close the CD Player window.

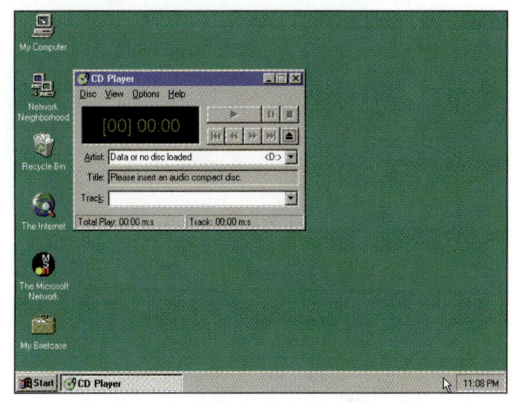

Figure 14-41

3 Understanding Multimedia Properties
Click the Start button on the taskbar, point to Settings menu, and then click Control Panel. Double-click the Multimedia icon in the Control Panel window. When the Multimedia Properties dialog box displays, click the Audio tab and then answer the following questions: (1) What is the Playback preferred device? (2) What is the Recording preferred quality? Click the Advanced tab. For each multimedia driver listed, if a plus sign (+) displays in the box to its left, click the plus sign to change it to a minus sign (–). For each device driver listed, write down the name(s) of the hardware device(s) installed on your system.

4 Using Help to Understand the Media Player
Click the Start button on the taskbar and then click Help on the Start menu. Click the Index tab, type `multimedia` in the text box, and then double-click playing multimedia files. Read and print the information. Click the arrow in the Help window to start Media Player. When the Media Player window displays, click Help on its menu bar and then click Help Topics. Double-click Playing Audio, Video, and Animation Files. Read and print each of these subtopics: Playing a multimedia file, Rewinding a multimedia file, and Fastforwarding a multimedia file. Close any open Help windows. Click File on the Media Player menu bar and then click Open. When the Open dialog box displays, be sure the Media folder is open in the Look in text box and then double-click Beethoven's 5th Symphony. Play the multimedia file. Close Media Player.

webWalk

inCyber | review | terms | yourTurn | hotTopics | outThere | winLabs | webWalk | exercises | news | home

INSTRUCTIONS: *To display this page from the Web, launch your browser and enter the URL, http://www.scsite.com/dc/ch14/walk.htm. Click the exercise link to display the exercise.*

1. Virtual Reality on the Web
To use a Web-based virtual reality application (Figure 14-42) developed using virtual reality modeling language (VRML), complete this exercise.

Figure 14-42

2. Animations and Graphics for Your Web Page
Graphics and animations often are used to reinforce Web page content. Complete this exercise to visit a Web page with hundreds of animations and graphics you can download free for your Web pages.

3. Multimedia on the Web
The World Wide Web was designed to be able to deliver multimedia through the Internet. To learn more about this and see the various media types used in a sophisticated multimedia Web site (Figure 14-43), complete this exercise.

Figure 14-43

4. Multimedia Authoring Software
New multimedia authoring software packages include tools for creating and delivering multimedia applications on the World Wide Web. To learn more about an authoring tool, complete this exercise.

5. Information Mining
Complete this exercise to improve your Web research skills by using a Web search engine to find information related to this chapter.

6. Sound Card
A sound card is a circuit board that houses processors used to provide both audio input and output. Complete this exercise to learn more about sound cards.

7. Video Capture Card
A video capture card is an expansion card, or adapter, that plugs into the computer's expansion slot and enables you to connect a videocamera or videocassette recorder to a computer and manipulate the video input. Complete this exercise to learn more about video capture cards.

8. Digital Cameras
Digital cameras work much like regular (film) cameras except they use a small reusable disk or internal memory to store digital photographs. To learn more about digital cameras, complete this exercise.

9. Web Chat
Complete this exercise to enter a Web Chat discussion related to the issues presented in the hotTopics exercise.

Virtual Reality

Virtual reality (VR) is the use of a computer to create an artificial environment that you can experience. The reality of the artificial environment and the extent you can interact with it depends on the software and the type of hardware used. **Desktop virtual reality** uses personal computers to display what appears to be a three-dimensional view of an environment such as an office or a home. Using a pointing device such as a mouse or joystick, you can simulate moving through the environment; for example, from room to room.

Immersion virtual reality uses additional equipment that makes you feel as though you are actually in the simulated environment. This additional equipment includes a head-mounted display (HMD) and also may include data gloves or complete body suits.

The following figures illustrate software and hardware used in virtual reality and some of the current applications.

14.44 VIRTUAL REALITY

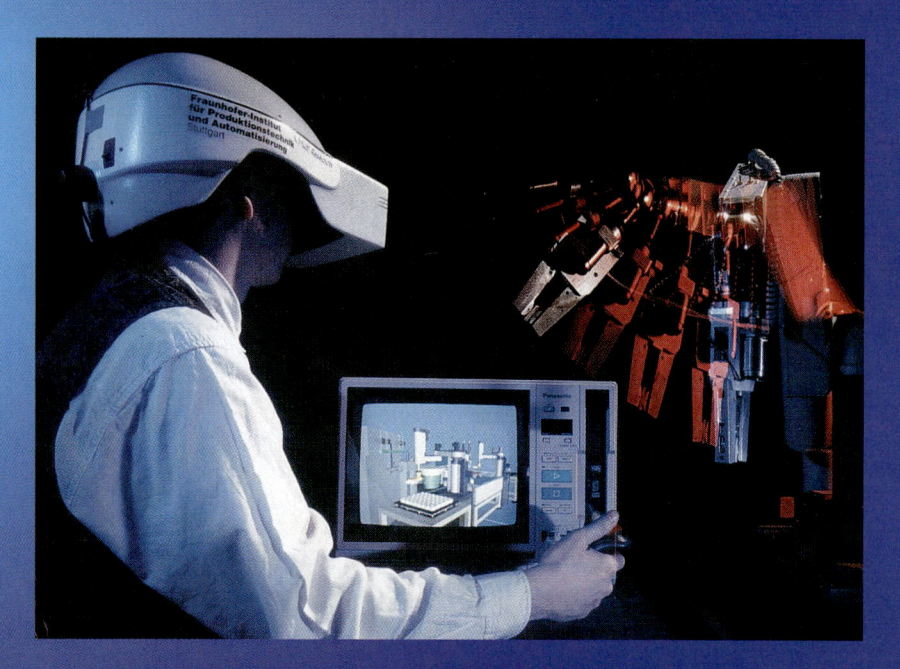

Figure 1
An engineer programs the motions of an industrial robot by viewing a VR display of the location where the robot will be installed.

Figure 2
This VR workbench displays an image of several planned buildings. The glasses worn by the participants allow them to see the buildings in 3-D. The data glove on the right hand of the person in the middle allows him to move the buildings.

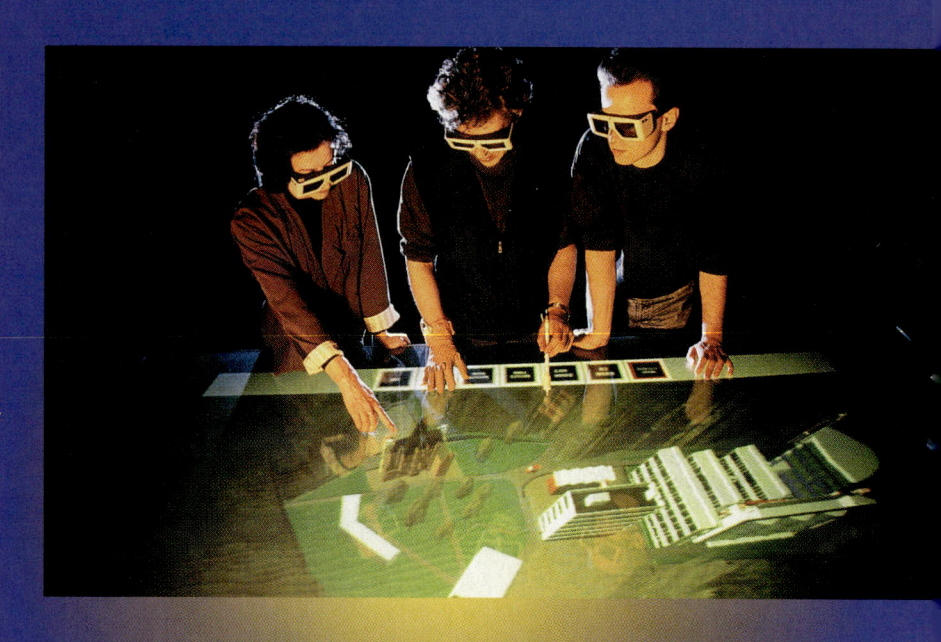

Figure 3
The head-mounted display and joystick allow this person to visualize a planned building from the outside or perform a walkthrough. As shown on the monitor, the rooms even can contain virtual furniture.

VIRTUAL REALITY 14.45

Figure 4
An astronaut trainee uses VR to simulate the tasks he will perform during an extra-vehicular exploration.

Figure 5
Ford Motor Company and other automobile manufacturers use VR to help design the interior of vehicles. The design engineer can sit in the virtual vehicle and touch where controls for the sound system, air conditioning, and other devices will be located.

Figure 6
This data suit transmits movement of the wearer's arms, legs, and torso to a computer that makes corresponding changes to the scene shown in the head-mounted display.

14.46 VIRTUAL REALITY

Figure 7
This woman explores a VR simulation of the Egyptian tomb of Nefertari, the wife of pharaoh Ramses II. The VR simulation allows researchers and others to study the tomb without visiting the actual site and possibly damaging the fragile interior.

Figure 8
An engineer uses a VR system to help design a nuclear power plant. The completed design later can be used as a reference for routine or emergency operations.

Figure 9
The device worn on the arm of this researcher allows him to experience the sense of touch while interacting with objects in a VR environment. The arm uses force-feedback to indicate the resistance of solid objects displayed on the VR screen.

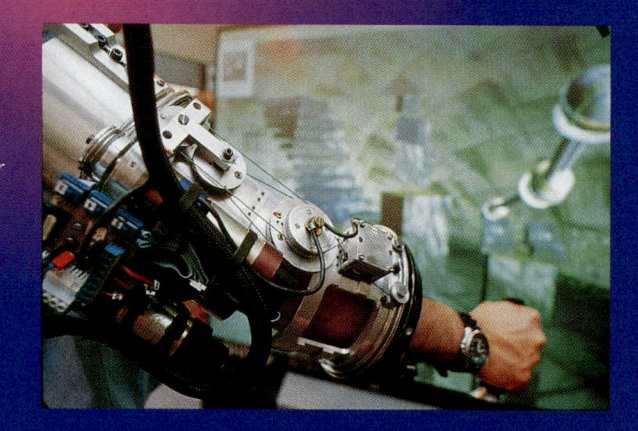

VIRTUAL REALITY **14.47**

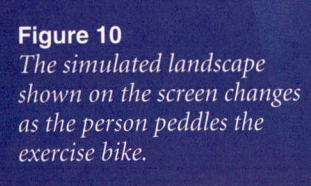

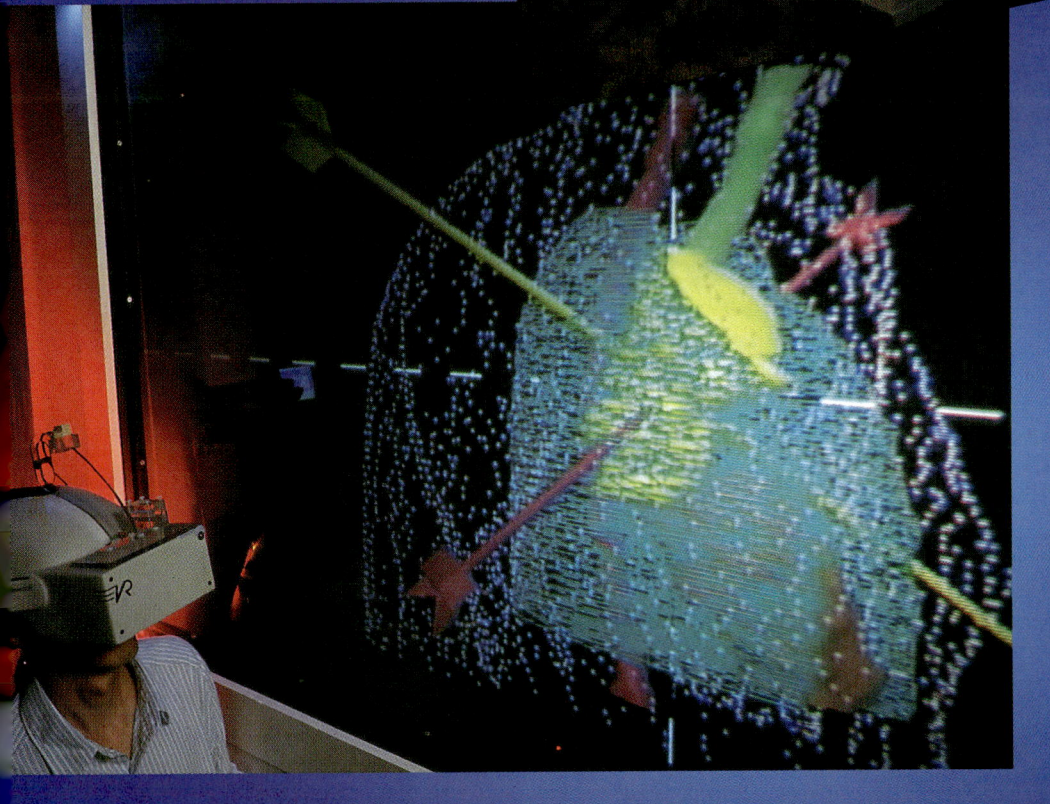

Figure 10
The simulated landscape shown on the screen changes as the person peddles the exercise bike.

Figure 11
VR is used to simulate many types of surgery. This simulation shows a doctor practicing eye surgery. Many medical students learn anatomy using virtual bodies.

14.48 VIRTUAL REALITY

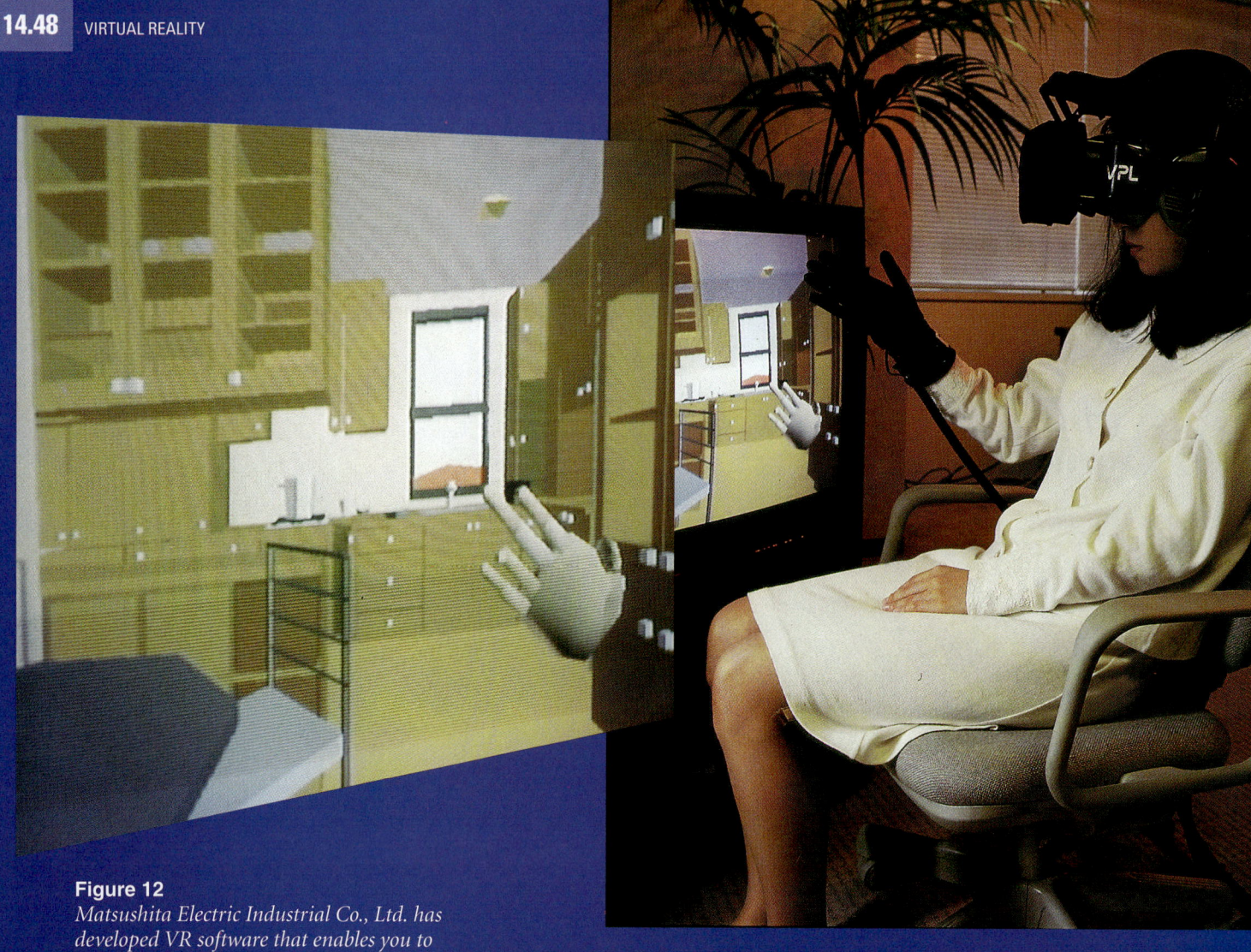

Figure 12
Matsushita Electric Industrial Co., Ltd. has developed VR software that enables you to experience home remodeling changes before they are made. Using a head-mounted display and a data glove, you can walkthrough the remodeled room, open cabinets, and place items on shelves. You navigate the room by pointing a finger in the direction you want to travel.

Figure 13
VR simulation is used in trials to recreate crime scenes. Simulation can show the actions of individuals, bullet trajectories, and the location of key evidence.

VIRTUAL REALITY   14.49

Figure 14
VR software from Division, Inc. was used by the Bechtol Corporation to review the design of the Dubai airport.

Figure 15
An experimental VR system is being developed to help flight controllers visualize aircraft taking off and landing.

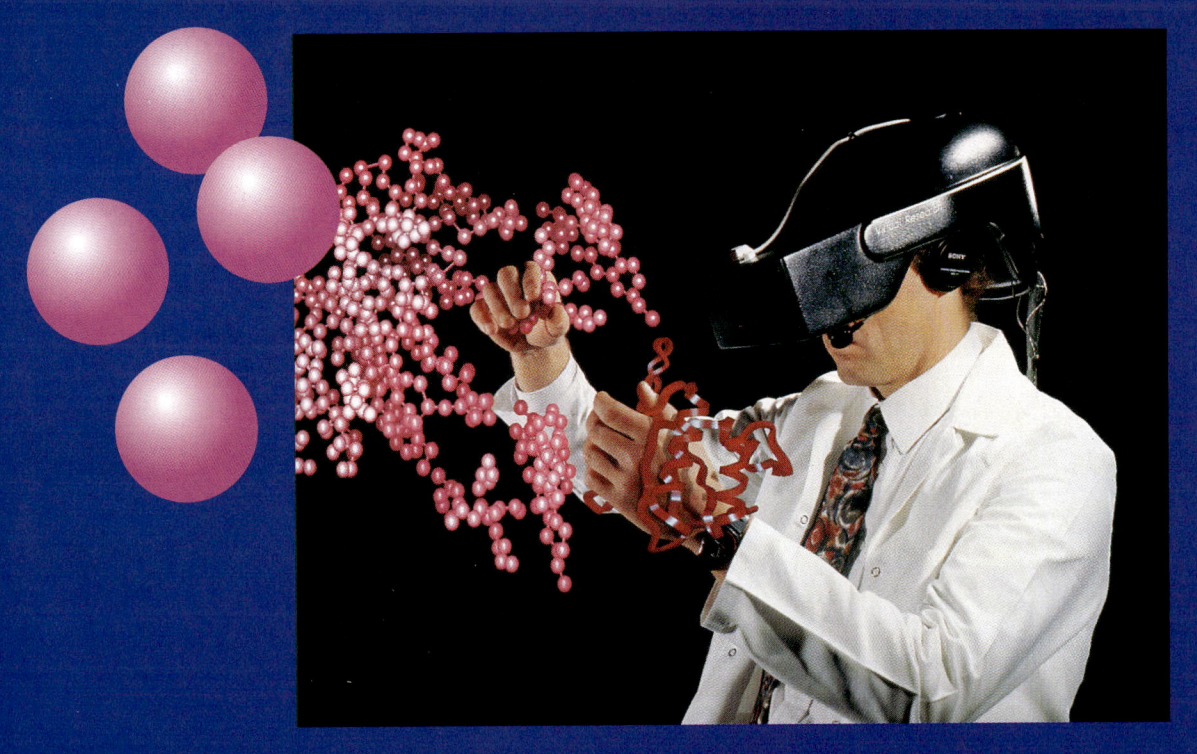

Figure 16
VR systems are used by biochemists to test the reaction of different molecules. The biochemist can pick up molecules, turn them around, and join them based on their chemical properties.

Figure 17
Kawasaki uses a VR system to simulate riding a motorcycle. The view seen by the rider is shown on the monitor to the left.

Figure 18
The armed forces use VR simulations for training on many types of equipment and for battle simulation. This VR battlefield shows air and ground forces. Moving a red circle on the map communicates a change in a landing zone or military objective.

Index

Absolute hyperlinks: Hyperlinks that move to another document on a different Internet computer. **7.8**
Absolute referencing: In spreadsheet programs, when a formula is copied to another cell, the formula continues to refer to the same cell location. **2.19**
Absolute referencing, used by graphics tablets, 4.11
Acceptance test: In information systems development, the check performed by end-users to make sure the new system works with the actual data. **11.30**
Access arms: Contain the read/write heads and move the heads across the surface of the disk. **5.10**
Access controls: Security measures defining who can access a computer, when they can access it, and what actions they can take while accessing the computer. **13.5**
Access privileges: Security measures established by a DBMS that allow different levels of access for each data field in database. **9.18**
Access speed: The time it takes to find data and retrieve it. **3.13-14**
Access time: The time required to locate data on floppy disk and transfer it to memory. **5.7**
  CD-ROM, 5.15
  floppy disk, 5.7
  hard disk, 5.10
Accounting department, 1.23
Accounting software: Software that is used by companies to record and report financial transactions. **2.30**
Accurate: Information that is correct; also a characteristic of data. **1.8, 1.19, 10.2, 10.11, 10.14**
Active Badge system: Small transmitters worn on outside of clothing that emit signals allowing wearer to be located. **13.30**
Active matrix: LCD screens that use individual transistors to control each crystal cell. **4.29**
Ada: Programming language developed in the late 1970s by the U.S. Department of Defense; can be used for business applications. **12.28**
Add-on HTML editor: Editing software tool that requires an existing software package, such as a word processor. **12.35**
Ad hoc report: Report created whenever needed to provide information that is not required on a scheduled basis; also called on-demand report. **4.24**
Advanced Research Projects Agency (ARPA), *see* **ARPA**
Agent software: Software that can independently carry out tasks on behalf of a user. **10.18**
Aldus Freehand, 2.13
Aldus Persuasion, 2.25
Alignment: Formatting of document, dealing with how text is positioned in relation to a fixed reference point, usually a right or left margin; also called justification. **2.9**
Alphanumeric: Type of field in database; data includes letters, numbers and special characters. **2.22**
AltaVista search tool, 7.17
American National Standards Institute (ANSI), 12.9, 12.16
America Online, 1.9, 2.26, 2.28, 6.7, 7.5, 7.28
American Standard Code for Information Interchange (ACSII): The most widely used coding system to represent data, primarily on personal computers and many minicomputers. **3.4**
Analog computers: Computers designed to process continuously variable data, such as electrical voltage. **3.3**
Analog signal: A signal used in communications lines that consists of a continuous electrical wave. **6.16**
Analysis phase: In information system development, the activities of conducting a feasibility study, and detailed analysis activities, consisting of studying how the current system works, determining the user's requirements, and recommending solutions. **11.2, 11.11-20, 14.23**
  multimedia application developing, 14.23
Analytical graphics: The charts provided by spreadsheet software. **2.20**
Animation: Moving graphic images that can make Web pages more visually interesting or draw attention to important information or links. **7.12, 14.5**
Animation, presentation graphics and, 2.24
Annotations: Editing feature of word processing programs; marks are made directly in document to make editing comments without changing document. **2.8**
Anonymous FTP: FTP site that allows anyone to log in and transfer some, if not all, available files. **7.20**
Antivirus program: Utility program that prevents, detects, and removes viruses. **8.20, 13.4**
Applets: To assist in running multimedia applications on the Web, small programs that can be downloaded and run in browser window. **7.11, 12.36**
Application generator: Program that allows an application to be built without writing extensive code in the programming language. **12.30**
Application server: Server computer that provides database information and runs all or part of the application software, such as a sales order entry program. **6.25**

Application software: Programs that tell a computer how to produce information, and reside permanently in storage, such as a disk. **1.18**
  accounting, 2.30
  communications, 2.26
  computer-aided design, 2.31
  database, 2.21-23
  desktop publishing, 2.12-14
  downward compatible, 8.14
  electronic mail, 2.27-28
  groupware, 2.30-31
  horizontal, 11.19
  illustration, 2.13
  integrated, 2.32-33
  learning aids, 2.36-37
  multimedia authoring, 2.32
  personal finance, 2.29
  personal information management, 2.28
  presentation graphics, 2.24-25
  project management, 2.29
  spreadsheet, 2.14-21
  support tools, 2.37
  upward compatible, 8.14
  user tools, 2.1-42
  vertical, 11.19
  Web browsers, 2.26
  word processing, 2.4-12
Application software packages: Programs purchased from computer stores or software vendors. **1.18, 2.4-37**
Archie: FTP search tool that is used to find files on a particular subject. **7.20**
Archie gateway: Web page that provides an easy-to-use interface to the Archie search function. **7.20**
Arithmetic/logic unit (ALU): Part of the CPU that performs math and logic operations. **1.6, 3.8**
Arithmetic operations: Numeric calculations performed by the arithmetic/logic unit in the CPU, that includes addition, subtraction, multiplication, and division. **3.8**
ARPA (Advanced Research Projects Agency): Agency of the U.S. Department of Defense; funded initial work on the Internet. **7.3**
ARPANET: The first Internet network. **7.3**
Arrow keys: Keys on a keyboard that move the cursor up, down, left, or right on the screen. **4.3**
Art, Web sites on, 7.42
Article: In a newsgroup, a previously entered message. **7.23**
Artificial intelligence (AI): A branch of computer science applying human intelligence to computer systems. **10.18**
Assembler: Program used to convert assembly language source program into machine language. **12.18**
Assembly language: Programming language written as symbols and codes; referred to as a symbolic programming language. **12.18**
Assistants, Office 97 and, 8.24
Asymmetric multiprocessing: Type of processing whereby application processes are assigned to a specific CPU in computers that have more than one CPU. **8.6**
Asynchronous transmission mode: Communications transmission mode that transmits data in individual bytes at irregular intervals; relatively slow method that is best used to send only small amounts of data. **6.16**
Attribute: Field in a relational database. **9.4, 9.17**
AT&T WorldNet, 7.28
Audio: Digitized sound that is stored in some form for replay. **14.5**
Audio files: Web applications consisting of individual sound files that must be downloaded before they can be played. **7.13**
Audio output: Consists of sounds, including words and music, produced by the computer; audio output device on the computer is a speaker. **4.25**
Authentication: Access control verifies that user is who he or she claims to be. **13.5**
Authoring: The use of multimedia authoring software by programmer or developer to combine media elements. **14.25**
Authorware: Multimedia application software package that uses a flowchart metaphor. **14.28-29**
AutoCAD, 2.31
AutoCorrect: Editing feature in word processing programs that corrects common spelling errors automatically in words as they are entered. **2.7**
AUTOEXEC.BAT: File containing hardware and software configuration information in earlier versions of Windows operating system. **8.13**
AutoFormat: Formatting feature in word processing programs; formats document automatically as it is being typed. **2.10**
Automatic teller machines (ATMs), 4.18
AutoSave: Feature that automatically saves open documents at specified intervals. **2.4**

AutoSum button: Used in spreadsheet program to automatically calculate totals. **2.16**
Auxiliary storage devices, *see* **Storage devices**

Backbones: High-speed communications lines connecting regional host computers to the major networks carrying most of the Internet communications traffic. **7.5**
Background: Jobs assigned a lower processing priority in a multitasking operating system. **8.5**
Backup: Procedures that provide for storing copies of program and data files so that in the event the files are lost or destroyed, they can be recovered. **5.12, 9.3, 13.15**
  database administrator and, 9.24
Backup plan: Step in disaster recovery plan that specifies how an organization will use backup files and equipment to resume information processing, **13.18**
Backup procedures: Procedures that specify a regular plan of copying and storing key data and program files. **13.15**
Backup software: Utility program that allows copying files or entire hard disk on tape or disk cartridges. **8.20**
Backward recovery: In DBMS recovery operations, process of computer keeping a log showing changes made to the database, and the log is used to reverse transactions that took place during a certain period of time, such as an hour; also called rollback. **9.19**
Band printer: Impact printer that uses a horizontal, rotating band and can print in the range of 600 to 2,000 lines per minute. **4.34**
Bandwidth: The range of frequencies that a communications channel can carry. **6.18**
Banking, online, 2.26, 6.6
Bar charts: Charts that display relationships among data with bars of various lengths. **2.20**
Bar code: A type of optical code consisting of vertical lines and spaces, found on most grocery and retail items; usually scanned to produce price and inventory information about the product. **4.14**
BASIC (Beginner's All-purpose Symbolic Instruction Code): Developed in the 1960s to be a simple, interactive problem-solving language; widely used on personal computers and minicomputers to develop business applications. **12.23**
Basic Input/Output System (BIOS): Set of instructions that provides the interface between the operating system and the hardware devices, stored on ROM chip. **8.12**
  loading operating system and, 8.12
Batch processing: Process in which data is collected, and at some later time, all the data that has been collected is processed as a group, or batch. **10.14**
Bay: An open area inside the system unit used to install additional equipment. **3.6, 3.18**
Benchmark test: Test on software that measures the time it takes to process a set number of transactions. **11.24**
Bernoulli disk cartridge: Removable hard disk storage device that works by using a cushion of air to keep the flexible disk surface from touching the read/write head. **5.11**
BigBook search tool, 7.17
Binary code, 5.7
Biological feedback input: Devices that work in combination with special software to translate movements, temperature, or even skin-based electrical signals into input; include devices such as gloves, body suits, and eyeglasses. **4.21**
Biometric device: Security device that verifies personal characteristics such as fingerprints, hand size, or signatures. **13.7**
Bit(s): An element of a byte that can represent one of two values, on or off. There are 8 bits in a byte. **3.3, 9.4**
  parity, 3.5, 6.17
Bits per inch (bpi): Number of bits that can be recorded on one inch of track on a floppy disk. **5.6**
Bits per second (bps): A measure of the speed of data transmission; the number of bits transmitted in one second. **6.18**
Blackout: Complete power failure. **13.13**
BLOB (binary large object): Media files such as graphic, video, or audio files consisting mainly of binary data. **9.5**
Board of directors: An advisory group that includes nonemployee members who meet periodically with the CEO and other officers to determine the overall direction of the organization. **10.6**
Book: The program or application built with ToolBook. **14.26**
Bookmark: The title and URL of a Web page, recorded in the browser so the user can return to the Web page in a future session. **7.11**
Books, electronic, 14.9-10
Booting: The process of loading an operating system into memory. **8.12-13**
Boot sector virus: Virus that replaces the boot program with a modified, infected version of the boot program, which, when run loads virus into the computer's memory. **13.3**

I.2 DISCOVERING COMPUTERS: A LINK TO THE FUTURE, WORLD WIDE WEB ENHANCED

Border: Decorative line or box used with text, graphics, or tables. **2.10**
Bridge: A combination of hardware and software that is used to connect similar networks. **6.22**
Brownout: Prolonged undervoltage. **13.13**
Buckets: The location on a disk where records in a direct file can be stored. **9.7**
Buffers: Areas of memory used to store data that has been read or is waiting to be sent to an output device. **8.7**
Bugs: Syntax or logic errors in a program. **12.15,** 12.38
Build-or-buy decision: In information systems development, the decision whether to buy a commercial software package from an outside source or build the entire system from scratch. **11.19,** 12.3
Built-in style: Feature of word processing program that allows font and format information to be saved so it can be applied to new documents. **2.10**
Bulletin board system (BBS): A computer system that maintains a centralized collection of information in the form of electronic messages, accessed using a personal computer and communications equipment. **6.5**
Bunny suits: Special protective clothing worn during chip manufacturing process in clean rooms. **3.26**
Bus: Any line that transmits bits between the memory and the input/output devices, and between memory and the CPU. **3.14**-15
Businesses
  network computers for, 7.25-26
  on World Wide Web, 7.30, 7.31
Business Web sites, 7.42
Bus network: A communications network that has all devices connected to and sharing a single data path. **6.28**
Button: Icon (usually a rectangular or circular shape) that when clicked, causes a specific action to take place. **2.3**
Byte: Each storage location within main memory, identified with a memory address. **3.3, 9.4**
  sync, 6.17

C: Powerful programming language originally designed to write system software. Today C is used to develop a wide variety of software, including operating systems and application software; most often used with UNIX. **12.26,** 12.36
C++: Object-oriented programming language, commonly used to develop application software. **12.26,** 12.36
Cache: High-speed memory between the CPU and the main RAM memory; stores the most frequently used instructions and data, and increases processing efficiency. **3.12**
  disk, 5.10
  RAM, 3.13
  speed and, 3.13
Cache memory chip, 3.7
Caching: Process of storing a copy of each Web page that is accessed in local storage by a proxy server. **7.18**
Cage: Two or more bays together. **3.18**
Callback system: Security feature to authenticate remote users that allows user to be connected to the computer system only after the computer calls the user back at a previously established telephone number. **13.8**
Career Web sites, 7.42
Carrier-connect radio, 6.12
Carrier sense multiple access with collision detection (CSMA/CD): Method used by Ethernet network protocol to detect data collisions and retransmit data. **6.30**
Cartridge tape: Frequently used storage medium for backup on personal computers, contains magnetic recording tape in a small plastic housing. **5.16**
CASE (computer-aided software engineering): Computer-based tools designed to support one or more phases of the SDLC. **11.28**
Case control structure: In structured design, control structure used when a condition can yield one of three or more possibilities. **12.7**
CASE workbench, 11.28-29
Cast window: The database of various media, used in Director software. **14.30**
Cathode ray tube (CRT): The large tube inside a monitor or terminal. **4.27,** 4.31
CD-E (compact disk-erasable): Erasable CD-ROM drive. **5.15**
CD-R (compact disk-recordable): Recordable CD-ROM drive. **5.15**
CD-ROM (compact disk read-only memory): A small optical disk that uses the same laser technology as audio compact disks; used for storage; able to hold almost 650 MB of data. 1.5, 1.7, 3.6, **5.14, 14.18**
  access time, 5.15
  hybrid, 14.33
CD-ROM drive: Storage device that uses a low-powered laser light to read data from removable.
Cell: Intersection of a row and column on a spreadsheet. **2.15**
Cellular telephone: A wireless telephone that uses radio waves to communicate with a local antenna assigned to a specific geographic area called a cell. **6.13**
Centered alignment: Alignment that divides text equally on either side of a reference point, usually the center of the page. 2.9
Central processing unit (CPU): Processing unit located on motherboard; contains a control unit that executes instructions that guide the computer through a task, and an arithmetic/logic unit that performs math and logic functions. These two components work together using the program and data stored in memory to perform the processing operations. **1.6,** 3.6, **3.8**-10
  components of, 3.8
  loading operating system and, 8.12
  microprocessor and, 3.7
  multimedia applications, 14.16-17
  multiple, 8.6
  multitasking and, 8.5
  superscalar, 3.21
  use of multiple, 3.21
  word size and, 3.9
Central processing unit (CPU) chip, 3.7
Central processing unit (CPU) upgrade sockets, 3.10
Certificates: Encrypted code that identifies a person, Web site, or company; also called digital Ids, or digital signatures. **13.26**
Chain of command, 10.10
Channel: Conversation group involved in Internet Relay Chat. **7.24**
Channel operator: The person who creates a channel for Internet Relay Chat, and has responsibility for monitoring the conversation. **7.24**
Characters per second (cps): Speed measurement of impact printers that have movable print heads. **4.33**
Chart: In spreadsheet software, a graphic representation of the relationship of numerical data. **2.20**
  presentation graphics, 2.24
Check disk, 5.20
Chief executive officer (CEO): The highest senior management position in an organization; chosen by and reports to the board of directors. **10.6**
Child record: In a hierarchical database, a record that is below the parent record. Each child record can have only one parent. **9.15**
Ciphertext: Unreadable characters that plaintext is converted into for security. **13.11**
CISC (complex instruction set computing/computers): Computers that have hundreds of commands in their instruction sets; describes most computers. **3.19**
Class: A larger category of objects. **12.22**
Clean rooms: Special laboratories where chips are manufactured to avoid contamination of the chip surface. **3.25-26**
Clicking: Describes process of pressing and releasing mouse button. **4.5**
Client-server: In information resource sharing on a network, process of the server completing some of the processing first, and then transmitting data to the requesting computer. **6.24**
Clip art: Previously created illustrations and pictures that are sold in collections, and inserted as graphics into word processing documents. **2.10,** 4.25
Clipboard: Temporary storage location for text during cut and copy operations. **2.6**
Clipper chip: Tamper-resistant microprocessor that has encryption formula implemented in chip. **13.12**
Cluster: Two to eight track sectors on a floppy disk; the smallest unit of floppy disk space used to store data. **5.5**
CMOS (complementary metal-oxide semiconductor): Type of memory used to store information about the computer system, such as the amount of memory, the type of keyboard and monitor, and the type and capacity of disk drives. **3.13**
Coaxial cable: A high-quality communications line consisting of a copper wire conductor surrounded by a nonconducting insulator that is in turn surrounded by a woven metal outer conductor, and finally a plastic outer coating. **6.9**-10
COBOL (COmmon Business Oriented Language): Developed in the 1960s and uses English-like statements; widely used programming language for business applications. **12.25**
  millennium bug and, 12.38
Code
  ASCII, 3.4
  binary, 5.7
  dead, 12.8, 12.15
  EBCDIC, 3.4
  HTML, 12.34-35
  object, 12.19
  operation, 3.20
  programming languages, 12.16-29
  thread, 8.5
  Unicode, 3.4-5
Codes of conduct: Written guidelines that help determine whether a specific computer action is ethical or unethical. **13.24**
Code standards: Standards developed by the American National Standards Institute to ensure that programs will run on many different types of computers. **12.13**
Coding: In developing programs, process of translating solution algorithm into a programming language, and entering the programming language code into the computer. **12.13**
Cold site: In disaster recovery, an empty facility that can accommodate the necessary computer resources. **13.18**
Collision: In a database, process that occurs with direct files when a hashing program generates the same disk location (called synonyms) for records with different key values. **9.8**
Collision: In data communications, describes occurrence of a transmitted packet of data running into another packet. **6.30**
Color libraries: Included in desktop publishing programs; standard sets of colors used by designers and printers to ensure that colors will print exactly as specified. **2.13**
Color monitor: Monitor that can display text or graphics in color. **4.28,** 4.31
Color Scanner: Used to convert images into a digitized format for use in multimedia applications. **14.20**
Columns: Data that is organized vertically on a spreadsheet. **2.15**
Command(s): Keywords and phrases input to direct the computer to perform certain activities. Commands are either chosen with a pointing device, entered from the keyboard, or selected using another type of input device. **2.3, 4.2**
Common carriers: Public wide area network companies such as the telephone companies. **6.26**
Command language: The set of commands used to interact with the computer in a command-line user interface. **8.3**
Command-line user interface: Type of user interface that has user enter keywords (commands) that cause the computer to take a specific action, such as copying a file or sending a file to the printer. **8.3,** 8.19
Commercial application software: Software that has been already developed and is available for purchase. **11.19**
Communications: The transmission of data and information between two or more computers using a communications channel such as a standard telephone line; also called data communications, or telecommunications. 1.8, **6.2**-36
  communications channels, 6.8-18
  equipment, 6.19-22
  line configurations, 6.14-16
  networks, 6.23-32
  software, 6.18
  transmission media, 6.8-14
Communications channel: The path that data follows as it is transmitted from the sending equipment to the receiving equipment in a communications system. **6.8**
  characteristics of, 6.16-18
  example of, 6.14
  Internet, 7.4, 7.5
  line configurations, 6.14-16
  transmission direction, 6.18
  transmission media, 6.8-14
  transmission modes, 6.17
  transmission rate, 6.18
  types of signals, 6.16-17
Communications Decency Act of 1996: Federal law making it a criminal offense to distribute indecent or patently offensive material online. **13.27**
Communications devices: Devices that enable a computer to connect to other computers; includes modems, and network interface cards. **1.7**
Communications satellites: Satellites that receive microwave signals from earth-based communications facilities, amplify the signals, and retransmit the signals back to the communications facilities. **6.11**
Communications software: Programs that perform data communications tasks such as dialing, file transfer, terminal emulation, and Internet access, allowing data to be transmitted from one computer to another. **2.26, 6.8, 6.19**
  Internet and, 7.29
Compiler: Process that converts the entire source program into machine language at one time. **12.19**
Component: Object. **12.33**
Compound document: In object linking and embedding applications, a document that contains objects from more than one application. **2.34**
CompuServe, 2.28, 6.6, 6.7, 7.28
Computer(s): An electronic device, operating under the control of instructions stored in its own memory unit that can accept data (input), process data arithmetically and logically, produce results (output) from the processing, and store the results for future use. **1.4**
  analog, 3.3
  categories of, 1.10-15
  components of, 1.4-7
  connectivity, 1.9
  digital, 3.3
  example of use, 1.20-25
  fault-tolerant, 8.6
  host, 6.15
  network, 7.25-27
  neural network, 3.22
  operations of, 1.7
  overview of using, 1.1-30
  power, 1.8
  proxy server, 7.18
  speed of, 3.9, 3.13-14
Computer-aided design (CAD): Design method that uses software to aid in product and structure design. 1.23, **2.31**
  graphics tablets used in, 4.11
Computer-aided software engineering, ***see*** **CASE**
Computer-assisted retrieval (CAR): Process in which microfilm readers perform automatic data lookup. **4.41**
Computer-based training: The use of computer-aided instruction to teach specific skills. **14.7**
Computer crime: Any illegal act involving a computer. **13.2**
Computer drawing programs: Graphics programs that allow an artistic user to create works of art. **4.25**
Computer ethics: The moral guidelines that govern the use of computers and information systems. **13.23**-24, 13.27

INDEX I.3

Computer graphics: Any nontext pictorial information. **4.25**
Computer literacy: Knowing how to use a computer. **1.2**
Computer output microfilm (COM): An output technique that records output from a computer as microscopic images on roll or sheet film. **4.41**
Computer program, *see* **Software**
Computer programmers: People who design, write, test, and implement programs necessary to direct the computer to process data into information. **1.16**
Computer security, 13.2-19
backup procedures and, 13.15-16
disaster recovery plan and, 13.17-18
hardware theft, 13.9
information theft, 13.11-12
Internet and, 13.25-26
software theft, 13.10-11
system failure and, 13.13-14
unauthorized access and use, 13.5-9
viruses and, 13.2-5
Computer security plan: Summary in writing of all safeguards that are in place to protect an organization's information assets. **13.19**
Computer security risk: Any event or action that could cause a loss of or damage to computer equipment, software, data and information, or processing capability. **13.2**
Computer system: Collection of devices that function together to process data. **1.4**
Computer virus, *see* **Virus(es)**
Computerized facial recognition (**CFR**): Computerized security system that developers claim will be as accurate as fingerprints. **13.31**
Computing Web sites, 7.43
Conditions
logic bomb detecting, 13.3
program design and, 12.6-8
CONFIG.SYS: File containing hardware and software configuration information in earlier versions of Windows operating system. **8.13**
Connectivity: The capability of connecting a computer to other computers. **1.9**
Connectors: Couplers contained in ports, used to attach cables to peripheral devices. 3.6, **3.16**-18
Constant angular velocity (CAV): Format for accessing information on a laser disk, allowing the display of single frames of video sequence or play of a clip slowly, frame by frame. **14.22**
Constant linear velocity (CLV): Format for accessing information on a laser disk that can store more information than CAV disks, but is not well-suited to showing single frames. **14.22**
Context diagram: Top level data flow diagram that identifies only the major process, or system being studied. **11.15**
Context-sensitive: Help information that is about the current command or operation being attempted. **2.36**
Context switching: Multitasking method in which multiple processes can be open but only one process is active; it happens when one process relinquishes control of the CPU and another starts. **8.5**
Contiguous clusters, 5.12
Continuous-form paper: A type of paper that is connected together for a continuous flow through the printer. **4.32**
Continuous-speech input: In voice recognition technology, limits spoken vocabulary to words stored in the computer system. **12.39**
Continuous-speech recognition: Voice input system that allows the user to speak in a flowing, conversational tone. **4.20**
Controlling: Management function of measuring performance, and if necessary, taking corrective action. **10.4**
Control program: The resident portion of the operating system, also called kernel, supervisor, monitor, executive, or master program. **8.2**
Control structure: A series of instructions that controls the logical order in which program instructions are executed. **12.6**
Control unit: Part of the CPU that repeatedly executes the fetching, decoding, executing, and storing operations, called the machine cycle. **1.6, 3.8**
Cookie: File that a Web server stores on user's computer when Web site is visited; gathers information about the user. **13.26**
Cooperative multitasking: Multitasking method in which multiple processes switch back and forth automatically when they reach logical break points, such as waiting for input; this method relies on the processes to relinquish control to other processes. **8.5,** 8.16
Coprocessor: A special microprocessor chip or circuit board designed to perform a specific task, such as numeric calculations. **3.14**
Copy: Makes a copy of marked text and stores it on the Clipboard, leaving original marked text where it was. **2.6**
Core competencies: What each partner in a virtual corporation does best. **10.21**
CorelDRAW!, 2.13
Corel Quattro Pro, 2.20
Cost/benefit feasibility, 11.5
Cost effective: Describes information that costs less to produce than the value of the information. **10.12**
Cost pressures, organizational competitiveness and, 10.3
Counter: Web site script that keeps track of the number of visits to the site. **12.36**
Courseware: Interactive training software. **14.7**
CPU, *see* **Central processing unit**
CPU utilization: The amount of time that the CPU is working and not idle, waiting for data to process. **8.10**
Crackers: People who try to access computer systems illegally. **13.5**
Crashing the system, test data used for, 12.14
CRT, *see* **Cathode ray tube**
Currency: Type of field in database; contains dollars and cents amounts. **2.22**
Current data, 9.9
Custom software: Applications software developed by the user or at the user's request. **11.20**
Cut: Removing portion of document and storing it on the Clipboard. **2.6**
Cyber corporation: A virtual corporation that uses the Internet and other networks to conduct much of its business; also called cybercorp. **10.21**
Cylinder: All the tracks on a disk that occupy the same position on the top and bottom of the disk that have the same number. **5.4**

Data: The raw facts, including numbers, words, images, and sounds, given to a computer during the input operation, that is processed to produce information. **1.7, 4.2**
access, 13.5-9
hierarchy of, 9.4-5
reading, 5.2
represented in computer, 3.3-5
writing or recording, 5.2
Data accuracy: Source of data is reliable and the data is correctly reported and entered; also called data integrity. **9.3,** 9.10, 9.14, 13.23
Database: Collection of data that is stored in related files. **2.21, 9.5, 9.12**-25
competition and, 10.3
employee, 10.3
generating, 9.15
guidelines for designing, 9.25
hierarchical, 9.15
network, 9.16
object-oriented, 9.18, 9.27
organization of, 9.15-18
reasons for using, 9.13-14
relational, 9.17
storage and, 9.27
Database administration, 9.22-24
Database administrator (DBA): The person responsible for managing an organization's computerized data and all database activities. **9.23**
Database design
database administrator and, 9.23
information systems development and, 11.25
Database management system (DBMS): The software that allows the user to create, maintain, and report data and file relationships. **9.2, 9.12,** 9.18-19
report generator, 12.21
Database server: Network server that provides selected information from files stored on the server, but does not run the application software; contrast with application server. **6.25**
Database software: Software that allows the user to create, maintain, and update the data that is stored in it. **2.21**-23
Data collection devices: Input devices used for obtaining data at the site where the transaction or event being reported takes place. **4.17**
Data compression: Method of storing data on a disk that reduces storage requirements by substituting codes for repeating patterns of data. **5.13,** 7.20
Data conversion: In information systems development, the process of converting existing manual and computer-based files so they can be used by new system. **11.32**
Data dictionary: In DBMS, feature that defines each data field that will be contained in the database files. **9.18**
Data dictionary: In structured analysis and design, section of the project dictionary that includes information about the characteristics of each data item. **11.18,** 11.25
Data distribution, database administrator and, 9.24
Data encryption standard (DES): Encryption method used by U.S. government. **13.12**
Data flow: In data flow diagram, shows the input or output of data or information in to or out from a process; represented by a line with an arrow. **11.15**
Data flow diagram (DFD): Graphic representation of the flow of data through a system. **11.15**
Data link, *see* **Communications channel**
Data maintenance: Procedures used to keep data current, called updating. **9.3,** 9.9-12
user role, 9.24
Data management, 9.2-3
Data mart: In a data warehouse, describes location that a subset of data is copied to in a separate database designed for a specific group of users. **9.26**
Data mining: Searching for patterns in data using sophisticated methods such as statistical analysis and rule-based reasoning. **9.26**
Data redundancy, 9.14
Data security: Protection of data to keep it from being misused or lost. **9.3,** 9.14
database administrator and, 9.24
DBMS and, 9.18
Data store: In data flow diagram, representation of a holding place for data and information, shown as two parallel lines. **11.15**
Data transfer rate: The time required to transfer data from disk to main memory. **5.7**
Data warehouse: A database that collects and organizes data from different sources, to provide information that decision makers need. **9.26**
Date: Type of field in database containing month, day, and year information. **2.22**
dBASE, 2.23
DBMS, *see* **Database management system**
Dead code: Code that is never executed in a program. **12.8,** 12.15
Debugging: Process of locating and correcting syntax and logic errors in a program. **12.15,** 12.20
Debug utility: Program that helps user identify syntax errors and find logic errors by examining program values while the program runs in slow motion. **12.15**
Decimal number system, 3.22-23
Decisions, 10.2
build-or-buy, 11.19, 12.3
on-the-job, 10.7
operational, 10.7
strategic, 10.6
systems development, 11.24
tactical, 10.7
Decision support system (DSS): A system designed to assist in decision making by summarizing or comparing data from internal and external sources. **10.16**
Decision tables: Table representing actions that should be taken under different decision-making conditions. **11.17**
Decision trees: Graphic representation of actions that should be taken under different decision-making conditions. **11.17**
Decoding: Control unit operation that translates the program instruction into the commands that the computer can process. **3.8**
Decompressing files, 7.20
Dedicated line: A communications line connection between devices that is always established. **6.15**
Dedicated word processing systems: Computers that are used only for word processing. **2.4**
Defining diagram, 12.4
Defragmentation: Storage method that reorganizes stored data so files are located in contiguous clusters, improving the speed of the computer. **5.12**
Delete: Removing text from a document. **2.6**
Deliverable: In project management, transmission on time and according to plan of a tangible item. **11.5**
Delphi: RAD tool that offers a drag-and-drop visual-programming environment. **12.33**
Design phase: Phase in information systems development consisting of acquiring essential hardware and software, if needed, and designing all the details of the system to be implemented. 11.2, **11.21**-29, **14.24**
multimedia applications development, 14.24
Desk checking: Process of stepping through the logic of the algorithm with test data. **12.12**
Desktop computer: The most common type of personal computer, designed to fit conveniently on the surface of a desk or workspace, and has separate keyboard and display screen. **1.13**
floppy disk drives in, 5.4
Desktop enhancer: Utility program that allows user to change the look and organization of a desktop (on-screen work area). **8.22**
Desktop publishing (DTP): Software that allows user to design and produce high-quality documents that contain text, graphics, and unique colors. **2.12**-14
Web authoring features, 7.8
Desktop video classroom: Distance learning where employees sit at computers in their offices or homes to attend class. **11.35**
Destination document: In object linking and embedding applications, the document into which to object is placed. **2.34**
Detailed analysis: In analysis phase of information systems development, studying the current system in depth, identifying user's requirements for the proposed system, and presenting alternative solutions to a problem and recommending a solution; sometimes called logical design. **11.12**
Detailed design specifications: In information systems development, specifying hardware and software for automated procedures. **11.25**
Detail report: A report in which each line usually corresponds to one record that has been processed. **4.23**
management use of, 10.7
Developing multimedia applications: Process of developing multimedia applications includes analysis, design, production, and use of multimedia authoring software. **14.23**-31
Device drivers: Programs used by the operating system to control input and output devices. **8.9**
Diagnostic program: Utility program that helps in determining if hardware and certain systems software programs are installed correctly and functioning properly. **8.21**

I.4 DISCOVERING COMPUTERS: A LINK TO THE FUTURE, WORLD WIDE WEB ENHANCED

Dialing: Communications software that stores, reviews, selects, and dials telephone numbers. **6.19**
Dialog authentication: User is asked to enter one of several items of personal information, which is chosen randomly from information on file. **13.7**
Dicing: Step in chip manufacturing process where wafers are cut into individual chips. **3.27**
Die: In chip manufacturing, name given to wafers that are cut into individual chips. **3.27**
Differential backup: Duplication only of the files that have changed since the last full backup. **13.15**
Diffusion oven: In chip manufacturing, oven that bakes first layer of material onto the wafer surface. **3.26**
Digital audio tape (DAT): Method of storing large amounts of data on tape using helical scan technology to write data at high densities across the tape at an angle. **5.18**
Digital cameras: Cameras that record photographs in the form of digital data that can be stored on a computer. **4.21, 14.21**
Digital computers: Computers that process data, including text, sound, graphics, or video, into a digital (numeric) value; describes most computers. **3.3**
Digital data service: Offered by telephone companies, communications channels specifically designed to carry digital signals. **6.17**
Digital signal: A type of signal for computer processing in which individual electrical pulses that represent bits are grouped together in bytes. **6.16**
Digital signal processing (DSP): In voice input systems, a board that is added to the computer to convert the voice into digital form. **4.20**
Digital video interleave (DVI): Video compression technology that reduces the file size while retaining image quality. **14.20**
Digitizer: Converts points, lines, and curves from a sketch, drawing, or photograph to digital impulses and transmits them to a computer. **4.10**
Digitizing: The process a computer uses to convert data into a digital form. **3.3**
DIMM (dual in-line memory module): Small circuit board that holds multiple RAM chips. **3.12**
Direct access: A database retrieval method in which the system can go directly to the record without having to read the preceding records; also called random access. **9.6**
Direct conversion: Process in implementing new information system that involves having users stop using the old system one day and begin using the new system the next. **11.31**
Direct file organization: File organization method that uses the key value of a record to determine the location on the disk where the record is stored; also called relative file organization, or random file organization. **9.7**-8
Director: Multimedia authoring program. **14.30**
Directory, formatting floppy disk, 5.5
Dirty data: Inaccurate input. **13.23**
Disaster recovery plan: Written plan describing steps an organization would take to restore computer operations in the event of a disaster. **13.17**-18
Disaster recovery test plan: Simulation of disasters to record an organization's ability to recover. **13.18**
Discrete speech input: Voice recognition technology feature that requires user to pause between spoken words so the computer can recognize the beginning and ending of words. **12.39**
Discrete-speech recognition: Voice input system that requires the user to pause slightly between each word spoken to the computer. **4.20**
Discussion database, 2.30, 2.31
Disk cache: An area of memory set aside for data most often read from the disk. **5.10**
Disk cartridges: Hard disk storage devices that can be inserted and removed from the computer, offering the storage and fast access features of hard disks and the portability of floppy disks. **5.11**
Disk compression programs, 5.13
Diskette, *see* **Floppy disk**
Disk management, operating system and, 8.11
Disk mirroring, *see* **Redundant array of inexpensive disks**
Display device: The visual output device of a computer, such as a monitor. **4.27**-31
Display terminals: A keyboard and a screen. **4.18**
Distance learning: The delivery of education at one location while the learning takes place at other locations, often using multimedia components and the World Wide Web. **11.35, 14.28**
Document
  hypermedia, 7.7
  hypertext, 7.7
Document, object linking and embedding applications
  compound, 2.34
  destination, 2.34
  source, 2.34
Documentation: Written materials produced as part of the information system life cycle. **11.6**
  program development and, 12.15
Domain: The range of values a field or attribute can have in a relational database. **9.17**
Domain name: The text version of the Internet protocol address. **7.6**
Domain name servers: Internet computers that use the domain name to look up the associated Internet protocol address. **7.6**
Domain name system (DNS): System that domain names are registered in. **7.6**
Dopants: Materials that are added to surface of wafer during chip manufacturing, and will conduct electricity. **3.26**
DOS (Disk Operating System): Several single tasking operating systems developed in the early 1980s for IBM-compatible personal computers; most widely used versions were MS-DOS and PC-DOS. **8.14**
Dot matrix printer: An impact printer that has a print head consisting of a series of small tubes containing pins that, when pressed against a ribbon and paper, print small dots closely together to form characters. **4.32**
Dot pitch: The distance between each pixel on the computer screen. **4.30**
Dots per inch (dpi): Measurement of laser printer resolution. **4.37**
Double-clicking: Pressing and releasing mouse button twice without moving the mouse. **4.5**
Do-until control structure: In structured design, control structure that tests the condition at the end of the loop. **12.8**
Do-while control structure: In structured design, control structure that repeats as long as the condition is true. **12.8**
Downlink: The transmission from a satellite to a receiving earth station. **6.11**
Downsize: In the information system department, a money-saving process that reduces the size of operations by moving applications from mainframe and minicomputer systems to networks of personal computers. **10.11**
Downward compatible: Describes application that is written for the new version of an operating system and can also run under the previous version. **8.14**
Dragging: Using mouse to move data from one location in document to another. **4.5**
Drivers, device, 8.9
Drum plotter: Plotter that uses a rotating drum, or cylinder, over which drawing pens are mounted. **4.38**
Dual scan: A type of passive matrix LCD screen frequently used on lower cost portable computers. **4.29**
Dumb terminal: A keyboard and a display screen that can be used to enter and transmit data to, or receive and display data from, a computer to which it is connected, and has no independent processing capability or secondary storage. **4.18**
DVD (digital video disk): Revised format for CD-ROM disks that eventually will increase the capacity of CD-ROM size disks to 4.7 gigabytes. **5.14**
Dye diffusion: Process used by a special type of thermal printer; chemically treated paper is used to obtain color print quality equal to glossy magazines. **4.37**
Dynamic RAM (DRAM): A type of RAM memory that has access to speeds of 50 to 100 nanoseconds; comprises most memory. **3.13**

EarthLink Network, 7.28
Earth stations: Communications facilities that contain large, dish-shaped antennas used to transmit and receive data from satellites. **6.11**
Ecco Pro, 2.28
Economic feasibility: Measures whether the lifetime benefits of the proposed system will exceed the lifetime costs; also called cost/benefit feasibility. **11.5**
Editing: Making changes and corrections to content of a document. **2.6**-8
Editing, sound, 4.19
Education, Web used for, 7.8, 7.31, 7.38
Education Web sites, 7.43
Edutainment: An experience meant to be both educational and entertaining, provided by multimedia products. **14.12**
Electronic books: Digitized text that use hyperlinks. **14.9**
Electronic data interchange (EDI): The direct electronic exchange of documents from one business's computer system to another. **6.4**
Electronic meetings, 6.3
Electronic reference: A type of electronic book used for reference, such as a multimedia encyclopedia. **14.9**
Electronic whiteboard: Input device that is a modified conference room whiteboard that uses a built-in scanner to record text and drawings in a file on an attached computer. **4.22**
Electrostatic plotter: Plotter in which the paper moves under a row of wires (styli) that can be turned on to create an electrostatic charge on the paper. **4.39**
E-mail (electronic mail): Electronic exchange of messages to and from other computer users. **6.2, 7.19**
  acronyms, 2.28
  emoticons, 2.28
E-mail etiquette, 2.28
E-mail software: Software that allows users to send messages to and receive messages from other computer users. **2.27**-28, 6.2
Embedded object: Object that user can make changes to in the destination document using tools from the application that originally created the object; only the destination document is changed, while the source document is not affected. **2.34**
Embedded processors: Unseen computers that are built into equipment such as radios, cellular telephones, ATMs, and automobiles. **3.28**
Emergency plan: Part of the disaster recovery plan that specifies the steps to be taken immediately after a disaster strikes. **13,17**
Employee(s)
  management, 10.6-7
  nonmanagement, 10.7
  organized by function, 10.8
  organized by process, 10.10
Employee database, 10.3
Employee monitoring: The use of computers to observe, record, and review an individual's use of a computer. **13.22**
Employment Web sites, 7.42
Empowered: Process of giving users the ability to write simple programs using program development tools. **12.21**, 12.31
Encapsulation: Packaging methods and attributes into a single object. **12.22**
Encryption: Process of converting readable data into unreadable characters. **13.11, 13.26**
  Web browser, 13.26
Encryption key: Code that converts plaintext to ciphertext. **13.11**
Enterprise computing: Connecting all of the computers in an organization into one network, so everyone in the organization can share computing resources. **6.33**
Entertainment, multimedia and, 14.12
Entertainment Web sites, 7.43
Entity: Object about which data is stored. **11.14**
Entity-relationship diagram (ERD): Tool used to represent graphically the associations between entities in a project. **11.14**
Entry point: The location where a program, module, or control structure begins. **12.9**
Environment, Web sites on, 7.44
Equal employment opportunity guidelines, 10.3
ESCAPE (ESC) key, 4.4
Etching: During chip manufacturing, process of removing channels in layers of materials on wafer. **3.26**
Ethernet: The most widely used network protocol for LAN networks; can transmit data at 10 Mbps. **6.30**
Eudora, 2.28
Even parity: The total number of on bits in the byte (including the parity bit) must be an even number. **3.5**
Event: Object-oriented programming term for message, such as pressing a key on the keyboard, or clicking the mouse. **12.23**
Exception report: A report containing information that is outside of normal user-specified values or conditions, called the exception criteria. **4.24**
  management use of, 10.6, 10.7
Excite search tool, 7.17
Executing: Control unit operation that processes the computer commands. **3.8**
Execution cycle: Together, executing and storing operations of the machine cycle. **3.8**
Executive information system (EIS): Management information system that has been designed for the information needs of senior management. 1.25, **10.15**, 10.20
Exit point: The location where a program, module, or control structure ends. **12.9**
Expanded markets, 10.2-3
Expansion board: Circuit board for add-on devices. 3.6, **3.15**
Expansion bus: Bus that carries data to and from the expansion slots. **3.14**
Expansion slot: A socket designed to hold the circuit board for a device, such as a sound card, that adds capability to the computer system. 3.6, **3.15**-16
Expert systems: Computerized systems that simulate a human expert's reasoning and decision-making processes; also called knowledge systems. **10.17**-18
Extended Binary Coded Decimal Interchange Code (EBCDIC): A coding system used to represent data, primarily on mainframes. **3.4**
External commands: Less frequently used instructions in the nonresident portion of the operating system. **8.2**
External modem: A separate, or stand-alone device attached to the computer with a cable and to the telephone outlet with a standard telephone cord. **6.19**
External report: A report used outside the organization. **4.23**
Extranets: Private networks that include more than one organization. **7.17**

FAQ: Stands for frequently asked questions, about the Internet. **7.24,** 7.45
Fast-Ethernet: A higher-speed version of Ethernet network protocol; can transmit data at 100 Mbps. **6.30**
Father: In three-generation backup, the second oldest copy of the file. **13.16**
Fault-tolerant computer: Computer built with redundant components to allow processing to continue if any single component fails. **8.6**
Favorites, 7.11
Fax (facsimile): Communications method that uses equipment to transmit and receive a document image over telephone lines. **4.42, 6.2**
Feasibility: Measurement of how suitable the development of a system will be to the organization. **11.5**

INDEX I.5

Feasibility study: In analysis phase of information systems development, study to determine if the problem identified in a project request is worth pursuing; also called preliminary investigation. **11.11**
Fetching: Control unit operation that obtains the next program instruction from memory. **3.8**
Fiber-optic cable: High-speed transmission media for communications channel that uses smooth, hair-thin strands of glass or plastic to transmit data as pulses of light. **6.10**
ISDN lines, 6.17
Fields: A special item of information, such as a name or Social Security number, in a record of a database file; a combination of one or more bytes and is usually the smallest item of meaningful data; also called attribute. **2.21, 9.4**
querying, 9.20-22
File(s): A collection of related records or data that is stored under a single name. **2.21, 9.4**
compressed, 5.13, 7.20, 8.20
database, 9.12-25
flat, 9.12
uncompressing, 5.13, 7.20, 8.20
video, 14.6
File allocation table (FAT): On personal computers, a directory that stores information such as the file name, file size, the time and date the file was last changed, and the cluster number where the file begins. **5.5**
File compression software: Utility program that reduces (compresses) the size of files. **8.20**
File conversion: Utility program that converts file from one format to another so the file can be used by another application. **8.20**
File management
operating system and, 8.11
utility programs, 8.19-21
File management system: Software that allows the user to create, maintain, and access one file at a time; sometimes called flat-file management system. **9.12**
File organization, 9.5-8
direct, 9.7-8
indexed, 9.6-7
sequential, 9.5-6
File-server: In information resource sharing on a network, method that uses a server to send an entire file at one time to a requesting computer, and then the requesting computer performs the processing. **6.24**
File transfer: Communications software that allows the user to move one or more files from one computer system to another. The software generally has to be loaded on both the sending and receiving computers. **6.19**
File transfer protocol, *see* **FTP**
File viewer: Utility program that lists the names and size of files. **8.19**
File virus: Virus that inserts virus code into program files. **13.3**
Finance: Organizational activities related to recording monetary transactions. **10.8**
Finance Web sites, 7.42
Financial transactions, accounting software and, 2.30
Firewall: Refers to both the hardware and software used to restrict access to data on a network. **7.18**
Firmware: Instructions that are stored in ROM memory; also called microcode. **3.13**
Fixed disks: Hard disks on minicomputers and mainframes; also called direct-access storage devices. **5.9**
Flagged record, 9.11
Flaming: Sending an abusive message on the Internet. **7.24**
Flash memory: Type of RAM that can retain data even when power is turned off, also called flash RAM. **3.11**
Flatbed plotter: Plotter that uses software to instruct the pens to move to the down position so the pens contact the flat surface of the paper. **4.38**
Flat file: In file-oriented systems, file that is independent and contains all the information necessary to process the records in that file. **9.12**
Flat-file management system, 9.12
Flat panel display: A thin display screen that uses liquid crystal display or gas plasma technology; often used in portable computers. **4.29**
Floppy disk: Type of small, removable magnetic disk storage consisting of a circular piece of thin mylar plastic, which is coated with an oxide material that is recorded on, storing data as magnetic areas. The plastic disk is enclosed in a rigid plastic shell for protection from debris; most widely used portable storage medium. **1.7, 5.3-8**
access time, 5.7
care of, 5.8
formatting, 5.4
storage capacity, 5.6
Floppy disk drive: Drive used to contain inserted floppy disk. 1.5, **1.7,** 3.6, 5.3, 5.6
Floptical: Floppy disk that combines optical and magnetic technologies to achieve high storage rates (currently up to 120 megabytes) on a disk similar to a 3fi-inch magnetic floppy disk. **5.15**
Flowchart, 12.9-10
Flow line: Graphical representation of the flow, or sequence, of action in the application. 12.10, **14.28**
Folder, *see* **Subdirectory**
Font: A specific combination of typeface and point size. **2.9**
Footers: Information printed at the bottom of every page. **2.10**
Foreground: In a multitasking operating system, describes process that is currently active or process that has the highest priority. **8.5**
Formalizing the solution: In program development, the programmer reviews the program code and all documentation. **12.15**
Formatting disk: Process that prepares a floppy disk for storage by defining the tracks, cylinders, and sectors on the surface of the floppy disk. **5.4**
Format/formatting documents: Changing the appearance of a document. **2.8**
word processing document, 2.8-11
Form builder: Program that allows the developer to design a form on the computer screen. **12.30**
Formulas: Perform calculations on the data in a spreadsheet. **2.15**
FORTRAN (FORmula TRANslator): Developed in the 1950s for scientific applications; one of the first high-level programming languages. **12.27**
Forward recovery: In DBMS recovery operations, describes process of a log being kept by the computer showing changes made to the database, and the log is used to automatically reenter transactions from the last time the system was backed up; also called rollforward. **9.19**
Four11 search tool, 7.17
Fourth-generation language: A nonprocedural language that uses English-like statements; very easy to use because the program has to be told only what to accomplish without explaining how. **12.20**
FoxPro, 2.23
Fragmented: File stored in clusters that are not next to each other; also describes the condition of a disk drive that has many files stored in noncontiguous clusters, slowing down the computer's speed. **5.12**
Frames: Division of screen into small windows that allow multiple files to be displayed on the screen at the same time. **8.16**
Front-end processor: A computer dedicated to handling the communications requirements of a larger computer. **6.21**
FTP (file transfer protocol): Internet standard that allows the exchange of files with other computers on the Internet. **7.20**
anonymous, 7.20
FTP sites: Computers that contain files available for transfer on FTP; many files can be downloaded at no cost. **7.20**
Full backup: Duplicates are made of all the files in the computer. **13.15**
Full-duplex transmission: Data transmission method in which data can be sent in both directions at the same time. **6.18**
Function(s): Stored formulas that perform common calculations in a spreadsheet. **2.16**
Function keys: A set of numerical keys preceded by an "F", included on keyboards as a type of user interface. Pressing a function key causes a command to take place in an application program. **4.4**

Games, 14.12
MOO (multiuser object oriented), 7.22
MUD (multiuser dimension), 7.22
virtual reality, 7.15
Web-based, 7.12
Gantt chart: A bar chart used for project management in which each bar represents a project phase or activity. **11.4**
Gas plasma: Screens that use neon gas deposited between two sheets of polarizing material. **4.29**
Gateway: A combination of hardware and software that allows users on one network to access the resources on a different type of network. **6.22**
Geosynchronous orbit: Orbit about 22,300 miles above the earth that communications satellites are placed in, causing the satellite to orbit at the same speed as the earth, so the dish antennas used to send and receive microwave signals remain fixed on the appropriate satellite at all times. **6.12**
Gestures: Special symbols made with a pen input device that issue commands to the computer. **4.8**
Ghosting, 8.22
Gigabyte (GB): A measurement of memory space, equal to a billion bytes, or one million kilobytes. **3.11,** 5.9
Gigaflops (GFLOPS): Billions of floating-point operations per second. **3.20**
Global positioning system (GPS): Communications system that uses satellites to determine the geographic location of earth-based GPS equipment; often used for tracking and navigation by all types of vehicles. **6.5**
Gopher: Menu-driven program that assists users in locating and retrieving files on the Internet. **7.21**
Gopher servers: Internet computers that maintain Gopher directories. **7.21**
Government regulation, 10.3
Government Web sites, 7.44
Grammar checker: Editing feature of word processors that is used to check for grammar, writing style, and sentence structure errors. **2.8**
Grandfather: In three-generation backup, the oldest copy of the file. **13.16**
Graphical user interface (GUI): A user interface that provides visual clues, such as symbols called icons, to help the user when entering data or running programs. **1.17, 2.2-3, 8.3**
browser-like features, 8.3
Macintosh, 8.17
multimedia and, 14.4
OS/2, 8.18
Windows 3.x, 8.15
Windows 95, 8.15
Windows NT, 8.17
Graphical Web browser, 7.9-11, 7.12
Graphics: The incorporation of pictures in documents; some graphics are included in word processing packages, but are usually created in separate applications, and imported (brought into) the word processing document, and can often be modified by the user; also describes designs and images used in Web pages to reinforce text messages. **2.10,** 4.25, **7.12, 14.4**
animated, 14.5
light pen used with, 4.10
multimedia use of, 14.4
Web page, 7.10, 7.12
Graphics objects, used in desktop publishing, 2.13
Graphics tablet: Converts points, lines, and curves from a sketch, drawing, or photograph to digital impulses and transmits them to a computer; also contains unique characters and commands. **4.11**
Gray scaling: Used by monochrome monitors to convert an image into pixels that are different shades of gray. **4.28**
Groupware: Software that helps multiple users work together by sharing information. **2.30**-31, **6.4**
intranets, 7.17

Hackers: Individuals who try to access computer systems illegally. **13.5**
Half-duplex transmission: Data transmission method that allows data to flow in both directions, but in only one direction at a time. **6.18**
Hand-held computers: Small computers used by workers who are on their feet instead of sitting at a desk, such as meter readers or inventory counters. **1.10**
Windows CE and, 8.16
Hand-held scanner, 4.13
Handshake: The process of establishing the communications connection on a switched line. **6.14**
Handwriting recognition software: Software that can be taught to recognize an individual's unique style of writing. **4.8**
Hard copy: Output that is printed. **4.23**
Hard disk(s): Storage devices containing high-capacity disk or disks, providing faster access time and greater storage capacity than floppy disks. **5.8**-11
access time, 5.10
hierarchical storage management using, 5.24
maintaining data stored on, 5.12-13
multimedia applications, 14.16-17
storage capacity, 5.9
Hard disk controller: Collection of electronic circuits that manage the flow of data to and from the hard disk. **5.10**-11
Hard disk drive: Secondary storage device containing nonremovable disks. 1.5, **1.7,** 3.6
disk cartridges, 5.11
Hardware: Equipment that inputs, processes, outputs, and stores data, consisting of input devices, a system unit, output devices, storage devices, and communications devices. **1.4**
acquiring in systems development, 11.21-23
communications, 6.19-22
configuration information, 8.13
device drivers, 8.9
Internet connection, 7.27, 7.29
multimedia, 14.16-22
network computers, 7.25-27
network connections, 6.14-15, 6.22, 6.27-29
operating system and, 8.8-9, 8.12
theft, 13.9
Hardware resource sharing: Used in local area networks, allowing each personal computer on a network to access and use devices that are too costly, or used too infrequently to provide to each user. **6.23**
Hashing: The process of using a formula or performing a calculation to determine the location (position) where a record will be placed on disk. **9.7**-8
Head crash: Describes process of a read/write head colliding with the hard disk surface, usually resulting in a loss of data. **5.10**
Headers: Information that is printed at the top of every page. **2.10**
Health Web sites, 7.44
Helical scan technology: Used by digital audio tape to record data at high densities across the tape at an angle. **5.18**
Helper application: Used for Web applications; allows multimedia to be run in a window separate from the browser. **7.11**
Hexadecimal (base 16): Number system that represents binary in a more compact form; used by the computer to communicate with a programmer when a problem with to program exists. **3.22**

I.6 DISCOVERING COMPUTERS: A LINK TO THE FUTURE, WORLD WIDE WEB ENHANCED

Hierarchical database: Database in which data is organized in a top-to-bottom series like a family tree or organization chart, having branches made up of parent and child records. **9.15**
Hierarchical file system: File system of most PCs; has different levels of files that start from the main file called the root directory; lower levels are called subdirectories. **9.16**
Hierarchical storage management (HSM): Process of automating the transfer of data by moving files from online devices to different categories and speeds of storage devices. **5.24**
Hierarchy chart: In top-down design, a tool used to represent program modules graphically. **12.5**
High-definition television (HDTV): Television sets designed for digital signals; may eventually replace computer screens. **4.26**
High-density (HD) floppy disk: Floppy disk that can store 1.44 megabytes on a 3fi-inch floppy disk; most widely used floppy disk. **5.6**
High-level language: Programming language that is machine-independent; able to run on different types of computers. **12.16**
Highlighting tool: Revision feature that allows user to mark text in color to call out key parts of a document for others. **2.8**
History, Web sites on, 7.45
History list: Records list of Web pages that are viewed during the time user is connected to the Web. **7.11**
Holographic storage, 5.25
Home, network computers for, 7.26
Home page: First page of information located at a Web site, located through the Internet. **1.8, 2.26**
Home page: The Web page designated as the page to display each time a browser is launched. **7.10**
Horizontal application software: Software packages used by many different types of organizations, such as accounting or word processing packages. **11.19**
Host computer: In a data communications system, a main computer that is connected to several devices, such as terminals or personal computers. **6.15**
number of, on Internet, 7.2
Hotlists, 7.11
Hot site: In disaster recovery, an alternate computer facility that has compatible computer resources. **13.18**
Hotwords: Text-based hypertext links. **14.3, 14.9**
How-to-guides: Multimedia applications that help users in their daily lives. **14.10**
HTML, *see* **Hypertext markup language**
http:// (hypertext transfer protocol): The communications standard used to transfer pages on the Web. **7.10**
Human resources: Activities involved in managing the people who work for an organization. 1.24, **10.9**
Humor Web sites, 7.45
Hybrid CD-ROM: Combining of CD-ROM application on a local system with an Internet application on the Web. **14.33**
Hyperlinks: In Web documents, built-in links to other related documents, allowing user to move quickly from one document to another. 1.8, **7.7**
absolute, 7.8
icons as, 8.16
relative, 7.8
target, 7.8
Hypermedia: Web document that contains text, graphics, video, or sound hyperlinks to other documents. **7.7,** 14.15
Hypertext: Web document that contains text hyperlinks to other documents. **7.7,** 14.15
Hypertext markup language (HTML): Set of special instructions used to create Web pages; the special instructions are called tags, or markups, that specify links to other documents and how the page is displayed. **7.8, 12.34**-35, 14.15

Icon: In a graphical user interface, on screen pictures that represent an application software program where data is stored. **1.17, 2.2**
as hyperlinks, 8.16
Identification: Access control verifying valid user. **13.5**
Ideograms: Symbols used by Asian and other foreign languages to represent multiple words and ideas. **3.4**
If-then-else control structure: Selection control structure that evaluates conditions to see if they are true or false, and takes action based on the result. **12.7**
Illustration software: Software that is designed for use by artists. **2.13**
Image, before and after, 9.19
Image libraries, 2.24
Imagemaps: Pictures that point to a URL and are used in place of, or in addition to, plain text hyperlinks. **12.36**
Image processing systems: In source data automation, systems that use scanners to capture and electronically file exact copies of documents. **4.13**
Image scanner: An input device that electronically captures an entire page of text or images such as photographs or art work, converting the information on the original document into digital data that can be stored on a disk and processed by the computer; also called page scanner. **4.13**
OCR software used with, 4.16
Impact printers: Printers that transfer images onto paper by some type of printing mechanism striking the paper, ribbon, and character together. **4.32**-**34**
Implementation phase: In information systems development, the phase of constructing, or building, the new system and then delivering it to the users. 11.2, **11.30**-32
Incremental backup: Duplication only of the files that have changed since the last full or incremental backup. **13.15**
Index: In a database, a file that consists of a list containing the values of one or more fields and the corresponding disk address for each record in a file. **9.6**
Indexed file organization: File organization method that uses a separate file, called an index, to record the location of a record on a storage device. **9.6**-7
Inference rules: In expert systems, rules that determine how the knowledge is used to make decisions. **10.17**
Infinite loop: Set of instructions that repeats indefinitely. **12.8**
Information: Data that has been processed by computer into a form that has meaning and is useful. **1.7**
accurate, 1.8, 1.19, 10.2, 10.11, 10.14
importance of, 10.2-3
qualities of valuable, 10.11-12
timely, 1.19, 9.3, 10.2, 10.12, 10.14
useful, 1.19, 10.12
Information appliance: Network computer for the home, that incorporates Internet access into a device normally found in the home, such as a television, telephone, or video game console; costs less than a personal computer. **7.26**
Information architecture: The way an organization provides information to different organization levels or groups; needs to match the organization architecture. **10.11**
Information hiding, 12.22
Information kiosk: Computerized information or reference center that allows user to select various options to find specific information or to browse through choices. **14.14**
Information literacy: Knowing how to find, analyze, and use information. **1.2**
Information privacy: The right of individuals and organizations to deny or restrict the collection and use of information about them. **13.20**-22
Internet and, 13.25-26
Information processing: The production of information by processing data on a computer. **1.7**
Information processing cycle: Input, process, output, and storage operations. Collectively, these operations describe the procedures that a computer performs to process data into information and store it for future use. **1.7**
Information requirements, changes in, 11.7
Information resource sharing: Allows LAN users to access the data stored on any other computer in the network. **6.24**
Information strategies, 10.2
Information system: Elements required for information processing, including software, hardware, data, users, procedures, and information systems personnel; provides support for the organization. **1.19,** 10.1, **10.6, 10.9**
development of, 11.1-35
elements of, 1.19
integrated, 10.18
interenterprise, 10.21
managers and, 10.4-7
personal computers and, 10.19
program development and, 12.1-16
prototype of, 11.27-28
types of, 10.13-18
Information systems department, 1.24
Information theft, 13.11-12
Infoseek search tool, 7.17
Infrared light wave transmission, 6.12
Inheritance: In object-oriented programming, the process of lower levels inheriting methods and attributes of higher levels. **12.22**
Ink: Describes the darkened location on screen where a pen input device touches it. **4.8**
Ink-jet printer: Nonimpact printer that forms characters by using a nozzle that shoots droplets of ink onto the page, producing high-quality print and graphics. **4.34**-**36**
Inoculation: Protection of program file from viruses by recording file size and file creation date information in a separate inoculation file. **13.4**
Input: First step in information processing cycle; the process of entering data (including numbers, words, images, and sounds), programs, commands, and user responses into memory of computer for processing. Input can also refer to the media (such as disks, tapes, and documents) that contain input data. **1.7, 4.2**-**22**
biological feedback, 4.21
digital camera, 4.21
keyboard, 4.2-4
mouse, 4.5
operating system management of, 8.8-9
pen, 4.8
pointing devices, 4.5-11
sound, 4.19
source data automation, 4.12-17
terminals, 4.18
video, 4.22I, 14.20
voice, 4.19-21
Input design, information systems development and, 11.26
Input devices: Hardware used to enter data into a computer, such as a keyboard and a mouse. **1.4**
storage devices used as, 5.2
Insert: Adding characters to existing text. **2.6**
Insertion point: A symbol such as an underline character, rectangle, or vertical bar that indicates where on the screen the next character entered will appear. **2.6, 4.3**
Insert mode, 2.6
Instruction cycle: Together, name given to fetching and decoding operations of the machine cycle. **3.8**
Instruction set: The collection of commands, such as ADD or MOVE, that the computer's circuits can directly perform. **3.19**
Integrated circuit (IC): A complete electronic circuit that has been etched on a thin slice of nonconducting material such as silicon; also called chip. **3.8, 3.25**
cache memory, 3.7
CPU, 3.7
manufacturing, 3.25-27
Integrated drive electronics (IDE): Controllers that can operate one or two hard disk drives. **5.11**
Integrated services digital network, *see* **ISDN**
Integrated software: Software that combines applications such as word processing, spreadsheet, database, and communications into a single, easy-to-use package. **2.32**-**33**
Integration test: In information systems development, the check of the application to be sure it works with other applications. **11.30**
Intelligent agent software, 10.20
Intelligent features, word processors with, 2.4
Intelligent terminal: Terminal that contains not only a keyboard and screen, but also has built-in processing capabilities and storage devices. **4.18**
Intel Pentium microprocessor, 1.6, 3.7, 3.12, 14.16
Iteration control structure, 12.7
Interactive links: Links that allow user to interact with multimedia application. **14.3**
Interactive multimedia: Multimedia application that accepts input from the user by a keyboard or pointing device and performs an action in response. **14.2**
Interenterprise information systems: Information systems used by cybercorporation partners to share all relevant information on a timely basis. **10.21**
Interlaced monitors: Monitors that display images by illuminating every other line and then return to the top to illuminate lines that were skipped. **4.31**
Internal commands: Instructions to the computer included in the resident portion of the operating system. **8.2**
Internal modem: A circuit board containing a modem that is installed inside the computer or inserted into an expansion slot. **6.20**
Internal report: Report used by individuals in the performance of their jobs and only by personnel within an organization. **4.23**
International markets, 10.2
Internet, The: Worldwide group of connected networks that allows the public access to information on thousands of subjects, gives users the ability to send messages, and obtain products and services. **1.3, 1.9, 6.7,** 7.1, **7.2**
addresses, 7.6
connecting to, 7.28-29
cybercorps and, 10.21
future of, 7.31
history of, 7.3
multimedia applications, 14.15
objectionable materials on, 13.27
operation of, 7.4-5
privacy, 13.25-26
security, 13.25-26
statistics, 7.2
traffic control, 7.5
Web sites about, 7.45
Internet access: Communications software feature that allows the computer to connect to the Internet. **6.19,** 7.5
Internet access provider, 7.9
Internet audioconferencing: Used by Web-based audio for conversations with other people over the Web; generally less expensive than regular telephone long-distance rates; also called Internet telephone service, or Internet telephony. **7.13**
Internet mailbox address: In e-mail, describes the combination of a user name and the domain that identifies the location of the mailbox computer. **7.19**
Internet organizer: Utility program that helps user manage and use list of favorite Web sites. **8.22**
Internet radio channel, 7.13
Internet Relay Chat (IRC): Service allowing user to join others in real-time conversations on the Internet; used by connecting to an Internet server with an IRC client program. **7.24**-25
Internet service provider (ISP): Company that has a permanent connection to the Internet, and offers access to the Internet as one of its services. 2.26, 2.28, **7.28**-29
e-mail and, 7.19
software, 7.29
Internet telephony, *see* **Internet audioconferencing**
Internet videoconferences, 7.14
Internet voice mail: Internet audioconferencing feature that enables the sending and retrieving of voice messages. **7.13**
Internetwork: Two or more networks joined together; also called internet. **7.2**
Interpreter: The translation of one program code statement at a time. **12.20**

INDEX I.7

Interviews, system development and, 11.7
Intranet: Internal networks that use Internet and Web technology. **7.17,** 10.7, 10.21
Intuit QuickBooks, 2.30
Investment information, online, 6.6
Ion implantation: Process of adding materials to the surface of a wafer that will conduct electricity. **3.26**
IP (Internet protocol) address: Addressing system for the Internet consisting of a four-part numeric address, identifying the geographic region, company, computer group, and the specific computer location. **7.6**
IPO chart: Chart used by programmer that identifies the inputs to the program, the outputs to be generated, and the processing steps required to transform the inputs into the outputs. **12.4**
IRC, *see* Internet Relay Chat
ISDN (integrated services digital network): An international standard for the transmission of both analog voice and digital data using different communications channels and companies. **6.17,** 7.29

JAD (joint-application design) session: A lengthy, structured, group work session where all involved in the SDLC, including users, discuss an aspect of the project. **11.7**
Java: Object-oriented scripting language used to develop multimedia on the Web. **7.11, 12.36,** 14.15
JavaScript: A simpler version of Java that runs directly in a Web browser. **12.36**
/join: Command used to participate in IRC channels. **7.25**
Join relational operation: In a relational database query, process used to combine two files (relations or tables). **9.21**
Joystick: Pointing device that uses the movement of a vertical stem to direct the pointer. **4.7**
Jughead: Program that searches Gopher directories for files on a specific subject. **7.21**
Justification, *see* Alignment
Justified alignment: Placement of text that aligns text with both the left and right margins. **2.9**

Kernel, *see* Control program
Keyboard: Input device that contains alphabetic, numeric, cursor control, and function keys. Used to enter data. **1.4,** 1.5, **4.2**-4
Key escrow: Government plan of using independent organizations that would have custody of private keys for decoding messages. **13.12**
Key field: A field containing unique data, such as a Social Security number, that is used to identify the records in a file. **9.4**
Kilobyte (K or KB): A measure of memory equal to 1,024 bytes, usually rounded to 1,000 bytes. **3.11**
Knowledge base: In expert systems, the combined subject knowledge of human experts. **10.17**
Knowledge systems, *see* Expert systems

Labels: Text that is entered in the cell of a spreadsheet. **2.15**
LAN, *see* Local area network
Landscape: Page orientation that is wider than it is tall. **2.11**
Language translators: Special-purpose systems software used to convert the programming instructions written by programmers into the binary code that a computer can understand. **8.23**
Laptop computers: Larger versions of notebook computers that weigh between 8 and 15 pounds. **1.13**
Laser
  holograms using, 5.25
  optical disk using, 5.14
Laser disks, multimedia and, 14.22
Laser printer: Nonimpact page printer that converts data from the computer into a laser beam aimed at a positively charged revolving drum. Each position on the drum touched by the beam becomes negatively charged and attracts toner, which is transferred and fused to paper by heat and pressure to create the text or image. **4.36**
Latency, *see* Rotational delay
Layout chart: During input and output design, the chart developed for the programmer that is technical and contains programming-like notations for data items. **11.26**
LCD projection panels: Data projection devices that use liquid crystal display (LCD) technology, and are designed to be placed on top of an overhead projector. **4.40,** 14.19
LCD projectors: Self-contained data projection devices that have their own light source, and do not require a separate overhead projector. **4.40**
LCS (liquid crystal shutters) printers, 4.36
Leading: Management activities involving instructing and authorizing others to perform the necessary work. **10.4**
Learning, hypermedia and, 7.8
Learning aids, software, 2.36-37
Leased line: A dedicated communications line provided by an outside organization; also called private line. **6.15**
LED (light emitting diode) printers, 4.36
Left alignment: Placement of text aligning it with left margin only. **2.9**
Level 1 (L1) cache: Cache memory built into the microprocessor chip; also called internal cache. **3.12**
Level 2 (L2) cache: Cache that is not part of the CPU chip; usually found on the motherboard. **3.12**
Light pen: Pen used as an input device by touching it on the display screen to create or modify graphics. **4.10**

Light wave transmission, 6.12-13
Line charts: Graphic charts that indicate a trend over a period of time by use of a rising or falling line. **2.20**
Line configurations: The types of line connections used in communications systems. The major line configurations are point-to-point and multidrop, or multipoint lines. **6.14**
  multidrop lines, 6.15-16
  point-to-point lines, 6.14-15
Line spacing: The vertical distance from the bottom of one line to the next line. **2.9**
Lines per minute (lpm): Measurement of the rate of printing of line printers. **4.33**
Lingo: Programming language for Director. **14.30**
Link(s)
  interactive, 14.3
  relational databases
Linked object: Object that user can make changes to in the source document, using the original software application, and the changes are reflected in both the source document and the linked destination document. **2.35**
Liquid crystal display (LCD): Type of flat panel display screen that has liquid crystal deposited between two sheets of polarizing material. When an electrical current passes between crossing wires, the liquid crystals are aligned so light cannot shine through, producing an image on the screen. **4.29**
/list: Command used to find IRC channels. **7.25**
Local area network (LAN): A communications network that covers a limited geographic area; consists of a communications channel connecting a series of computer terminals connected to a central computer, or connects a group of personal computers to one another. **6.23**
  intranets on, 7.17
  protocols for, 6.30-31
Local bus: An expansion bus that connects directly to the CPU. **3.14**
Logic: During program design, processing requirements identified by the systems analysis for each program in the system. **11.27**
Logical design, *see* Detailed analysis
Logical operations: Comparisons of data by the arithmetic/logic unit of the central processing unit, to determine if one value is greater than, equal to, or less than another. **3.8**
Logic bomb: Virus that is activated when a certain condition is detected. **13.3**
Logic error: The expected result and actual result do not match for each set of data. **12.12, 12.14**
Logon code: In multiuser operating systems, a code consisting of a word or series of characters must be entered correctly before a user is allowed to use an application program. **8.11,** 13.6
Longitudinal recording: Magnetic tape storage method used by quarter-inch-cartridge devices by recording data up and down the length of the tape. **5.18**
Loop, infinite, 12.8
Looping control structure, 12.7
Lossless compression, 5.13
Lossy compression, 5.13
Lotus 1-2-3, 2.20
Lotus cc:Mail, 2.28
Lotus Freelance Graphics, 2.25
Lotus Notes, 2.30, 2.31
Lotus Organizer, 2.28
Lotus SmartSuite, 2.33
Low-level language: Programming language that is machine-dependent; written to run on one particular computer. **12.16**
Lycos search tool, 7.17

Machine cycle: The four steps that the CPU carries out for each machine language instruction: fetch, decode, execute, and store. **3.8**
Machine-dependent: Languages that run only on the machine for which they were developed. 12.16, **12.17**
Machine-independent: High-level languages that can run on many different types of computers. 12.16, **12.19**
Machine language: Instructions to the computer that use a series of binary digits that correspond to the on and off electrical state of a computer; the only language the computer directly understands. **12.17,** 12.18
Machine language instructions: Program instructions are translated into a form that the electronic circuits in the CPU can interpret and convert into one or more of the commands in the computer's instruction set. **3.19**-20
Macintosh: Multitasking operating system first released with Macintosh computers in 1984; the first commercially successful graphical user interface. **8.17**
MacOS: Latest version of Macintosh operating system. **8.17**
Macro: A sequence of commands and keystrokes that are recorded and saved, to be performed when the macro is run. **2.16, 12.31**
Macro virus: Virus that uses the macro language of an application to hide virus code. **13.3**
Magazines, multimedia, 14.11
Magnetic disk: A round piece of plastic or metal, the surface of which is covered with a magnetic material; data is written to (recorded on) or read from the magnetic surface. The most widely used storage medium for all types of computers, offering high storage capacity, reliability, and fast access to data, include floppy disks, hard disks, and removable disk cartridges. **5.3**-13
Magnetic ink character recognition (MICR): Characters using a special ink that is magnetized during processing; used primarily by banking industry for processing checks. **4.17**
Magnetic tape: Sequential storage media consisting of a thin ribbon of plastic, coated on one side with a material that is magnetized to record bit patterns representing data; primary means of backup for most systems. **5.16**-18
  hierarchical storage management using, 5.24
Magneto-optical (MO): Drives that record data by using a magnetic field to change the polarity of a spot on a disk that has been heated by a laser. **5.15**
Mailbox: A file used to collect messages on an Internet computer, needed to receive e-mail over the Internet. **7.19**
Mainframes: Large computers that can handle hundreds of users connected at the same time, process transactions at a very high rate, and store large amounts of data; range in price from several hundred thousand to several million dollars. 1.10, **1.14**
  hard disks in, 5.9
Main memory, *see* RAM (Random Access Memory)
Main routine, 12.5
Maintaining a program: In program development, process of correcting errors and adding enhancements. **12.15**
Maintaining data, stored on disk, 5.12-13
Management information system (MIS): Any computer-based system that provides the timely and accurate information needed for managing an organization. **10.14**-15
Management pyramid, flattening, 10.10
Managers/management: The men and women responsible for directing the use of resources such as people, money, materials, and information so the organization can operate efficiently and prosper. Managers are responsible for of planning, organizing, leading, and controlling. **10.4**
  information use by, 10.4
  levels, 10.5-7
Manufacturing department, 1.22
Map software, 6.5
Margins: The space in the border of a page. **2.9**
Marketing, 1.20
  multimedia used for, 14.14-15
Markets, expanded, 10.2-3
Massively parallel processors (MPPs): Processors that use hundreds or thousands of microprocessor CPUs to perform calculations. **3.21**
Mass storage: Systems that provide automated retrieval of data from a library of storage media such as tape or cartridges. **5.21**
Master pages, 2.13
Master program, *see* Control program
MCI (media control interface) commands: Commands used to send instructions form the computer to the laser disk player. **14.22**
Meaningful: Information that is relevant to the person who receives it. **10.12**
Medicine Web sites, 7.44
Megabyte (MB): A measure of memory equal to one million bytes, or 1,000 kilobytes. **3.11,** 5.9
Megaflops (MFLOPS): Millions of floating-point operations per second. **3.20**
Megahertz (MHz): A measurement used to describe the speed of the system clock; it is equal to one million cycles (or pulses) per second. **3.9**
Member: In a network database, a child record. **9.16**
Memo: Type of field in database; contains freeform text of any type or length. **2.22**
Memory: Contained in the processor unit of the computer; temporarily stores data that can be retrieved and program instructions when they are being processed. **1.6, 3.11.**
  cache, 3.7, 3.12, 3.13
  CMOS, 3.13
  location of, 3.6
  nonvolatile, 3.13, 5.2
  operating system management of, 8.7-8, 8.10
  speed, 3.13-14
  volatile, 3.11, 5.2
Memory address: The location of a byte in memory. **3.11**
Memory buttons: Small storage devices the size of a dime that can be read or updated using a pen-like probe attached to a hand-held terminal. **5.21**
Menu: A screen display that provides a list of processing options for the user and allows the user to make a selection. **2.3**
Menu-driven user interface: User interface that uses menus to present a set of commands or options, selected with a keyboard or pointing device, that cause the computer to take a specific action. **8.3**
Menu generator: Application generator that allows the developer to create a menu, or a list of choices, for the application options. **12.30**
Message: Tells the object what to do. **12.22**
Method(s), *see* Operations
Metropolitan area exchanges (MAEs): Exchanges located in major cities, that carry Internet communications traffic; used to transfer data packets from one backbone provider to another. **7.5**
Metropolitan area network (MAN): A wide area network limited to the area surrounding a city. **6.26**

Microcode, *see* **Firmware**
Microcomputer, *see* **Personal computer(s)**
Microfiche: Sheet film used by computer output microfilm. **4.41**
Micro Focus Personal COBOL, 12.25
Microprocessor: The smallest processor, which is a single integrated circuit that contains the CPU, located on the motherboard. **3.7**
comparison of types, 3.10
Microsoft Access, 2.23, 9.20
Microsoft Corporation, 1.8
Microsoft Encarta, 14.9
Microsoft Excel, 2.20
Microsoft Explorer, 1.8
Microsoft Internet Explorer, 7.9, 7.11
Microsoft Mail, 2.28
Microsoft Money, 2.29
Microsoft Network, The, 2.26, The, 6.6, 6.7
Microsoft Office, 2.33
Microsoft Office 97 Office Assistant, 8.24
Microsoft PowerPoint, 2.25
Microsoft Project, 2.29, 11.5
Microsoft Schedule+, 2.28
Microsoft Windows: The most popular graphical user interface for personal computers. **2.2**
Microsoft Windows 95, 1.17
Microsoft Word, 2.12
Microwaves: Radio waves that can be used to provide high-speed transmission of both voice communications and digital signals. **6.11**-12
Middle management: Managers that make tactical decisions and are responsible for implementing the strategic decisions of senior management. **10.7**
MIDI, *see* **Musical instrument digital interface**
Millennium bug, 12.38
Millisecond: A thousandth of a second. **3.14**
Minicomputers: More powerful than personal computers and can support a number of users performing different tasks; cost from approximately fifteen thousand to several hundred thousand dollars. 1.10, **1.14**
hard disks in, 5.9
MIPS (million instructions per second): Measure of the processing speed of computers. **3.20**
MMX™ technology: An extension to the Pentium processor instruction set that yields a 50 to 100% improvement in the clarity and speed of audio, video, and speech. **14.16**
Mnemonics, *see* **Symbolic instruction codes**
Mobile workers, pen input devices used by, 4.8
Mockup: A sample of the input or output containing actual data; shown to users for their approval. **11.26**
Model: In decision support systems, model allows user to ask what-if questions by changing one or more of the variables to see what the projected results would be. **10.16**
Modem: Communications device that converts digital signals of a computer to analog signals, and converts analog signals back into digital signals that can be used by a computer; used to connect computers over telephone lines. 1.5, **1.7, 6.19**
external, 6.19
fax, 6.2
internal, 6.20
Internet connection, 7.29
speed of, 7.29
Moderator: Person who supervises a newsgroup by reading each article before it is posted to the newsgroup. **7.24**
Module: Section of a program dedicated to performing a single function. **12.5**
Monitor: Output display device that looks like a television and consists of a display surface, called a screen, and a plastic or metal case to house the electrical components. 1.5, **1.6, 4.27**-31
resolution of, 4.30
Monochrome monitor: Monitor that displays a single color such as white, green, or amber characters on a black background, or black characters on a white background. **4.28**
Monospacing: Each character on a page or screen takes up the same amount of horizontal space. **2.9**
MOO (multiuser object oriented): A type of MUD (role-playing game) that allows the user to create new characters and game locations. **7.22**
Motherboard: A circuit board that contains most of the electronic components of the system unit; also called the system board. **1.6**, 3.6, **3.7**
Mouse: Small, palm-sized input device that is moved across a flat surface, such as a desktop, to control the movement of the pointer on a screen. **1.4**, 1.5, **4.5**
Mouse pad: Rectangular piece of cushioned material that the mouse rests on, providing better traction for the mouse than a desktop. **4.5**
Mouse pointer: On screen symbol moved to select processing options or information; can be many shapes but is usually in the shape of an arrow. **1.4**
MPC level: Set of multimedia hardware and software standards; also called specifications. **14.16**
MPEG (Moving Pictures Experts Group): Standards for video compression and decompression. **14.6**
MS-BASIC, 12.23
MS-DOS (Microsoft DOS): A single tasking operating system originally developed by Microsoft Corporation for IBM personal computers. **8.14**
Multidrop line: Communications line configuration using a single line to connect multiple devices, such as terminals or personal computers to a main computer; also called multipoint line. **6.15**-16
Multifunction device (MFD): Output device that is a single piece of equipment that can print, scan, copy, and fax. **4.42**
Multimedia, 14.1-33
components of, 14.2-6
equipment, 14.16-22
Multimedia applications: Applications of multimedia technology for business, education, and entertainment. **14.7**-15
developing, 14.23-31
Multimedia authoring software: Software that allows user to create a presentation that can include text, color, graphics, video, sound, and animation. **2.32,** 14.15, **14.25**-31
Multimedia extensions: System software that operates in the background of a Windows application and is responsible for playing or displaying of media. **14.16**
Multimedia format: Format for presentation of information that integrates two or more of these elements: text, color, graphics, animation, audio, and video. **1.9, 14.2**
Web and, 7.11-15
Multimedia magazines: Magazines available with multimedia features, distributed on CD-ROM, or on the Web. **14.11**
Multimedia personal computer: Computer using special hardware and software components to input, process, and output the various types of media. **14.16**
Multimedia presentation: An interactive computer presentation created using multimedia authoring software, in which the user can choose what amount of material to cover and in what sequence it will be reviewed. **2.32**
Multimedia ToolBook, 2.32
Multiplexer (MUX): An electronic device that converts multiple input signals from several devices into a single stream of data that can be transmitted over a communications channel. **6.20**
Multiple zone recording (MZR): Storage method that records data a the same density on all tracks. **5.6**
Multiprocessing operating system: Operating system that coordinates the operations of computers with more than one CPU. **8.6**
Multiprocessors: Computers with more than one CPU. **8.6**
Multiscanning monitors: Monitors that are designed to work within a range of frequencies and thus can work with different standards and video adapters. **4.30**
Multistation access unit (MAU), *see* **Wiring hub**
Multisync monitors, *see* **Multiscanning monitors**
Multitasking: Operating systems that allow the computer to work on more than one process or task at a time. **8.4**
cooperative, 8.5, 8.16
preemptive, 8.5
virtual memory management, 8.7
Multithreading: Multitasking within a single program, allowing multiple threads to execute simultaneously within the same program, freeing the program to continue accepting commands. **8.5**
Multiuser timesharing: Operating systems that allow multiple users to run the same program at one time. **8.4**
Museum Web sites, 7.46
Musical instrument digital interface (MIDI): Serial port interface designed to be connected to a musical device such as an electronic music keyboard. **3.18**

Nanosecond: Measure of time equal to one billionth of a second. **3.13**
Narrative report: Report that is primarily text-based, but may contain some graphic or numeric information. **4.23**
Nassi-Schneiderman (N-S) chart: Program design tool used to show graphically the logic in a solution algorithm, using a series of rectangular boxes. **12.10**
National Science Foundation, 7.3
Natural language: A type of query language that allows the user to enter requests that resemble human speech; often is associated with expert systems and artificial intelligence. Natural languages are sometimes called fifth-generation languages. **12.21**
Natural language voice interface: Interface that allows the user to ask a question and have the computer not only convert the question to understandable words but interpret the question and give an appropriate response. **4.21**
Natural speech input: Voice recognition technology feature that places no limitations on speech; as user talks to computer, it understands to words. **12.39**
NautilusCD: A multimedia magazine. **14.11**
Near-line storage: Hierarchical storage management method consisting of high-capacity optical disks. **5.24**
NETCOM, 7.28
Netiquette: Guidelines developed for posting articles to newsgroups, and are also appropriate for other communications, such as e-mail. **7.24**
NetPC, *see* **Network personal computer**
Netscape Navigator, 7.9, 7.11
NetWare: Widely used network operating system designed for client-server networks, from Novell. **8.19**
Network: Collection of terminals, computers, and other equipment that uses communications channels to share data, information, hardware, and software. **1.7**, 1.9, **6.23**-32
configurations, 6.27-29
connected, 7.2
example of, 6.32
extranets, 7.17
intranets, 7.17
management decisions and, 10.7
operating system, 6.25
protocols, 6.29-31
security and, 7.17-18
servers, 1.10, 1.13
types of, 6.23-26
word processing documents shared on, 2.4
Network computers (NCs): Low-cost computers designed to work while connected to a network, but not as stand-alone computers. They have limited processing capability and little, if any, storage. **1.13, 7.25**-27
Windows CE and, 8.16
Network database: Similar to a hierarchical database except that each member can have more than one owner. **9.16**
Network interface card (NIC): Circuit card that fits in an expansion slot of a computer or other device, such as a printer, so the device can be connected to the network. **1.7, 6.21**
Network licenses: Special agreements, obtained from software vendors, that allow a software package to be shared by many users within the same organization. **6.24, 13.11**
Network MCI, 7.28
Network operating system (NOS): System software that makes it possible to implement and control a LAN and allows users to use the files, resources, and other services on that network. **6.25**
Network personal computer: Personal computer designed to work while connected to a network, primarily relying on a server for software and storage but has a hard disk used for storing some data and programs and able to run some programs; also called netPC. **7.26**
Neural network computers: Computers that use specially designed circuits to simulate the way to human brain processes information, learns, and remembers. **3.22**
Newbies: New users on the Internet. **7.24**
News, online, 6.6, 7.46
Newsgroups: A collection of news and discussion groups accessed via the Internet. **7.23**-24
Newsreader: Program used to access a newsgroup. **7.23**
Node: Device connected to a network, such as a computer or printer. **6.27**
Noise: An unwanted signal that is mixed with the normal voltage entering the computer. **13.13**
Nonimpact printing: Printing that occurs without having a mechanism strike against a sheet of paper. **4.34**-39
Noninterlaced monitors: Monitors that illuminate each line on screen sequentially so the entire screen is lighted in a single pass. **4.31**
Nonmanagement employees: Employees who need frequent information to make on-the-job decisions, includes production, clerical, and staff personnel. **10.7**
Nonprocedural language: Language in which the programmer has only to specify what is to be accomplished without explaining how, making coding easier. **12.20**
Nonvolatile: Type of memory (ROM) that retains its contents even when the computer is turned off. **3.13, 5.2**
Normalization: In relational databases, a process used to organize data into the most efficient and logical file relationships. **9.25**
Notebook computers: Personal computers that are small enough to be carried in a briefcase but are often transported in their own carrying case; they weigh between four and eight pounds. **1.11**
Novell, 8.19
NSFnet: Network operated by the National Science Foundation that served as the major U.S. Internet network from 1987 until 1995. **7.3**
NTSC (National Television System Committee): The organization that sets the standards for most video and broadcast equipment. **14.19**
NTSC converter: Device that connects the multimedia computer to a TV monitor. **14.19**
Number systems, 3.22-24
Numeric: Type of field in database containing number data only. **2.22**
Numeric keypad: Keypad, usually contained within the keyboard, where numeric keys are arranged in an adding machine or calculator format to aid the user with numeric data entry. **4.3**

Object: Any piece of information created with a Windows program, which is linked or embedded in another application. **2.34**
desktop publishing, 2.13
embedded, 2.34
linked, 2.35
3-D, 7.15
Object: In object-oriented programming, the single unit that the data and program (or procedure) is packaged into. **12.21**
Object code: The machine language version that results from compiling a third-generation language. **12.19**
Object instance: 12.22
Object linking and embedding (OLE): Describes ways to transfer and share information among software applications, by placing objects created in one application into another application. **2.34**-35

Object-oriented: Programming approach in which the programmer packages to data and the program (or procedure) into a single unit called an object. **12.21**-23

Object-oriented database: Database that keeps track of objects, entities that contain both data and the action that can be taken on the data; also designed to contain nontext data such as photographs, video, and audio clips. **9.18,** 9.27

Object-oriented programming (OOP) language: The event-driven programming language used to implement the design model if the object-oriented approach to program development is used. **12.23,** 12.33

Object program, *see* **Object code**

OCR (optical character recognition): Scanning devices that read typewritten, computer-printed, and in some cases hand-printed characters from ordinary documents, compare the characters with a predefined shape stored in memory, and convert the character into the corresponding computer code. **4.15**-16

OCR software: Software that is used with image scanners to convert text images into data that can be processed by word processing software. **4.16**

Odd parity: The total number of on bits in the byte (including the parity bit) must be an odd number. **3.5**

Office systems: Information systems that include software applications for administrative tasks that occur throughout the organization; sometimes referred to as productivity software. **10.13**

Offline storage: Hierarchical storage management method consisting of automated tape libraries. **5.24**

Offsite: Location different from computer site, used to store backup. **13.15**

On-demand report, *see* **Ad hoc report**

Online analytical processing (OLAP) systems: Decision support systems that include query languages, statistical analysis capabilities, spreadsheets, and graphics. **10.16**

Online Help: Feature of most applications software that evaluates questions from user and displays a list of related topics. **2.36**

Online information service, 1.9

Online research, 7.38

Online services: Information and services provided to users who subscribe to the services for a fee; accessed with communications equipment and software. 2.26, 2.28, **6.6,** 7.5, **7.28**

Online storage: Hierarchical storage management method usually consisting of hard disks, or sometimes RAM disks, providing fast, direct access to data. **5.24**

Online transaction processing (OLTP): Information systems that process transactions as they are entered, and all related records are updated at the same time. **10.14**

Online vendor support, 6.5

OpenScript: ToolBook programming language. **14.26**

Operand: Specifies the data or location of the data that will be used by machine language instructions. **3.20**

Operating environment: A graphical user interface between the user and the operating system. **8.15**

Operating system: Set of programs containing instructions that manage the operations of a computer such as loading, storing, and executing a program, and transferring data among the system devices and memory. **1.17, 2.2, 8.2-19**
functions of, 8.4-11
input and output management, 8.8-9
loading, 8.12-13
memory management, 8.7-8
multiprocessing, 8.6
multitasking, 8.4-5
network, 6.25
next-generation, 8.25
popular, 8.14-19
portable, 8.14
proprietary, 8.14
single tasking, 8.4
system administration, 8.10-11

Operation(s): Organizational functional area that carries out the primary activities of an organization. **10.8**

Operations(s): In object-oriented programming, the procedures in the object. **12.21**

Operational decisions: Decisions made by operational management that involve an immediate action such as accepting or rejecting an inventory delivery or approving a purchase order. **10.7**

Operational feasibility: Measurement of how well the final system will work in the organization. **11.5**

Operational management: Management level that makes operational decisions and provides supervision to the production, clerical, and nonmanagement staff. **10.7**

Operation code: First part of machine language instruction; tells the computer what to do and matches one of the commands in the instruction set. **3.20**

Optical codes: In source data automation, codes that use a pattern or symbol to represent data, such as a bar code. **4.14**

Optical disks: Storage medium in which data is written using lasers to burn microscopic holes on the surface of a hard plastic disk; able to store enormous quantities of information. **5.14**-15
hierarchical storage management using, 5.24

Optical mark recognition (OMR): Input devices that often are used to process questionnaires or test answer sheets. Carefully placed marks on the form indicate responses to questions that are read and interpreted by a computer program. **4.15**

Optical memory cards: Special purpose storage consisting of plastic cards the size of a credit card that can store up to 4.1 MB of digitized text or images using a laser beam. **5.22**

Optical recognition: Devices that use a light source to read codes, marks, and characters and convert them into digital data that can be processed by a computer. **4.14**-16

Organization
cyber corporation, 10.21
functional areas in, 10.8-9
virtual corporation, 10.21

Organized: Information that is arranged to suit user requirements. **10.12**

Organizing: Management function of identifying and bringing together the resources necessary to achieve the plans of an organization. **10.4**

OS/2: IBM's graphical user interface operating system designed to work with 32-bit microprocessors. **8.18**

Output: The data that has been processed into a useful form called information that can be used by a person or machine. **1.6, 1.7, 4.23-43**
audio, 4.25
computer output microfilm, 4.41
data projectors, 4.40
display devices, 4.27-31
fax, 4.42
multifunction devices, 4.42
operating system management of, 8.8-9
printers, 4.32-39
types of, 4.23-26
video, 4.26
voice, 4.25-26

Output design, information systems development and, 11.26

Output devices: Devices that convert the results of processing into a form that can be understood by users; most common devices are printers, monitors, and speakers. **1.6**
storage devices used as, 5.2

Outsourcing: The hiring of outside firms to provide information systems support for a contracted fee. **10.11**

Overhead projection system: System that uses overhead projection for presentation to large groups. **14.19**

Overtype mode, 2.6

Overvoltage: Incoming electrical power increases significantly above the normal 120 volts; also called power surge. **13.13**

Owner: In a network database, a parent record. **9.16**

Package: In chip manufacturing, ceramic or plastic case containing die that have passed all tests. **3.27**

Packets: Internet operation that divides data into separate parts including the data and the destination, origin, and sequence information, that is sent along the best route available to a destination computer, where the information is reassembled into the original message. **7.4**

Packet-switching: In communications networks, process of combining individual packets of data from various users and transmitting them over a high-speed channel. **6.26,** 7.4

Page: Each screen built using ToolBook multimedia authoring software. **14.26**

Page: In virtual memory management, the fixed number of bytes that are transferred from disk to memory each time data or program instructions are needed. **8.7**

Page composition and layout: In desktop publishing, the process of arranging text and graphics on a document page; also called page makeup. **2.12**

Page definition language: In desktop publishing, language describing the document to be printed that the printer can understand. **2.14**

Pages per minute (ppm): Measure of the speed of printers that can produce an entire page at one time. **4.37**

Paging: In virtual memory management, a fixed number of bytes (a page) is transferred from disk to memory each time data or program instructions are needed. **8.7**

Paint window: The drawing and painting program contained in Director software. **14.30**

Palmtop computers: Small computers that often have several built-in or interchangeable personal information management functions, such as a calendar and an address book; do not have disk storage devices and usually have a non-standard keyboard. **1.10**
Windows CE and, 8.16

Paradox, 2.23

Parallel conversion: Continuing to process data on the old system while some or all of the data is also processed on the new system. **11.32**

Parallel ports: Ports most often used to connect devices that send or receive large amounts of data such as printers or disk and tape drives. **3.16**

Parallel processing: The use of multiple CPUs, each with its own memory, that work on their assigned portion of a problem simultaneously. **3.21**

Parametric, 2.31

Parent record: In a hierarchical database, a record that has one or more child records. **9.15**

Parity, even, odd, 3.5
RAID technology, 5.20

Parity bit: One extra bit for each byte that is used for error checking. **3.5**
asynchronous transmission, 6.17

Partition(s): Portions of memory allocated by operating system into fixed areas. **8.7**

Partitioned disk: Separate areas that hard disk is divided into before it is formatted. **5.9**

Pascal: Programming language developed in the 1960s for the purpose of teaching structured programming concepts to students; currently used for scientific applications. **12.27**

Passive matrix: LCD screens that use fewer transistors, one for each row and column. **4.29**

Password: In multiuser operating systems, a value, such as a word or number, that must be entered correctly before a user is allowed to use an application program. **8.11,** 13.6-7

Paste: An option used after performing either the cut or copy command, where the selected data is placed elsewhere in the document. **2.6**

Path: In a hierarchical file system, the chain of directories from the root to a particular file. **9.16**

PC, *see* **Personal computer(s)**

PC Card: Small, credit-card sized device that fits into PCMIA expansions slots; often used with portable computers for storage, communications, and additional memory. **3.16,** **5.19**

PC-DOS (Personal Computer DOS): Single tasking operating system developed by Microsoft for IBM. **8.14**

PCMIA (Personal Computer Memory Card International Association): Association that developed specifications for PC Cards. **3.16**

Peachtree Accounting, 2.30

Peer-to-peer network: Local area network that allows any computer to share software, data, or hardware (such as a printer) located on any other computer in the network. **6.25**

Pen computers: Specialized personal computers that use a pen-like device to enter data, and have special software that allows the system to recognize handwritten input. **1.10**

Pen input: Input by device that can be used in three ways: to input data using hand-written characters and shapes that the computer can recognize, as a pointing device like a mouse to select items on the screen, and to gesture, which is a way of issuing commands. **4.8**

Pen plotter: Plotter used to create images on a sheet of paper by moving one or more pens over the surface, or by moving the paper under the top of the pens. **4.38**

Performance monitoring, database administrator and, 9.24

Periodic reports: Reports that are produced on a regular basis such as daily, weekly, or monthly; also called scheduled reports. **4.24**

Peripheral device: Any device connected to the system unit. **1.7**

PERL (Practical Extraction and Reporting Language): Scripting language that is object-oriented. **12.36**

Personal computer(s) (PCs): Small systems that have become widely used in recent years. Depending on their size and features, personal computer prices can range from several hundred to several thousand dollars. **1.10-13**
hard disks in, 5.8, 5.9
information systems and, 10.19
network, 7.26
terminal emulation software, 6.19
videoconferences using, 6.4

Personal digital assistant (PDA): Small pen input device designed for workers on the go; often has built-in communications capabilities that allows the PDA to use voice, fax, or data communications. **1.11**
pen input devices used with, 4.8

Personal finance software: Software used to track income and expenses, pay bills, complete online transactions, and evaluate financial plans. **2.29**

Personal identification number (PIN): Numeric password. **13.7**

Personal information management (PIM) software: Software that helps users keep track of miscellaneous bits of personal information, such as notes to self, phone messages, and appointment scheduling. **2.28**

Phased conversion: Used with larger systems that can be broken down into individual sites that can be implemented separately at different times. **11.32**

Phases: Steps in the system development life cycle. **11.2**

Photographs
digital camera, 4.21
multimedia applications, 14.4
used as graphics, 4.25 Photo CDs, 14.21

Photolithography: Process in chip manufacturing, where an image of the chip design, called a mask, is used as a negative. The photoresist is exposed to the mask using ultraviolet light. **3.26**

Photoresist: A soft gelatin-like emulsion that is added to the wafer during chip manufacturing. **3.26**

Pie chart: A graphic representation of proportions used for showing the relationship of parts to a whole, depicted as slices of a pie. **2.20**

Pilot conversion: The new system will be used by only one location in the organization so it can be tested. **11.32**

Pipelining: Describes the CPU starting a new instruction as soon as the preceding instruction moves to the next stage, providing rapid throughput. **3.21**

Pixel (picture element): On screen, the dots that can be illuminated. **4.30,** 4.31

PKZIP, 5.13

Placeholder, hierarchical storage management using, 5.24

Plaintext: Readable data that can be encrypted into ciphertext. **13.11**
Planning: Management function of establishing goals and objectives and establishing the strategies or tactics needed to meet the goals and objectives. **10.4**
Planning phase: In information systems development, the phase that begins when the steering committee receives a project request. 11.2, **11.9-10**
Platters: Part of hard disk that is coated with a material that allows data to be recorded magnetically on the surface; enclosed in an airtight, sealed case. **5.8**
Plotter: Output device used to produce high-quality line drawings and diagrams. **4.38**
Plug and Play technology: Technology that allows the operating system to recognize any new devices and assists in the installation of the device by automatically loading the necessary driver programs and checking for conflicts with other devices. **8.9**
Plug-ins: Applications that run multimedia within the browser window; can be downloaded from many sites on the Web. **7.11**
Point: Measure of character size, approximately equal to 1/72 of one inch. **2.8**
Pointing devices, 4.5-11
Pointing stick: Small input device shaped like a pencil eraser that moves the insertion point as pressure is applied to the device; also called isometric pointing device, or trackpoint. **4.7**
Point-of-sale (POS) terminal: Allows data to be entered at the time and place where the transaction with the consumer occurs, such as in fast-food restaurants or hotels. **4.18**
Point-to-point line: A line configuration used in communications that is a direct line between a sending and receiving device; may be a switched line or a dedicated line. **6.14-15**
Politics, Web sites on, 7.44
Polling: Used by front-end processor to check the connected terminals or computers to see if they have data to send. **6.21**
Polymorphic virus: Virus designed to modify its program code each time it attaches itself to another program or file. **13.4**
Port: A socket used to connect the system unit to a peripheral device such as a printer or a modem. 3.6, **3.16-18**
Portable computers
  floppy disk drives, 5.4
  input devices for, 4.6
Portable operating systems: Operating systems that will run on many manufacturers' computers. **8.14**
Portable programs, 12.29
Portrait: Page orientation that is taller than it is wide. **2.11**
Possessed object: Any item the user must carry to gain access to a computer facility, such as badges, cards, and keys. **13.7**
POST (Power On Self Test): Tests run by the BIOS chip when the computer is turned on to make sure the equipment is working properly. **8.12**
Post-implementation system review: In the support phase, a meeting with users to determine if the system is performing according to their expectations. **11.33**
Posting: Process of adding an article to a newsgroup. **7.23**
PostScript: A page definition language. **2.14**
PowerBuilder: A RAD tool that uses a proprietary language. **12.33**
Power supply: Converts the wall outlet electricity to the lower voltages used by the computer. 3.6, **3.18**
PPP (point-to-point protocol): A version of the Internet communications protocol TCP/IP, widely used by Internet service providers. **7.29**
Preemptive multitasking: Multitasking method in which the operating system prioritizes the processes to be performed and assigns a set amount of CPU time for the execution of each process. **8.5**
Preliminary investigation, see Feasibility study
Presentation graphics: Software that allows the user to create documents called slides that are used in making presentations before a group. **2.24-25**
Prime number: Number divisible without a remainder only by itself and 1. **9.7**
Printer/printing: Output device used to produce permanent hard copy. 1.5, **1.6, 4.32-39**
  impact, 4.32-34
  nonimpact, 4.34-39
  word processing document, 2.11
Print preview: Allows the user to see on the screen how a document will look when it is printed. **2.11**
Print spool: The reports stored on disk that are waiting to be printed. **8.9**
Privacy, information, 13.20-22
Problem analysis, program development and, 12.4
Problem definition, analysis phase of system development and, 11.11
Problem solving, management and, 10.6
Process/processing: Part of the information processing cycle; the procedures a computer performs to process data into information. **1.7**
  options, 2.2
Process: In data flow diagram, describes transformation of input data flow into an output data flow, drawn as a circle. **11.15**
Processing form: Form used to collect data from visitors to a Web site. **12.36**

Process management, operating system and, 8.4-6
Processor, see Central processing unit (CPU)
Process owner, 10.10
Prodigy, 6.6, 6.7
Product design department, 1.23
Production: In multimedia application development, the process of creating the various media elements used in the application, and putting them together using multimedia authoring software. **14.25**
Product life cycles, 10.3
Program(s): The detailed set of instructions that tells the computer exactly what to do, so it can perform the operations in the information processing cycle; also called program instructions, or software. **4.2**
  applets, 7.11
  coding, 12.13
  designing, 12.4-12
  design tools, 12.9-11
  maintaining, 12.15
  need to interface with other, 12.29
  object, 12.19
  testing, 12.13
  verbal development, 12.39
Program development, 12.1-16
Program development life cycle (PDLC): The process of developing programs or software, using these steps: analyzing the problem, designing the program, coding the program, testing the program, formalizing the solution, and maintaining the program. **11.30, 12.2-16**
Program development tools: Software tools that empower users in developing programs because they are easy to learn and use. **12.30-33**
Program files, virus in, 13.3
Program flowchart: Design tool used to show graphically the logic in a solution algorithm. **12.9**
Program generator, see Applications generator
Program logic, see Solution algorithm
Programmers, 11.3
  COBOL, 12.38
Programming grammar errors, 12.14
Programming language: Sets of words, symbols, and codes used to create instructions a computer can understand or recognize. **12.2, 12.16-29**
Programming standards, 12.29
Programming team: Team of programmers working on program development. **12.3**
Program specification package: Communication of program design requirements to the programmer. **11.27, 12.3**
Project dictionary (repository): Automated project notebook that contains all the documentation and deliverables associated with a project. **11.6, 11.16**
Project management: The process of planning, scheduling, and then controlling the individual activities during the system development life cycle. **11.4**
Project management software: Software that allows users to plan, schedule, track, and analyze the events, resources, and costs of a project. **2.29, 11.5**
Project notebook: The entire collection of documentation for a single project. **11.6**
Project plan: Plan of project activities in information systems development. **11.4**
Project relational operation: In a relational database query, specifies the fields (attributes) that appear on the query output. **9.21**
Project script: In multimedia application development, a written record of how the various media elements will be used in the production. **14.24**
Project team: Team formed to work on system development project. **11.4, 11.7**
Proper program: Program that is constructed in such a way tat the program has the following characteristics: no dead code, no infinite loops, one entry point, and one exit point. **12.8**
Proportional spacing: On a page or screen, wide characters, such as a W or M are given more horizontal space than narrow characters. **2.9**
Proprietary operating systems: Operating systems that are limited to a specific vendor or computer model. **8.14**
Protocol: In communications, a set of rules and procedures for exchanging information between computers. **6.29**
  FTP, 7.20
  hypertext transfer (http), 7.10
  Internet, 7.4, 7.20, 7.22, 7.29
  point-to-point, 7.29
  serial line Internet, 7.29
  TCP/IP, 7.4
  Telnet, 7.22
Prototype/prototyping: A working model of the proposed system. **11.27, 12.32**
Proxy server: A computer that is placed between two separate networks; used to implement a firewall that restricts access to data.
Pseudocode: A program design tool that uses an abbreviated form of English to outline program logic. **12.11**
Public key encryption: Method using two encryption keys. **13.11**
Push media, 7.38

Quality review
  information systems development and, 11.29
  program design and, 12.12
Quarter-inch-cartridge (QIC): Tape device, often used with PCs, that records data in narrow tracks along the length of the tape. **5.18**
Query: The ability to retrieve database information in a report, based on criteria specified by the user. **2.23, 9.20**
Query-by-example (QBE): A DBMS feature that helps the user construct a query by displaying a list of fields available in the files from which the query will be made, and the allows the user to specify selection criteria to limit the number of records displayed. **9.20**
Query language: A simple English-like language that allows users and programmers to specify the data from a database for a report or screen display. **9.19, 9.20-22, 12.20**
Query language, 12.20
QuickBASIC, 12.23
Quicken, 2.29

RAD, see Rapid application development
Radio, Internet, 7.13
Radio wave transmission, 6.12-13
RAID, see Redundant array of inexpensive disks
RAID levels, 5.19-20
Rails: Mounting brackets needed to install a device in a bay inside the system unit. **3.18**
RAM (Random Access Memory): Contained in the processor unit of the computer; temporarily stores data and program instructions when they are being processed. Also called main memory. **1.6, 3.11-12**
  multimedia applications, 14.16-17
RAM cache memory, speed and, 3.13
Rapid application development (RAD): The process of developing software with prototypes. **11.27, 12.32-33**
Reading data: The process of retrieving data. **5.2**
  from floppy disk, 5.7
Random file organization, 9.7
Read only memory, see ROM
Read/write head: Recording mechanism in the drive that rests on the top and bottom surface of the rotating disk, generating electronic impulses that change the polarity, or alignment of magnetic areas along a track on the disk. **5.7**
  floppy disk, 5.7
  hard disk, 5.10
  tape drives, 5.18
Reception, 1.20
Reciprocal backup relationship: Relationship with another firm; in case of disaster, one firm provides space and sometime equipment to the other. **13.18**
Record(s): Collection of related facts or fields in a database. **2.21, 9.4**
  adding, 9.9
  changing, 9.10
  child, 9.15, 9.16
  deleting, 9.11
  flagged, 9.11
  parent, 9.15, 9.16
  root, 9.15
  querying, 9.20-22
Record a macro: Process of beginning the macro recorder in the application and recording a series of actions. **12.31**
Recording data: The process of storing data. **5.2**
  on floppy disk, 5.7
Recording density: Number of bits that can be recorded on one inch of track on a disk, referred to as bits per inch. **5.6**
Recovery
  backward, 9.19
  database administrator and, 9.24
  DBMS and, 9.19
  forward, 9.19
Recovery plan: In disaster recovery, actions that are specified to be taken to restore full information processing operations. **13.18**
Redundant array of inexpensive disks (RAID): Storage technique that uses small disks which are connected into an integrated unit that acts like a single large disk drive. **5.19**
Reel-to-reel tape: Magnetic storage tape device that uses two reels: a supply reel to hold the tape to be read from or written to, and the take-up reel to temporarily hold portions of the supply reel tape as it is being processed. **5.17**
References, electronic, 14.9-10
Reference Web sites, 7.46
Refresh rate: Speed at which the entire screen is redrawn. **4.31**
Registers: Storage locations in the CPU that temporarily store specific data such as the address of the next instruction. **3.8**
Registry: Operating system files that contain information about which hardware and software is installed, and information about individual user preferences. **8.13**
Relation(s): In a relational database, data that is organized in tables. **9.17**
Relational database: Database that has data organized in tables called relations. **9.17**
Relational operations: Operations that are used to query a relational database; includes select, project, and join operations. **9.21**
Relative file organization, 9.7

INDEX I.11

Relative hyperlinks: Hyperlinks that move from one document to another document on the same Internet computer. **7.8**
Relative referencing: In spreadsheet programs, when a formula is copied to another cell, the formula is automatically updated to the new location. **2.19**
Reliability, 1.8
Reliable data entry: Process of entering all data into the computer correctly. **9.3**
Remembered information authentication: User is required to enter a word or series of characters that matches an entry in a security file in the computer, used for security. **13.6**
Remote workers, 2.28
Repetition control structure: Control structure used when a set of actions are to be performed repeatedly as long as a certain condition is met; also called looping, or iteration, control structure. **12.7**
Replace: Used with search feature, that allows substitution of new letters or words for the old. **2.6**
Replication: Process of distributing data to other computers. **9.19**
Report(s): Information presented in an organized form. **4.23**
database, 9.14, 9.20-22
detail, 10.7
exception, 10.6, 10.7
feasibility study, 11.11
management use of, 10.6, 10.7
Report generator: DBMS feature that allows access and display of data, and allows user to format query results professionally for output. **12.21,** 12.30
Report writer, *see* **Report generator**
Request for information (RFI): A less formal method using a standard form to request information about a product or service. **11.22**
Request for proposal (RFP): A written list of an organization's information system requirements that is given to vendors, for the vendors to select the products that meet the requirements and then quote prices. **11.22**
Request for quotation (RFQ): A written list of an organization's information system requirements that is given to vendors when the organization knows what products are needed, for the vendors to give price quotes. **11.22**
Rescue disk: Used to protect against viruses; contains an uninfected copy of certain operating system commands and information that enables the computer to restart correctly. **13.5**
Research, online, 7.38, 7.46
Resolution: Measure of a screen's image clarity, and depends on the number of individual dots (pixels) displayed on the screen, and the distance between each pixel. **4.30**
Response time: The amount of time measured from the moment data is entered into the computer until the computer responds. **8.10**
Restore: Process of reloading files on the computer in case of system failure. **13.15**
Restore programs, 8.20
Revision marks: Editing feature of word processing program that allows changes to be made directly in a document, by marking additions and deletions with underlines, strikethroughs, or different colors and fonts. **2.8**
Right alignment: Placement of text aligning it with right margin only. **2.9**
Right-size: Matching an organization's information processing requirements with an appropriate mix of computer systems. **10.11**
Ring network: Communications network that has a series of computers connected to one another in a continuous loop or ring. **6.29**
RISC (reduced instruction set computing): Technology that involves reducing the computer's instruction set to only those instructions that are most frequently used, allowing the computer to operate faster. **3.19**
Rollback, *see* **Backward recovery**
Rollforward, *see* **Forward recovery**
ROM (read only memory): Describes chips that store data or instructions that do not change. This data is permanently recorded in the memory when it is manufactured. ROM memory retains its contents even when the power is turned off. **3.13**
Root directory: In a hierarchical file system, the main file level. **9.16**
Root record: In a hierarchical database, the parent record at the top of the hierarchy. **9.15**
Rotational delay: The time it takes for the sector containing the data to rotate under the read/write head; also called latency. **5.7**
Router: An intelligent network connecting device that sends (routes) communications traffic directly to the appropriate network; used when several networks are connected together. **6.22**
Internet, 7.5
Routine, main, 12.5
Rows: Data organized horizontally on a spreadsheet. **2.15**
RPG (Report Program Generator): Nonprocedural programming language introduced in the 1960s by IBM; used for report generation, complex computations, and complicated file updating. **12.28**
Sales and marketing: Activities involved in selling and promoting an organization's product or service. 1.20, **10.8**
multimedia used for, 14.14-15
Satellites
communications, 6.11-12
global positioning system, 6.5
Scanners
hand-held, 4.13
image, 4.13, 4.16
optical character recognition, 4.15
Scanners, 14.20
Scheduled reports, *see* **Periodic reports**
Scheduling, group, 2.31
School, connecting to Internet through, 7.28
Science Web sites, 7.47
Scope: The range or extent of the project. **11.4**
Score window: The heart of Director multimedia software, used to direct application development. **14.30**
Screen(s): Term used to refer to both the surface of any display device and to any type of display device. **4.27**
touch, 4.9
Screen painter, *see* **Form builder**
Screen saver: Utility program that automatically displays a moving image on the screen if the computer remains idle for a certain period of time; primarily used for entertainment and security. **8.22**
Script: Short program that acts as a link between Web browser and the Internet server. **12.36**
Scrolling: The movement of screen data up or down one line or screen at a time. **2.6**
Scroll tips: Small page labels beside the scroll box, that show the current page during scrolling operations. **2.6**
SCSI (small computer system interface): Port that can be used to attach seven to fifteen different devices to a single port. **3.16**
SCSI (small computer system interface) controllers: Controllers that can support multiple disk drives or a mix of other SCSI-compatible devices. **5.11**
Search: Feature that allows user to find all occurrences of a particular character, word, or combination of words. **2.6**
Search tool: Software program that finds Web sites, Web pages, and Internet files that match one or more keywords that are entered by searching an index of Internet sits and documents. **7.16**-17, 12.36
FTP, 7.20-21
Sector: A pie-shaped section of the floppy disk. **5.4**
Secure Socket Layer (SSL): Internet encryption method that provides two-way encryption. **13.26**
Security
network, 7.18
operating system and, 8.11
Seek time: The time it takes to position the read/write head over the proper track. **5.7**
Selection control structure: Control structure used to tell the program which action to take, based on a certain condition. **12.6**
Select relational operation: In a relational database query, selection of certain records (rows or tuples) based on user-supplied criteria. **9.21**
Self-managed teams, 10.10
Senior management: The top managers in an organization, who make strategic decisions and are concerned with the long-range direction of the organization; also called executive or top management. **10.6**
executive information systems and, 10.15, 10.20
Sequence control structure: Control structure used to show a single action or one action followed sequentially by another. **12.6**
Sequential file organization: File organization method in which files are stored one after another, based on a value in the key field. **9.5**-6
Sequential storage: Name given to magnetic tape as storage media because the computer must write and read tape records one after another (sequentially). **5.16**
Serial port: Port that transmits data one bit at a time and is considerably slower than a parallel port. **3.18**
Serpentine recording, *see* **Longitudinal recording**
Server computers (servers): Computers designed to support a computer network that allow users to share files, application software, and hardware. 1.10, **1.13**
FTP, 7.20
operating system for, 8.18
proxy, 7.18
Web, 7.2
Set-top box: Home network computer that uses a device that looks and acts like a cable TV box, and uses a telephone line to connect to an Internet service provider. **7.26**
Shading: Formatting feature that allows darkening of the background area of a section of a document or table. **2.10**
Shadow mask, 4.31
Shareware: Program that can be downloaded from FTP sites and tried out for free, but a license fee must be paid if the programs are kept. **7.20**
Shelf storage: Hierarchical storage management method where data has been stored on a tape or other removable media and stored in a cabinet or rack. **5.24**
Shell: Program that acts as an interface between the user and the operating system, and offers a limited number of utility functions such as file maintenance. **8.15**
Shielded twisted-pair (STP) cable: Communications cable consisting of pairs of plastic-coated copper wires that are twisted together, covered by a foil wrapper around each wire to reduce electrical interference. B6.9
Shipping and receiving department, 1.22
Shockwave: Web browser plug-in that allows authorware applications to be viewed. **14.29**
Shopping
information kiosk and, 14.14
online, 2.26, 6.6, 7.30, 7.47
SHOUT!: Use of all capital letters in Internet communications. **7.24**
Shutter, floppy disk, 5.4
SIMM (single in-line memory module): Small circuit board that holds multiple RAM chips. **3.12**
Simplex transmission: Data transmission method in which data flows only in one direction, used when the sending device never requires a response from the receiving computer. **6.18**
Simulations: Computer-based models of real-life situations. **14.7**
Single tasking: Operating systems that allow only one user to run one program at one time. **8.4**
Site licenses, *see* **Network licenses**
SLEDs (single large expensive disks): Single large disk storage systems. **5.20**
Slides: Documents created by presentation graphics software that are used in making presentations before a group. **2.24**
SLIP (serial line Internet protocol): Older protocol that does not offer a high degree of error checking. **7.29**
Slots: In direct file organization, the division of buckets to hold more than one record. **9.7**
Small computer system interface, *see* **SCSI**
Smart cards: Special purpose storage devices about the size and thickness of a credit card that contain a thin microprocessor capable of storing data. **5.22**
Sniffer: Unauthorized programs that copy passwords as they are entered, and used later for unauthorized access. **13.7**
Social interface: Operating system interface that uses objects with human characteristics to deliver messages to users. **8.24**
Soft copy: Output displayed on a screen. **4.23**
Software: The detailed set of instructions that directs a computer to perform the tasks necessary to process data into information. **1.16**-18, **12.2**
acquiring in systems development, 11.21-24
communications, 6.8, 6.19
configuration information, 8.13
custom, 11.20
developing, 12.1-16
Internet service provider, 7.29
map, 6.5
network computers, 7.25-27
OCR, 4.16
sound editing, 4.19
system, 1.17
theft, 13.10-11
Web page authoring, 7.8
Software piracy: The unauthorized and illegal copying of copyrighted software. **13.10**
Software resource sharing: Describes sharing of software by multiple users; frequently used software is stored on the hard disk server in a LAN for access by users. **6.24**
Software suite: Individual applications are packaged in the same box and sold for a price that is significantly less than buying the applications individually. **2.33**
Software tools, 12.30-33
Solution algorithm: Graphic or written description of the step-by-step procedures for a module. **12.6**
desk checking, 12.12
programming language used to code, 12.16-29
Son: In three-generation backup, the most recent copy of the file. **13.16**
Sound, used in presentation graphics, 2.24
Sound board: Expansion board that enhances the sound-generating capacity of computer. **3.18**
lossy compression, 5.13
Sound card: Multimedia device containing electronics that captures sound data input and processes sound output; installed in the computer. **4.19, 14.17**
Sound editing software, 4.19
Sound files, audio Web applications and, 7.13
Sound input, 4.19
Source: In data flow diagram, representation of an entity outside the system that sends data into the system or receives information from the system; also called agent. **11.15**
Source data automation or **collection:** Procedures and equipment designed to make the input process more efficient by eliminating the manual entry of data; the equipment captures data directly from its original form such as an invoice or inventory tag. **4.12**-17
Source document: In source data automation, the original form that data is captured from. **4.12**
Source document: In object linking and embedding applications, the document from which the object originates. **2.34**
Source program: Program containing assembly language code. **12.18,** 12.19
Spacing: Describes how far apart individual letters and lines of text are placed. **2.9**

I.12 DISCOVERING COMPUTERS: A LINK TO THE FUTURE, WORLD WIDE WEB ENHANCED

Spamming: Process of posting an article (especially one soliciting business) to several inappropriate newsgroups. **7.24**
Speaker(s): Device used for audio output. 1.5, **1.6, 14.18**
Speaker dependent: Voice input system that has to be trained to recognize the speaker's individual speech pattern. **4.20**
Speaker independent: Voice input system that has voice templates for each word, so the system does not have to be trained to recognize the speaker's individual speech pattern. **4.20**
Special education, multimedia used for, 14.8
Special effects, presentation graphics, 2.24
Special-purpose terminal: Terminal that performs specific jobs and contains features uniquely designed for use in a particular industry, such as a point-of-sale terminal. **4.18**
Speed, 1.8
Spelling checker: Feature that allows user to review individual words, sections of a document, or the entire document for correct spelling. **2.6**
Spike: A momentary overvoltage, occurring when the power increase lasts for less than one millisecond. **13.13**
Spooling: Process in which a report is first written (saved) to the disk before it is printed; used to increase printer efficiency. **8.9**
Sports Web sites, 7.47
Spreadsheet: Organization of numeric data in a worksheet or table format, by spreadsheet software. Data is organized horizontally in rows, and vertically in columns. **2.14**
Spreadsheet software, 2.14-21
SPRYNET, 7.28
SQL, *see* **Structured Query Language**
Stackable hub: Communications wiring hub that can be connected to another hub to increase the number of devices attached to the server. **6.22**
Stand-alone HTML editor: HTML editor that is a complete editing software package. **12.35**
Star network: Communications network that contains a central computer and one or more terminals or computers connected to it, forming a star configuration. **6.27**
Static RAM: A type of RAM memory that is larger than dynamic RAM and has access times of 10 to 50 nanoseconds. **3.13**
Stealth virus: Virus that uses methods to avoid detection. **13.4**
Steering committee: Decision-making body for an organization; participates in planning phase for a project. **11.9,** 11.11, 11.24
Still graphic images: Graphics that contain no movement, such as photographs or drawings. **14.4**
Storage: Part of the information processing cycle in which data and programs are stored when not being processed; also called secondary storage, or auxiliary storage. **1.7,** 1.8, **5.2**-26
  CD-ROM, 5.14-15
  databases and, 9.14, 9.27
  holographic, 5.25
  magnetic disk, 5.3-13
  magnetic tape, 5.16-18
  mass systems, 5.21
  memory buttons, 5.21
  multimedia applications, 14.16-17
  optical disks, 5.14-15
  optical memory cards, 5.22
  PC Cards, 5.19
  RAID systems, 5.19-20
  smart cards, 5.22
Storage devices: Hardware that stores instructions and data when they are not being used by the system unit; often function as input source when previously stored data is read into memory. **1.7**
Storing: Control unit operation that takes place when the result of the instruction is written to memory. **3.8**
STRADIS: Commercial system development methodology. **11.34**
Strategic decisions: Decisions made by senior management that involve the overall goals and objectives of an organization. **10.6**
Strategies, information, 10.2
Streaming audio: Feature used by advanced audio Web applications that allows sounds to be heard as they are downloaded to the computer. **7.13**
Streaming video: Feature used by Web applications that allows viewing of longer or live video images as they are downloaded to the computer. **7.14**
Striping: Storage technique that divides a logical piece of data, such as a record or word into smaller parts and writes those parts on multiple drives. **5.20**
Structure chart, 12.5
Structured analysis and design: Graphics tools used to present the system analysis findings, using entity-relationship diagrams, data flow diagrams, and the project dictionary. **11.13**-18
Structured design: Program design methodology in which all program logic is constructed from a combination of three control structures or constructs: sequence, selection, and repetition control structures. **12.6**-8
Structured English: In project dictionary, style of writing that describes the steps in a process on the data flow diagram. **11.16**
Structured interview: Data gathering technique in information systems development that has the interviewer (systems analyst) direct the conversation by following a specific set of topics and asking predefined questions. **11.7**
Structured problems: Problems that are routine, involve specific facts, and have an established method of being resolved. **10.6**
Structured Query Language (SQL): A widely used query language. **9.22**
Structured walkthrough: In program design, a review of the solution algorithm by stepping through the program logic, to identify errors and check for improvements in program design. **12.12**
Structured walkthrough: In systems analysis, a step-by-step review of any deliverable by the project team, including reports, diagrams, and mockups, in order to identify errors. **11.29**
Style: Specific combination of features affecting the appearance of a document, such as bold, italic, or underline formatting, applied to a font to make it stand out. **2.9**
Subclasses: One or more lower levels of a class. **12.22**
Subdirectory or **folder:** In a hierarchical file system a lower-level file that contains other subdirectories or one or more data or program files. **9.16**
Subnotebook computers: Smaller versions of notebook computers that weigh less than 4 pounds. **1.13**
Summary report: Report that summarizes data, containing totals from detailed input data. **4.24**
  management use of, 10.6, 10.7
Superclass: Higher-level class. **12.22**
Supercomputers: The most powerful category of computers, and the most expensive; can process hundreds of millions of instructions per second, and cost several million dollars. 1.10, **1.15**
  NSFnet and, 7.3
Superscalar CPUs: CPUs that have two or more pipelines that can process instructions simultaneously. **3.21**
Supervisor, *see* **Control program**
Support phase: In system development life cycle, process of providing continuous assistance for a system and its users after it is implemented. 11.2, **11.33**
Support tools, software, 2.37
Surge protector: Device that uses special electrical components to smooth out minor voltage errors, provides stable current flow, and keeps an overvoltage from reaching the computer equipment; also surge suppressor. **13.14**
SVGA (super video graphics array): Standard for monitors and video adapter cards that display high resolutions, typically 800 x 600 or 1,024 x 768 pixels, producing images almost equivalent to the quality of a photograph. **4.30**
Swap file: In virtual memory management, the name given to the amount of disk space allocated for use as memory. **8.7**
Swapping: When using paging, the process of the operating system making room for additional pages by writing pages currently in memory back to the disk. **8.8**
Switched line: Point-to-point line using a regular telephone line to establish a communications connection. **6.14**-15
Symbol(s), program flowchart, 12.9-10
Symbolic addresses: Storage locations noted by symbolic name in assembly language. **12.18**
Symbolic instruction codes: In assembly language programming, meaningful abbreviations for program instructions; also called mnemonics. **12.18**
Symbolic programming language: Assembly language; instructions are written as symbols and codes. **12.18**
Symmetric multiprocessing: In computers that have more than one CPU, the process of assigning application tasks to whatever CPU is available. **8.6**
Sync bytes, 6.17
Synchronous transmission mode: Data communications method that transmits large blocks of data at regular intervals using timing signals to synchronize the sending and receiving equipment. **6.17**
Synonyms: The same disk location for records with different key values. **9.8**
Syntax: In program coding, the particular set of grammar or rules that specify how the instructions in a solution algorithm are to be written. **12.13,** 12.19
Syntax error: Program error that occurs when to code violates the syntax of the programming language. **12.14**
System administrator, 1.19
System administration, operating system and, 8.10-11
System clock: A chip used by the control unit to synchronize, or control the timing of all computer operations. **3.8**
System development, guidelines for, 11.3
System development life cycle (SDLC): An organized set of activities used to guide those involved through the development of an information system, including phases of planning, analysis, design, implementation, and support. **11.2**
  analysis phase, 11.2, 11.11-20
  design phase, 11.2, 11.21-29
  documentation, 11.6
  feasibility assessment, 11.5
  implementation phase, 11.2, 11.30-32
  initiation of, 11.7
  participants in, 11.3-4
  planning phase, 11.2, 11.9-10
  project management, 11.4-5
  support phase, 11.2, 11.33
System failure: The prolonged malfunction of a computer system. **13.13**
System flowchart: Used during program design, flowchart that shows a major process, the timing of the process, the outputs generated, database tables required, and the types of input devices that will provide data to the system. **11.27**
System operator (sysop): Person who maintains and updates the bulletin board system. **6.5**
System performance, measuring, 8.10
System proposal: A report that presents alternative solutions for the project. **11.19**
Systems analyst: Person who works with both the user and the programmer to determine and design the desired output of a program. **1.16,** 11.3, 12.15
System software: All the programs including the operating system that are related to controlling the operations of the computer hardware. **1.17, 8.2**-28
  language translators, 8.23
  multimedia applications, 14.17
  operating systems, 8.2-19
  utility programs, 8.19-23
System test: During implementation phase of information systems development, test that checks all programs in an application. **11.30**
System unit: Part of the computer containing the electronic circuits that cause the execution of program instructions and manipulation of data to occur; includes the central processing unit, memory, and other electronic components. 1.5, **1.6, 3.2**-28
  bays, 3.18
  buses, 3.14-15
  components of, 3.6-19
  connectors, 3.16-18
  coprocessors, 3.14
  CPU, 3.7-10
  expansion slots, 3.15-16
  machine language instructions, 3.19-20
  memory, 3.11-14
  microprocessor, 3.7-10
  motherboard, 3.7
  ports, 3.16-18
  power supply, 3.18
  sound components, 3.18
  types of processing, 3.21
  upgrade sockets, 3.10

T1: Digital communications line that transmits 1.5 megabits per second, costing several thousand dollars per month. **6.17**
T3: Digital communications line that transmits 45 megabits per second, costing more than $40,000 per month. **6.17**
Tables: Arrangement of information in rows or columns, allowing user to easily add and change table information and move the entire table as a single item, instead of as individual lines of text. **2.10**
Tables (database), *see* **Relation(s)**
Tactical decisions: Decisions made by middle management to implement specific programs and plans necessary to accomplish the stated objectives. **10.7**
Tags: Set of special instructions in HTML that specify links to other documents and how the Web page is displayed; also called markups. **7.8**
Tape density: The number of bits that can be stored on one inch of tape. **5.18**
Tape libraries, hierarchical storage management using, 5.24
Target hyperlinks: Hyperlinks that move from one location in a document to another location in the same document. **7.8**
Task: In operating system, a program or part of a program that can be executed separately; also called process. **8.4**
TCP/IP (transmission control protocol/Internet protocol): Communications protocol used for packet switching on the Internet. **7.4**
Team, programming, 12.3
Teamwork, 10.10
Technical feasibility: Measure of whether the organization has or can obtain the hardware, software, and people needed to deliver and then support the final system. **11.5**
Telecommunications, *see* **Communications**
Telecommuting: The capability of individuals to work at home and communicate with their offices by using personal computers and communications equipment and software. **6.2,** 7.29
Telephone
  cellular, 6.13
  dialing feature of communications software, 6.19
  fiber-optic cable, 6.10
  full-duplex transmission, 6.18
  modem and, 6.19
  switched line, 6.14
  voice mail, 6.2
Telephone companies, wide area networks and, 6.26
Telephone line, Internet connection and, 7.29
Telnet: An Internet protocol that enables user to log onto a remote computer on the Internet, and use the remote computer as if it were a direct, local connection. **7.22**
Template: Formatting feature of word processing software that uses a predefined style sheet, containing font, style, spacing, and formatting information, and usually includes text that is always used, such as title and headings. **2.10**
  desktop publishing, 2.13

INDEX I.13

10base2 cable, *see* **Thinnet**
10baseT cable, *see* **Unshielded twisted-pair (UTP) cable**
Terabytes, 5.9, 5.25
Terminal(s), *see* **Display terminals**
Terminal emulation: Communications software feature that allows a personal computer to act as a specific type of terminal so the personal computer can connect to another, usually larger, computer such as a mainframe. **6.19**
Terrestrial microwave: Earth-based microwave transmission; involves sending data from one microwave station to another in line-of-sight transmissions. **6.11**
Test: Fourth step in program development to ensure that the program runs correctly and is error-free; sample data is used that is valid and invalid to check for correct results. **12.13**-15
Test data: Sample data that simulates valid data the program might process when implemented, used when desk checking. **12.12**
Text: Fundamental component of most multimedia programs. **14.2**
The Microsoft Network, *see* Microsoft Network, The
Thermal printer: Printer that uses heat to transfer colored inks from ink sheets onto the printing surface; also called thermal transfer printer. **4.37**
Thermal transfer printer, *see* **Thermal printer**
Thesaurus: Allows the user to look up synonyms for words in a document. **2.8**
The Year 2000 Problem, 12.38
Thin-client, *see* **Network computer**
Thinnet: Coaxial cable with a small diameter often used with computer networks; also called 10base2 cable. **6.10**
Third-generation language (3GL): High-level programming language that uses program instructions written as a series of English-like words and arithmetic notations; also called procedural language. **12.19**
Thrashing: Process in a computer system with heavy workload and insufficient memory, where the system spends more time moving pages to and from the disk that it does processing data. **8.10**
Thread: In newsgroups, name given to the original article and all subsequent related replies. **7.23**
3-D objects, 7.15
Three-generation backup policy: Backup used in which important files are backed up separately, based on age of copies. **13.16**
Time bomb: Virus that is activated on a particular date; a type of logic bomb. **13.3**
Timeline, 1.36
Timely data: Data that has not lost its usefulness or legitimacy because time has passed. **9.3,** 10.2, **10.12,** 10.14
Time slice: Increments of CPU time. **8.5**
Toggle key: Key that switches, or toggles, the keyboard between two different modes, such as the CAPS LOCK key. **4.3**
Token: Electronic signal used for transmitting messages in a token ring network by constantly circulating around the network, allowing devices on the network to attach messages to the token. **6.31**
Token ring network: A type of ring network that constantly circulates an electronic signal, called a token, around the network, that allows devices on the network to send messages by taking the token and attaching it to data. **6.31**
Toolbar, 2.3
ToolBook: Widely used multimedia authoring software package that uses a graphical user interface and on object-oriented approach. **14.26**-28
Toolbox: In multimedia authoring, a fixed set of icons. **14.28**
Top-down chart, 12.5
Top-down design: Program design technique that takes the original set of program specification and breaks them down into smaller, more manageable components. **12.5**
Topology: The configuration, or physical layout, of the equipment in a communications network. **6.27**
Touchpad (trackpad): Input device with a flat rectangular surface that senses the movement of a finger on its surface to control the movement of the insertion point. **4.6**
Touch screen: Input device that allows user to touch areas on the screen to enter data. **4.9**
Tower computers: Personal computers in an upright case, that provides room for expanding the system and adding optional equipment. **1.13**
Track: A narrow recording band forming a full circle around the floppy disk. **5.4**
Trackball: Pointing device like a mouse, only with the sensing ball on top of the device, so the cursor can be moved by rotating the ball with a finger. **4.6**
Trackpad, *see* **Touchpad**
Trackpoint, *see* **Pointing stick**
Track sector: Section of track within a sector. **5.4**
Tracks per inch (tpi): The number of tracks on the recording surface of a floppy disk. **5.6**
Trade books: Books that are available to help users in learning to use the features of personal computer application packages, and can be found where software is sold and are usually carried in regular bookstores. **2.37**
Trade publications: Magazines written for specific businesses or industries. **11.19**
Training, computer-based, 14.7, 14.13
Transaction processing system (TPS): Information system that processes data generated by the day-to-day transactions of an organization. **10.13**-14
Transmission media: Physical materials or other means used to establish a communications channel. **6.9**-14
Transmission modes, of communications channels, 6.16
Travel planning, online, 6.6
Travel Web sites, 7.48
Triangulation: Technique used by global positioning systems to determine the precise geographical location of a GPS receiver on earth by comparing the time it takes for signals from three or more satellites to arrive. **6.34**
Trojan horse virus: Virus that hides within or is designed to look like a legitimate program. **13.3**
Tuples: Rows in a relational database. **9.17**
Turn-around documents: Documents designed to be returned to the organization that created them, and when returned (turned around), the data is read by an OCR device. **4.16**
Tutorials: Step-by-step instructions using real examples showing users how to use an application. 2.36
Twisted-pair cable: Communications cable consisting of pairs of plastic-coated copper wires that are twisted together. **6.9**
Typeface: A specific set of characters that are designed the same, such as Helvetica or Times New Roman. **2.8**
Typeover mode, 2.6

Unauthorized access: The use of a computer system without permission. **13.5**
Unauthorized use: The use of a computer system or data for unapproved or possibly illegal activities. **13.5**
Unclassified! Web sites, 7.48
Uncompressing data, 5.13
Undervoltage: Drop in electrical supply. **13.13**
Unicode: A 16-bit code that has the capacity to represent more than 65,000 characters and symbols; represents all the world's current languages. **3.4**-5
Uniform Resource Locator (URL): Address that points to a specific resource on the Internet; can indicate an Internet site, a specific document at a site, and a location within a document at a site. **7.10**
  guide to Web sites, 7.41-48
  pictures pointing to, 12.36
Uninstaller: Utility program that deletes unwanted software and any associated entries in system files. **8.21**
Uninterruptible power supply (UPS): Device that contains surge protection circuits and batteries that can provide power during a loss of power. **13.14**
Universal product code (UPC): Type of bar code, used for input information about grocery and retail items. **4.14**
Universal Serial Bus (USB): Bus that allows up to 128 devices to be connected to a serial port. **3.18**
UNIX: Multiuser, multitasking operating system developed in the early 1970s. **8.18**
Unshielded twisted-pair (UTP) cable: Communications cable consisting of pairs of plastic-coated copper wires that are twisted together; also called 10baseT cable. **6.9**
Unstructured interview: Data gathering technique in information systems development that relies on the interviewee (the user) to direct the conversation based on a general goal. **11.7**
Unstructured problems: Problems that do not have a clear method for their solution; the problem solver often has to rely on intuition and judgment. **10.6**
Updating: Data maintenance procedures for adding new data, changing existing data, and deleting old data. **9.3,** 9.10
Upgrade socket: Empty socket in motherboard that can be used to install more power CPUs. **3.10**
Uplink: The transmission to a satellite. **6.11**
Upward compatible: Describes application that is written for the old version of an operating system and can also run under the new version. **8.14**
URL, *see* **Uniform Resource Locator**
Useful: Information that results in an action being taken or specifically not being taken, depending on the situation; often improved through exception reporting. 1.19, **10.12**
Usenet: Collection of news and discussion groups accessed via the Internet. **7.23**-24
User(s): The people who either use the computer directly, or use the information it provides; also called computer users, or end users. **1.7**
  database system role, 9.24
  empowered, 12.21, 12.31
  information system development and, 11.3
  number of, 1.10
  system development and, 11.3
  training and educating in information systems development, 11.30
User coordination, database administrator and, 9.23
User-ID, *see* **User name**
User interface: Combination of hardware and software that allows user to communicate with a computer system. **1.17, 2.2, 8.3**
  types of, 8.3
User name: A unique combination of characters identifying user for e-mail; also called user-ID. **7.19, 8.11,** 13.6
User responses: The data that a user inputs to respond to a question or message from the software. **4.2**
User tools, 2.1-42
Utility programs (database): In a DBMS, programs that perform maintenance tasks including creating files and dictionaries, monitoring performance, copying data, and deleting unwanted records. **9.18**
Utility programs (system management): Programs that perform specific tasks related to managing computer resources or files; often contained in operating systems. **8.19**-23
  virus protection, 13.5

Vaccines: Antivirus programs that work by looking for viruses, and by inoculating existing program files from viruses. **13.4**
Validation: In database programs, the comparison of data entered against a predefined format or value. **2.23**
Validation rules: Valid codes, ranges, or values for the data item in the data dictionary. **11.18**
Value(s): Numerical data contained in the cells of a spreadsheet. **2.15**
Value-added carriers: Companies that lease channels from common carriers to provide specialized communications services. **6.26**
Value-added network (VAN): Network provided by companies that lease channels from common carriers to provide specialized communications services. **6.26**
Value-added reseller (VAR): A vendor that has resale agreements with computer manufacturers and takes full responsibility for equipment, software, installation, and training. **11.22**
Variables: The data elements in object-oriented programming. **12.21**
Vendors, 11.3
  evaluating proposals from, 11.23-24
  online support, 6.5
  soliciting proposals from, 11.22-23
Verbal program development, 12.39
Verifiable: Information that can be confirmed. **10.12**
Veronica: Search programs that search Gopher directories for files on a specific subject. **7.21**
Vertical application software: Software developed for a specific industry. **11.19**
Very small aperture terminal (VSAT): Satellite antenna measuring only one to three meters in size that can transmit up to 19,200 bits of data per second. **6.12**
VGA (video graphics array): Standard for monitors and video adapter cards that display resolutions of 640 x 480 pixels. **4.30**
Video: Photographic images that provide the appearance of motion in real-time. **14.6**
Video capture card: An expansion card, or adapter, that enables a video camera or VCR to be connected to the computer. **14.20**
Video card: Multimedia device containing electronics that capture and process video data; installed in the computer. **4.19**
Video compression: Compression of video files. **14.6**
Videoconferencing: The use of computers, television cameras, and communications software and equipment to conduct electronic meetings with participants at different locations. **6.3**-4
  Internet, 7.14
Video display: Important part of multimedia personal computer system, consisting of monitor and display adapter. **14.18**
Video display terminals (VDTs), ***see*** **Display terminals**
Video expansion board, lossy compression and, 5.13
Video files: Web applications that use individual video files such as movie clips that can be downloaded and played on a computer. **7.14**
Video input: Input to the computer using a video camera or a video recorder using previously recorded material, requiring tremendous amounts of storage space. **4.22**
Video output: Output consisting of visual images captured with a video input device, and directed to an output device, such as a monitor. **4.26**
Video overlay card: Allows the computer monitor to be used for multimedia presentations where the laser disk audio is connected directly to a stereo sound system or the computer's sound card. **14.22**
Video projector: For multimedia applications or presentations, a device with its own light source that is used to display images on screen. **14.19**
View: In a relational database, the subset of data from one or more files the user manipulates for a query. **9.21**
Virtual corporation: An alliance of individual companies that join together temporarily to offer goods and services. **10.21**
Virtual file allocation table (VFAT): File allocation table on Windows 95 systems. **5.5**
Virtual memory management: Process used by multitasking operating system that increases the amount of memory the operating system can use by allocating a set amount of disk space to be used to store items during processing, in addition to the existing memory. **8.7**

Virtual reality (VR): Creation of an artificial environment that can be experienced by the user as 3-D images that can be explored and manipulated interactively, using a pointing device. **7.15, 14.12**
Virtual reality modeling language, *see* **VRML**
Virus(es): A program that copies itself into other programs and files and spreads through multiple computer systems; can cause damage to files on the system where the virus is present. **8.21, 13.2-5**
Virus signature: Specific patterns of known virus code. **13.4**
Visual Basic: Windows application developed in the early 1990s to assist programmers in developing other event-driven Windows applications. **12.24, 12.33**
Visual table of contents, 12.5
Voice-aware: Programs that allow user to dictate the programming language syntax to create the program. **12.39**
Voice input: Input that allows the user to enter data and issue commands to the computer with spoken words. **4.19-**21
Voice mail: Verbal electronic mail that allows the caller to leave a message via telephone that is digitized so it can be stored on disk like other computer data, and accessed by the recipient. **6.2**
  Internet, 7.13
Voice output: Spoken words that are conveyed to the user from the computer. **4.26**
Voice recognition technology, 12.39
Voice synthesis: A type of voice generation that can transform words stored in memory into speech, which is played through speakers attached to the computer. **4.26**
Voice templates: Used by voice input systems to recognize patterns of sounds. **4.20**
Volatile: Describes RAM memory because the programs and data stored in RAM are erased when the power to the computer is turned off. **3.11, 5.2**
VRML (virtual reality modeling language: Language used by Web-based virtual reality applications that allows a developer to create a collection of 3-D objects. **7.15**

W3, *see* **World Wide Web**
Wafers: In chip manufacturing process, silicon ingot is sliced into wafers that eventually will become computer chips. **3.25**
Weather, online, 6.6, 7.48
Web, *see* **World Wide Web**
Web browser, *see* **Web browser software**
Web browser software: Software running on Internet-connected computers that interpret and display Web pages, enabling users to access Web sites that have text, graphics, video, and sound and have hypertext links to other information and Web sites. 1.8, **1.9, 2.26, 7.9-**11, 7.29, 14.4
  graphical, 7.9-11, 7.12
  script as link to Internet server, 12.36
  Windows and, 8.16
WebCrawler search tool, 7.17
Web page: Hypertext or hypermedia document residing on an Internet computer that contains text, graphics, video, or sound. **2.26, 7.7-**8
  bookmark, 7.11
  caching, 7.18
  code to design, 12.34-35
  creating using word processor, 2.12
  history list, 7.11
  home page, 7.10

Web page authoring software, 7.8
Web server computers, number of, 7.2
Web sites: Internet locations that contain hyperlinked documents. **1.9, 7.7**
  cybercorps and, 10.21
  domain names, 7.6
  guide to, 7.41-48
  list of favorite, 7.11, 8.22
Web site number of visitors, 12.36
  organized directories of, 7.16
Web surfing: Process of displaying pages one Web site after another; similar to using a television remote control to jump between channels. **7.8**
Welcome page: The first page on a Web site; often serves as a table of contents for the other pages on the site. 1.8, **7.10**
What-if analysis: The capability of a spreadsheet to recalculate when data is changed. **2.19**
What-if questions, 10.16
Wide area network (WAN): Communications network that covers a large geographical area, and uses telephone cables, microwaves, satellites, or a combination of communications channels. **6.26**
Widget Catalog: Catalog of widgets in ToolBook. **14.27**
Widgets: Graphical objects in ToolBook that are pre-scripted. **14.27**
Win 95, *see* **Windows 95**
Window: A rectangular area of the screen that is used to display information. **2.2**
Windows, program development tools, 12.24
Windows 95 (Win 95): Operating system developed by Microsoft for IBM-compatible personal computers that takes advantage of 32-bit processors. Windows 95 has an improved graphical user interface and supports preemptive multitasking. **8.16**
Windows 3.0: Operating system developed by Microsoft; the first widely used graphical user interface for IBM-compatible computers. **8.15**
Windows 3.1: Operating system that includes a number of improvements to Windows 3.0. **8.15**
Windows 3.x: Refers to these versions of Microsoft's Windows operating system: Windows 3.0, Windows 3.1, and Windows 3.11. **8.15**
Windows CE: Operating system used on wireless communication devices and smaller computers such as hand-helds, palmtops, and network computers; requires little memory. **8.16**
Windows for Workgroups: Networking version of Windows 3.1. **8.15**
Windows NT: Sophisticated graphical user interface operating system designed for client-server networks; uses a modular design. **8.17**
Wireless communications, Windows CE and, 8.16
Wireless transmission: In communications systems, used to connect devices in the same general area such as an office or business park, using one of three transmission techniques: infrared light beams, radio waves, or carrier-connect radio. **6.12**
Wiring hub: A central connecting point for devices such as computers, printers, and storage devices that are connected to the server; also called concentrator, or multistation access unit. **6.22**

Wizard: Automated assistant that helps user complete a task by asking questions and then automatically performing actions based on the given answers. **2.36**
Word processing: The most widely used computer application; involves the use of a computer to produce or modify documents that consist primarily of text. **2.4-**12
  creating Web pages using, 2.12
  dedicated systems, 2.4
  Web authoring features, 7.8
Word processing document
  creating, 2.4-6
  editing, 2.6-8
  formatting, 2.8-11
  printing, 2.11
WordPerfect, 2.12
Word size: The number of bits that the CPU can process at one time. **3.9**
Word wrap: An automatic line return that occurs when text reaches a certain position on a line in a document, such as the right-hand margin. **2.5**
Work, connecting to Internet through, 7.28
Workflow support, 2.31
Workgroup technology: Equipment and software that help group members communicate, manage activities, and make group decisions. **2.30, 6.4**
Worksheet, *see* Spreadsheet
Workstations: Personal computers connected to a network; often have powerful calculating and graphics capabilities and are frequently used by engineers. **1.13, 6.27**
World Wide Web (WWW), Web, W3: Portion of the Internet containing Web sites, where information can be accessed electronically; the collection of hyperlinked documents accessible on the Internet. **1.9,** 7.1, **7.7-**17
  authorware applications, 14.29
  connecting to, 7.28-29
  doing business on, 7.30
  expanded markets and, 10.3
  future of, 7.31
  guide to sites, 7.41-48
  multimedia on,
  multimedia applications, 7.11-15, 14.15
  searching for information on, 7.16-17
Worm: Virus program designed to copy itself repeatedly in memory or on a disk until no memory or disk space remains. **13.3**
Write-protect window: On a floppy disk, a small hole in the corner of the floppy disk that protects data from being erased accidentally. **5.5**
Writing data: The process of storing data; also called recording data. **5.2**
WWW, *see* **World Wide Web**
WYSIWIG: An acronym for What You See Is What You Get. A feature that displays the document on the screen exactly as it will look when it is printed. **2.5**

Yahoo! search tool, 7.16, 7.17

Zero insertion force (ZIF) socket, 3.10

Photo Credits

Cover Credits: Background, ticket, graduation cap, and diploma provided by PhotoDisc Inc © 1996; **Chapter 1:** *Chapter opener: upper left,* Sotographs/Liaison International; *right,* David Young Wolff/Tony Stone Images; *bottom right,* Greg Pease/Tony Stone Images; *Figure 1-1 upper right,* David Mason/Woodfin Camp & Associates; *Figure 1-1a bottom right,* Sotographs/Liaison International; *Figure 1-1b middle,* Charlie Westerman/Liaison International; *Figure 1-1d bottom left,* Courtesy of AST Research, Inc.; *Figure 1-1e upper left,* Mitch Kezar/Tony Stone Images; *Figure 1-3* Courtesy of Intel Corporation; *Figure 1-6a* Courtesy of Omnidata International, Inc.; *Figure 1-6b* Courtesy of Hewlett-Packard Company; *Figure 1-6c* Yoav Levy/Phototake, Inc.; *Figure 1-6d* Courtesy of U.S. Robotics; *Figure 1-6e* Courtesy of Texas Instruments, Inc.; *Figure 1-6f* Courtesy of International Business Machines Corporation; *Figure 1-6g* Courtesy of Toshiba America Information Systems, Inc.; *Figure 1-6h* Courtesy of Gateway 2000, Inc.; *Figure 1-6i* Courtesy of International Business Machines Corporation; *Figure 1-6j* Courtesy of Sun Microsystems, Inc.; *Figure 1-6k* Courtesy of International Business Machines Corporation; *Figure 1-7* Courtesy of Hewlett-Packard Company; *Figure 1-8* Courtesy of International Business Machines Corporation; *Figure 1-9* Courtesy of International Business Machines Corporation; *Figure 1-10* Courtesy of Cray Research, Inc.; *Figure 1-11* Courtesy of Minnesota Supercomputer Center; *Figure 1-14* Scott Goodwin Photography, Inc.; *Figure 1-15* International Business Machines Corporation; *Figure 1-16* Walter Hodges/Tony Stone Images; *Figure 1-17* Tom McCarthy/PhotoEdit; *Figure 1-18* David Young Wolff/Tony Stone Images; *Figure 1-19* Richard Pasley/Stock Boston; *Figure 1-21* Comstock, Inc.; *Figure 1-22* Courtesy of John Deere & Company; *Figure 1-23* Courtesy of Cannondale, Inc.; *Figure 1-24* Jeff Dunn/Stock Boston; *Figure 1-25* Courtesy of Hewlett-Packard Company; *Figure 1-26* Courtesy of International Business Machines Corporation; *Figure 1-27* Jose L. Pelaez/The Stock Market; *Page 1.33,* Anxious computer and carriage, Courtesy of Corel Professional Photos CD-ROM Image usage; **Timeline:** *1937* ABC, Courtesy of Iowa State University; *1937,* Dr. John Atanasoff, Courtesy of Iowa State University; *1937* Clifford Berry, Courtesy of Iowa State University; *1943* ENIAC, Courtesy of the University of Pennsylvania Archives; *1945* Dr. John von Neumann, Courtesy of the Institute for Advanced Studies; *1951* UNIVAC, Courtesy of Unisys Corporation; *1951* Newspaper, Courtesy of Unisys Corporation; *1952* Dr. Grace Hopper, Courtesy of Harvard University Archives; *1952* COBOL, Courtesy of the Department of the Navy; *1952* IBM Model 650, Courtesy of International Business Machines Corporation; *1952* Core memory, Courtesy of M.I.T. Archives; *1957* FORTRAN, Courtesy of the Department of the Navy; *1957* Vacuum tubes, Courtesy of International Business Machines Corporation; *1957* Transistor, Courtesy of M.I.T. Archives; *1964* IBM System/360, Courtesy of International Business Machines Corporation; *1964* Dr. John Kemeny, Courtesy of Dartmouth College News Service; *1964* DEC, Courtesy of Digital Equipment Corporation; *1964* Pascal, Shelly R. Harrison; *1970* LSI, Courtesy of International Business Machines Corporation; *1971* Dr. Ted Hoff, Courtesy of Intel Corporation; *1971* Pentium chip, Courtesy of Intel Corporation; *1971* Altair, Boston Computer Museum; *1975* Robert Metcalfe, Courtesy of *InfoWorld;* *1976* Apple logo, Courtesy of Apple Computer, Inc.; *1976* Steve Wozniak and Steve Jobs, Courtesy of Apple Computer, Inc.; *1976* Apple, Courtesy of Apple Computer, Inc.; *1979* VisCalc, Courtesy of Software Arts, Inc.; *1980* Bill Gates, Courtesy of Microsoft Corporation; *1981* IBM PC, Courtesy of International Business Machines Corporation; *1983* TIME magazine cover © 1982, Time, Inc.; *1983* Lotus 1-2-3, Courtesy of Lotus Development Corporation; *1983* Mitch Kapor, Courtesy of Lotus Development Corporation; *1984* IBM, Courtesy of International Business Machines Corporation; *1984* Apple Macintosh, Courtesy of Apple Computer, Inc.; *1987* Intel 80386, Courtesy of Intel Corporation; *1987* Intel 486, Courtesy of Intel Corporation; *1990* Windows, Courtesy of Microsoft Corporation; *1992* PDA, Courtesy of Apple Computer, Inc.; *1993* Pentium chip, Courtesy of Intel Corporation; *1993* Energy Star logo, Courtesy of the Environmental Protection Agency; *1995* Pentium Pro, Courtesy of Intel Corporation; *1996* Dr. Andrew Grove, Courtesy of Intel Corporation; *1997* Microsoft Office 97, Courtesy of Microsoft Corporation; **Chapter 2:** *Figure 2-8* Courtesy of T/Maker Company; *Figure 2-12* Courtesy of Corel Corporation; *Figure 2-25* Scott Goodwin Photography, Inc.; *Figure 2-41* Courtesy of International Business Machines Corporation; *Figure 2-48* Scott Goodwin Photography, Inc.; *Pages 2.44-45,* Chessmen, disk, pen, package, and giraffe, Courtesy of Corel Professional Photos CD-ROM Image usage; **Chapter 3:** *Chapter opener: upper right,* R. Ian Lloyd/West Light; *middle right,* Scott Goodwin Photography, Inc.; *lower right,* Scott Goodwin Photography, Inc.; *lower left,* David Parker/Seagate Microelectronics LTD/Science Photo Library/Photo Researchers, Inc.; *upper left,* Michael Rosenfeld/Tony Stone Images; *Figure 3-8* Courtesy of Intel Corporation; *Figure 3-9* Courtesy of Intel Corporation; *Figure 3-10* Courtesy of International Business Machines Corporation; *Figure 3-13* Scott Goodwin Photography, Inc.; *Figure 3-15* Scott Goodwin Photography, Inc.; *Figure 3-20* Scott Goodwin Photography, Inc.; *Figure 3-21* Scott Goodwin Photography, Inc.; *Figure 3-22* Scott Goodwin Photography, Inc.; *Figure 3-26* Scott Goodwin Photography, Inc.; *Figure 3-35* R. Ian Lloyd/West Light; *Figure 3-36* Alfred Pasieka/Peter Arnold, Inc.; *Figure 3-37* Charles D. Winters/Photo Researchers, Inc.; *Figure 3-38* Courtesy of Texas Instruments; *Figure 3-39* Dick Lurie/Tony Stone Images; *Figure 3-40* David Parker/Seagate Microelectronics LTD/Science Photo Library/Photo Researchers, Inc.; *Figure 3-41* Dr. Jeremy Burgess/Science Photo Library/Photo Researchers, Inc.; *Figure 3-42* John Maher/The Stock Market; *Figure 3-44* Dr. Jeremy Burgess/Science Photo Library/Photo Researchers, Inc.; *Pages 3.34-35,* Chip, calculator, brain, Courtesy of Corel Professional Photos CD-ROM Image usage; **Chapter 4:** *Chapter opener top,* Courtesy of International Business Machines Corporation; *lower left,* Courtesy of HEI, Inc.; *middle left,* Courtesy of NEC Technologies, Inc.; *Figure 4-1* Scott Goodwin Photography, Inc.; *Figure 4-4* Kevin Horan/Tony Stone Images; *Figure 4-5* Courtesy of NEC Technologies, Inc.; *Figure 4-6* Scott Goodwin Photography, Inc.; *Figure 4-7* Courtesy of International Business Machines Corporation; *Figure 4-8* Courtesy of Logitech, Inc.; *Figure 4-9* Scott Goodwin Photography, Inc.; *Figure 4-11* Courtesy of International Business Machines Corporation; *Figure 4-12* Courtesy of HEI, Inc.; *Figure 4-13* Courtesy of International Business Machines Corporation; *Figure 4-14* Peter Vadnai/The Stock Market; *Figure 4-16* Courtesy of Logitech, Inc.; *Figure 4-17* Courtesy of International Business Machines Corporation; *Figure 4-19a* John Coletti/Stock Boston; *Figure 4-19b* Jim Pickerell/Tony Stone Images; *Figure 4-19c* David Frazier/Tony Stone Images; *Figure 4-20* Courtesy of Scantron Corporation; *Figure 4-23* Scott Goodwin Photography, Inc.; *Figure 4-24* Courtesy of Hewlett-Packard Company; *Figure 4-25* Peter Vadnai/The Stock Market; *Figure 4-26* Tony Freeman/PhotoEdit; *Figure 4-28* Martin Schneider Associates; *Figure 4-30* Courtesy of VideoLabs, Inc.; *Figure 4-31* Courtesy of Softboard Microfield Graphics, Inc.; *Figure 4-37* AT&T Corporation; *Figure 4-38* Courtesy of Portrait Display Labs, Inc.; *Figure 4-39* Courtesy of NEC Technologies, Inc.; *Figure 4-40* Courtesy of International Business Machines Corporation; *Figure 4-41* Courtesy of International Business Machines Corporation; *Figure 4-43* Courtesy of Evans & Sutherland Computer Corporation; *Figure 4-45* Scott Goodwin Photography, Inc.; *Figure 4-50* Courtesy of Lexmark International Inc.; *Figure 4-52*

Courtesy of Epson America, Inc.; *Figure 4-53* Courtesy of Siemens Nixdorf Printing Systems, L.P.; *Figure 4-54* Courtesy of CalComp Inc.; *Figure 4-55* Courtesy of Hewlett-Packard Company; *Figure 4-56* Courtesy of CalComp Inc.; *Figure 4-57a* Courtesy of Seiko Instruments USA, Inc.; *Figure 4-57b* Courtesy of Zebra Technologies Corporation; *Figure 4-57c* Courtesy of Citizen America Corporation; *Figure 4-58* Courtesy of 3M Visual Systems Division; *Figure 4-59* Courtesy of In Focus Systems; *Figure 4-60* Courtesy of Eastman Kodak Co.; *Figure 4-61* Courtesy of Hewlett-Packard Company; *Figure 4-62* Courtesy of Hewlett-Packard Company; *Figure 4-64* James D. Wilson/Woodfin Camp & Associates; *Figure 4-65* © Jim Pickerell/West Light; *Pages 4.51-52*, Car, typewriter, and pen, Courtesy of Corel Professional Photos CD-ROM Image usage; **Chapter 5:** *Chapter opener: upper left,* Scott Goodwin Photography, Inc.; *middle left,* Courtesy of Drexler Technology Corporation; *middle,* Courtesy of GemPlus; *bottom left,* Courtesy of Imation Enterprises Corporation; *bottom right,* Courtesy of International Business Machines Corporation; *Figure 5-2* Scott Goodwin Photography, Inc.; *Figure 5-4* Scott Goodwin Photography, Inc.; *Figure 5-6* Scott Goodwin Photography, Inc.; *Figure 5-10* Courtesy of Western Digital Corporation; *Figure 5-11* Courtesy of International Business Machines Corporation; *Figure 5-14* Courtesy of Iomega Corporation; *Figure 5-18* Tony Cordoza/Liaison International; *Figure 5-19* Courtesy of Imation Enterprises Corporation; *Figure 5-20* Scott Goodwin Photography, Inc.; *Figure 5-21* Courtesy of International Business Machines Corporation; *Figure 5-22* Courtesy of Imation Enterprises Corporation; *Figure 5-24* Courtesy of Kingston Technology Corporation; *Figure 5-27* Rob Crandall/Folio, Inc.; *Figure 5-28* Courtesy of Dallas Semiconductor; *Figure 5-29* Courtesy of GemPlus; *Figure 5-30* Courtesy of Drexler Technology Corporation; *Pages 5.30-31,* Hand, disks, apple, optical disk, and movie board, Courtesy of Corel Professional Photos CD-ROM Image usage; **Chapter 6:** *Chapter opener: upper right,* Bob Krist/Tony Stone Images; *middle right,* Matthew Borkoski/Folio, Inc.; *middle,* Uniphoto, Inc.; *lower left,* Jeff Zaruba/The Stock Market; *Figure 6-1* Uniphoto, Inc.; *Figure 6-2* Robert Reichert/Liaison International; *Figure 6-3* Matthew Borkoski/Folio, Inc.; *Figure 6-4* Larry Mulvehill/Rainbow; *Figure 6-11* Jeff Zaruba/The Stock Market; *Figure 6-12* Harry M. Walker/Liaison International; *Figure 6-14* Scott Goodwin Photography, Inc.; *Figure 6-15* Courtesy of Motorola, Inc.; *Figure 6-16* Courtesy of Hewlett-Packard Company; *Figure 6-24* Scott Goodwin Photography, Inc.; *Figure 6-25* Courtesy of U.S. Robotics; *Figure 6-31* Bob Krist/Tony Stone Images; *Figure 6-39* David Parker/Science Photo Library/Photo Researchers, Inc.; *Pages 6.41-42,* Car, satellite, sign, pencil, hand, computers, lock, and file, Courtesy of Corel Professional Photos CD-ROM Image usage; **Chapter 7:** *Figure 7-3* Courtesy of Donna Cox and Robert Patterson/NCSA/UIUC; *Figure 7-19a* Catherine Noren/Stock Boston; *Figure 7-19b* Courtesy of Cray Research, Inc.; *Figure 7-19c* Courtesy of International Business Machines Corporation; *Figure 7-27* Courtesy of Sun Microsystems, Inc.; *Figure 7-28* Courtesy of Philips Consumer Electronics Company; *Figure 7-29a* Courtesy of Philips Consumer Electronics Company; *Figure 7-29b* Courtesy of Philips Consumer Electronics Company; *Figure 7-33* Courtesy of Donna Cox and Robert Patterson/NCSA/UIUC; *Pages 7.37-38,* Humor computer, striker, and world map; Courtesy of Corel Professional Photos CD-ROM Image usage; **Chapter 8:** *Figure 8-1* Courtesy of International Business Machines Corporation; *Figure 8-12* Courtesy of Microsoft Corporation; *Figure 8-13* Courtesy of Microsoft Corporation; *Figure 8-14* Fredrick D. Bodin; *Figure 8-15* Courtesy of International Business Machines Corporation; *Figure 8-20* Courtesy of Berkeley Systems, Inc.; *Page 8.30,* Television, Courtesy of Corel Professional Photos CD-ROM Image usage; **Buyers Guide:** *Figure a* Courtesy of International Business Machines Corporation; *Figure b* Courtesy of CompUSA; *Figure c* Scott Goodwin Photography, Inc.; *Figure f* Scott Goodwin Photography, Inc.; *Figure g* Courtesy of Toshiba America, Inc.; *Figure h* Scott Goodwin Photography, Inc.; *Figure i* Courtesy of Xircom, Inc.; *Figure k* Scott Goodwin Photography, Inc.; **Chapter 9:** *Figure 9-17* Courtesy of Microsoft Corporation; *Figure 9-20* Jon Riley/Tony Stone Images; *Figure 9-23 top right,* Courtesy of International Business Machines Corporation; *Pages 9.33-34,* Copyright symbol, car, bag, and magnifying glass, Courtesy of Corel Professional Photos CD-ROM Image usage; **Chapter 10:** *Chapter opener: top,* Mitch Kezar/Tony Stone Images; *Figure 10-8* Courtesy of International Business Machines Corporation; *Figure 10-9* Tim Brown/Tony Stone Images; *Figure 10-10* Courtesy of SAS Institute Inc.; *Figure 10-11* Mitch Kezar/Tony Stone Images; *Figure 10-12* R. Ian Lloyd/West Light; *Figure 10-13* Scott Goodwin Photography, Inc.; *Figure 10-15* Steve Chenn/West Light; *Pages 10.27-28,* Medical symbol and tech support art, Courtesy of Corel Professional Photos CD-ROM Image usage; **Chapter 11:** *Chapter opener: top,* Michael Rosenfeld/Tony Stone Images; *middle,* Frank Herholdt/Tony Stone Images; *bottom right,* William Taufic/The Stock Market; *Figure 11-2* Dan Bosler/Tony Stone Images; *Figure 11-4* David R. Frazier/Tony Stone Images; *Figure 11-5* Kaluzny/Thatcher/Tony Stone Images; *Figure 11-9* Frank Herholdt/Tony Stone Images; *Figure 11-20* William Taufic/The Stock Market; *Figure 11-28* Michael Rosenfeld/Tony Stone Images; *Pages 11.41-42,* Man and Revere, Courtesy of Corel Professional Photos CD-ROM Image usage; **Chapter 12:** *Figure 12-38* AT&T Corporation; *Pages 12.44-45,* Insect, nerd, coffee, and tree, Courtesy of Corel Professional Photos CD-ROM Image usage; **Careers:** *Figure 1* Charles Gupton/Stock Boston; *Figure 2* Tim Brown/Tony Stone Images; *Figure 4* Bonnie Kamin/PhotoEdit; *Figure 5* Steve Winter/Black Star; *Figure 6* Michael Newman/PhotoEdit; *Figure 11* Courtesy of Softbank COMDEX; *Figure 12* Scott Goodwin Photography, Inc.; **Chapter 13:** *Chapter opener: lower left,* © Kerry Klayman/U.C. Irvine; *middle right,* Courtesy of Cadix International; *Figure 13-5* Courtesy of Eyedentify, Inc.; *Figure 13-6* Yvonne Hemsey/Liaison International; *Figure 13-7* Courtesy of Cadix International; *Figure 13-8* Courtesy of Global Computer Supplies, Inc.; *Figure 13-13* Courtesy of American Power Conversion; *Figure 13-14* Courtesy of American Power Conversion; *Figure 13-19* Cynthia Satloff; *Figure 13-25* Olivetti Research Ltd; *Figure 13-26* © Kerry Klayman/U.C. Irvine; *Pages 13.37-38,* Computer and man, laptop, mortar, needle, and first aid symbol, Courtesy of Corel Professional Photos CD-ROM Image usage; **Chapter 14:** *Chapter opener: lower left,* Courtesy of Touchnet Systems, Inc.; *Figure 14-6* Mona Lisa/Leonardo da Vinci, Courtesy of Super Stock; *Figure 14-7* Courtesy of AMR Training Group; *Figure 14-14* Courtesy of Sense 8 Corporation; *Figure 14-15* Christian Zachariasen/Sygma; *Figure 14-16* Courtesy of Touchnet Systems, Inc.; *Figure 14-19* Courtesy of AST Research, Inc.; *Figure 14-21* Scott Goodwin Photography, Inc.; *Figure 14-22* Courtesy of In Focus Systems; *Figure 14-23* Courtesy of In Focus Systems; *Figure 14-24* Courtesy of Microtek, Inc.; *Figure 14-26* Courtesy of Canon Computer Systems, Inc.; *Figure 14-27* Courtesy of Corel Corporation; *Figure 14-28* Courtesy of Pioneer Electronics; *Figure 14-39* Courtesy of Ski America, Inc.; *Pages 14.39-40,* Frog, tools, batter, baseball and tickets, Courtesy of Corel Professional Photos CD-ROM Image usage; **Virtual Reality:** *Figure 1* Christian Zachariasen/Sygma; *Figure 2* Christian Zachariasen/Sygma; *Figure 3* Christian Zachariasen/Sygma; *Figure 4* Christian Zachariasen/Sygma; *Figure 5* Christian Zachariasen/Sygma; *Figure 6* Christian Zachariasen/Sygma; *Figure 7* PH. Plailly/Eurelios/Science Photo Library/Photo Researchers, Inc.; *Figure 8* PH. Plailly/Eurelios/Science Photo Library/Photo Researchers, Inc.; *Figure 9* PH. Plailly/Eurelios/Science Photo Library/Photo Researchers, Inc.; *Figure 10* Shahn Kermani/Liaison International; *Figure 11* Hank Morgan/ Science Source/ Photo Researchers, Inc.; *Figure 12a* M. Wada/Liaison International; *Figure 12b* M. Wada/Liaison International; *Figure 13* Alexander Jason/Liaison International; *Figure 14* Division, Inc.; *Figure 15* Geoff Tompkinson/Science Photo Library/Photo Researchers, Inc.; *Figure 16* Geoff Tompkinson/Science Photo Library/Photo Researchers, Inc.; *Figure 17* Kazuhiro Nogi/Agence France Presse/Corbis-Bettmann; *Figure 18* Geoff Tompkinson/Science Photo Library/Photo Researchers, Inc.